AMERICAN JOURNEY
THE QUEST FOR LIBERTY TO 1877

HISTORIAN REVIEWERS

Judy Chesen, Wilberforce University, Wilberforce, Ohio
Robert Ferrell, Indiana University, Bloomington, Indiana
Lori Ginzberg, Pennsylvania State University, University Park, Pennsylvania
Stephen Middleton, North Carolina State University, Raleigh, North Carolina
Kenneth Stampp, University of California, Berkeley, California

TEACHER REVIEWERS

Henry W. Dunbar, Canyon Hills Middle School, El Paso, Texas
Sharon Hamil, Resource Specialist, Secondary Social Studies,
Shawnee Mission, Kansas
Patricia T. Jordan, Hutchinson Junior High School, Lubbock, Texas
Judy Parsons, Social Studies Coordinator, Columbia, Missouri
Jewell Richey, Dallas Staff Development Center, Dallas, Texas
Donald G. Sasse, Dewitt Middle School, Dewitt, Michigan

ACCURACY PANEL

Susan Smulyan, Brown University, Providence, Rhode Island
With Joanne P. Melish, Brown University, Providence, Rhode Island

AMERICAN JOURNEY
THE QUEST FOR LIBERTY TO 1877

James West Davidson   Kathleen Underwood

PRENTICE HALL
Englewood Cliffs, New Jersey
Needham, Massachusetts

Supplementary Materials

Annotated Teacher's Edition
Teaching Resources File

ISBN 0-13-390568-3

10 9

PRENTICE HALL
A Division of Simon & Schuster
Englewood Cliffs, New Jersey

About the Cover

Front Cover   From top left: Iroquois chief Ki-on-twog-ky, known as Cornplanter; European explorers sailing to the Americas; colonial woman dyeing cloth; Spanish mission in the Southwest; early United States flag; canal boat; Frederick Douglass; wagon train moving west; miner panning for gold; steam engine; cotton boll; Civil War cannon.

Back Cover   Quotation from the diary of Amelia Stewart Knight who traveled the Oregon Trail in 1853. (See text page 452.)

Staff Credits

Editorial: Marion Osterberg, B'Ann Bowman, Naomi Kisch, Donna Disch, Frank Tangredi, Doug McCollum, Catherine Van Bemmel

Design: Susan Walrath, AnnMarie Roselli, Carmela Pereira, Leslie Osher

Production: Joan McCulley, Marlys Lehmann, Elizabeth Torjussen, Amy Fleming, Suse Cioffi

Publishing Technology: Andrew Grey Bommarito, Monduane Harris, Deborah Jones, Cleasta Wilburn, Gregory Myers

Marketing: Laura Asermily, Steve Lewin, Phillip Conklin, Lynda Scimeca

Pre-Press Production: Laura Sanderson, Laura Lamorte, Denise Herckenrath

Manufacturing: Rhett Conklin, Gertrude Szyferblatt

Credits for Voices and Visions and Other Excerpts

Every effort has been made to trace the copyright holders of the documents used in this book. Should there be any omission in this respect, we apologize, and shall be pleased to make the appropriate acknowledgment in any future printings. Acknowledgments appear immediately following each excerpt in Voices and Visions.

Illustration Credits

Frequently cited excerpts are abbreviated as follows: AMNH, American Museum of Natural History; LC, Library of Congress; MFA, Museum of Fine Arts, Boston; MMA, Metropolitan Museum of Art, New York; NA, National Archives; NG, National Gallery of Art, Washington, D.C.; NMAA, National Museum of American Art; NYHS, courtesy of the New York Historical Society, New York; NYPL, New York Public Library; NYSHA, New York State Historical Association, Cooperstown; SI, Smithsonian Institution; UPI, United Press International; WW, Wide World; Yale, Yale University Art Gallery

Key to position of illustrations:
b, bottom; *t,* top; *l,* left; *r,* right; *c,* center.

Page v NG; **vi** Henry Ford Museum, Greenfield Village, Dearborn, Michigan; **viii** NYSHA; **xi** Yale; **xii** The Granger Collection; **xiii** American-Jewish Historical Society; **xvii** U.S. Capitol Historical Society; **xviii** National Portrait Gallery

(continued on page 789)

CONTENTS

📖 **Voices and Visions**

📖 **Voices and Visions**

📖 **Voices and Visions**

UNIT 5 AN EXPANDING NATION 400

UNIT 6 — THE NATION TORN APART 512

VOICES AND VISIONS

First Person

Literature

◆ OF SPECIAL INTEREST ◆

Up Close

An American Portrait

Americans All

Eyewitness

Linking Past and Present

Geographic Connection

Life in America

Historical Re-creations

◆ SKILL LESSONS ◆

Map, Graph, and Chart Skills

Critical Thinking Skills

Research Skills

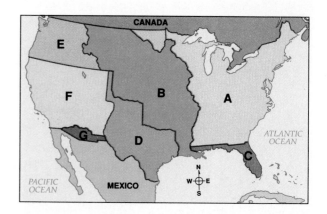

Recognizing Points of View

History Writer's Workshop

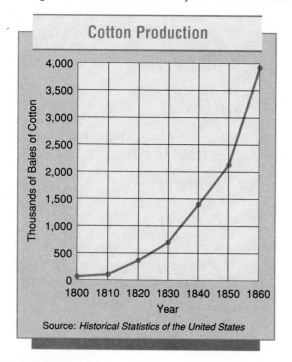

◆ MAPS ◆

Historical Atlas

Geographic Atlas

CHARTS, GRAPHS, AND TIME LINES

Causes and Effects

Historical Atlas

1820	1848	1850	1852	1854	1856	1858	1860

1820
Missouri
Compromise

1850
Compromise
of 1850

1852
Uncle Tom's
Cabin
published

1854
Kansas-
Nebraska Act

1858
Lincoln-
Douglas
debates

1861
Confederacy
founded;
fall of
Fort Sumter

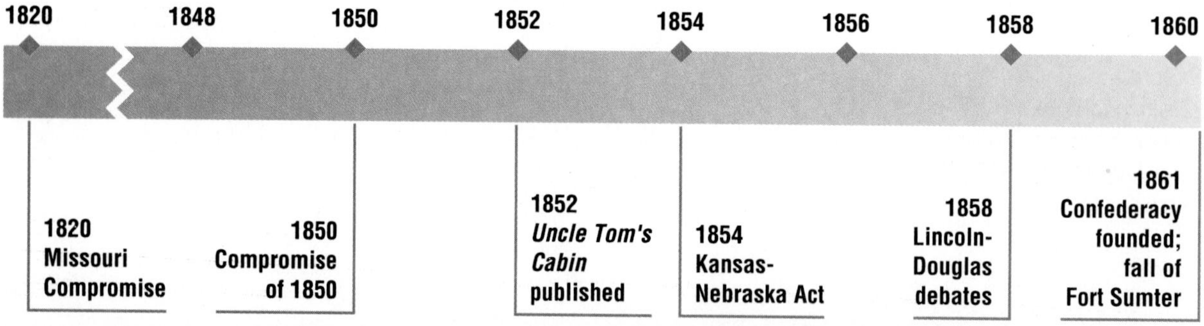

A LETTER FROM THE AUTHORS

Why Study History?

You are beginning a book about American history. It is hundreds of pages long and contains countless names, dates, and places. Why do you need to know about events that happened long before you were born? Why do you need to think about people you will never meet, streets you will never walk, times and places you can never visit?

History and You

You may think that you can do without history—until you stop and think how lost you would be without it. What if you woke up tomorrow morning having lost all your memory? Not knowing who you are? Not being able to remember the names of your parents or where you grew up? Not recalling what you have always believed most deeply?

All your memories are history. Your history. Without those memories, you would have no identity. Without them, your life would lack meaning.

Try an experiment. Walk down the halls of your school and listen to the conversations around you. How many people are telling histories? They might not necessarily be talking about George Washington or the Civil War. Chances are, however, they will be telling a "history" of something that has happened to them. The conversation might begin, "And then *he* said. . . ." Or, "And then I told *him*. . . ." And so on and so on. If you listen carefully, you will find that people are constantly telling stories about themselves. They are giving a personal history about who they are. And the more experiences they have, the more interesting they are to talk to.

Looking to the Past

What if you could actually sit in some whirring, darkened time machine, pull a few levers, and disappear into the past? How would it feel to visit the small lodgings in Philadelphia where Thomas Jefferson sits writing the Declaration of Independence? Or to join a pioneer family heading west with a wagon train along the Oregon Trail? What would it be like to huddle with American and Tejano volunteers inside the Alamo during the Texan war for independence, waiting for General Santa Anna's army to attack? What thoughts would you have if you could sit in a hushed hall, listening to the fiery words of former slave Frederick Douglass as he talks about ending the terrible evil of slavery—now!

Discovering Facts and Heroes

As yet, no one has invented a time machine. But you can travel back to the past, because Americans of the past have left behind records, diaries, and letters. Like the people you may overhear in the school halls, they have been eager to tell their own stories.

Some stories are worth hearing simply because they are interesting. How big were the lobsters that the early New England fishing people hauled into their boats? Three feet long? Four feet long? Five? You will find the answer on page 153. Why did French secret agents try to bribe the United States government in 1797? How did Americans respond to this "XYZ Affair"? You will find out on page 326. Why did bakers leave their bread in their ovens, and teachers and students leave their schools to rush to California in 1849? There is an explanation on page 449.

Other stories tell of the noble deeds of men and women. Thomas Jefferson, for example, risked his life when he wrote the Declaration of Independence. So too did John Hancock when he signed it. And thousands of ordinary Americans could have been hanged for joining the Continental Army during the Revolution. All played a part in winning freedoms not only for themselves but also for future generations, including yours.

In fact, Americans of all sorts have played a part in your history: A man named Benjamin Franklin, curious about lightning. Clergymen such as Moses Brown and Moses Seixas, leading the struggle to add the Bill of Rights to the Constitution. A Shoshone woman, Sacajawea, using her skills and knowledge to guide the Lewis and Clark expedition as it explored the

West. An escaped slave, Harriet Tubman, risking her life to lead other slaves to freedom.

Looking to the Future

One hundred years from now, you and your friends will be a part of the nation's history. A new generation of Americans will begin their lives. Somewhere, another class of students will open their history books. "Why study history?" they will ask. What will you tell them? What stories will you pass on? In the end, this history of America is your history, too.

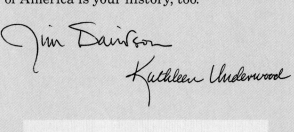

James West Davidson

James West Davidson has written many books and papers on American history. Among the works he has coauthored are *After the Fact: The Art of Historical Detection, The United States: A History of the Republic,* and *Nation of Nations.* He also has studied and written books and articles on religion in the colonial period. A former teacher at both the college and high school levels, Dr. Davidson has consulted on curriculum design for American history courses. In his spare time, Dr. Davidson is an avid canoeist and hiker. His works about canoeing include *One River Down,* a documentary film of a canoe trip in Labrador, and *Great Heart,* a true story of a 1903 canoe trip.

Kathleen Underwood

Kathleen Underwood is an Associate Professor of History at the University of Texas at Arlington. The recipient of a Spencer Fellowship from the National Academy of Education, Dr. Underwood is currently studying women teachers on the American frontier. Author of *Town Building on the Colorado Frontier,* Dr. Underwood recently coedited *Essays on Sunbelt Cities and Recent Urban America.* She is an active lecturer, panelist, and book reviewer. Her research interests include the American West, women's history, family history, and American social history.

American Journey: The Quest for Liberty to 1877 is organized into 6 units and 21 chapters. The Table of Contents lists the titles of the units and chapters. It also lists special features, skill lessons, and maps, charts, graphs, and time lines in the text. Finally, the Table of Contents provides a guide to the selected readings that form the Voices and Visions section, as well as to the Reference Section at the back of the book.

In Each Unit

Unit Opener Each unit opens with a colorful map and related pictures that illustrate major themes of the unit. Picture captions explain the connections between the map and the pictures. In addition, a time line presents major events and dates in American and world history covered in the unit. A multi-colored band in the time line shows the Presidents of the period.

Gazette An illustrated two-page Gazette offers fascinating but little-known stories and facts about people, places, and events of the period.

Unit Summary and Unit Review The Unit Summary and Unit Review help you to review and apply what you have learned. In addition, they feature:

◆ *Cause and Effect Chart* An easy-to-read chart traces the causes and effects of a major event in the unit.

◆ *Doing More* Suggestions for creative projects include many interesting ideas for exploring local history.

◆ *Recognizing Points of View* A guided reading of excerpts allows you to examine two opposing points of view about a major event or theme in American history.

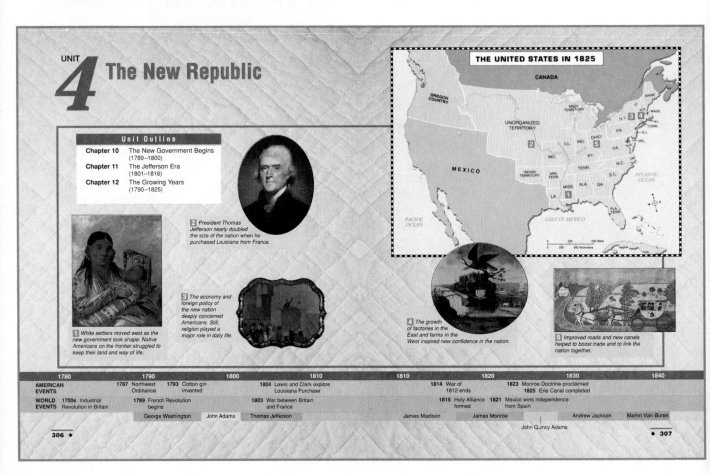

UNIT

4 The New Republic

THE UNITED STATES IN 1825

Unit Outline

Chapter 10 The New Government Begins (1789–1800)

Chapter 11 The Jefferson Era (1801–1816)

Chapter 12 The Growing Years (1790–1825)

2 President Thomas Jefferson nearly doubled the size of the nation when he purchased Louisiana from France.

3 The economy and foreign policy of the new nation deeply concerned Americans. Still, religion played a major role in daily life.

1 White settlers moved west as the new government took shape. Native Americans on the frontier struggled to keep their land and way of life.

4 The growth of factories in the East and farms in the West inspired new confidence in the nation.

5 Improved roads and new canals helped to boost trade and to link the nation together.

1780	1790	1800	1810	1810	1820	1830	1840
AMERICAN EVENTS	1787 Northwest Ordinance	1793 Cotton gin invented	1804 Lewis and Clark explore Louisiana Purchase		1814 War of 1812 ends	1823 Monroe Doctrine proclaimed 1825 Erie Canal completed	
WORLD EVENTS 1700s Industrial Revolution in Britain	1789 French Revolution begins		1803 War between Britain and France		1815 Holy Alliance formed 1821 Mexico wins independence from Spain		

George Washington | John Adams | Thomas Jefferson | James Madison | James Monroe | Andrew Jackson | Martin Van Buren

John Quincy Adams

306 ◆

◆ 307

In Each Chapter

Chapter Opener   A Chapter Spotlight helps to prepare you for reading the chapter. It includes The Big Picture, in which one of the authors offers insights into the chapter's major themes. A primary source sets the mood for the material that follows in the chapter.

To Help You Learn   Several features help you to read and understand the chapter:

 * *Find Out*   Questions at the beginning of each section guide your reading.
 * *Important Terms*   Vocabulary words are printed in blue type and clearly defined the first time they are used. Important historical terms are printed in **dark type.** These terms also appear in a Glossary at the back of the book.
 * *Section Reviews*   Questions test your understanding of what you have read and sharpen your critical thinking skills.
 * *Study Guide*   A summary of the main ideas of the chapter provides a guide for study and helps to prepare you for testing. A time line shows events covered in the chapter.

Of Special Interest   Three special features appear in each chapter. There are several kinds of special features throughout the book:

 * *Up Close*   provides an in-depth look at an interesting person or event in American history.
 * *An American Portrait*   is a short biography of an individual who is important to the period being studied.
 * *Americans All*   describes how Americans from a variety of backgrounds came together to shape a historical event or trend.
 * *Eyewitness*   presents a first-person account of an important historical event.
 * *Geographic Connection*   studies the ways in which land and climate have shaped American history.
 * *Life in America*   offers an account of daily life among a wide variety of Americans.

 * *Linking Past and Present*   explores the connection between events and places in the past and in the present.

Skill Lesson   A step-by-step skill lesson in each chapter helps you to understand and practice important skills.

Illustrations   Pictures and other graphics help you to understand major events:

 * *Pictures*   Works of fine art, photographs, cartoons and posters, and historical re-creations bring history to life. Picture captions include a question that encourages you to explore major themes of American history.
 * *Maps, Graphs, and Charts*   Maps, charts, and graphs help you to understand major historical developments and events. Captions provide important background information and also include questions to sharpen your map, graph, and chart skills.

Chapter Review   The Chapter Review helps you to review vocabulary and main ideas and to strengthen geography and critical thinking skills. The Chapter Review also includes the following feature of special interest:

 * *History Writer's Workshop*   This workshop helps you to develop writing and research skills needed for studying history.

Voices and Visions

This section at the back of the book offers excerpts from literature and first-person accounts that are keyed to the material in each chapter. The varied backgrounds of the authors make the excerpts appealing.

Reference Section

At the back of the book, you will find a section of reference materials for use throughout the course. It includes a Historical Atlas and a Geographic Atlas, charts with information about the 50 states and the Presidents, a Gazetteer of important places, a Chronology of American History, a Glossary, the Declaration of Independence, the Constitution of the United States, and an Index.

UNIT 1

The Americas

Unit Outline

Chapter 1 Geography of the Americas
(Prehistory–Present)

Chapter 2 The First Americans
(Prehistory–1600)

Chapter 3 European Exploration
(1000–1650)

ASIA

CHINA

EAST INDIES

AUSTRALIA

2 *Peoples of North America developed different ways of life. One group, the Micmacs, used porcupine quills and moosehair to make baskets and other items.*

1 *Powerful empires rose in Central and South America. Treasures of the Inca empire included golden sculptures of sacred animals.*

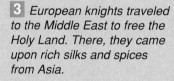

3 *European knights traveled to the Middle East to free the Holy Land. There, they came upon rich silks and spices from Asia.*

Prehistory		1400	1450	1500
AMERICAN EVENTS	**5,000 Years Ago** Farming begins	**1300s** Aztecs move into Valley of Mexico		**1492** Columbus reaches Americas
WORLD EVENTS		**1095** Crusades begin **Late 1300s** Renaissance begins		

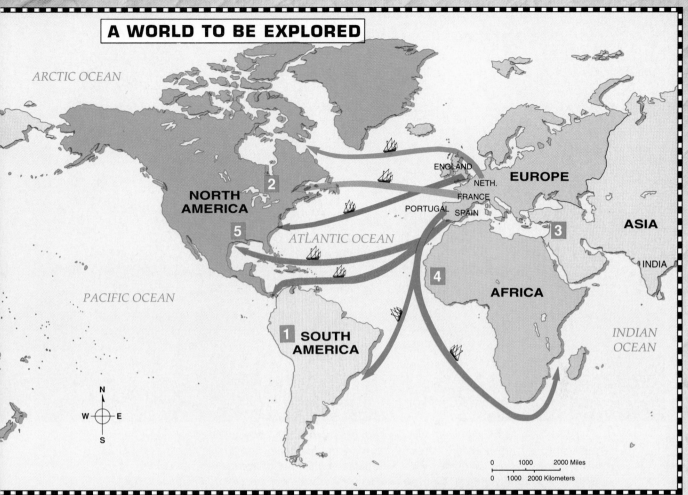

A WORLD TO BE EXPLORED

ARCTIC OCEAN

NORTH AMERICA

EUROPE

ENGLAND
NETH.
FRANCE
PORTUGAL   SPAIN

ASIA

INDIA

ATLANTIC OCEAN

PACIFIC OCEAN

AFRICA

SOUTH AMERICA

INDIAN OCEAN

1 2 3 4 5

N
W—E
S

0   1000   2000 Miles
0   1000   2000 Kilometers

4 Portugal explored the coast of Africa for a route to Asia. Traders soon brought back prized African sculpture—and slaves—to Portugal.

5 Explorers for Spain, England, and the Netherlands sailed west and reached the "new world" of the Americas. Hernando De Soto was the first European to see the Mississippi River.

1500	1550	1600	1650

1520 Magellan rounds South America

1500s League of Iroquois formed

1600s Search for northwest passage continues

1517 Protestant Reformation begins in Europe

1588 Spanish Armada defeated

The Sierra Nevada *Thousands of years ago, moving glaciers and rushing streams cut deep canyons in the granite mountains known as the Sierra Nevada. In this painting, Albert Bierstadt, an artist of the 1800s, captures the grandeur of this majestic mountain range of the American West.* **Economics** *How is the beauty of the Sierra Nevada an important economic resource? How might this endanger the beauty of the mountains?*

Geography of the Americas (Prehistory–Present)

Chapter Outline

1 Geography and History
2 Tools of Geography
3 Thinking Geographically
4 Landforms and Regions of the Americas
5 Climates of the Americas

C HAPTER SPOTLIGHT

The Big Picture

When Europeans first reached the Americas, geography was a major concern. Where? How far? How long? How high? they constantly asked. As settlers moved across the land, they, too, asked questions about geography. Soil, animals, trees, rivers, and climate all would affect where and how they lived.

Learning the geography of the Americas would be a slow process over hundreds of years. Today, as satellites in space take pictures of the Earth, Americans continue to learn about their land.

Jim Davidson

Of Special Interest

Focus On

◆ What themes help geographers study the Earth and its people?

◆ Why do we need different kinds of maps to study the Earth?

◆ Why are latitude and longitude useful?

◆ What landforms are found in the different regions of North America?

◆ How do climates differ across North America?

A s the summer sun scorched the desert, the Papago people of the American Southwest looked to the hills and sang of rain. Their songs, they felt sure, would bring life-giving moisture to the corn they had planted in the desert soil.

❝Clouds are standing in the east, they are approaching,
It rains in the distance,
Now it is raining here and the thunder rolls.

Green rock mountains are thundering with clouds.
With this thunder the Akim village is shaking.
The water will come down the [stream] and I will float on the water.
Afterwards the corn will ripen in the fields.❞

Throughout the Americas, other Native Americans adapted to other kinds of lands and climates. Some lived in deep valleys or on grassy plains. Others learned to survive in steaming jungles or ice-covered regions. As their songs and stories reveal, most respected the natural world around them.

These Native American groups were the first Americans. Later, people from Europe, Africa, and Asia reached North America and South America. They, too, adapted to the many landscapes and climates of the American land.

1 Geography and History

FIND OUT

◆ How did people first reach the Americas?

◆ How do geographers help historians understand the past?

◆ What are the five themes of geography?

◆ **VOCABULARY** geography, glacier, history, latitude, longitude, irrigate

If you read almost any newspaper today, you will find stories about the land around you. One story might point out that building a dam will be harmful to a river. Another might discuss the discovery of oil. Still another might tell of a revolution in a far-off country. To understand these and other issues, we need geographic knowledge.

Geography is the study of people, their environments, and their resources. Geographers ask not only where things are but why they are there. They ask how the natural environment affects the way we live and how we, in turn, affect the environment. By showing how people and the land are related, geography helps to explain both the past and the present.

The Last Ice Age

If you had flown over North America 15,000 years ago, you would have seen great masses of ice covering much of the continent. These thick sheets of ice, called glaciers, spread out from the arctic regions. According to scientists, the Earth has gone through four ice ages. The last one took place between 100,000 and 10,000 years ago.

During the last ice age, almost one third of the Earth was buried under glaciers. In North America, glaciers stretched across Canada and as far south as Kentucky.

Glaciers changed the lands they covered. They pushed soil, rocks, and huge boulders across the land. They created islands such as Long Island, New York, as well as Nantucket and Martha's Vineyard, off the coast of Massachusetts. Water from melting glaciers drained into channels, cre-

Cape Cod *Glaciers moving across the northern United States during the last ice age created new land masses. One of these is Cape Cod, a large hook-shaped peninsula that juts out into the Atlantic Ocean from the Massachusetts coast.*
Geography *Do you think that Cape Cod is still changing today? Explain.*

ating large rivers such as the Ohio and the Missouri.

The land bridge. Glaciers locked up water from the oceans, causing sea levels to drop. As a result, land appeared that had once been covered by water. Scientists think that during the last ice age, a land bridge was exposed between Siberia in Asia and Alaska in North America. Today, this land is under the Bering Sea.

According to scientists, the first people to reach the Americas arrived during the last ice age. These first Americans crossed the land bridge on foot or skirted its southern coast by boat. We do not know exactly when they first arrived in North America. They may have come as early as 70,000 years ago.

The first Americans may have been hunters who followed herds of wild animals such as woolly mammoths. Or they may have lived off fish they caught along the coast. Over thousands of years, they moved across North America into South America. They developed different ways of life. These differences were due in part to the geography of the Americas.

Temperatures get warmer. About 10,000 years ago, temperatures rose. Glaciers melted and flooded the land bridge between Siberia and Alaska. About the same time, the woolly mammoths and mastodons died out. The peoples of the Americas adapted to the new conditions. They hunted smaller game, gathered berries and grains, and caught fish.

About 5,000 years ago, some people learned to grow crops such as corn, beans, and squash. Farming changed people's lives. People who farmed no longer had to travel constantly in search of food. They built the first permanent villages in the Americas.

Themes of Geography

The ancient hunters who crossed into North America began the story of human life in the Americas. Since then, millions of people have migrated to North America and South America from around the world.

Why did people come to the Americas? How did they get here? What happened to them once they got here? How did they help make the Americas what they are today? Those are some of the questions that we ask historians. History is an account of what has happened in the development of a people, a nation, or a civilization.

History is closely linked to geography. Geography has two main branches: physical geography and human geography. Physical geography involves the study of natural features, climate, plants, animals, and resources. Human geography includes the study of ways that people use, depend on, and change their physical environment.

Both historians and geographers want to understand how the characteristics of a place affect people and events. They both ask the question, Why did this happen in this place?

To understand the link between the Earth and its people, geographers have developed five themes, or topics. The themes are location, place, interaction between people and their environment, movement, and region.

Location

Where did it happen? Both historians and geographers ask this question about an event. Finding out where something happened involves location.

Exact location. As you study American history, you will sometimes need to know the absolute, or exact, location of a place. For example, where exactly is Washington, D.C., our nation's capital?

To describe the exact location of Washington, D.C., geographers use a grid of numbered lines on a map or globe that measure latitude and longitude. Lines of latitude on a map or globe measure distance north and south from the Equator. Lines of longitude measure distance east and west from the Prime Meridian, which runs through Greenwich (GREHN ihch), England. (You will read more about latitude and longitude later in this chapter. See page 12.)

The exact location of Washington, D.C., is 39 degrees (°) north latitude and 77 degrees (°) west longitude. This location is shortened to 39°N/77°W. The Gazetteer on pages 723–729 of this book provides the exact location of other important places in American history. In each case, the latitude and longitude are given in their shortened form.

Relative location. Sometimes, you might find it more useful to know relative location, or where a place is located in relation to some other place. Is Washington, D.C., on the east or west coast of the United States? Is it north or south of Richmond, Virginia? Why was it chosen as our nation's capital? All these questions involve relative location.

Relative location includes knowing how places are connected to one another. Is a place located near a lake, river, or other water and transportation source? Is it a farming or industrial area? Answers to these kinds of questions help you see why cities grew where they did. Chicago, Illinois, for example, developed at the center of water, road, and railroad transportation in the Midwest.

Place

A second theme that geographers study is place. Geographers generally describe a place in terms of both physical and human characteristics.

Physical characteristics. The physical characteristics of a place include climate, soil, plant life, animal life, and bodies of water. For example, look at Jamestown, Virginia, in the 1600s.

When English settlers planted a colony in Jamestown, they found a mild climate and plenty of wild game to hunt. But the coastal swamplands were home to insects that brought disease and death to many colonists. In time, the colonists drained the swamps and planted crops such as tobacco.

Human characteristics. People help to shape the character of a place through their ideas and actions. The human characteristics of a place include the kinds of houses people build as well as their means of transportation, ways of earning a living, languages, and religion.

Think of the human characteristics of the American frontier. In the forests of the frontier, early settlers built log cabins. They traveled west in covered wagons. On the grassy plains, some settlers built their first homes out of sod.

"Apartment Houses" in Taos Pueblo *A place sometimes has a distinct style of homes. Taos Pueblo in New Mexico was built several hundred years ago. Native Americans still live in its apartment-like structures made of adobe, or sun-dried brick.* **Daily Life** *What do these houses tell you about the way of life of the people who lived in them?*

Interaction Between People and Their Environment

A third theme of geography is interaction between people and their environment. Throughout history, people have adapted to and altered different environments.

For example, some ancient hunters learned to grow food crops in the Americas. Later, Native Americans in the Southwest found ways to irrigate, or bring water to, the desert so that they could farm the land. In the 1850s, workers blasted through mountains and built bridges across rivers for railroads that linked the Atlantic and Pacific coasts.

Today, advanced technology allows people to alter their environment dramatically. People have invented ways to take oil from the ocean floor. They have cut down thick forests to build highways. They have wiped out pests that destroy food crops. Such changes have brought enormous benefits. But they have created new problems such as air and water pollution.

Movement

A fourth geographic theme involves the movement of people, goods, and ideas. Movement occurs because people and resources are scattered unevenly around the globe. To get what they need or want, people travel from place to place. As they meet with other people, they exchange goods as well as ideas and technology.

History provides many examples of the movement of people and ideas. The ancient hunters you read about followed animal herds across the land bridge into North America. Much later, millions of people migrated to the United States in search of political and religious freedom. These immigrants brought with them customs and beliefs that have helped shape American life.

Today, the movement of goods links the United States with all parts of the globe. We ship goods such as grain and computers to Europe and Africa, for example. In exchange, we rely on materials such as oil from other parts of the world.

Movement of People and Goods *The Golden Gate Bridge in California, shown at left, allows people and goods to cross San Francisco Bay. Below, cars from Korea arrive in an American port.* **Local History** *How have people in your state changed the land to improve transportation?*

Celebration in "Little Italy" *A region can be as small as a neighborhood. An example is New York City's "Little Italy." This area of about 20 blocks was home for many Italian immigrants in the early 1900s. Today, people of all backgrounds flock to Little Italy each year for the Feast of San Gennaro, shown here.* **Multicultural Heritage** *How do people celebrate their ethnic background in your area?*

Region

Geographers study regions. A region is an area of the world that has similar, unifying characteristics. The characteristics of a region may be physical, such as its climate or landforms. For example, the Great Plains is a region because it has fairly level land, very hot summers, very cold winters, and little rainfall.

A region's characteristics may also be human and cultural. San Francisco's Chinatown is a region because Chinese Americans there have preserved their language and culture.

As you can see, a region can be any size. It can be as large as the United States or as small as a neighborhood within a city.

SECTION 1 REVIEW

1. **Define:** (a) geography, (b) glacier, (c) history, (d) latitude, (e) longitude, (f) irrigate.
2. How did the last ice age affect the arrival of the first Americans?
3. Why is geography important to the study of history?
4. Describe briefly each of the five themes of geography.
5. (a) Name two benefits of interaction between people and their environment. (b) Name two problems that can result when people make major changes in their natural environment.
6. **Synthesizing Information** Why do you think understanding movement is important to the study of history?

2 Tools of Geography

FIND OUT

◆ How have maps become more accurate?

◆ What advantages do flat maps have over globes?

◆ What are three kinds of map projections?

◆ **VOCABULARY** cartographer, map projection

"I can see the whole state of Florida, just laid out like on a map," exclaimed astronaut John Glenn in 1962. Glenn recognized the shape of Florida from maps. But for the first time, he was looking at Florida from hundreds of miles above as he headed back to Earth from a voyage in space.

Today, space satellites help us create maps. They provide valuable information about the Earth and its resources.

Geographers and Cartographers

Since ancient times, people have wondered about the size and shape of the Earth. Early geographers used information from sailors, travelers, and legends to create maps of the world.

Early maps included many errors along with accurate information. Five hundred years ago, cartographers, or mapmakers, in Europe did not even know that North America and South America existed. They did not know the shape of Africa or Asia or the size of the world's oceans.

Since 1500, mapmaking has improved a great deal. Daring sailors such as Christopher Columbus brought Europeans information about newly discovered lands. Explorers studied ocean currents and wind patterns around the world. Scientists learned more about the Earth itself. With more information available, cartographers created more accurate maps.

Globes and Maps

To locate places, geographers use maps and globes. A map is a drawing of the Earth's surface. A globe is a sphere with a map of the Earth's landmasses and bodies of water pasted or printed on it. Because a globe

AN·AMERICAN·PORTRAIT

Gouverneur Kemble Warren: Mapmaker of the American West

What lay in the Great Unknown, the lands west of the Mississippi River? By 1850, railroad builders eager to link the east and west coasts wanted to know. So, too, did land-hungry settlers and the United States Army.

In 1850, Gouverneur Kemble Warren graduated from West Point after studying engineering. The young man soon received his orders: Develop an accurate map of the American West.

Warren faced a difficult task. For months, he pored over reports and sketchy maps. Often, one map or report contradicted another. Which information was correct? A report based on an Indian legend? Accounts of adventurers? A surveyor's drawings? To find answers, Warren went west to explore the Dakota country and the land along the Yellowstone and Powder rivers. He carefully recorded his findings.

Finally, in 1859, Warren published his map. At last, Americans had an accurate picture of the West—its landforms, lakes, and rivers, the locations of Indian villages and army forts, and the routes of wagon trails to the West. Thanks to the work of this young army engineer, the nation's huge interior was no longer the Great Unknown.

1. What Americans wanted to know about the Great Unknown?

2. **Evaluating Information** What skills and personal qualities do you think Warren needed to succeed in his project?

is the same shape as the Earth, it shows sizes and shapes accurately.

Even though a globe has this advantage, geographers often use flat maps rather than globes. Unlike a globe, a flat map allows you to see the Earth's surface at one time. It also can show more detail about a place. And it is easier to handle. Still, a flat map has the disadvantage that it distorts, or misrepresents, some part of the Earth.

Map Projections

Cartographers have developed dozens of map projections, or ways of drawing the Earth on a flat surface. Three map projections are shown on page 11.

Any given map projection has benefits and disadvantages. Some projections show the sizes of landmasses correctly but distort their shapes. Others give continents their true shapes but distort their sizes. Still other projections distort direction or distances.

Interrupted projection. A mapmaker who wants to show the correct sizes and shapes of landmasses might use the interrupted projection. But this projection cannot be used to measure distances across the oceans because of the cuts in the oceans.

Mercator projection. In 1569, Gerardus Mercator developed the Mercator projection, the best map in its day. For hundreds of years, sailors used the Mercator map. Mercator himself had boasted of his map:

> ❝If you wish to sail from one port to another, here is a chart, and a straight line on it, and if you follow this line carefully you will certainly arrive at your destination.❞

A Mercator map shows the true shapes of landmasses, but it distorts their relative sizes. On a Mercator map, for example, Greenland appears much larger than it is.

Robinson projection. Today, many geographers use the Robinson projection. It

MAP STUDY

Map projections make it possible for mapmakers to show a round world on a flat map.
1. *Which projections would you use to measure the distance across the Atlantic Ocean?*
2. *Which projections would you use to compare the size of North America and Europe?*
3. **Comparing** *Compare the landmasses on the Mercator and Robinson projections. (a) How are they similar? (b) How are they different?*

shows the correct sizes and shapes of landmasses for most parts of the world. This projection also gives a fairly accurate view of the relationship between landmasses and water. (About 71 percent of the Earth's surface is water.)

Kinds of Maps

Maps are part of our everyday lives. You have probably read road or bus maps. You may have drawn treasure maps. On the television news, you see weather maps.

As you study American history, you will use many other kinds of maps. Turn now to the Geographic Atlas on pages 714–721 in the reference section of this book. There, you will find five different kinds of very useful maps: political, physical, population, economic, and natural resource.

Each kind of map serves a specific purpose. A political map shows boundaries that people have set up to divide the world into countries and states. A physical map shows the natural features of the landscape, such as mountains, rivers, and islands. A population map lets you see how closely together people live in urban and rural areas. An economic map is useful because it shows how people make a living in a given area. A natural resource map helps you understand the links between the resources of an area and the way people use the land.

MAP PROJECTIONS

Interrupted Projection

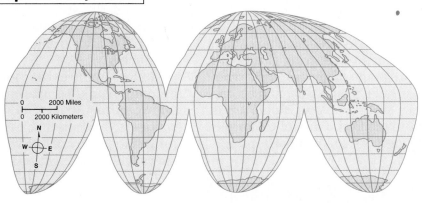

Mercator Projection

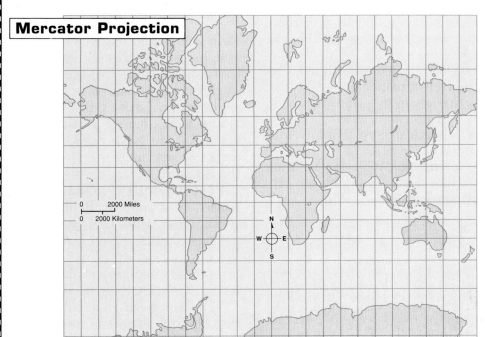

Robinson Projection

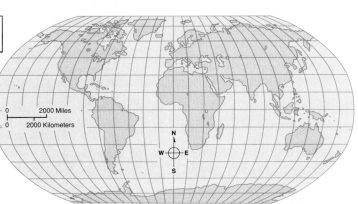

Still other kinds of maps you will use this year include climate maps, battle maps, and railroad maps. These maps also let you see the links between geography and history.

A Common Language

Like other scientists, geographers have their own language to describe the Earth. You use the language of geographers when you talk about hills, mountains, and oceans. For definitions of common geographic terms, you can refer to the Dictionary of Geographic Terms on pages 28–29 of this chapter.

SECTION 2 REVIEW

1. **Define:** (a) cartographer, (b) map projection.
2. Describe two ways that maps have become more accurate.
3. Why does a globe show the Earth more accurately than a flat map?
4. What are the advantage and disadvantage of the Mercator projection?
5. How does a political map differ from a physical map?
6. **Evaluating Information** Why do you think many historians prefer the Robinson projection for maps?

---

3 Thinking Geographically

FIND OUT

◆ How do latitude and longitude help us locate places on a map?

◆ Why is the world divided into time zones?

◆ **VOCABULARY** hemisphere, standard time zone, international date line

As the ship sails toward Puerto Rico, the captain listens carefully to radio reports of a hurricane forming in the Caribbean Sea. The voice on the radio announces that the center of the hurricane is currently located at 15°N/61°W.

The captain studies the charts and realizes that the storm is just north of Martinique. He then plots his own position at 25°N/75°W and decides to find a safe harbor quickly.

Sailors and weather forecasters are not the only people to use latitude and longitude to pinpoint locations. Miners, pilots, engineers, and other experts also have to think like geographers when they want to determine exact locations of places.

Using Latitude and Longitude

Both globes and maps use lines of latitude and longitude. The lines form a grid so that you are able to locate places exactly. Each line is measured in degrees (°).

Latitude. Look at the map on page 13. Notice that lines of latitude run east and west. As you have read, lines of latitude measure distances north and south from the Equator.

The **Equator** is an imaginary line that lies at 0° latitude. It divides the earth into two halves, called hemispheres.

The Northern Hemisphere lies north of the Equator. In the Northern Hemisphere, lines of latitude are numbered from 1°N to 90°N, where the North Pole is located.

The Southern Hemisphere lies south of the Equator. There, lines of latitude are numbered from 1°S to 90°S, where the South Pole is located. On the map, what continent lies mostly between 30°N and 30°S?

Longitude. Lines of longitude on a map or globe run north and south. They measure distances east and west from the **Prime Meridian**, which lies at 0° longitude.

Lines of longitude are numbered from 1° to 179° east or west longitude. The line of longitude at 180° lies directly opposite the Prime Meridian.

The circle formed by the Prime Meridian and 180° divides the Earth into the Eastern and Western hemispheres. The Eastern Hemisphere includes most of Europe, Africa, and Asia. The Western Hemisphere includes North America and South America. On the map below, through what continent or continents does 90°W run?

Locating. To locate places, you need to combine latitude and longitude. Look at the map below. The city of Chicago is located north of the Equator at about 42°N latitude. It lies west of the Prime Meridian at about 88°W longitude. In shortened form, its location is 42°N/88°W. Use the map on pages 716–717 to find the exact location of the capital of your state.

Time Zones

Lines of longitude are used to help travelers and business people determine what time it is in different parts of the world. Why does time differ from place to place?

The answer is that the Earth rotates on its axis. As the Earth moves, some places are turning toward the sun while others are turning away from the sun. Any given place on the Earth has a different time from places east or west of it. For example, Chicago, Illinois, has a different time from that of Denver, Colorado.

What time is it? "What time is it where you are?" someone in Houston might ask a friend telephoning from Los Angeles. To

MAP STUDY

Geographers use imaginary lines of latitude and longitude to locate places.
1. *What is the exact location of Beijing?*
2. *What city is located at about 55°N/35°E?*
3. **Applying Information** *Which continents are in both the Eastern and Western hemispheres?*

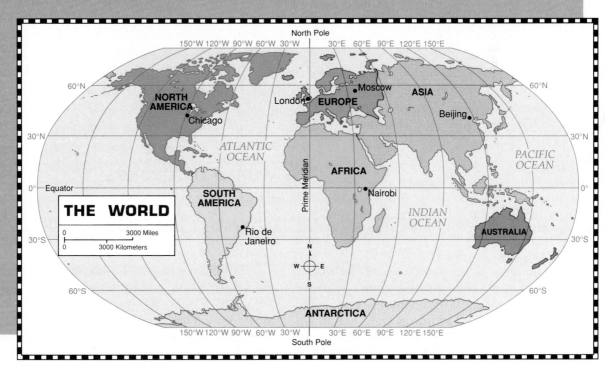

A system of 24 standard time zones allows business people and travelers to determine the time in different parts of the world. Airports, stock exchanges, and newspaper offices often have a series of clocks, like those at top, that show the time in major cities.

1. If it is 7:00 A.M. in Washington, D.C., what time is it in Cairo?
2. Where is it earlier: Beijing or Moscow?
3. **Drawing Conclusions** Why do you think that the boundaries of time zones are jagged lines?

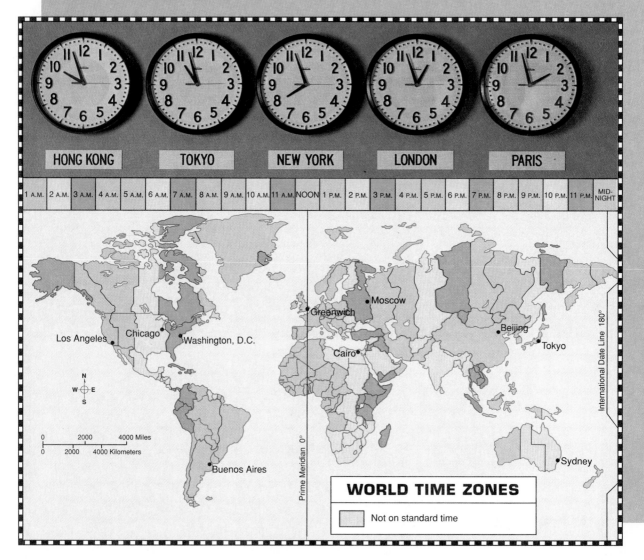

HONG KONG   TOKYO   NEW YORK   LONDON   PARIS

1 A.M. | 2 A.M. | 3 A.M. | 4 A.M. | 5 A.M. | 6 A.M. | 7 A.M. | 8 A.M. | 9 A.M. | 10 A.M. | 11 A.M. | NOON | 1 P.M. | 2 P.M. | 3 P.M. | 4 P.M. | 5 P.M. | 6 P.M. | 7 P.M. | 8 P.M. | 9 P.M. | 10 P.M. | 11 P.M. | MID-NIGHT

WORLD TIME ZONES

Not on standard time

make it easier to tell time around the world, a system of **standard time zones** was set up in 1884. Under this system, the world was divided into 24 time zones. Standard time is measured from the Prime Meridian, which runs through Greenwich, England.

Find Greenwich, England, on the map of world time zones above. Notice that when it is noon in Greenwich, places west of Greenwich have times before noon (A.M.) because they are turning toward the sun. Places east of Greenwich have times after noon (P.M.) because they are turning away from the sun.

International date line. If you travel east from Greenwich across Europe, Africa, or Asia, you add one hour as you move through each time zone. If you travel west from Greenwich across the Atlantic Ocean and North America, you subtract one hour as you move through each time zone.

If you travel halfway around the world from the Prime Meridian, you reach the international date line, which falls at 180° in the Pacific Ocean. At the international date line, you either gain a day or lose a day depending on the direction in which you are traveling.

Notice that the international date line does not follow a straight line. It jogs slightly so that eastern Siberia has the same date as the rest of the Soviet Union.

Changing time. In arctic areas, people do not use standard time because the sun either shines for weeks at a time or the area is in darkness for long periods. Instead, people use Greenwich Mean Time, the official time in Greenwich, England.

In other areas, people have made changes so that time works for their benefit. Many states of the United States, for example, use Daylight Savings Time (DST) from April to October of every year. This system was set up in World War II so that people would use less electricity.

SECTION 3 REVIEW

1. **Locate:** (a) Equator, (b) Prime Meridian.
2. **Define:** (a) hemisphere, (b) standard time zone, (c) international date line.
3. What is the purpose of lines of latitude and longitude on maps and globes?
4. If you are traveling east and cross the international date line, do you gain or lose a day?
5. **Drawing Conclusions** Why do you think the system of standard time zones is necessary in today's world?

4 Landforms and Regions of the Americas

FIND OUT

◆ What landforms are found in North America and South America?

◆ What are the seven physical regions of North America?

◆ What major rivers and lakes are important to the United States?

◆ **VOCABULARY** isthmus, mountain, elevation, hill, plain, plateau, tributary

"America is so vast," observed the writer James Farrell, "that almost anything said about it is likely to be true, and the opposite is probably equally true." The Americas are truly a land of opposites. For example, one of the world's highest mountains, Mount Aconcagua, is in Argentina. Yet one of the lowest points on the Earth is in Death Valley, California. You will find many examples of contrast as you read more about the American land.

Locating the Americas

North America and South America are the world's third and fourth largest continents. These two continents plus the islands in the Caribbean Sea make up the **Western Hemisphere.**

As the map on pages 714–715 shows, the Atlantic Ocean washes the eastern shores of North America and South America. The Pacific Ocean laps at their western shores. Far to the north lies the ice-choked Arctic Ocean. Far to the south is the Strait of Magellan (muh JEHL uhn), a water passage between the Atlantic and Pacific oceans. Joining the continents of North America and South America is an isthmus (IHS muhs), or narrow strip of land. It is called the **Isthmus of Panama.**

Four Basic Landforms

North America and South America have many landforms, or natural features. There are high mountains, rolling hills, and long rivers. There are grassy plains, dense forests, and barren deserts. Within these different landscapes, there are four basic landforms: mountains, hills, plains, and plateaus (pla TOHZ).

Mountains are high, steep, rugged land. They rise to an **elevation,** or height, of at least 1,000 feet (300 m) above the surrounding land. Few people can live on the steep, rocky sides of high mountains. Yet people often settle in valleys that lie between mountains.

Hills are also areas of raised land, but they are lower, less steep, and more rounded than mountains. More people live in hilly areas than on mountains because farming is possible there.

Plains are broad areas of fairly level land. Very few plains are totally flat. Most are gently rolling. Plains are usually not much above sea level. People often settle on plains because it is easy to build farms, roads, and cities on the level land.

Plateaus are large raised areas of flat or gently rolling land. The height of plateaus may range from a few hundred to many thousand feet above sea level. Plateaus can be good for farming if they get enough rain. Some plateaus are surrounded by mountains. Such plateaus are called basins. Basins are often very dry because the mountains cut off rainfall.

Physical Regions of North America

The mountains, hills, plateaus, and plains of North America* form seven major physical regions. The United States also includes an eighth region, the Hawaiian Islands, which lie in the Pacific Ocean. (See the map on page 18.)

---

*North America includes Canada, the United States, Mexico, and the seven nations of Central America.

Today, most Americans have heard of these regions. They recognize names such as Great Plains, Rocky Mountains, and Pacific Coast. Thanks to modern photography and transportation, many also get the chance to see the beauty and contrast of the regions. For most Americans of the 1800s, however, these regions were a mystery. (⬜ See "This Land Is Your Land" on page 626.)

U P CLOSE

An Artist Crosses the United States

By the 1850s, the United States stretched from the Atlantic Ocean to the Pacific Ocean. Americans were excited and curious about the vast lands of their young nation. Many had read about the wide prairies, rugged mountain ranges, and leaping waterfalls in newspapers or in letters from travelers. But few had actually seen these wonders.

An American artist named Albert Bierstadt (BEER stat) decided to take a trip across the country, painting what he saw. In 1863, he set out with a writer, FitzHugh Ludlow. They traveled by train from New York City, westward past the Appalachian Mountains, through farm country to St. Louis. These areas were familiar to many Americans.

Scenes west of the Mississippi. Then Bierstadt and Ludlow crossed the Mississippi River and boarded a stagecoach in Atchison, Kansas. At first, the Interior Plains region seemed lifeless to the two easterners.

The travelers soon discovered, however, that even the short grasses of the plains were full of life. Prairie dogs chattered and poked their heads up. They had dug so many holes that the stagecoach horses had to step carefully, to avoid sinking into them. Buffalo grazed on the plains, too. Bierstadt eagerly began to paint scenes of the flat grasslands.

As the stagecoach moved across the plains, a thunderstorm overtook them. Ludlow had never seen one so mighty in the East:

    ❝The lightning got broader, and its flashes quicker in succession. The thunder surpassed everything I have ever heard, or read, or dreamed of. Between explosions we were so stunned that we could scarcely speak to or hear each other.❞

Continuing west, Bierstadt and Ludlow soon approached the Rocky Mountains. "Mountain billows westward after mountain," reported Ludlow excitedly. Their peaks seemed quite different from the gentler shapes of the Allegheny Mountains. Bierstadt's dramatic colors captured the steep summits that stretched upward into the clouds.

The two travelers stopped at Salt Lake City, in the dry basin country between the Rockies and the far western mountains. By 1863, Mormon settlements had turned many Utah valleys into a world of "living green—green grass, green grain-fields, green gardens." Taking a swim in the Great Salt Lake, Ludlow was amazed that its salty waters kept him afloat. He could drift along even in water that was only six inches deep.

On the west coast, Bierstadt was most impressed by the canyons and mountains of California. But he traveled north, too, and painted Oregon's Willamette River in bright fall colors. A steamboat took him up to the raging falls of the Columbia River in Washington.

Americans take pride. Bierstadt returned home with paintings of the many grand landscapes he had seen. Americans were delighted and lined up to view the paintings. Another painter of the day,

Seal Rock *Albert Bierstadt's landscapes record the beauty and grandeur of the vast United States. Seal Rock, which captures the dramatic rock formations in San Francisco harbor, is typical of his work.* **Culture** *Why would Bierstadt's paintings be useful to a historian?*

Thomas Cole, explained why an American would take interest:

"For whether he beholds the Hudson [River] mingling waters with the Atlantic—explores the central wilds of this vast continent, or stands on the margin of the distant Oregon, he is still in the midst of American scenery. It is still his own land; its beauty, its magnificence . . . are all his!" ◆

From West to East

The seven physical regions of North America offer great contrasts. In some regions, the land is fertile. There, American farmers plant crops and reap rich harvests. Other regions have natural resources such as coal and oil.

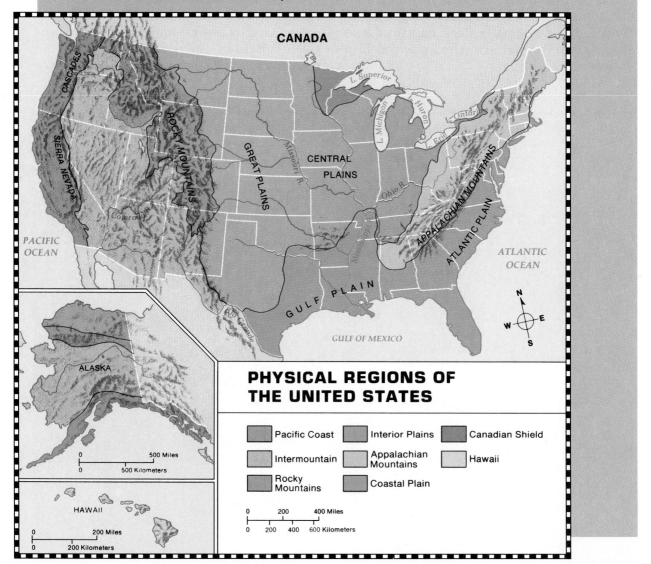

MAP STUDY

The United States can be divided into eight physical regions.
1. Which region is west of the Intermountain region?
2. Which physical region does the Missouri River flow through?
3. **Drawing Conclusions** Based on the map, would you describe the United States as a varied land? Explain.

CANADA

CASCADES
SIERRA NEVADA
ROCKY MOUNTAINS
GREAT PLAINS
Missouri R.
CENTRAL PLAINS
Colorado
Ohio R.
APPALACHIAN MOUNTAINS
ATLANTIC PLAIN
GULF PLAIN
Rio Grande
L. Superior
L. Michigan
Huron
Erie
Ontario

PACIFIC OCEAN

ATLANTIC OCEAN

GULF OF MEXICO

ALASKA

0   500 Miles
0   500 Kilometers

HAWAII

0   200 Miles
0   200 Kilometers

PHYSICAL REGIONS OF THE UNITED STATES

- Pacific Coast
- Intermountain
- Rocky Mountains
- Interior Plains
- Appalachian Mountains
- Coastal Plain
- Canadian Shield
- Hawaii

0   200   400 Miles
0   200   400   600 Kilometers

Pacific Coast. Beginning in the West, the first of the seven physical regions is the Pacific Coast. The highest and most rugged part of North America, it includes tall mountain ranges that stretch from Alaska to Mexico. In the United States, some of these western ranges hug the Pacific. The Cascades and **Sierra Nevada*** stand a bit farther inland. Some important cities of the Pacific Coast are Seattle, Portland, and San Francisco.

Intermountain region. East of the coast ranges is an area known as the Intermountain region. It is a rugged region of mountain peaks, high plateaus, deep canyons, and deserts. The Grand Canyon, which is more than one mile deep, and the Great Salt Lake are two natural features of this region. Salt Lake City and Phoenix are among the few major cities of the Intermountain region. (📖 See "Why We Need Wilderness" on page 628.)

Rocky Mountains. The third region, the Rocky Mountains, reaches from Alaska through Canada into the United States. Many peaks in the Rockies are more than 14,000 feet (4,200 m) high.** Throughout history, people have tried to describe their grandeur, including this gold prospector:

> ❝No, partner—if you want to see scenery see the Rockies: that's something to look at! Even the sea's afraid of them mountains—ran away from them: you can see 4,000 feet up where the sea tried to climb before it got scared!❞

The Rockies were a serious barrier to settlement of the United States. When settlers moved west in the 1800s, crossing the Rockies posed great hardships. In Mex-

Grandfather Mountain in the Appalachians *The Appalachians are the oldest mountains in North America, and their peaks are lower and more rounded than those of mountains in the West. The scene shown here is atop Grandfather Mountain, in the eastern Appalachians of North Carolina.* **Geography** *Why do mountains become more rounded as they grow older?*

ico, the Rocky Mountains become the Sierra Madre (MAH dray), or mother range.

Interior Plains. Between the Rocky Mountains in the West and the Appalachian Mountains in the East is a large lowland area called the Interior Plains. The dry western part of the Interior Plains is called the **Great Plains.** The eastern part is called the **Central Plains.**

According to scientists, the Interior Plains were once covered by a great inland sea. Today, some parts are rich in coal and petroleum.* Other parts have fertile soil, making them rich farmlands. Chicago, St. Louis, and Dallas are in the Interior Plains.

Appalachian Mountains. The fifth region, the Appalachian Mountains, runs

---

*Sierra (see EHR uh) is a name the Spanish use for a mountain range. Nevada is Spanish for snowy. Spanish explorers were the first Europeans to see these snow-covered mountains.

**The highest peaks in North America are in Alaska and the Yukon. Mt. McKinley, Alaska, rises to 20,320 feet (6,194 m).

---

*The map on page 721 shows where natural resources are located in the United States.

along the eastern part of North America. The Appalachians have different names in different places. For example, the Green Mountains, Alleghenies, Blue Ridge, and Great Smokies are all part of the Appalachian Mountains.

The Appalachians are lower and less rugged than the Rockies. The highest Appalachian peak is Mt. Mitchell in North Carolina, which is 6,684 feet (2,037 m) high. Still, early settlers had a hard time crossing these heavily forested mountains.

GEOGRAPHIC • CONNECTION

Death Valley

Half-dead, the prospectors struggled across the burning desert. They certainly would have agreed with Indians who called the land Tomesha, or "ground afire." But they had their own name for it: Death Valley. To them, it was

❝ the most God-forsaken country in the world, the Creator's dumping ground where he had left the worthless dregs after making a world, and the devil had scraped these together a little. **❞**

Death Valley lies on the border of southern Nevada and California. It covers 3,000 square miles (7,770 sq km), an area about twice the size of Rhode Island. The valley floor lies 282 feet (86 m) below sea level, making it the lowest point in the Americas.

In summer, temperatures soar above 100° Fahrenheit (40° C). In July 1913, Fur-

nace Creek had a record high of 134° Fahrenheit (57° C). The valley floor receives less than 2 inches (5 cm) of rainfall per year. Often, rain evaporates before reaching the ground. Despite these harsh conditions, plants and animals do survive there.

In the late 1800s, prospectors hunted for gold and silver among the valley's sand dunes, salt flats, and canyons. They left behind ghost towns with names such as Starvation Canyon, Deadman's Gulch, and Coffin Canyon. But the valley's greatest riches were huge deposits of borax, which is used as a cleansing agent. For many years, mule teams hauled out wagons loaded with borax.

1. Why did Death Valley attract people in the late 1800s?

2. **Evaluating Information** Would you expect many people to live in Death Valley today? Explain your answer.

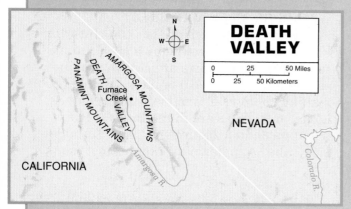

Geographic Facts About the United States

Largest states, by area	1. Alaska 2. Texas 3. California	591,004 square miles 266,807 square miles 158,706 square miles
Smallest states, by area	1. Rhode Island 2. Delaware 3. Connecticut	1,212 square miles 2,044 square miles 5,018 square miles
Largest states, by population (1990)	1. California 2. New York 3. Texas	29,287,000 17,868,000 17,053,000
Smallest states, by population (1990)	1. Wyoming 2. Alaska 3. Vermont	468,000 525,000 571,000
Longest rivers	1. Mississippi 2. Missouri 3. Rio Grande	2,348 miles 2,315 miles 1,885 miles
Highest mountain	Mount McKinley (Alaska)	20,320 feet
Lowest point	Death Valley (California)	282 feet below sea level
Largest lake	Lake Superior*	31,820 square miles
Deepest lake	Crater Lake (Oregon)	1,932 feet
Highest waterfall	Yosemite Falls (California)	2,425 feet
Largest island	Hawaii	4,038 square miles
Rainiest spot	Mt. Waialeale (Hawaii)	460 inches rainfall per year
Driest spot	Death Valley (California)	1.63 inches rainfall per year
Highest recorded temperature	Death Valley (California)	134° Fahrenheit (57° C), on July 10, 1913
Lowest recorded temperature	Prospect Creek (Alaska)	−80° Fahrenheit (−62° C), on January 23,1971

*Part of Lake Superior is located in Canada.

Sources: *Statistical Abstract of the United States;* National Geographic Society

CHART SKILLS *Everyone likes to know about extremes. What is the biggest? The smallest? The shortest? The longest? This chart shows some extremes in the geography of the United States.* ◆ *What is the longest river? The highest mountain? What was the highest temperature ever recorded in the United States?*

Contrasting Coastlines *American coastlines offer great contrasts in mood and beauty. Above, the still waters of a salt marsh on the Gulf Coast in Texas take on a golden glow in the light of an early morning sunrise. At left, waves crash against rugged rocks along the Pacific Coast near Carmel, California.* **Geography** *What other coastal area is found in the mainland United States?*

Canadian Shield. The sixth region is the Canadian Shield. It is a lowland area. Most of it lies in eastern Canada. The southern part extends into the United States. The region was once an area of high mountains. The mountains were worn away to low hills and plains. The Canadian Shield lacks topsoil for farming, but it is rich in minerals.

Coastal Plains. The seventh region is a lowland area called the Coastal Plains. Part of this region, the **Atlantic Plain,** lies between the Atlantic Ocean and the foothills of the Appalachians. It was once under water and is now almost flat. The Atlantic Plain is narrow in the North, where

Boston and New York City are located. It broadens in the South to include all of Florida.

Another part of the Coastal Plains is the **Gulf Plain,** which lies along the Gulf of Mexico. The Gulf Plain has large deposits of petroleum. New Orleans and Houston are major cities of the Gulf Plain.

Hawaiian Islands. The eighth physical region of the United States is made up of the Hawaiian Islands. They lie far out in the Pacific about 2,400 miles (3,860 km) west of California. There are eight large islands and many tiny islands.

The islands are the tops of volcanoes that erupted through the floor of the Pacific Ocean. Some volcanoes are still active. Mauna Loa on the island of Hawaii is an active volcano that rises to a height of 13,677 feet (4,169 m).

Rivers and Lakes

Great river systems crisscross North America. They collect the runoff from rains and melting snows and carry it into the oceans.

"What has four eyes and cannot see?" The Mississippi River, of course. Many students know the answer to this favorite American riddle long before they know the importance of the Mississippi to American geography and history.

The Mississippi and Missouri rivers make up the longest and most important river system in the United States. This river system flows through the Interior Plains into the Gulf of Mexico.

Many tributaries, or streams and smaller rivers, flow into the Mississippi. The Ohio, Tennessee, Arkansas, and Platte rivers are all tributaries of the Mississippi.

The Mississippi River carries moisture across the Interior Plains. It also serves as a means of transportation. Today, barges carry freight up and down the river. As in the past, people travel by boat along the river.

Political boundaries. The Rio Grande and the St. Lawrence River serve as political boundaries. They form parts of the borders between the United States and its neighbors, Mexico and Canada.

Five large lakes, called the **Great Lakes,** also form part of the border between the United States and Canada. The Great Lakes are Superior, Michigan, Huron, Erie, and Ontario. Today, canals connect the Great Lakes, forming an important inland waterway.

The Niagara River connects Lake Erie to Lake Ontario. But ships cannot use this fast-flowing river because at one point it plunges over broad cliffs, forming the spectacular Niagara Falls. Instead, ships travel through the Welland Canal, which connects these two Great Lakes.

To visitors, Niagara Falls is a remarkable sight. The author Charles Dickens once wrote:

> **❝**I think, in every quiet season now, still do those waters roll and leap, and roar and tumble all day long, still are the rainbows spanning them, a hundred feet below. Still when the sun is on them, do they shine and glow like molten gold. Still, when the day is gloomy, do they fall like snow.**❞**

Landforms of South America

Like North America, South America has a variety of landscapes. The Andes are a rugged mountain chain. They stretch along the western part of South America.

The tallest peaks of the Andes are much higher than those of the Rockies. The Andes plunge almost directly to the Pacific, leaving only a narrow coastal plain. Many people live in the high plateaus and valleys of the Andes.

To the east of the Andes is an interior plain. The plain is drained by three great river systems: the Orinoco, Amazon, and Paraná-Paraguay. The Amazon is the world's second longest river. It flows 4,000 miles (6,500 km) from the Andes Mountains to the Atlantic Ocean.

| SECTION | 4 | REVIEW |

1. **Locate:** (a) North America, (b) South America, (c) Atlantic Ocean, (d) Pacific Ocean, (e) Sierra Nevada, (f) Rocky Mountains, (g) Great Plains, (h) Appalachian Mountains, (i) Mississippi River.
2. **Identify:** (a) Western Hemisphere, (b) Isthmus of Panama.
3. **Define:** (a) isthmus, (b) mountain, (c) elevation, (d) hill, (e) plain, (f) plateau, (g) tributary.
4. (a) What are the eight physical regions of the United States? (b) Describe one feature of each.
5. Why are the Great Lakes important to the United States and Canada?
6. **Applying Information** What physical regions west of the Mississippi River did Bierstadt and Ludlow travel through?

5 Climates of the Americas

FIND OUT

♦ What factors influence climate?

♦ What climates are found in North America and South America?

♦ **VOCABULARY** weather, climate

❝Oh, what a blamed uncertain thing
This pesky weather is;
It blew and snew and then it thew,
And now, by jing, it friz.❞

Those lines by the poet Philander Johnson suggest our constant concern with weather. In fact, weather probably ranks highest in topics of conversation. People talk about weather because it affects their lives. Throughout history, people have adapted to different kinds of weather.

Factors Affecting Climate

Weather is the condition of the air at any given time and place. Often, when people talk about weather, they are referring to climate. **Climate** is the average weather of a place over a period of 20 to 30 years. Climate is important to people's lives because it is always there.

Climates have changed over time. During the last ice age, climates grew very cold. The extreme cold affected plants, animals, and people around the world.

Several factors affect climate. One factor is how far north or south of the Equator a region is located. Lands close to the Equator such as Hawaii generally have a tropical climate. They usually are hot and wet all year. Lands around the North and South poles have an arctic climate. They are cold all year. Alaska and northern Canada have a subarctic climate with long, cold winters and very short summers. Other lands have both warm and cold seasons.

A second factor that affects climate is altitude, or the height above sea level. In general, highland areas are cooler than lowland areas.

Ocean currents, wind currents, and mountains also influence climate. For example, when winds carrying moisture strike the side of a mountain, the air rises and cools rapidly. As moisture in the air cools, it falls as rain or snow. Plenty of moisture falls on one side of the mountain. The other side is usually quite dry because the winds have already dumped their moisture. The western sides of the Cascades, for example, have plenty of moisture while the eastern slopes are dry.

Climates of North America

Within North America, climates vary greatly. Many regions have mild temperatures and good rainfall. In such regions, Americans have successfully harvested many food crops.

The United States has ten major climates. Look at the map below and the chart on page 26. You have read about tropical, arctic, subarctic, and highland climates. The following text describes the other six climates of the United States.

Marine. The strip of land from southern Alaska to northern California is sometimes called the Pacific Northwest. This region has a mild, moist marine climate. The Pacific Northwest has many forests that make it the center of the busy lumber industry.

Mediterranean. Most of California has a Mediterranean climate. Winters are mild

MAP STUDY

The United States is a land of many climates.
1. *Name a state with a humid continental climate.*
2. *What type of climate or climates are found in your state?*
3. **Making Decisions** *Which climate would you least like to live in? Why?*

CLIMATES OF THE UNITED STATES

- Tropical
- Humid subtropical
- Humid continental
- Steppe
- Desert
- Mediterranean
- Marine
- Subarctic
- Arctic
- Highlands

Climates of the United States

Climate	Weather
Tropical	Hot, rainy, steamy
Humid subtropical	Humid summers; mild winters
Humid continental	Hot summers; cold winters; rainfall varies
Steppe	Very hot summers; very cold winters; little rainfall
Desert	Hot; very little rainfall
Mediterranean	Mild; wet winters; sunny, dry summers
Marine	Mild, rainy
Subarctic	Very short summers; long, cold winters
Arctic	Very cold winters; very short summers
Highlands	Seasons and rainfall vary with elevation

CHART SKILLS *This chart shows the weather found in each climate of the United States. Compare the chart with the map on page 25.* ◆ *What is the weather for your state?*

and moist. Summers are hot and dry. In many areas, the soil is good, but plants need to be watered in the summer. So farmers and fruit growers must irrigate the land.

Desert. On the eastern side of the Cascades and Sierra Nevada, the land has a desert climate. This dry region stretches as far east as the Rockies. In the deserts of Nevada, Arizona, and southeastern California, there is almost no rainfall. In many areas, people irrigate the land so that they can grow crops.

Steppe. East of the Rockies are the Great Plains. They have a steppe climate with limited rainfall. The short grasses that grow on the Great Plains are excellent for grazing. Huge buffalo herds grazed there for hundreds of years. In the 1800s, settlers brought cattle to graze on the plains. The famous song "Home on the Range" was set on the plains:

    ❝Oh, give me a home, where the
       buffalo roam,
    Where the deer and the antelope
       play;
    Where seldom is heard a
       discouraging word,
    And the skies are not cloudy all
       day.❞

Humid continental. The Central Plains and the northeastern United States have a humid continental climate. This climate has more rainfall than the steppe. Tall prairie grasses once covered the Central Plains. Today, American farmers raise much of the world's food in this region.

At one time, forests covered much of the northeastern United States. Early European settlers cleared the forests to grow crops. But many forests remain, and the lumber industry thrives in some areas.

Humid subtropical. The southeastern United States has a humid subtropical climate. Warm temperatures and regular rainfall make this region ideal for growing crops such as cotton, tobacco, and peanuts.

Climates of South America

South America has many climates. Thick tropical rain forests cover parts of southern Mexico, Central America,* and South Amer-

---

*Central America is the part of North America that lies between Mexico and South America. (See the map on pages 714–715.)

Varied Climates *American climates vary a great deal, as these two photographs show. At left, cactus thrive in the hot, dry desert climate of the Southwest. At right, heavy winter snows blanket the fields and make driving hazardous in the humid continental climate of the Central Plains.* **Technology** *How do you think the invention of air conditioning affected regions with a desert climate?*

ica. The huge area drained by the Amazon River is largely rain forest. Today, developers are rapidly cutting the forests down.

The Andes Mountains are a barrier to moist winds blowing from the east. The mountains force the winds to dump rain on the eastern slopes of the Andes. But the western slopes of the mountains are very dry. In fact, one of the driest deserts in the world, the Atacama Desert, stretches along the coast of Peru and northern Chile.

Large parts of Brazil have a savanna climate. These areas have a rainy season when huge amounts of moisture fall. The rainy season is followed by a dry season with no rainfall. Other countries in South America, such as Argentina, Uruguay, and Chile, have climates similar to those in the United States.

SECTION 5 REVIEW

1. **Define:** (a) weather, (b) climate.
2. Name two factors that affect climate.
3. List the ten major climates of the United States.
4. Describe two climates found in South America.
5. **Synthesizing Information** Why do you think climate is important to people's lives?

Dictionary of Geographic Terms

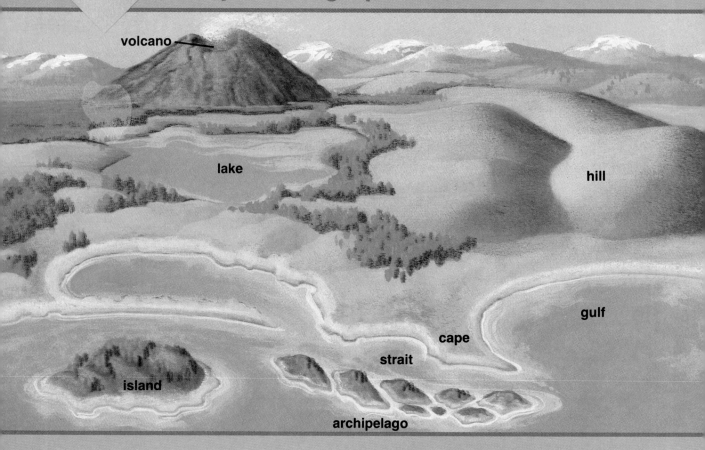

volcano

lake

hill

gulf

cape

strait

island

archipelago

The list below includes important geographic terms and their definitions. Sometimes, the definition of a term includes an example in parentheses. An asterisk (*) means that the term is illustrated above.

altitude height above sea level.

*archipelago chain of islands. (Hawaiian Islands)

basin low-lying land area that is surrounded by land of higher elevation; land area that is drained by a river system. (Great Basin)

*bay part of a body of water that is partly enclosed by land. (San Francisco Bay)

canal waterway made by people that is used to drain or irrigate land or to connect two bodies of water. (Erie Canal)

*canyon deep, narrow valley with high, steep sides. (Grand Canyon)

*cape narrow point of land that extends into a body of water. (Cape Canaveral)

climate pattern of weather in a particular place over a period of 20 to 30 years.

*coast land that borders the sea. (Pacific Coast)

coastal plain lowland area lying along an ocean. (Gulf Plain)

continent any of seven large landmasses on the Earth's surface. (Africa, Antarctica, Asia, Australia, Europe, North America, South America)

continental divide ridge along the Rocky Mountains that separates rivers that flow east from those that flow west.

*delta land area formed by soil that is deposited at the mouth of a river. (Mississippi Delta)

desert area that has little or no moisture or vegetation. (Painted Desert)

directional arrow arrow on a map that always points north.

downstream in the direction of a river's flow; toward a river's mouth.

elevation height above sea level.

fall line place where rivers drop from a plateau or foothills to a coastal plain, usually marked by many waterfalls and rapids.

foothills low hills at the base of a mountain range.

*gulf arm of an ocean or sea that is partly enclosed by land, usually larger than a bay. (Gulf of Mexico)

hemisphere half of the Earth. (Western Hemisphere)

*hill area of raised land that is lower and more rounded than a mountain. (San Juan Hill)

*island land area that is surrounded by water. (Puerto Rico)

*isthmus narrow strip of land joining two large land areas or

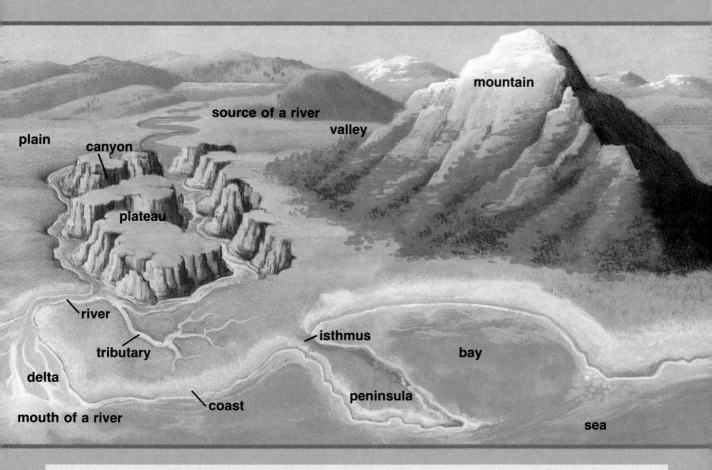

plain

source of a river

valley

mountain

canyon

plateau

river

tributary

isthmus

bay

delta

peninsula

mouth of a river

coast

sea

joining a peninsula to a mainland. (Isthmus of Panama)

*lake body of water surrounded by land. (Lake Superior)

latitude distance in degrees north or south from the Equator.

longitude distance in degrees east or west from the Prime Meridian.

marsh lowland with moist soils and tall grasses.

*mountain high, steep, rugged land area that rises sharply above the surrounding land. (Mount McKinley)

mountain range chain of connected mountains. (Allegheny Mountains)

*mouth of a river place where a river or stream empties into a large body of water.

ocean any of the large bodies of salt water that cover a large part of the Earth's surface. (Arctic,

Atlantic, Indian, and Pacific oceans)

*peninsula piece of land that is surrounded by water on three sides. (Delmarva Peninsula)

piedmont area of rolling land along the base of a mountain range.

*plain broad area of fairly level land that is generally close to sea level.

*plateau large area of high, flat, or gently rolling land.

prairie large area of natural grassland with few or no trees or hills.

*river large stream of water that empties into an ocean or lake or another river. (Pecos River)

*sea large body of salt water that is smaller than an ocean. (Caribbean Sea)

sea level average level of the ocean's surface from which the

height of land or depth of ocean is measured.

*source of a river place where a river begins.

steppe flat, treeless land with limited moisture.

*strait narrow channel that connects two larger bodies of water. (Straits of Florida)

*tributary stream or small river that flows into a larger stream or river.

upstream in the direction against a river's flow; toward a river's source.

*valley land that lies between hills or mountains. (Shenandoah Valley)

*volcano cone-shaped mountain formed by outpouring of lava–hot, liquid rock–from a crack in the Earth's surface. (Mount St. Helens or Mauna Loa)

weather condition of the air at any given time and place.

Maps are important tools used by historians and geographers. They have many uses. They show physical features such as lakes, rivers, and mountains. They show where people live, how people use the land, and where events took place.

A map shows part of the Earth's surface. Almost all maps are flat, but the Earth is not. Mapmakers have found ways to put the round Earth on flat paper. But all maps, except globes, have some distortion.

To use a map, you need to be able to read its different parts. Most maps in this book have a title, key, scale, and directional arrow. Some also show relief. **Relief** is the difference in height of land and is shown by using special colors. (See the color bands on the map on page 18.)

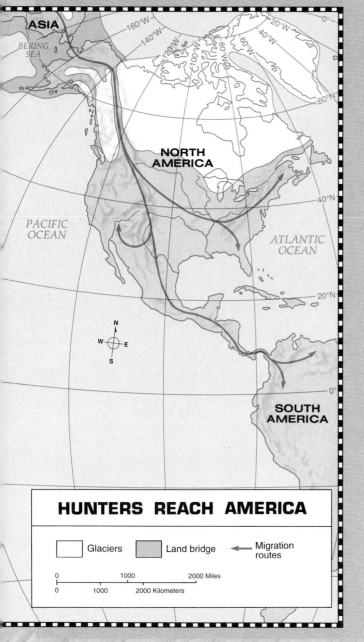

HUNTERS REACH AMERICA

| □ | Glaciers | ▨ | Land bridge | ← | Migration routes |

0   1000   2000 Miles
0   1000   2000 Kilometers

1 **Look carefully at the map to see what it shows.** The **title** tells you the subject of the map. The **key** explains the meaning of the colors or symbols. (a) What is the title of the map at left? (b) What color shows the land bridge from Asia to North America?

2 **Practice reading distances on the map.** The **scale** helps you read distances on the map in miles or kilometers. On a small-scale map, one inch might equal 500 miles. On a large-scale map, one inch might equal only 5 miles. The map at left is a small-scale map. (a) About how far in miles did glaciers stretch from north to south? (b) In kilometers?

3 **Study the map to read directions.** The **directional arrow** shows which way is north, south, east, and west. Generally, north is toward the top of a map, and south is toward the bottom. East is to the right, and west is to the left. (a) In what direction did early hunters travel to reach North America? (b) In what direction or directions did they move after they arrived here?

Use the Section Reviews and this Study Guide to review chapter content.

Main Ideas

The main ideas in each section of this chapter are summarized below.

SECTION 1 ■ Geography and History

◆ People first reached the Americas by crossing the land bridge between Asia and North America during the last ice age.
◆ Five themes of geography help historians understand the past: location, place, interaction between people and their environment, movement, and region.

SECTION 2 ■ Tools of Geography

◆ Flat maps show the Earth's surface at one time, are easy to handle, and can show details about a place.
◆ Three kinds of map projections are interrupted, Robinson, and Mercator.

SECTION 3 ■ Thinking Geographically

◆ Lines of longitude and latitude on a map form a grid that helps determine exact location of places.
◆ A system of time zones helps people know the time in different parts of the world.

SECTION 4 ■ Landforms and Regions of the Americas

◆ Four landforms in the Americas are mountains, hills, plains, and plateaus.

◆ The seven physical regions of North America are Pacific Coast, Intermountain region, Rocky Mountains, Interior Plains, Appalachian Mountains, Canadian Shield, and Coastal Plains.

SECTION 5 ■ Climates of the Americas

◆ Several factors affect climate.
◆ Major climates in the United States are marine, Mediterranean, desert, steppe, humid continental, humid subtropical, tropical, arctic, subarctic, and highland.

Key People and Terms

Refer to the Identify and Define questions in the Section Reviews on pages 8, 12, 15, 24, and 27. Use each person, term, and vocabulary word in a complete sentence. When possible, make connections between the people and terms by using more than one person or term in each sentence.

Time Line

1. Make a chart of events in time order. The chart will have two headings: Date, Event. Fill in the chart, using the events on the time line. Add the following events from the chapter: Mapmaking makes advances; Temperatures rise after the last ice age. (Refer to the chapter for dates.)
2. Which event in your chart led to farming in the Americas?

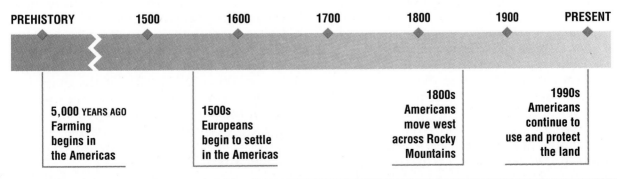

PREHISTORY	1500	1600	1700	1800	1900	PRESENT

5,000 YEARS AGO Farming begins in the Americas

1500s Europeans begin to settle in the Americas

1800s Americans move west across Rocky Mountains

1990s Americans continue to use and protect the land

CHAPTER 1 REVIEW

Understanding Vocabulary

Match each term at left with the correct definition at right.

1. latitude
2. cartographer
3. hemisphere
4. tributary
5. climate

a. mapmaker
b. stream or small river
c. half of the Earth
d. average weather over time
e. distance north or south from the Equator

Reviewing the Main Ideas

1. (a) Which theme of geography focuses on where an event happened? (b) What do the human characteristics of a place include?
2. How do map projections differ?
3. How do people use latitude and longitude?
4. (a) What are the four basic landforms of North and South America? (b) Describe each landform.
5. (a) What are the two parts of the Coastal Plains? (b) Describe one part.
6. Describe the weather in the following climates: (a) tropical; (b) arctic.

Thinking Critically

1. **Linking Past and Present** (a) How did the first Americans adapt to climate changes after the last ice age? (b) How do Americans today adapt to different climates?
2. **Applying Information** (a) How does technology affect both interaction and movement? (b) Give one example of the effect of technology on movement.
3. **Formulating Questions** What questions would you ask to learn about your state's physical geography?
4. **Drawing Conclusions** (a) Which American climates are probably the easiest to live in? (b) The hardest? (c) Why?

Applying Your Skills

1. **Outlining** An outline helps you summarize and review facts. It includes a list of topics, subtopics, and facts. To outline the first section of Chapter 1, write the topic —the numbered title on page 4. (See the sample below.) Below the topic, write the first subtopic—the subsection on page 4. Under the subtopic write at least two facts. Complete the outline for the first section of Chapter 1.

   I. Geography and History (main topic)
      A. The Last Ice Age (subtopic)
         1. Frozen land bridge between Asia and North America formed
         2. Rising temperatures produced floods that submerged land bridge

2. **Comparing** When you compare two or more things, you need to look for ways they are similar and ways they are different. Compare the Rocky Mountains and the Appalachians.
3. **Understanding the Parts of a Map** Review the map-reading steps in Skill Lesson 1 (page 30). Then study the map on page 25. (a) What is the title of the map? (b) What does the key tell you about the colors in the map? (c) How many miles does the scale represent? (d) According to the directional arrow, what climate is in the northeastern United States?

Thinking About Geography

Match the letters on the map with the places listed below.

1. North America
2. South America
3. Atlantic Ocean
4. Pacific Ocean
5. Isthmus of Panama
6. Great Lakes

Location What ocean lies to the east of North and South America?

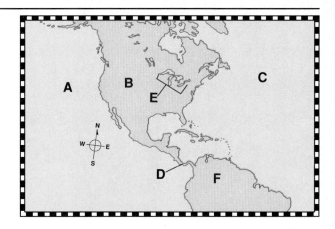

*H*istory *Writer's Workshop*

Analyzing a Question Before Writing

Before writing an answer to a question, study the question. Look for the key word and other clues in the question that will help you prepare a good answer.

The key word in a question tells you what to do with the topic. Often the key word is an instruction word. Some common instruction words and their meanings are listed below.

Explain:	tell how or why
Compare:	give similarities and differences
Describe:	give details or features
Summarize:	tell important ideas in as few words as possible

Sometimes the key word is a question word. Common question words and their meanings are *Why* (give reasons), *How* (tell in what way), and *What* (give examples).

Other clues in a question are words or phrases that limit the topic. A clue might tell you to limit the topic to a certain person, event, geographic area, or time period. Or it might tell you the number of examples or ideas you need to include.

Practice Analyze the following question: *What are the seven major physical regions of North America?*

1. What is the key word in the question?
2. What does the key word tell you to do?
3. What clue tells you how many regions you need to include?
4. What does the clue *of North America* tell you?

Writing to Learn

1. Write a poem about the American landscape. Before writing, list geographic terms and descriptive details. Decide on a central impression you want to make. In the poem, use as many sensory images as possible. Read your poem aloud as you revise, checking for word choice and figurative language. Proofread carefully, and make a final copy. Include your poem with those of your classmates in a magazine.
2. Write a paragraph that describes two climates of California. To prepare, use the map and chart on pages 25 and 26 to identify the climates and determine the weather. Begin the paragraph with a topic sentence that states the main idea. Group the weather details for each climate. Revise the paragraph for balance. Then, proofread it and make a final copy. Publish the paragraph in a bulletin board display about climate.

Pueblo Village *Native Americans developed many different cultures. This painting by Thomas Moran shows a Pueblo village in New Mexico. The Pueblos were one of the groups that adapted to the desert of the Southwest.* **Geography** *How can you tell from the painting that the village gets little rain?*

The First Americans (Prehistory–1600)

The Big Picture

In 1492, when Christopher Columbus reached the Americas, he thought that he had reached the East Indies. So he called the people he met Indians. This term is still used today to refer to Native Americans, the descendants of the peoples who first reached the Americas thousands of years ago.

Columbus's term is misleading for another reason. Indians of the Americas are not simply one large group. They were and are made up of many different peoples and nations. In this chapter, you will discover the variety of cultures in the Americas before Europeans arrived in the 1400s.

Jim Dawson

Of Special Interest

Focus On

◆ How do archaeologists learn about early cultures?

◆ What effects did geography have on Native American cultures of North America?

◆ What did the Maya, Aztec, and Inca empires achieve?

"In the beginning the earth was covered with water, and all living things were below in the underworld. . . . But now the earth was all dry, except for the four oceans and the lake in the center. . . .

All the people came up [from the underworld]. They traveled east until they arrived at the ocean. Then they turned south until they came again to the ocean. Then they went west to the ocean, and then they turned north. And as they went, each tribe stopped where it wanted to.

But the [Apaches] continued to circle around the hole where they had come up from the underworld. Three times they went around it. . . . [Their god] became displeased and asked them where they wished to stop. They said, 'In the middle of the earth.' So he led them to a place [in New Mexico] and left them. . . . There . . . the [Apaches] made their home."

For hundreds of years, a group of Native Americans known as the Apaches have handed down this story of the settlement of North America. Today, we know that the first humans to enter North and South America slowly spread across the land, much as the Apache legend says. We know this because early peoples left behind a trail of evidence, such as earthen burial mounds, stone cities, and pottery. By studying these physical remains, scientists have pieced together the story of the first Americans.

1 Uncovering the American Past

FIND OUT

◆ What do archaeologists study?

◆ Who were the Mound Builders?

◆ How did early peoples of the Southwest adapt to the desert?

◆ **VOCABULARY** archaeology, artifact, culture, adobe, pueblo, drought

In 1781, Thomas Jefferson—with a notebook, pencil, and shovel in hand—headed for a huge earthen mound near his home in Virginia. Jefferson sketched the mound and jotted down its height and width. For the next year, he dug into the mound, uncovering its contents layer by layer and taking careful notes. Based on his research, Jefferson concluded that early Native Americans had built the mound. **Native Americans** are the descendants of the first peoples to reach the Americas thousands of years ago.

Jefferson is best known as a founder of the American nation. But scientists also consider him the "father of American archaeology." His excavation was the first of many digs, or studies of places where early peoples lived, in North America.

The Study of Early Peoples

Like other early peoples of the world, the first Americans left no written records. But they did leave other clues about their lives, such as engraved stones or weapons. The study of evidence left by early peoples is known as **archaeology** (ahr kee AHL uh jee).

Imagine the evidence left behind at a campsite more than 6,000 years ago. Hunters cook animals over a fire and drop the charred bones on the ground. They throw away a broken clay pot or forget to pick up a stone tool. Along with bones, objects made by humans, known as **artifacts** (AHR tuh faktz), have become the building blocks of archaeology.

Learning from artifacts. Archaeologists, the scientists who study early peoples, use artifacts to re-create a picture of the past. A finely carved arrowhead suggests that a people knew how to make weapons and hunt. Woven plant fibers might show that they were skilled at making baskets.

From artifacts, archaeologists form theories about an early **culture**, or way of life. Culture includes the customs, ideas, and skills of a people. It also includes their homes, clothes, and government.

Often, archaeologists cannot completely piece together a culture. In many cases, too much evidence has been destroyed or lost over time. Sometimes, floods wipe out a site. Or a bulldozer crushes an ancient grave. Even so, archaeologists continue to find new evidence.

Collecting and studying evidence. The work of an archaeologist begins in the field, at the point where an object is found. After mapping the location of the object, the archaeologist removes the object with small picks to avoid damage.

At a laboratory, archaeologists analyze the object. By testing the level of carbon in a piece of pottery or a bone, they can date it within a few hundred years. They might also x-ray a bone, examine a kernel of corn through a microscope, or piece together a shattered pot. With study, each object can provide valuable information.

The Mound Builders

Archaeologists have learned much about early peoples known as the **Mound Builders.** Made up of separate groups, the Mound Builders lived at various times from about 2,800 years ago until the 1700s. The three main groups were the Adenas, Hopewells, and Mississippians.

These peoples built thousands of mounds in the present-day United States, from Oklahoma to the Atlantic coast. The

Mississippian Burial Mound *The early peoples known as Mound Builders left behind thousands of mounds of different shapes and sizes. This painting shows workers excavating a Mississippian burial mound.* **Technology** *The Mississippians had no horses or oxen and no wheeled vehicles. How do you think they moved the tons of earth, stone, and other materials needed to build the mound?*

simplest mounds looked like large hills. Others resembled flat-topped pyramids. Still others took the shape of animals, birds, or reptiles.

Purposes of the mounds. Some mounds served as burial grounds. Inside these mounds, archaeologists have found carved pipes, stone sculptures, and copper weapons, tools, and ornaments. They have also found shells from the Gulf of Mexico and turquoise from the Southwest. Based on this evidence, archaeologists believe that the Mound Builders traded with peoples from all over North America.

Mounds also might have been centers of religious ceremonies. For example, Mound Builders used the flat tops of pyramid mounds as bases for temples as well as homes for their upper class. The purpose of other mounds, such as those shaped like twisting serpents or soaring birds, remains a mystery.

A sprawling ancient city. Archaeologists are still dazzled by Cahokia (kah hoh KEE ah). This large settlement in Illinois was built between about 900 and 1250. At least 10,000 people lived there at one time.

Monk's Mound, the largest platform mound at Cahokia, covers 16 acres. Labor-ers carried tons of soil, basket by basket, to build it. Hundreds of other mounds surround Monk's Mound.

A wooden fence enclosed the city. Four circles of evenly spaced posts lay just beyond the fence. From the top of Monk's Mound, rulers could watch as the sun's rays cast shadows off the posts. Shorter shadows meant the approach of spring. Longer ones meant the coming of autumn. Were the posts an early calendar? Some archaeologists think so.

Peoples of the American Southwest

The deserts of the American Southwest seem like poor farmland. Annual rainfall is only 5 to 10 inches. Daytime temperatures soar to above 100° Fahrenheit (38° C). And cactus and sagebrush cover the desert floor. Yet, three major farming societies—the **Hohokams** (HOH hoh kahmz), **Mongollons** (mon GOHL lonz), and **Anasazis** (ah nuh SAH zeez)—made their homes there.

Farms in the desert. The Hohokams lived in present-day southern Arizona from about 2,400 years ago until 1400. Despite the dry climate, they found a way to grow crops. Using only stone and wooden tools, they dug the first irrigation ditches in the present-day United States. Water flowed into the ditches from the Salt and Gila rivers. The fields produced corn, squash, and beans.

About the same time, the Mongollons lived in the rugged mountains of present-day western New Mexico and eastern Arizona. They relied more on rainfall than on irrigation to grow their crops. They also hunted, and may have been the first people to use the bow and arrow. The Mongollons became best known for their beautiful pottery.

The Hohokams and Mongollons left behind few buildings. Yet more than 50,000 abandoned stone apartments dot the Southwest. Who built them? When archaeologists asked Navajos this question, they replied, the Anasazis. In Navajo language, Anasazis means "Ancient Ones."

Villages of stone and clay. The Anasazis built multistoried houses out of stone and sun-dried bricks, called adobe. When Spanish explorers arrived in the early 1500s, they called the houses pueblos (PWEHB lohz), the Spanish word for villages.

In Pueblo Bonito (Beautiful Village), New Mexico, the houses have as many as 800 rooms. The rooms are tiny, but the Anasazis spent much of their time in sunny, outer courtyards. The houses have no stairways or hallways. To reach rooms on the upper floors, people used ladders.

Between 1000 and 1200, the Anasazis sought protection from warlike neighbors. They built their adobe houses in the faces of cliffs. Toeholds cut into the rock allowed the Anasazis to climb up to and down from the top of the cliff, where they farmed and gathered water.

A network of roads connected Anasazi settlements. Along these roads, traders carried bundles of cotton, sandals made from yucca leaves, and blankets woven from turkey feathers. Some Anasazi traders headed into Mexico to trade with people there.

In the late 1200s, most Anasazis left their villages. Archaeologists offer several reasons why, including war with neighbors and loss of food supply. But many think a drought (drowt), or long dry spell, hit the lands. One legend describes what happened:

Anasazi Mugs *Anasazi craftworkers made fine objects of shell, bone, turquoise, and clay. These highly decorated mugs were found in the ruins of Pueblo Bonito, below.* **Geography** *Why do you think many early peoples made objects of clay?*

“Snow ceased in the north and the west; rain ceased in the south and the east; the mists of the mountains above were drunk up; the waters of the valleys below were dried up. . . . Our ancients who dwelt in the cliffs fled . . . when the rain stopped long, long ago.”

Some Anasazis may have returned later to their homes. Most of them, however, settled in different places of the Southwest and became part of other groups.

SECTION 1 REVIEW

1. **Identify:** (a) Native Americans, (b) Mound Builders, (c) Hohokams, (d) Mongollons, (e) Anasazis.
2. **Define:** (a) archaeology, (b) artifact, (c) culture, (d) adobe, (e) pueblo, (f) drought.
3. How do archaeologists collect and study evidence?
4. What evidence of their cultures did the Mound Builders and the Anasazis leave behind?
5. How did the Hohokams grow crops in the desert?
6. **Formulating Questions** Suppose that you are an archaeologist sent to study an Anasazi ruin. What questions might you ask about Anasazi houses?

2 Settling North America

FIND OUT

◆ What are the seven major Native American culture areas of North America?

◆ How did Native Americans adapt to their environment?

◆ What kinds of religion and rule did Native Americans develop?

◆ VOCABULARY culture area, igloo, kayak, totem pole, potlatch, wickiup, kiva, hogan, tipi, travois, long house, sachem

If Europeans had traveled across North America during the 1400s, they would have met with many different peoples and cultures. Memories of their journey might include Eskimos in skin boats skimming along frigid arctic waters, or a plentiful feast of salmon with Northwest Coast peoples, or farmers planting corn on deserts of the Southwest, or a risky buffalo hunt with people of the Plains.

In 1492, when Columbus reached the Americas, millions of Native Americans lived in North America. Native Americans north of Mexico spoke hundreds of languages. And they had as many different ways of life. The map on page 42 shows some of the major Native American culture areas of North America. A **culture area** is a region in which people share a similar way of life. (See "I'm Indian and That's It" on page 630.)

Peoples of the Far North

In the Far North, temperatures drop in winter to −30° Fahrenheit (−34° C). Snow stays on the ground well into the brief summer. Bitter winds, frozen seas, and icy, treeless plains make up the world of the **Eskimos,** the people who settled in the Far North.

The Eskimos adapted to the harsh arctic climate by using whatever the land had to offer. In summer, the Eskimos searched the ocean shores for driftwood to make tools and shelters. In winter, they built **igloos,** or houses of snow and ice.

Because food was scarce, the Eskimos moved in search of it throughout the year. In winter, they hunted in small family bands for polar bear, fox, and wolves. In spring, they followed herds of caribou and musk oxen. When the seas melted, the Eskimos climbed into **kayaks** (KĪ aks), or small skin boats, to hunt for seal, whale, and walrus. When the seas froze, they cut out holes in the ice and fished.

In their religion, the Eskimos showed concern for the animals they depended on for survival. The Eskimos believed that each animal had a spirit. So they offered presents to an animal they hoped to catch. Or they sang words of praise and thanks to the animal during the hunt.

Peoples of the Far West

The Far West was a land of contrasts. The peoples of the Northwest Coast enjoyed a favorable climate, a plentiful food supply, and time for leisure. But the peoples of the Intermountain region faced hunger and other hardships. Instead of seacoasts teeming with fish, they lived in deserts where food and water were scarce.

Peoples of plenty. The peoples of the Northwest Coast earned their living from the sea. They fished and traded with neighboring peoples. Each autumn, the rivers were full of salmon that could be caught by hand. To show their gratitude and respect, the people returned the salmon's skeletons to the water. They believed that the Salmon Beings would grow new bodies if their bones were returned to their source of life.

The Northwest Coast peoples also valued the dense inland forests. They cut down majestic cedar trees and brought them by way of the sea to villages. They then split the tree trunks into planks for houses and canoes. Using the soft inner bark, they made rope, baskets, and clothes. The magnificent forests also provided deer, moose, and bear.

Because food was plentiful, the peoples of the Northwest Coast did not have to search for food. They were able to stay in one place and have permanent dwellings. Families related by marriage built huge wooden houses. Outside each house stood a totem pole, or wooden post with animals or other figures carved in it. A totem pole told a family's history. Families might trace their descent from an eagle, a thunderbird, a bear, or a wolf.

Within each village, families won rank by how much they owned. Some families had grand oceangoing canoes that were 70 feet (21 m) long and could carry as many as 60 people. Slaves captured in war often paddled the boats of chiefs. Very rich families hired artists to make masks, headdresses, or cedar-bark coats. Dressed in this splendid attire, they proudly walked about the villages.

Families sometimes competed for rank. To improve their standing, they held a potlatch, or ceremonial dinner, to show off their wealth. A family invited many guests, and everyone received a gift. The more gifts a family gave away, the greater its fame. At one potlatch, which took years for the family to prepare, the gifts included 8 canoes, 54 elk skins, 2,000 silver bracelets, 7,000 brass bracelets, and 33,000 blankets.

Hardships in the Intermountain region. In the dry Intermountain region, peoples such as the Utes or Shoshones had little to give away. Without water, few plants or animals survived. People lived in brush huts called wickiups. Desperate for food, they beat sagebrush to drive rabbits out of hiding. Or they dug into the desert soil for roots. Sometimes, they climbed distant mountains in search of deer or goats. Because the land offered so little, families usually traveled alone to find food.

Peoples of the Southwest

The **Pueblos,** the Spanish name for peoples of the Southwest, are made up of 16 groups, including the Hopis, Acomas, Zuñis, and Lagunas. All groups trace their roots back to the Anasazis.

The Pueblo culture was already thousands of years old when Columbus reached North America in 1492. Only the Hopis continued to live on clifftops as the Anasazis had done. The rest of the Pueblos moved to villages along the Rio Grande and its tributaries.

Farmers of the Southwest. The Pueblos continued the ways of their ancestors. Like the Anasazis, they built adobe houses and grew corn, beans, and squash.

GEOGRAPHIC • CONNECTION

Shells as Money

The waters along the Pacific Coast offered an abundant variety of shellfish, including clams, oysters, and shrimp. The peoples of the Northwest Coast feasted on all of them. But one kind of shellfish—dentalia—served another purpose. Their tooth-shaped shells were used as money!

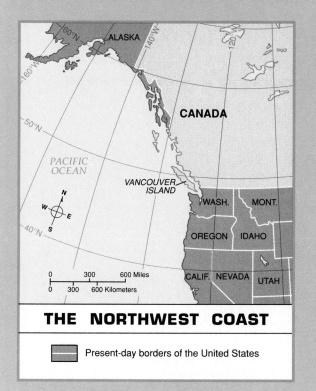

THE NORTHWEST COAST

Present-day borders of the United States

Dentalia shells had value as money because they were scarce. Dentalia lived in deep waters far offshore. Because they were hard to reach, they were a very difficult catch.

The Nootkans of Vancouver Island were the main suppliers of the highly prized dentalia shells. Off the island, dentalia lived in shallower waters. Using a long, broomlike device, Nootkans were able to reach the dentalia, trap them in the wood splints of the broom, and then lift them out of the water.

On shore, the Nootkans boiled out the flesh of the dentalia. Then they dried the shells and polished them with sand. Next, they grouped the shells according to size. Finally, they strung the shells together. The longer the string and the larger its shells, the greater its value.

1. Why did peoples of the Northwest Coast use dentalia shells as money?

2. **Linking Past and Present** How was the value of dentalia shells like the value of American money today?

The Pueblos also observed ancient religious practices based on farming. For example, most Pueblo villages had an underground chamber where men held religious ceremonies to please the spirits of nature, such as wind, rain, and thunder. The Pueblos called these chambers kivas.

Still another religious practice took place around planting or harvest time. A cry would go out among the Hopis and Zuñis. "The Kachinas are coming! The Kachinas are coming!" The **Kachinas** were masked dancers who represented the spirits. The Pueblos believed that such ceremonies would ensure rainfall and good crops.

The Pueblos traced their family lines through the woman's family. This custom gave women special importance. When a man married, he went to live with his wife's family. The wife owned most of the family property.

Hunters arrive. Around 1500, two other groups came to the Southwest: the Apaches and Navajos. Both groups lived as hunters. For many years, they raided Pueblo fields.

In time, the Navajos accepted many Pueblo ways. They learned to farm and build **hogans,** or houses made of mud plaster and wooden poles. But the Apaches remained a people who moved from place to place, following the hunt. They traded dried buffalo meat and animal skins with the Pueblos for corn and cloth.

MAP STUDY

By 1400, about 10 million Native Americans lived in North America north of Mexico. Historians group the Indians into seven major culture areas.
1. Name two groups that lived in the Southeast culture area.
2. About how many miles north to south did the California-Intermountain culture area extend?
3. **Synthesizing Information** In which culture areas could Native Americans probably depend on the sea for food? Explain.

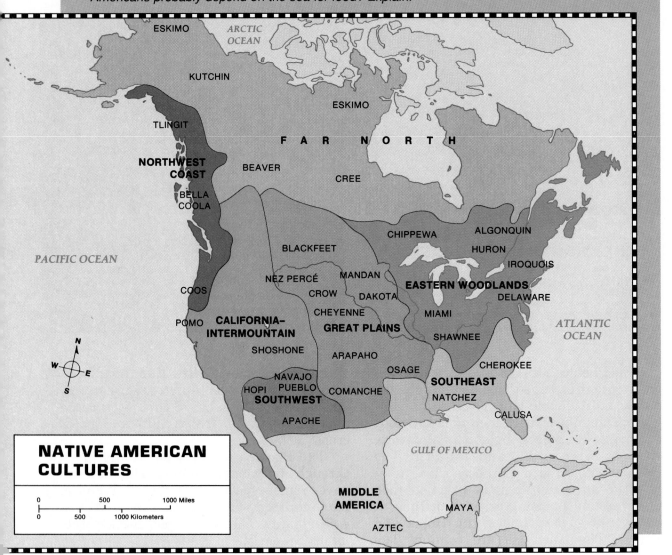

NATIVE AMERICAN CULTURES

Navajo Blanket *The Navajos believed that the world was made up of two kinds of beings: Earth Surface People and Holy People. Earth Surface People included the Navajos and other humans. Holy People included gods. The figures on this fine, old Navajo blanket represent two Holy People.* **Daily Life** *Why do you think that the blanket maker included a corn plant in the design?*

Peoples of the Great Plains

The sweeping grasslands of the Great Plains culture area stretched east from the Rocky Mountains to the Mississippi River. As artist George Catlin observed in the early 1800s, "The meadows roll on for as far as the eye can see and thought can travel."

Because there were few trees, Plains people built their homes of sod, or chunks of thickly matted grass. They also used buffalo hides to make cone-shaped tents called tipis.

People who lived along the edge of rivers farmed. In the spring, melting snow swelled the rivers, and the water overflowed the banks for a few days. While the ground was soft and easy to work, women used animal bones to break up the soil. They then planted corn, beans, squash, and sunflowers.

The grasslands drew an abundance of animals, including buffalo, antelope, elk, white-tailed deer, and bighorn sheep. Plains people hunted the animals on foot. In the winter, the men hunted animals near the village. In the summer, they went on long trips in search of buffalo.

Each village was ruled by a council made up of the best hunters. The chief was a council member respected by others because he spoke well and judged wisely. Sometimes, a village had several chiefs. Each chief served on a different occasion, such as hunting, farming, or going to war.

UP CLOSE

Horses Come to the Plains

Until the 1700s, the peoples of the Great Plains had no horses. The only species of horse in North America had died out thousands of years earlier. The Blackfeet, one group of Plains people, tell a story about their discovery of horses in Montana.

The Blackfoot story. A band of Blackfeet, led by Shaved Head, was crossing the Plains in search of Shoshone people. Shoshones had come out of the Rocky Mountains to hunt buffalo on Blackfoot land. Shaved Head and his men intended to stop them.

After several days of scouting, Shaved Head and his companions came upon a Shoshone camp. There, they saw what to them looked like a group of very large dogs. Dogs were part of Blackfoot everyday life. They hauled skin lodges, cooking pots, and other gear in a travois, or sled, whenever the Blackfeet moved camp.

But these "dogs" were different, Shaved Head and his men observed. They were as tall as men and more the size of elk. Quietly munching grass, several were tied with cords of buffalo hide to a tipi peg.

As the Blackfeet watched in awe, a band of Shoshones rode into the camp on yet more of these animals. The Blackfeet had never seen a man riding an animal. With great ease, the Shoshones brought

Warriors on Horseback *The use of horses transformed the way Plains people lived. On horseback, they traveled farther and faster. They became better hunters and so raised fewer crops. Horses also changed the way Plains people waged war. Here, rival warriors on horseback engage in fierce battle on the Plains.* **Technology** *What advantages would horses give to warriors in battle?*

the animals to a stop and then climbed off. The riders carefully removed pads of buffalo skin from the animals' backs and straps from their heads. Then they tethered the animals.

Shaved Head and his men were amazed. They must bring these marvelous creatures to their people, they agreed. When night fell and the Shoshones were asleep, the Blackfeet slipped into the camp. Quietly, they untied four horses and led them one by one out of the camp.

At a safe distance, a few of the Blackfeet mounted the animals. But when the horses began to walk, the men became frightened and jumped off. They decided to lead the animals home instead. The Blackfeet long remembered the arrival of Shaved Head and his band:

❝When the people heard that Shaved Head had brought back a pack of 'big dogs,' they gathered around the strange animals and looked at them in wonder. They put robes on the horses, but when the animals began to jump, they ran. After a time a woman said, 'Let's put a travois on one of them just like we do on our small dogs.' They made a larger travois and attached it to one of the gentler horses. It didn't kick or jump. They led the horse around with the travois attached. Finally, a woman mounted the horse and rode it.❞

According to history. This story has been passed down from one generation of Blackfeet to the next. Although the details may not be exact, historians do know that horses reached the northern Plains during the mid-1700s.

The Spanish brought the first horses to the Southwest during the 1500s. Native Americans there observed how the Spanish fed, outfitted, rode, and worked the horses. The use of horses soon spread from one Native American group to another. By the 1700s, many peoples of the Plains had acquired horses in much the same way as the Blackfeet.

A new way of life. In time, Plains people became skillful riders who could carry as many as 100 arrows. Galloping along, an expert rider could shoot them so rapidly that an arrow was always in the air.

On horseback, Plains people could travel farther and faster. They began to raise fewer crops and hunt more. They made larger tipis because horses could pull bigger travois. By the time white settlers reached the Great Plains in the early 1800s, horses had brought dramatic changes in the lives of Plains people. ◆

Peoples of the Southeast

More Native Americans lived in the Southeast than in any other culture area. The fertile soil, warm climate, and plentiful rains were well suited for farming.

Using the land. Farms surrounded each village. In the center of many villages was a "stomp ground." There, people held religious dances to ensure the success of crops. One crop was a multicolored corn with red, blue, and yellow kernels. Women pounded the corn into meal and baked it in cornhusks over hot stones. They also boiled corn into a thick mush known today as hominy grits.

More than 100 kinds of trees grew in the forests. The peoples of the Southeast used the trees to build pole houses. After splitting saplings, or young trees, into strips, they wove them into walls. Then they plastered the walls with a mixture of clay and dry grass.

A complex society. One Southeast people, the **Natchez** (NACH ihz), lived along the fertile Gulf Coast. The land provided resources for hunting and fishing. Dividing the year into 13 months, the Natchez named each month after a food harvested or hunted at that time. The names of months included Strawberry, Little Corn, Mulberry, Deer, Turkey, Bison, and Bear.

The Natchez organized their religion around worship of the sun. Priests kept a fire going day and night in a temple atop a great mound. The Natchez believed in an afterlife. For the faithful, there would be plenty of food and peace after they died. But the unfaithful would live in a swamp swarming with mosquitoes.

The Natchez were divided into social classes. At the top was the Great Sun, or chief. The Great Sun's feet never touched the ground. He rode in a litter or walked on mats. Only the Sun's wife could share his food. Below the Great Sun were other members of the chief's family, called Suns. Next came the Nobles and then the Honored People. The lowest class was the Stinkards.

Strict marriage laws bound the social classes together. Noble men and women had to marry Stinkards. Even the Great Sun chose a Stinkard as a wife. The Natchez traced inheritance through the woman's side of the family. So the male children of the Great Sun's sister, not the Great Sun's children, inherited the throne.

Peoples of the Eastern Woodlands

Many different groups made up the Eastern Woodlands culture area. In the forests and open lands, they hunted game such as

Young Indians at Play *This painting shows two young Indians of the Eastern Woodlands playing a game while a third looks on. Native Americans made good use of the natural resources of the Eastern Woodlands. The bark of birch trees, for example, made sleek, lightweight canoes, such as the one shown here.* **Geography** *What other use did the peoples of the Eastern Woodlands make of trees?*

deer, bear, and moose. Their crops included squash, pumpkins, and corn.

The Housebuilders. The most powerful people were the **Iroquois** (IHR uh kwoi), who lived in present-day New York State. The Iroquois called themselves Housebuilders. They used the region's forests to build long houses.

To make these houses, the Iroquois covered poles with slabs of bark. The typical long house was about 20 feet (7 m) wide and 150 feet (46 m) long. A hallway, with small rooms on either side, ran the length of the long house. Each room was a family's home. Families living across from each other shared a fireplace in the hallway.

Women held a special place in Iroquois life. Like a Pueblo man, an Iroquois man moved in with his wife's family when he married. Women owned all the property in the long house. They were in charge of planting and harvesting crops.

The Iroquois included five nations: the Mohawk, Seneca (SEHN ih kuh), Onondaga (ahn uhn DAH guh), Oneida (oh NĪ duh), and Cayuga (kay YOO gah). Each nation had its own ruling council. Iroquois women held a great deal of political power. They chose the sachems, or tribal chiefs, who served as council members. (📖 See "How Fire Came to the Six Nations" on page 631.)

See "How Fire Came to the Six Nations" on page 631.

CHART SKILLS *Native American groups adapted to their different environments by developing distinct ways of life. Three cultures are compared in the chart below.*
◆ *What did each group use for clothing? How would you explain the difference?*

Three North American Cultures

	Eskimos	Pueblos	Iroquois
Geography	Climate: Very cold winters; very short summers Location: Present-day Canada and Alaska	Climate: Hot; very little rain Location: Present-day Arizona and New Mexico	Climate: Hot summers; cold winters; rainfall varies Location: Present-day upper New York State
Settlement	No fixed home; roam for food	Settle in one place	Settle in one place
Shelter	Animal skin tents; snow-block houses called igloos	Four-story stone and adobe houses called pueblos	Wood pole and bark houses called long houses
Food	Polar bear, fox, wolves, seal, walrus, whale Wild berries, nuts	Deer, antelope Corn, beans, squash	Deer, bear, moose Corn, beans, squash, pumpkins, sunflowers, wild fruit, nuts
Clothing	Seal and caribou skin	Woven cotton	Deerskin
Religion	Honor ocean, wind, weather, and animal spirits	Honor earth, sky, and water spirits	Honor the "Good One," He-Who-Holds-the-Sky
Government	No system of rule	Heads of religious societies	Ruling council, or sachems, appointed by women
Art	Decorate tools and weapons	Decorate pottery; weave baskets and rugs	Decorate pottery and weapons

Peace among nations. A major problem facing the councils was the constant fighting among the Iroquois nations. Sometime around 1570, a religious prophet named Dekanawidah (deh khan ah WEE dah) began to preach against warfare. With the help of his follower, Hiawatha, he convinced the five nations to form a union, called the **League of the Iroquois**.

A council of 50 members, chosen by women, made decisions for the League. Each nation had one vote. The council could not take action unless all five nations agreed.

One legend recalled some words spoken upon the founding of the League of the Iroquois:

> ❝We bind ourselves together by taking hold of each other's hands. . . . Our strength shall be in union, our way the way of reason, righteousness, and peace. . . . Be of strong mind, O chiefs. Carry no anger and hold no grudges.❞

SECTION 2 REVIEW

1. **Identify:** (a) Eskimo, (b) Pueblo, (c) Kachina, (d) Natchez, (e) Iroquois, (f) League of the Iroquois.
2. **Define:** (a) culture area, (b) igloo, (c) kayak, (d) totem pole, (e) potlatch, (f) wickiup, (g) kiva, (h) hogan, (i) tipi, (j) travois, (k) long house, (l) sachem.
3. List the seven major Native American culture areas in North America.
4. What kinds of houses did the following groups build: (a) peoples of the Intermountain region, (b) peoples of the Plains, (c) the Iroquois of the Eastern Woodlands?
5. What were two religious practices of the Pueblos?
6. What system of political rule did the Iroquois of the Eastern Woodlands set up?
7. **Evaluating Information** Why do you think many peoples of the Plains developed stories about the arrival of horses?

---

3 Empires of the Americas

FIND OUT

◆ What three empires rose in the Americas?

◆ How did the people of each empire adapt to their environment?

◆ What were some accomplishments of each empire?

◆ **VOCABULARY** pictograph, aqueduct

Grand canoes often made their way along the Caribbean coast. Rowed by slaves, these boats cut swiftly through the blue waters. In the middle of each boat was "an awning of palm leaves," one observer wrote.

> ❝Under the awning were women, children, furniture, and merchandise. As provisions they had roots and grains, wines made of [corn], and axes made of good copper.❞

The canoes belonged to a people called the Mayas. At the height of Maya power, as many as 4,000 canoes sailed the seas. Maya traders carried jade statues, turquoise jewelry, brilliant parrot feathers, and cocoa beans. The Mayas were one of several Native American peoples who built empires in Central and South America.

The Mayas

The Maya culture began almost 3,000 years ago in the rain forests of present-day central Mexico. The rain forests were difficult and dangerous places to live. Poisonous snakes hung from trees. Jaguars prowled the forest floor. And disease-carrying mosquitoes buzzed above swamps.

The Mayas already knew about farming and stone architecture from earlier peoples. With this knowledge and much hard work, the Mayas tamed the rain forests.

MAP STUDY

The Mayas, Aztecs, and Incas built great empires in the Americas.
1. Which empire was farthest north?
2. What was the main city of the Maya empire?
3. **Drawing Conclusions** Why might the Incas have had trouble keeping their empire united?

GREAT EMPIRES OF THE AMERICAS

- Maya
- Aztec
- Inca

0   500   1000   1500 Miles

0   500   1000   1500 Kilometers

They dug canals to drain the swamps and cut down the jungle growth. On the cleared land, farmers grew beans, corn, and squash. They lived in houses with mud walls and thatch roofs.

An empire of cities. In time, the Mayas built great cities such as Tikal. These cities spread into present-day Belize, Guatemala, Honduras, and El Salvador.

Outside a Maya city, farming villages covered the countryside. Farmers took their crops into the city marketplace. There, they traded for woven baskets, blankets, pottery, and tools made of flint.

Towering above each city were huge stone pyramids, some ten stories high. Steep steps led to the top of each pyramid, where a temple stood. There, priests performed religious ceremonies.

A Maya city had tens of thousands of people. The people were divided into social classes. Priests were the highest class. Next came the nobles. Below them were the peasants, or farmers. At the bottom were the prisoners of war, who were slaves.

Visitors to a Maya city could easily spot priests and nobles. They wore gold jewelry, fancy headdresses, and colorful, soft cotton garments. Slaves attended to their every need.

Maya religion. Like Maya society, the Maya religion had many levels. The Mayas saw the Earth as a huge flat square where humans lived. Below was the dreaded 9-layered Underworld filled with evil gods and terror. Above the Earth was the 13-layered Heaven, home to the most important gods.

The Mayas believed that the Sun circled through all three of these worlds. So priests closely followed the Sun's movements and the passage of time. They also watched the stars and planets for other signs from the gods.

Maya achievements. Religious concerns about the heavens and time led the Mayas to make important advances. Priests developed a 365-day calendar that told farmers when to plant and when to harvest. They also invented a number system that was based on 20 and included zero.

The Mayas recorded their observations of the heavens in writing. Their writing consisted of pictographs, or pictures that represent objects. The Mayas carved these pictographs on stone tablets or painted them on paper made from tree bark. The pictographs were the first writing system in North America.

The Aztecs

In the 1300s, the Aztecs moved into the Valley of Mexico, a swampland between two mountain ranges. The Aztecs had long been wanderers, moving from place to place in search of food. Yet they believed that their future held greatness and glory.

According to legend, an Aztec god had told the Aztecs to look for a sign. When they saw an eagle on a cactus with a snake in its beak, the god said, it would be time to stop wandering. At that spot, they would build an empire. The Aztecs found such an eagle in a snake-filled lake, Texcoco (tehks COH coh), in the Valley of Mexico.

A floating city. The Aztecs built their capital city, **Tenochtitlán** (tay noch tee TLAHN), on an island in the middle of this lake. They built canals to drain the lake.

Farmers learned to grow crops on the swampland. Using wooden stakes, they secured reed mats to the bottom of the lake. Then they piled layers of mud on the mats and planted gardens. Farmers grew as many as seven crops a year on these floating gardens.

By the 1500s, the Aztec capital was the largest city in the Americas. Instead of streets, canals crisscrossed the city. Three raised roads linked the city to dry land. The roads had drawbridges that could be lifted if an enemy attacked.

Within the city, thousands of stone and mortar houses lined the canals. Magnificent palaces housed the nobles and priests. Towering above the city was the Great Temple. Here, many people lost their lives as sacrifices to the gods.

The emperor's appearance in the city was an impressive scene. The emperor held absolute power. Below him were the priests and nobles. As the emperor walked, nobles followed him. They threw flower petals in his path so that his feet would never touch the ground. Ordinary people, the farmers and merchants, lowered their eyes.

Aztec religion. Religion was central to Aztec life. Over 5,000 priests lived in Tenochtitlán. Like the Maya priests, they studied the heavens and made calendars. Their

Storing Food *The Aztecs were very careful to manage their food supply. To ensure good harvests, they irrigated their crops and took care not to wear out the soil. Most families kept corn and other crops in a storehouse in case of famine.* **Geography** *What conditions might cause a food shortage?*

calendars divided the year into 18 months. Each month was dedicated to a god.

The Sun god was the most important god. Nearly 20,000 people were sacrificed to the Sun each year. The Aztecs believed that the Sun battled its way across the heavens every day. They compared the Sun's battles to their own, calling themselves "warriors of the Sun."

The Aztecs compared human blood to flowers. To them, death in battle and sacrifices on altars were acts that honored the gods. One Aztec song declared, "There is nothing like death in war, nothing like the flowery death."

Aztec conquests. The Aztecs built a powerful empire. Their mighty armies conquered neighboring peoples. Aztec rule was harsh, and the conquered peoples suffered. The Aztecs taxed them to pay for the empire and used prisoners of wars as human sacrifices.

The conquered peoples were no match for the Aztecs. As one Aztec poet boasted, "Who could conquer Tenochtitlán? Who could shake the foundation of heaven?" As you will read in Chapter 3, the Spanish overthrew the Aztec empire in the 1520s.

The Incas

The Andes Mountains stretch along the western coast of South America. Peaks soar over 10,000 feet (3,048 m). At such high altitudes, the air is thin, making it difficult to breathe.

Yet in these mountains, the Incas built the largest empire in the Americas. By the 1400s, the Inca empire stretched about 2,500 miles (4,023 km) and had a population of 6 million. Its capital, Cuzco (KYOOS koh), was in present-day Peru.

Terraces for farming. The Incas were successful farmers. They set up gardens by carving terraces in the sides of the steep mountains. Rock walls stopped the topsoil from running off the terraces. Stone aqueducts, or canals, carried water to the terraces from distant rivers.

Most gardens produced two crops a year, including more than 100 varieties of potatoes. Farmers stored what they could not use in warehouses owned by the all-powerful Inca ruler, the Sapa Inca.

A system of roads and communication. To control and connect their sprawling empire, the Incas built a highway system. The system included paved roads, tunnels, and hanging rope bridges. The main highway ran 3,450 miles (5,552 km) along the Andes. Other roads linked the mountains to towns and to the coast.

Using the roads, teams of runners were able to carry messages across the empire quickly. A runner from Cuzco, for example, would carry a message to a village. From there, another runner would relay the message to the next village, and so on.

Achievements in stone. Inca temples and forts are considered wonders of the Americas. Some walls were made of stones 16 feet (5 m) high. Each stone weighed more than 200 tons (181 m tons). With no beasts of burden, the Incas moved the huge stones into place with ropes and wooden rollers. Then they chiseled the stones with stone tools. The blocks were joined so tightly that a knife blade could not fit between them. Yet during earthquakes, the blocks spread apart and then slid back into place.

Advances in medicine. Besides their success as farmers and engineers, the Incas made advances in medicine. They used quinine to treat malaria and discovered medicines that lessened pain.

Inca religion. As in the Aztec religion, the Sun held the highest place in the Inca religion. The Incas believed that their first ruler had been a child of the Sun god.

To honor the Sun, the Incas lined the walls of palaces and temples with sheets of gold. Nobles and priests adorned themselves with gold ornaments. One Sapa Inca ordered a garden filled with gold flowers and gold stalks of corn. The Incas called gold the "sweat of the gods."

The Inca empire reached its peak in the late 1400s. In the 1520s, a civil war

Pachacuti: Founder of the Inca Empire

Pachacuti was not born to lead the Incas. His eldest brother, Urcon, was heir to the throne. But about 1438, an enemy people, the Chancas, attacked the Inca capital of Cuzco. When it seemed that the Incas faced defeat, Viracocha, Pachacuti's father, and Urcon fled. Pachacuti rallied the Inca forces and defeated the Chancas. The grateful Incas soon made him their ruler.

With confidence and skill, Pachacuti planned for a grand future. His goal was to unite all the different lands and peoples of Peru into a single Inca empire. To achieve this, he sent out ambassadors to persuade the various peoples to join his empire. If this method failed, he sent soldiers to force them to join.

Inca power was soon unstoppable. Pachacuti united newly conquered peoples with the Incas by demanding that they all speak one language—Quechua. He resettled large groups of people in new areas, which produced food to feed his growing empire.

In his later years, Pachacuti devoted himself to making Cuzco a magnificent capital. One visitor from Spain wrote that Cuzco was "so beautiful and has such fine buildings, it would be remarkable even in Spain."

1. How did Pachacuti build his empire?

2. **Analyzing Information** Why would Pachacuti think that one language would help unite the empire?

broke out among the Incas. At about the same time, the European conquerors arrived. Mounted on horseback and armed with guns and iron swords, they rode up Inca highways to the golden city of Cuzco.

SECTION 3 REVIEW

1. **Locate:** (a) Mexico, (b) Tikal, (c) Tenochtitlán, (d) Andes Mountains, (e) Cuzco, (f) Peru.

2. **Define:** (a) pictograph, (b) aqueduct.
3. Where did the Mayas, Aztecs, and Incas build their empires?
4. How did each empire prepare land for farming?
5. Describe two Maya achievements.
6. How did the Incas control and connect their empire?
7. **Applying Information** One European explorer described Tenochtitlán, the Aztec capital, as "something out of a dream." Why might the city have seemed unreal to Europeans?

Historians use primary sources to learn about the past. A **primary source** is first-hand information about people or events of the past.

Paintings are one kind of primary source. They show how the people of a certain time and place saw themselves. Often, they give useful evidence about aspects of daily life such as food, clothes, and homes.

The picture below was painted on the walls of a Maya temple. Use the following steps to learn how to use a painting as a primary source.

1 Identify the subject of the painting. Study the painting carefully. (a) List three things the people are doing. (b) What kinds of plants and animals are shown? (c) What title would you give to this painting? (d) Explain why you chose this title.

2 Decide what the painting tells about the life of the people. Study the painting and review what you have read about the life of the Mayas. (a) Where was the painting found? (b) Describe the houses of the people. (c) From this painting, what conclusions can you draw about the daily life of the Mayas?

3 Decide if the painting is a reliable source. A painting does not always tell the full story. An artist may have painted it for a special reason or may have left out some details. You need to decide whether it is a reliable source of information. (a) Do you think that the artist showed everything exactly as it was? Explain. (b) Does this painting give you a complete idea of the daily life of the Mayas? Explain.

Use the Section Reviews and this Study Guide to review chapter content.

Main Ideas

The main ideas in each section of this chapter are summarized below.

SECTION 1 ■ Uncovering the American Past

◆ Archaeologists learn about early peoples by studying evidence they left behind.
◆ Mound Builders left thousands of mounds in the present-day United States.
◆ Early peoples of the Southwest desert hunted with bows and arrows, grew crops, and built villages of stone and clay.

SECTION 2 ■ Settling North America

◆ North America had seven major Native American culture areas.
◆ The peoples of each culture area used the area's resources for food, clothing, and shelter. For example, Eskimos of the Far North relied mainly on animals for food and built houses of snow and ice.
◆ Many Native American groups based their religions on nature. For example, the Natchez of the Southeast organized their religion around worship of the Sun.
◆ Native Americans often developed systems of rule. For example, each village of the Plains people was ruled by a chief and a council of hunters.

SECTION 3 ■ Empires of the Americas

◆ The Mayas cleared rain forests, dug canals, and built great cities. Other achievements were a calendar and pictographs.
◆ The Aztecs built canals and grew floating gardens. Their capital, Tenochtitlán, became the center of a powerful empire.
◆ The Incas built terraces for farming and aqueducts for irrigation. A system of roads and runners helped connect the empire.

Key People and Terms

Refer to the Identify and Define questions in the Section Reviews on pages 39, 47, and 51. Use each person, term, and vocabulary word in a complete sentence. When possible, make connections between the people and terms by using more than one person or term in each sentence.

Time Line

1. Make a chart of events in time order. The chart will have two headings: Date, Event. Fill in the chart, using the events on the time line. Add the following events from the chapter: Anasazis leave their villages; Horses reach the northern Plains. (Refer to the chapter for the dates.)
2. Which events on your chart concern Native American cultures north of Mexico?

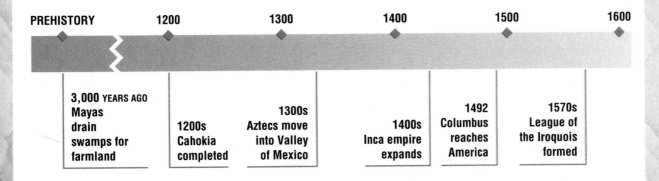

PREHISTORY	1200	1300	1400	1500	1600
3,000 YEARS AGO Mayas drain swamps for farmland	**1200s** Cahokia completed	**1300s** Aztecs move into Valley of Mexico	**1400s** Inca empire expands	**1492** Columbus reaches America	**1570s** League of the Iroquois formed

CHAPTER 2 REVIEW

Understanding Vocabulary

Match each term at left with the correct definition at right.

1. archaeology
2. culture
3. potlatch
4. travois
5. pictograph

a. way of life of a people
b. ceremonial dinner of peoples of the Northwest Coast
c. study of evidence left by early peoples
d. picture that represents an object
e. sled used to haul gear

Reviewing the Main Ideas

1. What evidence do archaeologists have that Cahokia might have had a calendar?
2. (a) Why did the Anasazis build their houses in cliffs? (b) Why did the Anasazis leave their homes in the late 1200s?
3. How did the need for food affect people of the following culture areas: (a) Northwest Coast; (b) Intermountain; (c) Southeast?
4. What role did women play in the following groups: (a) Pueblos; (b) Iroquois?
5. (a) What were the social classes of the Mayas? (b) Why did the Mayas develop a 365-day calendar? (c) What writing system did the Mayas develop?
6. (a) What were three achievements of the Aztecs? (b) What happened to people who were conquered by the Aztecs?
7. (a) Why were the Incas successful farmers? (b) Why were Inca temples and forts considered wonders of the Americas?

their different environments? Give three examples.
4. **Evaluating Information** What evidence shows that the Incas had a well-organized empire?

Applying Your Skills

1. **Outlining** Review the outlining steps on page 32. Then, outline the section "Uncovering the American Past" that begins on page 36.
2. **Using a Photograph as a Primary Source** A photograph, as well as a painting, can be used as a primary source. Review Skill Lesson 2 on page 52. Study the pictures on page 38. (a) What do they show? (b) Why do you think the Pueblos built houses of adobe and not of wood?
3. **Making a Generalization** A generalization is a true statement based on facts. Before making a generalization, you need to gather facts. Review what you read about peoples of the Northwest Coast. (a) List three facts about their way of life. (b) Make a generalization about their life based on these facts.
4. **Analyzing a Quotation** "Who could conquer Tenochtitlán? Who could shake the foundation of heaven?" What does this quotation by an Aztec poet tell you about the way Aztecs felt about their empire?

Thinking Critically

1. **Linking Past and Present** How does the work of archaeologists help us learn more about the past?
2. **Synthesizing Information** In what ways did Native American cultures north of Mexico show respect for nature? Give two examples.
3. **Analyzing Information** How did houses of Native Americans north of Mexico reflect

Match the letters on the map with the places listed below.

1. Maya empire
2. Aztec empire
3. Inca empire
4. Tenochtitlán
5. Tikal
6. Cuzco

Interaction How were the Aztecs able to grow crops on swampland?

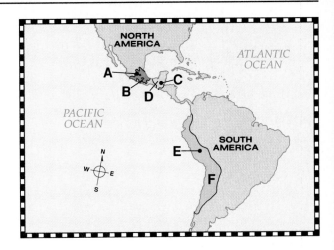

*H*istory *Writer's Workshop*

Identifying Parts of a One-Paragraph Answer

Study the following question. *How did the arrival of horses change the way of life of Plains people?* To answer the question, you might write a paragraph, or a group of sentences that together develop the main idea of the answer.

Begin the one-paragraph answer with a topic sentence that states the main idea of the answer. For example: *The arrival of horses changed the way of life of Plains people.*

Next, write detail sentences that give information to support the main idea. For example: *On horseback, people traveled farther and faster. They began to raise fewer crops and hunt more. They made larger tipis because the horses could pull bigger travois.*

Practice Study the following question. *What were the social classes of the Natchez?* Now study the following one-paragraph answer to the question.

The Natchez were divided into social classes. At the top was the Great Sun, or chief. Below the Sun were other members of the chief's family, called Suns. Next came the Nobles and then the Honored People. The lowest class was the Stinkards.

Identify the topic sentence and the detail sentences in the answer.

Writing to Learn

1. Imagine that you are an Iroquois who wants to stop the fighting among your people. Write a speech you would give to the League of the Iroquois. Before writing, list reasons why the fighting should stop. Begin the speech with a strong topic sentence that states your position. To support your stand, present your reasons in order of importance. In revising, make sure that the speech is persuasive. Then, proofread and make a final copy. Deliver the speech to your class.

2. Write a short report about one aspect of Eskimo life, such as religion, art, or hunting. Before writing, research and take notes. Begin the report with a thesis statement that summarizes your main points. Organize details and examples in a logical order. Revise for completeness and coherence. Then, proofread and make a final copy. Collect your classmates' reports and publish your own book about Eskimo life.

The Polos in China *Marco Polo's tales of his travels in the East made Europeans curious about the world. This illustration from a French manuscript of the 1300s shows Kublai Khan, the ruler of China, receiving members of the Polo family.* **Culture** *How does the artist show that Europeans valued religion and learning?*

CHAPTER

3

European Exploration (1000–1650)

Chapter Outline

1 Europe Reaches Out to a Wider World
2 Search for New Trade Routes
3 Explorers and Conquerors
4 Staking Claims in North America

CHAPTER SPOTLIGHT

The Big Picture

The exploration of the Americas after 1492 was a breathtaking period. Today, we might feel the same excitement if astronauts returned from space with tales of a new planet and different civilizations. The astronauts might describe strange customs, foods, plants, and animals. In the 1500s, European explorers returned home and described these very things.

For the first time in history, exploration of the world brought the peoples of Europe, Africa, and the Americas into lasting contact with one another. In this chapter, you will see how the civilizations of these continents would never again be the same.

Jim Davidson

Of Special Interest

Focus On

◆ How did the Crusades and Renaissance change life in Europe?

◆ Why did Europeans explore the Americas?

◆ How did the Spanish conquer empires in the Americas?

◆ What European nations were rivals for land in the New World?

"To this city of Peking [China] everything that is most rare and valuable in all parts of the world finds its way; and more especially does this apply to India, which furnishes precious stones, pearls, and various drugs and spices. . . . The quantity of merchandise sold [in Peking] exceeds also the traffic of any other place; for no fewer than a thousand carriages and pack-horses, loaded with raw silk, make their daily entry; and gold tissues and silks of various kinds are manufactured to an immense extent."

Accounts such as this one fill *A Description of the World*, Marco Polo's book about the 24 years he spent in China. In 1271, at age 17, Marco Polo set out with his father and uncle from Venice, Italy, for lands to the east, known as Asia. These lands included present-day India, China, and the East Indies.

Upon his return in 1295, Polo's handsome carpets, huge gems, and exotic spices such as clove, nutmeg, and cinnamon caused a sensation. Europeans wanted these and other Asian goods. But the Polos' overland route was too slow and dangerous. In the 1400s and 1500s, European vessels set sail to find an all-water route to Asia. It was these voyages that brought Europeans to the Americas.

1 Europe Reaches Out to a Wider World

FIND OUT

◆ Who were the first Europeans to reach the Americas?

◆ Why did Europeans of the Middle Ages look beyond their borders?

◆ How did attitudes toward learning change during the Renaissance?

◆ **VOCABULARY** saga, feudalism, manor, serf, clergy, magnetic compass, astrolabe

During the **Middle Ages,** a period from about 500 to 1350, many Europeans thought of the world as a disk floating on a great ocean. The disk was made up of three continents: Europe, Africa, and Asia.

Mapmakers called the waters bordering Europe the Sea of Darkness. Sailors who strayed into these waters often returned with tales of monsters. "One of these sea monsters," swore one sailor, "has terrible tusks. Another has horns, flames, and huge eyes 16 or 20 feet across."

Religious wars and reports by Marco Polo and other adventurers finally spurred Europeans to explore the unknown seas. Very few Europeans knew of earlier ocean journeys by people from the north called Vikings.

Viking Explorers

The **Vikings** were bold seafaring people from Scandinavia. Between 700 and 1000, their population grew steadily and food was scarce. So the Vikings turned their long boats west in search of new lands. In the mid-800s, they settled in Iceland.

From there, the Vikings pushed even farther west. In 982, a red-haired, great-bearded explorer named Eric the Red sailed to an island he called Greenland. Actually, Greenland had more ice and a harsher climate than Iceland. But Eric hoped the pleasant-sounding name of Greenland would attract farmers.

A voyage to North America. In 1001, Eric's son, Leif Ericsson, set sail to investigate reports of yet another new land. Leif's crew sailed west and south. In time, they

The Sea of Darkness *During the Middle Ages, most people believed that the oceans were full of sea monsters, such as the one shown here. Giant sea serpents did not really exist, but sea travel was still very dangerous.* **Culture** *Why do you think people believed in sea monsters in the Middle Ages?*

By 1300, a few bold Europeans had traveled to lands beyond Europe.
1. *Describe the route followed by the Vikings.*
2. *About how far did Marco Polo travel on his trip to China?*
3. Drawing Conclusions *Why do you think that most early Europeans traveled overland rather than across the ocean?*

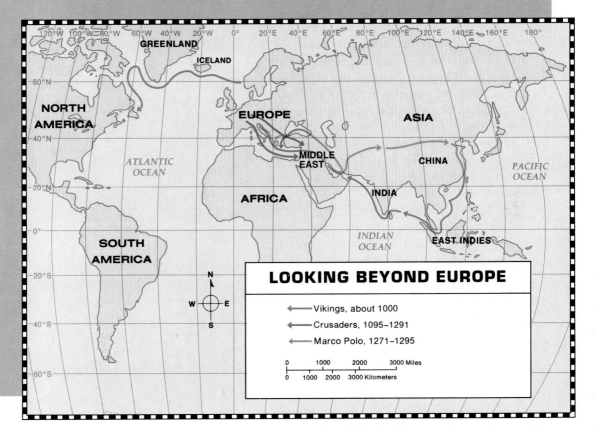

LOOKING BEYOND EUROPE

← Vikings, about 1000
← Crusaders, 1095–1291
← Marco Polo, 1271–1295

0   1000   2000   3000 Miles
0   1000 2000 3000 Kilometers

came to a place where wheat and grapes grew wild. Leif named it **Vinland,** or Wineland.

Viking **sagas,** or stories of brave deeds, described Vinland as a mild, plentiful land:

> **❝**This country was flat and wooded, with white sandy beaches. . . . And the land sloped gently down to the sea. . . . The weather was fine. There was dew on the grass, and . . . it seemed the sweetest thing [the Vikings] had ever tasted. . . . There was no lack of salmon in the river or the lake, bigger salmon than they had ever seen. The country seemed to them so kind that no winter [feed] would be needed for livestock. There was no frost in the winter, and the grass hardly withered.**❞**

Settlement in Vinland. According to sagas, Leif returned to Greenland. But one of his friends, Thorfinn Karlsefni (KAHRL sehf nee), decided to build a settlement in Vinland. He took a group of about 150 settlers with him.

For many years, historians wondered whether the Viking sagas were true. Then, in the 1960s, archaeologists discovered the remains of a Viking site in present-day L'Anse aux Meadows in Newfoundland. It proved that the Vikings were the first Europeans to settle in North America.

The Vikings left North America around 1013. No one is sure why. But sagas tell of fierce battles with the Skraelings (SKRAY lihngs), the Viking name for Eskimos. The next European voyage to the Americas did not take place until 1492.

Europe During the Middle Ages

Few people outside of Scandinavia knew of Viking voyages to North America. Even if other Europeans had known, they probably would not have risked exploring faraway seas and lands. Daily life was hard, and their main concern was survival.

Kings and lords. During the Middle Ages, weak European rulers could not defend themselves against invaders. So the kings divided their lands among powerful nobles. These nobles, or lords, had their own armies and courts but still owed loyalty to their king. This system of rule by lords who owe loyalty to a king is called **feudalism** (FYOOD 'l ihz 'm).

War was a way of life for many lords. They fought each other for power and land. Thousands of peasants died in the constant fighting. Many starved when their crops and homes were destroyed.

Life on a manor. The lord's manor was the center of life. The **manor** included the lord's castle, peasants' huts, and surrounding villages or fields. Most people on the manor were **serfs,** or peasants bound to the land for life.

Serfs worked for the lord and could not leave the manor without the lord's permission. But few serfs wanted to leave. Travel outside the manor often meant attack by robbers. Besides, there was no other place to live except on another manor.

Under feudalism, there were few merchants and traders. Almost no roads or towns existed. The manor produced nearly everything people needed. Serfs planted and harvested crops, raised sheep for wool, and wove wool into cloth. Cobblers made shoes, and blacksmiths made tools.

Most manors provided a place of worship, such as a church or small chapel. Here, serfs and lords heard teachings of the Roman Catholic Church.

Influence of Christianity. During the Middle Ages, Christians in Western Europe belonged to the Roman Catholic Church. The Church's power crossed political boundaries.

The Pope, leader of the Church, sent out **clergy,** or religious officials and priests, throughout Western Europe. In time, the Church's influence prompted Europeans to look to events beyond their manors.

The Crusades

In 1095, thousands of people gathered at Clermont in southern France. They had come to hear Pope Urban II speak. He called for a Truce of God in which all nobles would stop warring against one another. "Let all hatred depart from among you," pleaded the Pope, "all quarrels end, all wars cease."

The Holy Land. The Pope urged nobles to turn their attention toward the Holy Land, in the Middle East. Christians considered the Holy Land a sacred place because Jesus had lived and died there.

For years, the Holy Land had been controlled by Arab Muslims who followed the teachings of Muhammad. The prophet Muhammad had lived in the Holy Land, too, so it was also sacred to Muslims. Still, the Arabs allowed Christians to visit Jesus' tomb in the Holy Land.

A call to free the Holy Land. Then, in 1071, Seljuk Turks, who were also Muslims, conquered the Holy Land. The Turks closed the Holy Land to all Christians.

At the gathering in Clermont, Pope Urban called on Europeans to free the Holy Land from the Turks. "Start on the road to the Holy Sepulchre [tomb]," urged the Pope, "and free it from this wicked race!"

Upon hearing the Pope's speech, the crowd cried, "God wills it!" Across Europe, thousands of people joined the **Crusades,** or wars aimed at freeing the Holy Land. A white cross became their symbol. People sewed it on their shirts and on flags.

From 1100 to 1300, crusaders including kings and peasants, adults and children, marched east to the Holy Land. Thousands of Christians and Muslims died in the struggle. In the end, the Holy Land remained under Muslim control.

Leaving for the Holy Land *Thousands of Europeans joined the Crusades to free the Holy Land from the Turks. Here, a group of French crusaders board a ship bound for the Middle East.* **Economics** *Name two effects that the Crusades had on Europe.*

Effects of the Crusades

The Crusades did not regain the Holy Land. But they did change Europe in important ways.

New tastes and pleasures. For the first time, large numbers of Europeans had traveled beyond their small towns to the Middle East. They ate strange foods, such as rice, oranges, and dates. They tasted ginger, pepper, cloves, and other spices that both improved the taste of food and helped preserve it. Arab traders showed them shimmering silks, hand-painted porcelain dishes, and tightly woven, colorful rugs from Asia. All these goods offered new pleasures to Europeans.

An interest in trade. The Crusades also sparked an interest in trading these goods. Italian sea captains had transported crusaders across the Mediterranean Sea to the Holy Land. They realized that their ships could now transport goods from the Middle East to Europe. Soon, Italian traders became masters of commerce. Merchants from other nations looked on with envy.

Improvements in sailing. In the Middle East, Italian navigators took a keen interest in Arab sailing instruments. The Arabs had learned how to use a magnetic compass from the Chinese. The magnetic compass showed which direction was north. With a magnetic compass, a sea captain could steer a straight course.

From the Arabs, Europeans also learned about the astrolabe (AS truh layb), which measured the positions of stars. With it, a sailor could figure out his latitude at sea. Both the magnetic compass and the astrolabe helped make sailing less frightening.

Astrolabe *During the Middle Ages, Arab scholars made important advances in the fields of astronomy, mathematics, medicine, science, and philosophy. The astrolabe, shown here, made it possible for sailors to use the stars to determine their position at sea.* **Technology** *How would the astrolabe encourage sailors to sail farther away from land?*

A Rebirth of Learning

Increased trade and travel made Europeans more aware of the world and more curious about it. Scholars translated the works of ancient Greeks, Romans, and Arabs. They then made new, practical discoveries of their own in fields such as medicine, astronomy, and chemistry. This burst of learning was called the **Renaissance** (REHN uh sahns), a French word meaning rebirth. It started in the late 1300s and continued until about 1600.

One of the new inventions that helped spread the spirit of the Renaissance was the printing press. In the mid-1400s, Johannes Gutenberg (GOOT uhn berg) of Germany made small pieces of metal called movable type. He engraved each piece with a letter of the alphabet. These letters could be used and reused to form different words and sentences. In 1455, Gutenberg printed the Bible using movable type.

The printing press made it easier to spread information. In the past, few people knew how to read. Books were copied by hand, so only a few copies were available. But with the printing press, a large number of books could be printed at a low cost. With more books available, more people learned to read, which enabled them to learn more about the world.

Strong Nations Emerge

During the Renaissance, strong rulers gained control over feudal lords. These kings and queens built the foundations of nations we know today. In England and France, rulers increased their power as feudal lords killed one another in a long series of wars.

In Portugal and Spain, nation building was slower. During the Middle Ages, Arab Muslims had conquered Portugal and Spain. Christian knights fought for hundreds of years to drive out the Muslims. By 1249, the Portuguese had captured the last Muslim stronghold in Portugal.

In Spain, knights slowly forced the Muslims south. But the land remained divided among several rulers until the late 1400s. In 1469, Ferdinand, king of Aragon, and Isabella, queen of Castile, were married. Their marriage united much of Spain. The two rulers then joined forces against the Muslims.

By the late 1400s, powerful rulers in England, France, Portugal, and Spain looked for ways to increase their wealth. Huge profits could be made by trading silks from China and spices from the East Indies. But Arab and Italian merchants controlled the trade routes across the Mediterranean. Other Europeans realized that if they wanted a share of the silks and spices, they had to find another route to Asia.

A Renaissance Print Shop *By 1500, European printers, using presses such as the one shown here, had produced several million books. Information and new ideas could now reach a greater number of people in less time.* **Culture** *Why would the Renaissance produce a demand for books?*

1. **Locate**: (a) Iceland, (b) Greenland, (c) Europe, (d) Middle East, (e) Asia, (f) China, (g) East Indies.
2. **Identify**: (a) Middle Ages, (b) Vikings, (c) Eric the Red, (d) Leif Ericsson, (e) Vinland, (f) Pope Urban II, (g) Crusades, (h) Renaissance, (i) Johannes Gutenberg.
3. **Define**: (a) saga, (b) feudalism, (c) manor, (d) serf, (e) clergy, (f) magnetic compass, (g) astrolabe.
4. Why did the Vikings sail west to North America?
5. What changes did the Crusades bring to Europe?
6. **Understanding Causes and Effects** How did the invention of the printing press help spread the spirit of the Renaissance?

2 Search for New Trade Routes

FIND OUT

- How did Prince Henry encourage Portuguese exploration?
- How did Portugal expand its trade?
- What did Columbus find on his voyages?
- VOCABULARY navigation, caravel, colony

In 1400, a group of Italian traders returned from the city of Constantinople with a treasure. It was not a chest of rubies and sapphires, but a geography book written by the ancient Greek scholar Ptolemy (TOHL a mee). The book contained maps of the known world showing lines of latitude and longitude. These maps helped sailors plot distances more accurately.

Soon, the Portuguese and Spanish obtained Ptolemy's book. Both hoped that the book would help them find a sea route to the riches of Asia. Portugal believed that it could find a route by sailing south around the tip of Africa and then east to India. Spain, on the other hand, hoped to reach the East Indies by sailing west across the Atlantic Ocean.

Prince Henry the Navigator

The Portuguese were the first to explore the Atlantic. In the early 1400s, Prince Henry of Portugal encouraged sea captains to sail south along the coast of West Africa. To help them in their explorations, Henry founded an informal school for sailors at Sagres (SAH grehz), one of the westernmost points in Europe.

At Sagres, sailors studied navigation, or the practice of plotting a course at sea, and learned to use the magnetic compass and astrolabe. After each voyage, sea captains returned to the school at Sagres to report their observations. Their reports helped mapmakers draw more accurate maps of Africa.

Using a new type of ship, the Portuguese sailed even farther south. Most sailing ships of that day sailed with the wind. Sailors, therefore, feared strong head winds that would keep them from returning home. But the caravel (KAR uh vehl), with its rudder for steering and triangular sails, could sail against the wind.

When sailors angled the sails of the caravel a certain way, head winds actually moved the caravel sideways and forward. When they reangled the sails, the caravel moved sideways and forward in the opposite direction. This ability to sail against the wind inspired one Italian captain to call caravels "the best ships that [ever] sailed the seas."

Prince Henry himself never set sail. Even so, his work at Sagres won him the title of Prince Henry the Navigator. When he died in 1460, the Portuguese had not yet reached Asia. But they had come in contact with great kingdoms of Africa.

Ivory Carving From West Africa *West African artists produced many fine carvings. This ivory salt cellar was probably carved to order for a European merchant.* **Culture** *What objects did the artist include to show that the figures are Europeans?*

Kingdoms of Africa

In the 1400s, Europeans knew little about Africa or the many peoples who lived there. A Spanish map showed an African ruler in the middle of the Sahara desert. The caption read:

> ❝This Negro lord is called Musa Mali. So abundant is the gold in his country that he is the richest and most noble king in all the land.❞

In fact, Musa Mali's real name was Mansa Musa. He ruled Mali, a kingdom in West Africa. Mali reached its height between 1200 and 1400. In 1324, Mansa Musa traveled from Mali across North Africa to Egypt and the Middle East. He so dazzled the Egyptians with his wealth that news of his visit reached Europe.

Mali was only one of several advanced kingdoms that rose in West Africa. (See the map on page 65.) In the late 1400s, Songhai (SAWNG hī) became the most powerful kingdom in West Africa. Timbuktu, located on the Niger River, was a thriving center of trade and learning. The University of Sankore in Timbuktu produced many fine scholars.

Portuguese explorers did not visit these kingdoms in Africa's interior. But they traded with Africans along the coast. Europeans loaded their caravels with gold and ivory and statues of polished teak wood. Africans traded slaves for European goods and weapons.

In 1441, the Portuguese raided an African village. They captured about a dozen Africans and sold them as slaves in Europe. By 1460, about 1,000 Africans were sold each year in Portugal. An eyewitness described the scene:

> ❝Mothers would clasp their infants in their arms, and throw themselves on the ground to cover them with their bodies. They disregarded any injury to their own persons, so that they could prevent their children from being separated from them.❞

Many Europeans objected to the slave trade, but profits were high. Even though Prince Henry did not approve of slavery, he allowed it to continue. At the same time, he urged that all slaves be converted to Christianity. This early slave trade in Europe would later pave the way for slavery in South America in the 1500s and in North America in the 1600s.

India at Last

The Portuguese established a thriving trade in West Africa. Still, they continued their search for a route to Asia.

In 1488, Bartolomeu Dias (DEE uhsh) sailed around the southern tip of Africa. He saw a large body of water to the east and intended to sail on. But his crew, frightened by the rough seas, threatened mutiny. So Dias sailed back to Portugal, naming the tip of Africa the Cape of Storms. When King John of Portugal learned of the voyage, he realized that his nation may have found an all-water route to India. He renamed the Cape of Storms the **Cape of Good Hope.**

In 1497, Portugal sent off four ships under the command of Vasco da Gama. His orders were to "make discoveries and go in search of spices." In May 1498, after sailing around Africa and across the Indian Ocean, da Gama sailed into the bustling port of Calicut, India. From there, other Portuguese ships would go on to the East Indies, the source of spices. So ended a mission begun by Prince Henry nearly 80 years earlier. Within a few years, the Portuguese built a successful trading empire in Asia.

The Spanish Set Sail

The Spanish wanted a share of the spice trade, too. But first they had to drive out the Arab Muslims from Spain. In 1492, the armies of King Ferdinand and Queen Isabella crushed the last Arab stronghold. In that year, an Italian sea captain, Christopher Columbus, convinced Isabella to support a plan to sail west.

Captain Christopher Columbus. Columbus and other educated people believed

MAP STUDY

Portuguese sailors led the search for an all-water route to Asia.
1. Which explorer first rounded the southern tip of Africa? When?
2. Which explorer first reached India by sea? When?
3. **Drawing Conclusions** Based on the map, why do you think Portugal was a leader in sea exploration?

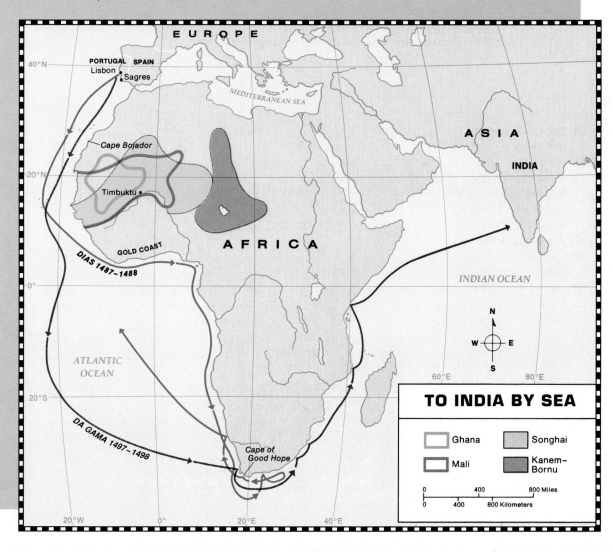

that the Earth was round. By sailing west, he reasoned, it should be possible to reach the East Indies, a group of islands off the coast of Asia. He calculated the distance from Europe to Asia to be about 3,000 miles (4,800 km). The voyage, he judged, would take less than two months.

Columbus thought that King John of Portugal would support him. But the king's advisers warned that Columbus was "full of fancies." The journey, they said, would take at least four months. Besides, the Portuguese preferred to explore the route around Africa. To Columbus's disappointment, King John turned him down.

Rejected by Portugal, Columbus tried Spain. He set his plan before Queen Isabella. But many members of her court thought him boastful and ridiculous. After six years of pleading, Columbus finally convinced the queen to finance his voyage.

The New World. On August 3, 1492, Columbus set sail with a crew of 90 sailors and three vessels. Columbus commanded the largest ship, the *Santa María*. The other ships were the *Niña* and the *Pinta*.

At first, the ships had fair winds. They stopped for repairs in the Canary Islands off the coast of Africa. On September 6, Columbus set his course due west. For a

The Santa María *Christopher Columbus had three ships on his first voyage to the New World in 1492—the* Niña, *the* Pinta, *and the* Santa María. *Like all ships of the time, these vessels were made of wood, had no engine, and provided few comforts. No one knows exactly what Columbus's ships looked like. This drawing of the flagship of the tiny fleet, the* Santa María, *is based on information about ships of the period.* **Technology** *How was the* Santa María *powered?*

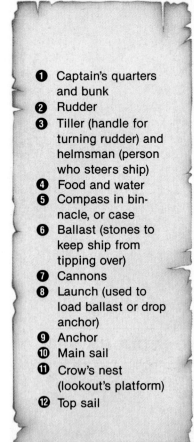

❶ Captain's quarters and bunk
❷ Rudder
❸ Tiller (handle for turning rudder) and helmsman (person who steers ship)
❹ Food and water
❺ Compass in binnacle, or case
❻ Ballast (stones to keep ship from tipping over)
❼ Cannons
❽ Launch (used to load ballast or drop anchor)
❾ Anchor
❿ Main sail
⓫ Crow's nest (lookout's platform)
⓬ Top sail

LINKING • PAST • AND • PRESENT

New Frontiers

Throughout history, people have explored the unknown. In the 1400s, Europeans dared to sail the world's uncharted oceans. Shown below, one such sailor, Christopher Columbus, set foot on the Americas in 1492. As Columbus reported to the king and queen of Spain, "Your Highnesses have an Other World here." Within a short time, other Europeans set sail across the Atlantic to explore these unknown lands.

Nearly 500 years later, Americans ventured into outer space. Shown at right, astronaut "Buzz" Aldrin in 1969 set foot on yet "an Other World"—the moon. In the future, many more space probes will explore outer

space to study yet other planets and other moons in the universe.

Why do people explore the unknown? What do they gain? Astronomer Carl Sagan explains it this way:

> ❝We are a species that needs a frontier. Every time humanity stretches itself, turns a corner, it receives a jolt of productive vitality that can last for centuries.❞

1. What are two examples of exploration of the unknown?

2. **Comparing** How did each exploration change people's view of the world?

---

month, the crew saw no land. They grew restless. Sailors had never been out of the sight of land for that long. Mutiny was in the air, but Columbus held firm.

On October 7, sailors saw flocks of birds flying southwest. Columbus changed course to follow the birds. A few days later, crew members spotted tree branches and flowers floating in the water. A storm blew up, but on the night of October 11, the moon shone brightly. At 2:00 A.M. on October 12, the

lookout on the *Pinta* spotted white cliffs shining in the moonlight. "Tierra! Tierra!" he shouted. "Land! Land!"

Admiral of the Ocean Sea

At dawn, Columbus rowed ashore. He planted the banner of Spain in what he believed was the East Indies. In fact, he had reached a group of islands in the Caribbean Sea, the present-day West Indies.

MAP STUDY

Christopher Columbus made four voyages to the Americas in the late 1400s and early 1500s.

1. *What West Indian islands did Columbus pass on his first voyage?*
2. *Locate the southernmost point reached by Columbus during his journeys to the Americas. What is the latitude and longitude of this point?*
3. **Comparing** *Like Dias and da Gama, Columbus was looking for a water route to the Indies. How was his route different from that taken by the Portuguese explorers? (See the map on page 65.)*

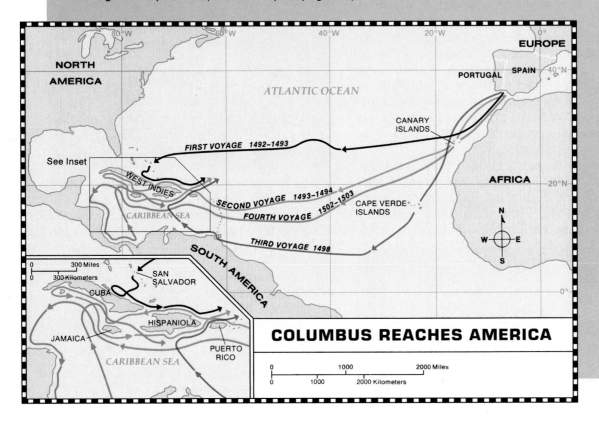

COLUMBUS REACHES AMERICA

The search for China continues. For three months, Columbus explored the nearby islands. He gave trinkets to the Native Americans, who called themselves Arawaks. Still convinced that he had reached the East Indies, he insisted on calling the Arawaks Indians. Sailing around the Caribbean, Columbus continued to look for the silks, spices, and golden cities of China.

As he traveled from island to island, Columbus met some Native Americans wearing gold ornaments. They pointed west when he asked them where they had found gold. Satisfied that China must be near, Columbus returned home.

A hero's welcome. In Spain, Columbus led a triumphant parade. On his way to the royal court, bystanders gaped at the strangely clothed Indians he had brought back with him.

At court, Columbus delighted the king and queen with gifts of pink pearls and brilliantly colored parrots. The royal couple listened intently to his descriptions of tobacco leaves, pineapples, and hammocks used for sleeping. As a reward, they named Columbus Admiral of the Ocean Sea and Viceroy of the Indies.

King Ferdinand and Queen Isabella also agreed to finance future voyages. Columbus made three more voyages to the West Indies. On each voyage, he continued to search for a passage to Asia. (See the map on page 68.)

From fame to disgrace. On his second voyage, Columbus discovered other islands, including present-day Puerto Rico. He founded the first Spanish colony in the Americas on an island named Hispaniola. A colony is a group of people who settle in a distant land and are ruled by the government of their native land.

On his third voyage to the Americas, Columbus met with trouble. He hanged some unruly settlers who enslaved Indians and insisted on searching for gold rather than building the colony.

Isabella sent an official to Hispaniola to report on the rumors of harsh rule. The official sent Columbus back to Spain in chains for trial. Isabella pardoned her admiral and granted him one last voyage. But she denied him the right to govern any territories.

When Columbus returned home in 1504, Isabella was dying. With her death that year, Columbus lost hope of setting sail again. Two years later, Columbus died a bitter man. He remained convinced that he had discovered part of Asia.

Naming the New World

Many explorers followed the routes that Columbus charted. In 1499, an Italian merchant named Amerigo Vespucci (vehs PYOOT chee) sailed along the northern coast of South America, mapping all that he saw on the way.

When Vespucci returned to Italy, he wrote a letter to a friend. "I have found a new continent, more densely peopled and full of animals than our Europe or Asia or Africa." Vespucci called the continent "a new world."

In 1507, a German mapmaker read Vespucci's letter. On a map, he labeled the new land America, after Amerigo. In this way, the Americas were named after Amerigo Vespucci, not Christopher Columbus.

SECTION 2 REVIEW

1. **Locate:** (a) Portugal, (b) Spain, (c) Sagres, (d) Mali, (e) Songhai, (f) Timbuktu, (g) Cape of Good Hope, (h) India, (i) West Indies, (j) Puerto Rico, (k) Hispaniola.
2. **Identify:** (a) Prince Henry, (b) Mansa Musa, (c) Bartolomeu Dias, (d) Vasco da Gama, (e) Christopher Columbus, (f) Queen Isabella, (g) Amerigo Vespucci.
3. **Define:** (a) navigation, (b) caravel, (c) colony.
4. How did exploration help to expand Portugal's trade?
5. (a) Where did Columbus think he landed in 1492? (b) Where did he actually land?
6. **Forecasting** Would you expect the African slave trade to increase after Europeans had reached the Americas? Explain.

3 Explorers and Conquerors

FIND OUT

◆ Where did Balboa and Magellan explore?

◆ How did Spain conquer Native American empires?

◆ What did explorers find in the Spanish borderlands?

◆ VOCABULARY conquistador, strait

"What a troublesome thing it is to discover new lands. The risks we took, it is hardly possible to exaggerate." So said Bernal Díaz del Castillo, one of the Spanish conquistadors (kohn KEES tah dohrs), or conquerors, who marched into the Americas. But when asked why conquistadors went there, Díaz explained, "We came here to serve God and the king and also to get rich."

In their search for glory and gold, the conquistadors made Spain one of the richest nations in Europe. But their arrival in the New World meant death for Aztecs, Incas, and other Native Americans.

Spain and Portugal Divide Up the New World

As Spain and Portugal explored the world, they sometimes claimed the same new lands. To prevent a war between the two nations, the Pope offered a settlement. He proposed a **Line of Demarcation** (dee mahr KAY shuhn) that divided up the world. (See the map on page 71.) Spain and Portugal agreed and signed the Treaty of Tordesillas (tor deh SEE yas) in 1494.

The treaty gave Spain the right to colonize and trade with the lands west of the line. Spain, therefore, claimed North and South America. To Portugal, the treaty gave the right to colonize and trade with the lands east of the line. Portugal, therefore, controlled trade with China and the East Indies.

In 1500, however, Portugal gained a foothold in South America. Pedro Álvares Cabral (kuh BRAHL) set sail for India around the tip of Africa. Strong winds forced his ship off course, and he landed on the eastern coast of present-day Brazil. Cabral realized that this was east of the Line of Demarcation. So he claimed the land for Portugal.

The Treaty of Tordesillas did not consider the rights of peoples living in lands claimed by Portugal or Spain. It also did not consider the claims of other European powers, such as England, France, and the Netherlands. In time, these nations, eager to build their own empires, would ignore the treaty.

Balboa Claims the Pacific

The Spanish continued their search for a western route to Asia. They explored the eastern coast of North and South America. These new lands blocked their way. The first person to discover a route across these large continents was Vasco Núñez de Balboa (bal BOH uh).

Balboa sought his fortune on the island of Haiti, a colony founded by Columbus. But Balboa's hot temper and quickness to use a sword got him into trouble with officials. To escape, he hid himself in a barrel of freight being shipped to a Spanish colony in present-day Colombia.

After his arrival, he learned from Native Americans that a large body of water

MAP STUDY

In the 1400s, Portuguese and Spanish sailors learned to use winds and ocean currents to help them navigate the ocean.
1. In which direction do the Northeast Trades blow?
2. In which direction does the Gulf Stream flow?
3. **Solving Problems** Imagine that you are the captain of a sailing ship in the 1400s. (a) What winds would you use to sail from Portugal to North America? (b) What winds and what ocean current would you use to sail back to Portugal?

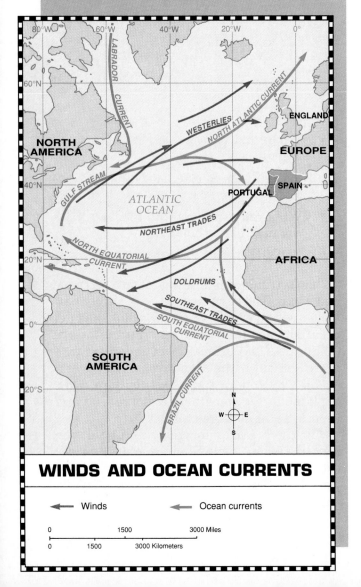

WINDS AND OCEAN CURRENTS

← Winds   ← Ocean currents

0   1500   3000 Miles

0   1500   3000 Kilometers

In the 1400s and 1500s, European sailors explored the oceans of the world. They wanted to find an easy sea route to Asia.

1. What continents did Magellan's expedition pass during its voyage?
2. What land did Portugal claim as a result of Cabral's voyage?
3. **Synthesizing Information** There was only one Line of Demarcation. Why do there seem to be two Lines of Demarcation on the map?

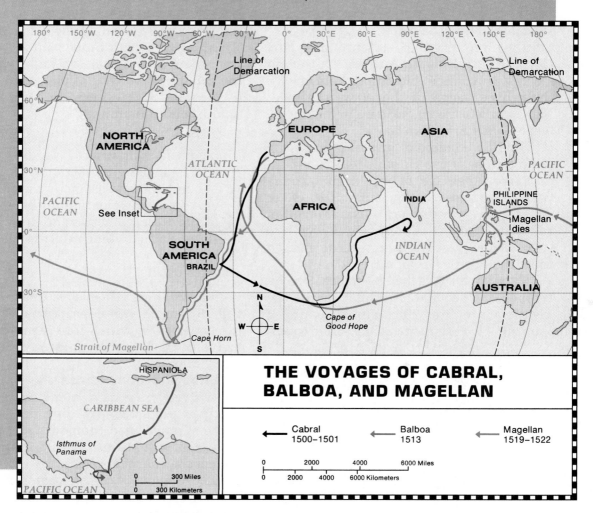

THE VOYAGES OF CABRAL, BALBOA, AND MAGELLAN

Cabral 1500–1501
Balboa 1513
Magellan 1519–1522

lay to the west. Anxious to win fame as an explorer, Balboa set out in 1513 with 190 Spaniards and hundreds of Indians. He intended to cross the Isthmus of Panama.

Balboa and his party hacked their way through 45 miles (72 km) of thick, steaming jungle. They waded through swamps swarming with mosquitoes and snakes. After 25 days, the men saw a huge sea.

In full armor, Balboa stood in the crashing surf and claimed the sea for Spain. He named it the Sea of the South because he thought it was south of Asia. In fact, he had found the Pacific Ocean.

Sailing Around the World

The Spanish had no idea how wide the Pacific was. But they hoped that it would provide a shorter route to China and India. A sea captain named Ferdinand Magellan (muh JEHL uhn) was determined to find this new route. On September 20, 1519, he left Spain with 5 ships and about 250 men. The first around-the-world voyage had begun.

A voyage west. After two months, Magellan's ships reached Brazil. Slowly, the fleet moved south along the coast. They looked for a passage to Balboa's Sea of the South. None appeared. Winter set in and storms battered the ships.

Magellan tried to sail around Cape Horn, the tip of South America. But again storms drove back his ships. Fearing for their lives, some of the crew mutinied. Magellan left the ringleaders to die on the bleak South American coast.

Finally, Magellan discovered a way around Cape Horn. He sailed into a strait, or narrow passage of water, that today bears his name. In November 1520, after 38 stormy, wave-tossed days, Magellan sailed into the peaceful waters Balboa had seen earlier. Greatly relieved, he named them the Pacific Ocean.

Magellan reaches the Philippines. On November 28, Magellan continued across the Pacific. Only three ships and one third of the crew's food remained. One sailor wrote:

> ❝We were 3 months and 20 days without getting any kind of fresh food. We ate biscuit, which was no longer biscuit, but powder . . . swarming with worms. . . . We drank yellow water that . . . stank strongly.❞

Sailors caught rats to eat. When there were no more rats, they ate sawdust and leather so tough that they had to soak it for days before it was soft enough to chew.

The explorers finally reached the Philippine Islands off the coast of Asia. (Find Magellan's route on the map on page 71.) Here, Magellan was killed in a battle with the local people.

Magellan's crew sailed on. In 1522, one ship and 18 sailors reached Spain. These survivors had found Spain's all-water route to Asia by sailing west. More important,

their voyage around the world had shown Europeans the true size of the Earth.

Building New Spain

While Spain looked for a western route to Asia, Spanish colonists in the Caribbean began to hear rumors of gold and other riches in nearby Mexico. At the same time, the Aztecs were learning about the Spanish.

In 1518, a man limped into Tenochtitlán, the Aztec capital. He had walked all the way from the Gulf of Mexico to deliver a message to his emperor, Montezuma (mahn tuh ZYOO muh):

> ❝Our lord and king, forgive my boldness. But when I went to the shores of the great sea [the Gulf of Mexico], there was a mountain range or a mountain floating in the midst of the water, and moving here and there without touching the shore. My lord, we have never seen the likes of this.❞

Montezuma's officials returned from the Gulf of Mexico with descriptions of a floating house filled with white men. The men had long, thick beards and wore clothing of many colors.

Strangers from across the sea. Were these strangers gods or men? Aztec sacred writings predicted that one day a great white-skinned god named Quetzalcoatl (keht sahl koh AH tuhl) would return from the east to rule the Aztecs.

These white strangers came from the east and were certainly powerful. They wore metal armor and had weapons (cannons) that shattered trees into splinters. The fair-skinned strangers rode "deer that carry them on their backs wherever they wish to go." (The "deer" the Spanish rode were actually horses.) Were these strangers the messengers of the Aztec god? Unsure, Montezuma invited them to visit Tenochtitlán.

The fall of the Aztecs. The Spanish leader, Hernando Cortés (kawr TEHZ), accepted

Montezuma's invitation. Like other conquistadors, Cortés wanted power and riches. An Indian woman the Spanish named Doña Marina had told Cortés about Aztec gold. With only 400 soldiers and 16 horses, Cortés set out to defeat the Aztecs. (📖 See "Cortés and Montezuma" on page 634.)

On November 8, 1519, Cortés marched into Tenochtitlán. Then, for six months, Cortés held Montezuma prisoner in his own city. Finally, the Aztecs attacked, driving out the Spanish. But Cortés soon returned. With the help of people the Aztecs had conquered, the Spanish captured and destroyed most of Tenochtitlán. The mighty Aztec empire had fallen.

Conquest of the Incas. A few years later, a conquistador named Francisco Pizarro (pee ZAHR oh) matched Cortés's conquest of the Aztecs. Pizarro had journeyed with Balboa through the jungles of Panama. There, he learned of the golden cities of the Incas.

In 1533, after killing the Inca ruler Atahualpa (at tah WAHL pah), Pizarro arrived in the Inca capital, Cuzco. There, Pizarro found the Incas divided by civil war. (See page 50.) By 1535, Pizarro had taken control of much of the Inca empire.

Reasons for the Spanish conquest. How did the conquistadors, so far from Spain and with only a handful of soldiers, conquer these two large empires? First, the Spanish fought with iron swords, guns, and cannons, while the Native Americans fought with bows, arrows, and spears. Second, the Aztecs and Incas, who had never seen horses, were frightened by the mounted Spanish knights. Third, many Indians, including the Aztecs and Incas, feared that the Spanish might be gods.

Finally, the Indians had no resistance to European diseases such as chicken pox, measles, and influenza. Millions died. Within 50 years, the population of Mexico

Aztecs Battle the Spanish *With their glass-tipped spears, the Aztecs were no match for Cortés's well-armed men, and by 1521 the mighty Aztec empire had fallen to the Spanish. But the Aztecs enjoyed a few victories. This picture shows traditionally dressed Aztec soldiers forcing the Spanish back into their quarters.* ***Economics*** *Why did Cortés want to conquer the Aztecs?*

Doña Marina: Adviser to a Conquistador

"After God, we owe the conquest of New Spain to Doña Marina," said the Spanish conquistador Hernando Cortés. Who was Doña Marina and how did she help Cortés to conquer the Aztec empire in the early 1500s?

In spite of her name, Doña Marina was not Spanish. She was born Malinche, heir to the throne of an Aztec chieftain in the highlands of

Mexico. But because her mother wanted Doña Marina's stepbrother to inherit the throne, Doña Marina was sold into slavery at age 12. Exiled to the eastern coast, she grew up far from her own people. At age 18, Doña Marina's owners gave her to Cortés.

Cortés soon realized how valuable Doña Marina was. Gifted in languages, she mastered Spanish in a short time. As Cortés's interpreter, she served as a bridge between him and Native Americans. She also advised Cortés on how best to deal with them. This advice proved crucial when Cortés wanted to convince people to rebel against Aztec rule. Cortés was most grateful to her, however, for warning him about a plot to kill him.

After serving Cortés, the former princess and slave girl journeyed to Spain. Welcomed at court, Doña Marina was rewarded with large land holdings and a position of deep respect.

1. Why was Doña Marina so valuable to Cortés?

2. **Evaluating Information** Do you think Cortés could have conquered the Aztecs without Doña Marina's help?

had dropped by 90 percent, mostly because of disease. The Spanish claimed that the hand of God was striking down the Aztecs.

Aztec and Inca treasures made the conquistadors rich. Spain grew rich, too, especially after the discovery of gold and silver mines in Mexico and Peru. Spanish treasure ships laden with thousands of tons of gold and silver sailed regularly across the Atlantic.

The Spanish Borderlands

While Cortés and Pizarro won riches in Central and South America, other conquistadors explored the southern half of the present-day United States. This area has been called the **Spanish borderlands.**

One adventurer, Juan Ponce de León (PAWN say day lay AWN), explored an island visited by Columbus. Sighting a beautiful bay north of the island, he called it Puerto Rico, or rich port. Later, Ponce de León put down a Taino (tay EEN yoh) Indian rebellion on Puerto Rico and became its first governor.

In 1513, Ponce de León decided to investigate an Indian story about a Fountain of Youth somewhere north of Puerto Rico. The Indians claimed that anyone who bathed in this magical fountain would remain young forever.

Ponce de León came upon a flower-filled peninsula, which he called Florida. But he found no fountain. In time, he returned to Puerto Rico, bringing back with him many Indians as slaves.

UP CLOSE

Adventures in the Spanish Borderlands

One remarkable journey across the Spanish borderlands began with disaster. In 1528, the conquistador Pánfilo Narváez (nahr VAH ehs) set off with 400 men for Florida. He proclaimed himself governor of

MAP STUDY

Conquistadors explored parts of North America in the 1500s. They mapped routes that Spanish missionaries and settlers later followed.
1. Which explorer was the first to visit Florida?
2. Which explorer crossed the Mississippi River?
3. **Comparing** (a) Which explorer traveled mostly overland? (b) Which explorers took water routes?

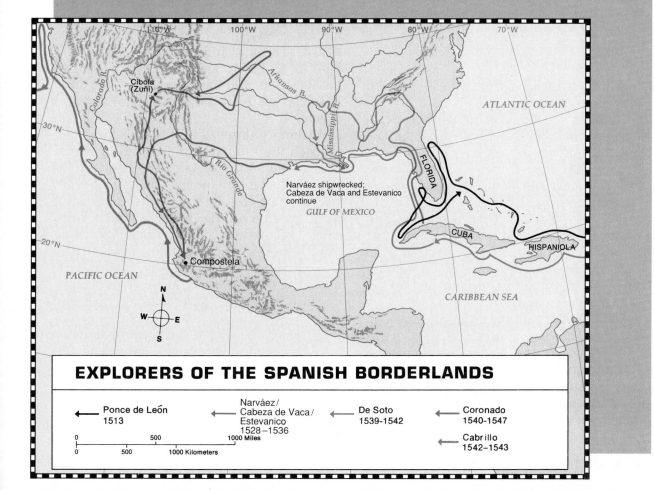

EXPLORERS OF THE SPANISH BORDERLANDS

← Ponce de León 1513

← Narváez/ Cabeza de Vaca/ Estevanico 1528–1536

← De Soto 1539-1542

← Coronado 1540-1547

← Cabrillo 1542–1543

0   500   1000 Miles
0   500   1000 Kilometers

Estevanico in the Spanish Borderlands *For three years, between 1533 and 1536, a tiny band of shipwreck survivors wandered through the Spanish borderlands, seeking a Spanish settlement—and rescue. Among these men was an African slave named Estevanico, pictured here during the journey.* **Daily Life** *What important skills did Estevanico have that helped the group to survive in the Spanish borderlands?*

the lands stretching from Florida to the Mississippi River.

Narváez was both reckless and inexperienced. When he attacked Native Americans and stole their food, they struck back. The Spanish were forced to retreat west along the coast and then across the mouth of the Mississippi River.

Sickness, battles with Indians, and shipwreck took a heavy toll, causing the death of nearly all of Narváez's men. One stormy night, Narváez himself, in a small boat, was blown into the Gulf of Mexico, never to be seen again.

Four survivors. In the end, only four men survived. The rugged Álvar Núñez Cabeza de Vaca became the leader. Estevanico, a tall and muscular African slave, became the group's translator and scout. Following the shipwreck, Cabeza de Vaca recalled how desperate they were.

❝[We] had lost everything. . . . It was November, bitterly cold, and we in such a state that every bone could be counted. . . . We looked like death itself.❞

The Charucco (chah ROO coh) Indians found the survivors and nursed them back to health. Much to the survivors' surprise, the Indians insisted that the four men act as healers. "[The Charuccos] cure illness by breathing on the sick . . . and they ordered us to do the same," Cabeza de Vaca reported.

At first, the survivors refused. But when the Indians deprived them of food they finally agreed to cooperate. "Our method," recalled Cabeza de Vaca, "was to bless the sick, breathing on them . . . praying with all earnestness to God our Lord that He would give health. . . ." When a number of the sick recovered, the Charuccos were impressed.

For nearly five years, the four men lived as slaves of the Charuccos. They ate mainly roots, spiders, worms, caterpillars, lizards, snakes, and ant eggs. Aside from healing the sick, the men were forced to gather, chop, and haul firewood. This labor left deep scars on the men's shoulders and chests.

A long journey. In 1533, the four men escaped their masters and set out in search of Spanish settlements to the west. Walking barefoot from Indian village to Indian village, they crossed the plains of Texas.

Throughout the journey, Estevanico communicated with the Indians. According to Cabeza de Vaca, "he inquired about the road we should follow, the villages—in short, about everything we wished to know." Hundreds of Indians flocked along with the four men, running ahead to the next village, bringing news of the great healers.

The journey continued across the Rio Grande and then south through the mountains and desert of Mexico. In 1536, the four men finally reached the Spanish settlement of Compostela (kahm poh STEH lah).

In Compostela, officials gave them beds and new clothes. But after eight years of living outdoors, the men "could not wear any [clothes] for some time, nor . . . sleep anywhere but on the ground."

It had been an astonishing journey of more than 1,000 miles. When Cabeza de Vaca returned to Spain, he wrote an account of his travels. Much of what we know today about early Native Americans in the Southwest, such as the Comanches, Apaches, and Sumas, comes from Cabeza de Vaca's report. ◆

Tales of Golden Cities

Two other conquistadors, Francisco Coronado (koh roh NAH doh) and Hernando De Soto, heard stories of the Seven Cities of Gold. Indians said that the streets were paved with gold and children played with emeralds. Since Aztec treasures had been so stunning, the conquistadors believed these stories.

In 1539, Coronado sent a scouting party north into present-day New Mexico. Because he could speak Indian languages, Estevanico was chosen as one of the leaders. But when his party reached a Zuñi village, Estevanico was killed in a battle. The next year, Coronado made his own journey. After great hardships, he found Zuñi villages, but no gold.

From 1539 to 1542, De Soto explored the southeast of the present-day United States. But he, too, died without finding gold. (Follow the routes taken by Ponce de León, Narváez/Cabeza de Vaca/Estevanico, Coronado, and De Soto on the map on page 75.)

At first, the conquistadors were welcomed by local Indians they met. But when the Spanish started to kill, rob, and enslave the Indians, the Indians fought back. Faced with fierce Indian resistance, Spain backed off from North America. Instead, Spain concentrated on its empire south of the borderlands. Before long, other nations began to explore and claim lands in North America.

SECTION 3 REVIEW

1. **Locate:** (a) Line of Demarcation, (b) Brazil, (c) Isthmus of Panama, (d) Pacific Ocean, (e) Philippine Islands, (f) Florida.
2. **Identify:** (a) Pedro Álvares Cabral, (b) Vasco Núñez de Balboa, (c) Montezuma, (d) Hernando Cortés, (e) Francisco Pizarro, (f) Spanish borderlands, (g) Juan Ponce de León, (h) Francisco Coronado.
3. **Define:** (a) conquistador, (b) strait.
4. Why was Magellan's voyage important?
5. Why did conquistadors explore the Spanish borderlands?
6. **Synthesizing Information** How did Cabeza de Vaca and his three companions survive for eight years in the Spanish borderlands?

4 Staking Claims in North America

FIND OUT

◆ What European nations searched for a northwest passage?

◆ How did the Protestant Reformation heighten rivalry between nations?

◆ How did England challenge Spain's control of the seas?

◆ **VOCABULARY** northwest passage

On August 6, 1497, a small ship docked in Bristol, England. The crew had just completed a 79-day voyage in the North Atlantic. A great crowd gathered to hear the report of the ship's captain, John Cabot. As one onlooker recorded, Cabot and his crew thought they had reached Asia:

> ❝They believe that brazilwood and silk are native there. . . . [On his next voyage,] Mr. Cabot . . . proposes to keep along the coast from the place at which he landed . . . until he reaches an island called [Japan]. Here he believes all the spices in the world have their origins, as well as jewels.❞

Cabot's voyage was one of many that Europeans made to North America. England, France, and the Netherlands all envied Spain's empire in the New World. They, too, wanted a share. Soon, they also outfitted voyages of discovery.

In Search of a Northwest Passage

Throughout the 1500s, European nations valued the riches of Asia more than land in North America. They saw North America as a barrier to these riches. But they did not want to use Magellan's long route around Cape Horn. Instead, they searched for a northwest passage, or waterway through or around North America.

John Cabot explores for England. Confident that he had reached Asia on his first voyage, the Italian sea captain John Cabot set sail from England in 1498 on a second voyage. On board his five vessels were a

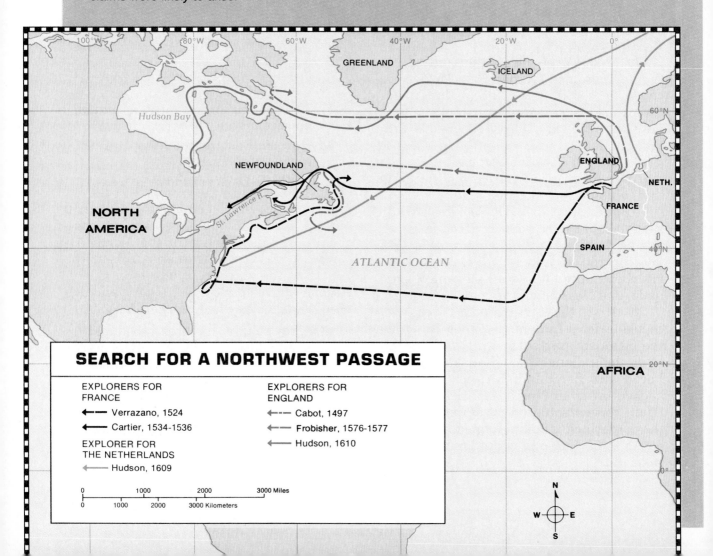

MAP STUDY

The search for a northwest passage sent explorers from many nations across the Atlantic.
1. For what nation did Hudson sail in 1610?
2. Which explorer sailed up the St. Lawrence River?
3. **Forecasting** Explorers usually claimed lands for the nation that had outfitted their voyage. Name two areas of North America where conflicts over land claims were likely to arise.

SEARCH FOR A NORTHWEST PASSAGE

EXPLORERS FOR FRANCE
- Verrazano, 1524
- Cartier, 1534-1536

EXPLORER FOR THE NETHERLANDS
- Hudson, 1609

EXPLORERS FOR ENGLAND
- Cabot, 1497
- Frobisher, 1576-1577
- Hudson, 1610

0   1000   2000   3000 Miles
0   1000   2000   3000 Kilometers

year's supply of food and many goods to trade with the Great Khan, the ruler of China.

Cabot explored the eastern coast of North America. Many think that he headed for Nova Scotia or perhaps present-day Maine. No one can be sure, for Cabot never returned. Even though he did not find Asia or a northwest passage, he led the way to exploration of the North Atlantic.

Verrazano and Cartier explore for France. In 1524, another Italian sailor, Giovanni da Verrazano (vehr rah TSAH noh), offered his services to the French. In search of a northwest passage, Verrazano probably sailed into New York harbor, where a bridge named after him stands today. Verrazano decided that the waterway was a dead end. (See "Scouting the Atlantic Coast" on page 636.)

France outfitted several more voyages. In the 1530s, Jacques Cartier (kahr tee YAY) sailed past Newfoundland and spotted the broad opening where the St. Lawrence River flows into the Atlantic. (See the map on page 78.) The opening looked as though it might lead to China.

Sailing up the St. Lawrence River, Cartier met a group of Iroquois. They told him about the kingdom of Saguenay (sag uh NAY), which they said had gold and silver mines. Some of Saguenay's people, the Iroquois added, hopped around on one leg or flew like bats.

Cartier believed these fabulous stories. In 1541, he left France again to search for Saguenay. Along the banks of the St. Lawrence, Cartier's men stumbled across what they believed to be diamonds and gold. They gathered more than 1,000 pounds of glittering stones and ten barrels of sparkling ore.

In the end, Cartier returned to France without finding Saguenay or a northwest passage. In France, he suffered another disappointment. The stones and ore he had brought back were not diamonds and gold, but quartz crystals and "fool's gold." Still, he had claimed many lands for France and had built the first French settlements in Canada.

Henry Hudson's Last Voyage *Rebellion by the crew was a constant threat on long voyages of discovery. This painting shows Henry Hudson and his son drifting among the icebergs after Hudson's men cast them out.* **Geography** *What was the purpose of Hudson's voyage?*

Frobisher and Hudson. In the late 1500s and early 1600s, the English tried again to find a northwest passage. Between 1576 and 1578, Queen Elizabeth I sent Martin Frobisher on three voyages of exploration. She encouraged Frobisher to explore parts of northern Canada. There, he found more fool's gold and met Eskimos. But he discovered no ice-free passage west.

Henry Hudson sailed for both the English and the Dutch. In 1609, while Hudson sailed for the Dutch, his ship, the *Half Moon,* headed into New York harbor. Hudson hoped that it was a northwest passage. Unlike Verrazano, he sailed some 150 miles (240 km) up the river that now bears his name.

Hudson made his final voyage for the English. He sailed into the far north, exploring what was later named Hudson Bay. Here, Hudson's crew rebelled. They put Hudson, his son, and seven loyal sailors into a small boat and set it adrift. The boat and its crew were never seen again.

Explorers kept looking for a northwest passage in the 1700s and 1800s. A route to the Pacific Ocean across the top of North America does exist. But it is blocked by ice for most of the year. The first successful trip through this passage was finally made in 1906.

Rivalries Among European Nations

Racing to gain more riches and trade, European nations became fierce rivals. Differences in religious beliefs heightened their rivalry. Until the 1500s, the Roman Catholic Church was the only church in western Europe. But in 1517, Catholics were divided by a new movement that called for religious reforms in the Church.

Protests against the Church. In that year, a German monk named Martin Luther nailed a list of 95 theses, or questions for debate, on a church door in Germany. These questions challenged practices of the Catholic Church. Luther said that the clergy should lead holier lives and study the Bible more closely.

Luther also objected to Church teachings on salvation, that is, how to gain eternal life. Catholic teaching emphasized the good works that believers should perform in order to be saved. Luther argued that, no matter how many good works a person performed, God's highest standard could never be met. People could be saved only by having faith that God would save them.

The followers of Luther became known as Protestants because of their protests against the Church. "Faith alone" became their rallying cry.

Catholics versus Protestants. The new movement, known as the **Protestant Reformation,** sharply divided Church members in Europe. Within a short time, the Protestants split, forming many different Protestant churches.

In the religious wars that followed, Catholics and Protestants tortured and killed one another. These religious wars became mixed up with political wars for power and territory. When European nations expanded to the Americas, they fought their religious and political wars there, too.

Spain versus England. In 1534, King Henry VIII became one of the first European rulers to break officially with the Pope in Rome. He declared himself the head of the Church of England and built a strong nation independent of Rome.

In the late 1500s, Spain was the strongest Catholic nation in Europe. England, on the other hand, was the strongest Protestant nation. The two nations became bitter enemies. When Henry's daughter Elizabeth became queen, the Spanish king, Philip II, tried to settle the matter by marrying her. But Queen Elizabeth turned him down. She feared that Philip would conquer England and force Protestants to return to the Catholic faith.

The Sea Dogs. Philip was insulted when Elizabeth declined his marriage proposal. But he was enraged when he learned that Elizabeth allowed English adventurers to rob Spanish treasure ships and raid Spanish colonies in the Americas. These adventurers were known in England as **Sea Dogs** —though the Spanish called them pirates! With Elizabeth's encouragement, the English Sea Dogs won fame and fortune.

Perhaps the boldest Sea Dog was Francis Drake. In 1577, Drake, called "the sea serpent" by the Spanish, took Magellan's route around Cape Horn. He attacked Spanish settlements in Peru. At one port, Drake forced helpless Spanish officials to dine with him on board his ship, the *Golden Hind.* As they dined, some of Drake's crew members played violins, while others snatched up Spanish treasure. Drake then continued farther up the Pacific coast before sailing west across the Pacific Ocean.

Drake returned to England in 1580, after sailing around the world. He received a hero's welcome, especially since the *Golden Hind* was filled with Spanish gold. Hearing the news, Philip demanded that Elizabeth seize Drake.

On April 4, 1581, Elizabeth boarded Drake's ship. To her Sea Dog she said, "His

The Court of Elizabeth I *During the reign of Elizabeth I, England enjoyed a period of great prosperity. The great wealth of Elizabeth's court is shown in this scene painted by a Flemish artist in 1600.* **Citizenship** *Why do you think kings and queens felt they needed splendid courts?*

majesty [Philip] has demanded Drake's head of me, and here I have a [golden] sword to strike it off." With these words, Elizabeth ordered Drake to kneel. In the presence of many European officials, Elizabeth touched each of Drake's shoulders with the sword. "I bid thee rise Sir Francis Drake," commanded Elizabeth. Now, her Sea Dog was an English nobleman.

Defeat of the Spanish Armada

In 1588, Philip struck back. To crush the English, he sent the **Spanish Armada,** the largest fleet in the world at that time. Even though the 130 Spanish ships far outnumbered the English, the small English ships were able to outsail the Armada.

The Sea Dogs led the fight, and many adventurous English fishermen joined them. During the battle, a violent storm scattered the Armada. Some Spanish ships fled up the Irish coast, where they were wrecked. Others narrowly made it back to Spanish ports. The Armada returned home in disgrace.

Defeat of the Armada did not end Spanish power in the Americas. But the English had clearly broken the Spanish hold on the Atlantic. In the years after 1588, England, France, and other nations began to establish their own colonies in North America.

SECTION 4 REVIEW

1. **Locate:** (a) Newfoundland, (b) St. Lawrence River, (c) Hudson Bay.
2. **Identify:** (a) John Cabot, (b) Jacques Cartier, (c) Henry Hudson, (d) Martin Luther, (e) Protestant Reformation, (f) Queen Elizabeth, (g) Sea Dogs, (h) Francis Drake, (i) Spanish Armada.
3. **Define:** northwest passage.
4. What Catholic practices and teachings did Martin Luther protest?
5. Why were Spain and England rivals in the late 1500s?
6. Why did King Philip send out the Spanish Armada against England in 1588?
7. **Analyzing a Quotation** One historian called the Sea Dogs the "conquistadors of the Atlantic." Do you agree? Explain.

Every major event in history has both causes and effects. **Causes** are events or conditions that produced the major event. They explain why the event happened. **Effects** are events or conditions that resulted from the causes.

One major event that historians study is the Columbian Exchange. It is named after Columbus, because his voyages to the Americas led to the movement, or exchange, of products, ideas, and even diseases between Europe and the Americas. The chart below lists some causes and effects. The arrows show the order of events, from causes of the exchange to its effects.

The following steps will help you to understand causes and effects. Rely on what you have read and the chart to answer the questions.

1 **Study events that took place before the major event to find causes.** (a) Which causes of the Columbian Exchange occurred after the Crusades? (b) Which causes occurred after Europeans sought new trade routes to Asia?

2 **Identify both immediate and long-range causes.** Immediate causes take place shortly before the major event and help trigger it. Long-range causes are underlying causes that build up over a longer period of time. (a) Which cause of the Columbian Exchange was most immediate? (b) Which cause was most long-range?

3 **Study events that took place after the major event to find effects.** (a) What religion spread in the New World as a result of the Columbian Exchange? (b) What affected farming methods?

4 **Identify both immediate and long-range effects.** Immediate effects take place shortly after the major event and are directly triggered by it. Long-range effects build up over a longer period of time. (a) Which effect of the Columbian Exchange was probably most immediate? (b) Why would European use of raw materials from the Americas in the late 1700s be a long-range effect?

5 **Analyze the causes and effects.** (a) Why was the settlement of European colonies in the Americas a cause of the Columbian Exchange? (b) Why did millions of Native Americans die from European diseases?

CAUSES

- Crusades broaden the European view of the world
- Europeans seek new trade routes to Asia
- Columbus explores the Caribbean
- European nations set up colonies in the Americas

THE COLUMBIAN EXCHANGE

EFFECTS

- New foods are introduced into European and Native American diets
- Introduction of European work animals affects farming methods in the Americas
- Millions of Native Americans die from "European" diseases
- Christianity spreads to the New World
- In the late 1700s, European industries use raw materials from the Americas

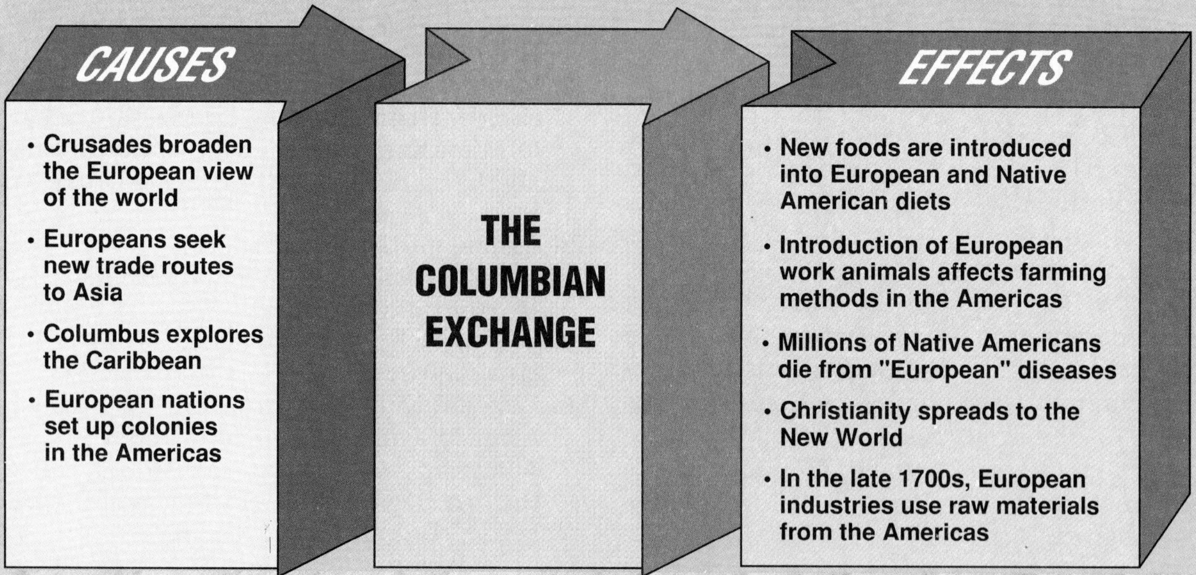

Use the Section Reviews and this Study Guide to review chapter content.

Main Ideas

The main ideas in each section of this chapter are summarized below.

SECTION 1 ■ Europe Reaches Out to a Wider World

◆ The Vikings were the first Europeans to settle in North America.
◆ From 1100 to 1300, Europeans joined the Crusades to free the Holy Land.
◆ During the Renaissance, the printing press helped spread new information.

SECTION 2 ■ Search for New Trade Routes

◆ Prince Henry the Navigator founded a school for sailors that encouraged Portuguese exploration.
◆ By the late 1400s, the Portuguese developed trade with Africa and Asia.
◆ In 1492, Columbus sailed west and reached the West Indies.

SECTION 3 ■ Explorers and Conquerors

◆ Spanish explorers discovered the Pacific Ocean and sailed around the world.
◆ In the 1500s, the Spanish conquered the Aztec and Inca empires.
◆ The Spanish explored the borderlands and came upon many different Native American peoples.

SECTION 4 ■ Staking Claims in North America

◆ The English, French, and Dutch made many voyages to North America in search of a northwest passage to Asia.
◆ After the Reformation, England became the strongest Protestant nation and Spain the strongest Catholic nation.
◆ In 1588, the English defeated the Spanish Armada, breaking Spain's hold on the Atlantic Ocean.

Key People and Terms

Refer to the Identify and Define questions in the Section Reviews on pages 63, 69, 77, and 81. Use each person, term, and vocabulary word in a complete sentence. When possible, make connections between the people and terms by using more than one person or term in a sentence.

Time Line

1. Make a chart of events in time order. The chart will have two headings: Date, Event. Fill in the chart, using the events on the time line. Add the following events from the chapter: Dias rounds tip of Africa; England defeats Armada; Renaissance begins. (Refer to the chapter for dates.)
2. Which event was a result of the Muslim conquest of the Holy Land?

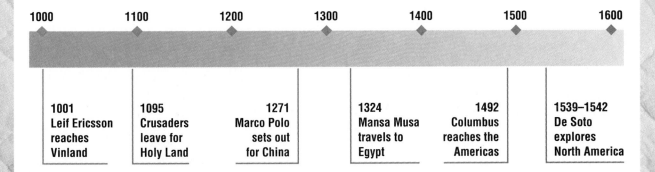

1000	1100	1200	1300	1400	1500	1600
1001 Leif Ericsson reaches Vinland	1095 Crusaders leave for Holy Land	1271 Marco Polo sets out for China		1324 Mansa Musa travels to Egypt	1492 Columbus reaches the Americas	1539–1542 De Soto explores North America

Understanding Vocabulary

Match each term at left with the correct definition at right.

1. feudalism
2. serf
3. caravel
4. conquistador
5. northwest passage

a. ship with triangular sails and a rudder for steering
b. system of rule by lords who owe loyalty to their king
c. Spanish conquerer
d. waterway through or around North America
e. peasant bound to the land for life

Reviewing the Main Ideas

1. Describe manor life during the Middle Ages.
2. (a) Why did the Pope urge Europeans to go on a Crusade? (b) What were three results of the Crusades?
3. What three improvements were made in sailing in the 1400s?
4. (a) Why did the Portuguese king refuse to help Columbus? (b) What ruler helped Columbus? (c) What did Columbus continue to seek on all his voyages?
5. Why were the Spanish able to conquer the huge Aztec and Inca empires?
6. (a) What was the Protestant Reformation? (b) How did the Reformation heighten rivalries among European nations?
7. (a) Why did European nations send explorers to North America? (b) Name the explorers who went to North America for England and France.

Thinking Critically

1. **Linking Past and Present** Compare the explorations of Columbus and other European adventurers with the explorations of today.
2. **Evaluating Information** Study Marco Polo's description of China on page 57. How might these words have influenced European ideas about Asia?

3. **Defending a Position** Review the story of Doña Marina on page 74. Do you think she was a traitor to her people or a heroine? Explain your position.
4. **Synthesizing Information** What personal qualities did European explorers share? Provide four descriptive words.

Applying Your Skills

1. **Understanding Causes and Effects** Review the definitions for causes and effects in Skill Lesson 3 on page 82. (a) What was one cause of the bitter rivalry between England and Spain? (b) What was one effect of their rivalry?
2. **Making a Review Chart** Make a chart with four headings: Explorer, Date(s) of Voyage(s), For What Country, Results of Voyage(s). Fill in the chart with all the explorers mentioned in this chapter.
3. **Ranking** Review the explorations of Balboa, Cartier, Columbus, Hudson, and Magellan. Then, rank them according to which you think was most important. In a few sentences, explain your ranking.
4. **Making a Generalization** Review what you read about Columbus. (a) List three facts about his life. (b) Make a generalization about his life based on the facts you listed.

Match the letters on the map with the places listed below.

1. Africa
2. Asia
3. Europe
4. China
5. India
6. East Indies
7. West Indies
8. Mediterranean Sea

Movement Why did Europeans want to reach Asia?

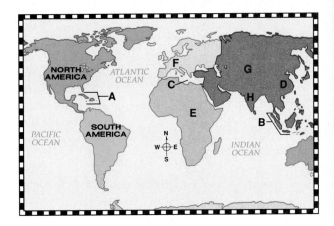

*H*istory *Writer's Workshop*

Rewording a Question as a Topic Sentence

The topic sentence in a one-paragraph answer states the main idea of the answer. You can often write a topic sentence by rewording the question.

Look at the following question: *How did the Crusades change Europe?* By rewording the question, you might write the following topic sentence. *The Crusades changed Europe in four important ways.*

Note that the topic sentence includes the clues in the question. The phrase *in four important ways* covers what the key word *How* in the question is telling you to do (tell in what way). The words *Crusades* and *Europe* are clues that limit the topic to a specific place and time.

You may reword the question as a topic sentence without covering the key word. For example: *The Crusades caused changes throughout Europe.* But keep the key word in mind when you later select information for detail sentences.

Practice Reword each of the following questions as a topic sentence for a one-paragraph answer.

1. Compare Cartier's and Hudson's searches for a northwest passage.
2. Why were Cortés and Pizarro able to conquer the Aztecs and Incas?

Writing to Learn

1. Imagine that you are one of Montezuma's messengers. Describe the Spanish conquistadors landing on your shores. Begin by freewriting about the events. Include facts, sense impressions, and reactions. In your first draft, capture your readers' interest with a dramatic topic sentence. Organize details in time order or order of importance. Revise your description for unity, and make a final copy. Then, share it with a classmate.

2. Write a short biography about one person in the chapter. First, research and record details about the person's life. Begin your first draft with a topic sentence that states the person's major accomplishments. Next, arrange the details in time order. Revise the biography for clarity and accuracy. Then, proofread and make a final copy. Publish a collection of historical biographies written by your classmates.

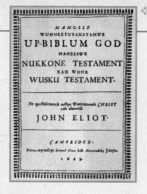

The First American Bible

John Eliot, a missionary from England, hoped to convert Native Americans to Christianity. So he translated the Bible into a dialect of Algonquin, a language of one of the peoples who lived in the Eastern Woodlands.

In 1661, his translation of the New Testament was printed, the first in North America. Today, no one can read Eliot's translation, however, because scholars understand little of the language.

Badlands

Strange shapes rise from the earth in the Badlands of South Dakota. The Dakota Indians first named this area *mako sica,* or land that was bad, because there was little good water. Wind, weather, and rivers carved startling shapes out of the Badlands and have revealed traces of the area's ancient history. Scientists have found the remains of giant turtles, camels, and saber-toothed tigers in deep layers of rock. Today, bear, elk, moose, and deer roam through the Badlands.

Over many years people have also tried to live there. Indians camped in the Badlands during buffalo hunts. Then, in the early 1900s, white settlers built homes there. But the lack of water constantly drove people out. It seems that nature has reserved this strange and beautiful place for itself.

A Lucky Oak

Many Native Americans of North America believed that oak trees were sacred and had many special powers because the trees were strong and tall. According to their traditions, the oak tree was home to the sky god or Great Spirit.

Touching the wood of the oak tree could be a prayer to the Great Spirit. A person might knock on the trunk of the tree to make a wish or to ask forgiveness for bragging. Today, the superstition of knocking on wood for luck is still with us.

A Relaxing Steambath

Native Americans living on the upper Missouri River knew how to relax in style. They took steambaths to relax sore muscles after a hunt or battle.

A tired hunter sat in his "sweatlodge" and carefully poured cold water onto hot rocks piled in a pit on the floor. The water hitting the rocks created a warm steam. Then the hunter closed the front flap of the lodge to keep the steam inside.

Medicine men also used sweatlodges for purification before sacred rituals.

The Land of Tomorrow

KENTUCKY
THE BLUEGRASS STATE

Many words in our language today were originally Native America words. *Skunk, raccoon, chipmunk, avocado,* and *pecan* are all Indian words. Even the word *buck* meaning dollar goes back to the days when Indians traded buckskins for other goods.

More than half of the states have Native American names. Did you know that in Cherokee, Kentucky means "the land of tomorrow" or "dark and bloody ground"? Mississippi is the Algonquin word for "big river." And in the Dakota language, Minnesota means "cloudy water."

Columbus's Secret Signature

Christopher Columbus was a very secretive man who signed his name in many different ways. One of his special signatures was a word puzzle. For his first name, he combined letters from both the Greek and Latin alphabets. The Greek *Xpo* means "Christ," and *ferens* is Latin for "bearing." According to one legend from the Middle Ages, St. Christopher had helped Christ carry the cross to his crucifixion. Columbus probably would have been happy to know that scholars spent many years studying his secret signature before they were able to understand it.

Footnotes to History

◆ The Pueblo of Acoma in New Mexico is the oldest continuously lived in settlement in the United States. Today, it appears almost the same as it did when Coronado saw it in the early 1500s.

◆ The Incas tied their vast empire together with more than 10,000 miles of roads. Well-trained teams of relay runners carried messages along these roads, often as far as 140 miles a day.

◆ Queen Isabella of Spain agreed to support Columbus's venture against the advice of her advisers.

◆ When Europeans arrived in the Americas, Native Americans spoke over 1,000 different languages.

UNIT *1* SUMMARY

Chapter 1 Geography of the Americas

History is closely linked to geography. The land and its resources affect the way people live and, in turn, the way a nation or a civilization develops. Geography describes where an event occurs (location), what the location is like (place), and how people have adapted to or altered the place (interaction). Geography also explains what happens when people need new resources (movement) and what makes an area unique (region).

Maps are among the most useful tools of geography. Cartographers have developed map projections to show the round Earth on the flat surface of a map. Each projection has benefits and disadvantages, showing one or more aspects of the Earth correctly but distorting others.

A grid of latitude and longitude lines is used to locate places on a map. Lines of latitude and longitude also divide the world into hemispheres. North America, South America, and the Caribbean islands are in the Western Hemisphere. Finally, lines of longitude divide the world into time zones.

Geographers have identified seven physical regions in North America. The regions differ from one another in their landforms, or natural features, and in their resources. The Pacific Coast, for example, is largely mountainous. The neighboring Intermountain region is marked by high plateaus, canyons, and deserts. The Canadian Shield has hills and plains that are rich in minerals.

Like the landscape, the climate of North America is varied. Several factors affect climate, including distance from the Equator, altitude, wind and ocean currents, and mountains. The United States itself has ten climates. They range from arctic in northern Alaska to tropical in southern Florida.

Chapter 2 The First Americans

The first Americans arrived in Alaska during the last ice age. Over thousands of years, their descendants moved across the continent, leaving behind pottery, tools, and other artifacts. Archaeologists study these remains to learn about early Native Americans.

Native Americans settled in groups throughout North America. The climate and resources of the land shaped their ways of life. Groups living in different regions developed different survival skills and different cultures.

Where the environment was harsh, life was hard. To survive in the frigid Far North, for example, Eskimos became nomadic hunters and built houses of ice and snow. In regions with favorable climates and plentiful resources, people built permanent settlements and organized communities.

In Central and South America, Native Americans built several large empires. Almost 3,000 years ago, the Mayas built great cities in the rain forests of Mexico. As their empire grew, the Mayas developed a calendar, a number system that included zero, and a system of writing. Farther north, the warrior Aztecs rose to power in the 1300s. From their splendid capital city, Tenochtitlán, they controlled the Valley of Mexico. The Inca empire in the Andes Mountains was even larger. Highly organized, the Incas were successful farmers and great builders. Their temples and forts are considered wonders of the Americas.

Chapter 3 European Exploration

About the year 1000, the Vikings reached North America. But European interest in the outside world was not awakened until the crusaders began returning from the

through deep snow to find their traps. Travel was especially hard when the weather suddenly warmed after a cold spell. One Frenchman wrote:

> “If a thaw came, dear Lord, what pain! . . . I was marching on an icy path that broke with every step I took; as the snow softened . . . we often sunk in it up to our knees and a few times up to the waist.”

In the spring, trappers loaded furs into canoes for the trip down the St. Lawrence. At the French settlements, they traded the furs for blankets, kettles, and other goods they needed for the next winter.

GEOGRAPHY AND HISTORY
“Father of the Waters”

French trappers and traders followed the St. Lawrence deep into the heart of North America. Led by Indian guides, they reached the Great Lakes. Here, Indians spoke of a mighty river, which they called Mississippi, or “Father of the Waters.”

Catholic missionaries often traveled with the fur traders. The missionaries were determined to convert the Indians to Christianity. They set up missions, drew maps, and wrote about the newly explored lands.

Marquette and Joliet. In 1673, a missionary named Father Jacques Marquette (mahr KEHT) and a fur trader named Louis Joliet (JOH lee eht) set out in canoes across Lake Michigan. Guided by Indians, they paddled south and then west until they reached the Mississippi. They were very excited by this discovery, thinking they had at last found a passage to Asia.

Marquette and Joliet followed the Mississippi for more than 700 miles (1,100 km). When they realized that the river emptied into the Gulf of Mexico, not into the Pacific, they were disappointed and turned back. In 1682, another explorer, Robert de La Salle (lah SAHL), completed the journey to the Gulf. La Salle claimed the entire Mississippi Valley for France. He named the region **Louisiana** in honor of the French king, Louis XIV.

Building forts for defense. To keep Spain and England out of Louisiana, the French built forts along the Mississippi. One of these was New Orleans, at the mouth of the river. New Orleans soon grew

Claiming the Mississippi Valley *Robert La Salle's journey to the mouth of the Mississippi took four months by canoe. In this painting, George Catlin shows the dramatic moment when La Salle claimed the entire Mississippi Valley for France.* **Multicultural Heritage** *How do you think La Salle's claim affected Native Americans, such as those in the painting?*

into a busy trading center. The French also built forts along the Great Lakes, in the north. One of these, Fort Detroit, was built by Antoine Cadillac near Lake Erie. ◆

New France Grows Slowly

New France was governed much like New Spain. The French king controlled the government directly, and settlers had little freedom. All decisions were made by a council appointed by the king.

The French try farming. In 1665, Louis XIV decided to encourage farming in New France. He appointed a new governor and sent him to the colony with 1,000 farmers. To develop family life, the governor included many young women in the group. Some were nobles. Others came from middle-class or peasant families. Most women were single, but they soon found husbands. Peasant women were in greatest demand because they were used to hard work.

Despite efforts to encourage farming, trappers still outnumbered farmers in New France. People made more money trapping than farming. Also, only nobles could own land. So farmers had to work for the nobles directly or else pay them rent.

By 1680, only about 10,000 people lived in New France. Of those, one third lived on farms along the St. Lawrence. Many more chose the life of the coureurs de bois, who lived largely free of government control.

Lasting French influence. As the coureurs de bois hunted for furs, they explored large parts of North America. Following Indian trails, they mapped routes from the Gulf of Mexico to northern Canada.

The French built towns and trading posts across a large expanse of land. French influence is seen today in place names such as Vermont (green mountain), Terre Haute (high land), and Baton Rouge (red stick).

Building New Netherland

In the 1600s, the Dutch set up the colony of **New Netherland** in North America. As you have read, the Dutch hired an English explorer, Henry Hudson, to search for a northwest passage. In 1609, Hudson found the mouth of the present-day Hudson River.

At first, the Dutch paid little attention to Hudson's discovery. Then, in January 1626, Peter Minuit (MIHN yoo wiht) led a group of Dutch settlers to North America. In a famous bargain, he bought Manhat-

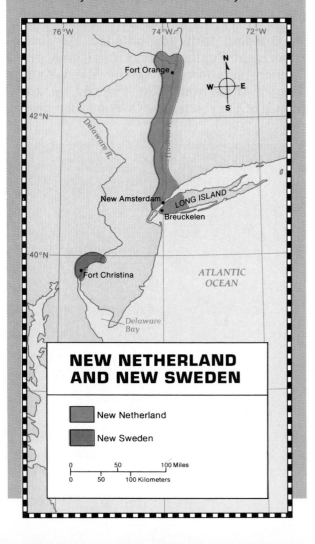

MAP STUDY

The Netherlands and Sweden both claimed lands in North America.
1. *Which country claimed the larger area?*
2. *(a) Along which river did the Netherlands claim lands? (b) Along which river did Sweden claim lands?*
3. **Linking Past and Present** *Determine the latitude and longitude of Fort Orange. Then, look at the map on pages 716–717. What city is located on this site today?*

NEW NETHERLAND AND NEW SWEDEN

- New Netherland
- New Sweden

0   50   100 Miles
0   50   100 Kilometers

$\mathcal{L}$INKING • PAST • AND • PRESENT

Wall Street

Wall Street is often the subject of today's financial news. But Wall Street had its beginnings more than 300 years ago in the Dutch settlement of New Amsterdam, shown in the map below.

In 1653, the Dutch decided to build a wall along New Amsterdam's northern boundary. They believed they needed it to protect their settlement against attack. The wall followed a winding cowpath called Broadway. It was built of wooden logs stood on end and tapered to sharp points at the top. The total cost was $1,350.

In time, the wall fell down, and people stole the logs for firewood. At last, the wall disappeared completely. But the path it had followed remained. The path was named Wall Street.

Today, Wall Street, above, is one of the world's best-known and most powerful financial centers. Major stock exchanges, brokerage houses, and banks operate there. In place of the wooden wall, soaring skyscrapers now rise high above both sides of the narrow street.

1. How did Wall Street get its name?

2. **Applying Information** What streets or other places in your community get their name from their location?

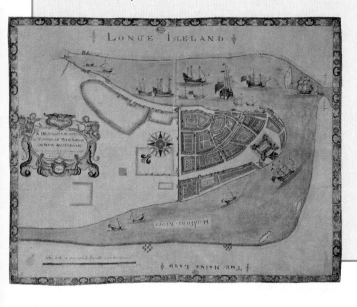

tan Island from local Indians. Minuit called his settlement New Amsterdam.

Settlers in New Amsterdam planted their first crops for harvest in the fall of 1626. These included grains new to the Americas—wheat, oats, and barley.

Rivalry over furs. In September 1626, the settlers sent a shipload of furs back to the Netherlands. The packing list included "the skins of 7,246 beaver, 853 otter, 81 mink, 36 cat lynx, and 34 small rats."

In the hunt for furs, the Dutch became fierce rivals of the French and their Indian allies, the Algonquins (al GAHN kwihnz). The Dutch made friends with the Iroquois, longtime enemies of the Algonquins. They gave guns to the Iroquois to fight the Algonquins. With Iroquois help, the Dutch brought furs down the Hudson to New Amsterdam. The French and Algonquins fought back. For many years, fighting raged among Europeans and their Indian allies.

The Dutch capture New Sweden. About 1640, Swedish settlers arrived in North America. They set up the colony of **New Sweden** along the Delaware River. The Swedes built a town where Wilmington stands today. Some Dutch settlers helped their Swedish neighbors, but most Dutch resented the nearby Swedish colony. Fighting broke out between the colonies. In 1655, the Dutch took over New Sweden.

Dutch Ways in North America

As you will read, England gained control of New Amsterdam in 1664. But by then the Dutch had left their mark on the area. New Amsterdam had grown into a bustling port for ships from all around the world. The Dutch welcomed people of many nations and religions to their colony. One Dutch governor boasted that more than 15 languages could be heard in the streets of New Amsterdam.

The Dutch liked to ice-skate, and in winter the frozen rivers and ponds filled with skaters. An English visitor described the scene. "It is admirable," he wrote, "to see men and women, as it were, flying upon their skates from place to place with [baskets] on their heads and backs."

Many Dutch customs became part of American culture. For example, every year on Saint Nicholas's birthday, children put out their shoes to be filled with presents. Later, "Saint Nick" became Santa Claus, and the custom of giving gifts was moved to Christmas Eve.

Some Dutch words entered the English language. A Dutch master was a "boss." The people of New Amsterdam sailed in "yachts." Dutch children munched on "cookies" and "crullers" and listened to ghost stories about "spooks."

Impact on Native Americans

The coming of Europeans to North America brought major changes for Native Americans. As in New Spain, European diseases killed thousands of Native Americans. Indians told one Dutch explorer that their people were "melted down" by disease. "Before the smallpox broke out among them," the explorer said, "they were ten times as numerous as they are now."

Rivalry over the fur trade brought increased Indian warfare as European settlers encouraged their Indian allies to attack one another. The scramble for furs also led to overtrapping. By 1640, trappers had almost wiped out the beavers on Iroquois lands in upstate New York.

The arrival of European settlers affected Native Americans in other ways. Missionaries tried to convert Indians to Christianity. Indians gave up hunting with bows and arrows in favor of muskets and gunpowder bought from Europeans. Alcohol sold by European traders had a terrible effect on Indian life.

The French, Dutch, and English influenced fewer Indians than the Spanish because there were fewer Indians where they settled. Even so, all these Europeans seized Indian lands. The displaced Indian nations then moved westward onto the lands of other Indians. In the end, all these European nations enslaved Native Americans and sold them to plantations in the West Indies.

SECTION 2 REVIEW

1. **Locate:** (a) Port Royal, (b) Quebec, (c) New France, (d) New Netherland, (e) New Sweden.
2. **Identify:** (a) Samuel de Champlain, (b) Jacques Marquette, (c) Louis Joliet, (d) Robert de La Salle, (e) Peter Minuit.
3. **Define:** coureur de bois.
4. Why did settlers in New France prefer trapping to farming?
5. How did the arrival of the French and Dutch lead to increased warfare among Native Americans?
6. **Comparing** (a) Name two ways New France differed from New Spain. (b) Name two ways they were similar.

3 The First English Colonies

FIND OUT

◆ What hardships did the Jamestown settlers endure?

◆ How did tobacco help save the Jamestown Colony?

◆ How did self-government begin in Virginia?

◆ **VOCABULARY** charter, joint stock company, capital, burgess, representative government, royal colony

❝If England possesses these places in America, Her Majesty will have good harbors, plenty of excellent trees for masts, good timber to build ships . . . all things needed for a royal navy, and all for no price.❞

Richard Hakluyt wrote these words to convince Queen Elizabeth I of England to plant colonies in North America. Hakluyt listed a total of 31 arguments in favor of settlement. "We shall," Hakluyt concluded, "[stop] the Spanish king from flowing over all the face . . . of America."

Hakluyt's pamphlet, written in 1584, appealed to English pride. England's rival, Spain, had built a great empire in the New World. England was determined to win a place in the Americas, too.

U P CLOSE

Mystery at Roanoke

The man who encouraged Hakluyt to write his pamphlet was Sir Walter Raleigh. Raleigh was a favorite of Queen Elizabeth. She presented him with special gifts and often had rich foods from the palace kitchens sent to his lodgings.

Looking for profit and fame, Raleigh asked Elizabeth to grant him a charter. A **charter** is a legal document giving certain rights to a person or company. Elizabeth's charter gave Raleigh the right to set up a colony in North America.

The first colonists arrive. By 1585, Raleigh had raised enough money to send seven ships and about 100 men across the Atlantic. They landed on Roanoke (ROH uh nohk), an island off the coast of present-day North Carolina. Among the settlers was an artist, John White, who made vivid drawings of the new land and its people.

For a year, the colonists searched without success for gold and silver. When they ran out of food, they demanded corn from nearby Indians. Fighting broke out. The settlers were tired, discouraged, and hungry. When an English ship stopped in the harbor the next year, the weary settlers climbed aboard and sailed for home.

A second attempt. In 1587, Raleigh asked John White to return to Roanoke with another group of colonists. To help the settlers set up a farming community, Raleigh sent along a number of women. Among the women was White's daughter, Ellinor Dare, who came with her husband.

American Wildlife *John White's skillful drawings, such as that of a box tortoise shown here, gave many Europeans their first glimpse of New World plants and animals.* **Geography** *Why do you think White's drawings would be valuable for people who planned to settle in the New World?*

In Roanoke, Ellinor gave birth to the first English child born in North America. She was christened Virginia Dare.

When supplies ran low, White returned to England. He left behind 117 colonists, including his daughter and granddaughter. Before sailing, White instructed the settlers carefully. If they moved to another place, the settlers were to carve the name of their new location on a tree. If they were attacked, they were to draw a cross.

White planned to return to Roanoke in a few months. But in England he found the whole nation preparing for war. Every available ship was being outfitted to defend England against the Spanish Armada. Not a single vessel could be spared to send help to the settlers at Roanoke.

Gone without a trace. It was three years before White was able to obtain a ship and set sail in search of his family. At Roanoke, he dropped anchor and rowed ashore. A sailor played a few English tunes on a trumpet to let the settlers know that help had arrived. There was no reply.

White proceeded to the fort. What he saw there only increased his fears. Houses stood empty and vines twined through the windows. Pumpkins sprouted from the earthen floors. White described the scene in his journal:

> ❝Several chests had been hidden, but dug up again. . . . My books were torn from the covers, the frames from my pictures and maps were rotted and broken by the rain, and my armor was almost eaten through with rust.❞

But there was still hope. No cross—the sign for an attack—was found. And the word *CROATOAN* was carved on a tree. White knew that Croatoan was the name of local Indians. It was also the name of a nearby island.

White was eager to set out for Croatoan. But a storm was blowing up, and the crew refused to make the trip. The waters around the island were too rough, they insisted. The next day, White stood sadly on board as the captain set course for England. White never saw his family again.

To this day, the fate of Roanoke's settlers remains a mystery. What happened to the "lost colony"? Did the settlers join the Croatoans? Did they starve to death? Were they killed by unfriendly Indians? No one knows. ◆

The Lost Colony *What happened to the settlers of Roanoke Colony? When John White returned from England, all the colonists, including White's family, were gone. The only trace of them was the word CROATOAN carved into the bark of a tree.*
American Traditions *What does the fate of the Roanoke settlers show about the problems of setting up colonies in the Americas?*

A Settlement at Jamestown

Nearly 20 years passed before England tried to set up a colony again. Then, in 1606, the **Virginia Company** of London received a charter from King James I. The charter gave the company the right to settle land to the north of Roanoke, between North Carolina and the Potomac River. The land was called Virginia. The charter guaranteed colonists the same rights as English citizens.

Raising money. To raise money for the colony, the Virginia Company organized a joint stock company, or private trading company that sold shares to investors. For years, merchants had used joint stock companies to finance, or pay for, trading voyages. In a joint stock company, a group of merchants pooled their funds to form a company. Each merchant got shares of stock for the money he put into the pool.

When the joint stock company raised enough capital, or money for investment, it outfitted ships for trading voyages. If the ships returned safely, the cargoes were sold. Each investor then received a share of the profits.

Hard times. In December 1606, the Virginia Company sent 144 men aboard three small ships to Virginia. In the spring of 1607, the 104 who survived the stormy journey sailed into the Chesapeake Bay and headed inland. They sailed up a river they called the James, after King James I, until they reached a wooded area. Here, they climbed ashore and began building homes. They named their tiny outpost Jamestown.

The colonists faced problems from the start. The land was swampy. Mosquitoes swarmed, and the water was undrinkable. Before long, many of the settlers died from disease.

Governing the colony also proved difficult. The Virginia Company had chosen a council of 13 men to rule the settlement. But members of the council quarreled with each other and did little to plan for the colony's future. Without guidance, most colonists spent their days hunting for gold instead of planting crops.

John Smith takes command. By the summer of 1608, the Jamestown Colony was on the edge of failure. Those settlers who had not died from disease or hardship were ready to give up and go home. It was Captain John Smith, a swashbuckling soldier, who saved the settlement from disaster. (See "John Smith Saves Jamestown" on page 638.)

John Smith thrived on adventure. Only 27 years old, he had already fought in France and the Netherlands and in wars against the Turks. He had taken part in battles at sea and had survived shipwrecks. Smith was determined not to let the colony fail.

Smith had little patience with most of the settlers. "No talk, no hope, nor work," he complained. People only wanted to "dig gold, wash gold, refine gold, load gold." But there was no gold to be found, and the colony was running out of food.

Smith visited nearby Indian villages to trade for food. Powhatan (pow uh TAN), a powerful chief who did not like the English, took Smith prisoner and ordered him put to death. According to Smith, Powhatan's 12-year-old daughter, Pocahontas (poh kuh HAHN tuhs), begged her father to spare Smith's life. Powhatan agreed and even sold corn to the English.

The hungry colonists rewarded Smith by putting him in charge of Jamestown. Smith set up stern rules:

> ❝Countrymen . . . You see that power now rests wholly with me. You must now obey this law, *that he that will not worke shall not eate* unless disabled by illness. For the labors of thirty or forty honest and industrious men shall not be consumed to maintain a hundred and fifty [lazy people].❞

This work-or-starve rule brought results. Life in the colony improved once colonists began to plant crops. But in 1609,

Smith badly injured his leg and had to return to England. The settlers returned to their old ways.

The Starving Time

As winter approached, the food supply dwindled. Settlers ate whatever they could find. They cooked "dogs, cats, snakes, toadstools, horsehides and what not." To keep warm, they broke up houses to burn as firewood. By spring, only 60 settlers were still alive.

When the Virginia Company learned of the disaster at Jamestown, it sent a stern army officer to act as governor. The new governor had power to make whatever laws he felt were needed.

The governor used his power harshly. He executed one settler for killing a chicken without permission. He chained another to a tree for stealing a few cups of oatmeal. The settler starved to death. Even so, matters at Jamestown did not improve.

Slaves From Africa *Tobacco helped the Jamestown Colony to survive and prosper. But it also led to the rise of slavery in the South. This picture of slaves on a tobacco plantation was used as a label for tobacco products around 1700.* **Daily Life** *Do you think that this picture shows slave life accurately? Explain.*

A Taste for Tobacco

Several events helped to change Jamestown's fortunes. The first major breakthrough came when the colonists began to grow tobacco.

Europeans had learned about tobacco and pipe smoking from the Indians. Then, in 1612, a settler named John Rolfe discovered that Jamestown's soil and climate were ideal for growing tobacco. But Virginia tobacco was too bitter for most European tastes. Rolfe sent for seeds from the West Indies and produced a milder tobacco that Europeans liked.

King James I considered smoking "a vile custom" and tobacco "a stinking weed." But the new fad caught on quickly. By 1620, England was importing more than 30,000 pounds of tobacco a year. At last, the Virginia Company had found a way to make a profit.

The First Africans

Growing tobacco was hard work. Settlers tried to force Native Americans to work on tobacco plantations. When the Indians fled to the forests, the settlers looked for other laborers.

In 1619, a Dutch ship arrived in Jamestown. Aboard were about 20 Africans whom the Dutch had seized in Africa. The Dutch sold the Africans to the colonists. These first Africans in Virginia may have worked as servants and earned their freedom. But by the late 1600s, Virginia planters had come to depend on a cruel system of slave labor to produce their crops. The system lasted for more than 200 years.

Beginnings of Self-Government

The second event that helped to save Virginia was the introduction of a new form of government. In 1619, the Virginia Company sent a governor to Jamestown with orders to consult settlers on all important matters. Male settlers who owned land were allowed to elect **burgesses,** or repre-

Women Colonists Arrive at Jamestown *The Virginia Company arranged for women to go to Jamestown to "help make the men more settled." Here, colonists warmly greet a boatload of women upon their arrival in Jamestown harbor.* **Daily Life** *Why would life be difficult for women in Jamestown?*

sentatives. The burgesses met in an assembly called the **House of Burgesses.** Together with the governor, they made laws for the colony.

The House of Burgesses marked the beginning of representative government in the English colonies. A representative government is one in which voters elect representatives to make laws for them. In Virginia, only male property owners could vote. Even so, the idea was planted that settlers had a right to have a say in the affairs of the colony.

A deeply rooted idea. The idea that people had political rights was not new to the English. In 1215, English nobles had forced King John to sign the **Magna Carta,** or Great Charter. This document said that the king could not raise taxes without first consulting the Great Council of nobles and church leaders. The Magna Carta showed that the king had to obey the law.

More people win rights. Over time, the rights won by nobles were extended to other English people. The Great Council grew into a representative assembly, called Parliament. By the 1600s, Parliament was divided into the House of Lords, made up of nobles, and an elected House of Commons. Only a few rich men had the right to vote. Still, the English had established that their king or queen must consult Parliament on money matters and must respect the law.

Arrival of Women

The arrival of women was the third event that helped to save the Jamestown Colony. The first English women in Jamestown had arrived aboard a supply ship in 1608. They were Anne Forest, who came with her husband, and Anne Burras, her young maid. And a small number of women were among the colonists during "the starving time." But for the most part, few women chose to live in Jamestown during its early years.

The Virginia Company realized that if Jamestown were to last, family life would have to grow. So in 1619, the investors sent 100 women to Virginia to "make the men more settled." This first shipload of women quickly found husbands in Jamestown. The Virginia Company charged each man who found a wife 150 pounds of tobacco.

Women did make the colony more settled. But life was still a day-to-day struggle. Women had to make everything from scratch—food, clothing, even medicines. Hard work and childbirth killed many at a young age. Still, settlers began to take hope that the colony might survive.

Pocahontas in England *The daughter of an Indian chief, Pocahontas brought food to hungry Jamestown settlers during "the starving time." Later, Pocahontas and her husband, John Rolfe, visited London, where an artist painted this portrait of her.* **Culture** *Why do you think the artist showed Pocahontas in English dress?*

An Uneasy Friendship

Jamestown's most famous marriage took place in 1614. John Rolfe had fallen in love with Pocahontas. Rolfe asked Powhatan for his daughter's hand in marriage. Powhatan agreed. A short time later, Pocahontas converted to Christianity and took the English name Rebecca. Rolfe believed that his marriage to Pocahontas would unite Native Americans and English "in one bond of love."

But relations between Indians and Europeans remained uneasy. Most English did not trust the Indians. They looked down on Indian customs, which were so different from their own. And they scorned the Indians' religion and tried to convert them to Christianity.

For their part, the Indians at first felt sorry for the half-starved white settlers and traded them corn and other food for axes, beads, and muskets. But the success of tobacco changed all that. Tobacco wore out the soil quickly, and settlers began to move onto Indian lands.

In 1622, Indians around Chesapeake Bay decided to drive out the English. In a surprise attack, they killed about 350 people. Striking back, the English killed or enslaved many Indians.

News of the attack soon reached England. King James decided that the colony had been badly run. In 1624, he took over management of the colony from the Virginia Company. Virginia became a royal colony, or a colony directly under the control of the king.

SECTION 3 REVIEW

1. **Locate:** (a) Roanoke, (b) Chesapeake Bay, (c) Jamestown.
2. **Identify:** (a) Sir Walter Raleigh, (b) John White, (c) Virginia Dare, (d) Virginia Company, (e) John Smith, (f) Pocahontas, (g) John Rolfe, (h) House of Burgesses, (i) Magna Carta.
3. **Define:** (a) charter, (b) joint stock company, (c) capital, (d) burgess, (e) representative government, (f) royal colony.
4. What problems did the Jamestown colonists face?
5. List three events that helped Jamestown to survive.
6. (a) How did Native Americans treat the Jamestown settlers at first? (b) Why did they change the way they felt about the English?
7. **Forecasting** How do you think reports about the "lost colony" of Roanoke would affect English settlement in the Americas?

4 A Haven for Pilgrims

FIND OUT

◆ Why did the Pilgrims start a colony in North America?

◆ What was the purpose of the Mayflower Compact?

◆ How did Native Americans help the Plymouth colonists?

In September 1620, another band of settlers set sail from England, aboard a small ship called the *Mayflower*. The travelers feared the long ocean voyage to North America. And they worried about finding food and keeping safe from Indian attacks in the new land. But as one of the settlers, William Bradford, later recalled, "They committed themselves to the will of God and resolved to proceed."

Two months later, the little group finally reached land. Bradford recorded the settlers' joy:

> **"**After a long beating at sea they . . . [reached] a land which is called Cape Cod. . . . Being thus arrived in a good harbor, and brought safe to land, they fell upon their knees and blessed the God of Heaven, who had brought them over the vast and furious ocean . . . and set their feet on the firm and stable earth.**"**

The group had arrived along a cold, bleak shore in present-day Massachusetts. Here they set up a colony, which they named Plymouth. The Plymouth colonists sought neither gold nor silver. They wanted only to practice their religion freely. They were known as **Pilgrims.**

In Search of Religious Freedom

In England, the Pilgrims belonged to a religious group known as Separatists. The Separatists wanted to separate from the official church, the Church of England, and start a new church.

Queen Elizabeth and her successor, King James I, opposed any group that refused to follow the Church of England. King James vowed to "harry [Separatists] out of the land." Separatists were persecuted, or attacked, for their beliefs.

A long journey. Many Separatists feared for their safety, and in the early 1600s, a group left England for Leyden, a city in the Netherlands. The Dutch allowed the newcomers to worship freely. But the Pilgrims missed their English way of life. They also worried that their children were growing up more Dutch than English.

A group of Pilgrims returned to England and, along with some other English people, won a charter to set up a colony in Virginia. In September 1620, more than 100 men, women, and children set sail on the *Mayflower.* Heavy storms tossed the tiny ship about the sea, and the captain could not hold course. The *Mayflower* landed near Cape Cod, far north of Virginia.

MAP STUDY

In the late 1500s and early 1600s, the English set up colonies in Roanoke, Jamestown, and Plymouth.
1. Which of these colonies was farthest south?
2. The labels in dark capital letters are the names of Indian nations. What Indians lived near the Plymouth colonists?
3. **Forecasting** Based on the map, why do you think the English settlers might come into conflict with the Indian nations?

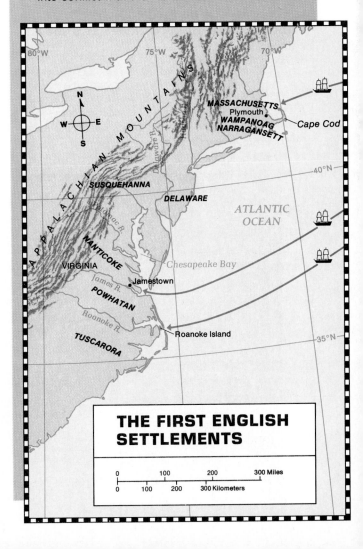

THE FIRST ENGLISH SETTLEMENTS

The Mayflower Compact. Exhausted by the sea voyage, the Pilgrims decided to travel no farther. But their charter was for a colony in Virginia. So before going ashore, they drew up the **Mayflower Compact.** The 41 signers agreed to consult each other about laws for the colony and promised to work together to make the colony succeed:

> ❝We, whose names are underwritten . . . Having undertaken for the Glory of God, and Advancement of the Christian Faith . . . a voyage to plant the first colony in the northern parts of Virginia . . . do enact, constitute, and frame, such just and equal Laws . . . as shall be thought most [fitting] and convenient for the general Good of the Colony.❞

Later, when the Plymouth Colony grew too large for everyone to consult together, the settlers chose representatives to an assembly. The assembly made laws for the colony.

Disaster—and Thanksgiving

The first winter at the Plymouth Colony was hard for the Pilgrims. They did not have time to build proper shelter, and most lived in sod houses quickly thrown together. According to William Bradford, a few settlers even scooped out caves that were "half a pit and half a tent of earth supported by branches . . . nasty, dank, and cold." The settlers had arrived too late in the year to plant crops. They lived off wild game and whatever food they had left from the voyage.

It seemed impossible that the colony could survive. As Bradford recalled:

> ❝[The Pilgrims] had no friends to welcome them, nor inns to entertain or refresh their weatherbeaten bodies. If they looked behind them, there was the mighty ocean which they had passed. . . . What could now sustain them, but the Spirit of God and his grace?❞

The Mayflower Compact *This painting shows the signing of the Mayflower Compact. Pilgrims signed this document before coming ashore in Massachusetts. In it, they promised to work together for the common good.* **Citizenship** *Why was the Mayflower Compact an important step toward developing self-government in the Americas?*

The First Thanksgiving *Gathering with Native Americans who helped them to survive the bitter winter, Pilgrims celebrated the first Thanksgiving. The menu probably included ducks, geese, deer, fish, corn bread, wild plums, and berries.* ***Culture*** *What does the first Thanksgiving tell you about Pilgrim beliefs?*

The Pilgrims' religious faith was strong, however. They believed that it was God's will for them to remain in Plymouth. Nearly half the settlers died of disease or starvation during that first harsh winter. But the other colonists carried on. (📖 See "The Seekers" on page 640.)

Native Americans offer help. In the spring, a Pemaquid Indian from Maine arrived at Plymouth. His name was Samoset. He had learned English earlier from explorers sailing along the coast. Samoset introduced the Pilgrims to Massasoit (mas uh SOYT), chief of the local Wampanoag (wahm puh NOH ahg) Indians. Massasoit and the Pilgrims made a treaty of peace.

The Indian who helped the Pilgrims most was a Wampanoag named Squanto. For a time, Squanto had lived among English sailors, and he spoke English well. He brought the Pilgrims seeds of native plants—corn, beans, and pumpkins—and showed them how to plant them. He also taught the settlers to stir up eels from the river bottoms and then snatch them with their

hands. The grateful Pilgrims called Squanto "a special instrument sent of God."

A good harvest. In the fall, the Pilgrims had a good harvest. Because they believed that God had given them this harvest, they set aside a day for giving thanks. In later years, the Pilgrims celebrated each harvest with a day of thanksgiving. Americans today celebrate **Thanksgiving** as a national holiday.

SECTION 4 REVIEW

1. **Locate:** (a) Cape Cod, (b) Plymouth.
2. **Identify:** (a) Pilgrim, (b) Mayflower Compact, (c) Samoset, (d) Massasoit, (e) Squanto, (f) Thanksgiving.
3. Why did the Pilgrims come to the Americas?
4. What did the signers of the Mayflower Compact agree to do?
5. List two ways that Squanto helped the colonists.
6. **Comparing** How were the reasons for founding Jamestown different from the reasons for founding Plymouth?

Historians use graphs to show trends, or developments over time. Graphs are a way of showing **statistics**, or facts in number form. The most commonly used kind of graph is a line graph. Other kinds are circle and bar graphs.

A line graph has a grid that is made up of horizontal and vertical lines. A **horizontal axis** runs across the bottom of the grid. A **vertical axis** runs up and down one side of the grid. Information is put on the grid with dots. The dots are then connected to make a **curve**. The curve shows changes taking place over a period of time.

The curve on a line graph shows a trend. If the curve goes up, the graph is showing an upward trend. If the curve goes down, the graph is showing a downward trend. On some line graphs, you might see both upward and downward trends.

Use the steps below to read the line graph at bottom left.

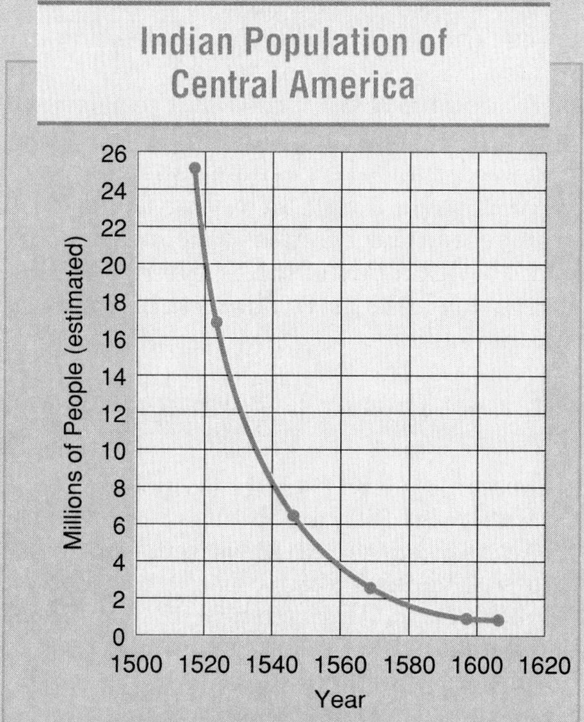

1 **Identify the type of information shown on the line graph.** Most graphs have a title, date, and source. The title tells you what the subject is. The date tells you what time period is covered. The source tells you where the information was found. (a) What is the title of the graph? (b) What time period does the graph cover? (c) What is the source of the graph?

2 **Study the labels on the graph.** Both the horizontal axis and the vertical axis have labels. (a) What do the numbers on the horizontal axis show? (b) What do the numbers on the vertical axis show?

3 **Practice reading the line graph.** The dates on the horizontal axis are spaced evenly. The numbers on the vertical axis are also spaced evenly and usually begin at zero. A line graph may show numbers in thousands or millions. (a) About how many Native Americans lived in Central America in 1520? (b) About how many lived there in 1540? In 1600? (c) During which period did the population fall the most?

4 **Draw conclusions from the information shown on the graph.** Use the line graph and your reading in this chapter to answer the following questions. (a) In your own words, describe what happened to the population of Native Americans living in Central America between 1520 and 1600. (b) Why did the Indian population in Central America decline so rapidly? (c) What effect do you think the death of so many people might have had on those who survived?

Indian Population of Central America

Source: Nicolas Sanchez-Albornoz, *The Population of Latin America*

Use the Section Reviews and this Study Guide to review chapter content.

Main Ideas

The main ideas in each section of this chapter are summarized below.

SECTION 1 ■ The Rise of New Spain

◆ Spain set up a government that firmly controlled its colonies in the Americas.
◆ Spanish settlers brought in slaves from Africa to work in mines and on plantations.
◆ A rich culture based on Spanish and Indian traditions grew up in New Spain.

SECTION 2 ■ The French and Dutch Look North

◆ French, Dutch, and Swedish settlers planted colonies in North America.
◆ The French and Dutch competed for control of the rich fur trade.
◆ The coming of Europeans to North America brought about major changes for Native Americans.

SECTION 3 ■ The First English Colonies

◆ The English built a settlement at Roanoke, Virginia, but it disappeared without a trace.
◆ The first permanent English settlement was made at Jamestown, Virginia.
◆ The Jamestown colonists faced terrible hardships at first, but growing tobacco helped the colony prosper.

◆ The House of Burgesses was the first representative assembly in the Americas.

SECTION 4 ■ A Haven for Pilgrims

◆ The Pilgrims set up the Plymouth Colony so that they could practice their religion.
◆ The Mayflower Compact set up rules for governing Plymouth.
◆ The Pilgrims faced great hardships, but were helped by Native Americans.

Key People and Terms

Refer to the Identify and Define questions in the Section Reviews on pages 103, 108, 114, and 117. Use each person, term, and vocabulary word in a complete sentence. When possible, make connections between the people and terms by using more than one person or term in each sentence.

Time Line

1. Make a chart of events in time order. The chart will have two headings: Date, Event. Fill in the chart, using the events on the time line. Add the following events from the chapter: Africans arrive in Virginia; House of Burgesses set up; New Amsterdam settled; Quebec settled. (Refer to the chapter for dates.)
2. What two events happened in the same year?

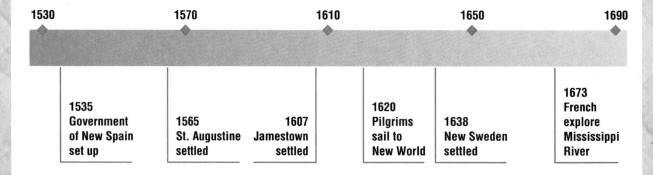

1530	1570	1610	1650	1690
1535 Government of New Spain set up	1565 St. Augustine settled / 1607 Jamestown settled	1620 Pilgrims sail to New World	1638 New Sweden settled	1673 French explore Mississippi River

CHAPTER 4 REVIEW

Understanding Vocabulary

Match each term at left with the correct definition at right.

1. creole
2. plantation
3. coureur de bois
4. charter
5. representative government

a. document giving certain rights to a person or company
b. person born in the Americas to Spanish parents
c. runner of the woods
d. government in which voters elect representatives to make laws for them
e. large estate farmed by many workers

Reviewing the Main Ideas

1. Describe the three kinds of settlements in New Spain.
2. (a) What four social classes did the Laws of the Indies set up? (b) What did each group do for a living?
3. Why did the Dutch and French become rivals in North America?
4. Name three major changes that the arrival of Europeans brought to Native Americans in North America.
5. How did the Virginia Company raise money to finance the Jamestown Colony?
6. (a) What was the House of Burgesses? (b) Why was it important?
7. Why did the Pilgrims remain in Plymouth despite terrible hardships?

Thinking Critically

1. **Defending a Position** Do you agree or disagree with the following statement: In trying to help Native Americans, Bartolomé de Las Casas did more harm than good. Defend your position.
2. **Linking Past and Present** Identify one American tradition or idea that can be traced to each of the following: (a) Native Americans; (b) Spanish; (c) French; (d) Dutch; (e) English.
3. **Analyzing Information** Review the discussions of government in New Spain and Jamestown. Which colony gave settlers more say in their government? Explain your answer.
4. **Comparing** Compare the first years of the Jamestown and Plymouth colonies. (a) How were the experiences of settlers similar? (b) How were they different?

Applying Your Skills

1. **Making a Generalization** Review the description of relations between Europeans and Native Americans on pages 97–99, 108, and 114. (a) Make a generalization about how Europeans treated Native Americans. (b) List three facts to support your generalization.
2. **Analyzing a Quotation** Review the excerpt from the Mayflower Compact on page 116. (a) Why did the Pilgrims want to plant a colony? (b) What kinds of laws did they plan to enact for the colony?
3. **Reading a Line Graph** Review Skill Lesson 4 on page 118. (a) What is the subject of the graph? (b) What is the label on the horizontal axis? (c) In what 20-year period was the Indian population greatest? Smallest? (d) Based on the graph, what generalization can you make about the Indian population of Central America?

Thinking About Geography

Match the letters on the map with the places listed below.

1. New Spain
2. Peru
3. Brazil
4. New France
5. English colonies
6. Mexico City
7. Quebec
8. Jamestown

Place (a) What mineral resources in Mexico and Peru attracted the Spanish? (b) What animal resource brought the French to New France?

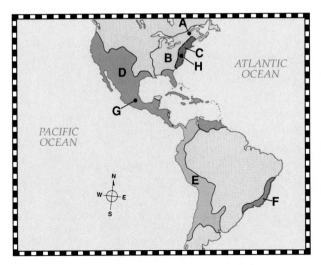

History Writer's Workshop

Selecting Supporting Information

Detail sentences in a one-paragraph answer give information to support the main idea. The information may be details, facts, examples, reasons, or incidents. The topic sentence often helps you decide what kind of information you need.

Look at the following topic sentence. *John Smith helped the Jamestown colonists in several ways.* The information you need is ways Smith helped the colonists. For example: *Smith traded with Indians for food. He also made colonists plant crops.*

Make sure you have enough information. Also make sure the information supports the main idea. Look at the following topic sentence. *The Laws of the Indies divided people into four social classes.* The following detail would not support the main idea. *The laws provided for three kinds of settlements in New Spain.* It is not information about the four social classes.

Practice Look at the following topic sentence. *The Pilgrims suffered hardships in their early days at Plymouth.*

1. What kind of information should the detail sentences give?
2. Select information for detail sentences.

Writing to Learn

1. Imagine you are a coureur de bois along the St. Lawrence River. Write a diary entry about a typical day. Before writing, list details about the area and your tasks, problems, and reactions. Begin with a topic sentence that captures the feeling you want to give. Organize the details logically. Revise to make sure the details are realistic. Then, proofread and make a final copy. Read the entry to classmates.
2. Write a paragraph that compares how Spain and England treated their colonies. Before writing, make a chart of similarities and differences. Begin with a topic sentence that summarizes your main point. Organize details by presenting a point about Spain and then a point about England. Revise, making sure that each point supports the topic sentence. Proofread and make a final copy. Exchange papers with a friend.

Farm Settlement in Pennsylvania *Settlers came to the English colonies for many reasons. Bethlehem, Pennsylvania, shown in this 1757 painting, was founded by Germans seeking religious freedom. In a few short years, they turned the wilderness into orderly farms.* **Geography** *How do you think geography affected the kinds of settlements that colonists built?*

The 13 English Colonies (1630–1750)

Chapter Outline

CHAPTER SPOTLIGHT

The Big Picture

Why did men and women—even whole families—leave their homes in England to settle in the Americas? Some were lured by the promise of profits from selling tobacco, rice, fish, and furs. Plentiful land attracted farming families. Other colonists came for religious freedom. Finally, some newcomers had no choice. They were brought unwillingly as slaves.

The settlers transformed the lands along the Atlantic coast. By 1750, the newcomers had built 13 colonies stretching from New Hampshire to Georgia.

Of Special Interest

Focus On

◆ How did religion influence the New England Colonies?

◆ Why did a wide variety of people settle in the Middle Colonies?

◆ How were the Southern Colonies founded?

◆ How did England rule its colonies?

"**M**y Faithful and Dear Wife, It pleases God, that you should once again hear from me before our departure. . . . Our boys are well and cheerful, and have no [thought] of home. . . .

We are preparing (by God's assistance) to set sail in the morning. . . . We have spent now two [Sundays] on shipboard very comfortably (God be praised) and are daily more and more encouraged to look for the Lord's presence to go along with us on our long and troublesome passage [across the Atlantic]."

John Winthrop wrote these lines to his wife in March 1630 before sailing to North America. Several Winthrop children traveled with him aboard the *Arbella*. Winthrop was sad that the family would be separated, but he had faith that God would reunite them in the New World.

More than 700 men, women, and children sailed with Winthrop. They were Puritans, and they were leaving England to escape religious persecution. They planned to found a colony in the Americas where they could "live together under a proper form of civil and church government . . . in order to serve the Lord . . . [and] to increase and comfort the church of which we are members."

In this chapter, you will read about the colony that the Puritans planted at Massachusetts Bay. You will also read about the colonies planted by other English settlers in North America.

1 Puritan New England

FIND OUT

◆ Why did Puritans set up the Massachusetts Bay Colony?

◆ Who founded the colonies of Connecticut and Rhode Island?

◆ Why did conflicts arise between settlers and Indians?

◆ **VOCABULARY** emigrate, toleration

In 1614, a group of English merchants hired John Smith to explore the northern Atlantic coast of North America, from Cape Cod to Maine. Smith wrote glowing reports about the area, which he named "New England." He praised the excellent fishing and described the abundant beaver and otter whose furs were sure to fetch handsome prices in England.

But it was not the promise of wealth that drew the first settlers to New England. They came instead for religious freedom. As you have read, the Pilgrims planted a colony at Plymouth in 1620 so that they could worship as they pleased. Another religious group, the Puritans, soon followed them.

Puritans Plan to Leave England

The **Puritans** wanted to reform the Church of England. In this way, they were different from the Pilgrims, who had wanted to separate from the English Church. The Puritans called for simpler forms of worship. They wanted to do away with practices borrowed from the Catholic Church, such as organ music and special clothes for priests.

Puritans were a powerful group in England. Many were well-educated merchants or landowners. Some held seats in the House of Commons. Few Puritans had any

reason to **emigrate,** or leave their country and settle elsewhere.

But King James I disliked Puritans as much as he disliked Pilgrims. His son, Charles I, who became king in 1625, proved to be an even greater threat. Charles took strong action against the Puritans. He took away many Puritan business charters and had Puritans expelled from universities. Some Puritans were even jailed.

Puritans and their supporters in Parliament tried to fight back. In response, Charles dismissed Parliament, saying he would rule without it. Some Puritan leaders decided that England had fallen on "evil and declining times." They made plans to form a company and set up a colony in North America.

Massachusetts Bay: "A City Upon a Hill"

In 1629, royal officials granted a group of Puritans a charter to form the Massachusetts Bay Company. Luckily for the Puritans, the charter did not name a particular place for company meetings. Acting quickly, the directors voted to take the charter and move the company to New England. There, away from the watchful eye of the king, they would run their colony as they pleased.

The Puritans sent a small advance party to North America in 1629. The next year, 17 ships carrying more than 1,000 men, women, and children sailed for the **Massachusetts Bay Colony,** as the Puritan settlement was called. They were led by John Winthrop, who had been chosen the colony's first governor.

The Puritans had a bold dream. They wanted to build a new society based on the laws of God as they appeared in the Bible. Sailing west across the Atlantic, John Winthrop addressed his fellow voyagers. Their colony, he said, would set an example to the world:

❝The Lord will make our name a praise and glory, so that men shall say of succeeding [colonies]: 'The

Lord make it like that of New England.' For we must consider that we shall be like a City upon a Hill. The eyes of all people are on us.**"**

Once ashore, Winthrop set an example for others. Even though he was governor of the colony, he worked as hard as anyone to build a home, clear land, and plant crops. "He so encouraged us," Israel Stoughton remarked in a letter to his brother, "that there was not an idle person to be found in the whole [colony]."

The Great Migration

Under the leadership of Winthrop and other Puritans, the Massachusetts Bay Colony grew and prospered. Between 1629 and 1640, more than 20,000 men, women, and children journeyed from England to Massachusetts. This movement of people is known as the **Great Migration.** Many of the newcomers settled in Boston, which grew into the colony's largest town. (📖 See "Forefathers' Song" on page 642.)

Some of the new arrivals to Massachusetts Bay came for economic rather than religious reasons. They were not Puritans escaping persecution but people looking for land. In England, the oldest son usually inherited his father's estate. Younger sons had little hope of owning land. To these people, Massachusetts Bay offered cheap land or a chance to start their own business.

Governing Massachusetts Bay

At first, Winthrop tried to govern the colony according to its charter. Under the charter, only stockholders who had invested money in the Massachusetts Bay Company had the right to vote. But most settlers were not stockholders. They resented taxes and laws passed by a government in which they had no say.

Winthrop and other stockholders quickly realized that the colony would run more smoothly if other settlers could take part. On the other hand, the Puritan leaders

The Puritans *Relying on faith and hard work, the Puritans built a thriving colony at Massachusetts Bay. The Puritan spirit is captured in this powerful bronze statue by Augustus Saint-Gaudens, the foremost American sculptor of the 1800s.* **Culture** *How did their religious beliefs help the Puritans to succeed?*

were determined to keep non-Puritans out of government. As a result, they granted the right to vote for governor to all men who were church members. Later, male church members were also allowed to elect representatives to an assembly called the **General Court.**

Settling Connecticut

Although the Puritan leaders allowed settlers some say in the government of Massachusetts Bay, they believed that the power of the people should be limited. "If the people be the governors," asked the

Puritan minister John Cotton, "who shall be the governed?"

Hooker opposes Puritan rule. But some Puritans felt that the leaders of the Massachusetts Bay Colony had too much power. Thomas Hooker argued that an official might mean well but still govern badly. Hooker called for laws to limit the governor's power. The power of government, Hooker said, rests upon "the free consent of the people."

Rivalry grew up between Hooker and Winthrop. Finally, Hooker and about 100 followers decided to leave Massachusetts Bay. A handful of Puritans had already pushed west into the fertile Connecticut River valley. In May 1636, Hooker and his supporters set out to join them. They drove their cattle, goats, and pigs along Indian trails that cut through the forests. When they reached the Connecticut River, they built a town, which they called Hartford. Other settlers followed, setting up more towns in Connecticut.

A plan of government. In 1639, the Connecticut settlers wrote a plan of government called the **Fundamental Orders of Connecticut.** The Fundamental Orders set up a government much like that of Massachusetts, but with two important differences. First, the Fundamental Orders gave the vote to all men who were property owners, including men who were not church members. Second, the Fundamental Orders limited the governor's power. In this way, the Fundamental Orders expanded the idea of representative government in the English colonies.

In 1662, Connecticut became a separate colony. In that year, the towns along the Connecticut River joined together under the Fundamental Orders of Connecticut, and the king chartered them as the colony of Connecticut.

Journeying to Connecticut *Thomas Hooker and his followers left Massachusetts Bay to set up the colony of Connecticut. This painting by Frederick Church shows the group during the journey to Hartford.* **Citizenship** *Hooker believed that the power of government rests upon "the free consent of the people." How did this belief cause him to leave Massachusetts Bay?*

Religious Toleration in Rhode Island

Another Puritan who disagreed with Governor Winthrop was Roger Williams. A young minister in the village of Salem, Williams was a gentle, good-natured man. Almost everyone, including Winthrop, liked him. But in 1635, Williams found himself in trouble. The General Court had declared him guilty of spreading "new and dangerous opinions."

"New and dangerous opinions." One of Williams's opinions was that the business of church and state should be completely separate. The state, said Williams, should maintain order and peace. It should not support a particular church.

Williams also believed in religious toleration. Toleration means willingness to let others practice their own beliefs. In Puritan Massachusetts, non-Puritans were not permitted to worship freely. Williams wanted to change that. He also wanted to let men who were not church members vote for government officials.

Williams's ideas about the Indians worried Puritan leaders as much as his religious views did. According to Williams, the king of England had no right to give land to settlers in North America. The land, he argued, belonged to the Indians. Europeans who wished to settle on land in the Americas should be required to buy it from the Indians.

In 1635, the General Court ordered Williams to return to England. Governor Winthrop took pity on the young man and secretly advised him to flee. Williams escaped to Narragansett Bay and spent the winter with Indians there. In the spring, the Indians sold him land for a settlement.

Rogue's Island. In 1644, Williams obtained a charter for his colony from England. At first, the colony was called the Providence Plantations. Later, Providence and other towns joined together in the colony of **Rhode Island.**

In Rhode Island, Williams put into practice his ideas about religious toleration. He

The New England Colonies were among the first colonies the English set up in North America.
1. Name the four New England Colonies.
2. To whom did Maine belong?
3. **Drawing Conclusions** Based on the map, why do you think fishing became important in the New England Colonies?

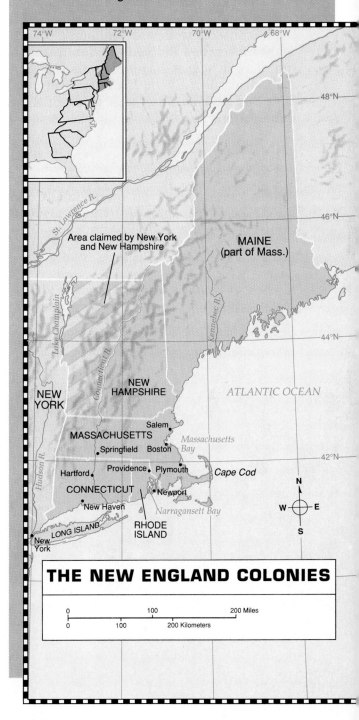

THE NEW ENGLAND COLONIES

allowed complete freedom of religion, even for Jews and Catholics. He did not set up a state church or require settlers to attend church services. And he gave all white men the right to vote.

Before long, settlers who disliked the strict Puritan rule of Massachusetts were flocking to Rhode Island. Puritan leaders in Massachusetts scoffed at Williams's colony. They nicknamed it Rogue's Island, implying that it was a haven for misfits and scoundrels. But Rhode Islanders were not bothered. Indeed, they took pride in their independent ways.

Anne Hutchinson: An Independent-Minded Woman

Among the people who found shelter in Rhode Island was Anne Hutchinson. Hutchinson and her husband, William, had settled in Boston in 1634. She worked as a midwife, helping to deliver babies. Hutchinson herself had 14 children.

A mind of her own. Hutchinson was an intelligent, God-fearing person. But her religious views and independent mind angered Puritan officials.

Hutchinson sometimes held Bible readings in her home. And she and her friends often gathered after church to discuss the minister's sermon. Puritan leaders questioned Hutchinson's right to hold such meetings. They believed that only the clergy were qualified to explain God's law. When Hutchinson claimed that many ministers explained God's law incorrectly, she was put on trial.

On trial. At her trial, Hutchinson answered all the questions put to her by Governor Winthrop. Time after time, she revealed weaknesses in his arguments. He could not prove that she had broken any Puritan laws or religious teachings.

Then, after two days of questioning, Hutchinson made a serious mistake. She said that God had spoken directly to her. The Puritans believed that God spoke only through the Bible, not to individuals. The General Court declared that Hutchinson was "deluded by the Devil" and ordered her out of the colony.

In 1638, Hutchinson, along with her family and some friends, went to Rhode Island. Later, she moved to the Dutch colony of New Netherland. In 1643, she and most of the members of her family were killed by Indians.

Clashes With Indians

From Massachusetts, settlers fanned out across New England. Some built trading and fishing villages along the coast north of Boston. In 1680, the king of England made these coastal settlements into a separate colony called **New Hampshire.**

Most colonists believed that they had a right to settle these lands, even though Indians had lived there for thousands of years. In their view, the Indians did not

Anne Hutchinson Preaches at Home *Anne Hutchinson's independent views angered the leaders of Massachusetts Bay, and in 1638 they ordered her to leave the colony. Here, Hutchinson defies Puritan leaders by preaching in her Boston home.*
Citizenship *Why do you think Hutchinson moved to Rhode Island after leaving Massachusetts Bay?*

make good use of the land and so did not deserve to keep it. As Governor Winthrop said:

> **❝**The Natives of New England . . . enclose no land [with fences], have no settled homes, nor any tame cattle to improve the land. . . . So if we leave sufficient [land] for their use, we may take the rest.**❞**

In fact, most Indians did farm the land, even though they did not grow crops the way Europeans did. The Indians also depended on the land for hunting, which provided them with meat. But the Puritans did not understand Indian customs and rejected them as either strange or unimportant.

War with the Pequots. As English settlements expanded, fighting broke out with Indians. In 1637, the English accused the Pequots (PEE kwahts) of killing two white traders in the Connecticut Valley. Colonists decided to punish the Pequots. Waiting for a time when most Indian men would be away, colonists attacked a Pequot town and killed about 400 unarmed men, women, and children.

In the war that followed, most Pequots were killed. The English then took over the rich lands of the Connecticut Valley.

Metacom takes a stand. In 1675, a Wampanoag leader, Metacom, stood up to the English who were moving onto Indian lands near Plymouth. Metacom was called King Philip by the English settlers, and the war that he waged against them is known as **King Philip's War.**

King Philip's War lasted 15 months and set the land in flames. Indians burned the homes of white settlers who had come onto their lands. Bands of white settlers tracked down and killed Indians and burned their farmlands. In the end, Metacom was captured and killed. The English sold his family and about 1,000 other Indians into slavery in the West Indies. Many other Indians were forced from their homes and died of starvation.

The pattern of English expansion followed by war between settlers and Indians

Metacom *Native Americans in New England watched with alarm as settlers moved onto Indian lands. More than 10,000 Indians joined the Wampanoag leader, Metacom, in a war against the New England Colonies. Colonists nicknamed Metacom King Philip because he referred to England's King Charles II as "my brother."* **Multicultural Heritage** *Do you think the Wampanoags would have been willing to sell their land?*

was repeated throughout the colonies. And it would continue even after the colonies won independence.

SECTION 1 REVIEW

1. **Locate:** (a) New England Colonies, (b) Massachusetts, (c) Connecticut, (d) Rhode Island, (e) New Hampshire.
2. **Identify:** (a) Puritans, (b) John Winthrop, (c) Great Migration, (d) General Court, (e) Fundamental Orders of Connecticut, (f) Roger Williams, (g) Anne Hutchinson, (h) King Philip's War.
3. **Define:** (a) emigrate, (b) toleration.
4. How did the Puritans govern the Massachusetts Bay Colony?
5. (a) Why did Thomas Hooker and Roger Williams leave the Massachusetts Bay Colony? (b) Where did each of them go?
6. Why did white settlers believe that they had a right to Indian lands?
7. **Evaluating Information** Did the Puritans succeed in building their "city upon a hill"? Explain.

Settling the Middle Colonies

FIND OUT

◆ How did New Netherland become New York?

◆ How was New Jersey founded?

◆ What was William Penn's "holy experiment"?

◆ Why was Delaware formed?

◆ VOCABULARY patroon, proprietary colony

In 1627, trumpet blasts startled Pilgrims working in their fields in Massachusetts. Looking up, they saw a strange ship at anchor in Plymouth harbor. The curious Pilgrims hurried down to the shore, where they were greeted by a group of colorfully dressed men. The strangers' velvet waistcoats, balloon-like red pants, and wooden shoes contrasted sharply with the simpler clothing of the Pilgrims.

The visitors came from New Netherland, the Dutch colony south of New England. Local Indians had told them about the English settlement at Plymouth, and they had decided to visit. Governor William Bradford welcomed the Dutch. But he warned them that the king of England would not be as friendly if he learned of their presence.

As the Dutch visitors knew, their country and England were fierce rivals for trade and colonies. That rivalry would later lead England to seize New Netherland. In time, England came to have four colonies in the region south of New England—New York, New Jersey, Pennsylvania, and Delaware. Because of their location between New England and the Southern Colonies, these colonies were known as the Middle Colonies.

Dutch Rule in New Netherland

As you have read in Chapter 4, the Dutch set up the colony of New Netherland along the Hudson River. In the colony's early years, settlers engaged in a lively fur trade with Indians and built the settlement of New Amsterdam into a thriving port. Later, the Dutch sought to "open up the country with agriculture."

The patroon system. To encourage farming in New Netherland, Dutch officials granted large parcels of land to a few rich families. A single land grant could stretch for miles. Indeed, one grant was as big as Rhode Island! Owners of these huge estates, or manors, were called **patroons.** In return for the grant, each patroon promised to settle at least 50 European farm families on the land.

Patroons had enormous power. They decided how much land each family would farm and how much rent each would pay. They held their own courts and punished people they found guilty of crimes. Because few farmers wanted to live under such harsh rule, the population of New Netherland remained small.

Settlers from many lands. Most settlers lived in the trading center of New Amsterdam. They came from all over Europe. Many were attracted by the chance to practice their religion freely.

Most Dutch colonists were Protestants who belonged to the Dutch Reformed Church. But they allowed people of other religions, including Catholics, French Protestants, and Jews, to buy land. "People do not seem concerned what religion their neighbor is," wrote a shocked visitor from Virginia. "Indeed, they do not seem to care if he has any religion at all."

"Old Silver Nails." New Netherland was owned by the Dutch West India Company. The company gave the governor of the colony almost complete power over settlers. Company officials believed that strict rule was needed to make the colony produce high profits.

Peter Stuyvesant (STĪ vuh suhnt) was an especially tough-minded governor. While serving as a soldier in the West Indies, Stuyvesant had lost his right leg. In its place, he wore a wooden peg, which he decorated with silver nails and bands. For this reason, Stuyvesant was called "Old Silver Nails."

Stuyvesant ruled New Netherland harshly. He punished lawbreakers with heavy fines or public whippings. When angry settlers demanded a voice in the government, Stuyvesant turned them down. His authority, he said, came "from God and the West India Company, not from the pleasure of a few ignorant subjects."

L I F E • I N • A M E R I C A

The First Jewish Settlement in North America

In the summer of 1654, the *St. Charles* sailed into New Amsterdam harbor. The ship had just completed a long and stormy voyage from Brazil, in South America. Among those aboard was a small group of Jews—"23 souls, big and little," as the ship's captain called them. These "23 souls" were the first Jews to settle in North America.

The Jews had journeyed to New Amsterdam seeking freedom from persecution. In the late 1400s, their ancestors had been driven out of Spain and Portugal, where they had lived for centuries. After a brief stay in the Netherlands, some had settled in a Dutch-ruled town in Brazil. But in 1654, Portuguese captured the town. Once again, the Jews needed to find a home.

Remembering that the Dutch had been tolerant, the group set out for New Amsterdam. But no sooner had they set foot on shore than Governor Peter Stuyvesant ordered them to leave. The newcomers appealed to the Dutch West India Company, which welcomed all settlers. Company officials overruled the governor. The Jews were granted the right to stay.

The settlers worked hard to build a Jewish community in New Amsterdam. Many were desperately poor because they had sold all their belongings to pay for the voyage. But they had a variety of skills and knew how to read and write. Many of them had business contacts in Europe. They used these advantages to become successful merchants, traders, and craftworkers. By 1697, the small Jewish community was able to build a synagogue—the first in what had now become the English town of New York.

1. Why did Jews go to New Amsterdam in 1654?

2. **Applying Information** How do you think being able to read and write helped the Jews to succeed?

New Netherland Becomes New York

In 1664, the rivalry between England and the Netherlands for trade and colonies led to war in Europe. English traders who wanted control of the vast lands between New England and Virginia urged King Charles II to send a fleet to New Amsterdam. As the English ships entered the harbor, they trained their guns on the town.

"Hoist a white flag at your fort," the English commander ordered. Governor Stuyvesant refused, vowing to fight. But he had few weapons and little gunpowder. Worse still, discontented settlers refused to support the governor. In the end, Stuyvesant had to surrender without firing a shot.

King Charles then gave New Netherland to his brother, the Duke of York, and the colony was renamed **New York** in his honor. For a time, the Duke of York ruled the colony much as the Dutch had. But New Yorkers, especially Puritans who moved to New York from New England, protested. They demanded the right to choose an assembly to make laws for the colony. In 1683, the Duke of York finally gave in and allowed New York to have a representative assembly.

Founding New Jersey

When King Charles gave New York to his brother, it stretched as far south as the Delaware River. The new owner soon realized that his colony was too big to govern easily. So he gave some of the land to friends, Lord Berkeley and Sir George Carteret. These men arranged to set up a proprietary (pruh PRĪ uh tehr ee) colony, which they called **New Jersey.**

In a proprietary colony, the king gave land to one or more people, called proprietors. In return, the proprietors made a yearly payment to the king. Proprietors were free to divide the land and rent it to others. They made laws for the colony but had to respect the rights of colonists under English law.

Like New York, New Jersey attracted people from many lands. English Puritans, French Protestants, Scots, Irish, Swedes, Dutch, and Finns mingled in the colony.

For a time, the colony was divided into East Jersey and West Jersey. But in 1702, the two settlements were joined as a single royal colony under the control of the English crown. The colony's charter protected religious freedom and the rights of an assembly that voted on local matters.

William Penn:
A Quaker on Trial in England

Religious freedom also played a key part in the founding of Pennsylvania. That colony came into being thanks to the talents of a remarkable man, William Penn.

Penn came from a well-to-do English family. His father was an admiral in the English navy and a friend of King Charles II. As a boy, Penn received a good education and was sent on a grand tour of France and Italy. Like other fashionable gentlemen, he dressed in colorful silks and learned to fight with a sword.

Admiral Penn had high ambitions for his son, hoping to win him a place at court. But first, he had to arrange for William to meet the king. So one night, as the fleet prepared to sail, Admiral Penn sent William to the royal palace with a secret letter for King Charles II. Riding through the night, William reached the palace at dawn.

Servants led the messenger to the royal bedchamber. Penn was surprised to find the king "skipping out of his bed . . . in his gown and slippers." The two men talked for more than half an hour, beginning a friendship that would later serve Penn well.

But just as Penn's future seemed assured, he made a decision that put everything at risk. In 1667, at age 22, Penn became a Quaker—one of the most despised religious groups in England.

Quaker teachings. Like the Pilgrims and Puritans, the **Quakers** were Protestant reformers. But their beliefs went further than those of other Protestants. The Quakers believed that all people—men and women, nobles and commoners—were equal in God's sight. They saw no need for ministers or priests. They refused to pay taxes to the Church of England, spoke out against war, and refused to serve in the army.

To most English people, Quaker beliefs seemed wicked. The government persecuted Quakers harshly. In both England and New England, Quakers were arrested, fined, and even hanged for their beliefs.

The trial. Penn's father was deeply angry when William joined the Quakers. And Penn's friends scorned his decision. But William Penn remained firm.

As a Quaker, Penn stopped wearing fine silk clothes. He gave away his sword and spoke publicly in support of Quaker teachings. In 1670, he was arrested and thrown into jail. The charge was vague: disturbing the peace.

When Penn's case came to trial, the government expected an easy victory. But Penn knew the laws of England well. Standing proudly in the crowded courtroom, he demanded to know what specific law he had broken. The prosecutor had trouble answering, as can be seen in the following dialogue adapted from the court record:

> **"***Prosecutor:* You're a fancy fellow. It is enough for you to know you've broken the Common Law of England.
>
> *Penn:* This answer is very short of my question. For if the Law be Common, it should not be so hard to produce.

William Penn *Wealthy young William Penn seemed destined for a life of luxury at the English court. Instead, he joined the Quakers, one of the most despised religious groups in England. Penn risked everything for what he believed. In time, he put his ideas to work in the colony of Pennsylvania.* **Culture** *Which Quaker belief do you think might trouble the English king most? Explain.*

> *Prosecutor:* It is not for the honor of the court to suffer you to go on!
>
> *Penn:* I have asked you but one question, and you have not answered me, though the rights and privileges of every Englishman be concerned in it.
>
> *Prosecutor:* If I should [allow] you to ask questions till tomorrow morning, you would never be the wiser.
>
> *Penn:* That depends on the answers.**"**

Penn's quick response made the spectators laugh. Enraged, the prosecutor had Penn locked in a small iron cage before continuing the trial. But Penn's arguments had impressed the jury, which found him "not guilty." ◆

Penn's Woodlands

Although William Penn was eventually freed, persecution of Quakers continued. Penn became convinced that the Quakers must leave England. He turned for help to his friend, King Charles II. He told Charles that he wanted to start a colony in the Americas.

The king granted Penn a charter for a large tract of land in North America. Penn named his colony Sylvania, meaning woodlands. But the king changed the name to **Pennsylvania,** or Penn's woodlands, to honor Penn's family. In 1682, William Penn journeyed to Pennsylvania.

Penn's plan for his colony. Penn drew up a **Frame of Government** for Pennsylvania. Under the Frame of Government, Penn appointed a governor and a council of advisers to make laws for the colony. A representative assembly accepted or rejected these laws. Later, the assembly won the right to make laws on its own. Any white Christian man who owned property or paid taxes could vote.

Penn sent pamphlets with copies of the Frame of Government all over Europe. Soon, settlers from England, Scotland, Wales, the Netherlands, France, and Germany began to cross the ocean to Pennsylvania. Among the new arrivals were large numbers of German-speaking Protestants. They became known as the Pennsylvania Dutch, because people could not pronounce the word Deutsch (doich), which means German.

A "holy experiment." Penn thought of his colony as a "holy experiment." He wanted it to be a model of religious freedom, peace, and Christian living. The Frame of Government promised freedom of worship to anyone who believed in God. Protestants, Catholics, and Jews went to Pennsylvania to escape persecution.*

Penn's Quaker beliefs also led him to oppose slavery and to speak out for fair treatment of Native Americans. Like Roger Williams in Rhode Island, Penn believed that the land belonged to the Indians. He said that settlers should pay for the land. Native Americans respected Penn for this policy. As a result, colonists in Pennsylvania enjoyed many years of peace with their Indian neighbors.

---

*Later, English officials forced Penn to turn away Catholic and Jewish settlers.

William Penn Lands in Pennsylvania *William Penn believed in fair treatment for Native Americans, and Pennsylvania enjoyed friendly relations with its Indian neighbors. This painting shows Penn greeting a Native American upon Penn's arrival in Pennsylvania.* **Citizenship** *Why do you think Pennsylvania attracted settlers from many backgrounds?*

City of brotherly love. Penn traveled up and down the Delaware River looking for a place to build the capital of his colony. He had grown up in London, a dirty city with houses so close together that fires often destroyed whole neighborhoods. Penn wanted Pennsylvania's capital city to be "high, dry, and healthy . . . a green country town, which will never be burnt and always be wholesome."

Penn named his capital Philadelphia, a Greek word meaning "brotherly love." He drew up a detailed plan for the city so that it would grow in an orderly way. In 1710, an English visitor wrote that Philadelphia "is the most noble, large, and well-built city I have seen."

Delaware Is Formed

Pennyslvania had no outlet to the Atlantic Ocean. So William Penn asked the Duke of York to give up some land along the lower Delaware River. The duke agreed, and Penn took over what were known as the Lower Counties.

But settlers in the Lower Counties protested. They did not want to send delegates to a far-away assembly in Philadelphia. Penn responded by allowing them to elect their own assembly in 1701. Later, the Lower Counties broke away to form the colony of **Delaware.**

SECTION 2 REVIEW

1. **Locate:** (a) Middle Colonies, (b) New York, (c) New Jersey, (d) Pennsylvania, (e) Philadelphia, (f) Delaware.
2. **Identify:** (a) Peter Stuyvesant, (b) William Penn, (c) Quakers, (d) Frame of Government, (e) Pennsylvania Dutch.
3. **Define:** (a) patroon, (b) proprietary colony.
4. Why was it easy for England to take over New Netherland?
5. (a) From which colony was New Jersey formed? Why? (b) How was Delaware created?

MAP STUDY

The Middle Colonies were set up south and west of New England.
1. *What were the four Middle Colonies?*
2. *Name three rivers that flowed through the Middle Colonies.*
3. **Drawing Conclusions** *Why do you think these colonies were called the Middle Colonies?*

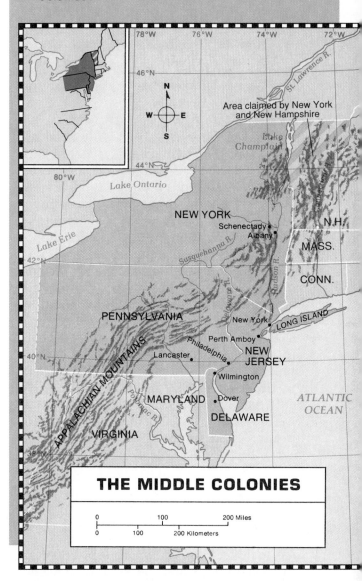

THE MIDDLE COLONIES

6. What was William Penn's goal for his colony?
7. **Applying Information** Which Quaker belief do you think influenced William Penn's attitude toward Native Americans?

3 Early Days of the Southern Colonies

FIND OUT

◆ Why was Maryland founded?

◆ What was Bacon's Rebellion?

◆ How did Carolina become two separate colonies?

◆ Why did James Oglethorpe set up the colony of Georgia?

In 1632, Sir George Calvert convinced his good friend, King Charles I, to grant him land for a colony in the Americas. Seven years earlier, Calvert had ruined his career in Protestant England by becoming a Roman Catholic. Now, he was going to build a colony, **Maryland,** where Catholics would be free to practice their religion. But Sir George died before the king could sign the charter. It was up to his son Cecil, Lord Baltimore, to fulfill his dream of Maryland.

The new colony was to be located along the upper Chesapeake Bay, across from England's first Southern Colony, Virginia. By the mid-1700s, England ruled five Southern Colonies. Besides Maryland and Virginia, there were North Carolina, South Carolina, and Georgia. (See the map on page 138.)

GEOGRAPHY AND HISTORY

Maryland: A Land of Plenty

Late in 1633, Lord Baltimore sent 200 colonists aboard two ships, the *Ark* and the *Dove,* to Maryland. They arrived at the mouth of the Potomac River four months later, in the spring of 1634.

The land that the king had granted to Lord Baltimore's father was rich and beautiful. Father Andrew White, a Catholic priest who traveled with the first group of settlers, described its resources:

The soil appears particularly fertile. Strawberries, vines, sassafras, hickory nuts, and walnuts, we tread upon every where. . . . The soil is dark and soft, a foot in thickness, and rests upon a rich and red clay. Every where there are very high trees. . . . An abundance of springs afford water. . . . There is an [endless] number of birds, . . . [such] as eagles, herons, swans, geese, and partridges. From which you may infer, there is not [anything] wanting to the region.

Maryland was truly a land of plenty. Chesapeake Bay was full of fish, oysters, and crabs. Across the bay, Virginians were already growing tobacco for profit. Marylanders hoped to do the same.

Remembering the early problems at Jamestown, the newcomers avoided the swampy lowlands. They made sure to build their first town, which they named St. Mary's, in a healthful location. ◆

A Careful Plan

Lord Baltimore never visited Maryland, but he planned the colony carefully. He appointed a governor and a council of advisers. He gave colonists a role in government by creating an elected assembly.

Lord Baltimore was eager to attract settlers to Maryland. So he offered 100 acres of land to anyone who brought over a healthy male servant. For each woman or child brought to the colony, he offered 50 acres. A settler who brought five male servants received 1,000 acres at a low yearly rent.

Women set up plantations. A few women took advantage of Lord Baltimore's offer of land. Two sisters, Margaret and Mary Brent, arrived in Maryland in 1638 with nine male servants. They set up two plantations of 1,000 acres each. Later, they brought more settlers from England.

In 1647, when the governor lay dying, he asked Margaret Brent to take charge of his estate. She did. She also helped prevent a rebellion among the governor's soldiers. The Maryland assembly praised her efforts, saying that "the colony's safety at any time [was better] in her hands than in any man's." But when Brent asked for a place in the assembly, they turned her down because she was a woman.

Religious toleration. To ensure Maryland's continued growth, Lord Baltimore welcomed Protestants as well as Catholics to the colony. Later, he came to fear that the Protestants might try to deprive Catholics of their right to worship freely. In 1649, he asked the assembly to pass an **Act of Toleration.** The act provided religious freedom for all Christians. As in many colonies, however, this freedom did not extend to Jews.

The Virginia Frontier

Meanwhile, many settlers had gone to Virginia, lured by the promise of profits from tobacco. The best lands near the coast were soon divided among wealthy planters. Newcomers had to push inland, onto Indian lands. (📖 See "A Complaint From Virginia" on page 644.)

Conflict with Indians. As in New England, conflict over land led to fighting between settlers and Indians. In the 1640s, Indian and white leaders met to restore peace. They reached an agreement to divide the land. But the truce did not last. New waves of settlers ignored the agreement, and fighting broke out once again.

After several bloody clashes, settlers called on the governor to take action against the Indians. The governor refused. Frontier settlers were furious. They accused the governor of refusing to take action because he profited from his own fur trade with Indians.

Settlers rebel. Finally, in 1676, Nathaniel Bacon, a 29-year-old planter, organized men and women on the frontier. He raided

The Founding of Maryland *Maryland was founded as a haven where Catholics could practice their religion freely. This painting by Emanuel Leutze shows the first group of settlers giving thanks after their long sea voyage.* **Geography** *What kind of land did Maryland offer for settlement?*

Indian villages. Bacon and his followers then marched on Jamestown and burned the capital.

Bacon's Rebellion lasted only a short time. When Bacon died suddenly, the revolt fell apart. The governor hanged 23 of Bacon's followers. But he could not stop the movement of settlers onto Indian lands along the frontier.

South to the Carolinas

From Virginia, some settlers moved south in search of land. They traveled along rough trails into Carolina, a vast region stretching from Virginia to Spanish Florida.

A grand scheme. Carolina was named for Charles I. In 1663, King Charles II had given the region to eight nobles, who made lofty plans to found a colony there. People who bought land would be given high-sounding titles, such as baron and lord high chamberlain. They would have

The Southern Colonies stretched from Maryland to Georgia.
1. Name the Southern Colonies.
2. What natural barrier formed the western boundary of the Southern Colonies?
3. **Forecasting** Which southern colony do you think faced possible conflict with Spain? Explain.

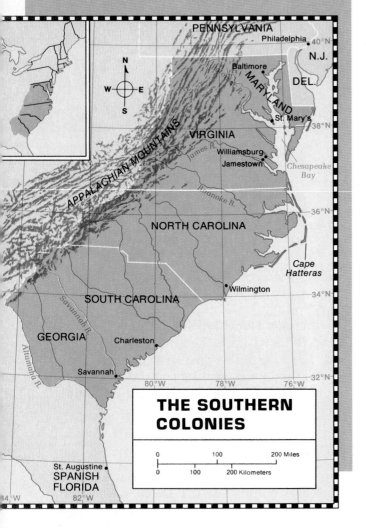

THE SOUTHERN COLONIES

olina set up a government like that of Virginia and Maryland, with a governor and an elected assembly.

Two areas of settlement. Settlement in Carolina took place in two separate areas. The areas were far apart, and people had little contact with one another. In the north, settlers were mostly poor tobacco farmers who had drifted south from Virginia. They tended to have small farms.

In the south, settlers built Charles Town, later shortened to Charleston. At first, they tried to grow grapes, oranges, and lemons. They also tried to raise silkworms, in the hopes of setting up a silk industry. But their efforts failed. Then, around 1685, a few planters discovered that rice grew well in the swampy lowlands along the coast. Before long, Carolina rice was a valuable crop traded around the world.

Planters in the south needed large numbers of workers to grow rice. At first, they tried to enslave local Indians. But many Indians died of disease or mistreatment. Others escaped into the forests.

Like the Spanish in New Spain, planters then turned to slaves from Africa. By 1700, most newcomers to the southern area were African men and women brought there against their will. The northern area of Carolina had fewer slaves. Differences between the two areas of Carolina led to the division of the colony into **North Carolina** and **South Carolina** in 1712.

Georgia: A Haven for Debtors

The last of England's 13 colonies was carved out of the southern part of South Carolina. Called **Georgia** in honor of King George II, it was founded in 1732 by James Oglethorpe. Oglethorpe was a respected soldier and energetic reformer. He saw Georgia as a place where people jailed for debt in England could make a new start.

Land "to feed all the poor of England." Under English law, debtors could be jailed until they paid what they owed. Conditions in prisons were terrible. And when debtors

serfs and slaves to work for them. And the eight proprietors would grow rich from selling land!

The plan did not work. Many people were eager to become wealthy nobles in Carolina. But almost no one wanted to go there as a slave or serf. In the end, the settlers in Car-

AN·AMERICAN·PORTRAIT

James Oglethorpe: Defender of England's Debtors

London, 1728. Several well-dressed gentlemen left the House of Commons. They walked briskly along narrow streets to Fleet Prison. Entering the prison, they picked their way among dirty, ragged, and hungry men, women, and children. Many of the prisoners were sick. Most were there for the simple reason that they owed money.

James Oglethorpe had a strong reason for leading this grisly tour. Oglethorpe wanted his fellow members of Parliament to see firsthand the misery of England's imprisoned debtors. He hoped in this way to persuade them to change the laws that jailed people because they could not pay their debts. Two years later, Parliament acted to correct the worst abuses.

Encouraged by this success, Oglethorpe persuaded King George II to charter a colony, Georgia, "for the settling of the poor persons of London." In 1732, Oglethorpe left his comfortable home in England to lead the first group of settlers to Georgia. Oglethorpe spent ten years helping settlers make a new beginning in Georgia. Even after he returned to England, he remained committed to "the Georgia idea"—that poor people with a little help could improve their lives.

1. Why did Oglethorpe lead his fellow members of Parliament to Fleet Prison?

2. **Applying Information** What arguments might Oglethorpe have made to support his plan to send debtors to Georgia rather than to prison?

finally got out of jail, they often had no money and no place to live.

Oglethorpe offered to pay for debtors and other poor people to travel to Georgia. "In America," he said, "there are enough fertile lands to feed all the poor of England." He dreamed that settlers in Georgia would "cut down trees, build houses, fortify towns, dig and sow the land."

In 1733, Oglethorpe and 120 settlers reached Georgia. They built the colony's first settlement at Savannah, above the

Oglethorpe and Chief Tomo-Chi-Chi in London
In 1734, James Oglethorpe brought a group of Native Americans to England to spark interest and support for his colony. In this painting, Oglethorpe presents the chief of the Yamacraw Indians to the Lord Trustees of Georgia. **Citizenship** *Why did Oglethorpe set up the colony of Georgia?*

Savannah River. Savannah was a planned city, built according to a design drawn up by Oglethorpe and William Bull.

Oglethorpe set strict rules for the colony. Farms could be no bigger than 50 acres, and slavery was forbidden. No one could sell rum in the colony.

Under these rules, Georgia grew slowly. Some settlers moved to other colonies, where they could own large plantations and buy slaves to work them. When Oglethorpe eased the rules to allow slavery, the colony grew more quickly.

Fighting the Spanish in Florida. Georgia was important to King George II because he needed a strong English colony on the border of Spanish Florida. Spain and England were still rivals in the Americas, and both countries claimed the land between South Carolina and Florida.

In 1739, England declared war on Spain. Putting his military talents to work, Oglethorpe led forces against the Spanish in Florida. The Spanish responded by invading Georgia. Aided by Creek Indians, Oglethorpe forced the Spanish to retreat.

Relations with Indians. A woman named Mary Musgrove greatly helped Oglethorpe during this period. Musgrove was the daughter of a Creek mother and an English father. She had married an English planter, John Musgrove, and together they managed a successful plantation.

Because Musgrove spoke both Creek and English, she helped to keep peace between the Creeks and settlers in Georgia. She also gave Oglethorpe useful information about Spanish movements along the Georgia border. Musgrove's efforts did much to allow the colony of Georgia to develop in peace.

SECTION 3 REVIEW

1. **Locate:** (a) Southern Colonies, (b) Maryland, (c) Virginia, (d) Charleston, (e) North Carolina, (f) South Carolina, (g) Georgia, (h) Savannah.
2. **Identify:** (a) George Calvert, (b) Cecil Calvert, (c) Margaret Brent, (d) Act of Toleration, (e) Bacon's Rebellion, (f) James Oglethorpe, (g) Mary Musgrove.
3. (a) Why did Lord Baltimore's father want to set up a colony? (b) Why did Lord Baltimore ask the assembly to pass the Act of Toleration?
4. What caused Bacon's Rebellion?
5. (a) How did most settlers in the northern area of Carolina earn a living? (b) How did most settlers in southern Carolina earn a living?
6. (a) What plans did James Oglethorpe have for Georgia? (b) Why was Georgia important to King George II?
7. **Applying Information** Imagine that you had to advertise for settlers for one of the Southern Colonies. What facts would you include to attract people to that colony?

4 Ruling the Colonies

FIND OUT

◆ Why did colonists resent the Navigation Acts?

◆ How did the Glorious Revolution in England help the colonists?

◆ How was self-rule strengthened in the colonies?

◆ **VOCABULARY** mercantilism, import, export, enumerated article, legislature, indentured servant

In 1750, Philadelphia bustled with activity. Young men drove cattle and sheep to market along narrow cobblestone streets. On the docks, sailors unloaded large barrels of molasses from the West Indies, while children gazed at ships arriving from distant ports.

Philadelphia was the largest and busiest seaport in the colonies. But by the 1700s, trade flourished all along the Atlantic coast. As trade increased, England began to take a new interest in its colonies.

England Regulates Trade

In the mid-1600s, events in England kept the government from paying attention to its colonies in North America. In 1649, King Charles I was overthrown in a civil war and executed. For 11 years, Parliament ruled the country. The revolution finally ended in 1660, when Parliament asked the king's son to return to England and be crowned King Charles II.

The theory of mercantilism. With a king once again in power, England turned its attention to its colonies in the Americas. Like other European nations at the time, England believed that its colonies existed solely for the benefit of the home country. This belief was part of an economic theory known as **mercantilism** (MER kuhn tihl ihz'm). According to this theory, a nation became strong by building up its gold supply and expanding its trade.

Trade occurs when goods are exchanged. **Imports** are goods brought into a country. **Exports** are goods sent to markets outside a country. Because exports help a country earn money, mercantilists thought that a country should export more than it imports.

Laws restrict colonial trade. In the 1660s, Parliament passed a series of laws to regulate trade between England and its colonies. The laws were known as the **Navigation Acts.** The purpose of the Navigation Acts was to strengthen England and make it richer.

Under the laws, only ships built in England or the colonies were allowed to

---

A Flourishing City *Almost from its founding in 1682, Philadelphia was a thriving port. This painting by Peter Cooper shows the busy Philadelphia waterfront in 1720.* **Economics** *Why did ports become the major cities of the colonies?*

carry goods to and from the colonies. Also, most sailors on the ships had to be from England or the colonies. These laws were designed to allow England to control trade. They also helped to ensure that England had trained sailors who could serve in the navy during wartime.

One law required any ship carrying European goods to America to stop first in England. Before the ship continued on to the colonies, the English collected taxes on the goods it carried. In this way, England profited from any trade its colonies had with other nations.

Still another law listed certain goods from the colonies that could be sold only in England. These restricted goods were called enumerated articles and included items such as tobacco, cotton, and sugar. England passed this law to ensure that English merchants and workers had a plentiful supply of raw materials to turn into finished goods.

Colonists Resent the Navigation Acts

In many ways, the Navigation Acts helped the colonies as well as England. The law that required the use of English or colonial ships encouraged colonists to build their own ships. New England became a center for shipbuilding, and New England shipbuilders made good profits.

The laws benefited the colonies in other ways, too. Colonial merchants did not have to compete with foreign merchants because they had a sure market for their goods in England. And colonists could rely on the English navy to protect their ships.

Still, many colonists resented the Navigation Acts. In their view, the laws favored English merchants. They also complained that they paid more for European goods because of English taxes on them.

In the end, many colonists ignored the Navigation Acts or found ways to get around them. Smuggling flourished. Many colonial merchants made large profits by secretly importing goods from Europe and the West Indies. At first, English officials did little to stop the smuggling. But as more and more foreign ships sailed boldly into colonial ports, England took steps to enforce the Navigation Acts.

The "Glorious Revolution"

When Charles II died in 1685, his brother James II became king. King James tried to exercise tighter control over the colonies. He was especially concerned about Massachusetts and Rhode Island, where smuggling had become a way of life.

In 1686, James combined all the colonies from Massachusetts to New Jersey into the **Dominion of New England.** He dismissed their assemblies and appointed Sir Edmund Andros as governor. Andros detested Puritans and soon made many enemies in New England.

The colonists angrily protested the change. But before they could take further action, good news came from England. In 1688, Parliament began a movement called the Glorious Revolution. In the revolt, Parliament ousted King James and asked William and Mary of the Netherlands to rule. The new king and queen ended the Dominion of New England and restored elected assemblies to the colonies.

The Glorious Revolution had another result for the colonies. In 1689, William and Mary signed the **English Bill of Rights.** It protected the rights of individuals and gave anyone accused of a crime the right to a trial by jury. It outlawed cruel and unusual punishments. Finally, it said that a ruler could not raise taxes or an army without the approval of Parliament. As English citizens, colonists were protected by the bill.

Strengthening the Tradition of Self-Rule

In the years after the Glorious Revolution, English monarchs did not interfere with colonial assemblies. But they did take over

Founding of the Colonies

Colony/Date Founded	Leader	Reasons Founded
New England Colonies		
Massachusetts 　Plymouth/1620 　Massachusetts Bay/1630	William Bradford John Winthrop	Religious freedom Religious freedom
New Hampshire/1622	Ferdinando Gorges John Mason	Profit from trade and fishing
Connecticut 　Hartford/1636 　New Haven/1638	Thomas Hooker	Expand trade; religious and political freedom
Rhode Island/1636	Roger Williams	Religious freedom
Middle Colonies		
New York/1624	Peter Minuit	Expand trade
Delaware/1638	Swedish settlers	Expand trade
New Jersey/1664	John Berkeley George Carteret	Profit from land sales; religious and political freedom
Pennsylvania/1682	William Penn	Profit from land sales; religious and political freedom
Southern Colonies		
Virginia/1607	John Smith	Trade and farming
Maryland/1632	Lord Baltimore	Profit from land sales; religious and political freedom
The Carolinas/1663 　North Carolina/1712 　South Carolina/1712	Group of eight proprietors	Trade and farming; religious freedom
Georgia/1732	James Oglethorpe	Profit; home for debtors; buffer against Spanish Florida

CHART SKILLS *The 13 English colonies were founded for many different reasons.*
◆ *Which colonies were founded by people seeking religious freedom? Which were founded by people seeking to expand trade?*

the powers that proprietors had in many colonies. In time, all colonies, except Pennsylvania, Delaware, Maryland, Connecticut, and Rhode Island, became royal colonies.

Governors, councils, and legislatures. The governments of the colonies were similar. Each was headed by a governor. The governor enforced the laws and appointed a council of advisers to help him rule.

Each colony also had a legislature. A legislature is a group of people who have the power to make laws. In most colonies, the legislature had an upper house and a lower house. The upper house was made

A Colonial Assembly *Each of the 13 English colonies had an elected assembly. This picture shows a meeting of Virginia's assembly, the House of Burgesses.* **Linking Past and Present** *How were colonial assemblies elected? How are state legislatures elected today?*

up of the governor's council. The lower house was an elected assembly.

The assembly approved laws and protected the rights of citizens. Just as important, it had the right to approve or disapprove any taxes the governor wanted. This "power of the purse," or right to raise or spend money, was an important check on the governor's power. Any governor who ignored the assembly risked losing his salary.

The right to vote. Each colony had its own rules about who could vote. In all 13 English colonies, only white Christian men over age 21 could vote. In some, only Protestants or members of a particular church could vote. All voters had to own property. Colonial leaders believed that only property owners knew what was best for a colony. A newcomer had to live in the colony for a certain time before he could vote.

There were fewer rules for local elections. Often, any law-abiding white man could vote for local officials.

On election day, voters and their families gathered in towns and villages. A buzz of excitement filled the air as people exchanged news and gossip. Candidates shook hands with voters and slapped them heartily on the back. In some areas, they offered to buy them drinks.

When things quieted down, the sheriff called the voters together. One by one, he read out their names. When called, each voter announced his choice in front of everyone. The candidate often thanked the voter for his support. One observer made notes of a typical election-day scene:

    ❝*Sheriff:* Mr. Blair, whom do you
       vote for?
    Mr. Blair: John Marshall.
    Mr. Marshall: Your vote is appreciated, Mr. Blair.
    Sheriff: Whom do you vote for, Mr. Buchanan?
    Mr. Buchanan: For Mr. John Clopton.

Mr. Clopton: Mr. Buchanan, I shall treasure that vote in my memory. It will be regarded as a feather in my cap forever. **"**

Few Rights for Blacks, Indians, and Women

At a time when most of Europe was ruled by strong kings and queens, English citizens at home and in the colonies were proud of their rights. Even so, only a few white men enjoyed these rights. Blacks and Indians had almost no rights. Neither did women or white servants.

Like women in Europe, colonial women had few legal rights. A woman's father or husband was supposed to protect her. Women were expected to marry at an early age. A married woman could not start her own business or sign a contract unless her husband approved it.

In most colonies, unmarried women and widows had more rights than married women. They could make contracts and sue in court. In Maryland and the Carolinas, women settlers who headed families could buy land on the same terms as men. As you have read, Margaret and Mary Brent managed two huge plantations.

Indentured Servants

Many men and women who were eager to settle in the colonies did not have enough money to pay for the voyage. Some of these people became indentured servants. An **indentured servant** promised to work without wages for four to seven years for whoever would pay for his or her ocean passage. When they completed their term of service, indentured servants received "freedom dues": a set of clothes, tools, and 50 acres of land.

A pamphlet written by a Maryland tobacco farmer to attract indentured servants described the advantages an "industrious servant" might enjoy:

"Those servants who will be industrious during their service can gain a fair amount of property by the time they are freed. . . . There is almost no master who will not allow his servant a piece of cleared land in which to plant some tobacco for himself. . . . When a ship arrives, he may exchange his tobacco for [goods], and in the summer sell them for a profit and get a sow pig or two. . . . With one year's increase of pigs the servant may purchase a calf or two, and by that time he will have gained his freedom. Then he may have cattle, hogs, and tobacco of his own, and come to live fashionably.**"**

More men than women were indentured servants. Because there were so few women in the English colonies, women were often able to shorten their terms of service by marrying. Thousands of men, women, and children who completed their terms of service became farmers, merchants, and craftworkers. Some rose to positions of respect in the colonies.

SECTION 4 REVIEW

1. **Identify:** (a) Navigation Acts, (b) Dominion of New England, (c) English Bill of Rights.
2. **Define:** (a) mercantilism, (b) import, (c) export, (d) enumerated article, (e) legislature, (f) indentured servant.
3. List three ways in which the Navigation Acts helped England.
4. How did the English Bill of Rights affect colonists?
5. How were governments of the colonies organized?
6. **Analyzing a Quotation** Review the description on this page of the advantages an indentured servant might enjoy. Do you think the description is completely accurate? Explain.

Among the many kinds of primary sources are written records. Written records are primary sources if they are firsthand accounts by people who were involved in an event. Letters, diaries, contracts, laws, and treaties are all primary sources.

The excerpt below is adapted from Gottlieb Mittelberger's *Journey to Pennsylvania.* The book was published after a trip in 1750.

1 **Identify the source by asking who, what, when, and where.** (a) Who wrote the source? (b) What is it about? (c) About when was it written? (d) Where does the event described take place?

2 **Recognize the author's point of view.** Many eyewitnesses have a particular reason for writing about an event. Often, they want to persuade the reader to share their views. When you read a primary source, you need to recognize the author's point of view. (a) What is Mittelberger's opinion about the journey to Pennsylvania? (b) What words or phrases show you that he feels strongly about the journey?

3 **Decide whether the source is reliable.** (a) Do you think that Mittelberger gives an accurate view of the journey? Why? (b) Do you think that there is anything left out of his account? (c) Would you say that this is a reliable source for learning about crossing the Atlantic in the mid-1700s? Explain.

Journey to Pennsylvania

❝When the ships have weighed anchor, the real misery begins. Unless they have good wind, ships must often sail 8, 9, 10 or 12 weeks before they reach Philadelphia. Even with the best wind, the voyage lasts 7 weeks. . . . During the voyage people suffer terrible misery, stench, many kinds of seasickness, fever, dysentery, boils, scurvy, cancer, and the like, all of which come from old, sharply-salted food and meat and from very bad, foul water so that many die miserably.

Add to this misery, the lack of food, hunger, thirst, frost, heat, dampness, and fear. The misery reaches a peak when a gale rages for two or three nights and days so that every one believes that the ship will go to the bottom with all human beings on board.

When ships land at Philadelphia after the long voyage, only those who have paid for their passage are allowed to leave. Those who cannot pay must stay on board until they are bought and released from the ships by their buyers. . . . The sale of human beings in the market on board ship goes like this. English, Dutch, and Germans come on board to choose among the healthy passengers and bargain with them how long they will serve for their passage money. Adults bind themselves to serve anywhere from 3 to 6 years. Young people must serve until they are 21 years old.

Many parents must sell and trade away their children like so many head of cattle. It often happens that whole families are sold to different buyers.

Work and labor in this new and wild land are very hard. Work mostly consists of cutting wood, felling oak trees, and clearing large tracts of forest.❞

Use the Section Reviews and this Study Guide to review chapter content.

Main Ideas

The main ideas in each section of this chapter are summarized below.

SECTION 1 ■ Puritan New England

◆ The Puritans hoped to make Massachusetts Bay Colony a society based on God's laws.
◆ Thomas Hooker broke with Massachusetts leaders and founded Connecticut.
◆ Roger Williams set up Rhode Island to put religious toleration into practice.
◆ Indians and colonists clashed when settlers moved onto Indian lands.

SECTION 2 ■ Settling the Middle Colonies

◆ The English took over New Netherland and renamed it New York.
◆ Part of New York became New Jersey.
◆ William Penn founded Pennsylvania as a model of religious freedom and peace.
◆ The Lower Counties of Pennsylvania became Delaware.

SECTION 3 ■ Early Days of the Southern Colonies

◆ Lord Baltimore founded Maryland so that Catholics could have religious freedom.
◆ Conflict with Indians over land on the Virginia frontier led to Bacon's Rebellion.
◆ Settlement in Carolina took place in two separate areas.

◆ James Oglethorpe founded Georgia as a haven for debtors.

SECTION 4 ■ Ruling the Colonies

◆ England passed the Navigation Acts to regulate trade in the colonies.
◆ Colonists were protected by the English Bill of Rights.
◆ Each colony was governed by a governor, council, and legislature.

Key People and Terms

Refer to the Identify and Define questions in the Section Reviews on pages 129, 135, 140, and 145. Use each person, term, and vocabulary word in a complete sentence. When possible, make connections between the people and terms by using more than one person or term in each sentence.

Time Line

1. Make a chart of events in time order. The chart will have two headings: Date, Event. Fill in the chart, using the events on the time line. Add the following events from the chapter: Bacon's Rebellion; Charles I crowned king of England; Massachusetts Bay Colony founded. (Refer to the chapter for the dates.)
2. Which event on your chart helped lead to the founding of the Massachusetts Bay Colony? Explain your answer.

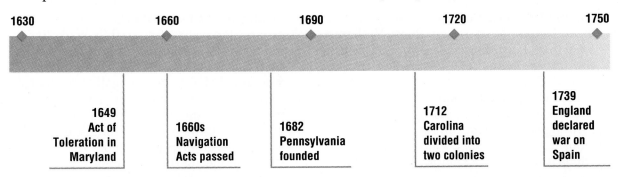

1630	1660	1690	1720	1750
1649 Act of Toleration in Maryland	1660s Navigation Acts passed	1682 Pennsylvania founded	1712 Carolina divided into two colonies	1739 England declared war on Spain

CHAPTER 5 REVIEW

Understanding Vocabulary

Match each term at left with the correct definition at right.

1. toleration
2. proprietary colony
3. mercantilism
4. import
5. legislature

a. economic theory that says a nation becomes strong by building up its gold supply and expanding its trade
b. group of people with the power to make laws
c. willingness to let others practice their own beliefs
d. land granted by the king to one or more people in exchange for a yearly payment
e. trade good brought into a country

Reviewing the Main Ideas

1. (a) How were Puritans different from Pilgrims? (b) Describe the religious beliefs held by Puritans.
2. (a) How did Dutch officials encourage farming in New Netherland? (b) Were they successful? Explain.
3. (a) What beliefs did Quakers hold? (b) How did those beliefs influence William Penn when he set up Pennsylvania?
4. (a) What was the purpose of the Act of Toleration? (b) Why did Lord Baltimore feel that the act was needed?
5. (a) List the rules James Oglethorpe made for the colony of Georgia. (b) How did he later change those rules? Why?
6. (a) What did the Navigation Acts provide? (b) Why did colonists resent them?

Thinking Critically

1. **Linking Past and Present** (a) Why do you think Puritan leaders saw Roger Williams as a threat to Massachusetts? (b) Would the government today consider him a threat? Explain.
2. **Synthesizing Information** (a) Which colony or colonies were founded by people seeking religious freedom? (b) Do you think religious toleration was widespread in the 1600s and 1700s? Explain your answer.

3. **Forecasting** How do you think the settlers' desire for more land would affect relations with the Indians?

Applying Your Skills

1. **Using a Primary Source** Review Skill Lesson 5 on page 146. Then study the letter by John Winthrop on page 123. (a) To whom is the letter addressed? (b) Where was it written? (c) What is it about? (d) Is the letter a good source for learning about Puritan experiences? Explain.
2. **Analyzing a Quotation** James Oglethorpe believed that once debtors reached Georgia, they could work "in a land of liberty and plenty, where . . . they are unfortunate indeed if they can't forget their sorrows." What do you think he meant?
3. **Identifying the Main Idea** Each paragraph or group of paragraphs in this book has a main idea. The main idea is a generalization that underlies all the facts and examples. Read the subsection called "Colonists Resent the Navigation Acts" on page 142. (a) What is the main idea of each paragraph? (b) Give two facts that support the main idea of each paragraph. (c) What is the main idea of the subsection?

Thinking About Geography

Match the letters on the map with the places listed below.

1. New England Colonies
2. Middle Colonies
3. Southern Colonies
4. Massachusetts
5. Pennsylvania
6. Virginia

Region Name the five Southern Colonies.

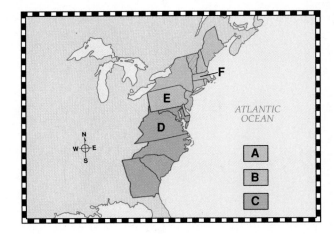

History Writer's Workshop

Arranging Supporting Information

Arrange supporting information for detail sentences in a logical order. The order you use will depend on your topic sentence and the supporting information you have selected. Common orders for arrangement of supporting information include time order, comparison order, order of importance, and cause-and-effect order. Each of these orders is described below.

Time order is arrangement of supporting information in the order it occurred. **Comparison order** is arrangement according to the similarities and differences between two or more things. **Order of importance** is arrangement of information from most important to least important, or vice versa. **Cause-and-effect order** is arrangement of information to show a chain reaction of causes and effects.

Practice Look at the following topic sentence. *The 13 English colonies were founded over a 125-year period.* The following is supporting information. *Roger Williams founded Rhode Island in 1636. James Oglethorpe set up the last colony, Georgia, in 1732. Virginia, the first colony, was founded by John Smith in 1607.*

1. Which order might be best to arrange the supporting information?
2. Arrange the information in the order that you selected.

Writing to Learn

1. Imagine that you are a new colonist in Pennsylvania. Write a letter to your family in Europe. Before writing, list details of your journey to the New World and your first impressions after you arrived. Begin your letter with a topic sentence that summarizes your main impressions. Organize supporting details in time order. Revise to make sure that you have given a complete picture. Proofread and make a final copy. Read your letter to the class.
2. Write a newspaper editorial that takes a stand on William Penn's "holy experiment." Before writing, make a list of arguments for and against Penn's model of religious freedom. Compose a topic sentence that summarizes your position. Organize supporting reasons in order of importance. Revise the editorial, making sure that you have answered the arguments of the other side. Proofread and make a final copy. Publish the editorial in a class newspaper.

Colonists Gather to Work and Play *From quilting bees to barn-raisings, colonists found ways to make social occasions out of hard work. This painting, done in the 1800s, shows what a flax-scutching bee was like. Settlers used wooden paddles, or scutches, to separate the fibers of the flax plant so that they could be spun into linen.* **Daily Life** *Why do you think colonists got together to do chores?*

CHAPTER

6

Colonial Life (1630–1775)

Chapter Outline

1 The Hard-Working New England Colonies
2 The Prosperous Middle Colonies
3 Two Ways of Life in the Southern Colonies
4 New Ideas and Beliefs
5 The Colonies Grow and Prosper

CHAPTER SPOTLIGHT

The Big Picture

Sometimes, the 13 English colonies seemed a hodgepodge of cultures and voices. Not only English, but Dutch, Germans, French, Scotch-Irish, Swedes, and Africans made up the population. Each group had its own language, customs, and traditions. Because the settlers were so varied, the colonies developed different ways of living.

Something else was happening, too. More and more children were born and raised in the colonies. They left behind the old ways of Europe and Africa. Slowly, a new American culture was taking root.

Jim Davidson

Focus On

◆ What was life like in the New England Colonies?

◆ Why did the Middle Colonies prosper?

◆ Why did two ways of life grow up in the Southern Colonies?

◆ What new ideas and beliefs did colonists develop?

◆ How did the colonies grow and change in the 1700s?

"If ever two were one, then surely we.
If ever man were lov'd by wife, then thee;
If ever wife was happy in a man,
Compare with me, ye women, if you can.
I prize thy love more than mines of gold,
Or all the riches the East [does] hold."

Anne Bradstreet wrote these lines for her husband, Simon, in the 1640s. Anne and Simon had married in England in 1628. Two years later, they crossed the Atlantic and settled in Massachusetts. There, they cleared a farm out of the forest and raised eight children.

Anne Bradstreet never intended her poems for the public. But her brother-in-law took them to England and had them printed in 1650. A second volume of her poetry was published in Boston six years after her death, in 1678.

Bradstreet was America's first important poet. Her poems reflect her deep Puritan faith, her love of husband and children, and the beauty of the New England countryside. By the early 1700s, people throughout the colonies knew Bradstreet's works.

The poems of Anne Bradstreet helped colonists learn about life in New England. But the Middle Colonies and the South each had its own special character, too. In this chapter, you will learn about the different ways of life that grew up in the English colonies.

1 The Hard-Working New England Colonies

FIND OUT

◆ What resources did colonists find in New England?

◆ How did New Englanders earn a living?

◆ Why were towns important in New England life?

◆ VOCABULARY subsistence farmer, surplus, stocks

For a child waking up in the New England Colonies, there was much to do. A young Connecticut girl described her day's chores as follows:

> ❝Fixed gown . . . mended Mother's Ridinghood, spun short thread, fixed two gowns for Welsh's girls . . . spun linen, worked on cheesebasket, [combed] flax with Hanna, we did 51 lbs. apiece. Pleated and ironed, read a sermon of Dodridge's, spooled a piece, milked the cows, spun linen, did 50 knots, made a broom of guinea wheat straw, spun thread to whiten, set a red dye, [visited with] two scholars from Mrs. Taylor's, I carded two pounds of whole wool [and then] spun harness twine and scoured the pewter.❞

New England was a difficult land for colonists. Both adults and children had to work hard to survive. But the Puritans who settled New England were hard workers. They believed that daily labor honored God as much as prayer. Rising to many challenges, they built a thriving way of life.

GEOGRAPHY AND HISTORY

A "Wild, Woody Wilderness"

One of the first Puritans to arrive in New England described the land as a "remote, rocky, barren, bushy, wild, woody wilderness." Settlers soon discovered that New England was, indeed, a land of forests and rocks. They formed groups to clear away trees and haul off large boulders that dotted the land.

Farming is hard. New England's rocky soil was poor for farming, and early settlers feared that they would not have enough to eat. But Indians taught the settlers to plant corn. This Native American food grew better than European grains on the roughly cleared land. Settlers also grew other Native American crops, including beans, squash, and pumpkins.

Settlers used crude farming methods and wore out the soil quickly. As a result, they needed to chop down more forests and clear more fields every few years.

Because the soil was poor, most settlers were subsistence farmers. That is, they had small plots of land on which they grew enough food for their own needs. When they did produce a surplus, or an amount more than needed, they traded it for goods such as tools and kettles.

The New England climate was often harsh. During the short growing season, families worked from dawn to dusk in the fields. Winters were long, and deep snows sometimes cut towns off from one another.

Finding food in the forests. New Englanders also found food in the forests. Deer bounded through the woods, and flocks of turkeys ran wild. In the fall, settlers hunted hogs that they had let loose to run in the forest. In the spring, they set up maple-sugar camps to collect the sweet sap that dripped from gashes cut in the trees.

Products From the Seas and Forests

The soil and climate of New England had been a disappointment to early settlers. New Englanders soon found that the real wealth of the region lay in its forests, seas, and rivers.

Harvesting the seas. Although most New Englanders were farmers, many fished the coastal waters. Fishing people hauled in huge catches of cod, halibut, and other fish. Foot-long oysters and lobsters up to six feet in length were not unusual. "Those a foot long," one host recommended, "are better for serving at a table." Larger ones often hung off the edge!

Fishing was hard and dangerous work. When the fish were running, fishing people worked tirelessly, seldom taking time to eat or sleep. After the fishing boats returned to shore, settlers dried and salted the fish. They kept some fish for themselves. The rest of the fish they packed in barrels and sent to other colonies or to England.

In the 1600s, New Englanders also began to hunt whales. Whales supplied them with products such as oil for lamps and ivory. In the 1700s and 1800s, whaling grew into a big business.

Turning trees into ships. New Englanders used the products of the forests to create a profitable shipbuilding industry. Settlers in forested areas cut down trees and floated them to sawmills near port cities such as Boston, Massachusetts, or Portsmouth, New Hampshire. Here, major shipbuilding centers grew.

England encouraged shipbuilding in the colonies. English officials marked the best trees for use in the royal navy. White pines, which grew especially tall and straight, were prized as masts for the English fleet. New England forests also provided other products used in shipbuilding, such as tar, pitch, and turpentine. ◆

Towns: Centers of New England Life

Puritans believed that people should worship and take care of local matters as a community. For this reason, New England became a land of tightly knit towns and villages.

A typical town. What did a New England town look like? At the center was the common, an open field where cattle grazed. Nearby was the meetinghouse, which almost always faced south, "to be square with the sun at noon."

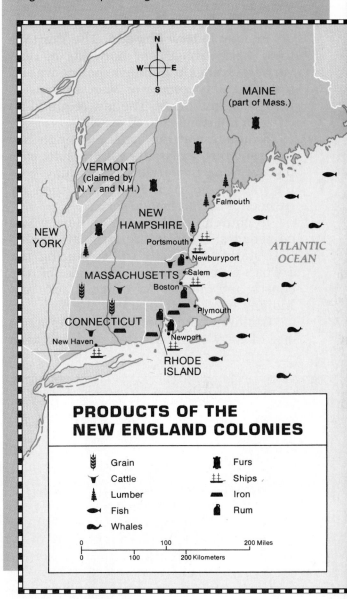

Shipbuilding, fishing, and fur trapping were among the major economic activities of New England colonists.
1. Name two cities where ships were built.
2. What products did Connecticut produce?
3. **Understanding Causes and Effects** How did New England's geography encourage the growth of shipbuilding?

PRODUCTS OF THE NEW ENGLAND COLONIES

Grain		Furs	
Cattle		Ships	
Lumber		Iron	
Fish		Rum	
Whales			

The meetinghouse was the most important building in the town. As one New Englander remarked, it was "built by our own vote, framed by our own hammers and saws, and by our own hands set in the most convenient place for all." The town meetinghouse served as the church where Puritans worshipped. It was also used for town meetings.

Wooden houses with steep roofs lined both sides of the town's narrow streets. Often, the second floor of a house was built out over the street. This overhang gave second-floor rooms more space. It also protected first-floor walls from rain and snow.

Sunday in New England. The Puritans took their Sabbath, or holy day of rest, very seriously. On Sundays, no one was allowed to play games or visit taverns to joke, talk, and drink. The law required all citizens to attend church services.

Sunday morning, the meetinghouse bell rang out across the countryside, calling everyone to worship. At midday, people had an hour for lunch and then returned for the afternoon service.

In church, Puritans sat on hard wooden benches. The wealthy sat apart in boxlike stalls with high walls. During the 1600s, women sat on one side of the church and men on the other. Blacks and Indians stood in a balcony at the back.

Children had separate pews. An adult often kept watch, but it was hard to keep children quiet during the long services. Boys and girls who "sported and played" or made "wry faces [that] caused laughter" were punished. Sometimes a few bold children sneaked away from church to run in the open air.

Town meetings. Church services were solemn occasions, but town meetings could be noisy. Citizens met to discuss questions that affected the town: What roads should be built? What fences needed repair? How much should the schoolmaster be paid? Townspeople debated and then voted on the issues.

Town meetings gave New Englanders a chance to speak their minds. Unlike Spanish or French colonists in the Americas, the English colonists had a say in how they were governed. This early experience encouraged the growth of democratic ideas in New England.

In a New England Home

New England families gathered each evening around the kitchen fireplace. The fireplace was very large, often occupying an entire wall. Yet the room was still cold

New Englanders on the Way to Church *Religion was the center of New England life. Here, colonists make their way through the snow to church.* **Daily Life** *Why do you think the men are carrying guns to church?*

because winds blew down the chimney. One New Englander described how the ink on his pen froze as he sat writing in his kitchen.

The bedrooms were even colder. Heavy drapes around the beds helped to keep out the cold. Before going to sleep, people put a metal warming pan filled with hot coals in their beds to heat the sheets.

In the 1600s, New Englanders sat to eat "at the board." This was a long, narrow plank set on sawhorses close to the fireplace. The family sat on benches without backs and ate from hollowed-out blocks of wood called trenchers. Two diners shared a trencher, picking from it with their fingers. Forks and china dishes did not come into common use until the 1700s.

At mealtimes, adults ate first. Children stood silently by the table, waiting to be offered food. One book of manners offered children the following advice:

> **❝**Never sit down at the table till asked, and after the blessing. Ask for nothing; [wait] till it be offered thee. Speak not. Bite not the bread but break it. Take salt only with a clean knife. . . . Look not earnestly at any other that is eating.**❞**

The Family

The Puritans saw children as a blessing of God and welcomed large families. The average family had seven or eight children.

New Englanders tended to live long, often reaching age 70. As a result, many children grew up knowing both their parents and their grandparents. This did much to make New England towns closely knit communities.

Feeding and clothing a large family required hard work. Men worked in the fields, planting and harvesting crops. Sometimes women worked with the men. More often, women ground corn, skinned and cleaned animals, and dried fruits and vegetables. Many families kept geese, and

The Mason Children *Artists often traveled from place to place in colonial times, painting portraits for families who could afford them. This portrait of David, Joanna, and Abigail Mason was painted by an unknown Massachusetts artist around 1670.*
Daily Life *Do you think that colonial children dressed like this every day? Explain.*

women plucked goose feathers for pillows and mattresses.

In the fall, women made candles for the long winter evenings ahead. They also made clothes for the family. They began with wool from sheep and flax from a plant. Wool had to be dyed, degreased, and combed before it was spun into yarn. Flax had to be cut, beaten, combed, and sorted before it was spun into linen thread.

Justice in New England

Puritan laws were strict, and lawbreakers faced severe punishment. About 15 crimes carried the death penalty. One crime punishable by death was witchcraft. In 1692, 20 men and women were executed as witches in Salem Village, Massachusetts.

Less serious crimes brought other punishments. People found guilty of offenses such as swearing or public drunkenness were made to sit in the stocks for a few hours, or even a few days. Stocks were wooden frames with holes for a person's arms and legs. They were usually set up on the town common. Passersby laughed at prisoners and sometimes threw rotten eggs or stones at them.

SECTION 1 REVIEW

1. **Define:** (a) subsistence farmer, (b) surplus, (c) stocks.
2. How did the land and resources of New England affect the way colonists earned a living?
3. Name two activities that took place in the meetinghouse.
4. What jobs did New England women do?
5. **Linking Past and Present** How was the life of a child in the New England Colonies different from the life of a child today?

2 The Prosperous Middle Colonies

FIND OUT

◆ Why were the Middle Colonies known as the Breadbasket Colonies?

◆ What peoples settled in the Middle Colonies?

◆ What was life like in the Pennsylvania backcountry?

◆ VOCABULARY cash crop, tenant farmer, backcountry

In the summer of 1744, a well-known Maryland doctor toured the Middle Colonies. Doctor Hamilton was amazed at the variety of people he met. Describing an evening in Philadelphia, he wrote:

&&I dined at a tavern with a very mixed company of different nations and religions. There were Scots, English, Dutch, Germans, and Irish. There were Roman Catholics, Church [of England] men, Presbyterians, Quakers, . . . Moravians, . . . and one Jew.JJ

As the doctor observed, the Middle Colonies had a much greater mix of peoples than either New England or the Southern Colonies. Its geography was different, too. Blessed with ideal land and climate, farmers in the Middle Colonies enjoyed a prosperous way of life.

Thriving Farms and Workshops

Farmers found more favorable conditions in the Middle Colonies than in New England. Where New England soil was thin and rocky, the broad Hudson and Delaware River valleys were rich and fertile. Winters were milder than they were in New England. Summers were warmer, and the growing season lasted longer.

Food to spare. Unlike the subsistence farmers of New England, farmers in the Middle Colonies produced surpluses of wheat, barley, and rye. These were **cash crops**, or crops that are sold for money on the world market. The Middle Colonies exported so much grain that they became known as the **Breadbasket Colonies.**

Farmers of the Middle Colonies also raised herds of cattle and pigs. Every year, they sent tons of beef, pork, and butter to the ports of New York and Philadelphia. From there, the goods were shipped to New England and the South or to the West Indies, England, and other parts of Europe.

A comfortable life. Visitors to the Middle Colonies remarked on the comfortable life enjoyed by farm families. A New Englander who stayed with a Quaker family in Philadelphia observed that the people dressed simply, according to Quaker custom. But, he noted, the supper he was served was anything but simple. It included "ducks, hams, chickens, beef, pig, tarts, creams, custards, [and] jellies."

A center of manufacturing and crafts. The Middle Colonies produced many kinds of manufactured goods. One visitor to Pennsylvania reported that workshops turned out "most kinds of hardware, clocks, watches, locks, guns, flints, glass, stoneware, nails, [and] paper." Pennsylvania became a center of manufacturing and crafts, in part because William Penn encouraged German settlers with valuable skills to set up shop there.

Settlers in the Delaware River valley used rich deposits of iron ore to make household and farm tools. First, they heated the ore in special furnaces to turn it into pig iron. Then, in forges, or smaller furnaces, ironworkers hammered the pig iron into nails, tools, and parts for guns.

Tenant Farmers in New York

In Delaware, Pennsylvania, and New Jersey, farmers earned a legal right to land by clearing, planting, and living on the land. But in New York, a different system of farming grew up.

As you have read, Dutch patroons owned huge manors along the Hudson River in New York. Tenant farmers worked the land and paid rent to the landowner. Even after England took over New Netherland, the manor system remained.

Many tenant farmers were unhappy with the manor system. Tenants felt that rents were too high. They resented using their own oxen to plow the landowner's fields. And they thought it unfair that they had to harvest the landowner's crops before they could harvest their own.

New Englanders who moved to New York especially objected to the manor system, which was new to them. In 1757, they persuaded Dutch and German tenants to join them in refusing to pay rents. Mobs formed and attacked manor houses. There was even talk of marching on New York City. The rebels ended their protest only after the arrival of English troops armed with a cannon.

Many tenant farmers simply left New York. They moved to Pennsylvania or New Jersey, where they could work their own land. Others went north to the land later known as Vermont.

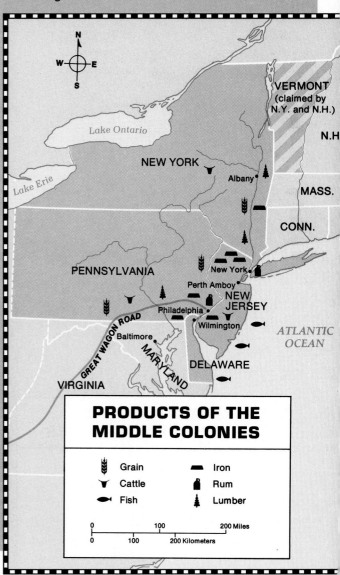

MAP STUDY

The Middle Colonies produced a variety of products, including iron and grain.
1. What was the main product of New Jersey?
2. Where was grain produced in the Middle Colonies?
3. **Analyzing Information** Based on the map, why do you think Philadelphia would be a trading center?

PRODUCTS OF THE MIDDLE COLONIES

Grain		Iron	
Cattle		Rum	
Fish		Lumber	

0   100   200 Miles
0   100   200 Kilometers

The 13 colonies grew larger and more populated in the 1600s and 1700s.
1. *In which direction did settlers move as the colonies grew?*
2. *What barriers to settlement did settlers have to overcome?*
3. **Drawing Conclusions** *What role do you think rivers played in determining areas of new settlement?*

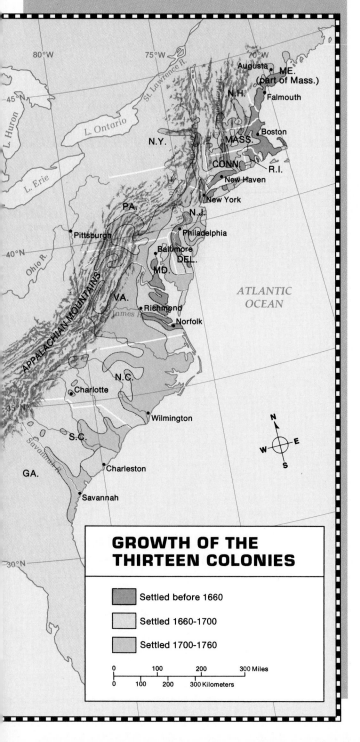

GROWTH OF THE THIRTEEN COLONIES

- Settled before 1660
- Settled 1660–1700
- Settled 1700–1760

0   100   200   300 Miles
0 100 200 300 Kilometers

Log Cabins and Brick Houses

Farms in the Middle Colonies were usually larger than those in New England. Houses were of a variety of styles, depending on the background of the settlers who built them. Because houses tended to be fairly far apart in the Middle Colonies, towns were less important than in New England.

The different groups who settled the Middle Colonies had their own favorite ways of building. Swedish settlers introduced log cabins to the Americas. Sweden was a land of forests, and log cabins had been popular there for hundreds of years.

The Dutch used red bricks to build narrow, high-walled houses in the towns and cities of New York. At each end of the house, walls rose above the roof in a series of little steps. At the top, a weathervane showed which way the wind was blowing. In front of the house, the Dutch built a wooden porch, or stoop. Here, they set two benches where the family could relax and talk to passersby.

German settlers in Pennsylvania developed a new kind of woodburning stove. It heated a home better than a fireplace, and other colonists soon copied it. Often, a German family would place an Indian figure made of iron on the roof to show that they had paid Indians for the land.

Heading Into the Backcountry

In the 1700s, thousands of German and Scotch-Irish settlers arrived in the Middle Colonies. Many had read pamphlets written by William Penn urging them to come to Pennsylvania. From Philadelphia, they headed west into the backcountry, the area of land along the eastern slopes of the Appalachian Mountains. Settlers heading into the backcountry followed an old Iroquois trail that became known as the **Great Wagon Road.**

Wagons travel west. Like most roads of the time, the Great Wagon Road was rough and rutted with deep mudholes. To

Moving West *Thousands of pioneers set out on the Great Wagon Road to the land along the Appalachian Mountains. This picture shows a Pittsburgh-bound family stopping to rest.* **Geography** *Why do you think the travelers chose to stop at this spot?*

carry goods along the road, settlers built **Conestoga** (kahn uh STOH guh) wagons. These wagons had large wheels that raised goods high above the road, keeping them from getting wet as the wagons bumped through mudholes. The floor curved up at both ends so that goods would not fall out as the wagon went up or down steep hills. A cloth cover stretched over hoops of wood kept out rain and snow.

Taming the land. Settlers moving into the backcountry had to clear thick forests before they could farm the land. To do this, they girdled the trees, a method they borrowed from Indians. Using axes, they "cut a notch in the bark a hand broad round about the tree, which pull[ed] off and the tree [would] sprout no more." Once sun-

light began to shine between the dead branches, farmers planted seeds beneath them. After a year or two, they cleared away the remains of the dead trees.

Forests provided settlers with many of their needs. From Indians, settlers learned how to use knots from pine trees as candles to light their homes. They made wooden dishes from logs, gathered honey from hollows in trees, and hunted wild animals for food. German gunsmiths developed a lightweight rifle for use in forests. Sharpshooters boasted that the "Pennsylvania rifle" could hit a rattlesnake between the eyes at 100 yards.

Conflict with Indians. Many settlers arriving in the backcountry moved onto Indian lands. Pennsylvania officials worried that this might lead to war with Indians. One official commented:

> **❝**The Indians . . . are alarmed at the swarm of strangers. We are afraid of a [fight] between them for the [Scotch] Irish are very rough to them.**❞**

Disputes between settlers and Indians resulted in violence on occasion.

SECTION 2 REVIEW

1. **Locate:** (a) Hudson River, (b) Delaware River, (c) Appalachian Mountains, (d) Great Wagon Road.
2. **Identify:** (a) Breadbasket Colonies, (b) Conestoga wagon.
3. **Define:** (a) cash crop, (b) tenant farmer, (c) backcountry.
4. How did the land and climate of the Middle Colonies help farmers to prosper?
5. What groups of people settled the Middle Colonies?
6. Why did backcountry settlers come into conflict with Indians?
7. **Applying Information** Why do you think the manor system did not work in the Middle Colonies?

---

3 Two Ways of Life in the Southern Colonies

FIND OUT

◆ How did geography help to shape life in the Southern Colonies?

◆ What was the Middle Passage?

◆ What was life like on a southern plantation?

◆ **VOCABULARY** slave code, racism

In 1763, two English mathematicians, Charles Mason and Jeremiah Dixon, began to survey the 244-mile boundary between Pennsylvania and Maryland. The boundary had been in dispute since 1681. For four years, Mason and Dixon carefully laid stone markers on the border between the two colonies. On the sides of the markers facing Pennsylvania, the letter *P* was inscribed. The sides facing Maryland were inscribed with the letter *M*. In 1767, the **Mason-Dixon Line** was complete.

But the Mason-Dixon Line was more than just the boundary between Pennsylvania and Maryland. It also divided the Middle Colonies from the Southern Colonies. Below the Mason-Dixon Line, the Southern Colonies developed a way of life very different from that of the other English colonies.

GEOGRAPHY AND HISTORY

Two Kinds of Land

The Southern Colonies enjoyed warmer weather and a longer growing season than their northern neighbors. As you have read, tobacco thrived in the Virginia climate. But planting tobacco year after year on a small plot of land wore out the soil.

Virginia farmers soon found that it was more profitable to produce tobacco on large plantations. Plantation owners could rotate crops and leave part of the land idle each year. In this way, the soil did not wear out so quickly.

Settlers in other Southern Colonies followed Virginia's example. In the 1700s, Maryland and parts of North Carolina became major tobacco-growing areas. Rice and indigo, a plant used to make a blue dye, thrived on plantations in South Carolina and Georgia.

Tidewater plantations. Geography affected where southerners built plantations. Along the coastal plain was an area of low land that stretched like fingers among broad rivers and creeks. Because the land was washed by ocean tides, the region was known as the **Tidewater.** The gentle slopes and banks of the Tidewater offered rich farmland for plantations.

Inland, planters settled along rivers because they provided an easy way to get goods to market. At harvest time, planters brought their crops to the river bank. There, the crops were loaded on ships bound for the West Indies and Europe. Later, the ships returned carrying English manufactured goods and other luxuries for the planter and his family.

Most Tidewater plantations had their own docks, and merchant ships picked up crops and delivered goods directly to them. For this reason, few large seaport cities developed in the Southern Colonies.

The southern backcountry. West of the Tidewater was a very different landscape. Here, at the base of the Appalachian Mountains, the land was hilly and covered with thick forests. As in the Middle Colonies, this inland area was called the backcountry. Two ways of life grew up in the Southern Colonies, one in the Tidewater and the other in the backcountry. ◆

The Rise of Slavery

Plantations needed large numbers of workers to be profitable. At first, Tidewater planters brought indentured servants from England to work their land. But indentured servants earned their freedom after a few years. A slave cost more than an indentured servant, but a planter controlled the slave and the slave's children forever.

By 1700, slave labor had become important to plantation farming in the Southern Colonies. Slaves cleared the land, worked the crops, and tended the livestock. They showed white colonists how to grow rice. Slaves helped the Southern Colonies to prosper.

But slaves resented their lot. Some tried to escape. Others protested their condition by attacking their owners or damaging crops and tools.

A Tidewater Plantation *This painting shows a typical Tidewater plantation. The Great House of the planter and his family dominates the scene. Slave cabins, barns, and warehouses dot the hillside below the mansion.* **Geography** *Why do you think the painting shows all roads leading down to the river?*

Farm products and lumber were important to the economy of the Southern Colonies.

1. *What were the major products of the Tidewater, or coastal areas?*
2. *What were the major products of the backcountry?*
3. **Comparing** *Compare this map with the map on page 157. (a) How were the products of the Southern Colonies similar to those of the Middle Colonies? (b) How were they different?*

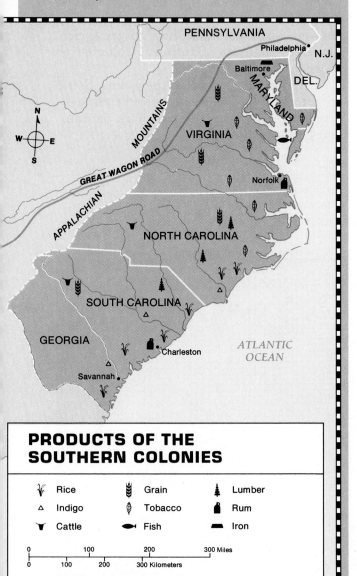

PRODUCTS OF THE SOUTHERN COLONIES

🌾 Rice	🌾 Grain	🌲 Lumber
△ Indigo	🌾 Tobacco	🍶 Rum
⛊ Cattle	🐟 Fish	▬ Iron

Slaves as property. Colonists passed slave codes, or laws that controlled the behavior of slaves and denied them their basic rights. Slaves were seen not as human beings but as property—no different from horses or plows.

Most English colonists accepted slavery. They did not question the justice of owning slaves because they believed that black Africans were inferior to white Europeans. The belief that one race is superior to another is called racism. Those colonists who felt the need to defend their actions claimed to be helping slaves by introducing them to Christianity.

A handful of colonists clearly saw the evils of slavery. In 1688, Quakers in Germantown, Pennsylvania, became the first group of colonists to call for an end to slavery. Pennsylvania Quakers also criticized New England merchants who grew rich from the slave trade.

The Middle Passage

With demand so high, the slave trade became a profitable business. White slave traders set up posts along the African coast. They offered guns and other goods to African rulers who brought them slaves. When the slave merchants had a large enough "cargo," the slaves were loaded aboard Portuguese, Dutch, Spanish, English, and French ships headed for the Americas. By the 1700s, about 100,000 slaves were arriving in the Americas each year.

The trip from Africa to the Americas was called the **Middle Passage.** Conditions were horrible. Slaves were crammed into small spaces below deck with hardly enough room to sit up. Often, they were chained together, two by two. Once or twice a day, they were taken up on deck to eat and exercise.

Some Africans fought for their freedom during the trip. Others refused to eat. But slaves were too valuable to be allowed to starve. Sailors pried open their mouths and forced food down their throats. Some

Terrors of the Middle Passage

Among the thousands of Africans who endured the horrors of the Middle Passage from Africa to the Americas was Olaudah Equiano (oh LAW dah ehk wee AH no). Equiano was only 11 years old when he was kidnapped from his home in Nigeria and sold to a slave trader. In time, Equiano was able to buy his freedom. Under his slave name, Gustavus Vassa, he wrote a book about his life. The following excerpt describes the Middle Passage:

❝The first object which saluted my eyes when I arrived on the coast was the sea, and a slaveship. . . . These filled me with astonishment, [then] terror. . . .

I was soon put down under the decks, and there I received such a salutation in my nostrils as I have never experienced in my life. . . . I became so sick and low that I was not able to eat. . . . On my refusing to eat, [a white man] held me fast by the hands and tied my feet, while [another] flogged me severely. . . .

The closeness of the place, and the heat of the climate, added to the number in the ship, which was so crowded that each had scarcely room to turn himself, almost suffocated us. . . .

The shrieks of the women, and the groans of the dying, rendered the whole a scene of horror almost [impossible to believe]. . . . One day . . . two of my wearied countrymen who were chained together . . . jumped into the sea; immediately another quite dejected fellow . . . followed their example. . . . Two of the wretches were drowned, but [the ship's crew] got the other, and afterwards flogged him unmercifully for thus attempting to prefer death to slavery.❞

1. What conditions on the ship frightened Equiano?

2. **Drawing Conclusions** Why do you think the traders tried to keep the slaves alive, yet at the same time treated them so poorly?

captives leaped overboard, choosing to die rather than live as slaves.

The number of slaves who did not survive the voyage was high. Dr. Alexander Garden, an inspector for the port of Charleston, South Carolina, reported:

❝There are few ships that come here from Africa but have had many of their Cargoes thrown overboard. Some [lost] one fourth [of their slaves], some lost half. And I have seen some that have lost two thirds of their slaves. . . . I have never been on board one [a slave ship] that did not smell [of disease]. . . . It is a wonder any escape with Life. **"**

Living on a Southern Plantation

Most white southerners did not own plantations. Still, planters set the style of life in the South. William Byrd, a wealthy planter, wrote to a friend describing plantation life:

" . . . Besides the advantage of pure air, we . . . who have plantations abound in all kinds of provisions. . . . I have my flocks and my herds, my bondmen and bondwomen, and every sort of trade among my own servants. . . . I live in . . . independence of everyone but [Heaven]. **"**

As Byrd's letter suggested, many plantations were self-sufficient. That is, people on the plantation produced most of the food and other goods they needed. The greatest part of the work was done by anywhere from 20 to 100 slaves. Most of them worked in the fields. A few were skilled workers, such as carpenters, barrelmakers, or blacksmiths. Still other slaves worked as cooks, servants, or housekeepers.

The Great House. Plantation life centered around the Great House, where the planter and his family lived. These stately homes were built in the style of English manor houses. Besides elegant quarters for the family, the mansion usually had a parlor for visitors, a dining room, and guest bedrooms. Some houses also had ballrooms for dancing. The kitchen was often a separate building. As one planter explained, "The Smell of . . . [food]" was "offensive in hot Weather."

Planters and wives. Planters made all important decisions about the plantation. They decided which fields to plant, what crops to grow, and when to harvest the crops and take them to market. They also decided what to do with profits earned from cash crops. Most planters used the money to buy more land and more slaves.

Planters' wives kept the household running smoothly. They were in charge of the house slaves and made sure daily tasks were done. These tasks included weeding the vegetable garden, milking cows, and collecting eggs. Wives ran the plantation if their husbands were away or had died.

A Planter and His Wife *This portrait of a prominent Charleston planter and his wife is by John Singleton Copley, the foremost painter of colonial times. As the portrait shows, wealthy planters often copied the elegant manners and fashions of the English upper class.* **Economics** *Do you think that the couple in the portrait were typical of southern colonists? Explain.*

A Rougher Life in the Southern Backcountry

As you have read, a stream of settlers headed into the Pennsylvania backcountry along the Great Wagon Road. Often, the newcomers pushed beyond Pennsylvania. Attracted by the rich soil of the Shenandoah Valley, they settled in western Maryland, Virginia, and the Carolinas. This was the southern backcountry.

The backcountry was more democratic than the Tidewater. Few rich families lived on the frontier, and settlers treated one another as equals. As one visitor noted, "Every man . . . calls his wife, brother, neighbor, or acquaintance by their proper name of Sally, John, James, or Michael." By contrast, Tidewater people used terms such as "My dear sir," "Madam," or "Mister." Also, backcountry people wore simple clothes suited to frontier life. Their long linen shirts and moccasins contrasted sharply with the silks and velvets of the Tidewater people.

A Day in the Life of a Backcountry Woman

What was life like for a woman in the backcountry? Peggy, the woman in the following account, never actually lived. But the description of her life is based on diaries and other records left by real women of the southern backcountry in the 1700s.

Peggy lived in a log cabin a few miles from the Great Wagon Road with her husband, Tom, and five children, three boys and two girls. The family was Scotch-Irish.

Time to get up. In the morning, Peggy knew it was time to get up when light began to leak through cracks in the cabin walls. Rising, she stirred the glowing embers in the fireplace. When the fire was hot, she cooked the family breakfast of cornmeal mush mixed with milk.

Hard Work in the Backcountry *From sunup to sundown, life for a backcountry woman was an endless round of chores. Here, a woman on the Carolina frontier fetches water from a well.* **Daily Life** *What qualities do you think a backcountry woman needed?*

After breakfast, Tom and the boys went off to the fields, and the women turned to their chores. Peggy and her younger daughter milked the cows, then churned milk and cream to make butter and cheese. Peggy set her older daughter to spinning wool for the family's clothes. She was also to keep an eye on Baby Brother, who crawled about the cabin floor.

Afternoon. Sometime between noon and three, the men came back for the big meal of the day. Peggy served a stew, an easy dish because it bubbled away without too much tending. Another favorite dish was hominy grits, boiled corn—sometimes with beans and milk.

After the meal, there were more chores. On this day, Peggy "pulled flax." She beat the flax plants and pulled their fibers apart. Later, she would use the fiber to make shirts for Tom and the boys. The shirts were scratchy, but the family could not afford to buy anything fancier. Besides, there was no market nearby.

Different chores every day. Peggy's chores were different every day. If Tom had killed a hog, she smoked the meat to keep it from spoiling. In the summer, the garden behind the kitchen needed tending. And once in a while, Peggy and Tom cleaned the chimney to keep it from catching fire. They did this by dropping a chicken down the chimney. The trapped bird squawked and flapped its wings, trying to get out. In the meantime, it knocked a lot of soot off the chimney walls.

During the harvest, Peggy joined Tom and the boys in the field, gathering corn or cutting tobacco and hanging up the leaves to dry. There was too much to be done to worry about whether it was proper "woman's work." A visitor from the East was amazed by the activities of a backcountry woman:

> ❝[S]he will carry a gunn in the woods and kill deer, turkeys &c., shoot down wild cattle, catch and tye hoggs, knock down [cattle] with an ax, and perform the most manfull Exercises as well as most men.❞

Peggy looked forward to the special occasions that provided her only break from work. Now and then, a minister passed through to hold church services. And a few times a year, Peggy visited neighbors, a day's ride down the road. Families got together to husk corn or help each other raise barns.

Bedtime. But most days, work continued until dusk. When darkness fell, the entire family went to bed. Peggy and Tom stretched out on a bumpy mattress, stuffed with old rags and corn cobs, and quickly fell asleep.

Life in the backcountry was not easy. But the hardships served to bring families closer. Kinfolk, a family's relations, looked out for one another. Spread out in the forests and fields along the edge of the Appalachians, these hardy families felled trees, grew crops, and changed the face of the land. ◆

SECTION 3 REVIEW

1. **Identify:** (a) Mason-Dixon Line, (b) Tidewater, (c) Middle Passage.
2. **Define:** (a) slave code, (b) racism.
3. (a) Where were most plantations located? (b) Why?
4. Why did southern planters turn to slave labor?
5. What jobs did each of the following do on a plantation: (a) planters; (b) planters' wives; (c) slaves?
6. **Forecasting** Why do you think tensions might develop between the backcountry and the Tidewater?

4 New Ideas and Beliefs

FIND OUT

◆ How did colonists educate their children?

◆ What was the Enlightenment?

◆ What were some accomplishments of Benjamin Franklin?

◆ How did the Great Awakening increase religious toleration?

◆ VOCABULARY public school, apprentice, gentry, almanac

In 1743, Benjamin Franklin, a leading citizen of Philadelphia, made a proposal to the English colonists. It began:

> ❝The first drudgery of settling new colonies . . . is now pretty well over, and there are many in every province . . . [who have time] to cultivate the finer arts, and improve the common stock of knowledge.❞

Franklin wanted colonists to put their newly found spare time to good use. He invited them to join together in a society to promote "USEFUL KNOWLEDGE among British [colonies] in America." Thanks to

Franklin's efforts, the American Philosophical Society was born.

Franklin's new society was only one sign that the English colonies were coming of age. By the mid-1700s, they had developed a culture different from that of England. This new culture, created by the many peoples of the colonies, was uniquely American.

Educating the Children

From the start, colonists had to decide how to educate their children. New Englanders were the most concerned about education. Puritans believed that all people had a duty to study the Bible. If settlers did not learn to read, how would they fulfill this duty? As one Massachusetts leader explained, "It is the chief project of that old deluder, Satan, to keep men from Knowledge of the Scriptures."

New England sets up public schools. In 1647, the Massachusetts assembly passed a law ordering all parents to teach their children "to read and understand the principles of religion." Beyond that, they required all towns with 50 families to hire a schoolteacher. Towns with 100 families had to set up a grammar school that prepared boys for college.

In this way, Massachusetts set up the first public schools, or schools supported by taxes. Public schools were important because they allowed both rich and poor children to get an education.

The first New England schools had only one room for students of all ages. Parents paid the schoolteacher with corn, peas, or other foods. Each child was expected to bring a share of wood to burn in the stove. Students who forgot would find themselves seated in the coldest corner of the room!

Books were scarce in the colonies, so many New England pupils learned their ABC's from hornbooks. These small wooden boards had lessons printed on one side. A thin layer of transparent horn kept the boards clean.

A Colonial Textbook *Colonial children learned both reading and religion from books such as the one shown here. The rhymed verses provided lessons for leading a moral life.* **Daily Life** *Why did the Puritans value education?*

Schools in the Middle and Southern colonies. In the Middle Colonies, churches and individual families set up private schools. Pupils paid to attend, so only wealthy families could afford to send their children.

In the Southern Colonies, most people lived too far apart to bring children together in one building. Many planters hired tutors, or private teachers. The wealthiest planters sent their sons to school in England. From time to time, a school was set up in a tobacco shed in the fields. Children rode on horseback or rowed up a river to these "field schools."

Higher Education

In 1636, Massachusetts set up a college to train Puritan ministers, because "our present Ministers shall soon lie in the dust." Two years later, a minister named John Harvard left his library to the college, which then took his name. In 1693, Virginia founded the College of William and Mary to train ministers of the Church of England. In 1701, Connecticut opened the doors of Yale College. While most colleges began as training places for ministers, before long they also graduated lawyers, doctors, and teachers.

Learning by Doing

Many children in the colonies received no formal schooling. They learned the skills they needed as they went along. In farm families, children learned from parents and older brother and sisters.

Children also served as apprentices (uh PREHN tihs ehz). An apprentice worked for a master craftsman to learn a trade or craft. For example, when a boy reached age 12 or 13, his parents might apprentice him to a master glassmaker. The young apprentice lived in the glassmaker's home for six or seven years. The glassmaker gave him food and clothing and treated him like a member of the family. He was also supposed to teach the boy how to read and write and provide him with religious training.

In return, the apprentice worked without pay in the glassmaker's shop and learned the skills needed to become a master glassmaker. He was then ready to start his own glassmaking shop. Boys were apprenticed in many trades, including papermaking, printing, and leather tanning.

Learning a Craft *Being an apprentice was usually hard work, as shown here. But for most colonial boys, it was the only way to learn a craft or trade.* **Linking Past and Present** *How do young people today learn a craft or trade?*

Education for Girls

In New England, some girls attended dame schools, or private schools run by women in their own homes. But most schools in the colonies accepted only boys. Girls learned skills from their mothers, who taught them to spin wool, weave, and embroider. If they were lucky, they also learned to read and write.

Sometimes, girls became apprentices, although they had a smaller choice of trades than boys did. A girl's parents might send her to become a cook or a housemaid. Women also learned trades from their fathers, brothers, or husbands. They worked as shoemakers, silversmiths, and butchers. Quite a few women became printers. A woman often took over her husband's business upon his death.

Wigs and Other Fashions

Colonists enjoyed more social equality than people in England. Still, class differences did exist. At the top of society stood the gentry. They included wealthy planters, merchants, ministers, successful lawyers, and royal officials. Below the gentry was the middle class. It included farmers who worked their own land, skilled craftworkers, and some tradespeople. The lowest class included hired farmhands, indentured servants, and slaves.

People dressed according to their class. The gentry was wealthy enough to follow the latest fashions from England. But not everyone approved of the new styles. In 1701, an older Bostonian made the following entry in his diary:

> ❝Having last night heard that Josiah Willard cut off his hair (a very full head of hair) and put on a Wigg, I went to him this morning. . . . I inquired of him what Extremity had forced him to put off his own hair, and put on a Wigg?❞

The gentleman tried to argue Willard out of his new fashion, saying that it was

1 Red poppies (pain killer)
2 Balsam (healing salve)
3 Buckthorn (laxative)
4 Wormwood (remedy for worms)
5 Compound soap liniment (bruise ointment)
6 Myrrh (germ killer)·
7 Rhubarb (stomach soother)
8 Tobacco
9 Alum (stops external bleeding)
10 Chamomile flowers (cramp remedy)
11 Wild valerian root (sedative)
12 Wooden pill case
13 Book of formulas
14 Mortar (bowl) and pestle (grinding instrument)
15 Beeswax (base for ointment)

Apothecary's Shop *Health care in colonial times was poor by today's standards. There were few trained doctors or nurses. Medicines, usually made of herbs or roots, were made and sold by an apothecary, or druggist, in a shop like the one pictured here.* **Linking Past and Present** *How does this shop compare with a drugstore today?*

against "God's Laws." Even so, fashionable men and women throughout the colonies began to wear long, curly wigs or fancy white, powdered wigs. Poorer colonists often called these gentry "bigwigs."

The middle and lower classes dressed more simply, wearing garments of homespun linen and cowhide shoes. Men wore their hair long and tied back with a ribbon.

An Age of Reason

During the 1700s, European scholars and scientists tried to use reason and logic to find out how the world worked. They developed theories and then performed experiments to test them. In doing so, they discovered many laws of nature. Isaac Newton, for example, explained how the force of gravity kept the planets from flying out of their orbits. Because these thinkers believed in the light of human reason, the movement that they started is known as the **Enlightenment.**

Educated colonists eagerly took up the "new learning." The colonies were growing and prospering, their people becoming richer and more numerous. So colonists were quick to believe that human reason could help to promote progress and improve society.

Benjamin Franklin: Home-Grown Genius

The best example of the Enlightenment spirit in the colonies was Benjamin Franklin. Franklin was born in 1706, the son of a poor Boston soap and candle maker. A strong believer in self-improvement, Franklin worked his way from poverty to become an important colonial leader.

Hard-working printer. Franklin was one of 17 children. He had to leave school at age 10 to help in his father's shop. When he was 12 years old, he was apprenticed to his brother James, a printer. Although Franklin had only two years of formal schooling, he never stopped learning. He used his spare time to read and to study literature, mathematics, and foreign languages.

At age 17, Franklin ran away to Philadelphia. There, through hard work, he built up a printing business. He published pamphlets, newspapers, and almanacs, or books containing calendars and other useful information. His most popular publication was *Poor Richard's Almanac.* Many of its sayings are still quoted today:

> **"**A penny saved is a penny earned.
> Never leave that till tomorrow which you can do today.
> God helps those that help themselves.**"**

Scientist and inventor. From an early age, Franklin tried to find ways to improve things. In 1740, he invented the Franklin stove. It burned less wood and heated homes better than other stoves. Another Franklin invention was the bifocal lens, which let people wear one pair of glasses for both distance and close work.

In 1752, Franklin proved that lightning was a form of electricity. To do this, he flew a kite during a thunderstorm. A bolt of lightning struck a wire fastened to the kite and caused an electric spark. Applying this knowledge, Franklin then invented the lightning rod to protect buildings against "mischief from . . . lightning."

Energetic public servant. Franklin had ideas for improving his adopted city of Philadelphia. He convinced city officials to pave the streets with cobblestones, organize a police force, and set up a fire company. Eager to promote education, Franklin set up the first lending library in the Americas and an academy that later became the University of Pennsylvania.

Benjamin Franklin's contributions went far beyond Philadelphia, as you will read later. His practical inventions and his public service earned him worldwide fame. Colonists had good reason to be proud of

Fireman Franklin *Benjamin Franklin always sought ways to improve life in his adopted hometown of Philadelphia. Here, Franklin is shown wearing the helmet of the fire company he founded in 1736. Members ran to fires with water buckets, carrying bags in which they packed rescued goods.*
Daily Life *What other improvements did Franklin make in Philadelphia?*

their home-grown genius. (📖 See "A Striking Sun Dial" on page 646.)

A Renewal of Faith

In the 1730s and 1740s, a religious movement known as the **Great Awakening** swept through the colonies. Like the Enlightenment, the Great Awakening started in Europe. But while the Enlightenment affected only educated colonists, the Great Awakening touched people of all backgrounds.

Most colonists were ready for the Great Awakening. As the colonies had grown, religion had weakened as a force in daily life. By the early 1700s, many colonists, especially New Englanders, longed for the deep religious feelings that the first settlers had experienced.

A New England preacher named Jonathan Edwards set off the Great Awakening in the colonies. Edwards called on people to examine their lives. In powerful sermons, he warned listeners that they were "sinners in the hands of an angry God," headed for the fiery torments of hell.

In 1739, when an English minister named George Whitefield (WIHT feeld) arrived in the colonies, the movement spread like wildfire. Whitefield drew huge crowds to outdoor meetings from Massachusetts to Georgia. His voice rang with feeling as he called on sinners to reform. Jonathan Edwards's wife described the impact Whitefield had on listeners:

> ❝[Whitefield] casts a spell over an audience. . . . I have seen upwards of a thousand people hang on his words with breathless silence, broken only by an occasional half-suppressed sob.❞

The Great Awakening aroused bitter debate. People who supported it often split away from their old churches to form new ones. Opponents warned that the movement was too emotional. Still, the growth of new churches forced colonists to become more tolerant of people with different beliefs.

The Church as Center of Colonial Life *Many colonial women sewed scraps of cloth to make elaborate quilts. The designs on the quilts often reflected important themes of the period. The lovely quilt shown here emphasizes the idea of the church as the center of colonial life.* **Culture** *Why were many colonists ready for the Great Awakening?*

SECTION 4 REVIEW

1. **Identify:** (a) Enlightenment, (b) Benjamin Franklin, (c) *Poor Richard's Almanac,* (d) Great Awakening, (e) Jonathan Edwards, (f) George Whitefield.
2. **Define:** (a) public school, (b) apprentice, (c) gentry, (d) almanac.
3. Why did the Puritans support public education?
4. What goals did Enlightenment thinkers have?
5. List three contributions of Benjamin Franklin.
6. **Applying Information** Why do you think there was greater social equality in the colonies than there was in England?

5 The Colonies Grow and Prosper

FIND OUT

◆ How did the colonists improve travel and communication?

◆ What items did the colonies trade?

◆ How did cities influence colonial culture?

◆ VOCABULARY triangular trade

During the 1690s, New England merchants brought in a strange new product from the East Indies—tea. Puzzled colonists were not sure what to do with the shredded brown leaves. They tried boiling the leaves in water, until the water turned brown. Then they threw out the water, put butter and salt on the leaves, and ate them. Only later did they learn that tea leaves were used to make a drink!

A Colonial Mail Carrier *Colonial mail carriers often announced their arrival by blowing a horn. As mail service improved, colonists learned more about their neighbors.* **Daily Life** *How did the relay system help to move mail more quickly?*

For many years, the English colonists were cut off from the rest of the world. Often, they learned about new products like tea long after everyone else. But as the colonies grew, foreign trade increased. Contact among the colonies also increased. By the mid-1700s, many colonists found that they had much in common.

Improving Travel and Communication

In the 1600s and early 1700s, travel was slow and difficult, and most colonists stayed close to home. The few roads that existed were dusty in summer and muddy in winter. Worst of all, there were no road signs. One traveler recalled a trip:

> ❝We missed the road, although we were upon it, and could not find that or any other plantation, and meanwhile it became dark. . . . We were utterly [confused] and [lost]. We followed the roads as we found them, now easterly and then westerly, now a little more on one side, and then a little more on the other, until we were completely tired out.❞

Often, there were no bridges over streams and rivers. Visitors to Boston took a ferry across the Charles River. But their carriages could not fit on the ferry unless they were taken apart. Carriage horses had to swim behind the boat! (📖 See "By Horseback From Boston" on page 648.)

Milestones mark the distance. In the mid-1700s, colonists tried to improve road travel. Benjamin Franklin had milestones placed along the road between Boston and Philadelphia so that people could see how far they had traveled. To do so, Franklin invented a machine that recorded distances as it was wheeled behind his wagon. At each mile, he dropped a large stone on the ground. Later, roadworkers pounded the stone firmly into place.

Delivering the mail. Because road conditions were so poor, relatives and friends

John Peter Zenger: Fighter for Freedom of the Press

On November 1, 1733, a new newspaper, *The New York Weekly Journal,* appeared in the colonies. It was published by a printer named John Peter Zenger.

Zenger had come to the colonies from Germany at age 13. Lacking formal education as well as writing ability, he seemed an unlikely publisher. But Zenger had another important quality: He had courage.

Zenger had a special mission for his paper. He wanted to expose the dishonesty and greed of New York's governor, William Cosby. Furious at Zenger's attacks, Cosby ordered a public burning of the *Journal.* Then, charging that Zenger had no right to criticize him in print, Cosby threw the printer into jail.

For eight months, Zenger remained in a cell. A poor printer could not afford bail. But Zenger's wife, Anna, took up his cause. Through her efforts, the *Journal* continued to appear.

In the end, Zenger was brought to trial. His lawyer argued that the press must have the right to point out the faults of government. How else are the people to be protected, he asked. The jury took only 10 minutes to reach a verdict: "Not guilty."

Zenger won his freedom. But Zenger's trial represented a much greater victory. In the words of a later American leader, "The trial of Zenger in 1735 was the germ of American freedom, the morning star of that liberty which subsequently revolutionized America."

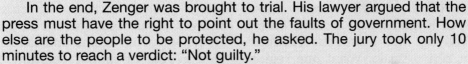

1. What was Zenger's mission for his newspaper?

2. **Defending a Position** A free press is an important part of democracy. Do you agree or disagree with this statement? Why?

in different colonies rarely heard from one another. A postal system was set up, but it was slow. In 1717, it took one month for a letter to get from Boston to Williamsburg, Virginia. In winter, it took two months.

In 1753, Benjamin Franklin became postmaster general for the colonies. He set up relay stations along the post roads, as the roads used by mail carriers were called. At the relays, mail carriers exchanged tired horses for fresh ones. The relay system helped mail to move more quickly.

Spreading the news. As roads and mail service improved, colonists learned more about their neighbors. Families built taverns along main roads and in towns and cities. Colorful signs out front attracted customers, who stopped to rest and to exchange news and gossip with local people.

Colonial printers spread news and ideas by turning out pamphlets and newspapers. The first printing press was set up at Harvard College in 1639. Presses later appeared in most major cities. They printed religious books and travelers' stories.

By the mid-1700s, all the colonies except New Jersey and Delaware had at least one weekly newspaper. Newspapers took several months to travel from colony to colony or from England to the colonies. But even though the news was old, colonists read it eagerly.

Exchanging Goods

As you have read, different colonies produced different goods. New England was known for fish, lumber, and furs. The Middle Colonies produced grains, cattle, and flour. And the South was important for tobacco, rice, and indigo.

Colonial trade. Colonists sold these goods both to England and to each other. Ships moved up and down the Atlantic coast in an active trade. What one region did not produce, it bought from another. Southerners ate New England cod, and New Englanders smoked southern tobacco.

Merchants from New England dominated colonial trade. They were known as **Yankees,** a nickname that implied they were clever and hard-working. Yankee traders won a reputation for always getting a good buy and profiting from any deal.

Molasses, rum, and slaves. Merchants developed many trade routes. One route was known as the triangular trade because the three legs of the route formed a triangle. (See the map on page 175.) On the first leg of the journey, New England ships carried fish, lumber, and other goods to the West Indies. There, they picked up sugar and molasses, a dark brown syrup made from sugar cane. New Englanders used molasses to make rum.

On the second leg, merchants carried rum, guns, gunpowder, cloth, and tools from New England to West Africa. In Africa, they traded these goods for slaves. On the final leg, traders carried slaves from Africa to the West Indies. With the profits from selling the slaves, traders bought more molasses.

Many New England merchants grew wealthy from the triangular trade. In doing so, they often disobeyed the Navigation Acts. (See pages 141–142.) Traders were supposed to buy sugar and molasses only from English colonies in the West Indies. But the demand for molasses was so high that New Englanders bought from the Dutch, French, and Spanish West Indies. Although this trade was illegal, bribes made customs officials look the other way.

Cities: Centers of News and Ideas

Even though most colonists lived on farms, cities greatly influenced culture. The newest ideas from Europe appeared first in city drawing rooms and taverns. By the mid-1700s, all major colonial cities had their own theaters. City dwellers also enjoyed singing societies, traveling circuses, and horse races. Some communities established libraries stocked with the latest books from the colonies and Europe.

The major colonial cities—Boston, New York, Philadelphia, Charleston—were seaports. As trade expanded, so, too, did the cities. Boston was one of the busiest ports in the colonies, with 40 wharves where ships loaded and unloaded goods.

The fastest-growing city was Philadelphia. By 1760, it had the largest population of any city in North America. Thanks to Benjamin Franklin, it boasted the only hospital on the continent. Philadelphia also had three libraries and three newspapers, including one in German.

Colonists traded extensively with the rest of the world.
1. *Find the triangular trade route between the colonies, Africa, and the West Indies. What goods were traded at each point along the route?*
2. *(a) What goods did the colonies export to England? (b) What goods did England send to the colonies?*
3. **Comparing** *Make a generalization comparing the types of goods exported by the colonies and England.*

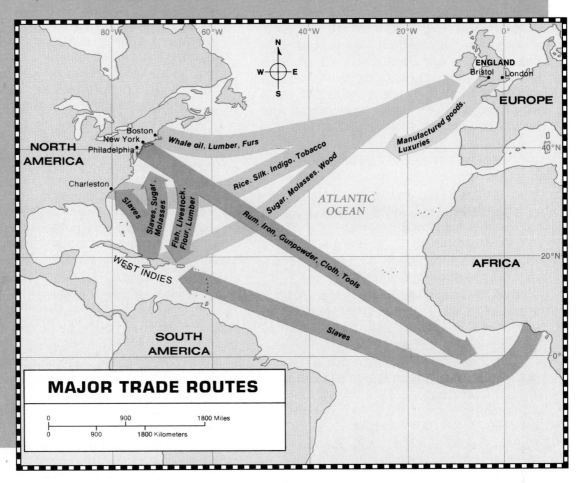

MAJOR TRADE ROUTES

| 0 | 900 | 1800 Miles |
| 0 | 900 | 1800 Kilometers |

---

1. **Locate:** (a) West Indies, (b) Africa, (c) Boston, (d) New York, (e) Philadelphia, (f) Charleston.
2. **Identify:** Yankee.
3. **Define:** triangular trade.
4. Describe travel in the colonies in the 1700s.

5. What goods were traded by each of the following: (a) New England Colonies; (b) Middle Colonies; (c) Southern Colonies?
6. How did the growth of trade cause colonial cities to grow?
7. **Synthesizing Information** How do you think improvements in travel and communication helped to create a uniquely American culture?

As you learned in Skill Lesson 4 (page 118), graphs show statistics in picture form. A bar graph is useful because it shows changes in one or more sets of numbers over time. The bar graph below shows the growth of trade between England and the 13 colonies during the period from 1700 to 1750.

There are two kinds of bar graphs. In a vertical bar graph, the bars go up and down. In a horizontal bar graph, the bars go from side to side. Some bar graphs have two or more bars in different colors so that you can make comparisons.

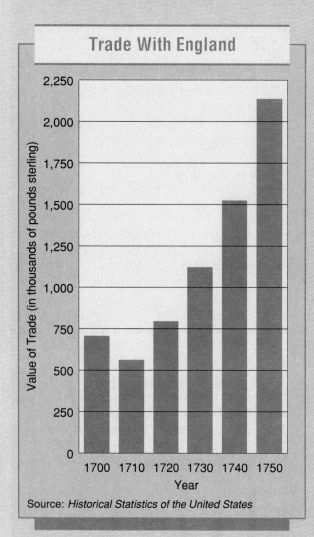

Trade With England

Value of Trade (in thousands of pounds sterling)

Source: *Historical Statistics of the United States*

Study the bar graph on this page. Then use the following steps to read the graph.

1 **Identify the subject of the bar graph.** Like a line graph, a bar graph has a title as well as a horizontal axis and a vertical axis. Each axis is labeled with numbers or dates. Often, a label says that the numbers are in thousands. In this case, you add three zeros to the numbers shown. If the numbers are in millions, you add six zeros. (a) What is the title of the graph? (b) What do the numbers on the vertical axis show? (c) What dates are shown on the horizontal axis? (d) What is the source of the information shown on this graph?

2 **Practice reading the facts on the bar graph.** Notice that the intervals, or spaces, between the numbers and dates are always equal. Also, the lowest number on the vertical axis is zero. (a) What are the intervals between the dates on the graph? (b) What was the value of trade with England in 1700? (c) What was its value in 1740? (d) In what year was trade worth most? (e) In what year was it worth least?

3 **Make a generalization based on the bar graph.** Study the graph to find facts to support a generalization. (a) Between what years did trade with England increase the most? (b) Between what years did it decrease? (c) Make a generalization about trade with England between 1710 and 1750.

4 **Interpret the information.** Use the bar graph, the map on page 175, and your reading in the chapter to interpret the information about trade between England and the colonies. (a) Why do you think trade was important to England? (b) Why do you think it was important to the colonies? (c) What goods were traded between England and the colonies?

Use the Section Reviews and this Study Guide to review chapter content.

Main Ideas

The main ideas in each section of this chapter are summarized below.

SECTION 1 ■ The Hard-Working New England Colonies

◆ New Englanders were subsistence farmers, fishers, whalers, and shipbuilders.
◆ Towns were centers of New England life.

SECTION 2 ■ The Prosperous Middle Colonies

◆ Farmers in the Middle Colonies produced surpluses of grain.
◆ People from many countries settled the Middle Colonies.

SECTION 3 ■ Two Ways of Life in the Southern Colonies

◆ Tidewater planters owned large plantations.
◆ Life in the southern backcountry was rougher than in the Tidewater.
◆ Plantation owners used African slaves.

SECTION 4 ■ New Ideas and Beliefs

◆ Massachusetts set up public schools.
◆ Benjamin Franklin was the best example of the Enlightenment spirit in the colonies.
◆ The Great Awakening resulted in increased religious toleration.

SECTION 5 ■ The Colonies Grow and Prosper

◆ As roads and mail service improved, the colonists found that they had much in common.
◆ The colonies traded many different goods with England and with each other.
◆ The major colonial cities were centers of news and ideas.

Key People and Terms

Refer to the Identify and Define questions in the Section Reviews on pages 156, 160, 166, 171, and 175. Use each person, term, and vocabulary word in a complete sentence. When possible, make connections between the people and terms by using more than one person or term in each sentence.

Time Line

1. Make a chart of events in time order. The chart will have two headings: Date, Event. Fill in the chart, using the events on the time line. Add the following events from the chapter: Mason-Dixon Line completed; Quakers call for end of slavery; Tenant farmers attack manor houses in New York. (Refer to the chapter for the dates.)
2. Which events on your chart show that colonists were concerned about education?

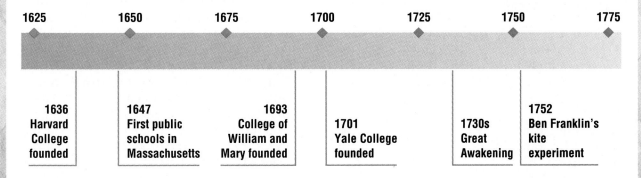

| 1625 | 1650 | 1675 | 1700 | 1725 | 1750 | 1775 |

1636 Harvard College founded

1647 First public schools in Massachusetts

1693 College of William and Mary founded

1701 Yale College founded

1730s Great Awakening

1752 Ben Franklin's kite experiment

Understanding Vocabulary

Match each term at left with the correct definition at right.

1. subsistence farmer
2. cash crop
3. slave code
4. apprentice
5. triangular trade

a. colonial trade route involving New England, the West Indies, and West Africa
b. person who works without pay for a master craftsman to learn a trade or craft
c. crop sold for money on the world market
d. person who grows just enough food to live on
e. laws that controlled the behavior of slaves and denied them basic rights

Reviewing the Main Ideas

1. How did New England colonists use the coastal waters to earn a living?
2. Why was the town the center of Puritan life?
3. Why did Pennsylvania become a center of manufacturing?
4. (a) What was the land like in the Tidewater? (b) In the southern backcountry?
5. List three ways that girls were educated in the colonies.
6. What were two results of the Great Awakening?
7. (a) How did Benjamin Franklin improve mail service in the 1700s? (b) How did improved mail service affect the colonies?
8. What goods were traded along the triangular trade route?
9. How did cities influence colonial culture?

Thinking Critically

1. **Linking Past and Present** Review the description of New England homes and family life on pages 152–156. How was life in colonial New England different from life today?
2. **Drawing Conclusions** Why do you think New Englanders came to dominate trade in the colonies?

3. **Evaluating Information** Do you think racism was a major or minor factor in the growth of slavery? Explain.
4. **Comparing** Compare the ways of life of Tidewater planters and people living in the southern backcountry.

Applying Your Skills

1. **Using a Painting as a Primary Source** Study the painting on page 161. (a) Which building do you think was the Great House? Why? (b) Which building or buildings do you think were the slaves' houses? Why? (c) How do the hill and the houses on it show the different classes in the South?
2. **Analyzing a Quotation** In 1748, Benjamin Franklin gave the following advice to a young tradesman: "Remember, time is money." Give an example to show what Franklin meant.
3. **Reading a Bar Graph** Review Skill Lesson 6 on page 176. Use the bar graph to answer the following questions. (a) What was the value of trade with England in 1720? In 1750? (b) Make a generalization about colonial trade with England between 1720 and 1750.

Match the letters on the map with the places listed below.

1. Virginia
2. Maine
3. Boston
4. New York City
5. Philadelphia
6. Baltimore
7. Charleston
8. Great Wagon Road

Movement Why did settlers follow the Great Wagon Road?

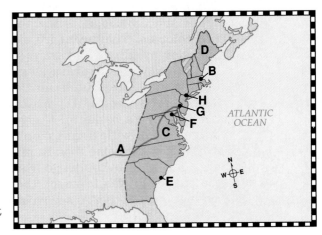

ATLANTIC OCEAN

History Writer's Workshop

Arranging Information in Time Order

Time order is order of occurrence. You often can arrange supporting information in time order when the information is events or steps in a process.

Look at the following topic sentence for a paragraph. *Among the colonies, New England led the way in education.* In writing detail sentences for the paragraph, you might arrange the supporting information in time order. For example: *In 1636, Harvard College was set up. In 1647, Massachusetts required all towns with 50 families to hire a schoolteacher for their children. In 1701, Yale College was founded in Connecticut.* Note that the dates show the time order.

You need not always give dates. You can use other transitions, or connecting words or phrases, to show time order. Some common transitions for time order include *after, afterward, at last, before, earlier, finally, first, formerly, last, later, meanwhile, next, now, previously, soon, then, until,* and *while.*

Practice Rewrite each of the detail sentences above. Replace the dates with transitions to show time order. Make sure the transitions you use adequately connect the ideas in the

paragraph. For example: *First, Harvard College was set up.*

Writing to Learn

1. Imagine that you are a magazine writer interviewing Benjamin Franklin about his career. Brainstorm questions to ask about Franklin's accomplishments. The answers to your questions will be the information to include in your article. Begin the article with a topic sentence that will capture your readers' attention. Organize the information in time order. Revise for unity. Then, proofread and make a final copy. Publish the interview in a class newspaper.

2. Imagine that you are one of the people in the painting on page 150. Write a brief story about something you experienced during the flax-scutching bee. Begin by freewriting about your sense impressions during the event. Then, write a topic sentence that will draw your readers into the action. Select the details for the story. Revise to make sure the story holds together. Proofread and make a final copy. Read the story to your classmates.

Ninepins and Easter Eggs

Dutch settlers introduced many pastimes and amusements to the English colonies. They went ice skating and sleigh riding, and they played golf and ninepins, which was similar to bowling. The Dutch also introduced Easter eggs. At Easter, the family boiled a basketful of eggs and colored them with bright paints and dyes. Then everyone took a bunch of eggs and went to challenge friends— the challenge was to knock the eggs against one another to see whose egg would crack first.

An Early "No Smoking" Sign

Early English settlers first learned about smoking the tobacco weed from Native Americans in Virginia. By the early 1600s, the habit was spreading throughout England and Europe. When Sir Walter Raleigh visited Virginia, he tried smoking some Virginia tobacco. His servant thought Raleigh was on fire and doused him with a bucket of water. It took Raleigh a few moments to recover and then a few more to explain to his servant that he was not on fire.

Everyone a Doctor

Early American settlers were often their own doctors. If they were bitten by a rattlesnake or stricken by fever, there were few trained doctors to turn to.

In the New England Colonies, schoolmasters and ministers often served as local doctors.

On large plantations in the Southern Colonies, the planter and his wife doctored both family and slaves. For medical advice, they often turned to the book *Every Man his own Doctor; or, the Poor Planter's Physician.*

A Pesty Pirate

For many years in the early 1700s, the coast of North Carolina had been a haven for Atlantic pirates. Shifting sandbars and shallow sounds provided great hiding places for pirate ships.

The most famous pirate of that time was Edward Teach, known as Blackbeard.

Blackbeard captured many trading ships in the waters off South Carolina. However, when he ventured up the coast to Virginia, he ran into trouble. In November 1718, Virginians set off in two armed ships to find Blackbeard and get rid of him once and for all. Lieutenant Robert Maynard's ship finally trapped the pirate, killing him and many of his crew. Maynard and his men tied Blackbeard's hairy head to the bow of their ship and sailed home in victory.

A Poetic Exception

Few black men and women were able to get a formal education in colonial America. Phillis Wheatley was an exception. She had been brought to Boston from West Africa as a slave at age eight.

With the support of her owners, the Wheatleys, she

learned to read English, Greek, and Latin. Wheatley wrote poetry that made her famous throughout the colonies and in England as well.

In a poem about George Washington, she wrote, "A crown, a mansion, and a throne that shine,/With gold unfading, Washington be thine."

Comic Curls

In colonial times, well-dressed men spent hours on their appearance. One of the most important parts of the dressing routine was the fashionable wig. Most gentlemen wore wigs, and barbers were kept busy dressing these hairpieces.

When a man selected a wig, he had a huge variety of styles from which to choose. He could pick the pigeon's wing, the comet, the cauliflower, the rose, the long bob, the snail back, or any of a number of others. The gentleman could then instruct the barber to sprinkle the wig with grey or blue perfumed powder.

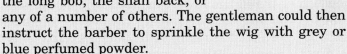

Footnotes to History

- The Mayflower was 90 feet long and 25 feet wide. It carried a crew of 34 and had 101 passengers, including 2 pet dogs.
- A Massachusetts law of 1639 stated that no garment could be made with short sleeves "whereby the nakedness of the arms may be discovered."
- Benjamin Franklin set up the first lending library in Philadelphia in 1732.

UNIT 2 SUMMARY

Chapter 4 Colonizing the Americas

During the 1500s, Spain faced the task of ruling its empire in the Americas. In New Spain, a viceroy appointed by the king enforced a code of laws called the Laws of the Indies. These laws regulated daily life, provided for three kinds of settlements, and divided the people into four social classes.

Under the encomienda system, Spanish settlers forced the lowest class, the Indians, to work on plantations and in mines. Later, the Spanish brought slaves from Africa to fill their need for cheap labor.

The French colony, New France, grew more slowly. In the early 1600s, French explorer Samuel de Champlain established the first successful settlements, Port Royal and Quebec. Although King Louis XIV tried to encourage farming, most French colonists were trappers and traders.

Settling along the Hudson River in 1626, the Dutch in New Amsterdam competed with the French in the hunt for furs. Both groups encouraged their Indian allies to attack one another.

The first permanent English settlement was founded at Jamestown in 1607. Led by John Smith, Jamestown survived its first years, but when Smith returned to England, the colony faced disaster. Jamestown began to prosper only after John Rolfe planted tobacco. In 1619, the colonists set up a representative assembly. That same year, the first Africans arrived in the colony.

In 1620, a group of Pilgrims arrived in Plymouth, Massachusetts. The Pilgrims were fleeing religious persecution in England. Before going ashore, they drew up the Mayflower Compact, an agreement for self-government. Despite great hardships, the Plymouth Colony survived its first year with the help of Native Americans.

Chapter 5 The 13 English Colonies

Like the Pilgrims, the Puritans came to New England for religious freedom. In 1630, they set up the Massachusetts Bay Colony. Led by John Winthrop, the colony prospered.

But the Puritans did not welcome people with other points of view. Thomas Hooker, who opposed the leaders of Massachusetts Bay, left to form a colony in Connecticut. Roger Williams, who was ordered out of Massachusetts Bay for his "new and dangerous opinions," founded Rhode Island. As settlers fanned out across New England, they clashed with Native Americans.

During the 1600s, England came to have four colonies in the region south of New England. In 1664, England took over the Dutch colony of New Netherland and renamed it New York. The colony's new owner gave some of the land to friends, who set up the proprietary colony of New Jersey. As a "holy experiment," Quaker William Penn founded Pennsylvania. In time, the Lower Counties of Pennsylvania broke away to form Delaware.

By the mid-1700s, English rule extended to five Southern Colonies. Maryland was founded by Lord Baltimore as a refuge for Catholics. The Carolinas were settled by Virginians who moved south in search of land. Carved out of South Carolina, Georgia was founded by James Oglethorpe as a haven for debtors. As in New England, conflict over land in the South led to fighting between settlers and Native Americans.

As the colonies prospered, England passed laws to control colonial trade. Many colonists resented trade restrictions and ignored the laws. Angered by colonial smuggling activity, King James II dismissed elected assemblies in colonies north of New Jersey. After James was ousted, the assemblies were restored.

Each colony had an appointed governor and council and an elected assembly. As English citizens, colonists were also protected by the English Bill of Rights.

Chapter 6 Colonial Life

Distinctive ways of life developed in the New England, Middle, and Southern colonies. While most New Englanders were subsistence farmers, colonists also engaged in fishing, whaling, and shipbuilding. New England colonists lived in close-knit communities, and social life revolved around church services and town meetings.

Settlers in the Middle Colonies generally enjoyed a prosperous way of life. Blessed by rich land and mild climate, farms thrived and produced cash crops. Towns were less important than in New England. The Middle Colonies also produced many kinds of manufactured goods.

Tidewater planters set the style of life in the South. Many plantations were self-sufficient communities. To meet the need for large numbers of workers, plantation owners relied on slaves from Africa, and the slave trade soon became a profitable business. Backcountry farmers lived rougher lives than Tidewater planters.

Despite differences, colonists developed a uniquely American culture by the mid-1700s. Education was important, especially in New England. Although class differences existed, colonists enjoyed more social equality than did people in England.

As roads and mail service improved, colonists shared news and ideas. Colonists also exchanged goods with one another and with England. As trade prospered, seaports grew into major cities and cultural centers.

Understanding Causes and Effects *The English colonies developed their own governments.* ◆ *What were two causes for the development of self-government? Which effect of self-government do you think was least democratic? Explain.*

CAUSES

- England has a representative assembly
- English Bill of Rights protects English men and women
- England leaves the colonies to themselves

SELF-GOVERNMENT IN THE ENGLISH COLONIES

EFFECTS

- Each colony has its own government and voting rules
- Each colony has a legislature
- Elected assembly approves laws and taxes and protects citizens' rights
- White Christian men over age 21 can vote
- Spirit of independence grows

UNIT 2 REVIEW

Reviewing the Main Ideas

1. How did Spain bring order to its colonies in the Americas?
2. What skills did the coureurs de bois learn from Native Americans?
3. How did each of the following help to save Jamestown: (a) tobacco; (b) House of Burgesses; (c) arrival of women?
4. What role did religion play in the founding of the English colonies?
5. Describe relations between Native Americans and English colonists during the early years of settlement.
6. How did the Glorious Revolution that shook England in 1688 affect settlers in the English colonies?
7. (a) Why did people become indentured servants? (b) What did an indentured servant promise to do?
8. Describe a typical New England town.
9. What was life like in the colonial backcountry?
10. What new European ideas and beliefs influenced colonists in the 1700s? Explain.

Thinking Critically

1. **Understanding Causes and Effects** (a) What were two causes for the introduction of African slaves in New Spain? (b) What were two effects?
2. **Forecasting** After the Glorious Revolution, English kings stopped interfering with colonial assemblies. Do you think that they also gave up control of colonial trade? Why or why not?
3. **Comparing** (a) How did the settlers earn a living in the New England Colonies? (b) The Middle Colonies? (c) The Southern Colonies?
4. **Defending a Position** Colonial society was democratic. Do you agree or disagree with this statement? Explain.

Applying Your Skills

1. **Identifying the Main Idea** Review the subsection "A Class System," on page 97. (a) Write a statement that tells the main idea of the subsection. (b) Write four detail sentences that support the main idea.
2. **Outlining** Review the outlining skill on page 32. Then, outline the section "A Haven for Pilgrims," on pages 114–117.
3. **Analyzing a Quotation** Reread Dr. Hamilton's description of his evening in Philadelphia, on page 156. (a) Why do you think Dr. Hamilton was amazed at the variety of people he met? (b) Why was there such a great mix of people?
4. **Making a Review Chart** Make a chart with three columns and three rows. Title the columns New England Colonies, Middle Colonies, Southern Colonies. Title the rows Land, Climate, Products. Fill in the chart using the information in the unit. (a) How was the land in New England different from the land in the Middle Colonies? (b) What crops were produced only in the South? (c) How do you think land and climate affected crops and products that the three regions produced?

Doing More

1. **Creating a Map** On an outline map of North and South America, show the lands claimed around 1650 by Spain, France, the Netherlands, Sweden, and England. Use a different color for each nation's colonies. Include a key, explaining the meaning of the colors. Label the main cities or towns in each colony.
2. **Illustrating a Story** Use pictures to tell the story of the founding and settlement of one of the 13 English colonies. Use the information in Chapter 4 or Chapter 5 to make a list of events related to your story.

List the events in time order. Illustrate the most important events. Publish your picture history as a story board or in a bound book.

3. **Writing a Dialogue** Imagine that you are a settler from the Southern Colonies visiting New England in 1730. Write a dialogue that you might have with a New Englander about the ways people earn a living in each region. Before you begin writing, choose names and occupations for yourself and the New Englander. Jot down observations that each of you might make. In your first draft, try to convey two clear points of view. As you revise, check that each speaker has a distinct voice. Be sure to write in the form of a dialogue. Proofread your work before making a final copy. With the help of a classmate, present your dialogue to the class.

4. **Exploring Local History** Visit your local library to find out which groups settled your community in its early days. Then make a poster that shows how each group left its mark. Consider styles of houses, names of streets, kinds of stores, types of crafts, and local parades or celebrations.

During the 1600s, settlers in the English colonies had widely different opinions about freedom of worship. Below are excerpts from documents written by two New England clergymen of the period. Read the excerpts and answer the following questions.

1. (a) Does Nathaniel Ward believe the government should allow freedom of religion? (b) What argument does he use to support his position?
2. (a) Does Roger Williams believe the government should allow freedom of religion? (b) What argument does he use to support his position?
3. According to Ward, why does anyone tolerate a religion besides his own?
4. According to Williams, what results from lack of toleration?
5. In what way are the arguments of the two men similar?
6. What is the position of the United States government today on the issue of religious toleration? Explain.

Should the government allow freedom of religion?

Nathaniel Ward

❝I dare [declare] that God does nowhere in His word tolerate Christian [governments] to give toleration to such [enemies] of His truth, if they have power in their hands to suppress them. . . . To authorize an untruth by a toleration of state is to build a [fort] against the walls of heaven, to batter God out of His Chair. . . . He that is willing to tolerate any religion . . . besides his own . . . either doubts of his own or is not sincere in it.❞

Roger Williams

❝It is the will and command of God that . . . a permission of the most pagan, Jewish, Turkish, or anti-Christian . . . worships be granted to all men in all nations and countries. . . . God requires not a uniformity of religion to be enacted and enforced in any civil state. . . . Such enforced uniformity . . . is the greatest [cause] of civil war, . . . persecution of Christ Jesus in his servants, and . . . destruction of millions of souls.❞

3 From Revolution to Republic

Unit Outline

3 After six long years, Americans overcame the powerful British army and navy. John Paul Jones led the small American navy in surprising victories at sea.

1 The 13 colonies protested British rule for many years and finally declared independence. Delegates used the inkstand shown here for the signing of the Declaration.

2 The war for independence from Britain was hard fought throughout the states. In New York and other Middle States, American troops endured food shortages and bitter winters.

1740	1750	1760	1770
AMERICAN EVENTS	**1740s** English settlers move into Ohio Valley	**1754–63** French and Indian War	**1765** Stamp Act
WORLD EVENTS	**1700s** Age of Enlightenment	**1756–63** Seven Years' War in Europe	

THE UNITED STATES IN 1783

CANADA

(Claimed by N.Y. and N.H.)

MAINE (part of Mass.)

LOUISIANA

WESTERN LANDS

Lake Superior

Lake Michigan

Lake Huron

Lake Ontario

Lake Erie

Ohio River

Mississippi River

APPALACHIAN MOUNTAINS

VT.

N.H.

N.Y.

MASS.

CONN.

R.I.

PA.

N.J.

MD.

DEL.

VA.

N.C.

S.C.

GA.

1

2

3

4

ATLANTIC OCEAN

SPANISH FLORIDA

N
W E
S

| 0 | 125 | 250 Miles |
| 0 | 125 | 250 Kilometers |

4 *Americans were proud of their new nation and its symbols. From Maine to Georgia, they displayed the eagle as a symbol of the nation's freedom and power.*

| 1770 | 1780 | 1790 | 1800 |

1775 American Revolution begins

1788 Constitution ratified

1783 Treaty of Paris

1778 France recognizes American independence from Britain

George Washington

John Adams

The Boston Massacre *No one knows exactly what happened in Boston on March 5, 1770. But this engraving by Paul Revere, which shows British soldiers firing into an innocent crowd, helped to fuel colonial resentment of Britain.* **Citizenship** *Why do you think Revere showed a sign on the customs house reading "Butcher's Hall"?*

CHAPTER

7

The Road to Revolution (1745–1775)

Chapter Outline

1 Rivals for North America
2 The French and Indian War
3 A Storm Over Taxes
4 The Quarrel Deepens
5 To Arms!

The Big Picture

The second half of the 1700s saw a quick turnabout in relations between England and the 13 colonies. In 1760, England defeated France, its chief rival, in North America. That same year, George III became king of England. From Boston to Savannah, colonists proudly celebrated their English heritage.

By 1775, everything had changed. Colonial newspapers accused Parliament and King George of trying to enslave the colonists. Ordinary people prepared to take up arms against the parent country. In 15 short years, England and the colonies had moved from friendship to the edge of war.

Jim Davidson

Of Special Interest

Focus On

◆ Why was the Ohio Valley a center of conflict?
◆ How did the French and Indian War affect North America?
◆ Why did colonists protest British taxes?
◆ Why did the quarrel deepen between Britain and the 13 colonies?
◆ How did fighting begin in 1775?

"**Y**esterday Morning at break of day was discovered hanging upon a tree in the street of the town a [likeness] . . . of Mr. Andrew Oliver. . . . That night a mob carried the effigy to . . . Mr. Oliver's house where they burnt the effigy in a bonfire. . . . The mob finding the doors of the house [blocked] . . . beat in all the doors and windows. . . . As soon as they got possession they searched about for Mr. Oliver, declaring that they would kill him. **"**

In this letter, Massachusetts Governor Francis Bernard described an attack on Andrew Oliver by an angry Boston mob in 1765. Who was Andrew Oliver? What had stirred the mob's anger?

The mob unleashed its fury on Oliver because he was a tax collector for the English government. A series of wars had left England deeply in debt. To raise money, Parliament decided to tax the colonies. Colonists were outraged. They saw Parliament's action as an attack on their liberties.

As time went by, the anger of colonists grew. By 1775, it became clear to many that only war could settle the quarrel with England.

1 Rivals for North America

FIND OUT

◆ What nations were rivals for North America?

◆ How did the French prevent expansion of the English colonies?

◆ Why did Native Americans become involved in the struggle between France and England?

In June 1749, the governor of New France sent a group of men to claim the Ohio Valley. As the men traveled along the shores of the Ohio and Allegheny rivers, they stopped from time to time to dig a hole in the ground. In each hole, they buried an engraved lead plate proclaiming that the land belonged to France.

About the same time, Christopher Gist, a Virginia fur trader working for the Ohio Company, roamed the Ohio Valley. King George II of England had given the Ohio Company a huge tract of land in the valley. The company sent Gist to find a good spot for settlement. He chose a site where the Ohio and Allegheny rivers meet. On a rock beside the water, he carved these words:

The Ohio Company
FEBy 1751
By Christopher Gist

The stage was set for a battle between France and England. At stake was more than control of the Ohio River valley. Each nation hoped to drive the other out of North America.

Trading With Native Americans *French traders exchanged a variety of goods with Native Americans in return for furs. Here, Native Americans inspect a blanket being offered in trade.* **Economics** *Why did the French keep friendly relations with Native Americans?*

Competing Claims

By the mid-1700s, the nations of Europe were locked in a worldwide struggle for empire. England, France, Spain, and the Netherlands were competing for trade and colonies in far-flung corners of the globe. The 13 English colonies in North America soon became caught up in the contest.

Spanish claims. By the late 1600s, England had two rivals in North America: Spain and France. The major threat from Spain was in the West Indies and along the border between Georgia and Spanish Florida. England and Spain clashed often in these areas.

Spain also had settlements in present-day New Mexico, Texas, and Arizona. But these settlements lay far away from England's colonies on the Atlantic coast. So the English paid little attention to them.

French claims. The threat from France was much more serious. France claimed a vast area in North America. French land claims stretched west along the St. Lawrence River all the way to the Great Lakes and south to the Gulf of Mexico. (See the map at right.)

To protect their lands, the French built a system of forts. One line of forts, in the north, gave them control of the rich fishing grounds off Newfoundland and the fur trade around the Great Lakes. Another string of forts, stretching from the Great Lakes to New Orleans, prevented English colonists from expanding west.

Conflict in the Ohio Valley

At first, most English settlers were content to remain along the Atlantic coast. But by the 1740s, traders from New York and Pennsylvania were crossing the Appalachian Mountains in search of furs. Pushing into the Ohio Valley, they tried to take over the profitable French trade with the Indians.

The French were determined to stop the English from intruding on their terri-

MAP STUDY

In 1753, France and Spain claimed land to the north, south, and west of the 13 English colonies in North America.
1. Which nation claimed land along the Mississippi River?
2. Which nation controlled Florida?
3. **Drawing Conclusions** Notice the location of French forts in North America. Why do you think the French built forts at these places?

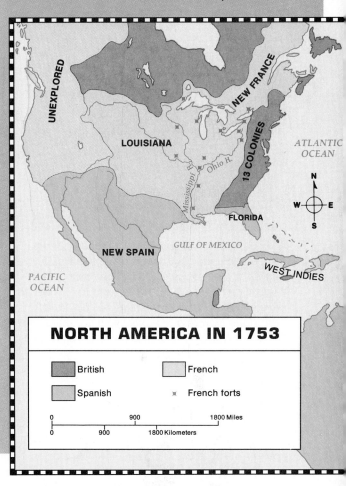

NORTH AMERICA IN 1753

| British | French |
| Spanish | × French forts |

0   900   1800 Miles
0   900   1800 Kilometers

tory. The Ohio River was especially important to them because it provided a vital link between their lands in Canada and the Mississippi River. In 1751, the French government sent the following orders to its officials in New France:

> **"**Drive from the Ohio River any European foreigners, and do it in a way that will make them lose all taste for trying to return.**"**

A Mohawk Ally *Joseph Brant, a Mohawk chief, helped persuade the Iroquois nations to side with the English in their struggle against the French. In later years, Brant became a Christian and translated the Bible into the Mohawk language.* **Multicultural Traditions** *How does the painting show that Brant combined Native American and English cultures?*

French soldiers and their Indian allies burned the cabins of English traders. But the English were not scared off. So the governor of New France, the Marquis Duquesne (mahr KEE doo KAYN), had a line of forts built in the Ohio River valley. The new forts were meant to keep the English out of French lands.

Indians Choose Sides

Native Americans had hunted and grown crops in the Ohio Valley for centuries. They did not want to give up the land to European settlers, French *or* English. One Native American protested to an English trader:

"You and the French are like the two edges of a pair of shears. And we are the cloth which is to be cut to pieces between them."

However, some Native Americans decided that the only way to protect their way of life was to take sides in the struggle.

Competing for allies. Both France and England tried to make Indian allies because Indians controlled the fur trade in the heart of North America. The French expected the Indians to side with them. Most French in North America were trappers and traders, not farmers. They did not destroy hunting grounds by clearing forests for farms. Also, many French trappers married Indian women and adopted Indian ways.

In contrast, English settlers were mostly farm families. They ignored Indian rights when they cleared land for crops, and they looked down on Indian ways. Indians fought back as the English moved onto their lands.

Algonquins, Hurons, and Iroquois. In the end, both France and England found allies among the Indians. The French gained the support of the Algonquins and Hurons. The English won over the powerful Iroquois nations, who were old enemies of the Algonquins.

An English trader and official named William Johnson helped gain Iroquois support for England. Johnson was one of the few English settlers with an Indian wife. He was married to Molly Brant, daughter of a Mohawk chief. The Iroquois respected Johnson and listened carefully when he urged them to side with the English.

Some Indians supported the English because they charged lower prices for trade goods than the French did. Many Indians began to buy goods from English rather than French traders. The loss of Indian trade angered the French, who were determined to defend their claims in the Ohio Valley.

1. **Locate:** (a) Ohio River, (b) St. Lawrence River, (c) Great Lakes, (d) Gulf of Mexico, (e) New Orleans, (f) Canada, (g) Mississippi River.
2. (a) Name three European nations that claimed lands in North America. (b) Where did conflict between these nations occur?
3. How did France protect its lands in North America?
4. (a) Which Indians sided with the English? (b) Why?
5. **Making Decisions** Imagine that you are an Indian leader in the Ohio Valley in 1750. Would you support the French or the English? Why?

2 The French and Indian War

FIND OUT

◆ What were the causes of the French and Indian War?

◆ What advantages did each side have in the war?

◆ How did the Treaty of Paris affect North America?

Captain Joncaire had just sat down to dinner on December 4, 1753, when a soldier entered. A party of Englishmen, the soldier explained, wished to see the French captain at once.

A tall young man in a buff-and-blue uniform strode into the room. He introduced himself as Major George Washington. The young officer had a letter from Governor Dinwiddie of Virginia to the commander of the French forces in the Ohio Valley.

Joncaire told Washington where the commander could be found and then invited him to dine. As they ate, Joncaire boasted, "It is our absolute design to take possession of the Ohio, and by God, we will do it!" The remark made Washington pause. Governor Dinwiddie's letter, he knew, warned the French to get out of the Ohio Valley. A conflict between England and France seemed certain.

Opening Shots

Three times between 1689 and 1748, France and Great Britain* had fought for power in Europe and North America. English colonists named the wars after the king or queen who ruled at the time. There was King William's War, Queen Anne's War, and King George's War. Each war ended with an uneasy peace. In 1754, fighting broke out again. The long conflict that followed was called the **French and Indian War.**

Major Washington. Scuffles between France and Britain in the Ohio River valley triggered the opening shots of the French and Indian War. Young Major Washington played an important part as fighting began.

George Washington grew up on a plantation in Virginia, the son of wealthy parents. At age 15, he began work as a surveyor. His job took him to unexplored frontier lands in western Virginia. When Governor Dinwiddie wanted to warn the French in Ohio in 1753, Washington offered to deliver the message.

The grateful governor promoted Washington. He also sent him west again. This time, Dinwiddie ordered Washington to take 150 men and build a fort where the Monongahela and Allegheny rivers meet. (See the map on page 196.) The fort was to protect Virginian land claims in the upper Ohio River valley.

---

*In 1707, England and Scotland were officially joined into the United Kingdom of Great Britain. After that date, the terms Great Britain and British were used to describe the country and its people. However, the terms England and English were still used throughout much of the 1700s.

Washington Meets With Iroquois Chiefs *Young George Washington played an important part in the opening skirmishes of the French and Indian War. Here, Major Washington confers with chiefs of the Iroquois nations.* **Geography** *What region was at the heart of the conflict that triggered the French and Indian War?*

Trapped at Fort Necessity. In May 1754, Washington and his party headed for Ohio country. Along the way, they heard disturbing news. The French had just completed Fort Duquesne at the fork of the Monongahela and Allegheny rivers —the precise spot where Washington was to build a British fort.

Determined to carry out his orders, Washington continued on. Indian allies revealed that a French scouting party was camped in the woods ahead. Marching quietly through the night, Washington surprised and scattered the French.

But Washington's success was short-lived. Hearing that the French were planning to counterattack, he and his men quickly built a makeshift stockade. They named it **Fort Necessity.** A huge force of French and Indians surrounded the fort. Trapped and heavily outnumbered, the Virginians were forced to surrender. Soon after, the French released Washington, and he returned home to Virginia.

The British quickly saw the importance of the skirmish. "The volley fired by this young Virginian in the forests of America," a British writer noted, "has set the world in flames."

The Albany Congress

While Washington was defending Fort Necessity, delegates from seven colonies gathered in Albany, New York. The delegates met for two reasons. They wanted to persuade the Iroquois to help them against the French. And they wanted to plan a united defense.

Iroquois leaders listened patiently to the delegates. But they were wary of the request for help. The British and French "are quarreling about lands which belong to us," pointed out Hendrik, a Mohawk chief. "And such a quarrel as this may end in our destruction." The Iroquois left without agreeing to help the British. But they did not join the French either.

The delegates in Albany knew that the colonists needed to work together if they were to defeat the French. Benjamin Franklin, the delegate from Pennsylvania, proposed the **Albany Plan of Union.** The plan called for a Grand Council with representatives from each colony. The council would make laws, raise taxes, and set up the defense of the colonies.

The delegates voted to accept the Plan of Union. But when the plan was submitted to the colonial assemblies, not one approved it. None of the colonies wanted to give up any of its powers to a council. In the words of the disappointed Franklin:

> ❝Everyone cries a union is necessary. But when they come to the manner and form of the union, their weak noodles are perfectly distracted.❞

Early Years of the War

At the start of the French and Indian War, the French enjoyed several advantages over the British. Since the English colonies could not agree on a united defense, 13 separate colonial assemblies had to approve all decisions. New France, on the other hand, had a single government that could act quickly when necessary. Also, the French had the support of many more Indian allies than the British did.

But Britain also had strengths. The English colonies, which were clustered along the coast, were easier to defend than the widely scattered French settlements. At the same time, the population of the 13 English colonies was about 15 times greater than that of New France. And while most Indians sided with the French, the British did have some Indian allies. Finally, the British navy ruled the seas.

"Bulldog" Braddock. In 1755, General Edward Braddock led British and colonial troops in an attack against Fort Duquesne. The general boasted that he would sweep the French from the Ohio Valley.

Braddock was a stubborn man, called "Bulldog" behind his back. He knew how to fight a war in the open fields of Europe. But he knew little about how to fight in the wilderness of North America.

Braddock's men moved slowly because they had to clear a road through thick forests for their cannons and other heavy gear. George Washington, who went with Braddock, was upset by the slow pace. Indian scouts warned Braddock that he was headed for trouble. But he ignored them.

Disaster for the British. As the British neared Fort Duquesne, the French and their Indian allies launched a surprise attack. Sharpshooters hid in the forest and picked off British soldiers, whose bright red uniforms made them easy targets. Braddock had five horses shot out from under him before he fell, fatally wounded. Washington was luckier. As he later reported, he "escaped without a wound, although I had four bullets through my coat."

Almost half the British were killed or wounded. Washington and other survivors returned to Virginia with news of Braddock's defeat. Washington was now put in command of a small force of men. For the rest of the war, he had the almost impossible task of guarding the long Virginia frontier against Indian attack.

During the next two years, the war continued to go badly for the British. British attacks against several French forts ended in failure. Meanwhile, the French won important victories, capturing Fort Oswego on Lake Ontario and Fort William Henry on Lake George. (See the map on page 196.) To English colonists, the situation looked grim. In the words of Massachusetts minister Jonathan Edwards:

> ❝God indeed is remarkably frowning upon us every where; our enemies get up above us very high, and we are brought down very low: They are the Head, and we are the Tail. . . . What will become of us God only knows.❞

A Bold Leader Takes Charge

In 1757, William Pitt became head of the British government. Pitt was a bold leader. "I believe that I can save this nation and that no one else can," he declared with great confidence.

Pitt set out to win the war in North America. Once that was done, he argued, the British could focus on victory in other parts of the world.* Pitt sent Britain's best generals to North America. To encourage colonists to support the war, he promised

---

*By 1756, fighting between the French and British had broken out in Europe. There, it became known as the Seven Years' War. The British and French also fought in India. In the early years of the war, the British suffered setbacks on every front.

MAP STUDY

During the French and Indian War, Britain and France battled for control of North America.

1. Which French forts were located on Lake Ontario?
2. About how many miles did advancing British troops travel from Louisbourg to Quebec?
3. **Analyzing Information** Based on the map, do you think naval power was important in fighting the French and Indian War? Explain.

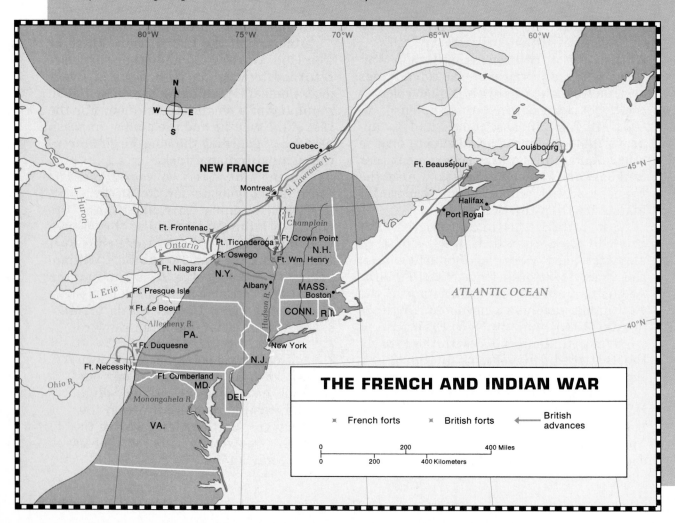

THE FRENCH AND INDIAN WAR

Battle of Louisbourg
The British capture of Louisbourg was a turning point in the French and Indian War. In this engraving, cannonballs fly as British ships shell the fort. **Geography** *Locate Louisbourg on the map on page 196. Why do you think this fort was so important?*

large payments for military services and supplies.

Under Pitt's leadership, the tide of battle turned. In 1758, Lord Jeffrey Amherst captured **Louisbourg,** the most important fort in French Canada. That year, the British also won more Iroquois support.

The Iroquois persuaded the Delawares at Fort Duquesne to abandon the French. Without the Delawares, the French could no longer hold the fort. Acting quickly, the British seized Fort Duquesne, which they renamed **Fort Pitt.** The city of Pittsburgh later grew up on the site.

The Fall of New France

The British enjoyed even greater success in 1759. By summer, they had pushed the French from Fort Niagara, Crown Point, and Fort Ticonderoga (ti kahn duh ROH guh). Now, Pitt sent General James Wolfe to take **Quebec,** capital of New France.

Battle for Quebec. Quebec was vital to the defense of New France. Without Quebec, the French would be unable to supply their forts farther up the St. Lawrence River. But Quebec was well defended. The city sat atop a steep cliff above the St. Lawrence. An able French general, the Marquis de Montcalm, was prepared to fight off any British attack.

General Wolfe devised a daring plan. Late one night, he ordered British troops to move quietly in small boats to the foot of the cliff. Under cover of dark, the soldiers swarmed ashore and scrambled to the top. The next morning, Montcalm awakened to see 4,000 British troops drawn up on the **Plains of Abraham,** a grassy field just outside the city.

Montcalm quickly marched out his own troops. A fierce battle followed. When it was over, both Montcalm and Wolfe were dead. Moments before Wolfe died, a soldier gave him the news that the British had won. Wolfe reportedly whispered, "Now, God be praised, I will die in peace."

News of the capture of Quebec set off wild celebrations in the 13 colonies. Church bells rang out the victory, while colonists toasted the king of England and lit bonfires.

Treaty of Paris. The fall of Quebec sealed the fate of New France. In 1760, the British took Montreal, and the war in North America ended. Fighting dragged on in Europe until Britain and France signed the **Treaty of Paris** in 1763.

The Treaty of Paris marked the end of French power in North America. Under the treaty, Britain gained Canada and all French lands east of the Mississippi River. (See the map on page 198.) France was allowed to keep only a few sugar-growing

The Treaty of Paris of 1763 greatly changed the map of North America.

1. Which countries shared control of North America in 1763?
2. Which country controlled the land west of the Mississippi?
3. **Comparing** Compare this map with the map on page 191. How was North America in 1763 different from North America in 1753?

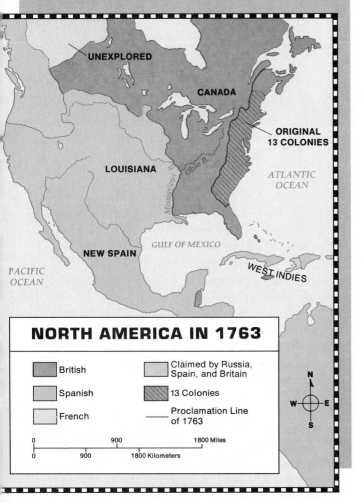

NORTH AMERICA IN 1763

- British
- Spanish
- French
- Claimed by Russia, Spain, and Britain
- 13 Colonies
- Proclamation Line of 1763

| 0 | 900 | 1800 Miles |
| 0 | 900 | 1800 Kilometers |

islands in the West Indies. Spain, which had entered the war on the French side in 1762, gave up Florida to Britain. In return, Spain received all French lands west of the Mississippi.

After years of fighting, peace returned to North America. But in a few short years, a new struggle would break out. This struggle would pit Britain against its own colonies.

1. **Locate:** (a) Fort Necessity, (b) Louisbourg, (c) Fort Pitt, (d) Quebec.
2. **Identify:** (a) French and Indian War, (b) George Washington, (c) Albany Plan of Union, (d) Edward Braddock, (e) William Pitt, (f) James Wolfe, (g) Marquis de Montcalm, (h) Plains of Abraham, (i) Treaty of Paris.
3. Why did the British and French go to war in North America in 1754?
4. List two strengths of the British in the French and Indian War.
5. What lands did Britain gain under the Treaty of Paris?
6. **Evaluating Information** Under the Albany Plan of Union, the Grand Council could "draw on the fund in the Treasury of any Colony" in time of war. Why might colonial assemblies object to that part of the plan?

3 A Storm Over Taxes

FIND OUT

◆ Why did Britain issue the Proclamation of 1763?

◆ What steps did Britain take to raise money to repay its war debts?

◆ How did colonists protest the Stamp Act?

◆ **VOCABULARY** boycott, repeal

As Britain celebrated the victory over France, a few officials in London expressed concern. Now that the French were no longer a threat, would the 13 colonies become too independent? Might they even unite one day against Great Britain? Benjamin Franklin, who was visiting London at the time, gave his opinion:

❝If [the colonies] could not agree to unite for their defense against the French and Indians, . . . can it reasonably be supposed there is any danger of their uniting against their own nation? . . . I will venture to say, a union amongst them for such a purpose is not merely improbable, it is impossible. **"**

But Franklin added a word of caution. "When I say such a union is impossible," he explained, "I mean without the most grievous tyranny." Franklin hardly expected tyranny, or unjust rule, from Britain. But he misjudged the situation. After the French and Indian War, new British policies toward the colonies brought cries of tyranny from Massachusetts to Georgia.

New Troubles on the Frontier

Even before the war between France and Britain ended, trouble flared in the Ohio Valley. For many years, fur traders had sent back glowing reports of the land beyond the Appalachian Mountains. Now, English colonists eagerly headed west to claim the former French lands for farms.

Relations with Indians worsen. But Native American nations already lived in the Ohio Valley. They included the Senecas, Delawares, Shawnees, Ottawas, Miamis, and Hurons. Many had sided with the French and were uneasy about the future.

After scattered incidents between settlers and Indians, the British sent Lord Jeffrey Amherst to the frontier to keep peace. French traders had always treated Native Americans as friends, holding feasts for them and giving them presents. Amherst refused to do this. He raised the price of British goods traded to the Indians. And he allowed English settlers to build forts on land given to the Indians by treaties.

Discontented Native Americans found a leader in Pontiac, an Ottawa chief who had fought with the French. An English trader described Pontiac as "a shrewd, sensible Indian of few words" who commanded great respect among his people. In April 1763, Pontiac spoke out against the British, calling them "dogs dressed in red, who have come to rob [us] of [our] hunting grounds and drive away the game."

Fighting on the frontier. Soon after, Pontiac led an attack on British troops at Fort Detroit. Other Indians joined the fight, and in a few months they captured most British forts on the frontier. British and colonial troops struck back and regained much of what they had lost.

Pontiac's War, as it came to be called, did not last long. In October 1763, the French informed Pontiac that they had signed the Treaty of Paris. Without hope of French aid, the Indian nations stopped fighting and returned home. "All my young men have buried their hatchets," Pontiac sadly observed. By December, Britain again controlled the frontier.

Proclamation of 1763

Pontiac's War convinced the British to close western lands to settlers. To do this, the British government issued the **Proclamation of 1763.** The proclamation drew a line along the crest of the Appalachian Mountains. Colonists were forbidden to settle west of the line. The proclamation ordered all settlers already west of the line "to remove themselves" at once. To enforce the law, Britain sent 10,000 troops to the colonies. Few troops went to the frontier, however. Most stayed in cities along the Atlantic coast.

The proclamation angered colonists. Some colonies, including New York, Pennsylvania, and Virginia, claimed lands in the West. Also, colonists had to pay for the additional British troops that had been sent to enforce the law. In the end, many settlers simply ignored the proclamation and moved west anyway.

Britain's Empty Treasury

The French and Indian War had plunged Britain deeply into debt. As a result, the tax bill for citizens in Britain rose sharply. The British prime minister, George Grenville, decided that colonists in North

America should help share the burden. After all, he reasoned, it was the colonists who had gained most from the war.

In 1764, Grenville asked Parliament to pass a new tax on molasses. Molasses, you will remember, was a valuable item in the triangular trade. (See page 174.)

The **Sugar Act** replaced an earlier tax on molasses that had been in effect for years. That tax was so high that merchants could not afford to pay it and still stay in business. Most merchants simply avoided the tax, either by smuggling molasses into the colonies or by bribing tax collectors to look the other way.

The Sugar Act of 1764 cut the molasses tax almost in half. But Grenville demanded that the smuggling and bribes end. He was determined that the new tax be paid.

The following year, Grenville persuaded Parliament to pass the **Stamp Act.** The new law put a tax on legal documents such as wills, diplomas, and marriage papers. It also taxed newspapers, almanacs, playing cards, and even dice. All items named in the law had to carry a stamp showing that the tax had been paid. Stamp taxes were used in Britain and other countries to raise money. But Britain had never used such a tax in its colonies.

Stamp Act Crisis

When British officials tried to enforce the Stamp Act, they met with stormy protests. Riots broke out in New York City, Newport, and Charleston. Angry colonists threw rocks at agents trying to collect the unpopular tax or tarred and feathered them. In Boston, as you read, a mob burned an effigy, or likeness, of Andrew Oliver and then destroyed his home.

The outrage was felt throughout the colonies. As John Adams, a Massachusetts lawyer, wrote:

> **"**Our presses have groaned, our pulpits have thundered, our legislatures have resolved, our towns have voted, the crown officers everywhere trembled.**"**

Why were colonists angry? The fury of the colonists shocked people in Britain. After all, Britain had spent a great deal of money to protect the colonies against the French. And British citizens paid much higher taxes than colonists did.

The average citizen in Britain paid about 26 shillings a year in taxes. By contrast, most colonists paid only about 1 shilling. Why, the British asked, were the colonists so angry about the Stamp Act?

No taxation without representation! Colonists replied that the taxes imposed by the Stamp Act were unjust. The taxes, they claimed, went against the principle that there should be no taxation without representation. That principle had its roots in English traditions dating back to the Magna Carta. (See page 113.)

Colonists Protest the Stamp Act *Colonists reacted violently to the Stamp Act of 1765. In this engraving, they have strung up one British tax collector from a Liberty Pole and are preparing to tar and feather another.* **Citizenship** *In what other ways did colonists protest the Stamp Act?*

The Stamp Act Is Repealed *The repeal of the Stamp Act in 1766 sent a wave of joy throughout the colonies. In Britain, however, the reaction was quite different. This British cartoon shows mournful members of Parliament carrying the dead act to its grave.* **Economics** *Do you think that repeal of the Stamp Act was likely to end problems between Britain and the colonies? Explain.*

Colonists insisted that only they or their elected representatives had the right to pass taxes. Since the colonists did not elect representatives to Parliament, Parliament had no right to tax them. The colonists were willing to pay taxes—but only if the taxes were passed by their own colonial legislatures.

The colonial assemblies firmly defended the idea of no taxation without representation. In heated debates, members of the assemblies denounced the Stamp Act as an attack on colonial liberties.

A Call for Unity

The Stamp Act brought a sense of unity to the colonies. Critics of the law called for delegates from every colony to meet in New York City. The purpose of the meeting was to consider action against the hated Stamp Act.

In October 1765, nine colonies sent delegates to what became known as the **Stamp Act Congress.** The delegates drew up petitions, or letters, to King George III and to Parliament. In these petitions, they rejected the Stamp Act and asserted that Parliament had no right to tax the colonies. But Parliament paid little attention.

The colonists took other steps to change the law. They joined together to boycott British goods. To boycott means to refuse to buy certain goods and services. The boycott of British goods took its toll. Trade fell off by 14 percent. British merchants suffered. So, too, did British workers who made goods for the colonies.

Finally, in 1766, Parliament repealed, or canceled, the Stamp Act. At the same time, however, it passed the Declaratory Act. In this act, Parliament claimed that it still had the right to make laws and raise taxes in "all cases whatsoever."

Colonists were so overjoyed by the repeal of the Stamp Act that they paid little attention to the Declaratory Act. But the dispute over taxes had not been settled. Another crisis would soon erupt when Parliament tried to tax the colonists again.

SECTION 3 REVIEW

1. **Locate:** Appalachian Mountains.
2. **Identify:** (a) Pontiac's War, (b) Proclamation of 1763, (c) Sugar Act, (d) Stamp Act, (e) Stamp Act Congress.
3. **Define:** (a) boycott, (b) repeal.
4. (a) What were the terms of the Proclamation of 1763? (b) What event convinced Britain to issue the proclamation?
5. Why did colonists object to the Stamp Act?
6. **Evaluating Information** Study the statement by Benjamin Franklin on pages 198–199. Based on what you have read, do you think that Britain's treatment of the colonies was "grievous tyranny"? Explain.

4 The Quarrel Deepens

FIND OUT

◆ How did colonists resist the Townshend Acts?

◆ What was the Quartering Act?

◆ Why did the Boston Massacre occur?

◆ **VOCABULARY** writ of assistance, nonimportation agreement, committee of correspondence

After Parliament repealed the Stamp Act, a group of British merchants sent an open letter to the colonists. "You must be sensible," they advised. They urged colonists to "express Gratitude to your Parent Country" for all it had done for them.

When George Mason of Virginia read these words, he was furious. The merchants, he thought, sounded like parents scolding naughty children:

> ❝We have . . . got you excused this one time; pray be a good boy for the future, do what your papa and mama bid you . . . and then all your acquaintances will love you, and praise you, and give you pretty things.❞

"Is not this a little ridiculous?" asked Mason. The colonists, he said, were only claiming their rights as British citizens. But Parliament did not agree. Within a year, it enacted new taxes on the colonists and the battle began once again.

New Taxes

In May 1767, Parliament resumed the debate over taxing the colonies. George Grenville, now a member of Parliament, challenged Charles Townshend, who was in charge of the British treasury. The following exchange resulted:

> ❝*Grenville:* You are cowards, you are afraid of the Americans, you dare not tax America!
> *Townshend:* Fear? Cowards? I dare tax America!
> *Grenville:* Dare you tax America? I wish I could see it!
> *Townshend:* I will, I will!❞

The next month, Parliament passed the **Townshend Acts,** which taxed goods such as glass, paper, silk, lead, and tea. The taxes were low, but colonists still objected. The principle, they felt, was the same: Parliament did not have the right to tax them without their consent. (📖 See "What Should Colonists Do?" on page 650.)

The Townshend Acts set up new ways to collect taxes. Customs officers were sent to colonial ports with orders to stop smugglers. They used legal documents known as **writs of assistance.** A writ of assistance gave a customs officer the right to inspect a ship's cargo without giving a reason. Some customs officers used these writs to keep ships from leaving port until merchants paid them bribes.

Colonists protested that the writs violated their rights as British citizens. Under British law, an official could not search property without giving a good reason for suspecting the owner of a crime.

Colonists Fight Back

The colonists' response to the Townshend Acts was loud and clear. From New Hampshire to Georgia, merchants and planters signed **nonimportation agreements.** In these agreements, they promised to stop importing goods taxed by the Townshend Acts. The colonists remembered that a boycott of British goods had helped win repeal of the unpopular Stamp Act. They hoped that the new boycott would secure the same fate for the Townshend Acts.

Colonists supported the boycott in various ways. Men and women refused to buy cloth made in Britain. Instead, they wore

❶	Type case	❻	Paper soaked before printing	⓫	Platen (part of press that holds paper against inked type)
❷	Metal type	❼	Apprentice	⓬	Press bar
❸	Composing stick to adjust type	❽	Inker and puller (pulls on press bar)	⓭	Master printer
❹	Typesetter	❾	Leather-covered ink balls	⓮	Drying rack
❺	Frame to lock columns of type into place	❿	Printing press		

Colonial Print Shop *Colonial printers did more than operate printing presses. They were also the colonies' first publishers of newspapers, books, and magazines. This picture shows a typical American print shop of the 1700s.* **Citizenship** *How do you think colonial printers helped to unite colonists against the British?*

clothes made of fabric spun at home, or homespun. A popular Boston ballad encouraged women to avoid British cloth:

> **❝**Young ladies in town, and those that live round
> Wear none but your own country linen;
> Of economy boast; let your pride be the most
> To show clothes of your own make and spinning.**❞**

To avoid buying British paper, Harvard College printed its graduation program on coarse paper made in the colonies. And colonial newspapers printed letters warning colonists of the danger of letting Parliament tax them.

Some angry colonists joined the **Sons of Liberty.** This group was first formed during the Stamp Act crisis. Women set up their own group, known as **Daughters of Liberty.**

In cities from Boston to Charleston, Sons and Daughters of Liberty placed lanterns in large trees. Gathering around these Liberty Trees, as they were called, they staged mock hangings of cloth or straw figures dressed like British officials.

The hangings were meant to show tax collectors what might happen to them if they tried to collect the unpopular taxes.

Sons and Daughters of Liberty also used other methods to strengthen their cause. Some visited merchants urging them to sign the nonimportation agreements. A few even threatened people who continued to buy British goods.

Leaders in the Struggle

During the struggle over taxes, leaders emerged in all the colonies. Men and women in the New England colonies and Virginia were especially active in the colonial cause.

In Massachusetts. Samuel Adams of Boston stood firmly against Britain. Sam Adams seemed an unlikely leader. He was a failure in business and a poor public speaker. But he loved politics. He was always present at Boston town meetings and Sons of Liberty rallies.

A Fiery Leader *Throughout New England, wherever protests erupted, Sam Adams was usually at the center. Here, the fiery leader is shown in a portrait by John Singleton Copley.* **Citizenship** *What actions did Adams take to win colonists to his cause?*

Adams worked day and night to unite colonists against Britain. He published pamphlets and wrote letters to newspapers. But his greatest talent was organizing people. Sam Adams knew how to work behind the scenes, arranging protests and stirring public support.

Sam's cousin John was another important leader in Massachusetts. John Adams was a skilled lawyer. More cautious than Sam, he weighed evidence carefully before acting. His knowledge of British law earned him much respect.

Mercy Otis Warren and other women also aided the colonial cause. (See page 205.) Warren published plays that made fun of British officials. She formed a close friendship with Abigail Adams, wife of John Adams. The two women used their pens to spur the colonists to action.

Young men from Virginia. Virginia contributed many leaders to the struggle against taxes. In the House of Burgesses, George Washington joined other Virginians to protest the Townshend Acts.

A young firebrand, Patrick Henry, gave speeches that moved listeners to both tears and anger. In one speech, Henry attacked Britain with so much fury that some listeners cried out, "Treason!" Henry boldly replied, "If this be treason, make the most of it!"

At the time, a 22-year-old law student named Thomas Jefferson stood at the back of the assembly hall, quietly listening. Later, Jefferson, too, joined the ranks of colonial leaders.

Centers of Protest

Port cities such as Boston and New York were centers of protest. At wharves and docks, customs officers inspected cargoes and collected the hated taxes.

In New York, a dispute also arose over the **Quartering Act.** Under that law, colonists had to provide housing, candles, bedding, and beverages to British soldiers stationed in the colonies. In 1766, the New York assembly refused to obey the Quarter-

AN·AMERICAN·PORTRAIT

Mercy Otis Warren: Crusader for Liberty

From Boston to Philadelphia, colonists gathered to read about the latest adventures of the brave patriot Brutus and the evil tyrant Rapatio. Colonists who opposed British rule admired the heroic Brutus. But few knew that he and Rapatio were the creation of Mercy Otis Warren, a Massachusetts poet and playwright.

Warren strongly supported the cause of liberty. Her brother, James Otis, shared her beliefs. Otis was a lawyer and leading figure in the struggle against Britain. In 1769, supporters of King George III brutally beat Otis. He suffered periods of insanity for the rest of his life.

Mercy Otis Warren vowed to carry on her brother's work. Her weapon was her pen. She had received a fine education and had learned to write well. In 1772, she wrote her first play featuring Rapatio and Brutus. Colonists quickly recognized Rapatio as Governor Hutchinson of Boston. Brutus was James Otis.

In four more plays, Warren used humor to make the British look ridiculous. Colonists laughed at Brigadier Hate-All, Sir Sparrow Spendall, Hum Humbug, and Simple Sapling. They easily identified each character as one of the king's allies.

Warren's plays helped win support for the colonial cause. "Her energies and abilities," wrote John Adams, "were exerted by the use of her pen . . . in promoting the principles that resulted in the Independence of America."

1. How did Mercy Otis Warren help the colonists' cause?

2. **Analyzing Ideas** Why do you think humor sometimes can be a powerful weapon of protest?

ing Act. New Yorkers argued that the law was just another way of taxing them without their consent. When news of New York's action reached Britain, royal officials dismissed the assembly.

In Boston, too, tempers were rising. In 1768, the Massachusetts assembly petitioned Parliament to repeal the Townshend Acts. In response, the royal governor dismissed the assembly. Soon after, two regiments of British soldiers arrived in Boston to protect customs officers from outraged citizens.

To many Bostonians, the soldiers' tents set up on Boston Common were a daily reminder that Britain was trying to bully them into paying unjust taxes. When British soldiers walked along the streets of Boston, they risked insults or even beatings. The time was ripe for disaster.

The Boston Massacre

On the night of March 5, 1770, a crowd gathered outside the Boston customs house. Colonists shouted insults at the "lobsterbacks," as they called the redcoated British who guarded the building. Then they began to throw snowballs, oyster shells, and chunks of ice at the soldiers.

The soldiers stood their ground. Suddenly, a shot rang out—no one knows whether from the soldiers or the crowd. The soldiers fired into the crowd. When the smoke from the musket volley cleared, five people lay dead or dying. Among them was Crispus Attucks, a black sailor who was active in the Sons of Liberty.

The Burning of the Gaspee *In 1772, Rhode Island merchants set fire to the* Gaspee, *a British ship. The British had sent the* Gaspee *to colonial waters to prevent smuggling. When the British investigated the incident, Rhode Islanders claimed to know nothing about it. The incident greatly increased tensions between Britain and the colonies.* **Economics** *How might each side have defended its action?*

Sam Adams quickly wrote to other colonists about the shooting, which he called the **Boston Massacre.** Paul Revere, a Boston silversmith, made an engraving of the event. The engraving vividly showed the dead and wounded colonists. (See page 188.) As news of the Boston Massacre spread, colonists' outrage grew.

The soldiers were arrested and tried in court. John Adams agreed to defend them, saying that they deserved a fair trial. He wanted to show the world that the colonists believed in justice, even if the British government did not. At the trial, Adams argued that the crowd had provoked the soldiers. His arguments convinced the jury, and the British soldiers received very light sentences.

Repeal of the Townshend Acts

By strange chance, on the day of the Boston Massacre, Parliament voted to repeal most of the Townshend Acts. The nonimportation agreements hurt British merchants, and they pressured Parliament to end the Townshend taxes. But King George III asked Parliament to keep the tax on tea. "There must always be one tax to keep up the right [to tax]," argued the king. Parliament agreed.

News of the repeal delighted the colonists. Most people dismissed the remaining tax on tea as not important and ended their boycott of British goods. For a few years, calm returned.

Doubts About the Future

For many colonists, the recent events raised serious doubts about the future. They feared that at any time Parliament might again threaten colonial liberties.

To keep colonists informed of British actions, Sam Adams set up a **committee of correspondence.** The committee wrote letters and pamphlets reporting on events in Massachusetts. The idea worked well, and soon there were committees of correspondence in every colony. The committees played an important role in uniting the colonists against Britain.

1. **Identify:** (a) Townshend Acts, (b) Sons of Liberty, (c) Sam Adams, (d) Mercy Otis Warren, (e) Patrick Henry, (f) Quartering Act, (g) Crispus Attucks, (h) Boston Massacre.
2. **Define:** (a) writ of assistance, (b) nonimportation agreement, (c) committee of correspondence.
3. What actions did colonists take to protest the Townshend Acts?
4. Why did colonists oppose the Quartering Act?
5. Why were Bostonians gathered outside the customs house on the night of the Boston Massacre?
6. **Making Decisions** Do you think the Stamp Act was unjust? Explain.

5 To Arms!

FIND OUT

◆ Why did Britain pass the Tea Act?

◆ What was the Boston Tea Party?

◆ How did colonists respond to the Intolerable Acts?

◆ What was the shot heard 'round the world?

◆ **VOCABULARY** militia, minuteman

One night in July 1774, John Adams stopped at a tavern in eastern Massachusetts. After riding more than 30 miles, he was hot and dusty, and his body ached with fatigue. Adams asked the innkeeper for a cup of tea. He would have to drink coffee, she said. She did not serve tea. In a letter to his wife, Adams later praised the innkeeper's conduct. "Tea," he wrote, "must be . . . [given up]" by all colonists.

He promised to break himself of the habit as soon as possible.

Why did colonists like John Adams give up tea? The answer was taxes. When Parliament decided to enforce a tea tax in 1773, a new crisis exploded. This time, colonists began to think the unthinkable. Perhaps they should reject British rule and declare independence.

Uproar Over Tea

Tea became popular after it was brought to the colonies in the early 1700s. By 1770, at least 1 million Americans brewed tea twice a day. People "would rather go without their dinners than without a dish of tea," a visitor to the colonies noted.

Parliament passes the Tea Act. Most tea was brought to the colonies by the British East India Company. The company sold its tea to colonial tea merchants. The merchants then sold the tea to the colonists.

In the 1770s, however, the British East India Company found itself in deep financial trouble. More than 15 million pounds of its tea sat unsold in British warehouses. Parliament tried to help the company by passing the **Tea Act** of 1773. The act did away with some taxes paid by the company. It also let the company bypass the tea merchants and sell directly to colonists. These steps were meant to lower prices and thus encourage colonists to buy more tea.

To the surprise of Parliament, colonists protested the Tea Act. Colonial tea merchants were angry because they had been cut out of the tea trade. If Parliament ruined tea merchants today, they warned, what would prevent it from turning on other businesses tomorrow? Even tea drinkers, who would have benefited from the law, scorned the Tea Act. They believed that it was a British trick to make them accept Parliament's right to tax the colonies.

Boycott the "accursed STUFF"! Once again, colonists responded with a boycott. One colonial newspaper warned:

❝Do not suffer yourself to sip the accursed, dutied STUFF. For if you do, the devil will immediately enter into you, and you will instantly become a traitor to your country. **"**

Daughters of Liberty and other women led the boycott. They served coffee or made "liberty tea" from raspberry leaves. Sons of Liberty enforced the boycott by keeping the British East India Company from unloading cargoes of tea.

The Boston Tea Party

In late November 1773, three ships carrying tea arrived in Boston harbor. Governor Thomas Hutchinson ordered the captain to pay the required taxes, unload, and sell

MAP STUDY

Much of the early protest against the British was centered in the city of Boston. This map shows Boston in the 1770s.

1. *(a) At which building did colonists gather before the Boston Tea Party?*
   (b) On what street was it located?
2. *At what place did the Boston Tea Party take place?*
3. **Drawing Conclusions** *Why would taxes on trade be especially unpopular in cities like Boston?*

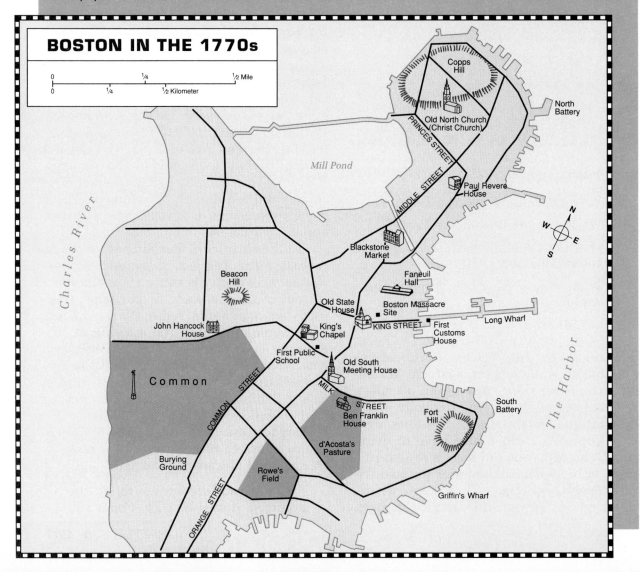

BOSTON IN THE 1770s

the tea as usual. If the taxes were not paid within 20 days, he would seize the cargo and have it sold. The deadline was Thursday, December 16.

A demand that the tea ships leave. That day, Boston seethed with excitement. Townspeople roamed the streets, wondering what the Sons of Liberty would do. Farmers and workers from nearby towns joined the crowds. "Committee Men & Mob Men were buzzing about in Swarms, like Bees," reported a nephew of Governor Hutchinson.

By 10 A.M., thousands of people had made their way along Milk Street to the Old South Meetinghouse. Sam Adams was there, directing affairs. So was the wealthy merchant John Hancock. At the meeting, colonists voted that the tea ships should leave Boston that afternoon—without unloading. Runners were sent to the customs house to voice the colonists' demand.

By afternoon, word came back. Customs officers would not act without the governor. Messengers then set off to see Governor Hutchinson. Once again, the colonists in the meetinghouse settled down to wait.

Then, as darkness fell, a voice suddenly rang out: "Fire! Fire!" Panic-stricken, people pushed toward the door. The town clerk had to shout over the uproar to calm the crowd. It was a false alarm, he said. A few British officers had created the disturbance hoping to break up the meeting.

Nervously, Sam Adams waited. So did the 5,000 people who had gathered in and around the meetinghouse. Finally, the messengers returned. The governor would not let the ships sail. The crowd's angry roar echoed far down the streets of Boston.

"Boston harbor a teapot tonight!" Adams waved for silence. "This meeting can do nothing further to save the country," he announced. Suddenly, as if on cue, a group of men with darkened faces burst into the meetinghouse. Wrapped in blankets like Mohawk Indians, they waved hatchets in the air. The crowd stirred. What was this? From the gallery above,

The Boston Tea Party *Under cover of darkness, colonists dressed as Mohawk Indians boarded British ships and dumped 342 chests of tea into Boston harbor. Some colonists cheered the Boston Tea Party. Others worried that it would encourage lawlessness.* **Economics** *Why were colonial tea merchants angered by the Tea Act?*

voices cried, "Boston harbor a teapot tonight! The Mohawks are come!"

George Hewes was one of the "Mohawks" poised for action. He later reported:

> **❝**I [had] dressed myself in the costume of an Indian, equipped with a small hatchet after having painted my face and hands with coal dust in the shop of a blacksmith. . . . When I first appeared in the street after being thus disguised, I fell in with many who were dressed, equipped and painted as I was, and . . . marched in order to the place of our destination.**❞**

That place was Griffin's Wharf, where the tea ships lay at anchor. About 50 or 60 people disguised as Indians were there. Some were carpenters and barbers. Others were doctors and merchants. In the cold, crisp night, under a nearly full moon, the men worked quickly. They boarded the ships, split open the tea chests, and dumped the tea into the harbor. On shore, the crowd watched silently. The only sounds were the chink of hatchets and the splash of tea landing in the water. (▢ See "Johnny Tremain" on page 652.)

By 10 P.M., the job was done. The **Boston Tea Party,** as it was later called, had ended. But the effects would be felt for a long time to come. ◆

Britain Strikes Back

Did Sam Adams organize the Boston Tea Party? He never said so publicly, but he very likely knew that it was planned. Whoever led the tea party, however, made sure that the protest was orderly. Only tea was destroyed. No other cargo was touched. The Boston Tea Party was meant to show Britain that the colonists would act firmly.

Colonists had mixed reactions to the event. Some cheered the action. Others worried that it would encourage lawlessness in the colonies. But even those who condemned the Boston Tea Party were shocked at Britain's response to it.

Punishment for Massachusetts. The British were outraged by what they saw as Boston's lawless behavior. In 1774, Parliament, encouraged by King George III, acted to punish Massachusetts. First, Parliament shut down the port of Boston. No ship could enter or leave the harbor—not even a small boat. The harbor would remain closed until the colonists paid for the tea and showed that they were sorry for what they had done.

Second, Parliament forbade colonists to hold town meetings more than once a year without the governor's permission. In the past, colonists had called town meetings whenever they wished.

Third, Parliament allowed customs officers and other officials charged with major crimes to be tried in Britain instead of in Massachusetts. Colonists protested. They said that a dishonest official could break the law in the colonies and avoid punishment "by being tried, where no evidence can pursue him."

Fourth, Parliament passed a new Quartering Act. No longer would redcoats camp in tents on Boston Common. Instead, British commanders could force citizens to house troops in their homes. The colonists called these laws the **Intolerable Acts** because they were so harsh.

Quebec Act. About the same time, Parliament passed the **Quebec Act.** It set up a government for Canada and protected the rights of French Catholics. The Quebec Act also redrew the boundaries of Canada to include land between the Ohio and Mississippi rivers. The act angered colonists, who claimed these western lands as their own.

Colonists support Boston. The committees of correspondence spread news of the Intolerable Acts and the Quebec Act. People from other colonies responded quickly to help the people of Boston, who faced hunger while their port was closed. Carts rolled into the city with rice from South Carolina, corn from Virginia, flour from Pennsylvania, and sheep from Connecticut.

In the Virginia assembly, Thomas Jefferson suggested that a day be set aside to mark the shame of the Intolerable Acts. The royal governor of Virginia rejected the idea and dismissed the assembly. But the colonists went ahead anyway. On June 1, 1774, church bells tolled slowly. Merchants closed their shops. Many colonists prayed and fasted all day.

The First Continental Congress

In response to the Intolerable Acts, colonial leaders called a meeting in Philadelphia. In September 1774, delegates from 12 colonies gathered at what became known as the **First Continental Congress.** Only Georgia did not send delegates.

The delegates had different views about what the Continental Congress should do. Some hoped to patch up the quarrel with

AMERICANS • ALL

Four Who Challenged the British

Step by step, colonists moved toward a final break with Britain. Thousands of men and women played a part. Each challenged the British in his or her own way.

Peter Timothy of South Carolina was one of those challengers. The son of a French father and a Dutch mother, Timothy used his newspaper, *The South Carolina Gazette,* to blast Parliament and King George III. He urged his readers to resist unjust laws like the Stamp Act and called on them to support freedom and liberty instead. When the Revolution came, the British arrested Timothy and held him as a prisoner of war.

Haym Salomon of New York also took a stand against the British. Salomon had been born into a Jewish-Portuguese family living in Poland. He came to the colonies to escape religious persecution. In his adopted homeland, he continued to fight for freedom, joining the Sons of Liberty almost as soon as he arrived. Years later, Salomon made a fortune in business and then spent it all to support the colonists' fight for independence from Britain.

Paul Revere is one of the most famous Sons of Liberty. But few people know that

Paul Revere's father fled to the colonies from France to escape religious persecution. He changed his name to make it easier for colonists to pronounce. Imagine! If he had not, his son's nighttime journey might be known today as "the midnight ride of Apollos Rivoire"!

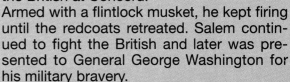

One colonist who heeded Paul Revere's call to action was a minuteman named Peter Salem. A former African slave, Salem marched with his company to face the British at Concord. Armed with a flintlock musket, he kept firing until the redcoats retreated. Salem continued to fight the British and later was presented to General George Washington for his military bravery.

1. How did Timothy, Salomon, Revere, and Salem each help move the colonies toward the final break with Britain?

2. **Drawing Conclusions** What does the story of these four people tell you about the colonists who fought the British to gain liberty?

Britain by getting Parliament to guarantee their rights. Others argued that the Intolerable Acts proved that Britain was determined to take away their rights. They urged firm, united action.

After much debate, the delegates passed a resolution backing Massachusetts in its struggle against the Intolerable Acts. They agreed to boycott all British goods and to stop exporting goods to Britain until the harsh laws were repealed. They urged each colony to set up and train its own militia (muh LIHSH uh). A **militia** is an

army of citizens who serve as soldiers during an emergency.

Before leaving Philadelphia, the delegates agreed to meet again the following May. Little did they know that by May 1775 an incident in Massachusetts would have changed the fate of the colonies forever.

The Shot Heard 'Round the World

In Massachusetts, newspapers called on citizens to prevent what they called "the Massacre of American Liberty." Volunteers known as minutemen trained regularly. Minutemen got their name because they kept their muskets at hand, prepared to fight at a minute's notice. Meanwhile, Britain built up its forces. More troops arrived in Boston, bringing the total number in that city to 4,000.

Early in 1775, General Thomas Gage, the British commander, learned that minutemen had a large store of arms in Concord, a village 18 miles (29 km) from Boston. General Gage planned a surprise march to Concord to seize the arms.

On April 18, about 700 British troops quietly left Boston under cover of darkness. But the Sons of Liberty were watching. As soon as the British set out, they hung two lamps from the Old North Church in Boston as a signal that the redcoats were on the move.

Sounding the alarm. Paul Revere and other colonists saw the signal. They mounted their horses and galloped through the night toward Concord. "The British are coming! The British are coming!" shouted Revere as he passed through each sleepy village along the way.

At dawn on April 19, the redcoats reached Lexington, a town near Concord. There, waiting for them on the village green, were 70 minutemen commanded by Captain John Parker. The British ordered the minutemen to go home. The colonists refused. A shot rang out through the chill morning air. No one knows who fired it. But in the brief struggle that followed,

MAP STUDY

The fighting at Lexington and Concord lasted only a few minutes. But the battles ended any hope that Britain and its colonies could solve their problems without war.
1. *What towns did the British pass through on their way to Concord?*
2. *In what direction did Paul Revere ride when he left Charlestown?*
3. **Comparing** *Compare the routes Dawes and Revere took.*

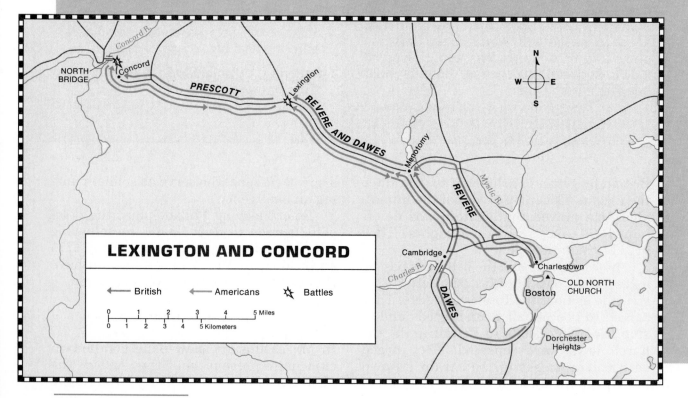

LEXINGTON AND CONCORD

← British   ← Americans   ✦ Battles

The Battle of Concord On April 19, 1775, British troops and colonial minutemen clashed outside Concord, Massachusetts. There, the "embattled farmers . . . fired the shot heard round the world." This detailed engraving of British troops near Concord cemetery was made from a sketch by minuteman Amos Doolittle. **Citizenship** Do you think that the fighting at Lexington and Concord could have been avoided? Explain.

eight colonists were killed, and one British soldier was wounded.

The British pushed on to Concord. Finding no arms in the village, they turned back to Boston. On a bridge outside Concord, they met 300 minutemen. Again, fighting broke out. This time, the British were forced to retreat. As they withdrew, colonial sharpshooters took deadly aim at them from the woods and fields. By the time they reached Boston, the redcoats had lost 73 men. Another 200 were wounded or missing.

A turning point. News of the battles at Lexington and Concord spread swiftly. To many colonists, the fighting ended all hope of reaching an agreement with Britain. Only war would decide the future of the 13 colonies.

More than 60 years after the battles, a monument was set up in Concord. A well-known New England poet, Ralph Waldo Emerson, wrote a poem to be sung at the opening ceremony. In the "Concord Hymn," he created a vivid picture of the clash at Concord. It begins:

> **❝**By the rude bridge that arched the flood,
> Their flag to April's breeze unfurled,

> Here once the embattled farmers stood,
> And fired the shot heard round the world.**❞**

The "embattled farmers" faced long years of war. But at the war's end, the 13 colonies would stand firm as a new, independent nation.

SECTION 5 REVIEW

1. **Locate:** (a) Boston, (b) Concord, (c) Lexington.
2. **Identify:** (a) Tea Act, (b) Boston Tea Party, (c) Intolerable Acts, (d) Quebec Act, (e) First Continental Congress, (f) Paul Revere.
3. **Define:** (a) militia, (b) minuteman.
4. Why was Parliament surprised at the colonists' reaction to the Tea Act?
5. How did the Intolerable Acts help unite the colonies?
6. Describe the events that led to fighting at Lexington.
7. **Linking Past and Present** Compare the way colonists protested an unpopular action by Parliament with the way Americans protest unpopular government actions today.

Historians study events that happened in the past. They often look at these events in **chronological order,** or the order in which they occurred. In this way, they can judge whether or not events might be related.

A **time line** is one way to show the order in which events took place. A time line also shows the dates when events happened.

A time line appears at the beginning of each unit and in the Study Guide at the end of each chapter in this book. These time lines are called horizontal time lines because they set out dates and events on a line from left to right.

Study the time line below. Then, use these steps to read the time line.

1 **Identify the time period covered in the time line.** (a) What is the earliest date shown on the time line below? (b) What is the latest date? (c) What is the period covered by this time line?

2 **Decide how the time line is divided.** Time lines are always divided into equal parts or time periods. Some time lines are divided into 10-year periods. A 10-year period is called a **decade.**

Some time lines are divided into 100-year periods. A 100-year period is called a **century.** The period from 1701 to 1800, for example, is called the 18th century. We live in the 20th century, or the period from 1901 to 2000. (a) List the dates that appear on the top of the time line below. (b) How many years are there between each date? (c) What events occurred during the decade of the 1760s? (d) What century is shown on this time line?

3 **Study the time line to discover how events might be related.** Use your reading in this chapter and the time line to answer these questions. (a) When did the Boston Tea Party take place? (b) Was the Tea Act passed before or after the Boston Tea Party ? (c) Was there a relationship between these two events? Explain your answer.

4 **Draw conclusions.** Compare the time line below to the one on page 215. Then, use your reading in this chapter and the two time lines to draw conclusions about the events taking place during this period. (a) What time period is shown in the time line on page 215? (b) Which time line shows the longer period of time? (c) What events took place between 1745 and 1763? (d) How do you think these events affected what happened after 1763?

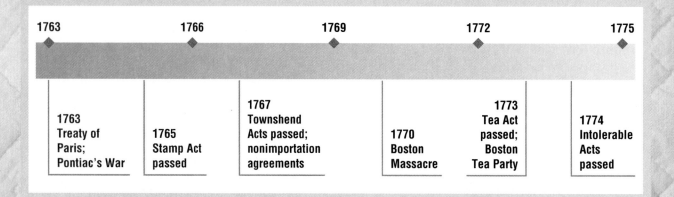

1763	1766	1769	1772	1775

| 1763 Treaty of Paris; Pontiac's War | 1765 Stamp Act passed | 1767 Townshend Acts passed; nonimportation agreements | 1770 Boston Massacre | 1773 Tea Act passed; Boston Tea Party | 1774 Intolerable Acts passed |

Use the Section Reviews and this Study Guide to review chapter content.

Main Ideas

The main ideas in each section of this chapter are summarized below.

SECTION 1 ■ Rivals for North America

◆ By the late 1600s, England had two rivals in North America: France and Spain.
◆ Both France and England enlisted Indian allies to help them.

SECTION 2 ■ The French and Indian War

◆ Rivalry between France and England in the Ohio Valley led to war.
◆ Under the Treaty of Paris of 1763, Britain gained most French lands in North America.

SECTION 3 ■ A Storm Over Taxes

◆ Britain closed western lands to settlers in the Proclamation of 1763.
◆ To help repay its huge war debts, Britain decided to tax the colonies.
◆ Colonists protested that there should be no taxation without representation.

SECTION 4 ■ The Quarrel Deepens

◆ Colonists protested the Townshend Acts by boycotting British goods.
◆ The Quartering Act required colonists to house British soldiers.

Tensions between colonists and British soldiers erupted in the Boston Massacre.

SECTION 5 ■ To Arms!

◆ Colonists protested the Tea Act by dumping British tea into Boston harbor.
◆ To punish colonists, Parliament passed the Intolerable Acts.
◆ In response to the Intolerable Acts, colonial leaders met at the First Continental Congress in September 1774.
◆ In April 1775, minutemen and British troops clashed at Lexington and Concord.

Key People and Terms

Refer to the Identify and Define questions in the Section Reviews on pages 198, 201, 207, and 213. Use each person, term, and vocabulary word in a complete sentence. When possible, make connections between the people and terms by using more than one person or term in each sentence.

Time Line

1. Make a chart of events in time order. The chart will have two headings: Date, Event. Fill in the chart, using the events on the time line below and on page 214.
2. (a) Which event was a cause of Pontiac's War? (b) Which event was a result?

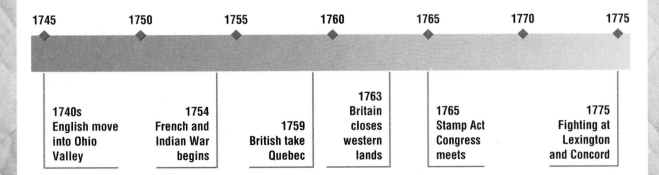

1745   1750   1755   1760   1765   1770   1775

1740s
English move into Ohio Valley

1754
French and Indian War begins

1759
British take Quebec

1763
Britain closes western lands

1765
Stamp Act Congress meets

1775
Fighting at Lexington and Concord

Understanding Vocabulary

Match each term at left with the correct definition at right.

1. boycott
2. repeal
3. writ of assistance
4. militia
5. minuteman

a. army of citizen soldiers
b. refusal to buy certain goods and services
c. volunteer who trained to fight the British
d. legal document granting a customs officer the right to make a search
e. cancel

Reviewing the Main Ideas

1. Why did Native Americans take sides in the struggle between France and Britain?
2. (a) Why did George Washington lead troops into the Ohio Valley in 1754? (b) Why was his clash with the French at Fort Necessity important?
3. (a) Why did Pontiac fight the British? (b) How did Pontiac's War affect British policy in the colonies?
4. What were the main results of the Treaty of Paris of 1763?
5. (a) List three ways Parliament tried to tax the colonies. (b) How did colonists respond to each?
6. (a) How did colonists protest the Tea Act? (b) What did Britain do in response?
7. What actions did the First Continental Congress take?
8. (a) Why did General Gage send troops to Concord? (b) What happened when they reached Lexington?

Thinking Critically

1. **Linking Past and Present** How might the lives of Americans today be different if France, not England, had won the French and Indian War?
2. **Forecasting** (a) How did Britain try to prevent clashes between Native Americans and settlers on the frontier? (b) Do you think this policy was likely to succeed? Explain.
3. **Evaluating Information** The dictionary defines a massacre as the cruel and violent killing of large numbers of people. Why do you think Sam Adams called the incident in Boston a massacre when only five people were killed?

Applying Your Skills

1. **Analyzing a Quotation** Review the following statement made by a Native American to an English trader in the mid-1700s: "You and the French are like the two edges of a pair of shears. And we are the cloth which is to be cut to pieces between them." (a) What did the speaker mean by these words? (b) Do you think he felt hopeful about the chances of Native Americans to hold out against the British and French? Explain.
2. **Using a Time Line** Review Skill Lesson 7 on page 214. Then, study the time line on page 215. (a) What is the earliest date on the time line? (b) What is the latest date on the time line? (c) In what year did the French and Indian War begin? (d) In what year did the British take Quebec? (e) How did the British victory at Quebec affect the French and Indian War?

Thinking About Geography

Match the letters on the map with the places listed below.

1. Spanish lands (1763)
2. British lands (1763)
3. Original 13 colonies
4. Mississippi River
5. Ohio River

Location What body of water formed the western boundary of British lands in North America in 1763?

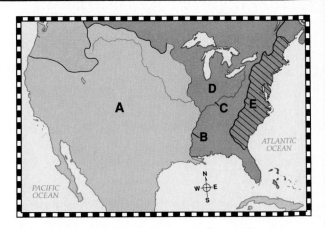

History Writer's Workshop

Arranging Information for Comparison

Comparison order is arrangement of supporting information according to similarities and differences. One way to group the information is by subject.

Look at the following topic sentence. *The British and the colonists had different points of view about taxes.* The subjects being compared are the points of view of the British and the colonists. In the detail sentences for the paragraph, first present all the information about the British view of taxes. For example: *The British believed that colonists should help pay for the French and Indian War. They also believed that Parliament represented all British subjects, including the colonists, and so had a right to tax them.*

Then, using a transition, present all the information about the colonists' view. Be sure to omit any information that does not directly support the topic sentence.

Common transitions for differences include *but, however, in contrast, instead, on the contrary, on the other hand, yet, whereas,* and *unlike.* Common transitions for similarities include *both, like, likewise, similarly,* and *similar to.*

Practice Using the instructions above, complete the comparison by writing detail sentences about the colonists' view of taxes. (See pages 200–201 for information.)

Writing to Learn

1. Imagine that you are a delegate to the Albany Congress. Decide whether you will vote for or against Benjamin Franklin's proposed Plan of Union. Make a list of reasons for your decision. Compose a topic sentence that summarizes your position. Then, write detail sentences stating your reasons in order of importance. Revise your paragraph for persuasive power and logic. Proofread and make a final copy. Share your argument with a classmate who has an opposing point of view.

2. Explain in an essay why the Boston Tea Party was, as John Adams put it, "a turning point in history." Before writing, list the causes and effects of the event. Then, compose a topic sentence stating the main point of your argument. In detail sentences, describe causes and effects of the event. You may present either the causes or the effects first. When you revise, be sure that each point supports the topic sentence. Proofread and make a final copy. Submit your essay to a historical magazine.

Battle of Princeton *In 1775, the colonies and Britain went to war. The fighting lasted for more than six years. When it was over, the 13 English colonies had become the independent United States of America. This painting shows the Battle of Princeton in 1777.* **Local History** *Were any battles of the Revolution fought in your area?*

CHAPTER

8

The War for Independence (1775–1783)

CHAPTER SPOTLIGHT

The Big Picture

In the Declaration of Independence, delegates from the 13 English colonies announced that the colonies were now an independent nation. John Hancock signed the Declaration first. "There must be no pulling different ways," Hancock said. "We must all hang together."

To the delegates in 1776, signing the Declaration was a fateful step. If the British ever captured them, they would most likely pay with their lives. For the signers, as for other colonists, creating an independent nation involved dangers and hardships.

Jim Davidson

Of Special Interest

Focus On

◆ What problems faced Americans in the early days of the war?
◆ What goals did the Declaration of Independence set for Americans?
◆ Why were 1777 and 1778 difficult years for Americans?
◆ How did different groups contribute to the American cause?
◆ How did the United States achieve its goal of independence?

"**G**entlemen may cry, 'Peace! peace!'—but there is no peace. The war is actually begun! . . . Our brethren are already in the field! Why stand we here idle? . . . Is life so dear, or peace so sweet, as to be purchased at the price of chains and slavery? Forbid it, Almighty God! I know not what course others may take; but as for me, give me liberty or give me death!**"**

Patrick Henry's words rang out through St. John's Church in Richmond, Virginia. It was March 1775, and the 13 colonies stood on the brink of war.

Delegates from across Virginia had gathered to debate a course of action. Some wanted to give Britain one last chance to change its conduct toward the colonies. Others, like Henry, wanted to take up arms to protect colonists' rights. "There is no longer any room for hope," cried Henry. "We have done everything that could be done to [prevent] the storm which is coming on us now."

Similar debates raged in other colonies. As British troops poured into Boston, colonists faced a hard decision: Should they give in to Britain? Or should they fight for their liberties? On July 4, 1776, the final break was made. One by one, colonial leaders voted to form a new nation, the United States of America.

1 Early Battles

FIND OUT

◆ What actions did the Second Continental Congress take?

◆ What were the strengths and weaknesses of the Americans and British?

◆ How did Americans oppose the British in Boston?

◆ **VOCABULARY** blockade

As darkness fell, the redcoats limped into Boston from Lexington and Concord. All along the route, rebel musket fire had taken its toll. The events of April 19, 1775, left the British stunned. How had a ragtag band of rebels forced 700 redcoats to retreat? What did such resistance to the king's authority mean? That night, the British watched uneasily as rebels set up a ring of campfires around Boston.

In the weeks and months ahead, the rebel campfires remained. They were a clear sign that the long-smoldering quarrel between Britain and its colonies had blazed into war. Many Americans still hoped for a peaceful solution. But the rebels outside Boston were determined not to back down.

The Green Mountain Boys

In 1775, the colonies did not have a united army—or even a united government. But in each colony, bands of rebels took daring action. Ethan Allen, a Vermont blacksmith known for his strength and fierce temper, flew into a rage when he learned of events in Massachusetts. "I read with horror," he later wrote, of the "bloody attempt at Lexington to enslave America."

Allen led a group of Vermonters, known as the **Green Mountain Boys,** in a surprise attack on Fort Ticonderoga. The fort was a British outpost at the southern tip of Lake Champlain. (See the map on page 223.) Allen knew that the fort had many cannons that the Americans badly needed.

Soldiers at Fort Ticonderoga did not suspect an attack. They had not even heard about the fighting at Lexington and Concord. So on May 10, the Green Mountain Boys slipped easily through the morning mists at Fort Ticonderoga. They quickly overpowered the guard on duty and entered the fort. Allen headed straight to the room where the British commander slept. "Come out, you old rat!" he shouted.

Ethan Allen Captures Ticonderoga *In May 1775, Ethan Allen and the Green Mountain Boys made a bold surprise attack on Fort Ticonderoga. Here, Allen waves his sword over his head and demands that the British commander surrender. The capture of the fort gave colonists their first victory of the Revolution.* **Geography** *Why was Fort Ticonderoga important?*

The commander pulled on his uniform and demanded to know on whose authority Allen acted. "In the name of [God] and the Continental Congress!" Allen replied. The commander had no choice but to surrender the fort with its cannons and valuable supply of gunpowder. The Americans also won control of a water route into Canada. "We are now masters of Lake Champlain!" cried Allen.

Last Efforts for Peace

While the Green Mountain Boys celebrated their victory, delegates from the 13 colonies met at the Second Continental Congress in Philadelphia. The situation was very different from what it had been when they met in 1774. Now, colonists were actually fighting the British.

Still, delegates were divided over what to do. A few, like Sam and John Adams, secretly wanted the colonies to declare independence. But most delegates hoped to avoid a final break with Britain.

After much debate, the Continental Congress voted to try to patch up the quarrel with Britain. Delegates sent King George III the **Olive Branch Petition.** In it, they declared their loyalty to the king. They also asked him to repeal the Intolerable Acts and end the fighting.

The Congress took another, bolder step. It set up the **Continental Army.** John Adams nominated George Washington as commander. Adams proposed the Virginia colonist with the following words:

> ❝I [have] in my mind for that important command . . . a gentleman whose skill and experience as an officer, whose independent fortune, great talents, and excellent universal character would command the [approval] of all America.❞

Washington was present during Adams's nomination speech. Embarrassed by the praise, he quietly slipped out of the room. All delegates voted in favor of his appointment as commander.

Strengths and Weaknesses

In late May, Washington left Philadelphia to take charge of the militia around Boston. He faced an uphill struggle. American troops were a motley assortment of untrained men. In addition, the Americans had few cannons and little gunpowder. And they had no navy at all.

The British, on the other hand, had well-trained troops, experienced in fighting. And Britain's navy was the most powerful in the world. Its ships could move soldiers quickly up and down the coast.

But Britain faced serious problems, too. Its soldiers were fighting 3,000 miles (4,800 km) from home. News took months to travel from Britain to North America. And it took months for supplies and fresh troops to reach North America from Britain. Also, British soldiers were in enemy territory, likely to be attacked by colonists once they ventured into the countryside.

The Americans had other advantages. They had every reason to fight because they were defending their own homes, farms, and shops. Reuben Stebbins of Williamstown, Massachusetts, was typical of many farmers. When he heard the British were near his home, he rode off to battle. "We'll see who's goin' t' own this farm!" he cried.

Although few Americans were trained as soldiers, many owned rifles and were good shots. Also, Americans were fortunate to have a leader like George Washington. He had never commanded such a large force, but he learned quickly. He demanded—and received—respect from his troops.

The First Major Battle

While Washington rode north to take command, the Americans tightened their circle around the British in Boston. They wanted to keep the British from leaving the city.

"Dig, men, dig." At sunset on June 16, 1775, Colonel William Prescott led 1,200 American troops to take up a position on Bunker Hill in Charlestown, across the

MAP STUDY

Early in the American Revolution, several battles took place in and around Boston.

1. (a) At what place on the map did the first major battle of the Revolution take place? (b) Who won the battle?
2. Which side captured Dorchester Heights?
3. **Solving Problems** Based on the map, what action did Washington take to keep the British from marching west out of Boston?

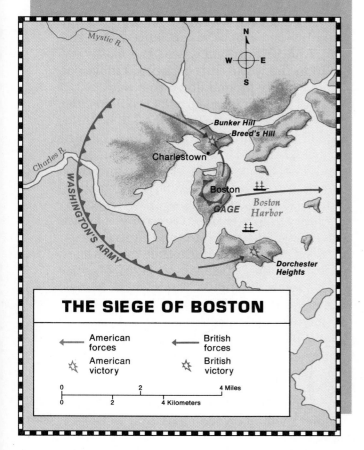

THE SIEGE OF BOSTON

← American forces

← British forces

American victory

British victory

0   2   4 Miles
0   2   4 Kilometers

river from Boston. (See the map above.) From the hill, they could fire on British ships in Boston harbor.

But Prescott soon saw that nearby Breed's Hill was a better position. So he put his men to work digging trenches there. "Dig, men, dig," he urged. Prescott knew that the trenches must be finished before dawn. Otherwise, the British might force the Americans off the hill.

At sunrise, the British general, William Howe, spotted the Americans. He ferried about 2,400 redcoats across the harbor to Charlestown. There, the British had to cross rough fields broken by fences to climb Breed's Hill. Each soldier carried a heavy pack that weighed about 125 pounds. It was hot, exhausting work, and the soldiers moved slowly.

From their trenches, the Americans watched the British struggle up the hill. Because the colonists had only a small amount of gunpowder, the American commanders warned, "Don't shoot until you see the whites of their eyes!"

The British push over the top. As the enemy advanced, colonists "gave them such a hot fire that they were obliged to retire nearly 150 yards before they could rally," recalled Colonel Prescott. Twice, the British advanced up the hill. Twice, they had to retreat from American musket fire.

On the third try, the British pushed over the top. By then, the Americans had run out of gunpowder. The British took both Bunker and Breed's hills. But they paid a high price. More than 1,000 redcoats lay dead or wounded. The Americans lost 400.

The **Battle of Bunker Hill** was the first major battle of the war. It proved that Americans could fight bravely in battle. It also showed that the British would not be easy to defeat.

The British Retreat

Washington finally reached Boston in midsummer. There, he found a Continental Army greatly pleased with its defense of Bunker Hill. In fact, however, the men were raw recruits, badly in need of training. About 16,000 troops camped in huts and tents sprawled at the edge of the city. Their weapons ranged from frontier rifles to swords made by local blacksmiths.

Washington started work at once turning this ragtag band into a trained army. His job was made harder by the mistrust of soldiers from different colonies. "Connecticut wants no Massachusetts men in her corps," he wrote. And "Massachusetts thinks there is no necessity for a Rhode Islander to be introduced into her [ranks]." Slowly, Washington won the respect of the troops. Slowly, they learned to take orders and work together.

By January 1776, the Continental Army was firmly dug in around Boston. From Ticonderoga, soldiers had dragged cannons on sleds across the mountains. Washington had the cannons placed on Dorchester Heights, overlooking Boston and its harbor. General Howe realized that he could not defeat the strong American force. So in March 1776, he decided to move his troops north from Boston to Halifax, Canada.

Although the British left New England, they had not given up. King George III ordered a blockade of all colonial ports. A **blockade** is the shutting off of a port by ships to keep people or supplies from moving in or out. The king also hired Hessian troops from Germany to help fight the colonists.

Disaster in Canada

Some Americans wanted to attack the British in Canada. They hoped that the French Canadians, who were not happy under British rule, would support the Patriot cause.

In late 1775, two American armies moved north into Canada. (See the map at right.) One army, led by Richard Montgomery, started out from Fort Ticonderoga. The other, led by Benedict Arnold, moved north through Maine.

Montgomery seized Montreal in November 1775. He then moved down the St. Lawrence River toward the city of Quebec, where he hoped to join forces with Benedict Arnold.

Arnold and his troops, however, had a terrible journey through the Maine woods in winter. Rainstorms followed by freezing nights coated their clothing with ice that was "a pane of glass thick." Supplies ran very low. Soldiers survived by eating boiled candles, bark, and shoe leather. Finally,

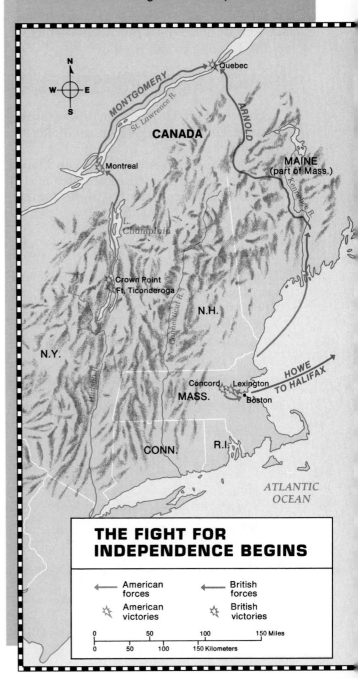

MAP STUDY

The first clashes of the Revolution took place in the northern colonies and in Canada.
1. In what direction did Benedict Arnold march to reach Quebec?
2. About how far did Montgomery have to travel from Fort Ticonderoga to Quebec?
3. **Analyzing Information** Based on the map, which American commander would have had a harder time reaching Quebec? Explain.

THE FIGHT FOR INDEPENDENCE BEGINS

← American forces
← British forces
American victories
British victories

0   50   100   150 Miles
0   50   100   150 Kilometers

Arnold reached Quebec. But to the Americans' disappointment, French Canadians did not rush to support them.

On December 31, 1775, during a blinding snowstorm, the Americans attacked. Montgomery was killed, and Arnold was wounded. The Americans failed to take the city. They stayed outside Quebec until May 1776, when the British landed new forces in Canada. At last, weakened by disease and hunger, the Americans withdrew, leaving Canada to the British.

SECTION 1 REVIEW

1. **Locate:** (a) Fort Ticonderoga, (b) Boston, (c) Bunker Hill, (d) Breed's Hill, (e) Montreal, (f) Quebec.
2. **Identify:** (a) Ethan Allen, (b) Green Mountain Boys, (c) Olive Branch Petition, (d) Continental Army, (e) Battle of Bunker Hill, (f) Benedict Arnold.
3. **Define:** blockade.
4. Name three actions taken by the Second Continental Congress.
5. What did the Battle of Bunker Hill reveal about each side?
6. **Comparing** Compare the strengths and weaknesses of the British and Americans at the start of the war.

2 Independence Declared

FIND OUT

◆ How did *Common Sense* help move Americans toward independence?

◆ What are the main ideas of the Declaration of Independence?

◆ How did Americans respond to the Declaration of Independence?

◆ VOCABULARY traitor

When George III learned of the Olive Branch Petition, he refused to look at it. The colonies, he raged, are in a "desperate [plot] to establish an independent empire!" He vowed to "bring the traitors to justice."

News of the king's response reached the colonies in November 1775. Few Americans wanted to declare independence. Most still hoped the quarrel with Britain could be settled peacefully. But attitudes toward independence were changing.

The Common Sense of Thomas Paine

In January 1776, a pamphlet appeared on the streets of Philadelphia. "In the following pages," announced the author, "I offer nothing more than simple facts, plain arguments, and common sense." The pamphlet, *Common Sense,* stunned readers. The "plain arguments" boldly urged the colonies to declare independence.

The author of *Common Sense* was Thomas Paine. Paine had only recently arrived from England, but he quickly embraced the American cause. In *Common Sense,* he told Americans that they had been patient with England long enough:

> ❝[It is foolish] . . . to be always running three or four thousand miles with a tale or petition, waiting four or five months for an answer, which when obtained requires five or six more to explain it in.❞

Since King George had just rejected the Olive Branch Petition, that argument made sense to many Americans.

More important, Paine attacked the idea of having kings and queens as rulers. What right did monarchs have to rule, he asked. One honest man was worth more "in the sight of God than all the crowned ruffians that ever lived."

In *Common Sense,* Paine wrote so clearly and with such energy that he won many colonists to the idea of independence. In six months, more than 500,000 copies were printed and sold. "*Common Sense* is working a powerful change in the minds of men," George Washington observed. The pamphlet even changed the general's own

Down With King George III! *By mid-1776, many colonists were ready to heed the "plain arguments" of* Common Sense *and throw off British rule. Here, New Yorkers express their anger by toppling a statue of King George III.* **Citizenship** *What opinion of kings and queens did Thomas Paine offer in* Common Sense?

habits. Until 1776, Washington always drank a toast to the king at official dinners. After reading Paine's pamphlet, he dropped this custom.

The Fateful Step

Common Sense had an effect on the Continental Congress, too. Richard Henry Lee of Virginia wrote to Washington, "I am now convinced . . . of the necessity for separation." In June 1776, Lee offered a resolution saying that "these United Colonies are, and of right ought to be, free and independent States." It was a tense moment. Delegates knew there would be no turning back once they declared independence. If Britain won the war, they would be hanged as traitors. A traitor is a person who betrays his or her country.

The delegates acted bravely. They appointed a committee to draw up a declaration of independence. The committee included John Adams, Benjamin Franklin, Thomas Jefferson, Robert Livingston, and Roger Sherman. Their job was to tell the world why the colonies were taking such a drastic step. The committee asked Jefferson to write the document.

Jefferson was one of the youngest delegates to the Congress. Tall, slender, and quiet, he spoke little at formal meetings. But among friends, he liked to sprawl in a chair with his long legs stretched out and talk for hours. In late June, Jefferson completed the declaration, and it was read to the Congress.

On July 2, the Continental Congress voted that the 13 colonies were "free and independent States." Two days later, on July 4, 1776, the delegates accepted the **Declaration of Independence.** Since then, Americans have celebrated July 4th as Independence Day.

The Declaration

Across the colonies, Americans gathered to read the Declaration of Independence. The document has three main parts. (The Declaration of Independence is printed on pages 749–752.)

The first section of the Declaration explains the basic rights on which the nation was founded. In bold, ringing words, Jefferson wrote:

❝We hold these truths to be self-evident, that all men are created

Fourth of July

On July 4, 1776, delegates to the Continental Congress approved the Declaration of Independence. From Philadelphia, John Adams wrote to his wife, Abigail:

❝[Independence Day] ought to be [remembered] as the Day of Deliverance . . . with Pomp and Parade, with Shows, Games, Sports, Guns, Bells, Bonfires, and Illuminations from one End of this Continent to the other from this Time forward forever more.❞

Americans agreed with Adams. A year later, on July 4, 1777, people paraded and

watched fireworks. Patriots put lighted candles in their windows. Throughout the land, cannons boomed and church bells rang out from every steeple.

Today, Americans still celebrate the Fourth of July with "Pomp and Parade." One of the most spectacular celebrations took place on July 4, 1986. On that

day, Americans mounted a giant display of "illuminations," not only to remember the signing of the Declaration but to wish a happy 100th birthday to another symbol of American freedom—the Statue of Liberty.

1. How did John Adams believe Independence Day should be remembered?

2. **Analyzing Ideas** Why do you think John Adams believed Independence Day should be celebrated "forever more"?

equal, that they are endowed by their Creator with certain unalienable rights, that among these are life, liberty, and the pursuit of happiness.❞

How could people protect these basic rights? By forming governments, the Declaration says. Governments could exist only if they had the "consent of the governed." If a government took away its citizens' rights, then it was the people's "right [and] duty,

to throw off such government, and provide new guards for their future security."

The second part of the Declaration lists the wrongs committed by Britain. Point by point, Jefferson showed how George III had abused his power. He condemned the king for disbanding colonial legislatures and sending over cruel customs agents. He attacked the king for sending troops to the colonies in times of peace. The list went on, backing up the colonists' argument that they had a right to revolt.

The last part of the Declaration announces that the colonies had become "the United States of America." All ties with Britain were cut. As a free and independent nation, the United States could make alliances and trade with other countries.

Choosing Sides

John Dunlap of Philadelphia printed the Declaration of Independence on July 4, 1776. Later, Mary Katherine Goddard, a Baltimore printer, produced the first copies that included the names of all the signers. Colonists carefully studied the document. They had to decide whether to support the new nation or remain loyal to Britain.

The nation was divided. On one side were **Patriots,** people who supported independence. On the other were **Loyalists,** people who remained loyal to the British king. Many families were split. Ben Franklin, for example, was a Patriot. His son, the royal governor of New Jersey, supported King George. Loyalists included merchants and farmers as well as royal officials.

During the war for independence, thousands of Americans supported the British. There were more Loyalists in the Middle States and the South than in New England. But life was difficult for Loyalists everywhere. Patriots tarred and feathered people who spoke in favor of Britain. Many Loyalists fled to England or Canada. Those who fled lost their homes, stores, and farms.

SECTION 2 REVIEW

1. **Identify:** (a) Thomas Paine, (b) Richard Henry Lee, (c) Thomas Jefferson, (d) Declaration of Independence, (e) Mary Katherine Goddard.
2. **Define:** traitor.
3. What arguments did Thomas Paine offer in favor of independence?
4. Describe the three main parts of the Declaration of Independence.
5. **Comparing** Compare the viewpoints of Patriots and Loyalists.

3 Desperate Days

FIND OUT

◆ What battles were fought in the Middle States?

◆ Why was the Battle of Saratoga important?

◆ How did people from other nations help the American cause?

◆ **VOCABULARY** cavalry

One summer morning at the end of June 1776, rifleman Daniel McCurtin gazed out at New York harbor. Suddenly, his eyes widened. From his second-floor window, he saw "something resembling a wood of pine trees trimmed." It was like a forest far out on the water. No, it was not a forest. It was the masts of ships!

❝I could not believe my eyes . . . when in about ten minutes, the whole bay was full of shipping as ever it could be. I declare that I thought all London was afloat.**❞**

By noon, a fleet of British warships were anchored offshore. Continental soldiers like McCurtin shivered with fear and excitement. The redcoats, led by General Howe, had arrived in force!

With the arrival of the British fleet in New York, the war entered a new stage. Most early battles of the Revolution had been fought in New England. Now, in mid-1776, the heavy fighting shifted to the Middle States. For the next two years, the Americans battled the British in New York, New Jersey, and Pennsylvania. These were the worst days of the war.

Campaign in New York

Washington had expected Howe's attack. So he had marched his army south from Boston to defend New York City. But the

British Ships Sail Up the Hudson *In 1776, the Continental Army was no match for British forces—especially the British navy. Here, British ships move unharmed up the Hudson River while Washington's troops watch from either shore.* **Economics** *Why do you think it was hard for the Americans to build a navy?*

Americans faced a grim situation. Howe had 34,000 troops and 10,000 sailors. He also had 30 warships and 400 smaller boats to ferry his army ashore. Washington had fewer than 20,000 poorly trained, untested troops. Worse, he had no navy.

Washington did not know exactly where Howe would mount his attack. So he divided his troops. He sent some to Long Island. Others he sent to Manhattan.

In August, the British made their move, landing boatload after boatload of soldiers on Long Island. In the **Battle of Long Island,** more than 1,400 Americans were killed, wounded, or captured. The rest retreated across the East River to Manhattan. The British followed. (See "A Teenage Prisoner of War" on page 654.)

A narrow escape. To avoid capture, Washington headed north. All through the fall, he fought running battles with Howe's army. In November, he crossed the Hudson River into New Jersey. With the British in pursuit, the Americans retreated across the Delaware River into Pennsylvania. (See the map on page 230.)

Nathan Hale. While Washington was battling for New York, he needed information about Howe's forces. Nathan Hale, a young Connecticut officer, offered to go behind British lines. Hale got the information but was captured soon after. The British tried and condemned him to death.

According to reports, Hale's last words before he stepped to the gallows were "I only regret that I have but one life to lose for my country."

New Hope for Americans

December 1776 was a low point for the Continental Army. Washington described his troops as sick, dirty, and "so thinly clad as to be unfit for service." Every day, soldiers left the army to return home. In a letter to his brother, Washington confided, "I am wearied to death. I think the game is pretty near up."

Thomas Paine had marched with Washington's army as it retreated through New Jersey. During these gloomy days, he picked up his pen and wrote *The Crisis*. In it, he called on Americans to support the brave men who fought for them:

> ❝These are the times that try men's souls. The summer soldier and the sunshine patriot will, in this crisis, shrink from the service of his country; but he that stands it now deserves the love and thanks of man and woman.❞

Grateful for the inspiring words, Washington had *The Crisis* read aloud to his troops.

A bold move. The Americans needed more than words to help their cause. Washington decided on a bold move—a surprise attack on Trenton.

On Christmas night, Washington secretly led his troops across the icy Delaware River. Soldiers shivered as spray from the river froze on their faces. Reaching shore, the troops marched through swirling snow. "Soldiers, keep by your officers," Washington urged.

Early on December 26, the Americans surprised the Hessian troops guarding Trenton and took most of them prisoner. An American summed up the **Battle of Trenton:** "Hessian population of Trenton at 8 A.M.—1,408 men and 39 officers; Hessian population at 9 A.M.—0."

Victory at Princeton. The British quickly responded by sending General Charles Cornwallis to trap Washington. On the night of January 2, 1777, Cornwallis saw the lights of Washington's campfires. "At last we have run down the old fox," he said, "and we will bag him in the morning."

But Washington fooled Cornwallis. He left the fires burning and slipped behind British lines to attack Princeton. There, Washington led his army to another victory. From Princeton, he moved to Morristown, where the army spent the winter. Washington's victories at Trenton and Princeton gave the Americans new hope.

A New British Strategy

In London, British officials were upset by the army's failure to crush the colonial rebels. Early in 1777, a handsome and confident general, John Burgoyne (buhr GOIN), presented King George III with a new plan for victory. If British troops cut off New England from the other colonies, argued General Burgoyne, the war would soon be over.

Burgoyne's plan called for three British armies to march on Albany from different directions. The three forces were to meet in Albany and crush the Americans there. Then, in control of the Hudson River, the British could keep soldiers and supplies from flowing to Washington from New England.

Brandywine and Germantown. General Burgoyne's plan called for General Howe to march on Albany from New York City. But King George III ordered Howe to capture Philadelphia first. This might not have been a problem if Howe had captured the city quickly. But sadly for the British, he did not.

In July 1777, Howe sailed from New York to the Chesapeake Bay. (See the map on page 230.) As Howe marched toward Philadelphia, Washington tried to stop him. At the **Battle of Brandywine,** Howe defeated the Americans.

Washington at Princeton
After the American victories at Trenton and Princeton, the British viewed the Continental Army with new respect. In the words of a British lieutenant, "They are now become a [powerful] enemy." Here, General Washington, on a white horse, leads the attack at Princeton. **American Traditions** *How did Washington fool the British at Princeton?*

In 1776 and 1777, American and British forces fought many battles over a large land area. An American victory at the Battle of Saratoga in October 1777 marked a major turning point of the war.

1. *What route did Burgoyne's army take to reach Saratoga?*
2. *Who won the Battle of Brandywine?*
3. **Understanding Causes and Effects** *Based on the map, why do you think many Patriots left Philadelphia in 1777?*

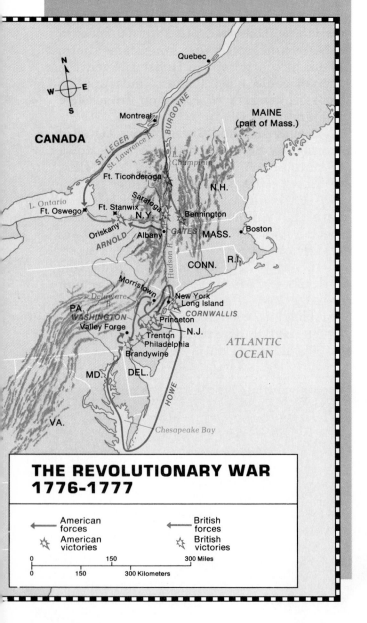

THE REVOLUTIONARY WAR 1776–1777

← American forces
← British forces
☆ American victories
☆ British victories

0   150   300 Miles
0 150   300 Kilometers

Howe entered Philadelphia in late September. Washington again attacked the redcoats, this time at Germantown, just outside Philadelphia. At the **Battle of Germantown,** the Americans again met defeat. Washington retreated to Valley Forge, where he set up winter quarters.

While Howe rested in Philadelphia, two other British armies under Barry St. Leger (lay ZHAIR) and Burgoyne moved south from Canada on their way to Albany. St. Leger tried to take Fort Stanwix. However, Benedict Arnold drove him back with a strong American army.

Success at Saratoga. Only Burgoyne was left to march on Albany. His army moved slowly because it had to drag heavy baggage carts through the woods. Americans made the work harder by blocking the route with trees and damming streams to create swampy bogs.

Burgoyne's army did retake Fort Ticonderoga. The general then sent soldiers into Vermont to find food and horses. Patriots fell on these troops. Nearly 1,000 British were wounded or captured at the **Battle of Bennington.**

Burgoyne's troubles grew. The Green Mountain Boys hurried into New York to help American forces led by General Horatio Gates. At the village of Saratoga, Gates surrounded the British. Twice, Burgoyne tried to break through the American lines. Each time, Benedict Arnold beat him back. Realizing that he was trapped, Burgoyne surrendered his entire army to the Americans on October 17, 1777.

A Powerful Ally

The American victory at the **Battle of Saratoga** was a turning point in the war. It ended the British threat to New England. And it boosted American spirits at a time when Washington's army was suffering defeats in Pennsylvania. But most important, it convinced France to sign a treaty with the United States.

In 1776, the Continental Congress had sent Benjamin Franklin to Paris to persuade the French king, Louis XVI, to help the Americans. The Continental Army sorely needed weapons and other supplies. The Congress wanted France to declare war on Britain. France had a strong navy that could be used against the British.

The French were still fuming about their defeat by Britain in the French and Indian War. But Louis XVI did not dare to help the Americans openly until he had proof that they could win. The Battle of Saratoga gave him that proof.

In February 1778, France became the first nation to sign a treaty with the United States. In it, Louis XVI recognized the new nation and agreed to give it military aid.

Valley Forge

French aid came too late to help Washington and his army at Valley Forge. During the long, cold winter of 1777–1778, the Continental Army suffered hardships at their makeshift quarters in Pennsylvania. Meanwhile, in Philadelphia, the British soldiers were warm, comfortable, and well fed.

At Valley Forge, American soldiers shivered in huts. Many slept on the frozen ground. They had little or no warm clothing. Some soldiers stood on guard wrapped only in blankets. Many had no shoes and wrapped bits of cloth around their feet. As winter wore on, soldiers suffered from frostbite and disease. A Rhode Island officer, writing to the governor to ask for help, described his troops as "the naked regiment."

When news of the army's suffering spread, Americans sent food and clothing to Valley Forge. Women gathered medicine, food, clothing, and ammunition for the army. They raised money to buy other supplies. Some, including General Washington's wife, Martha, went to Valley Forge to help the sick and wounded.

Help From Abroad

People from other nations also helped the American cause. In 1777, the Marquis de Lafayette (lah fih YET), a French noble, brought professional soldiers to the United States. Lafayette fought at Brandywine and spent the winter with Washington at Valley Forge. The young Frenchman became a trusted friend of Washington.

Two Polish officers joined the American cause. They were Thaddeus Kosciusko (kahs ee UHS koh) and Casimir Pulaski (poo LAHS kee). Kosciusko, an engineer, helped build forts and other defenses. Pulaski helped to train cavalry, or troops on horseback.

Help came from New Spain, too. Bernardo de Gálvez, governor of the Spanish lands of Louisiana, threw his support behind the Americans. Gálvez supplied the Continental Army with cattle from Spanish herds in Texas. He also attacked the British in Florida. (See "An American Portrait" on page 232.)

Friedrich von Steuben (STOO buhn) from Prussia helped train the American army. Von Steuben had served in the Prussian army, considered the best in Europe. A lively man, Von Steuben kept everybody in good spirits. Among the skills he taught the Continental Army was how to use bayonets. Most American soldiers had been using them to roast meat over the fire!

Although Von Steuben spoke little English, he soon taught Washington's troops how to march. He ordered each soldier to put his left hand on the shoulder of the man in front of him. Then, Von Steuben called out in his German accent: "Forward march! One, Two, Three, Four!"

By the spring of 1778, the army at Valley Forge was more hopeful. A New Jersey soldier observed:

❝The army grows stronger every day. The troops are instructed in a new and so happy a method of

Bernardo de Gálvez: Champion of the Patriot Cause

Bernardo de Gálvez was born in Spain in 1746, the son of an ancient noble family. In 1777, he was appointed governor of Spanish Louisiana. At the time, Spain was officially neutral in the war between Britain and its colonies. But Gálvez favored the Patriots and did whatever he could to help them.

At first, Gálvez acted secretly. From New Orleans, he sent medicine, cloth, muskets, and gunpowder up the Mississippi and Ohio rivers to Fort Pitt and other western outposts. George Rogers Clark used Gálvez's gunpowder to take Vincennes. (See page 234.)

In 1779, Spain entered the war against Britain, and Gálvez joined the fight openly. Leading Spanish troops, he captured British forts along the Mississippi and the Gulf of Mexico. He also drove the British out of West Florida. His actions tied up thousands of British soldiers, keeping them from joining British efforts against the Americans.

After the Revolution, the United States government thanked Gálvez. Bernardo de Gálvez was never an American citizen. But his generous support for the Patriot cause earned him the gratitude of Americans and caused them to honor him as one of their own. In Texas, the city and bay of Galveston were named for this Spanish hero of the American Revolution.

1. Why were Americans grateful to Bernardo de Gálvez?

2. **Evaluating Information** Do you think Bernardo de Gálvez took risks in helping the Americans? Explain.

marching that they will soon be able to advance with the utmost regularity, even without music and on the roughest grounds. "

While soldiers drilled, Washington and his staff planned new campaigns against the British.

SECTION 3 REVIEW

1. **Locate:** (a) New York, (b) Delaware River, (c) Princeton, (d) Albany, (e) Brandywine, (f) Saratoga, (g) Valley Forge.

2. **Identify:** (a) Battle of Long Island, (b) Nathan Hale, (c) Battle of Trenton, (d) John Burgoyne, (e) Battle of Saratoga, (f) Marquis de Lafayette, (g) Thaddeus Kosciusko, (h) Bernardo de Gálvez, (i) Friedrich von Steuben.

3. **Define:** cavalry.

4. What were three results of the Battle of Saratoga?

5. How did France become a supporter of the Patriot cause?

6. **Analyzing Ideas** Why do you think that people from other nations, such as Lafayette, Pulaski, and Gálvez, worked for the American cause?

4 Other Battlefronts

FIND OUT

◆ What role did Native Americans play in the American Revolution?

◆ What battles did Americans win in the West and at sea?

◆ How did African Americans and women contribute to the war?

◆ VOCABULARY neutral

Flying Crow, a Seneca chief, looked sternly at the British officers seated before him. "If you are so strong, Brother, and they but a weak Boy, why ask our assistance?"

Like many other Native American leaders, Flying Crow did not want to become involved in a war between the "weak Boy" —the United States—and Britain. But Native Americans were not able to avoid the struggle. The Revolution was fought not only in the East, but on the western frontier, often on Indian lands. It was also fought at sea.

Fighting on the Frontier

During the Revolution, white settlers continued to push west of the Appalachians. In Kentucky, they named a new settlement Lexington, after the first battle of the Revolution. They called another Louisville, after the American ally, King Louis XVI of France. As settlers moved west, they clashed with Native Americans, whose lands they were invading.

Native Americans choose sides. When the Revolution began, most Indians tried to stay **neutral,** or not fight for either side. "It is a family affair," said an Iroquois chief. He told whites that he preferred "to sit still and see you fight it out."

But as the war spread, Indians were drawn into the struggle on one side or the

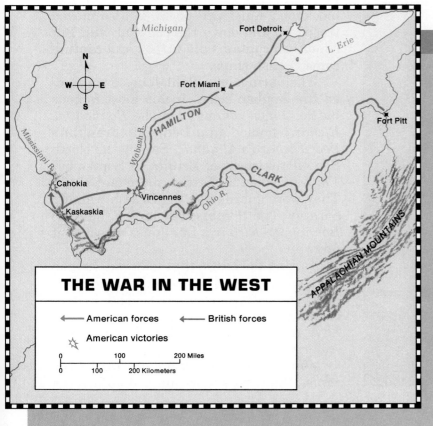

THE WAR IN THE WEST

← American forces   ← British forces

☆ American victories

0   100   200 Miles
0   100   200 Kilometers

MAP STUDY

American and British forces fought for control of lands west of the Appalachian Mountains in 1778 and 1779.

1. *Along what river did Clark's men travel after setting out from Fort Pitt?*
2. *What British forts did Clark capture?*
3. *Applying Information Why was control of lands west of the Appalachians important to Americans?*

other. The Iroquois nations were divided, although most helped the British. In Massachusetts, the Algonquins supported the Patriots. West of the Appalachians, many Indians joined the British to protect their lands from American settlers.

In Tennessee, most Cherokees stayed neutral at first or favored the Patriots. Nancy Ward, a Cherokee leader, warned American settlers of a raid planned by a small group of Cherokees. Settlers responded by attacking all the Cherokees.

George Rogers Clark *When George Rogers Clark and his tiny band of soldiers reached Vincennes, they were exhausted and had been without food for two days. But the British commander had no way of knowing this and surrendered the fort to the Americans.* **Geography** *How did Clark use the geography of the area around Vincennes to surprise the British?*

Feeling betrayed, the Cherokees joined the British.

Victories in the West. In 1778, George Rogers Clark led Virginia frontiersmen against the British in the Ohio Valley. With the help of Miami Indians, Clark captured British forts at Kaskaskia and Cahokia. (See the map on page 233.)

Next, Clark plotted to take Vincennes. Because British forces there outnumbered his own, he planned a surprise attack. During the winter, he marched 150 miles through heavy rains, swamps, and icy rivers. When Clark's small band reached the fort, they spread out through the woods to make their numbers appear greater than they really were. The strategy worked. The British commander thought it was useless to fight so many Americans. He surrendered Vincennes in February 1779.

Fighting on the High Seas

The Americans could do little to fight the powerful British navy. The British fleet blockaded American ports. It also moved troops up and down the coast at will. But American captains did attack and capture some British ships.

The daring John Paul Jones even raided the English coast. In his most famous battle, Jones commanded the *Bonhomme Richard,* named after Benjamin Franklin's *Poor Richard's Almanac.* Sailing the North Sea off the coast of Britain in September 1779, he spied 39 British merchant ships. They were guarded by the British warship *Serapis.* The *Serapis* was larger than the *Bonhomme Richard,* but Jones attacked it anyway.

During the battle that followed, British cannonballs ripped through the *Bonhomme Richard,* setting it on fire. The British commander called on Jones to surrender. "I have not yet begun to fight!" replied the American captain.

Jones sailed his ship close to the *Serapis.* American sailors jumped aboard the enemy ship and defeated the British in hand-to-hand combat. The victory made Jones a hero.

African Americans Join the Effort

When the Revolution began, the Continental Congress refused to let slaves or free blacks join the army. The British, on the other hand, offered freedom to any male slave who served the king. Thousands of slaves joined the British. In response, Washington allowed free blacks to join the Continental Army.

Comrades in arms. More than 5,000 African Americans took part in the fighting. At least seven blacks stood with the minutemen at Lexington and Concord. Peter Salem, a free black, was a hero at the Battle of Bunker Hill. Some free blacks and slaves formed black regiments. Others served in white regiments as drummers, fifers, spies, and guides. Slaves hoped to win freedom by serving in the Continental Army.

White soldiers recognized the courage of their black comrades. An eyewitness told this story of bravery:

> ❝*Three times in succession,* [African American soldiers] were attacked . . . by well-disciplined and veteran [British] troops, and *three times* did they successfully repel the assault, and thus preserve our army from capture.❞

Are not all men created equal? Black Patriots hoped that the Revolution would bring an end to slavery. After all, did not the Declaration of Independence proclaim that "all men are created equal"? Some white Americans supported the idea of freedom for slaves. James Otis wrote that "the colonists are by the law of nature free born, as indeed all men are, white or black."

By the 1770s, slavery was declining in the North, where a number of free blacks lived. During the Revolution, several states

Peter Williams *Americans performed many heroic acts, large and small, during the Revolution. New York merchant and preacher Peter Williams, shown here, risked his life to save an outspoken Patriot clergyman from British officers.* **Citizenship** *What British action prompted Washington to allow free blacks to serve in the Continental Army?*

moved to end slavery, including Vermont, Massachusetts, New Hampshire, and Pennsylvania. Other states debated the issue.

Women in the War

Women contributed greatly to the American cause. When men left the farms to fight, women took over their work. Women planted and harvested the crops that fed the Continental Army. They also made guns and other weapons. One woman, known as "Handy Betsy the Blacksmith," was famous for supplying cannons and guns to the army.

Women made shoes and wove cloth for blankets and uniforms. Betsy Ross of Philadelphia sewed flags for Washington's army. Legend claims that Washington asked

"Molly Pitcher" at the Cannon *Some American women went to war with their husbands. This print shows Mary Ludwig Hays taking her fallen husband's place at a Patriot cannon during the Battle of Monmouth.* **American Traditions** *How else did women help the Patriot cause?*

Ross to make the first American flag of stars and stripes. But the story cannot be proved.

Many women also joined their soldier-husbands at the front. There, they washed clothes, cooked, and cared for the wounded. Martha Washington joined her husband whenever she could.

A few women took part in battle. During the Battle of Monmouth in 1778, Mary Ludwig Hays carried water to her husband and other soldiers. The soldiers called her "Moll of the Pitcher," or Molly Pitcher. When her husband was wounded, she took his place, loading and firing a cannon. Deborah Sampson of Massachusetts dressed as a man and fought in several battles. Later, she wrote about her life in the army.

UP CLOSE

A Young Girl's War

Most colonists were not involved in the actual fighting of the Revolution. For them, daily life went on much as it had before. But when war swirled through an area, no one escaped its effects.

For 16-year-old Sally Wister of Philadelphia, the war brought both excitement and fear. In 1777, Sally and her family fled as the British approached Philadelphia. The Wisters were Quakers and did not believe in war. But they favored the Patriot cause, so they settled in a country house behind American lines, about 15 miles outside Philadelphia.

Headquarters for Patriots. One autumn day, two Patriot officers rode up to the house to warn the Wisters of British troops nearby. "About seven o'clock we heard a great noise," Sally reported in her diary.

    " To the door we all went. A large number of waggons, with about three hundred of the Philadelphia Militia [were outside]. They begged for drink, and several pushed into the house. **"**

Even though the men were Patriots, Sally rushed out the back door, "all in a shake with fear; but after a while, seeing the officers appear gentlemanly . . . my fears were in some measure dispelled, tho' my teeth rattled, and my hand shook like an aspen leaf."

For a time, Patriot General William Smallwood and his officers used the Wister home as their headquarters. "How new is our situation!" Sally wrote. "I feel in good spirits, though surrounded by an Army, the house full of officers, the yard alive with soldiers—very peaceable sort of men, tho'."

Many Patriot officers came from other colonies. Sally "took great delight in teasing" two Virginians about their strange accents. They, in turn, talked to her of life at home and told her "how good turkey hash and fryed hominy is."

Handsome Major Stoddert. Sally's favorite soldier was Major William Stoddert, a handsome young man from Maryland. But the 19-year-old officer was "vastly bashful" at first and said little to her except "Good morning," and "Your servant, madam."

One night, Major Stoddert stood by the dining room table, holding a candle so that General Smallwood could read his newspaper. Sally managed to strike up a conversation. "We talked and laughed for an hour. He is very clever, amiable, and polite. He has the softest voice, never pronounces the *R* at all."

Before long, the militia had to march on. Major Stoddert went with them. "Goodbye, Miss Sally," he said, in a voice so "very low" that Sally guessed he was sorry to leave her. In the next weeks, the Wisters heard "the beating of the distant drum" but saw no fighting.

A month later, Major Stoddert returned. He could "scarcely walk," reported Sally, and "looked pale, thin, and dejected." He had caught a fever. The Wisters looked after him until he recovered, and then he was off to war once more. Sally never saw him again.

Home again. Sally Wister's experience of war was like that of many Americans. Armies marched and drilled around them.

The Home Front *Most Americans did not take part in the actual fighting of the Revolution. But they did whatever they could to support the Patriot cause. Here, a young Quaker woman gives news of British troop movements to one of General Washington's aides.* **American Traditions** *In what other ways could the home front aid the Continental Army?*

Musket and cannon fire sounded in the distance. Then life returned to normal. By mid-1778, the British had left Philadelphia, and Sally Wister returned to city life and "the rattling of carriages over the streets." By then, the field of battle had shifted from the Middle States to the South. ◆

<hr>

SECTION 4 REVIEW

1. **Locate:** (a) Kaskaskia, (b) Cahokia, (c) Vincennes.
2. **Identify:** (a) Nancy Ward, (b) George Rogers Clark, (c) John Paul Jones, (d) Peter Salem, (e) Mary Ludwig Hays, (f) Deborah Sampson.
3. **Define:** neutral.
4. Why did Native Americans on the western frontier help the British?
5. Why did many African Americans join the Continental Army?
6. **Linking Past and Present** Imagine that you are living in a country at war today. Do you think that your experience of war would be similar to that of Sally Wister during the American Revolution? Explain.

5 The World Turned Upside Down

FIND OUT

◆ Why did the fighting shift to the South?

◆ Why did the British surrender at Yorktown?

◆ What were the terms of the Treaty of Paris?

◆ VOCABULARY ratify

On October 7, 1780, 16-year-old Thomas Young set out with 900 other rebels up King's Mountain in South Carolina. Although most were barefoot, they moved quickly up the wooded hillside, shouldering their old muskets. The band of Patriots was determined to capture the mountain from the thousand Loyalists dug in at the top.

Whooping and shouting, Young and his fellow Patriots ran from tree to tree, dodging bullets and firing rapidly. Suddenly, Thomas heard the cry "Colonel Williams is shot!"

“I ran to his assistance for I loved him as a father. He had ever been kind to me and almost always carried a cake in his pocket for me and his little son Joseph. They . . . sprinkled some water in his face. He revived, and his first words were, 'For God's sake boys, don't give up the hill!' . . . I left him in the arms of his son Daniel, and returned to the field to avenge his fate.”

The Patriots captured King's Mountain. The victory boosted morale after a string of Patriot defeats in the South.

War in the South

Scattered fighting had taken place in the South since the start of the Revolution. In February 1776, North Carolina Patriots defeated a Loyalist army at the **Battle of Moore's Creek Bridge.** This battle is sometimes called the Lexington and Concord of the South.

After France entered the war, the British decided to shift their efforts to the South. They counted on Loyalists there to support them. The Patriots suffered one blow after another. In December 1778, the British seized Savannah, Georgia. They later took Charleston, South Carolina. "I have almost ceased to hope," wrote Washington when he learned of the losses.

An American traitor. In the summer of 1780, Washington received more bad news. Benedict Arnold, one of his best generals, had joined the British. Arnold had fought bravely in many battles. One soldier recalled that Arnold always led—never followed—his men into battle. "It was 'Come on, boys!' not 'Go on, boys!' He didn't care for nothin'. He'd ride right in."

Washington had made Arnold the commander of the key fort at West Point. But Arnold was not satisfied. He felt that he had not received credit for his victories. He also needed money. So he secretly offered to turn over West Point to the British. By chance, American soldiers captured the messenger carrying Arnold's offer. Although Arnold escaped to join the British, West Point was saved.

The Patriots rally. The victory at King's Mountain in October 1780 helped rally Patriots to the cause. Slowly, the tide turned in their favor.

Patriots organized hit-and-run attacks on the British. Francis Marion of South Carolina led a small band of men who slept by day and traveled by night. Marion was known as the Swamp Fox. He appeared suddenly out of the swamps, attacked the British, and then retreated into the swamps. His attacks kept the British off balance. (□ See "Marion's Men" on page 656.)

Two American generals, Daniel Morgan and Nathanael Greene, led the Patriots to victory in the South. Morgan, a Virginian, was a big, bull-necked man. His leather-shirted company of riflemen had served well in the Battle of Saratoga. In January 1781, he defeated a British army at the **Battle of Cowpens** in South Carolina.

General Greene used the same hit-and-run tactics as Marion. Even though Greene won few outright victories, his sniping wore down the British. So did attacks by fierce bands of backcountry Patriots, who struck frequently and without warning. The harassed British general, Charles Cornwallis, decided to take his army north into Virginia.

Victory at Last

Cornwallis moved across Virginia in the spring of 1781. He sent Loyalist troops to attack Charlottesville, where the Virginia legislature was meeting. The Loyalists almost captured the lawmakers, including Virginia's governor, Thomas Jefferson.

American troops under the Marquis de Lafayette fought back. Although Lafayette had only a small force, he launched many raids against the British. When fresh troops arrived to help the Americans, Cornwallis retreated toward the coast. He camped at Yorktown, on a peninsula that juts into the Chesapeake Bay.

Cornwallis felt safe at Yorktown, where the British navy could supply his troops. Imagine his dismay when a French fleet

A Victory at Cowpens
Americans under General Daniel Morgan's command dealt the British a "very unexpected and severe blow" at Cowpens, in South Carolina. This painting of the Battle of Cowpens is by William Ranney, well-known for his scenes of the Revolution. **Citizenship** *Why did the British decide to shift their efforts to the South?*

under Admiral de Grasse sailed into the bay. The French drove the British ships out of the Chesapeake Bay. With the French fleet in control of the bay, Cornwallis was cut off not only from his supplies but from his escape route by sea.

Meantime, French troops under the Comte de Rochambeau (roh shahm BOH) had landed in Rhode Island. They joined General Washington in New York. Washington saw his chance to strike. He rushed his combined army into Virginia, trapping Cornwallis.

Cornwallis held out for three weeks before he surrendered his army on October 17, 1781. Two days later, the defeated British soldiers turned their muskets over to the Americans. During the ceremony, the British army band played the tune "The World Turned Upside Down."

Making Peace

Americans rejoiced at the surrender of Cornwallis. But in London, the news shocked the British. "It is all over," cried the British prime minister, Lord North. Pressured by Parliament, he agreed to peace talks with the Americans.

Peace talks began in Paris in 1782. Congress sent Benjamin Franklin and John Adams, along with John Jay of New York and Henry Laurens of South Carolina, to work out a treaty. Because Britain was eager to end the war, the Americans achieved most of what they wanted.

Under the **Treaty of Paris,** Britain recognized the United States as an independent nation. The borders of the new nation extended from the Atlantic Ocean to the Mississippi River. The southern border stopped at Florida, which belonged to Spain again.

For their part, the Americans agreed to ask state legislatures to pay Loyalists for the property they had lost in the war. In the end, however, most state legislatures ignored Loyalist claims. On April 15, 1783, Congress ratified, or approved, the Treaty of Paris. It was eight years to the month since the opening shots were fired at Lexington and Concord.

MAP STUDY

The final battles of the Revolution were fought in the South. The Americans suffered a string of defeats between 1778 and 1780, but the tide slowly turned. Finally, trapped at Yorktown in 1781, the British surrendered.

1. *Name three British victories that took place in the South.*
2. *(a) Who commanded American troops at Yorktown? (b) Who commanded British troops?*
3. **Analyzing Information** *How did the French fleet contribute to the American victory at Yorktown?*

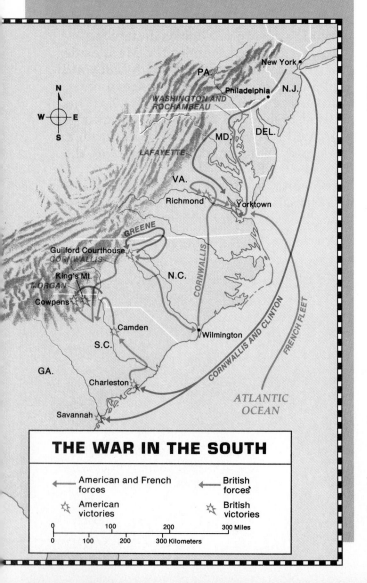

THE WAR IN THE SOUTH

← American and French forces
← British forces
☆ American victories
☆ British victories

0 100 200 300 Miles
0 100 200 300 Kilometers

Washington's Farewell

Americans had won a war against a much more powerful nation. Money, arms, and soldiers from France helped them win major battles. But the strength and courage of leaders like Washington held the Patriots together.

On December 4, 1783, General Washington bid farewell to his officers at Fraunces Tavern in New York City. Colonel Benjamin Tallmadge recalled the event:

> ❝Such a scene of sorrow and weeping I had never before witnessed. . . . The simple thought that we were then about to part from the man who had conducted us through a long and bloody war, and under whose conduct the glory and independence of our country had been achieved, and that we should see his face no more in this world, seemed to me utterly [unbearable].❞

All along Washington's route home to Mount Vernon, Virginia, crowds greeted the hero of American independence. The new nation still faced difficult tests, however. Americans would call on Washington to lead them again.

SECTION 5 REVIEW

1. **Locate:** (a) Savannah, (b) Charleston, (c) King's Mountain, (d) Cowpens, (e) Yorktown.
2. **Identify:** (a) Battle of Moore's Creek Bridge, (b) Benedict Arnold, (c) Francis Marion, (d) Daniel Morgan, (e) Nathanael Greene, (f) Admiral de Grasse, (g) Comte de Rochambeau, (h) Treaty of Paris.
3. **Define:** ratify.
4. Why did the British move their forces to the South in 1778?
5. Why was Cornwallis forced to surrender at Yorktown?
6. What were the boundaries of the United States in 1783?

MAP STUDY

Under the Treaty of Paris of 1783, Britain recognized the United States as an independent nation.
1. What nation held land west of the new United States?
2. What natural feature formed the western border of the United States?
3. **Comparing** Compare this map with the map on page 198. (a) According to the maps, what was the major difference between North America in 1783 and 1763? (b) Name one way that North America was the same in 1783 and 1763.

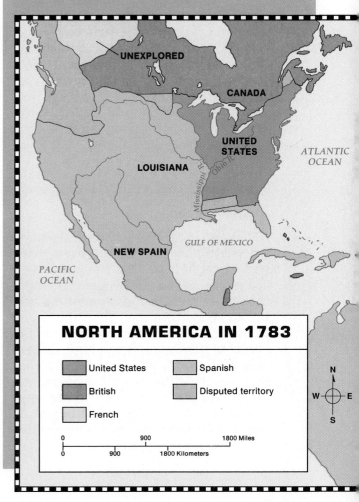

NORTH AMERICA IN 1783

- United States
- British
- French
- Spanish
- Disputed territory

7. **Analyzing Ideas** Why was "The World Turned Upside Down" a fitting tune to be played at the British surrender at Yorktown?

As you learned in Skill Lesson 5 (page 146), people usually have a reason for writing about events or developments in which they are involved. As a result, a primary source, or firsthand account, reflects the author's point of view. Two people writing about the same subject can have different points of view.

The letters below were written by Abigail and John Adams. During the Revolution, John Adams was away from home for long periods. His wife, Abigail, wrote to him often. She kept him informed about their children and their farm, which she kept going. When the Continental Congress was preparing the Declaration of Independence, she wrote her husband the first letter reprinted below. The second letter is John Adams's reply to his wife.

Read the letters. Then, compare the two points of view.

1 **Study the contents of each source.** (a) What does Abigail Adams want her husband to do? (b) What is John Adams's response to her request? (c) Who does John Adams mean when he says "another tribe, more numerous and powerful than all the rest"?

2 **Compare the points of view.** (a) What does Abigail Adams think men are like? (b) Does John Adams agree with his wife's view of men? Explain.

3 **Evaluate the usefulness of the sources.** (a) What do these letters tell you about American society in 1776? (b) Do you think these letters are a reliable source of information? Explain.

Abigail Adams wrote:

❝I long to hear that you have declared independence. And by the way, in the new code of laws that I suppose you will make, I wish you would remember the ladies and be more generous and favorable to them than your ancestors. Do not put such unlimited power in the hands of husbands. Remember, all men would be tyrants if they could. If particular care and attention is not paid to the ladies, we are determined to stir up a rebellion and will not regard ourselves as bound by any laws in which we have had no voice or representation.❞

John Adams replied:

❝As to your extraordinary code of laws, I can't help laughing. We have been told that our struggle has loosened the bonds of government everywhere, that children and apprentices were disobedient, that schools and colleges had grown turbulent, that Indians slighted their guardians and negroes grow insolent to their masters. But your letter was the first hint that another tribe, more numerous and powerful than all the rest, had grown discontented.

Depend upon it, we know better than to repeal our masculine systems. Although they are in full force, you know they are little more than theory. . . . In practice, you know, we are the subjects. We have only the title of masters, and rather than give this up, which would subject us completely to the power of the petticoat, I hope General Washington and all our brave heroes would fight.❞

CHAPTER 8 STUDY GUIDE

Use the Section Reviews and this Study Guide to review chapter content.

Main Ideas

The main ideas in each section of this chapter are summarized below.

SECTION 1 ■ Early Battles

- The Second Continental Congress asked King George III to repeal the Intolerable Acts.
- When the American Revolution began, Americans faced an uphill struggle.
- At Bunker Hill, Americans showed that they would defend their liberties.

SECTION 2 ■ Independence Declared

- The Declaration of Independence set out the principles of the United States and explained why the colonists had broken away from Britain.
- The nation was divided between Patriots and Loyalists.

SECTION 3 ■ Desperate Days

- In mid-1776, the fighting shifted from New England to the Middle States.
- The American victory at Saratoga convinced France to aid the United States.

SECTION 4 ■ Other Battlefronts

- Fierce fighting took place on the western frontier as well as at sea.
- Native Americans, African Americans, and women helped the American war effort.

SECTION 5 ■ The World Turned Upside Down

- After 1778, Britain focused its efforts on winning control of the South.
- In 1781, Cornwallis surrendered to Washington at Yorktown.
- In the peace treaty, Britain recognized the independence of the United States.

Key People and Terms

Refer to the Identify and Define questions in the Section Reviews on pages 224, 227, 232, 238, and 241. Use each person, term, and vocabulary word in a complete sentence. When possible, make connections between the people and terms by using more than one person or term in each sentence.

Time Line

1. Make a chart of events in time order. The chart will have two headings: Date, Event. Fill in the chart, using the events on the time line. Add the following events from the chapter: Battle of Bunker Hill; *Common Sense* is published; Howe lands on Long Island; Washington's troops winter in Valley Forge. (Refer to the chapter for the dates.)
2. Describe a cause-and-effect relationship between at least two events on your chart.

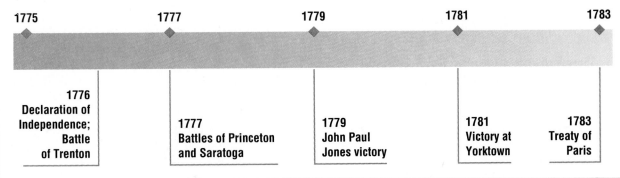

1775	1777	1779	1781	1783
1776 Declaration of Independence; Battle of Trenton	**1777** Battles of Princeton and Saratoga	**1779** John Paul Jones victory	**1781** Victory at Yorktown	**1783** Treaty of Paris

Understanding Vocabulary

Match each term at left with the correct definition at right.

1. blockade
2. traitor
3. cavalry
4. neutral
5. ratify

   a. not fighting for either side in a war
   b. someone who betrays his or her country
   c. shutting off of a port to keep supplies from moving in or out
   d. approve
   e. troops on horseback

Reviewing the Main Ideas

1. (a) Why did John Adams think Washington was a good choice for commander of the Continental Army? (b) What problems did George Washington face in 1775?
2. How did the pamphlet *Common Sense* influence colonists?
3. (a) Why was the winter of 1777–1778 a bad time for the Americans? (b) Describe conditions at Valley Forge.
4. Why was the Battle of Saratoga a turning point in the American Revolution?
5. How did each of the following people help the Patriot cause: (a) Nancy Ward, (b) George Rogers Clark, (c) Mary Ludwig Hays?
6. Why did African Americans find hope in the Declaration of Independence?
7. How did France help the Americans win the Battle of Yorktown?
8. Describe the major points of the Treaty of Paris of 1783.

Thinking Critically

1. **Defending a Position** Loyalists believed that colonists were betraying their country by declaring independence. Do you agree? Explain.
2. **Evaluating Information** What qualities do you think the commander of the Continental Army needed to succeed?

3. **Drawing Conclusions** How do you think the British blockade affected Americans?
4. **Linking Past and Present** Review the Declaration of Independence printed on pages 749–752. (a) What basic rights does the Declaration guarantee? (b) Do Americans today enjoy these rights? Explain.

Applying Your Skills

1. **Comparing Points of View** Review the discussion of the Olive Branch Petition on pages 221 and 224. (a) What was the subject of the Olive Branch Petition? (b) How do you think colonists viewed the petition? (c) How did King George III respond to the petition? (d) How might each side defend its point of view?
2. **Analyzing a Quotation** Reread the quotation from *The Crisis* on page 228. (a) What did Paine mean by the words, "These are the times that try men's souls"? (b) What are "sunshine patriots"? (c) What do you think Washington's soldiers thought of Paine's words?
3. **Outlining** Review the outlining skill you learned on page 32. Then, prepare an outline of Sections 1 and 2 on pages 220–227. Using your outline, write a summary of what happened during the early years of the American Revolution.

Thinking About Geography

Match the letters on the map with the places listed below.

1. Bunker Hill
2. Trenton
3. Saratoga
4. Vincennes
5. Cowpens
6. Savannah
7. Yorktown

Movement Why was British control of the Chesapeake Bay important to Cornwallis at Yorktown?

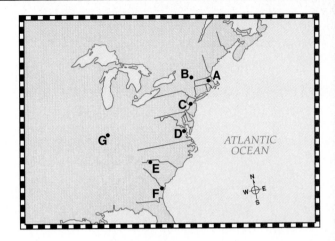

ATLANTIC OCEAN

History Writer's Workshop

Arranging Information to Show Cause and Effect

A cause is an event that produces an effect, another event. Often, that effect becomes a cause. It produces still another event. To show this chain reaction, you would arrange supporting information in order of cause and effect.

Look at the following topic sentence. *Many African Americans joined the Continental Army.* In a paragraph, you might arrange in cause-and-effect order the events leading to African Americans joining the Continental Army. The following diagram of events shows the chain reaction of cause and effect.

(first event)	Declaration of Independence statement that "all men are created equal"

causes

(second event)	Slaves to believe they will be freed if Americans win Revolution

causes

(third event)	African Americans to join Continental Army

Transitions to show cause and effect include *as a result, because, therefore, thus,* and *so.*

Practice Use the diagram to write detail sentences that support the topic sentence. (See page 235 for information.)

Writing to Learn

1. Write a short biography of a lesser-known hero of the American Revolution, such as Laura Wolcott, Salem Poor, Peter Francisco, or Sybil Ludington. Before writing, research the person's accomplishments. Begin your biography with a topic sentence evaluating the person's influence. Support your evaluation with details arranged in time order. Revise your biography for accuracy. Then, proofread and make a final copy. Publish your biography in a collection with others from your class.

2. Imagine that you are a neutral reporter during the American Revolution. Write an article predicting who will win the war. Before writing, list the strengths and weaknesses of the Americans and the British. In your first draft, compose a topic sentence that makes your prediction clear. Support it with details comparing the two sides. Revise for logical organization and clear transitions. Then, proofread and make a final copy. Publish your article in a class newspaper.

Celebrating a New Plan of Government *Americans celebrated ratification of the Constitution with huge parades and other festivities. People from all walks of life took part. The banner shown here was carried by the Society of Pewterers, makers of pots and pans.* **Citizenship** *The United States is still governed under the Constitution that was adopted in 1788. What does that tell you about the document?*

CHAPTER

9

Creating a Republic (1776–1790)

The Big Picture

When the United States declared independence in 1776, Americans talked about *these* United States, not *the* United States. They saw the 13 states as individual nations that had joined in a loose alliance.

The Continental Congress drew up a government for *these* United States. Under that government, the states had more power than the national government. Nearly 10 years and many crises later, Americans realized that the country needed a stronger central government. In 1787, delegates met to draw up a new constitution.

Jim Davidson

Of Special Interest

Focus On

◆ Why did the Articles of Confederation give so little power to the national government?
◆ What problems did the United States face?
◆ What compromises were worked out at the Constitutional Convention?
◆ What framework of government did the Constitution set up?
◆ Why was the Bill of Rights added to the Constitution?

"The American war is over: but this is far from being the case with the American revolution. On the contrary, nothing but the first act of the great drama is closed. It remains yet to establish and perfect our new forms of government."

Those words, spoken by Dr. Benjamin Rush in January 1787, reflected the feelings of many Americans in the years after the Revolution. Like Dr. Rush, they knew that winning the war against Britain had been only a beginning.

Rush was a respected doctor. In Philadelphia, he set up the nation's first free medical clinic. At the University of Pennsylvania, he taught students the latest medical theories.

Rush was also an outspoken Patriot. In 1775, he urged Thomas Paine to write a pamphlet in favor of independence and suggested the title *Common Sense*. As a member of the Continental Congress, Rush signed the Declaration of Independence. And with his fellow Patriots, he celebrated the signing of the Treaty of Paris in 1783.

By 1787, however, Rush was worried about the health of the nation. Could the United States succeed in its bold experiment at self-government? During the war, Americans had set up their first government. Rush believed that the government was too weak to hold the 13 states together. Others agreed. In May 1787, a special convention met in Philadelphia. There, the curtain rose on the next act of the American Revolution.

1 A Confederation of States

FIND OUT

◆ What kinds of government did the states set up?

◆ How did the Articles of Confederation limit the power of Congress?

◆ How did Daniel Boone help to open western lands to settlers?

◆ **VOCABULARY** constitution, execute, bill of rights

One afternoon in January 1776, a Patriot mob aimed a cannon at the home of John Wentworth, governor of New Hampshire. Wentworth, a Loyalist, did not wait to find out what the mob would do. Moving quickly, he fled to safety in a nearby British fort.

As war approached, royal officials throughout the colonies fled. Colonists were suddenly without a government. "The sudden and abrupt departure of our late Governor," announced the New Hampshire assembly, "creates the necessity of establishing a [new] form of government."

In May 1776, the Continental Congress asked each colony to set up a government to protect "the lives, liberties, and properties" of its citizens. Two months later, in July 1776, the Congress set about the more difficult task of organizing a new national government.

State Constitutions

During the Revolution, most states wrote their own constitutions. A **constitution** is a document that sets out the laws and principles of a government. States wanted written constitutions for two reasons. First, a written constitution would spell out the rights of all citizens. Second, it would set limits on the power of government.

In writing their constitutions, states often followed the basic form of their old colonial charters. These, in turn, were based on English law. Some states simply kept the charters but struck out all refer-

Exeter, New Hampshire *Most American towns, like Exeter, New Hampshire, shown here, had their own way of doing things in the late 1700s. A strong local government handled daily problems. Larger problems were handled by the state. Few people saw any reason to give up control to a national government.* **Linking Past and Present** *Do you think towns like Exeter could manage today without help from the national government? Explain.*

ences to the king. Others wrote new constitutions, which voters approved.

Dividing power. Colonists felt that the British government had abused its power. They wanted to prevent similar abuses in the future. So they divided the power of state governments between a legislature and an executive.

Every state had a legislature that passed laws. Lawmakers were elected by voters. Power within the legislature was divided between an upper house, called a senate, and a lower house. All states except Pennsylvania had a governor, who executed, or carried out, the laws.

Protecting freedoms. Virginia further limited the power of government by including a bill of rights in its constitution. A bill of rights lists freedoms the government promises to protect. In Virginia, the bill of rights protected freedom of speech, freedom of religion, and freedom of the press. Citizens also had the right to a trial by jury. Other states followed Virginia's example and included bills of rights in their own constitutions.

Expanding the right to vote. Under state constitutions, more people had the right to vote than in colonial times. To vote, a citizen had to be male and over age 21. He had to own a certain amount of property or pay a certain amount of taxes. For a time, some women in New Jersey could vote. In a few states, free black men could vote. But slaves could not vote in any state.

Forming a National Government

While the states formed 13 separate governments, the Continental Congress drafted a plan for the nation as a whole. Without a well-organized national government, many Americans felt, the Patriot cause could not succeed.

The first national constitution. Writing a constitution that all the states would approve was difficult. In 1776, few Americans thought of themselves as citizens of one nation. Instead, they felt loyal to their

Women at the Polls *Even after the Revolution, voting rights were limited. For a time, New Jersey let women vote, but this practice ended in 1807, only 17 years after it began. This picture by Howard Pyle shows New Jersey women at the polls.* **Citizenship** *What other people were denied the right to vote?*

own states. "Virginia, Sir, is my country," said Thomas Jefferson. "Massachusetts is our country," John Adams told a friend.

The states were unwilling to turn over much power to the national government. They were not fighting Britain in order to be ruled by another strong power. In 1777, after much debate on this and other issues, the Continental Congress completed the first American constitution, known as the **Articles of Confederation.**

The Articles of Confederation created a "firm league of friendship" among the 13 states. The states agreed to send delegates to a Confederation Congress. Each state had one vote in Congress. But the Articles limited the power of Congress by giving the states final authority over all decisions.

Congress could pass laws, but at least 9 of the 13 states had to approve a law before it went into effect. Congress could not regulate trade between states or even between states and foreign countries. Nor could it pass any laws regarding taxes. To raise money, Congress had to ask the states for it. And no state could be forced to contribute.

Under the Articles, Congress could declare war, appoint military officers, and coin money. Congress was also responsible for foreign affairs. But these powers were few compared to those of the states.

A loose alliance. The Articles created a loose alliance among the 13 states. The national government was weak. The Articles did not provide for a president to carry out laws. It was up to the states to enforce laws passed by Congress.

Despite these weaknesses, the Articles might have worked if the states had been able to agree about what needed to be done. But many disputes arose. And there was no way of settling them because the Articles did not set up a system of courts. As Noah Webster, a teacher from New England, warned:

❝So long as any individual state has power to defeat the measures of the other twelve, our pretended union is but a name, and our confederation, a cobweb.❞

Disputes Over Western Lands

The first dispute between the states arose even before the Articles of Confederation went into effect. Most states quickly ratified the Articles. Maryland, however, refused to ratify. It would not sign the Articles of Confederation, it said, until all the lands between the Appalachian Mountains and the Mississippi River were turned over to Congress.

Virginia and several other states claimed lands in the West. (See the map at left.) As a small state, Maryland worried that states such as Virginia would become too powerful if they were allowed to keep the western lands. Also, what if Virginia sold its western lands to gain income? Then, Virginia would not need to tax its citizens. What would prevent people and businesses in Maryland from flocking to Virginia to escape taxes?

At first, Virginia and the other "landed" states rejected Maryland's demand. But Thomas Jefferson and other Virginia leaders strongly believed that a national government was needed. So they convinced Virginia lawmakers to give up the state's claims to western lands. Other states followed Virginia's lead. Finally, in

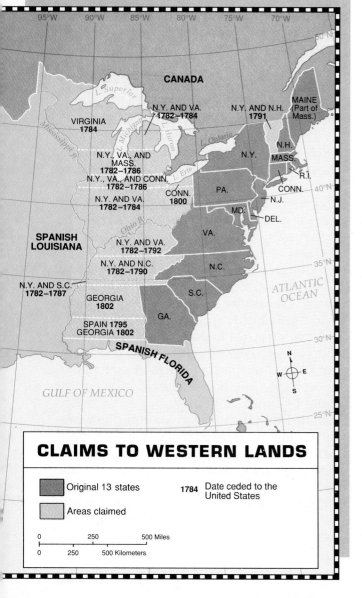

MAP STUDY

By 1783, a number of states claimed lands west of the Appalachians.
1. Which state claimed land directly south of Lake Superior?
2. Which states had no claims to western lands?
3. **Solving Problems** Why did Thomas Jefferson, a Virginian, persuade Virginia to give up its claims to western lands?

CLAIMS TO WESTERN LANDS

- ▓ Original 13 states
- ☐ Areas claimed
- 1784 Date ceded to the United States

0   250   500 Miles
0   250   500 Kilometers

1781, Maryland ratified the Articles of Confederation, and the first American government went into effect.

Through the Cumberland Gap With Daniel Boone

While states debated the issue of western land claims, settlers streamed into those lands. Before and even during the Revolution, hardy pioneers trekked across the Appalachians to hunt deer, bear, and other animals or to trade with Indians. They returned home with tales of the beautiful country beyond the mountains.

Roaming the wilderness. Among the early pioneers was Daniel Boone. In the 1750s, Boone settled his family in a cabin in the Yadkin Valley of North Carolina. From there, he roamed the wilderness. At night, Boone found shelter in a mountain cave. By day, he hunted deer and other animals at salt licks, or natural salt deposits. After several months, Boone would return home with skins to sell. The skin of a male deer, or buck, sold for a dollar. So "buck" became slang for "dollar."

One winter, John Finley, an old friend, visited Boone. The two had served as wagon drivers for General Braddock during the French and Indian War. Finley told fantastic stories about the country to the west, known as Kentucky. In the spring of 1769, Boone, Finley, and four companions set off to explore the western lands.

Following a Cherokee trail, Boone and his party crossed through a steep, rocky opening in the mountains, called the **Cumberland Gap.** Ahead lay Kentucky. And what riches they found there! Deer, elk, and even buffalo came to the salt licks. Grapevines heavy with fruit clung to the trees. Strawberries were so plentiful along the ground that the horses' legs turned bright red from the juice.

Encounter with the Shawnees. Boone and his party traveled cautiously because Indians had rights by treaty to the land. From north of the Ohio River, Shawnees regularly came to hunt in Kentucky. The Cherokees, too, claimed Kentucky as their hunting grounds.

Boone set up camp well back from Indian trails. To hide his tracks, he sometimes walked in a stream, as the Indians did. Or he might swing through the trees on vines. He cooked only at night, when smoke from his fire could not be seen.

One day, Boone and another hunter were trailing an animal through a thicket of tall grass. Suddenly, a party of Shawnees appeared on horseback. The Shawnees took the white men's deerskins, horses, and guns. Captain Will, the Shawnee chief, gave them a friendly warning:

> ❝Now, brothers, go home and stay there. Don't come here any more, for this is the Indians' hunting ground, and all the animals, skins, and furs are ours; and if you are so foolish to venture here again you may be sure the wasps and yellow-jackets will sting you severely.❞

Boone silently vowed to get his horses back. On foot, he trailed the Shawnees. Finally catching up with them, he quietly recovered several horses. Off he rode as fast as possible. A few days later, Captain Will appeared once again. "Steal hoss, ha?" said Captain Will, laughing. He took back the horses and left Boone unharmed. This time Boone did not follow.

Boonesborough. Two years after he left for Kentucky, Boone returned home. His tales of rich land and plentiful game attracted both hunters and farmers. In 1775, as the Revolution began, Boone led a group of settlers through the Cumberland Gap. Aided by dozens of men armed with axes, he cut a trail to the Kentucky River.

Daniel Boone in Kentucky *Of all the pioneers who helped open the frontier to settlement, Daniel Boone was most famous. Here, Boone and his party have just made their way through the Cumberland Gap. Ahead lies the land of Boone's dreams— Kentucky!* **Geography** *What is a mountain gap? Why were mountain gaps important to early pioneers?*

There, the party built the settlement of Boonesborough.

Settlers soon flooded along the trail Boone cut, which became known as the **Wilderness Road.** Once more, Americans pushed their frontiers westward in search of land. But would the young United States be able to bring the new western lands into the Union? The answer to that question was not yet clear. ◆

| SECTION | 1 | REVIEW |

1. **Identify:** (a) Articles of Confederation, (b) Daniel Boone, (c) Cumberland Gap, (d) Wilderness Road.
2. **Define:** (a) constitution, (b) execute, (c) bill of rights.
3. Why did most of the states want written constitutions?
4. Why did the states want a weak national government?
5. **Evaluating Information** (a) What did the incident between Boone and Captain Will show about the Indians? (b) About Boone?

2 Growing Pains

FIND OUT

◆ What problems did the nation face in its early years?

◆ How did the Northwest Ordinance provide for the growth of the United States?

◆ What were the causes and results of Shays' Rebellion?

◆ **VOCABULARY** economic depression

The United States had won independence. But the government of the new nation had no money. It owed millions of dollars but had no way to repay its debts. Robert Morris, superintendent of finance during the Revolution, had worked miracles raising money to buy supplies for Washington's army. By 1783, however, Morris had reached the end of his resources.

Money was only one of many problems the new nation faced after the Revolution. From 1783 to 1787, Americans had good reason to doubt whether their new country could survive.

Serious Problems Under the Articles of Confederation

Under the Articles of Confederation, Congress could ask the states for money. But the states had the right to turn down Congress's request. And they often did.

Troubles with money and trade. During the Revolution, the Continental Congress solved the problem of raising funds by printing paper money. With the crank of a printing press, plain paper was turned into Continental dollars. But without gold or silver to back up the paper money, it had little value. Before long, Americans began to describe any useless thing as "not worth a Continental." (See "Comments From a German Visitor" on page 658.)

As the Continental dollars became worthless, states were printing their own paper money. This caused confusion. How much was a North Carolina dollar worth? Was a Virginia dollar as valuable as a Maryland dollar? Most states refused to accept the money of other states. As a result, trade between states became difficult.

Other troubles. The new nation faced other troubles. Massachusetts, New Hampshire, and New York all claimed Vermont. But under the Articles of Confederation, these states had no way to settle their dispute.

Foreign countries took advantage of the new government's weakness. Britain, for example, refused to withdraw its troops from the Ohio Valley, as it had agreed to do under the Treaty of Paris. Spain, too, challenged the United States. It closed its port in New Orleans to American farmers in the western lands. This was a serious blow to western farmers, who had used the port to ship their products to markets in the East.

GEOGRAPHY AND HISTORY

A Far-sighted Policy for the Western Lands

Settlers in the western lands posed still another problem. The Articles of Confederation said nothing about admitting new states to the United States. Feeling neglected, some settlers in the West took matters into their own hands. At Boonesborough, settlers formed the state of Transylvania. In eastern Tennessee, people set up a government called the State of Franklin and applied for admission to the United States.

Congress realized the desperate need to provide for local governments in the western lands. Thousands of settlers already lived in these lands. And every year, many more headed west to clear land for farms.

To meet the challenge, Congress passed two laws. Both concerned the Northwest

A Rhode Island Bank Note *After the Revolution, each state issued its own money. In the financial confusion that followed, trade between states became difficult. The $3 bill pictured here was issued by Rhode Island in 1780.* **Economics** *Give an example of how your life would be affected if each state issued its own money today.*

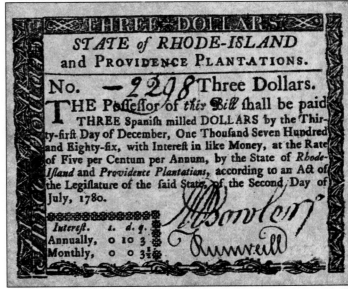

Territory,* lands lying north of the Ohio River and east of the Mississippi. (See the map below.) The principles set out in the two laws were later applied to other areas of settlement.

———

*Americans used the word territory to mean an area of the United States that was not organized into a state.

Townships and sections. The first law, the **Land Ordinance of 1785,** set up a system for settling the Northwest Territory. The law called for the territory to be surveyed and then divided into townships. Each township would have 36 sections. A section was one square mile and contained 640 acres. (See the diagram below.) Congress planned to sell sections to settlers for

MAP STUDY

In the 1780s, Congress set up a system for settling and governing the Northwest Territory.
1. *Which states were carved out of the Northwest Territory?*
2. *(a) What was the size of a township? (b) A section?*
3. **Analyzing Information** *How does the chart of a township show that Congress was concerned about education?*

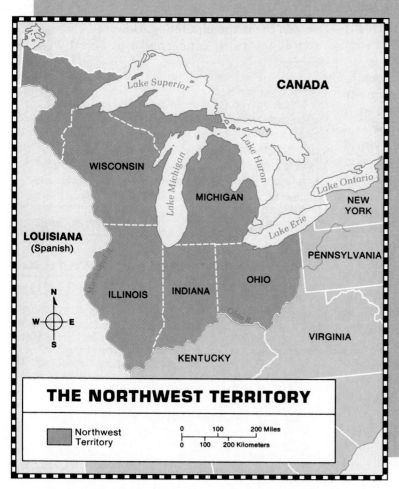

THE NORTHWEST TERRITORY

Northwest Territory

0   100   200 Miles
0   100   200 Kilometers

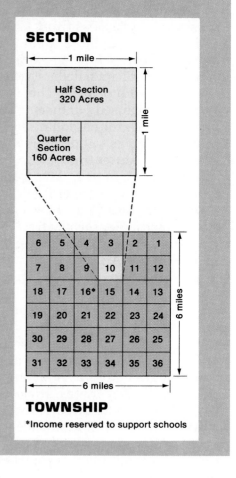

SECTION

Half Section
320 Acres

Quarter
Section
160 Acres

6	5	4	3	2	1
7	8	9	10	11	12
18	17	16*	15	14	13
19	20	21	22	23	24
30	29	28	27	26	25
31	32	33	34	35	36

TOWNSHIP

*Income reserved to support schools

$640 each. One section in every township was set aside to support public schools.

A plan for new states. The second law, passed in 1787, was the **Northwest Ordinance.** It set up a government for the Northwest Territory and outlawed slavery there. It also provided for the vast region to be divided into three to five separate territories in the future.

When a territory had a population of 60,000 free citizens, it could ask Congress to be admitted as a new state. The newly admitted state would be "on an equal footing with the original states in all respects whatsoever."

The Northwest Ordinance was important because it provided a way for new states to be admitted to the United States. It guaranteed that new states would be treated the same as the original 13 states. In time, five states were carved from the Northwest Territory: Ohio, Indiana, Illinois, Michigan, and Wisconsin. ◆

A Farmers' Revolt

After the Revolution, the nation suffered an *economic depression.* An economic depression is a period when business activity slows, prices and wages fall, and unemployment rises.

Hard times for farmers. The depression hit farmers especially hard. During the war, the demand for farm products had been high. Eager to produce more food, farmers borrowed money for land, seed, animals, and tools. Now, as prices for farm goods fell, many farmers could not repay their loans.

In Massachusetts, matters were made even worse when the state raised farmers' taxes. The courts seized the farms of people who could not pay their taxes or loans. Angry farmers protested what they considered unfair treatment.

Rebellion in Massachusetts. In 1786, discontent ignited into rebellion. Daniel Shays, a Massachusetts farmer who had fought at Bunker Hill and Saratoga, was determined to save his debt-ridden farm. Shays gathered a force of nearly 2,000 farmers. The ragged band traveled around the state, attacking courthouses and preventing the sale of property as payment for debts. When they tried to raid a warehouse full of rifles and gunpowder, the alarmed Massachusetts legislature sent the militia to drive them off. **Shays' Rebellion** was over.

Time for action. Shays' Rebellion worried many Americans. They saw it as a sign that the Articles of Confederation did not work. George Washington shared their concern. He felt that a desperate crisis was in store for the nation:

> ❝No day was ever more clouded than the present. . . . I predict the worst consequences from a half-starved, limping government, always moving upon crutches and tottering at every step.❞

Leaders from several states called for a convention to discuss ways of revising the Articles of Confederation. They decided to gather in Philadelphia in May 1787. The action they took when they met, however, went far beyond what many had imagined.

SECTION 2 REVIEW

1. **Locate:** Northwest Territory.
2. **Identify:** (a) Land Ordinance of 1785, (b) Northwest Ordinance, (c) Shays' Rebellion.
3. **Define:** economic depression.
4. List three weaknesses of the Articles of Confederation.
5. (a) What were the terms of the Northwest Ordinance? (b) Why was it important?
6. **Analyzing Ideas** "I like a little rebellion now and then," wrote Thomas Jefferson when he heard about Shays' Rebellion. "The spirit of resistance to government is so valuable on occasion that I wish it to be always kept alive." Do you think Shays' Rebellion was good for the United States? Explain.

3 A Grand Convention

FIND OUT

◆ Why did the Constitutional Convention meet in secret?

◆ How did the delegates settle the question of representation?

◆ What other issues did the Convention resolve?

◆ **VOCABULARY** legislative branch, executive branch, judicial branch, compromise

An air of mystery hung over the Pennsylvania State House in Philadelphia during the summer of 1787. Between May and September, Philadelphians watched curiously as the nation's greatest leaders passed in and out of the building. Eleven years earlier, some of the same men had signed the Declaration of Independence there. What, people asked, was going on now? Susannah Dillwyn wrote her father about the excitement:

❝There is now sitting in this city a grand convention, who are to form some new system of government or mend the old one. I suppose it is a body of great consequence, as they say it depends entirely upon their pleasure whether we shall in the future have a congress.❞

What would this "grand convention" decide? No one knew. For almost four months, Americans waited for an answer.

Work Begins

Delegates to the **Constitutional Convention** faced a difficult task. Soon after the meeting began, they decided to do more than revise the Articles of Confederation. They chose instead to write an entirely new constitution for the nation. Between May and September 1787, they forged a document that has been the basis of American government ever since.

The framers. Every state except Rhode Island sent delegates to the Convention. The 55 delegates were well qualified for the job of designing a new government. As a Philadelphia citizen noted:

❝Many of them were part of that band of patriots who, with halters round their necks, signed the Declaration of Independence on the Fourth of July 1776. Many of them were distinguished in the [battle] field and some of them bear the marks of wounds they received in our late contest for liberty.❞

At age 81, Benjamin Franklin was the oldest delegate. He was wise in the ways of government and human nature. George Washington traveled north from his home in Mount Vernon, Virginia. Washington was so well respected that the delegates at once elected him president of the Convention.

A number of delegates were young men in their 20s and 30s. Among them was Alexander Hamilton of New York. During the Revolution, Hamilton had served for a time as Washington's private secretary. Hamilton was outspoken in his dislike for the Articles of Confederation. "The nation," he wrote, "is sick and wants powerful remedies." The powerful remedy he prescribed was a strong national government.

James Madison keeps notes. The best-prepared delegate was 36-year-old James Madison of Virginia. At first glance, Madison was not impressive. He was short and thin and spoke so softly that he was often asked to speak up. But few wanted to miss what the scholarly Madison had to say.

Madison had served in Congress and in the Virginia legislature. Before leaving for Philadelphia, he collected the latest books on government and politics. Madison arrived in Philadelphia a week early so that he would have time to read and to organize

AN • AMERICAN • PORTRAIT

Richard Allen: Leader of the American Black Church

"You must get up—you must not kneel here," the white usher whispered to the black man.

"Wait until prayer is over," replied the black man, "and I will get up and trouble you no more." Angrily, several white ushers pulled the kneeling man to his feet.

Both blacks and whites attended services at St. George's Church in Philadelphia. But in 1787, whites made blacks sit apart—even to hear the popular black preacher Richard Allen. "We all went out of the church in a body," Allen later wrote, "and [the whites] were no more plagued with us in the church."

The incident took place just a month after the Constitutional Convention ended. To Allen, it showed that African Americans must set up their own churches. In 1794, he organized the Bethel Church, one of the first black churches in the United States.

Allen continued to preach while working to unite black congregations. In 1816, 16 black churches from several cities formed the African Methodist Episcopal Church. They chose the Reverend Allen as bishop. Although the church included the word "African" in its name, it was an American church. In Bishop Allen's words:

> **"**This land, which we have watered with our tears and our blood, is now our mother country.**"**

1. Why did Richard Allen set up a black church?

2. **Forecasting** What problems do you think Allen might have faced in setting up an independent black church?

---

his thoughts. Once the Convention began, Madison kept detailed notes on the debates. The notes, he felt, would be an important record for future generations.

Behind closed doors. Delegates decided to keep their talks secret so that they could speak their minds freely. "My wish," wrote Washington, "is that the Convention may . . . probe the defects of the Constitution to the bottom, and provide radical cures." He and the other delegates wanted to explore every issue and solution, without pressure from outside.

To ensure secrecy, guards stood at the door. Only delegates were permitted to enter. The windows were left closed to keep passersby from overhearing the debates. But the closed windows made the room very hot. As it was, that summer was the hottest in many years. New Englanders in their woolen suits suffered terribly. Southerners, who were more used to hot weather, wore lighter clothes.

Hopelessly Divided

Each day, delegates gathered in a large, square room. They sat in groups of three or four around tables covered with green cloth. In a high-backed chair at the front of the room was the president of the Convention, George Washington.

Virginia makes a proposal. Early on, Edmund Randolph and James Madison, both from Virginia, put forward a plan for the new government. It became known as the **Virginia Plan.** In the end, much of the plan was included in the new constitution.

The Virginia Plan called for a strong national government with three branches: the legislative, the executive, and the judicial (jyoo DIHSH uhl). In general, the legislative branch of government passes the laws. The executive branch carries out the laws. And the judicial branch, or system of courts, decides if laws are carried out fairly.

The Virginia Plan also called for a two-house legislature. Seats in both houses would be awarded to each state on the basis of population. Thus, in both houses, larger states would have more representatives than smaller ones. This differed from the Articles of Confederation, which gave every state, regardless of population, one vote in Congress.

Small states object. Small states objected strongly to the Virginia Plan. They feared that the large states could easily outvote them. In response, supporters of the Virginia Plan argued that it was only fair for a state with more people to have more representatives.

After two weeks of debate, William Paterson of New Jersey presented a plan that had the support of the small states. The **New Jersey Plan** also called for three branches of government. But it provided for a legislature that had only one house. Each state, no matter what the size of its population, would have one vote in the legislature.

Breaking the Deadlock

The two sides deadlocked. Tempers flared in the summer heat, and for a while it seemed that the Convention would fall

Pennsylvania State House *The Constitutional Convention took place at the Pennsylvania State House in Philadelphia, shown here. The building was already well-known to Americans because the Declaration of Independence was signed there in 1776. Today, the Pennsylvania State House is known as Independence Hall.* **Local History** *What historic buildings are located in your city or state?*

apart without adopting any plan. Finally, Roger Sherman of Connecticut worked out a compromise between the large and small states. A compromise is a settlement in which each side agrees to give up some of its demands.

Sherman's compromise called for a legislature with a lower and an upper house. Members of the lower house, known as the House of Representatives, would be chosen by all men who could vote. Seats in the lower house would be awarded to each state according to its population. This idea, which resembled the Virginia Plan, was popular with the larger states.

Members of the upper house, called the Senate, would be chosen by state legislatures. Each state, no matter what its size, would have two senators. This part of Sherman's compromise appealed to the smaller states.

On July 16, the delegates narrowly approved Sherman's plan, which became known as the **Great Compromise.** Each side gave up some demands to preserve the nation as a whole. If the delegates had not compromised, the Convention might have broken up without solving the nation's pressing problems.

Compromises Between the North and South

The Great Compromise raised another thorny issue. Would slaves be counted as part of a state's population? The answer to this question was important because it affected the number of votes a state would have in the House of Representatives.

Should slaves be counted? The question of slavery led to bitter arguments between the North and South. Southerners wanted to include slaves in the population count even though they would not let slaves vote. Northerners protested. If slaves were counted, southern states would have more representatives than northern states. Northerners argued that since slaves could not vote, they should not be counted.

Once again, debate raged on until the delegates compromised. They agreed that three fifths of the slaves in any state would be counted. In other words, if a state had 5,000 slaves, 3,000 of them would be included in the state's population count. This agreement was known as the **Three-Fifths Compromise.**

The slave trade. Northerners and southerners also disagreed over another issue related to slavery. By 1787, some northern states had banned the slave trade within their borders. They wanted the new Congress to ban the slave trade in the entire nation. Southerners warned that such a ban would ruin their economy.

In the end, the two sides compromised. Northerners agreed that the slave trade could continue for at least 20 years. After that, Congress could regulate the trade if it wished.

Signing the Constitution

As summer drew to a close, the weary delegates struggled with other difficult questions. How many years should the President, head of the executive branch, serve? How should the courts be organized? Would members of Congress be paid?

Finally, on September 17, 1787, the Constitution was ready. Gathering for the last time in the State House, delegates listened quietly as the final document was read aloud. James Wilson then read a speech written by the aged Benjamin Franklin, who was too weak to deliver it himself:

> ❝Mr. President . . . It . . . astonishes me, Sir, to find this system approaching so near perfection as it does. . . . Thus I consent, sir, to this constitution because I expect no better, and because I am not sure it is not the best.❞

Franklin then rose shakily to his feet and moved that the Constitution be approved. One by one, delegates came forward to sign the document. They had done

Signing the Constitution
On September 17, 1787, the work of the Constitutional Convention was done. Here, George Washington looks on as delegates sign the new Constitution of the United States. Benjamin Franklin, holding a cane, is seated in the foreground. **Citizenship** *Why was it important that delegates to the Constitutional Convention were willing to compromise?*

something truly remarkable. In just a few months, they had set up the framework for a lasting government.

SECTION 3 REVIEW

1. **Identify:** (a) Constitutional Convention, (b) James Madison, (c) Virginia Plan, (d) New Jersey Plan, (e) Roger Sherman, (f) Great Compromise, (g) Three-Fifths Compromise.
2. **Define:** (a) legislative branch, (b) executive branch, (c) judicial branch, (d) compromise.
3. (a) How did the Virginia Plan arrange for seats to be awarded in the legislature? (b) Why did the small states object to this arrangement?
4. What compromises did the North and South reach?
5. **Defending a Position** James Madison said that "no Constitution would ever have been adopted by the Convention if the debates had been made public." Do you agree or disagree? Explain.

4 A More Perfect Union

FIND OUT

◆ How did Enlightenment ideas influence the Constitution?

◆ How was power divided between the federal government and the states?

◆ How did the framers of the Constitution limit the power of government?

◆ **VOCABULARY** republic, separation of powers, federalism, electoral college, checks and balances, bill, veto, override, impeach

As the Constitutional Convention ended, a woman rushed up to Benjamin Franklin. "Well, Doctor," she asked, "what have we got, a republic or a monarchy?" "A republic," he replied. "If you can keep it."

A **republic** is a nation in which voters elect representatives to govern them. "We, the people of the United States," the preamble, or introduction, to the Constitution begins. Those words make clear that the power of government comes from the people. As Franklin pointed out, it was up to the people to make their new government work.

Ideas That Shaped the Constitution

Americans were the first people to write a constitution setting up a government. But many ideas in the Constitution had come to the United States from Europe.

The idea of limiting the power of the ruler, for example, was included in England's Magna Carta. (See page 113.) From England, too, came the idea of representative government. Since the mid-1200s, representatives in Parliament had made laws for the country. And since 1689, the English Bill of Rights had protected the rights of individuals. (See page 142.)

The Constitution reflects Enlightenment ideas, too. During the Enlightenment, as you recall, thinkers believed that people could improve society through the use of reason. These thinkers also wanted to apply reason to studying and improving governments. Many of the Constitution's framers had read the works of Enlightenment thinkers, such as John Locke and the Baron de Montesquieu (MAHN tuhs kyoo).

John Locke. In 1690, John Locke published *Two Treatises on Government*. In it, he stated two important ideas.

First, Locke declared that all people had natural rights to life, liberty, and property. Second, he explained that government is an agreement between the ruler and the ruled. The ruler must enforce the laws and protect the people. If a ruler violates the people's natural rights, the people have a right to rebel.

Locke's ideas were popular among Americans. Thomas Jefferson included the idea of natural rights in the Declaration of Independence. The framers of the Constitution also wanted to protect the natural rights of the people and limit the power of government. So they drew up the Constitution as a contract between the people and their government.

Montesquieu. In the 1700s, the French thinker Montesquieu published *The Spirit of Laws*. In it, he urged that the power of government be divided among three separate branches: the legislative, executive,

The Scales of Justice *In this tavern sign of the late 1700s, a woman holds the scales of justice. The idea of justice was not new to Americans. It had its roots in ancient civilizations. Still, Americans made establishing justice a goal of the Constitution.* **Linking Past and Present** *In what ways does the government establish justice today?*

and judicial. Such a division prevented any individual or group from gaining too much power. This principle became known as the **separation of powers.**

Montesquieu stressed the importance of the rule of law. The powers of government, he said, should be clearly defined. This would prevent individuals or groups from using government power for their own purposes. In the Constitution of the United States, the framers set out the basic laws of the nation, defining and limiting the powers of the government.

A Federal System

The need to limit government power was only one of the issues Americans debated in 1787. Just as important, they had to decide how to divide power between the national government and the states.

Under the Articles of Confederation, the states had more power than the Congress. The new Constitution changed that. Under the new Constitution, the states delegated, or gave up, some of their powers to the national government. At the same time, the states reserved, or kept, other powers. This sharing of power between the states and the national government is called **federalism.** (See the chart on page 287 in the Civics Overview.)

Federalism has given Americans a flexible system of government. The people elect both national and state officials. The federal, or national, government has the power to act for the nation as a whole. And the states have power over many local matters.

What powers does the federal government have? The Constitution spells out the powers of the federal government. For example, only the federal government can coin money or declare war. The federal government can also regulate trade between the states and with other countries. Under the Articles, the states controlled those areas of government.

What powers do states have? Under the Constitution, states have the power to regulate trade within their borders. They decide who can vote in state elections. They also have power over education and local governments.

Furthermore, the Constitution says that powers not given to the federal government belong to the states. This point pleased people in small states, who were afraid that the federal government might become too powerful.

What powers are shared? The Constitution lists some powers that are to be shared by federal and state governments. Both governments, for example, can build roads and raise taxes.

"The supreme law of the land." The framers of the Constitution had to decide how the states and the federal government would settle any disagreements. They did so by making the Constitution "the supreme law of the land." In other words, in any dispute, the Constitution is the final authority.

Separation of Powers

The Constitution set up a strong federal government. To keep the government from becoming too powerful, the framers relied on Montesquieu's idea of separation of powers. In the Constitution, they created three branches of government and then defined the powers of each. (See the chart on page 263.)

The legislative branch. Congress is the legislative branch of government. It is made up of the House of Representatives and the Senate. Members of the House are elected for two-year terms. Senators are elected for six-year terms. The main function of Congress is to make laws.

Under the Constitution, voters in each state elect members of the House of Representatives. Delegates to the Constitutional Convention wanted the House to represent the interests of ordinary people. At first, the Constitution provided for senators to be chosen by state legislatures. In 1913, this was changed. Today, senators are elected in the same way as House members.

Article 1 of the Constitution sets out the powers of Congress. These include the power to collect taxes and to regulate foreign and interstate trade. In foreign affairs, Congress has the power to declare war and to "raise and support armies."

The executive branch. Some delegates in Philadelphia objected to the idea of a strong executive branch. They remembered the power that King George III had exercised over the colonies. But Madison argued that a strong executive was needed to balance the legislature. Otherwise, a headstrong Congress might pass "tyrannical laws" and then execute them "in a tyrannical way." His arguments prevailed.

Article 2 of the Constitution sets up the executive branch of government. It is headed by the President. The executive branch also includes the Vice President

CHART SKILLS *The Constitution set up three branches of government. Each has its own powers. ◆ Who heads the executive branch? What is the role of the legislative branch?*

Separation of Powers

Legislative Branch
(Congress)

Passes laws
Can override President's veto
Approves treaties and presidential appointments
Can impeach and remove President and other high officials
Creates lower federal courts
Appropriates money
Prints and coins money
Raises and supports the armed forces
Can declare war
Regulates foreign and interstate trade

Executive Branch
(President)

Carries out laws
Proposes laws
Can veto laws
Negotiates foreign treaties
Serves as commander in chief of the armed forces
Appoints federal judges, ambassadors, and other high officials
Can grant pardons to federal offenders

Judicial Branch
(Supreme Court and
Other Federal Courts)

Interprets laws
Can declare laws unconstitutional
Can declare executive actions unconstitutional

and any advisers appointed by the President. The President and Vice President serve four-year terms.

The President is responsible for carrying out all laws passed by Congress. The President is also commander in chief of the armed forces and is responsible for foreign relations.

The judicial branch. Article 3 of the Constitution calls for a Supreme Court. This article also allowed Congress to set up other federal courts under the Supreme Court. The Supreme Court and other federal courts hear cases that involve the Constitution or any laws passed by Congress. They also hear cases arising between two or more states.

Electing the President

During the Constitutional Convention, a Philadelphia newspaper reported that the delegates wanted a king to head the new government. For once, the Convention broke its rule of secrecy. "While we cannot tell you what we are doing," it announced, "we can tell you what we are not doing: we never once thought of a king."

Delegates took great pains to ensure that the President would not become too strong. Some delegates feared that if the President were elected directly by the people, he might become too independent of Congress and the states.

The delegates had another worry. In the late 1700s, news traveled slowly. How would voters know a candidate who lived outside their area? New Englanders would probably know little about a candidate from the South. And a candidate from Pennsylvania might be unknown to voters in Massachusetts or South Carolina.

To solve these problems, delegates set up the electoral college. The electoral college would be made up of electors from each state. State legislatures would decide how to choose their electors. Every four years, the electors would meet as a group and vote for the President and Vice President of the United States.

The framers of the Constitution expected that the electors would be well-informed citizens who were familiar with the national government. They believed that such men would choose a President and Vice President wisely. The electoral college still meets today, but its function has changed somewhat.

A System of Checks and Balances

The Constitution set up a system of checks and balances. Under this system, each branch of the federal government has some way to check, or control, the other two branches. The system of checks and balances is another way in which the Constitution limits the power of government. (See the chart on page 289.)

Checks on the Congress. The system of checks and balances works in many ways. For example, to do its work, Congress passes bills, or proposed laws. A bill then goes to the President to be signed into law. (See the chart on page 303.) The President can check the power of Congress by vetoing, or rejecting, a bill. Congress can check the President by overriding, or overruling, the President's veto. To override a veto, two thirds of both houses of Congress must vote for the bill again.

Checks on the President. Congress has other checks on the President. The President appoints officials such as ambassadors. But the Senate must approve these appointments. The President can negotiate treaties with other nations. But two thirds of the Senate must approve a treaty.

Congress can remove a President from office if it finds the President guilty of a crime or serious misbehavior. First, the House of Representatives must impeach, or bring charges against, the President. A trial is then held in the Senate. If two thirds of the senators vote for conviction, the President must leave office.

The Articles of Confederation and the Constitution

The Articles	The Constitution
1. Legislative branch: Congress is made up of one house	1. Legislative branch: Congress is made up of two houses—Senate and House of Representatives
2. Each state has one vote in Congress	2. Each state has two votes in Senate; each state has one or more votes in House of Representatives, depending on population
3. At least 9 of 13 states must approve a law	3. A majority of each house must approve a law
4. No executive branch	4. Executive branch, headed by President, carries out laws
5. No judicial branch	5. Judicial branch, headed by Supreme Court, interprets laws
6. Only states can tax	6. Congress can tax
7. Each state can coin its own money	7. Only Congress can coin money
8. Each state can regulate trade with other states	8. Only Congress can regulate trade between states
9. Each state can act independently	9. States accept Constitution as supreme law of land

CHART SKILLS *The Constitutional Convention met to revise the Articles of Confederation. Instead, the delegates wrote a completely new document—the United States Constitution.* ◆ *Compare the way the two documents treat each of the following: (a) legislative branch; (b) executive branch; (c) power to tax.*

Checks on the courts. Congress and the President have checks on the power of the courts. The President appoints judges, who must be approved by the Senate. If judges misbehave, Congress may remove them from office.

A Living Document

The Constitution carefully balances power among three branches of the federal government and between the states and the federal government. This system has worked for more than 200 years, longer than any other written constitution in the world. The Constitution has survived because it is a living document. As you will read in this and later chapters, it can be changed to meet new conditions in the United States.

SECTION 4 REVIEW

1. **Identify:** (a) John Locke, (b) Baron de Montesquieu.
2. **Define:** (a) republic, (b) separation of powers, (c) federalism, (d) electoral college, (e) checks and balances, (f) bill, (g) veto, (h) override, (i) impeach.
3. Name two Enlightenment ideas that influenced the Constitution.
4. Why did the framers of the Constitution set up a system of federalism?
5. **Applying Information** How did the following ideas limit government: (a) separation of powers, (b) checks and balances?

5 Ratifying the Constitution

FIND OUT

◆ How did the views of Federalists and Antifederalists differ?

◆ How can the Constitution be amended?

◆ What rights does the Bill of Rights protect?

◆ **VOCABULARY** amend, due process

Praising the Constitution *In rallying support for the Constitution, George Washington noted that it protected the "greatest interests of every true American." Here, Americans from all walks of life join to praise the new plan of government.* **Citizenship** *What was the main argument used by Antifederalists against the Constitution?*

At home and in town squares, Americans discussed the new Constitution. Many supported it. Many others did not. Its critics especially worried that the Constitution had no bill of rights. In Virginia, Patrick Henry sounded the alarm:

> ❝Show me an age and country where the rights and liberties of the people were placed on the sole chance of their rulers being good men, without a consequent loss of liberty!❞

Was a bill of rights necessary? Did the new Constitution give too much power to the federal government? In the autumn of 1787, citizens debated the Constitution sentence by sentence. The Constitutional Convention had done its work. Now it was up to the states to decide whether or not to ratify the new frame of government.

A Vigorous Battle

The framers of the Constitution sent the document to Congress along with a letter from George Washington. "In our deliberations," wrote Washington, "we kept steadily in view . . . the greatest interests of every true American." He then called on Congress to support the plan.

The framers had set up a process for the states to decide on the new government. At least 9 of the 13 states had to ratify the Constitution before it could go into effect. In 1787 and 1788, voters in each state elected delegates to special state conventions. These delegates then met to decide whether or not to ratify the Constitution.

Heated debate. In every state, heated debates took place. Supporters of the Constitution called themselves **Federalists.** They called people who opposed the Constitution **Antifederalists.**

Federalists favored a strong national government. The best-known Federalists were James Madison, Alexander Hamilton, and John Jay. They wrote a series of essays, called *The Federalist Papers,* defending the Constitution. They signed the essays "Publius," the name of an ancient Roman statesman. Most people knew who the essay writers were. But it was the custom of the time to use pen names.

Antifederalists opposed the Constitution for many reasons. They felt that it

Thinking About Geography

Match the letters on the map with the places listed below.

1. Original 13 states
2. Northwest Territory
3. Spanish Louisiana
4. Spanish Florida
5. Canada

Movement Why did settlers travel to the Northwest Territory?

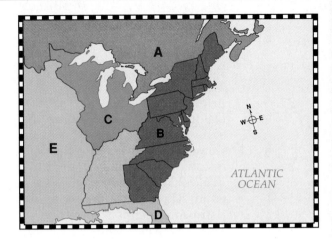

ATLANTIC OCEAN

History Writer's Workshop

Checklist for Writing a One-Paragraph Answer

You may use the following checklist to prepare and write a one-paragraph answer. Refer to earlier lessons if you need help.

1. Analyze the question. Determine what the key word is telling you to do. Take note of the topic limits set by other clues.
2. Write a topic sentence that states the main idea of the answer. Try to reword the question as a topic sentence.
3. Select information that supports the main idea. Keep in mind the key word and the topic limits. You might make a list of possible supporting information and then cross out items that you cannot use. Make sure you have enough information.
4. Arrange the supporting information in a logical order. Consider time order, comparison order, order of importance, or cause-and-effect order. The topic sentence or supporting information might suggest a logical order.
5. Write detail sentences to present the supporting information. Use transitions to show the order you are using.
6. Check your answer for smoothness. Correct grammar and spelling mistakes.

Practice Using the checklist, write a one-paragraph answer for the following question. *Explain the importance of the Great Compromise.* (See page 259 for information.)

Writing to Learn

1. Write a short play about the Constitutional Convention. To prepare, outline an incident you want to portray. Include notes on the setting and characters. As you write the play, be sure to include realistic dialogue and action. Revise the script for liveliness and clear stage directions. Proofread and make a final copy. Ask students to perform the play in class.
2. Write a newspaper editorial taking a stand for or against ratifying the Constitution. To prepare, list arguments for each side. In your first draft, compose a topic sentence summarizing your point of view. Write detail sentences, organizing your reasons in order of importance. In the editorial, be sure to disprove the arguments of the other side. Revise for persuasive power and balance. Then, proofread and make a final copy. Publish your editorial in a class newspaper.

Not a Typical Soldier

American soldier Robert Shurtleff begged to be left in the field to die of a leg wound—not because the wound was so serious, but because a trip to the field hospital would certainly reveal Shurtleff's true identity. Shurtleff was really Deborah Sampson, who, in 1782, disguised herself as a man and enlisted in the Fourth Massachusetts Regiment. Sampson escaped discovery that time, but later she was taken, with a fever and unconscious, to the hospital and her secret was uncovered. She received an honorable discharge, and in 1805 the United States government granted her a disability pension.

DONT TREAD ON ME

Early American settlers were loyal to their home colony, often at the expense of unity among the colonies. A flag showing a snake cut into pieces was popular in the colonies for years. It symbolized the 13 separate colonies, and the words "Join or Die" were a plea for unity.

By the mid-1770s, new flags were appearing. The one shown here portrays a unified snake with the words, "Don't tread on me." This was a clear warning to the British that the colonies would resist any violation of their rights.

In 1777, after the beginning of the Revolutionary War, the Continental Congress passed a resolution calling for a flag with 13 stripes of red and white to stand for the 13 original colonies. The new flag was designed by Francis Hopkinson, a lawyer. Three years later, he presented the Congress with a bill for the design.

A True American Language

Noah Webster, a teacher from Goshen, New York, wrote a book that became a best seller in 1783. The book was not an adventure story or a biography of a famous person. It was an elementary spelling book! Webster later published other books on what he considered a new American language.

Webster wanted English spelling to be simplified. He thought that borrowing from other languages had turned it into a senseless hash. Webster thought that the word "head" should be spelled "hed" and the word "laugh" should be "laf."

Not all of his proposals did catch on. But Americans did change words like "theatre" to "theater" and "plough" to "plow."

A Secret Weapon

It may not look like much, but this is a sketch of the very first submarine, which was invented by David Bushnell during the American Revolution. Called the *Turtle,* the tiny one-person submarine was made of wood and had a propeller operated by hand. On the outside of the small ship was an egg-shaped time bomb. The operator used an iron screw to break through the hull of an enemy ship and attach the bomb.

The first mission of the *Turtle* took place in New York Harbor in August 1776. First Sergeant Ezra Lee guided his submarine alongside the British *Eagle,* a 64-gun warship under the command of Admiral Howe. But alas, the hull of the *Eagle* was covered with copper and Lee was unable to attach the bomb. With the failure of the mission, Congress denied any more money for the project.

The American Turkey?

The Constitutional Convention picked the bald eagle as the national bird. It had appeared on the Great Seal of the nation since 1782. For most delegates, the power and proud bearing of the eagle made it a worthy symbol of the new nation. But Benjamin Franklin disagreed. He thought the bald eagle was too common and that it had a bad character: "He does not get his living honestly; you may see him perched on some dead tree, where, too lazy to fish for himself, he watches the labor of the fishing hawk [hoping to steal its food]." Franklin preferred a native American bird that had been important to the early settlers—the wild turkey.

Footnotes to History

- The Boston Marathon takes place on Patriot's Day, which commemorates the battles of Lexington and Concord.
- Brown Betty, the horse Paul Revere rode on his famous ride, had been borrowed from Deacon John Larkin of Charlestown.
- The average age of the delegates to the Constitutional Convention was 43.

Yankee Doodle Dandy

In the 1750s, British merchants called New England traders "Yankees." They used the word as an insult to mean greedy people. During the French and Indian War, a British army officer had penned the words to the song "Yankee Doodle" to poke fun at colonial soldiers. What a surprise when after the Battle of Bunker Hill, American soldiers themselves began to sing the song with some new verses added. They were proud to be called Yankees. "Yankee Doodle" soon became a popular patriotic tune.

Chapter 7 The Road to Revolution

In the mid-1700s, colonists were caught up in the English-French competition for empire. In North America, the Ohio Valley became the center of conflict. As English traders pushed into the valley in search of furs, the French expanded their line of forts. In the struggle for power, both sides enlisted Indian allies.

Scuffles in the Ohio Valley triggered the French and Indian War. Although the English greatly outnumbered the French, the French and their Indian allies won several early victories. The tide of battle turned in 1757. By 1763, the English had driven the French out of North America.

Pontiac's War in 1763 convinced the British to issue a proclamation closing western lands to settlers. The proclamation angered colonists who claimed lands in the West. Colonists were further angered by the Stamp Act, which imposed taxes to help repay Britain's war debts. Outraged colonists organized to oppose the taxes and boycott British goods.

In 1767, Parliament passed the Townshend Acts, taxing glass, paper, silk, lead, and tea. Once again, colonists protested by boycotting British goods. Port cities such as New York and Boston became centers of protest. In 1770, British troops killed five colonists in what became known as the Boston Massacre.

When Parliament decided to enforce a tea tax in 1773, angry colonists dumped a shipload of English tea into Boston harbor. As punishment, Parliament passed the Intolerable Acts. In response, delegates from 12 colonies met in 1774 in the First Continental Congress. They planned to meet again in May 1775. In the meantime, colonial minutemen and British troops clashed at Lexington and Concord.

Chapter 8 The War for Independence

The Second Continental Congress met in Philadelphia in May 1775. Hoping to avoid a final break with Britain, the Congress petitioned King George III to repeal the Intolerable Acts. It also set up the Continental Army and named George Washington as commander. Washington set out for Boston, but before he arrived, Americans and British had fought the first major battle of the Revolution, at Bunker Hill.

As skirmishes continued in the Boston area, the Continental Congress learned that King George III rejected its petition. Influenced by Thomas Paine's pamphlet *Common Sense,* the Congress appointed a committee to draw up a document declaring independence. Thomas Jefferson's eloquent Declaration of Independence was adopted by Congress on July 4, 1776.

The American Revolution was fought on many fronts. Americans drove the British from Boston, but failed to take Canada. With the arrival of the British fleet in New York, fighting shifted to the Middle States. While New York fell to the redcoats, victories at Trenton and Princeton gave Americans new hope. The American victory at the Battle of Saratoga was a turning point in the war. Assured that Americans could win, France recognized the new nation and agreed to give it military aid.

The final battles of the Revolution took place on the western frontier, at sea, and in the South. With the help of Miami Indians, Virginians captured British forts in the Ohio Valley. American captains attacked British ships at sea. In the South, Patriots organized hit-and-run attacks. Finally, trapped at Yorktown, the British surrendered in 1781. Under the Treaty of Paris of 1783, Britain recognized the United States as an independent nation.

Chapter 9 Creating a Republic

After declaring independence in 1776, Americans had to govern themselves. The states formed 13 separate governments, each with its own constitution. For the nation as a whole, the Continental Congress drafted the Articles of Confederation. The Articles created a loose alliance among the states. Because states were not willing to give up power, the national government set up by the Articles was weak.

Under the Articles of Confederation, Congress could not impose taxes, regulate trade, or resolve disputes between states. Although Congress successfully set up a system for settling and governing the Northwest Territory, it could not solve other important political and economic problems. Shays' Rebellion in 1786 convinced lawmakers of the need for a stronger national government.

In May 1787, delegates to the Constitutional Convention faced the difficult task of writing a new national constitution. Arguments over representation in Congress nearly doomed the Convention to early failure. Finally, however, Roger Sherman of Connecticut worked out a compromise between large and small states. And northern and southern states reached a compromise on the way slaves would be counted.

The new Constitution defined the powers of government and set up a system for limiting those powers. Certain powers are delegated to the national government. Other powers are reserved for the states. Still other powers are shared by the states and the national government. The national government is divided into three separate branches: legislative, executive, and judicial. Each branch can check the power of the other two branches.

To become law, the Constitution had to be ratified by 9 of the 13 states. In every state, heated debates took place between Federalists and Antifederalists. One by one, states voted to ratify. Americans held their first election under the Constitution in January 1789. The first Congress added ten amendments to the Constitution. These ten amendments are known as the Bill of Rights.

Understanding Causes and Effects *Protests against British rule turned into armed resistance.* ◆ *List two effects of the American Revolution. What effects do you think a British victory might have had?*

CAUSES

- Proclamation of 1763 stops colonists from moving west
- Parliament taxes the colonies to pay British war debts
- Intolerable Acts set up harsh rule in Massachusetts

THE AMERICAN REVOLUTION

EFFECTS

- Colonies declare independence
- Britain recognizes United States independence
- United States borders extend to Florida and to the Mississippi River
- United States sets up a government under the Constitution

UNIT **3** REVIEW

Reviewing the Main Ideas

1. (a) What advantages did the French have over the British at the beginning of the French and Indian War? (b) How did William Pitt help to turn the tide of battle?
2. What new British policies after the French and Indian War outraged colonists?
3. (a) Why did the First Continental Congress meet? (b) What actions did it take?
4. How did colonists respond to the Declaration of Independence?
5. (a) How did British General John Burgoyne plan to end the American Revolution? (b) What spoiled his plans?
6. What was the role of each of the following in the American Revolution: (a) Native Americans; (b) African Americans; (c) women?
7. Why did the nation face serious problems under the Articles of Confederation?
8. Why was the Great Compromise needed at the Constitutional Convention?
9. How does the Constitution limit the power of the government?

Thinking Critically

1. **Drawing Conclusions** Do you think that conflict between the French and the British in the Ohio Valley could have been avoided? Explain.
2. **Solving Problems** How might Parliament have better handled disputes over taxes in the colonies?
3. **Analyzing Information** Britain was one of the world's most powerful nations, with a strong army and navy. Why do you think the Americans were able to defeat the British and win the Revolution?
4. **Defending a Position** Without the Constitution, the United States would not have survived as a nation. Do you agree or disagree with this statement? Explain.

Applying Your Skills

1. **Using Visual Evidence** Based on the evidence in the maps and pictures in Chapter 8, write five statements that describe the American Revolution.
2. **Ranking** Based on your reading of Unit 3, who do you think was most important in shaping American history from 1745 to 1790? Choose five people discussed in the unit. Then, rank them in order of importance. Explain your ranking.
3. **Constructing a Time Line** Make a time line for the period from 1745 to 1790. Include dates and events from Chapters 7, 8, and 9 that show how the United States became an independent nation. Use the time lines in the chapter Study Guides for help. Which pairs of events have a cause-and-effect relationship?

Doing More

1. **Preparing a Newspaper Advertisement** Write an ad for a 1765 newspaper urging colonists to boycott British goods. To get started, jot down reasons for the boycott. In your ad, use an attention-grabbing opener. Focus on the reason or reasons most likely to make your readers take action. As you revise, make sure that your message is clear. Proofread the ad, and publish it on a piece of oaktag for a bulletin board display.
2. **Eyewitness Reporting** Do library research to learn more about one of the Revolutionary War battles described in Chapter 8. Then, write an eyewitness report for a local newspaper. You might use one of the pictures of a battle scene as a springboard for your account. Jot down words that describe what you see. In your first paragraph, answer the questions *who, what, when, where, why,* and *how.* Add support-

ing information in the paragraphs that follow. As you revise your report, check that your facts are accurate. Proofread before making a final copy. Share your report with classmates.

3. **Making Flash Cards** As a group project, make a set of flash cards that illustrate the Constitution at work. On one side of each card, write a bold-faced word from Chapter 9. On the other side, paste a newspaper headline that provides an example of the word. A headline about the President's veto of a tax bill, for example, might be pasted on the back of the card for *veto*. Challenge classmates to identify the term illustrated by each headline.

4. **Exploring Local History** Consult your school or local library to find out how your state government is organized. Using the chart on page 263 for reference, prepare a chart to show the organization.

Using the chart on page 263 for reference

Recognizing Points of View

As the colonies prepared for war in 1774 and 1775, colonists debated the wisdom of fighting against the British. Below are excerpts from statements by two influential colonists. Read the excerpts and answer the following questions.

1. What arguments does Daniel Leonard give against fighting Britain?
2. How does Patrick Henry respond to Daniel Leonard's arguments?
3. Based on the excerpts, which of the two men do you think made the following statement: "The battle . . . is not to the strong alone; it is to the vigilant, the active, the brave." Explain.
4. If you had lived in the English colonies in 1775, which position would you have taken? Explain.

Should colonists take up arms against Britain?

Daniel Leonard

❝Do you expect to conquer in war? War is no longer a simple, but a [complicated] science, not to be learned from books or two or three campaigns, but from long experience. You need not be told that His Majesty's generals . . . are possessed of every talent [needed by] great commanders, matured by long experience in many parts of the world. . . .

Alas! My friends, you have nothing to oppose to this force but a militia unused to service, impatient of command, and [lacking] resources. . . . Nothing short of a miracle could gain you one battle.❞

Patrick Henry

❝They tell us, sir, that we are weak; unable to cope with [such a powerful enemy]. But when shall we be stronger? Will it be the next week, or the next year? Will it be when we are totally disarmed, and when a British guard shall be stationed in every house? . . .

Sir, we are not weak if we make proper use of those means which . . . God . . . has placed in our power. Three millions of people armed in the holy cause of liberty, and in such a country as we possess, [cannot be beaten]. . . . Besides, sir, we shall not fight our battles alone. There is a just God who . . . will raise up friends to fight our battles for us. . . .

Besides, sir, we have no [choice]. If we were [dishonorable] enough to desire it, it is now too late to [turn back from war].❞

Trial by Jury *The Constitution both sets up a national government and guarantees the rights of the people. In this painting, artist Thomas Hart Benton pays tribute to the precious legal right of trial by jury.* **Citizenship** *Why do you think the right to trial by jury is so important?*

ivics **O**verview

The Constitution at Work

Outline

1 The Goals of the Constitution
2 Five Principles of the Constitution
3 A Living Constitution
4 The National Government at Work
5 Citizenship at Work

Imagine what your life might be like if there were no Constitution. For example, suppose you plan to visit a neighboring state. Without the Constitution, you might need a passport. Or the state might deny you entry because of your race or religion.

Now suppose that you send a letter to your local newspaper criticizing your governor. Without the Constitution, the newspaper might ignore your letter because it prints only what the state government approves. Or the governor might order your arrest and imprisonment without a trial.

As you can see, the Constitution affects you personally. Under its protection, you are free to express your opinion. It also guarantees you equal opportunity under the law, whatever your religion, sex, or race. Most important, the Constitution allows you to make your own choices about how to live your life.

The Constitution has remained the framework of our government for more than 200 years. It endures in part because it guarantees people their rights. At the same time, it has allowed the people to further define and extend those rights.

Of Special Interest

Focus On

- What are the goals of the Constitution?
- What are the five principles of the Constitution?
- Why do we say that we have a "living" Constitution?
- How does our national government work?
- What are citizens' rights and responsibilities?

1 The Goals of the Constitution

FIND OUT

- How does the national government help to unify the nation?
- Why is a national system of courts necessary?
- How does the Constitution provide for defense?
- How does the Constitution protect the rights of the people?
- **VOCABULARY** justice, domestic tranquillity, general welfare, liberty

"We, the people of the United States, in order to form a more perfect Union, establish justice, ensure domestic tranquillity, provide for the common defense, promote the general welfare, and secure the blessings of liberty to ourselves and our posterity, do ordain and establish this Constitution for the United States of America."

Those words are the **Preamble,** or opening statement, of the Constitution. In the Preamble, the people proudly announce that they have established the Constitution. They have done so, they declare, to achieve certain goals. As you read about these goals, think about their importance to you.

Contents of the Constitution

CHART SKILLS *The Constitution includes a preamble, 7 articles, and 26 amendments. To find where they appear in this book, see the page numbers in the chart.* ◆ *On what pages is the Bill of Rights printed?*

Form a More Perfect Union

What do the words "my country" mean to you? You probably will say the United States. But if you lived in the 1780s, you probably would have answered Virginia, Massachusetts, or whatever state you came from.

Indeed, under the Articles of Confederation, the United States was a loose alliance of independent, quarreling states. Many states acted like separate nations. The framers of the Constitution, however, saw the need for states to work together as part of a single, united nation.

How does the Constitution try to achieve "a more perfect union"? It provides the national government with the powers that it needs to unify and strengthen the nation.

For example, Congress, one part of the national government, has powers important to a healthy national economy. It can raise taxes and regulate trade between the states. It also has the sole power to coin and print money.

Other parts of the national government also have powers that help to unify the nation. The President is responsible for carrying out all the laws of the nation. And national courts ensure fair treatment of all people under one system of law.

Establish Justice

A second goal of the Constitution is to establish justice, or fairness. The Constitution gives this task to a national system of courts.

The national courts deal with a broad range of cases. They hear cases involving the Constitution, national laws, treaties, foreign ambassadors, and ships at sea. They also decide disputes between individuals, between individuals and the national government, and between the states.

When the national courts decide cases, they often interpret, or explain, the law. The Supreme Court, the highest court in the land, can rule that a law is not permitted by the Constitution.

Why is a national system of courts necessary? Without it, state or local courts would interpret national laws. Judges in some states might refuse to act on laws they did not like. Disputes about the meaning of certain laws would remain unsettled. The result would be confusion and injustice.

Ensure Domestic Tranquillity

In 1786, Daniel Shays marched on a Massachusetts courthouse with nearly 2,000 other protesters. Upon hearing about Shays' Rebellion, George Washington warned, "We are fast verging to [absence of government] and confusion!" The uprising made it clear that the national government must have the means to ensure domestic tranquillity, or peace at home.

The Constitution allows for means to keep the peace. State and local governments have the power to use their own police to enforce national laws. But when crime crosses state borders, national police agencies can step in to help protect life and property.

Have you ever watched a news broadcast about a civil emergency, such as a riot or a flood? If so, you probably saw members of the National Guard keeping the peace. The President can summon such aid if a state or local community cannot or will not respond to the emergency.

Provide for the Common Defense

After the American Revolution, the United States could not defend its new borders. Without a national army, it could not force British troops to leave the frontier. Lacking a navy, it was unable to prevent Spain from closing part of the Mississippi River to American trade.

The framers of the Constitution realized that strong armed forces are important to a nation's foreign policy. Military power helps not only to prevent attack by other nations but also to protect economic and political interests.

The Constitution gives Congress the power to "raise and support Armies" and to "provide and maintain a Navy." Today, the armed forces of the United States include the Army, Navy, Air Force, Marine Corps, and the Coast Guard.

Promote the General Welfare

The Constitution gives the national government the means to promote the general welfare, or well-being of all the people. The national government has the power to collect taxes. It also has the power to set aside money for programs that will benefit the people.

In the workplace. The workplace provides many examples of how the national

Medical Care *Health care for older people has become a major concern. Medicare and other government programs enable senior citizens who need financial assistance to pay medical bills.* ***Daily Life*** *What other government programs do you think promote the general welfare?*

government—often in cooperation with state governments—has acted to promote the general welfare. Factory owners are required to meet safety standards for work areas. Workers who are disabled or unemployed receive financial support. And thanks to Social Security, all workers are entitled to income upon retirement.

In the school. Another area in which the national government helps to promote the general welfare is education. Education helps to prepare people to become responsible citizens. It also provides tools and training for employment.

Support for education takes many forms. The national government pays for school nutrition programs in local school districts. Many students receive money to help pay the costs of a college education.

In the laboratory. The national government supports scientific research and development to improve the quality of life. For example, researchers at the National Institutes of Health lead the fight against many diseases. And scientists at the Department of Agriculture help farmers to improve their crops as well as to develop better livestock.

ISSUE • FOR • TODAY

Government Spending

The federal government spends $1 trillion each year on various programs. Deciding the amount for each program often stirs fierce debate among Americans.

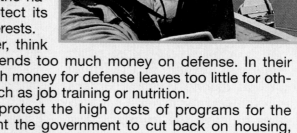

Most people agree that the United States needs a strong defense. Troops, weapons, planes—all are needed to defend the nation's borders and to protect its political and economic interests.

Some people, however, think that the United States spends too much money on defense. In their view, setting aside so much money for defense leaves too little for other important programs, such as job training or nutrition.

Still other Americans protest the high costs of programs for the general welfare. They want the government to cut back on housing, medical, and other programs. Local governments and private groups should fill these needs, they say, not the federal government.

1. How much does the federal government spend on various programs?

2. **Defending a Position** Do you think that the nation benefits more from programs that promote the general welfare or programs that provide defense? Explain.

Secure the Blessings of Liberty

Protection of liberty was a major reason why colonists fought the American Revolution. It is no wonder, then, that the framers made securing liberty a major goal of the Constitution. Liberty is the freedom to live as you please, as long as you obey the law and respect the freedom of others.

One way that the Constitution ensures liberty is to limit the powers of government. For example, the **Bill of Rights,** the first 10 amendments to the Constitution, lists the liberties that Americans have. The amendments present these liberties as basic rights and freedoms that the government may not take away.

The Constitution provides yet another safeguard of liberty—the right to vote. The people can select the leaders who make the laws. At the same time, they can remove from office those leaders who have done a poor job.

The "blessings of liberty" have been extended to more Americans since the Constitution was written. Changes in the Constitution have been made to ensure that all Americans—no matter what sex or race—have the same rights to voting, education, housing, employment, and other choices in life.

Voting to Protect Liberty *The ballot box has long been a symbol of liberty. Through the vote, Americans are able to safeguard their rights and have a say in government decisions.* **Citizenship** *How does the Bill of Rights protect the "blessings of liberty" for Americans?*

SECTION 1 REVIEW

1. **Identify:** (a) Preamble, (b) Bill of Rights.
2. **Define:** (a) justice, (b) domestic tranquillity, (c) general welfare, (d) liberty.
3. List two powers of the national government that help to form a more perfect union.
4. Why would confusion and injustice result without a national court system?
5. List two ways that the national government helps workers.
6. **Evaluating Information** Which goal of the Constitution do you think is most important? Explain.

2 Five Principles of the Constitution

FIND OUT

◆ What is popular sovereignty?

◆ What is limited government?

◆ How does federalism divide power?

◆ How does the separation of powers limit government?

◆ How does the system of checks and balances prevent abuse of power?

◆ **VOCABULARY** representative government, ratify, tyranny, federal, veto, override, bill, unconstitutional

The Constitution sets up a strong national government. At the same time, it safeguards the liberty of the people. Five basic principles, or rules, support this delicate balance. They are popular sovereignty, limited government, federalism, separation of powers, and checks and balances. In large part, the framers drew on European ideas for these principles. (See Chapter 9, pages 261–262.) As you read about the basic principles of the Constitution, think about how they help to protect you.

Popular Sovereignty Means the People Rule

The first three words of the Constitution, "We, the people," express the principle of popular sovereignty. According to this principle, the people rule. They hold the final authority, or ruling power, in government.

A contract with the government. The Constitution is a contract, or formal agreement, between the people and their government. In it, the people grant the government the powers it needs to achieve its goals. At the same time, they limit the power of government by spelling out what the government may not do.

The people vote. How does popular sovereignty work? In a large society, people cannot always take part directly in government. Instead, they exercise their ruling power indirectly. The people elect public officials to make laws and other government decisions for them. This practice is called representative government.

The people elect public officials by voting in free and frequently held elections. Americans today have the constitutional right to vote for members of the House of Representatives (Article 1, Section 2) and for members of the Senate (Amendment 17). The people also elect the members of the electoral college, who, in turn, choose the President (Article 2, Section 1).

The right to vote has been gradually expanded over time. When the Constitution was ratified, or approved, only white men over age 21 who owned property could vote. As the chart above right shows, other Americans have won the right to vote since then. Today, if you are a citizen, you are eligible to vote at age 18.

The Right to Vote

Year	People Allowed to Vote
1789	White men over age 21 who met property requirements (state laws)
Early 1800s–1850s	All white men over age 21 (state laws)
1870	Black men (Amendment 15)
1920	Women (Amendment 19)
1961	People in the District of Columbia in presidential elections (Amendment 23)
1971	People over age 18 (Amendment 26)

CHART SKILLS *The right to vote has expanded since the Constitution first went into effect.* ◆ *Who could vote in 1789? In 1971? Which amendment granted women the right to vote?*

The Government's Power Should Be Limited

The framers of the Constitution remembered well the harsh rule of the British king. Like most Americans, they feared tyranny, or cruel and unjust government. But the failures of the Articles of Confederation made it clear that the national government had to be strong.

How could the framers strike a balance between too much government and too little government? The answer was limited government, or a government by law. According to this principle, the government does not have complete power. It has only the powers that the people have granted it.

Limits on power. The Constitution states the powers of the national government. You and every other citizen can tell what powers Congress, the President, and the courts have. The Constitution also states what powers the government does not have. This list of denied powers puts still more limits on the government.

Guarantees to the people. The most important limits on government are set out in the Bill of Rights. In these amendments, the Constitution guarantees the individual freedoms of the people. One of the 10 amendments states that the people have other rights, even though they are not listed in the Constitution (Amendment 9). Still another amendment gives the states or the people any powers not granted to the national government (Amendment 10).

Limited government is also known as the "rule of law." The Constitution is the law of the land. No person—not you, not the highest government official—is above it.

Federalism Results in a Sharing of Power

The framers of the Constitution faced a difficult conflict. They saw the need for a strong national government. At the same time, they did not want to take away all power from the states. Like most Americans, they believed that state governments would better understand the special needs and concerns of their citizens.

The framers choose federalism. The framers solved this conflict by basing the government on the principle of federalism. Under federalism, power is divided between the **federal,** or national, government and the state governments. The national government has the power to deal with national issues. The states have the power to meet local needs.

CHART SKILLS *The system of federalism divides power between the national government and the state governments.* ◆ *Name two powers reserved to the states. Who has the power to raise taxes?*

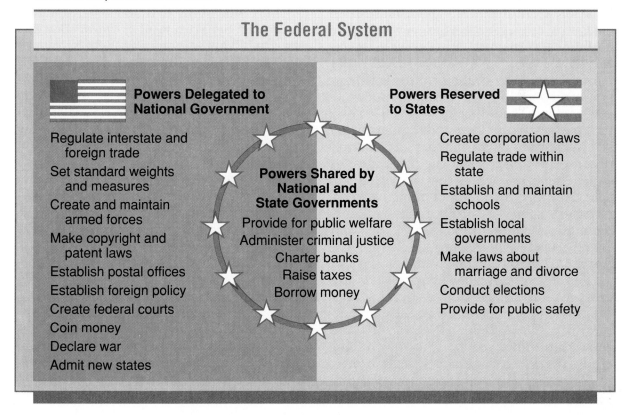

The Federal System

Powers Delegated to National Government

- Regulate interstate and foreign trade
- Set standard weights and measures
- Create and maintain armed forces
- Make copyright and patent laws
- Establish postal offices
- Establish foreign policy
- Create federal courts
- Coin money
- Declare war
- Admit new states

Powers Shared by National and State Governments

- Provide for public welfare
- Administer criminal justice
- Charter banks
- Raise taxes
- Borrow money

Powers Reserved to States

- Create corporation laws
- Regulate trade within state
- Establish and maintain schools
- Establish local governments
- Make laws about marriage and divorce
- Conduct elections
- Provide for public safety

Public Schools *Powers reserved to the states include the power to establish and maintain schools. Today, the federal government provides funds to help support education, but Americans still insist on local control over schools.* **Citizenship** *Why do you think Americans want to keep local control over education?*

A division of power. The Constitution delegates, or assigns, certain powers to the national government. Other powers are reserved, or left, to the states. Still other powers, sometimes called concurrent powers, are shared by the national and state governments. The chart on page 287 shows how powers are divided under federalism.

The powers of the states. The Constitution does not clearly list the powers of the states. Instead, it states that all powers not specifically granted to the national government are reserved to the states (Amendment 10). At the same time, it makes clear exactly what powers are denied to the states (Article 1, Section 10).

Besides reserved powers, the Constitution makes other guarantees to the states. All states must be treated equally in matters of trade (Article 1, Section 9). And each state must respect the laws of the others (Article 4, Section 1). Perhaps most important of all, states are given representation in the national government.

National supremacy. Federalism creates a working partnership between the national government and the state governments. But when a dispute arises between them, there is no doubt where the final authority lies. The Constitution is the "supreme law of the land" (Article 6, Section 2). And only national courts can settle the dispute.

Separation of Powers Further Limits the Government

In 1787, nearly every government in Europe was a monarchy. The king or queen made and enforced the laws and appointed judges to interpret the laws. This system was dangerous. It put political power entirely in the hands of a few people.

Three branches of government. In the United States, the Constitution prevents one person or group from having all the power. It separates the national government into three branches: the legislative, the executive, and the judicial. Each branch has its powers and responsibilities. This division of the national government is known as separation of powers. (See the chart in Chapter 9 on page 263.)

The legislative branch. Article 1 of the Constitution sets up the legislative branch. This branch, called Congress, makes the laws. It has two houses: the House of Representatives and the Senate. Its many powers include the power to tax, to coin money, and to declare war.

The executive branch. Article 2 describes the executive branch, which carries out the laws. The President heads the executive branch and appoints advisers and other officials to assist him.

The executive branch plays an important role in foreign affairs. As commander in chief, the President has broad military powers. The President also can make treaties.

The judicial branch. Article 3 creates the Supreme Court to head the judicial branch. This branch interprets and explains the laws. Congress may set up lower courts as necessary.

Checks and Balances Prevent Abuse of Power

The Constitution divides the powers of government among three branches. But how does it prevent one branch of government from having too much power? The answer lies in a system of checks and balances. Each branch of the government can check, or control, the power of the other two branches.

How does the system of checks and balances work? The chart below shows some of the checks that the Congress, the President, and the Supreme Court have on each other.

Checks on Congress. Congress has the power to pass laws. But the President can check Congress by **vetoing**, or rejecting, a proposed law. Congress, in turn, can check the President by **overriding**, or setting aside, a presidential veto. In this way, a

CHART SKILLS *Through the system of checks and balances, each branch of government has checks, or controls, on the power of the other branches.* ◆ *Name one check that the President has on Congress. How can the Supreme Court check Congress?*

System of Checks and Balances

Executive Branch (President carries out laws)	Checks on the Legislative Branch	Checks on the Judicial Branch
	Can propose laws Can veto laws Can call special sessions of Congress Makes appointments Negotiates foreign treaties	Appoints federal judges Can grant pardons to federal offenders

Legislative Branch (Congress makes laws)	Checks on the Executive Branch	Checks on the Judicial Branch
	Can override President's veto Confirms executive appointments Ratifies treaties Can declare war Appropriates money Can impeach and remove President	Creates lower federal courts Can impeach and remove judges Can propose amendments to overrule judicial decisions Approves appointments of federal judges

Judicial Branch (Supreme Court interprets laws)	Check on the Executive Branch	Check on the Legislative Branch
	Can declare executive actions unconstitutional	Can declare acts of Congress unconstitutional

Principles of the Constitution

Principle	Definition
Popular sovereignty	Principle of government in which the people hold the final authority or power
Limited government	Principle that the government is not all powerful but can do only what the people say it can do
Federalism	Division of power between the national government and the state governments
Separation of powers	Division of the operations of the national government into three branches, each with its own powers and responsibilities
Checks and balances	Means by which each branch of the national government is able to check, or control, the power of the other two branches

CHART SKILLS *The Constitution is based on five principles.* ◆ *According to the principle of limited government, what can the government do? Which principle calls for dividing power between the national government and the state governments?*

bill, or proposed law, can become a law without the signature of the President.

The Supreme Court also can have a say in lawmaking. It can declare a law passed by Congress unconstitutional, or not permitted by the Constitution. That law then cannot take effect.

Checks on the President. The President has broad powers, especially in matters of foreign policy. As the chart shows, however, Congress has several checks on these powers.

For example, the President has the power to make treaties with foreign nations. But the Senate must ratify treaties. Also, the President is commander in chief of the armed forces. But Congress, not the President, holds the power to declare war.

The President also faces possible checks by the Supreme Court. The Court has the power to declare that an act of the President is unconstitutional.

Checks on the courts. Both the President and the Congress have several checks on the power of the judiciary. The Presi-

dent appoints all federal judges. Yet the Senate must approve the President's appointments. And Congress can remove federal judges from office if they are found guilty of wrongdoing. Congress may also propose a constitutional amendment to overrule a judicial decision.

SECTION 2 REVIEW

1. **Define:** (a) representative government, (b) ratify, (c) tyranny, (d) federal, (e) veto, (f) override, (g) bill, (h) unconstitutional.
2. According to the principle of popular sovereignty, who holds the final ruling power?
3. Why is limited government known as the "rule of law"?
4. What is federalism?
5. (a) List the three branches of government. (b) Name one power of each.
6. How can Congress check the President's power to make treaties?
7. **Analyzing Ideas** Explain the following statement: The Constitution sets up a government of law, not of people.

3 A Living Constitution

FIND OUT

◆ How can the Constitution be formally changed?

◆ What is the purpose of the Bill of Rights?

◆ What informal changes have been made in the Constitution?

◆ **VOCABULARY** amendment, precedent, cabinet, judicial review

"I do not think we are more inspired, have more wisdom, or possess more virtue than those who will come after us," said George Washington. The framers of the Constitution agreed with Washington. They also realized that the nation would grow and change. As a result, they provided future Americans with a living Constitution—one that could be adapted and altered to meet new conditions and challenges.

The Constitution Provides for Formal Changes

The Constitution allows amendments, or formal written changes, to the Constitution. But amending the Constitution is not easy. The process requires two difficult steps: proposal and ratification. (See the chart below.)

Proposing an amendment. Article 5 describes two methods for proposing amendments. Two thirds of each house of Congress can vote to propose an amendment.

CHART SKILLS *The amendment process requires proposal and ratification.*
◆ *Name one way to propose an amendment. Name one way to ratify an amendment.*

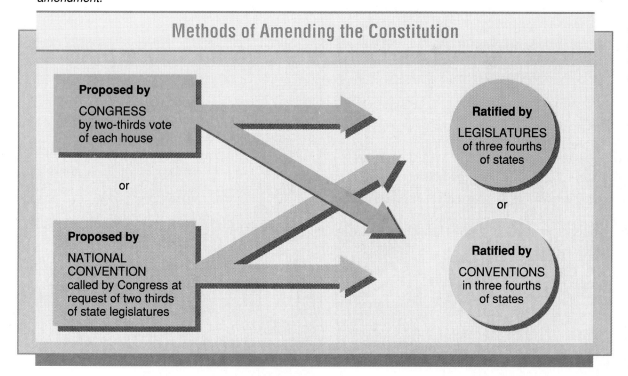

Methods of Amending the Constitution

Proposed by
CONGRESS
by two-thirds vote
of each house

or

Proposed by
NATIONAL
CONVENTION
called by Congress at
request of two thirds
of state legislatures

Ratified by
LEGISLATURES
of three fourths
of states

or

Ratified by
CONVENTIONS
in three fourths
of states

Or, two thirds of the state legislatures can demand that Congress summon a national "convention for proposing amendments."

So far, only the first method—a vote by Congress—has been used. As experts have warned, the Constitution does not give guidelines for a national convention. Who should set the agenda? How should delegates be selected? Those and other questions probably would cause much delay and confusion.

Ratifying an amendment. Article 5 also outlines two methods of ratifying a proposed amendment. Either three fourths of the state legislatures, or three fourths of the states meeting in special conventions, must approve the amendment.

Congress decides which method of ratification will be used. At present, all but one amendment have been ratified by state legislatures.

In recent years, Congress has set a time limit for ratification of amendments. The time limit today is seven years, but it can be extended.

The Constitution Has 26 Amendments

As you can see, the amendment process is a difficult one. Since 1789, more than 9,000 amendments have been introduced in Congress. Yet only 26 amendments have been ratified.

Bill of Rights. The original Constitution did not list basic freedoms of the people. In fact, several states refused to approve the Constitution until they were promised that a bill of rights would be added. Those states wanted to ensure that the national government could not take away basic freedoms.

The Bill of Rights, which includes the first 10 amendments to the Constitution,

The Right to Assemble and to Vote *Amendments to the Constitution include guarantees of individual rights. At left, deaf students from Gallaudet College exercise their First Amendment right to assemble in a peaceful protest. At right, an 18-year-old exercises his right to vote, a right granted by the Twenty-sixth Amendment.* **Citizenship** *Which amendments were passed to protect the rights of African Americans? What rights do they protect?*

was ratified in 1791. See the chart on page 282 for a list of the amendments in the Bill of Rights.

You will easily recognize many of the freedoms in the Bill of Rights. For example, the First Amendment protects your right to worship freely, to speak freely, to write freely, to hold peaceful meetings, and to ask the government to correct wrongs. The Fourth Amendment protects you from "unreasonable" search and seizure of your home and property. And the Sixth Amendment guarantees you the right to a trial by jury and to a lawyer.

Amendments 11 through 26. Only 16 amendments have been ratified since 1791. Several of these amendments reflect changes in ideas about equality.

Amendments 13 through 15—the so-called Civil War amendments—were passed to protect the rights of former slaves. The Thirteenth Amendment ended slavery. The Fourteenth Amendment guaranteed citizenship and constitutional rights to African Americans. And the Fifteenth Amendment guaranteed African Americans the right to vote.

Equality was also the goal of two later amendments. The Nineteenth Amendment gave women the right to vote. And the Twenty-sixth Amendment set age 18 as the minimum voting age.

The chart on page 282 includes a list of Amendments 11 through 26. For more information about the amendments, refer to the Constitution printed on pages 753–774.

Language and Tradition Allow Informal Changes

The language of the Constitution provides a general outline rather than specific details about the national government. Over time, this flexible language has allowed each branch of government to fulfill its role and meet the changing needs of the nation.

"Necessary and proper." The framers knew that they could not foresee what life would be like in the future. So Article 1,

An Age of Air Travel *Because the framers used flexible language, Americans have been able to make informal changes in the Constitution. Congress has used the Commerce Clause to pass laws dealing with airplane safety and traffic.* **Citizenship** *What other clause of the Constitution has allowed Congress to extend its powers?*

Section 8, Clause 18, gives Congress the power to make all laws that shall be "necessary and proper" to carry out the powers of the national government. This so-called **Elastic Clause** has allowed Congress to stretch its power to pass laws.

"Regulate commerce." Still another clause of the Constitution has allowed Congress to extend its powers. Article 1, Section 8, Clause 3, gives Congress the power to "regulate" trade with other nations and between the states.

Armed with this **Commerce Clause** and the Elastic Clause, Congress has been able to keep pace with many changes. For example, it has passed laws that regulate the airline industry, television, nuclear energy, and genetic engineering.

A more powerful executive branch. The Constitution does not describe in detail the powers of the President. But some Presidents have taken action or made decisions that set a precedent, or example, for later Presidents.

George Washington set one such precedent. The Constitution does not state that the President may appoint a cabinet, or group of close advisers. But President Washington assumed the power to do so on his own. Every President since then has followed his lead.

In times of national emergency, Presidents have expanded their constitutional role. During the Great Depression, for example, President Franklin Roosevelt expanded the size and power of the executive branch to propose and carry out programs to restore the national economy.

A broader role for the judiciary. The Supreme Court can decide whether acts of a President or laws passed by Congress are unconstitutional. Another name for this power is judicial review.

But the Constitution does not list judicial review as a power of the judicial branch. Like the unstated powers of the President, judicial review is implied in the words and structure of the Constitution. In the case of *Marbury* v. *Madison,* an early Supreme Court decision interpreted Article 3, Section 2, to mean that the Supreme Court has the right to decide whether a law violates the Constitution.

SECTION 3 REVIEW

1. **Identify:** (a) First Amendment, (b) Sixth Amendment, (c) Thirteenth Amendment, (d) Fourteenth Amendment, (e) Fifteenth Amendment, (f) Nineteenth Amendment, (g) Twenty-sixth Amendment, (h) Elastic Clause, (i) Commerce Clause, (j) *Marbury v. Madison*.
2. **Define:** (a) amendment, (b) precedent, (c) cabinet, (d) judicial review.
3. What two steps are required in the amendment process?
4. List four rights protected by the Bill of Rights.

5. (a) How did George Washington expand the powers of the President? (b) How did Franklin Roosevelt expand the role of the President during the Great Depression?
6. **Drawing Conclusions** Why have there been more informal changes than formal changes in the Constitution?

4 The National Government at Work

FIND OUT

◆ Why has Congress set up committees?

◆ What roles does the President play?

◆ How is the federal court system organized?

◆ VOCABULARY appropriate, standing committee, joint committee, impeach, constituent, executive agreement, jury, appeal

The Constitution establishes three branches of government, each with its own clearly defined powers. But they work together to accomplish the same goal: a government of laws. Together they make, carry out, and interpret the laws of the United States.

The Legislative Branch Makes the Laws

Congress, the legislative branch of government, is made up of two houses: the House of Representatives and the Senate. Together, the two houses have the power to make the laws that govern all 50 states. But at the same time, the states have a say in making those laws.

House of Representatives. The larger house, the House of Representatives, seats 435 members. Representatives serve two-year terms and are elected on the basis of a state's current population. The more people that live in a state, the greater is its number of representatives. Each state, however, is guaranteed at least one representative.

Senate. In contrast to the House, the Senate has only 100 members. Each state has two senators, no matter how large or small the population of the state. Senators serve for six-year terms. But the terms are staggered. As a result, one third of the Senate is up for election every two years.

Power to spend money. The chief purpose of Congress is to make the nation's laws. But Congress has yet another important power. It decides what laws or programs will receive funds.

The federal government cannot spend money unless Congress has appropriated it, or set aside the money for a special purpose. In this way, Congress controls how much money the government spends on military aircraft, school lunches, national highways, and other programs.

How a bill becomes a law. A bill is a proposal for a new law. It must be passed by both houses of Congress and signed by the President to become law. The chart on page 303 shows the many steps a bill must pass through before becoming law.

Congress Relies on Committees

During the first session of Congress, 31 bills were proposed by both houses. Today, thousands of bills are introduced each year in Congress.

It would be impossible for each of the 535 members of Congress to study and make recommendations about every bill. This job is reserved for committees, or special groups, that work on legislation.

Committees in each house. The House of Representatives and the Senate each have standing committees, or permanent committees. These committees study special subjects such as agriculture, labor, and energy. They are often broken up into subcommittees that study certain problems in depth.

Committees of both houses. Congress sometimes creates joint committees, or

groups made up of both House and Senate members. One of the most important joint committees is the conference committee. Its task is to settle differences between the House and Senate versions of the same bill. Members of a conference committee try to find a middle ground and to agree on the language of the bill. Very often, compromise is difficult.

A Vote in the House *An electronic voting board keeps track of the votes cast by the House of Representatives. A bill passes if the majority of the representatives votes "yes."* **Citizenship** *Who else must approve the bill before it becomes law?*

Passing a bill requires the cooperation of many individuals. For example, a recent trade bill was 1,000 pages long. It required the efforts of 200 members of Congress, working in 17 subcommittees, to get it passed. But most bills introduced in Congress do not meet with such success. In fact, more than 90 percent of all the bills introduced are defeated in committees.

Congress Plays Other Roles

Members of Congress have duties other than serving on committees and making laws. They also guard the public trust and respond to the special needs of their states.

A "watchdog." For example, the House of Representatives can impeach, or bring a formal charge of wrongdoing, against the President or another federal official. The Senate acts as a court to try the accused. Congress also acts as a "watchdog" by supervising the way the executive branch carries out the laws.

The people "back home." Responsible representatives and senators must remember their constituents, or the people who elect them. Therefore, members of Congress actively support bills that promote new post offices, improve highways, and help pay for education programs for the people "back home."

The President Has Several Roles

The framers created an executive branch to carry out the laws. But they left out details about the President's powers. Over the years, the powers of the President have been increased or decreased, depending on the needs of the time. Still, Americans expect the President to fill certain roles.

Chief executive. The main role of the President is to carry out the nation's laws. As chief executive, the President oversees the many departments, agencies, and commissions that help to deal with the burden.

Chief of state. The President is the living symbol of the nation. In this role, the President represents all American citizens at many occasions. For example, the President greets visiting foreign leaders and gives medals to national heroes.

Chief diplomat. The President directs the nation's foreign policy. Three important powers allow the President to influence relations with other countries. They are the powers to appoint ambassadors, make treaties, and enter into executive agreements. Executive agreements are informal agreements with other heads of state, usually dealing with trade. Unlike treaties, they do not require Senate approval.

Commander in chief. The President is the highest ranking officer in the armed forces. As commander in chief, the President can appoint and remove top military commanders. The President may also use the armed forces to deal with crises both at home and abroad.

Chief legislator. The President suggests new laws and works for their passage. In this role, the President often meets with members of Congress to win their support. Sometimes, the President campaigns for public support through television speeches and press conferences.

The President also can use persuasion to oppose a bill. But in this case, the most powerful weapon is the power to veto a bill.

The President Carries Out the Laws

The nation's laws cover a broad range of concerns—defense, housing, crime, and pollution, to name a few. To carry out these laws and to perform other duties, the President needs the help of millions of government workers. These workers make up five major groups.

Executive Office. One group of assistants, the Executive Office, includes many agencies and individuals. They range from the Office of Management and Budget, which prepares the total budget of the

The President at Work *The Constitution assigns the President the role of commander in chief. At left, President Reagan boosts morale by shaking hands with American troops. The President also serves as chief of state. At right, President Bush plays host to President Collor of Brazil on his visit to the United States.* **Citizenship** *Describe two other roles of the President.*

United States, to the Vice President. In all, the Executive Office has about 1,600 workers.

Executive departments. The President's cabinet, called secretaries, are the heads of executive departments. President Washington had only four departments. Today, the President relies on 14 executive departments—among them, the Departments of Defense, Commerce, Justice, Labor, and Energy. Each department has many concerns. For example, the Department of Agriculture deals with food quality, crop improvement, and nutrition.

Independent executive agencies. More than 30 independent executive agencies also help the President carry out duties. For example, the Central Intelligence Agency (CIA) provides the President with secret information about the world's trouble spots. The National Aeronautics and Space Administration (NASA) is in charge of the nation's space program.

Independent regulatory commissions. The fourth group of workers, 11 independent regulatory commissions, enforce national laws. They set down specific rules, rates, and standards for trade, business, science, and transportation. For example, a law of Congress forbids "false or misleading advertising." But it was the Federal Trade Commission (FTC) that ruled that cigarettes may not be advertised as "kind" to your throat.

Government corporations. There are at least 60 government corporations today. Also independent agencies, they include the United States Postal Service, the Tennessee Valley Authority, and the National Passenger Corporation, known as Amtrak.

The Judicial Branch Interprets the Laws

Article 3 of the Constitution gives the judicial power of the United States to the Supreme Court and to lower courts that Congress may set up. Under the Judiciary Act of 1789, Congress created the system of federal courts that still operates today.

District courts. Most federal cases begin in the district courts. These courts are placed in 91 districts around the country. The cases may involve matters of criminal law, such as kidnapping, or matters of civil law, such as bankruptcy. Decisions are made by either a judge or a jury, a panel of citizens.

Circuit courts. Every citizen has the right to appeal a decision, or ask that it be reviewed by a higher court. These higher courts of appeal are called circuit, or appellate, courts. The United States is divided into 12 judicial districts, or circuits.

Circuit courts operate differently from district courts. A panel of three judges reviews each case. The judges decide if rules of trial procedure were followed in the original trial. If errors did occur, the circuit court may reverse, or overturn, the original decision. Or it may send back the case to the district court for a new trial.

Supreme Court. The Supreme Court is the highest court in the land. It is made up of a Chief Justice and eight Associate Justices.

CHART SKILLS *The Constitution details the number, length of term, method of selection, and requirements of officeholders in the three branches of government.*
◆ *What are the requirements for the President? A senator? Which officeholders are elected directly by the voters?*

Federal Officeholders

Office	Number	Term	Selection	Requirements
Representative	At least 1 per state; based on state population	2 years	Elected by voters of congressional district	Age 25 or over Citizen for 7 years Resident of state in which elected
Senator	2 per state	6 years	Original Constitution— elected by state legislature Amendment 17— elected by voters	Age 30 or over Citizen for 9 years Resident of state in which elected
President and Vice President	1	4 years	Elected by electoral college	Age 35 or over Natural-born citizen Resident of U.S. for 14 years
Supreme Court judge	9	Life	Appointed by President	No requirements in Constitution

The Supreme Court *The Chief Justice and eight Associate Justices of the Supreme Court interpret the law. A majority of five votes can determine a Supreme Court decision. In recent years, many Supreme Court cases have involved the protection of individual rights.* **Citizenship** *What kinds of issues does the Supreme Court hear?*

Only two kinds of cases can begin in the Supreme Court. The first kind involves disputes between states. The second involves foreign ambassadors.

Otherwise, the Supreme Court serves as a final court of appeals. It hears cases that have been tried and appealed as far as law permits in federal and state courts.

The Supreme Court hears only issues about the Constitution, federal law, or treaties. It selects only about 120 cases from the 4,000 or more requests it receives each year. Most of the cases involve laws written in unclear language. The Court must decide what each law means, whom it affects, and whether it is constitutional.

A Supreme Court decision rests on a simple majority vote of at least five Justices. It is a final decision. There are no other courts of appeal. But if Congress strongly disagrees with a Supreme Court decision, it can pass a modified version of the law or propose an amendment to the Constitution.

SECTION 4 REVIEW

1. **Identify:** (a) House of Representatives, (b) Senate, (c) Supreme Court.
2. **Define:** (a) appropriate, (b) standing committee, (c) joint committee, (d) impeach, (e) constituent, (f) executive agreement, (g) jury, (h) appeal.
3. Name three programs for which Congress might appropriate money.
4. (a) What duties does the President perform as chief executive? (b) As chief legislator?
5. (a) What is the role of circuit courts? (b) What is the role of the Supreme Court?
6. **Analyzing Ideas** Should judges be required to run for office? Explain.

5 Citizenship at Work

FIND OUT

◆ How did the Fourteenth Amendment help to expand rights?

◆ What responsibilities do citizens have?

◆ **VOCABULARY** due process of law

The Constitution and its amendments guarantee rights to you and every other American citizen. But along with these rights of citizenship come responsibilities.

Citizens Have Rights

Americans first proclaimed their rights in the Declaration of Independence. "All men are created equal," the Declaration states, and they have "certain unalienable rights,"

CHART SKILLS *The First Amendment to the Constitution guarantees some basic individual liberties.* ◆ *Name two freedoms it protects. Which freedom allows you to hold and attend meetings?*

Liberties Protected by the First Amendment

Freedom of the Press

Freedom of Religion

Freedom of Petition

Freedom of Assembly

Freedom of Speech

including "life, liberty, and the pursuit of happiness." Since the birth of the nation, Americans have struggled to reach this ideal of basic rights for all citizens.

The first step. The original Constitution protected some individual rights by limiting government actions. For example, Article 6, Section 3, prevents government from making religion a requirement for public service. And Article 1, Section 9, forbids passing any law that makes someone guilty of a crime without a trial.

Bill of Rights. As you have read, many Americans demanded a more specific list of rights. The first 10 amendments to the Constitution further spell out rights. For example, the First Amendment forbids government actions that limit freedom of religion, speech, press, assembly, and petition. (See the chart on page 282.)

The Bill of Rights applied only to the national government, however. It did not affect the actions of state governments. As a result, states were able to limit or deny basic rights of many Americans, including African Americans, Asian Americans, Native Americans, and women. The federal government sometimes restricted basic rights, too, through laws and in court decisions.

Fourteenth Amendment. An amendment passed in 1868 paved the way for a major expansion of rights. The Fourteenth Amendment states that persons born or naturalized in the United States are citizens of both the nation and their state. No state, the amendment says, may limit the rights of citizens or deny citizens "due process of law" and "equal protection of the laws."

Court decisions. Beginning in the 1920s, the Supreme Court interpreted the Fourteenth Amendment in a long series of cases. Over the years, it decided that the Fourteenth Amendment's guarantee of "due process" and "equal protection" included rights listed in the Bill of Rights. For example, in the 1960s, the Court ruled that due process of law, or fair rules in all cases brought to trial, includes the Sixth Amendment rights to a speedy trial by jury

Voter Registration

Every election day, the polls are open from early morning until early evening. Often, however, fewer than one half of the eligible voters vote. Many people offer the excuse that they are not registered. That is, they have not signed up in advance of the election as required by state law.

Under the Constitution, states have the right to set voting requirements. They require voter registration to prevent people from voting more than once in the same election. In the past, some people used another person's name in order to vote a second time.

Voters must register only once, unless they move or fail to vote for a long period. Yet many Americans think it is a bother to register. Some reformers want to end registration entirely. Others want to make it more convenient. They propose registration by mail or at the polls on election day. Or perhaps, they suggest, officials could make home visits to register citizens.

1. Why do state laws require voter registration?

2. Forecasting Do you think registration reform would increase the number of people who vote? Explain.

---

and to a lawyer. States could not deny citizens the protections of the Bill of Rights.

Ideas of liberty grow. As the Ninth Amendment states, the people have rights beyond those described in the Constitution. Americans still strive to define and guarantee those rights. Many believe that their rights include the opportunity to pursue a good education, to find a job, and to live in decent housing.

Citizens Have Responsibilities

You and every other citizen must do your part to safeguard your rights. That role includes responsibilities.

Learn about your rights. You cannot protect your rights unless you know what they are. Books, government pamphlets, and groups such as the League of Women Voters and Legal Aid Society can give you information about your rights and the law.

Respect the rights of others. Your rights are only as safe as your neighbor's. If you abuse or allow others to abuse another citizen's rights, your rights might also be at risk someday.

Express your views. The First Amendment guarantees you the freedom to speak, write, sign petitions, and meet with others freely. You can use those freedoms not only to defend your rights but to take a stand on political and community issues. But remember that such expressions should be truthful and peaceful.

Learn about community and national issues. As a responsible citizen, keep informed about issues critical to the nation and to your community. Besides reading newspapers and magazines, attend local meetings. At a town council meeting, for example, you might learn about proposed solutions to pollution problems. Or the League of Women Voters might offer a debate among candidates for political office.

Vote. Good government depends on good leaders. Therefore, citizens have the responsibility to exercise their right to vote and select the best candidate. If citizens have studied the candidates and the issues in an election, they will be able to make a responsible decision.

A Neighborhood Cleanup *Responsibilities of citizens include caring for the community. Helping to clean up the neighborhood benefits you as well as others.*
Daily Life *What do you think you could do to improve your community?*

Obey laws. Citizens enter into a contract with the government. They give the government the power to make certain laws. In return, they expect government to protect the health and well-being of society. As part of this contract, the government has the power to set penalties if laws are broken.

Like other citizens, you have a responsibility to obey the laws that safeguard your rights and the rights of others. For example, you should not steal, damage the property of others, or harm someone physically.

Serve on juries. The Bill of Rights guarantees citizens the right to a trial by jury. Every citizen, in turn, has the responsibility to serve on juries when called.

Serving on a jury is a serious duty. Jurors must take time out from their work and personal life. Listening to evidence can be tiring. And deciding the guilt or innocence of the accused can be difficult.

Volunteer. Responsible citizens offer their time and talents to help others and to improve the community. For example, you can join or start a group to clean up parks or to serve food to senior citizens. Or you can take part in a walk-a-thon or bike-a-thon to raise money for a worthy cause.

Defend the nation. At age 18, all young men must report their name, age, and address to the government. In time of war, the government may draft, or choose, them to serve in the armed forces. Some young citizens feel the duty to enlist in, or join, the military on their own.

SECTION 5 REVIEW

1. **Define:** due process of law.
2. What are the five basic freedoms of the First Amendment?
3. What does the Fourteenth Amendment guarantee?
4. List three responsibilities of citizenship.
5. **Applying Information** Why has the Fourteenth Amendment been called the "nationalization" of the Bill of Rights?

A flow chart gives a lot of information in a simple, easy-to-understand way. It shows a process or development step by step. For example, under the Constitution, Congress can pass a bill and the President can sign it into law. Over the years, a complicated process has developed whereby a bill actually becomes a law.

1 **Identify the parts of the flow chart.** (a) What is the title of the flow chart? (b) What does each of the four columns show? (c) What do the black arrows show? (d) What color shows House action? Senate action?

2 **Practice reading the flow chart.** (a) Where is a bill usually introduced? (b) What happens to a bill after it has been introduced? (c) What happens after the House and Senate have both passed their own forms of a bill? (d) What is the last step a bill goes through before it becomes a law?

3 **Evaluate the information shown on the flow chart.** Every year, about 10,000 bills are introduced in Congress. Only about 1,000 ever make it through the many steps to become laws. (a) Why do you think House and Senate committees hold hearings on bills that have been introduced? (b) Using the flow chart, why do you think only a few bills actually become laws?

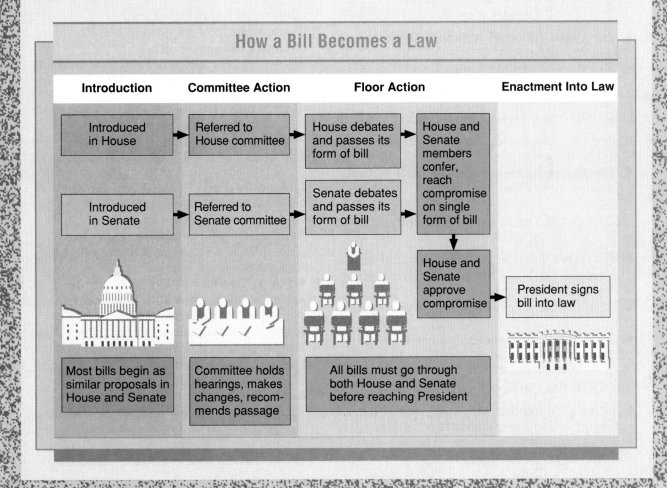

How a Bill Becomes a Law

Introduction	Committee Action	Floor Action	Enactment Into Law
Introduced in House	Referred to House committee	House debates and passes its form of bill	House and Senate members confer, reach compromise on single form of bill
Introduced in Senate	Referred to Senate committee	Senate debates and passes its form of bill	
			House and Senate approve compromise
			President signs bill into law
Most bills begin as similar proposals in House and Senate	Committee holds hearings, makes changes, recommends passage	All bills must go through both House and Senate before reaching President	

CIVICS REVIEW

Use the Section Reviews and this Review to study the Civics Overview.

Summary

The main ideas in each section of this Overview are summarized below.

SECTION 1 ■ The Goals of the Constitution

◆ The people have established the Constitution to achieve certain goals.
◆ The national government has the power to accomplish those goals.

SECTION 2 ■ Five Principles of the Constitution

◆ The Constitution is based on five important principles.
◆ The five principles support a strong but limited national government.

SECTION 3 ■ A Living Constitution

◆ The Constitution has adapted to changes in the nation.
◆ The Constitution allows for both formal and informal changes.

SECTION 4 ■ The National Government at Work

◆ The three branches of the national government work together to achieve a government of laws.
◆ Each branch of government plays a separate role.
◆ Over time, the branches have expanded their roles and powers.

SECTION 5 ■ Citizenship at Work

◆ Through amendments, the Constitution has extended basic rights to all citizens.
◆ To safeguard their rights, citizens must assume responsibilities.

Reviewing the Main Ideas

1. List two goals of the Constitution. Describe one way that the national government helps to achieve each goal.
2. List the branches of the national government. Describe the role of each branch.
3. How can the President and the Supreme Court check the power of Congress to pass laws?
4. Describe two methods of proposing an amendment to the Constitution.
5. Describe two ways that the language of the Constitution has allowed informal changes.
6. (a) Describe standing committees and joint committees. (b) What task does a conference committee have?
7. What three powers enable the President to direct foreign policy?
8. How did the Fourteenth Amendment pave the way for a major expansion of individual rights?

Thinking About the Constitution

1. **Linking Past and Present** Are the goals of the nation today the same as those set out in the Preamble? Explain.
2. **Synthesizing Information** How are the principles of popular sovereignty and limited government related?
3. **Making Decisions** Do you think the amendment process should be made simpler? Explain your answer.
4. **Analyzing Information** Former Chief Justice Hughes said, "We are under a Constitution, but the Constitution is what the judges say it is." What did Hughes mean?
5. **Evaluating Information** What are the advantages and disadvantages of the process by which a bill becomes a law?
6. **Comparing** Describe the differences between district courts and circuit courts.

Applying Your Skills

1. **Outlining** Review the outlining steps you learned on page 32. Then, outline the section "Five Principles of the Constitution" that begins on page 285.
2. **Reading a Chart** Review the chart on page 287. (a) Name three powers delegated to the national government. (b) Name three powers shared by the national government and state governments.
3. **Reading a Chart** Review the chart on page 298. Write a paragraph about Supreme Court Justices based on the information in the chart.
4. **Making a Generalization** Review the subsection "The President Carries Out the Laws" that begins on page 296. Make a generalization about the size of the executive branch. List three facts to support your generalization.
5. **Ranking** Review the subsection "The President Has Several Roles" on page 296. List the roles of the President. Then, rank the roles in order of importance. Explain your ranking.
6. **Reading a Flow Chart** Refer to the Skill Lesson on page 303. (a) At what two points do the Senate and House act separately? (b) At what point do they act jointly?

Doing More

1. **Making a Poster** Make a poster that shows government activities related to one of the goals of the Constitution.

2. **Organizing a Debate** As a group project, organize a debate on the following proposal for a constitutional amendment: The terms of United States representatives should be four years instead of two years.
3. **Researching a Report** Research and write a report on the executive departments. Identify their secretaries and explain their roles. List the departments in order of importance. Check your final copy for punctuation and grammar.
4. **Making a Poster** Make a poster urging citizens to take part in their community. Possible subjects include voting and cleaning up neighborhoods.
5. **Writing a Letter** Write a letter to your senator or representative expressing your views on a national issue such as drugs or education. Brainstorm a list of your concerns and organize them in order of importance. Check your final copy for spelling and punctuation errors.

Using the Time Line

1. Make a chart of events in time order. The chart will have two headings: Date, Event. Fill in the chart, using the events on the time line. Add the following events from the Overview: Amendment 13 ratified; Amendment 15 ratified. (Refer to pages 768 and 769 for the dates.)
2. (a) Which events on your chart took place during the 1860s? (b) How did they affect African Americans?

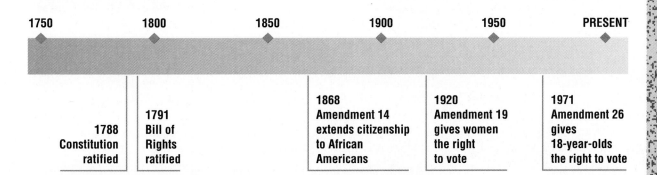

| 1750 | 1800 | 1850 | 1900 | 1950 | PRESENT |

1788 Constitution ratified

1791 Bill of Rights ratified

1868 Amendment 14 extends citizenship to African Americans

1920 Amendment 19 gives women the right to vote

1971 Amendment 26 gives 18-year-olds the right to vote

UNIT 4 The New Republic

Unit Outline

2 President Thomas Jefferson nearly doubled the size of the nation when he purchased Louisiana from France.

1 White settlers moved west as the new government took shape. Native Americans on the frontier struggled to keep their land and way of life.

3 The economy and foreign policy of the new nation deeply concerned Americans. Still, religion played a major role in daily life.

	1780	1790	1800	1810
AMERICAN EVENTS		**1787** Northwest Ordinance	**1793** Cotton gin invented	**1804** Lewis and Clark explore Louisiana Purchase
WORLD EVENTS	**1700s** Industrial Revolution in Britain	**1789** French Revolution begins	**1803** War between Britain and France	

George Washington · John Adams · Thomas Jefferson

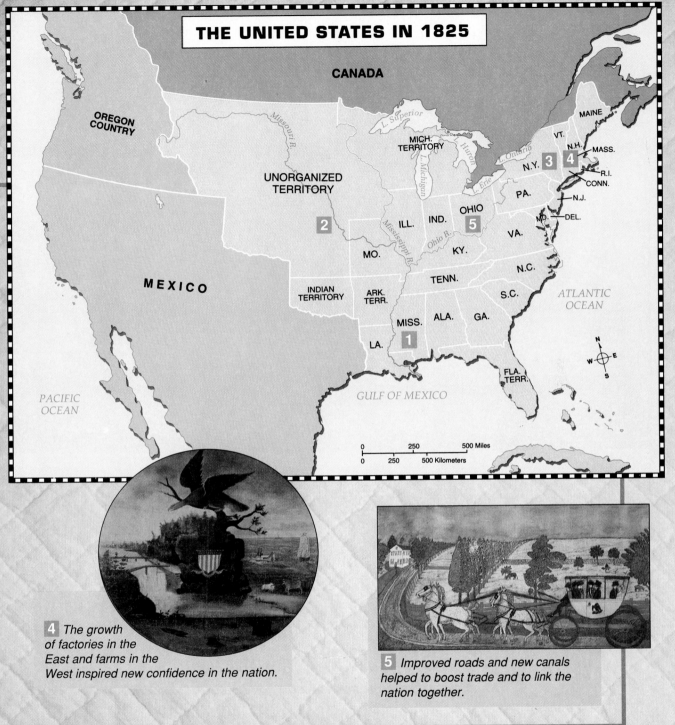

THE UNITED STATES IN 1825

CANADA

OREGON COUNTRY

UNORGANIZED TERRITORY

MEXICO

PACIFIC OCEAN

Missouri R.

MICH. TERRITORY

L. Superior

L. Michigan

L. Huron

L. Ontario

L. Erie

MAINE

VT.

N.H.

MASS.

N.Y.

R.I.

CONN.

PA.

N.J.

ILL.

IND.

OHIO

MD. — DEL.

Mississippi R.

Ohio R.

VA.

MO.

KY.

N.C.

INDIAN TERRITORY

ARK. TERR.

TENN.

S.C.

MISS.

ALA.

GA.

LA.

ATLANTIC OCEAN

FLA. TERR.

GULF OF MEXICO

N E S W

2

3

4

5

1

0   250   500 Miles
0   250   500 Kilometers

4 The growth of factories in the East and farms in the West inspired new confidence in the nation.

5 Improved roads and new canals helped to boost trade and to link the nation together.

1810	1820	1830	1840

1814 War of 1812 ends

1823 Monroe Doctrine proclaimed

1825 Erie Canal completed

1815 Holy Alliance formed

1821 Mexico wins independence from Spain

James Madison

James Monroe

Andrew Jackson

Martin Van Buren

John Quincy Adams

The Nation's First President *To Americans, George Washington was a symbol of the patriotism they felt for their new country. In this painting, crowds cheer Washington as he arrives in New York City to be inaugurated as the nation's first President.* **Citizenship** *Why did Americans have confidence in President Washington?*

10

The New Government Begins (1789–1800)

Chapter Outline

1 Washington Leads the Nation
2 Avoiding War
3 The First Political Parties
4 John Adams As President

The Big Picture

Historians often talk about learning from the "lessons of history." In 1789, the "lessons" that the framers of the Constitution studied were not encouraging. In all recorded history, no republican government had ever survived for long. Some turned into dictatorships. Others broke up in quarrels.

In 1789, no one knew that the United States would become the longest-lasting republic in the history of the world. Washington and other leaders who helped to form the republic did not know that they were writing a new "lesson" in history. They knew only that the odds of creating a successful republic were against them.

Jim Davidson

Focus On

◆ How was the new government organized?

◆ How did the young republic avoid war?

◆ Why did political parties form?

◆ What caused the Federalist party to split?

Most Americans looked on George Washington as a great hero. They were proud that he would be their first President. In his biography of Washington, Mason Weems describes the excitement of the crowds that gathered as Washington rode to New York City to take the oath of office:

❝As soon as it was officially notified to him, in the spring of 1789, that he was unanimously elected President of the United States . . . he set out for [New York]. Then all along the roads where he passed . . . it was only said, 'General Washington is coming.' . . . The inhabitants all hastened from their houses to the highways, to get a sight of their great countryman; while the people of the towns, hearing of his approach, sallied out . . . to meet him. In eager throngs, men, women and children pressed upon his steps.❞

Americans continued to adore Washington throughout his two terms in office. Still, the President faced serious problems. How should he handle a rebellion of backcountry farmers? How could he keep political parties from splitting the nation into two opposing groups? To add to his concerns, a few critics insulted him in words "as could scarcely be applied . . . even to a common pickpocket."

In this chapter, you will read about the difficult years of the country's first two Presidents, George Washington and John Adams. Their decisions as leaders were important to the success of the new nation.

1 Washington Leads the Nation

FIND OUT

◆ Who served in Washington's cabinet?

◆ What was Hamilton's two-step plan to repay the national debt?

◆ How did Hamilton propose to strengthen the economy?

◆ **VOCABULARY** precedent, cabinet, bond, national debt, speculator, tariff

In the spring of 1789, the new House of Representatives and Senate echoed with an unusual debate. The debate had nothing to do with taxes or foreign policy. For three solid weeks, Congress argued about how to address the President of the United States.

Members of the House thought that the President should be referred to simply as "President Washington." But some senators thought that this form of address lacked dignity. "What will the common people of foreign countries, what will the sailors and soldiers say?" sputtered Vice President John Adams. "'George Washington, President of the United States?' They will despise him to all eternity." Instead, the Senate suggested calling him "His Elective Highness," or even "His Highness the President of the United States and Protector of the Rights of the Same."

The House finally won the debate. Since Washington was not a king, members of Congress did not wish to make him one. This lengthy debate would be one of many that the young republic would face as it took shape.

President Washington

George Washington took the oath of office as President on April 30, 1789. He looked "grave, almost to sadness," one witness

The Washington Family
After the Revolution, George Washington returned to Mount Vernon, eager to enjoy the quiet pleasures of country life. But the nation called once again, and Washington sadly left his home to take up the duties of President. Here, Washington is shown with his wife, Martha, and two of his stepchildren. **Linking Past and Present** *Why might it have been harder to be the first President than to be President today? How might it be harder to be President today?*

310 ◆ CHAPTER 10

said. Washington felt more at ease commanding the Continental Army than heading the new government. But the young nation looked to him to solve its problems.

Setting an example. As the first President, Washington had no one to imitate. Even though the Constitution provided a framework for the new government, it did not explain how the President should govern from day to day. Washington, therefore, had to make many new and important decisions. "There is scarcely any part of my conduct," he said solemnly, "which may not hereafter be drawn into precedent." A precedent (PREHS uh duhnt) is an act or decision that sets an example for others to follow.

Washington set one important precedent in 1796, near the end of his second term. Though friends tried to persuade him to run for reelection, Washington firmly refused. His refusal to seek a third term set a precedent that later Presidents followed until 1940.

The President's cabinet. The Constitution also said little about how the executive branch should be organized. But it was clear that the new President needed people to help him carry out his duties. When the first Congress met in 1789, it quickly created five new departments. These included the State Department, Treasury Department, War Department, and the offices of Attorney General and Postmaster General.

Washington chose some of the best-known people in the country to head these departments. Thomas Jefferson became Secretary of State, Alexander Hamilton was Secretary of the Treasury, and Henry Knox served as Secretary of War. The Attorney General was Edmund Randolph, and Samuel Osgood served as Postmaster General. The heads of the five departments were called the cabinet. Often, cabinet members gave Washington advice.

Creating federal courts. The Constitution called for a Supreme Court. But it left to Congress the job of organizing the federal court system. In 1789, Congress passed the **Judiciary Act.** The act said that the Supreme Court should have one Chief Justice and five Associate Justices.* It also set up district courts and circuit courts throughout the nation. Decisions made in these lower courts could be appealed to the Supreme Court, the highest court in the land.

Washington asked John Jay to be the first Chief Justice of the Supreme Court. Jay had worked hard for ratification of the Constitution and believed in a strong federal government. Like judges in Britain, Jay and the other justices wore black and scarlet robes. But Thomas Jefferson convinced them not to wear white wigs as British judges did.

Paying the Nation's Debts

As Secretary of the Treasury, Alexander Hamilton wanted to build a strong economy. But the nation faced major problems. One of Hamilton's concerns was government debts.

Repaying government bonds. During the Revolution, both the national government and individual states needed money to pay soldiers and buy supplies. They borrowed money from foreign countries and ordinary citizens.

Then, as now, governments borrowed money by issuing bonds. A bond is a certificate that promises to pay the holder its face value plus interest on a certain date. For example, if a person buys a bond for $100, the government agrees to pay back $100 plus interest in five or ten years. The money that a government owes is called the national debt.

By 1789, most southern states had paid off their debts from the Revolution. But other states and the federal government had not. Hamilton insisted on repaying all these debts. After all, he said, who would lend money to the United States in the future if the country did not pay its old debts?

---

*Today, the Supreme Court has eight Associate Justices.

Veterans Return From the War *The Revolution was over, and veterans, like those pictured here, headed home. But when they arrived, they found that the nation they fought to create had no money to pay them their wages.* **Economics** *To whom else did the new United States owe money?*

Hamilton's plan. Hamilton soon devised a two-step plan to repay both the national and state debts. First, he wanted to buy up all old bonds issued by the government before 1789. Hamilton would then sell new bonds to pay off the old debt. Second, he wanted to buy up all state bonds and pay them off in the same way.

Many Americans, including bankers and investors, approved of Hamilton's plan. Other Americans, however, felt that the plan was unfair.

Opposition to Hamilton's Plan

In Congress, James Madison led the opposition to Hamilton's plan. Madison pointed out that during the Revolution, soldiers and other citizens had been paid with government bonds. Many of these bondholders needed cash to survive during the war. So they sold their bonds to speculators. A speculator is someone willing to invest in a risky venture on the chance of making a big profit.

Madison's objections. Speculators had bought up most of the bonds issued during the Revolution. But they paid only 10 or 15 cents for a bond worth one dollar. If the government repaid the bonds at their full value, speculators stood to make large profits. Speculators should not be paid full value and allowed such profits, Madison argued.

Hamilton believed otherwise. In his view, the new government needed the support of speculators and other investors. By paying back the bonds at full price, the United States would win their loyalty. After much debate, Hamilton convinced Congress to accept his plan and to repay the national debt in full. (📖 See "Great Little Madison" on page 662.)

Many southern states were bitterly opposed to the second part of Hamilton's plan. It called for buying up and repaying state debts. Having already paid their debts, southern states had little to gain. Once again, Madison led the fight against Hamilton. When Hamilton saw that most of Congress supported Madison, he offered the South a deal.

Hamilton's compromise. Hamilton knew that many southerners wanted to move the nation's capital from New York to Virginia. He offered to persuade his northern friends to vote for a new capital in the South. In turn, he asked southerners to support his plan to pay off state debts.

Madison and other southerners finally agreed to Hamilton's compromise. In July 1790, Congress passed a bill taking over state debts and making plans for a new capital city.

Congress decided that the new capital should not be part of any state. Instead, Congress set aside a piece of land on the Potomac River between Maryland and Virginia. It called the area the District of Columbia. Congress hoped that the new capital, called Federal City, would be ready by 1800. In the meantime, Congress made Philadelphia the nation's capital. (□ See "Moving Into a New House" on page 664.)

GEOGRAPHIC • CONNECTION

Building the Nation's Capital

After choosing an area in the South for the nation's capital, Congress asked President Washington to select the location. He picked a ten-square-mile site along the Potomac River. Centrally located, the site was not a part of any state, yet was easily within reach of all the states.

Hoping to turn this wilderness into a beautiful city, Washington hired the French architect Pierre L'Enfant (lahn FAHN). Making the city "magnificent enough to grace a great nation" was L'Enfant's goal.

L'Enfant planned a city of broad avenues. Like spokes on a wheel, these avenues radiated outward from two major centers. One center was for Congress House, later known as the Capitol. The oth-

er, one mile down the grand boulevard of Pennsylvania Avenue, was for the President's Palace, later called the White House. L'Enfant's plans also included many public parks and fountains.

Construction of the capital was costly and slow. Still, in 1800, President Adams and all three branches of government moved to present-day Washington, D.C. Instead of a magnificent city, they found a muddy village with unfinished buildings. But Abigail Adams, the President's wife, saw its promise. "It is a beautiful spot. . . . The more I view it, the more I am delighted with it."

1. What two major centers did L'Enfant include in his plan?

2. **Making Decisions** Do you think it was wise not to locate the nation's capital in any one state? Explain.

Strengthening the Economy

Hamilton had more ideas about how to strengthen the nation's economy. He wanted the United States to have a national bank, as Britain did. In 1791, Congress passed a bill setting up the **Bank of the United States.** The government deposited taxes it raised in the Bank. The Bank then issued paper money to pay the government's bills. The Bank also made loans to farmers and businesses. In this way, Hamilton argued, the Bank would help new businesses grow.

The new government had many expenses. It had to pay its employees, build the new Federal City, and maintain an army and navy. As Secretary of the Treasury, Hamilton's job was to raise money for these expenses. The Constitution, as you have read, gave Congress the power to pass tax laws. So Hamilton asked Congress to approve several taxes. (See the chart below.)

One of the laws put a tariff, or tax, on all foreign goods brought into the country. The tariff raised the price of these imports. By making foreign goods cost more than American products, Hamilton hoped to encourage people to buy products made in the United States. The tariff would also raise money for the government, since some people would still buy imports and pay the tax.

Many northerners supported the tariff, but most southerners did not. In the North, small factories were growing. The tariff protected these manufacturers from foreign competition. But in the South, most people were farmers. They bought more foreign goods than northerners did. For them, the tariff only made these goods more expensive.

The Whiskey Tax

In 1794, Congress also passed a bill that taxed all liquor made and sold in the United States. Hamilton wanted this tax to raise money for the government. Settlers in the backcountry, however, bitterly opposed the tax.

Like many other American farmers, backcountry farmers raised corn. But in the backcountry, far from good roads or cities, corn was too bulky to haul to markets in the East. So farmers turned their corn into whiskey, which could be shipped easily in barrels.

Backcountry farmers were furious when they heard about the "excise" tax on whiskey, as it was called. They compared it to the unfair taxes that Britain forced the colonists to pay in the 1760s. Many refused to pay the tax. One backcountry poet wrote:

> ❝Some chaps whom freedom's
> spirit warms

CHART SKILLS *As Secretary of the Treasury, Alexander Hamilton had to set up a plan for the government to meet its expenses.* ◆ *What was the government's income in 1789? How much did it owe?*

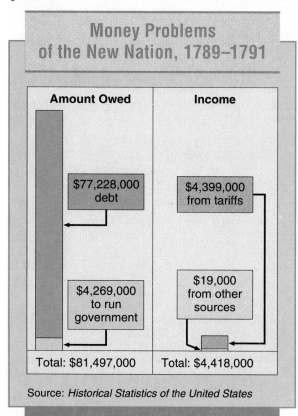

Money Problems of the New Nation, 1789–1791

Amount Owed	Income
$77,228,000 debt	$4,399,000 from tariffs
$4,269,000 to run government	$19,000 from other sources
Total: $81,497,000	Total: $4,418,000

Source: *Historical Statistics of the United States*

Are threatening hard to take up arms. . . .
Their liberty they will maintain,
They fought for't, and they'll fight again. **"**

The Whiskey Rebellion

When tax collectors appeared in western Pennsylvania, they faced angry farmers. One of the most well-known tax collectors was John Neville.

One spring morning, Neville and his wife were riding home from Pittsburgh. When Mrs. Neville's saddle began to slip off, Neville stopped to adjust it. He heard the clip-clop of an approaching horse, and then a voice.

"Are you Neville, the excise officer?"

Still busy with his wife's saddle, Neville replied, "Yes," without turning around.

"Then I must give you a whipping!" yelled the stranger, who grabbed Neville by the throat.

The two men struggled. In the end, Neville threw his attacker to the ground and frightened him into running off. But the incident left no doubt: Neville was an unpopular man in the backcountry.

William Miller receives a summons. Farmers around Pittsburgh were not only angry because they had to pay the whiskey tax. According to the law, they also had to appear in court if they did not pay.

William Miller, a farmer who distilled whiskey, soon found out about that part of the law. One hot day in July 1794, a stranger arrived at Miller's door. The man explained that he was the sheriff from Philadelphia and had come to serve Miller legal papers. Next to the sheriff stood the tax collector, John Neville.

Miller read the court summons. It ordered him to set aside "all manner of busi-

ness and excuses" and appear before the court in little more than a month. To appear, Miller would have to make a long journey east, just when he was planning to sell his farm. Even worse, the court papers seemed to say that he owed the government $250, a very large sum. Miller recalled his anger:

> **"**I felt myself mad with passion. I thought $250 would ruin me; and to have to go [to] the federal court at Philadelphia would keep me from going to Kentucky this fall after I had sold my plantation. . . . I felt my blood boil at seeing General Neville along to pilot the sheriff to my very door.**"**

Farmers rebel. The rumor quickly spread that a sheriff had come to take Miller to Philadelphia. Within a short time, 60 angry farmers marched down the road toward Neville and the sheriff. Some had muskets, and others had pitchforks. The sheriff and Neville retreated. But the following day, farmers and Neville clashed again. This time, Neville opened fire and killed a man. Several other farmers were wounded.

Elsewhere, other mobs formed. At one point, thousands of farmers marched through Pittsburgh. Supporters of this so-called **Whiskey Rebellion** set up Liberty Trees and sang revolutionary songs.

News of the rebellion spread quickly. When Alexander Hamilton heard the report, he was shocked. The rebellion, he said, "was treason against society, against liberty, against everything that ought to be dear to a free, enlightened, and prudent people." President Washington acted quickly. Calling up the militia in several states, he marched out to review the troops.

When the rebels heard that an army of 13,000 was marching against them, they ended all talk of taking up arms. In fact, the army took only a handful of prisoners. Hamilton wanted to execute two men

Washington Reviews the Troops *When Pennsylvania farmers rioted against the whiskey tax, George Washington called out the state militias to restore order. Here, Washington reviews troops that had assembled at Fort Cumberland, Maryland.* **Citizenship** *Why do you think Washington acted quickly to put down the Whiskey Rebellion?*

convicted of treason, but Washington disagreed and pardoned them. The President felt that the government had already shown its strength.

Many Americans compared the Whiskey Rebellion with Shays' Rebellion just eight years earlier. (See page 255.) The speedy end of the Whiskey Rebellion proved, they said, that their new government was strong and efficient. ◆

SECTION 1 REVIEW

1. **Identify:** (a) Judiciary Act, (b) Bank of the United States, (c) Whiskey Rebellion.
2. **Define:** (a) precedent, (b) cabinet, (c) bond, (d) national debt, (e) speculator, (f) tariff.
3. List the five members of Washington's cabinet.
4. Describe Hamilton's two-step plan to repay the national and state debts.
5. List two of Hamilton's ideas for strengthening the economy.
6. Why did some Americans oppose a tariff?

7. **Analyzing Ideas** Why do you think people who had taken part in the American Revolution still looked on the Whiskey Rebellion as "treason"?

2 Avoiding War

FIND OUT

◆ What effect did the French Revolution have on the United States?

◆ What was the purpose of the Neutrality Proclamation?

◆ Why did settlers and Indians fight in the Northwest Territory?

◆ What was Washington's advice in his Farewell Address?

Late in 1789, French ships arriving at American ports brought startling news. On July 14, 1789, a mob in Paris had attacked the Bastille (bah STEEL), a huge prison. The mob freed the few prisoners in the Bastille and then tore it down, brick by brick. This attack marked the beginning of the **French Revolution.**

The French Revolution took place a few years after Americans won their own revolution. In fact, the American Revolution had inspired the people of France. Yet the French Revolution would heat up political quarrels already simmering in the United States.

Revolution in France

The French had many reasons to rebel against their king and nobles who ruled them. French peasants paid very heavy taxes. They wanted a constitution and rights similar to those that Americans had won after 1776.

At first, most Americans favored the French Revolution. They knew what it meant to struggle for liberty. They also remembered that France had been their ally against Britain. Should not Americans now support the Marquis de Lafayette and others in their struggle to make France a republic?

But the French Revolution took a violent turn in the 1790s. The revolutionary government beheaded the French king, Louis XVI, and his family. Thousands of other executions soon followed.

The Reign of Terror in France split American opinion. Thomas Jefferson and

Storming the Bastille *This engraving shows the storming of the Bastille, the event that marked the beginning of the French Revolution. At first, most Americans supported the French Revolution, but the violence that followed split opinion in the United States.* **United States and the World** *Why would the French expect Americans to support their revolution?*

others condemned the terror, but felt that the French had a right to overthrow nobles and even to use violence. "Rather than it should have failed," Jefferson later said of the revolution in France, "I should have seen half the earth devastated."

Alexander Hamilton and his followers strongly disagreed. They believed that the French Revolution was doomed to fail. John Adams claimed that the French could no more create a democracy "than a snowball can exist in the streets of Philadelphia under a burning sun."

The United States Stays Neutral

The French Revolution also shocked the kings and nobles of Europe. They feared that revolutionary ideas would spread to their own countries and inspire uprisings. To prevent this, Britain, Austria, Prussia, Holland, and Spain joined forces to crush the French Revolution. French armies fought back bravely. Fighting continued on and off in Europe from 1792 to 1815.

War in Europe threatened to draw in the United States. In 1778, the United States and France had signed a treaty of friendship. The treaty said that France could use American ports. Now at war, the French hoped to supply their ships in American ports and attack British ships.

Washington and his cabinet were unsure what to do. Honoring the French treaty could easily lead to war with Britain. Hamilton argued that the treaty was no longer binding because Louis XVI, who signed it, was dead. But Jefferson thought that France should be allowed to use the ports. President Washington wanted above all to keep his young nation out of war. "It is the sincere wish of United America," Washington said, "to have nothing to do with . . . the squabbles of European nations."

In April 1793, Washington issued the **Neutrality Proclamation.** It stated that the United States would not support either side in the war. It also forbade Americans from taking any warlike action against either Britain or France.

An Unpopular Treaty

Despite the Neutrality Proclamation, Washington's troubles did not end. American merchants wanted to trade with both countries. But Britain and France each tried to stop Americans from trading with the other nation.

In 1793, the British began to attack American ships that traded with French colonies in the West Indies. Off the small island of St. Eustatius, the British captured 130 American ships. When Americans learned of Britain's bold action, many wanted to declare war. Washington knew that the United States was in no position to fight a war. So he sent Chief Justice John Jay to Britain for talks.

Jay worked out a treaty with Britain in 1794. In it, the British agreed to pay damages for American ships captured in the West Indies. But they refused to promise that they would stop the attacks. Jay also demanded that Britain give up forts it still held in the Ohio Valley. The British agreed to leave the forts, and the Americans agreed to pay debts owed to British merchants since the Revolution.

Many Americans disliked **Jay's Treaty.** They felt that they were giving up more than Britain was. In 1795, the Senate finally approved the treaty, mainly because Washington believed that the United States should avoid war with Britain. "Such is the popularity of the President," Jefferson commented after the treaty was approved, "that the people will support him in whatever he will do."

War in the Northwest Territory

Another conflict brewed closer to home. Thousands of Americans had moved into the Northwest Territory in the 1790s. This wave of white settlers caused serious problems. The United States had signed treaties with the Indian nations who lived there.

Signing the Treaty of Greenville *In the Treaty of Greenville, Native Americans agreed to give up the southern half of present-day Ohio. They received a payment of about 1/8 cent per acre. Here, Indian leaders meet with General Wayne to discuss the terms of the treaty.* **Linking Past and Present** *How do you think future generations of Native Americans would view the terms of the treaty?*

But most settlers ignored the treaties and took land wherever they pleased.

Clashes with Indians. Native Americans resented these newcomers who invaded their lands. Settlers and Indians clashed along the frontier. Indians attacked white families living far from a fort. White settlers, in turn, took revenge on Indians, even on those who had not taken part in the attacks. Violence spread.

In 1791, the Miamis in Ohio joined other Indian nations. Together they drove settlers from Indian lands. Little Turtle, a skilled fighter, led the Miamis. Armed with rifles and gunpowder from British troops in the Ohio Valley, the Miamis drove most white settlers from the area.

When President Washington heard the news, he sent General Arthur St. Clair and 3,000 soldiers to Ohio. Little Turtle and the Miamis defeated St. Clair and routed his troops. Washington then replaced St. Clair with General Anthony Wayne.

Battle of Fallen Timbers. Wayne's troops were well trained. In 1794, he marched his army into Miami territory. Blue Jacket, a Shawnee leader, had taken over from Little Turtle. He gathered his forces at a place called Fallen Timbers in Ohio. Blue Jacket thought that Wayne would have trouble fighting there because it was covered with trees blown down in a storm. But Wayne's army pushed through the tangled logs and defeated the Indians.

In 1795, the Miamis and 11 other Indian nations signed the **Treaty of Greenville** with the United States. They agreed to give up about 25,000 square miles

George Washington: An "American Star" *George Washington retired from public life in 1797. He had served his country loyally and well for more than 20 years. This painting by Baltimore artist Frederick Kemmelmeyer symbolizes the devotion and respect that Americans felt for the man known as "Father of His Country."* **American Traditions** *What symbols of the nation did the artist place around Washington?*

(65,000 square km) of land. In return, they received $20,000 and a promise of more money if they kept the peace.

Washington's Parting Advice

While war raged across Europe, Washington kept the United States at peace. He hoped that future Presidents would follow his example of avoiding war to build a prosperous nation. In his **Farewell Address** of 1796, Washington urged that the United States remain neutral in its relations with other countries:

> **❝**Observe good faith and justice towards all nations. Cultivate peace and harmony with all. . . . Nothing is more essential than that permanent, [habitual hatred] against particular nations and passionate attachments for others should be excluded.**❞**

Washington warned against becoming involved in European affairs. "'Tis our true policy to steer clear of permanent alliances with any portion of the foreign world," the President said. Washington did favor trade with other countries. But he advised against joining alliances that might pull the United States into war. This advice became a guiding principle of American foreign policy for many years.

Washington also cautioned Americans not to quarrel so bitterly about politics. He feared that disagreements between Hamilton and Jefferson would lead to a lasting political division. Despite Washington's warning, a split did occur. The nation had many different regions and interests, and everyone could not agree.

SECTION 2 REVIEW

1. **Identify:** (a) French Revolution, (b) Neutrality Proclamation, (c) Jay's Treaty, (d) Treaty of Greenville, (e) Washington's Farewell Address.
2. How did Americans view the revolution in France?
3. Why did Washington issue the Neutrality Proclamation?
4. What problems with Britain and France arose after the Neutrality Proclamation?
5. What events led to the Battle of Fallen Timbers?
6. **Synthesizing Information** How might the location of the United States make it possible for the nation to "steer clear of permanent alliances" with European nations?

3 The First Political Parties

FIND OUT

◆ Why did political parties form in the United States?

◆ What were the opposing views of Hamilton and Jefferson?

◆ How did newspapers influence the growth of political parties?

◆ Who became President after Washington?

◆ **VOCABULARY** unconstitutional

In 1797, Thomas Jefferson worried about tensions within the government. Congress was divided into two groups. On one side were those who agreed most often with Alexander Hamilton. On the other side were supporters of Jefferson and James Madison.

Feelings on both sides had turned bitter. Jefferson described the unpleasant mood at that time in Philadelphia:

❝Men who have been intimate all their lives cross streets to avoid meeting, and turn their heads another way, lest they should be obliged to touch their hats.❞

This split was an abrupt change from 1789, when Washington began his first term in office. At that time, the country had no political parties. But when Washington left office in 1797, two parties competed for power.

A Distrust of Political Parties

The Constitution of the United States does not mention political parties. In fact, the framers of the Constitution had hoped political parties would not form. They saw how parties worked in Britain. The parties were made up of a few people who schemed to win favors from the government. These party members were more interested in personal profit than public good.

Most Americans did not want political parties either. They feared that parties would pit one group of Americans against another. By turning every decision into a squabble, parties would keep politicians from thinking about the good of the whole country. Parties, George Washington had warned, would lead only to "jealousies and false alarms."

Disagreements between two of Washington's advisers, however, spurred the growth of two political parties in the 1790s. One party was led by Secretary of the Treasury Alexander Hamilton. The other party was headed by Secretary of State Thomas Jefferson.

Side by side, the two men contrasted sharply. Hamilton was short and slender. He dressed in fine clothes and spoke forcefully. Energetic, brilliant, and restless— Hamilton was a political man.

Jefferson, on the other hand, was tall and a bit gawky. Although he was a Virginia aristocrat, he dressed and spoke informally. As one senator recalled:

❝His clothes seem too small for him. He sits in a lounging manner, on one hip commonly, and with one of his shoulders elevated much above the other. His face has a sunny aspect. His whole figure has a loose, shackling air. . . . He spoke almost without ceasing. [His conversation] was loose and rambling; and yet he scattered information wherever he went.❞

Clashing Views

Hamilton and Jefferson disagreed about many issues. At the root of their quarrels were different views about what was good for the nation then and for the future.

Manufacturing versus farming. Hamilton wanted the United States to become more like Britain. He urged the growth of trade, cities, and manufacturing. In his view, the federal government should help the nation's economy grow.

Jefferson believed that farmers were the backbone of the nation. "Cultivators of the earth," he wrote, "are the most valuable citizens." He feared that an industrial economy might corrupt American life. "Let our workshops remain in Europe," Jefferson wrote. "The mobs of the great cities add just so much to the support of pure government, as sores do to the strength of the human body."

Federal versus state governments. Hamilton and Jefferson also had opposing views about which level of government should have more power. Hamilton wanted the federal government to be stronger than state governments. Jefferson, on the other hand, believed that state governments had to be stronger than they were. Otherwise,

A Pennsylvania Farm *Thomas Jefferson envisioned a nation of quiet, self-sufficient farms, such as the one in this painting by Edward Hicks. Small, independent farmers were the backbone of American democracy, Jefferson believed, and he wanted them to have control in running the country.* **Citizenship** *How did this differ from Hamilton's vision of the nation?*

the federal government would swallow up the powers that the Constitution gave to the states.

Strict versus loose interpretation. As you have read, Hamilton helped to establish the Bank of the United States. Jefferson opposed the Bank because it gave too much power to the federal government and wealthy investors who helped to run it. Jefferson said that the law that created the Bank was unconstitutional, that is, not permitted by the Constitution.

Jefferson's objection to the Bank was based on a strict interpretation of the Constitution. Nowhere, he said, did the Constitution give Congress the power to create a Bank. Jefferson believed that any powers not specifically given to the federal government belonged to the states.

Hamilton, on the other hand, thought that the words of the Constitution should be interpreted more loosely. According to him, the Constitution gave Congress the power to make all laws "necessary and proper" to carry out its duties. Hamilton argued that the Bank was needed to make government work efficiently.

Britain versus France as an ally. Finally, Hamilton favored Britain as an important trading partner. Jefferson favored France, an ally during the American Revolution and a nation struggling for its own liberty.

A Widening Rift

As members of Washington's cabinet, Hamilton and Jefferson at first disagreed only in private. But when Congress began to pass Hamilton's program, Jefferson and his friend James Madison decided to organize support for their views.

Jefferson and Madison traveled to New York State in 1791. They told people that they were going to study its wildlife. In fact, Jefferson was an amateur scientist and did study the state's plants and animals. But he and Madison also met with important New York politicians, including Governor George Clinton and Aaron Burr. Both men opposed Hamilton's programs.

The Virginians asked Clinton and Burr to persuade New Yorkers to vote for Jefferson's supporters in the coming elections. With more votes in Congress, Jefferson hoped to defeat Hamilton's economic plan.

Parties take shape. Soon, leaders in other states began to side with either Hamilton or Jefferson. Jefferson's supporters called themselves **Democratic Republicans.** Often, they shortened the name to Republicans.* Supporters of Republicans included small farmers, craftworkers, and some wealthy planters.

---

*Jefferson's Republican party was not the same as today's Republican party. In fact, his party later grew into the Democratic party.

CHART SKILLS *By the 1790s, two political parties had formed—the Federalist party and the Republican party.* ◆ *Who led each party? What were two differences between the parties on economic issues?*

The First Political Parties

Federalists	Republicans
1. Led by A. Hamilton	1. Led by T. Jefferson
2. Wealthy and well-educated should lead nation	2. People should have political power
3. Strong central government	3. Strong state governments
4. Emphasis on manufacturing, shipping, and trade	4. Emphasis on agriculture
5. Loose interpretation of Constitution	5. Strict interpretation of Constitution
6. Pro-British	6. Pro-French
7. Favored national bank	7. Opposed national bank
8. Favored protective tariff	8. Opposed protective tariff

AN·AMERICAN·PORTRAIT

Benjamin Banneker: American Genius

"Each day in living is an adventure in learning." This philosophy always guided Benjamin Banneker. He was born in Maryland in 1731, the grandson of an enslaved African prince and the son of a freed slave.

In his boyhood, Banneker borrowed textbooks and taught himself math and science. At age 22, he memorized the working parts of a pocket watch. Then, he created his own clock, carving all of its pieces out of wood. For 50 years, the clock kept nearly perfect time.

Throughout his long life, Banneker continued to challenge his mind. He learned to survey land and was appointed by George Washington to lay out the boundaries of the District of Columbia. He created and published mathematical puzzles, a popular form of entertainment at the time. And much later in life, he taught himself astronomy.

In 1791, Banneker found a way to combine all his knowledge. He began to issue yearly almanacs. The almanacs were filled with weather forecasts, tide calculations, proverbs, health remedies, and suggestions for good and peaceful living. Along with his other achievements, Banneker's almanacs earned him fame and respect as an American genius.

1. What information appeared in Banneker's almanacs?

2. **Applying Information** How was Banneker's life "an adventure in learning"?

Hamilton and his supporters were called **Federalists** because they favored a strong federal government. Federalists drew support from merchants in coastal cities like Boston and New York as well as from some southern planters.

Newspapers fan the flames. Both Republicans and Federalists used newspapers to rally people to their cause. Between 1790 and 1800, American newspapers more than doubled—from about 100 to more than 230.

Newspaper publishers of the 1790s argued for the political issues and politicians they supported. John Fenno, publisher of the *Gazette of the United States* in Philadelphia, defended Alexander Hamilton. Jefferson's friend Philip Freneau (fruh NOH) started a rival paper called the *Na-*

tional Gazette. It vigorously supported Republicans. These newspapers played a major role in the new nation. They kept people informed and helped to shape public opinion.

In Washington's Footsteps

The new political parties played an important part in choosing George Washington's successor. In 1796, Republicans chose Thomas Jefferson to run for President and Aaron Burr for Vice President. Federalists nominated John Adams for President and Thomas Pinckney for Vice President.

The election had an unexpected outcome. According to the Constitution, the person who received the most electoral votes became President. The person with the next highest total was Vice President. John Adams, a Federalist, became President in 1797. But Thomas Jefferson came in second. So Jefferson, the leader of Republicans, became Adams's Vice President.

With a President and Vice President from different parties, political conflict was sure to continue. In fact, during John Adams's term, tensions between Republicans and Federalists reached a new height.

SECTION 3 REVIEW

1. **Identify:** (a) Democratic Republicans, (b) Federalists.
2. **Define:** unconstitutional.
3. Why did many Americans distrust political parties?
4. On what issues did Hamilton and Jefferson disagree?
5. How did newspapers contribute to the growth of political parties?
6. What was the outcome of the election of 1796?
7. **Drawing Conclusions** Why do you think political parties emerged even though many Americans opposed them?

---

4 John Adams as President

FIND OUT

◆ Why did many Americans want war with France?

◆ Why did Adams become unpopular with his own Federalist party?

◆ What were the Alien and Sedition acts?

◆ **VOCABULARY** alien, sedition, nullify

Years after serving as President, John Adams began to write his autobiography. He knew that Washington, Franklin, and Jefferson were widely admired as heroes of the Revolution. But he himself received very little recognition. Feeling ignored, Adams wrote proudly of his own deeds:

❝I have done more labor, run through more and greater dangers, and made greater sacrifices than any man . . . living or dead, in the service of my country.❞

Still, Adams found it hard to write at length about his achievements. In the end, he gave up. "I am not, never was, and never shall be a great man," Adams concluded.

In both cases, Adams exaggerated. He may not have been a popular President or a heroic man. But Americans would remember him as an honest, able leader. In a crisis, he tried to act in the best interests of the nation, even if it threatened his political future.

The XYZ Affair

Soon after becoming President, Adams faced a crisis in foreign policy. France had strongly objected to Jay's Treaty between the United States and Britain. French ships began to capture American ships in the West Indies, just as the British had done.

Once more, there was a cry for war, this time against France. President Adams hoped to arrive at a peaceful solution with France, as Washington had with Britain.

France asks for a bribe. In 1797, Adams sent three ambassadors to Paris to discuss neutral rights. The French foreign minister, Charles Maurice de Talleyrand, said that there would be delays before talks could begin. Talleyrand was shrewd but not very honest. He sent three secret agents to offer the three Americans a deal.

The French agents stated bluntly what would stop the attacks. "You must pay money," they said. "You must pay a great deal of money." Talleyrand wanted $250,000 for himself and a loan to France of $10 million. "Not a sixpence!" replied one of the Americans.

The Americans reported this incident to President Adams. He told Congress about the bribe, but he kept secret the names of the three French agents. Instead, Adams referred to them as X, Y, and Z.

When the **XYZ Affair** became public in 1798, most Americans were outraged. People took up the slogan "Millions for defense, but not one cent for tribute!" Americans were willing to spend money to defend their country, but refused to pay a bribe to another nation.

Adams avoids war. For a time, the XYZ Affair united Federalists and Republicans. Even Americans who strongly supported the French Revolution were insulted by the incident.

Despite strong pressure, President Adams refused to ask Congress to declare war on France. But he did strengthen the American navy. Shipyards built nearly a dozen frigates, fast sailing ships with many

---

The Adamses *John and Abigail Adams were the first presidential couple to live in the White House. They moved into the unfinished building in 1800. A lively and intelligent woman, Abigail Adams was one of the most influential First Ladies in the history of the United States.* **United States and the World** *Describe the crisis in foreign policy that John Adams faced after becoming President.*

guns. This show of strength convinced France to cease their attacks on American ships. Talleyrand assured Adams that if American ambassadors returned to France, he would treat them with respect.

The Federalist Party Splits

Many Federalists did not like the way Adams handled the French crisis. Some, led by Alexander Hamilton, wanted to go to war with France. They thought that a war would weaken support for Jefferson and the Republicans, who had always favored France. Going to war would also force the United States to build up its army and navy. A strong military meant a stronger federal government, which was exactly what Federalists wanted.

President Adams was a Federalist, but he disagreed with Hamilton's desire for war. The disagreement between Adams and Hamilton led to a split in the Federalist party. Hamilton and his supporters were called **High Federalists.**

Over Hamilton's opposition, Adams sent a new group of ambassadors to France. When they arrived, they found a young army officer, Napoleon Bonaparte, in charge. Napoleon planned to expand French power in Europe. He did not want to risk war with the United States at the same time. So Napoleon signed an agreement to stop seizing American ships in the West Indies. The agreement was known as the **Convention of 1800.**

Adams, like Washington, had kept the nation out of war. But making peace cost him the support of many Federalists and split his party.

Strict Federalist Laws

While peace talks with France were taking place in 1798, High Federalists in Congress passed several important laws. The laws were known as the Alien and Sedition acts.

Alexander Hamilton *Along with other High Federalists, Alexander Hamilton disagreed with President Adams over the issue of war with France. This portrait of Hamilton is by the well-known American painter John Trumbull.* **United States and the World** *What position did Hamilton and his supporters take toward France? Why?*

The **Alien Act** allowed the President to expel any alien, or foreigner, who he thought was dangerous to the country. Another law made it harder for immigrants to become citizens. Before 1798, white males who came to the United States could become citizens after living in the country for 5 years. The new law made the waiting period 14 years.

High Federalists said that the laws were needed to protect the United States from spies in case of war. But they also wanted the laws for political reasons. Many French people had come to the United States. They supported Jefferson and Republicans and often criticized Federalists for being pro-British. With the new laws, these immigrants would not be able to vote for many years. The immigrants could even be expelled if the President thought that they were troublemakers.

These measures angered Republicans, but a final law made them furious. This was the **Sedition Act.** Sedition (sih DIHSH uhn) means stirring up rebellion against a government. The new law said that citizens could be fined or jailed if they criticized elected officials.

Republicans argued that the Sedition Act violated the Constitution. After all, the First Amendment protected every American's freedom of speech. One Republican charged that the new law would make it a crime "to laugh at the cut of a congressman's coat, [or] to give dinner to a Frenchman."

The worst fears of Republicans were quickly confirmed. Several Republican newspaper editors, and even members of Congress, were fined and jailed for their opinions. Jefferson saw the beginning of the end of American democracy in the new laws:

> **"**If this goes down, we shall immediately see attempted another act of Congress, declaring that the President shall continue in office during life, and after that other laws giving both the President and the Congress life terms in office.**"**

The Rights of States

Most Republicans believed that the Alien and Sedition acts were unconstitutional. But few of them expected that the Supreme Court would overturn the laws. This was because most Supreme Court justices were Federalists.

Instead of turning to the courts, Thomas Jefferson called on the states to act. Jefferson argued that states had the right to nullify, or cancel, a law passed by the federal government.

With advice from Jefferson and James Madison, two states claimed that they had the right to nullify federal laws. Kentucky and Virginia passed resolutions in 1798 and 1799. They declared that each state "has an equal right to judge for itself" whether a law is constitutional or not. If a state decides a law is unconstitutional, the **Kentucky and Virginia resolutions** said, it can nullify that law within its borders.

For Jefferson, nullification gave states a way to resist the growing power of the federal government. But the Kentucky and Virginia resolutions raised a difficult question. Did the states, or the federal government, have the final say over whether or not a law was constitutional?

The question was not answered in Jefferson's lifetime. Within a few years, the Alien and Sedition acts were changed or dropped. But the issue of a state's right to nullify federal laws would come up again in the 1830s.

Election of 1800

As the election of 1800 drew near, the fear of war with France faded. Republicans had high hopes that they could now sweep the Federalists out of office. In their campaign, they focused on two issues. The Federalists had raised taxes to prepare the country for war with France. And the Federalists had pushed the unpopular Alien and Sedition acts through Congress.

Republicans chose Thomas Jefferson to run for President and Aaron Burr, a New Yorker, for Vice President. Even though John Adams had lost support, he was the Federalist candidate, along with Charles Pinckney for Vice President.

A deadlocked vote. Republicans won many seats in Congress in 1800. In the race for President, Republicans also beat the Federalists. But when the electoral college voted, Jefferson and Burr each received 73 votes. Who would be President?

According to the Constitution, the House of Representatives decides the elec-

A Victory Flag for Thomas Jefferson *Republicans rejoiced at the election of Thomas Jefferson, which signaled the end of the Federalist era. This picture shows a hand-painted flag celebrating Jefferson's victory. Note the words on the banner: "T. Jefferson President of the United States of America. John Adams Is No More."* **Citizenship** *Why did Americans reject the Federalists in 1800?*

tion if there is a tie vote. But the House, too, was evenly split. It voted 35 times, and each time the vote was a tie. Finally, the tie was broken. The House made Jefferson President, and Burr became Vice President. Congress then passed the Twelfth Amendment, which required electors to vote separately for President and Vice President. The amendment was ratified by the states in 1804.

Federalists lose favor. With the election of Thomas Jefferson in 1800, the Federalist era ended. Federalists won fewer seats in Congress. In 1804, the leader of the High Federalists, Alexander Hamilton, was killed in a duel with Aaron Burr.

Many Americans believed that the Federalists lost power because they distrusted the ordinary citizen. Hamilton once said, "The turbulent and changing people seldom judge or determine right." Voters were not likely to elect candidates who distrusted them so much.

Yet the Federalist party left its mark. Federalists helped the nation during its early years. President Adams had kept the country out of war. And, as you will read, Republican Presidents kept most of Hamilton's economic program.

SECTION 4 REVIEW

1. **Identify:** (a) XYZ Affair, (b) High Federalists, (c) Convention of 1800, (d) Alien Act, (e) Sedition Act, (f) Kentucky and Virginia resolutions.
2. **Define:** (a) alien, (b) sedition, (c) nullify.
3. Why did many Americans demand war with France?
4. What caused High Federalists to split with John Adams?
5. Why did Republicans oppose the Sedition Act?
6. **Applying Information** How do you think the Kentucky and Virginia resolutions fit in with Jefferson's views on government?

Many primary sources, such as letters, diaries, and speeches, express the opinions of the people who wrote them. Therefore, when historians study primary sources, they have to recognize fact and opinion. A **fact** is something that actually happened. It is known to be true because it can be proved or observed. An **opinion** is a judgment that reflects a person's beliefs or feelings. It is not necessarily true.

Often, writers present a series of facts to back up an opinion. For example, in the Declaration of Independence, Jefferson listed facts to support the opinion that George III had tried to establish "an absolute tyranny over these states."

In the letter below, Alexander Hamilton writes about political differences between himself and the party led by Madison and Jefferson.

1 **Determine which statements are facts.** Remember that facts can be checked and thereby can be proved. Use your reading in this chapter to help answer these questions. (a) Choose two statements of fact in Hamilton's letter. (b) How might you prove that each statement is a fact?

2 **Determine which statements are opinions.** Writers often show that they are giving an opinion by saying "in my view" or "I think" or "I believe." (a) Choose two statements in which Hamilton gives his opinion. (b) How can you tell that each is an opinion?

3 **Determine how a writer mixes fact and opinion.** Reread the last sentence of the letter. (a) What did Hamilton mean by a "womanish attachment to France and a womanish resentment against Great Britain"? (b) Is it true that Jefferson supported France and opposed Britain? (c) What country did Hamilton want the United States to support? (d) Why do you think Hamilton mixed fact and opinion in the statement?

Alexander Hamilton wrote:

"It was not until the last session of Congress that I became completely convinced that Mr. Madison and Mr. Jefferson are at the head of a faction that is hostile toward me. They are motivated by views that, in my judgment, will undermine the principles of good government and are dangerous to the peace and happiness of the country.

Freneau, the present publisher of the *National Gazette,* was a known Antifederalist. It is certain that he was brought to Philadelphia by Mr. Jefferson to be the publisher of a newspaper. At the same time as he was starting his paper, he was also a clerk in the Department of State. His paper is devoted to opposing me and the measures that I have supported. And the paper has a general unfriendly attitude toward the government of the United States.

On almost all questions, great and small, which have come up since the first session of Congress, Mr. Jefferson and Mr. Madison have been found among those who want to limit federal power. In respect to foreign policy, the views of these gentlemen are, in my judgment, equally unsound and dangerous. They have a womanish attachment to France and a womanish resentment against Great Britain."

Use the Section Reviews and this Study Guide to review chapter content.

Main Ideas

The main ideas in each section of this chapter are summarized below.

SECTION 1 ■ Washington Leads the Nation

◆ In 1789, George Washington chose a cabinet to head the executive departments.
◆ Alexander Hamilton devised a plan to pay off government debts.
◆ To strengthen the economy, Hamilton proposed a national bank and taxes.

SECTION 2 ■ Avoiding War

◆ Political quarrels over the French Revolution heated up between Thomas Jefferson and Alexander Hamilton.
◆ The Neutrality Proclamation of 1793 stated that the United States would not support either France or Britain in their war.
◆ Settlers and Native Americans in the Northwest Territory clashed.
◆ Washington's Farewell Address urged Americans to avoid foreign alliances.

SECTION 3 ■ The First Political Parties

◆ The Republican and Federalist parties formed in the 1790s.
◆ Alexander Hamilton and Thomas Jefferson had opposing views on industry and a strong federal government.

◆ In 1797, John Adams, a Federalist, became President, and Jefferson, a Republican, became Vice President.

SECTION 4 ■ John Adams As President

◆ As a result of the XYZ Affair, many Americans wanted war with France.
◆ The Federalist party split because Adams refused to declare war on France.
◆ In 1798, the High Federalists passed strict new laws, the Alien and Sedition acts.

Key People and Terms

Study the Identify and Define questions in the Section Reviews on pages 316, 320, 325, and 329. Use each person, term, and vocabulary word in a complete sentence. When possible, make connections between the people and terms by using more than one person or term in each sentence.

Time Line

1. Make a chart of events in time order. The chart will have two headings: Date, Event. Fill in the chart, using the events on the time line. Add the following events from the chapter: Congress passes bill for a national bank; French Revolution begins; Washington issues Neutrality Proclamation. (Refer to the chapter for the dates.)
2. Which event on your chart was a direct result of the French Revolution?

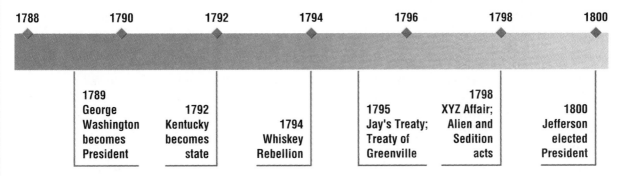

1788	1790	1792	1794	1796	1798	1800

1789 George Washington becomes President

1792 Kentucky becomes state

1794 Whiskey Rebellion

1795 Jay's Treaty; Treaty of Greenville

1798 XYZ Affair; Alien and Sedition acts

1800 Jefferson elected President

Understanding Vocabulary

Match each term at left with the correct definition at right.

1. cabinet
2. tariff
3. unconstitutional
4. nullify
5. sedition

a. tax
b. not permitted by the Constitution
c. cancel
d. stirring up rebellion against a government
e. group of officials who head executive departments

Reviewing the Main Ideas

1. Why did Hamilton think that each of the following would strengthen the nation's economy: (a) national bank; (b) tariffs?
2. What caused the Whiskey Rebellion?
3. Why did Washington issue the Neutrality Proclamation?
4. (a) What was one cause of the war in the Northwest Territory in the 1790s? (b) What was one result?
5. (a) How did political parties develop? (b) Who supported the Federalists? (c) Who supported the Republicans?
6. Describe two results of the XYZ Affair.
7. What important issue was raised by the Kentucky and Virginia resolutions?

Thinking Critically

1. **Linking Past and Present** (a) What advice did Washington give in his Farewell Address? (b) Do you think Americans today would agree? Explain.
2. **Making Decisions** (a) Why would speculators make large profits from Hamilton's plan to repay government debts? (b) Do you agree with his plan? Explain.
3. **Defending a Position** Do you think the Alien and Sedition acts were necessary to protect the nation? Explain.
4. **Synthesizing Information** What problems did the first Presidents face?

Applying Your Skills

1. **Skimming a Chapter** Skimming is reading quickly for the general idea. To skim a chapter in this book, first look at the Chapter Outline at the beginning of each chapter. Note that the Chapter Outline lists the section titles. Next, look at the boldface headings that show the main topics in each section. Finally, quickly read the first and last sentence of each paragraph. Skim the first half of this chapter (pages 308–320). (a) What does the Chapter Outline tell you about the chapter? (b) List the main topics in the section "Avoiding War." (c) What do you think is the general idea of this section?
2. **Analyzing a Quotation** After George Washington became President, he said, "There is scarcely any part of my conduct which may not hereafter be drawn into precedent." What do you think he meant by this statement?
3. **Distinguishing Fact From Opinion** Study the quotation on page 309. Then, study the following statement by Thomas Jefferson about President Washington: "Such is the popularity of the President that the people will support him in whatever he will do." (a) Which quotation contains facts? (b) Identify two of those facts. (c) How would you prove that they are facts? (d) Which quotation expresses an opinion? (e) What is the opinion? (f) Why is it an opinion and not a fact?

Thinking About Geography

Match the letters on the map with the places listed below.

1. New York City
2. Philadelphia
3. Washington, D.C.
4. Virginia
5. Kentucky

Location On what river is Washington, D.C., located?

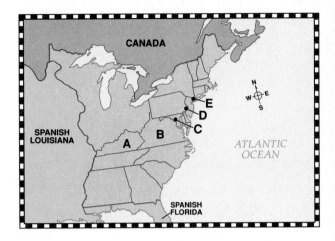

History Writer's Workshop

Writing an Essay Answer

An essay is a group of paragraphs written to communicate one main point. An essay includes an introductory paragraph and two or more body paragraphs. In an essay, a thesis statement presents the main point in the same way that a topic sentence presents the main idea in a paragraph.

You may use the following checklist to prepare and write an essay answer.

1. Analyze the question and try to answer it in one basic sentence. This sentence will be the thesis statement.
2. Brainstorm for facts and details that will support and develop the thesis statement. Group these ideas into a logical outline.
3. Guided by the outline and thesis statement, begin writing the essay. Include the thesis statement in the first paragraph. Be sure the body paragraphs answer the question fully and provide enough supporting facts, details, and reasons.
4. Finish the essay with a clear and logical conclusion that refers back to the thesis statement.
5. Check your essay answer for errors in grammar, spelling, and punctuation.

Practice Write an essay answer to the following question: *On what important issues did Jefferson and Hamilton disagree?*

Writing to Learn

1. Imagine that you are a backcountry farmer who took part in the Whiskey Rebellion. Write a letter to a friend about this incident. First, freewrite about what occurred and how President Washington responded. Begin the first draft of your letter with a topic sentence that summarizes your reactions. Organize the details in time order. Revise for clarity. Proofread and make a final copy. Then, have classmates read your letter.
2. Pretend that you are a reporter for the *National Gazette.* Write an editorial defending Jefferson's political beliefs. First, brainstorm a list of topics and supporting details. In your first draft, summarize your position in a topic sentence. Then, organize the details in logical order. When you revise, check for unity, coherence, and persuasive power. Then, proofread and make a final copy. Publish your editorial in a class newspaper.

The Battle of Lake Erie *The War of 1812 increased the pride of Americans in their nation. In this painting, Captain Oliver Hazard Perry rescues the United States colors from a sinking ship at the Battle of Lake Erie.* **Linking Past and Present** *How is the flag in the painting different from the American flag today? Explain.*

The Jefferson Era (1801–1816)

Chapter Outline

The Big Picture

Today, a presidential election does not seem remarkable. Thomas Jefferson, however, referred to his election as the "Revolution of 1800." In many ways, it was revolutionary, or new and unusual. For the first time in the United States, power passed peacefully from one political party to another.

In 1800, a peaceful change in political power was unusual. Just a few years earlier, French revolutionaries had beheaded the French king. Members of rival political parties were tried and executed. But Jefferson's "revolution" proved that a nation could change course without violence.

Jim Davidson

Of Special Interest

Focus On

◆ How did Jefferson make the government more democratic?
◆ What lands doubled the United States in size?
◆ Why did Jefferson want to avoid war with France and Britain?
◆ What finally drew the United States into a second war with Britain?
◆ What was the outcome of the War of 1812?

"**E**ducate and inform the whole mass of the people. Enable them to see that it is their interest to preserve peace and order, and they will preserve them. . . . They are the only [ones to rely on] for the preservation of our liberty. . . . This reliance cannot deceive us, as long as we remain [good]; and I think we shall . . . as long as agriculture is our principal object. . . . When we get piled upon one another in large cities, as in Europe, we shall become corrupt as in Europe, and go to eating one another as they do there."

In this letter to James Madison, written in 1787, Thomas Jefferson expressed his faith in the American people. At that time, nearly nine out of ten Americans were farmers. This fact gave Jefferson confidence in the nation's future. For even though he was a member of the upper class, Jefferson was convinced that ordinary people, especially farmers, would best preserve the nation's peace, order, and liberty.

As the nation's President, Jefferson wanted to represent these ordinary citizens. He believed that John Adams and Alexander Hamilton had been more concerned about the good of the wealthy few than about the majority of farmers. In this chapter, you will learn how Jefferson changed the direction of the new nation.

1 Republicans in Power

FIND OUT

◆ How did Jefferson's policies differ from Federalist policies?

◆ Why did Federalists control the federal courts?

◆ Why was *Marbury* v. *Madison* an important case?

◆ **VOCABULARY** democratic, laissez faire, judicial review

In 1801, Thomas Jefferson was the first President to be inaugurated in Washington, D.C., the nation's new capital. Most visitors to the half-built capital criticized

Thomas Jefferson *Thomas Jefferson, third President of the United States, was a man of wide-ranging talents and interests. In this portrait by Thaddeus Kosciusko, Jefferson wears a headband of myrtle leaves, symbolizing his achievements as a scholar.* **Citizenship** *What were Jefferson's goals for the government?*

it. The city was located on swampy land near the Potomac River. Dense forests encircled the capital, making it difficult for visitors to find.

Thomas Jefferson, however, was happy with the new capital. He disliked the old cities of Europe and made fun of people who were afraid of new things. The fact that Washington was being carved out of a wilderness pleased him.

Jefferson felt that the success of the American republic signaled the dawning of an age of liberty. "This whole chapter in the history of man is new," he said after his election. To him, it was fitting that the United States should have its capital in a new, planned city.

A New Style of President

Jefferson saw himself as different from Washington and Adams. Because he strongly believed in the good sense of ordinary people, Jefferson wanted to make the government more democratic. **Democratic** means ensuring that all people have the same rights.

An informal air. Most Americans expected Jefferson to bring a new style to the capital, and he did. The new President preferred informal dinner parties to the formal parties given by Washington and Adams. He greeted people by shaking hands instead of bowing. Jefferson also wore more casual clothes. His informal ways showed that he considered himself the equal of ordinary citizens.

Easing Federalist fears. Some Federalists worried about how Jefferson would govern. In his inaugural address, he tried to quiet their fears. He had no plan to treat Federalists harshly. As a minority, they "possess their equal rights, which equal law must protect," Jefferson told the nation. He called for an end to the bitter political quarrels of past years. "We are all Republicans, we are all Federalists," the President said.

Digging Up a Creature From the Past *Thomas Jefferson was intrigued by natural history. As head of the American Philosophical Society, he financed a project to dig up the bones of a mastodon, a prehistoric elephant-like animal, in New York. This picture of the excavation is by American scientist-painter Charles Willson Peale.* **Culture** *Why are excavations like this one useful?*

Republican changes. Although Jefferson had no wish to punish Federalists, he made clear that he would change Federalist policies. In his view, the Federalists had made the national government too large and powerful. He wanted to cut the federal budget and reduce taxes.

Jefferson believed in an idea known as laissez faire (lehs ay FAYR), which comes from the French term for "let alone." He believed that government should intervene as little as possible in economic affairs. Laissez faire was very different from the Federalist idea of government. Alexander Hamilton, you recall, wanted government to promote trade, commerce, and manufacturing.

A Frugal and Simple Government

Jefferson chose a cabinet that would help him reach his goals. He appointed Albert Gallatin as Secretary of the Treasury. A wizard at finances, Gallatin helped Jefferson cut government expenses. For Secretary of State, he chose his friend and Virginia neighbor, James Madison. Together the two men had built the Republican party. Madison agreed with Jefferson that, under the Federalists, the national government had taken on powers that really belonged to the states.

Limits on federal power. As President, Jefferson asked Congress to repeal the unpopular whiskey tax. He then fired all federal tax collectors. "It may be the pleasure and pride of an American to ask," Jefferson later remarked, "what farmer, what mechanic, what laborer, ever sees a tax-gatherer of the United States."

In his first years in office, Jefferson changed other Federalist policies. He stopped prosecutions under the Sedition Act. He even pardoned those who had been convicted under the act. Jefferson also asked Congress to return to the law that allowed immigrants to become citizens after five years.

Cuts in federal spending. Jefferson cut the size of the federal government and the cost to run it. With Congress's approval, he reduced the size of the navy and halted the construction of new ships. He also reduced the army from 4,000 soldiers to 2,500. The President meant to bring about the "frugal and simple government" he had promised Americans in his campaign.

Some Federalist policies remain. Jefferson and his cabinet maintained some of the Federalist programs. Gallatin convinced Jefferson that the Bank of the United States was worthwhile. And the federal government continued to pay off state debts that it had taken over during Washington's presidency.

Federalists in the Courts

Congress passed Jefferson's programs because many Republicans had been elected to Congress in 1800. But Federalists remained powerful in the federal courts. Before the new Republican Congress met, Federalists passed a bill creating more judges for the federal court system.

Just before President Adams left office, he appointed many Federalists to fill those positions. In fact, on his last night as President, Adams stayed up late to finish filling the jobs. Republicans charged that these tactics were an unfair way to keep Federalist influence in the courts.

Among the judges that Adams appointed was John Marshall, Chief Justice of the Supreme Court. In some ways, Marshall was like Thomas Jefferson. He was a rich Virginia planter with a brilliant mind. But unlike Jefferson, Marshall was a staunch Federalist. He wanted to make the federal government stronger.

Marshall arrived in Washington in 1801. The Supreme Court building had not yet been built. So the six justices met in the basement of the Capitol. Members of Congress scarcely knew the justices, who lived together in a small boardinghouse and rarely attended parties. Once, President Jefferson and Justice William Paterson traveled all day on the same stagecoach without recognizing one another!

A Stronger Supreme Court

The framers of the Constitution expected the federal courts to balance the powers of the President and Congress. But John Marshall found the courts to be the weakest branch of government. In his view, it was not clear what powers the federal courts had. In 1803, Marshall decided a case that both defined and strengthened the power of the Supreme Court.

As you have read, President Adams appointed a number of judges just before leaving office. One of them was William Marbury. But before Marbury could take office, Adams's term ended. James Madison, the new Secretary of State under Jefferson, refused to hand over the official papers appointing Marbury. So Marbury sued Madison. The case went before the Supreme Court because the Judiciary Act of 1789 said that the Court must decide any case brought against a federal official.

Chief Justice Marshall *John Marshall grew up in frontier Virginia and served in the American Revolution. Under his strong leadership as Chief Justice, the Supreme Court gained prestige and power.* **Citizenship** *How did Marshall's decision in* Marbury v. Madison *strengthen the power of the Supreme Court?*

In writing the decision for **Marbury v. Madison,*** Marshall ruled that the Judiciary Act was unconstitutional. Nowhere, he said, did the Constitution give the Supreme Court the right to decide cases brought against federal officials. Therefore, Congress could not give the Court that power by passing the Judiciary Act. Marbury could not become a judge because the Court refused to rule on his appointment.

Marshall's decision was one of the most important in American history. It established a key precedent—the right of the Supreme Court to make the final decision on whether federal or state laws should be allowed under the Constitution. The right of the Court to judge laws passed by Congress is called judicial review.

Jefferson disliked Marshall's decision because it gave more power to the Supreme Court, where Federalists such as Marshall were still strong. Even so, the President and Congress accepted the right of the Supreme Court to overturn laws. Today, judicial review is one of the most important powers of the Supreme Court.

SECTION 1 REVIEW

1. **Identify:** (a) Albert Gallatin, (b) John Marshall, (c) *Marbury* v. *Madison.*
2. **Define:** (a) democratic, (b) laissez faire, (c) judicial review.
3. (a) Name two Federalist policies that Jefferson changed. (b) Name two Federalist policies he allowed to continue.
4. How did Federalists keep control of the federal courts?
5. What precedent did *Marbury* v. *Madison* set?
6. **Analyzing a Quotation** "We are all Republicans, we are all Federalists." What did Jefferson mean by this statement?

---

*Every case brought before a court has two parties. One is the plaintiff, or person with a complaint. The other is the defendant, or person who must defend against the complaint. The plaintiff's name appears first, followed by the defendant's name. The v. means versus, or against.

2 The Louisiana Purchase

FIND OUT

◆ Why were western farmers concerned about control of the Mississippi River?

◆ How did the United States acquire Louisiana?

◆ What did Lewis and Clark accomplish on their expedition?

◆ **VOCABULARY** continental divide

One day during his second term in office, President Jefferson received several packages. The packages were from Lewis and Clark, explorers of newly bought lands west of the Mississippi River. They had promised to send Jefferson samples from this little-known region.

Inside the boxes, the President found the hides and skeletons of an antelope, a weasel, a wolf, a prairie dog, and a bear. Also included were the horns of a mountain ram and a tin box full of insects. Cages containing live birds and squirrels followed, as well as gifts from Plains Indians. Besides a bow and arrow from the Mandans, there was a buffalo hide with a battle scene painted on it from the Sioux.

For Jefferson, the contents of the boxes were treasures. As both a scientist and President, he was eager to learn about the nation's vast new lands.

"The Mississippi Is to Them Everything"

By 1800, almost 1 million Americans lived between the Appalachians and the Mississippi River. Most were farmers. The cheapest way to get their goods to markets in the East was to ship them down the Mississippi to New Orleans. Wheat, corn, and other goods were then stored in warehouses. From there, they were loaded onto ships

GEOGRAPHIC • CONNECTION

New Orleans

In the early 1800s, New Orleans bustled with activity. Located on the Mississippi River, just 110 miles upriver from the Gulf of Mexico, it was the gateway for goods being shipped from the West to markets in the East.

New Orleans also owed its vitality to a rich mixture of peoples. Along its streets strolled creoles, the descendants of French and Spanish settlers. African Americans were everywhere, too, most of them free. Some were descendants of African slaves who arrived as early as 1718. Others had come from the West Indies. Adding a dash of danger to this diverse population were pirates and other fugitives from the law.

The mix of people in New Orleans created a unique culture. Both the architecture and food reflected their native lands. From West Africa came "shotgun houses," one room wide and three or four rooms deep. From the West Indies came graceful homes with intricate iron grillwork. To this day, people enjoy African gumbos, or stews made

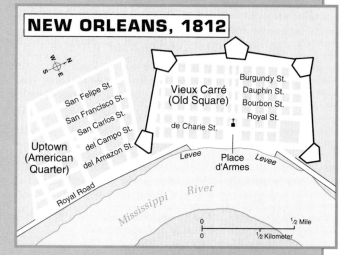

NEW ORLEANS, 1812

Vieux Carré (Old Square)
Uptown (American Quarter)
San Felipe St.
San Francisco St.
San Carlos St.
del Campo St.
del Amazon St.
Burgundy St.
Dauphin St.
Bourbon St.
Royal St.
de Charie St.
Levee
Place d'Armes
Levee
Royal Road
Mississippi River
0   ½ Mile
0   ½ Kilometer

with chicken or seafood. Creole cooking, a spicy blend of French and Spanish dishes, also remains popular. New Orleans was, and still is, truly an American melting pot.

1. What groups lived in New Orleans in the early 1800s?

2. **Synthesizing Information** Why does a variety of people enrich a culture?

market folks

that took them around Florida and up the Atlantic coast.

From time to time, Spain threatened to close the port of New Orleans to Americans. Being cut off from their eastern markets worried the farmers. As James Madison said of these westerners, "The Mississippi is to them everything. It is . . . all the navigable rivers of the Atlantic states formed into one stream."

In 1795, President Washington sent Thomas Pinckney to Spain to find a way to keep the port of New Orleans open. Pinckney negotiated a treaty with Spain. In the **Pinckney Treaty,** Spain agreed to let Americans ship their goods down the Mississippi and store them in New Orleans. The treaty also settled a dispute over the northern border of Spanish Florida.

For a time, Americans sent their goods to New Orleans without problem. Then, in 1800, Spain signed a secret treaty with Napoleon Bonaparte, the ruler of France. The treaty gave Louisiana back to France. When President Jefferson heard about the treaty, he was alarmed. Napoleon had already set out to conquer Europe. Jefferson feared that Napoleon might now attempt to build an empire in North America.

The Haitian Revolt

Jefferson had good reason to worry. Napoleon did have plans to build an empire in North America. He wanted to grow food in Louisiana and ship it to French islands in the West Indies. But his plan was thwarted by events in Haiti.*

Haiti was the richest French colony in the Caribbean. There, black slaves worked sugar plantations that made French planters wealthy. During the French Revolution, slaves in Haiti were inspired to fight for their liberty. Heading the rebel forces was Toussaint L'Ouverture (too SAN loo vehr TYOOR). By 1801, L'Ouverture had forced the French out of Haiti.

Napoleon sent troops to recapture Haiti. He expected his army to win easily, but the Haitians fought back fiercely. Many French soldiers died in battle and from yellow fever. Although the French captured L'Ouverture, they were not able to regain control of the island. In 1804, Haitians declared their independence. Haiti became the second republic in the Americas, after the United States.

---

*Haiti occupies the western half of Hispaniola, one of the islands Columbus explored.

Toussaint L'Ouverture *A self-educated former slave, Toussaint L'Ouverture led slaves in Haiti in a revolt against French rule. L'Ouverture was captured and later died in a French prison. For enslaved blacks throughout the Americas, however, he became a symbol of the struggle for liberty.* **United States and the World** *Why would President Jefferson be concerned about the revolt in Haiti?*

The Nation Doubles in Size

About the time that the French lost Haiti, President Jefferson decided to try to buy New Orleans from Napoleon. Jefferson wanted to be sure that American farmers would always be able to ship their goods through the port of New Orleans. The President sent Robert Livingston and James Monroe to France as ambassadors. His orders were to offer Napoleon up to $10 million for New Orleans.

A surprising proposal. Livingston and Monroe talked to Talleyrand, the French foreign minister. Talleyrand, you remember, was the shrewd diplomat who had caused the XYZ Affair. (See page 326.)

At first, Talleyrand showed little interest in the offer. Then, events quickly changed. Napoleon's dream of an empire in the Americas ended when L'Ouverture drove the French out of Haiti. Also, Napoleon needed money to finance his wars in Europe. Talleyrand now asked Livingston an unexpected question: "What will you give for the *whole* of Louisiana?"

Livingston was shocked and delighted. France was willing to sell all of Louisiana, not just New Orleans. Livingston offered $4 million.

"Too low!" said Talleyrand. "Reflect, and see me tomorrow."

Livingston and Monroe debated the matter. They had no authority to buy all of Louisiana. But they knew Jefferson wanted control of the Mississippi. Before getting the President's approval, they agreed to pay the French $15 million. Neither the French nor the Americans asked the various Indian nations in Louisiana about the purchase.

Was the purchase constitutional? Jefferson was pleased by the news from France. But did the Constitution give him the power to buy land? After all, Jefferson had always said that the federal government had only those powers spelled out in the Constitution. And the document said nothing about a President's power to purchase territory.

After much thought, Jefferson decided that he could buy Louisiana. The Constitution, he reasoned, allowed the President to make treaties. The Senate quickly approved a treaty making the **Louisiana Purchase.**

In 1803, the United States took control of the vast new lands west of the Mississippi. Jefferson predicted proudly that the new territory would become "an empire of freedom." (See "The Man Without a Country" on page 666.)

Lewis and Clark's Assignment

The United States now owned Louisiana. But few Americans knew what this new territory included. In 1803, Congress provided money for an army expedition to study the new lands. Jefferson chose Meriwether Lewis, his private secretary, to head the team. Lewis asked another Virginian, William Clark, to join him. About 40 men made up their band, known as the "Corps of Discovery."

Jefferson gave Lewis and Clark careful instructions. "Your observations are to be taken with great pains and accuracy," the President said. He even reminded them to write neatly so that others could read their notes. Jefferson asked the men to map a route to the Pacific. He also wanted them to learn all that they could about Native Americans they met.

Signing the Louisiana Purchase *This bronze plaque by Karl Bitter honors the signing of the Louisiana Purchase. American ambassadors James Monroe, far left, and Robert Livingston, seated, look on as Maurice de Talleyrand signs the document for France.* **Geography** *What important river did the Louisiana Purchase include?*

Many Indian nations lived in the rugged new lands. For decades, these Native Americans had carried on a busy trade with English, French, and Spanish merchants. Jefferson hoped that the Indians could be convinced to trade with Americans instead. For this reason, he urged Lewis and Clark to tell the Indians of "our wish to be neighborly, friendly, and useful to them."

The explorers also were told to study the climate, wildlife, soil, and mineral resources of the new lands. Jefferson requested the following specifics:

❝Climate as characterized by the thermometer, by the proportion of rainy, cloudy, and clear days, by lightning, hail, snow, ice . . . by the winds prevailing at different season, the dates at which particular plants put forth or lose their flowers, or leaf, times of appearance of particular birds, reptiles or insects.❞

GEOGRAPHY AND HISTORY

The Expedition Begins

In May 1804, Lewis and Clark started up the Missouri River from St. Louis. In time, their trip would take them to the Pacific Ocean. (Follow their route on the map on page 360.)

At first, their progress was slow as they traveled against the Missouri's swift current. One night, the current tore away the riverbank where they were camping. The party had to scramble into boats to avoid being washed downstream.

Soon, the travelers met people from various Indian nations. Since it was an Indian custom to exchange gifts, Lewis and Clark brought many presents for Native Americans. The explorers carried medals stamped with the United States seal, mirrors, beads, knives, and blankets, as well as more than 4,000 sewing needles and some 3,000 fish hooks.

As winter approached, Lewis and Clark decided to stay with the Mandans near present-day Bismarck, North Dakota. The Mandan villages had been trading centers for at least 100 years. Crows, Cheyennes, Arapahoes, and other Indians traveled hundreds of miles to trade with the Mandans. British and French traders also visited the villages. The Mandans traded corn, beans, and squash for horses and leather clothing from the Southwest. Sioux Indians sold buffalo meat and hides for British rifles and bullets. The Mandan trading network impressed Lewis and Clark.

Over the Rockies

The Rocky Mountains were hundreds of miles to the west. Still, the explorers were worried about how they would cross them. Luckily, they met Sacajawea (sahk uh juh WEE uh), a Shoshone Indian woman who was staying with the Mandans that winter. The Shoshones (shoh SHOH neez) lived in the Rockies, so Sacajawea knew the mountains well. She offered to be a guide and interpreter for Lewis and Clark. Her husband, a French Canadian, would go with them.

In early spring, the party set out. On April 22, 1805, Lewis made the following entry in his journal:

❝I ascended to the top of the bluff this morning, from whence I had a most delightful view of the country, the whole of which except the valley formed by the Missouri is void of timber or underbrush, exposing to the first glance of the spectator immense herds of buffalo, elk, deer, and antelope feeding in one common and boundless pasture.❞

In the foothills of the Rockies, the landscape and wildlife changed. Bighorn sheep ran along the high hills. The thorns of

Sacajawea: Guide to Lewis and Clark

Sacajawea was just a young girl when Hidatsa Indians captured her. Swooping down on her Shoshone camp in the Rocky Mountains, they took her to North Dakota, far to the east. There, she was sold as a slave to a French Canadian trader, whom she later married.

In 1805, Sacajawea and her husband joined the Lewis and Clark expedition. She was to serve as both guide and interpreter. In that same year, Sacajawea gave birth to a son. Strapping him to her back, she continued the journey west.

Sacajawea contributed greatly to the success of the expedition. Besides doing the laundry and cooking, she gathered wild vegetables and advised the men where to fish and hunt game. Because of her knowledge of herbs, the expedition relied on her to be nurse and doctor.

Sacajawea's courage and leadership never faltered. When a canoe overturned in the icy Missouri River, she leaped in to retrieve precious instruments, papers, and medicines. When the party reached her homeland in the Rocky Mountains, she persuaded her Shoshone relatives to supply the expedition with the food and horses it needed to continue.

Lewis and Clark appreciated Sacajawea's help. "Our journey would have ended in failure without her aid," they said.

1. How did Sacajawea help the expedition?

2. **Synthesizing Information** What evidence shows that Sacajawea was dedicated and loyal to the expedition?

---

prickly pear cactus jabbed the explorers' moccasins. Grizzly bears roamed about. Lewis was once chased by a grizzly while he was exploring alone.

When the party reached the mountains, Sacajawea recognized the lands of her people. One day, Lewis met some Shoshone leaders and invited them back to camp. Sacajawea began "to dance and show every mark of the most extravagant joy." One of the leaders was her brother. The Shoshones told Lewis and Clark the best route to take over the Rockies.

Reaching the Pacific

As they crossed the Rockies, the explorers saw that the rivers flowed west, toward the Pacific. They had crossed the continental divide. A continental divide is a mountain ridge that separates river systems. In North America, the continental divide is located in the Rocky Mountains. Rivers east of the divide flow into the Mississippi, which drains into the Gulf of Mexico. West of the divide, rivers flow into the Pacific Ocean.

Entering the Pacific Northwest. After building canoes, Lewis and Clark's party floated down the Columbia River. It carried them into the Pacific Northwest. There, they met the Nez Percé (NEHZ puhr SAY) Indians.

Lewis and Clark wanted to learn about the Nez Percés. But every one of their questions had to be translated four times. First, their English words were translated into French for Sacajawea's husband. He then translated the French into Mandan. Sacajawea translated the Mandan into Shoshone. Then, a Shoshone, who lived with the Nez Percés, translated the question into Nez Percé. Each answer went through the same process in reverse.

A view of the west coast. On November 7, 1805, Lewis and Clark reached their goal. Lewis wrote in his journal: "Great joy in camp. We are in view of the . . . great Pacific Ocean which we have been so long anxious to see." On a nearby tree, Clark carved, "By Land from the U. States in 1804 & 5."

The return trip to St. Louis took another year. In 1806, Americans celebrated the return of Lewis and Clark. The explorers

MAP STUDY

Traveling on horseback, Lewis and Clark, accompanied by Sacajawea, crossed the continental divide in August 1805.

1. At what place did Lewis and Clark cross the continental divide?
2. Does the continental divide form a straight line? Explain.
3. **Analyzing Information** How do you think the continental divide influenced the way settlers could travel to the West?

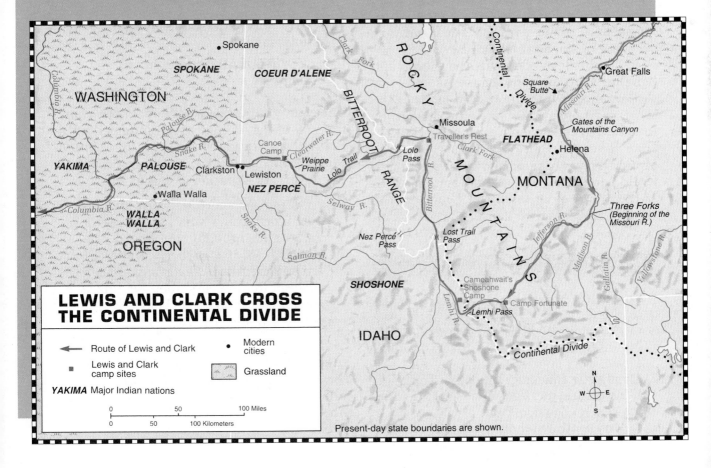

LEWIS AND CLARK CROSS THE CONTINENTAL DIVIDE

→ Route of Lewis and Clark
■ Lewis and Clark camp sites
● Modern cities
Grassland
YAKIMA Major Indian nations

0   50   100 Miles
0   50   100 Kilometers

Present-day state boundaries are shown.

brought back much useful information about the Louisiana Purchase. Except for one small battle, their meetings with Native Americans were peaceful.

Pike Explores the West

Before Lewis and Clark returned, another explorer set out from St. Louis. From 1805 to 1807, Zebulon Pike explored the upper Mississippi River, the Kansas and Arkansas rivers, and parts of present-day Colorado and New Mexico. On Thanksgiving Day in 1806, Pike saw a mountain peak rising above the Colorado plains. Today, this mountain is known as Pikes Peak. (See the map on page 360.)

Later, Pike headed south into Spanish lands in the Southwest. In New Mexico, the Spanish arrested him as a spy and escorted him across Texas to the Spanish-American border at Natchitoches, Louisiana. Pike was released in 1807, but Spanish officials kept his maps and notes. Still, Pike brought back with him valuable information about trade and military strength in the Spanish lands.

The journeys of Lewis and Clark and Zebulon Pike excited Americans. But few settlers moved into the rugged lands of the West right away. As you will read, they first settled the region closest to the Mississippi River. Within a short time, the area around New Orleans had a large enough white population to apply for statehood. In 1812, this area entered the Union as the state of Louisiana. ◆

| SECTION 2 REVIEW |

1. **Locate:** (a) Mississippi River, (b) New Orleans, (c) Haiti, (d) Louisiana Purchase, (e) St. Louis, (f) Missouri River, (g) Rocky Mountains, (h) Columbia River, (i) Pikes Peak.
2. **Identify:** (a) Pinckney Treaty, (b) Toussaint L'Ouverture, (c) Lewis and Clark, (d) Sacajawea, (e) Zebulon Pike.
3. **Define:** continental divide.

4. Why was New Orleans important to many American farmers?
5. Why did France offer to sell Louisiana to the United States?
6. (a) What did Jefferson instruct Lewis and Clark to do on their expedition? (b) What did Lewis and Clark learn about the Mandan Indians?
7. **Synthesizing Information** Was Jefferson's decision to purchase Louisiana based on a strict or loose interpretation of the Constitution? Explain.

3 Protecting American Neutrality

FIND OUT

◆ What dangers did American ships face in the early 1800s?

◆ Why did British warships seize sailors?

◆ Why was Jefferson's embargo unpopular?

◆ **VOCABULARY** impressment, embargo

The young American sailor's letter came from overseas. It had been smuggled off a British ship and carried to the United States. The handwritten message described the desperate situation of James Brown:

❝Being on shore one day in Lisbon, Portugal, I was [seized] by a gang and brought on board the [British ship] *Conqueror*, where I am still confined. Never have I been allowed to put my foot on shore since I was brought on board, which is now three years.❞

Brown's case was not unusual. Thousands of American sailors were forced to serve on British ships in the early 1800s. This was only one of many dangers that Americans faced as their sea trade began to thrive.

Yankee Ships Trade Around the World

In the years after the Revolution, American overseas trade grew rapidly. Ships sailed from New England ports on voyages that sometimes lasted three years. Everywhere they went, Yankee captains kept a sharp lookout for new goods to trade and new markets in which to sell. One clever trader sawed up winter ice from New England ponds, packed the slabs deep in sawdust, and transported them to India. There, he traded the ice for silks and spices.

Yankee traders cruised the world. In 1784, the *Empress of China* became the first American ship to trade with China. Other New England traders followed and built a profitable China trade. Yankee ships carried ginseng, a plant that grew wild in New England, to trade for Chinese tea and silks. The Chinese made medicine from ginseng root.

Yankee merchants sailed up the Pacific coast of North America in the 1790s. In fact, Yankee traders visited the Columbia River more than ten years before Lewis and Clark. For a time, traders from Boston were so common in the Pacific Northwest that Native Americans called every white man "Boston." Traders bought furs from Native Americans. They then sold the furs for large profits in China.

The Tripoli Pirates

To make a good profit, American traders ran great risks, especially in the Mediterranean Sea. For many years, pirates along the coast of North Africa attacked vessels from Europe and the United States. The North African nations were called the **Barbary States.** To protect American ships, the United States paid a yearly tribute, or bribe, to the rulers of the Barbary States.

In the early 1800s, the ruler of Tripoli, one of the Barbary States, demanded a larger bribe than usual. When President Jefferson refused to pay, Tripoli declared war on the United States. In response, Jefferson ordered the American navy to blockade the port of Tripoli.

During the blockade, the American ship *Philadelphia* ran aground near Tripoli. Pirates from Tripoli boarded the ship and imprisoned the crew. The pirates planned to use the *Philadelphia*. But Stephen Decatur, the captain of another American ship, thwarted their plan. Very late one night,

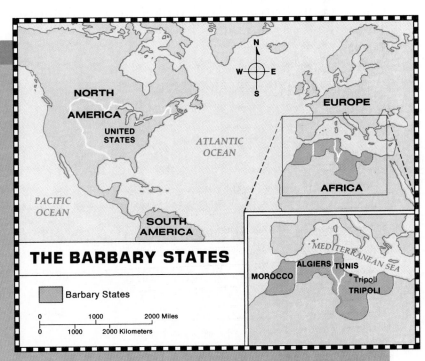

MAP STUDY

President Jefferson wanted to end the practice of paying tribute to the Barbary States.

1. *What bodies of water bordered the Barbary States?*
2. *About how far from the United States were the Barbary States?*
3. **Making Decisions** *Use this map and the map on pages 714–715 to describe routes American traders might have used to avoid the Barbary States. What advantage would these routes have? What disadvantage?*

THE BARBARY STATES

Barbary States

0   1000   2000 Miles
0   1000   2000 Kilometers

Decatur and his crew quietly sailed into Tripoli harbor. When they reached the captured ship, they set it on fire so that the pirates could not use it.

Meanwhile, a force of American marines landed in North Africa. The marines marched 500 miles (800 km) to launch a surprise attack on Tripoli. The war with Tripoli lasted until 1805. In the end, the ruler of Tripoli signed a treaty promising to let American ships alone.

American Ships Under Attack

In 1803, Britain and France went to war again. As in the 1790s, the European war gave a boost to American trade. British and French ships were so busy fighting that they could not carry goods for trade. So American merchants made good profits trading with both sides.

Violating American neutrality. But neither Britain nor France wanted America to provide needed supplies to its enemy. Americans claimed they were neutral, or not supporting either side in the war. But Britain and France ignored the claim, just as they had in the 1790s. Each tried to cut off American trade with the other. Napoleon seized American ships bound for England, and the British nabbed Yankee traders on their way to France. Between 1805

and 1807, hundreds of American ships were captured.

American sailors seized. Britain went beyond taking American ships. As you have read, the British navy also snatched American sailors and forced them to serve on British ships. This practice of forcing people into service, called impressment, was common in Britain. For centuries, impressment gangs had raided villages and forced young men to serve in the navy.

Because of the war with France, the British navy needed all the men it could find. British warships stopped and searched private American vessels. Often, they found British sailors on board. British sailors preferred to work on American ships because wages were higher and discipline was milder.

When a British officer found British sailors on an American ship, he forced them to serve in the British navy. British officers ignored sailors who claimed that they had become American citizens. "Once an Englishman, always an Englishman," the British said. Even worse, the British impressed thousands of American sailors.

A Ban on Trade

Americans were furious with the British for attacking their ships and impressing

Seizing Young Men to Be Sailors *Long before they began seizing sailors off American ships, the British forced their own young citizens into the Royal Navy. This picture shows an English family pleading to save their son from impressment.* ***United States and the World*** *Why did Britain need sailors in the early 1800s?*

their sailors. Many wanted to go to war with Britain. But Jefferson, like Washington and Adams, hoped to avoid war. He knew that the small American fleet was no match for the British navy, the most powerful in the world. Indeed, Jefferson's budget cuts had left the American navy unprepared for war.

A ban on all foreign trade. Jefferson convinced Congress in 1807 to pass the Embargo Act. An embargo is a ban on trade with another country. The **Embargo Act** forbade Americans to export or import any goods. Jefferson hoped that the embargo would hurt France and Britain by cutting off supplies they needed. "Our trade is the most powerful weapon we can use in our defense," one Republican newspaper wrote. If France and Britain agreed to respect American neutrality, then Jefferson would lift the embargo.

The embargo hurt Britain and France. But Americans suffered even more. Exports dropped from $108 million in 1807 to $22 million in 1808. American sailors had no work. Farmers lost money because they could not ship wheat overseas. Docks in the South were piled high with cotton and tobacco. The Embargo Act hurt New England merchants most of all, and they protested loudly.

A limited embargo. After more than a year, Jefferson admitted that the embargo had failed. In 1809, Congress replaced the embargo with the **Nonintercourse Act.** Under the act, Americans could trade with all nations except Britain and France. The new act also allowed the President to restore trade with Britain or France, if either nation agreed to stop seizing American ships and sailors.

The Embargo Act was the most disliked measure of Jefferson's term in office. Still, the Republicans remained very popular. In 1808, Jefferson followed the precedent set by Washington and refused to run for a third term. His friend, James Madison, ran and easily won. When Madison took office in 1809, he hoped that Britain

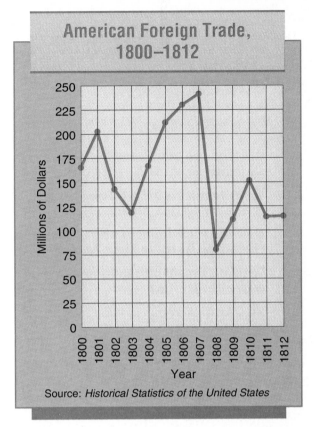

American Foreign Trade, 1800–1812

Source: *Historical Statistics of the United States*

GRAPH SKILLS *In the early 1800s, trade was important to the new nation, especially to New Englanders. ◆ Why do you think trade decreased sharply between 1807 and 1808?*

and France would soon agree to stop violating American neutrality.

SECTION 3 REVIEW

1. **Locate:** Tripoli.
2. **Identify:** (a) *Empress of China,* (b) Barbary States, (c) Embargo Act, (d) Nonintercourse Act.
3. **Define:** (a) impressment, (b) embargo.
4. Why did the United States and Tripoli go to war?
5. How did the renewed war in Europe in 1803 affect American overseas trade?
6. (a) What was the purpose of the Embargo Act? (b) Why did it fail?
7. **Linking Past and Present** Do countries today use an embargo to achieve political goals? Explain.

4 The Road to War

FIND OUT

◆ Why did the South and West want war with Britain?

◆ What problems did white settlers create for Native Americans?

◆ How did the Prophet and Tecumseh try to stop white settlements?

◆ Why did President Madison agree to war with Britain?

◆ VOCABULARY nationalism

As Britain and France continued their struggle in Europe, it seemed more likely that the United States might be drawn into a war. Some leaders were concerned about the state of American armed forces. In 1802, the army had only 3,300 soldiers. That small number could not defend American cities from an invasion, much less launch an attack. In 1808, Congress finally increased the size of the army.

Republican leaders, however, appointed their friends to be army officers. Since many of these officers knew little about the military, their troops did not respect them. Neither did Winfield Scott, who later became a well-known general. Scott said that many of his fellow officers were "imbeciles and ignoramuses." A member of Congress who studied the army agreed. "The state of that Army," he said, "is enough to make any man who has the smallest love of country wish to get rid of it."

The War Hawks

Despite the weakness of the American army and navy, many Americans strongly favored going to war. But whom should they fight? Both Britain and France were seizing American ships.

Then, in 1810, Napoleon promised to respect the rights of American ships. So the United States continued to trade with France. When Britain refused to make a similar promise, the United States restored its embargo against Britain.

Like earlier Presidents, James Madison wanted to avoid war. But other Americans were less cautious. Except in New England, where merchants wanted to restore trade with Britain, anti-British feeling ran strong. Members of Congress from the South and the West clamored for war with Britain. They were known as **War Hawks.**

War Hawks had a strong sense of nationalism. Nationalism is pride in or devotion to one's country. War Hawks felt that Britain was treating the United States as if it were still a British colony. "If we submit [to Britain]," warned one War Hawk, "the independence of this nation is lost."

Henry Clay of Kentucky was the most outspoken War Hawk. Clay wanted war for two reasons. He wanted revenge on Britain for attacking American ships. And he wanted an excuse to conquer Canada. "The militia of Kentucky are alone [able] to place Montreal and Upper Canada at your feet," Clay boasted to Congress. Canadians, Clay believed, would be happy to leave the British empire and join the United States.

Federalists disagreed. They claimed that an attack on Canada would be unjust. One member of Congress from Massachusetts pointed out that Canada had done nothing wrong:

> **"**[Canada] has not impressed our seamen, taken our ships, confiscated our property, nor in any other respect treated us ill. All the crime alleged against Canada or the Canadians, is that, without any act of their own, they are connected with . . . a nation which has injured us on the ocean.**"**

Conflicts in the West

There was still another reason that War Hawks wanted to fight Britain. They claimed that Britain was arming Indians on the frontier and encouraging them to attack white settlers. In fact, the British, who held military forts in Canada, did hope to take advantage of troubles along the frontier.

White settlers push west. But a much more important reason for troubles on the frontier was ever increasing white settlement. As you have read, in 1795 the Treaty of Greenville forced Indians to sell much of their land in Ohio. (See page 319.) Ohio joined the Union in 1803. By then, thousands of settlers were pushing beyond Ohio into Indiana Territory. The War Hawks believed strongly that neither the British nor Native Americans should stop the westward march of white settlers.

As settlers poured into the frontier, Indians were introduced to the white people's way of life. Many Native Americans came to depend on white trade goods from the East. Most Indian hunters in Ohio, for example, preferred to use rifles instead of Indian bows and arrows. Indian women cooked with iron pots and kettles bought

MAP STUDY

As settlers moved west, they took over Indian lands.
1. *Which Indian groups lost their lands between 1784 and 1810?*
2. *When did the Natchez lose their land?*
3. **Forecasting** *Notice the areas of the map shaded tan. Based on what you have learned about settlers' treatment of Native Americans, what do you think happened to Indian lands in these areas? Explain.*

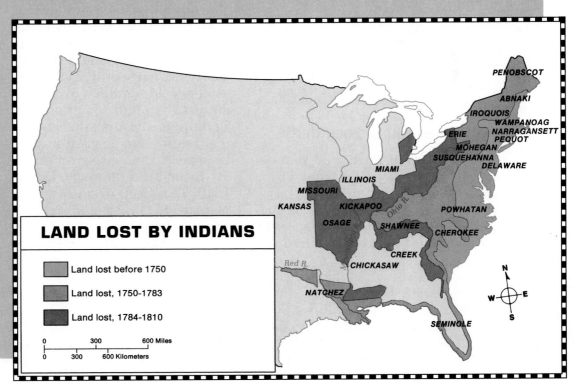

LAND LOST BY INDIANS

Land lost before 1750

Land lost, 1750-1783

Land lost, 1784-1810

from white traders. Because Native Americans depended on these items, they found it difficult not to deal with the whites.

The flood of settlers created serious problems for Native Americans. Whites built farms on land reserved for Indians. They hunted deer and birds that Indians depended on. "Stop your people from killing our game," Shawnee chiefs asked the federal government. "They would be angry if we were to kill a cow or hog of theirs. The little game that remains is very dear to us."

Indians try to resist. Sometimes, one or another Indian nation protested white settlements to the federal government. Other times, small bands attacked white settlers to drive them off the land. But Indians found it difficult to unite with one another to oppose white settlements. Indian rivals who had once been enemies did not easily become allies.

During the same years that Americans were pulled toward war with Britain, many Indians became determined to halt white settlers. They were led by two remarkable Shawnee brothers, the Prophet and Tecumseh.

P CLOSE

Two Shawnee Brothers Seek Unity

One winter evening in 1804, a 30-year-old Shawnee sat cross-legged in front of his wigwam fire. As he lifted a burning stick from the fire to light his long pipe, he suddenly gasped. Dropping the blazing twig, he fell to his side as if dead. Terrified, his wife ran for help.

Families from the other lodges came running. They knew this man—his name was Tenskwatawa (ten SKWA tah wah). To their amazement, the supposedly dead man stirred.

When Tenskwatawa was able to speak, he reported that he had a strange vision. His soul, he said, had taken a journey to the spirit world. There, he learned the path that all Indians must take if they were to live happily. In the weeks that followed, Tenskwatawa told his experiences to those who came to listen. He became known as the Prophet.

The Prophet's message. According to the Prophet, Indians must give up white ways. They must no longer trade for cloth, rifles, axes, or whiskey. If Indians returned to the old ways, they would gain power to resist the whites from the East.

In 1808, the Prophet built a village for his followers along Tippecanoe Creek in Indiana. From as far away as Missouri, Iowa, and Minnesota, Indians traveled to hear the Prophet's message. To many, his religious teachings brought hope.

Tecumseh (tih KUM suh), the Prophet's older brother, visited other Indian nations. Tall, handsome, and energetic, Tecumseh organized many Native Americans into a confederation, or league. While the Prophet was the spiritual leader of the confederation, Tecumseh became its spokesperson. He said all Indians must unite "in claiming a common right in the land."

In 1809, William Henry Harrison, governor of the Indiana Territory, signed a treaty with several Indian leaders. The leaders sold 3 million acres of Indian land for less than half a cent an acre. Enraged, Tecumseh said that the chiefs who signed the treaties had no right to sell the land. It belonged to all Native Americans.

Tecumseh's message. In the summer of 1810, Tecumseh decided to deliver a firm message to Governor Harrison. He and 75 warriors marched to Vincennes, Indiana. Awaiting their arrival, Governor Harrison arranged chairs on his front porch for the meeting. Tecumseh objected. He insisted that they meet on the grass of the forest— on Indian ground.

Harrison was impressed with Tecumseh's proud manner. "He is one of those uncommon geniuses which spring up occasionally to produce revolutions and over-

Shawnee Leaders *Tecumseh, above, and the Prophet, at right, believed that the land belonged to all Indians. No nation had the right to sell any part of it unless all agreed. "Sell a country?" asked Tecumseh. "Why not sell the air, the clouds, and the great sea? . . . Did not the Great Spirit make them all for the use of its children?"* **Multicultural Heritage** *What did the Prophet say Indians must do?*

turn the established order of things," Harrison commented.

As Tecumseh addressed the governor, he warned of the need for change:

> **❝**You are continually driving the red people [from their land,] when at last you will drive them into the [ocean] where they can't either stand or work. Brother. You ought to know what you are doing with the Indians. . . . It is a very bad thing and we do not like it.**❞**

Tecumseh insisted that Harrison give his message to President Madison. The governor agreed, but warned that it was not likely to change Madison's mind. Tecumseh stared grimly. He knew that if whites did not stop moving onto Indian land, war would surely come. ◆

A Showdown at Tippecanoe

Rivalries among different Indian nations kept Tecumseh from uniting all Native Americans east of the Mississippi River. Still, white settlers were alarmed at his success. "I am inclined to believe that a crisis is fast approaching," said Governor Harrison. In 1811, he decided to march with 1,000 soldiers to Prophetstown, on Tippecanoe Creek. He knew that Tecumseh was organizing Indians in the South. His brother, the Prophet, was in charge.

The Prophet learned of Harrison's approach. He decided to meet the danger with a surprise night attack on Harrison's troops. In the battle that followed, neither side won a clear victory. But whites in the East celebrated the **Battle of Tippecanoe** as a major victory.

In 1812, Tecumseh went to Canada to speak with the British. By that time, war between Britain and the United States seemed likely. Tecumseh offered to lead his Indian confederation against the United States if war broke out.

Congress Declares War

The Battle of Tippecanoe marked the beginning of a long and deadly war on the frontier. Fighting between Native Americans and white settlers spurred the War Hawks to call even louder for war with Britain. Convinced that the British were arming the Indians, one newspaper called the war, "purely BRITISH."

War Hawks saw other advantages of going to war with Britain. South of the United States, Florida belonged to Spain, Britain's ally. If Americans went to war with Britain, the War Hawks said, the United States could seize Florida from Spain.

President Madison at last gave in to the war fever. In June 1812, he asked Congress to declare war on Britain. The House vote was 79 to 49 in favor of war, and the Senate vote 19 to 13. This was the closest vote ever recorded in American history on a declaration of war. Americans soon discovered that winning the war would not be as easy as the War Hawks thought.

SECTION 4 REVIEW

1. **Locate:** (a) Canada, (b) Ohio, (c) Indiana Territory, (d) Spanish Florida.
2. **Identify:** (a) War Hawks, (b) Henry Clay, (c) the Prophet, (d) Tecumseh, (e) Battle of Tippecanoe.
3. **Define:** nationalism.
4. Why did Henry Clay and other War Hawks want to fight the British?
5. How did white settlements affect Native Americans?
6. Why did President Madison finally ask Congress to declare war on Britain?
7. **Comparing** How was the Prophet's message different from Tecumseh's?

5 The War of 1812

FIND OUT

◆ How did Americans prepare for the War of 1812?

◆ What were the American and British victories in the war?

◆ What part did Native Americans play in the fighting?

◆ What was the outcome of the war?

Many Republicans welcomed the news of war with Britain. In some cities, they fired cannons and rifles and danced in the street. One New Jersey man wrote a song calling for a swift attack on Canada:

  ❝On to Quebec's embattled halls!
Who will pause, when glory calls?
Charge, soldiers, charge, its lofty walls.
And storm its strong artillery.**❞**

Other Americans were less enthusiastic. Many New Englanders strongly opposed fighting Britain again. They talked scornfully of "Mr. Madison's war." In fact, before the war ended, some New Englanders would plot to leave the Union and make a separate peace with England.

Preparing for War

The United States was not ready for war. As you have read, the American army was small and poorly trained. The navy had only 16 ships to fight against the huge and well-equipped British fleet.

Since there were few regular troops, the government relied on volunteers to fight the war. Congress voted to give them $124 and 360 acres of land for their service. This was high pay at the time—equal to a year's salary for most workers. Lured by the reward of owning their own farm, young men eagerly enlisted.

Although many men joined the army, few had much training. Most had served in their town militias, which trained only one day a year. And that day was as much a party as a day for drilling. As a result, American troops were not well disciplined. Many soldiers deserted after a few months. Others would not fight unless they were paid promptly. One officer complained that his men "absolutely refused to march until they had [received] their pay."

By the end of the war, the Americans had become good soldiers. More than 500,000 men served in the army between 1812 and 1815. To pay their salaries, the federal government borrowed $98 million. The Republicans got the war they wanted. But it meant the end of Jefferson's thrifty government.

Fighting at Sea

Because the British were busy fighting Napoleon, the American declaration of war took them by surprise. The British navy could not spare many ships to fight the United States. But they used a number of them to blockade American ports.

The American navy was too small to break the blockade. Yet several young sea captains won stunning victories. One famous battle took place early in the war. Isaac Hull, captain of the *Constitution,* spotted the British frigate *Guerrière* (gair ee AIR) in August 1812. For close to an hour, the two ships tried to close in on each other. The *Guerrière* fired on the *Constitution* several times. But Captain Hull ordered his cannons to hold their fire.

A Major Sea Battle *The battle between the U.S.S.* Constitution *and the British frigate* Guerrière *was a key victory for the Americans in the War of 1812. In this painting by famed marine artist Thomas Birch, the* Constitution *levels a broadside blast at the crippled* Guerrière. **Technology** *Why was the American navy unable to break the British blockade?*

The War of 1812 was fought on several fronts.
1. *What battles took place in or near Canada?*
2. *(a) Name two American victories shown on the maps. (b) Name two British victories.*
3. **Comparing** *Compare the American invasion of Canada in the Revolution with the invasion of Canada in the War of 1812. (See pages 223–224.) Were they similar or different? Explain.*

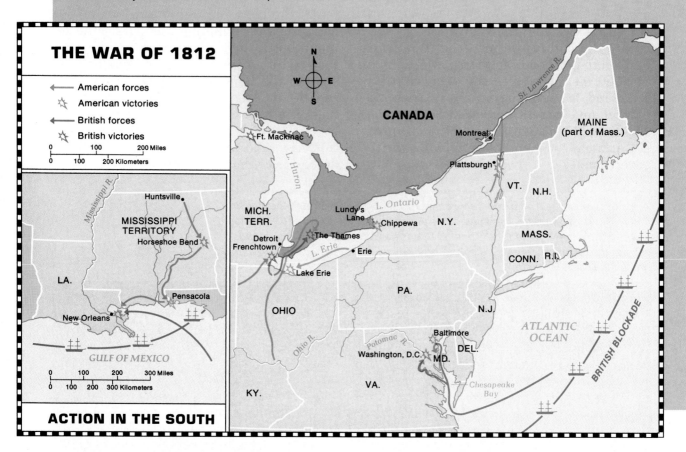

When Hull was close enough to the enemy, he bent over and shouted to the sailors on the deck below: "Now, boys, you may fire!" The cannons on the *Constitution* roared. They tore holes in the sides of the *Guerrière* and shot off both masts.

When the smoke cleared, Hull asked the British captain if he had "struck" his flag—that is, surrendered by lowering his flag. "Well, I don't know," replied the stunned British captain. "Our mizzenmast is gone, our mainmast is gone. And, upon the whole, you may say we *have* struck our flag."

American sea captains won other victories at sea. Even though these victories cheered Americans, they did little to win the war.

War in the West

As you have read, one goal of the War Hawks was to conquer Canada. The United States planned to invade Canada at three points: Detroit, Niagara Falls, and Montreal. Americans were hopeful that Canadians would welcome the chance to throw off British rule. Instead, the Canadians fought back and forced the Americans to retreat.

Americans invade Canada. William Hull led American troops into Canada from Detroit. The Canadians had only a few untrained troops to fight the invasion.

To trick the Americans, General Isaac Brock paraded his soldiers in red cloaks. This made Hull think that well-trained British troops were helping the Canadians. Brock also let a false "secret" message fall into Hull's hands. It said that more than 5,000 Indians were fighting on Brock's side. The real number was far less. But raids on Hull's troops by Tecumseh, Brock's ally, made the message believable.

Brock's tricks worked, and Hull retreated from Canada. The British followed him and captured Detroit. Since British ships controlled Lake Erie, the Americans could not retake Detroit. The invasion of Canada was a failure.

Struggle over Lake Erie. In 1813, the Americans set out to win control of Lake Erie. Captain Oliver Hazard Perry was in charge of the American attack, but he had no ships. Perry had to design and build his own fleet. In September 1813, he sailed his tiny force into battle against the British.

The British bombarded Perry's ship. Perry took his flag and rowed over to another American vessel. There, he hoisted his colors and continued to fight. The battle ended with an American victory. Perry wrote a famous message of victory on the back of an envelope: "We have met the enemy and they are ours."

Tecumseh's last battle. When the Americans gained control of Lake Erie, Tecumseh and the British were forced to abandon Detroit. William Henry Harrison, hero of Tippecanoe and now a general in the army, pursued them into Canada. The Americans won a decisive victory at the **Battle of the Thames.** Tecumseh died in battle. Without Tecumseh, the Indian confederation he had worked so hard to form fell apart.

The Creeks surrender. The Creeks, Tecumseh's allies in the South, were involved in a bloody war against white settlers. A Tennessee officer, Andrew Jackson, took command of American troops in the Creek War.

In 1814, Jackson led his forces into battle. With the help of the Cherokees, Jackson won a decisive victory at the **Battle of Horseshoe Bend.** The leader of the Creeks walked alone into Jackson's camp to surrender:

> ❝I am in your power. Do unto me as you please. . . . If I had an army I would yet fight, and contend to the last. . . . But your people have destroyed my nation.❞

For the time being, the fighting ended. But once again, Native Americans were forced to give up land to whites.

The British Burn Washington, D.C.

In 1814, Britain and its allies finally defeated France. Now, Britain could send its best troops and ships to America.

That summer, British ships sailed into Chesapeake Bay. They put soldiers ashore about 30 miles (48 km) from Washington, D.C. Americans tried to stop the British at Bladensburg, Maryland. President Madison himself rode out to watch the battle, carrying a set of dueling pistols in case of trouble. But the battle-hardened British quickly scattered the untrained Americans, leaving the capital undefended.

In the President's mansion, Dolley Madison waited for her husband to return. Her guard of soldiers disappeared. Hastily, she scrawled a note to her sister:

> ❝Will you believe it, my sister? We have had a battle or skirmish near Bladensburg and here I am still within sound of the cannon! Mr. Madison comes not. May God protect us. Two messengers covered with dust come bid me fly. But here I mean to wait for him.❞

Soon after, British troops marched into the capital. Dolley Madison gathered up important papers of the President and a portrait of George Washington. Then, she fled south. The British took Washington, D.C., and burned the President's mansion and other buildings before leaving.*

From Washington, D.C., the British marched north toward nearby Baltimore. The key to Baltimore's defense was Fort McHenry. From evening on September 13 until dawn on September 14, British rockets bombarded the harbor. But when the early morning fog lifted, the "broad stripes and bright stars" of the American flag still waved over Fort McHenry. Finally, the British gave up the attack. Soon after, Francis Scott Key wrote "The Star-Spangled Banner," a poem telling of his night's watch of the bombardment.

———

*When Washington, D.C., was rebuilt after the fire, the President's mansion was given a coat of whitewash to cover the charred wood. After that, it was called the White House.

———

"The Flag Was Still There" *Rockets and shells lit up the night sky as the British bombarded Fort McHenry. Francis Scott Key watched the bombardment from the harbor. When dawn came and the American flag still flew above the fort, Key was inspired to write the verses of "The Star-Spangled Banner."* **Geography** *Why was Fort McHenry important?*

Jackson Defends New Orleans

Meanwhile, the British prepared to attack New Orleans. Control of New Orleans would allow the British to cut off American trade on the Mississippi. From there, the British hoped to sail up the Mississippi.

Andrew Jackson, however, was waiting for the British. Jackson's forces included thousands of frontiersmen, many of them expert riflemen. Hundreds of African Americans from New Orleans also volunteered to defend their city.

Jackson's troops dug trenches to defend themselves. On January 8, 1815, the British tried to overrun Jackson's line. Again and again, British soldiers charged the American trenches. More than 2,000 British fell. Only seven Americans died.

All over the United States, Americans celebrated their victory at the **Battle of New Orleans.** Andrew Jackson became an overnight hero, second only to George Washington. (See "At the Battle of New Orleans" on page 669.)

Jackson's fame did not dim even when Americans later learned that the long and bloody battle could have been avoided. The battle took place two weeks after the United States and Britain had signed a peace treaty.

Peace at Last

In the early 1800s, it took weeks for news to cross the Atlantic. By the winter of 1814, Americans knew that peace talks had begun. But no one knew how long they would last. While Jackson prepared to fight the British at New Orleans, New Englanders met to protest "Mr. Madison's War."

A threat to the Union. Delegates from around New England met in Hartford, Connecticut, in December 1814. Most were Federalists. They disliked the Republican President and the war. The British blockade had hurt New England's sea trade. Also, many New Englanders felt that the South and the West had more to gain if the United States won land in Florida and Canada.

Battle of New Orleans
The Battle of New Orleans gave the United States its greatest victory of the War of 1812. But it decided nothing. Although neither side knew it, the war was already over. In this engraving, Andrew Jackson, on a white horse, spurs the Americans on to victory. **Geography** *Why did the British want to gain control of New Orleans?*

If new states were carved out of these lands, New England would lose its influence.

Delegates to the **Hartford Convention** threatened to leave the Union if the war continued. While the delegates talked, news of the peace treaty arrived. Since the war was over, the Hartford Convention quickly ended. But the threat to leave the Union made Federalists very unpopular. The Federalist party, which had regained some strength during the war, died out completely after the War of 1812.

"Nothing was settled." Peace talks had been held in Ghent, Belgium. The **Treaty of Ghent** was signed on December 24, 1814. John Quincy Adams, one of the Americans at Ghent, summed up the treaty in one sentence: "Nothing was adjusted, nothing was settled."

Both sides agreed to return matters to the way they had been before the war. The treaty said nothing about impressment or American neutrality. But since Britain was no longer at war with France, these conflicts had faded. Other issues were settled later. In 1818, the two countries agreed to set much of the border between Canada and the United States at 49°N latitude.

Looking back, some Americans believed that the War of 1812 had been a mistake and nearly a disaster. Others said that Europe would now treat the young republic with more respect. The victories of Oliver Hazard Perry and Andrew Jackson had given Americans pride in their country. "The people are now more American," one Republican said. "They feel and act more as a nation."

SECTION **5** REVIEW

1. **Locate:** (a) Detroit, (b) Montreal, (c) Lake Erie, (d) Horseshoe Bend, (e) Chesapeake Bay, (f) Washington, D.C., (g) Baltimore, (h) Hartford.
2. **Identify:** (a) Oliver Hazard Perry, (b) Battle of the Thames, (c) Andrew Jackson, (d) Battle of Horseshoe Bend, (e) Dolley Madison, (f) Battle of New Orleans, (g) Hartford Convention, (h) Treaty of Ghent.
3. What problems did Americans face in preparing for war?
4. What part did Tecumseh play in the War of 1812?
5. What were two positive outcomes of the War of 1812 for Americans?
6. **Analyzing Information** Why do you think the War of 1812 has been referred to as the Second War of American Independence?

SKILL LESSON 11

MAP, GRAPH, AND CHART SKILLS
Following Routes on a Map

Every map tells a story. Many maps in this book tell the story of explorers moving across the land and sea. Other maps show the movements of troops or ships during a war. The map below shows the routes of Lewis and Clark and of Pike as they explored the lands of the Louisiana Purchase.

1 **Study the map to see what it shows.** (a) What is the subject of this map? (b) What color shows the route of Lewis and Clark?

2 **Practice reading directions on the map.** To follow a route on a map, you need to determine in what direction or directions the route goes. Find the directional arrow that shows N, S, E, and W.

Sometimes, you need to combine directions. For example, when explorers travel in a direction between north and east, they are said to be traveling northeast (NE). They could also travel northwest (NW), southeast (SE), or southwest (SW). (a) In what direction did Lewis and Clark travel after they left St. Louis? (b) In what direction did they travel along the Columbia River?

3 **Describe movements on a map in terms of direction.** Maps like this one show movement. (a) Describe the directions in which Pike traveled during 1806 and 1807. (b) What city did he reach at the end of his trip?

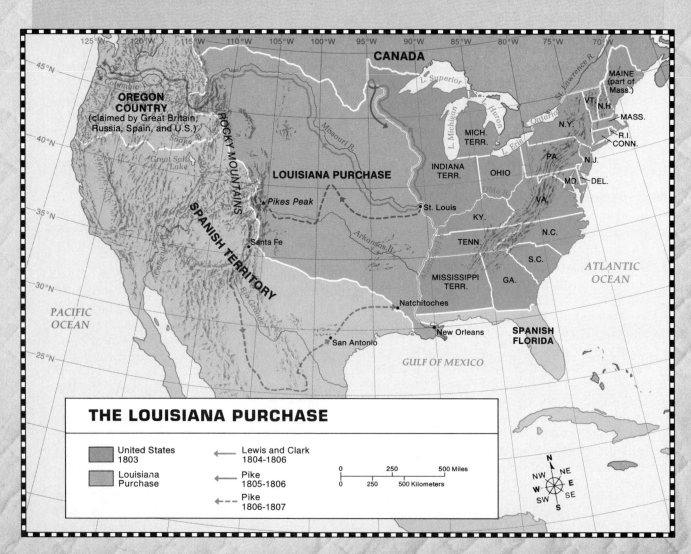

THE LOUISIANA PURCHASE

CHAPTER 11 STUDY GUIDE

Use the Section Reviews and this Study Guide to review chapter content.

Main Ideas

The main ideas in each section of this chapter are summarized below.

SECTION 1 ■ Republicans in Power

◆ President Jefferson cut the federal budget and reduced taxes.
◆ *Marbury* v. *Madison* established the principle of judicial review.

SECTION 2 ■ The Louisiana Purchase

◆ New Orleans was an important port to western farmers.
◆ President Jefferson bought Louisiana from France in 1803.
◆ Lewis and Clark's expedition mapped the Louisiana Purchase.

SECTION 3 ■ Protecting American Neutrality

◆ During their war, France and Britain each tried to cut off American trade with the other.
◆ Britain seized American ships and sailors.
◆ The Embargo Act of 1807 cut off foreign trade.

SECTION 4 ■ The Road to War

◆ By 1810, the South and West were eager for war with Britain.
◆ White settlers pushed west and threatened the way of life of Native Americans.

◆ In 1812, President Madison asked Congress to declare war on Britain.

SECTION 5 ■ The War of 1812

◆ The government trained and paid a volunteer army to fight in the War of 1812.
◆ Native Americans took sides in the war.
◆ In the Treaty of Ghent, Britain and the United States agreed to return to pre-war conditions.

Key People and Terms

Refer to the Identify and Define questions in the Section Reviews on pages 339, 346, 349, 354, and 359. Use each person, term, and vocabulary word in a complete sentence. When possible, make connections between the people and terms by using more than one person or term in each sentence.

Time Line

1. Make a chart of events in time order. The chart will have two headings: Date, Event. Fill in the chart, using the events on the time line. Add the following events from the chapter: Battle of New Orleans; Battle of Tippecanoe; *Marbury* v. *Madison*; Thomas Jefferson becomes President. (Refer to the chapter for the dates.)
2. Which events on your chart took place while Jefferson was President?

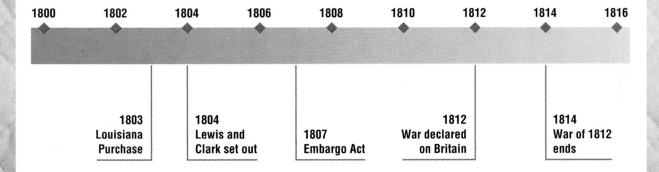

| 1800 | 1802 | 1804 | 1806 | 1808 | 1810 | 1812 | 1814 | 1816 |

1803
Louisiana
Purchase

1804
Lewis and
Clark set out

1807
Embargo Act

1812
War declared
on Britain

1814
War of 1812
ends

CHAPTER 11 REVIEW

Understanding Vocabulary

Match each term at left with the correct definition at right.

1. laissez faire
2. continental divide
3. impressment
4. embargo
5. nationalism

a. practice of forcing people into service
b. mountain ridge that separates river systems
c. devotion to one's country
d. ban on trade with another country
e. let alone

Reviewing the Main Ideas

1. (a) Describe Jefferson's style as President. (b) How did Jefferson's belief in laissez faire differ from the Federalist idea of government?
2. (a) Why did Jefferson decide to buy New Orleans? (b) How did the Senate help Jefferson purchase Louisiana?
3. (a) How did American overseas trade grow after the Revolution? (b) Why did Jefferson blockade Tripoli?
4. (a) Why did the French and British seize American ships? (b) Why did the British seize American sailors?
5. Why did the War Hawks want war?
6. Why were each of the following important to Native Americans in the West: (a) the Prophet; (b) Battle of Tippecanoe; (c) Battle of Horseshoe Bend?
7. (a) Why did an American invasion of Canada fail? (b) How did Britain's defeat of France affect Britain's war against the Americans?
8. (a) What was the Hartford Convention? (b) What did the delegates threaten to do? (c) What was the effect of the War of 1812 on the Federalist party?

Thinking Critically

1. **Synthesizing Information** (a) How did the Louisiana Purchase affect the size of the United States? (b) What did the journey of Lewis and Clark prove? (c) How might these two events have affected the view Americans had of their country?
2. **Making Decisions** Do you think President Madison was right to give in to pressure from the War Hawks and declare war on Britain? Explain.
3. **Linking Past and Present** Reread the paragraphs on pages 358–359 about the Hartford Convention. (a) What did the delegates threaten to do if the war continued? (b) How do state representatives react today if they oppose government actions?

Applying Your Skills

1. **Skimming a Chapter** Review the steps on skimming a chapter on page 332. Then, skim this chapter. (a) What are the main topics? (b) What is the main idea of the section "Republicans in Power"?
2. **Analyzing a Quotation** What did Tecumseh mean when he said that all Native Americans must unite in "claiming a common right in the land"?
3. **Following Routes on a Map** Study the map on page 360. (a) How does the map show Pike's route during 1805 and 1806? (b) During 1806 and 1807? (c) In what directions did Pike travel in 1805 and 1806? (d) In what direction was Pike headed when he crossed the Rio Grande?

Thinking About Geography

Match the letters on the map with the places listed below.

1. Canada
2. Battle of Lake Erie
3. Battle of the Thames
4. Battle of Horseshoe Bend
5. Battle of New Orleans
6. Baltimore
7. British blockade

Movement How did the British blockade hurt the United States?

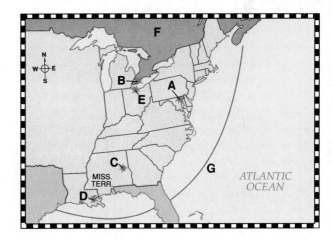

Ꮋistory *Writer's Workshop*

Writing a Report

Like an essay, a report presents information on a single topic. It has a title, an introduction with a thesis statement, body paragraphs, and a conclusion. When you write reports, you can use many of the same skills you learned in writing paragraphs and essays. However, reports also have special features of their own.

A report is based on information from books, magazine articles, encyclopedias, and other reference sources. It brings together facts and examples that you have found through research. The main point should always be your own idea, with supporting information from other sources.

In the report, you must give credit for information from other sources by including footnotes and a bibliography. Footnotes show the sources of specific pieces of information within the report. The bibliography lists all the sources at the end of the report.

Practice Plan a report on one of the following topics: Jefferson's policy of laissez faire, John Marshall, the Haitian Revolution, or the Louisiana Purchase.

1. Jot down all the ideas that you have about the topic.

2. In the library, locate two sources of information—a book and an encyclopedia entry—about the topic.

Writing to Learn

1. Imagine that you are a member of the Lewis and Clark expedition. Write a diary entry about your experiences. First, brainstorm several places you explored. Include specific sense details as well as what occurred. In your first draft, write a topic sentence that captures your reactions. Then, organize your details in time order. Revise for unity and coherence. Then, proofread and make a final copy. Publish your diary entry by making a bulletin board display.

2. Imagine that you are a journalist assigned to write a magazine article about Sacajawea and her contribution to the Lewis and Clark expedition. First, do some research. Begin the first draft of your article with a topic sentence that will capture your readers' interest. Next, organize your material in time order or order of importance. Revise for unity and clarity. Then, proofread and make a final copy. Publish your article in a class magazine.

A Changing Landscape *The Industrial Revolution changed the face of the nation. This painting shows an early factory set among the church spires and green fields of a New England town.* **Daily Life** *How do you think the factory affected the life of the townspeople?*

12

The Growing Years (1790–1825)

Chapter Outline

1 A Bloodless Revolution
2 Growth of Industry
3 A People on the Move
4 A Sense of National Unity
5 The Spirit of Independence Spreads

CHAPTER SPOTLIGHT

The Big Picture

On July 4, 1826—exactly 50 years after the Declaration of Independence was signed—both Thomas Jefferson and John Adams died. Americans remarked on the twist of fate. Both men had helped to shape events during the Revolution. Both had served the new nation as President. Their deaths, it seemed, marked the end of an era.

By the 1820s, the United States was growing and expanding. Thousands of settlers headed west. Canals and steamboats sped the movement of goods across the nation. And a new generation of Americans looked to the future with hope and confidence.

Of Special Interest

Focus On

◆ How did the early Industrial Revolution change the nation?

◆ Why did industry grow in the United States?

◆ What changes helped to improve transportation?

◆ What laws did Congress pass to help the economy?

◆ How did neighboring nations gain independence?

Clang-clang-clang-clang! Every morning at dawn, the factory bell awoke 11-year-old Lucy Larcom. Rising quickly, she ate breakfast and set out for work. Lucy worked at the Lowell mills, a Massachusetts factory that turned raw cotton into cloth. Years later, Lucy described the room where she worked:

❝I never cared much for machinery. The buzzing and hissing and whizzing of pulleys and rollers and spindles and flyers around me often grew tiresome. . . .

The last window in the row behind me was filled with flourishing houseplants. . . . Standing before that window, I could look across the room and see girls moving backwards and forwards among the spinning frames, sometimes stooping, sometimes reaching up their arms, as their work required. . . .

On the whole, it was far from being a disagreeable place to stay in. . . . [But] in the sweet June weather I would lean far out of the window, and try not to hear the unceasing clash of sound inside. Looking away to the hills, my whole stifled being would cry out, 'Oh, that I had wings!'❞

Like Lucy Larcom, many Americans left family farms to work in factories in the early 1800s. Across the land, new factories sprang up, and cities grew up around them. In this chapter, you will learn how the growth of industry transformed life in the young United States.

1 A Bloodless Revolution

FIND OUT

◆ What inventions led to the Industrial Revolution?

◆ How did the Industrial Revolution reach the United States?

◆ **VOCABULARY** spinning jenny, cotton gin, capitalist, factory system

Shortly before his death in 1790, Benjamin Franklin wrote to a friend:

> **❝**I wished it had been my destiny to have been born two or three centuries [later]. For invention and improvement are everywhere. The present progress is nothing less than astounding.**❞**

Although Franklin did not live to see it, a new revolution was about to sweep the United States. Unlike the revolution against British rule, this one had no battles and no fixed dates. Instead, it was a long, slow process that completely changed the way goods were produced. It is known as the **Industrial Revolution.**

From Homes to Factories

Before the Industrial Revolution, most goods were produced by hand at home or in workshops. Women, for example, spun thread on spinning wheels and wove cloth on hand looms. As the Industrial Revolution got under way, machines replaced hand tools. And new sources of power, such as steam and electricity, replaced human and animal power.

But the Industrial Revolution did more than change the way goods were made. It also affected the way people lived and worked. The new machines were too large and too expensive for the average person to

set up at home. Instead, business owners set up factories and hired people to work in them. People left jobs on the farm and moved to cities, where the factories were located. In the early 1800s, most Americans still worked on farms, but manufacturing played a growing part in the economy.

Britain Takes the Lead

The Industrial Revolution began in Great Britain in the mid-1700s. It was triggered by a series of inventions that transformed Britain's textile industry.

A series of inventions. In 1764, James Hargreaves developed a machine he named the **spinning jenny,** probably after his wife. With a spinning jenny, a worker could spin several threads at once, not just one thread as on a spinning wheel. Richard Arkwright took the process a step further. In 1769, he invented a machine that held 100 spindles of thread. Because this machine required too much strength to operate by hand, Arkwright used water power to turn it. The new machine was called the water frame.

Other inventions speeded up the process of weaving. In the 1780s, Edmund Cartwright built a loom powered by water. Using this power loom, a worker could produce 200 times more cloth in a day than was possible before.

In 1793, Eli Whitney, an American, gave a further boost to the textile industry. Whitney invented the **cotton gin,** a machine that speeded up the process of cleaning cotton fibers. (You will read more about the cotton gin in Chapter 15.)

The first factories. Machines like the water frame had to be set up near rivers because they needed running water to power them. Water flowing rapidly downstream or over a waterfall turned a water wheel that produced the power to run the machines.

The new machines were expensive and had to be housed in large buildings. Most were owned by **capitalists,** people with

A Factory Powered by Water *The swift-moving streams of New England were an ideal source of power for early factories. The textile mill in this painting— the building with the smokestack—was built above the rushing waters of Rhode Island's Blackstone River.* **Technology** *How was the rushing water used to power the machines?*

capital, or money, to invest in business to make a profit. Early capitalists built spinning mills and hired hundreds of workers to run the machines.

The spinning mills were the beginning of a new system of production in Britain. Instead of spinning and weaving in their homes, people went to work in factories. The factory system brought workers and machines together in one place to produce goods. In factories, everyone had to work a certain number of hours each day. Workers were paid daily or weekly wages.

An Idea Crosses the Atlantic

Other nations wanted to build machines like those the British had invented. But Britain tried to keep its inventions secret. In the late 1700s, Parliament passed a law forbidding anyone to take plans of Arkwright's water frame out of the country. It also forbade factory workers to leave Britain.

Arrival of Samuel Slater. Samuel Slater soon proved that those laws were impossible to enforce. Slater was a mechanic in one of Arkwright's mills. When he heard that Americans were offering rich rewards for plans of British factories, he decided to

seek his fortune across the Atlantic. In 1789, Slater booked passage on a ship bound for New York. He knew that British officials often searched the baggage of people sailing to the United States. So he memorized the design of Arkwright's mill before he sailed.

In New York, Slater learned that Moses Brown, a Quaker merchant, wanted to build a spinning factory in Rhode Island. Slater wrote to Brown. "If I do not make as good yarn as they do in England," he claimed confidently, "I will have nothing for my services, but will throw the whole of what I have attempted over the bridge." Brown replied at once: "If thou canst do what thou sayest, I invite thee to come to Rhode Island."

The first American mill. Slater and Brown quickly built the spinning mill. It opened on December 20, 1790, a cold winter's day. Chopping ice off the water wheel, Slater started the 2 water frames and 72 spindles. Brown breathed a sigh of relief as the machinery cranked into motion.

In the next few years, the two men improved the mill. Hannah Slater, wife of Samuel Slater, developed a way to make thread stronger so that it would not snap

LINKING • PAST • AND • PRESENT

From Machines to Robots

Some 200 years ago, Samuel Slater and Moses Brown used technology borrowed from Britain to build the first factory in the United States. In doing so, they forever changed the way Americans lived and worked. For the first time, large numbers of people were brought together under a single roof to produce goods.

In factories of the 1800s, machines needed constant tending. Many workers were required just to keep the operation running smoothly. And machines were dangerous. Their wheels and gears had no safety devices. Unless workers were quick and careful, they could lose fingers, hands, or even arms.

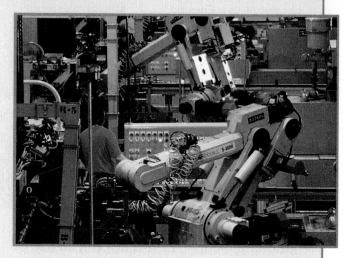

Today, technology has produced a new revolution in the way goods are made. In modern factories, robots directed by computers perform many tasks once performed by humans. These mechanical workers with electronic brains never get tired or bored with routine jobs. And they can do tasks that are difficult or dangerous for human workers.

1. How did factories change the way goods were made in the 1800s?

2. **Analyzing Information** What kinds of tasks might robots not be able to do?

on the spindles. Before long, other American manufacturers began to build mills, using Slater's ideas.

SECTION 1 REVIEW

1. **Identify:** (a) Industrial Revolution, (b) Samuel Slater, (c) Moses Brown.

2. **Define:** (a) spinning jenny, (b) cotton gin, (c) capitalist, (d) factory system.

3. (a) Name two inventions of the Industrial Revolution. (b) How did each change the way goods were produced?

4. How did Samuel Slater bring Arkwright's mill to the United States? Explain.

5. **Linking Past and Present** What inventions would astonish Benjamin Franklin today?

2 Growth of Industry

FIND OUT

◆ How did the War of 1812 spur the growth of American industry?

◆ Why was Lowell a showplace of American industry?

◆ What were working conditions like in early factories?

◆ **VOCABULARY** interchangeable parts

During colonial times, Americans had little industry of their own. Colonists depended on British manufacturers for many of their needs. If a colonial family wanted a cooking pot or a farm tool, it had to buy one made in Britain. In the early 1800s, new inventions made British industry even more advanced. Could Americans ever catch up?

The War of 1812 provided the answer. By blockading the Atlantic coast, Britain cut the United States off from foreign manufactures. Americans had to do without manufactured goods or make the goods themselves. American industry began to grow. In a few short years, it became a major force in the economy.

The Lowell Experiment

As in Britain, the greatest early advances were made in the textile industry. Before the War of 1812, a Boston merchant, Francis Cabot Lowell, had toured Britain's textile mills. The British, he saw, spun thread in one factory and wove it in another. Lowell had a better idea. Why not combine spinning and weaving under one roof?

Lowell's idea cost money. No one had ever built a factory on such a large scale. In 1813, Lowell and several partners formed the **Boston Associates.** They raised about $1 million—a huge sum in those days—to build a textile factory in Waltham, Massachusetts. The new factory had all the machines needed to turn raw cotton into finished cloth. The machines were powered by water from the nearby Charles River.

A showplace of American industry. Lowell died in 1817, but the Boston Associates continued. Now, the partners began an even more ambitious project. Along the Merrimack River, they built an entire town to support their factory. They named the town after Francis Lowell.

When it was first begun in 1821, Lowell, Massachusetts, was a village of five farm families. By 1836, it had become a model town and a showplace of American industry. It boasted 18,000 people, numerous factories, banks, schools, stores, a library, and a church. A visitor described Lowell in glowing terms:

> ❝There are huge factories, five, six or seven stories high, each capped with a little white belfry . . . which stands out sharply against the dark hills on the horizon. There are small wooden houses, painted white, with green blinds, very neat, very snug, very nicely carpeted, and with a few small trees around them.❞

"Lowell girls." The Boston Associates hired young women from nearby farms to work in the Lowell mills. Usually, the "Lowell girls" moved to town and worked for a few years, then returned home to marry. They sent their wages home to help their families. Some might save a bit of money for the time when they set up their own homes.

At first, farm families hesitated to let their daughters work in the textile mills. To reassure parents, the Boston Associates built neat boardinghouses for their employees. They hired housemothers to manage the houses. The company also planted thousands of shade trees, built a

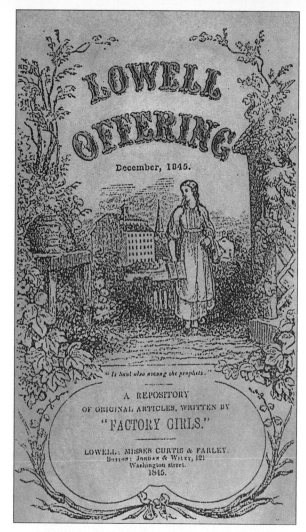

The Lowell Offering The "Lowell girls" had their own magazine, the Lowell Offering. In it, they published stories and poems about the "toilsome" life in the mills. **Daily Life** How did working conditions at Lowell compare with those in later factories?

church, and made rules to both protect and attract the young women.

Working in the Mills

In Lowell and other mills, owners hired women and children to do most of the work. They had good reasons for this. Women and children worked for half what men were paid.

Child workers. Children were especially useful in the mills. Because they were quick and small, they could scamper easily around the large machines, changing spindles. Such children were called "doffers." They doffed, or took off, full spindles of thread and replaced them with empty ones. "I can see myself now," recalled a woman who worked in a mill as a child, "carrying in front of me a [spindle] bigger than I was."

Today, it seems cruel that children as young as seven years old worked long hours in factories. But in the 1800s, boys and girls usually worked long hours on family farms. To most parents, it did not seem very different to ask children to work in a factory. After all, the child's wages were needed to help pay for the family's food and housing.

From dawn till dusk. Working hours in the mills were long—12 hours a day, 6 days a week. True, people worked long hours on farms, too. But while the workload on farms was lighter during winter, mill workers kept up the same pace no matter what the season.

Winter was "lighting up" time in the factory. Then, work began before daylight and ended after dark. Whale-oil lamps cast a dim glow and filled the long rooms with smoke.

Conditions in early mills like those at Lowell were better than in most European factories at the time. But as the factory system spread and competition increased, employers took less interest in the welfare of their employees. As a result, wages dropped and conditions in American factories grew increasingly harsh.

10 Muskets in 10 Minutes

In the early 1800s, Eli Whitney came up with an idea that transformed the way goods were produced. At the time, most manufactured goods were made with painstaking care by skilled workers. A gunsmith, for example, spent many hours making the stock, barrel, and trigger of a rifle. Each rifle was slightly different from the next because each part was made by hand. If a rifle part broke, a gunsmith had to make a new part to fit that gun. This method of making and repairing goods was very slow.

Whitney wanted to build machines to make the parts of a gun. The machine-made parts would be exactly alike. All the stocks would be the same size and shape. All the barrels would be the same length. If a trigger broke, it could easily be replaced with another machine-made trigger. Using Whitney's idea of interchangeable parts, it would be possible to put together and repair guns more quickly and cheaply than before.

Because the government bought thousands of rifles, Whitney took his idea to Washington. At first, officials laughed at his scheme. But Whitney was not easily put off. Quickly, he laid out parts for 10 muskets, sorted into separate piles. At Whitney's request, an official selected one part from each of the piles. In minutes, the first musket was assembled. The process was repeated until all 10 muskets were assembled and fired. The response, reported one observer, was "sheer amazement."

The idea of interchangeable parts spread rapidly. Inventors designed machines to make parts for locks, knives, and other items. Before long, factories were using interchangeable parts to produce goods faster and more cheaply than ever before.

UP CLOSE

A Yankee Clockmaker

Clockmakers quickly saw the benefits of using interchangeable parts. One Yankee clockmaker, Chauncey Jerome, took advantage of this new method of production to earn a fortune and to spread his name throughout the world.

10 clocks a year. Born in 1793, Chauncey Jerome grew up on a farm in western Connecticut. As a child, he sometimes saw

a local clockmaker ride by. Packed in each of the man's saddlebags was a clock. A third clock, with "the dials in plain sight," was tied on behind. The man was on his way to New York State to sell his clocks.

The clocks were made of wood. Connecticut clockmakers used oak, apple, and cherry wood. Slowly and carefully, they sawed out each tiny part and gear that fit inside the clock. Then, they shaped each piece with files. An experienced clockmaker could finish 10 clocks a year.

200 clocks? Impossible! When Jerome was 14 years old, he went to work for Eli Terry, a clockmaker in a nearby village.

A Clock by Chauncey Jerome *Chauncey Jerome yearned for fame and fortune. He achieved both by using interchangeable parts to make a brass clock that everyone could afford.* **Technology** *How would the use of interchangeable parts change the way clocks were made?*

Terry was the subject of much gossip. He had promised to make 200 clocks for a local merchant to sell. Impossible, declared many villagers. Terry "never would live long enough to finish them," they said. Chauncey swallowed hard when he heard the comments but took the job with Terry anyway.

Eli Terry knew that he could make the 200 clocks. In 1807, he built a factory to make clock parts. In it, he placed machines that he had designed. The machines let workers make the same part quickly, over and over again. Within a few years, Terry was producing not hundreds but thousands of clocks a year.

Going into business. Jerome learned about clockmaking from Terry. Before long, he went into business for himself. Copying Terry's production methods, he made and sold wooden clocks. The clocks were called one-day clocks because they had to be rewound each day. A few companies made eight-day clocks out of brass. But few people could afford them.

For several years, Jerome's business flourished. But like other clockmakers, he had problems with wooden clocks. Often, he could not get the right wood for the gears. Then, too, if the wood got wet or the air was too damp, the wooden wheels swelled, and the clock stopped.

"I knew there was a fortune in it." Jerome kept thinking about how to improve his clocks. In 1837, he was traveling through the South on business when he had an idea:

> **"**I was looking at the wood clock on the table and it came into my mind instantly that there could be a cheap one-day brass clock that would take the place of the wood clock. . . . I lay awake nearly all night thinking this new thing over. I knew there was a fortune in it.**"**

Eager to try out his idea, Jerome hurried home to Connecticut. Within a year, he was producing and selling thousands of one-day brass clocks at low prices. "This successful state of things set all of the wood clockmakers half crazy," he recalled, "and they went into it one after another as fast as they could."

Before long, Chauncey Jerome could report that clocks with his nameplate on them could be found all over the world. "Travelers have mentioned seeing them in the city of Jerusalem, in many parts of Egypt, and in fact, everywhere," he reported proudly. ◆

Growing Cities

As factories grew, so did towns and cities where they were located. By today's standards, cities in the 1800s were small. A person could walk from one end of any American city to the other in 30 minutes. Buildings were only a few stories high. Houses were built of wood, heated by fireplaces, and lit by oil lamps.

Problems. Growing cities had many problems. The dirt and gravel streets turned into mudholes when it rained. There were no sewers, and people threw garbage into the streets. An English visitor to New York reported:

> **"**The streets are filthy, and the stranger is not a little surprised to meet the hogs walking about in them, for the purpose of devouring the vegetables and trash thrown into the gutter.**"**

Because people lived in dirty, crowded conditions, disease spread easily. Yellow fever and cholera (KAHL er uh) epidemics raged through cities, killing hundreds.

Fire posed another threat. If a sooty chimney caught fire, the flames quickly spread from one wooden house to the next. In most cities, people set up volunteer fire departments. Volunteer companies often competed to be first to the scene of a blaze. Sometimes, the rivals engaged in fistfights, brawling while the fire burned.

Attractions. Despite problems, cities had much to offer. There were plays to see and museums to visit. In New York, P. T.

1 Slipper-style shoes (for men as well as women)
2 Parasol
3 Taffeta dress with silk cape
4 Beaver skin hat
5 Coat with long tails (favored by older men)
6 Checkered suit with short tails (favored by young men)
7 Red cravat, or bow tie, for daytime wear (white for evening dress)
8 Fingerless full-length gloves
9 Fan
10 Muslin dress with crewelwork, or hand-embroidered, border
11 Cotton play suit
12 Spurs (style set by Andrew Jackson)

The Latest Fashions *In the cities of the early 1800s, fine stores sold the latest fashions. This drawing shows a group of stylishly dressed city dwellers enjoying a quiet afternoon in the park.* **Daily Life** *What major change occurred at this time in the way some men's clothing was made? What do you think would be the effect of this change?*

Barnum made a fortune showing unusual animals and other attractions in his American Museum. Circuses came to town from time to time, and racetracks attracted large crowds.

Cities also had fine stores that sold the latest fashions. Some offered modern "ready-to-wear" clothing. A New York store boasted that "gentlemen can rely upon being as well fitted from the shelves as if their measures were taken." Women still sewed most of their own clothes, but they enjoyed visiting china shops, "fancy-goods" stores, and shoe stores.

SECTION 2 REVIEW

1. **Identify:** (a) Francis Cabot Lowell, (b) Boston Associates, (c) Eli Whitney.
2. **Define:** interchangeable parts.
3. How did the War of 1812 speed up the Industrial Revolution in the United States?
4. How did the Boston Associates make the Lowell mills attractive to workers?
5. Why were mill owners eager to hire women and children?
6. **Applying Information** How did capitalists like Chauncey Jerome and Eli Terry contribute to the Industrial Revolution?

3 A People on the Move

FIND OUT

◆ How did settlers travel to the West?

◆ What steps did Americans take to improve roads?

◆ How did steamboats and canals change transportation?

◆ **VOCABULARY** turnpike, corduroy road, canal

In the 1790s, a visitor from Ireland traveled through Maryland by stagecoach. He did not enjoy the ride. He described the terrors of the trip in his journal:

GRAPH SKILLS *During the early 1800s, the nation's population increased steadily. As the population grew, so too did the demand for better transportation.* ◆ *About how much did the population increase between 1810 and 1820?*

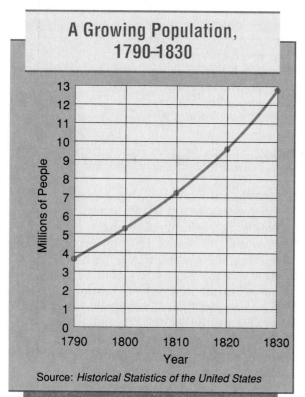

A Growing Population, 1790–1830

Millions of People

Year

Source: *Historical Statistics of the United States*

❝The driver frequently had to call to the passengers in the stage, to lean out of the carriage first at one side, then at the other, to prevent it from oversetting in the deep ruts with which the road abounds: 'Now gentlemen, to the right,'. . . 'Now gentlemen, to the left,' and so on.❞

In the young United States, travel was as difficult as it had been in colonial times. Most roads were simply mud tracks. On rivers, boats slowly pushed upstream against strong currents. As the nation grew, Americans felt the need for better transportation.

GEOGRAPHY AND HISTORY

Heading West

During the early 1800s, thousands of settlers headed west, to the land between the Appalachians and the Mississippi. "Old America seems to be breaking up and moving westward," noted a visitor in 1817. By 1820, so many people had packed up and moved that the population in most of the original 13 states had declined.

Pioneers followed a number of paths west. A well-traveled route was the Great Wagon Road through Pennsylvania that was used in colonial times. (See page 158.) Some settlers continued south and west along the road to the Cumberland Gap, following Daniel Boone's trail into Kentucky.

Others pushed on to Pittsburgh. There, they loaded their animals and wagons onto flatboats and poled down the Ohio River to Indiana, Kentucky, and Illinois. Flatboats were well suited to the shallow waters of the Ohio River. Even with heavy loads, these raftlike barges did not sink far below the river's surface.

Pioneers from Georgia and South Carolina followed other trails west, carving out plantations in the rich, black soil of Alabama and Mississippi.

In the north, New Englanders, "Yorkers," and Pennsylvanians pushed into the

A Bumpy Ride *Passengers who traveled by stagecoach on the nation's rocky, mud-filled roads took it for granted that they would be "crushed, shaken, thrown about . . . and bumped." This painting, by a visitor from Russia, shows the* Diligence *on its regular run between Philadelphia, Pennsylvania, and Trenton, New Jersey.* **Linking Past and Present** *Who built new roads in the early 1800s? Who builds roads today?*

Northwest Territory along several routes. One route ran from Albany, New York, west along the Mohawk River through a gap in the Appalachians. (See the map on page 376.) Some travelers then followed Indian trails west around Lake Erie. Others took boats across Lake Erie into Ohio.

With the flood of settlers, it was not long before the western lands had enough people to apply for statehood. Between 1792 and 1819, eight new states joined the Union: Kentucky (1792), Tennessee (1796), Ohio (1803), Louisiana (1812), Indiana (1816), Mississippi (1817), Illinois (1818), and Alabama (1819).

Better Roads

Settlers heading west faced a rough journey. What Americans called roads were little more than narrow trails, not wide enough even for a single wagon. One pioneer wrote of "rotten banks down which horses plunged" and streams that "almost drowned them." The need for better roads was obvious.

Turnpikes and covered bridges. Perhaps the best road in the United States at the time was the **Lancaster Turnpike.** Built in the 1790s by a private company, it linked Philadelphia and Lancaster in Pennsylvania. The road was set on a bed of gravel, so rains drained off easily. It was topped with smooth, flat stones.

Private companies built other gravel and stone roads. To pay for the roads, the companies collected tolls. At various places along the road, a pole, called a pike, blocked the road. After a wagon driver paid a toll, the pike was turned aside. These toll roads came to be called **turnpikes,** or pikes, for short.

Gravel and stone roads were expensive to build. Many roads were made of logs instead. Such roads were called **corduroy roads** because the logs set side by side looked like corduroy cloth. Corduroy roads had fewer ruts and potholes than dirt roads, but they made for a noisy and bumpy ride.

Road builders faced a problem when they reached a stream or river. Stone bridges were costly to build, but wooden ones rotted quickly. A clever Massachusetts carpenter designed a wooden bridge with a roof. The roof protected the bridge from the weather. The new covered bridges lasted much longer than open ones.

The National Road. Some states set aside money to improve roads and build new ones. In 1806, for the first time, Congress approved spending money to build a road. The National Road was to run from

Cumberland, Maryland, to Wheeling, in western Virginia. The War of 1812 halted work on the National Road, but it was finally completed in 1818. Later, it was extended across Ohio and Indiana into Illinois. (📖 See "Traveling Westward" on page 671.)

Travel increases. As roads improved, people began to travel more. All day, heavy freight wagons rumbled along well-traveled routes. As many as eight horses pulled these vehicles, piled high with boxes, barrels, and crates.

Small farm wagons drawn by one or two horses also plodded along, moving quickly aside when stagecoaches sped recklessly past them. From October to December, the nation's roads were filled with animals being driven to market. Herders, called drovers, used dogs to keep hogs, cattle, sheep, and even turkeys moving. ◆

Steamboats Everywhere

Many Americans preferred river travel to overland travel by wagon. After all, floating downstream on a flatboat was a lot easier than bumping along rutted roads.

But river travel also presented problems. How could a boat move rapidly upstream against the current? A boat leav-

MAP STUDY

In the early 1800s, settlers took new roads to the West. Some were turnpikes built by private companies. Others were built by states or the national government.
1. Through which states did the National Road run?
2. Which road connected Albany and Buffalo?
3. **Synthesizing Information** Why were so many new roads built in the early 1800s?

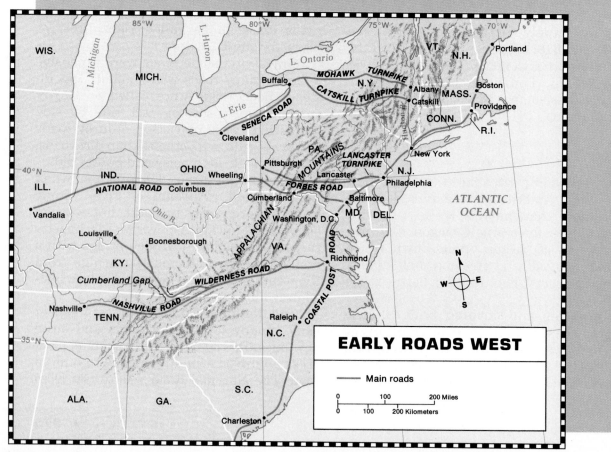

EARLY ROADS WEST

—— Main roads

0   100   200 Miles
0   100   200 Kilometers

Loading a Steamboat at New Orleans *Great flat-bottomed steamboats turned the rivers of the West into busy routes for traders and travelers. Here, workers load goods onto the steamboat* Gipsy *at New Orleans.* **Geography** *How was the design of these steamboats suited to western rivers?*

ing Pittsburgh traveled downstream to New Orleans in six weeks. But the return trip upstream to Pittsburgh took *at least 17 weeks!* Moving upstream was very hard work. Boatmen used paddles or long poles to push boats upstream against the current. Or they hauled boats upstream from the shore with ropes. Neither method worked well.

Fitch and Fulton. The Industrial Revolution provided a solution to the problem of river travel—the steam engine. In 1787, a Connecticut Yankee named John Fitch used a steam engine to propel a boat along the Delaware River, in Philadelphia. Soon after, Fitch set up a ferry service on the river. But few people used it, and Fitch went out of business.

Twenty years later, Robert Fulton succeeded where Fitch had failed. Fulton grew up in Philadelphia and probably saw Fitch's steamboat. In 1807, he launched his own steamboat, the *Clermont*, on the Hudson River. On his first run, Fulton carried passengers from New York City upriver to Albany and back again. The *Clermont* made the 300-mile (480-km) round trip in just 62 hours—a record for the time. Within three months, the *Clermont* was making a profit for its owner.

Fulton's success ushered in the steamboat era. Soon, steamboats were ferrying passengers up and down the Atlantic coast and around the Great Lakes. But steamboats were most important in the West. There, they turned the Mississippi, Ohio, and Missouri rivers into busy routes for trade goods and travelers.

"Floating palaces." Western rivers were shallow compared with those in the East. They needed a special kind of boat. Henry Shreve, a steamboat captain, designed a flat-bottomed steamboat. It could carry heavy loads without getting stuck on sandbars.

By the mid-1800s, some western steamboats had become "floating palaces." Those who could afford the fare relaxed on vessels that had three separate decks and a saloon for eating. Along the walls of the saloon were double-decker berths, where men slept. Women had a separate "ladies' parlor." They entered the saloon only for meals. Poor travelers sailed on rougher boats with leaking roofs and pillows stuffed with corn husks.

Steamboat travel could be dangerous. Sparks from smokestacks sometimes kindled fires. Western steamboats used high-pressure boilers. As steamboat captains raced each other up and down the river, boilers sometimes exploded. Between 1811 and 1851, 44 steamboats collided, 166 burned, and more than 200 exploded.

The Canal Boom

Rivers helped to move people and their goods. But rivers do not exist wherever people need them. So Americans built canals to travel. A **canal** is a channel dug by people and filled with water to allow ships to cross a stretch of land.

The first canals were only a few miles long. Some provided routes around water-falls on a river. Others linked a river to a nearby lake. In the early 1800s, however, Americans began building longer canals.

"Little short of madness." Some New Yorkers dreamed of building a canal to link the Great Lakes with the Mohawk and Hudson rivers. Such a canal would let western farmers ship their goods east to the port of New York. It would bring business and riches to all the towns and cities along a route stretching hundreds of miles. (See the map below.)

For years, the **Erie Canal,** as the project was called, seemed far-fetched. When a New Yorker told President Jefferson about it, the President remarked:

"Why, sir, you talk of making a canal 350 miles through the wilderness—it is little short of madness to think of it at this day!**"**

MAP STUDY

The success of the Erie Canal, completed in 1825, set off an age of canal building.
1. *About how long was the Erie Canal?*
2. *What two bodies of water were linked by the Ohio and Erie Canal?*
3. **Synthesizing Information** *Use the map to describe an all-water route from Evansville, Indiana, to New York City.*

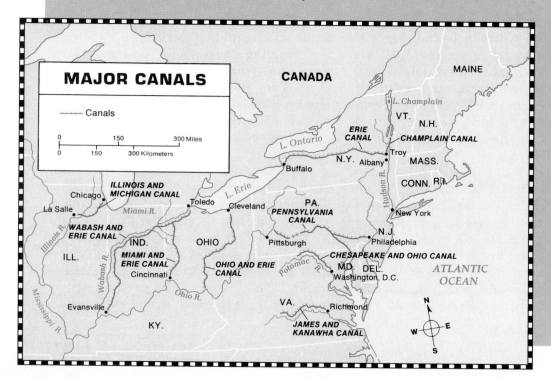

AN·AMERICAN·PORTRAIT

De Witt Clinton: Promoter of the Erie Canal

For years, Americans laughed at De Witt Clinton's plan to build the Erie Canal. "Clinton's Ditch," they called it mockingly.

But Clinton was not put off by opposition. During his long and varied political career, he had embraced many unpopular causes. He fought for free public education and against slavery. He worked to improve conditions for the poor and called for an end to the practice of jailing debtors.

The Erie Canal was Clinton's biggest battle. From the beginning, he had championed the canal, which would connect the Great Lakes with the Atlantic Ocean. When he became governor of New York in 1817, he devoted himself to making the canal a reality.

Eight years later, on November 4, 1825, Clinton's dream came true. Standing proudly aboard the canal boat *Seneca Chief,* the governor was towed through New York harbor.

"From whence came ye?" signaled a nearby ship.

". . . From Lake Erie!" came the reply.

"Where bound?"

"To the Atlantic!"

With great ceremony, Clinton poured a small keg of fresh Lake Erie water into the salt sea. The act symbolized the "wedding of the waters"—the joining of the Great Lakes to the Atlantic Ocean. As cannons boomed, Clinton declared:

❝May the God of the heavens and the earth smile . . . on this work and [make it serve] the best interests of the human race.❞

1. What causes did De Witt Clinton support?

2. **Applying Information** How did leaders like Clinton help the nation to grow?

Digging the waterway. Governor De Witt Clinton of New York disagreed with President Jefferson. He convinced the state legislature to provide money for the Erie Canal.

In 1817, workers began to dig the waterway by hand. To speed up the job, the canal company invented new equipment.

One machine was a stump-puller. It could pull out nearly 40 tree stumps a day. In two places, the canal had to cross over rivers. Workers built stone aqueducts, or bridges, to carry the canal over the rivers.

By 1825, the immense job was finished. At the opening celebrations, a cannon in Buffalo, New York, fired a volley.

When the sound reached the next town along the route, it, too, fired a cannon. Then, the next town and the next fired its cannon—all the way to New York City. The thunderous salute took 80 minutes to complete. The booming sound announced that the Erie Canal was open for business.

An instant success. The Erie Canal was an instant success. In a single day, more than 50 canal boats might be seen moving up and down its length. A traveler described the scene from one of the bridges that crossed the canal:

> **"**It is an impressive sight to gaze up and down the canal. In either direction, as far as the eye can see, long lines of boats can be observed. By night, their flickering head lamps give the impression of swarms of fireflies.**"**

The Erie Canal brought many benefits. Along the canal, the cost of shipping goods dropped. Just as important, travel time declined. By canal, it took only 8 days to send goods from Buffalo to New York instead of 20. The canal helped to make New York City a center of commerce. (📖 See "Low Bridge, Everybody Down" on page 673.)

The success of the Erie Canal encouraged other states to build canals. These canals helped to link the nation together.

SECTION 3 REVIEW

1. **Locate:** National Road.
2. **Identify:** (a) Lancaster Turnpike, (b) Robert Fulton, (c) *Clermont*, (d) Henry Shreve, (e) Erie Canal, (f) De Witt Clinton.
3. **Define:** (a) turnpike, (b) corduroy road, (c) canal.
4. What different means of transportation did settlers use to move west?
5. (a) How did road travel improve in the early 1800s? (b) How did river travel also improve?
6. **Understanding Causes and Effects** (a) Name two immediate effects of the Erie Canal. (b) Name two long-range effects.

---

4 A Sense of National Unity

FIND OUT

◆ What was the Era of Good Feelings?

◆ What three leaders emerged in Congress?

◆ How did Congress help the economy?

◆ Why did Henry Clay propose the American System?

◆ **VOCABULARY** dumping, protective tariff

The crowd of nearly 8,000 craned their necks eagerly. They could just make out the cavalry escorting James Monroe along the dusty street to the platform outside the Capitol. The date was March 4, 1817. In a few minutes, Monroe would take the oath of office as fifth President of the United States.

This was the first time the inauguration was held outdoors. Usually, the President took the oath of office in the House of Representatives. But when senators insisted on bringing their fancy red armchairs to the ceremony, the House refused. The solution was to hold the inauguration ceremony outdoors.

In his Inaugural Address, the new President spoke of the sense of national unity that was emerging. After the War of 1812, Americans took great pride in their nation. More and more, they felt and acted like one people.

An Era of Good Feelings

In 1816, the Republicans nominated James Monroe to succeed Madison as President. The Federalists put up a weak candidate. For years, their party had been declining. Some Federalists even joined the Republican party.

Monroe easily won the election. He received 183 electoral votes. His opponent,

Rufus King of New York, polled only 34. Republicans also held a majority of seats in Congress.

In the summer of 1817, James Monroe visited Boston. Along the streets of the city, people turned out to see the new President. They were curious about this tall, dignified man in his old-fashioned clothes and three-cornered hat. He looked like a figure out of the past—like one of the heroes of the American Revolution. In fact, the 59-year-old Monroe belonged to the generation of Jefferson and Adams.

Boston newspapers expressed surprise at the welcome Monroe received. After all, Boston had been a Federalist stronghold. Monroe was a Republican from Virginia. Yet even longtime Federalists seemed charmed by the President. A local newspaper wrote that the United States was entering an "Era of Good Feelings." The period of bitter disputes between political parties seemed to have ended.

When Monroe ran for a second term in 1820, no one ran against him. The easy Republican victory marked the end of the Federalist party.

Three Political Giants

Although conflict between political parties declined, disputes between different sections of the nation increased. In Congress, three bright young men took center stage. Each came from a different section of the United States. They were John C. Calhoun of South Carolina, Daniel Webster of Massachusetts, and Henry Clay of Kentucky. The three men played critical roles in Congress for more than 30 years.

John C. Calhoun spoke for the South. He knew its ways well. He had grown up on a farm on the South Carolina frontier, where he picked cotton in the hot summer sun. Later, he went to Yale College in Connecticut. There, he learned to think his ideas through clearly. Slim and handsome, Calhoun had deep-set eyes, a high forehead, and immense energy. His way of speaking was so intense that some people felt uncomfortable in his presence.

Daniel Webster spoke for the North. His dark hair and eyes earned him the nickname "Black Dan." Webster was an impressive sight in Congress. When he

New Political Leaders *A new generation of leaders rose to prominence in the early 1800s. Among them were Daniel Webster, at left, and Henry Clay. The two men had differed sharply on the War of 1812. But in the 1820s, both urged the government to take a larger role in developing the nation's economy.* **Citizenship** *Who was the third major political leader of the period?*

spoke, he stood straight as a ramrod, with shoulders thrown back. The hall would fall silent. "He will not be outdone by any man, if it is within his power to avoid it," observed a friend. Webster served as a representative in the House and later as a senator from Massachusetts.

From the West came Henry Clay of Kentucky. As you have read, Clay was a War Hawk in 1812. He had grown up on a backcountry farm and was a man of action. As a young lawyer, Clay was once fined for getting into a fistfight with an opposing lawyer. Usually, however, Clay charmed both friends and rivals. He enjoyed staying up late to talk about politics or play cards. Like Calhoun and Webster, Clay could move people to laughter or tears with his speeches.

A New National Bank

Leaders like Webster, Calhoun, and Clay faced many problems in the years after the War of 1812. The nation was growing, but its economy remained weak. One problem was the lack of a national bank.

In 1811, the charter for the first Bank of the United States ran out. The Bank had loaned money and regulated the nation's money supply. Without it, the economy suffered. State banks made loans and issued money. But they put too much money into circulation, which caused prices to rise rapidly.

Republicans like Jefferson and Madison had opposed a national bank. After all, it was a Federalist rival, Alexander Hamilton, who first proposed it. But by 1816, many Republicans in Congress felt that a national bank was needed. So they supported a law to charter the second Bank of the United States. By lending money to individuals and restoring order to the money supply, the Bank helped American businesses to grow.

Competition From Abroad

Another problem the nation faced after the War of 1812 was foreign competition, especially from Britain. During the early 1800s, when Britain and France were at war, American industry grew quickly. First the Embargo Act and then the War of 1812 kept most British goods out of the United States. As a result, textile mills like those of Samuel Slater and Francis Cabot Lowell prospered. Other American manufacturers also set up mills and factories.

Imported Goods for Sale
After the War of 1812, American manufacturers raised an outcry as foreign goods poured into the country. In this advertisement, a Philadelphia merchant offers a wide variety of European goods for sale at "lowest market prices." **Economics** *Why had there been very little foreign competition during the early 1800s?*

British goods pour in. In 1815, British goods again poured into the United States. The British could make and sell goods more cheaply than Americans, who had to pay for building their new factories. As a result, American goods often cost more.

During the war, British factories had stored up a lot of cloth. Now, they began to ship the cloth to the United States, where they sold it at low prices. Sometimes, they sold the cloth for even less than it cost to make. The practice of selling goods in another country at very low prices is called dumping. By dumping their goods, British manufacturers hoped to force American factories out of business.

Congress protects American industry. Dumping caused dozens of New England businesses to fail. Angry factory owners turned to Congress for help. They asked for a law that would put a high tariff on all goods imported from Europe.

Congress responded by passing the Tariff of 1816, which increased tariffs on foreign goods to 25 percent. The increase made goods imported from Europe more expensive than American-made goods. (See the diagram at right.) This kind of tariff is called a protective tariff because it is meant to protect a country's industries from foreign competition.

An outcry from the South. In 1818 and 1824, Congress passed even higher tariffs. Some Americans, especially southerners, protested. Southerners had built few factories, so the tariff did not help them. Indeed, southerners had bought cheaper British goods for many years. Now, the tariff forced them to buy expensive American-made goods, which cost them more. To southerners, the tariff made northern manufacturers rich at the expense of the South.

Henry Clay's Grand Design

The bitter debate over the tariff pointed up a major threat to the Union. Some laws, such as protective tariffs, helped one section but hurt another. As a result, sectional

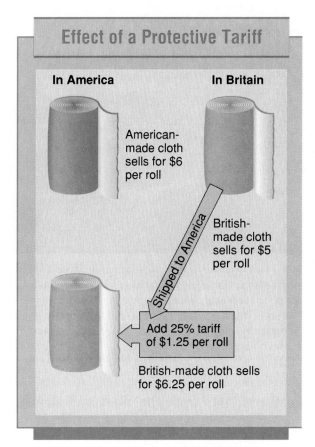

CHART SKILLS *In 1816, the government passed a protective tariff to help American factory owners. As this chart shows, the tariff made British goods more expensive than American goods.* ◆ *Why did southerners object to the tariff?*

conflict grew. Americans identified themselves as southerners, northerners, and westerners. At home and in Congress, southerners argued against laws they felt favored the North. People from the West, who had their own interests, sometimes quarreled with easterners.

Henry Clay looked for a way to meet the economic needs of all sections of the country. In 1824, he set out his ideas, which became known as the **American System.** Under the American System, tariffs on imports would be kept high. High tariffs would help northern factories expand. With wealth from growing industry, northerners would have the money to buy

Steaming up the Hudson *Americans debated the value of spending money for internal improvements. Those who supported the idea believed that improved transportation was vital to the growth of the nation. Here, the* Paragon, *one of Robert Fulton's boats, steams up the Hudson River to Albany and the Erie Canal.* **Geography** *Why did many southerners oppose spending money for internal improvements?*

farm products from the West and South. To those who protested the tariff, Clay replied:

> ❝And what is this tariff? It seems to have been regarded as a sort of monster, huge and deformed . . . with tremendous powers of destruction. . . . But let us calm our passions, and deliberately survey this alarming, this terrific being. The sole object of the tariff is to tax the produce of foreign industry, with the view of promoting American industry.❞

Clay also wanted to help all sections by encouraging internal improvements—the building of roads, bridges, and canals. He urged Congress to spend money earned from the tariff on such improvements. Internal improvements, he said, would help the West and South by making it easier for farmers there to ship goods to markets in the cities.

Clay's American System never went into effect. Tariffs stayed high, but Congress did not spend much money for internal improvements. Southerners especially disliked Clay's plan. Why should the South support the building of roads and canals? With its many excellent rivers, southerners pointed out, the South could easily ship most goods by water.

SECTION 4 REVIEW

1. **Identify:** (a) John C. Calhoun, (b) Daniel Webster, (c) Henry Clay, (d) American System.
2. **Define:** (a) dumping, (b) protective tariff.
3. Why did some people call the period after Monroe became President the Era of Good Feelings?
4. Explain how Congress tried to solve each of the following: (a) problems with the money supply; (b) dumping.
5. Why did sectional differences grow during the tariff debate?
6. **Defending a Position** Do you think Clay's American System was a good plan for the nation? Explain.

5 The Spirit of Independence Spreads

FIND OUT

◆ How did Canada become a self-governing nation?

◆ How did revolutions change Latin America?

◆ Why did the United States issue the Monroe Doctrine?

In 1812, a rebel army was gathered in Caracas, in present-day Venezuela. For two years, they had been fighting to free their land from Spanish rule. They seemed to have a good chance of winning.

Then, without warning, on Thursday, March 26, the earth trembled and rolled. Buildings that housed the rebel troops collapsed, killing thousands. Only a few miles away, Spain's army was nearly untouched.

Simón Bolívar (see MOHN bohl EE vahr), a young rebel officer, leaped onto the rubble. "If nature thwarts us and our plans," he cried defiantly, "we will fight her and force her to obey us!"

Bolívar and his forces were not the only ones trying to throw off colonial rule. As the United States went to war with Britain in 1812, its neighbors in the Western Hemisphere sought independence. To the north, Canada followed a peaceful route to self-rule. In the Spanish colonies to the south, rebels had to fight long, bloody wars before they won independence.

Canadians Gain Self-rule

In the early 1800s, Canada was a country of farmers, fishers, and fur traders. A few Canadians also earned their living as merchants. Canada was under British rule, although Indian nations controlled much of the land in the north and west.

As you have read in Chapter 4, the French settled the lands along the lower St. Lawrence River. In 1763, however, the British won control of Canada. During and after the American Revolution, more than 40,000 Loyalists fled to Canada from the United States. They settled mainly in Nova Scotia, New Brunswick, Prince Edward Island, and the area north of the Great Lakes.

Two cultures. The British conquest left Canada a troubled land. French Canadians and English Canadians distrusted one another. They not only spoke different languages but also practiced different religions. Most English settlers were Protestants. Most French settlers were Catholics.

Britain decided to rule the two groups separately. In 1791, it divided Canada into Upper and Lower Canada. Upper Canada included the area around the Great Lakes settled by English-speaking people. Lower Canada included lands along the lower St. Lawrence River settled by the French. Each province was given its own government. But Britain made the important decisions for the colony.

During the early 1800s, reformers in Canada pressed for change. They were upset that a few wealthy families controlled Canadian affairs. In 1837, rebellions broke out in both Upper and Lower Canada. But the British had learned from their experience in the American Revolution. Faced with bands of armed "patriots," they looked for a peaceful solution to the crisis.

In the end, Britain accepted the recommendations of Lord Durham, the governor of Canada. He urged that Canadians be given complete control over local affairs. He also proposed that Upper and Lower Canada be united. The Durham Report became the basis for Canadian self-rule.

The Dominion of Canada. The plan proceeded slowly. But at last, in 1867, the provinces of Nova Scotia, New Brunswick, Ontario, and Quebec were joined into the **Dominion of Canada.** Some time later,

Prince Edward Island, Manitoba, Alberta, Saskatchewan, and British Columbia also joined the Dominion.

By slow and generally peaceful means, Canada became a nation. The government of Canada was similar to the British government. Canadians had an elected parliament and a prime minister. A governor general represented the British ruler but had little power.

MAP STUDY

The wars of independence in Latin America led to the creation of many new nations.
1. *Which new nation was farthest north?*
2. *Which places remained European colonies?*
3. **Linking Past and Present** *Use the map on pages 714–715 to name the nations that were eventually carved out of the United Provinces of Central America.*

NEW NATIONS IN LATIN AMERICA

☐ New nations   ☐ European colonies

0   1000   2000 Miles
0   1000   2000 Kilometers

Upheavals in Latin America

During the early 1800s, revolutions broke out in Spain's colonies in Latin America.* People living under Spanish rule had many reasons to fight for independence. Most had no say in government. The American and French revolutions encouraged the people in Latin America to seek the right to control their own affairs.

By the late 1700s, Spain had already put down several revolts in Latin America. In Peru, Indians had battled Spanish officials. In New Granada (present-day Colombia), almost 20,000 colonists had marched in protest against high taxes.

The early rebellions failed. The rebels came mostly from the lower classes—Indians and mestizos. Creoles refused to join them. Without the help of the creoles, the wars for independence could not succeed.

Independence for Mexico

On a Sunday morning in September 1810, the people of Dolores, a small town in Mexico, heard the church bell ring. The church bell always rang on Sundays, but this time it pealed longer and louder than usual. Hurrying to the square, the townspeople found their priest, Father Miguel Hidalgo (mee GEHL ih DAHL goh), in the midst of a stirring speech. No one knows the exact words, but Mexicans remembered his message:

> ❝My children . . . Will you free yourselves? Will you recover the lands stolen 300 years ago from your forefathers by the hated Spaniards? We must act at once. . . . Will you not defend your religion and your rights as true patriots? Long live our Lady of Guadalupe! Death to bad government!❞

---

*Latin America refers to the parts of the Western Hemisphere where Latin languages such as Spanish, French, and Portuguese are spoken. It includes Mexico, Central and South America, and the West Indies.

Father Hidalgo's speech became known as the *Grito de Dolores,* or Cry of Dolores. It sounded the call to revolution. Thousands of Native Americans responded to the call and joined Hidalgo.

Marching through the countryside, the rebels gained control of several Mexican provinces. Hidalgo then tried to set up a government. It outlawed slavery and ordered lands to be returned to the Indians.

In 1811, Hidalgo was captured and executed by troops loyal to Spain. José Morelos (hoh ZAY moh RAY lohs), another priest, took up the fight. Morelos boldly proclaimed that all races should be treated equally. He began a program to give land to poor peasants. Wealthy creoles opposed his ideas and helped Spanish troops to capture him.

By 1821, however, many creoles had decided to support independence. Under Agustín de Iturbide (ah goos TEEN day ee toor BEE day), an army forced Spain to give up Mexico. A few years later, Mexican leaders wrote a constitution that made Mexico a republic.

The Liberator

Perhaps the best-known revolutionary leader in Latin America was Simón Bolívar. Because he fought so long and hard for independence, Bolívar became known as the Liberator.

Bolívar was born into a wealthy creole family in Venezuela. As a young man, he took up the cause of Latin American independence. "I will never allow my hands to be idle," he vowed, "nor my soul to rest until I have broken the shackles which chain us to Spain."

Bolívar visited the United States because he admired its form of government. He also spent time in France after the French Revolution. He came to have a high regard for the French leader Napoleon, admiring his military genius and ability to lead. Bolívar hoped that he could act as strongly in Latin America.

Leader for Mexican Independence *Mexicans fought for more than 10 years to win independence from Spain. Father José Morelos, shown here, was an important leader in the struggle. Betrayed by the creoles, Morelos was captured and put to death by the Spanish.* **Citizenship** *Why do you think the creoles opposed Morelos?*

Returning to Venezuela, Bolívar commanded rebel armies during the long struggle against Spain. In August 1819, he led his men on a daring march from Venezuela over the ice-capped Andes Mountains into Colombia. The troops waded through rivers, where killer fish lurked, and crept cautiously across narrow bridges high above deep gorges.

In Colombia, Bolívar defeated the Spanish. Soon after, he became president of the independent Republic of Great Colombia. It included today's nations of Venezuela, Colombia, Ecuador, and Panama.

Other New Nations

Elsewhere in Latin America, people also sought freedom. José de San Martín (san mahr TEEN) led Argentina in its struggle for independence. Argentina won its freedom in 1816. San Martín also helped

Chile, Peru, and Ecuador to win their independence.

In 1821, the people of Central America declared their independence from Spain. Two years later, they formed the United Provinces of Central America. It included present-day Nicaragua, Costa Rica, El Salvador, Honduras, and Guatemala.

The Portuguese colony of Brazil also won independence—but without having to fight for it. Instead, the people asked Prince Pedro, son of the Portuguese king, to be their ruler. He accepted. In 1822, Pedro declared Brazil's independence.

By 1825, most colonies in Latin America had thrown off European rule. Spain, however, held on to Puerto Rico and Cuba. The new republics modeled their constitutions on that of the United States. Yet their experience after independence was very different from that of their neighbor to the north.

Unlike the 13 colonies, the colonies of Latin America did not unite into a single country. Instead, they set up many different nations. In part, the geography of South America made unity difficult. The high, rugged Andes Mountains, for example, form a serious barrier to travel and communication. Also, the Spanish colonies were spread out over a huge area.

The new Latin American republics had a hard time setting up stable governments. Spain had not allowed its colonies to elect assemblies as the 13 English colonies had done. So Latin Americans had no experience in self-government. Also, deep divisions between social classes and economic problems fueled discontent. As a result, many of the new nations were unable to achieve their goal of democratic rule.

Invasion of Florida

While Spain fought to hold on to its colonies in Latin America, it faced another challenge in Florida. Americans, especially in the South and West, wanted to make Florida part of the United States.

Georgia planters, for example, were angry because runaway slaves found safety in Spanish Florida. Also, Creek Indians who had been forced off their lands in Georgia had fled to Florida. There, they joined with the Seminoles to attack settlements in Georgia. And Spain did little to stop pirates who used ports in Florida as bases for raids on American ships.

To end the Indian attacks, the American border commander, General Andrew Jackson, invaded Florida in 1818. President Monroe did not give Jackson formal permission to invade Spanish territory. But he did not stop Jackson either. Jackson captured several Spanish towns and executed two British citizens, claiming that they had helped the Indians fight the Americans.

A Seminole Attack *From time to time, Seminole Indians living in Spanish Florida crossed the border to attack American settlements in Georgia. This picture shows a Seminole attack on an American fort.* **United States and the World** *Why do you think Spanish officials did not try to stop the Indian attacks?*

Spain protested. But it was too busy fighting rebels in Latin America to risk war with the United States. In the end, Spain agreed to peace talks. John Quincy Adams, son of the second President of the United States, was Monroe's Secretary of State. Adams worked out a treaty with Spain that went into effect in 1821. In the **Adams-Onís Treaty,** Spain gave Florida to the United States in return for a payment of $5 million.

The Monroe Doctrine

Americans were very pleased with the Adams-Onís Treaty. They also cheered the success of Latin American nations in their battle for independence from Spain. But European rulers were uneasy about events in Latin America. To them, the wars of independence were like the French Revolution—threats to their power. To crush any new European revolutions, Russia, Prussia, Austria, and France formed the Holy Alliance in 1815.

President Monroe and Secretary of State Adams worried that the Holy Alliance might try to help Spain regain its colonies in Latin America. Russia also claimed lands on the Pacific coast of North America.

The British, too, worried about other European nations meddling in the affairs of North and South America. They suggested that the United States join with them to issue a statement. The statement would guarantee the freedom of the new nations of Latin America.

Adams advised Monroe to issue his own statement. Joining with the British, he warned, would make the United States appear "to come in as a [tiny] boat in the wake of the British man-of-war." Monroe agreed.

In a message to Congress in 1823, the President made a statement on foreign policy that is known as the **Monroe Doctrine.** The United States, he said, would not interfere in the affairs of European nations or European colonies in the Americas. At the same time, he warned European nations not to interfere with the newly independent nations of Latin America. Finally, he added:

> **❝**The American continents, by the free and independent condition which they have assumed . . . are henceforth not to be considered as subjects for future colonization by any European powers. . . . We owe it, therefore, to . . . declare that we should consider any attempt on their part to extend their system to any portion of this hemisphere as dangerous to our peace and safety.**❞**

The Monroe Doctrine showed that the United States was determined to keep European nations from building new colonies in the Americas. In 1823, the United States did not have the power to enforce the Monroe Doctrine. But Britain supported the President's message. Its powerful navy could stop European nations from seizing new colonies in the Americas.

SECTION 5 REVIEW

1. **Locate:** (a) Peru, (b) Mexico, (c) Great Colombia, (d) Argentina, (e) Chile, (f) United Provinces of Central America, (g) Brazil.
2. **Identify:** (a) Dominion of Canada, (b) Miguel Hidalgo, (c) Simón Bolívar, (d) José de San Martín, (e) Adams-Onís Treaty, (f) Monroe Doctrine.
3. (a) Why did rebellions break out in Canada? (b) What were the recommendations of Lord Durham?
4. (a) How did the *Grito de Dolores* spark a revolt in Mexico? (b) What other Latin American nations won independence from Spain?
5. Why did the United States issue the Monroe Doctrine?
6. **Comparing** How did the wars of independence in Latin America differ from the American Revolution?

Circle graphs are one way of showing statistics. A circle graph is sometimes called a pie graph because it is divided into wedges, like a pie. Each wedge, or part, can be compared to every other part. A circle graph shows the relationship between each of the parts and the whole.

To compare information over time, two or more circle graphs can be used. A circle graph can also be used with a line or bar graph. (See Skill Lesson 4 on page 118 and Skill Lesson 6 on page 176.)

1 Identify the information shown on the graphs. (a) What year does the circle graph on the left show? (b) What do the colors represent? (c) What year does the circle graph on the right show? (d) What do the colors represent?

2 Practice reading the graphs. In a circle graph, you can compare any part with every other part or with the whole graph.

The graph shows each part as a percentage of the whole. The whole graph is 100 percent. (a) What percent of the population lived in the North in 1800? (b) Which section of the country had the largest percent of the population in 1800? (c) Which section had the smallest percent of the population in 1800? (d) What percent of the population lived in the West in 1830? In the North? In the South?

3 Compare the two graphs. (a) Which section of the country had the largest percentage gain in population between 1800 and 1830? (b) Which section of the country lost the greatest percent in this period? (c) Why do you think this section did not grow as fast as the West in this period? (d) Using your reading in the chapter and these graphs, make a generalization about what was happening to the population of the United States between 1800 and 1830.

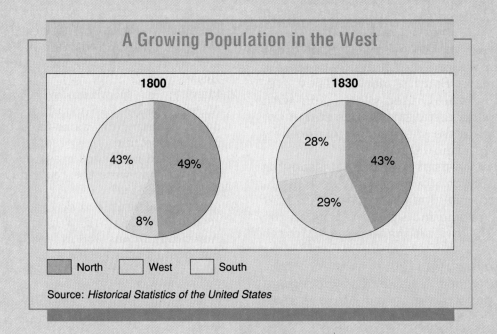

A Growing Population in the West

1800 — North 49%, West 43%, South 8%

1830 — North 43%, West 28%, South 29%

Legend: North — West — South

Source: *Historical Statistics of the United States*

Use the Section Reviews and this Study Guide to review chapter content.

Main Ideas

The main ideas in each section of this chapter are summarized below.

SECTION 1 ■ A Bloodless Revolution

◆ The Industrial Revolution started in Britain and spread to the United States.
◆ Samuel Slater and Moses Brown built the first factory in the United States.

SECTION 2 ■ Growth of Industry

◆ The War of 1812 spurred the growth of industry in the United States.
◆ Factory owners in the early 1800s hired women and children to do most of the work.

SECTION 3 ■ A People on the Move

◆ In the early 1800s, many Americans risked the dangers of travel to move west.
◆ New roads and canals and the use of steamboats helped improve transportation.

SECTION 4 ■ A Sense of National Unity

◆ During the Era of Good Feelings, conflict between political parties declined.
◆ In Congress, John Calhoun, Daniel Webster, and Henry Clay spoke for different sections of the country.
◆ To help the economy, Congress chartered the second Bank of the United States and passed protective tariffs.

◆ Henry Clay proposed the American System to help all sections of the country.

SECTION 5 ■ The Spirit of Independence Spreads

◆ Canada achieved self-rule peacefully.
◆ In Latin America, Spanish colonies fought hard for their freedom.
◆ In the Monroe Doctrine, the United States warned European nations to stay out of the affairs of the Western Hemisphere.

Key People and Terms

Refer to the Identify and Define questions in the Section Reviews on pages 368, 373, 380, 384, and 389. Use each person, term, and vocabulary word in a complete sentence. When possible, make connections between the people and terms by using more than one person or term in each sentence.

Time Line

1. Make a chart of events in time order. The chart will have two headings: Date, Event. Fill in the chart, using the events on the time line. Add the following events from the chapter: Brown opens first factory in United States; Clay proposes American System; Lowell mills open. (Refer to the chapter for the dates.)
2. Which events on your chart are part of the Industrial Revolution?

1790	1795	1800	1805	1810	1815	1820	1825

1793 Cotton gin invented

1790s Lancaster Turnpike built

1806 Congress votes money for National Road

1807 *Clermont* launched

1817 Era of Good Feelings begins

1825 Erie Canal completed

CHAPTER 12 REVIEW

Understanding Vocabulary

Match each term at left with the correct definition at right.

1. capitalist
2. interchangeable parts
3. turnpike
4. dumping
5. protective tariff

a. selling goods in another country at very low prices
b. road built by a private company that charged tolls
c. person with money to invest in business to make a profit
d. tax to help home industries against foreign competition
e. identical parts of a tool that are made by machine

Reviewing the Main Ideas

1. How did the Industrial Revolution come to the United States?
2. What new idea did Francis Cabot Lowell introduce to the textile industry?
3. Describe how interchangeable parts improved the way goods were produced.
4. (a) Why did Americans need better transportation? (b) Describe three ways that transportation improved in the early 1800s.
5. (a) Why did northern manufacturers want a protective tariff? (b) Why did southerners oppose the tariff?
6. Why did some Americans want Florida to become part of the United States?
7. (a) Why did the United States fear that European nations might interfere in the Western Hemisphere? (b) What other nation supported the Monroe Doctrine? (c) Why was this support important?

Thinking Critically

1. **Applying Information** (a) How did inventions such as the spinning jenny and water frame lead to the factory system? (b) Why were early factories set up near rivers?
2. **Linking Past and Present** (a) What were the problems of city life in the early 1800s? (b) What advantages did cities offer? (c) Do cities today still have the same problems and advantages? Explain.

3. **Analyzing Ideas** (a) How did geography make travel to the West difficult? (b) How did Americans overcome these problems?
4. **Comparing** (a) Compare the way Canada won its independence with the way the Spanish colonies won theirs. (b) Suggest some reasons why their experiences were different.

Applying Your Skills

1. **Analyzing a Quotation** Reread the quotation on page 365. (a) What did Lucy dislike about factory life? (b) Why did Lucy Larcom enjoy looking out the window? (c) Did Lucy think factory life was completely bad? Explain.
2. **Reading a Circle Graph** Review Skill Lesson 12 on page 390. (a) Why is a circle graph sometimes called a pie graph? (b) What relationship does a circle graph show? (c) In each Skill Lesson graph, what does the whole graph represent? (d) What do the parts represent? (e) What evidence in the chapter supports the information in the graphs?
3. **Identifying the Main Idea** Reread the first paragraph on page 366 under the heading "Britain Takes the Lead." (a) What is the main idea of the paragraph? (b) What facts in the next paragraph support the main idea?

Thinking About Geography

Match the letters on the map with the places listed below.

1. Wheeling, Virginia
2. New York City
3. Cumberland Gap
4. Lancaster Turnpike
5. National Road
6. Erie Canal
7. Wabash and Erie Canal

Interaction What obstacles did Americans overcome in building the Erie Canal?

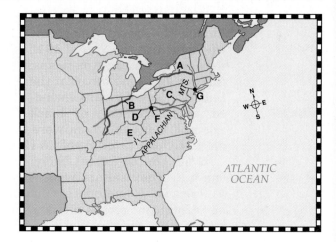

History Writer's Workshop

Writing Footnotes for a Report

A report should include footnotes that identify all outside sources of information. You will need footnotes:

1. When you quote a source.
2. When you put someone else's ideas into your own words.
3. When you include unusual facts.

To write a footnote, place a number right after and slightly above the quotation, idea, or fact you are using. Then, identify the source at the bottom of the page or in a numbered list at the end of the report. Study the examples of footnotes that follow.

Source	Footnote
Book	[1]Chauncey Jerome, *History of the American Clock Business*, p. 55.
Encyclopedia article	[2]*The World Book Encyclopedia*, 1990 ed., "Bolívar, Simón."
Magazine article	[3]E. Moreno, "Bolivarian Ideals Reawakened," *Americas*, September/October, 1988, p. 53.

Practice Locate in the library a book and an encyclopedia article about De Witt Clinton and the Erie Canal. Write a sample footnote for each source.

Writing to Learn

1. Write a one-paragraph essay about the changes caused by the Industrial Revolution. To prepare, brainstorm a list of problems and benefits resulting from the Revolution. Write a topic sentence that summarizes the effects of the Industrial Revolution. Then, write sentences to organize the listed details in logical order. When you revise, be sure you have supported each of your points with specific examples. Proofread and make a final copy. Then, share your essay with a group of classmates.

2. Imagine that you are a reporter sent to observe the Lowell mills. Write a newspaper article about conditions there. To prepare, make a chart of sense impressions that you might have experienced. Write a topic sentence that summarizes your observations and reactions. Then, organize your details logically. Revise for specific word choice and realistic details. Then, proofread and make a final copy. Publish your article in a class newspaper.

Valiant Sailors and Soldiers

Among the brave Americans who fought in the War of 1812 were many African Americans. Andrew Jackson's forces at the Battle of New Orleans included two battalions of black soldiers, many of whom were veterans of L'Ouverture's revolt in Haiti.

In the United States Navy, about one out of six sailors were African Americans. Commodore Chauncey, an American naval officer, spoke highly of the black sailors he served with, noting that these men were "not surpassed by any seamen we have in the fleet, and I have yet to learn that the color of the skin or the cut and trimmings of the coat can affect a man's qualifications or usefulness."

Launching the Ship *Fame*

George Ropes, who was born unable to hear or speak, worked as a sign painter and carriage decorator. But he is known to us today for his fine paintings. Seaside scenes were a favorite subject for Ropes, who grew up in Salem, Massachusetts. Like many early American artists, he was also commissioned to make paintings of current events, such as the launching of a new ship.

The Star-Spangled Banner

Francis Scott Key was an unexpected witness to the British attack on Fort McHenry in September 1814. He had gone on board a British warship near Baltimore to negotiate the release of an American prisoner.

The flag he saw so proudly waving after the long night of shelling was the second flag of the United States. As the official flag from 1795 to 1818, it had 15 stripes and 15 stars, one for each state. The flag flying over Fort McHenry, which measured 42 feet by 30 feet, had been sewn by Mary Young Pickersgill. What remained of the flag after the battle, pictured here, hangs in the Smithsonian Institution in Washington, D.C.

Uncle Sam

The great, tall man with striped pants, stars on his shirt, and a high hat whom we know as Uncle Sam had very humble beginnings. The real Uncle Sam was Samuel Wilson of Troy, New York, who sold meat to the United States Army during the War of 1812. Wilson sent each barrel to a supply officer in the army named Elbert Anderson. So Wilson would stamp each barrel "U.S.—E.A." which stood for "United States—Elbert Anderson."

Once when asked what the initials U.S. stood for, however, one of Wilson's employees replied, "Uncle Sam", meaning Uncle Sam Wilson. The idea that food, uniforms, and other supplies came from Uncle Sam caught on. At first, Uncle Sam appeared in cartoons as a young man with stars and stripes on his shirt. In the 1840 cartoon here, he has the familiar top hat and tails. Later cartoonists added the gray hair and beard.

Red Barns

High-tech pictures of solar panels on the roof of a futuristic house might lead you to believe that solar energy is something new. Throughout history, however, people have found ways to take advantage of heat from the sun. American farmers in the early 1800s did just that. They found out that deep red colors absorbed the sun's rays. This meant that if barns were painted red, they would stay warmer during cold winter months. These clever farmers made their paint from a mixture of skim milk and shavings from rusty nails and metal fences.

Footnotes to History

- From 1790 to 1800, the number of newspapers in the United States rose from 100 to more than 230.
- Among Thomas Jefferson's many inventions were a dumbwaiter and a quartet music stand that could hold the music for four musicians.
- As a result of the Louisiana Purchase, the United States acquired over 800,000 square miles of land at about 3 cents an acre.
- Today the National Road is part of U.S. Highway 40.

UNIT 4 SUMMARY

Chapter 10 The New Government Begins

In 1789, George Washington took office as the first President of the United States. He and Congress worked together to organize a national government. Washington chose able leaders to serve in his cabinet and on the Supreme Court. His Secretary of the Treasury, Alexander Hamilton, devised a two-step plan to repay national and state debts. To strengthen the economy, Hamilton proposed a national bank and several taxes. The tax on whiskey led farmers to rebel in 1794. Washington's swift response showed the government's strength.

War raged across Europe during the 1790s, but Washington worked hard to keep the United States at peace. Washington tried to avoid taking sides in the French Revolution by issuing the Neutrality Proclamation. When the British attacked American ships that traded with French colonies, he sent John Jay to Britain to work out a treaty. Closer to home, settlers and Native Americans clashed in the Northwest Territory.

After serving two terms, Washington left office. He warned Americans not to quarrel about politics. By 1796, however, disagreements between Hamilton and Thomas Jefferson already formed the basis of two political parties. Hamilton's Federalists favored a strong federal government, an industrial economy, and a loose interpretation of the Constitution. Jefferson's Republicans favored strong state governments, an agricultural economy, and a strict interpretation of the Constitution.

In 1796, a Federalist, John Adams, was elected President. Despite pressure from members of his own party, Adams refused to go to war with France over the XYZ Affair. As a result, the party split. High Federalists passed the unpopular Alien and Sedition Acts, threatening freedom of speech. In 1798 and 1799, Kentucky and Virginia claimed the right to nullify the acts within their borders. In 1800, Americans voted the Federalists out of office.

Chapter 11 The Jefferson Era

Republican Thomas Jefferson, the new President, wanted a more democratic nation. Jefferson worked with Congress to limit the power of the federal government, cut government spending, and reduce taxes. In the meantime, Chief Justice John Marshall worked to strengthen the federal courts.

Although Jefferson believed in a strict reading of the Constitution, he did use his power to buy Louisiana from France in 1803. In so doing, he kept the port of New Orleans open to farmers. He also doubled the size of the nation. Jefferson organized the expedition of Lewis and Clark to explore the new territory.

Jefferson spent his last years in office trying to stay out of the new war between France and Britain. Since neither nation wanted the United States to trade with its enemy, both seized American ships. The British also impressed American sailors. Jefferson convinced Congress to ban foreign trade until Britain and France agreed to respect American neutrality.

Jefferson's successor, James Madison, gave in to pressure from War Hawks and asked Congress to declare war against Britain.

Neither the United States nor Britain won the War of 1812. The British lost many battles at sea, but successfully blockaded the coast. There was fierce fighting on the frontier where Indians tried to defend their lands against settlers. Americans under Andrew Jackson won a stunning victory at New Orleans two weeks after the war was officially over.

Chapter 12 The Growing Years

The early 1800s were a period of growth and expansion. Using Richard Arkwright's design to build a spinning mill in Rhode Island, Samuel Slater helped to bring the Industrial Revolution to the United States. Steam-powered machines soon replaced hand tools. Industry moved from homes to factories.

The War of 1812 helped to spur the growth of American industry. Cut off from foreign manufactures by the British blockade, Americans began to produce more and more of their own goods. Eli Whitney's idea of interchangeable parts increased production. As factories grew, so did the towns and cities where they were located.

Americans traveling west felt the need for improved transportation. In 1818, the National Road linking Maryland to Virginia was completed. River travel improved with the invention of the steamboat. The success of New York's Erie Canal in 1825 encouraged other states to build canals.

The election of James Monroe as President in 1816 ushered in an era of national pride and unity. To strengthen the economy, Congress chartered a new national bank. To protect American industry, Congress passed high tariffs on imports. Debate over the tariffs pointed up growing sectional conflict. Henry Clay proposed the American System to meet the economic needs of all sections of the country.

As the nation prospered, its neighbors sought independence. Canada followed a peaceful route to self-rule in 1867. After bloody revolutions, most Spanish colonies in Latin America gained independence by 1825. To guarantee the freedom of the new nations, President Monroe issued a statement warning Europeans not to interfere in the affairs of the Western Hemisphere.

Understanding Causes and Effects *The Industrial Revolution was a time of great change.* ◆ *What inventions and ideas helped to produce the Industrial Revolution? Do you think the Industrial Revolution was a change for the better? Explain.*

CAUSES

- British ideas of a spinning mill and power loom reach the United States
- Eli Whitney invents the cotton gin
- War of 1812 prompts Americans to make their own goods
- Eli Whitney introduces the idea of interchangeable parts

THE INDUSTRIAL REVOLUTION IN THE UNITED STATES

EFFECTS

- Factory system spreads
- Young women and children from nearby farms work in mills
- Growing cities face problems of fire, sewage, garbage, and disease

Reviewing the Main Ideas

1. How did the first Congress help to organize the executive branch of government?
2. (a) Name the first two American political parties. (b) How did the parties differ?
3. How did the XYZ Affair affect relations between Federalists and Republicans?
4. List three policies Jefferson introduced as President.
5. Describe the events that led to the Louisiana Purchase.
6. (a) How did the Battle of New Orleans affect the outcome of the War of 1812? (b) How did it affect Andrew Jackson's reputation? Explain.
7. What was the Lowell experiment?
8. (a) What was the American System? (b) Why did Henry Clay propose it?
9. How did the United States help to guarantee the freedom of new Latin American nations?

Thinking Critically

1. **Making Decisions** One of the first issues that the new Congress debated in 1789 was whether to address the President of the United States simply as President Washington or to use a more elegant title. Congress decided to stay with the simpler term. How might a different decision have affected the nature of the presidency?
2. **Applying Information** How did the advice Washington gave to the nation about foreign policy in his Farewell Address affect the actions of the Presidents that followed him?
3. **Analyzing Ideas** Thomas Jefferson strongly believed in the rights and freedom of the individual. He once said, "The minority possess their equal rights, which equal law must protect." How can a government elected by majority vote still protect the rights of minorities?

4. **Comparing** (a) Compare the way muskets were made by a skilled gunsmith with the way they were made using interchangeable parts. (b) How did the concept of interchangeable parts affect the production of goods?
5. **Defending a Position** Did James Monroe really usher in an "Era of Good Feelings"? Review the events that occurred during his presidency. Then, state and defend your position.

Applying Your Skills

1. **Making a Generalization** Review the discussion of the spread of independence in Latin America on pages 386–388. (a) Based on your reading, write two generalizations about the independence movement in Latin America. (b) Give two facts to support each generalization.
2. **Understanding Sequence** The United States purchased Louisiana in 1803. (a) What happened in 1801 that helped make the purchase possible? (b) Do you think that the United States could have bought Louisiana ten years earlier? Explain.
3. **Making a Review Chart** To review early inventions leading to the Industrial Revolution, set up a chart with four columns. Label the columns Year, Inventor, Invention, Importance. Then, use the information in Chapter 12 to complete the chart.

Doing More

1. **Creating Headlines** Each of the first five Presidents faced difficult problems during his term in office. For each President, select a newsworthy issue and write a newspaper headline describing it. Try to draft a headline that both captures attention and summarizes the story. Revise for conciseness, making sure each word counts. After proofreading, print each headline,

line for line, as it would appear on the front page of a newspaper.

2. **Illustrating a Story** The national anthem of the United States was written during the British attack on Fort McHenry in 1814. Research the story of "The Star-Spangled Banner." Locate and study the words of the song. Then draw a picture of the scene Francis Scott Key described.

3. **Organizing a Debate** As a group project, organize a debate on Henry Clay's American System. In preparing for the debate, consider the effect of the plan on each section of the country. Draw up a list of arguments for and against the plan. Be prepared to support your assigned point of view and to disprove your opponents' points of view.

4. **Exploring Local History** Research the first factories in your community. Find out when each factory was opened, who owned it, and who worked there. Present the information as an oral report or in the form of a poster.

Recognizing Points of View

One of the first issues to separate Thomas Jefferson and Alexander Hamilton was that of a national bank. Each man defended his point of view in a letter to President George Washington. Below are excerpts from both letters. Read the excerpts and answer the following questions.

1. What is Jefferson's main argument in support of the idea that the establishment of a national bank is unconstitutional?

2. Under the Constitution, Congress has the power to make all laws "necessary" to carry out delegated powers. (a) How does Hamilton define "necessary"? (b) How could Hamilton use his definition of "necessary" to build an argument in support of a national bank?

3. Review Clause 18—the "elastic clause"—of Article 1, Section 8, of the Constitution on page 758. Do you think that lawmakers should follow Jefferson or Hamilton in interpreting the clause? Explain.

According to the Constitution, can a national bank be created?

Thomas Jefferson

❝The incorporation of a bank, and the powers assumed by this bill [establishing the bank], have not, in my opinion been delegated to the United States by the Constitution. They are not among the powers specially [listed]. . . . Nor are they within either of the general phrases. . . . It has been [argued] that a bank will give great . . . convenience in the collection of taxes. Suppose this were true: yet the Constitution allows only the means which are 'necessary,' not those which are merely 'convenient' for [putting into effect] the [listed] power.❞

Alexander Hamilton

❝It is essential to the being of the national government that [such a great misunderstanding] of the meaning of the word 'necessary' be [disproved]. . . . Necessary often means no more than needful, . . . useful, or [helpful]. . . . And [this] is the true [sense] in which it is to be understood as used in the Constitution. The whole [purpose] of the clause containing it indicates that it was the intent of the [Constitutional] Convention . . . to [provide freedom] to exercise the specified powers.❞

UNIT

5 An Expanding Nation

2 Pioneers crossed the Missouri River to make the long journey to Oregon and other parts of the West.

1 A democratic spirit swept the nation. In the new western states as well as in the East, the common people gained a say in politics and government.

3 Texans won a war of independence from Mexico. In gratitude for sparing his life, the Mexican leader gave his snuff box to Sam Houston, the Texan commander.

1816	1824	1832	1840
AMERICAN EVENTS	**1820s** More white men gain right to vote	**1828** Andrew Jackson elected President **1830** Indian Removal Act	
WORLD EVENTS	**1822** Liberia set up in West Africa	**1832** Santa Anna comes to power in Mexico	
	James Monroe	Andrew Jackson	Martin Van Buren
	John Quincy Adams		

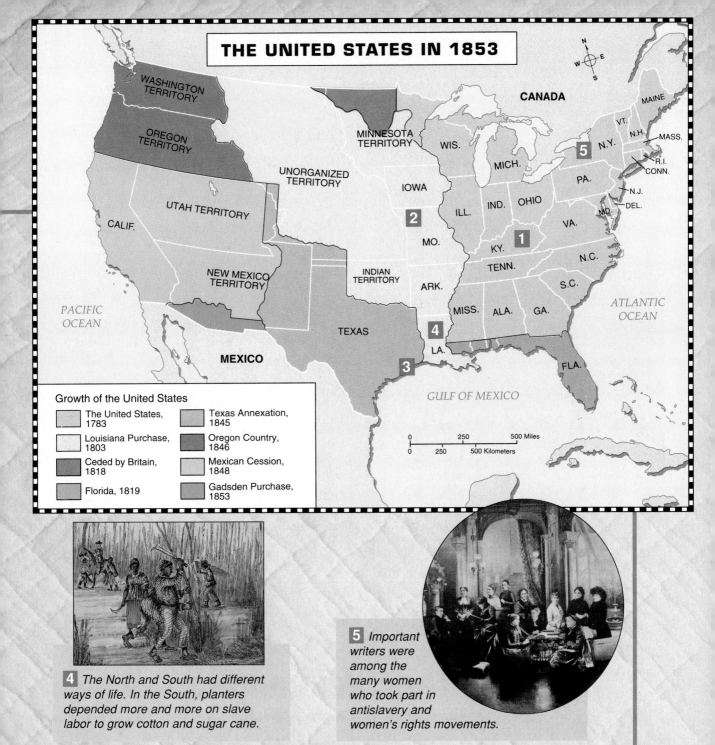

THE UNITED STATES IN 1853

WASHINGTON TERRITORY

OREGON TERRITORY

CANADA

MINNESOTA TERRITORY

UNORGANIZED TERRITORY

UTAH TERRITORY

CALIF.

NEW MEXICO TERRITORY

MEXICO

TEXAS

WIS.

IOWA

MICH.

ILL. IND. OHIO

MO.

INDIAN TERRITORY

ARK.

KY.

TENN.

MISS. ALA. GA.

LA.

FLA.

PACIFIC OCEAN

GULF OF MEXICO

ATLANTIC OCEAN

N.Y.

PA.

VA.

N.C.

S.C.

MAINE
VT.
N.H.
MASS.
R.I.
CONN.
N.J.
DEL.
MD.

1 **2** **3** **4** **5**

Growth of the United States

- The United States, 1783
- Louisiana Purchase, 1803
- Ceded by Britain, 1818
- Florida, 1819
- Texas Annexation, 1845
- Oregon Country, 1846
- Mexican Cession, 1848
- Gadsden Purchase, 1853

0   250   500 Miles
0   250   500 Kilometers

4 The North and South had different ways of life. In the South, planters depended more and more on slave labor to grow cotton and sugar cane.

5 Important writers were among the many women who took part in antislavery and women's rights movements.

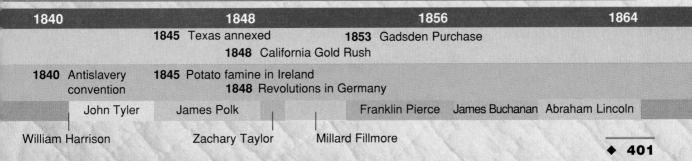

1840	1848	1856	1864

1845 Texas annexed   **1853** Gadsden Purchase

1848 California Gold Rush

1840 Antislavery convention

1845 Potato famine in Ireland

1848 Revolutions in Germany

John Tyler   James Polk   Franklin Pierce   James Buchanan   Abraham Lincoln

William Harrison   Zachary Taylor   Millard Fillmore

◆ **401**

On the Campaign Trail *A democratic spirit swept the nation during the Jackson era. This painting by George Caleb Bingham shows a political candidate campaigning for votes on the frontier.* **Linking Past and Present** *How do candidates campaign for votes today?*

13

The Jackson Era (1824–1840)

Chapter Outline

1 The People's President
2 New Mood in the White House
3 Jackson Proves His Strength
4 Jackson's Successors

CHAPTER SPOTLIGHT

The Big Picture

In the early 1800s, a democratic spirit swept the nation. State after state dropped property requirements for voting. By the late 1840s, nearly all white men had won the right to vote. Still, for women, Native Americans, and African Americans, voting and other rights would require many more years of struggle.

The new voters elected Andrew Jackson, a new kind of President. To a greater degree than previous Presidents, Jackson spoke for the common people. And more so than other Presidents, he tested and strengthened the powers of the executive branch.

Kathleen Underwood

Of Special Interest

Focus On

◆ How did democracy expand in the 1820s?

◆ Why did President Jackson veto the Bank of the United States?

◆ Why did South Carolina threaten to secede from the Union?

◆ What economic problems did Jackson's successors face?

"**Y**esterday the President's house was open at noon. . . . The old man stood in the center of a little circle . . . and shook hands with anybody that offered. . . . There was a throng of apprentices, boys of all ages, men not civilized enough to walk about the rooms with their hats off; the vilest . . . [group] that ever [gathered] in a decent house; many of the lowest gathering around the doors, pouncing . . . upon the wine and refreshments, tearing the cake . . . all fellows with dirty faces and dirty manners; all the [trash] that Washington could turn forth from its workshops and stables.**"**

George Bancroft, the well-to-do visitor who described this scene at the White House in 1831, did not like what he saw. To him, the young men waiting to see President Jackson were roughnecks. But to Andrew Jackson, they were the backbone of the new American republic. Perhaps they were hungry and a bit dirty, but they were honest, thrifty, and hard working. Jackson treated the workers with respect, shook their hands, and offered them food and drink.

No President before Jackson had welcomed such ordinary folk to the White House. Jackson was a new breed of President. His victory in the election of 1828 showed how quickly the United States was growing and changing. Whether or not they liked Jackson, most Americans understood that his election was the start of a new era.

1 The People's President

FIND OUT

◆ Why did the election of 1824 cause dispute?

◆ How did President Adams plan to improve the nation?

◆ How did the nation become more democratic during the 1820s?

◆ VOCABULARY suffrage, caucus, nominating convention

In November 1824, just before the presidential election, a New England schoolteacher named Harry Ward was visiting Cincinnati, Ohio. He was amazed by the excitement that one candidate stirred up among Ohioans. "Strange! Wild! Infatuated! All for Jackson!" Ward wrote to a friend. "It is like an influenza."

Ward was right. That November, more people voted for Andrew Jackson than for any other candidate. Still, Jackson did not become President in 1824.

The 1824 Election

As you have read, the Federalist party faded in the 1820s. With no political parties to choose candidates, four men ran for President in 1824. Each drew support from a different part of the country. John Quincy Adams of Massachusetts was most popular in New England. Henry Clay and Andrew Jackson had strong support in the West. William Crawford was favored in the South, but he was too ill to campaign.

Adams, Clay, and Jackson. John Quincy Adams came from a rich, famous New England family. He was the son of Abigail and John Adams, the nation's second President. A Harvard graduate, he had served as Secretary of State under President James Monroe. People admired Adams for his intelligence and strict morals.

Henry Clay, a Kentuckian, did not come from a notable family as Adams did. But Clay was charming and shrewd. His talents had won him the powerful position of Speaker of the House of Representatives. In Congress, Clay proved to be a skillful negotiator and brought about many important compromises. Still, Clay was never as well liked as the other candidate from the West, Andrew Jackson.

Most Americans knew Andrew Jackson as General Jackson, the hero at New Orleans during the War of 1812. But to many, he was also an example of someone who rose from poverty to wealth. Farmers and workers especially admired Jackson as a self-made man. Since Jackson had gained success, they felt, perhaps one day they could, too.

The "corrupt bargain." On election day, Jackson won a majority of the popular vote. But no candidate won a majority of electoral votes. In such a case, the Constitution states, the House of Representatives must choose the President from among the top three candidates. Henry Clay, who finished fourth, could not be elected. But as Speaker of the House, he could influence who did win.

With Clay's help, John Quincy Adams was made President by the House. The new President then named Henry Clay as Secretary of State. Jackson and his supporters were furious. To them, it seemed that Adams and Clay had made a "corrupt bargain" to steal the election. But they could not deny that the election had been decided as the Constitution said. (See "The President's Lady" on page 674.)

Adams Loses Support

President Adams knew that his election had upset many Americans. He hoped, however, that his programs to improve the nation would "bring the whole people together." But his plan backfired. His programs were so unpopular that he united the people against him.

John Quincy Adams *President John Quincy Adams had great plans for improving the nation. He lacked the political skill, however, to win support for his programs.* **Citizenship** *Why did Americans oppose Adams's projects?*

Programs for national growth. President Adams was strongly influenced by old Federalist ideas. Like Alexander Hamilton, he thought that the federal government should help the economy of the young republic to grow. He wanted the government to pay for new roads and canals. These would help farmers to get their goods to market.

Adams had other programs in mind. They included a national university, an observatory for astronomers, and various projects to improve farming, manufacturing, science, and the arts. If governments in Europe supported these kinds of programs, his supporters reasoned, why should the American republic not do the same?

Most Americans, however, did not want to spend large sums of money on such programs. They also feared that the federal government would become too powerful. In the end, Congress approved money for a national road and some canals. But it turned down nearly all of Adams's other programs.

Adams and Jackson run again. Even though he was unpopular, Adams ran for reelection in 1828. This time, Andrew Jackson was his only opponent.

The campaign turned into a name-calling contest. Jackson supporters reminded Americans of the "corrupt bargain" to make Adams President four years earlier. They attacked Adams for being an aristocrat, a member of the upper class. In turn, supporters of Adams called Jackson a "military chieftain." They warned that Jackson could become a dictator like Napoleon Bonaparte.

In November, Jackson won a landslide victory. His supporters called the outcome

MAP STUDY

In the election of 1828, Andrew Jackson ran against President John Quincy Adams.
1. *Who won the election?*
2. *What area of the country supported Adams?*
3. **Solving Problems** *(a) What does the map show about the vote in New York? In Maine? (b) How did the mapmaker show this information?*

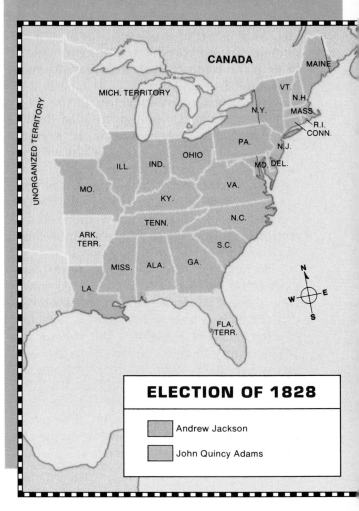

ELECTION OF 1828

Andrew Jackson

John Quincy Adams

a victory for the common people. By common people, they meant farmers in the West and South and working people in the cities of the East. A bitter Adams supporter, on the other hand, felt that Jackson had been swept into office by "the howl of raving Democracy."

Democracy Expands

The election of 1828 showed how the United States was changing. The nation was growing quickly. In 1828, three times more people voted than in 1824.

New voters in the West and East. Many new voters lived in the frontier states between the Appalachians and the Mississippi River. Life on the frontier had encouraged a democratic spirit. People there were a rugged group. Most began life very poor, but prospered through hard work. Also, there were fewer rich, old families than in the East. So most white men in the West were on an equal footing. This democratic spirit showed in the voting laws of the western states. Any white man over age 21 could vote.

There were also new voters in the East. Several eastern states had dropped the requirement that voters own land. For the first time, shopkeepers and craftworkers won suffrage, the right to vote.

Many cannot vote. Despite these changes, many Americans still did not have the right to vote. They included women, Native Americans, and most African Americans. Slaves had no political rights at all.

In fact, while many white Americans gained the right to vote in the 1820s, many free black Americans lost it. Most northern states had allowed African Americans to vote in the early 1800s. But during the 1820s, many of these states took the vote away. By 1830, free African Americans could vote only in a few New England states.

Political parties form again. The growing number of voters helped to spark the growth of new political parties. By 1832, two new parties had begun to form. They took shape around the sharp differences between John Quincy Adams and Andrew Jackson.

People who had supported Adams and his programs for national growth first called themselves National Republicans and later **Whigs.*** Business people in the East and large planters in the South often became Whigs. They wanted the federal government to spur the economy.

Jackson and his supporters also formed a new party. They called themselves **Democrats.** Today's Democratic party can trace its roots to the party of Andrew Jackson. Most support for the Democratic party came from frontier farmers in the West and craftworkers and factory workers in the East.

New ways to choose candidates. Soon, the democratic spirit of the time changed the way of choosing candidates for President. Earlier, the most powerful members of each party held a caucus, or private meeting. At the caucus, these party leaders chose the candidate. Many people felt that the caucus system was unfair because so few people took part in it.

By the 1830s, both parties began to hold nominating conventions. Delegates from each state went to their party's convention. The delegates then selected the party's candidate for President. This process gave people a more direct voice in choosing their future leaders. Today, the major political parties still choose their candidates at conventions.

A Growing Spirit of Equality

The democratic spirit of the time affected more than politics. Attitudes of Americans toward one another also changed. Ordinary people no longer looked up to the rich.

---

*Supporters of Adams took the name Whig from a political party in England that opposed King George III. The Whigs called Jackson "King Andrew I," because they thought he, like George III, had too much power.

"Does a man become wiser, stronger or more virtuous and patriotic because he has a fine house?" asked one Democrat.

In the United States, servants expected to be treated as equals. Butlers and maids refused to be called with bells, as in Europe. One coach driver complained that his employer "had had private meals every day and not asked him to the table." Europeans considered American demands for equality downright rude.

This new mood was made clear at Andrew Jackson's inauguration in March 1829. For the first time, thousands of common people flooded the capital to witness a President taking the oath of office. "It is beautiful! It is sublime!" one Jackson supporter said of the crowd.

After taking the oath of office, Jackson went to the White House for a reception. The crowd followed. One horrified onlooker described the scene:

“A rabble, a mob, of boys, negros, women, children, scrambling, fighting, romping. What a pity, what a pity! No arrangements had been made, no police officers on duty, and the whole house had been [filled] by the rabble mob. We came too late. The President, after having been literally nearly pressed to death and almost suffocated and torn to pieces by the people in their eagerness to shake hands . . . had retreated through the back way.”

The Common People Turn Out for Jackson *The election of Andrew Jackson as President in 1828 was seen as a triumph for the common people. Here, Jackson doffs his hat to an admiring crowd as he journeys to his inauguration in Washington, D.C.* **American Traditions** *How did Jackson's inauguration reflect the growing spirit of equality?*

Opponents of Jackson said that the inauguration was proof that "King Mob" now ruled the nation. Jackson supporters disagreed. "It was a proud day for the people," one pro-Jackson newspaper wrote of the inauguration. "General Jackson is their own President."

SECTION 1 REVIEW

1. **Identify:** (a) John Quincy Adams, (b) Henry Clay, (c) Whigs, (d) Democrats.
2. **Define:** (a) suffrage, (b) caucus, (c) nominating convention.
3. What was the outcome of the election of 1824?
4. Why did most Americans disagree with John Quincy Adams's programs for the nation?
5. How had the nation become more democratic by the 1820s?
6. **Applying Information** "Does a man become wiser, stronger or more virtuous and patriotic because he has a fine house?" How do you think a Jackson supporter might have responded to this question?

2 New Mood in the White House

FIND OUT

◆ How did Jackson earn the nickname Old Hickory?

◆ Why did Jackson appoint many new officeholders?

◆ Why did Jackson battle the Bank of the United States?

◆ **VOCABULARY** spoils system, kitchen cabinet, pet bank

During the 1828 election campaign, many voters swapped stories about Andrew Jackson. Like the following story, many stories told of Jackson's courage and grit.

Long before he ran for President, Jackson was a judge on the Tennessee frontier. One day, an outlaw named Russell Bean came to town. Bean scared the townspeople so badly that the sheriff ran off rather than face him. But not Andrew Jackson. When Jackson strode out of the courthouse, Bean "looked [Jackson] in the eye and saw shoot." Bean left town rather than face Jackson's wrath. The same strong will that scared off outlaws made Jackson a powerful President.

As Tough as Hickory

Andrew Jackson was the President of the common people. Like many of them, he was born in a log cabin on the frontier—in his case, on the Carolina frontier. Both his parents, immigrants from Ireland, died before Jackson reached age 14. Life was indeed hard for young Andrew, and he grew up quickly.

"He would never stay throwed." By his teens, Jackson had already become a fierce opponent. Even though he was slight of build, he was strong and tireless. As one friend who wrestled with him said, "I could throw him three times out of four, but he would never stay throwed."

Even in more dangerous situations, Jackson showed a tough will. At age 13, he fought as a Patriot in the American Revolution. Early on, he was captured by the British. When a British officer ordered the young prisoner to clean his boots, Jackson proudly refused. The officer slashed his hand and face with a sword. Jackson bore the scars for the rest of his life.

The self-made man. As a young man, Jackson studied law in North Carolina. Later, he moved to the Tennessee frontier and began a law practice. He was soon wealthy enough to buy land and slaves. While still in his twenties, Jackson was elected to Congress.

As you have read, Jackson won national fame during the War of 1812. Under his command, United States troops crushed the British at New Orleans. To settlers on the frontier, Jackson was also a hero of wars against Native Americans. He defeated the Creek Indians at Horseshoe Bend, forcing them to give up millions of acres of land in Georgia and Alabama.

As a general, Jackson was a strong leader with a forceful personality. The Creeks that Jackson defeated called him Sharp Knife. But his own troops gave him another nickname—**Old Hickory.** To them, he was hard and tough as the wood of a hickory tree. The name stuck, and Americans would call him Old Hickory even after he became President.

The Spoils System

President Jackson knew that Americans had high hopes for his administration. "The people expected reform," the new President said. "This was the cry from Maine to Louisiana."

"To the victor belong the spoils." After taking office, Jackson fired many federal employees. Some had held their jobs since the time of George Washington. Jackson replaced them with his own supporters.

Critics said that Jackson gave jobs to Democrats who had helped to elect him, not to people who could do the job well. But Jackson defended the practice. He was giving more people a chance to serve their government, he said.

Jackson also felt that ordinary people could serve their country just as well as the educated and well-bred. "The duties of all public officers," declared Jackson, "are . . . so plain and simple that men of intelligence may readily qualify themselves for their performance."

Jackson was not the first President to give jobs to supporters. But he did so on a larger scale than ever before. One Jackson supporter explained that "to the victor belong the spoils." Spoils are profits or benefits. The name caught on, and the practice of giving jobs to loyal supporters was called the **spoils system.**

Old Hickory *Andrew Jackson was a strong, self-confident man. As President, he greatly increased the prestige and power of the national government.* ***American Traditions*** *What qualities of Jackson's prompted his troops to call him Old Hickory?*

The spoils system helped the Democrats, and later the Whigs, to build up their new political parties. Loyal supporters helped to elect candidates and received jobs in return. For the first time, citizens in cities and towns became full-time politicians. Soon, both political parties relied on these politicians to win elections.

Jackson's cabinet. Jackson rewarded some of his supporters with cabinet jobs. Some critics complained that only Secretary of State Martin Van Buren was qualified for his post.

Jackson seldom met with his official cabinet. Instead, he relied on advice from Democratic leaders and newspaper editors.

The group met in the White House kitchen and soon became known as the kitchen cabinet.

The members of the kitchen cabinet chewed tobacco and spat at the woodstove while they talked over the issues of the day. Despite their rough manners, these men had a good sense of the nation's mood. Some Americans felt that the kitchen cabinet helped Jackson to reach his goal of being President of all the people.

Jackson Battles the Bank

During his first term, President Jackson waged a major battle over the Bank of the United States. Like many people from the West, Jackson disliked the Bank. He thought that it was too powerful.

Jackson's objections. The Bank of the United States controlled loans made by state banks. When the Bank's directors felt that state banks were making too many risky loans, they cut back on the money these banks could loan. The cutbacks hurt farmers, merchants, and others who wanted to borrow money. Westerners especially suffered because they wanted loans to help finance new farms and businesses.

Jackson also objected to the way the Bank was run. Even though Congress had created the Bank for the public good, private bankers directed it. Jackson especially disliked Nicholas Biddle, president of the Bank since 1823.

Biddle stood for everything Jackson and the Democrats mistrusted. He was very well educated, rich, and from a prom-

A Meeting of the Kitchen Cabinet *As President, Jackson relied for advice on an informal group of advisers. A meeting of Jackson's kitchen cabinet, as the group was commonly called, is shown in this cartoon from the period.* **Citizenship** *What was the cartoonist's opinion of Jackson's kitchen cabinet? Explain.*

LIFE · IN · AMERICA

Artist of the American Frontier

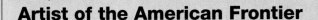

The artist George Caleb Bingham grew up in frontier Missouri during the 1820s. Two great rivers, the Missouri and the Mississippi, gave his home state a sense of endless movement—people and goods constantly coming and going.

Life on the rivers became one of Bingham's favorite subjects. In one of his best-known works, *Fur Traders Descending the Missouri,* two trappers enjoy a quiet moment as they bring their wares to market. Other paintings are action-filled scenes. For example, in *The Jolly Flatboatmen,* shown at right, boatmen on the Mississippi take time out for music and dance.

Politics on the frontier was another of Bingham's favorite subjects. As a citizen, he ran for and won several state offices. As a painter, he captured the drama of frontier elections—the winning and losing, the happiness and despair. In *Canvassing for a Vote,* on page 402, a political hopeful seeks support from local voters.

Whether showing river life or political life, George Caleb Bingham captured the mood of the West. As one art historian said, "More than any other single individual, Bingham gave artistic form to the spirit of the western frontier."

1. What rivers inspired Bingham's work?
2. **Drawing Conclusions** Why are Bingham's paintings important to the study of the history of the frontier?

---

inent family. Jackson was convinced that Biddle used the Bank to profit himself and his rich friends. He was also angry because Biddle used his power to influence members of Congress.

The Bank war. Biddle and other Whigs knew that Jackson disliked the Bank. They feared that the President might find a way to destroy it. Two Whig senators, Henry Clay and Daniel Webster, devised a scheme to save the Bank and weaken Jackson at the same time.

The Bank's charter was not due for renewal by Congress until 1836. But Clay and Webster wanted to make the Bank an issue in the 1832 election. They convinced Biddle to apply for renewal early.

The Whigs were sure that most Americans supported the Bank. Surely, they thought, the people realized that the Bank helped to keep the economy stable. If Jackson vetoed a bill to renew the Bank's charter, he would anger many voters—and, the Whigs believed, lose the election.

Clay pushed the recharter bill through Congress in 1832. Jackson was sick in bed when he heard that Congress had renewed the Bank's charter. "The Bank . . . is trying to kill me," Jackson fumed, "but I will kill it!"

Jackson's veto. Jackson vetoed the Bank bill as soon as it reached his desk. His veto message terrified his foes and thrilled his supporters. In fact, when Nicholas Biddle read the veto message, he said it was like "the fury of a chained panther biting the bars of his cage."

In the message, Jackson gave two reasons for his veto. First, even though the Supreme Court had ruled the Bank constitutional, it was in his opinion not constitutional. Only states, not the federal government, had the right to charter banks. Second, the Bank gave advantages to people who already had wealth and power. It was wrong for government to allow this, Jackson warned:

> ❝When the laws undertake . . . to make the rich richer and the potent more powerful, the humble members of society—the farmers, mechanics, and laborers—who have neither the time nor the means of securing like favors to themselves, have a right to complain of the injustice of their government.❞

The Whigs were sure that Jackson's veto was a blunder. To make the most of the Bank issue, they chose Henry Clay to run against Jackson in 1832. But when the votes were counted, the Whigs were stunned. Jackson won the election by a huge margin. Americans stood behind Jackson's veto of the Bank bill.

The end of the Bank. With its charter vetoed, the Bank was due to close its doors in 1836. But Jackson wanted to send the Bank to an early grave. He ordered the Secretary of the Treasury, Roger Taney, to stop putting government money in the Bank. Taney deposited federal money in state banks instead. These became known as pet banks because Taney and his friends controlled many of them. The loss of federal money crippled the Bank of the United States. As you will read, it also helped to cause an economic crisis in 1837.

SECTION 2 REVIEW

1. **Identify:** (a) Old Hickory, (b) Nicholas Biddle, (c) Roger Taney.
2. **Define:** (a) spoils system, (b) kitchen cabinet, (c) pet bank.

3. List two achievements of Andrew Jackson as a young man.
4. Why did Jackson's critics object to the spoils system?
5. Why did Jackson dislike the Bank of the United States?
6. **Analyzing a Quotation** See the quotation from Jackson's veto message at left. Why do you think the common people might have applauded this part of Jackson's message?

---

3 Jackson Proves His Strength

FIND OUT

◆ Why did the South object to the tariffs of 1828 and 1832?

◆ How did Andrew Jackson respond to the Nullification Crisis?

◆ Why were Native Americans forced to resettle west of the Mississippi River?

◆ VOCABULARY nullification, states' rights, secede

President Jackson's battle against the Bank made him more popular than ever. "The Jackson cause is the cause of democracy and the people," boasted one Democrat. Another supporter praised Jackson's determination:

> ❝Who but General Jackson would have had the courage to veto the bill rechartering the Bank of the United States, and who but General Jackson could have withstood the overwhelming influence of that corrupt Aristocracy?❞

By vetoing the Bank, Jackson showed that he was a strong President. Jackson would face new tests of strength in his second term. His bold actions left the executive branch stronger than when he was elected.

A Strong Leader *Andrew Jackson showed his strong will long before he became President. As a general during the War of 1812, he jailed a judge who challenged his actions. After the war, the judge cited Jackson for contempt of court. Here, Jackson answers the charges.* **Citizenship** *Name an incident from Jackson's presidency that reflects his strong will.*

The Tariff of Abominations

The first crisis of President Jackson's second term centered around the tariff bill passed by Congress in 1828. The tariff was the highest in the nation's history. Southerners called it the **Tariff of Abominations.** An abomination is something that is hated.

Like earlier tariffs, the tariff of 1828 helped northern manufacturers. It made goods imported from Europe cost more than American goods. (See page 383.) But the tariff hurt southern planters. They sold their cotton in Europe and bought European goods in return. The high tariff meant that southerners paid more for these imports.

Calhoun for states' rights. Vice President John C. Calhoun led the South's fight against the tariff. He drew on an idea that Thomas Jefferson had used in the Kentucky and Virginia resolutions. (See page 328.) Like Jefferson, Calhoun argued that a state had the right to cancel a federal law that it considered unconstitutional.

The idea of a state declaring a federal law illegal is called nullification.

Calhoun raised a serious question. Could the states limit the power of the federal government? Or did the federal government have final power over the states? Calhoun pointed out that states had existed *before* the Constitution was ratified in 1788. Since states had in fact created the national government, Calhoun argued, then the states had final authority. He supported states' rights, the right of the states to limit the power of the federal government.

Webster for the Union. Daniel Webster disagreed with Calhoun. In 1830, he attacked nullification on the Senate floor. If states had the right to nullify federal laws, Webster insisted, the national government would be powerless. The states would no longer be united, and the nation would fall apart. The last words of Webster's speech quickly became famous: "Liberty and Union, now and forever, one and inseparable."

Calhoun challenges Jackson. As anger over the tariff grew in the South, people eagerly awaited President Jackson's response. Many southerners hoped that he would support states' rights. After all, Jackson was born in the South and had lived in the West. Both areas strongly supported states' rights. Also, the leading spokesperson for states' rights was Calhoun, Jackson's Vice President.

Jackson's position on states' rights soon became clear. In 1830, Jackson and Calhoun attended a dinner party at the home of a southern member of Congress. Several guests made toasts that praised states' rights. Finally, Jackson rose. The room fell silent. Old Hickory raised his glass, looked Vice President Calhoun in the eye and said, "Our Federal Union—it must be preserved!"

The drama continued when Calhoun raised his glass. "The Union—next to our liberty, most dear," he replied. With these words, Calhoun clearly challenged Jackson. To him, the liberty of a state was more important than saving the Union.

The debate between supporters of states' rights and defenders of the Union would rage on for years. Because he did not agree with Jackson, Calhoun resigned from the office of Vice President. He was then elected senator from South Carolina. Martin Van Buren became Jackson's Vice President in 1833.

A Crisis Over Nullification

Congress passed a new tariff in 1832. It was slightly lower than the Tariff of Abominations, but South Carolina was not satisfied. It passed the Nullification Act, which declared the tariffs of 1828 and 1832 illegal. At the same time, the state prepared to defend itself. It threatened to secede, or withdraw, from the Union if challenged.

Jackson was enraged when he heard the news from South Carolina. "If one drop of blood be shed there in defiance of the laws of the United States," he declared, "I will hang the first man of them I can get my hands on to the first tree I can

find." Jackson knew that nullification threatened to destroy the nation. "It leads directly to civil war and bloodshed," he said privately.

Officially, the President was more practical. He supported a compromise tariff that Henry Clay had proposed. The bill called for lower tariffs. But at the same time, Jackson asked Congress to pass a force bill. The bill allowed him to use the army, if necessary, to enforce the law in South Carolina.

Jackson's firm stand worked. Faced with the threat of war, no other state supported South Carolina. Calhoun gave in and agreed to Clay's compromise tariff. And South Carolina repealed the Nullification Act.

Because of the President's strong leadership, the **Nullification Crisis** passed. Yet the differences between the North and South would only increase. In the next great crisis, 30 years later, South Carolina would not stand alone.

Tragedy for Native Americans

Jackson's firm stand on another issue had tragic results for Native Americans. Since Europeans first arrived in North America, they had steadily pushed Native Americans off their land. From New York to Florida, Indians were forced to move west. Indian leaders like Pontiac and Tecumseh tried to stop settlers from invading their lands. But these efforts ended in defeat, and the long retreat continued.

The Southeast nations. By the 1820s, only about 125,000 Indians still lived east of the Mississippi. Most belonged to the Creek, Chickasaw, Cherokee, Choctaw, and Seminole nations. The people of these five nations lived on the fertile lands of the Southeast. Many had adopted customs of white settlers.

Sequoyah (sih KWOI uh), a Cherokee born in Tennessee, created a written alphabet for his people. Using Sequoyah's letters, Cherokee children learned to read and write. The Cherokees also used his alphabet to write a constitution and publish a newspaper.

The Cherokees and other Indians hoped to live in peace with their white neighbors. But the land they owned and lived on was ideal for growing cotton. Land-hungry settlers wanted to cultivate that valuable land for themselves.

President Jackson sympathized with the settlers and took actions to help them. Early in his first term, he urged Congress to set aside land west of the Mississippi for Native Americans. The southeastern Indians, Jackson believed, would then "voluntarily" move to the lands reserved for them.

The Cherokees win a lawsuit. Not long after Jackson took office, the state of Georgia claimed the right to seize Cherokee lands. The Cherokees went to court to defend their land. William Wirt, one of the nation's best lawyers, handled their case.

In court, the Cherokees pointed out that they had signed a treaty with the federal government that protected their land. Therefore, they argued, Georgia had no right to take their property. When the case reached the Supreme Court, Chief Justice John Marshall and the Court upheld the right of the Cherokees to keep their land.

In the Nullification Crisis, Jackson strongly supported the power of the federal government. But this time, he defended states' rights. He said that the federal government could not stop Georgia from moving Native Americans. "John Marshall has made his decision," Jackson reportedly said. "Now let him enforce it." The President then refused to use his power to carry out the Court's decision and protect the Cherokees.

Congress supports removal. Since the Supreme Court ruling was not enforced, Native Americans had no protection. In 1830, Congress passed the **Indian Removal Act.** It stated that Native Americans had to move west of the Mississippi. Most Americans had heard that land there was a vast desert. So they did not mind turning it over to the Indians.

Removal or Death

The Cherokees and other Indian nations did not want to move west of the Mississippi. But they had no choice. Between 1835 and 1838, the United States army forced them to leave at gunpoint. Their long, sorrowful journey west became known as the **Trail of Tears.** One eyewitness described the scene:

The Trail of Tears *The Supreme Court ruled that the Cherokees had a right to keep their land. But President Jackson disagreed. Here, the Cherokees make their way west on the Trail of Tears.* **Citizenship** *How did Jackson justify his refusal to enforce the Court's ruling?*

"The Cherokees are nearly all prisoners. They had been dragged from their homes and encamped at the forts and military places, all over the nation. In Georgia especially, multitudes were allowed no time to take anything with them except the clothes they had on. . . . The property of many has been taken and sold before their eyes for almost nothing."

Native Americans marched hundreds of miles to lands they had never seen before. (See the map below.) They had little food or shelter. Thousands perished during the march, mostly children and the elderly.

In Florida, the Seminole Indians fought fiercely against removal. They were led by Chief Osceola (ahs ee OH luh). The Seminoles battled the United States army from 1835 to 1842. In the end, they were defeated. But the **Seminole War** was the most

MAP STUDY

In the 1830s, some 100,000 southeastern Indians were driven from their homes and forced to march to Indian Territory, west of the Mississippi.
1. What five southeastern nations marched to Indian Territory?
2. How many miles (km) did the Cherokees have to walk on this Trail of Tears?
3. **Geography** Why were many Americans willing to give Native Americans the land called Indian Territory?

INDIAN REMOVAL

A N • AMERICAN • PORTRAIT

Osceola: Fighter Against Indian Removal

In 1813, Osceola, then 10 years old, watched young Creek men leave his village in Alabama. Sometime earlier, the great Shawnee chief Tecumseh had visited the boy's people. Tecumseh urged the Creeks to fight white settlers and to defend their homelands. Now his people were going off to war. How the boy wished he could go, too!

In the battles that followed, General Andrew Jackson's forces outnumbered the Creeks. The Creek people were forced by the federal government to give up two thirds of their land and live elsewhere. Osceola fled with his mother and joined the Seminoles in Florida.

Over the years, Osceola became a bold leader. In 1835, when the federal government ordered the Seminoles to leave Florida, Osceola took a firm stand. He vowed to lead his warriors in a fight against yet another removal. Florida soon became a battleground for Seminoles and United States troops.

By 1837, Osceola's men were exhausted. Waving a white flag of surrender, Osceola approached an army fort to make a truce. He was promptly captured and put in prison. There, he became ill and died. In time, Seminole resistance crumbled, too.

1. Why did Osceola resettle in Florida with the Seminoles?

2. **Making Decisions** Why do you think Osceola decided to fight rather than leave Florida?

costly battle the government fought to gain Indian lands. By 1844, only a few thousand Native Americans still lived east of the Mississippi River.

SECTION 3 REVIEW

1. **Locate:** (a) South Carolina, (b) Georgia, (c) Mississippi River.
2. **Identify:** (a) Tariff of Abominations, (b) John C. Calhoun, (c) Nullification Crisis, (d) Indian Removal Act, (e) Trail of Tears, (f) Seminole War.
3. **Define:** (a) nullification, (b) states' rights, (c) secede.
4. Why did the South oppose high tariffs?
5. What action did President Jackson take in the Nullification Crisis?
6. (a) How did the Cherokees try to protect their land? (b) Why did they fail?
7. **Making Decisions** Why do you think Andrew Jackson supported states' rights in the Cherokee case but not in the Nullification Crisis?

4 Jackson's Successors

FIND OUT

◆ What caused an economic depression in 1837?

◆ What were the effects of the depression?

◆ Why did William Henry Harrison's campaign for President succeed?

◆ What problems did President Tyler face?

After serving two terms, a weary Andrew Jackson retired from politics. Jackson's close friend and Vice President, Martin Van Buren, followed him into the White House.

When Van Buren took the oath of office in March 1837, Jackson stood at his side. Onlookers fixed their gaze on the outgoing President, not on Van Buren. As Old Hickory stepped down from the platform, a rousing cheer rose from the crowd. In that roar, the people expressed their respect and admiration for Andrew Jackson.

Even though he was a Democrat, Martin Van Buren was very different from Jackson. He was famous as a shrewd politician, not as a war hero. Davy Crockett, a member of Congress from Tennessee, once described Van Buren as "an artful, cunning, intriguing, selfish, speculating lawyer." But as President, Van Buren would face a crisis that not even the sharpest politician could solve.

The Economy Collapses

Martin Van Buren entered office on a wave of popular support. But within two months, he faced the worst economic crisis the nation had known—the **Panic of 1837.**

Causes of the Panic. Several factors caused the Panic of 1837. Besides the tariff, land sales were the main source of government income at the time. During the 1830s, the government sold millions of acres of public land in the West. Farmers bought some land, but speculators bought even more.

To pay for the land, speculators borrowed money from state banks, especially in the West. As you have read, there was no longer a national bank to limit lending because Jackson had vetoed the renewal of the Bank of the United States.

To meet the demand for loans, state banks printed more and more paper money. Often, the paper money was not backed by gold or silver. So the paper money was no longer as valuable or secure as it had been under the national Bank.

In 1836, President Jackson had become alarmed at the wild land speculation. To slow it down, he ordered that anyone buying public land had to pay with gold or silver, not with the less secure paper money. Speculators and others rushed to trade their paper money for gold and silver. But they found that the banks did not have enough gold and silver.

The Panic. Very quickly, the Panic began. More and more people hurried to banks to try to exchange paper money for gold and silver. In New York, one bank "was jammed with depositors crying 'Pay, pay!'" a witness said. Hundreds of banks failed, leaving depositors empty-handed.

The Panic was made worse by another factor. The price of cotton was falling because of an oversupply. Cotton planters, who often borrowed money before they sold their crop, were unable to pay back the loans. As a result, more banks failed. Business slowed, and the nation plunged into a deep economic depression.

Three years of depression. In the worst days of the economic depression, 90 percent of the nation's factories were closed. Thousands of people were out of work. In

The Long Bill *Ordinary people suffered greatly because of the Panic of 1837. People had bought on credit, confident that they could pay later. Now, many people, like the general-store customer shown here, faced a "long bill" that they did not know how to pay.* **Economics** *How did the sale of western lands contribute to the Panic of 1837?*

some cities, hungry crowds broke into warehouses and stole food.

Even though he was a skillful politician, Van Buren could not avoid blame for the Panic. A die-hard Democrat, he refused to interfere with the economy, even during hard times. So Van Buren did little to ease the impact of the Panic.

To show his concern, Van Buren did cut back expenses at the White House. For example, when he entertained guests, they were served simple dinners. But as the depression dragged on, Van Buren became less popular.

William Henry Harrison for President

The Whigs had learned a lesson from their defeats by Andrew Jackson in the elections of 1828 and 1832. To win a presidential election, they would need the vote of the common people. So in 1840, the Whigs chose a popular war hero, William Henry Harrison of Ohio, to run for President. Harrison was well-known for winning the Battle of Tippecanoe. (See page 353.) As their candidate for Vice President, the Whigs chose John Tyler.

The Democrats renominated President Van Buren, even though he had lost a great deal of support. By 1840, Vice President Richard Johnson had grown so unpopular that he failed to gain renomination. Van Buren became the only candidate for President to seek election without a running mate.

The Log Cabin Campaign of 1840

With a candidate as popular as William Henry Harrison, the Whigs were sure that they could win the election of 1840. Chanting the slogan "Tippecanoe and Tyler too," they set out to win the office of President from Martin Van Buren.

Attacks on Van Buren. Much of the Whig attack consisted of name-calling. Martin Van "Ruin," Whigs charged, had brought on the Panic of 1837 and the depression that followed. "King Mat," they sneered, was a "democratic peacock, plumed, perfumed, and strutting around the White House." Daniel Webster, a Whig supporter, joked that the Democrats had replaced "Old Hickory" Jackson with "Slippery Elm" Van Buren.

Half-truths or lies were still another tactic. One Whig paper spread the lie that

Van Buren spent "thousands of the people's dollars" to install a *bathtub* in the White House.

Harrison, the common man. At the same time, Whigs presented their candidate, William Henry Harrison, as a man of the people. Harrison, they boasted, was not only a military man, but a frontiersman—a humble Ohio farmer who lived in a log cabin. In fact, Harrison was a wealthy and educated man from Virginia who lived on an estate.

The log cabin quickly became the symbol of the Whig campaign. One typical Whig cartoon showed Harrison as the "log cabin, hard cider" candidate. In the cartoon, Harrison stands before his log cabin and greets Van Buren and his aides:

❝Gentlemen. . . . If you will accept the fare of a log cabin, with a western farmer's cheer, you are welcome. I have no champaigne but can give you a mug of good cider, with some ham and eggs, and good clean beds. I am a plain backwoodsman. I have cleared some land, killed some Indians, and made the Red Coats fly in my time.**❞**

Harrison's campaign trail. Harrison was the first candidate for President to make his own campaign speeches. He traveled across the nation, greeting the voters. They, in turn, admired his informal style.

Along the campaign trail, Whigs built log cabins for their headquarters, even in

General Harrison's Log Cabin March *With the slogan "Tippecanoe and Tyler too," William Henry Harrison set out to capture the presidency from Martin Van "Ruin." The symbol of Harrison's campaign was the log cabin, meant to show that the wealthy, rather elegant Harrison was a man of the people.* **Linking Past and Present** *Could the techniques of the Harrison campaign be used today? Explain.*

large cities like New York. In parades, they sometimes carried the log cabins on wagons. Everywhere the campaign went, there was plenty of free cider for all.

"Keep the ball rolling." The people themselves often took part in Harrison rallies. They gave speeches and marched in parades. Many enjoyed joining in a campaign song:

> **"**The times are bad, and want curing;
> They are getting past all enduring;
> So let's turn out Martin Van Buren
> And put in old Tippecanoe!**"**

From one town to the next, Harrison supporters rolled huge balls down the streets. The balls were 12 feet in diameter, made of twine, and covered with slogans. "Keep the ball rolling," supporters chanted as they marched.

For many, campaign souvenirs were an attraction. Merchants sold badges, handkerchiefs, and even shaving cream bearing the slogan "Tippecanoe and Tyler too!" Among the most popular souvenirs was a bottle shaped like a miniature log cabin.

Even though they could not vote, women played a major role in the Harrison campaign. They wrote pamphlets, sewed banners, rode on floats, and paraded with brooms to "sweep" the Democrats out of office. The sashes of many a young woman read, "Whig husbands or none."

A Whig victory at last. The Democrats tried to stem the tide of Harrison's popularity with their own clever insults. "Granny Harrison, the Petticoat General," had resigned from the army before the War of 1812 even ended, Democrats teased. Using another nickname, they accused "General Mum" of not speaking out on the issues. Should Harrison be elected? Democrats asked voters. "Read his name spelled backwards," they advised. "No sirrah."

In the end, the Whig strategy succeeded. Harrison won easily and forced the Democrats out of the White House for the first time in 12 years. "We have taught them how to conquer us!" lamented one Democrat. "We've been sung down," another complained.(📖 See "Campaign Hoopla" on page 676.) ◆

Whigs in the White House

The Whigs arrived in Washington with a clear-cut program. They wanted to create a new Bank of the United States. With federal money, they planned to improve roads and canals. And they wanted a high tariff.

Whig hopes soon were dashed. After less than a month in office, President Harrison died of pneumonia. John Tyler became the first Vice President to succeed a President who had died in office.

As President, Tyler bitterly disappointed the Whigs. Tyler had once been a Democrat. He disagreed with Whig plans for the government to develop the economy. When Whigs in Congress passed a bill to revive the Bank of the United States, Tyler vetoed it. This reminded Whigs of their enemy, Andrew Jackson.

Soon, Tyler's whole cabinet resigned, except for Daniel Webster. The Whigs even ousted Tyler from their party. Democrats were delighted to see the Whigs squabbling. "Tyler is heartily despised by everyone," reported one. "He has no influence at all." With few friends in either party, Tyler could do little during his one term in office.

SECTION 4 REVIEW

1. **Identify:** Panic of 1837.
2. How did President Jackson's actions help to cause the Panic of 1837?
3. How did the oversupply of cotton deepen the depression?
4. Why did the Whigs select William Henry Harrison as their candidate for President in 1840?
5. How did John Tyler disappoint the Whigs?
6. **Synthesizing Information** Why do you think the log cabin was a successful campaign symbol for Harrison?

Political cartoons can tell you a great deal about the past. For many years, cartoonists have tried to influence public feeling about important issues.

To help present their views, cartoonists may exaggerate the facts. For example, a cartoonist might draw a nose too large in order to focus on a well-known person's physical features. For this reason, a cartoon can often make a point more strongly than words alone can.

Study the cartoon at left, which was published in the 1830s. Ask yourself what point the cartoonist was trying to make about Andrew Jackson. Then, answer the following questions.

BORN TO COMMAND.

VETO.

CONSTITUTION of the UNITED STATES of America

Internal Improvements

U.S. Bank

KING ANDREW THE FIRST.

1 **Identify the symbols used in the cartoon.** Cartoons often use symbols. A **symbol** is something that stands for something else. For example, a skull and crossbones is a symbol for death. A dove is a symbol for peace. To understand a cartoon, you must know what its symbols mean.

Figure out what the symbols in this cartoon stand for. (a) Who is pictured in the cartoon? (b) What is he holding in each hand? (c) What do these symbols stand for? (d) What is he wearing on his head? (e) What does this symbol stand for? (f) What is he standing on?

2 **Analyze the meaning of the symbols.** Use your reading of this chapter and the cartoon to decide what the symbols refer to. (a) What incident is probably referred to by the object in Jackson's left hand? (b) What event might the cartoonist have had in mind when he showed Jackson standing on the Constitution?

3 **Interpret the cartoon.** Draw conclusions about the cartoonist's point of view. (a) What do you think the cartoonist thought of President Jackson? Why? (b) How was the cartoonist trying to influence the public's attitude toward Jackson? (c) Does the cartoon give a balanced view of Jackson as President? Explain.

Use the Section Reviews and this Study Guide to review chapter content.

Main Ideas

The main ideas in each section of this chapter are summarized below.

SECTION 1 ■ The People's President

◆ The House of Representatives chose John Quincy Adams for President.
◆ Congress turned down most of President Adams's programs for national growth.
◆ In the 1820s, all white men over age 21 gained the right to vote in several states.

SECTION 2 ■ New Mood in the White House

◆ President Andrew Jackson was a self-made man, a war hero, and a strong leader.
◆ Through the spoils system, Jackson rewarded supporters with government jobs.
◆ Jackson vetoed the bill to recharter the Bank of the United States.

SECTION 3 ■ Jackson Proves His Strength

◆ The tariffs of 1828 and 1832 helped the North and hurt the South.
◆ Congress passed a compromise tariff and a force bill when South Carolina threatened to secede.
◆ The Indian Removal Act supported land-hungry settlers and forced Native Americans to move west of the Mississippi.

SECTION 4 ■ Jackson's Successors

◆ After the Panic of 1837, the nation slipped into an economic depression.
◆ William Henry Harrison won the vote of the common people in the election of 1840.
◆ President John Tyler disagreed with Whig plans for government to develop the economy.

Key People and Terms

Refer to the Identify and Define questions in the Section Reviews on pages 408, 412, 417, and 421. Use each person, term, and vocabulary word in a complete sentence. When possible, make connections between the people and terms by using more than one person or term in a sentence.

Time Line

1. Make a chart of events in time order. The chart will have two headings: Date, Event. Fill in the chart, using the events on the time line. Add the following events from the chapter: Daniel Webster attacks nullification; Martin Van Buren takes oath as President; three times more people vote than in 1824; Trail of Tears begins. (Refer to the chapter for the dates.)
2. Which event on your chart was the cause of the Trail of Tears?

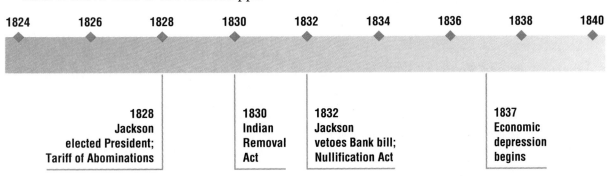

1824 1826 1828 1830 1832 1834 1836 1838 1840

1828
Jackson
elected President;
Tariff of Abominations

1830
Indian
Removal
Act

1832
Jackson
vetoes Bank bill;
Nullification Act

1837
Economic
depression
begins

CHAPTER 13 REVIEW

Understanding Vocabulary

Match each term at left with the correct definition at right.

1. suffrage
2. caucus
3. nullification
4. states' rights
5. secede

a. private meeting to choose a candidate
b. right to vote
c. right of states to limit federal power
d. idea of declaring a federal law illegal
e. withdraw

Reviewing the Main Ideas

1. (a) What were President John Quincy Adams's programs for national growth? (b) Were his plans carried out? Explain.
2. (a) What political parties had formed by 1832? (b) Who supported each party?
3. (a) What is a nominating convention? (b) Why is it more democratic than a caucus?
4. How did Jackson defend his practice of giving government jobs to supporters?
5. What role did each of the following play in the battle over the Bank of the United States: (a) Henry Clay; (b) Nicholas Biddle; (c) Andrew Jackson?
6. (a) What was the Nullification Crisis? (b) How did President Jackson handle the crisis?
7. (a) Why did settlers want to force Native Americans to move west? (b) How did Andrew Jackson help the settlers achieve their goal?
8. (a) What were the causes of the Panic of 1837? (b) What was its effect?

Thinking Critically

1. **Linking Past and Present** (a) What group of Americans gained more rights in the 1820s? (b) What groups have gained more rights since then?
2. **Synthesizing Information** Why was Jackson considered the people's President? Explain.
3. **Distinguishing Fact From Opinion** Study the quotation about General Jackson on page 412 at bottom right. Is this statement a fact or an opinion? Explain.
4. **Making Decisions** Why do you think Jackson decided that the Union must be preserved at all cost? Explain.

Applying Your Skills

1. **Reading a Political Cartoon** Review Skill Lesson 13 on page 422. Then, study the cartoon on page 410. (a) Where does the cartoon take place? (b) What symbols does the cartoonist use to identify the place? (c) Who are the people in the cartoon? (d) What are they doing? (e) How might the cartoon have influenced public opinion?
2. **Comparing** Prepare a chart with two columns and three rows. Label the columns John Quincy Adams and Andrew Jackson. Label the rows Family, Education, Experience in Public Life. Fill out the chart. (a) What were the differences between Adams and Jackson? (b) How do the differences show the changes in American politics in the 1820s?
3. **Identifying the Main Idea** Review the subsection "A Growing Spirit of Equality" on pages 406–408. (a) What is the main idea of each paragraph? (b) What is the main idea of the entire subsection?

Thinking About Geography

Match the letters on the map with the places listed below.

1. Indian Territory
2. Chickasaw
3. Choctaw
4. Creek
5. Cherokee
6. Seminole

Place Why did settlers want Cherokee land in the Southeast?

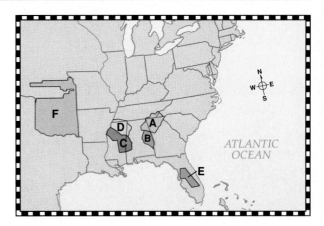

History Writer's Workshop

Writing a Bibliography for a Report

A report should include a bibliography. The bibliography is a list of all sources used in preparing the report or quoted in it. It is usually written on a separate page and placed at the end of the report.

List the sources in your bibliography in alphabetical order by authors' last names. When there is more than one source by the same author, arrange these sources alphabetically by title under the author's name. Also alphabetize unsigned books or articles by title. Be sure to include complete information about each source.

Study the sample bibliography entries for style and punctuation. Note the indent after the first line of each entry.

Source	Bibliography entry
Book	Josephy, Alvin M., Jr. *Indian Heritage of America.* New York: Knopf, 1968.
Encyclopedia article	*The World Book Encyclopedia,* 1990 ed., "Cherokee."
Magazine article	Maddox, C. "On the Cherokee Trail of Tears." *Southern Living,* September 1988, p. 18.

Practice Locate in the library two books and an encyclopedia article about Andrew Jackson. Write a bibliography entry for each.

Writing to Learn

1. Imagine that you are a Cherokee on the Trail of Tears. Write a brief story about your experiences. First, freewrite about what occurred and how you reacted. In your first draft, compose a topic sentence that will arouse a reader's curiosity. Then, organize your details logically. Revise for unity and coherence. Then, proofread and make a final copy. Read your story to the class.

2. Imagine that you are President John Quincy Adams. Write a short speech that defends federal government spending on a national university and an observatory for astronomers. Begin by brainstorming a list of benefits these projects would offer. In your first draft, write a topic sentence that states why the government should fund these projects. Then, organize the benefits in order of importance. When you revise, be sure that all your points support your topic sentence. Proofread and make a final copy. Then, deliver your speech to the class.

Westward Ho! *Attracted by the promise of rich farmland, thousands of Americans packed up their belongings in covered wagons and headed west. Here, a wagon train stops for rest.* **Daily Life** *How do you think pioneers got food and water along the journey?*

CHAPTER

14

From Sea to Shining Sea (1820–1860)

The Big Picture

In the 1800s, thousands of Americans left their homes and moved west. Some traveled to Oregon or California. Others colonized Texas. Still others moved into the area between the Rocky Mountains and the Sierra Nevada. In time, the boundaries of the United States stretched to the Pacific Ocean.

This movement of pioneers had other effects, too. Native Americans and people of Spanish descent had long made their homes in the Southwest and West. With the arrival of large numbers of Americans, the way of life of these peoples was disrupted forever.

Kathleen Underwood

Of Special Interest

Focus On

◆ Who settled Oregon Country?

◆ How was the Republic of Texas formed?

◆ What was the Manifest Destiny of the United States?

◆ What happened during the Mexican War?

◆ What drew settlers to Utah and California?

"Last spring, 1846, was a busy season in the city of St. Louis. Not only were emigrants from every part of the country preparing for the journey to Oregon and California, but an unusual number of traders were making ready their wagons and outfits for Santa Fe. The hotels were crowded, and the gunsmiths and saddlers were kept constantly at work in providing arms and equipments for the different parties of travellers. Steamboats were leaving the [dock] and passing up the Missouri, crowded with passengers on their way to the frontier."

As American historian Francis Parkman noted in this opening of *The Oregon Trail,* St. Louis bustled with activity in the spring of 1846. Like Parkman, thousands of Americans had gathered in the city, ready to head west.

Moving west was not at all new to Americans. After all, the nation had begun as a string of colonies dotting the Atlantic coast. As the colonies grew, they spread inland, across the Appalachians to the Mississippi.

By the 1830s, Americans had filled up the land east of the Mississippi and were looking for new frontiers. Hardy settlers pushed west once more, into Texas, New Mexico, California, and Oregon. By 1850, Americans had expanded the borders of the United States until they reached "from sea to shining sea."

1 Oregon Fever

FIND OUT

◆ Why did the United States and Britain agree to share Oregon Country?

◆ Why did Mountain Men go to the Far West?

◆ What hardships did travelers face on the Oregon Trail?

◆ **VOCABULARY** rendezvous

In 1846, a New York newspaper editor named Horace Greeley published an article titled "To Aspiring Young Men." In it, Greeley offered the following advice:

> ❝If you have no family or friends to aid you, . . . turn your face to the great West and there build up your home and fortune.❞

Greeley's advice exactly suited the spirit of the times. Soon, his statement was shortened to four simple words: "Go West, young man." Thousands of Americans rallied to the cry "Westward Ho!"

GEOGRAPHY AND HISTORY

Oregon Country: A Varied Land

By the 1820s, Americans occupied much of the land between the Appalachians and the Mississippi River. Families in search of good farmland continued to move west. Few, however, settled on the Great Plains between the Mississippi and the Rockies. Instead, they were drawn to lands in the Far West.

Americans first heard about Oregon Country in the early 1800s. **Oregon Country** was the huge area beyond the Rockies. Today, this land includes Oregon, Washing-ton, Idaho, and parts of Wyoming, Montana, and Canada. (See the map on page 432.)

The land early settlers called Oregon Country has a varied geography. Along the Pacific coast, the soil is fertile and rainfall is plentiful. The Pacific Ocean keeps temperatures mild all year round. Early white settlers found fine farmland in the Willamette River valley and the lowlands around Puget Sound. Trappers were lured by bear and beaver that filled the dense forests of coastal mountains farther inland.

Between the coastal mountains and the Rockies is a high plateau. This Intermountain region is much drier than the coast and has some desert areas. Temperatures are also more extreme here.

The Rocky Mountains formed the eastern boundary of Oregon Country. As in the coastal range, beaver and other fur-bearing animals roamed the Rockies in the 1800s. As a result, trappers flocked to the area. ◆

Competing Claims

In the early 1800s, four countries claimed Oregon. They were the United States, Great Britain, Spain, and Russia. Of course, Native Americans who lived in Oregon believed that the land belonged to them. They had lived in Oregon and controlled those lands for thousands of years. But the United States and competing European nations gave no thought to Indian rights.

The United States based its claim to Oregon on the voyage of Robert Gray, a sea captain from Boston. Gray visited the coast of Oregon and named the Columbia River in 1792. Americans pointed to the journey of Lewis and Clark through Oregon as further support for their claims to the land.

In 1811, an American fur trader named John Jacob Astor sent a shipload of men and supplies around South America to Oregon. The men built the town of Astoria at the mouth of the Columbia River. Astor's fur traders stayed only a short time, but they gave Americans another claim to Oregon.

The British claim to Oregon dated back to a visit by Sir Francis Drake in 1579. By the early 1800s, many British fur traders had made their way to Oregon. And Fort Vancouver, built by the British close to present-day Portland, was the only permanent outpost in Oregon Country.

In 1818, the United States and Britain reached an agreement. The two countries would occupy Oregon jointly. Citizens of each nation would have equal rights in Oregon. Spain and Russia had few settlers in the area and agreed to drop their claims.

Fur Trappers in the Far West

At first, the only Europeans or Americans who settled in Oregon Country were a few hardy trappers. These adventurous men hiked through Oregon's vast forests, trapping animals and living off the land. They were known as **Mountain Men.**

Lives filled with danger. Mountain Men could make a small fortune trapping beaver in Rocky Mountain streams. But they led dangerous lives. Bears, wildcats, and poisonous snakes lurked in the forests where they hunted. And Indians sometimes attacked Mountain Men for trapping on Indian hunting grounds.

Mountain Men were usually young and fearless. They wore shirts and trousers made of animal hides and decorated with porcupine quills. Their hair hung to their shoulders, and pistols and tomahawks peeked out from their belts. Around their necks dangled a "possibles sack," filled with a pipe, some tobacco, a mold to make bullets, and other items of "possible" use.

Living off the land. In warm weather, when game was plentiful, Mountain Men gorged themselves with food. A trapper remembered one meal of "buffalo tongues, dry buffalo meat, fresh venison, wheat flour cakes, buffalo marrow (for butter), sugar, coffee, and rum." But during lean times, trappers ate almost anything. "I have held my hands in an anthill until they were covered with ants, then greedily licked them off," another Mountain Man recalled.

Trappers often spent winters in Native American villages. In fact, they learned many of their trapping skills and survival methods from Indians, especially the Indian women they married.

Trading furs. During the fall and spring, Mountain Men tended their traps. Then, in July, they tramped out of the wilderness, ready to meet the fur traders. They headed to a place chosen the year before, called the

Trading at Fort Laramie *Fort Laramie, on the Platte River, was an important trading site. This painting by Alfred Jacob Miller shows the interior of the fort.* ***Geography*** *Why do you think a fort was a good meeting place for trappers and traders?*

AN·AMERICAN·PORTRAIT

James Beckwourth: Mountain Man, Scout, Pioneer

James Beckwourth was one of the boldest and most daring Mountain Men. Beckwourth was born in 1798, the son of a Virginia slave woman and a wealthy white planter. All during his boyhood, he thrilled to stories of his father's exploits as a major in the American Revolution. At age 20, yearning for adventures of his own, Beckwourth set out for the West.

Beckwourth soon excelled in all the skills the wilderness demanded—marksmanship, hunting, trapping, and tracking. Sometimes, he worked as a fur trapper and trader. Other times, he guided wagon trains traveling west.

One day, Beckwourth and a band of traders found themselves surrounded by a war party of Crow Indians. Luckily, the Crows mistook Beckwourth for a chief's son who had been kidnapped as a baby. Instead of killing the trappers, the Crows made Beckwourth a chief and took him to live with them for the next 10 years!

After leaving the Crows, Beckwourth served as an army scout and ran trading posts in the Rocky Mountains. Around 1850, he discovered a pass in the Sierra Nevada. Beckwourth Pass, as it is still called, opened a major route to California.

In later years, Beckwourth finally settled down in a cabin at Beckwourth Pass. Each night, he entertained visitors with stories of his "career of wild adventure and thrilling romance." In the late 1860s, when he felt his life ebbing, Beckwourth returned to the Crows and died among them.

1. What skills helped Beckwourth to survive in the wilderness?

2. **Linking Past and Present** Why are mountain passes less important for travel today than in the 1800s?

rendezvous (RAHN day voo). Rendezvous is a French word meaning get-together.

For trappers, the first day of the rendezvous was a time to have fun. A visitor to one rendezvous captured the excitement:

❝[The trappers] engaged in contests of skill at running, jumping, wrestling, shooting with the rifle, and running horses. . . . They sang, they laughed, they whooped; they tried to out-brag and out-lie each other in stories of their adventures and achievements. Here the . . . trappers were in all their glory.❞

After the "laughing and whooping" were done, trappers settled down to bargain with the traders. Beaver hats were in great demand in the East and in Europe, so the

Mountain Men got a good price for their furs. "With their hairy bank notes, the beaver skins, they can obtain all the luxuries of the mountains, and live for a few days like lords," one visitor said of the trappers.

Still, traders charged high prices for the bullets, fishhooks, knives, scissors, and other goods they hauled to the rendezvous. Often, trappers spent more than their furs were worth.

By the late 1830s, the fur trade was dying out. Trappers had killed so many beavers that the animals grew scarce. Also, beaver hats went out of style. But the Mountain Men found that their skills and knowledge were still in demand. Some took on a new job—leading settlers across the rugged trails into Oregon.

Mountain Men Explore New Lands

In their search for furs, Mountain Men explored much new territory in the West. They often followed Indian trails across the Rockies and through mountain passes. Later, they showed these trails to settlers moving west.

For example, Jedediah Smith led white settlers across the Rockies through South Pass, in present-day Wyoming. Manuel Lisa, a Spanish American trapper, led a trip up the Missouri River in 1807. He founded Fort Manuel, the first outpost on the upper Missouri. At least one Mountain "Man" was a woman. Marie Dorion, an Iowa Indian, first went to Oregon with fur traders in 1811. She won fame across the nation for her survival skills.

Missionaries in Oregon

The first white Americans to build permanent homes in Oregon Country were missionaries. Among these, Marcus and Narcissa Whitman led the way. The couple married in 1836 and set out for Oregon, where they planned to convert local Native Americans to Christianity. The seven-month journey to the West was their honeymoon.

Few white women before Narcissa Whitman had crossed the Rocky Mountains. In a letter to her mother, Whitman told about hardships on the trail. She woke before dawn, rode all day, ate dry buffalo meat, and slept on the ground. But Whitman added:

> ❝Do not think I regret coming. No, far from it. I would not go back for a world. I am contented and happy notwithstanding I get very hungry and weary.❞

Arriving in Oregon, the Whitmans built their mission near the Columbia River. They set out to work with the Cayuse (KĪ oos) Indians. Marcus Whitman was a doctor. Narcissa Whitman ran the mission school. Soon, other settlers joined the Whitmans. They took over Indian lands for their houses and farms.

In 1847, tragedy struck. An outbreak of measles among the settlers spread to the Indians. Dr. Whitman tended both white and Indian children, but many Cayuses died. The Cayuses blamed the settlers for

Narcissa Whitman *Narcissa Whitman and her missionary husband were among the first white settlers of Oregon Country. Their homestead was a welcome sight for the thousands of pioneers who soon followed on the Oregon Trail.* **Geography** *How did the land and climate of Oregon Country make it favorable for settlement?*

bringing the disease, which was new to them. A band of angry Cayuses attacked the mission, killing the Whitmans and 12 other settlers.

A Flood of Settlers

Despite the Whitmans' deaths, the settlement in Oregon grew. News about Oregon Country trickled back to the United States. There, farmers marveled at stories of wheat that grew taller than a man and Oregon turnips five feet around. "Oregon Fever" broke out. Soon, pioneers clogged the trails west. Beginning in 1843, wagon trains left every spring for Oregon. The route they followed was called the **Oregon Trail.** (See the map on page 441.)

Families planning to go west met at Independence, Missouri, in the early spring. They camped outside town with their cattle and other animals. When enough families had gathered, they formed a wagon train. Each group elected leaders to make decisions along the way.

Wagon Trains West

Oregon-bound pioneers hurried to leave Independence in May. Timing was important. Travelers had to reach Oregon by early October, before snow began to fall in the mountains. This meant that pioneers had to cover 2,000 miles (3,200 km) on foot in five months!

Life on the trail. Once on the trail, pioneer families woke to a bugle blast at dawn. Each person had a job to do. Young girls helped their mothers prepare breakfast. Men and boys harnessed the horses and oxen. By 6:00 A.M., the cry of "Wagons Ho!" rang out across the plains.

Wagon trains stopped for a brief meal at noon. Then, it was back on the trail until 6:00 or 7:00 P.M. At night, wagons were drawn up in a circle to keep the cattle from wandering off.

Most pioneer families set out on the journey west with a lot of heavy gear. But they soon found that it was dangerous to cross streams and scale mountains with overloaded wagons. So travelers often threw things away. Soon, the Oregon Trail was littered with junk. One traveler found the trail strewn with "blacksmiths' anvils, ploughs, large grind-stones, baking ovens, kegs, barrels, harness, [and] clothing." Some pioneers changed dirty clothes for clean sets found along the trail. Others used the "plains library." They picked up a book, read it, then left it beside the trail for later travelers to read.

Rain, snow, and disease. The long trek west held many dangers. During spring

MAP STUDY

Oregon Country was the first area in the Far West to draw settlers from the United States.
1. What two rivers did the Oregon Trail follow as it wound into Oregon Country?
2. What line of latitude marked the northern boundary of Oregon Country?
3. **Analyzing Information** Why do you think the Oregon Trail often followed the course of a river?

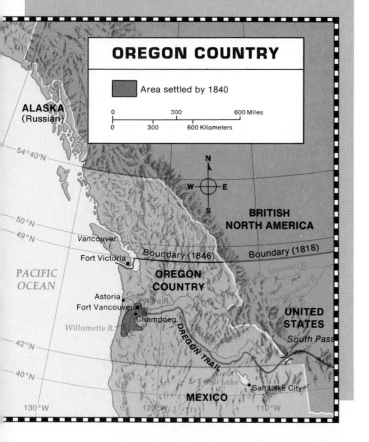

rains, travelers risked their lives floating wagons across swollen rivers. In the summer, they faced blistering heat on the treeless plains. Early snowstorms often blocked passes through the mountains.

But the biggest threat was sickness. Cholera and other diseases could wipe out whole wagon trains. Because the travelers lived so close to one another, germs spread quickly.

Trading with Native Americans. As they moved west toward the Rockies, pioneers often saw Indians. At times, Indians attacked the whites trespassing on their land. But such incidents were rare. A guidebook published in 1845 warned that pioneers had more to fear from their own guns than from Indians: "We very frequently hear of emigrants' being killed from the accidental discharge of firearms; but we very seldom hear of their being killed by Indians."

Many Native Americans traded with the wagon trains. Hungry pioneers were grateful for food the Indians sold. "Whenever we camp near any Indian village," a traveler said, "we are no sooner stopped than a whole crowd may be seen coming galloping into our camp. The [women] do all the swapping."

Oregon at last! Despite the hardships, more than 50,000 people reached Oregon between 1840 and 1860. Their wagon wheels cut so deeply into the plains that the ruts can still be seen today.

By the 1840s, Americans greatly outnumbered the British in Oregon. As you have read, the two nations agreed to occupy Oregon jointly in 1818. Now, many Americans began to feel that Oregon should belong to the United States alone.

SECTION 1 REVIEW

1. **Locate:** (a) Oregon Country, (b) South Pass, (c) Oregon Trail, (d) Independence.
2. **Identify:** (a) John Jacob Astor, (b) Mountain Man, (c) Jedediah Smith, (d) Manuel Lisa, (e) Marie Dorion, (f) Marcus and Narcissa Whitman.
3. **Define:** rendezvous.

4. (a) What four nations claimed Oregon Country? (b) What agreement did they reach?
5. How did Mountain Men help open the Far West?
6. Why did settlers pour into Oregon Country?
7. **Understanding Causes and Effects** (a) What was an immediate cause for the Cayuse attack on the Whitmans' mission? (b) What was a long-range cause?

---

2 A Country Called Texas

FIND OUT

◆ Why did Mexico want Americans to settle in Texas?

◆ How was the Republic of Texas set up?

◆ Why did the United States refuse to annex Texas?

◆ VOCABULARY annex

In late 1835, the word spread like wildfire: Americans in Texas had rebelled against Mexican rule! Joseph Barnard, a young doctor, later recalled:

❝I was at Chicago, Illinois, practicing medicine, when the news of the Texan revolt from Mexico reached our ears, in the early part of December, 1835. They were in arms for a cause that I had always been taught to consider sacred, [that is,] Republican principles and popular institutions.❞

Dr. Barnard took a steamship down the Mississippi and made his way to Texas. Like hundreds of other Americans, he risked his life to help win independence for Texas.

Americans in Mexican Texas

Since the early 1800s, American farmers had looked eagerly at the vast region called Texas, far to the southwest. At the

A Texan Ranch *In the 1820s, thousands of Americans poured into Texas. They built prosperous farms and ranches, such as the one shown here.* **Citizenship** *Why do you think the arrival of so many Americans might be of concern to Mexico?*

time, Texas was part of the Spanish colony of Mexico.

At first, Spain refused to let Americans move into the region. Then, in 1821, Spain gave Moses Austin a land grant in Texas. Austin died before he could set up a colony, but his son Stephen took over the project.

Meanwhile, Mexico had won its independence from Spain. (See pages 386–387.) The new nation agreed to let Stephen Austin lead settlers into Texas. Only about 4,000 Mexicans lived there. Mexico hoped that the Americans would help develop the area.

The new government of Mexico also hoped that American settlers might help control Indian attacks in Texas. Thousands of Indians lived in the area. For 200 years, Spanish priests had tried to convert these Indians to Christianity. But they had little success. In fact, some Indians fiercely resisted the missionaries.

Mexico gave Stephen Austin and each settler a large grant of land. In return, the settlers agreed to become citizens of Mexico, obey its laws, and worship in the Roman Catholic Church. Austin carefully chose 300 families to move to Texas with him. He looked for hard-working people who knew how to take care of themselves. In 1821, the first Americans moved into Texas. Under Austin's wise leadership, the colony grew. By 1830, more than 20,000 Americans had resettled in Texas.

Some parts of Texas were ideal for raising cattle. Other areas were good for growing cotton. Many of the Americans who went to Texas came from the South. Some built large cotton plantations and brought thousands of slaves to work the land.

Mexico Tightens Its Laws

Stephen Austin and his settlers had agreed to become Mexican citizens and Catholics. But other Americans who flooded into Texas felt no loyalty to Mexico. They spoke only a few words of Spanish, the official language of Mexico. And most were Protestants. Conflict soon erupted between the newcomers and the Mexican government.

In 1830, Mexico passed a law forbidding any more Americans to move to Texas. Mexico feared that the Americans wanted to make Texas part of the United States. This fear had some basis. The United States had already tried to buy Texas, once in 1826 and again in 1829.

Mexico also decided to make Texans obey Mexican laws they had ignored for years. One law banned slavery in Texas. Another required Texans to worship in the Catholic Church. Texans resented the laws and the Mexican troops who came north to enforce them.

In 1832, General Antonio López de Santa Anna came to power in Mexico. Two years later, Santa Anna threw out the Mexican constitution. Rumors spread wildly. Santa Anna, some said, intended to drive all Americans out of Texas.

Texans Take Action

Americans in Texas felt that the time for action had come. In this, they had the support of many **Tejanos** (teh HAH nohs), Mexicans who lived in Texas. The Tejanos did not necessarily want independence from Mexico. But they hated General Santa Anna, who ruled as a military dictator, and wanted to be rid of him.

In October 1835, Texans in the town of Gonzales (gon ZAH lehs) clashed with Mexican troops. (See the map on page 436.) The Texans defeated the Mexicans, forcing them to withdraw. The battle, which is known as "the Lexington of Texas," inspired Stephen Austin and convinced him that Texans must continue the fight for independence. Austin wrote to a friend:

> ❝My friend—All goes well and glorious for Texas—the whole country is in arms and moved by one spirit, which is to . . . drive all the military out of Texas. *This is as it should be*—no halfway measures now. . . . No more doubts—no submission. *I hope to see Texas forever free from Mexican domination.*❞

AMERICANS • ALL

Winning Independence for Texas

Many brave fighters took part in the Texan struggle for independence. But fighters did not win the struggle alone. Many others helped them along the way.

A fighting force must have supplies. In 1835, Texan volunteers battling for San Antonio were dangerously short of food and other supplies. Giuseppe Cassini, a merchant who had come to Texas from Italy, furnished all that they needed. With Cassini's help, the Texans kept going until they recaptured the city.

William Goyens, a prosperous black businessman in Nacogdoches (nak uh DOH chehz), also provided valuable aid. As a trader, Goyens had learned several Native American languages. He had also earned the trust of local Indians. When fighting began, commander in chief Sam Houston asked Goyens to talk to his Indian friends. As a result of Goyens's effort, the Cherokees promised to remain neutral, and Texan fighters faced fewer enemies in battle.

Many Texan fighters were grateful to Albert Moses Levy. When he learned that war had broken out in Texas, this young Jewish doctor left his comfortable practice in Virginia to join the struggle "with both scalpel and sword." Dr. Levy's untiring work on the battlefield saved countless Texan lives.

Once independence was won, Texas needed a well-planned government. José Antonio Navarro helped the new Republic of Texas in this important task. Navarro was born in San Antonio when Texas was still ruled by Spain. He worked for independence first from Spain and then from Mexico. Navarro was a signer of the Texas declaration of independence. Later, Navarro helped draft a constitution for Texas.

1. What activities besides fighting helped Texas win independence?

2. **Drawing Conclusions** Based on the text, what can you conclude about the kinds of people who supported the cause of Texan independence?

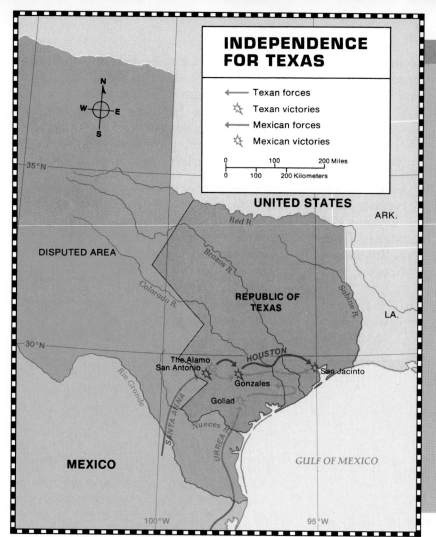

INDEPENDENCE FOR TEXAS

← Texan forces
✦ Texan victories
← Mexican forces
✦ Mexican victories

0   100   200 Miles
0   100   200 Kilometers

UNITED STATES

ARK.

DISPUTED AREA

Red R.

Brazos R.

Colorado R.

Sabine R.

REPUBLIC OF
TEXAS

LA.

The Alamo
San Antonio

HOUSTON

San Jacinto

Rio Grande

Gonzales

Goliad

Nueces R.

URREA

MEXICO

GULF OF MEXICO

100°W   95°W

35°N

30°N

SANTA ANNA

MAP STUDY

The Texan war for independence was brief but bloody.

1. Where did Santa Anna's army first fight the Texans?
2. Who won the battle at Gonzales?
3. **Comparing** Refer to the map of the present-day United States on pages 716–717. How do the boundaries of the Republic of Texas compare with the boundaries of Texas today?

Two months later, Texans stormed and took San Antonio. Santa Anna was furious. Determined to crush the rebellion, he marched north with a large army.

While Santa Anna massed his troops, Texans met at Washington-on-the-Brazos (BRAH zohs). There, on March 2, 1836, they declared their independence from Mexico and set themselves up as a new nation called the **Republic of Texas.** Appointing Sam Houston as commander of their army, Texans prepared to fight.

By the time Santa Anna arrived in San Antonio, many of the Texans who had taken the city had drifted away. Fewer than 200 Texans remained as defenders. Despite the odds against them, the Texans refused to give up. Instead, they retired to an old Spanish mission called the **Alamo.**

UP CLOSE

Remember the Alamo!

The Spanish built the Alamo in the mid-1700s. Like other missions, it included a church, corrals, barracks, storage rooms, and a blacksmith shop. Surrounded by walls 12 feet high and 5 feet thick, it was like a small fort. The Alamo, said an observer, was "a strong place."

But the Texan defenders who gathered in the Alamo in the winter of 1835–1836 were ill-prepared to fight. Supplies of ammunition and medicine were low. Food consisted of some beef and corn, and access to water was limited. As for warm clothing, many of the men had only a blanket and a single flannel shirt! Of most concern, however, was the fact that there were only 187 Texans in the Alamo—not nearly enough to defend it against 6,000 Mexican troops.

William Travis—hardly more than a boy—commanded the Texan troops. Volunteers inside the mission included the famous frontiersmen Jim Bowie and Davy Crockett. Several Tejano families, two Texan women, and two young male slaves were also present. They later helped to nurse the sick and wounded.

"Victory or death." On February 23, 1836, a Texan lookout spotted the gleam of swords in the sunlight. Santa Anna's army had arrived!

The first shots from the Alamo were rapid and deadly and took the Mexicans by surprise. To cut down on reloading time, Commander Travis placed three or four rifles by each man's side. In that way, a Texan could fire three or four shots in the time it took a Mexican to fire one.

Still, Travis knew that unless he received help, he and his men were doomed. On February 24, he sent a Texan through the Mexican lines with a message. It was addressed "to the People of Texas and all the Americans in the World":

> ❝Fellow Citizens and Compatriots—I am besieged by a thousand or more of the Mexicans under Santa Anna. I have sustained a continual bombardment for 24 hours and have not lost a man. The enemy have demanded a surrender. . . . I have answered the demand with a cannon shot and our flag still waves proudly from the walls.
>
> *I shall never surrender or retreat.*
>
> I call on you in the name of Liberty, of patriotism, and of everything dear to the American character to come to our aid with all dispatch. The enemy are receiving reinforcements daily. . . . If this call is neglected, I am determined to sustain myself as long as possible & die like a soldier who never forgets what is due to his own honor or that of his country. *Victory or Death!*
>
> W. Barret Travis❞

Travis also sent both Texan and Tejano scouts to seek additional soldiers and provisions. About 60 men were able to sneak through enemy lines and join the fighters in the Alamo. But no large force ever arrived.

The final siege. Daily, the Mexicans bombarded the Alamo. For 12 days, the defenders bravely held them off. Then, at dawn on March 6, 1836, Mexican cannon fire broke through the Alamo walls. Thousands of Mexican soldiers poured into the mission. When the bodies were counted, 182 Texans and 600 Mexicans lay dead. The five Texan survivors, including Davy Crockett, were promptly executed at Santa Anna's order.

Siege at the Alamo *Fewer than 200 Texans held the Alamo for 12 days against almost 6,000 Mexican troops. Almost all the defenders were killed, but their heroic effort inspired Texans. Throughout Texas, the cry rang out: "Remember the Alamo!"* **Multicultural Heritage** *Why did many Tejanos support the revolt against Mexican rule?*

The slaughter at the Alamo angered Texans and set off cries for revenge. The fury of the Texans grew even stronger three weeks later, when Mexicans murdered several hundred Texan soldiers at Goliad after they had surrendered. Volunteers flooded into Sam Houston's army. Men from the United States also raced south to help the Texan cause. ◆

Texan Independence

While the Mexicans were busy at the Alamo, Sam Houston organized his army. Six weeks later, on April 21, 1836, Houston decided that the moment had come to attack.

Santa Anna was camped with his army near the San Jacinto (jah SEEN toh) River. With cries of "Remember the Alamo!" the Texans charged the surprised Mexicans. The Battle of San Jacinto lasted only 18 minutes. Although they were outnumbered, Texans killed 630 Mexicans and captured 700 more. The next day, Texans captured Santa Anna himself. They forced the general to sign a treaty granting Texas its independence.

The Lone Star Republic

In battle, Texans carried a flag with a single white star. After winning independence, they nicknamed their nation the **Lone Star Republic.** They drew up a constitution based on that of the United States and elected Sam Houston president.

Problems for the republic. The new country faced huge problems. First, Mexico refused to accept the treaty signed by Santa Anna. Mexicans still claimed Texas as part of their country. Second, Texas was nearly bankrupt. Most Texans thought that the best way to solve both problems was for Texas to become part of the United States.

In the United States, however, Americans were divided about whether to annex Texas. To annex means to add on. Most white southerners favored the idea. But many northerners were against it. At issue was slavery. Antislavery feeling was growing in the North in the 1830s. Knowing that many Texans owned slaves, northerners did not want to allow Texas to join the Union. President Andrew Jackson also worried that annexing Texas would lead to war with Mexico. As a result, the United States refused to annex Texas.

Texas prospers. Still, the Republic of Texas survived and prospered. During the Panic of 1837, thousands of Americans moved to Texas to find new land and to start businesses. Throughout the Southwest, people left the following brief message on their doors: "GTT"—"Gone to Texas."

Settlers from Germany also swelled the population. By the 1840s, there were 140,000 people in Texas, including many Tejanos and African Americans.

Both free blacks and slaves fought for Texan independence. After independence, however, slave owners wanted to drive free blacks out of the new country. Like slaveholders in the South, they claimed that free blacks caused unrest among slaves. Despite the pressure to leave, some free blacks chose to stay in Texas.

SECTION 2 REVIEW

1. **Locate:** (a) Mexico, (b) Gonzales, (c) San Antonio, (d) Republic of Texas.
2. **Identify:** (a) Stephen Austin, (b) Antonio López de Santa Anna, (c) Tejano, (d) Sam Houston, (e) Alamo, (f) Lone Star Republic.
3. **Define:** annex.
4. (a) Who were the first settlers from the United States to move into Texas? (b) Why did Mexico encourage Americans to settle in Texas?
5. Why did Americans in Texas come into conflict with the Mexican government?
6. (a) Why did northerners and southerners disagree about annexing Texas? (b) Why did President Jackson hesitate to annex Texas?
7. **Drawing Conclusions** How was the defeat at the Alamo also a victory for Texans?

MAP STUDY

Texas attracted settlers from many lands and of many ethnic backgrounds.
1. **What group settled in Nacogdoches?**
2. **Name two cities where Mexicans settled.**
3. **Analyzing Information** *Which area of Texas had the greatest mix of peoples?*

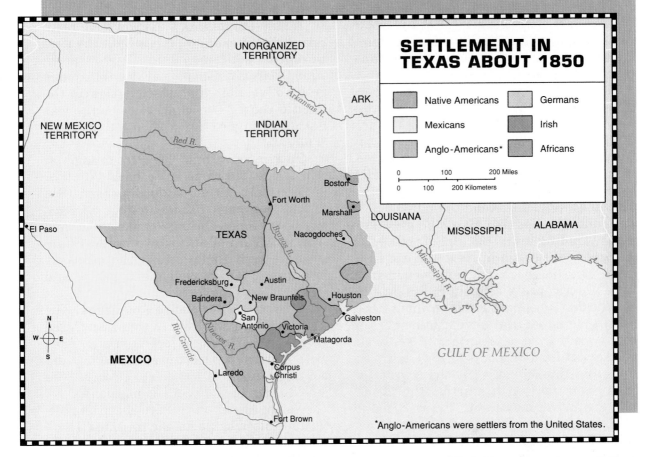

SETTLEMENT IN TEXAS ABOUT 1850

- Native Americans
- Mexicans
- Anglo-Americans*
- Germans
- Irish
- Africans

*Anglo-Americans were settlers from the United States.

---

3 Manifest Destiny

FIND OUT

◆ Who were the first white settlers in New Mexico and California?

◆ What was mission life like for Native Americans?

◆ What did Americans mean by Manifest Destiny?

Americans who took up ranching in Texas in the early 1800s adopted a yearly spring ritual: cattle branding. The red-hot iron that burned a "Lazy Z" or "Running A" on- to a young calf's hide created proof that the calf was the rancher's property.

In the 1840s, Americans moved farther west, into New Mexico and California— both part of Mexico. Like the Texan ranch- ers, these Americans wanted to stamp their nation's "brand" on the lands they now called home. The thousands who moved to the Far West came to feel that it was the "destiny" of the United States to expand all the way to the Pacific Ocean.

New Mexico Territory

In the 1840s, the entire Southwest be- longed to Mexico. This huge region was called **New Mexico Territory.** It included most of the present-day states of Arizona

CHAPTER 14 ◆ **439**

and New Mexico, all of Nevada and Utah, and parts of Colorado. The capital of New Mexico Territory was Santa Fe.

The Southwest is hot and dry. In some areas, thick grasses grow, while other areas are desert. Before the arrival of the Spanish, Pueblo and Zuñi Indians irrigated and farmed the land. Other Native Americans, such as the Apaches, lived by hunting.

Santa Fe. As you have read, the Spanish explorer Juan de Oñate traveled across New Mexico in 1598. He built the region's first white settlement north of present-day Santa Fe. When Spanish settlers arrived, they set up huge sheep ranches. A few rich families owned the ranches and employed Native Americans to tend the herds.

Under the Spanish, Santa Fe grew into a busy trading town. But Spain refused to let Americans settle in New Mexico. Only after Mexico won its independence in 1821 were Americans welcome in Santa Fe.

The first Americans arrive. William Becknell, a merchant and adventurer, was the first American to head for Santa Fe. Becknell set out from St. Louis in 1821, carrying tools and rolls of cloth. He led a group of traders on the long trip across the plains. When they reached Santa Fe, they found Mexicans eager to buy their goods. Other Americans soon followed Becknell's route. It became known as the **Santa Fe Trail.** (See the map on page 441.)

Early Years in California

California, too, belonged to Mexico in the early 1840s. Spain had claimed the region 100 years before English colonists built homes in Jamestown. In the years that followed, Spanish and Native American culture shaped life in California.

A land of contrasts. California is a land of dramatic contrasts. Two tall mountain ranges slice through the region. One range hugs the coast. The other sits inland on the border of Nevada and Arizona. Between these two ranges is California's fertile central valley.

Northern California receives plenty of rain. But in the south, water is scarce, and much of the land is desert. California enjoys mild temperatures all year, except high in the mountains.

A string of missions. As you have read, Spanish soldiers and priests built the first European settlements in California. In 1769, Captain Gaspar de Portolá led a group of soldiers and missionaries up the Pacific coast. The chief missionary was Father Junípero Serra (hoo NEE peh roh SEHR rah).

Father Serra built his first mission at San Diego. He went on to build 20 other missions along the California coast. (See the map on page 102 in Chapter 4.) Each mission claimed the surrounding land and soon took care of all its own needs. Spanish soldiers built forts near the missions. The missions supplied meat, grain, and other foods to the forts.

Mission life for Native Americans. The California Indians lived in small, scattered groups rather than in large nations. They were generally peaceful people. They did not offer much resistance to soldiers who forced them to work for the missions.

Native Americans herded sheep and cattle and raised crops for the missions. In return, they lived at the missions and learned the Catholic religion. Many missionaries were truly concerned with converting the Native Americans to Christianity.

But mission life was hard for Native Americans. Thousands died from overwork and disease. And after Mexico won its independence, conditions grew even worse. The new Mexican government offered mission land to ranchers. Some of the ranchers cruelly mistreated the Indians. If Indians tried to run away, ranchers hunted them down. One American reported:

❝ The natives [in California] . . . are in a state of absolute [slavery], even more degrading, and more oppressive than that of our slaves in the South.❞

Americans followed a number of trails to the West.
1. Which trails ended in cities in California?
2. About how long was the Mormon Trail?
3. **Analyzing Information** (a) What would be the best route for a pioneer family to take from Independence, Missouri, to Sutter's Fort, California? (b) What mountains would they cross? (c) In what town might they seek shelter along the way?

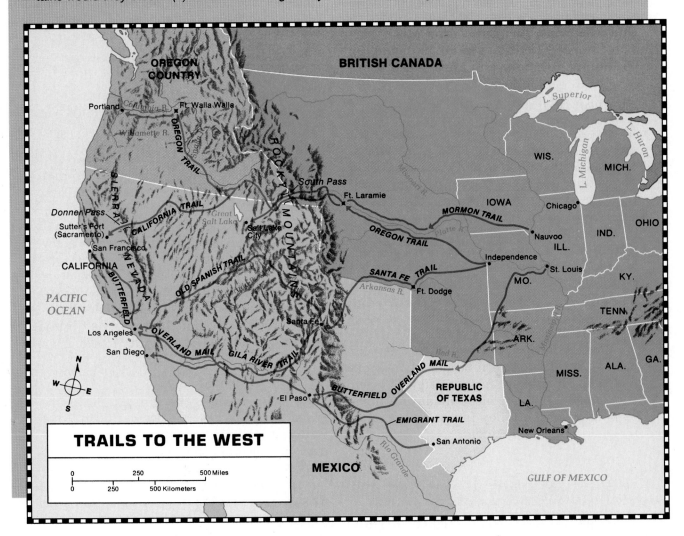

TRAILS TO THE WEST

These harsh conditions had a deadly effect. Between 1770 and 1850, the Native American population of California decreased from 310,000 to 100,000.

Expansion: A Right and Duty

As late as the mid-1840s, only about 700 people from the United States lived in California. But each year, more and more Americans looked toward the West.

Americans believed that their democratic government was the best in the world. Many thought that the United States had the right and duty to spread its rule all the way to the Pacific Ocean.

In the 1840s, a New York newspaper coined a phrase for this belief. The phrase was **Manifest Destiny.** Manifest means clear or obvious. Destiny means something that is sure to happen. Americans who believed in Manifest Destiny thought that the United States was clearly meant to expand to the Pacific.

But Manifest Destiny had another side, too. Many Americans believed that they were better than Native Americans and Mexicans. For these Americans, racism justified taking over lands belonging to "inferior" Indians and Mexicans.

Election of 1844

Manifest Destiny played an important part in the election of 1844. The Whigs nominated Henry Clay for President. Clay was a famous and respected national leader. The Democrats chose a little-known man named James K. Polk.

But voters soon knew Polk as the candidate who favored expansion. Polk demanded that Texas and Oregon be added to the United States. He made Oregon a special campaign issue. Even though the United States had agreed to share Oregon with Britain, Polk now insisted on the whole region for the United States—all the way to its northern border at latitude 54°40'N. "Fifty-four forty or fight!" cried the Democrats. On election day, Americans showed that they favored expansion by electing Polk President.

| SECTION 3 REVIEW |

1. **Locate:** (a) Santa Fe, (b) Santa Fe Trail, (c) San Diego.
2. **Identify:** (a) New Mexico Territory, (b) William Becknell, (c) Junípero Serra, (d) Manifest Destiny, (e) James K. Polk.
3. How did mission life affect Native Americans in California?
4. Why did Americans elect James Polk President in 1844?
5. **Synthesizing Information** Why do you think Americans in the 1840s believed that their government was the best in the world?

4 The Mexican War

FIND OUT

◆ How did the United States gain Oregon?

◆ What events led to war with Mexico?

◆ What lands did the United States gain from the Mexican War?

◆ How did Spanish and Indian traditions blend in the new lands?

◆ **VOCABULARY** cede

In 1845, President Polk rode into the White House on a wave of popular support. Americans eagerly endorsed his promise to expand the United States from sea to sea.

Fulfilling that promise was a difficult task. First, the new President faced a showdown with Britain over the issue of Oregon. Happily for the nation, he resolved this issue peacefully. But Polk also was determined to add Texas to the United States. To fulfill this dream, he took the United States into a bloody war with Mexico.

Annexing Texas

As you have read, the United States refused to annex Texas in 1836. But by 1844, many Americans had changed their minds. As Polk's election showed, expansionist feelings were strong in the United States.

In 1844, Sam Houston, the president of Texas, signed a treaty of annexation with the United States. But the Senate refused to ratify the treaty. Senators still feared that annexing Texas would cause a war with Mexico.

Sam Houston did not give up. To persuade Americans to annex Texas, he pretended that Texas might become an ally of Britain. The trick worked. Americans did not want an ally of Europe's greatest power on their western border. In 1845, Congress passed a joint resolution admitting Texas to the Union.

Annexing Texas led at once to a dispute with Mexico. Texas claimed that its southern border was the Rio Grande. Mexico argued that it was the Nueces (noo AY says) River. The Nueces was some 200 miles (320 km) north of the Rio Grande. (See the map on page 444.) The United States supported Texan claims. Trouble with Mexico seemed likely.

Dividing Oregon

The quarrel over Texas was not the only problem Polk faced when he took office in March 1845. As he had promised in his campaign, Polk acted to gain control of Oregon. It seemed that Britain and the United States would go to war.

Despite his expansionist beliefs and campaign slogans, President Polk did not really want a war with Britain. So in 1846, he agreed to a compromise. Oregon was divided at latitude 49°N. Britain got the lands north of the line, and the United States got the lands south of the line. The United States named its portion the Oregon Territory. The Oregon Territory was later made into three states: Oregon (1859), Washington (1889), and Idaho (1890).

War With Mexico

Meanwhile, the United States and Mexico stood on the brink of war. Mexico had never accepted the independence of Texas. Now, the annexation of Texas made Mexicans furious. They also were concerned that the example of Texas might encourage Americans in California and New Mexico to rebel.

Americans, in turn, were angry with Mexico. President Polk offered to pay Mexico $30 million for California and New Mexico. But Mexico strongly opposed any further loss of territory and refused the offer. Americans felt that Mexico stood in the way of Manifest Destiny.

In January 1846, Polk ordered General Zachary Taylor to cross the Nueces River and set up posts along the Rio Grande. Polk knew that Mexico claimed this land

Sam Houston, Texan Leader *As president of the Republic of Texas, Sam Houston worked hard to convince Congress that the United States should annex Texas.* **Citizenship** *In what other ways had Houston proven himself a leader in Texas?*

and that the move might spark a war. In April 1846, Mexican troops crossed the Rio Grande and fought briefly with the Americans. Soldiers on both sides were killed.

President Polk claimed that Mexico had "shed American blood on American soil." At his urging, Congress declared war on Mexico. But Americans were divided over the war. Many people in the South and West wanted more land and so were eager to fight. But northerners opposed the war. They saw it as a southern plot to add slave states to the Union.

Still, many Americans joined the war effort. Since the army was small, thousands of volunteers were needed. When the call for recruits went out, the response was overwhelming.

Fighting in Mexico

As the **Mexican War** began, the United States attacked on several fronts. General Zachary Taylor crossed the Rio Grande into northern Mexico. There, he won several battles against the Mexican army. In

Fighting on the Texan border triggered the Mexican War.
1. What two rivers border the area disputed by the United States and Mexico at the start of the war?
2. What American commanders fought in the war?
3. **Analyzing Information** *Based on the map, was sea power important to the United States in the Mexican War? Explain.*

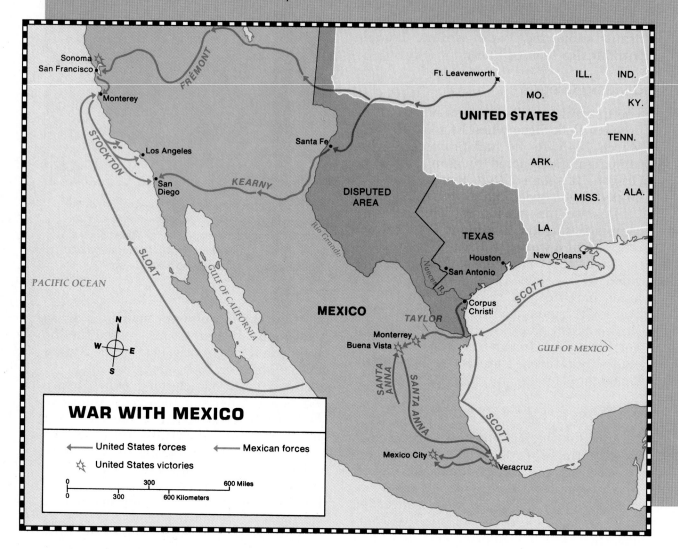

WAR WITH MEXICO

← United States forces ← Mexican forces
☆ United States victories

0 300 600 Miles
0 300 600 Kilometers

February 1847, he defeated General Santa Anna at the Battle of Buena Vista. (See the map above.)

Meanwhile, General Winfield Scott landed another American army at the Mexican port of Veracruz. After a long battle, the Americans took the city. Scott then marched west toward the capital, Mexico City. He followed the same route taken by Hernando Cortés 300 years earlier.

Rebellion in California

A third army, led by General Stephen Kearny, headed west along the Santa Fe Trail. His army captured Santa Fe without firing a shot. After setting up a temporary government in Santa Fe, Kearny hurried on to San Diego. After several battles, Kearny took control of southern California early in 1847.

Even before hearing of the Mexican War, Americans in northern California had risen up against Mexican rule. John Frémont and a band of frontiersmen led the rebels. On June 14, 1846, they declared California an independent republic. The rebels raised a handmade flag showing a grizzly bear. They called their new nation the **Bear Flag Republic.** Later in the Mexican War, Frémont joined forces with the United States army.

A Nation's Dream Come True

By 1847, the United States controlled all of New Mexico and California. Meanwhile, General Scott had reached the outskirts of Mexico City. He hoped to take the Mexican capital without bloodshed, but his troops faced a fierce battle. Young Mexican soldiers made a heroic last stand at Chapultepec (chah POOL tuh pek), a fort just outside Mexico City. Like the Texans who died at the Alamo, the Mexicans at Chapultepec fought to the last man. Today, Mexicans honor these young men as heroes.

The Mexican Cession. With the American army in Mexico City, the Mexican government had no choice but to make peace. In 1848, Mexico signed the Treaty of Guadalupe Hidalgo (gwah duh LOOP ay ih DAHL goh). Under the treaty, Mexico ceded, or gave, all of California and New Mexico to the United States. These lands were called

MAP STUDY

By 1848, the United States stretched all the way from the Atlantic Ocean to the Pacific Ocean.
1. *What area on this map was the last to be added to the United States?*
2. *How did Oregon Country become part of the United States?*
3. **Comparing** *Refer to the map on pages 716–717. When and in what way did your state become part of the United States?*

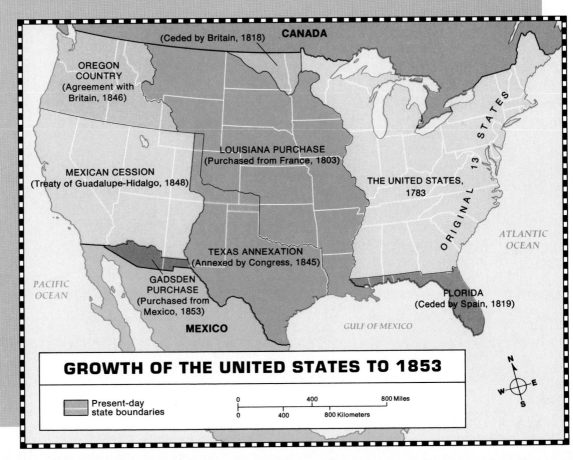

GROWTH OF THE UNITED STATES TO 1853

the **Mexican Cession.** (See the map on page 445.) In return, the United States paid Mexico $15 million. Americans also agreed to respect the rights of Spanish-speaking people in the Mexican Cession.

A final addition. A few years after the Mexican War, the United States completed its expansion across the continent. In 1853, it agreed to pay Mexico $10 million for a strip of land in present-day Arizona and New Mexico. The land was called the **Gadsden Purchase.** Americans rejoiced. Their dream of Manifest Destiny had come true.

A Rich Heritage

Texas, New Mexico, and California added vast new lands to the United States. In these lands, Americans found a rich cul-ture that blended Spanish and Native American traditions. (📖 See "Death Comes for the Archbishop" on page 678.)

A mix of cultures. English-speaking settlers who poured into the Southwest brought their own culture with them, including ideas about democratic government. At the same time, Americans learned a great deal from the older residents of the region. Mexican Americans taught the newcomers how to irrigate the soil. They also showed the Americans how to mine silver and other minerals. Many Spanish and Indian words became part of the English language. They included stampede, buffalo, soda, and tornado.

Americans kept some Mexican laws. One law said that a husband and wife owned property together. In the rest of the United States, married women could not

Fiesta in California *Spanish traditions were strong in the American Southwest. Here, a settlement in California holds a* fiesta, *a celebration marked by singing, dancing, and displays of horsemanship.* **Multicultural Heritage** *What groups other than the Spanish influenced the culture of the Southwest?*

own property. Another law said that landowners could not cut off water to their neighbors. This law was important in the Southwest, where water was scarce.

Mexican Americans and Indians. Americans often did not treat Mexican Americans and Indians well. The older residents struggled to protect their traditions and rights. But Americans often ignored their claims. The family of Guadalupe Vallejo (vah YAY hoh) lived in California for decades before the Americans arrived. Vallejo noted bitterly:

> ❝In their dealings with the rancheros, [Americans] took advantage of laws which they understood, but which were new to the Spaniards, and so robbed the latter of their lands.❞

When Mexican Americans went to court to defend their property, they found that American judges rarely upheld their claims. "The Americans say they have come for our good," one Mexican American commented. "Yes, for all our goods."

SECTION 4 REVIEW

1. **Locate:** (a) Rio Grande, (b) Nueces River, (c) Buena Vista, (d) Mexico City, (e) Mexican Cession, (f) Gadsden Purchase.
2. **Identify:** (a) Zachary Taylor, (b) Mexican War, (c) Stephen Kearny, (d) John Frémont, (e) Bear Flag Republic, (f) Chapultepec, (g) Treaty of Guadalupe Hidalgo.
3. **Define:** cede.
4. What event sparked the Mexican War?
5. What were the terms of the Treaty of Guadalupe Hidalgo?
6. (a) Name two things that English-speaking settlers learned from Mexican Americans in the Southwest. (b) Name one tradition that English-speaking settlers brought to the Southwest.
7. **Drawing Conclusions** Why do you think the United States was willing to make a boundary compromise with Britain but not with Mexico?

5 Surge to the Pacific

FIND OUT

◆ How did the Mormons set up a successful community in Utah?

◆ How did the discovery of gold affect life in California?

◆ What mix of peoples helped California to grow and prosper?

◆ VOCABULARY forty-niner, vigilante

In 1848, James Marshall was helping John Sutter build a sawmill on the American River, north of Sacramento, California. On January 24, Marshall set out to inspect a ditch his crew was digging. He later told a friend what he saw:

> ❝It was a clear, cold morning; I shall never forget that morning. As I was taking my usual walk, . . . my eye was caught with the glimpse of something shining in the bottom of the ditch. There was about a foot of water running then. I reached my hand down and picked it up; it made my heart thump, for I was certain it was gold.❞

Word of Marshall's find spread quickly. From all over the nation, prospectors flocked to California. The California Gold Rush had begun!

But gold was not the only thing that attracted settlers to the West in the mid-1800s. California, New Mexico, Oregon, Texas—all were now part of the United States. Restless pioneers, always eager to try something new, headed into these lands to build homes and a new way of life.

Mormons Seek Refuge in Utah

The largest group of settlers to move into the Mexican Cession were the **Mormons.** Mormons belonged to the Church of Jesus

Christ of Latter-day Saints. The church was founded by Joseph Smith in 1830. Smith, a farmer who lived in upstate New York, won many followers.

Troubles with neighbors. Smith was an energetic and popular man. But his teachings angered many non-Mormons. For example, Mormons at first believed that property should be owned in common. Smith also said that a man could have more than one wife.* Angry neighbors forced the Mormons to leave New York for Ohio. From Ohio, they were later forced to move to Missouri, and from there to Illinois.

In the 1840s, the Mormons built a town called Nauvoo in Illinois. United by their faith, the Mormons worked for the good of their community. They ran successful farms, shops, and factories. By 1844, Nauvoo was the largest town in Illinois. Neat brick houses lined its clean streets.

––––––––

*In 1890, Mormons gave up the practice of allowing a man to have more than one wife.

But before long, neighbors again made trouble for the Mormons. In 1844, an angry mob killed Joseph Smith. The Mormons quickly chose Brigham Young as their new leader.

Brigham Young realized that the Mormons needed a home where they would be safe. He had read about a valley between the Rocky Mountains and the Great Salt Lake in Utah. Young decided that the isolated valley would make a good home for the Mormons.

A difficult journey. To move 15,000 men, women, and children from Illinois to Utah in the 1840s was an awesome challenge. But relying on faith and careful planning, Brigham Young achieved his goal.

In 1847, Young led an advance party into the Great Salt Lake valley. Wave after wave of Mormons followed. For the next few years, Mormon wagon trains struggled across the plains and over the Rockies to Utah. When they ran short of wagons and oxen, thousands made the long trip pulling their gear in handcarts.

Mormons Move West *Thousands of Mormons trekked west to Utah. Many like C.C.A. Christensen, who painted this picture, walked the whole way, pulling their belongings in handcarts.* **Multicultural Heritage** *Which other areas of the United States were settled by people seeking religious freedom?*

The Mormons prosper in the desert. In Utah, the Mormons had to survive in a desert climate. Once again, Young proved to be a gifted leader. He planned an irrigation system to bring water to farms. He also drew up plans for a large city, called **Salt Lake City,** to be built in the desert.

The Mormon settlement in Utah grew quickly. Like other whites, Mormons took over thousands of acres of Native American land, usually paying nothing for it.

Congress recognized Brigham Young as governor of the Utah Territory in 1850. Trouble later broke out when non-Mormons moved to the area. In the end, peace was restored, and Utah became a state in 1896.

Gold!

While the Mormons trekked to Utah, thousands of other Americans were racing to California. They all had a single objective: Gold!

Sutter's Mill. As you have read, James Marshall found gold at Sutter's Mill in California in January 1848. In a few days, word of the gold strike spread to San Francisco. Carpenters threw down their saws. Bakers left bread in their ovens. Schools emptied as teachers and students joined the rush to the gold fields.

The news spread outward from San Francisco. Thousands of Americans caught gold fever. People in Europe and South America joined the rush as well. More than 80,000 people made the long journey to California in 1849. They became known as **forty-niners.**

In the California gold fields. The first miners needed little skill. The gold was near the surface of the earth, and miners were able to dig it out with knives. Soon, they found a better way. They loaded sand and gravel from the riverbed into a washing pan. Then, they held the pan under water and swirled it gently. The water washed away lighter gravel, leaving the heavier gold in the pan. This process was known as "panning for gold."

MAP STUDY

In 1849, tens of thousands of people flocked to California hoping to strike it rich.
1. *Name two ways that people traveled to California.*
2. *What symbol is used on the map to show gold mines?*
3. **Drawing Conclusions** *Name two cities on the map that might have grown as a result of the Gold Rush. Explain.*

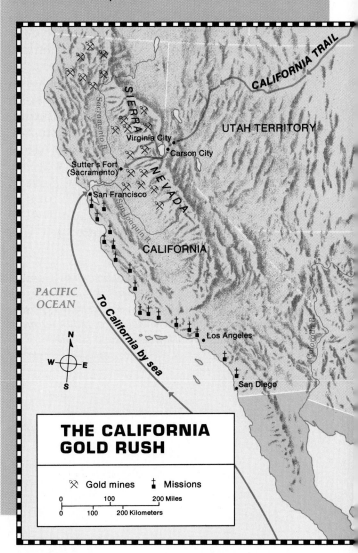

THE CALIFORNIA GOLD RUSH

⚒ Gold mines   ✝ Missions

0   100   200 Miles
0   100   200 Kilometers

But only a few miners struck it rich. Most went broke trying to make their fortunes. Many miners left the gold fields but stayed in California. These unsuccessful miners took other jobs and helped to build up California's economy. (📖 See "In the Gold Fields of California" on page 680.)

A new state. The Gold Rush changed life in California. Almost overnight, San Francisco grew from a sleepy town to a bustling city. But the Gold Rush also created problems. Greed turned some forty-niners into criminals. Murders and robberies plagued many mining camps. To fight crime, miners formed vigilance committees. Vigilantes (vihj uh LAN teez), self-appointed law enforcers, dealt out punishment even though they had no legal power to do so. Sometimes, an accused criminal was lynched, or hanged without a legal trial.

Californians realized they needed a government to stop the lawlessness. In 1849, they drafted a state constitution. They then asked to be admitted to the Union. Their request caused an uproar in the United States. The issue was whether or not the new state would allow slavery. As you will read in Chapter 17, after a heated debate, California was admitted to the Union in 1850 as a free state.

California's Unique Culture

Most mining camps included a mix of peoples. One visitor to a mining town met runaway slaves from the South, Native Americans, and New Englanders, as well as people from Hawaii, China, Peru, Chile, France, Germany, Italy, Ireland, and Australia. But most of the miners were white Americans. During the wild days of the Gold Rush, they often ignored the rights of other Californians.

Native Americans. Indians fared worst of all. Many were driven off their lands and died of starvation or disease. Others were murdered. In 1850, about 100,000 Indians lived in California. By the 1870s, there were only 17,000 Indians left in the state.

Mexican Americans. As you have read, Mexican Americans often lost land they had owned for generations. But many fought to preserve the customs of their people. José Carillo (cah REE yoh) was from one of the oldest families in California. In part through his efforts, the state's

Prospecting for Gold *The lure of gold drew prospectors to California from all over the world. Most gold was found in the form of gold dust or flakes. Sometimes, however, a lucky miner found a solid gold nugget weighing 5, 10, or even 25 pounds, such as the one shown here.* **Multicultural Heritage** *How did the Gold Rush contribute to California's unique culture?*

Tent City in San Francisco *Sleepy San Francisco became a booming city almost overnight after gold was discovered at nearby Sutter's Mill. Here, tents put up by gold-hungry forty-niners dot San Francisco's Telegraph Hill.* **Economics** *How did the forty-niners help to build California's economy?*

constitution was written in both Spanish and English.

Chinese Americans. Chinese settlers began to arrive in California in 1848. Since California needed workers, the Chinese were welcomed at first. But when the Chinese staked claims in the gold fields, white miners often drove them off. Still, many Chinese Americans stayed in California and helped the state to grow. They farmed, irrigated, and reclaimed vast stretches of land.

African Americans. Like other forty-niners, free blacks rushed to the California gold fields hoping to strike it rich. Some did become wealthy. By the 1850s, in fact, California had the richest African American population of any state. Yet African Americans still faced discrimination. For example, California law denied blacks the right to testify against whites in court. After a long struggle, blacks won repeal of the law in 1863.

In spite of these problems, California thrived and grew. Settlers continued to arrive in the state. By 1860, it had 100,000 citizens. The mix of peoples in California gave it a unique culture.

SECTION 5 REVIEW

1. **Locate:** (a) Sacramento, (b) Nauvoo, (c) Salt Lake City, (d) San Francisco.
2. **Identify:** (a) Mormons, (b) Joseph Smith, (c) Brigham Young.
3. **Define:** (a) forty-niner, (b) vigilante.
4. Why did Brigham Young lead the Mormons to Utah?
5. What problems did the Gold Rush create for California society?
6. What problems did each of the following face in California: (a) Native Americans; (b) Mexican Americans; (c) Chinese Americans; (d) African Americans?
7. **Comparing** Compare the settling of Utah with the settling of California.

A diary is often a useful primary source because it tells what the writer saw, heard, said, thought, and felt. It gives firsthand information about people, places, and events. Because diaries are private, writers often say what they honestly think.

The excerpts below are taken from a diary that was kept by Amelia Stewart Knight. With her husband and children, Knight traveled west along the Oregon Trail in 1853. Her diary tells about the hardships the family faced on their way to a new life in Oregon Country.

1 Identify the primary source. (a) Who wrote the diary? (b) When was the diary written? (c) Under what conditions was it written? (d) Why do you think the writer wrote it?

2 Analyze the information in the primary source. Study the diary for information about how the writer lived. (a) What does Knight say about hardships on the Oregon Trail? (b) Describe the geography of the area the Knight family traveled through. (c) What chores did Amelia Knight do? (d) What chores did the children do?

3 Draw conclusions about the writer's point of view. Decide how the writer felt about making the overland journey west. (a) How do you think she felt about the hardships of the journey? (b) How might keeping the diary have helped Knight face these hardships? (c) What personal qualities did a person need to make the journey?

Amelia Stewart Knight's Diary

"Monday, April 18th Cold; breaking fast the first thing; very disagreeable weather; wind east cold and rainy, no fire. We are on a very large prairie, no timber to be seen as far as the eye can reach. Evening—Have crossed several bad streams today, and more than once have been stuck in the mud.

Saturday, April 23rd Still in camp, it rained hard all night, and blew a hurricane almost. All the tents were blown down, and some wagons capsized. Evening—It has been raining hard all day; everything is wet and muddy. One of the oxen missing; the boys have been hunting him all day. (Dreary times, wet and muddy, and crowded in the tent, cold and wet and uncomfortable in the wagon. No place for the poor children.) I have been busy cooking, roasting coffee, etc. today, and have come into the wagon to write this and make our bed.

Friday, May 6th We passed a train of wagons on their way back, the head man had drowned a few days before, in a river called the Elkhorn, while getting some cattle across. With sadness and pity I passed those who a few days before had been well and happy as ourselves.

Friday, August 19th After looking in vain for water, we were about to give up, when husband came across a company of friendly Cayuse Indians, who showed him where to find water. The men and boys have driven the cattle down to water and I am waiting to get supper. We bought a few potatoes from an Indian, which will be a treat for our supper.*"*

Use the Section Reviews and this Study Guide to review chapter content.

Main Ideas

The main ideas in each section of this chapter are summarized below.

SECTION 1 ■ Oregon Fever

◆ The United States and Britain agreed to occupy Oregon jointly.
◆ Mountain Men roamed the Far West trapping animals and living off the land.
◆ Thousands of settlers traveled to Oregon along the Oregon Trail.

SECTION 2 ■ A Country Called Texas

◆ In the 1820s, Americans began to move into Texas.
◆ Texans rebelled against Mexican rule and set up the Republic of Texas in 1836.
◆ Despite a request by Texans, the United States refused to annex Texas.

SECTION 3 ■ Manifest Destiny

◆ The Spanish built a string of missions along the California coast.
◆ Americans believed it was their Manifest Destiny to expand to the Pacific.

SECTION 4 ■ The Mexican War

◆ In 1846, the United States and Britain divided Oregon.
◆ After the United States annexed Texas, war broke out with Mexico.

◆ Under the treaty ending the Mexican War, the United States gained California and New Mexico.
◆ Spanish and Indian traditions blended in the new American lands.

SECTION 5 ■ Surge to the Pacific

◆ The Mormons set up a successful community in Utah.
◆ Thousands of people rushed to California after gold was discovered at Sutter's Mill.
◆ A unique mix of peoples helped California to grow and prosper.

Key People and Terms

Refer to the Identify and Define questions in the Section Reviews on pages 433, 438, 442, 447, and 451. Use each person, term, and vocabulary word in a complete sentence. When possible, make connections between the people and terms by using more than one person or term in each sentence.

Time Line

1. Make a chart of events in time order. The chart will have two headings: Date, Event. Fill in the chart, using the events on the time line. Add the following events from the chapter: Bear Flag Republic proclaimed; California statehood; Siege at Alamo. (Refer to the chapter for the dates.)
2. What event on the chart was a long-range effect of the Gold Rush? Explain.

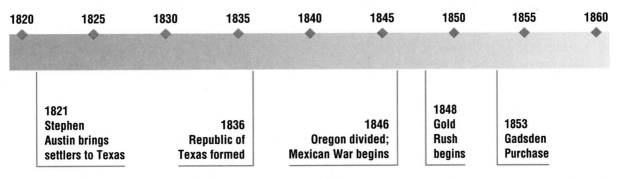

| 1820 | 1825 | 1830 | 1835 | 1840 | 1845 | 1850 | 1855 | 1860 |

1821
Stephen Austin brings settlers to Texas

1836
Republic of Texas formed

1846
Oregon divided; Mexican War begins

1848
Gold Rush begins

1853
Gadsden Purchase

Understanding Vocabulary

Match each term at left with the correct definition at right.

1. rendezvous
2. annex
3. cede
4. forty-niner
5. vigilante

a. give
b. person who went to California during the Gold Rush
c. add on
d. get-together
e. self-appointed law enforcer

Reviewing the Main Ideas

1. (a) What attracted settlers to Oregon Country in the mid-1800s? (b) How did they travel there?
2. What action by Santa Anna convinced Texans to fight for independence?
3. (a) Describe the life of Native Americans on missions in California. (b) How did their lives change after Mexico gained independence from Spain?
4. What role did the idea of Manifest Destiny play in the election of 1844?
5. (a) What problem did the Mormons face in Utah? (b) How did Brigham Young help the Mormons to solve this problem?
6. Why did thousands of people come to California in 1849?

Thinking Critically

1. **Comparing** Compare the American Revolution and the struggle of Texas for independence. (a) How were they similar? (b) How were they different?
2. **Understanding Causes and Effects** Review the events leading up to the Mexican War. (a) What was the immediate cause of war with Mexico? (b) What were the long-range causes?
3. **Solving Problems** Do you think that the United States could have avoided war with Mexico in 1846? Explain.

4. **Linking Past and Present** (a) Why do you think forty-niners risked their savings and lives looking for gold in California? (b) Can you think of people today who take great risks to make a fortune? Explain.

Applying Your Skills

1. **Making a Review Chart** Make a chart with four columns and two rows. Title the chart American Expansion. Label the columns Oregon, Texas, Mexican Cession, Gadsden Purchase. Label the rows Date Added, How Added. Use the material in the chapter to complete the chart.
2. **Using a Diary as a Primary Source** This excerpt is from the diary of a Mormon woman traveling to Utah: "To start out on such a journey in the winter and in our state of poverty, it would seem like walking into the jaws of death. But we put our trust in [our heavenly father], feeling that we were his chosen people." (a) What does the writer think the trip will be like? Explain. (b) Why is she willing to face the hardships of the trip?
3. **Outlining** Review the outlining skill on page 32. Then, prepare an outline of Section 2 of this chapter. Using your outline, write a summary of events leading up to Texan independence.

Thinking About Geography

Match the letters on the map with the places listed below.

1. Louisiana Purchase
2. Gadsden Purchase
3. Oregon Country
4. Florida
5. The United States, 1783
6. Texas Annexation
7. Mexican Cession

Location At what latitude did the United States and Britain agree to divide Oregon?

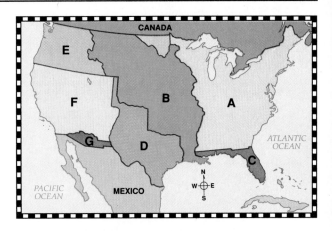

History Writer's Workshop

Choosing a Topic for a Report

Finding a topic is the first step in the prewriting process for preparing a report. Choose a topic that you want to read and write about and one for which you can find at least three good sources of information.

To begin, make a list of several possible topics. Then, visit your library to discover what resources are available for each. Look up the topics in encyclopedias, the library card catalog, and the *Readers' Guide to Periodical Literature*. If you find little information on a topic, you probably should not use it. If you find a great deal of information, you may have to narrow the topic so that you can cover it in a short report.

Practice Choose two topics from the following list. Then, write a sentence describing an aspect of each topic that you would like to research.

1. Mountain Men
2. The Oregon Trail
3. Stephen Austin
4. The Alamo
5. The Republic of Texas
6. The Mormons
7. The California Gold Rush

Writing to Learn

1. Write the lyrics to a song that the Mountain Men might have sung during a rendezvous. Begin by listing some problems Mountain Men probably endured in their daily lives, some benefits they might have enjoyed, and their feelings about their way of life. Write a different verse for each of these areas. As you write, try to give a feeling of what the life of a typical Mountain Man was like. Revise your lyrics for specific and realistic detail. After you proofread and make a final copy, read your lyrics to the class.

2. Write a dialogue between a Mexican and an American about Manifest Destiny. Before you begin to write the dialogue, list the possible positions each side might take on the issue. Then, write a topic sentence for each person that summarizes his or her views on the issue. Write supporting statements for each person, organized in order of importance. Revise to include the ideas of each person in dialogue form. Then, proofread and make a final copy of your dialogue. Ask two classmates to deliver the dialogue in class.

The "Iron Horse" *A flurry of inventions boosted the northern economy during the 1800s. Perhaps the most important improvement, however, was the growth of railroads. Here, an early "iron horse" pulls into the station at Stratford, Connecticut.* **Economics** *How do you think the growth of railroads affected life in the North?*

CHAPTER SPOTLIGHT

The Big Picture

In the mid-1800s, a surge of inventions brought on many changes in the United States. New machines as well as new methods improved farming, industry, and communication. Factories expanded and railroads stretched across the nation. With these changes came a wave of prosperity.

Despite this progress, the United States held on to slavery, a very old and inhumane practice. In 1860, whites owned 4 million African Americans. Clearly, there was need for drastic change. But to many Americans, the right to liberty and the pursuit of happiness was for some, not for all.

Kathleen Underwood

Of Special Interest

Focus On

◆ How did inventions change the northern economy?

◆ What was life like in the industrial North?

◆ How did cotton come to dominate the southern economy?

◆ What was life like for white and black Americans in the South?

"I was born in 1844. . . . First [thing] I remember was my ma and us [children] being sold off the [auction] block to Mistress Payne. When I was . . . too little to work in the field, I stayed at the big house most of the time and helped Mistress Payne feed the chickens, make scarecrows to keep the hawks away and put wood on the fires. After I got big enough to hoe, I went to the field same as the other[s]. . . . In the summer after the crop was laid by I helped to cut wood for winter, build fences, cut bushes and drive a wagon. . . . I never earned any money for myself. . . . I didn't hardly know what money looked like."

In this excerpt, Jack Payne recalls his life as a slave in Texas. Throughout the South, millions of African Americans like him suffered the anguish of slavery. Toiling from dawn to dusk, they had neither freedom nor rights.

By the 1840s, cotton was the South's major cash crop. Cotton plantations and slavery spread from the east coast to the Mississippi River and beyond. From the plantations worked by slaves, thousands of bales of cotton were shipped to the North.

In the North, new factories and new cities grew. Workers toiled long hours at low wages to make cotton into thousands of rolls of cloth. So it was that the North and South, very different in ways of life, were linked by cotton—and the evil of slavery.

1 The Growth of Industry in the North

FIND OUT

◆ What new inventions changed farming in the North?

◆ How did the telegraph help business?

◆ How did steam power and railroads help industry grow?

◆ VOCABULARY telegraph, clipper ship

In 1846, Elias Howe made a bold challenge. He claimed that he had built a machine that could sew faster than the five best seamstresses in Boston. A clothing maker accepted Howe's dare and arranged a contest.

During the showdown, Howe sat at a small table, calmly pumping the foot pedal that drove his machine. Nearby, the seamstresses worked feverishly with needle and thread. In the end, all agreed that Howe had won. When tailors in Boston heard about Howe's invention, they cried, "Death to sewing machines or death to tailors!"

Sewing machines did not die. Clothing makers bought hundreds of them. Workers could now make dozens of jackets faster than a tailor could sew one by hand. The cost of clothing dropped. Many tailors had to find new ways to earn a living. The sewing machine was one of many new inventions that changed life in the North after 1820.

Farming Inventions

In the 1800s, the North was a seedbed for new inventions. "In Massachusetts and Connecticut," a French visitor exclaimed, "there is not a laborer who has not invented a machine or a tool."

Several inventions made work easier for farmers. John Deere invented a light-weight plow made of steel. Earlier plows were made of wood or iron. They weighed so much that they had to be pulled by slow-moving oxen. A horse pulling a new steel plow could prepare a field for planting much faster.

In 1847, Cyrus McCormick opened a factory in Chicago that made mechanical reapers. The reaper was a horse-drawn machine that mowed wheat and other grains. McCormick's reaper could do the work of five people using hand tools.

The reaper and the steel plow helped farmers raise more grain with fewer hands. As a result, thousands of farm workers left the countryside. Some went west to start farms of their own. Others found jobs in new factories in northern cities.

The Telegraph

In 1837, Samuel F. B. Morse invented his "talking wire," or telegraph. The telegraph was a device that sent electrical signals along a wire. The signals were based on a code of dots, dashes, and spaces. Each group of dots and dashes stood for a letter. Dot-dash, for example, stood for "A." Later, this code was called the Morse code.

Congress gave Morse funds to run 40 miles of wire from Washington, D.C., to Baltimore. On May 24, 1844, Morse set up his telegraph in the Supreme Court chamber in Washington. He tapped out a short message: "What hath God wrought!" A few seconds later, the operator in Baltimore tapped back the same message. The telegraph worked!

Morse's invention was an instant success. Telegraph companies sprang up everywhere and strung thousands of miles of wire. Businesses especially gained from being able to send messages over long distances in minutes. Using the telegraph, factory owners, merchants, and farmers could find out instantly about supply, demand, and prices of goods in different areas. For example, western farmers might

Cyrus McCormick: Inventor and Business Leader

While growing up on a Virginia farm, Cyrus McCormick spent hours tinkering with tools. As a young man, he turned his talents to developing a machine to harvest wheat. McCormick was well aware of the advantages such a machine would have. At harvest time, farmers had to hire a crew to cut their wheat. If he could design a machine that mowed wheat, McCormick realized, he could save farmers money—and make a fortune for himself.

In 1831, McCormick created a "mechanical reaper." He hitched the reaper to a horse that pulled it through a wheat field. The weird-looking device actually cut wheat.

McCormick then wanted to sell his reaper to as many farmers as possible. In 1847, he built his first factory in Chicago. When the reapers were ready, he told farmers that they could buy one for $30 down and take six months to pay the balance of $100.

Within a short time, 19 more McCormick factories opened, turning out reapers by the hundreds. Through inventiveness, hard work, and business skill, Cyrus McCormick helped to make the Great Plains the greatest food producer in the world.

1. Why would a reaper save farmers money?

2. **Solving Problems** Why was McCormick's payment plan a good idea for farmers who could not afford $130 to buy a reaper?

learn of a wheat shortage in New York and ship their grain east to meet the demand.

The First Railroads

A further boost to the economy came as transportation improved. Americans continued to build new roads and canals. But the greatest change came with railroads.

The first railroads were built in the early 1800s. They ran on wood rails covered with strips of iron. Horses or mules slowly pulled the cars along the rails. Then, in 1829, an English family developed a steam-powered engine to pull rail cars. The engine, called the *Rocket,* barreled along at 30 miles (48 km) per hour, an amazing speed at the time.

In the United States, some people laughed at the noisy clatter of these "iron horses." Others watched in horror as sparks flew from the smokestack, burning holes in passengers' clothing and setting barns on fire. Many Americans believed that horse-drawn rail cars were safer and faster than trains pulled by steam engines. In 1830, a race was held to settle the question.

A huge crowd gathered in Baltimore to watch a horse-drawn rail car race the *Tom Thumb,* a steam-powered engine. One onlooker said that the *Tom Thumb* looked like "a teakettle on a truck." At first, the horse struggled to keep up with the steam engine. Suddenly, *Tom Thumb* broke down. The crowd cheered as the horse crossed the finish line first. But *Tom Thumb*'s defeat did not mean the end of the steam engine.

Engineers soon designed better engines and rails. Private companies began to build railroads, often with help from state governments. By the 1850s, railroads linked eastern cities to Cincinnati and Chicago in the Midwest. Cities at the center of railroad hubs grew rapidly. (📖 See "American Notes" on page 682.)

Yankee Clippers

Railroads boosted business inside the United States. At the same time, trade also increased between the United States and other nations. At seaports in the North-

An Unusual Race *In 1830, the steam-powered engine* Tom Thumb *raced a horse-drawn rail car. To the delight of horse fanciers, who jeered at the "teakettle on a truck," the horse won. But the race convinced many Americans that railroads were the transportation of the future.* **Technology** *Why did people oppose steam-powered engines at first? What do you think caused them to change their minds?*

east, captains loaded their ships with cotton, fur, wheat, lumber, and tobacco. They then sailed to the four corners of the world.

Speed was the key to successful trade at sea. In 1845, an American named John Griffiths launched the *Rainbow,* the first of the clipper ships. These sleek vessels had tall masts and huge sails that caught every gust of wind. Their narrow hulls clipped swiftly through the water.

In the 1840s, American clipper ships broke every speed record. One clipper sped from New York to Hong Kong in 81 days, flying past older ships that took five months to reach China. The speed of the clippers helped the United States win a large share of the world's sea trade in the 1840s and 1850s. This trade brought wealth to port cities like Boston, New York, and Philadelphia.

The golden age of the clipper ship was brief. In the 1850s, Britain launched the first ocean-going steamships. These sturdy iron vessels carried more cargo and traveled faster than clippers.

The steamship helped to open markets in Japan to American traders. In 1852, President Millard Fillmore sent Commodore Matthew Perry to win access to Japanese ports. These ports had long been closed to foreign merchants. When Japanese officials saw the black smoke belching from the stacks of Perry's warships, they were impressed. They decided that the United States was a power they should respect. In 1854, Perry persuaded the Japanese to grant trading privileges to the United States.

The Northern Economy Expands

In 1834, a young French engineer, Michael Chevalier, toured the North. He was most impressed by the burst of industry there—the textile factories, shipyards, and iron mills. In describing the North, he wrote:

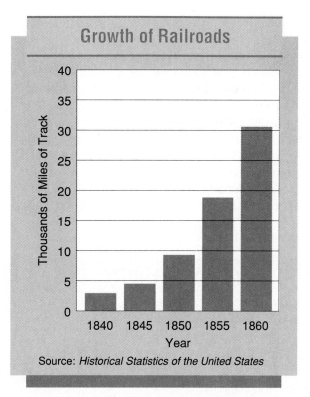

Growth of Railroads

Source: *Historical Statistics of the United States*

GRAPH SKILLS *Railroads expanded rapidly after 1840. The South built thousands of miles of railroads. But most new railroad track was laid in the North and the Midwest.* ◆ *According to the graph, in what year was the country's total railroad mileage more than 20,000 miles? How do you think the growth of factories in the North affected the building of railroads there?*

"Everywhere is heard the noise of hammers, of spindles, of bells calling the hands to their work, or dismissing them from their tasks. . . . It is the peaceful hum of an industrious population, whose movements are regulated like clockwork."

Northern industry did, in fact, grow steadily in the mid-1800s. That growth was largely due to new methods, inventions, and developments.

Steam power. By the 1830s, factories began to use steam power instead of water power. Steam-driven machines were powerful and cheap to run. Also, steam power allowed factory owners to build factories almost anywhere, not just alongside swift-flowing rivers.

New machines. At the same time, new machines cut the cost of manufacturing many goods. The lower-priced goods attracted eager buyers. Families no longer made clothing and other goods in their homes. Instead, they bought factory-made products. As demand rose, owners built larger factories and hired more workers.

Railroads. Railroads allowed factory owners to ship raw materials and finished goods cheaply and quickly. Also, as railroads stretched across the nation, towns that once were hard to reach now were linked to cities and factories. These towns became new markets for factory goods.

Railroads also affected northern farming. Since colonial days, farmers in New England had scratched a living from the poor, rocky soil. Now railroads brought grain and other foods from the West. New Englanders could not compete with this new source of cheap food. Many left their

MAP STUDY

Farming remained vital to the northern economy, but industry grew in importance every year.
1. *Which states produced textiles?*
2. *What products did Ohio produce?*
3. **Applying Information** *Which states would be helped by the invention of new farm tools? Explain.*

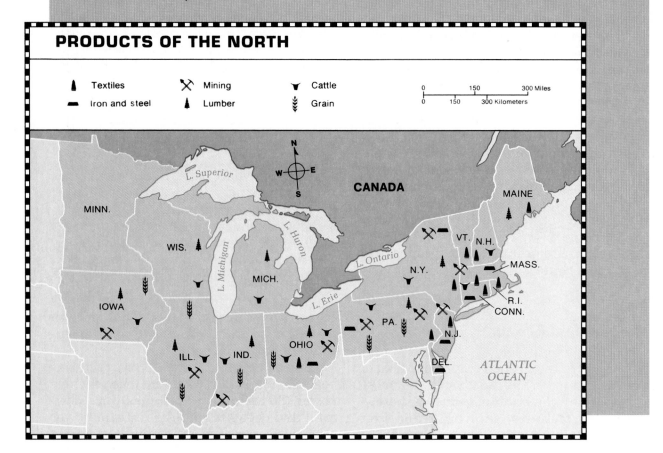

A Northern Iron Foundry *Growth in one area of manufacturing promoted growth in other industries. The spread of railroads, for example, led to an increased need for iron. This, in turn, stimulated mining in areas where ore was plentiful. Great furnaces produced iron in foundries such as the one shown here.* **Technology** *Name two developments that encouraged the growth of northern industries.*

farms to find new jobs as factory workers, store clerks, and sailors. More and more, New Englanders turned to manufacturing and trade.

SECTION 1 REVIEW

1. **Identify:** (a) Elias Howe, (b) John Deere, (c) Cyrus McCormick, (d) Samuel F. B. Morse, (e) John Griffiths.
2. **Define:** (a) telegraph, (b) clipper ship.
3. (a) What new inventions made work easier for farmers? (b) How did these inventions affect farm workers?
4. How did many businesses benefit from the telegraph?
5. How did each of the following help industry grow: (a) steam power; (b) railroads?
6. **Drawing Conclusions** Samuel F.B. Morse invented the telegraph. But he tapped out, "What hath God wrought!" when he demonstrated the device. What does this show about religious belief at the time?

2 Life in the Industrial North

FIND OUT

◆ How did working conditions change in factories and shops?

◆ Why did skilled workers form unions?

◆ What newcomers arrived in the United States in the mid-1800s?

◆ What was life like for African Americans in the North?

◆ **VOCABULARY** skilled worker, trade union, strike, unskilled worker, immigrant, famine, nativist, discrimination

On her thirteenth birthday, Alzina Parsons suffered a terrible experience at the factory where she worked. It began when Alzina caught her right hand in a spinning machine, badly mangling her fingers. Without giving medicine for the pain, the factory doctor cut off one of her fingers. Then, the foreman sent the young girl back to work without notifying her family.

In the early 1800s, this horrible incident probably would not have occurred. Even though the work day was hard, mill owners treated workers like human beings. But by the 1840s, life in the factories had changed. Factory owners no longer faced a labor shortage. Many now treated workers like machines.

Factory Conditions Worsen

Factories of the 1840s and 1850s were very different from earlier mills. Besides being larger, they used steam-powered machines. More laborers worked longer hours for lower wages.

The cities where the factories were located also changed. Factory owners no longer built planned villages with boardinghouses and parks. Instead, ugly buildings surrounded the factories. The workers' homes often stood in the shadow—and smoke—of the factory.

Families in factories. As more factories sprang up, the demand for workers increased. Owners began to hire entire families, including mothers and children. In some cases, a family signed a contract to work for one year. If even one family member broke the contract, the entire family might be fired.

The factory day began early. A whistle sounded at 4:00 A.M. Father, mother, and children dressed in the dark and headed off to work. At 7:30 A.M. and at noon, the whistle blew again to announce breakfast and lunch breaks. The day did not end until 7:30 P.M. when a final whistle sent workers home.

Hazards at work. During their long day, factory workers faced discomfort and danger. Owners often ignored poor working conditions. Few factories had windows or heating systems. In summer, the heat and humidity were stifling. In winter, the cold contributed to sickness.

The factory's whirling, pounding machines had no safety devices. From time to time, machines crushed workers' hands or arms, as happened to Alzina Parsons. But owners paid little attention to the hazards. At that time, the courts did not fine factory owners for injuries or unsafe conditions. Injured workers, however, paid a heavy price. They lost their jobs and received no money to make up for lost wages.

Workers as machines. In 1855, a visitor to a textile mill in Fall River, Massachusetts, asked the manager of the mill how he treated his workers. The manager's reply was harsh but honest:

> ❝I regard people just as I regard my machinery. So long as they can do my work for what I choose to pay them, I keep them, getting out of them all I can.❞

Yet despite the long hours and dangers, factory workers in America were better off than those in Europe. At least American workers could find jobs and earn regular wages. European workers often had no work at all.

Craftworkers Become Laborers

By the 1830s, the work life of many craftworkers, or skilled workers, was changing. Skilled workers are people who have learned a trade, such as carpentry or shoemaking.

In 1831, Jesse Hatch described a shoemaker's shop in Rochester, New York:

> ❝It was customary for the boss, with the younger apprentices, to occupy the room in front where, with bared arms and leather aprons, they performed their work and met their customers.❞

The young apprentices Hatch described were learning from a craftworker how to

"R": Letter From a Factory Girl, 1847

The magazine Voice of Industry *asked readers to describe working in a factory. One worker, or "operative," sent this account. She signed her name "R" out of fear that she might be fired for her remarks.*

"Dear Sir:

Since I was between seven and eight years old, I have been employed almost without intermission in a factory, which is almost 18 years. During that time I have not attended school more than one year. . . .

The time we are required to labor is altogether too long. . . . If any one doubts it, let them come to our mills on a summer's day, at five . . . in the afternoon, and see the drooping, weary persons moving about, as though their legs were hardly able to support their bodies. . . . There is nothing more common amongst operatives than the remark that 'their legs ache so, it seems as though they would drop off.' . . . Many times have I had girls faint in the morning . . . the air being so impure in the mill. . . .

We commence to work as soon—and work as long as we can see almost the year round, and for nearly half the year we work by lamp light, at both ends of the day. . . . As to wages, [they do not] exceed $1.50 per week.

Yours for the right, R"

1. What does "R" dislike about factory work?

2. **Drawing Conclusions** Why do you think "R" mentions that she attended school for only one year?

---

make shoes. They hoped one day to become expert shoemakers and open their own shops.

But within ten years, the shoe trade had changed completely. No longer did young apprentices learn to make an entire shoe. Instead, the boss hired workers to do only one part of the job. One worker sewed the sole, for example, while another tacked on the heel. No longer either did apprentices work with the boss in the front room of a shop. Instead, workers crowded in the back room of a small factory.

After 1830, many other trades changed as shoemaking did. Why did these changes take place? Shop owners and others saw that they could produce goods more cheaply if they hired workers with less skill and paid them lower wages. More and more, laborers rather than craftworkers produced shoes, clocks, barrels, and other goods.

Skilled Workers Unite

Craftworkers had always taken pride in their skill and independence. The growing factory system threatened to rob them of both. As more shops turned into small factories, skilled workers fought back. By the 1830s, skilled workers in each trade were uniting to form trade unions.

The unions called for a shorter work day, higher wages, and better working conditions. Sometimes, unions pressed their demands by going on strike. In a strike, union workers refuse to do their jobs. But at the time, strikes were illegal in the United States. Strikers faced fines or jail sentences. And strike leaders often were fired from their jobs.

Slowly, however, workers made progress. In 1840, they won a major victory when President Van Buren approved a 10-hour workday for government employees. Most people still worked 12 to 15 hours a day. But they pressed their demand for the same hours as government workers. Workers celebrated another victory in 1842 when a Massachusetts court declared they had the right to strike.

Skilled workers won better pay because of their value to factory owners. Unskilled workers, however, were unable to bargain for better wages. Unskilled workers did jobs that required little or no training. Because these workers were easily replaced, employers were unwilling to listen to their demands.

Women Workers Organize

The success of trade unions encouraged unskilled workers to organize. Workers in New England textile mills especially were eager to protest cuts in wages and unfair work rules. As you have read, many of these workers were women.

Women workers faced special problems. First, they had always earned less money than men. Second, most union leaders did not want women in their ranks. Unions shared the belief that women should not work outside the home. In fact, the goal of many unions was to raise men's wages so that their wives could leave the factories.

Women also faced another problem. People thought it was wrong for a woman to be a public speaker. Sarah Bagley, a labor

Women Workers on Strike
Like men in trade unions, unskilled women workers used strikes to make their demands clear. In this drawing by an eyewitness, women shoemakers in Lynn, Massachusetts, march to protest unfair treatment.
Economics *The women are carrying a banner that reads "Give Us a Fair Compensation." What does this refer to?*

leader for women in the Lowell mills, encouraged women to overcome this obstacle:

> ❝For the last half century, it has been [considered] a violation of woman's [role] to appear before the public as a speaker; but when our rights are trampled upon and we appeal in vain to legislators, what shall we do but appeal to the people?❞

Despite the problems, women continued their protests. They staged several strikes at Lowell in the 1830s. But as working conditions at the mills worsened, fewer native-born women took factory jobs. By the late 1840s, newcomers from Europe were replacing women in the factories.

Millions of New Americans

Many workers in the new factories of the North were immigrants. An immigrant is a person who enters a new country in order to settle there. In the 1840s and 1850s, about 4 million immigrants arrived in the United States. They supplied much of the unskilled labor that helped to build the nation's growing industries.

The Irish. People from Ireland had been coming to the United States for many years. But in the 1840s, a disease rotted the potato crop across Europe. The loss of the crop caused a famine, or food shortage, especially in Ireland. Between 1845 and 1860, over 1.5 million Irish fled to the United States.

Most of the Irish immigrants were too poor to buy farmland. So they settled in the cities where their ships landed. In New York and Boston, thousands of Irish crowded into poor neighborhoods. They took any job they could find.

The Germans. Another wave of immigrants came from Germany. Nearly one million Germans arrived between 1850 and 1860. Revolutions had broken out in several parts of Germany in 1848. The rebels fought for democratic government. When the uprisings failed, thousands had to flee for their lives. Many other Germans came simply to make a better life for themselves. Those with enough money often bought farms in the Midwest. Others settled in eastern cities.

Contributions. Newcomers from many lands helped the American economy grow. In New England, Irish men and women took the factory jobs that native-born women were giving up. Coal miners and iron workers from Britain and Germany brought useful skills to American industry.

Each group left an imprint on American life. The Irish brought their lively music and dances. Germans brought the custom of decorating trees at Christmas. Immigrants from Norway, Sweden, and other countries also enriched the United States with their language, food, and customs.

A Reaction Against Immigrants

Not everyone welcomed the flood of newcomers. Some Americans, called nativists, wanted to preserve the country for native-born, white citizens. Using the slogan "Americans must rule America," they called for laws to limit immigration. They also wanted to keep immigrants from voting until they had lived in America for 21 years. At the time, newcomers could vote after only 5 years.

Nativists gave several reasons for disliking immigrants. Some felt that newcomers "stole" jobs from native-born Americans by working for lower pay. Others blamed immigrants for crime in the growing cities. Still others mistrusted the many Irish and German newcomers who were Catholics. Until the 1840s, nearly all Americans were Protestants.

In the 1850s, nativists formed a political party. It was called the **Know-Nothing party** because members said "I know nothing" when asked about the party. Many of the party's meetings and rituals were kept secret from those who were not members.

In 1856, the Know-Nothing candidate for President won 21 percent of the popular vote. Soon after, however, the party died. Still, many Americans continued to blame the nation's problems on immigrants.

African Americans in the North

Slavery was once legal in the North. But by the early 1800s, all the northern states had abolished slavery. As a result, thousands of free African Americans lived throughout the North.

Selling Oysters in Philadelphia *Free blacks in the North often had to work at unskilled jobs for very low wages. Still, the North offered blacks more opportunity than the South did. Here, a Philadelphia man sells oysters outside the Chestnut Street Theater.* **Citizenship** *In what other ways were African Americans discriminated against in the North?*

Although they were free, African Americans in the North still faced discrimination. **Discrimination** is a policy or an attitude that denies equal rights to certain people. One writer pointed out that African Americans were denied "the ballot-box, the jury box, the halls of the legislature, the army, the public lands, the school, and the church."

Even skilled African Americans had trouble finding decent jobs. One black carpenter was turned away by every furniture maker in Cincinnati. A study on free blacks reported one of his disappointments:

> **❝**At last he found a shop carried on by an Englishman, who agreed to employ him—but on entering the shop, the workmen threw down their tools and declared that he should leave or they would.**❞**

Despite discrimination, some free African Americans moved ahead. James Forten grew rich by manufacturing sails. Other free blacks became lawyers, actors, and scientists. Many of those who gained success risked their fortunes and lives to speak out against slavery in the South.

SECTION 2 REVIEW

1. **Identify:** (a) Know-Nothing party, (b) James Forten.
2. **Define:** (a) skilled worker, (b) trade union, (c) strike, (d) unskilled worker, (e) immigrant, (f) famine, (g) nativist, (h) discrimination.
3. (a) How did working conditions in factories worsen in the 1840s and 1850s? (b) How did the work life of skilled workers change?
4. (a) Name two groups of immigrants who arrived in the 1840s and 1850s. (b) Why did nativists dislike the immigrants?
5. What problems did free African Americans face in the North?
6. **Linking Past and Present** Why do you think tens of thousands of immigrants still come to the United States each year?

3 Cotton Becomes King

FIND OUT

◆ How did the cotton gin affect the growth of slavery?

◆ Why did cotton planters move westward?

◆ Why did the South have less industry than the North?

In 1827, an Englishman named Basil Hall traveled through much of the South aboard a riverboat. He complained that southerners were interested in only one thing—cotton:

> ❝All day and almost all night long, the captain, pilot, crew and passengers were talking of nothing else; and sometimes our ears were so wearied with the sound of cotton! cotton! cotton! that we gladly hailed fresh . . . company in hopes of some change—but alas! . . . 'What's cotton at?' was the first eager inquiry.❞

Cotton became even more important to the South in the years after Hall's visit. Even though southerners grew other crops, cotton was the region's leading export. Cotton plantations—and the slave system they depended on—shaped the way of life in the South.

The Cotton Gin

As you have read, New Englanders built the first American textile mills in the 1790s. These mills, along with British factories, needed raw cotton to manufacture cloth.

At first, southern planters could not keep up with the demand. They could grow the cotton easily because the soil and cli-

mate were ideal. But removing the seeds from the cotton pods was a slow task. To make a profit, planters needed a better way to clean the cotton.

In 1793, a young Connecticut school teacher named Eli Whitney traveled to Georgia. He planned to take a job as a tutor on a plantation. But when Whitney learned of the problem facing planters, he put his mind to building a gin, or machine, to clean cotton.

In only ten days, Whitney came up with a model. His cotton gin had two rollers with thin wire teeth. The teeth pulled the seeds and fibers apart, leaving the cotton ready to be spun.

The cotton gin was simple, but its effects were enormous. A worker using a gin could do the work of 1,000 people cleaning cotton by hand. Because of the gin, planters could now grow cotton at a huge profit.

The Cotton Boom

Planters soon found that soil planted with cotton year after year wore out. They needed new land to cultivate. After the War of 1812, cotton planters began to move west. Often, the sons and daughters of planters set off for new land on the frontier. By the 1850s, the Cotton Kingdom had spread in a wide band from South Carolina through Alabama and Mississippi into Texas. (See the map on page 470.)

As plantations spread across the South, cotton production increased at a rapid rate. In 1792, cotton planters grew only 6,000 bales of cotton a year. By 1820, the South produced over 400,000 bales. By 1850, the figure was over 2 million bales.

The cotton boom had a tragic side. As the Cotton Kingdom spread, so did slavery. Even though cotton could now be cleaned by machine, it still had to be planted and picked by hand. The result was a cruel cycle. Slaves grew and picked the cotton that brought profits. Planters used the profits to buy more land and more slaves.

The United States had made the slave trade with Africa illegal after 1807. But planters in the new cotton regions still were able to buy slaves from the eastern states. As their land wore out, eastern planters there sold the slaves they did not need. In many cases, these sales broke up slave families.

No Place for Industry

Cotton was the South's biggest cash crop. But tobacco, rice, and sugar cane also made money for planters. Southerners raised much of the nation's livestock, too.

Some southerners wanted to encourage industry in the South. William Gregg, for ex-

MAP STUDY

By the mid-1800s, cotton had become king in the South. It overshadowed other important goods, such as tobacco, rice, and livestock.
1. *To what areas did cotton growing spread between 1840 and 1860?*
2. *What were the main products of Virginia?*
3. **Comparing** *Compare this map with the map on page 462. (a) What products did the North and South both produce? (b) What products did the South alone produce?*

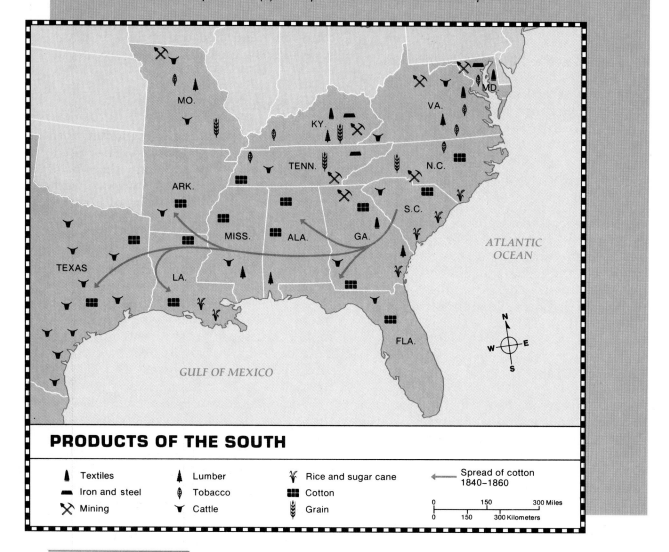

PRODUCTS OF THE SOUTH

- Textiles
- Iron and steel
- Mining
- Lumber
- Tobacco
- Cattle
- Rice and sugar cane
- Cotton
- Grain
- Spread of cotton 1840–1860

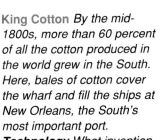

King Cotton *By the mid-1800s, more than 60 percent of all the cotton produced in the world grew in the South. Here, bales of cotton cover the wharf and fill the ships at New Orleans, the South's most important port.* **Technology** *What invention encouraged southern planters to grow more cotton? Explain.*

ample, modeled his cotton mill in South Carolina on the mills in Lowell, Massachusetts. Gregg built houses and gardens for his workers and schools for their children.

Even so, the South lagged behind the North in manufacturing. Rich planters invested their money in land and slaves rather than factories. Also, slavery reduced the demand for goods. In the North, most farmers had enough money to buy manufactured goods. But in the South, millions of slaves could buy absolutely nothing. This greatly reduced the number of products the South used and hurt southern industry.

With little industry, the South depended on the North and Europe for goods such as cloth, furniture, and tools. Many southerners resented this fact. One southerner described a burial to show how the South depended on the North for many goods in the 1850s:

“The grave was dug through solid marble, but the marble headstone came from Vermont. It was in a pine wilderness but the pine coffin came from Cincinnati. An iron mountain overshadowed it but the coffin nails and the screws and the shovel came from Pittsburgh. . . . A hickory grove grew nearby, but the pick and shovel handles came from New York. . . . That country, so rich in underdeveloped resources, furnished nothing for the funeral except the corpse and the hole in the ground.”

Still, most southerners were proud of their booming cotton industry. As long as cotton remained king, southerners looked to the future with confidence.

SECTION 3 REVIEW

1. **Locate:** (a) South Carolina, (b) Alabama, (c) Mississippi, (d) Texas.
2. **Identify:** (a) Eli Whitney, (b) William Gregg.
3. What effect did the cotton gin have on the southern economy?
4. Why did cotton planters move farther west?
5. Why did the South lag behind the North in manufacturing?
6. **Forecasting** How do you think southerners would have reacted to a threat to the cotton industry?

4 Life in the Cotton Kingdom

FIND OUT

◆ What three groups made up white society in the South?

◆ What was life like for free blacks in the South?

◆ How did slaves endure hardships on the plantations?

◆ VOCABULARY extended family

Solomon Northup learned his first lesson in picking cotton at age 32. Northup was born a free African American in New York. In 1841, however, two white men kidnapped him and sold him as a slave in the South. For the next 12 years, Northup worked on a plantation in Louisiana. Like other slaves, he toiled in the fields from "can see to can't see," or from dawn to dusk. For supper, he ate cold bacon and corn meal. His bed was a "plank twelve inches wide and ten feet long."

A Plantation Mistress *The wife of a planter enjoyed wealth and social position. But she also had many duties, including nursing the sick and overseeing the work of the house slaves.* **Economics** *Why were wealthy southern families called the "cottonocracy"?*

Northup was not the only free black to be captured and sold into slavery. But he was one of the few who escaped and told his story. His book *12 Years a Slave* gave northerners a firsthand look at the slave system.

White Southerners

The Old South is often pictured as a land of vast plantations worked by hundreds of slaves. Such grand estates did exist in the South. But most white southerners were not rich planters. In fact, a large majority of whites owned no slaves at all.

The "cottonocracy." A planter was someone who owned at least 20 slaves. In 1860, there were about 2 million white families in the South. Of them, only 1 in 40, or a total of about 50,000, were families of planters. These wealthy families were called the "cottonocracy" because they made their money from cotton. Even though they were few in number, their views and way of life dominated the South.

The richest planters built elegant homes and filled them with fine European furniture. They entertained lavishly, dressing and behaving very much like European nobility.

Planters had responsibilities, too. They had to make important decisions about planting and harvesting their crops. Because of their wealth and influence, many planters became political leaders. They devoted many hours to local, state, and national politics. To run day-to-day affairs on their plantations, planters hired overseers to manage the work of slaves.

Small farmers. Most southern whites were small farmers. These "plain folk," as they called themselves, owned some land and perhaps one or two slaves. Unlike planters, plain folk worked alongside their slaves in the cotton fields.

Small farmers in the South were not so well off as those in the North. As a result, they helped each other out. "People who lived miles apart counted themselves as neighbors," wrote a farmer in Mississippi.

Virginia Wedding *Most southern whites were "plain folk" who lived on small farms and worked hard to make a living. They socialized modestly with friends and neighbors. This painting by William Ranney shows a wedding procession arriving at a farm in Virginia.* **Economics** *Why did small farmers who owned no slaves themselves support slavery?*

One man from Georgia described what happened when a family lost its home in a fire:

> **❝**The neighbors came bearing gifts, food, dishes and clothes, and quilts, and even furniture. They contributed logs and lumber, helped to rebuild the house and barn, and brought wagon loads of fodder to feed the stock.**❞**

Even though most small farmers owned no slaves, they firmly supported slavery. Many hoped to make enough money to become planters themselves some day.

Poor whites. At the bottom of the social ladder was a small group of poor whites. They did not own the land they farmed. Instead, they rented it, often paying the owner with part of their crop. Many barely kept their families from starving.

Poor whites often lived in the hilly, wooded areas of the South. They planted corn, potatoes, and other vegetables. Like their better-off neighbors, they herded cattle and pigs. Despite their hard lives, poor whites enjoyed rights denied to free blacks and slaves.

African Americans in the South

Both free blacks and slaves lived in the South. Although legally free, free blacks faced harsh discrimination. And slaves had no rights at all.

Free blacks. Most free blacks were descendants of slaves freed during and after the American Revolution. Others had bought their freedom. In 1860, over 200,000 free blacks lived in the South. Most lived in Maryland and Delaware, where slavery was in decline. But others lived in cities like New Orleans, Richmond, and Charleston.

Slave owners did not like free African Americans living in the South. They feared that free blacks encouraged slaves to rebel. Also, slave owners justified slavery on the basis that blacks could not take care of themselves. Free black workers proved this idea wrong.

To discourage free African Americans, southern states passed laws that made life even harder for them. Free blacks were not allowed to vote or travel. In some southern states, they either had to leave the state or become slaves.

Despite these limits, free African Americans made valuable contributions to southern life. Norbert Rillieux (RIHL yoo), a free black in New Orleans, invented a machine that revolutionized sugar making. Henry Blair patented a seed planter.

Slaves. Four million slaves made up one third of the South's population by 1860. Most worked as field hands on cotton plantations. Both men and women did the backbreaking labor of clearing new land, planting, and harvesting crops. Children helped by pulling weeds, collecting wood, and taking water to the field hands. By the time they were teenagers, they too worked between 12 and 14 hours a day.

Slave Craftworkers *Most plantation slaves worked in the fields. But some were skilled carpenters, barrelmakers, quilters, potters, and spinners. The goods they made were both beautiful and practical.* **Daily Life** *Why do you think slave craftworkers were important to a plantation?*

On large plantations, some slaves became skilled workers, such as carpenters and blacksmiths. Planters often hired these workers out to other farms. A few slaves worked in cities and lived almost as if they were free blacks. But their earnings belonged to their owners.

Older slaves, especially women, worked as house servants on big estates. They cooked, cleaned, and took care of children under the direction of the planter's wife.

Slave Laws

Southern states passed laws known as slave codes to keep slaves from either running away or rebelling. (See page 162.)

These laws denied slaves basic human rights. Under the codes, slaves were forbidden to gather in groups of more than three. They could not leave their owner's land without a written pass. They were not allowed to own guns.

Slave codes also made it a crime for slaves to learn how to read and write. By limiting education for slaves, owners hoped to keep them from escaping. If slaves did run away, they often had trouble making their way north. Because of their poor education, few could use maps or read train schedules.

Some laws were meant to protect slaves, but only from the worst forms of abuse. Even so, slaves did not have the right to testify in court. So they were not able to bring charges against owners who abused them. Slaves had only one real protection against mistreatment. Owners looked on their slaves as valuable property. Most wanted to keep this human property healthy and productive.

The Slave's World

The slave's life varied from plantation to plantation. Some owners made sure their slaves had decent food, clean cabins, and warm clothes. Other planters spent as little as possible to feed, clothe, and shelter slaves. Even the best owners insisted that slaves work long, hard days.

Long days, short nights. Slaves often toiled in the fields until the sun set. Frederick Douglass, an escaped slave, described working for one harsh master:

> ❝We worked in all weathers. It was never too hot or too cold; it could never rain, blow, hail, or snow too hard for us to work in the field. Work, work, work. . . . The longest days were too short for him and the shortest nights too long for him.❞

Owners and overseers whipped slaves to get a full day's work. But the worst part of slavery was not the beatings. It was the complete loss of freedom. "It's bad to belong to folks that own you soul an' body," one slave said.

Family life. It was hard for slaves to keep families together. Southern laws did not recognize slave marriages. Owners could sell a husband and wife to different buyers. Children were taken from their parents and sold.

On large plantations, many slave families did stay together. For those slaves, the family provided strength, pride, and love. Grandparents, parents, children, aunts, uncles, and cousins formed a close-knit group. This custom of an **extended family** among slaves had its roots in Africa.

Slaves preserved other African customs as well. Parents taught their children old stories and songs. Many African cultures used folktales as a way to pass on their history and moral beliefs.

Importance of religion. By the 1800s, nearly all slaves were devout Christians. Planters often arranged for white ministers to preach to their slaves. But slaves had their own preachers and beliefs. Black preachers emphasized hope in the future. The beautiful spirituals sung by slaves reflected this strong hope. Like many other spirituals, one spoke of a coming day of freedom:

> ❝Old Satan thought he had me fast,
> Broke his old chain and free at last.❞

In later years, much popular American music would emerge from these African

Hauling in the Cotton *For slaves of all ages, life was a constant round of hard work. This picture shows a slave family "hauling the whole week's picking" of cotton.* **Daily Life** *Why did slave owners want to discourage free blacks from living in the South?*

American spirituals. Jazz, blues, and rock 'n' roll all had their roots in the songs slaves sang as they worked in the cotton fields.

Resisting Slavery

Slaves struck back against the system that denied them both freedom and wages. Some broke tools, destroyed crops, and stole food.

Many slaves dared to run away. Some wanted desperately to see a loved one on a nearby plantation. They left for only a few days and then returned. But most runaways wanted to reach the North. In the end, very few of them made it to freedom. The journey was long and dangerous. Every county had slave patrols and sheriffs ready to question an unknown black. It took courage and a great deal of luck to make it through.

Flight for Freedom

What was it like to run away from slavery? The escaped slave in the following account never actually lived. But the description of his flight is based on reports of real runaways who made their way to freedom.

In the dark, on an early Sunday morning, 20-year-old Jesse Needham slipped out of his shabby cabin into the nearby cotton fields. Sunday was the best day to escape. Slaves did not work on Sunday, and there was a good chance he would not be missed for 24 hours.

In an extra shirt, Jesse carried a chunk of bacon and some cornbread, stolen from the cook house. Not much food for the 300-mile journey ahead, Jesse worried.

When he reached the edge of his master's land, Jesse crossed into the woods beyond. As he well knew, without a pass, he had already broken the law.

Finding new courage. By dawn, Jesse was eight miles from the plantation. Traveling by daylight was easier, but it was too risky. He curled up under an old spruce tree and tried to sleep. But his mind would not rest. When dogs began barking at a nearby plantation, Jesse leapt to his feet. His heart pounded and his knees buckled. He was sure that the slave patrol's hounds had picked up his scent. To his relief, no one came.

At dusk, Jesse set out again. The countryside was becoming more and more unfamiliar. Jesse had never been so far from the plantation before. Making his way through the moonlit woods, he thought about life on the plantation—the weariness, the hunger, his bed of straw and rags. He would never go back, he vowed—never.

Thinking things through. Stopping to rest and eat a little, Jesse thought about the men who would soon be hunting him. Today, or tomorrow, newspapers would announce his escape. Handbills with his description would be posted and slave patrols alerted. Jesse could read—just a little—and he remembered a newspaper ad for a runaway slave:

> **❝**TWENTY DOLLARS REWARD—the slave HERCULES. 36 years old, 5 feet 7 or 8 inches high, badly scarred with the whip. I will pay the reward if delivered to me, or lodged in jail, so that I get him.**❞**

His mind racing, Jesse tried to form a plan. Perhaps he could steal some corn and roast it. No, he decided, a fire might draw attention. He had better eat the corn uncooked. Maybe other slaves would give him food. But going near slave quarters was a sure way to get caught, he reminded himself. Patrols usually kept a close eye on the quarters.

The way north. As Jesse plotted, he remembered the words of a spiritual he often sang: "Follow the North Star, up to the land of freedom." Jesse looked up. There was nothing but clouds. Cold, alone, and helpless, he suddenly wondered if he was walking in a circle.

Moving on, Jesse soon spied a rutted country lane. He would leave the woods and follow it, he decided. After all, there probably would be few travelers at that hour. But at every sound, Jesse ducked back into the woods, trembling.

Dawn was breaking as Jesse came to a crossroads. There, he spelled out a mileage stone: Richmond 27 miles (43 km). His master's brother lived in Richmond, Jesse recalled. Jesse took a deep breath. He was, indeed, headed north.

As the sun rose, Jesse returned to the woods. Kneeling at a stream, he washed and took a long drink. Then, looking up at the bright sky, he folded his hands and prayed that Jesus would help him find his way to freedom.

Did Jesse make it to the North? Like many other runaways, he was captured and returned to his owner. Now considered a troublemaker, he was sold to another slave owner. Other Jesses, however, would run from slavery. Despite the nearly hopeless odds, they would risk all to reach freedom. ◆

Slave Revolts

A few slaves used violence to resist the brutal system they faced. Denmark Vesey, a free black, planned a revolt in 1822. Vesey was betrayed before the revolt began. He and 35 others were executed.

In 1831, a slave preacher named Nat Turner led the biggest revolt in the South. Turner led his followers through Virginia, killing more than 60 whites. Terrified whites hunted the countryside for Turner. They killed many innocent blacks before catching and hanging him.

Nat Turner's revolt increased southern fears of a slave uprising. But revolts were rare. Since whites were cautious and well-armed, a revolt had almost no chance of success.

As slavery grew, the economic ties between the North and South became stronger. Northern mill owners needed southern

Running Away *Thousands of blacks fled north each year to escape slavery. Very few reached freedom. Most were caught by packs of hunting dogs or by people who made a business of catching runaways. In this painting by Thomas Moran, two fugitives are pursued through a swamp by bloodhounds.*
Daily Life *How else did slaves resist slavery?*

cotton. And southerners relied on goods from northern factories. Yet Americans in both regions knew that the North and South had very different ways of life. The key difference seemed to be slavery. (📖 See "Contrasting North and South" on page 684.)

| SECTION **4** REVIEW |

1. **Identify:** (a) Norbert Rillieux, (b) Henry Blair, (c) Denmark Vesey, (d) Nat Turner.
2. **Define:** extended family.
3. What classes formed among white society in the South?
4. Why was life difficult for free African Americans in the South?
5. How did African culture and religion help slaves endure the hardships of plantation life?
6. **Analyzing Information** What concerns did runaway slaves like Jesse Needham have in their flight to freedom?

Historians use graphs to show trends, or developments over time, as you learned in Skill Lesson 4 (page 118). Often, historians use two or more graphs to compare different kinds of information. They can compare a line graph and a circle graph. They can also use two line, bar, or circle graphs.

By comparing graphs, historians can begin to draw conclusions about two or more developments. For example, suppose one graph shows an increase in population during a certain period. Another graph shows a decrease in disease for the same period. Historians looking at the graphs might think that population increased because disease decreased. They would need more information before they could be certain, however.

The graphs below are both line graphs. Each shows a trend that took place over a number of years. By comparing the two graphs and thinking about what you read in this chapter, you can draw conclusions about the two developments. Use the following steps to compare the graphs.

1 **Identify the information shown on the graphs.** (a) What is the title of the graph at left? (b) What is the title of the graph at right? (c) What do the numbers on the horizontal axis and vertical axis of the graph at left show? (d) What do the numbers on each axis of the graph at right show?

2 **Practice reading the graphs.** Notice that the numbers given on the vertical axis are in the thousands. (a) About how many thousands of bales of cotton were produced in 1830? In 1860? (b) What was the slave population in 1830? In 1860?

3 **Compare the information shown on the graphs.** Use the graphs and your reading of this chapter to answer these questions. (a) Was there an upward or downward trend in cotton production between 1800 and 1860? (b) Was there an upward or downward trend in slave population in the same period? (c) How do you think the trend in cotton production is related to the trend in slave population?

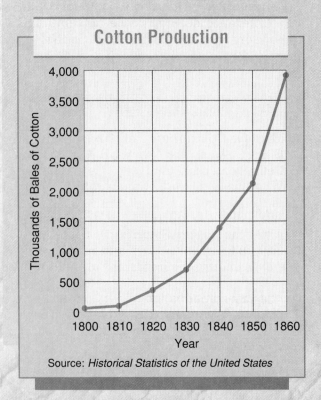

Cotton Production

Thousands of Bales of Cotton

Year

Source: *Historical Statistics of the United States*

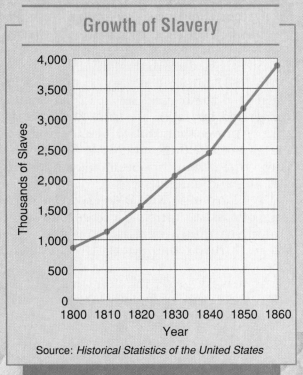

Growth of Slavery

Thousands of Slaves

Year

Source: *Historical Statistics of the United States*

Use the Section Reviews and this Study Guide to review chapter content.

Main Ideas

The main ideas in each section of this chapter are summarized below.

SECTION 1 ■ The Growth of Industry in the North

◆ New inventions helped farmers raise more grain with fewer workers.
◆ The telegraph allowed businesses to send and receive messages instantly.
◆ The clipper ship boosted sea trade in the 1840s and 1850s.
◆ Steam power and railroads helped the northern economy grow.

SECTION 2 ■ Life in the Industrial North

◆ Factory conditions worsened in the 1830s and 1840s.
◆ Skilled workers formed trade unions to fight for better conditions and wages.
◆ Irish and German immigrants poured into the United States in the mid-1800s.
◆ Free African Americans in the North faced discrimination.

SECTION 3 ■ Cotton Becomes King

◆ The cotton gin boosted cotton production and slavery in the South.
◆ Cotton planters pushed farther west as soil in the east wore out.
◆ Unlike the North, the South had very little industry.

SECTION 4 ■ Life in the Cotton Kingdom

◆ White southerners included rich planters, small farmers, and poor whites.
◆ Free African Americans in the South had few rights.
◆ Slaves took pride in their families, religion, and African culture.
◆ Some African Americans resisted slavery by running away or leading revolts.

Key People and Terms

Refer to the Identify and Define questions in the Section Reviews on pages 463, 468, 471, and 477. Use each person, term, and vocabulary word in a complete sentence. When possible, make connections between the people and terms by using more than one person or term in a sentence.

Time Line

1. Make a chart of events in time order. The chart will have two headings: Date, Event. Fill in the chart, using the events on the time line. Add the following events from the chapter: First clipper ship launched; Howe invents sewing machine; *Tom Thumb* competes with a horse; Whitney invents cotton gin. (Refer to the chapter for the dates.)
2. Which events on your chart affected the South more than the North?

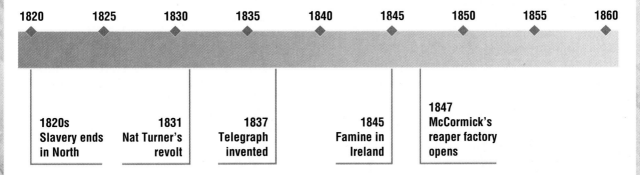

| 1820 | 1825 | 1830 | 1835 | 1840 | 1845 | 1850 | 1855 | 1860 |

1820s Slavery ends in North

1831 Nat Turner's revolt

1837 Telegraph invented

1845 Famine in Ireland

1847 McCormick's reaper factory opens

Understanding Vocabulary

Match each term at left with the correct definition at right.

1. telegraph
2. trade union
3. immigrant
4. famine
5. nativist

a. person who leaves his or her homeland to settle in another country
b. severe food shortage
c. organization of skilled workers
d. person who wanted to limit immigration
e. device that sends electrical signals along a wire

Reviewing the Main Ideas

1. How did the invention of labor-saving devices for farmers spur industry?
2. (a) How did clipper ships help the United States capture sea trade? (b) What cut short the age of clipper ships?
3. What goals did early trade unions have?
4. Why did Irish and German immigrants come in large numbers to United States in the 1840s and 1850s?
5. How did slavery slow the growth of industry in the South?
6. Describe the way of life of small farmers in the South.
7. Why was it difficult for slave families to stay together?
8. What African customs did slaves keep alive in the South?

Thinking Critically

1. **Linking Past and Present** Review the description of inventions on pages 458–460. What recent inventions have changed American life?
2. **Understanding Causes and Effects** How do you think life might have changed in a small Ohio town after a railroad linked it to New York City in the 1840s?
3. **Drawing Conclusions** Few southerners were planters. Why do you think this small group was able to dominate the political and social life of the South?

Applying Your Skills

1. **Making a Generalization** Read the excerpt about apprentices in a New York shoemaker's shop on page 464. Based on the excerpt and your reading in this chapter, write a generalization about the relationship between a boss and his apprentices before the 1830s.
2. **Analyzing a Quotation** In the 1840s, a southerner wrote this description of a southern gentleman: "See him with northern pen and ink, writing letters on northern paper, and sending them away in northern envelopes, sealed with northern wax, and impressed with a northern stamp." What point about the South do you think the writer was making?
3. **Comparing Two Line Graphs** Review Skill Lesson 15 on page 478. Use the line graphs to answer the following questions. (a) What was cotton production in 1800? (b) What was the slave population in 1800? (c) Why were there already many slaves in the South at a time when cotton production was low?
4. **Using a Painting as a Primary Source** Study the painting on page 456. (a) What does the painting show? (b) How can you tell that the scene portrayed is after 1829? (c) What means of transportation besides train travel does the painting show? (d) Based on the painting, make a generalization about transportation in the North in the early 1800s.

Match the letters on the map with the places listed below.

1. Northern states
2. Southern states
3. Massachusetts
4. New Hampshire
5. Alabama
6. Mississippi

Region (a) What was the basis of the North's economy? (b) Of the South's economy?

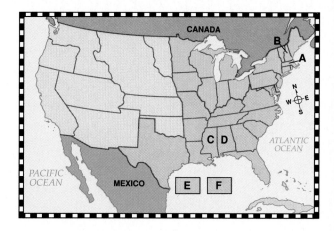

$\mathcal{H}$istory Writer's Workshop

Considering Areas for Research

After choosing a topic, the next step in preparing a report is to find information. You will often be able to find information listed under more than one topic.

For example, suppose your report is about the effects of the cotton gin on southern agriculture. After looking at sources listed under the topic *cotton gin,* think of topics that deal with the time period, the geographic location, and other related subjects. For example, you might look into the following topics: *Eli Whitney, Technological History,* and *Slave Labor.* Books about the history of agriculture in the South might also provide helpful information.

If you cannot think of related topics, look in an encyclopedia for an article on your original topic. Often, the article will include a bibliography as well as a list of related topics.

Practice List two related areas of research for each of the following topics.

1. The Expansion of Industry in the 1800s
2. The Labor Movement in the 1800s
3. Slave Revolts
4. Irish Immigration in the 1800s

Writing to Learn

1. Write a one-page description of Nat Turner's revolt. Before writing, ask *who, what, where, when, why,* and *how* about the event. In your first draft, write a topic sentence that summarizes the significance of the revolt. Organize the information in time order. Make sure that your points support the topic sentence. Revise your description for adequate detail and coherence. Proofread and make a final copy. Share your description by reading it to a classmate.

2. Imagine that you are a free black living in the South in 1831. Write a persuasive letter asking President Andrew Jackson to end slavery throughout the nation. Before writing, brainstorm a list of persuasive arguments. Then, in your first draft, write a topic sentence summarizing your position. Next, organize your points in order of importance. Be sure to use specific examples. Revise your letter for persuasive power and unity. Then, proofread and make a final copy. Publish your letter by making a bulletin board display or by adding it to a class collection.

Getting Out of School *A spirit of reform swept the nation in the mid-1800s. One result was that more American children attended school. Here, a group of children get out of school after the day's lessons.* **Linking Past and Present** *How do you think that the school in the picture compares with schools today?*

16

A Reforming Age (1820–1860)

Chapter Outline

CHAPTER SPOTLIGHT

The Big Picture

The idea that people can improve society has deep roots in American history. The Puritans came to New England to build a perfect society based on the laws of God. As the nation grew, Americans of different religions and cultures continued to believe that people can *be* better and *do* better.

In the mid-1800s, Americans worked for change in many areas. They called for better schools, basic rights for women, a ban on alcohol, and an end to slavery. In a wave of reform, Americans banded together to reshape society.

Kathleen Underwood

Of Special Interest

Focus On

◆ How did Americans work to end slavery?
◆ What progress did women make in gaining equal rights?
◆ Why did the spirit of reform sweep the nation?
◆ How did American culture flower in the 1800s?

"**W**e are all a little wild here with numberless projects for social reform," wrote the New England author and philosopher Ralph Waldo Emerson in 1840. "But," Emerson continued, "what is man born for but to be a Reformer, a Re-maker of what man has made . . . a restorer of truth and good?"

Many Americans in the mid-1800s shared Emerson's feelings. They were proud of what the United States had accomplished. But they believed that much remained to be done to fulfill the ideals on which the nation was founded.

The years between 1820 and 1860 were a period of great idealism in the United States. Countless reform movements sprang up to cure the nation's ills. Reformers worked to end slavery, win equal rights for women, and ensure kind treatment of prisoners and the mentally ill. They battled the evils of alcohol and fought to improve education for the nation's children. By the time this age of reform was over, Americans had worked to change every aspect of society. "Our ultimate aim," said newspaper editor Charles A. Dana, "is nothing less than Heaven on Earth."

1 Liberty for All

FIND OUT

◆ What were the roots of the antislavery movement?

◆ What did reformers do to combat slavery?

◆ How did Americans react to the antislavery movement?

◆ VOCABULARY abolitionist, underground railroad

❝Some people of color say that they have no home, no country. I am not among that number. . . . America is my home, my country. . . . I love every inch of soil which my feet pressed in my youth, and I mourn because the accursed shade of slavery rest[s] upon it. I love my country's flag, and I hope that soon it will be cleansed of its stains, and be hailed by all nations as the emblem of freedom and independence.❞

Henry Highland Garnet, a black minister and escaped slave, spoke these emotional words at a meeting of women reformers in 1848. At the time, some African Americans were losing hope of ever winning full equality in the United States. Garnet urged free blacks to stay in the United States and to fight against slavery and for equal rights.

Garnet was one of a growing number of Americans—black and white—who spoke out against slavery in the mid-1800s. Like Garnet, these Americans loved their country but wanted to make it better. Only by ending slavery, they believed, would the United States fulfill its promise to provide liberty and equality for all.

The Issue of Slavery

The election of Andrew Jackson in 1828 unleashed a wave of democratic feeling in the United States. (See pages 406–407.) Americans pointed proudly to the growth of democracy. More people could vote and take part in government than ever before.

Yet some Americans felt that democracy was far from complete. After all, would a democracy allow people to own slaves? An English visitor summed up the American dilemma in a few words: "You will see [Americans] with one hand hoisting the cap of liberty, and with the other flogging their slaves."

A spirit of democracy. The idea that slavery was wrong had two separate elements. One was political. The other was religious.

The political reasons for opposing slavery went back to the American Revolution. In the Declaration of Independence, Thomas Jefferson wrote that "all men are creat-

GANG OF 25 SEA ISLAND
COTTON AND RICE NEGROES,
By LOUIS DE SAUSSURE.

On THURSDAY the 25th Sept., 1852, at 11 o'clock, A.M., will be sold at RYAN'S MART, in Chalmers Street, in the City of Charleston,

A prime gang of 25 Negroes, accustomed to the culture of Sea Island Cotton and Rice.

CONDITIONS.—One-half Cash, balance by Bond, bearing interest from day of sale, payable in one and two years, to be secured by a mortgage of the negroes and approved personal security. Purchasers to pay for papers.

Slaves for Sale *By the mid-1800s, many Americans believed that slavery was wrong. But in the South, slavery continued. This 1852 notice advertises a slave auction in Charleston, South Carolina.* **Citizenship** *How do you think people justified the sale of human beings?*

Slave Auction *Despite growing antislavery feeling, a brisk trade in slaves continued. Here, a Virginia auctioneer takes bids for a young slave woman while traders lounge about inspecting blacks still to be sold.* **Culture** *How do you think that paintings like this one helped the antislavery cause?*

ed equal." Yet many white Americans, including Jefferson, did not think that the statement applied to slaves. Reformers in the 1800s disagreed.

A spirit of revival. The second motive for opposing slavery was religious. Since colonial times, Quakers had spoken out against slavery. All men and women were equal in the eyes of God, they said. It was a sin for one human being to own another.

Other religious groups also began to speak out against slavery. In the early 1800s, a powerful religious movement known as the **Second Great Awakening** swept the nation. One of its leaders was a minister named Charles Grandison Finney.

At first, Finney asked the faithful to purify their own lives. He warned them to give up sin and "walk with God." Later, he urged his followers to broaden their outlook and take up the banner of reform. Especially, he called on Christians to join a crusade to stamp out the evil of slavery:

> ❝It is a great national sin. . . . Let Christians of all denominations meekly but firmly come forth . . . and wash their hands of this thing.

Let them give forth and write on the head and front of this great [evil], SIN. ❞

Slavery ends in the North. The campaign against slavery succeeded in the North. By 1804, all states from Pennsylvania north had promised to free their slaves. Of course, there were only 50,000 slaves in the North in 1800, compared to nearly 1 million in the South.

A Colony in Africa

The **American Colonization Society,** founded in 1817, proposed to end slavery by setting up a colony in Africa for freed slaves. Many prominent Americans supported this idea. In 1822, President Monroe helped the society to establish the independent nation of **Liberia** in western Africa. The name Liberia comes from the Latin word meaning free. The American Colonization Society helped free blacks move to Liberia.

Many white southerners supported the colonization movement. They were pleased that the society did not call for an end to all slavery. Instead, it promised to pay slave owners who freed their slaves.

Black Americans, on the other hand, had mixed feelings about Liberia. Some, like Paul Cuffe, thought blacks should go to Africa because they would never have equal rights in the United States. Cuffe spent $4,000 of his own money to help settle 38 free blacks in Liberia.

But most blacks opposed colonization. They wanted to stay in the United States. After all, nearly all American blacks—slave and free—had been born in the United States, and it was their homeland. In the end, only a few thousand free blacks settled in Liberia.

A Call to End Slavery

Supporters of colonization did not attack the practice of slavery directly. But another group of Americans did. They were

Frederick Douglass *A slave for 21 years, Frederick Douglass became one of the most effective speakers for the abolitionist cause.* **Citizenship** *Douglass once said, "No man can put a chain about the ankle of his fellow man without at last finding the other end fastened about his own neck." What do you think he meant?*

abolitionists, people who wanted to end slavery in the United States.

Some abolitionists supported a gradual end to slavery. They thought slavery would die out if it were kept out of the western territories. Other abolitionists did not want to wait. They demanded that slavery end everywhere, and at once.

Black abolitionists. From the start, African Americans played an important part in the abolitionist movement. Blacks tried to end slavery through lawsuits and petitions. In the 1820s, Samuel Cornish and John Russwurm set up an antislavery newspaper, *Freedom's Journal.* They tried to turn public opinion against slavery by printing stories about the brutal treatment of slaves. James Forten and other wealthy blacks gave generously to the paper as well as to other antislavery efforts.

In 1829, David Walker, one of the most outspoken black abolitionists, published *Appeal to the Coloured Citizens of the World.* In it, he blasted the idea of slavery and called on slaves to throw off their chains by any means necessary.

Frederick Douglass speaks out. The best-known black abolitionist was Frederick Douglass. Douglass was born a slave in Maryland. As a child, he defied the slave codes and taught himself to read. Because slaves could not own books, the young Douglass often picked through "the mud and filth of the gutter" to find discarded newspapers.

In 1838, Douglass escaped and made his way to Boston. One day at an antislavery meeting, Douglass felt a powerful urge to speak. Rising slowly to his feet, he talked about the sorrows of slavery and the meaning of freedom. The audience was moved to tears. Soon, Douglass was traveling throughout the United States and Britain, lecturing against slavery. In 1847, he began publishing an antislavery newspaper, the *North Star.*

The *Liberator.* The most outspoken white abolitionist was a fiery young man named William Lloyd Garrison. Garrison

AN·AMERICAN·PORTRAIT

William Whipper: Black Abolitionist

Not long ago, buried in the clutter of an old Massachusetts barn, a painting from the 1830s was found. That painting, shown here, pictured a prosperous black man identified only as "W. W." In time, historians figured out that W. W. was William Whipper. Whipper was a successful merchant and an early leader of the antislavery movement.

Although his wealth allowed Whipper to live comfortably, he never forgot the fate of other African Americans. He gave his time and money freely to fight against slavery. Whipper helped to support slaves who had come north on the underground railroad. He also organized abolitionist societies and founded an antislavery newspaper. He wrote:

> ❝I would prefer to be penniless in the streets, rather than have withheld a single hour's labor or a dollar from the sacred cause of liberty, justice, and humanity.❞

Whipper worked hard to win freedom for southern slaves. But he also struggled to gain equal rights for free blacks, who faced constant discrimination in the North.

1. What goals did William Whipper support?
2. **Making Decisions** Why do you think William Whipper decided to devote his time and money to fight against slavery?

launched his antislavery paper, the *Liberator,* in 1831. In it, he proclaimed that slavery was an evil to be ended immediately. On the first page of the first issue, Garrison revealed his commitment:

> ❝I will be as harsh as truth, and as uncompromising as justice. . . . I am in earnest. . . . I will not excuse—I will not retreat a single inch—AND I WILL BE HEARD.❞

A year after starting his paper, Garrison helped to found the **New England Anti-Slavery Society.** Members included Theodore Weld, a young minister connected with Charles Grandison Finney. Weld brought the energy of a religious revival to antislavery meetings.

The Grimké sisters. Many women joined the abolitionist cause. Angelina and Sarah Grimké were the daughters of a wealthy slaveholder in South Carolina. They came to hate slavery and moved to Philadelphia to work for abolition. Their lectures about the evils of slavery drew large crowds.

Some people, including other abolitionists, objected to women speaking out in

CHAPTER 16 ◆ **487**

public against slavery. But the Grimkés defended their right to do so. "To me," said Sarah, "it is perfectly clear that whatsoever it is morally right for a man to do, it is morally right for a woman to do." As you will read, this belief led the Grimkés and others to start a crusade for women's rights.

Railroad to Freedom

Most abolitionists pursued their goals through the press and public debate. But some risked prison and even death by helping slaves escape from the South.

These men and women formed the underground railroad. This was not a real railroad. The **underground railroad** was a network of abolitionists that secretly helped runaway slaves to reach freedom in the North and in Canada.

Whites and free blacks served as "conductors" on the underground railroad. They guided runaway slaves to "stations" where they could spend the night. Some stations were houses of abolitionists. Others were churches, or even caves. Conductors sometimes hid slaves in wagons with false bottoms and under loads of hay.

One daring conductor, Harriet Tubman, was an escaped slave herself. Slave owners offered $40,000 for Tubman's capture. But Tubman paid no heed. Risking her freedom and her life, Tubman returned to the South 19 times. She conducted more than 300 slaves to freedom. On one of her last trips, Tubman led her aged parents to freedom. (📖 See "Conductor on the Underground Railroad" on page 686.)

The Nation Reacts

Abolitionists like Douglass and Garrison made enemies in both the North and the South. Northern mill owners, bankers, and merchants depended on cotton from the South. They saw attacks on slavery as a threat to their livelihood. Some northern

Destroying an Abolitionist Printing Press *Some proslavery groups used violence to halt the spread of abolitionist ideas. Here, an angry band of slavery supporters breaks up an abolitionist printing press.* **Citizenship** *Why do you think a proslavery group would attack a printing press?*

workers also opposed the abolitionists. They feared that if slavery ended, free blacks would come north and take their jobs by working for low pay. Henry Highland Garnet condemned northerners who "admit that Slavery is wrong in the abstract, but when we ask them to help us overthrow it, they tell us it would make them beggars!"

In New York and other northern cities, mobs sometimes broke up antislavery meetings and attacked the homes of abolitionists. At times, the attacks backfired and won support for the abolitionists. One night, a Boston mob dragged William Lloyd Garrison through the streets at the end of a rope. A doctor who saw the scene wrote, "I am an abolitionist from this very moment."

The antislavery movement failed to gain a foothold in the South. In fact, many slave owners reacted to the crusade by defending slavery even more. One slave owner wrote that if slaves were well-fed, well-housed, and well-clothed, they would "love their master and serve him cheerfully, diligently, and faithfully." Other owners argued that slaves were better off than northern workers—whom they called wage slaves—who worked long hours in dusty, airless factories.

Even southerners who owned no slaves defended slavery. To them, slavery was essential to the southern economy. In fact, they hoped to be wealthy planters and own slaves one day, too. Many southerners exaggerated the extent of northern support for the antislavery movement. They began to believe that northerners wanted to destroy their way of life.

SECTION 1 REVIEW

1. **Locate:** Liberia.
2. **Identify:** (a) Henry Highland Garnet, (b) Second Great Awakening, (c) American Colonization Society, (d) Frederick Douglass, (e) William Lloyd Garrison, (f) New England Anti-Slavery Society, (g) Theodore Weld, (h) Angelina and Sarah Grimké, (i) Harriet Tubman.
3. **Define:** (a) abolitionist, (b) underground railroad.
4. Give two reasons why Americans opposed slavery.
5. (a) Why did many southerners support the goals of the American Colonization Society? (b) Why did most blacks oppose it?
6. How did the abolitionist movement affect the way the South viewed northerners?
7. **Drawing Conclusions** Why do you think ending slavery was easier for the North than for the South?

2 Women Are Created Equal

FIND OUT

◆ How did the antislavery crusade spur the women's rights movement?

◆ What rights did women want?

◆ What did the Seneca Falls Convention demand?

◆ How did opportunities for women improve in the mid-1800s?

In 1840, a group of Americans sailed to London to attend the World Antislavery Convention. Among them were two young women—Lucretia Mott and Elizabeth Cady Stanton.

The Americans got a shock when they arrived in London. The convention refused to let women take part in the proceedings. Convention officials even forced female delegates, including Mott and Stanton, to sit behind a curtain, hidden from view. Mott had prepared a speech but was not allowed to give it.

Lucretia Mott and Elizabeth Cady Stanton stayed in London for several weeks. At their hotel each evening, they debated the issue of women's rights. One

The "True Woman" *According to the popular view in the 1800s, the "true woman" was a homemaker, happy to devote herself to her husband and children. Public life and the business world were to be left to men. The young bride in this painting— shy, gentle, submissive—has many qualities that Americans of the 1800s thought proper for a woman.* **Daily Life** *Do you think that most women of the 1800s fit the ideal of the "true woman"? Explain.*

day, the two women took a long walk to- gether. "[We] agreed to hold a women's rights convention," Stanton later recalled. "The men . . . had [shown] a great need for some education on that question." It was eight years, however, before the convention took place.

An Uphill Struggle

The treatment that Mott and Stanton faced in London was not unusual for the mid-1800s. Women had few political or le- gal rights at the time. They could not vote or hold office. When a woman married, her husband became owner of all her prop- erty. If a woman worked outside the home, her wages belonged to her husband. A husband also had the right to hit his wife as long as he did not badly injure her.

"Unnatural" women. Many women had joined the abolitionist movement. As these women worked to end slavery, they real- ized that they lacked full social and politi- cal rights themselves. Among the first to speak out on the subject were Angelina and Sarah Grimké.

As you have read, the boldness of the Grimkés shocked audiences in the North. In a newspaper editorial, a group of New England ministers scolded the sisters. "When [a woman] assumes the place and tone of a man as a public reformer," they wrote, "her character becomes unnatural."

But the Grimkés and other women reformers rejected such ideas. More determined than ever, they continued their crusade. Only now, they lectured about women's rights as well as abolition. Said Angelina Grimké:

> ❝The investigation of the rights of the slave has led me to a better understanding of my own.❞

"Ain't I a woman?" Black women joined the struggle for women's rights. Sojourner Truth was born into slavery in New York. She ran away from her owner just before state law would have freed her. Truth became active in the crusade against slavery.

At an antislavery meeting in 1851, Truth listened to a minister speak about women's need to be protected. Wives and mothers should stay in the safety of their home, he said. When he was done, Truth leaped to her feet with this stinging reply:

> ❝The man over there says women need to be helped into carriages and lifted over ditches, and to have the best place everywhere. Nobody ever helps me into carriages, or over puddles, or gives me the best place. And ain't I a woman? I have ploughed and planted and gathered into barns. . . . And ain't I a woman? . . . I have borne thirteen children, and seen most of 'em sold into slavery, and when I cried out with my mother's grief, none but Jesus heard me! And ain't I a woman?❞

Others call for equal rights. After returning home from the World Antislavery Convention (see page 489), Lucretia Mott and Elizabeth Cady Stanton took up the cause of women's rights with new zeal. Mott was a Quaker minister and the mother of five children. A quiet speaker, she won the respect of many listeners with her logic.

Elizabeth Cady Stanton was the daughter of a well-known New York judge. When she was growing up, clerks in her father's law office teased Stanton by reading her laws that denied basic rights to women. This teasing helped make Stanton a lifelong foe of inequality.

Another energetic organizer was Susan B. Anthony. She was ready to go anywhere at any time to speak for the cause. Even when audiences heckled her and threw eggs, Anthony finished her speech. Lucy Stone and Abby Kelley also gave their energies to the movement.

Sojourner Truth *Born Isabella Baumfree, Sojourner Truth took her new name in 1827, claiming that God had sent her to "declare truth unto people." She became a powerful speaker for abolition and women's rights.* **Daily Life** *Name two arguments Truth used to show that women are as capable as men.*

A Historic Meeting

As you have read, in 1840, Lucretia Mott and Elizabeth Cady Stanton decided to hold a national women's rights convention. They wanted to draw attention to the problems women faced. Eight years later, in 1848, in Seneca Falls, New York, that convention finally took place.

About 200 women and 40 men attended the **Seneca Falls Convention.** At the meeting, leaders of the women's rights movement presented a Declaration of Sentiments. Modeled on the Declaration of Independence, it proclaimed, "We hold these truths to be self-evident: that all men and women are created equal."

The women and men at Seneca Falls voted for resolutions that demanded equality for women at work, at school, and in church. All the demands passed without a no vote, except one. It demanded that women be allowed to vote in elections. Even the bold women at Seneca Falls hesitated to make this demand. In the end, it passed by a slim majority.

Founder of Mount Holyoke *Mary Lyon was determined to establish a school devoted to "the training of young women for usefulness." She achieved her goal in 1837, when she founded Mount Holyoke Female Seminary.* **Daily Life** *What argument did people raise against advanced education for women?*

The Seneca Falls Convention marked the start of an organized women's rights movement. In the years after 1848, women worked for change in many areas. They won more legal rights in some states. New York passed laws allowing women to keep property and wages after they married. But progress was slow. Many men and women opposed the goals of the women's rights movement. The struggle for equal rights would last many years.

New Opportunities for Women

The women at Seneca Falls believed that education was a key to equality. At the time, women from poor families had little hope of learning even to read and write. And while young middle-class women were often sent to school, they were taught dancing and drawing rather than mathematics and science, like their brothers. After all, people argued, women were expected to devote themselves to marriage and children. Why did they need an education?

Reformers like Emma Willard and Mary Lyon worked hard to improve education for women. Willard opened a high school for girls in Troy, New York. Here, young women studied "men's subjects," such as mathematics, physics, and philosophy.

Mary Lyon spent years raising money to build Mount Holyoke Female Seminary in Massachusetts. She did not call the school a college because she knew that many people thought it was wrong for women to attend college. But Mount Holyoke, which opened in 1837, was the first women's college in the United States.

At about the same time, a few men's colleges began to admit women. And as women's education improved, women found jobs teaching, especially in grade schools.

A few women tried to enter fields such as medicine. Elizabeth Blackwell applied to medical school at Geneva College in New York. She was admitted, although school officials thought that she would fail. To their surprise, Blackwell graduated first in her class. Women had practiced medicine since colonial times, but Blackwell was the first woman in the United States with a medical degree. She later set up the first nursing school in the nation.

SECTION 2 REVIEW

1. **Identify:** (a) Lucretia Mott, (b) Elizabeth Cady Stanton, (c) Angelina and Sarah Grimké, (d) Sojourner Truth, (e) Susan B. Anthony, (f) Seneca Falls Convention, (g) Emma Willard, (h) Mary Lyon, (i) Elizabeth Blackwell.
2. What rights were denied to women in the early 1800s?
3. What steps did delegates at Seneca Falls take?
4. What type of education did most women receive in the mid-1800s?
5. **Understanding Causes and Effects** How was the women's rights movement a long-range effect of the antislavery movement?

3 Reform Sweeps the Country

FIND OUT

◆ What reforms did Dorothea Dix seek?

◆ How did Americans improve public education in the mid-1800s?

◆ Why did some Americans want to ban the sale of alcohol?

◆ **VOCABULARY** temperance movement

In the mid-1800s, the spirit of reform even made its way into the classroom. In McGuffey's *Eclectic Reader,* the most widely used textbook of the period, children read the following poem:

    ❝Beautiful hands are they that do
    Deeds that are noble, good, and true;
    Beautiful feet are they that go
    Swiftly to lighten another's woe.❞

Many young women and men took these words to heart. They devoted themselves to helping those Americans who could not help themselves.

Some reformers turned their attention to what one minister called the "outsiders" in American society—criminals and the mentally ill. One of the most vigorous reformers was a Boston schoolteacher named Dorothea Lynde Dix.

UP CLOSE

Dorothea Dix: Helping the Helpless

Dorothea Dix was born on the Maine frontier in 1802. At age 12, her parents sent her to live with her grandmother in Boston. There, Dorothea attended school to become a teacher.

A strict teacher. Dix loved to read and did well in school. After completing eighth grade, she was qualified to teach, by the standards of the time. So at age 14, Dix opened her own grade school.

Dix's pupils found her a good but strict teacher. She punished one student by making her wear a sign that said "A very bad girl, indeed." A few years later, Dix opened another, larger school as well as a free school for poor children.

Although her health was never good, Dix amazed people with her energy and hard work. She awoke each day at 4 or 5 A.M. She read, wrote, and studied until well after midnight. When the available textbooks did not provide enough material on history and science, Dix wrote her own book. Teachers throughout the nation were soon using it.

A new mission. One day in March 1841, Dix got an urgent message. A young Harvard University student had been asked to set up a Sunday School class for women in the jail at Cambridge, near Boston. The young man could not keep order among the prisoners. Did Dix know anyone who could help?

Dorothea Dix *The sight of "harmless lunatics" locked in a cold, dark cell touched Dorothea Dix's heart and prompted her to action. Largely through Dix's efforts, 28 states had established special hospitals for the care of the mentally ill by 1860.* **Citizenship** *How did Dix go about the task of achieving reform?*

Dix took the job herself. At the Cambridge jail, she found 20 women prisoners. Some were there for stealing, others for drunkenness. But the prisoners who caught Dix's attention had committed no crime. These women had been jailed because they were mentally ill.

The jailer locked the mentally ill prisoners in small, dark cells at the rear of the jail. There was no heat in the cells, and the women were half-frozen. Dix demanded to know why these women were treated so cruelly. The jailer replied that "lunatics" did not feel the cold.

That moment changed Dorothea Dix's life forever. By the time she left the jail, she knew she had to take action.

During the next 18 months, Dix visited every jail, poorhouse, and hospital in Mas-sachusetts. She submitted a detailed report to the state legislature. Most legislators were shocked by her blunt words:

> **❝**I proceed, gentlemen, briefly to call your attention to the present state of Insane Persons confined within this Commonwealth, in cages, closets, cellars, stalls, pens! Chained, naked, beaten with rods, and lashed into obedience.**❞**

Still, the legislators hesitated to raise taxes to build a new mental hospital. So Dix offered her report to the newspapers. In the end, the legislature voted for the hospital.

Dix knew her work was not done. She inspected jails and poorhouses in Vermont, Connecticut, and New York. In time, she traveled as far as Louisiana and Illinois. In North Carolina, an angry official told Dix that "nothing can be done here." She replied, "I know no such word." In nearly every state, her reports convinced legislatures to treat the mentally ill as patients, not criminals.

Reforming prisons. Dix did not limit her efforts to treatment of the mentally ill. She also spoke out against conditions in the prisons she visited. Men, women, and children were often crammed into cold, damp rooms. If food was in short supply, prisoners went hungry unless they had money to buy meals from jailers.

In the 1800s, people were put in jail for minor offenses, such as owing money. In 1830, five out of six people in northern jails were debtors. To Dix, jailing debtors made no sense. How could debtors earn money to pay back debts when they were behind bars?

Dix and other reformers called for changes in the prison system. As a result, some states built new prisons with only one or two inmates to a cell. Cruel punishments were banned, and people convicted of minor crimes received shorter sentences. And slowly, states stopped treating debtors as criminals. ◆

Educating a Free People

"If a nation expects to be ignorant and free, it expects what never was and never will be."

Thomas Jefferson wrote these words in 1816. Jefferson knew that a democracy needs educated citizens. Reformers agreed. As more men won the right to vote in the 1820s, reformers acted to see that they were well informed.

Before the 1820s, few American children attended school. Public schools were rare. And those that did exist were usually old and run-down. Teachers were poorly trained and ill-paid. Students of all ages crowded together in a single room.

New public schools. New York State led the way in reforming public education. In the 1820s, the state ordered every town to build a grade school. The new public schools were not completely free. Parents had to pay a fee for their children to attend. But it was a start. Before long, other northern states also required towns to support public schools.

In Massachusetts, Horace Mann led the fight for better schools. Mann became head of the state board of education in 1837. For 12 years, he hounded legislators to provide more money for education. Under his leadership, Massachusetts built new schools, extended the school year, and gave teachers higher pay. The state also opened three colleges to train teachers. (📖 See "How Americans Shortchange Their Children" on page 689.)

(See "How Americans Shortchange Their Children" on page 689.)

Reformers in other states urged their legislatures to follow the lead of Massachusetts and New York. By the 1850s, most northern states had set up free,

A One-Room Schoolhouse *Many Americans in the 1800s received their education in one-room schoolhouses, such as the one in this painting by Winslow Homer. The single room housed all grades, and older students often helped younger ones with their lessons.* **Citizenship** *Why is education important in a democracy?*

tax-supported elementary schools. Schools also improved in the South, but more slowly. In both the North and South, schooling ended in the eighth grade. There were very few public high schools.

Education for African Americans. In most areas, free black children had little chance to attend school. A few cities, like Boston and New York, set up separate schools for black students. But these schools received less money than schools for white students did. Even so, some African Americans got good educations at private colleges such as Harvard, Dartmouth, and Oberlin. In the 1850s, several colleges for African Americans opened in the North. The first was Lincoln University, in Oxford, Pennsylvania.

Teaching the disabled. Some reformers took steps to improve education for the physically disabled. In 1817, the Reverend Thomas Gallaudet (gal uh DEHT) set up a school for the deaf in Hartford, Connecticut. He showed that the deaf could learn like others. A few years later, Dr. Samuel Gridley Howe became director of the first school for the blind. Howe invented a way to print books with raised letters. Blind students could read the letters with their fingers.

Battling "Demon Rum"

In 1854, Timothy Shay Arthur published a book called *Ten Nights in a Barroom and What I Saw There.* It told the story of how an entire village was destroyed by "demon rum." A play based on the novel soon followed. In its opening lines, a little girl pleaded with her drunken parent:

Giving Up "Demon Rum" *The temperance movement called on Americans to give up "demon rum" before it destroyed their homes and families. Here, an ashamed father swears on the Bible to give up alcohol as his thankful family looks on.*
Linking Past and Present *Are there groups today that fight against the drinking of alcohol? Explain.*

"Father, dear father, come home
with me now,
The clock in the belfry strikes
one."

To modern audiences, *Ten Nights in a Barroom* seems somewhat silly. But the play addressed a serious problem of the 1800s. Alcohol abuse was widespread at the time. At political rallies, weddings, and even funerals, men, women, and sometimes children drank heavily. Craftworkers and apprentices often drank alcohol in their workshops. In cities, men could buy a glass of whiskey in groceries, candy stores, and barber shops as easily as at taverns.

Reformers linked abuse of alcohol to crime, the breakup of families, and mental illness. In the late 1820s, reformers began a campaign against drinking. It was known as the temperance movement. Some temperance groups tried to persuade people to drink less. Others demanded that states ban the sale of alcohol.

In the 1850s, temperance groups won a major victory when Maine banned the sale of alcohol. Eight other states soon passed "Maine laws." But many Americans resented the new laws, and most states later repealed them. Still, temperance crusaders pressed on. They gained new strength in the late 1800s.

Reform movements improved life for many Americans. States built new schools and provided better care for the mentally ill. The public became aware of the dangers of alcohol. Not all the reforms succeeded. But Americans renewed their faith that they could make society better. The reformers of the mid-1800s served as a model for others who would come later.

SECTION 3 REVIEW

1. **Identify:** (a) Dorothea Dix, (b) Horace Mann, (c) Thomas Gallaudet, (d) Samuel Gridley Howe.
2. **Define:** temperance movement.
3. What conditions did Dorothea Dix find in Massachusetts prisons?
4. Why did reformers seek to expand public education in the 1820s?
5. Why did temperance groups want to end the drinking of alcohol?
6. **Evaluating Information** What qualities do you think made Dorothea Dix successful as a reformer?

4 New Voices, New Visions

FIND OUT

◆ Who were some of the writers and artists of the 1800s?

◆ How did American writers express the unique spirit of the nation?

◆ What styles did American painters develop?

In 1820, a Scottish minister named Sydney Smith blasted the lack of culture in the United States:

"In the four quarters of the globe, who reads an American book? Or goes to an American play? Or looks at an American picture or statue? What does the world yet owe to Americans?"

Any American artist or writer of worth, Smith went on, had been trained in Europe. The best the United States could offer, he said, was "a galaxy . . . of newspaper scribblers."

But even as Smith wrote these scornful words, a group of American writers and artists was breaking free of European traditions. These men and women created a voice and a vision that were truly American.

American Storytellers

Until the early 1800s, most American writers depended on Europe for their ideas and inspiration. In the 1820s, however,

Americans began to write stories with American themes.

The first flowering. One of the most popular American writers of the early 1800s was Washington Irving, a New Yorker. Irving first became known for *The Sketch Book,* a collection of tales published in 1820. Two of the best-loved tales are "Rip Van Winkle" and "The Legend of Sleepy Hollow."

"Rip Van Winkle" is based on an old Dutch legend. Rip is a simple farmer who lives in the days before the American Revolution. One afternoon, a magic spell puts him to sleep. He sleeps for 20 years. When he wakes at last, everything has changed. His quiet village is now a bustling town. People buzz with talk about "rights of citizens—elections—members of Congress—Bunker's Hill, heroes of seventy-six—and other words, which . . . bewildered Van Winkle." Rip, it turned out, had slept through the entire American Revolution!

Irving's stories amused people. They also gave Americans a sense of the richness of their past. But Irving's appeal went beyond the United States. Irving was the first American writer to enjoy fame in Europe as well as at home.

James Fenimore Cooper, another New Yorker, also published novels set in the past. Cooper's stories took place on the American frontier in upstate New York. In *The Deerslayer* and *The Last of the Mohicans,* Cooper gave a romantic, or idealized, view of relations between whites and Native Americans. But his stories were so full of excitement and adventure that few readers cared whether or not they were true to life.

Later writers. Nathaniel Hawthorne drew on the history of Puritan New England to create his novels and short stories. The Puritan past fascinated Hawthorne. His best-known novel, *The Scarlet Letter,* was published in 1850. It explores the forces of good and evil in a Puritan New England town.

In 1851, Herman Melville published *Moby Dick.* In this novel, Melville takes the reader on a wild voyage aboard the whaling ship *Pequod.* The crazed captain, Ahab, has vowed revenge against the white whale that years earlier bit off his leg. *Moby Dick* had only limited success when it was first published. Today, however, critics see the story of the great whale hunt as a symbolic struggle between good and evil. They rank *Moby Dick* among the finest American novels ever written.

William Wells Brown published *Clotel,* a novel about slave life, in 1853. Brown was the nation's first published black novelist and the first African American to earn his living as a writer.

Women Writers

By the mid-1800s, a growing number of women were publishing books. Margaret Fuller, a friend of Emerson's, wrote *Woman in the Nineteenth Century.* The book was an important influence on the movement for women's rights.

Many of the best-selling novels of the period were written by women. These novels often told about young women who gained wealth and happiness through honesty and self-sacrifice. Some novels were more true to life. They showed the hardship faced by widows and orphans.

Few of these novels are read today. But writers like Catharine Sedgwick and Fanny Fern earned far more money than Nathaniel Hawthorne or Herman Melville. In fact, Hawthorne complained bitterly about the success of women writers. "America is now wholly given over to a . . . mob of scribbling women," he once said.

Poetic Voices

John Greenleaf Whittier, a Quaker from Massachusetts, wanted to write poems about the colonial past. But his friend, the

LIFE • IN • AMERICA

The Abolitionist Poetry of John Greenleaf Whittier

With the nation gripped by a spirit of idealism, it is not surprising that American writers lifted their voices to call for reform. Poet John Greenleaf Whittier was deeply committed to the abolitionist movement. Some of the most fiery antislavery writing came from his pen.

In 1843, an incident involving an escaped slave aroused Whittier's fury. The runaway, from Virginia, was tracked down in Boston and returned to his master in the South. What right, demanded Whittier, did Virginia have to send slave catchers into Massachusetts, a free state? "Massachusetts to Virginia," his response to the incident, is one of the most stirring of his poems against slavery. A few lines of the poem appear below.

> **"**Hold, while ye may, your struggling slaves, and burden God's free air
> With woman's shriek beneath the lash, and manhood's wild despair; . . .
> But for us and for our children, the vow which we have given

For freedom and humanity is registered in heaven;
No slave-hunt in our borders,—no pirate on our strand!
No [chains] in [Massachusetts],—no slave upon our land!**"**

1. What inspired Whittier to write "Massachusetts to Virginia"?

2. **Analyzing Information** To whom is Whittier referring with the words "for us and for our children"? What "vow" do you think they have given?

abolitionist William Lloyd Garrison, urged him to use his pen to serve the antislavery cause. In many poems, Whittier sought to make his readers aware of the evils of slavery.

The favorite poet of Americans in the mid-1800s was Henry Wadsworth Longfellow. Longfellow based many of his poems on events from the nation's past. Perhaps his best-known poem is "Paul Revere's Ride." Set at the beginning of the American Revolution, it describes Paul Revere's ride through the night to alert colonists that "the British are coming!" Today, many Americans can still recite the opening lines of Longfellow's poem:

> "Listen, my children, and you
> shall hear
> Of the midnight ride of Paul
> Revere,
> On the eighteenth of April in
> Seventy-five;
> Hardly a man is now alive
> Who remembers that famous day
> and year."

Among Americans today, Walt Whitman is probably read more than any other poet of the 1800s. Whitman published only one book of poems, *Leaves of Grass*. But he added to it over a period of 31 years. Whitman believed in the common people. He put bold emotions in the everyday language of the time. His poetry celebrated democracy and the many different people that made the nation great.

Some of the best poems of the period were written by Emily Dickinson. Like Walt Whitman, Dickinson broke with past styles and created new forms. Dickinson wrote more than 1,700 poems, but only seven were published in her lifetime. She called her poetry "my letter to the world." Today, Dickinson is considered one of the nation's greatest poets.

Emerson and Thoreau: Following the "Inner Light"

The American writer who probably had the greatest influence in the mid-1800s was Ralph Waldo Emerson. People flocked to hear him read his essays stressing the importance of the individual. Each person, Emerson said, has an "inner light" that is part of God. He urged people to use this inner light to guide their lives.

Emerson's friend and neighbor, Henry David Thoreau (THOR oh), believed that the growth of industry and the rise of cities were ruining the nation. He tried to live as simply as possible. A person's wealth, Thoreau said, is measured by the number of things he or she can do without.

Thoreau's best-known work is *Walden*. In it, he tells of a year spent alone in a remote cabin on Walden Pond in Massachusetts. Like Emerson, Thoreau believed that each person must decide what is right or wrong:

> "If a man does not keep pace with
> his companions, perhaps it is be-
> cause he hears a different drum-
> mer. Let him step to the music he
> hears."

Thoreau's "different drummer" told him that slavery was wrong. He was a fierce abolitionist and served as a conductor on the underground railroad.

Walt Whitman *This picture of Walt Whitman was done by Thomas Eakins, one of the great American portrait painters. Eakins did not try to flatter his subjects, and many of them complained about the results. Whitman, however, liked this portrait and remarked that he would "stick by it like molasses to the jug."* **Culture** *What did Whitman write about in his poems?*

American Landscapes

Before the 1800s, American painters traveled to Europe to study art. Benjamin West of Philadelphia, for example, settled in London. In 1772, he was appointed historical painter to King George III.

Many American painters journeyed to London to study with West. They included Charles Willson Peale, Gilbert Stuart, and John Singleton Copley, among the best American portrait painters of the time. Both Peale and Stuart painted well-known pictures of George Washington.

By the mid-1800s, American artists began to develop their own style. The first group to do so became known as the **Hudson River School** because they painted landscapes of New York's Hudson River region. Two of the best-known painters of the Hudson River School were Thomas Cole and Asher Durand.

Other American artists painted scenes of hard-working farm families and country people. George Caleb Bingham was inspired by his native Missouri. His paintings show frontier life along the rivers that feed the great Mississippi.

Several painters tried to capture the culture of Native Americans on canvas. George Catlin and Alfred Jacob Miller traveled to the Far West. Their paintings record the daily life of Indians on the Great Plains and in the Rocky Mountains.

Artists of the 1800s celebrated the vast American landscape. They expressed confidence in Americans and their future. This confidence was shared by reformers in the East and by the thousands of Americans opening up new frontiers in the West.

Catskill Scene *Artists of the Hudson River School celebrated the gentle beauty of New York's Catskill Mountain region. This painting is by Thomas Doughty, one of the early members of the school. According to a magazine of the time, Doughty's pictures were filled with "all that is quiet and lovely, romantic and beautiful in Nature."* **Culture** *Name two other painters of the Hudson River School.*

SECTION 4 REVIEW

1. **Identify:** (a) Washington Irving, (b) Nathaniel Hawthorne, (c) Herman Melville, (d) William Wells Brown, (e) Margaret Fuller, (f) Henry Wadsworth Longfellow, (g) Walt Whitman, (h) Emily Dickinson, (i) Ralph Waldo Emerson, (j) Henry David Thoreau, (k) Hudson River School, (l) George Catlin.

2. What kinds of books did women write in the mid-1800s?

3. What important theme did each of the following stress in his work: (a) John Greenleaf Whittier; (b) Walt Whitman; (c) Ralph Waldo Emerson; (d) Henry David Thoreau?

4. What subjects did artists paint in the 1800s?

5. **Drawing Conclusions** Why do you think artists and writers did not develop a unique American style until the mid-1800s?

You will sometimes need to research information using books in the library. Most libraries have a card catalog. The card catalog helps you find the books you need.

1 **Study the parts of the card catalog.** The **card catalog** is a set of drawers holding small cards. The cards are in alphabetical order. Every nonfiction, or factual, book has at least three cards. The author card lists the book by the author's last name. The title card lists the book by its title. The subject card lists the book by its subject—for example, Baseball or American History.

You can tell what kind of card you are looking at by reading the top line. The top line will show either the author's last name, the title of the book, or the subject heading. Sometimes, author and title cards are kept together in one set of drawers and the subject cards are kept in a separate set of drawers.

Look at Card A. (a) Is this an author, title, or subject card? (b) Who is the author of the book? (c) What is the title of the book?

2 **Practice using the call number.** Every card for a nonfiction book has a number in the top left corner. This is the call number of the book. The **call number** tells you where you will find the book on the library shelves. Each nonfiction book has its call number printed on the spine, or narrow back edge. Nonfiction books are arranged on the shelves in numerical order. The letters after the number are the first letters of the author's last name. Look at Card A. (a) What is the call number of the book? (b) What do the letters "Wal" printed below the call number mean?

3 **Use other cards in the card catalog.** Look at Cards B and C. (a) Is Card B an author, title, or subject card? (b) Is Card C an author, title, or subject card? (c) Why do Cards A, B, and C have the same call number?

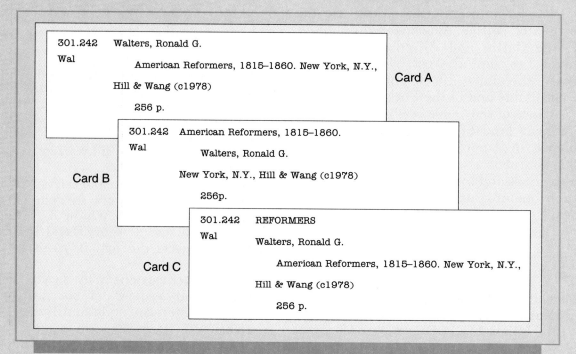

```
301.242   Walters, Ronald G.
Wal
              American Reformers, 1815–1860. New York, N.Y.,
       Hill & Wang (c1978)
              256 p.
```
Card A

```
301.242   American Reformers, 1815–1860.
Wal
              Walters, Ronald G.
       New York, N.Y., Hill & Wang (c1978)
              256p.
```
Card B

```
301.242   REFORMERS
Wal
              Walters, Ronald G.
              American Reformers, 1815–1860. New York, N.Y.,
       Hill & Wang (c1978)
              256 p.
```
Card C

CHAPTER ◆ 16 ◆ STUDY GUIDE

Use the Section Reviews and this Study Guide to review chapter content.

Main Ideas

The main ideas in each section of this chapter are summarized below.

SECTION 1 ■ Liberty for All

◆ Between 1820 and 1860, a wave of reform swept the United States.
◆ Abolitionists opposed slavery for both political and religious reasons.
◆ Some abolitionists helped slaves escape on the underground railroad.
◆ Slavery ended in the North in the early 1800s, but the antislavery movement failed to gain a foothold in the South.

SECTION 2 ■ Women Are Created Equal

◆ Women working to end slavery became aware that their own rights were limited.
◆ At the Seneca Falls Convention in 1848, women drew up a list of demands.
◆ In the mid-1800s, women gained opportunities in education and other areas.

SECTION 3 ■ Reform Sweeps the Country

◆ Dorothea Dix campaigned to improve conditions for prisoners and the mentally ill.
◆ Reformers argued that Americans needed to be better educated to vote wisely.
◆ Reformers who blamed alcohol for crime and family problems organized the temperance movement.

SECTION 4 ■ New Voices, New Visions

◆ After 1820, American writers began to use American themes in novels and poems.
◆ Some American writers, such as John Greenleaf Whittier, devoted their works to the antislavery cause.
◆ American painters developed new styles and celebrated the beauty of the landscape in the mid-1800s.

Key People and Terms

Refer to the Identify and Define questions in the Section Reviews on pages 489, 493, 497, and 501. Use each person, term, and vocabulary word in a complete sentence. When possible, make connections between the people and terms by using more than one person or term in each sentence.

Time Line

1. Make a chart of events in time order. The chart will have two headings: Date, Event. Fill in the chart, using the events on the time line. Add the following events from the chapter: Douglass begins publishing *North Star;* Gallaudet sets up school for the deaf; Mott and Stanton attend World Antislavery Convention. (Refer to the chapter for the dates.)
2. Which events on the chart are connected with the abolitionist movement?

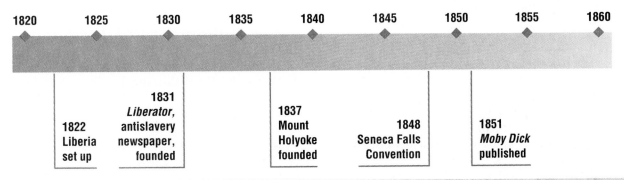

1820   1825   1830   1835   1840   1845   1850   1855   1860

1822 Liberia set up

1831 *Liberator,* antislavery newspaper, founded

1837 Mount Holyoke founded

1848 Seneca Falls Convention

1851 *Moby Dick* published

CHAPTER 16 ◆ **503**

Understanding Vocabulary

Match each term at left with the correct definition at right.

1. abolitionist
2. underground railroad
3. temperance movement

a. network of people who helped runaway slaves reach freedom
b. campaign against the drinking of alcohol
c. person who wanted to end slavery

Reviewing the Main Ideas

1. (a) What were the political ideas behind the antislavery movement? (b) What were the religious ideas?
2. How did abolitionists try to end slavery?
3. (a) Why were some northerners opposed to the antislavery movement? (b) How did southerners justify slavery?
4. What did women at the Seneca Falls Convention demand?
5. What role did each of the following play in the movement for women's rights: (a) Sojourner Truth; (b) Elizabeth Cady Stanton; (c) Mary Lyon?
6. (a) What were American public schools like in the early 1800s? (b) How did schools improve in the mid-1800s?
7. Why was Washington Irving's writing important for Americans?
8. What themes did American painters take up in the mid-1800s?

Thinking Critically

1. **Linking Past and Present** (a) What did abolitionists do to win public support? (b) How do reform leaders today try to win support for their causes?
2. **Understanding Causes and Effects** Why do you think former slaves were especially effective speakers for the abolitionist cause?
3. **Drawing Conclusions** (a) Why do you think leaders in the women's rights movement believed that education was a key to winning equality? (b) What effect do you think the opening of new schools for women had on the women's rights movement?
4. **Analyzing Information** American writers in the 1800s stressed the importance of the individual. How does American history help explain this stress?

Applying Your Skills

1. **Making a Review Chart** Make a review chart with five columns and three rows. Label the columns Abolition, Women's Rights, Care for the Mentally Ill, Prison Reform, Education Reform. Label the rows Problems to Solve, Leaders, Achievements. Then, complete the chart. Which movement do you think achieved the most? Explain.
2. **Identifying the Main Idea** Reread the statement by Henry Highland Garnet on page 484. Then, write one or two sentences summarizing the main idea.
3. **Using the Card Catalog** Review Skill Lesson 16 on page 502. (a) In what order are cards arranged in the card catalog? (b) What is the purpose of a call number? (c) In Skill Lesson 16, what kind of card is Card A? Card B? Card C?

Thinking About Geography

Match the letters on the map with the places listed below.

1. Massachusetts
2. New York
3. South Carolina
4. Maryland
5. Connecticut
6. Maine

Movement Why would a slave in South Carolina want to escape to Maine?

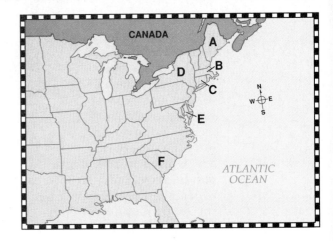

History Writer's Workshop

Taking Notes for a Report

Once you complete all the prewriting steps outlined in the previous chapters, you are ready to take notes for your report. Begin by making a list of questions about your topic and by writing a rough thesis statement. As you read your research sources, take notes on information that answers your questions and that relates to your thesis statement.

Use the following checklist to take notes:

1. Take notes on cards. Use one card for each new subject or source. Write on the front of the card only. Be sure your notes are legible.
2. In the upper left corner of each card, write the author, title, and publishing information you will need for your footnotes and bibliography.
3. In the upper right corner, write the subject of the information on that card.
4. Write each quotation, idea, or fact on your cards. Copy quotations word for word and set them off with quotation marks. Always include the page number where you found the information.
5. Keep the note cards from each of your sources together.

Practice Write a sample note card on the subject "American Writers in the Mid-1800s." Use your textbook as the source.

Writing to Learn

1. Imagine that you are an art critic. Write a review of the painting on page 501 for a newspaper. First, list the characteristics of the painting, such as color, mood, and realistic detail. Write a topic sentence summarizing your reaction to the painting and how it depicts the American landscape. Organize your support logically. Revise for effective word choice. Then, proofread and make a final copy. Publish your review in a bulletin board display.
2. Choose a leader of the women's rights movement, such as Lucretia Mott or Susan B. Anthony. Write a report about the contributions of the woman you select. First, research her life. Write a topic sentence summarizing her influence. Organize your details in time order or in order of importance. Revise for unity and coherence. Then, proofread and make a final copy. Publish your report in a class collection of biographies.

The opening of the West meant new jobs for brave young men—at least for a while. In March of 1860, western newspapers ran the following ad: "WANTED —YOUNG, SKINNY, WIRY FELLOWS not over 18. Must be expert riders, willing to risk death daily. Orphans preferred." A new company called the Pony Express had placed the ad. It had a bold plan—to carry mail about 2,000 miles from St. Joseph, Missouri, to Sacramento, California in only 10 days. At the time, it took weeks for mail to reach the West by stagecoach or ship.

The Pony Express used a relay system. Every 10 miles along the route there was a relay station at

Orphans Preferred

which the rider jumped off his weary horse and quickly mounted a fresh one. After changing horses eight times, the rider tossed the mailbag, called a mochila, to a new rider. The new rider sped off. In this way, the mail never stopped moving.

Young men scrambled to join the Pony Express despite the hardships and dangers because the pay was good and riders were admired for their bravery. The success of the Pony Express was short-lived, however. When telegraph wires reached across the country, messages could cross the plains and mountains in seconds. In October 1861, the Pony Express went out of business.

Bloomers Become Fashionable

Women in the mid-1800s wore long skirts and corsets that made it difficult to breathe, much less do anything practical. Amelia Bloomer, a temperance and women's rights activist, believed that women were imprisoned by these fashions. She advocated more comfortable clothing, particularly long, loose trousers worn under a short dress. For a short time, these trousers were very popular. Critics made fun of them, calling them "bloomers," and the name stuck.

The Divisible State

Only one state in the Union has the right to subdivide itself—Texas. According to the congressional resolution annexing Texas in 1845, the state can divide itself into as many as five states, at any time. If the Texas legislature ever decided to break up the state into five new states, the region would have a total of 10 senators instead of 2.

G·A·Z·E·T·T·E

A Surprising Legacy From Santa Anna

Following the Mexican War, General Santa Anna settled in the United States. In 1866, he was living on Staten Island, New York. One day, his interpreter and secretary, James Adams, noticed that the general was chewing on slices of chicle, which he had brought from Mexico.

Adams had an idea. Chicle, made from the milky juice of the sapodilla tree, is tasteless. If he added flavoring to the chewy chicle, maybe people would buy it. Adams experimented with sweeteners and flavors until he found the right combination. Later, he founded the Adams Chewing Gum Company.

Gone Broke

When gold was discovered at Sutter's Mill in 1848, the gold rush was on. People flocked from all over the country and the world as word spread of the riches to be had. Over $350 million of gold was mined by the middle of the 1850s. Yet, ironically, miners ruined John Sutter's mill and land, and he was left bankrupt. For compensation, the territorial government of California awarded him a pension of $250 per month.

Goodyear's Lucky Blunder

Charles Goodyear was determined. Somehow, there had to be a way to make rubber that would not get sticky or melt in hot weather. Raw rubber was cheap because no one had found a practical use for it. So Goodyear bought a bunch and began experimenting. He mixed it with everything he could think of—castor oil, witch hazel, and even cream cheese. Nothing worked. One day in 1839, he was experimenting with rubber and sulfur when he accidently spilled some onto the hot stove. To his surprise, the mixture did not melt.

The process of vulcanization he had discovered made rubber flexible, but it did not make Goodyear rich. In fact, he spent many years in court trying to defend his patent.

Footnotes to History

- Martin Van Buren was the first President born in the United States rather than in the English colonies.
- In the 1820s, both Presidents Adams and Jackson tried to buy Texas from Mexico.
- Samuel Colt's invention, the revolver, a gun with a revolving cylinder that held the bullets, was first used during the Mexican War.
- In 1830, less than 30 percent of books sold in the United States were printed here. But by 1840, almost 70 percent were.

Reviewing the Main Ideas

1. (a) How did democracy expand during the Jackson era? (b) Which groups were not included?
2. How did the federal government help white settlers to acquire Indian lands in the 1830s and 1840s?
3. How did land speculation help to cause the Panic of 1837?
4. Why did Tejanos support the Americans in their struggle for independence from Mexico?
5. What role did the idea of Manifest Destiny play in the Mexican War?
6. What attracted Americans to each of the following areas: (a) Oregon Country; (b) Texas; (c) Utah; (d) California?
7. List three developments that contributed to the growth of northern industry in the mid-1800s.
8. How did factories of the 1840s and 1850s differ from earlier mills?
9. (a) How did the cotton boom in the South promote the growth of slavery? (b) Why did slavery spread westward?
10. What led women abolitionists like Lucretia Mott and Elizabeth Cady Stanton to take up the cause of women's rights?
11. What changes were made in education in the mid-1800s?
12. How did American writers and artists of the mid-1800s break free of European traditions?

Thinking Critically

1. **Defending a Position** Andrew Jackson was a firm believer in states' rights. Do you agree or disagree? Explain.
2. **Analyzing Ideas** How do you think each of the following groups reacted to the idea of Manifest Destiny: (a) Native Americans; (b) Mexicans; (c) eastern farmers?
3. **Linking Past and Present** Many Irish and German immigrants came to the United States in the mid-1800s. (a) Why did nativists want to limit immigration? (b) What reasons do people give today for putting limits on immigration?
4. **Analyzing Information** Review the discussion of slave codes on pages 474–475. How did the codes prevent slave uprisings?

Applying Your Skills

1. **Outlining** Review the outlining skill on page 32. Then prepare an outline of Chapter 13, Section 4, "Jackson's Successors." How were Jackson's successors affected by Jackson's actions during his presidency?
2. **Analyzing a Quotation** Review the following statement made by a Mexican American in the Southwest in the mid-1800s: "The Americans say they have come for our good. Yes, for all our goods." What did he mean?
3. **Ranking** Skim Chapter 15 for information about inventions that changed the northern economy in the mid-1800s. Rank the inventions according to their importance to the growth of the nation as a whole. Explain your ranking.
4. **Identifying the Main Idea** Reread the statement by Sojourner Truth on page 491. Then write one or two sentences summarizing the main idea.

Doing More

1. **Making a Poster** Make a poster to rally Texans to fight for independence from Mexico. In your poster, appeal to patriotism and love of liberty.
2. **Drawing a Political Cartoon** Draw a cartoon that comments on an important political issue in American life between 1820 and 1860. Make sure that your cartoon clearly shows your point of view.

3. **Writing a Speech** Imagine that you have been asked to speak at an antislavery, women's rights, or temperance meeting in 1850. Write the speech that you will deliver. First, choose your topic, purpose, and point of view. Then, outline the main points you would like to make. Use your textbook to find supporting details. Begin with an opening statement that will capture the attention of the audience. Close with a summary statement. Revise your speech for clarity. Proofread, and make a final copy.

4. **Exploring Local History** Check your local library for an exhibit of the works of community artists, past or present. Study the paintings to discover if the artists make a statement about life in your community. Share your findings with classmates.

Recognizing Points of View

In the mid-1800s, Americans were divided over the issue of slavery. Below are excerpts from the works of two writers of the period. Read the excerpts and answer the following questions.

1. (a) What is William Lloyd Garrison referring to when he mentions "compromises ... made to secure the adoption of the Constitution"? (b) Why does Garrison believe that compromise is not possible on the issue of slavery?
2. (a) According to George Fitzhugh, what is the result of liberty and equality? (b) How does Fitzhugh defend slavery?
3. Do you think it would be possible for either Garrison or Fitzhugh to win over the other man to his point of view? Explain.

hould the United States allow slavery?

William Lloyd Garrison

❝Let us confess the sin of our fathers, and our own sin as a people, in conspiring for the . . . enslavement of the colored race among us. Let us be honest with the facts of history, and acknowledge the compromises that were made to secure the adoption of the Constitution, and the consequent establishment of the Union. . . .

It was pleaded at the time of [the Constitution's] adoption, it is pleaded now, that without such a compromise there could have been no union. . . .

To this we reply: The plea [that compromise was necessary] is as [wrong] as the [compromise] was tyrannical. . . . It assumes . . . that there can be freedom with slavery, union with injustice, and safety with blood-guiltiness. . . . A partnership between right and wrong is wholly wrong.❞

George Fitzhugh

❝Liberty and equality are new things under the sun. The free states of [old] abounded with slaves. . . . Liberty and equality throw the whole weight of society on its weakest members; they combine all men in oppressing precisely that part of mankind who most need sympathy, aid, and protection. . . .

The bestowing upon men equality of rights, is but giving [permission] to the strong to oppress the weak. . . . It [creates] the [most shocking] inequalities. . . .

There is no rivalry, no competition to get employment among slaves, as among free laborers. Nor is there a war between master and slave. . . . The slaves are all well fed, well clad, have plenty of fuel, and are happy. They have no dread of the future—no fear of want.❞

UNIT 6 The Nation Torn Apart

2 *Both North and South won public support. Some northerners wore badges from Abraham Lincoln's presidential campaign to show support for the Union cause.*

1 *The issue of slavery divided the North and South. After civil war broke out, southerners proudly carried the Confederate flag into battle.*

3 *Most battles took place in the South. This Confederate camp was in Mississippi, which became a battleground for control of the Mississippi River.*

1820	1830	1840	1850
AMERICAN EVENTS 1820 Missouri Compromise			**1848** Mexican Cession
WORLD EVENTS	**1830s** Slavery abolished in British Empire		

James Monroe   Andrew Jackson   Martin Van Buren   John Tyler   James Polk

John Quincy Adams   William Harrison   Zachary Taylor

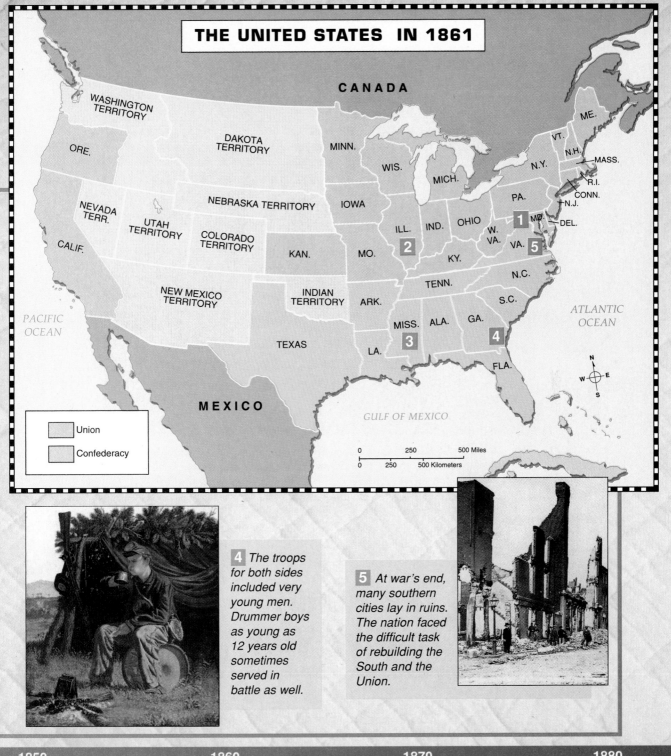

THE UNITED STATES IN 1861

CANADA

WASHINGTON TERRITORY

ORE.

DAKOTA TERRITORY

MINN.

WIS.

MICH.

ME.

VT.

N.H.

MASS.

N.Y.

R.I.

CONN.

PA.

N.J.

NEVADA TERR.

UTAH TERRITORY

NEBRASKA TERRITORY

IOWA

ILL.

IND.

OHIO

1 MD.

DEL.

CALIF.

COLORADO TERRITORY

KAN.

MO.

W. VA.

VA.

5

2

KY.

N.C.

NEW MEXICO TERRITORY

INDIAN TERRITORY

ARK.

TENN.

S.C.

PACIFIC OCEAN

TEXAS

MISS.

ALA.

GA.

ATLANTIC OCEAN

3

4

LA.

FLA.

MEXICO

GULF OF MEXICO

N W E S

Union

Confederacy

0   250   500 Miles

0   250   500 Kilometers

4 The troops for both sides included very young men. Drummer boys as young as 12 years old sometimes served in battle as well.

5 At war's end, many southern cities lay in ruins. The nation faced the difficult task of rebuilding the South and the Union.

1850	1860	1870	1880
1850 Compromise of 1850	**1860** Lincoln elected	**1870** Fifteenth Amendment	**1877** End of Reconstruction
	1861–65 Civil War		
	1861 Russian ruler frees serfs	**1870** Italy unified	
		1871 Germany unified	

Millard Fillmore   Abraham Lincoln   Ulysses Grant   Rutherford Hayes

Franklin Pierce   James Buchanan   Andrew Johnson

A Slave Market *By the mid-1800s, the issue of slavery sharply divided the North and South. In the meantime, however, the traffic in slaves continued. Here, an auctioneer describes the skills of the men, women, and children he has for sale.* **Citizenship** *How do you think the entry of new states into the Union affected the slavery debate?*

CHAPTER

17

The Road to Civil War (1820–1861)

Chapter Outline

1 Slavery or Freedom in the West
2 Saving the Union
3 Bloodshed in Kansas
4 Republicans Challenge Slavery
5 The South Breaks Away

CHAPTER SPOTLIGHT

The Big Picture

Events sometimes force people to make difficult decisions. By the late 1840s, the nation's borders stretched beyond the Mississippi River to the Pacific Ocean. Americans now had to decide whether slavery would be allowed in the new territories of the West.

At first, compromise seemed possible. But as the debate and violence increased, Americans came to realize that the nation could not continue half slave and half free. In the end, the issue would be decided by war.

Kathleen Underwood

Of Special Interest

Focus On

◆ Why did new territories raise the slavery question?
◆ How did the North and South compromise on the slavery question?
◆ Why did tension over the slavery question increase in the 1850s?
◆ What new political party emerged in 1854?
◆ What events triggered the Civil War?

On June 16, 1858, a lawyer named Abraham Lincoln spoke before a crowded convention hall in Springfield, Illinois:

❝A house divided against itself cannot stand. I believe this government cannot endure permanently half-slave and half-free. I do not expect the Union to be dissolved—I do not expect the house to fall—but I do expect it will cease to be divided. It will become all one thing, or all the other. Either the opponents of slavery will arrest the further spread of it . . . or its [supporters] will push it forward till it shall become . . . lawful in all the states, old as well as new, North as well as South.❞

Lincoln had just been chosen to run as the Republican candidate for the Senate. Few people outside Illinois had heard of him. But his speech became famous. Soon, many northerners were repeating the phrase "a house divided . . . cannot stand." They agreed that the nation could not go on half slave and half free.

By the 1850s, more and more northerners had turned against slavery. They strongly opposed southern attempts to open the new territories of the West to slavery. Time after time, the North and South clashed over this issue.

By 1861, when Abraham Lincoln became President, Americans were worried. Could the Union that had existed for nearly a century remain whole?

1 Slavery or Freedom in the West

FIND OUT

- Why did the issue of slavery flare up in 1819?
- What was the Missouri Compromise?
- What was the goal of the Free Soil party?
- **VOCABULARY** sectionalism, popular sovereignty

By 1820, 77-year-old Thomas Jefferson had tired of politics. He vowed "never to write, talk, or even think of politics." Still, the former President voiced alarm when he learned of a fierce debate in Congress. The issue was slavery. Jefferson feared that the quarrel would tear the country apart:

> **"** In the gloomiest moment of the revolutionary war, I never had any [fears] equal to what I feel from this source. . . . Every new irritation will make it deeper and deeper. . . . We have a wolf by the ears, and we can neither hold him nor safely let him go. **"**

The Missouri Question

The debate that alarmed Jefferson in 1820 concerned the spread of slavery. As you have read, the first state carved out of the Louisiana Purchase was Louisiana. Because slavery was well established there, few protested when Louisiana joined the Union as a slave state in 1812. But when Missouri asked to join the Union as a slave state in 1818, there was an uproar.

The problem was that the admission of Missouri as a slave state would upset the balance of power in the Senate. In 1819, there were 11 free states and 11 slave states. Each state had two senators. If Missouri joined the Union as a slave state, the South would have a majority in the Senate. Determined not to lose power, northerners fought against letting Missouri enter as a slave state.

The argument over Missouri lasted many months. Finally, Senator Henry Clay proposed a compromise. During the long debate, Maine had applied to become a state. Clay suggested admitting Missouri as a slave state and Maine as a free state. His plan, called the **Missouri Compromise,** kept the number of slave and free states equal.

As part of the Missouri Compromise, Congress drew an imaginary line across the southern border of Missouri at latitude 36°30'N. Slavery was permitted in the part of the Louisiana Purchase south of that line. But it was banned north of the line. Missouri itself was the only exception. (See the map on page 525.)

Slavery in the Mexican Cession

The Missouri Compromise applied only to the Louisiana Purchase. In 1848, the Mexican War added a vast stretch of western land to the United States. Once again, the question of slavery in the territories arose. Would slavery be allowed in the Mexican Cession?

A plan to ban slavery. As you have read in Chapter 14, many northerners had opposed the war with Mexico. They thought that the South wanted to push slavery into the West.

A few months after the Mexican War began, a young member of Congress from Pennsylvania, David Wilmot, raised the slavery question. Wilmot called on Congress to outlaw slavery in any land won from Mexico. Southerners were furious. They said that Congress had no right to ban slavery in the territories.

In 1846, the House passed Wilmot's measure, called the **Wilmot Proviso.** But the Senate defeated it. As a result, Americans continued to argue about slavery in the West even while their army fought in Mexico.

On to Liberty *In this painting, a group of slave women lead their children on the dangerous journey to freedom in the North. Southern slave owners were enraged when northerners refused to return such runaways to their masters.* **Daily Life** *How does the artist show that the journey was dangerous?*

Americans take sides. The Mexican War strengthened feelings of sectionalism in the North and South. Sectionalism means that people feel loyalty to their state or section, instead of to the whole country. Southerners were united by their support for slavery. To them, the North was a growing threat. Many northerners saw the South as a foreign country where American rights and liberties did not exist.

As the debate over slavery in the West heated up, people found it hard not to take sides. Northern abolitionists demanded that slavery be abolished throughout the country. They insisted that slavery was morally wrong. By the late 1840s, a growing number of northerners agreed with them.

On the other hand, southern slave owners thought that slavery should be allowed in any territory. They also demanded that slaves who escaped to the North be returned to them. Many white southerners agreed with these ideas, even though they owned no slaves.

Moderate views. Between these extreme views were more moderate positions. Some moderates argued that the Missouri Compromise line should be extended across the Mexican Cession to the Pacific. Any new state north of the line would be free. Any state south of the line could have slavery.

Other moderates supported the idea of popular sovereignty. Popular sovereignty means control by the people. In other words, voters in a new territory would decide for themselves whether or not to allow slavery. Slaves, of course, could not vote.

A new party. Debate over slavery in the territories led to the birth of a new political party. By 1848, many northerners in both the Whig and Democratic parties strongly opposed the spread of slavery. But the leaders of both parties refused to take a stand on the question. If they came out against slavery, they would give up any chance of winning votes in the South. Some leaders feared that the slavery issue would split the nation.

In 1848, antislavery members of both parties met in Buffalo, New York. There, they founded the **Free Soil party.** Their slogan was "Free soil, free speech, free labor, and free men." The party's main goal was to keep slavery out of the western territories. Only a few Free Soilers were abolitionists who wanted to end slavery in the South.

The Free Soil Challenge

The 1848 campaign for President took place while Americans debated the slavery question. Free Soilers named Martin Van

A Three-way Race *Slavery was an important issue in the 1848 presidential election. In this cartoon, the candidates race for the finish as their supporters cheer from the sidelines. Zachary Taylor rides a bloodhound, Martin Van Buren is astride a buffalo, and Lewis Cass is on a bicycle.* **Citizenship** *What position on slavery did each candidate represent?*

Buren as their candidate. Democrats chose Lewis Cass of Michigan. Whigs selected Zachary Taylor, a hero of the Mexican War.

For the first time, slavery was an important election issue. Cass supported popular sovereignty. Because Taylor was a slave owner from Louisiana, many southerners assumed that he supported slavery. Van Buren called for a ban on slavery in the Mexican Cession.

In the end, Zachary Taylor won the election. But Van Buren took 10 percent of the popular vote, and 13 other Free Soilers won seats in Congress. After only three months of work, the Free Soilers had made a strong showing. Their success showed that slavery had become a national issue.

SECTION 1 REVIEW

1. **Locate:** (a) Missouri, (b) Maine, (c) Missouri Compromise line.
2. **Identify:** (a) Missouri Compromise, (b) Wilmot Proviso, (c) Free Soil party, (d) Martin Van Buren, (e) Lewis Cass, (f) Zachary Taylor.
3. **Define:** (a) sectionalism, (b) popular sovereignty.
4. Why did Missouri's request to join the Union cause debate in Congress?
5. How did the Mexican Cession affect the slavery question?

6. **Analyzing Ideas** The slogan of the Free Soil party was "Free soil, free speech, free labor, and free men." Why might this slogan have appealed to voters in the North?

2 Saving the Union

FIND OUT

◆ Why did the slavery question flare up again in 1850?

◆ How did the North and South reach another compromise?

◆ How did the issue of fugitive slaves divide the North and South?

◆ **VOCABULARY** fugitive, civil war

The question of slavery in the West further divided the North and South in 1850. That year, California asked to join the Union as a free state. Tempers flared as members of Congress tried to reach another compromise.

One outburst in Congress nearly ended in violence. Senator Thomas Hart Benton of Missouri, a slave owner himself, had represented the slave state of Missouri for 30 years. Still, he supported California's request to enter as a free state. In his view, the Missouri Compromise had to be upheld, and most of California lay on the free side of the compromise line.

One day, Benton addressed the Senate. In a fit of rage, he denounced a fellow southerner, Senator Foote of Mississippi, for helping to block California's admission. Insulted, Foote angrily rose from his seat, drew a pistol, and pointed it at Benton's chest. As other senators watched in horror, Benton roared: "Let him fire! Stand out of the way and let the assassin fire!"

No blood was shed in the Senate that day. But the fierce debates in Congress over slavery worried leaders. Was a peaceful solution to the slavery question possible?

Seeking a Compromise

For a time after the Missouri Compromise, both slave and free states entered the Union peacefully. Between 1821 and 1850, Michigan, Iowa, and Wisconsin entered as free states. Arkansas, Florida, and Texas came in as slave states. (See the graph at right.)

But in 1850, the admission of California as a free state once more threatened the balance of power in the Senate. Southerners did not want to give the North a majority in the Senate. They also feared that more free states might be carved out of the huge Mexican Cession and further upset the balance. Some southerners even talked about seceding from the Union.

Clay pleads for compromise. To resolve this crisis, Congress turned to Senator Henry Clay. Clay had won the nickname "Great Compromiser" for working out the Missouri Compromise. Now, 30 years later, the 73-year-old Clay was frail and ill. But his power and charm returned as he pleaded for the North and South to reach an agreement. If they failed to do so, Clay warned, the nation could fall apart.

Calhoun replies. Senator John C. Calhoun of South Carolina prepared the South's reply to Clay. Calhoun was dying of tuberculosis and could not speak loudly

enough to address the Senate. Wrapped in a heavy cloak, he glared at his northern foes while another senator read his speech.

Calhoun refused to compromise. Slavery *must* be allowed in the western territories, he insisted. The slave system could not be changed. Calhoun also demanded that fugitive, or runaway, slaves be returned to their owners in the South. The fugitives, in fact, were few in number and not the real issue. What Calhoun really wanted was northerners to admit that southerners had the right to get their "property" back.

GRAPH SKILLS *Both the North and South were determined to maintain the delicate balance in the Senate between slave and free states. ◆ How did the admission of California affect this balance?*

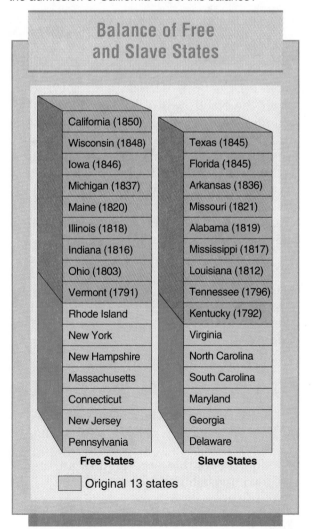

Balance of Free and Slave States

Free States	Slave States
California (1850)	
Wisconsin (1848)	Texas (1845)
Iowa (1846)	Florida (1845)
Michigan (1837)	Arkansas (1836)
Maine (1820)	Missouri (1821)
Illinois (1818)	Alabama (1819)
Indiana (1816)	Mississippi (1817)
Ohio (1803)	Louisiana (1812)
Vermont (1791)	Tennessee (1796)
Rhode Island	Kentucky (1792)
New York	Virginia
New Hampshire	North Carolina
Massachusetts	South Carolina
Connecticut	Maryland
New Jersey	Georgia
Pennsylvania	Delaware

☐ Original 13 states

A Great Debate *The Senate debated Henry Clay's proposed Compromise of 1850 for six months. Here, Clay appeals to his fellow senators to support his plan. Daniel Webster, resting his head on his hand at left, and white-haired John Calhoun, at the far right, listen.* **Citizenship** *What was Calhoun's view of slavery in the territories?*

If the North would not agree to his demands, Calhoun told the Senate, "let the states . . . agree to part in peace. If you are unwilling that we should part in peace, tell us so, and we shall know what to do." Everyone knew what Calhoun meant. If an agreement could not be reached, the South would secede from the United States, using force if necessary.

Webster calls for unity. Daniel Webster of Massachusetts spoke next. Webster had been Clay's rival for decades. But now he supported Clay's plea to save the Union. Webster stated his position clearly before Congress:

❝I speak today not as a Massachusetts man, nor as a northern man, but as an American. . . . I speak today for the preservation of the Union. . . . There can be no such thing as a peaceable secession. Peaceable secession is an utter impossibility.❞

There was no doubt in Webster's mind. The states could not separate without a civil war. A **civil war** is a war between people of the same country.

Like many northerners, Webster now saw slavery as evil. But he felt that disunion was worse. To save the Union, Webster was willing to compromise with the South. He would not agree to continue the slave trade in Washington, D.C. He would, however, support the South's demand that escaped slaves be returned.

A Compromise at Last

In 1850, while the debate raged, Calhoun died. His last words were "The South! The South! God knows what will become of her!" President Taylor also died in the summer of 1850. Taylor had opposed Clay's compromise plan. But the new President, Millard Fillmore, supported it. An agreement finally seemed possible.

Henry Clay gave more than 70 speeches in favor of a compromise. At last, he became too sick to carry on. Stephen Douglas, a young and energetic senator from Illinois, took up the fight for him. Douglas tirelessly guided each part of Clay's plan, called the **Compromise of 1850,** through Congress.

The Compromise of 1850 had four parts. First, California entered the Union as a free state. Second, the rest of the Mexican Cession was divided into the territories of New Mexico and Utah. In each territory, voters would decide the slavery question according to popular sovereignty. Third, the slave trade was ended in Washington, D.C. But Congress declared that it had no power to ban the slave trade between slave states. Fourth, a strict new fugitive slave law was passed.

The North and South had reached a compromise. But neither side got all it wanted. The new Fugitive Slave Law was especially hard for northerners to accept.

The Fugitive Slave Law of 1850

Most northerners had ignored the old Fugitive Slave Law, passed in 1793. As a result, fugitive slaves often lived as free blacks in northern cities. But northerners could not ignore the **Fugitive Slave Law of 1850.** The new law demanded that all citizens help to catch runaway slaves. People who let fugitives escape could be fined $1,000 and jailed for six months.

The new law also set up special courts to hear the cases of runaways. Northern judges received $10 if a person was sent to the South, but only $5 for setting a person free. Thus, for some judges, it paid to send blacks to the South, whether or not they were runaways. After the law passed, thousands of free blacks fled to Canada, fearful that they would be kidnapped and enslaved.

The Fugitive Slave Law pleased southerners, but enraged northerners. By forcing them to catch runaways, the law made

Speaking Out Against the Fugitive Slave Law *Many northerners condemned the Fugitive Slave Law as an "outrage to humanity" that should be "disobeyed at all hazards." Here, a newspaper engraving shows a crowd gathered in Boston Common to hear abolitionist Wendell Phillips speak out against the hated law.* **Citizenship** *What were the terms of the Fugitive Slave Law of 1850?*

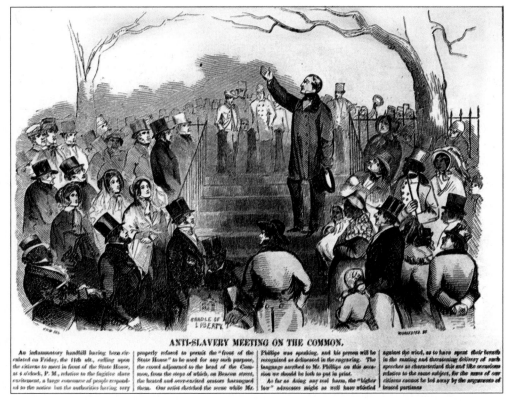

ANTI-SLAVERY MEETING ON THE COMMON.

northerners feel like part of the slave system. In several northern cities, crowds tried to rescue fugitive slaves from their captors. Calhoun had hoped the Fugitive Slave Law would force northerners to admit the rights of slave owners. Instead, each time the law was enforced, it convinced more northerners that slavery was evil.

An Antislavery Bestseller

An event in 1852 added to the growing antislavery mood of the North. That year, Harriet Beecher Stowe published a novel called **Uncle Tom's Cabin.** Stowe wrote the novel to show the evils of slavery and the injustice of the Fugitive Slave Law.

Stowe told the story of Uncle Tom, a kind, deeply religious slave. Tom's owners are in debt and sell him to raise money. In time, a cruel planter named Simon Legree buys Tom. Legree treats his slaves brutally and finally beats Tom to death.

The book had wide appeal in the North. In its first year, Stowe's novel sold 300,000 copies. In addition, the novel was published in many different languages. Soon, a play based on the novel appeared in cities not only in the North but also around the world.

Southerners claimed that *Uncle Tom's Cabin* did not give a true picture of slave life. Indeed, Stowe had seen little of slavery firsthand. Yet the book helped to change the way thousands of northerners felt about slavery. They no longer thought of it as a political problem for Congress to settle. Slavery now seemed to be a moral problem that touched everyone. More

Uncle Tom's Cabin *Harriet Beecher Stowe's story about the evils of slavery convinced millions of northerners to rally to the abolitionist cause. This poster advertising a stage production of* Uncle Tom's Cabin *shows a fugitive slave being chased by bloodhounds.* **United States and the World** *How do you think Stowe's book affected world opinion of the United States?*

Harriet Beecher Stowe: Author of *Uncle Tom's Cabin*

As a young woman, Harriet Beecher Stowe wrote stories. Her sister-in-law found them amusing, but not very important. "If I could use a pen as you can," she told Stowe, "I would write something that will make this whole nation feel what an accursed thing slavery is."

Stowe took up the challenge. She wrote a short story about a slave named Uncle Tom. The story slowly grew into a novel. In 1851, *Uncle Tom's Cabin* ran as a serial in an abolitionist newspaper. Readers praised it, so Stowe published it as a book in 1852.

No one could have foreseen what followed. The first 5,000 copies sold out in two days. Soon, Stowe's publisher had three power presses running day and night to meet the demand. Men, women, and children wept as they read about the cruel treatment Uncle Tom suffered. Support for abolitionist societies grew, and Stowe became famous.

During the Civil War, Stowe met President Lincoln. Lincoln, who recognized the impact of *Uncle Tom's Cabin,* is said to have commented, "So this is the little woman who made this big war."

1. Why did Harriet Beecher Stowe write *Uncle Tom's Cabin?*

2. Understanding Causes and Effects Why do you think Stowe's novel had such an impact on northerners?

Americans began to ask how one human being could own another. For this reason, *Uncle Tom's Cabin* was one of the most important books in American history. (📖 See "Uncle Tom's Cabin" on page 691.)

SECTION 2 REVIEW

1. Locate: (a) California, (b) New Mexico Territory, (c) Utah Territory.

2. Identify: (a) Thomas Hart Benton, (b) Henry Clay, (c) John C. Calhoun, (d) Daniel Webster, (e) Stephen Douglas, (f) Compromise of 1850, (g) Fugitive Slave Law of 1850, (h) Harriet Beecher Stowe, (i) *Uncle Tom's Cabin.*

3. Define: (a) fugitive, (b) civil war.

4. Why did California's request for statehood raise the slavery issue again?

5. Why did northerners and southerners support the Compromise of 1850?

6. What did northerners dislike about the Fugitive Slave Law of 1850?

7. Forecasting Do you think the Compromise of 1850 offered a lasting solution to the slavery question? Explain.

3 Bloodshed in Kansas

FIND OUT

◆ What events made the issue of slavery emerge again in 1854?

◆ Why did proslavery and antislavery forces move into Kansas?

◆ Why did northerners think that the Dred Scott decision was unjust?

In 1854, Congress passed a bill that allowed settlers in Kansas to vote for or against slavery in that territory. Members of Congress knew that the bill would lead to a political uproar in Kansas between antislavery and proslavery forces. One northern senator challenged his southern colleagues:

> ❝Come on then, Gentlemen of the Slave States. . . . We will engage in competition for the . . . soil of Kansas, and God give the victory to the side which is stronger in numbers as it is in right.❞

But the contest in Kansas quickly became violent. Northerners and southerners struggled fiercely for control of the territory. Kansas was soon the scene of stolen elections, gunfights, and murder.

Kansas-Nebraska Act

Americans had hoped that the Compromise of 1850 would end debate over slavery in the West. But in 1854, the issue of slavery in the territories surfaced again.

In January 1854, Illinois Senator Stephen Douglas introduced a bill to set up a government for the Nebraska Territory. The new territory stretched from Texas north to Canada, and from Missouri west to the Rocky Mountains. (See the map on page 525.)

Douglas wanted to organize the territory so that a railroad, running from Illinois to California, could be built across it. A railroad would open the West to new settlers. It would also make Chicago the gateway to the West and thereby help Douglas win votes in Illinois.

Undoing the Missouri Compromise. Douglas knew that southerners did not want to add another free state to the Union. So he proposed dividing the Nebraska Territory into two territories, Kansas and Nebraska. The question of slavery in each would then be decided by popular sovereignty.

Douglas's bill, called the **Kansas-Nebraska Act,** seemed fair to many people. After all, the Compromise of 1850 had applied popular sovereignty in New Mexico and Utah. But others felt that Kansas and Nebraska were different. The Missouri Compromise had already banned slavery in those areas, they insisted. The Kansas-Nebraska Act would, in effect, undo the Missouri Compromise.

Most southerners supported the Kansas-Nebraska Act. They were sure that slave owners from neighboring Missouri would move across the border into Kansas. In time, they hoped, Kansas would become a slave state.

President Franklin Pierce, a Democrat elected in 1852, also supported the bill. With the President's help, Douglas pushed the Kansas-Nebraska Act through Congress.

Northern outrage. Northern reaction to the Kansas-Nebraska Act was swift and angry. Opponents of slavery called the act a "criminal betrayal of precious rights." Slavery could now spread to areas that had been free for over 30 years.

Northerners protested by challenging the Fugitive Slave Law. Two days after Congress passed the Kansas-Nebraska Act, slave catchers in Boston seized Anthony Burns, a fugitive slave. Citizens of Boston poured into the streets to keep Burns from being sent to the South. It took two companies of soldiers to stop the crowd from freeing Burns. Such incidents showed that antislavery feeling was rising in the North. Events in Kansas soon proved that slavery could stir people to violence.

Kansas Explodes

The Kansas-Nebraska Act made Kansas a testing ground for popular sovereignty.

Stephen Douglas hoped that Kansas settlers would decide the slavery question in a quiet vote on election day. But this was not to be. Both proslavery and antislavery forces sent settlers to Kansas ready to fight for control of the territory.

Rushing to Kansas. Most of the new arrivals were farmers from neighboring states. Their main interest in Kansas was cheap land. But abolitionists also helped

MAP STUDY

The issue of whether or not to allow slavery in the territories created tension between the North and South.

1. Which territories were opened to slavery under the Compromise of 1850?
2. Which territories were opened to slavery in 1854?
3. **Analyzing Information** Locate the Missouri Compromise line. What happened to the Missouri Compromise after 1854? Explain.

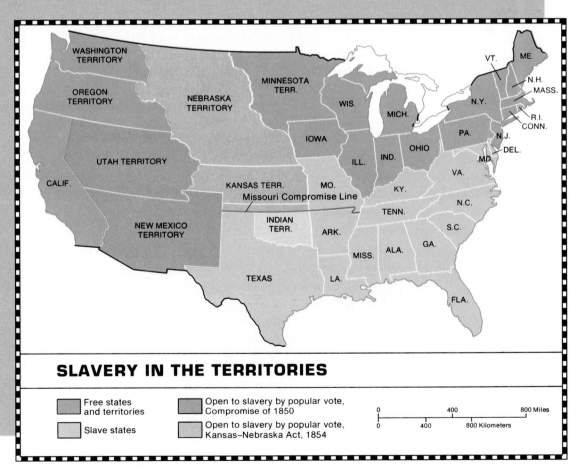

SLAVERY IN THE TERRITORIES

- Free states and territories
- Slave states
- Open to slavery by popular vote, Compromise of 1850
- Open to slavery by popular vote, Kansas–Nebraska Act, 1854

more than 1,000 people move to Kansas from New England.

Proslavery settlers moved into Kansas as well. They wanted to make sure that antislavery forces did not overrun the territory. Proslavery bands from Missouri, called **Border Ruffians,** often rode across the border. They battled the antislavery forces in Kansas.

Divided Kansas. In 1855, Kansas held elections to choose lawmakers. Hundreds of Border Ruffians crossed into Kansas and voted illegally. They helped to elect a proslavery legislature.

The new legislature quickly passed laws to support slavery. One law said that people could be put to death for helping slaves escape. Another made speaking out against slavery a crime punishable by two years of hard labor.

Antislavery settlers refused to accept these laws. They elected their own governor and legislature. With two rival governments, Kansas was in chaos. Armed gangs roamed the land looking for trouble. Abraham Lincoln predicted that they would find it:

❝Bowie-knives and six-shooters are seen plainly enough; but never a glimpse of a ballot-box. And, really, what is to be the result of this? . . . Is it not probable that the contest will come to blows, and bloodshed?❞

The first shots. In 1856, a drunken band of proslavery men raided the town of Lawrence, an antislavery stronghold. The attackers destroyed homes and smashed the press of a Free Soil newspaper.

John Brown, an abolitionist, decided to strike back. Brown had moved to Kansas to help make it a free state. He claimed that God had sent him to punish supporters of slavery.

After the attack on Lawrence, Brown rode with his four sons and two other men to the town of Pottawatomie (pot uh WOT uh mee) Creek. In the middle of the night, Brown and his followers dragged five proslavery settlers from their beds and murdered them.

The killings at Pottawatomie Creek sparked more violence. Both sides fought

Border Ruffians Cross Into Kansas *Proslavery leaders encouraged bands of men from Missouri, a slave state, to cross the border into Kansas. These Border Ruffians voted illegally in Kansas elections and stirred up trouble for antislavery settlers there.* **Citizenship** *Why were two rival governments set up in Kansas?*

Bleeding Kansas *The struggle between proslavery and antislavery forces for control of Kansas erupted into violence. Here, the two sides battle at the town of Hickory Point.* **Citizenship** *How was the violence in Kansas related to the Kansas-Nebraska Act?*

fiercely. By late 1856, more than 200 people had been killed. Newspapers called the territory **Bleeding Kansas.**

Bloodshed in the Senate

Even before the murders at Pottawatomie Creek, the battle over Kansas spilled into the Senate. Charles Sumner of Massachusetts was the leading abolitionist senator. In one speech, Sumner denounced the proslavery legislature in Kansas. Then, he sharply criticized his southern foes. His attack singled out Andrew Butler, an elderly senator from South Carolina.

Butler was not in the Senate on the day Sumner spoke. But two days later, Congressman Preston Brooks, Butler's nephew, marched into the Senate chamber. Using a heavy cane, Brooks beat Sumner until he fell, bloody and unconscious, to the floor.

Many southerners felt that Sumner got what he deserved. Hundreds sent canes to Brooks to show their support for him. To northerners, the brutal act was just more proof that slavery led to violence.

Dred Scott Decision

With Congress in an uproar, many Americans looked to the Supreme Court to settle the slavery issue and restore peace. In 1857, the Court agreed to rule on a case involving a slave named Dred Scott. Instead of bringing harmony, however, the Court's decision pushed the North and South further apart.

Dred Scott had lived in Missouri for many years. Later, he moved with his owner to Illinois and then to Wisconsin Territory, where slavery was not allowed. When Scott's owner died, antislavery lawyers helped him to file a lawsuit. They argued that since Scott had lived in a free territory, he should be a free man. In time, the case reached the Supreme Court.

The Court decided the case in a surprising way. First, it ruled that Scott could not even file a lawsuit because, as a black, he was not a citizen. The Court also agreed that slaves were property.

The judges did not stop there. They went on to make a sweeping decision. The Court ruled that Congress did not have the power to outlaw slavery in a territory. Only when a territory was ready for statehood could it ban slavery. The ruling meant that the Missouri Compromise, in effect from 1820 to 1854, was unconstitutional.

White southerners rejoiced at the **Dred Scott decision.** It meant that slavery was legal in all the territories—just what southerners had been demanding for years.

Northerners were shocked and angry. Many believed that slavery would die out if it were restricted to the South. But now, the government said that slavery could spread throughout the West. Even northerners who disliked abolitionists felt that the Dred Scott ruling was wrong. "We are

EYEWITNESS

An Attack on the Dred Scott Decision

Dred Scott, shown below, filed a lawsuit for his freedom. When the Supreme Court handed down the Dred Scott decision, no one criticized the ruling more powerfully than black abolitionist Frederick Douglass. The following passages are from a speech he gave in 1857.

❝This infamous decision of . . . the Supreme Court maintains that slaves . . . are property in the same sense that horses, sheep, and swine are property; . . . that slavery may go in safety anywhere under the star-spangled banner; . . . that [people] of African descent are not and cannot be citizens of the United States.

You will readily ask me how I am affected by this devilish decision. . . . My answer is. . . my hopes were never brighter than now. . . .

By all the laws of nature, of civilization, and of progress, slavery is a doomed system. . . . I base my sense of the certain overthrow of slavery, in part, upon the nature of the American government, the Constitution, the tendencies of the age, and the character of the American people. . . . All I ask of the American people is that they live up to the Constitution, adopt its principles, [take in] its spirit, and enforce its provisions. When this is done . . . liberty . . . will become the inheritance of all the inhabitants of this highly favored country.❞

1. According to Douglass, what did the Dred Scott ruling say?

2. Analyzing Ideas Why did Douglass believe that slavery could not last, in spite of the Dred Scott decision?

now one great . . . slaveholding community," a Cincinnati newspaper declared. A New England paper asked, "Where will it all end?"

| SECTION | 3 | REVIEW |

1. **Locate:** (a) Kansas Territory, (b) Nebraska Territory.
2. **Identify:** (a) Kansas-Nebraska Act, (b) Franklin Pierce, (c) Border Ruffians, (d) John Brown, (e) Bleeding Kansas, (f) Charles Sumner, (g) Dred Scott decision.
3. How did the Kansas-Nebraska Act undo the Missouri Compromise?
4. Why did popular sovereignty lead to fighting in Kansas?
5. Why did the Dred Scott decision please southerners?
6. **Analyzing a Quotation** After the Kansas-Nebraska Act was passed, Stephen Douglas claimed that "the struggle for freedom was forever banished from the halls of Congress to the western plains." What did Douglas mean?

4 Republicans Challenge Slavery

FIND OUT

◆ Why did a new political party take shape in the mid-1850s?

◆ How did Abraham Lincoln view slavery?

◆ How did the North and South react to the raid on Harpers Ferry?

◆ **VOCABULARY** arsenal

In the mid-1850s, people who opposed slavery in the territories were looking for a political voice. Neither the Whig party nor the Democratic party would take a strong stand against slavery. Disgust with the two parties peaked when the Kansas-Nebraska Act became law. "We have submitted to slavery long enough, and must not stand it any longer," an Ohio Democrat said.

Angry Free Soilers, northern Democrats, and antislavery Whigs met in towns and cities across the North. In 1854, a group gathered in Michigan to form a new political party, the **Republican party.** By 1856, the Republicans were ready to enter politics.

The Republican Party

The main goal of the Republican party was to keep slavery out of the western territories. A few Republicans were abolitionists and hoped to end slavery in the South as well. Most Republicans, however, expected only to stop the spread of slavery.

The Republican party grew quickly. In 1856, Republicans selected John Charles Frémont to run for President. Frémont was a frontiersman who had fought for California's independence. (See page 445.) He had never held office, but he opposed the spread of slavery. In northern cities, Republicans marched through the streets singing Frémont's campaign song:

> **❝**Arise, arise ye brave!
> And let our war-cry be,
> Free speech, free press, free soil,
> free men,
> Fré-mont and victory!**❞**

Since the Whig party had become very weak, Frémont's main opponent was Democrat James Buchanan. Buchanan was a northerner from Pennsylvania, but he sympathized with the southern position on slavery. Democrats hoped that he would win votes in both the North and South.

Supported by southerners and many northerners, Buchanan did win the election. Still, the Republicans made a strong showing. Frémont nearly won the election without the support of a single southern state. Southerners worried that their influence in the national government was fading fast.

Abe Lincoln of Illinois

The next test for the new Republican party came in 1858. That year, a race in Illinois captured the attention of the whole nation. Abraham Lincoln, a Republican, was challenging Stephen Douglas for his seat in the Senate. The race was important because most Americans thought that Douglas, a Democrat, would run for President in 1860.

A self-starter from Kentucky. Abraham Lincoln was born in the backwoods of Kentucky. Like many frontier people, his parents moved often to find better land. The family lived in Indiana and later in Illinois. As a child, Lincoln spent only a year in school. But he taught himself to read and spent hours reading by firelight.

After Lincoln left home, he opened a store in Illinois. There, he studied law on his own and launched a career in politics. After spending eight years in the state legislature, Lincoln served one term as a member of Congress. Bitterly opposed to the Kansas-Nebraska Act, he decided to run for the Senate in 1858.

"Just folks." When the race began, Lincoln was not a national figure. But people in Illinois knew him well and liked him. To them, he was "just folks"—someone who enjoyed picnics, wrestling contests, and all their other favorite pastimes.

People also admired his honesty and wit. His plainspoken manner made him a good speaker. Even so, a listener once complained that he could not understand one of Lincoln's speeches. "There are always some fleas a dog can't reach" was Lincoln's reply.

UP CLOSE

The Lincoln-Douglas Campaign Trail

One sunny day in August 1858, a train sped across the Illinois prairie. Inside his private railroad car sat Senator Stephen Douglas. Banners draped outside the car proudly announced the "Little Giant," as Douglas, only five feet tall, was called. Behind the senator's car was a flatcar mounted with a brass cannon. Whenever the train approached a station, two young men in uniforms fired the cannon. Senator Douglas was coming to town!

Abraham Lincoln was traveling on the same train. But Lincoln sat in a public car with other passengers. Lincoln knew that on his own he could never draw big crowds as Senator Douglas did. So Lincoln followed his opponent around the state, answering him speech for speech.

The Lincoln-Douglas debates begin. To get more attention, Lincoln challenged Douglas to a series of debates. Though reluctant, Douglas agreed. During the campaign, the two men debated seven times.

Lincoln and Douglas held their first debate in Ottawa, Illinois. It was a broiling hot day. Dust clouds rose as farmers drove their wagons to town. Others eager to hear the debate floated down the Illinois River in flatboats. Nobody minded the heat because this Senate election was especially important. Besides, politics was a favorite entertainment for Americans.

Douglas speaks. Standing before a crowd of 10,000, Douglas began his attack. Lincoln, he declared in a booming voice, was a hot-headed abolitionist who wanted blacks and whites to be complete equals— even to socialize with one another! Even worse, Douglas warned, Lincoln's call for an end to slavery would lead to war between the North and South.

Douglas then reminded the audience of his own views on slavery. Popular sovereignty, he urged, was the best way to solve the slavery crisis. Even though he personally disliked slavery, he did not care whether people in the territories voted "down or up" for it.

Lincoln replies. Lincoln rose to reply. He seemed unsure what to do with his long arms and big hands. But Lincoln's voice carried clearly to the edge of the

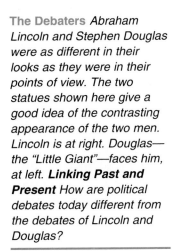

The Debaters *Abraham Lincoln and Stephen Douglas were as different in their looks as they were in their points of view. The two statues shown here give a good idea of the contrasting appearance of the two men. Lincoln is at right. Douglas—the "Little Giant"—faces him, at left.* **Linking Past and Present** *How are political debates today different from the debates of Lincoln and Douglas?*

crowd. If slavery was wrong, he said, Douglas and other Americans could not ignore it. They could not treat it as an unimportant question to be voted "down or up." To the contrary, if slavery was evil, it should be kept out of the territories.

Like nearly all whites of his day, Lincoln did not believe in "perfect equality" between blacks and whites. But he still took the position that slavery was wrong. Slavery, he said, denied to the African American

> ❝all the natural rights [listed] in the Declaration of Independence, the right to life, liberty and the pursuit of happiness. I hold that he is as much entitled to these as the white man. . . . In the right to eat the bread . . . which his own hand earns, *he is my equal and the equal of Judge Douglas, and the equal of every living man.*❞

The debate went on for three hours. When it ended, Douglas supporters marched away with their hero. A crowd of Republicans carried Lincoln on their shoulders, his long legs dangling nearly to the ground.

A leader emerges. Week after week, the campaign went on. Both men spoke nearly every day to large crowds. Newspapers reprinted their speeches. The more northerners heard and read Lincoln's speeches, the more they thought about slavery. Many could no longer agree with Douglas that slavery was simply a political issue. Like Lincoln, they believed that "if slavery is not wrong, nothing is wrong." (📖 See "Lincoln's Warning" on page 694.)

The election results brought Douglas victory by a slim margin. But Lincoln was now known throughout the country. In 1860, Lincoln and Douglas would both seek the office of President. In the meantime, more bloodshed pushed the North and South further apart. ◆

John Brown's Raid

In 1859, abolitionist John Brown carried his campaign against slavery to the East. Brown and a group of followers, including five African Americans, slipped into Harpers Ferry, Virginia. There, the band raided a federal arsenal, or gun warehouse. Brown thought that slaves would flock to the captured arsenal. He planned to give them weapons and then lead a slave revolt.

The Last Moments of John Brown *John Brown was executed on December 2, 1859. This painting shows Brown being led from jail, as northerners imagined the scene. Abolitionist Horace Greeley reported in his newspaper: "A black woman with a little child . . . stood by the door. [Brown] stopped a moment, and stooping, kissed the child." The fact is that neither Greeley nor the black woman was there—only the soldiers waiting to lead Brown to the gallows.* **Culture** *How do you think southerners might have responded to this painting?*

Brown quickly gained control of the arsenal, but no slave uprising took place. Instead, troops led by Robert E. Lee killed 10 of the raiders and captured Brown.

Most people, in both the North and South, thought that Brown's plan to lead a slave revolt was insane. There were few slaves in Harpers Ferry. And not many would have risked their lives for a man they did not even know. But at his trial, Brown seemed perfectly sane. He sat quietly as the court found him guilty of murder and treason and sentenced him to death. Even the governor of Virginia admitted that Brown was "a bundle of the best nerves I ever saw."

Because he showed great dignity during his trial, Brown became a hero to many northerners. On the morning he was hanged, church bells rang solemnly throughout the North. In years to come, New Englanders would sing a popular song telling how "John Brown's body lies a mold'ring in the grave, but his soul is marching on."

To southerners, the northern response to John Brown's death was outrageous. To criticize slavery was bad enough. But to sing the praise of a man who had hoped to lead a slave revolt was intolerable! Many southerners became convinced that the North wanted to destroy slavery and the South along with it. The nation was poised for a violent clash.

SECTION 4 REVIEW

1. **Identify:** (a) Republican party, (b) John Charles Frémont, (c) James Buchanan, (d) Abraham Lincoln, (e) John Brown.
2. **Define:** arsenal.
3. What was the main goal of the Republican party?
4. Why did Americans pay attention to the 1858 Senate race in Illinois?
5. Why did John Brown raid an arsenal at Harpers Ferry?
6. **Comparing** Compare Lincoln's and Douglas's views on slavery.

5 The South Breaks Away

FIND OUT

◆ How did the South react to Lincoln's victory in 1860?

◆ What were the Confederate States of America?

◆ What events led to the outbreak of the Civil War?

In May 1860, hundreds of delegates and thousands of spectators swarmed into Chicago for the Republican convention. They filled the city's 42 hotels. When beds ran out, they slept on billiard tables and on couches in hotel lobbies.

No one was sure who would win the Republican nomination for President. The two front-runners were William Seward of New York and Abraham Lincoln of Illinois. On the third day of the convention, a delegate rushed to the roof of the hall. There, a man stood waiting next to a cannon. "Fire the salute," ordered the delegate. "Old Abe is nominated!"

As the cannon fired, crowds surrounding the hall burst into cheers and danced in the streets. Inside the hall, delegates roared their approval. Amid the celebration, a delegate from Kentucky struck a somber note. "Gentlemen, we are on the brink of a great civil war."

The Election of 1860

Soon after the Republicans nominated Lincoln, Democrats held their convention in Charleston, South Carolina. There, the party split in two. Southerners wanted the party to support slavery in the territories. But northern Democrats refused to do so. One exclaimed, "Gentlemen of the South, you mistake us—you mistake us! We will not do it!"

In the end, northern Democrats chose Stephen Douglas to run for President. Southern Democrats met separately and picked John Breckinridge of Kentucky.

Some Americans tried to smooth over the split between the North and South by forming a new party. The Constitutional Union party chose John Bell of Tennessee, a Whig, to run for President. Bell was a moderate who simply wanted to keep the Union together. His appeal to reason was not popular, although he received support in a few southern states that were still seeking a compromise.

With the Democratic party split, Republican victory seemed certain. Alexander Stephens of Georgia saw the nation rushing toward civil war. When a friend asked why, Stephens explained:

> ❝Because there are not [goodness] and patriotism and sense enough in the country to avoid it. Mark me, when I repeat that in less than twelve months we shall be in the midst of a bloody war. What is to become of us then God only knows.❞

The Union Is Broken

When the votes were counted, Lincoln had carried the North and won the election. Southern votes did not affect the election at all. Northerners outnumbered southerners and simply outvoted them. In fact, Lincoln's name was not even on the ballot in 10 southern states.

To many southerners, Lincoln's election meant that the South no longer had a voice in national government. They believed that the President, the Senate, and the House were now all set against their interests, especially slavery.* Even before Lincoln's victory, the governor of South

———
*The North had a large majority in the House and a small one in the Senate. Even so, most northern members of Congress did not wish to force the South to end slavery.

Carolina had written to other southern governors. If Lincoln won, he wrote, it would be their duty to leave the Union.

Trying to save the Union. Senator John Crittenden of Kentucky made a last effort to save the Union. In December 1860, he introduced a bill to extend the Missouri Compromise line to the Pacific. But slavery in the West was no longer the issue. Southerners felt that the North had put an abolitionist in the White House. Secession was their only choice, they believed.

The first state to secede was South Carolina. On December 20, 1860, delegates to a special convention in Charleston voted for secession. By February 1, 1861, six more southern states had left the Union. They were Alabama, Florida, Georgia, Louisiana, Mississippi, and Texas. (See the map on page 543.)

A new nation. The seven states that had seceded held a convention in Montgomery, Alabama, in early 1861. There, they formed a new nation and named it the **Confederate States of America.** Jefferson Davis of Mississippi was named president of the Confederacy.

Many southerners were joyful and confident about the future. They believed that they had every right to secede. After all, the Declaration of Independence said that "it is the right of the people to alter or to abolish" a government that denies the rights of its citizens. Lincoln, they believed, would deny white southerners their right to own slaves.

Most southerners did not think that the North would fight to keep them in the Union. But if war did come, southerners were certain that they would win quickly.

The War Comes

When Lincoln took the oath of office on March 4, 1861, he faced a dangerous crisis. Lincoln warned that "no state . . . can lawfully get out of the Union." But he also pledged that there would be no war unless the South started it.

Federal forts in the South. The Confederacy, however, had already started seizing federal forts in the South. It felt that the forts were a threat because the United States was now a "foreign" power.

President Lincoln faced a difficult decision. Should he let the Confederates take over federal property? If he did, he would seem to be admitting that states had the power to leave the Union. But if he sent troops to hold the forts, he might start a war. He might also lose the support of the eight slave states that had not seceded.

In March 1861, the Confederacy forced Lincoln to make up his mind. By then, Confederate troops had taken over nearly all the forts, post offices, and other federal buildings in the Confederacy. The Union held only three forts off the Florida coast and Fort Sumter in South Carolina.

Opening shots. President Lincoln knew that food supplies at **Fort Sumter** were

Inauguration of Jefferson Davis *Southerners chose Jefferson Davis to be president of the Confederate States of America. Here, a crowd watches as Davis takes the oath of office outside the state house in Montgomery, Alabama.* **Citizenship** *How was this moment a turning point for the South?*

Flags Over Fort Sumter *On April 13, 1861, Confederate troops shot down the Union flag, at right, that flew over Fort Sumter. For almost four years after, until February 1865, Confederate flags flew over the fort. In the painting above, the Second National Flag of the Confederacy proclaims Confederate control of Fort Sumter in 1863 as Union ships blockade Charleston Harbor.*
Citizenship *Why did Lincoln refuse to send troops to hold federal forts in the South?*

low. Lincoln sent a message to the governor of South Carolina. It said that a northern ship would carry only food to the troops at Fort Sumter. Lincoln promised not to send any troops or weapons.

Fort Sumter was important to the Confederacy because it guarded Charleston Harbor. The fort could not be left in Union hands. On April 12, 1861, the Confederates asked for the fort's surrender. Major Robert Anderson, the Union commander, refused to give in. Confederate guns then opened fire. Anderson and his troops quickly ran out of ammunition. On April 13, Anderson surrendered the fort.

The Confederate cannons had nearly destroyed Fort Sumter. Amazingly, no one was injured. People in Charleston gathered on their rooftops to watch the shelling. To many, it seemed like a huge fireworks display. No one knew that the fireworks marked the beginning of a terrible war that would last four years.

SECTION **5** REVIEW

1. **Identify:** (a) John Breckinridge, (b) John Bell, (c) John Crittenden, (d) Confederate States of America, (e) Jefferson Davis, (f) Fort Sumter.
2. Why did the Democratic party split in two in 1860?
3. What did Lincoln's victory in the 1860 election mean to southerners?
4. What difficult decision did Lincoln face when he became President?
5. Why was Fort Sumter important to the Confederacy?
6. **Solving Problems** Do you think that the country could have avoided war if the North and South had reached an agreement about slavery in the territories? Explain.

Maps can show different kinds of information. The election map below shows the results of the 1860 presidential election.

Presidential election maps are useful because they show which states each candidate won. Most presidential election maps are accompanied by circle graphs to show what percent of the popular vote and electoral vote each candidate won.

Use the election map and circle graphs below to learn more about the election of 1860.

1 Decide what is shown on the map and graphs. (a) What is the subject of the map? (b) What do the four colors stand for? (c) What does the graph at bottom left show? (d) What does the graph at bottom right show?

2 Practice using information from the map and graphs. (a) Which party won nearly all the northern states? (b) Which party won nearly all the southern states? (c) What percent of the popular vote did the Republican party receive? (d) What percent of the electoral vote did the Republican party receive? (e) Who was the candidate of the Constitutional Union party? (f) Which states did he win?

3 Draw conclusions about the election. Based on the map and graphs, draw conclusions about the election of 1860. (a) How does the map show that sectionalism was important in the election? (b) What did the election seem to show about the political voice of voters in the South?

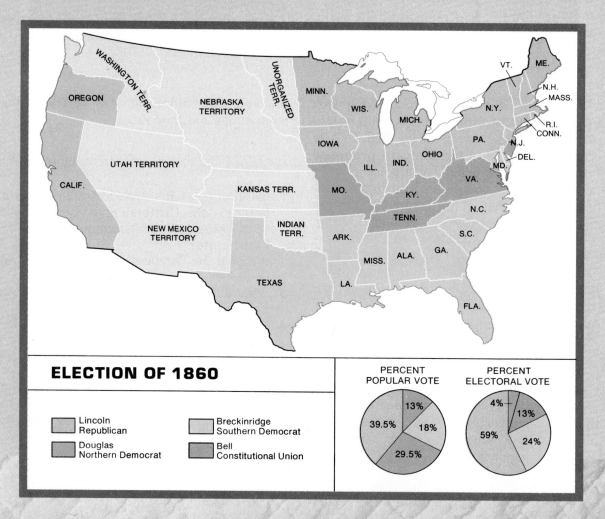

ELECTION OF 1860

- Lincoln Republican
- Douglas Northern Democrat
- Breckinridge Southern Democrat
- Bell Constitutional Union

PERCENT POPULAR VOTE

13%
39.5%
18%
29.5%

PERCENT ELECTORAL VOTE

4%
13%
59%
24%

Use the Section Reviews and this Study Guide to review chapter content.

Main Ideas

The main ideas in each section of this chapter are summarized below.

SECTION 1 ■ Slavery or Freedom in the West

◆ The Missouri Compromise banned slavery in the Louisiana Purchase north of latitude 36°30'N.
◆ The Mexican Cession reopened the debate about slavery in the West.

SECTION 2 ■ Saving the Union

◆ Under the Compromise of 1850, slavery in the New Mexico and Utah territories would be decided by popular sovereignty.
◆ The Fugitive Slave Law demanded that northerners return runaway slaves.

SECTION 3 ■ Bloodshed in Kansas

◆ Proslavery and antislavery groups fought over whether Kansas would have slavery.
◆ The Dred Scott decision further divided the North and South.

SECTION 4 ■ Republicans Challenge Slavery

◆ The Republican party was formed to keep slavery out of the territories.
◆ Senate candidate Abraham Lincoln became known for his antislavery position.

◆ Abolitionist John Brown won northern sympathy after he tried to lead a slave revolt in Virginia.

SECTION 5 ■ The South Breaks Away

◆ Lincoln's election alarmed southerners.
◆ Seven southern states seceded and formed the Confederate States of America.
◆ The Civil War began when the Confederacy bombarded Fort Sumter.

Key People and Terms

Refer to the Identify and Define questions in the Section Reviews on pages 518, 523, 529, 532, and 535. Use each person, term, and vocabulary word in a complete sentence. When possible, make connections between the people and terms by using more than one person or term in a sentence.

Time Line

1. Make a chart of events in time order. The chart will have two headings: Date, Event. Fill in the chart, using the events on the time line. Add the following events from the chapter: Dred Scott decision; Fugitive Slave Law; Raid on Harpers Ferry; Republican party formed. (Refer to the chapter for the dates.)
2. Which events between 1850 and 1860 on your chart angered northerners?

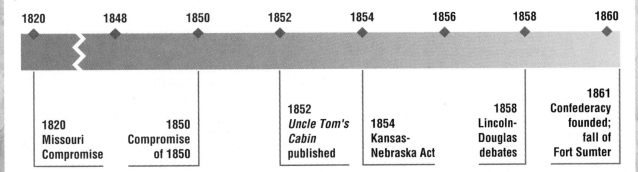

| 1820 | 1848 | 1850 | 1852 | 1854 | 1856 | 1858 | 1860 |

1820
Missouri
Compromise

1850
Compromise
of 1850

1852
Uncle Tom's Cabin
published

1854
Kansas-
Nebraska Act

1858
Lincoln-
Douglas
debates

1861
Confederacy
founded;
fall of
Fort Sumter

CHAPTER 17 REVIEW

Understanding Vocabulary

Match each term at left with the correct definition at right.

1. sectionalism
2. popular sovereignty
3. fugitive
4. civil war
5. arsenal

a. runaway slave
b. war between people of the same country
c. gun warehouse
d. loyalty to state or region instead of country
e. control by the people

Reviewing the Main Ideas

1. (a) Why did the Mexican War raise the question of slavery in the territories? (b) What were two moderate plans to settle the question of slavery in the Mexican Cession?
2. List the four main parts of the Compromise of 1850.
3. (a) Why did proslavery and antislavery settlers rush to Kansas after 1854? (b) What was the result?
4. (a) What was the Dred Scott decision? (b) How did northerners and southerners view the decision?
5. (a) What were the Lincoln-Douglas debates? (b) What impact did they have on northerners?
6. How did John Brown's death further divide the North and South?
7. Why did seven southern states secede after Lincoln won the presidential election of 1860?
8. (a) Why did the Confederacy seize federal forts in the South? (b) Why did Lincoln hesitate to send troops to hold the forts?

Thinking Critically

1. **Linking Past and Present** (a) Why do you think it took months for Congress to reach both the Missouri Compromise and the Compromise of 1850? (b) What issues are difficult for Congress to agree on today?
2. **Defending a Position** If the United States had not expanded to the Pacific Ocean, a civil war would not have occurred. Do you agree with this statement? Explain.
3. **Forecasting** Lincoln said that "no state . . . can lawfully get out of the Union." Why do you think the North would be unwilling to let the South secede peacefully?

Applying Your Skills

1. **Reading an Election Map** Review Skill Lesson 17 on page 536. (a) Did Lincoln get electoral votes from states south of the Missouri Compromise line? (b) Did states on the West Coast vote the same way as the North or the South? (c) What evidence is there that border states between the North and South had a unique political outlook?
2. **Analyzing a Quotation** Review Lincoln's response to Stephen Douglas on page 531. (a) According to Lincoln, what rights were slaves denied? (b) What does Lincoln mean by "the right to eat the bread . . . which his own hand earns"?
3. **Identifying the Main Idea** Review the subsection "The Missouri Question" on page 516. (a) What is the main idea of each paragraph? (b) Give one fact that supports the main idea of each paragraph. (c) What is the main idea of the subsection?

Thinking About Geography

Match the letters on the map with the places listed below.

1. Missouri
2. Maine
3. California
4. Kansas Territory
5. Nebraska Territory
6. New Mexico Territory
7. Utah Territory

Region Which area listed above was admitted to the Union as a free state in 1850?

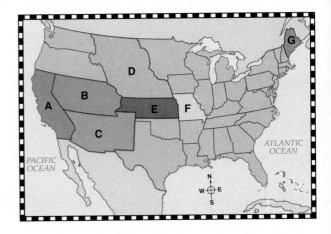

History Writer's Workshop

Writing a Topic Outline

In a report, the final step before writing is to arrange ideas and information in a topic outline. Select two or more aspects of your thesis statement to develop in the body of the report. These will be your subtopics. Group your note cards according to the subtopics, discarding any that do not fit. Then, choose a logical order for the subtopics.

Begin your outline with the introduction. List all introductory ideas and your revised thesis statement. Next, write down each subtopic, and list supporting information under it. Finally, outline your conclusion.

The following is the beginning of a topic outline. Note that subtopics are labeled with roman numerals and supporting information with capital letters.

I. Introduction
  A. In 1850s, slavery becomes more unpopular in North
  B. Thesis statement: Antislavery sentiment among northerners increased because of Fugitive Slave Law and *Uncle Tom's Cabin.*
II. Subtopic 1: Effects of Fugitive Slave Law
  A. Northerners could be fined and jailed
  B. Some free blacks were kidnapped
  C. Free blacks fled to Canada
III. Subtopic 2: Effects of *Uncle Tom's Cabin*

Practice Complete the topic outline for the report by adding supporting information for Subtopic 2 and the conclusion. (See pages 522–523 for information.)

Writing to Learn

1. Write a brief story about Kansas in 1855. First, freewrite about what it was like to be among Border Ruffians and antislavery settlers. Include vivid details about the difficulties and your reactions to them. In your first draft, write a topic sentence that draws your readers into the action. Organize supporting information in a logical order. Revise for clarity and coherence. Then, proofread and make a final copy. Read your story to the class.

2. Write a newspaper editorial for or against John Brown's raid on Harpers Ferry. Begin by listing the arguments for and against Brown's actions. In your first draft, compose a topic sentence that summarizes your position. Then, organize your reasons in order of importance. When you revise, be sure that you have disproved the arguments of the opposing side. Check for accuracy and fairness. Then, proofread and make a final copy. Publish your editorial in a class newspaper.

Prisoners From the Front *The Civil War was long and bloody. More Americans died in it than in any other war. In this painting,* Prisoners From the Front, *Winslow Homer captures some of the sadness of the war.* **American Traditions** *Why do you think soldiers on both sides would have mixed feelings about the war?*

CHAPTER

18

Torn by War (1861–1865)

Chapter Outline

1 Preparing for War
2 The Struggle Begins
3 Freedom
4 Hardships of War
5 Victory at Appomattox

CHAPTER SPOTLIGHT

The Big Picture

Why do democracies work better than governments ruled by a king? One reason is that in a democracy ordinary people have a say in the government. They can debate and change government policies.

But sometimes, even democracy fails. The North and South, for example, could not settle their dispute over slavery by political means. Instead, they went to war.

The Civil War was long and bloody. Still, when it was over, the Union was stronger. And for the first time, African Americans took their place as citizens of the nation they had done so much to help build.

Kathleen Underwood

Of Special Interest

Up Close
Lee at Gettysburg, *page 561*

An American Portrait
David Glasgow Farragut: Bold Commander of the Union Fleet, *page 549*

Americans All
Fighting for the Blue and the Gray, *page 555*

Voices and Visions
The Red Badge of Courage, *page 696*
Lee, Dignified in Defeat, *page 698*

Skill Lesson 18
Reading a Chart, *page 566*

Focus On

◆ How did the North and South prepare for war?

◆ What were the early battles of the war?

◆ How did the Emancipation Proclamation change the North's goals?

◆ What hardships did each side suffer?

◆ Why did Lee surrender at Appomattox?

"I have just . . . heard a sermon . . . to the graduating class [of West Point]. . . . There is a certain hymn that is always sung . . . the last Sunday that graduates attend church here. It commences 'When shall we meet again?' . . . And everyone felt the truth of the concluding words, 'Never, no more,' for in all probability in another year, the half of them may be in their graves. . . ."

Tully McCrea, an 18-year-old cadet, included this moving account in a letter to his sweetheart, Belle. President Lincoln had recently issued a call for troops to put down what he considered a revolt in the South. Now, the graduating class at West Point, the academy where army officers were trained, was preparing to take up arms. But the young men who had studied together would be enemies. Some would fight for the Union. Others joined the Confederacy.

Tully McCrea's own family was deeply divided in its loyalties. Orphaned at a young age, Tully and a brother grew up with relatives in Ohio. Another brother and a sister grew up on a plantation in Louisiana. "My sister and aunt would rather see me dead in my grave than see me remain in the North," wrote Tully. "We are destined to have a long and bloody civil war, in which brother will be fighting against brother," he predicted.

Tully McCrea's prediction proved correct. The Civil War lasted four violent years. More Americans died in it than in any other war the nation has fought.

1 Preparing for War

FIND OUT

- How did the states choose sides?
- What resources for war did each side have?
- Who were the leaders of each side?
- **VOCABULARY** martial law

A few days after Fort Sumter fell, President Lincoln called for 75,000 volunteers to serve as soldiers for 90 days in a campaign against the South. The response to Lincoln's call was overwhelming. At war meetings in towns and villages throughout the North, crowds cheered the Stars and Stripes and booed the southern "traitors." Wrote one New Englander:

> **"**The whole population, men, women, and children, seem to be in the streets. . . . The people have gone stark mad!**"**

In the South, the scene was much the same. Southerners rallied to the Stars and Bars, as they called the new Confederate flag. Volunteers flooded into the Confederate army.

With flags held high, soldiers on both sides marched off to war. Most felt certain that a single, gallant battle would resolve the issue. Few suspected that the North and South would be locked in civil war for four long years—the most destructive war in the nation's history.

A Nation Divided

As war began, each side was convinced of the justice of its cause. Southerners believed that they had the right to leave the Union. In fact, they called the conflict the War for Southern Independence. Northerners just as firmly believed that southerners had betrayed their country by seced-ing. People in the North felt that they had to fight to save the Union.

Choosing sides was most difficult in the eight slave states that were still in the Union in April 1861. (See the map on page 543.) "We must either identify ourselves with the North or the South," said one newspaper in the undecided states.

Four of the eight undecided states—Virginia,* North Carolina, Tennessee, and Arkansas—quickly joined the Confederacy. But the four remaining states—Delaware, Kentucky, Missouri, and Maryland—had many citizens who favored the Union. These states are known as the border states. From the start, Delaware threw its support behind the Union. Kentucky, Missouri, and Maryland wavered between the North and the South.

Maryland was especially important to the Union. Maryland borders on Washington, D.C. If Maryland sided with the Confederacy, the Union capital would be surrounded by Confederate territory.

When a pro-Confederate mob attacked Union troops in Baltimore, in April 1861, President Lincoln acted quickly. Sending federal troops to occupy the city, he declared martial law. **Martial law** is rule by the army instead of by elected officials. Many people who sided with the South were arrested. With most Confederate supporters in prison, the Maryland legislature decided to stay in the Union. In time, Kentucky and Missouri also decided to remain in the Union.

The Two Sides

In 1861, neither the North nor the South was prepared to fight a war. As the two sides rushed to build their armies, each had advantages and disadvantages. (See the chart on page 566.)

---

*In the western part of Virginia, many people supported the Union. When Virginia seceded, the westerners formed their own government. They joined the Union as West Virginia in 1863.

The South. The South had the key advantage of fighting a defensive war. If the North did not attack and defeat the South, the Confederacy would become a separate country. "All we ask," Jefferson Davis said, "is to be left alone."

Defending their homeland gave southerners a strong reason to fight. "Our men must prevail in combat," one Confederate said, "or they will lose their property, country, freedom—in short, everything."

Southerners also had skills that made them good soldiers. Hunting was an important part of southern life. From an early age, boys learned to ride horses and use guns. Wealthy young men often went to military school. Before the Civil War, southern graduates of West Point were the best officers in the United States Army.

The South, however, also had serious weaknesses. It had few factories to make guns, cannons, railroad tracks, and other vital supplies. Before the war, southerners bought most manufactured goods from the North or from Europe. In addition, the South had few railroads to move troops and supplies. And the railroads they had often did not connect to one another. Tracks simply ran between two points and then stopped.

MAP STUDY

In April 1861, eight slave states were still in the Union. As war began, these states had to choose sides in the struggle.
1. Which states eventually seceded?
2. Which states stayed in the Union?
3. **Forecasting** How do you think that the decision of some slave states to remain in the Union might have affected Union goals in the war? Explain.

*West Virginia separated from Virginia in 1861 and was admitted to the Union in 1863.

CHOOSING SIDES

- Union states
- Confederate states
- States that stayed in the Union after April 1861
- States that joined the Confederacy after April 1861
- —— Confederate States of America

0   400   800 Miles
0   400   800 Kilometers

Finally, the South had a small population. Only about 9 million people lived in the Confederacy, compared with 22 million in the Union. And more than one third of the population were slaves. So there were far fewer people to become soldiers and support the war effort in the South.

The North. The North had almost four times as many free citizens as the South. Thus, it had a large source of volunteers. It also had many people to grow food and to work in factories making supplies.

Industry was the greatest resource of the North. Northern factories turned out 90 percent of the nation's manufactured goods. These factories supplied Union armies with guns, bullets, cannons, boots, and uniforms. The North also had more than 70 percent of the nation's rail lines.

A strong navy combined with a large fleet of private trading vessels provided another major advantage for the North. Early in the war, President Lincoln ordered naval ships to blockade the Confederacy. The blockade cut off the South's trade with Europe. With few warships and only a small commercial fleet, the South could do little to break the blockade.

Despite these advantages, the North faced a difficult military challenge. To bring the South back into the Union, northern soldiers had to conquer a huge area. Instead of defending their homes, they were invading unfamiliar land.

Wartime Leaders

The outcome of the war also depended on leadership. The two presidents directing the war—Abraham Lincoln in the North and Jefferson Davis in the South—as well as military leaders on both sides played key roles in determining who won the war.

President Davis. When the war began, many people thought Jefferson Davis, the Confederate president, was a better leader than Abraham Lincoln. Davis had gone to West Point and served as an officer in the Mexican War. Later, he served as Secretary of War under President Franklin Pierce. Davis was widely respected for his honesty and courage.

Marching Off to War
Patriotic feeling was strong on both sides as the Civil War began. Here, the 7th New York Regiment, responding to President Lincoln's call for volunteers, marches proudly off to war. **Citizenship** *Name two advantages the North had as war began.*

Lee and His Generals
Strong military leadership was one of the South's chief advantages in the Civil War. Here, Confederate generals meet on a hillside. Robert E. Lee is at the center, on a white horse. **Citizenship** *Why did Lee refuse when Lincoln asked him to command the Union army?*

Davis, however, did not like to turn over the details of day-to-day military planning to others. And when Davis made a decision, he "could not understand any other man coming to a different conclusion," in the words of his wife. As a result, Davis wasted time worrying about small matters and arguing with his advisers.

President Lincoln. At first, some northerners had doubts about Abraham Lincoln's ability to lead. He had little experience in national politics or military matters. This lack of experience led him to make mistakes. But he learned from his errors. In time, Lincoln proved to be a patient but strong leader and a fine war planner.

Day by day, Lincoln gained the respect of those around him. Many especially liked his sense of humor, noting that Lincoln even accepted criticism with a smile. When Secretary of War Edwin Stanton called Lincoln a fool, Lincoln commented, "Did Stanton say I was a fool? Then I must be one, for Stanton is generally right and he always says what he means."

The generals. After Fort Sumter fell, army officers in the South had to make a choice. They could stay with the Union army and fight against their home states. Or they could join the Confederate forces.

Robert E. Lee faced such a decision when Virginia, his home state, seceded. President Lincoln asked Lee to command the Union army. Although he disliked slavery and had opposed secession, Lee refused. "With all my devotion to the Union, I have not been able to make up my mind to raise my hand against my relatives, my children, my home," he explained. Lee later became commander of the Confederate army.

Many of the army's best officers sided with the Confederacy. As a result, Lincoln had trouble finding generals who were a match for the South's military leaders. He replaced the commander of the Union army several times before the North began to win battles.

SECTION 1 REVIEW

1. **Locate:** (a) Virginia, (b) Delaware, (c) Kentucky, (d) Missouri, (e) Maryland.
2. **Identify:** (a) Jefferson Davis, (b) Edwin Stanton, (c) Robert E. Lee.
3. **Define:** martial law.
4. (a) Name the eight slave states that were still in the Union in April 1861. (b) Which of these states remained in the Union?
5. Name two strengths and two weaknesses that each of the following had as a leader: (a) Jefferson Davis; (b) Abraham Lincoln.
6. **Comparing** (a) Compare the advantages and disadvantages of the North and South at the beginning of the war. (b) Which side do you think was better equipped to fight a long war? Explain.

2 The Struggle Begins

FIND OUT

◆ What were the military aims of each side?

◆ Who won the early battles of the war?

◆ How did the Union achieve two of its three war aims?

In the summer of 1861, the armies of both the North and the South marched off to war with flags flying and drums rolling. Each side expected to win and to win quickly. The reality of war soon shattered this dream. Abner Small, a volunteer from Maine, described a scene that would be repeated again and again:

> ❝I can see today, as I saw then, the dead and hurt men lying limp on the ground. . . . The faces near me were inhuman. From somewhere across the field a battery pounded us; in the hot, still air the smoke of the cannon clung to the ground before it lifted; and through the smoke, straight ahead of us, flashed and crackled rebel [guns]. . . . We wavered, and rallied, and fired blindly; and men fell writhing.❞

Hundreds of thousands of troops massed to fight for the North and South. Both sides soon discovered that there would be no quick, easy end to the war. Leaders in both the North and the South began to plan for a long and difficult struggle.

Strategies for Victory

Fighting during the Civil War took place in three major areas: the East, the West, and at sea. Union war plans involved all three areas.

Union plans. First, the Union planned to blockade southern ports. This would cut off the South's supply of manufactured goods by halting its trade with Europe. Second, in the West, the Union planned to seize control of the Mississippi River. This would keep the South from using the river to supply its troops. It would also separate Arkansas, Texas, and Louisiana from the rest of the Confederacy. Finally, in the East, Union generals wanted to seize Richmond, Virginia, and capture the Confederate government headquartered there.

Confederate plans. The South's strategy was simpler: It would fight a defensive war. Southerners hoped to hold out against the Union invaders. Northerners, they believed, would quickly tire of fighting. If the war became unpopular in the North, President Lincoln would have to give up the effort to bring the South back into the Union.

Southerners counted on European money and supplies to help fight the war. Southern cotton was important to the textile mills of England and other countries. Confederates were confident that Europeans would quickly recognize the South as an independent nation and continue to buy southern cotton for their factories.

Forward to Richmond!

"Forward to Richmond! Forward to Richmond!" Every day for more than a month, the influential *New York Tribune* blazed this "Nation's War-Cry" across its front page. Throughout the North, people were impatient. Sure of a quick victory, they called for an attack on Richmond, the Confederate capital.

A clash of untrained troops. Responding to popular pressure, President Lincoln ordered the attack. In July 1861, Union soldiers set out from Washington, D.C., for Richmond, about 100 miles (160 km) away. They clashed with the Confederates soon after they left. The battle took place near a small stream called Bull Run. (See the map on page 547.)

July 21, 1861, was a lovely summer day, and hundreds of Washingtonians came out to watch the battle. They came in carriages, wagons, buggies, and on horseback.

Many brought picnic baskets of food and drink with them. In a holiday mood, they spread out on a grassy hilltop overlooking Bull Run. They were eager to see Union troops crush the Confederates.

But the spectators were disappointed. Southern troops did not turn and run. Led by General Thomas Jackson, they formed a strong line and held their ground. A Confederate officer remarked that Jackson was standing "like a stone wall." From then on, the general was known as "Stonewall" Jackson.

In the end, it was Union troops that retreated. One observer reported:

> ❝Off they went . . . across fields, toward the woods, anywhere, everywhere, to escape. The farther they ran the more frightened they grew. . . . To enable them better to run, they threw away their blankets, knapsacks, canteens, and finally muskets, cartridge-boxes, and everything else.❞

The Confederates did not press their advantage by pursuing the fleeing Union army. Had they done so, they might even have captured Washington, D.C. Instead, they remained behind to gather the gear thrown away by the panicked Union troops. The **Battle of Bull Run** showed both sides that their soldiers needed training. It also showed that the war would be very long and bloody.

"All quiet along the Potomac." After the disaster at Bull Run, President Lincoln appointed General George McClellan as commander of the Union armies. McClellan was a superb organizer. In six months, he transformed a mob of raw recruits into an army of trained soldiers.

But McClellan was very cautious and delayed leading his troops into battle. Newspapers reported "all quiet along the Potomac" so often that the phrase became a national joke. Finally, President Lincoln lost patience. "If McClellan is not using the army," the President snapped, "I should like to borrow it."

In March 1862, McClellan was at last ready to move. He and most of the Union army left Washington by steamboat and sailed down the Potomac River for Richmond. (See the map below.) The rest of the army stayed in Washington.

Landing south of Richmond, McClellan began inching slowly toward the Confederate capital. Learning of the Union approach, General Robert E. Lee launched a

MAP STUDY

Early in the war, General Lee led the Confederate army to one victory after another in the East.
1. *What victories did Lee win in the East in 1862?*
2. *Who claimed victory at Antietam?*
3. **Applying Information** *Based on the subsection "Battle of the Ironclads" on page 548, locate Hampton Roads, Virginia, on the map.*

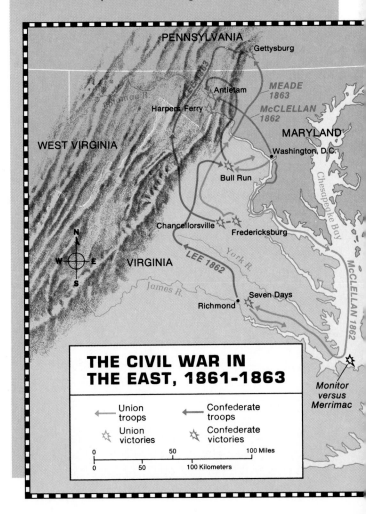

THE CIVIL WAR IN THE EAST, 1861-1863

← Union troops   ← Confederate troops
☆ Union victories   ☆ Confederate victories

0   50   100 Miles
0   50   100 Kilometers

series of brilliant counterattacks. Lee also sent Stonewall Jackson north to threaten Washington, thus preventing Lincoln from sending the rest of the Union army to help McClellan. Cautious as usual, McClellan decided to abandon the attack. He retreated to Washington with his troops, and, once again, there was a lull in the war in the East.

The Union Blockade

Early in the war, Union ships blockaded southern ports. At first, enterprising southerners slipped through the blockade in small, fast ships. These "blockade runners" brought everything from matches to guns into the Confederacy.

In time, however, the blockade became more effective, and trade through southern ports dropped by more than 90 percent. "The blockade," complained one southerner, "has closed us in like a prison gate." The South desperately needed a way to break the Union blockade. One method it tried was the ironclad ship.

Blockade Runner *Swift sailing ships, like the* C.S.S. Armstrong *shown here, slipped through the Union blockade more than 8,000 times. Still, the large numbers of Union ships offshore made it almost impossible for the South to carry on ordinary trade.* **Economics** *What was the goal of the Union blockade?*

Battle of the Ironclads

At the start of the war, the Union abandoned a warship named the *Merrimac* near Portsmouth, Virginia. Confederates covered the ship with iron plates four inches thick, renamed it the *Virginia,* and sent it into battle against the Union navy. On March 8, 1862, the *Merrimac* sank one Union ship, drove another aground, and forced a third to surrender. Their cannonballs bounced harmlessly off the *Merrimac's* metal skin.

The Union countered with its own ironclads. One of these, the *Monitor,* struck back at the *Merrimac* in the waters off Hampton Roads, Virginia. The Confederate ship had more firepower, but the *Monitor* moved more swiftly. In the end, neither ship seriously damaged the other, and both withdrew.

Ironclad ships changed naval warfare. Both sides rushed to build more of them. But the South never mounted a serious attack against the Union navy. The Union blockade held throughout the war.

Lee Takes the Offensive

In September 1862, General Lee went on the offensive and marched his troops north into Maryland. He believed that a southern victory on northern soil would be a great blow to northern morale. But luck was not on Lee's side. A Confederate messenger lost Lee's battle plans. A Union soldier found them and turned them over to McClellan.

Once again, McClellan moved slowly. He finally attacked Lee's main force at Antietam (an TEET uhm) on September 17. In the daylong battle that followed, more than 24,000 Union and Confederate soldiers fell dead or wounded.

On the night of September 18, Lee ordered his troops to slip back into Virginia. The Confederates breathed a sigh of relief when they saw that McClellan was not pursuing them. McClellan, remarked one

David Glasgow Farragut: Bold Commander of the Union Fleet

Sea power was one of the North's most effective weapons. The Union used its ships to blockade the South and to seize the Mississippi River. No sea captain helped the North more than David Glasgow Farragut.

Farragut was born in 1801 in Tennessee. His father was a Spanish sea captain who fought with the Patriots in the American Revolution. Young David went to sea before he was 10. By age 12, he had made a name for himself in the naval battles of the War of 1812.

Even though he was a southerner, Farragut decided to fight with the Union when the Civil War began. He quickly proved his daring. Commanding a squadron of warships, Farragut headed for New Orleans. Two Confederate forts guarded the city, but Farragut was determined to get past them. In the dead of night, April 24, 1862, he steamed up the Mississippi. The artillery fire that broke out seemed like "all the earthquakes in the world, and all the thunder and lightnings . . . going off at once," but the ships got through. Shortly after, New Orleans surrendered.

Farragut's greatest moment came at the Battle of Mobile Bay in 1864. Several forts protected Mobile Bay. The Confederates had also placed torpedoes, or mines, across the entrance to the bay. Even so, Farragut attacked fearlessly. One Union ship hit a mine and blew up. "Torpedoes!" an officer warned. "Damn the torpedoes! Full speed ahead!" Farragut replied. His crew could hear mines scraping the ship's hull as they surged forward. But none exploded, and Farragut won the battle.

1. How did Farragut react to the Confederate mines guarding the entrance to Mobile Bay?

2. **Evaluating Information** What facts support the idea that Farragut was a bold commander?

---

southern officer, "lacked that divine spark which impels a commander, at the right moment, to throw every man on the enemy and grasp at complete victory."

Neither side won a clear victory at the **Battle of Antietam.** But since Lee had withdrawn his forces, the North claimed a victory for itself.

Winning the Mississippi

While McClellan hesitated in the East, Union forces gained ground in the West. As you have read, the Union war plan called for the North to gain control of the Mississippi River. General Ulysses S. Grant began moving toward that goal. (See the map on page 563.) In February 1862, Grant attacked and captured Fort Henry and Fort Donelson in Tennessee. These Confederate forts guarded two important tributaries of the Mississippi.

"Glorious war." Grant now pushed south to Shiloh, a small village located on the Tennessee River. At Shiloh, on April 6, he was surprised by Confederate forces, and only after reinforcements arrived was Grant able to beat back the enemy. It was an important victory, for it allowed the Union to gain control of the northern Mississippi.

The **Battle of Shiloh,** with its many dead and wounded, was typical of Civil War battles. More Americans died in one day at Shiloh than in the American Revolution, the War of 1812, and the Mexican War combined. One Confederate soldier wrote:

❝I never realized the 'pomp and circumstance' of the thing called glorious war until I saw this. Men . . . lying in every conceivable position; the dead . . . with their eyes wide open, the wounded begging piteously for help.❞

MAP STUDY

After several unsuccessful attempts, Grant finally captured Vicksburg in July 1863.
1. *Describe Grant's movements during the campaign of Vicksburg.*
2. *What victories did Union troops win on the way to Vicksburg?*
3. **Evaluating Information** *Based on the map, why was the Confederate army unable to escape at Vicksburg?*

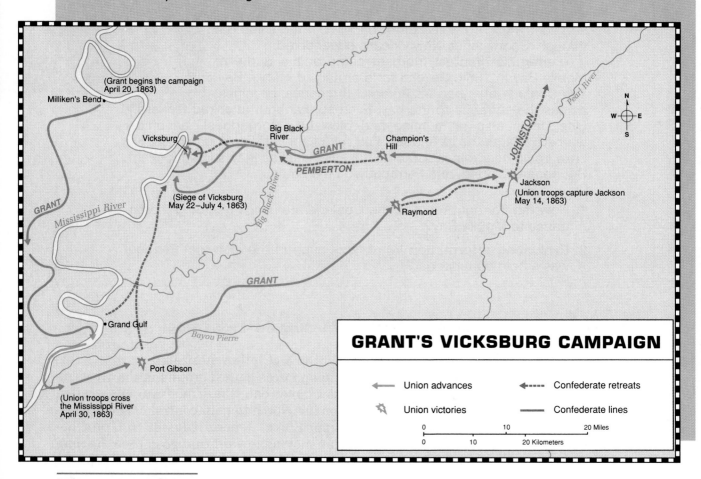

GRANT'S VICKSBURG CAMPAIGN

← Union advances   ←---- Confederate retreats

⚡ Union victories   —— Confederate lines

0   10   20 Miles
0   10   20 Kilometers

The fall of Vicksburg. While Grant was fighting at Shiloh, along the northern Mississippi, the Union navy moved to seize the southern part of the river. In April 1862, Union gunboats captured the port city of New Orleans. Other ships seized Memphis, Tennessee. The Union now controlled both ends of the great river. The South could no longer use the Mississippi as a supply line.

But the North could not safely use the river, either. Confederates still held Vicksburg, Mississippi. **Vicksburg** sat on a cliff high above the river. Cannons there could shell boats traveling between New Orleans and Memphis.

Early in 1863, Grant's forces tried again and again to seize Vicksburg. The Confederates held out bravely. At last, Grant devised a brilliant plan. Skirting Vicksburg, he marched his troops inland to Jackson, Mississippi. After taking that city by surprise, Grant turned and attacked Vicksburg from the rear. The people of Vicksburg held out for six weeks. Finally, on July 4, 1863, the city surrendered.

The Union had achieved two of its military goals. First, its naval blockade had cut off the South's trade with Europe. Second, by taking control of the Mississippi, the Union had split the Confederacy in two.

SECTION 2 REVIEW

1. **Locate:** (a) Mississippi River, (b) Richmond, (c) Washington, D.C., (d) Potomac River, (e) Fort Henry, (f) Fort Donelson, (g) New Orleans, (h) Memphis, (i) Vicksburg.
2. **Identify:** (a) "Stonewall" Jackson, (b) Battle of Bull Run, (c) George McClellan, (d) *Merrimac,* (e) *Monitor,* (f) Battle of Antietam, (g) Ulysses S. Grant, (h) Battle of Shiloh.
3. How did the North plan to defeat the South in three areas?
4. (a) What did both sides learn from the Battle of Bull Run? (b) Why was the Battle of Shiloh important?
5. **Analyzing Ideas** "The South could win the war by not losing, but the North could win only by winning." What does this statement mean?

---

3 Freedom

FIND OUT

◆ Why did Lincoln issue the Emancipation Proclamation?

◆ How did Union war goals change?

◆ How did African Americans contribute to the Union war effort?

◆ **VOCABULARY** emancipate

In 1861 and 1862, Union troops pushed into Louisiana, Tennessee, and other areas of the Confederacy. Thousands of slaves flocked to the Union camps and—they hoped—to freedom. They were sorely disappointed. Not knowing what to do with these runaways, Union officers often held them prisoner until their masters arrived to take them back to slavery.

At first, the Civil War was not a war against slavery. Indeed, President Lincoln was careful to avoid adopting abolition as an official war goal. Union, he insisted, not slavery, was the main issue of the war. Yet wherever Union troops went, slaves rushed to their side, expecting to be freed. The issue of slavery, it seemed, could not be avoided.

Some northerners began to raise new questions. Would the North support slavery by sending runaways back to their owners? Was slavery not the root of the conflict between the North and South? Had tens of thousands of men died to bring a slaveholding South back into the Union? Because of questions such as these, the mood of the North began to change.

"Forever Free"

The Civil War began as a war to restore the Union, not to end slavery. President Lincoln made this clear in the following statement:

> **❝**If I could save the Union without freeing *any* slave, I would do it; and if I could save it by freeing *all* the slaves, I would do it; and if I could do it by freeing some and leaving others alone, I would also do that.**❞**

Lincoln had a reason for handling the slavery issue cautiously. As you have read, four slaves states remained in the Union. The President did not want to do anything that might cause these states to shift their loyalty to the Confederacy. After all, the resources of these border states might allow the South to turn the tide of the war.

Addressing the issue of slavery. By mid-1862, Lincoln came to believe that he could save the Union only by broadening the goals of the war. He decided to free slaves living in the Confederacy. In the four loyal slave states, however, slaves would not be freed. Nor would slaves be freed in Confederate lands that had already been captured by the Union, such as New Orleans.

In part, Lincoln's cautious approach to freeing the slaves stemmed from practical reasons. He wanted to weaken the Confederacy without angering slave owners in the Union. Then, too, Lincoln was not sure whether most northerners would support freedom for slaves. He hoped to introduce the idea slowly, by limiting it to territory controlled by the Confederacy.

But the President had another motive, too. As you have read in Chapter 17, Lincoln believed that slavery was wrong. When he felt that he could act to free slaves without threatening the Union, he did so.

Lincoln was concerned about the timing of his announcement. He did not want Americans to think he was freeing slaves as a last, desperate effort to save a losing Union cause. So he waited for a Union victory to announce his plan. The Battle of Antietam gave Lincoln his chance.

Issuing the Proclamation. On September 22, 1862, Lincoln issued a preliminary proclamation. It warned that on January 1, 1863, anyone held as a slave in a state still in rebellion against the United States would be freed.

Then, on January 1, 1863, Lincoln issued the formal **Emancipation Proclamation**. To emancipate means to set free. The Emancipation Proclamation declared:

> **❝**On the 1st day of January, in the year of our Lord 1863, all persons held as slaves within any state or . . . part of a state [whose] people . . . shall then be in rebellion against the United States, shall be then, thenceforward, and forever free.**❞**

Since the rebelling states were not under Union control, no slaves were actually set free on January 1, 1863. Even so, the Emancipation Proclamation changed the character of the war. Now, when Union troops marched into the Confederacy, they

Abraham Lincoln and Son Tad *President Lincoln changed the nature of the Civil War when he issued the Emancipation Proclamation. Now, northerners were fighting to end slavery as well as to save the Union.* **Citizenship** *What were Lincoln's motives for issuing the Emancipation Proclamation?*

Free at Last! Northerners had mixed reactions to the Emancipation Proclamation. And the South viewed it as the act of a "fiend." But slaves, as shown here, rejoiced with song and prayer when they learned that they were "thenceforward, and forever free." **Citizenship** *Which slaves were affected by the Emancipation Proclamation? Which were not affected?*

were fighting to end slavery as well as to save the Union.

The Proclamation was applauded by many Europeans, especially workers. As a result, it became less likely that Britain or any other European country would come to the aid of the South. And the Proclamation prompted a wave of support for the Union from free blacks.

African Americans Take Up Arms

When the war began, thousands of free blacks volunteered to fight for the Union. At first, federal law forbade blacks to serve as soldiers. But when Congress repealed that law in 1862, both free blacks and escaped slaves enlisted in the Union army.

The army assigned black volunteers to all-black units, commanded by white officers. For more than a year, the black troops earned only half the pay of white soldiers. Even so, about 200,000 African Americans fought with the Union during the war. Nearly 3,000 died in action.

Massachusetts was one of the first states to organize all-black regiments. One of them, the 54th, attacked Fort Wagner near Charleston in the summer of 1863. Under heavy fire, nearly 100 soldiers forced their way into the fort and engaged the Confederate troops in hand-to-hand combat. The commander, most of the offi-cers, and almost half the men of the regiment were killed in the assault. The courage of regiments like the 54th Massachusetts helped to win respect for African American soldiers.

Both free blacks and escaped slaves made good soldiers. Like other Union troops, they went to war to save the United States. But they also fought to free their people from slavery. In a letter to President Lincoln, Secretary of War Stanton wrote that blacks "have proved themselves among the bravest of the brave, performing deeds of daring and shedding their blood with a heroism unsurpassed by soldiers of any race." Lincoln agreed. "The emancipation policy and use of [black] troops," the President said, "constitute the heaviest blow yet dealt to the rebellion."

African Americans Behind Confederate Lines

As news of emancipation filtered into the South, slaves found it hard to hide their joy. One slave woman heard the news just before she was to serve her master's dinner. She asked to be excused so that she could fetch water from a nearby spring. When she reached the quiet of the spring, she shouted: "Glory, glory hallelujah to Jesus! I'm free! I'm free!"

Despite the Proclamation, slaves still had to work on plantations while whites were away fighting. But many slaves slowed down their work in the fields. This was one way to undermine the South's war effort. They knew that when Union troops arrived in their area, they would be free.

SECTION 3 REVIEW

1. **Identify:** (a) Emancipation Proclamation, (b) 54th Massachusetts Regiment.
2. **Define:** emancipate.
3. Why was Lincoln cautious about making abolition a war goal?
4. (a) Which areas of the nation were affected by the Emancipation Proclamation? (b) What slaves were actually freed when the Proclamation was issued? Explain.
5. (a) How did free blacks and escaped slaves help the Union? (b) How did slaves help to undermine the Confederacy?
6. **Drawing Conclusions** What did the treatment of blacks in the Union army reveal about northern attitudes toward African Americans?

4 Hardships of War

FIND OUT

◆ What was life like in the Union and Confederate armies?

◆ What problems did each side face during the war?

◆ How did women participate in the war effort?

◆ **VOCABULARY** civilian, bounty, draft, habeas corpus, inflation, profiteer, tax-in-kind

In 1863, a Virginia woman wrote a letter to President Davis. In it, she pleaded with the Confederate president to send her son home from the war. "If you don't send [my son] home, I am bound to lose my crop and come to suffer," she wrote. "I am eighty-one years of age."

As this letter shows, the Civil War caused hardships not only for soldiers but for people at home as well. Southerners especially suffered from the war, since most of the fighting took place in the South.

On both sides, civilians, or people not in the army, worked on farms and labored in factories to back the war effort. They used their mules to move troops and supplies. They tended the wounded. And as their hardships increased, so did their opposition to the war.

The Blue and the Gray

Early in the war, soldiers on each side came up with nicknames for the enemy. Union troops wore blue uniforms. They were called blues or Billy Yanks, short for Yankees. Gray was the color of the Confederacy. Southern soldiers were called grays or Johnny Rebs, short for rebels.

The test of battle. Soldiers on both sides were young, most under 21 years old. But war quickly turned gentle boys into tough men of experience.

Soldiers put in long hours drilling and marching. They slept on the ground even in rain and snow. But nothing toughened "fresh fish," as new recruits were called, like combat. Boys of 18 learned to stand firm while cannon blasts shook the earth and bullets whizzed past their ears. (📖 See "The Red Badge of Courage" on page 696.)

Friendly enemies. At times, Rebs and Yanks could be friendly enemies. Before one battle, a Confederate hailed a Union soldier. "Say, Yank," he said, "got something to trade?" After swapping Union coffee for southern tobacco, the soldiers shook hands. "Good luck, Yank!" said the southerner. "I hope you won't get hurt in any of our fights."

Deadly weapons. New technology added to the horror of Civil War battles. Cone-shaped bullets, which made rifles twice as

Fighting for the Blue and the Gray

More than any other war in the nation's history, the Civil War touched all Americans. The armies of both the North and South were cross sections of the diverse American people. Men born in Shanghai fought alongside soldiers from Hamburg, Dublin, Warsaw, and Moscow. All had become Americans. Each group had its heroes, as the following examples show.

John Ericsson served in the Swedish navy before coming to the United States. Ericsson used his knowledge of naval design to help the Union to build the *Monitor*. Thanks to Ericsson, the ironclad ship was completed in only 100 days—just in time to face the South's *Merrimac*.

Sergeant William H. Carney fought with the all-black 54th Massachusetts Regiment, shown at right. During the assault on Fort Wagner (see page 553), his company's flag bearer was shot. Although wounded himself, Carney seized the falling banner and led his men forward. "The old flag never touched the ground," Carney later said proudly. For his bravery, Carney won the Congressional Medal of Honor.

The last battle of the Civil War was fought in Texas. During the battle, Colonel Santos Benavides (bay nah VEE dehs) led Confederate forces against invading Union troops near Brownsville. Benavides and his men defeated the Yankees. But although they fought bravely, their victory had no effect on the South's fortunes. The Texans did not know it, but Lee had already surrendered at Appomattox.

• •

1. Why did William Carney win the Congressional Medal of Honor?

2. **Analyzing Information** Do you think Colonel Benavides and his men were heroes even though their victory had no effect on the war? Explain.

accurate, replaced round musket balls. New cannons could hit targets several miles away. As a result of these new, deadly weapons, one quarter or more of the soldiers in most battles were casualties. A casualty is a soldier who is killed or seriously wounded.

Before one battle, Union troops knew that they were greatly outnumbered. Each soldier wrote his name on a slip of paper and pinned it to his uniform. The soldiers wanted to make sure that their bodies could be identified when the battle was over.

Medical Station *Both the Union and Confederate governments did their best to provide proper medical care for their soldiers. But good medical care simply did not exist in the 1860s. Many soldiers believed that if they were taken to a medical station, such as the one shown here, they "might as well say good-bye."* **Linking Past and Present** *What kind of medical care do you think a combat soldier receives today? Explain.*

Crude medical care. Soldiers who were sick, wounded, or captured faced other horrors. Medical care on the battlefield was crude. Not having any better technique to deal with injuries, surgeons routinely cut off the injured arms and legs of wounded men. Many minor wounds became infected. Since there were no medicines to fight infections, more than half the wounded died. Diseases like malaria and pneumonia swept through the camps, killing even more men than bullets or cannon shells.

Prisoners of war on both sides faced appalling conditions. At Andersonville, a prison camp in Georgia, more than one out of three Union prisoners died of disease and starvation. One prisoner wrote:

❝There is no such thing as delicacy here. . . . In the middle of last night I was awakened by being kicked by a dying man. He was soon dead. I got up and moved the body off a few feet, and again went to sleep to dream of the hideous sights.❞

Discord in the North

Not everyone in the North supported the war. Some northerners thought the South should be allowed to leave the Union. Others favored calling a peace conference to work out a compromise with the South. Supporters of the war called these people

Copperheads, after the poisonous snake. Other northerners wanted to save the Union but opposed the way Lincoln was handling the war. And in the border states, many slave owners openly supported the South.

Filling the ranks. By 1863, with no end of the war in sight, northerners grew discouraged. Soon, there were not enough volunteers to fill the ranks of the Union army. From the start, the Union had given $100 **bounties,** or payments, to men who enlisted in the army. Now, it raised the bounty to more than $300. But still, there were not enough volunteers. The government decided to take new measures.

In 1863, Congress passed a draft law. The **draft** required all able-bodied males between the ages of 20 and 45 to serve in the military if they were called. But a man could avoid the draft by paying the government $300 or by hiring someone to serve in his place. This angered many common people, who began to see the Civil War as "a rich man's war and a poor man's fight."

Draft riots. The draft law went into effect just a few months after President Lincoln signed the Emancipation Proclamation. As a result, some northerners believed that they were being forced to fight to end slavery. Riots broke out in several cities.

The worst riot, in New York City during July of 1863, lasted four days. White workers turned their anger against African Americans, murdering almost 100 free blacks. The rioters also attacked rich New Yorkers who had paid to escape serving in the army.

Lincoln moved to stop the draft riots and other "disloyal practices." Several times, he suspended **habeas corpus** (HAY bee uhs KOR puhs), the right to have a hearing before being jailed. When people protested his action, Lincoln referred them to the Constitution. It gave him the power, he said, to deny people their rights "when in the cases of rebellion or invasion, the public safety may require it."

Trouble in the Confederacy

The Confederacy had its share of problems, too. In some areas of the South, such as eastern Tennessee, thousands of citizens opposed the war.

As Jefferson Davis worked to create a strong federal government, he too ran into trouble. Southerners believed strongly in the idea of states' rights. Throughout the

A Confederate Regiment *The Confederate draft law required all white men between the ages of 18 and 35 to serve in the war. Some soldiers were even younger. The flag bearer in this picture, for example, was a mere boy—not even 16 years old.* **Citizenship** *How did the Union raise soldiers to fill out the ranks of its armies?*

war, Davis had trouble getting the Confederate states to pay taxes and cooperate on military matters. Governor Joseph Brown of Georgia, for example, refused to provide state troops to help defend Atlanta because he feared that they would be placed under Confederate control. Indeed, at one point, Georgia threatened to secede from the Confederacy!

Like the North, the South faced a shortage of soldiers. As early as 1862, the South passed a draft law. Under the law, men who owned or supervised more than 20 slaves did not have to serve in the army. This caused much resentment among the South's small farmers, most of whom owned no slaves, or only a few slaves. They felt it was unfair that they had to fight to preserve slavery while slave owners did not.

Toward the end of the war, the South was unable to replace soldiers killed or wounded in battle—or the thousands who deserted. There simply were not enough white men to fill the ranks. Robert E. Lee urged the Confederacy to let slaves serve as soldiers. The Confederate congress finally agreed to Lee's plan, but the war ended before any slaves put on gray uniforms.

Paying for the War

The Civil War cost far more than any earlier war. The need to pay for the war affected the economies of the North and South in different ways.

The Union. In 1861, Congress passed the nation's first income tax law. It required workers to pay a small part of their wages to the federal government. The North also raised money by taxing luxuries like carriages, jewelry, and billiard tables. And the Union issued bonds worth millions of dollars to help finance the war. People who bought bonds were in effect lending money to the Union.

But even with new taxes and bonds, the Union did not have enough money to pay for the war. So the North printed more than $400 million in paper money. People called these dollars "greenbacks" because of their color. The flood of greenbacks led to inflation, a rise in prices caused by an increase in the amount of money in circulation. As the money supply increases, each dollar is worth less. So merchants charge more for their goods. During the war, prices for goods nearly doubled in the North.

In some ways, however, the war helped the North's economy. As more and more farmers went off to fight, the people left to tend the farms began to use machines to plant and harvest crops. Northern farmers bought 165,000 reapers during the war, compared to a few thousand the year before the war began. Farm production actually went up during the war.

Wartime demand for clothing, shoes, guns, and other goods brought a boom to many northern industries. Some northern manufacturers made fortunes by profiteering. Profiteers overcharged the government for goods desperately needed for the war.

The Confederacy. The South had even greater trouble raising money than the North. The Confederate congress passed an income tax as well as a tax-in-kind. The tax-in-kind required farmers to turn over one tenth of their crops to the government. The government decided to take crops because it knew that southern farmers had little cash to spare.

Like the North, the South also printed paper money. It printed so much, in fact, that wild inflation set in. By 1865, one Confederate dollar was worth only two cents in gold.

The southern economy suffered greatly because of the war. This was especially true of the cotton trade, the South's main source of money. Early in the war, Jefferson Davis halted cotton shipments to Britain. He was sure that the British would side with the South in order to get southern cotton. But the tactic backfired. Britain simply bought more cotton from Egypt and India. By stopping the export of cotton, Davis succeeded only in cutting the South's income.

Hard Times in the South

The Union blockade slowly strangled the southern economy. It created severe shortages for both soldiers and civilians. By 1865, famine stalked the Confederacy. Even the wealthy went hungry. "I had a little piece of bread and a little molasses today for my dinner," wrote South Carolina plantation mistress Mary Boykin Chesnut in her diary for March 1865.

The South spent precious dollars buying weapons in Europe. But the blockade kept most from being delivered. When southern troops won a battle, they had to scour the field for guns and unused bullets. Southerners hurried to build weapons factories, but the shortages continued.

Even when supplies were available, the South had trouble getting them to their troops. Union armies ripped up railroad tracks, and the South had few parts to make repairs. Soldiers sometimes waited weeks for food and clothing.

Women at War

In both the North and South, women took over jobs as men left for the battlefields. "Women were in the field everywhere," wrote a northern traveler in 1863. They were "driving the reapers . . . and loading grain . . . a very unusual sight [before the war]." As the northern economy geared up for war production, women also took jobs in factories.

Soldiers and spies. Some women helped the war effort more directly. In April 1861, Susan Lear wrote to the governor of Virginia:

> **❝**Send me a good Musket, Rifle, or double barrel Shot Gun. I think I would prefer the latter as I am acquainted with its use. I believe, Sir, if a Regiment of Yankees were to come we [women] would drive them away.**❞**

A few women disguised themselves as soldiers and fought in battle. Others served as spies.

Nursing the wounded. Many women on both sides volunteered as nurses. Women

Family Life in a Union Camp
Women on both sides visited relatives at army camps in the early days of the war. This 1861 photograph shows a Union soldier who has been joined in camp by his wife and children. **Daily Life** *What false view of the war would have encouraged families to join soldiers in camp in 1861?*

had served as nurses during the Revolution and in the Mexican War. But these women were untrained. During the Civil War, doctors were unwilling at first to permit even trained nurses to work in military hospitals. But when wounded men began to swamp army hospitals, this attitude changed.

Dorothea Dix, famous for her work reforming prisons and mental hospitals, became superintendent of nurses for the Union army. Dix set strict rules but toiled day and night alongside the women she enlisted. She cleaned wounds and helped surgeons to perform their grisly tasks. From time to time, she would take a brief nap in a nearby tent, then return to help more wounded until she was exhausted once again.

Clara Barton earned fame as a Civil War nurse and founder of the American Red Cross. Barton kept records on hundreds of wounded soldiers. She helped many families to trace sons and husbands who were missing in action. Sojourner Truth, the antislavery leader, worked in Union hospitals and in camps for freed slaves.

In the South, Sally Louisa Tompkins opened a hospital in Richmond, Virginia. Of the 1,333 patients treated in Tompkins's hospital, only 73 died—an excellent record for the time.

SECTION 4 REVIEW

1. **Identify:** (a) Copperhead, (b) Dorothea Dix, (c) Clara Barton, (d) Sojourner Truth, (e) Sally Louisa Tompkins.
2. **Define:** (a) civilian, (b) bounty, (c) draft, (d) habeas corpus, (e) inflation, (f) profiteer, (g) tax-in-kind.
3. How did new technology make Civil War battles more deadly than battles of earlier wars?
4. (a) Why did many northerners see the Civil War as "a rich man's war and a poor man's fight"? (b) Why did many southerners oppose the draft?
5. How did the Union blockade affect the South?
6. **Drawing Conclusions** Why do you think northerners who opposed the war were called Copperheads?

5 Victory at Appomattox

FIND OUT

◆ What ideals did Lincoln express in the Gettysburg Address?

◆ What strategies did Grant use to defeat the Confederacy?

◆ How did the war end?

As you have read, the Union claimed victory at Antietam in September 1862. But General Lee was not ready to give up and go home. In the months that followed, the Confederates won several dazzling victories. "There never were such men in an army before," Lee said of his soldiers. "They will go anywhere and do anything if properly led."

These were gloomy days in the North. Few people realized that in a short time the tide of war would turn and the Union would be victorious.

Confederate Victories

The two stunning victories that gave Lee hope came in late 1862 and 1863. (See the map on page 547.) Lee won by outsmarting the Union generals who fought him.

Fredericksburg. In December 1862, Union forces set out once again on a drive toward Richmond. This time, they were led by General Ambrose Burnside. Encountering Robert E. Lee's army outside Fredericksburg, Virginia, Burnside ordered his troops to attack. But after the two sides traded fire, Lee had his soldiers fall back, leaving the town to Burnside.

With his troops, Lee dug in at the crest of a treeless hill above Fredericksburg. There, they waited for the Yanks.

As the Union soldiers advanced, Confederate guns mowed them down by the thousands. Six times Burnside ordered his men to charge. Six times the rebels drove them back. Southerners could hardly believe the bravery of the doomed Union troops. "We forgot they were fighting us," one Southerner wrote, "and cheer after cheer at their fearlessness went up along our lines." The battle was one of the Union's worst defeats.

Chancellorsville. The following May, Lee, aided by Stonewall Jackson, again outwitted the Union army to score a brilliant victory. This time, the battle was fought on thickly wooded ground near Chancellorsville, Virginia. Lee and Jackson defeated the Union troops in three days.

Although the South won the battle, it suffered a severe loss. At dusk, a nervous Confederate sentry fired at what he thought was a Union soldier riding toward him. The "Union soldier," it turned out, was Stonewall Jackson. Jackson died of blood poisoning several days later. Lee said sadly, "I have lost my right arm."

Still, Lee decided to keep the Union off balance by moving north into Pennsylvania. He hoped to take the Yankees by surprise in their own backyard. If he was suc-

cessful in Pennsylvania, Lee planned to swing south and capture Washington, D.C.

UP CLOSE

Lee at Gettysburg

By accident, on June 30, some of Lee's men stumbled on Union soldiers at the small town of Gettysburg, Pennsylvania. The two sides scrambled to bring in additional troops. In the battle that followed on the next day, Confederates drove the Union forces out of town. But the Yanks took up strong positions on Cemetery Ridge, overlooking Gettysburg.

Cemetery Ridge. The next morning, July 2, General James Longstreet trained his field glasses on Cemetery Ridge. Longstreet, one of Lee's right-hand men, studied the tents, campfires, and lines of soldiers that dotted the ridge. He did not like what he saw. The Union position looked too strong to risk a battle.

Lee disagreed. He was eager to attack. "The enemy is there," Lee said, pointing to the distant hill, "and I am going to attack him there."

"If he is there," Longstreet replied, "it will be because he is anxious that we should attack him; a good reason, in my

The Armies Clash at Gettysburg *The Battle of Gettysburg was a major turning point in the war. This painting by James Walker shows almost the entire Gettysburg battlefield on the final day. The view is from the center of the Union line.*
Geography *What was General Longstreet's opinion of the Union position? What was General Lee's position?*

judgment, for not doing so." Longstreet urged Lee to march south, drawing the Union army after him. Then, Lee could choose more favorable ground for battle.

Lee's plan. But Lee's mind was made up. His soldiers wanted to fight, not retreat. Lee hoped to destroy the Union army once and for all.

Lee ordered an attack on both ends of the long Union line. Southern troops fought hard and suffered heavy casualties. But when the sun set after a day of savage fighting, the Union line had not broken.

Next morning, Longstreet again argued that Lee should move south. But Lee was convinced that a direct assault could overwhelm the troops on Cemetery Ridge. He sent 15,000 men under General George Pickett to charge the center of the Union line on Cemetery Ridge. To reach the Yankees, the men would have to cross an open field and then run up a steep slope.

Pickett's Charge. Pickett's men waited in a shady grove as Confederate cannons tried to soften up the Union line. At 3 P.M., an unhappy Longstreet gave Pickett the signal to proceed. "My heart was heavy," Longstreet recalled. "I could see the desperate and hopeless nature of the charge and the hopeless slaughter it would cause."

Pickett gave the order to charge, and the men rushed forward. For once, there was no rebel yell—Pickett ordered the men to be silent until they closed in on Union lines.

Suddenly, Union rifles opened fire. Bullets and shells rained down upon the desperate attackers. Row after row of Confederates dropped bleeding on the ground. Still, the wave of gray-uniformed men surged forward. "Home, boys, home!" called one rebel lieutenant. "Remember, home is over beyond those hills." But the merciless hail of lead kept all but a few southerners from reaching the top of Cemetery Ridge. Those who did faced even further horrors. A Union soldier described the terrible scene at the crest:

66Men fire into each other's faces not five feet apart. There are bay-

onet thrusts, saber strokes, pistol shots, men going down on their hands and knees, spinning round like tops, throwing out their arms, gulping blood, falling, legless, armless, headless. There are ghastly heaps of dead men.99

In the end, **Pickett's Charge** failed. As the surviving rebel troops limped back, Lee rode among them. "It's all my fault," he admitted humbly.

Lee had no choice but to retreat. The Confederates would never again invade the North. The war had reached its turning point. ◆

Honoring the Dead at Gettysburg

The Battle of Gettysburg left more than 40,000 dead or wounded. When the soldiers who died there were buried, their graves stretched as far as the eye could see. On November 19, 1863, northerners held a ceremony to dedicate this cemetery.

President Lincoln attended, but he was not the main speaker. At the time, his popularity was quite low. Lincoln sat with his hands folded as another speaker talked for two hours. Then, the President rose and spoke for just three minutes.

In his **Gettysburg Address,** Lincoln said that the Civil War was a test of whether or not a democratic nation could survive. He reminded Americans that their nation was founded on the belief that "all men are created equal." Looking out at the thousands of graves, Lincoln told the audience:

66We here highly resolve that these dead shall not have died in vain—that this nation, under God, shall have a new birth of freedom— and that government of the people, by the people, for the people, shall not perish from the earth. 99

Few in the audience listened to Lincoln. Newspapers gave his speech little attention. "It is a flat failure," Lincoln said of his speech. "The people are disappointed."

But later generations have honored Lincoln's brief address as a profound statement of American ideals.

Total War

For three years, Lincoln had searched for a general who could lead the Union to victory. More and more, his eye fell on Ulysses S. Grant, who continued to win battles in the West. In 1864, after Grant's victory at Vicksburg, Lincoln appointed him commander of the Union forces.

Sheridan in the Shenandoah. Grant had a plan for ending the war. He wanted to destroy the South's ability to keep fighting. Grant sent General Philip Sheridan and his cavalry into the rich farmland of Virginia's Shenandoah Valley. He instructed Sheridan:

MAP STUDY

Union forces in the West enjoyed success early in the war. From the West, Union troops under General Sherman pushed into Georgia and the Carolinas.
1. What coastal city did Sherman capture after marching from Atlanta?
2. In what bodies of water did the Union set up a naval blockade?
3. **Drawing Conclusions** Based on the map, why would the South be hurt more than the North, no matter who won the war?

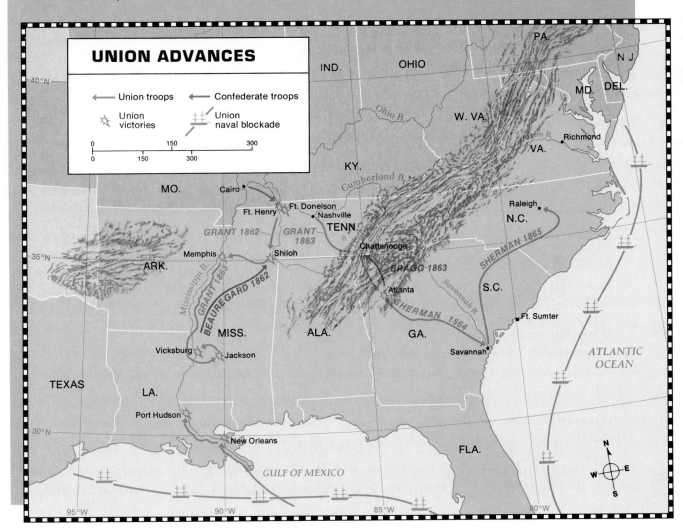

Ulysses S. Grant *President Lincoln chose Ulysses S. Grant to lead the Union troops in 1864. Grant had a scruffy, nonmilitary look, and many northerners questioned Lincoln's choice. But Lincoln believed in Grant and his ability to win. "I can't spare this man,"* he said. *"He fights."* **Citizenship** *How did Grant wage total war against the South?*

❝Leave nothing to invite the enemy to return. Destroy whatever cannot be consumed. Let the valley be left so that crows flying over it will have to carry their rations along with them.**❞**

Sheridan obeyed. In the summer and fall of 1864, he marched through the valley, destroying farms and livestock.

Marching through Georgia. Grant also sent General William Tecumseh Sherman to capture Atlanta, Georgia, and then march to the Atlantic Ocean. Like Sheridan, Sherman had orders to destroy everything useful to the South. After burning Atlanta in September 1864, Sherman began his "march to the sea."

Sherman's men ripped up railroad tracks, built bonfires from the ties, then heated and twisted the rails. They burned barns, homes, and factories. Looking over the destruction, Sherman said: "We have devoured the land. . . . To realize what war is one should follow in our tracks."

A new type of combat. Grant, Sherman, and Sheridan had created a new type of combat called total war. In the past, only soldiers were involved in wars. But in total war, everyone was affected as the army destroyed food and equipment that might be useful to the enemy. As a result of the Union decision to wage total war, civilians in the South suffered the same hardships as soldiers.

Lincoln Is Reelected

In 1864, Lincoln ran for reelection. At first, his defeat seemed, in his own words, "extremely probable." Before the capture of Atlanta, Union chances for victory looked bleak. Lincoln knew that many northerners were unhappy with his handling of the war, and he expected that he would lose.

The Democrats nominated General George McClellan to oppose Lincoln. Although he had commanded the Union army, McClellan was much more willing to compromise with the South. If peace could be achieved, he was ready to restore slavery.

When Sherman took Atlanta in September, the North rallied around Lincoln. Sheridan's smashing victories in the Shenandoah Valley in October increased Lincoln's popular support. In the election in November, the vote was close, but Lincoln remained President.

The War Is Over

Grant had begun a drive to capture Richmond in May 1864. Throughout the spring and summer, he and Lee fought a series of costly battles. Northerners read with horror that Grant had lost 60,000 dead and wounded in a single month at the battles of the Wilderness, Spotsylvania, and Cold Harbor. (See the map on page 565.) Still,

Grant pressed on. He knew that the Union could replace both men and supplies. The South could not.

Richmond falls. As Grant knew, Lee's army was shrinking. To prevent further losses, Lee dug in at Petersburg, a town that guarded the entrance to Richmond. Here, Grant kept Lee under siege for nine months. At last, with a fresh supply of troops, Grant took Petersburg on April 2, 1865. The same day, Richmond fell. But Jefferson Davis and his cabinet had slipped out of the city.

Lee surrenders. Lee and his army withdrew from Petersburg to a small Virginia town called Appomattox Courthouse. There, a week later, they were trapped by Union troops. Lee knew that his men would be slaughtered if he kept fighting. On April 9, 1865, Lee surrendered. (📖 See "Lee, Dignified in Defeat" on page 698.)

At Appomattox, Grant offered the Confederates generous terms of surrender. Soldiers had to turn over their rifles, but officers could keep their pistols. Soldiers who had horses could keep them. Grant knew that southerners would need the animals for spring plowing. As the Confederates surrendered, Union soldiers began to cheer. Grant ordered them to be silent. "The war is over," he said. "The rebels are our countrymen again."

SECTION 5 REVIEW

1. **Locate:** (a) Fredericksburg, (b) Chancellorsville, (c) Gettysburg, (d) Atlanta, (e) Appomattox Courthouse.
2. **Identify:** (a) Pickett's Charge, (b) Gettysburg Address, (c) Ulysses S. Grant, (d) Philip Sheridan, (e) William Tecumseh Sherman.
3. (a) What victories in late 1862 and early 1863 encouraged the Confederates? (b) What battle marked the turning point of the war?
4. What was Grant's plan for ending the war?
5. Why was Grant better able than Lee to withstand tremendous losses?

MAP STUDY

The last battles of the war pitted Grant against Lee in Virginia. Grant attacked again and again, and finally, on April 9, 1865, Lee surrendered at Appomattox Courthouse.

1. *Where did Grant hold Lee under siege for nine months?*
2. *Which battle took place first: Cold Harbor or Spotsylvania? Explain.*
3. **Solving Problems** *Why did Grant press his attacks despite huge Union losses in men and supplies?*

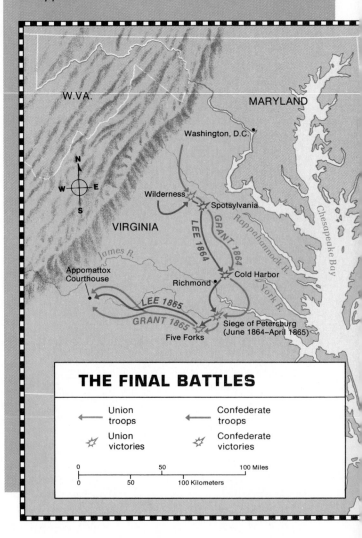

THE FINAL BATTLES

| ← Union troops | ← Confederate troops |
| ☆ Union victories | ☆ Confederate victories |

0   50   100 Miles
0   50   100 Kilometers

6. **Making Decisions** How might Lee's brilliant successes at Fredericksburg and Chancellorsville have contributed to his defeat at Gettysburg?

SKILL LESSON 18

MAP, GRAPH, and CHART SKILLS
Reading a Chart

A chart is used to present information in a way you can understand quickly and easily. Charts often present numbers or statistics. The numbers are set up in columns and rows.

The chart below compares the resources of the North and South in 1861. For both the North and South, the chart shows the amount of the resource and the percent of the national total. Studying the chart can help you to understand why the North won the Civil War.

Use the following steps to read and interpret the chart.

1 **Identify the information in the chart.** Note that the resources in the chart are measured in different ways. For example, population is measured in thousands of people. (a) What is the title of the chart? (b) How is farmland measured in the chart? (c) How is railroad track measured?

2 **Read the information in the chart.** Note that the chart has five columns. The first column shows what each resource is—farmland, railroad track, and so on. The second and third columns give the amount and percent of each resource that the North had. The fourth and fifth columns give the same information for the South. (a) How many factories did the South have? (b) What percent of the national total of factories did the South have? (c) What percent of the nation's railroad track did the North have?

3 **Compare the information in the chart.** Use the chart to compare the resources of the North and South. (a) Which side had more workers in industry, the North or the South? (b) How many acres of farmland did each side have? (c) In which resource did the South come closest to equaling the North?

4 **Interpret the information based on your reading.** Interpret the information in the chart based on your reading of the chapter. (a) Which side had the advantage in each of the resources shown? (b) How might these advantages have helped that side during the war? (c) Which resource do you think was the most important during the war? Explain.

Resources of the North and South, 1861

Resources	North		South	
	Number	Percent of Total	Number	Percent of Total
Farmland	204 million acres	51%	200 million acres	49%
Railroad Track	21,847 miles	71%	8,947 miles	29%
Value of Manufactured Goods	$1,794,417,000	92%	$155,552,000	8%
Factories	119,500	85%	20,600	15%
Workers in Industry	1,198,000	92%	111,000	8%
Population	22,340,000	63%	9,103,000 (3,954,000 slaves)	37%

Source: *Historical Statistics of the United States*

Use the Section Reviews and this Study Guide to review chapter content.

Main Ideas

The main ideas in each section of this chapter are summarized below.

SECTION 1 ■ Preparing for War

◆ As war began, the eight undecided slave states had to take sides.
◆ Neither side was prepared for war, but the North enjoyed important material advantages.

SECTION 2 ■ The Struggle Begins

◆ The North had three war goals: to blockade the southern ports, to control the Mississippi, and to capture Richmond.
◆ The South planned to fight a defensive war.
◆ Early battles were fought at Bull Run, Antietam, and Shiloh.

SECTION 3 ■ Freedom

◆ Lincoln broadened Union war goals by issuing the Emancipation Proclamation.
◆ More than 200,000 African Americans fought with the Union.

SECTION 4 ■ Hardships of War

◆ New technology made combat more deadly than in earlier wars.
◆ Both sides experienced divisions over the war, resentment concerning the draft, and inflation.

◆ Women on both sides supported the war effort by working in farms and factories and serving as battlefield nurses.

SECTION 5 ■ Victory at Appomattox

◆ At Gettysburg, the Union halted Lee's drive north, turning the tide of the war.
◆ Grant, Sherman, and Sheridan waged a total war against the South.
◆ Soon after Richmond fell in 1865, Lee surrendered at Appomattox.

Key People and Terms

Refer to the Identify and Define questions in the Section Reviews on pages 545, 551, 554, 560, and 565. Use each person, term, and vocabulary word in a complete sentence. When possible, make connections between the people and terms by using more than one person or term in each sentence.

Time Line

1. Make a chart of events in time order. The chart will have two headings: Date, Event. Fill in the chart, using the events on the time line. Add the following events from the chapter: Fall of Vicksburg; 54th Regiment attacks Fort Wagner; Gettysburg Address. (Refer to the chapter for dates.)
2. Which events on your chart were setbacks for the Confederacy?

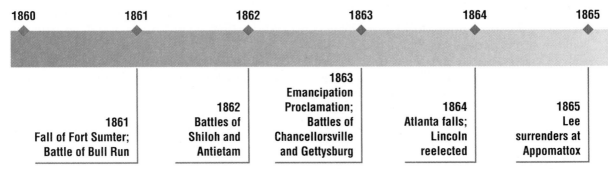

1860	1861	1862	1863	1864	1865

| | 1861 Fall of Fort Sumter; Battle of Bull Run | 1862 Battles of Shiloh and Antietam | 1863 Emancipation Proclamation; Battles of Chancellorsville and Gettysburg | 1864 Atlanta falls; Lincoln reelected | 1865 Lee surrenders at Appomattox |

Understanding Vocabulary

Match each term at left with the correct definition at right.

1. martial law
2. emancipate
3. civilian
4. draft
5. inflation

a. law requiring service in the military
b. person not in the army
c. decrease in value of money and rise in prices
d. rule by the army, not by elected officials
e. set free

Reviewing the Main Ideas

1. (a) What advantages did each side have as war began? (b) What weaknesses?
2. (a) What were the war goals of the North? (b) How did the South hope to win the war?
3. (a) What battles did Grant win in the West? (b) Which war goals had the North achieved by 1863?
4. (a) What did the Emancipation Proclamation provide? (b) How did it change the nature of the war?
5. Why did some northerners oppose the war?
6. (a) How did each side raise money to fight the war? (b) How did the war affect the economy of each side?
7. How did women on each side contribute to the war effort?
8. How did the Union wage total war on the South in 1864 and 1865?

Thinking Critically

1. **Comparing** Compare Abraham Lincoln, Jefferson Davis, George McClellan, Robert E. Lee, and Ulysses S. Grant. (a) What characteristics did each have that made him a good leader? (b) What characteristics weakened their leadership abilities?
2. **Linking Past and Present** (a) What advances in technology made Civil War battles deadly? (b) How would a war today be even more deadly?

3. **Drawing Conclusions** Why were free blacks eager to fight for the Union?
4. **Making Decisions** Some people believe that Grant's decision to wage total war on the South was wrong because it hurt civilians as much as it hurt Confederate soldiers. Do you agree or disagree? Explain.

Applying Your Skills

1. **Reading a Chart** Review Skill Lesson 18 on page 566. (a) What resources does the chart show? (b) Which side had more factories? (c) Which side had more workers in industry? (d) What percent of the nation's manufactured goods did each produce, in terms of value? (e) How do you think these factors affected the war?
2. **Analyzing a Quotation** In 1861, the antislavery leader Frederick Douglass declared: "This is no time to fight with one hand when both are needed. This is no time to fight with only your white hand, and allow your black hand to remain tied!" (a) What was Douglass referring to in this statement? (b) What evidence from the chapter shows that the government came to agree with Douglass?
3. **Making a Review Chart** Make a chart with three columns labeled Battle, Date, Outcome. Use the information in the chapter to complete the chart.

Thinking About Geography

Match the letters on the map with the places listed below.

1. Atlanta
2. Bull Run
3. Vicksburg
4. Gettysburg
5. Appomattox
6. Confederate states
7. Union states

Location Which battles shown on the map were fought in the Confederate states?

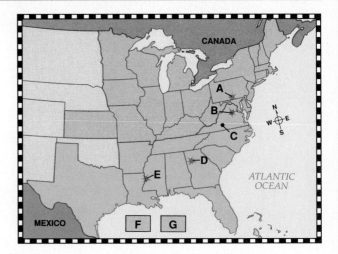

History Writer's Workshop

Writing and Revising the First Draft of a Report

You are now ready to write the first draft of your report. Start by jotting down ideas for an introduction, a conclusion, and a title. Then, write the first draft of your report, using these ideas, your outline of the body paragraphs, and your note cards. As you write, remember to present your information clearly and accurately. Connect your ideas with transitions, and write footnotes when you use sources.

Begin your report with an introductory paragraph that has a clear thesis statement. Develop the thesis statement with effective supporting information in the body paragraphs. Then, write a conclusion. Finally, prepare a bibliography and add a title.

Use this checklist to revise your report:

1. Does the thesis statement present the main point clearly?
2. Does any information not develop the statement? Is there other information you could add?
3. Did you write footnotes for quotations, borrowed ideas, and little-known facts?
4. Do your footnotes and bibliography follow the correct form?

Practice Research and write a first draft of a report on one of these topics:

1. Robert E. Lee
2. Ulysses S. Grant
3. The Emancipation Proclamation
4. African Americans in the Civil War

Writing to Learn

1. Write a paragraph comparing the resources of the North and South at the beginning of the Civil War. First, list the resources of each side in order of importance. Then, write a topic sentence stating your main idea. Compose supporting sentences, giving specific examples. Revise for balance and clarity. Then, proofread and make a final copy. Finally, exchange papers with a classmate.
2. Imagine that you are a Confederate soldier. Write a letter to a brother fighting for the Union. Brainstorm your reasons for supporting the Confederacy. Begin your letter with a topic sentence that makes your position clear. Organize your supporting details in order of importance. Revise the letter for clarity. Then, proofread and make a final copy. Publish your letter by reading it to several classmates.

The Death of Lincoln *Abraham Lincoln's assassination stunned the nation. Lincoln had brought the Union through the Civil War. Now, Americans faced the difficult task of rebuilding without him. Here, family and friends gather by the bedside of the dying President.* **Daily Life** *What problems might the nation face after the Civil War?*

19

Rebuilding the Union (1864–1877)

CHAPTER SPOTLIGHT

The Big Picture

The Civil War gave a firm answer to the question of whether a state could leave the Union. But after the war, other questions loomed. Would the Confederates be punished? Should the North help the South to rebuild its ruined economy? Now that they were free, what rights would African Americans have?

These questions were important. Most urgent, however, Americans in 1865 wondered how the South would rejoin the Union. How would the United States be "United" once more?

Kathleen Underwood

Of Special Interest

Focus On

◆ What steps did the nation take toward reunion in the first years after the Civil War?
◆ How did Congress gain control of Reconstruction?
◆ What were the successes and failures of Reconstruction?
◆ How did Reconstruction end?

"**W**ith malice toward none; with charity for all; with firmness in the right, as God gives us to see the right, let us strive on to finish the work we are in; to bind up the nation's wounds; to care for him who shall have borne the battle and for his widow, and his orphan—to do all which may achieve and cherish a just and lasting peace among ourselves, and with all nations."

President Abraham Lincoln spoke these words on March 4, 1865, as part of his second inaugural address. In the South, cannons still roared, and soldiers still died on the battlefield. Yet Americans knew that the Civil War was nearly over. Soon, it would be time to rebuild and reunite the nation.

Lincoln wanted all Americans to work together at this huge task. In his speech, he urged northerners to forgive the South. And he called on northerners and southerners to build a "union of the hearts."

But northerners did not all share Lincoln's forgiving spirit. The South had caused the Civil War, they said, and the South should be punished for it. Some wanted Confederate leaders to stand trial for treason. Others wanted to seize southern plantations, break them up, and give the land to newly freed slaves.

Americans faced hard decisions in the years following the Civil War. The fighting ended in 1865, but the North and the South still had many problems to resolve before they could be truly reunited.

1 First Steps Toward Reunion

FIND OUT

◆ What hardships did the South face after the Civil War?

◆ What was President Lincoln's plan for reunion?

◆ Why did Congress oppose President Johnson's Reconstruction plan?

◆ **VOCABULARY** freedman

The North lost more soldiers in the Civil War than the South did. But northern farms and cities were hardly touched by the war, and northern industry had boomed. As one returning Union soldier remarked, "It seemed . . . as if I had been away only a day or two, and had just taken up . . . where I had left off."

For Confederate soldiers returning home, however, there was no chance of taking up where they had left off. The problems facing the South after the war were staggering. Southern cities and farmlands lay in ruins, and a whole way of life was ended. All southerners—rich and poor, black and white—faced a long, uphill struggle to rebuild their lives out of the wreckage.

The Defeated South

Shortly after the Civil War ended, an Englishman visited the South. He was horrified by the destruction he saw:

> ❝[The land consists of] plantations in a state of semi-ruin, and plantations of which the ruin is for the present total and complete. . . . The trail of war is visible . . . in burnt-up [cotton gins], ruined bridges, mills, and factories . . . and in large tracts of once cultivated land stripped of every vestige of fencing. The roads, long neglected, are in disorder, and . . . in many places . . . impassable.❞

Except for the battles of Gettysburg and Antietam, all the fighting of the war took place in the South. In some areas, every house, barn, and bridge had been destroyed. Two thirds of the South's railroad tracks had been turned into twisted heaps of scrap. The cities of Charleston, Richmond, Savannah, and Atlanta had been leveled. A quarter of a million Confederate soldiers died in the war. Thousands more were disabled by their wounds.

The war wrecked the South's financial system. After the war, Confederate money was worthless. People who lent money to the Confederacy were never repaid. Many southern banks closed, and depositors lost their savings.

Southern society was changed forever by the war. No longer were there white owners and black slaves. Nearly 4 million **freedmen,** men and women who had been slaves, now lived in the South. Most had no land, no jobs, and no education. Under slavery, they had been forbidden to own property and to learn to read and write. What would become of them?

Rival Plans for the South

Even before the war ended, President Lincoln worried about rebuilding the South. He wanted to make it reasonably easy for southerners to rejoin the Union. The quicker the nation was reunited, Lincoln believed, the faster the South would be able to rebuild.

As early as 1863, Lincoln outlined a plan for **Reconstruction.** Reconstruction refers to the period when the South was rebuilt, as well as to the federal government's program to rebuild it. Under Lincoln's **Ten Percent Plan,** as it was called, a southern state could form a new government after 10 percent of its voters swore an oath of loyalty to the United States. Once it was formed, the new government had to abolish slavery. After these steps were complet-

Ruins of Richmond *At war's end, the South lay in ruins. This photograph shows the desolation of Richmond, Virginia, the Confederate capital.* **Daily Life** *Why was the South more badly hurt than the North during the Civil War?*

ed, voters could elect members of Congress and the state could once again take part in the national government.

Many Republicans in Congress opposed Lincoln's plan. They thought it was too generous toward the South. In 1864, these Republicans passed the **Wade-Davis Bill,** which outlined a rival plan for Reconstruction. It required a majority of white men in the South to swear loyalty to the United States. It denied the right to vote or hold office to any southerner who had volunteered to fight for the Confederacy.

Help for Freedmen

Lincoln refused to sign the Wade-Davis Bill because he felt it was too harsh. But Congress and the President did agree on one step. A month before Lee surrendered, Congress passed a bill creating the **Freedmen's Bureau.** Lincoln quickly signed it.

Providing food and clothing. The Freedmen's Bureau provided food and clothing to former slaves. It also tried to find jobs for freedmen. Because so many southerners were needy after the war, the bureau helped poor whites as well. It provided medical care for more than a million people. One former Confederate was amazed to see "a Government which was lately fighting us with fire, and sword, and shell, now generously feeding our poor and distressed."

Setting up schools. The bureau's most important work was in setting up schools and providing teachers for freed slaves throughout the South. By 1869, about 600,000 African Americans attended bureau schools. For teachers, the bureau relied mainly on volunteers—often women—from the North.

Teachers found both old and young students eager to learn. Grandmothers and granddaughters sat side by side in the classroom. One bureau agent in South Carolina observed that freedmen "will starve themselves, and go without clothes, in order to send their children to school."

The Freedmen's Bureau laid the foundation for the South's public school system. It set up more than 4,300 grade schools. It also created four universities for black students: Howard, Morehouse, Fisk, and Hampton Institute. The schools gave black students a chance to get a higher education. Many graduates became teachers themselves, and by the 1870s, blacks were teaching in grade schools throughout the South.

Learning to Read
"My Lord, Ma'am, what a great thing learning is!" a South Carolina freedman told a northern teacher. This painting by Winslow Homer, Sunday Morning in Virginia, *shows a family of freedmen using their new skills to read from the Bible.* **Citizenship** *How did the Freedmen's Bureau help African Americans to get an education?*

UP CLOSE

Charlotte Forten and Black Education

For former slaves, attending school was one of freedom's most precious gifts. Even before the Freedmen's Bureau set up schools, newly freed slaves built schools on their masters' abandoned lands. Many teachers from the North came to help in these schools. Among them was a young woman named Charlotte Forten.

Forten volunteers. Charlotte Forten came from a wealthy black Philadelphia family. As a young girl, she was educated by private tutors. Later, she attended a teacher training school. A strong abolitionist, Forten dedicated her life to helping poor blacks improve the quality of their lives through education.

During the Civil War, Forten was eager to serve. She got her chance early in the war, after Union troops captured the Sea Islands, off the coast of South Carolina. Plantation owners fled, but their slaves refused to go with them. With their masters gone, the slaves planted crops, built a church, and established a school. In 1862, Charlotte Forten, age 25, joined a group of northern teachers who came to help the Sea Islanders run their school.

The Sea Islands. Forten found the Sea Islands beautiful but badly neglected. The abandoned plantation house she stayed in had little furniture and no beds. But Forten was undaunted by these hardships. "I have never felt more hopeful, more cheerful, than I do now," she wrote.

Forten faced a stiff challenge. She was to teach reading, writing, spelling, history, and arithmetic. But there were few books or supplies. Classes were large and included students of all ages. Still, Forten was excited by the willingness and enthusiasm of her students. She wrote:

&&I never before saw children so eager to learn. . . . They come here as other children go to play. The older ones . . . work in the fields . . . and then come to school, after their hard toil in the hot sun, as bright and as anxious to learn as ever. . . . It is wonderful how a people who have been so long crushed to the earth . . . can have so great a desire for knowledge, and such a capacity for attaining it. 🎙🎙

Forten loved her work as a teacher, and her students made good progress. She assisted the tiny community in other ways, too. She cared for sick babies, and from time to time even tended a local store.

Recruiting for the Freedmen's Bureau. After two years, poor health forced Charlotte Forten to return to the North. There, after the Civil War, she helped to recruit teachers for the Freedmen's Bureau schools opening throughout the South. The diary she kept of her experiences on the Sea Islands was later published as a book. ◆

Lincoln Assassinated

President Lincoln hoped to convince Congress to accept his Reconstruction plan. Whether he would have succeeded will never be known. On April 14, 1865, just five days after Lee's surrender at Appomattox, the President attended a play at Ford's Theater in Washington, D.C. As Lincoln watched the performance, an actor named John Wilkes Booth crept into the President's box. Booth, a southerner, blamed Lincoln for the South's crushing defeat. Now, taking careful aim, he shot Lincoln in the head. Within a few hours, the President was dead. (📖 See "O Captain! My Captain!" on page 700.)

The relief that greeted the end of the war suddenly turned to shock. Millions mourned Lincoln's death. Booth, meanwhile, fled Washington. He was caught and killed in a barn outside the city.

A New President, A New Plan

Vice President Andrew Johnson became President when Lincoln died. Johnson, a southerner, had been born poor, and was a fierce enemy of what he called aristocratic planters. A Democrat in the mold of Andrew Jackson, Johnson had served as governor of Tennessee and had represented that state in Congress.

When Tennessee seceded in 1861, Johnson remained loyal to the Union. In 1864, the Republicans offered Johnson the vice presidential nomination. They needed him to attract Democratic votes in order to help Lincoln win reelection.

At first, many Republicans in Congress were pleased that Johnson had become President. They believed that he would support a strict Reconstruction plan, as they did. After all, Johnson had stated that "traitors must be punished." But the Republicans soon learned they were wrong. Johnson's plan for Reconstruction was almost as mild as Lincoln's.

Johnson called for a majority of voters in each southern state to pledge loyalty to the United States. He also demanded that

Andrew Johnson *Andrew Johnson was born into a poor southern family and for many years supported himself as a tailor. He rose to political power in Tennessee by portraying himself as the champion of the people against the wealthy planter class—the "stuck-up aristocrats," he liked to call them.* **Citizenship** *Why did many people think that Johnson would favor a strict Reconstruction plan?*

each state ratify the **Thirteenth Amendment,** which banned slavery throughout the nation. Congress had passed the Thirteenth Amendment in January 1865. Now, most southern states ratified the amendment, and it became part of the Constitution in December 1865.

Rebellion in Congress

The southern states did what Johnson had asked. So in late 1865, the President approved the new state governments that southerners had set up. Southern voters then elected new members of Congress. Many of those elected had held high office in the Confederacy. Alexander Stephens, the former vice president of the Confederacy, was elected senator from Georgia.

Republicans in Congress were outraged. The men who had led the South out of the Union were now being elected to the House and Senate. Also, nowhere in the South had African Americans been allowed to vote.

When Congress met in December 1865, many Republicans felt they could not approve Johnson's handling of the South. They refused to let southern representatives take their seats. Instead, Republicans set up a Joint Committee on Reconstruction to draw up a new plan for the South. The stage was set for a showdown between Congress and the President.

| SECTION 1 REVIEW |

1. **Identify:** (a) Reconstruction, (b) Ten Percent Plan, (c) Wade-Davis Bill, (d) Freedmen's Bureau, (e) Charlotte Forten, (f) Andrew Johnson, (g) Thirteenth Amendment.
2. **Define:** freedman.
3. Name two problems the South faced after the Civil War.
4. What did the Freedmen's Bureau do?
5. Why did Republicans in Congress refuse to seat the South's representatives?
6. **Drawing Conclusions** Would Charlotte Forten have been able to teach blacks in the South to read and write before the Civil War? Explain.

2 Congress Takes Charge

FIND OUT

◆ How did white southerners try to limit the rights of blacks?

◆ What were the goals of Radical Republicans?

◆ Why did Congress try to remove President Johnson from office?

◆ What were the Fourteenth and Fifteenth amendments?

◆ VOCABULARY black code

In the spring of 1866, disturbing reports trickled in to the Joint Committee on Reconstruction. In some southern cities, peddlers openly sold Confederate flags. A New Orleans restaurant featured "Stonewall Jackson soup" and "Confederate hash." And throughout the South, people sang a new song called "The Good Old Rebel." "I'm a good old rebel," it declared, "and I don't want no pardon for anything I done."

These reports confirmed what the committee had suspected. Under President Johnson's plan, there was "evidence of an intense hostility to the federal union and an equally intense love of the late Confederacy." "The rebellion has not ended," declared one angry Republican. "It has only changed its weapons!"

A New Kind of Bondage in the South

Most southern states had ratified the Thirteenth Amendment, which banned slavery. But white southerners did not want to give blacks real freedom. Southern legislatures passed **black codes,** laws that severely limited the rights of freedmen.

Black codes forbade African Americans to vote, own guns, or serve on juries. In some states, blacks were permitted to work only as servants or farm laborers. In others, the

Auctioned Off to the Highest Bidder
Under the black codes, freedmen found idle or unemployed could be fined. If they did not pay the fine, their services could be sold. Here, a freedman in Florida is auctioned off to work for the highest bidder. **Citizenship** *What did the black codes reveal about the South's attitude toward the idea of freedom for African Americans?*

codes required freedmen to sign contracts agreeing to work for a year at a time. Blacks without contracts could be arrested and sentenced to work on a plantation.

Black codes were not as harsh as slave codes before the Civil War. For example, blacks could legally marry and own some kinds of property. But the codes were clearly meant to keep freedmen from gaining political or economic power. As one black veteran wrote, "If you call this Freedom, what do you call Slavery?"

The North Reacts

Republicans were angered by the black codes and the election of former Confederate leaders to Congress. The Joint Committee on Reconstruction sent President Johnson a report condemning southern practices. "There is yet among the southern people," the report said, "a desire to preserve slavery in its original form as much and as long as possible." When Johnson ignored the report, members of Congress vowed to take Reconstruction out of the President's hands.

Radicals. Those who led the opposition to Johnson were called **Radical Republi-**cans, often shortened to Radicals.* Congressman Thaddeus Stevens of Pennsylvania led the Radicals in the House. Charles Sumner of Massachusetts was the chief Radical Republican voice in the Senate.

Radical Republicans had two main goals. First, they wanted to break the power of the rich planters who had ruled the South for years. These "aristocrats," Radicals believed, had caused the Civil War. Thaddeus Stevens urged Congress to break up big plantations and give the land to former slaves. "Strip a proud nobility of their bloated estates," Stevens thundered, "send them forth to labor . . . and you will thus humble the proud traitors." Second, Radicals wanted to ensure that freedmen received the right to vote.

Moderates. Radical Republicans did not control Congress. To accomplish anything, they needed the help of moderate Republicans, who formed the largest group in Congress. Although moderates and Radicals did not agree on all issues, they shared a common goal that encouraged them to work together: they wanted to stay in power.

---

*A radical is a person who wants to make drastic changes in society.

The Republicans had a strong political motive for demanding a strict policy toward the South. Most southerners were Democrats. With southerners barred from Congress, Republicans easily controlled both the House and Senate. If southern congressmen were seated, Republicans might lose their majorities and their power.

The President and Congress Clash

The conflict between President Johnson and Congress came to a head in 1866. In April, Congress passed the Civil Rights Act. The act gave citizenship to African Americans. By passing it, Congress hoped to combat the black codes and secure for blacks the rights denied them by the southern states.

Thaddeus Stevens *Like other Radical Republicans, Thaddeus Stevens wanted to secure basic rights for African Americans. Stevens argued that unless Reconstruction altered "the whole fabric of southern society, . . . all our blood and treasure have been spent in vain."* **Citizenship** *How did Radical Republicans try to secure political rights for African Americans?*

President Johnson vetoed the bill. But Republicans in Congress overrode the veto.

Citizenship for African Americans. Some Republicans worried that the Supreme Court might declare the Civil Rights Act unconstitutional. They remembered that in the Dred Scott decision in 1857, the Court had ruled that blacks were not citizens. Hoping to forestall any problems, Republicans now proposed the Fourteenth Amendment to the Constitution.

The **Fourteenth Amendment** granted citizenship to all persons born in the United States. This included nearly all African Americans. It also guaranteed all citizens "equal protection under the law" and declared that no state could "deprive any person of life, liberty, or property without due process of law." This provision made it illegal for states to discriminate against an individual on unreasonable grounds such as the color of a person's skin.

In addition, the Fourteenth Amendment provided that any state that denied African Americans the right to vote would have its representation in Congress reduced. This clause was included to encourage states to let blacks vote. Republicans believed that freedmen would be able to defend their rights if they could vote.

With the Fourteenth Amendment, Republicans tried to secure basic political rights for southern blacks. In fact, the nation had far to go before all Americans achieved equality. Over the next 100 years, citizens would seek to obtain their rights by asking the courts to enforce the Fourteenth Amendment.

Election of 1866. President Johnson was furious. He violently opposed the Fourteenth Amendment and urged the former Confederate states to reject it. In time, all did so except Tennessee.

Johnson decided to make the Fourteenth Amendment an issue in the November 1866 congressional elections. Traveling through the North, the President called on voters to reject the Radical Republicans and endorse his plan for Reconstruction.

EYEWITNESS

A Freedman Writes to His Former Owner

During Reconstruction, some freedmen stayed with their former masters and toiled for shares of the crop. Others left the South to seek a better way of life. In this 1865 letter, Jourdon Anderson explains to his former owner why he chose to live in the North.

"To my old Master, Colonel P. H. Anderson, Big Spring, Tennessee

SIR: I got your letter, and was glad to find that you had not forgotten Jourdon, and that you wanted me to come back and live with you. . . .

I am doing tolerably well here. I get twenty-five dollars a month . . . have a comfortable home for Mandy—the folks call her Mrs. Anderson—and the children . . . go to school and are learning well.

Mandy says she would be afraid to go back without some proof that you were disposed to treat us justly and kindly; and we have concluded to test your sincerity by asking you to send us our wages for the time we served you. . . . If you fail to pay us for faithful labors in the past, we can have little faith in your promises for the future. . . .

In answering this letter, please state . . . if there has been any schools opened for the colored children in your neighborhood. The great desire of my life now is to give my children an education. . . .

Say howdy to George Carter, and thank him for taking the pistol from you when you were shooting at me.

From your old servant,
JOURDON ANDERSON"

1. Why does Anderson feel he is doing well?

2. **Analyzing Ideas** In what way does Anderson's letter quietly make fun of his former owner?

In many towns, the President was heckled by the audience. Losing his temper, Johnson yelled right back. In Cleveland, Ohio, a heckler shouted out that Johnson should hang Jefferson Davis. "Why not hang Thad Stevens?" the President replied. Johnson's behavior shocked many northerners, who thought it undignified for a President.

In July, white mobs rioted in New Orleans, Louisiana, killing 34 African Americans. This convinced many northerners that Johnson's policies were not succeeding. To them, the riot showed that measures were needed to protect freedmen.

The election results were a disaster for Johnson. Republicans won majorities in both houses of Congress. They also won every northern governorship and majorities in every northern state legislature.

The Radical Program

Republicans in Congress now prepared to take charge of Reconstruction. With overwhelming majorities in both the House and Senate, they could override Johnson's veto. The President, one Republican said, was the "dead dog in the White House." The period that followed is often called **Radical Reconstruction.**

Taking the life out of the rebels. Congress passed the first **Reconstruction Act** over Johnson's veto in March 1867. The Reconstruction Act threw out the southern

---

Lining Up to Vote *Throughout the South, freedmen proudly exercised their right to vote. In this engraving, freedmen line up to cast their first ballot.* **Citizenship** *Why do you think most freedmen supported the Republican party?*

state governments that had refused to ratify the Fourteenth Amendment—all the former Confederate states except Tennessee. It divided the South into five military districts. Each district was commanded by an army general. Only when the states did what Congress demanded could they rejoin the Union. Said one Radical senator:

> **❝**This bill sets out by laying its hand on the rebel governments and taking the very life out of them . . . it puts the bayonet at the [chest] of every rebel in the South. . . . It leaves in the hands of Congress, utterly and completely, the work of reconstruction.**❞**

The Reconstruction Act required the former Confederate states to write new constitutions. Congress also required the new state governments to ratify the Fourteenth Amendment before rejoining the Union. Most important, the act stated that blacks must be allowed to vote in all southern states.

Elections in the South. Once the new constitutions were in place, the reconstructed states held elections to set up new state governments. To show their disgust with Radical Reconstruction policies, many white southerners stayed away from the polls. Freedmen, on the other hand, proudly turned out to exercise their new right to vote. As a result, Republicans gained control of the new southern state governments.

Congress passed several more Reconstruction acts, each time over Johnson's veto. It was Johnson's duty, as President, to enforce these laws. But many Republicans feared he would not do so. Republicans in Congress decided to remove the President from office.

Showdown

On February 24, 1868, the House of Representatives voted to impeach President Johnson. As you have read, to impeach means to bring formal charges of wrong-

Senate Trial of President Johnson *The Senate galleries buzzed with spectators at the trial of President Andrew Johnson. Johnson, who did not appear at the trial, was acquitted by a single vote.* **Linking Past and Present** *What disputes have divided the President and Congress in recent years?*

doing against an elected official. According to the Constitution, the House can impeach the President only for "high crimes and misdemeanors." The case is tried in the Senate. The President is removed from office only if found guilty by two thirds of the senators.

Thaddeus Stevens read the charges against President Johnson on the Senate floor. During the trial, it became clear that the President was not guilty of high crimes and misdemeanors. Even Charles Sumner, Johnson's bitter foe, admitted that the charges were "political in character."

In the end, the Senate vote was 35 to 19. This was just one vote short of the two-thirds majority needed to remove Johnson from office. Despite intense pressure, seven Republicans refused to vote for conviction. They knew that Johnson was not guilty of any crime. The Constitution, they believed, did not intend for a President to be removed because he disagreed with Congress. Johnson served out the few months left in his term.

Grant Becomes President

In 1868, Republicans nominated General Ulysses S. Grant as their candidate for President. Grant was the Union's greatest hero in the Civil War.

By election day in November 1868, most of the southern states had rejoined the Union. As Congress demanded, the new southern governments allowed African Americans to vote. About 700,000 blacks went to the polls in the 1868 election. Nearly all cast their votes for Grant. He easily defeated his opponent, Democrat Horatio Seymour of New York.

African Americans Gain the Right to Vote

Republican politicians quickly saw that black votes had brought them victory in the South. If blacks could vote in the North as well, the politicians realized, they would help Republicans to win elections there, too. In 1869, Republicans in Congress proposed another amendment to the Constitution. The **Fifteenth Amendment** forbade any state from denying African Americans the right to vote because of their race.

Some Republican politicians supported the Fifteenth Amendment only because they wanted to win elections. But many Americans remembered the great sacrifices made by black soldiers in the Civil

War. They felt it was wrong to let blacks vote in the South but not in the North. For these reasons, the Fifteenth Amendment was ratified in 1870. Finally, all African American men over age 21 received the right to vote.

SECTION 2 REVIEW

1. **Identify:** (a) Radical Republicans, (b) Thaddeus Stevens, (c) Charles Sumner, (d) Fourteenth Amendment, (e) Radical Reconstruction, (f) Reconstruction Act, (g) Fifteenth Amendment.
2. **Define:** black code.
3. How did southern legislatures limit the rights of freedmen?
4. Describe the Reconstruction plan adopted by Congress in 1867.
5. (a) Why did Republicans impeach Johnson? (b) What was the result?
6. **Analyzing Ideas** A senator who voted against the removal of President Johnson later said that he did not vote in favor of Johnson but in favor of the presidency. What do you think the senator meant?

3 The Reconstruction South

FIND OUT

◆ What groups dominated southern politics during Reconstruction?

◆ How did some white southerners use terror to regain control of the South?

◆ What did Reconstruction governments do to rebuild the South?

◆ What was life like for freedmen and poor whites during Reconstruction?

◆ **VOCABULARY** scalawag, carpetbagger, sharecropper

By 1867, life in the South had changed dramatically. Gone forever were slave auctions and the hated slave patrols. Blacks were free—free to work for themselves, to vote, and to run for office. Many freedmen took an active part in politics. In Alabama, a group of freedmen drew up this ringing declaration:

> ❝We claim exactly *the same rights, privileges and immunities as are enjoyed by white men*—we ask nothing more and will be content with nothing less. . . . The law no longer knows white nor black, but simply men, and consequently we are entitled to . . . hold office, sit on juries and do everything else which we have in the past been prevented from doing solely on the ground of color.❞

Before the Civil War, a small group of rich planters controlled southern politics. But during Reconstruction, new groups dominated state governments. They tried to reshape the politics of the South.

New Forces in Southern Politics

The state governments created during Radical Reconstruction were different from any the South had known before. The leaders of the old South had lost much of their influence. Three groups stepped in to take their place. These were white southerners who supported the Republicans, northerners who moved to the South after the war, and freedmen.

Scalawags and carpetbaggers. Some white southerners supported the new Republican governments. Many were business people who had opposed secession in 1860. Now, they wanted to forget the war and get on with rebuilding the South. Many whites felt that any southerner who helped the Republicans was a traitor. They called white southern Republicans scalawags, a word used for a small, scruffy horse.

Northerners who moved south after the war were another important force during Reconstruction. White southerners called these northerners carpetbaggers. They said that carpetbaggers had left in a hurry to get rich in the South. They had time only to fling a few clothes into cheap cloth suitcases, called carpetbags.

In fact, northerners went south for a number of reasons. A few were fortune hunters who hoped to profit as the South was being rebuilt. Many more were Union soldiers who had grown to love the South's rich land. Others, including many northern blacks, were reformers who wanted to help the freedmen. And many were volunteers who traveled south to teach in schools for men, women, and children who had been forbidden to learn under slavery.

Blacks in public life. Freedmen were the third major group in southern politics during Reconstruction. As slaves, blacks had no voice in southern politics. Now,

AN · AMERICAN · PORTRAIT

Blanche K. Bruce: African American Senator

The life of Blanche K. Bruce is a story of courage and hard work. Bruce was born into slavery in Virginia in 1841. Although it was a crime for slaves to get an education, Bruce dared to learn to read and write. When the Civil War erupted, the young man risked his life escaping to the North.

Bruce helped to set up a school for freedmen in Missouri. Later, he enrolled at Oberlin College in Ohio. There, he distinguished himself among better-prepared students, making up for his lack of formal training with long hours of study. After the war, Bruce returned to the South, where he worked hard and prospered as a planter in Mississippi.

Like other blacks who had been educated in the North, Bruce decided to enter politics. He was elected to the United States Senate in 1874 and was the first African American to serve a full term there. Bruce earned the respect of the Senate for his energy and intelligence. He tried to increase trade along the Mississippi River by building new railroads and new shipping lines. He also spoke out in favor of improved education.

As Reconstruction wore on, Bruce became especially concerned about the increased use of violence against black voters. He warned that white terrorism was threatening the new-found political rights of blacks. Still, Bruce never lost hope. He said:

> ❝I have confidence not only in my country and her institutions, but in the endurance, capacity and destiny of my people.❞

1. Name two causes that Bruce worked for in the Senate.

2. Making Decisions Do you think it required courage for Bruce to speak out against white violence? Explain.

they were not only voting in large numbers but also running for office and winning elections.

Blacks became sheriffs, mayors, and legislators in the South's new local and state governments. A few African Americans were elected to Congress: Hiram Revels and Blanche Bruce, both of Mississippi, won seats in the United States Senate. But blacks did not control the Reconstruction South. Only in South Carolina did African Americans have a majority in the legislature.

Many white Americans in both the North and the South had doubts about the ability of blacks to govern. But black officials soon proved themselves. "The [black]

men who took seats in both the Senate and the House," one white said, "were as a rule studious, earnest, ambitious men whose political conduct . . . would be honorable to any race."

White Southerners Fight Back

From the start, most southerners who had held power before the Civil War resisted Reconstruction. Nearly all were Democrats. These white southerners, known as **Conservatives,** wanted the South to change as little as possible. They were willing to let blacks vote and hold a few offices so long as real power remained in the hands of whites.

Other white southerners took a harsher view. Some were wealthy planters who wanted to force blacks back to work on plantations. Others were small farmers and laborers who felt threatened by the millions of freedmen who now competed with them for land and power. These whites declared war on anyone who worked with the Republican party. As Senator Ben Tillman of South Carolina recalled:

> ❝We reorganized the Democratic party with one plank, and only one plank, namely, that 'this is a white man's country, and white men must govern it.' Under that banner we went to battle.❞

A reign of terror. White southerners formed secret societies to help them regain power. The most dangerous was the **Ku Klux Klan,** or KKK. The Klan worked to keep blacks and white Republicans out of office.

Dressed in white robes and hoods to hide their identity, klansmen rode at night to the homes of black voters, shouting threats and burning wooden crosses. When threats did not work, the Klan used violence. Klan members murdered hundreds of blacks and their white allies.

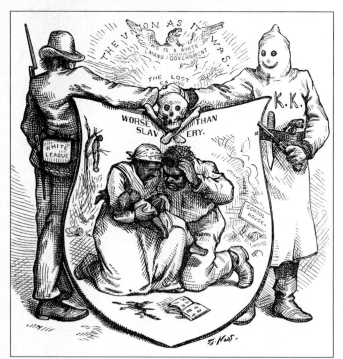

Spreading Terror *Secret societies used floggings, hangings, and other acts of violence to frighten blacks and their white supporters. In this 1874 cartoon by Thomas Nast, the Ku Klux Klan and the White League join to keep blacks in a state "worse than slavery."* **Citizenship** *What effect did the secret societies have on African American voters?*

Congress responds. Many moderate southerners condemned the violence of the Klan. But they could do little to stop the Klan's reign of terror. Freedmen turned to the federal government for help. In Kentucky, black voters sent a letter to Congress. They wrote:

❝We believe you are not familiar with the Ku Klux Klan's riding nightly over the country spreading terror wherever they go by robbing, whipping, and killing our people without provocation.❞

Congress acted to stop the Klan's violence. In 1870, Congress made it a crime to use force to keep people from voting. As a result, Klan activities decreased, but the threat of violence lingered. Some blacks continued to risk their lives by voting and holding office, but many others stayed away from the ballot box.

The Difficult Task of Rebuilding

Despite political problems, Reconstruction governments tried to rebuild the South. They built public schools for both black and white children. Many states gave women the right to own property. They improved care for the mentally and physically ill.

In addition, Reconstruction governments rebuilt railroads, telegraph lines, bridges, and roads. Between 1865 and 1879, the South laid 7,000 miles (11,200 km) of railroad track.

Rebuilding the economy. Cotton production, long the basis of the South's economy, recovered slowly. Not until 1880 did planters grow as much cotton as they had in 1860. That same year, 158 textile mills operated in the South.

Other types of industry also grew during Reconstruction. Birmingham, Alabama, founded in 1871 on the site of an old cotton field, became an important iron and steel center, often called the "Pittsburgh of the South." Still, the South lagged behind the rest of the nation in industry. In 1900, the South actually produced a smaller part of the nation's manufactured goods than it had produced in 1860.

Problems of taxes and corruption. Rebuilding cost money. Before the war, southerners had paid very low taxes. Now, Reconstruction governments raised taxes sharply. Higher taxes created discontent among many southern whites.

Southerners were further angered by widespread corruption in the Reconstruction governments. One state legislature, for example, voted $1,000 to cover a member's bet on a horse race. Other items billed to the state included hams, perfume, clothing, champagne, and a coffin.

But corruption was not limited to governments of the South. Dishonesty plagued state and local governments after the Civil War in the North as well. In fact, most southern officeholders served their states well and honestly.

A Cycle of Poverty

In the first months after the war, freedmen left the plantations on which they had lived and worked. For many, moving away from their former owners was a way to prove that they were free. As one woman said, "I must go. If I stay here, I'll never know I am free." Freedmen found few opportunities, however. Frederick Douglass noted bitterly that the former slave "was free from the old plantation, but he had nothing but the dusty road under his feet."

"Nothing but freedom." Some Radical Republicans talked about giving each freedman "40 acres and a mule." Thaddeus Stevens suggested breaking up big plantations to distribute the land. Most Americans opposed the plan, however. In the end, former slaves received—in the words of a freedman—"nothing but freedom." Through hard work or good fortune, some freedmen did manage to become landowners. But most former slaves had little choice but to

Back to the Plantation *For many freed slaves, life did not change much after the Civil War. Without education or money, freedmen were forced to remain on plantations doing the same kind of work they had done as slaves.* **Daily Life** *Do you think that these freedmen were better off than before the Civil War? Explain.*

return to the area where they had lived in slavery. Lizzie Atkins, a former slave from Texas, explained:

> ❝We was almost forced to stay on there with [Master], because no other white man would hire us or give us a place to stay.❞

Sharecropping. Some large planters had held onto their land and wealth through the war. Now, they had huge amounts of land but no slaves to work it. In the hard times of Reconstruction, many freedmen and poor whites went to work for the large planters. They farmed the planters' land, using seed, fertilizer, and tools that the planters provided. In return, they gave the landowners a share of the crop at harvest time. For this reason, these landless farmers were called **sharecroppers.**

Sharecroppers hoped to own their own land one day. But most faced a day-to-day struggle just to survive. They were doing well if they had enough food for themselves and their families.

Even farmers who owned land faced hard times. Each spring, farmers received supplies on credit from a store owner. In the fall, they had to pay back the store. Often, the harvest did not cover the whole debt. As they sank deeper into debt, many farmers lost their land and became sharecroppers themselves. Much of the South became locked into a cycle of poverty.

| SECTION 3 REVIEW |

1. **Identify:** (a) Blanche Bruce, (b) Hiram Revels, (c) Conservatives, (d) Ku Klux Klan.
2. **Define:** (a) scalawag, (b) carpetbagger, (c) sharecropper.
3. What role did blacks play in Reconstruction governments?
4. (a) What were two accomplishments of Reconstruction governments? (b) What were two problems?
5. Why did many blacks and poor whites in the South become sharecroppers?
6. **Drawing Conclusions** Why do you think groups like the Ku Klux Klan did not exist before the Civil War?

4 End of an Era

FIND OUT

◆ Why did northerners lose interest in Reconstruction?

◆ What happened in the election of 1876?

◆ How did white Conservatives tighten their control over the South?

◆ What did the Supreme Court rule in *Plessy* v. *Ferguson*?

◆ **VOCABULARY** poll tax, literacy test, grandfather clause, segregation

In 1876, millions of Americans traveled to a great Centennial Exposition held in Philadelphia. The exposition celebrated the first hundred years of the United States. Visitors to Philadelphia gazed at the wonders of modern industry, including a giant steam engine four stories high. They marveled at new devices like the telephone and the elevator.

As Americans looked to the future, they lost interest in Reconstruction and the rights of former slaves. By the late 1870s, conservative whites had regained control of the South. "The long controversy over the black man," one Chicago newspaper stated, "seems to have reached a finality."

Radicals in Decline

By the 1870s, Radical Republicans were losing power in Congress. Thaddeus Stevens died in 1868, and Charles Sumner died in 1874. Many northerners grew weary of trying to change the South. It was time to forget the Civil War, they believed, and let southerners run their own governments—even if that meant blacks might lose the rights they had so recently gained.

Republicans were also hurt by widespread corruption in the government of President Grant. The President had appointed many friends to office. Some used their jobs to steal money. Grant managed to win reelection in 1872, but many northerners lost faith in Republican leaders and policies.

Congress reflected the North's new mood. In 1872, it passed a law pardoning Confederate officials. As a result, nearly all white southerners could vote again. They voted solidly Democratic. At the same time, southern whites terrorized blacks who tried to vote. One by one, the Republican governments in the South fell. By 1876, only three southern states were still under Republican control: South Carolina, Florida, and Louisiana. (See "Abandoning Black Citizens" on page 702.)

The End of Reconstruction

The end of Reconstruction came with the election of 1876. Democrats nominated Samuel Tilden, governor of New York, for

President. Tilden was known for fighting corruption. The Republican candidate was Rutherford B. Hayes, governor of Ohio. Like Tilden, Hayes vowed to fight dishonesty in government.

A disputed election. When the votes were tallied, Tilden had 250,000 more popular votes than Hayes. But Tilden had only 184 electoral votes—one short of the number needed to win. Twenty votes were in dispute, however. The election hung on these votes.

All but one of the disputed votes came from Florida, Louisiana, and South Caroli-

MAP STUDY

The election of 1876 was one of the closest in American history. Samuel Tilden won the popular vote. But Rutherford B. Hayes became President when a congressional commission awarded him the disputed electoral votes of three southern states.
1. *In which three southern states were election results disputed?*
2. *Which candidate won in the other southern states?*
3. **Analyzing Information** *Based on the map, do you think that the end of the Civil War brought an end to sectionalism? Explain.*

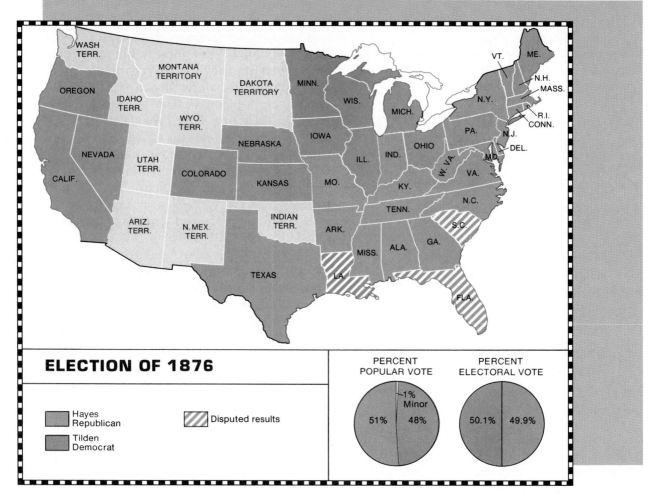

ELECTION OF 1876

- Hayes Republican
- Tilden Democrat
- Disputed results

PERCENT POPULAR VOTE

1% Minor
51%   48%

PERCENT ELECTORAL VOTE

50.1%   49.9%

na—the three southern states still controlled by Republicans. In each of these states, Tilden had won. But Republicans claimed that many people, especially blacks, had been kept from voting for Hayes. The Republicans in the three southern states filed a second set of electoral votes—for Hayes.

Hayes wins. Inauguration day drew near, and the nation had no one to swear in as President. Congress set up a special commission to settle the crisis. A majority of the commission members were Republicans. All the disputed electoral votes went to Hayes.

Southern Democrats could have fought the election of Hayes. But Hayes had privately agreed to end Reconstruction. Once in office, he removed federal troops from South Carolina, Florida, and Louisiana. Reconstruction was over.

Separate But Not Equal

With the North out of southern affairs, white Conservatives tightened their grip on southern governments. Some whites continued to use violence to keep blacks from voting or holding office. But southern states found other ways to keep blacks from exercising their rights.

Voting restrictions. By the late 1880s, many southern states had passed poll taxes. Poll taxes required voters to pay a fee each time they voted. As a result of the poll taxes, poor freedmen could rarely afford to vote.

Literacy tests required voters to read and explain a difficult part of the Constitution. Since freedmen had little education, such tests kept them away from the polls. Many southern whites, however, were poor and illiterate, too. Some were kept from voting. Others were allowed to register anyway by friendly white officials.

To allow more whites to vote, states passed grandfather clauses. If a voter's father or grandfather had been eligible to vote on January 1, 1867, the voter was excused from a poll tax or literacy test. Since no southern blacks could vote then, grandfather clauses were a way to ensure that only white men could vote.

Jim Crow. At the same time that African Americans were losing the right to vote, segregation became the law of the South. Segregation means separating people of different races. Southern states passed laws that separated blacks and whites in schools, restaurants, theaters, trains, streetcars, playgrounds, hospitals, and even cemeteries. They were called **Jim Crow laws.**

Blacks brought lawsuits to challenge segregation. But in 1896, the Supreme Court upheld segregation in ***Plessy v. Ferguson.*** The Court ruled that segregation was legal so long as facilities for blacks and whites were equal. In fact, facilities were rarely equal. For example, southern states spent much less on schools for blacks than on schools for whites.

Reconstruction was a time of both success and failure. Southerners, especially blacks, faced hard times during and after Reconstruction. But at last, all black Americans were citizens. And laws passed during Reconstruction became the basis of the civil rights movement almost 100 years later.

SECTION 4 REVIEW

1. **Identify:** (a) Samuel Tilden, (b) Rutherford B. Hayes, (c) Jim Crow laws, (d) *Plessy* v. *Ferguson.*
2. **Define:** (a) poll tax, (b) literacy test, (c) grandfather clause, (d) segregation.
3. Why did Republicans lose support in the North?
4. How did Rutherford B. Hayes gain southern support in the election of 1876?
5. **Evaluating Information** Do you think African Americans in the South benefited from Reconstruction? Explain.

SKILL LESSON 19

RESEARCH SKILLS
Finding Information in the Library

You can find information in the library in many sources, such as books, encyclopedias, and magazines. In Skill Lesson 16 (page 502), you learned how to use the card catalog to find books in the library. Most libraries have several encyclopedias. Encyclopedias present useful overviews of many subjects. **Periodicals,** or magazines, offer up-to-date articles on many subjects.

1 **Find information in an encyclopedia.** Encyclopedias contain articles on many subjects. The articles are arranged in alphabetical order. Imagine that you are writing a report on President Andrew Johnson. Under JOHNSON, ANDREW, you would find the main article. It tells about his life and term in office. At the end of the article are **cross-references** that tell you which other articles in the encyclopedia have information about Andrew Johnson.

Using an encyclopedia in your classroom or library, look up Andrew Johnson.(a) Are there any cross-references at the end of the article?(b) What articles do the cross-references refer you to?

2 **Practice using the Readers' Guide.** The Readers' Guide to Periodical Literature is an index, or list, of articles that appear in popular magazines. The Readers' Guide lists every article at least twice, once by the author's last name and again by the subject. Look at the sample from the Readers' Guide below. (a) What subject entry is shown? (b) How many articles are listed under the subject entry? (c) Which article appears under an author entry?

3 **Look for information in the Readers' Guide.** Each subject entry in the Readers' Guide tells you the title of the article and the author's name. It gives the title of the magazine in which the article appears. The entry lists the volume number of the magazine, the first page number of the article, and the date of the magazine. The date is in abbreviated form. At the front of the Readers' Guide is a list that tells you what the abbreviation stands for.

Look at the sample from the Readers' Guide. (a) In which volume of Ebony did the article "The 100 most influential black Americans" appear? (b) On what page did the article begin? (c) In what magazine did the article "Hailing a hero" appear? (d) What was the date of the magazine in which the article appeared? (e) What date do you think is indicated by the abbreviation My '90?

Volume: page number

Abbreviated date (July 2, 1990)

Magazine title

BISHOP, RACHAEL
Rescuing oily birds. *The Atlantic* 265:36
My '90

BLACK LEADERSHIP
Hailing a hero. M. Whitaker. *Newsweek*
116:20 Jl 2 '90

The 100 most influential black Americans.
Ebony 45:84 My '90

---

590 ◆ CHAPTER 19

Use the Section Reviews and this Study Guide to review chapter content.

Main Ideas

The main ideas in each section of this chapter are summarized below.

SECTION 1 ■ First Steps Toward Reunion

◆ The South lay in ruins after the Civil War.
◆ Lincoln urged generous treatment for the South but was assassinated before his plan was adopted.
◆ Republicans in Congress rejected Johnson's mild Reconstruction plan.

SECTION 2 ■ Congress Takes Charge

◆ Southern legislatures passed black codes limiting the freedom of former slaves.
◆ Congress took over Reconstruction.
◆ Congress impeached Johnson but failed to remove him from office.

SECTION 3 ■ The Reconstruction South

◆ Three new groups dominated southern politics during Reconstruction: scalawags, carpetbaggers, and freedmen.
◆ Some whites used terror to regain control of southern governments.
◆ Reconstruction governments made slow progress in rebuilding the South.
◆ Lack of money and land forced many poor blacks and whites to become sharecroppers.

SECTION 4 ■ End of an Era

◆ Republicans lost power in Congress, and interest in Reconstruction declined.
◆ Conservative Democrats gained control of most southern states.
◆ The election of Rutherford Hayes brought the end of Reconstruction.
◆ Segregation was upheld by the Supreme Court in *Plessy* v. *Ferguson*.

Key People and Terms

Refer to the Identify and Define questions in the Section Reviews on pages 576, 582, 587, and 589. Use each person, term, and vocabulary word in a complete sentence. When possible, make connections between the people and terms by using more than one person or term in each sentence.

Time Line

1. Make a chart of events in time order. The chart will have two headings: Date, Event. Fill in the chart, using the events on the time line. Add the following events from the chapter: Federal troops withdrawn from Florida, South Carolina, and Louisiana; Grant elected President; *Plessy* v. *Ferguson*. (Refer to the chapter for the dates.)
2. Which events on the chart are evidence of Republican power in Congress?

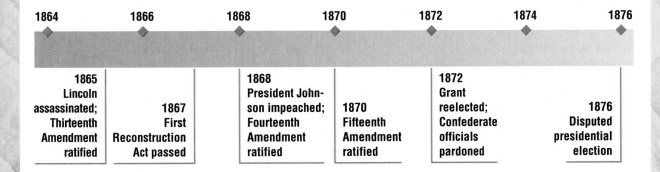

1864	1866	1868	1870	1872	1874	1876

| 1865 Lincoln assassinated; Thirteenth Amendment ratified | 1867 First Reconstruction Act passed | 1868 President Johnson impeached; Fourteenth Amendment ratified | 1870 Fifteenth Amendment ratified | 1872 Grant reelected; Confederate officials pardoned | | 1876 Disputed presidential election |

Understanding Vocabulary

Match each term at left with the correct definition at right.

1. black code
2. carpetbagger
3. sharecropper
4. grandfather clause
5. segregation

a. northerner who moved south after the Civil War
b. law that severely limited the rights of freedmen
c. separating people of different races
d. farmer who worked another person's land in return for a share of the crop
e. law that excused certain voters from poll taxes and literacy tests

Reviewing the Main Ideas

1. (a) What was Lincoln's plan for Reconstruction? (b) Why did some Republicans oppose it?
2. What did Radical Republicans want to achieve during Reconstruction?
3. What did the Reconstruction Act provide?
4. Why did Congress try to remove President Johnson from office?
5. What three groups dominated southern governments during Reconstruction?
6. What problems did freedmen face?
7. Why did northerners finally lose interest in Reconstruction?
8. How did Hayes win the election of 1876 even though he received fewer popular votes than Tilden did?

Thinking Critically

1. **Forecasting** How might the history of Reconstruction have been different if Lincoln had not been assassinated?
2. **Linking Past and Present** Many white southerners were angered by high taxes imposed by Reconstruction governments. (a) How do voters today feel about paying high taxes for services? (b) Are there services that should be provided even if they require high taxes? Explain.
3. **Understanding Causes and Effects** Read statements a–c that follow. Decide which one is an effect and which two are causes.

Explain how the causes and the effect are connected.
(a) Southern states passed black codes.
(b) Southern states elected former Confederates to Congress.
(c) Republicans opposed Johnson's plan to readmit southern states.

Applying Your Skills

1. **Making a Generalization** Reread the discussion of conditions in the South after the Civil War on page 572. (a) List three facts about the South after the war. (b) Based on your list, make a generalization about the South after the war.
2. **Finding Information in the Library** Review Skill Lesson 19 on page 590. Using an encyclopedia in your classroom or school library, look up Hiram Revels. (a) What is Revels's birth date? (b) Death date? (c) From which state was he elected to the Senate? (d) Are there cross-references? If so, what do they refer you to?
3. **Making a Review Chart** Make a chart with three columns. Label the columns Lincoln, Johnson, Radical Republicans. Then, list the major points of the Reconstruction plan each proposed. (a) Which plan(s) was strictest? (b) Which plan(s) was least strict? (c) Based on what you have read, how would you explain the differences?

Match the letters on the map with the places listed below.

1. South Carolina
2. Florida
3. Louisiana
4. Ohio
5. New York

Region What were the only states in the South under Republican control in 1876?

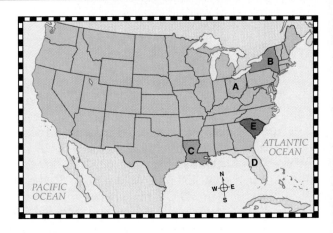

History Writer's Workshop

Proofreading a Report

Proofreading is the final step in writing a report. Proofreading involves making corrections in spelling, capitalization, punctuation, and grammar.

Use the following checklist to help you proofread your report.

1. Does your report have any errors in sentence structure (for example, fragments or run-ons)?
2. Have you used verbs and pronouns in your sentences correctly?
3. Have you capitalized properly?
4. Have you used periods, commas, apostrophes, quotation marks, and other punctuation marks where they are needed?
5. Have you checked the spelling of any words that do not look right or that you often misspell?

When you have finished proofreading and correcting your report, recopy it neatly, if necessary.

Practice Proofread the following paragraph. Then, recopy the corrected version.

Lincolns plan for reconstrucsion was generous toward the South. according to the presidents' plan ten percent of voters in each southern state had to swear an oath of loyalty, once the loyalty othe was sworn, each state could form a new goverment. As soon as the new goverment abolished slavery the state could elect members of Congress and take part in the nacional goverment again.

Writing to Learn

1. Imagine that you are a member of Congress after the Civil War. Write a plan to rebuild the South. Begin by listing what has to be done and how it can be accomplished. Write a topic sentence summarizing your goals for Reconstruction. Then, organize your ideas chronologically. Revise your proposal for clarity and completeness. Proofread and make a final copy. Then, present your plan to your classmates, and discuss its possibilities.

2. Do some research about the Freedmen's Bureau. Then, select one aspect of the bureau and write a report. For example, you could report on the people involved in the bureau or on the bureau's achievements. Take notes on your selected topic, and then write a thesis statement that summarizes your main point. Organize your information logically. When you revise, check for coherence and be sure you have included specific examples. Proofread and make a final copy. Finally, present your information as an oral report.

Society Spy

No one suspected that Rose Greenhow was a Confederate spy. She had lived in Washington, D.C., for years. And her close friends included senators and cabinet members.

Greenhow, however, was secretly loyal to the South. She was surprised at how easy it was to collect information from her unsuspecting Union friends.

Early in the war, Mrs. Greenhow told Confederate leaders when Union General McDowell was leaving Washington. This enabled the Confederates to stop the Union troops at Bull Run.

Eventually, Greenhow was discovered. After a brief prison term, she was freed on condition that she return to the South. Jefferson Davis, President of the Confederacy, greeted her in Richmond: "But for you, there would have been no battle of Bull Run."

A First-Class Package

Henry Brown of Richmond, Virginia, decided to make a daring escape from slavery. He had himself crated in a large shipping box and mailed to abolitionists in the North. Clearly marked on the side of the box was the instruction: "This side up with care." Despite this direction, Brown spent much of the trip on his head with his eyes "almost swollen out of their sockets and the veins on his temple . . . ready to burst."

Should he call out for help? No, Brown decided that freedom was too important and that he would risk death to win it. But luck was with him. After a steamship ride on his head and a jolt that nearly broke his neck, Henry "Box" Brown reached Philadelphia and freedom.

Sinterklaas

Sinterklaas—Santa Claus—almost the same but very different. Sinterklaas is the Dutch name for St. Nicholas, a bishop who was believed to appear around December 6 to leave gifts on the doorsteps of good children. Dutch settlers brought the myth of Sinterklaas with them to America in the 1600s. Over the years, his name and appearance changed. In 1863, cartoonist Thomas Nast depicted Santa Claus as the round, jolly fellow we know today.

Up, Up, and Away

Both the Union and the Confederacy used hot-air balloons during the Civil War. High above the trees, lookouts could watch for enemy troop movements.

Usually, the balloons were tied to the ground with ropes. One time, the Union launched a balloon from a ship to search for enemy vessels, making the ship the world's first aircraft carrier.

Since there was a wartime shortage of materials, one Confederate balloon was sewn from silk dresses donated by women. The balloon was "a great patchwork ship of many and varied hues."

Baseball's Lucky Stretch

On June 19, 1846, the New York Nine played the Knickerbocker Club in the first baseball game between two organized clubs. Baseball mania was catching.

Traditions grew with the game. About 1860, for example, the seventh-inning stretch became part of the game when baseball began to be played in larger stadiums with plenty of seats for spectators.

It served both a practical and a superstitious purpose. Fans stood to stretch their legs. But the number seven is also considered lucky. Thus, the fans stood to give their team luck in the "lucky seventh" inning.

Footnotes to History

- In the 1860s, "shoddy" meant recycled wool from old rags. During the Civil War, profiteers sold "shoddy" uniforms, and the word came to mean low-quality goods.
- General Burnside wore his whiskers from his ears all the way to his chin. The word "sideburns" refers to whiskers such as these and comes from the name of the general who wore them.
- The first desegregated jury in the United States met in May 1867 to try Jefferson Davis, the president of the defeated Confederacy. Eventually, however, Davis was released without going to trial.

The Real McCoy

In 1872, Canadian-born engineer Elijah McCoy invented a device that constantly oiled the moving parts of a machine. Soon, no machine was considered good unless it could oil itself.

Inspectors and buyers began asking for "the real McCoy." Gradually, the phrase came to mean "the real thing."

Chapter 17 The Road to Civil War

As settlers pushed west, the issue of slavery caused a growing strain in the nation. In 1820, Congress passed the Missouri Compromise to balance the number of free and slave states to be created from the Louisiana Purchase. The question of slavery in the Mexican Cession divided the nation during the 1840s. The request of California to enter the Union as a free state in 1850 caused some southerners to talk about secession.

To resolve the crisis, Henry Clay proposed the Compromise of 1850. While admitting California as a free state, the Compromise established the principle of popular sovereignty in New Mexico and Utah. The Compromise also included a strict fugitive slave law. This law enraged northerners and led Harriet Beecher Stowe to write *Uncle Tom's Cabin* in 1852.

In 1854, Congress again angered northerners by passing the Kansas-Nebraska Act. Reversing the Missouri Compromise, the act established popular sovereignty in Kansas and Nebraska. Kansas "exploded," as proslavery and antislavery forces battled for control. The Dred Scott decision heightened sectional tensions.

The Republican party, formed in 1854, gave a political voice to those who opposed slavery in the territories. Campaigning for the Senate in 1858, Republican Abraham Lincoln debated Democrat Stephen Douglas on the issue of slavery. John Brown's 1859 raid in protest of slavery brought the nation to the brink of war.

Abraham Lincoln was elected President in 1860. By February 1861, seven southern states had seceded and formed the Confederate States of America. The Confederate attack on Fort Sumter in April marked the start of the Civil War.

Chapter 18 Torn by War

Neither side was prepared to fight a long war. The North lacked the able soldiers and the fine military leaders of the South. The South lacked the population, factories, rail lines, and navy of the North.

As the war began, the North had three goals: to blockade southern ports, to control the Mississippi, and to capture Richmond. Southerners hoped to hold out against the Union invaders until they tired of fighting. Confederate Generals Robert E. Lee and Stonewall Jackson prevented the capture of Richmond. But Union forces under Ulysses S. Grant won the Mississippi. The Union blockade held throughout the war.

In 1862, General Lee went on the offensive and marched his troops north. They were greeted by Union troops, who claimed a victory at the Battle of Antietam. Lincoln used this victory to issue the Emancipation Proclamation freeing slaves in the Confederacy. As a result, the war to restore the Union also became a war to end slavery.

On the battlefield, new technology made weapons deadly. Medical care was crude. As the war dragged on, public support dwindled. People on both sides resented the draft. Both sides had difficulty paying for the war. But the war boosted the economy in the North, while causing increasing hardship in the South.

In 1862 and 1863, the South won several important victories. Lee moved north into Pennsylvania, hoping to surprise the Yankees. But the Battle of Gettysburg ended his plans, and he retreated.

Northern forces invaded the South in 1864, waging total war. After a bloody, year-long campaign, Grant captured Richmond in April 1865. Lee surrendered soon after.

Chapter 19 Rebuilding the Union

The Civil War left the South in ruins. President Lincoln was assassinated before he could put his Reconstruction plan into effect. Andrew Johnson, who became President upon Lincoln's death, proposed a moderate plan of Reconstruction. But Republicans in Congress objected.

Radical Republicans drew up their own plan for the South. After the election of 1866, they had enough votes in Congress to carry it out.

Under Radical Reconstruction, the South was divided into military districts. Before they could rejoin the Union, the former Confederate states had to write new constitutions, ratify the Fourteenth Amendment, and allow African Americans to vote.

The Radical Republicans impeached Andrew Johnson, but he was acquitted.

Reconstruction continued under Ulysses S. Grant, who was elected President in 1868. Dramatic changes were made in the South. Republicans controlled the state legislatures. Many freedmen took an active role in politics, and resentful whites formed secret societies such as the Ku Klux Klan. Facing hard times, many former slaves and poor whites became sharecroppers.

By the 1870s, northerners had lost interest in Reconstruction. Congress pardoned Confederate officials in 1872. President Rutherford B. Hayes withdrew federal troops from the South in 1877, and Reconstruction ended. Conservative white Democrats used poll taxes and literacy tests to keep blacks from voting. Jim Crow laws segregated blacks from whites.

Understanding Causes and Effects *The Civil War pitted the North against the South for four long years.* ◆ *What effect did the war have on the northern economy? Which side suffered most from the war? Explain.*

CAUSES

- South fears that it will lose power in the national government
- Issue of slavery in the territories divides the North and South
- Northerners hate the Fugitive Slave Law
- Southern states secede after Lincoln's election
- Confederates bombard Fort Sumter

THE CIVIL WAR

EFFECTS

- Lincoln issues the Emancipation Proclamation
- Northern economy booms
- South loses its cotton trade with Britain
- Blockade creates southern shortages
- Total war destroys the South
- Hundreds of thousands of Americans killed
- Lee surrenders at Appomattox
- Reconstruction attempts to rebuild the South and reunite the nation

Reviewing the Main Ideas

1. Why did northern Whigs and Democrats form the Free Soil party in 1848?
2. How did each of the following heighten sectional tensions in the 1850s: (a) *Uncle Tom's Cabin;* (b) Kansas-Nebraska Act; (c) Dred Scott decision?
3. (a) Why were there two Democratic candidates for President in 1860? (b) How did the election results show the sectional split?
4. What did the Union gain from each of the following Civil War battles: (a) Vicksburg; (b) Gettysburg; (c) Petersburg?
5. (a) According to Lincoln, what was the main issue of the war? (b) Why did he address the issue of slavery in 1862?
6. (a) How did the Civil War help the North's economy? (b) What effect did the war have on the South's economy?
7. What was the most important work of the Freedmen's Bureau?
8. What were the two main goals of the Radical Republicans?
9. How did southern states keep blacks from exercising their rights after 1877?

Thinking Critically

1. **Making Decisions** If you had been a member of Congress in the 1840s, what position would you have taken on slavery in the territories? Give reasons to support your decision.
2. **Defending a Position** Based on the information in Unit 6, do you think that Abraham Lincoln was an abolitionist? Give facts to support your position.
3. **Drawing Conclusions** Why might Lincoln's death be considered a tragedy for the South?
4. **Comparing** (a) How was life as a freedman in the South different from life as a slave? (b) In what ways was it similar?

Applying Your Skills

1. **Constructing a Time Line** Make a unit time line for the period from 1820 to 1876. Include the events listed on the time lines in the chapter Study Guides. Add other events that you think are important. (a) Which events are related to the national debate on slavery? (b) Which events benefited freedmen and northern blacks? (c) Which events were setbacks for freedmen?
2. **Analyzing a Quotation** John C. Calhoun died during the debate over slavery in the Mexican Cession. His final words were: "The South! The South! God knows what will become of her!" What did Calhoun fear? Why?
3. **Making a Generalization** General Robert E. Lee said of his soldiers: "There never were such men in an army before. They will go anywhere and do anything if properly led." List two facts to show that this generalization might also apply to Union forces.

Doing More

1. **Creating Headlines** For each of the following events, write two headlines, one to appear in a northern newspaper, the other to appear in a southern newspaper: (a) Dred Scott decision; (b) John Brown's raid; (c) election of 1860; (d) Johnson's veto of the Reconstruction Act. Try to capture the way each side would view the event. As you revise, eliminate all unnecessary words. After you proofread, print each headline, line for line, as it would appear on the front page of a newspaper.
2. **Creating a Map** Create an illustrated map of Civil War battle sites. First, on an outline map, label the sites of important battles. Use different colors to identify Union and Confederate victories, and include a key. In a box, briefly explain the importance of each battle.

3. **Writing a Letter** Imagine that you are a Union or Confederate soldier stationed away from home. Write a letter to a family member in which you describe your experiences during a battle. Skim Chapter 18 to help you choose a side and a battle. Then, put yourself in the soldier's place, and jot down your impressions. In the body of the letter, include vivid details about what you saw and how you felt. Revise for clarity. Then, proofread and make a final copy. Exchange letters with a classmate.

4. **Exploring Local History** Do research to identify the first minority public officials in your community. Find out who they were, what jobs they held, when they were elected, and what they accomplished. Share your findings with classmates.

Recognizing Points of View

The Radical Republicans battled Andrew Johnson over Reconstruction policy. One issue on which they differed was voting rights. Below are excerpts from statements made by Thaddeus Stevens and President Johnson. Read the excerpts and answer the questions.

1. List three reasons that Stevens gives to support his opinion that freedmen should vote in the Reconstruction South.
2. (a) Which of Johnson's statements are facts? (b) Which are opinions? Explain.
3. (a) Which arguments are motivated by idealism? (b) Which arguments are motivated by practical reasons?
4. Which man do you think is more persuasive: Stevens or Johnson? Explain.

 ho should vote in the Reconstruction South?

Thaddeus Stevens

"There are several good reasons for the passage of this bill [for reconstructing the South].

In the first place, it is just. I am now confining my argument to Negro suffrage in the rebel states. Have not loyal blacks quite as good a right to choose rulers and make laws as rebel whites? In the second place, it is a necessity in order to protect the loyal white men in the seceded states. . . .

Another good reason is, it would insure the [power] of the [Republican] Party. . . . I believe, on my conscience, that on the continued [power] of that party depends the safety of this great nation.

If impartial suffrage is excluded in the rebel states, then every one of them is sure to send a solid rebel representative delegation to Congress."

Andrew Johnson

"It is . . . [clearly] the object of these laws [proposed by Congress] to confer upon negroes the privilege of voting and to [take the vote from] such a number of white citizens as will give the [negroes] a clear majority at all elections in Southern States. . . . The plan of putting the Southern States wholly and the General Government partially into the hands of negroes is proposed at [an especially unfavorable] time. . . . The foundations of society have been broken up by civil war. Industry must be reorganized, justice reestablished, public credit maintained, and order brought out of confusion."

A "Teeming Nation" *The United States is a "teeming nation of nations," wrote poet Walt Whitman. This painting of New York's Central Park in the early 1900s shows some of the many peoples who helped to give the country its strength and life.* **Multicultural Traditions** *What area of the world did your family come from?*

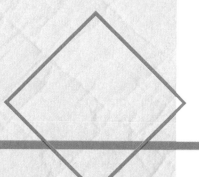

The Journey Continues (1877–Present)

The Big Picture

Since the Civil War, the world has changed dramatically. For example, consider travel time. In 1873, not long after the Civil War, readers looked on Jules Verne's adventure story of an 80-day trip around the world as fantasy. Today, in fact, astronauts circle the Earth in 80 minutes.

The United States has taken part in many changes in the world. Millions of immigrants have arrived from every part of the globe. American farmers and manufacturers have increased their trade with far-flung nations. And the government of the United States has played an important role in world affairs.

Jim Davidson

Of Special Interest

Up Close
A Young Filipino in America,
page 603

Focus On

◆ What changes have affected American culture?

◆ How did the United States become an industrial giant?

◆ What rights have citizens gained?

◆ How has the United States become a world leader?

For days on end, Sarah Asher had been shut up inside a steamer crossing the Atlantic Ocean from Europe. Outside, a storm raged, with 30-foot waves rocking the ship so violently that it nearly sank. On the seventeenth day, the Statue of Liberty came into view. Sarah described the sight:

"Well, she was beautiful with the early morning light. Everybody was crying. The whole boat bent toward her because everybody went out, everybody, everybody was in the same spot. We had been sinking and we survived and now we were looking at the Statue of Liberty. She was beautiful with the sunshine so bright."

The tears of the immigrants were tears of relief—and joy. So many of the newcomers had heard of "the lady with the torch." Now, she was before them, welcoming them to a new land and life.

The millions of immigrants who came to the United States in the late 1800s and early 1900s would see the nation undergo great change. Large, bustling cities sprang up in all parts of the country. New factories transformed the United States into a modern industrial giant. More and more, the nation became involved in world affairs. This chapter highlights the remarkable American journey from the end of the Civil War to the present.

1 A Nation of Nations

FIND OUT

◆ What immigrants have come to the United States?

◆ How did cities change after the Civil War?

◆ How have advances in technology and communication affected American life?

"The United States themselves are essentially the greatest poem." So wrote Walt Whitman, the author of *Leaves of Grass.* In this volume of poetry, published in 1855, Whitman hailed the bustling, growing United States. His praise included the many different peoples and regions that gave the nation its strength and life.

"Here is not merely a nation but a teeming nation of nations," Whitman said. In *Leaves of Grass*, he celebrated all Americans who made up the "teeming nation":

> ❝The spinning-girl retreats and
> advances to the hum of the big
> wheel, . . .
> The machinist rolls up his
> sleeves, . . .
> The groups of newly-come
> immigrants cover the wharf
> or levee, . . .
> The squaw wrapt in her yellow-
> hemmed cloth is offering
> moccasins and bead bags for
> sale, . . .
> The President holding a cabinet
> council is surrounded by the
> great Secretaries, . . .
> The Missourian crosses the
> plains toting his wares and his
> cattle, . . .
> And of these one and all I weave
> the song of myself.❞

In the years since the Civil War, the United States has continued to live up to Whitman's vision. Still a "teeming nation of nations," it reflects the influence of many cultures and backgrounds. The result has been the creation of a unique people—Americans.

The Tide of Immigration

After the Civil War, immigrants continued to enter the United States. In the 1880s, the number of newcomers rose sharply to almost half a million a year.

The "new" immigrants. Many of these immigrants came from countries in South-

GRAPH SKILLS *The United States is often called a nation of immigrants. ◆ Where did the largest number of immigrants come from in the period between 1871 and 1890? Between 1971 and 1990?*

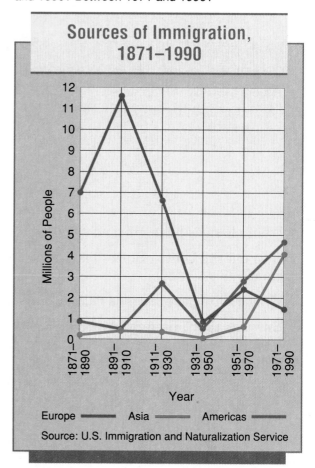

Sources of Immigration, 1871–1990

Europe ——— Asia ——— Americas ———

Source: U.S. Immigration and Naturalization Service

New Americans From Abroad *More than 25 million immigrants, most of them from Europe, came to the United States between 1866 and 1915. The painting at left shows a Hungarian steelworker on the day he became a citizen. The picture at right shows Margarathe Tiedermann, who came to the United States in 1903. At age 101, she is visiting Ellis Island with her daughter.* **Linking Past and Present** *Where do many immigrants come from today?*

ern and Eastern Europe, such as Italy, Poland, Russia, and Hungary. They included many Catholics, as well as Jews fleeing persecution in Eastern Europe.

The "new" immigrants from Southern and Eastern Europe faced great hardships to reach the United States. Uprooted from their families and homes, they flocked to European ports, sometimes sneaking past guarded borders. And like Sarah Asher, many endured a rough voyage across the Atlantic.

Ports of entry. The most famous port for European immigrants was Ellis Island, located near the Statue of Liberty in New York. But thousands of other immigrants arrived elsewhere.

As immigration increased in the 1900s and 1910s, the city of Galveston, Texas, took many immigrants that Ellis Island could not handle. On the West Coast, immigrants from China, Japan, and Korea entered through San Francisco, California, as well as Seattle, Washington, and Oahu, Hawaii. From Mexico, families traveled north to El Paso and Laredo in Texas.

The pain of discrimination. Like the Irish and German immigrants who arrived in the 1840s and 1850s, the new immigrants faced discrimination. Their religious beliefs, customs, and languages seemed "strange" to Americans. In the 1920s, Congress cut back sharply the number of immigrants who were allowed to enter the United States.

Despite the new restrictions, people from all over the world still dreamed of coming to the United States. They, too, wanted to share in the American dream of freedom and opportunity.

A Young Filipino in America

In the 1920s, the United States governed the Philippines as a territory. During those years, young Filipinos came to work in the United States. One, Carlos Bulosan, later wrote a book about his experiences. Not all

Carlos Bulosan *In* America Is in the Heart, *Carlos Bulosan writes about the hardships and discrimination that Filipinos faced in the United States. Still, he praises the American dream. "America," he tells readers, "is not a land of one race or one class. . . . We are all Americans."* **American Traditions** *What famous American inspired "Carlos" in Bulosan's book?*

of the events described in it actually happened to Bulosan himself. But they give a vivid picture of what life was like for Filipinos like "Carlos."

Dreams of America. Growing up as a young boy in the Philippines, Carlos worked as a houseboy for an American woman. In time, he learned more and more about the United States—or America, as it was commonly called.

In his spare hours, Carlos often walked to a nearby lake with his friend Dalmacio (dahl MAH see oh). There, Carlos and Dalmacio shared their dream of starting a new life in America. The two boys practiced their English by reading aloud to each other from a book about Abraham Lincoln.

"Who is this Abraham Lincoln?" Carlos asked.

"He was a poor boy who became President of the United States," replied Dalmacio. "He was born in a log cabin and walked miles and miles to borrow a book so that he would know more about his country." The story about Lincoln fascinated Carlos. Determined to learn more, Carlos began to borrow other books from the local library.

In the golden land. By age 17, Carlos had saved enough money to buy a ticket to Seattle, Washington. But he had to ride with 200 other Filipinos in steerage—the hot, dark lower section of the boat.

Carlos arrived in Seattle in June 1930, with only 20 cents. For a day or two, he stayed at a hotel in Chinatown. When he could not pay for his room, the hotel owner appeared with an older Filipino.

"You are working for me now," the man told Carlos. "Get your hat and follow me." The man sent him to Alaska to work in a fish-canning factory.

The jobs in Alaska required long hours and hard work. Sometimes, they were dangerous. One day, Carlos saw a worker lose his arm in a cutting machine. Still, he and other workers found some enjoyment. Because summer days were very long in Alaska, they stayed up very late to play baseball after work.

Carlos had arrived in the United States during the Great Depression of the 1930s. Jobs were scarce. After returning from Alaska, he and other Filipinos took whatever work they could find. In the Yakima Valley of Washington, they picked apples. In California, they gathered winter peas and oranges.

Too often, Carlos and other workers met with discrimination. When Carlos tried to rent an apartment in a "whites only" district in Los Angeles, the landlady pulled down the "For Rent" sign. Another time, he was beaten by anti-union people for trying to join a farm workers' union.

America Is in the Heart. Eventually, Bulosan himself found good American friends. When he fell ill from tuberculosis, they encouraged him to write about his experiences.

In 1943, Bulosan completed his book, *America Is in the Heart.* He wanted his Filipino friends and all Americans to understand that everyone could contribute to "this vast land"—just as Abraham Lincoln had:

> "America is not a land of one race or one class. . . . We are all Americans that have toiled and suffered and known oppression and defeat, from the first Indian that offered peace in Manhattan to the last Filipino peapickers. America is not bound by geographical latitudes. America is not merely a land or an institution. America is in the hearts of men that died for freedom; it is also in the eyes of men that are building a new world." ◆

Recent Newcomers

In 1965, Congress revised the immigration laws so that more people could enter the country. Many more immigrants from Latin America arrived, including Mexicans and Cubans.

During the 1970s and 1980s, the number of immigrants from Asia rose sharply as well. Most were Filipinos, Chinese, and Koreans. During and after the Vietnam War, many Vietnamese and Cambodians also sought new homes in the United States.

In the 1980s, about 6 million immigrants entered the United States legally. Another 3 to 5 million crossed American borders without official papers. Together, those totals are higher than in any previous decade in American history.

In 1986, Congress took steps to control illegal immigration. An amnesty or pardon, however, was granted to illegal aliens who had been in the country before January 1, 1982.

Each wave of immigrants has enriched American life. In the late 1800s and early 1900s, immigrants helped to build railroads, subways, and factories. They brought their foods, songs, stories, and customs with them. Today, more recent newcomers contribute their labor, talents, and traditions, too. Over the years, the different ethnic groups have woven rich and varied threads into the fabric of American culture.

The Rise of Cities

The growth of cities in the past 100 years also brought changes in American life. At the end of Reconstruction, less than one quarter of all Americans lived in cities. Between 1880 and 1900, the number of people living in cities doubled. By 1920, a majority of Americans made their homes in cities or suburbs.

The Morning News *Big-city newspapers of the early 1900s attracted readers with stories of crime, sports, and gossip. Here, New Yorkers crowded into a trolley eagerly read the morning news.* **Linking Past and Present** *How do people keep informed about the news today?*

The move to the cities changed American culture. City newspapers printed more interesting—and sometimes more sensational—news stories. Huge department stores such as Macy's in New York offered goods of every type. Subways and trolleys whisked people from one side of town to the other. Professional sports, especially baseball, became popular pastimes.

Cities and suburbs continued to grow through the mid-1900s. Then, in the 1970s, the trend changed. For the first time since 1820, small towns and rural areas gained population faster than cities and suburbs.

Older cities of the East and Midwest actually lost population. People left those regions and moved to the Sunbelt, as the states of the Southeast and Southwest are called. Many went in search of jobs. But the sunny climate with mild winters also was an attraction. By the 1980s, three of the ten largest cities in America were in Texas: Dallas, Houston, and San Antonio.

A People and Their Music

The richness of American life has always been expressed in music. Since colonial times, folk songs have been popular. Some were the ballads of Irish and Scotch immigrants. Some were spirituals sung in slave quarters. Others were banjo tunes from the gold fields of California.

As the United States changed, its music changed. In the early 1900s, a new kind of music, called jazz, was heard in the South. It drew on the rhythms brought from West Africa by slaves. African American composers like Scott Joplin and "Jelly Roll" Morton were the founders of jazz.

In the 1950s, another sound swept the nation—rock 'n' roll. Artists like Chuck Berry, Little Richard, and Bill Haley pioneered rock 'n' roll. Buddy Holly and Elvis Presley also became teenage favorites.

During the 1960s, 1970s, and 1980s, popular music took many forms. Americans of all ages and backgrounds enjoyed country and western, rhythm and blues, heavy metal, new wave, jazz, and rap. Music superstars like Michael Jackson, Bruce Springsteen, Whitney Houston, and Queen Latifah sold millions of albums.

Radio, Film, and Television

Advances in the field of communication have also shaped American culture. Radio, film, and television all have become part of everyday life.

Radio. During the 1920s, radio stations began to broadcast across the nation. They brought news, sports, and entertainment into American homes. Today, radios and cassette recorders almost as small as a credit card allow people to listen to music anywhere.

Movies. Motion-picture film revolutionized American culture as well. The first movie theaters opened in the early 1900s. Until 1927, movies were silent—that is, they had no sound track. Audiences read subtitles to follow the plot. Today, some movie theaters offer not one movie, but a choice of seven or eight.

Television. Television began in the United States in the late 1940s. By the 1950s, millions of Americans began to buy television sets. Today, almost every home has at least one set. Also, more people now buy VCRs, or videocassette recorders, which allow them to record programs or buy or rent movies to watch at home.

Radio, movies, and television allow Americans to share experiences. They also help to inform the public. For example, millions of Americans can watch candidates for President debate on television. Viewers may then use this information to help them decide for whom they will vote in an upcoming election.

Cable TV. At the same time, the growing number of radio stations and television channels have increased the variety of programs available. Cable television offers programs for country-and-western music fans, home shoppers, and comedy lovers. Local channels allow ordinary citizens a chance to air their own programs. Channels like the Spanish Information Network (SIN) serve a variety of audiences and groups.

Technology and Tomorrow

In July 1969, American astronaut Neil Armstrong stepped out of a lunar landing craft onto the surface of the moon. "That's one small step for a man, one giant leap for mankind," he announced. Armstrong was the first person to walk on the moon. The moon landing was only one example of the effects of high technology.

Since the 1940s, a revolution in processing information by computer has affected every part of American life. Businesses use computers to print documents, keep bank records, or program factory robots. Doctors can look inside the brain and other organs using computer-assisted X-ray scanning—CAT scan, for short. Personal computers in the home help students to write papers and parents to balance checkbooks and keep records.

Technology has helped to tie together a diverse nation. As American society becomes more complex, the nation needs ways to weave together its many different regions, groups, and traditions. Even more than in Walt Whitman's day, we are a "teeming nation of nations."

Traffic Report *Advances in communication have changed the way Americans live. Here, a helicopter pilot reports on traffic conditions for station KRON-TV during rush hour in San Francisco.* **Daily Life** *How have improved communications helped to bring Americans together?*

SECTION 1 REVIEW

1. **Locate:** (a) Italy, (b) Poland, (c) Russia, (d) Hungary, (e) China, (f) Korea, (g) Vietnam, (h) Philippine Islands.
2. **Identify:** (a) Carlos Bulosan, (b) Neil Armstrong.
3. Why did immigrants of the late 1800s face discrimination?
4. Why did people move to the Sunbelt in the 1970s and 1980s?
5. How have computers affected American life?
6. **Comparing** How are Walt Whitman's and Carlos Bulosan's views of America similar?

2 The New Industrial America

FIND OUT

◆ How did railroads boost industry?

◆ What changes in business took place after the Civil War?

◆ How have jobs changed in the 1900s?

◆ VOCABULARY corporation, monopoly

At the end of the Civil War, taking a train usually meant inconvenience and delay. Passengers had no place to eat or sleep. And more often than not, they would have to wait while workers fixed a derailed car or repaired a broken bridge ahead.

Less than 20 years later, American railroads had been transformed. T. S. Hudson, a British tourist, boasted about his "scamper through America." In 1882, he boarded a train outfitted with luxurious Pullman sleeping cars. For seventy-five cents, he bought on board a breakfast of hot breads, eggs, sausage, oysters, and trout. One new river bridge after another allowed the train to speed westward without delay.

The much-improved railroads benefited businesses as well as passengers. By the 1900s, the United States had become a leader in industry. Able to move equipment and products quickly from one place to another, railroads were the key to linking together distant sections of the new industrial nation.

Linking the Nation Together

After 1865, the railroad system expanded quickly. Railroad owners combined small lines with large systems. Cornelius Vanderbilt, for example, bought up all the rail lines between New York City and Chicago. This meant that goods loaded in Chicago rode on the same car of the New York Central Railroad all the way to New York City.

As a result, the cost of shipping freight by rail dropped sharply.

Transcontinental railroads. In 1869, the first railroad to span the country was completed. Heading west, workers for the Union Pacific Railroad laid tracks from Omaha, across the Great Plains, and through the Rocky Mountains. Meanwhile, crews of the Central Pacific Railroad began in Sacramento and hacked through the granite peaks of the Sierra Nevada. The two railroads joined their routes at Promontory Point, Utah.

By 1893, five cross-country railroads spanned the nation. These railroads opened the West to settlement by cattle ranchers and farmers. As settlers from the East moved onto the Great Plains, war broke out with Native Americans living there. In the end, the United States Army was victorious. Forced to move onto reservations, Plains Indians suffered a painful end to their way of life.

The expanding rail system gave a boost to industry. Just building the railroads created a huge demand for coal, iron, steel, and lumber. And the railroads opened up

Searching for a New Home *The arrival of white settlers on the Great Plains meant the end of a way of life for Native Americans living there. This painting by Charles Russell shows Indian women riding the plains in search of a new home.* **Economics** *How did the growth of railroads help to end the way of life of Plains Indians?*

new markets in towns and villages across the nation.

The automobile. A second revolution in transportation came in the 1900s, with the coming of automobiles, trucks, and airplanes. In 1900, cars were still novelties. Only 4,000 "horseless carriages" chugged along America's dirt roads. But Henry Ford developed an assembly line that made it possible to put cars together quickly and efficiently. He compared making a car with making any other product:

> **❝**The way to make automobiles is to make one automobile like another automobile . . . just as one pin is like another pin when it comes from a pin factory, or one match is like another match when it comes from a match factory.**❞**

The assembly line reduced costs, so more people could afford a car. "Better and cheaper," said Ford. "We'll build more of them, and cheaper." By 1920, more than 9 million cars were on the roads. By the mid-1980s, that number had skyrocketed to more than 320 million.

The airplane. In 1903, two bicycle mechanics, Orville and Wilbur Wright, made history by building the first successful airplane. The first passenger airline in the United States began service in 1914. Airplanes were also used during World War I (1914–1918).

After the war, planes moved more and more mail, freight, and passengers. During World War II (1939–1945), jet engines were first developed. Today, jets carry goods and people to all parts of the world in record time. Wide-bodied jumbo jets carry 500 people at one time. Military jets fly faster than the speed of sound.

A Flood of Inventions

The automobile and airplane were only two of the many inventions that changed

Making Steel in Birmingham, Alabama *The Bessemer process revolutionized the steel industry. This painting by Alabama artist Richard Coe shows the fiery might of the blast furnaces that transformed pig iron into high-grade steel.* **Technology** *What was the advantage of the Bessemer process?*

American life. During the late 1800s, a flood of inventions fueled the development of American industry. From 1790 to 1860, the United States patent office issued 36,000 patents for new inventions. But from 1860 to 1890, the number jumped to more than half a million.

A boost for the steel industry. Some inventions, such as the automobile, led to the creation of new industries. Others made it possible to produce vital goods more quickly and cheaply. For example, in the 1850s, a new way to produce steel was developed. With the Bessemer process, as it was called, high-grade steel could be made much more cheaply than before.

Cheaper high-grade steel found many uses. Long-lasting steel rails replaced iron

A Nation of Inventors

Inventor	Date	Invention
Anna Baldwin	1878	milking machine
Thomas Alva Edison	1879	incandescent bulb
James Ritty	1879	cash register
Jan E. Matzeliger	1882	shoemaking machine
Lewis E. Waterman	1884	fountain pen
Elihu Thomas	1886	electric welding machine
Granville Woods	1887	automatic air brake
King C. Gillette	1888	safety razor with throw-away blades
George H. Wheeler and Jesse W. Reno	1892	escalator
Charles and J. Frank Duryea	1893	gasoline-powered car
Leo H. Baekeland	1909	plastic
Willis Carrier	1911	air conditioner
Vladimir Kosma Zworykin	1923	video camera
Bell Telephone Laboratories	1947	transistor
Edwin Herbert Land	1947	instant camera
Francis Melvin Rogallo	1948	hang glider
Clarence Birdseye	1949	food-dehydrating process
IBM	1965	word processor
Raymond Zukauskas	1980	self-cleaning gutter
Robert Jarvik	1982	artificial heart

CHART SKILLS *Americans have been pioneers in scientific research and practical inventions.* ◆ *Which invention shown on the chart do you think had the greatest impact on American life? Explain.*

rails on the nation's railroads. Strong steel girders supported skyscrapers, or buildings of 20 stories or more. Steel also was used for smaller items such as nails, screws, needles, bolts, barrel hoops, and barbed wire. Today, steel remains an important material in cars and buildings as well as in consumer goods such as stainless-steel pans and tableware.

Advances in the laboratory. No one did more to organize inventing into a scientific system than Thomas Alva Edison. During the late 1800s, Edison set up the first modern research laboratory.

Out of the laboratory came hundreds of new products, including the phonograph, sound motion picture, and electric light bulb. Edison also developed the first electric power plant. Soon, streets, businesses, and houses were brightened by electric lights. Today, many companies have huge research laboratories that produce thousands of inventions every year.

New Business Ways

Before the Civil War, most businesses were small and often run by a single family. They usually sold their products in their own or neighboring villages, towns, and cities. After the Civil War, demands for products caused businesses to grow.

A new age of corporations. During the late 1800s, businesses developed new ways to run more efficiently. Many businesses became corporations. A corporation is a business owned by investors who buy shares of stock. By allowing thousands of investors to buy stock, corporations could raise the millions of dollars they needed to build huge factories and hire hundreds of workers.

The rapid growth of industry in the late 1800s caused problems, however. In many industries, single companies became large enough to force almost all other companies out of business. When one company gained control of a certain industry, it became a monopoly. Monopolies dominated steel, oil, and sugar production, as well as other industries.

Government regulation. Reformers in the late 1800s and early 1900s fought for government regulation of industry to prevent the abuses of monopolies. Many monopolies were broken up under Presidents Theodore Roosevelt, William Howard Taft, and Woodrow Wilson.

Today, government regulations prevent any one company from gaining a monopoly in an industry. Yet many modern companies are far larger than the monopolies of the late 1800s. Often, a single corporation owns a large number of smaller companies in different fields. For example, one conglomerate, as it is called, might own a bus company, a cosmetic company, a toy company, a frozen-food company, and a football team.

The Labor Force

The rise of large industries changed the daily lives of American workers. Many of the new factories were dangerous places to work. They were poorly lighted and had few windows, so there was little fresh air. Textile workers inhaled dust and fibers. In steel mills, workers stood only inches away from vats of hissing, molten steel. Children often worked long hours in strenuous jobs like coal mining.

The first labor unions. Like business leaders, workers pioneered new organizations. To protect themselves against poor working conditions and long hours, some workers joined together in labor unions. The first national union of skilled and unskilled workers, the Knights of Labor, was founded in 1869.

The early labor unions were unpopular with factory owners and much of the American public. Strikers in the late 1800s often were arrested—and sometimes fired at—by police or army troops.

Slowly, unions won acceptance in many industries. In 1935, during the Great Depression, Congress passed a law making it legal for workers to form unions to bargain with factory owners. By 1940, there were 9 million workers in unions. Large labor unions, like large corporations, became an accepted part of American business.

A shifting job market. Today, economic changes are again affecting the work that people do. In some industries, computers direct the operation of labor-saving robots. Skilled workers program the computers

At Work in a Textile Mill *Factory work—and factory workers—have changed greatly since the late 1800s. Early factories were dangerous places to work, and the labor force was often made up of children. Today, improvements in technology have made factory work safer, and child labor is forbidden by law. These pictures of a textile mill of the late 1800s, at left, and a similar mill today show some of the changes that have occurred.* **Technology** *How has technology made factory work safer? How has it made factory work more dangerous?*

and maintain the equipment. In other industries, newly developed chemicals are possible hazards for workers. Often, the long-range health effects of new products are not known for many years.

More people today are working in white-collar, or professional, occupations and service jobs. They sell insurance, videocassette recorders, and automobiles. They program computers, repair washing machines, work in restaurants, maintain jetliners, and deliver newspapers.

Foreign Competition

In the 1900s, the United States developed a healthy foreign trade. It exported far more goods than it imported.

During the 1980s, however, American industries faced strong competition from other countries. In Japan, for example, factories were newer and more efficient. Also, wages were lower. So Japan was able to produce and sell goods more cheaply.

American industries have taken steps to overcome foreign competition. Many have improved their plants and products. Some have asked the government to limit foreign imports by imposing tariffs.

SECTION 2 REVIEW

1. **Identify:** (a) Henry Ford, (b) Orville and Wilbur Wright, (c) Thomas Alva Edison, (d) Knights of Labor.
2. **Define:** (a) corporation, (b) monopoly.
3. (a) How did transcontinental railroads affect the West? (b) How did railroads boost industry?
4. (a) How did monopolies grow? (b) Why are there no monopolies today?
5. Why did labor unions form in the late 1800s?
6. What changes have affected the work that people do today?
7. **Synthesizing Information** How did inventions affect economic growth?

3 A Changing Government

FIND OUT

◆ How have the rights of African Americans changed since the Civil War?

◆ How did women gain suffrage?

◆ Why did the federal government expand its role in the economy?

◆ VOCABULARY initiative, referendum, recall

In December 1916, President Woodrow Wilson appeared in the House of Representatives to read his annual message to Congress. The members sat listening quietly. Suddenly, in the front row of the visitors' gallery above, six women leaned over the edge of the balcony. They unrolled a yellow banner in front of Wilson. In bold letters, the banner read, "Mr. President, what will you do for woman suffrage?"

Wilson smiled faintly and then continued with his speech. But the doorkeeper for the House took action. Running up the aisle, he jumped up to pull the banner down. On the third try, he yanked it from the women. But the protesters had made their point. Newspapers carried the story across the nation.

These and other actions by women finally convinced President Wilson to join the campaign for woman suffrage. In the years after the Civil War, many citizens worked to ensure individual rights and bring about other reforms in government.

Winning the Full Rights of Citizenship

Today, all American citizens over age 18 have the right to vote. In 1860, however, only white men age 21 or over could vote. Winning the right to vote, as well as other rights of citizenship, for other groups of Americans became an ongoing struggle.

Rights for African Americans. The Fifteenth Amendment, ratified in 1870, stated that an adult male citizen could not be prevented from voting because of his race.

Moving North *African Americans have faced discrimination in many areas. This painting by Jacob Lawrence shows a group of African Americans setting out in search of a better life.* **Citizenship** *Which amendment guaranteed African Americans the right to vote?*

This officially extended the right to vote to black men.

After Reconstruction, however, southern states passed laws to make it difficult or impossible for African Americans to vote. Other laws kept blacks and whites from associating in public places. In the North, too, African Americans faced discrimination in many areas.

Even though many could not vote, African Americans fought for their country in World War I and World War II. But they were forced to serve in segregated regiments. Not until 1948 was the military integrated, by order of President Harry Truman. In the Korean War, blacks and whites fought side by side in the same regiments.

San Francisco's Chinatown *San Francisco, California, is home to one of the largest Chinese communities outside Asia. Many of the city's first Chinese came during the California Gold Rush in 1849. Thousands of others arrived in the 1860s to help build the nation's railroads. This painting shows a street market in San Francisco's Chinatown in the mid-1800s.* **Citizenship** *How were Asians treated differently from other immigrants?*

Civil rights movement. Beginning in the 1950s and 1960s, African Americans began a new campaign for equal treatment under the law. The Reverend Martin Luther King, Jr., led nonviolent protests against segregation. His marches often met violent opposition. But that only increased his support. Time after time, King encouraged his followers to keep up their efforts:

“If we protest courageously, and yet with dignity and Christian love, when the future history books are written, somebody will have to say, 'There lived a race of people, of black people, of people who had the moral courage to stand up for their rights.'”

In response, Congress passed civil rights laws to help end racial segregation and discrimination. The Voting Rights Act of 1965 protected African Americans who wanted to register to vote. In 1964, only 35 percent of southern blacks were registered to vote. By 1969, almost 65 percent were registered. In 1984, Jesse Jackson became the first black man to seek the presidential nomination of a major party. Jackson tried again in 1988, encouraging many black Americans to register and vote.

Citizenship for Asian immigrants. Most immigrants who came to the United States could become naturalized citizens after a number of years. But a law passed in 1790 allowed only "white" immigrants to become naturalized citizens.

Under this system, Asian immigrants were denied full participation in American life. Unlike other immigrants, they could not become citizens and vote. In states that allowed only citizens to own property, Asian immigrants could not own houses, farms, or businesses.

Takao Ozawa, a Japanese immigrant who had lived in the United States more than 20 years, challenged the law as unfair. But in 1922, the Supreme Court ruled against him. Only in 1952 did Congress allow Asian immigrants to become naturalized citizens.

Women's rights. Women won the right to vote when the Nineteenth Amendment was ratified in 1920. But the struggle had begun much earlier. The Seneca Falls Convention in 1848 passed a resolution demanding suffrage for women. (See page 492.) During the late 1800s and early 1900s, women's organizations continued the campaign for the vote.

The campaign was often long and hard. Women organized protests in Congress and around the White House. Across the country, "suffragettes" tried to win support wherever they could. One suffragette told of her campaign on a train trip in Kansas:

> **❝**About a dozen passengers were in the caboose . . . and we held a meeting and discussion which lasted about 45 minutes. Upon reaching Osborne at three o'clock I found about 100 people assembled for an auction sale in the middle of the street. . . . The temptation to hold a meeting overcame fatigue. I jumped into an automobile nearby and had a most interested crowd until the auctioneer came.**❞**

By 1919, women in many states could vote in state and local elections. The Nineteenth Amendment gave women the right to vote in presidential elections as well.

During the 1960s, women won greater civil and economic rights. Federal laws made it illegal to favor men over women when hiring or paying wages. In the 1970s and 1980s, women made important gains in politics. The candidacy of Geraldine Ferraro for Vice President in 1984 reflected the growing strength of women in politics.

The vote for 18-year-olds. In March 1971, Congress passed the Twenty-sixth Amendment. This amendment guaranteed the right to vote to persons age 18 or older. At the time, soldiers as young as age 18 were fighting and dying in the Vietnam War. The amendment won wholehearted support, and it was ratified in less than four months.

Representative Angie Perez *Women have made important gains in many areas in recent years. Here, Angie Perez, a member of the New Mexico state assembly, reviews plans for a health care facility.* **Local History** *What women hold political office in your state?*

A Growing Role for Voters

As new groups of Americans gained the right to vote, voters also won new powers. In some states, voters today can introduce a bill to the legislature by collecting signatures on a petition. This process is called an **initiative.** In a **referendum,** people vote directly on a bill. In some states, voters also have the power to remove a person from office in a **recall** election.

The initiative, referendum, and recall were ideas supported by reformers in the early 1900s. These reformers were called Progressives. Progressives also supported primary elections and direct election of senators. In a primary, voters from each political party decide who will be their party's candidate in the general election. The creation of primaries meant that political bosses could no longer handpick candidates.

The Constitution originally called for senators to be chosen by state legislatures. The Seventeenth Amendment, which was ratified in 1913, gave voters in each state the right to elect two senators.

Research for Space and Ecology *In the airtight chamber shown here, NASA space scientists are developing a "closed-loop life support system." Just by breathing, astronauts will supply enough carbon dioxide to sustain a collection of plants. The plants, in turn, will give off enough oxygen to sustain the astronauts. Closer to home, this project offers valuable insights into ways to protect the Earth's fragile ecology.* **Daily Life** *What other steps have Americans taken to protect the environment?*

A More Active Federal Government

As the nation has expanded, the role of the federal government has grown. Often, the government has stepped in to help or protect Americans.

Regulation of business. In the late 1800s, for example, the growth of industry created large new businesses worth millions of dollars. These new businesses sometimes used their power and influence unfairly. Reformers called on Congress to regulate large businesses and protect ordinary workers and citizens. Congress created the Interstate Commerce Commission, or ICC, in 1887. The ICC looked into complaints and took some big companies to court.

Government-sponsored programs. During the 1900s, the government became increasingly involved in the lives of Americans. One of the major turning points grew out of the Great Depression of the 1930s. During the depression, millions of workers were thrown out of work, and many farmers lost their land.

In 1933, when the depression was at its worst, Franklin Delano Roosevelt became President. With the help of Congress, he set up many new programs to relieve the suffering of the unemployed. The government also sponsored public-works programs. These put unemployed men and women to work on projects such as the creation of dams, schools, and parks.

Questions about regulation. Since the 1930s, government has been faced with other questions. Should it regulate the dangerous gases that pour from factory smokestacks? Should it protect consumers from foods and medicines that might be harmful? Should it inspect shops and factories to make sure they are safe for workers? The federal government now regulates each of these areas, as well as many others.

In the 1980s, new areas of environmental concern raised additional questions. Americans debated whether the government should act to curb acid rain that can damage crops and trees. They also wondered whether human activities such as cutting down forests and burning gas, oil, and coal are causing a dangerous increase in the Earth's temperatures. Whatever the answers to these questions, Americans realized that the way they live has long-term effects on the Earth.

Americans also began to worry about the high costs of government programs and of enforcing government regulations. They worried, too, that the federal government had too much power. In 1980 and again in 1984, Americans elected Ronald Reagan to be President in part because he promised to cut taxes and reduce government regulation. Still, the government continues to play an active role in many areas of American life.

4 Looking Abroad

FIND OUT

◆ Why did the United States become more active in world affairs?

◆ What part did the United States play in the two world wars?

◆ How has American foreign policy changed since the end of World War II?

In 1858, three years before the Civil War, New Yorkers paraded through their city streets amid bonfires and fireworks. The celebration was in honor of Cyrus Field, who had just laid the first successful wire cable across the Atlantic Ocean.

For the first time, telegraph messages passed instantly between England and the United States. But the celebration had begun too soon. A few weeks later, the telegraph was silent. Somewhere in the deep Atlantic, the cable had broken.

The Civil War disrupted Field's plans to lay a stronger cable. But in 1866, he hired the largest steamship in the world, the *Great Eastern*. Powered by huge paddle wheels, the ship steamed east from Ireland. Carefully, it lowered a total of 1,900 miles (3,058 km) of wire into the ocean. This time, the line did not break.

In the years after the Civil War, Field's transatlantic cable drew the nations of the world together. Railroads and oceangoing steamers also cut travel time on land and sea. Because of these and other changes, the United States became more involved in world affairs.

Growing Involvement in World Affairs

During its first 100 years, the United States paid little attention to world affairs. Washington, Jefferson, and other Presidents hoped that the nation could grow and prosper without becoming entangled in foreign wars or other disputes.

Foreign trade. In time, however, the United States began to export food and manufactured goods to foreign countries. Europe was the most important market. But after the Civil War, trade with China, Japan, Korea, and the countries of Latin America also grew.

In 1853, for example, Isaac Singer opened a factory that manufactured sewing machines. He soon saw that his machines would be in demand in Europe as well as in the United States. Before long, sewing-machine sales representatives began to travel to China and the islands of the South Pacific. By 1900, more than 60,000 Singer machine agents were located throughout the world.

Trade with Asia. As American trade was growing, European countries were building empires in Africa and Asia. These empires increased the power and wealth of European nations. Americans feared that they would be squeezed out of many foreign markets. More and more, they began to look toward Asia. In Congress, Senator Albert Beveridge of Indiana urged an increase in trade:

> **"**Our largest trade henceforth must be with Asia. The Pacific is our ocean. . . . China is our natural customer. . . . That statesman commits a crime against American trade . . . who fails to put America where she may command that trade.**"**

In 1898, the United States annexed Hawaii, whose fine harbors provided a base for the American navy. From there, trading ships could sail to Asia. This meant that the United States could open and protect markets in Asia.

New territories. The Spanish-American War of 1898 also gave the United States new territories. The war broke out as a result of a dispute over Spanish actions in Cuba. American troops quickly defeated the Spanish.

Under the peace treaty, the formerly Spanish islands of Puerto Rico in the Caribbean and Guam and the Philippines in the Pacific became territories of the United States. Cuba became an independent nation.

Relations With Latin America

The United States also took a more active role in Latin America. In 1901, Theodore Roosevelt became President. His motto was "Speak softly, but carry a big stick." By this, he meant that the United States would strive for peace but not shy away from using force when necessary.

Roosevelt used the "big stick" in Latin America. Several European countries were trying to influence Venezuela and the Dominican Republic. Roosevelt reminded them that under President Monroe, the United States had warned against European powers meddling in the Americas. (See page 389.) Roosevelt was the second President to use the Monroe Doctrine as an active policy in the region.

Throughout the 1900s, the United States has intervened in Latin America in

Teddy Roosevelt Wields the "Big Stick" *President Theodore Roosevelt believed that the United States had the "regrettable but necessary . . . duty" to act as an international policeman. In this 1904 cartoon, TR, as he was called, uses his "big stick" to maintain order around the world.* **United States and the World** *How do Americans feel today about the policies of a "big stick"?*

Americans in World War II
World War II was fought in both Europe and the Pacific. This painting shows the landing of American troops on the tiny island of Corregidor, in the Philippines. **United States and the World** *What event led the United States to enter World War II?*

order to protect American interests. President William Howard Taft, for example, sent troops into Nicaragua and Honduras. President Woodrow Wilson sent marines to Haiti. President Ronald Reagan ordered troops to invade Grenada. And more recently, President George Bush ordered troops into Panama.

Over the years, Americans have debated the policies of a "big stick." Opponents argue that the United States has made enemies by intervening in the internal affairs of weaker nations. Supporters respond that the United States has served as a needed police officer in the area.

The World at War

In 1914, World War I broke out in Europe. At first, President Wilson declared neutrality. But in 1917, the United States entered the war on the side of Britain and its allies. When peace came in 1918, many Americans no longer wanted to be involved in world affairs. These people were called isolationists.

In the 1930s, the nations of Europe again moved toward war. In Germany, the dictator Adolf Hitler ruled with absolute power. In 1939, war broke out when Hitler invaded neighboring Poland. Italy and Japan sided with Hitler, forming the Axis powers. They fought against the Allies, which included Britain, France, and the Soviet Union.

Again, the United States tried to remain at peace. But on December 7, 1941, the Japanese launched a surprise attack on Pearl Harbor in Hawaii. Congress declared war on the Axis powers. After four years of war and millions of deaths, the Allies defeated Germany and Italy. The war against Japan did not end until American planes dropped atomic bombs on the Japanese cities of Hiroshima and Nagasaki.

The United States as a World Power

At the end of World War II, much of Europe lay in ashes. Homes had no heat, city streets were dark, and the war-weary were starving. To help Europe's battered economy, the United States created the Marshall Plan. Under the plan, the United States gave billions of dollars to rebuild factories and railroads in Europe.

Rivalry with the Soviet Union. Soon after the end of World War II, the United States became concerned about the Soviet Union. The two nations had been allies during the war. But after the war, the Soviets helped communists to take over countries in Eastern Europe. To contain Soviet influence, the United States and the nations of Western Europe formed the North Atlantic Treaty Organization, or NATO.

Rivalry between the United States and the Soviet Union never broke out into armed conflict. With nuclear missiles pointed at each other, that prospect became too frightening. But the tension and hostility between the two superpowers became known as the Cold War.

Wars in Asia. Twice, American troops fought wars to contain communist expansion. From 1950 to 1953, American troops under United Nations command turned back an invasion of South Korea by communist North Korea.

In the 1960s and 1970s, American soldiers fought in Vietnam against communist rebels. Many Americans, especially young people, protested. They said that the conflict in Vietnam was a civil war and that it did not threaten American security. In the early 1970s, the troops finally returned home. But more than 57,000 Americans had lost their lives in the nation's longest war.

Hopes for peace and democracy. After 1985, superpower tensions began to ease as Premier Mikhail Gorbachev (mee kah EEL gor buh CHAWF) promised economic and democratic reforms in the Soviet Union. In 1989, countries in Eastern Europe rejected their communist governments. But as the 1990s began, the peoples of Eastern Europe and the Soviet Union still struggled to bring more freedom to their economies and political systems.

Regional Involvement

The United States has been involved in other troubled regions of the world. In the Middle East, it has tried to bring about peace between its chief ally in the region, Israel, and Israel's Arab neighbors.

In 1990, new tensions broke out in the Middle East. Iraq invaded the oil-rich kingdom of Kuwait. The United Nations set up an embargo, closing off Iraq's foreign trade. When Iraq refused to withdraw from Kuwait, the United States and its allies went to war with Iraq in January 1991.

Americans have tried to help other peoples of the Third World. The Third World includes many countries in Africa, Asia,

American Troops in the Persian Gulf *In 1990, hundreds of thousands of American troops were sent to Saudi Arabia to pressure Iraq to withdraw from Kuwait. Here, President Bush visits the troops before the outbreak of war.* **United States and the World** *What action did the United Nations take to convince Iraq to withdraw from Kuwait?*

Ready for the Future *The United States faces many challenges as it approaches a new century. Still, Americans, like these people proudly displaying the flag, look to the future with confidence in themselves and their nation.* **Citizenship** *What do you think is the greatest challenge the nation faces in the next century? How can Americans meet the challenge?*

and Latin America that are beginning to industrialize. Most are very poor. The United States gives billions of dollars every year to help Third World nations develop their economies. But the problems of these countries are hard to solve.

The United States has given foreign aid in part because poverty can cause political problems. In poor countries, rebels have often won the support of the people by promising to distribute the wealth more evenly. In 1959 in Cuba, Fidel Castro led a successful revolution. After winning power, he angered the United States because he made Cuba a strong ally of the Soviet Union. Today, some Americans still fear that communism will take hold in Central America.

As citizens of a superpower, Americans face a world filled with difficult problems. People do not always agree on what action to take. But Americans no longer expect to return to the days when a nation could ignore events in the rest of the world.

The Journey of a Free People

In this book, you have read about the American journey to 1877. At times, the journey was hard. But the same spirit that sent sailors like Christopher Columbus across the Atlantic Ocean continued to inspire Americans to face new challenges and launch new ventures.

Since 1877, people of many backgrounds have contributed to the history of our nation. They have helped to make the United States an industrial power and a world leader. As the American journey continues, each generation builds in its own way on the proud traditions of a free people.

SECTION 4 REVIEW

1. **Locate:** (a) Hawaii, (b) Puerto Rico, (c) Cuba, (d) Soviet Union, (e) Israel, (f) Iraq, (g) Kuwait.
2. **Identify:** (a) Cyrus Field, (b) Theodore Roosevelt, (c) Adolf Hitler, (d) Mikhail Gorbachev.
3. How did the United States acquire Puerto Rico, Guam, and the Philippines?
4. What was President Theodore Roosevelt's policy in Latin America?
5. (a) How did Americans feel about world involvement after World War I? (b) How did the United States help Europe after World War II?
6. **Synthesizing Information** Do you think it is possible for the United States to be isolationist today? Explain.

Presidents of the United States, 1877–Present

President	Dates	Major Events
Rutherford B. Hayes	1877–1881	Reconstruction ends; light bulb invented; millions of European immigrants arrive
James A. Garfield	1881	Booker T. Washington founds Tuskegee Institute; Garfield assassinated
Chester A. Arthur	1881–1885	First electric power plant and skyscraper; Civil Service Commission curbs spoils system
Grover Cleveland	1885–1889	Statue of Liberty unveiled; Interstate Commerce Commission orders railroads to set "reasonable and just rates"
Benjamin Harrison	1889–1893	Sherman Antitrust Act prohibits monopolies
Grover Cleveland	1893–1897	Cuba revolts against Spain; Supreme Court upholds racial segregation in *Plessy* v. *Ferguson*
William McKinley	1897–1901	United States acquires Philippines, Guam, and Puerto Rico; McKinley assassinated
Theodore Roosevelt	1901–1909	Roosevelt defends striking coal workers; Panama grants United States the Canal Zone; Pure Food and Drug Act protects consumers
William H. Taft	1909–1913	National Association for the Advancement of Colored People founded; Pan American Union (21 republics) acts on mutual concerns
Woodrow Wilson	1913–1921	Panama Canal opened; World War I
Warren G. Harding	1921–1923	Harlem Renaissance flourishes; Harding dies
Calvin Coolidge	1923–1929	Lindbergh flies Atlantic; Kellogg-Briand Pact outlaws war except in self-defense
Herbert C. Hoover	1929–1933	Stock market crashes; Great Depression begins; Hitler gains power in Germany
Franklin D. Roosevelt	1933–1945	New Deal creates employment; World War II; Roosevelt dies
Harry S. Truman	1945–1953	United Nations seeks peaceful solutions to international disputes; NATO provides mutual defense for some European nations; Korean War
Dwight D. Eisenhower	1953–1961	Civil rights sit-in movement begins
John F. Kennedy	1961–1963	First American in space; Cuban missile crisis; John Kennedy assassinated
Lyndon B. Johnson	1963–1969	Civil Rights Act bans job discrimination; bombing of North Vietnam begins; Martin Luther King, Jr., and Robert Kennedy assassinated
Richard M. Nixon	1969–1974	Moon landing; Vietnam cease-fire; Watergate hearings; Nixon resigns
Gerald R. Ford	1974–1977	Ford pardons Nixon; South Vietnam falls to North Vietnam
Jimmy Carter	1977–1981	Egypt and Israel sign Camp David peace agreement; Iranians seize American hostages
Ronald W. Reagan	1981–1989	First woman justice appointed to Supreme Court; United States and Soviet Union reduce nuclear forces
George Bush	1989–	Eastern European nations seek democracy; Iraq invades Kuwait; Persian Gulf War

CHART SKILLS *This chart shows the Presidents from Reconstruction to the present.* ◆ *Who was President during World War I? World War II?*

CHAPTER ◇ REVIEW

Understanding Vocabulary

Match each term at left with the correct definition at right.

1. corporation
2. monopoly
3. initiative
4. referendum
5. recall

a. business owned by investors
b. process by which people vote directly on a bill
c. company that controls a certain industry
d. process allowing voters to introduce a bill
e. method of removing a person from office

Reviewing the Main Ideas

1. (a) What "new" immigrants arrived in the late 1800s and early 1900s? (b) What new waves of immigrants arrived in the 1960s, 1970s, and 1980s? (c) How have immigrants contributed to the United States?
2. What advances in communication have affected American culture?
3. How did the Bessemer process affect American industry?
4. What changes have taken place in American business?
5. How did each of the following amendments extend voting rights: (a) Fifteenth; (b) Nineteenth; (c) Twenty-sixth?
6. How has the federal government expanded its role in the economy since the Civil War?
7. Why did the United States seek to increase trade with Asia in the late 1800s?
8. (a) What role did the United States play in World War I and World War II? (b) How has the United States tried to help Third World countries?

Thinking Critically

1. **Linking Past and Present** Compare the dangers that workers faced in factories of the late 1800s and the hazards that workers face today.

2. **Analyzing Ideas** The Reverend Martin Luther King, Jr., led nonviolent protests against segregation. Why do you think this method of protest was successful?
3. **Defending a Position** Do you think the United States should follow a "big stick" policy in Latin America? Explain.
4. **Synthesizing Information** Imagine that you lived in the United States in the late 1800s. What changes would you see taking place in the nation?

Applying Your Skills

1. **Skimming a Chapter** (a) What does the chapter outline tell you about this chapter? (b) List the main topics in Section 3.
2. **Using Photographs as a Primary Source.** Study the photographs on page 612. (a) What is the subject of the photographs? (b) Describe the workers and the machinery shown in the photographs. (c) Based on the photographs, do you think factory conditions are better today than they were 100 years ago? Explain.
3. **Ranking** Make a list of 10 events since the Civil War. Rank them according to the impact you think each has had on American history, beginning with the one with the greatest impact.

◆ VOICES AND VISIONS ◆

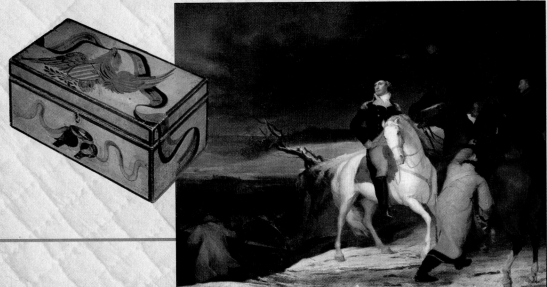

The Americas

A Majestic Landscape *Among the many striking features of the diverse North American landscape are snow-capped mountains, thick pine forests, and breathtaking canyons. This painting by Karl Bodmer captures the rugged beauty and grandeur of the high plains.* **Linking Past and Present** *This picture was painted during the 1800s. How might this landscape have changed since the picture was painted? Why?*

Geography of the Americas

1-1   This Land Is Your Land

 LITERATURE

◆ **INTRODUCTION** Anyone who has ever traveled across America has been impressed by the country's immense size and beauty and by the tremendous variety of its geographic features. During his youth, songwriter Woody Guthrie visited many parts of America. In this song, "This Land Is Your Land," Guthrie draws upon his memories of those travels. The song provides a sense of the scope of America and praises the beauty of its mighty rivers, towering mountains, and fertile valleys.

◆ **VOCABULARY** Before you read the selection, find the meaning of these words in a dictionary: rambled, chanting.

As I was walking that ribbon of highway
I saw above me that endless skyway
I saw below me that golden valley
This land was made for you and me.

Chorus: This land is your land
    This land is my land from Cali-
      fornia to the New York island
    From the red wood forest to the
      Gulf Stream waters
    This land was made for you and
      me.

I've roamed and rambled and followed my
  footsteps
to the sparkling sands of her diamond
  deserts

And all around me a voice was sounding
This land was made for you and me.

Chorus: This land is your land
This land is my land from California to the New York island
From the red wood forest to the Gulf Stream waters
This land was made for you and me.

When the sun comes shining and I was strolling
and the wheat fields waving and the dust clouds rolling
As the fog was lifting a voice was chanting
This land was made for you and me.

Chorus: This land is your land
This land is my land from California to the New York island
From the red wood forest to the Gulf Stream waters
This land was made for you and me.

Source: Woody Guthrie, "This Land Is Your Land" © 1956 (renewed), 1958, 1970 New York: Ludlow Music, Inc. Used by permission.

THINKING ABOUT THE SELECTION

1. How does the songwriter convey a sense of America's vast size?
2. Which physical regions of North America are mentioned in the song?
3. **Applying Information** Use the map on pages 716–717 to locate places named or referred to in "This Land Is Your Land."

The Rugged Coast of Maine *Many features of the American landscape reveal the tremendous power of nature. In this painting, Paul Dougherty portrays the beauty and ruggedness of the Maine coast.* **Geography** *How do you think the harshness of the Maine landscape affected the lives of the people who settled there?*

◆ **INTRODUCTION** Americans like to speak of conquering the wilderness. Indeed, after Europeans began settling North America, that is what they did, from the coastal plains bordering the Atlantic Ocean to the mountain ranges along the Pacific. But many beautiful areas of wilderness remain. Here Minnesota writer Paul Gruchow, who has hiked throughout the West, explains why we need to preserve these empty places.

◆ **VOCABULARY** Before you read the selection, find the meaning of these words in a dictionary: pika, evoke, perseveres, parsimonious, persistence, arduous, void.

Walkers use the . . . maps published by the United States Department of the Interior Geological Survey, on which five and a quarter inches represent a mile. These maps are marvels of clarity and economy. They are printed in four colors: black for place names, brown for contour lines, blue for water, green for forests. The contour lines record every forty-foot change in elevation. Where the going gets rough, the brown lines crowd more and

Traveling by Dog Sled *To survive in the American wilderness, people had to adapt to their environments. As this painting by Paul Kane shows, Native Americans on the northern plains sometimes traveled over the snow-covered land by dog sled.* **Geography** *Why were dog sleds an especially effective method of transportation for people living in northern climates?*

more closely together; in the steepest places, they make almost solid bands of brown. The places I look for on the topographic maps are the ones with lots of brown lines and no green. They will prove rugged and rocky, flowerful in summer and swarming with insects, boggy with meltwater in places and still snow-covered in others, ringing with the bright whistles of pikas.

The maps, I suppose, compromise the idea of wilderness even as they help to evoke it. How absolutely wild can a place be that has already been reduced symbolically to . . . a topographic map? But the maps reassured us that we were headed, at least, toward houseless, roadless, trailless places, toward empty places.

In empty places life perseveres against harsh restrictions of climate or topography. In a sense they always were empty. The places that survive now as wilderness are by nature demanding, uncompromising, parsimonious. The green and rich wilderness places have long since been claimed for human purposes. I like the brittle and severe qualities of the places that remain empty. I like life that has braved the odds, made the best of little, come to terms with conditions that frustrate life in general.

I see, too, an appealing youthfulness in such places. Most of the places on the maps that remain empty are, by geologic measure, very young. The sparse North American grasslands, the Nebraska sandhills, the Sonoran desert, the tundra-covered mountaintops: all are communities that have developed in the recent geologic past. . . .

I like too the idea of life lived at the edge. A spruce tree at the upper limits of a mountain treeline, thick and misshapen, shorn of its branches on its windward side, no more than shoulder high although it may be a century old, such a spruce speaks powerfully of the persistence of life. Every person who enters the wilderness goes in search of the same speech. A journey into the wilderness is a test of the will against the odds. Going into the wilderness, any wilderness, is a way of opening yourself to the possibility of danger and to the likelihood of discomfort, at the least. There is the possibility of getting lost, of being trapped in a storm, of confronting an angry animal, of falling. There are the certain hardships of arduous walks, of exposure to cold, heat, wind, rain, of sleeping on the ground, of solitude. To be alone is sometimes the most difficult challenge of all. . . . Just as the tortured spruce tree at the edge of the upper forest enlarges and frees the world for trees, so our encounters with wilderness widen and free us.

Empty: unoccupied. . . . Empty is one of those words that reveals unspoken attitudes. Lacking people, it means. No humans equals nothing. . . .

Nevertheless some value and meaning clearly resides in such places, as in all places. Despite ourselves and our beliefs, some among us continue . . . to seek them out. We go to a mountaintop, or retreat to the desert, or . . . to some lonely cove along the wide and empty sea. We are drawn toward wildness as water is toward the level. And there we find that something that we cannot name. We find ourselves, we say. But I suppose that what we really find is the void within ourselves, the loneliness, the surviving heart of wildness, that binds us to all the living earth.

Source: Paul Gruchow, *The Necessity of Empty Places* (New York: St. Martin's Press, 1988).

THINKING ABOUT THE SELECTION

1. How does Gruchow use the map to plan where he will hike?
2. What does the author like about wilderness regions?
3. **Expressing an Opinion** What are your feelings about "empty places"? Why?

The First Americans

2-1   "I'm Indian and That's It"   FIRST PERSON

◆ **INTRODUCTION** Among many Native American groups, the old customs died out after Europeans came to America. Some peoples, however, preserved their traditions—not just ways of doing things, but also ways of thinking and believing. Among them are the Chippewa (or Ojibwa), who lived, and still live, near the shores of Lake Superior. Elizabeth Gurno, a Chippewa, was born in Minnesota in the early 1900s. In this selection, she talks about some Native American traditions and what they mean.

◆ **VOCABULARY** Before you read the selection, find the meaning of these words in a dictionary: mainstay, eyesore.

The Indians survived with their hunting and their garden produce. And years ago there was plenty of wild rice. . . . Wild rice has always been our mainstay of life. If you have rice, you are not hungry. Indians believed that at one time or another, we came from the water. Therefore, anything in the water is edible. You can eat it if you know how to cook it.

And then we made maple sugar. . . . Indians took things from Mother Earth. She gave us maple syrup. But with the left hand, we thanked her. I still do this in my family. We had quite a ceremony about that when I was growing up. Same with rice. Even if you don't ask everybody on the reservation to come in and join you, you ask a few people to come in and you give thanks. And with this wild rice, you save up enough maple syrup or sugar to mix with it. Just the two things mixed

together. You eat that. That's a thanksgiving for what Mother Nature has given to you. . . .

There are many things in Indian life that nowadays you'd say don't make sense. We are associated with drums and feathers and that sort of thing. . . . [A] feather in our culture has to be earned. We are born with one feather. That is a gift from our parents. Now my father told me he was given a feather at his birth, and a blanket. And the blanket did not come from J. C. Penney. It was homemade out of rabbit hide. And the mother took nine months to make it. She finished her last stitch the day the baby was born. That was her gift to the baby. . . .

And now these feathers weren't just crow feathers or robin. They were eagle. Years ago, eagles were plentiful, but as the non-Indians moved in with all their concrete, the eagles went other places. . . .

And then we decorated things with porcupine quills. Those quills are very dangerous, but then they were used to decorate anything made out of birch bark. The ends have to be bent. They can go through human flesh. . . . They were dyed with chokecherries and raspberries for red, or pitch from the base of a balsam tree or a beech tree. . . . My grandmother had an art with birch bark that she chewed a design into the thin bark that my uncle would then in turn sew onto another basket. . . .

And she worked in the true Indian spirit. An Indian always has several things in mind when he does things: first, that he's busy with his hands doing some-

A Rich Artistic Tradition
Many Native American groups looked to nature for art as well as survival. This elaborately decorated coffin is the work of the Haidas, a group that lives in what is now Alaska and British Columbia. **Culture** *What do you think might be the purpose of the face carved into the coffin? Explain.*

thing and not wasting his or anybody else's time. Then that he's making something useful and something beautiful to look at—not just an eyesore. And then that he's making something that will tell a story. It had to have meaning. . . .

The sacred colors are white, red, black, yellow, and blue. White is for the north, for the white snow. That, in turn, gives you strength. Red is the east for the sun. Yellow is for the south—for the heat that ripens our staff of life, the corn. And black is for the west. If a storm is coming, look to the west and there will be black clouds. The storm originates in the west. And blue represents man. So in doing any type of work, we try to include one or all of the colors depending on what we're making. . . .

Years back, it was a downright sin to be known as an Indian. It was something to be ashamed of. I couldn't go along with that because my grandmother spoke nothing but Chippewa. I lived in an Indian home. That's the way I breathed. The others picked up English. Then they in turn didn't want their children to speak Chippewa because the government agent told us that was wrong: "You don't look like a white man, but you got to live like one. You have to live like a white man now."

But I'm an Indian. I believe Indian ways. They know I'm Indian and that's it. I cannot erase me. I'm here to stay.

Source: Elizabeth Gurno, "Red is the east for the sun," in Eliot Wigginton, ed., *"I wish I could give my son a wild raccoon."* (Garden City, NY: Anchor Press/Doubleday, 1976).

THINKING ABOUT THE SELECTION

1. What Native American customs involving food does the author describe?
2. According to Gurno, what is the "true Indian spirit" of workmanship?
3. **Analyzing a Quotation** In speaking of her Native American heritage, Gurno says "That's the way I breathed." What do you think she means by that? In what, if any, traditional way do you "breathe"?

2-2   How Fire Came to the Six Nations   LITERATURE

◆ **INTRODUCTION** Information about the lives and beliefs of Native Americans is provided by their legends and folk tales. These stories were passed by word of mouth from generation to generation.

Often, such legends were told to explain forces in nature that are difficult to understand. The Mohawks, one of the Iroquois nations, told the following tale about how humans discovered fire. As you read the selection, you will see that it supplies many details about the Mohawk way of life.

◆ **VOCABULARY** Before you read the selection, find the meaning of these words in a dictionary: attained, ceaseless, balsam, resinous.

Three Arrows was a boy of the Mohawk tribe. Although he had not yet seen fourteen winters he was already known among the Iroquois for his skill and daring. His arrows sped true to their

---

An Algonquin of the Carolinas *Much information about the clothing and traditions of the Algonquin people was preserved in a series of watercolors by John White, an early English settler. In this painting, White shows an Algonquin man in typical clothing.* **Local History** *Why are paintings and sketches an effective means of preserving history?*

---

mark. His name was given him when with three bone-tipped arrows he brought down three flying wild geese from the same flock. He could travel in the forest as softly as the south wind and he was a skillful hunter, but he never killed a bird or animal unless his clan needed food. He was well-versed in woodcraft, fleet of foot, and a clever wrestler. His people said, "Soon he will be a chief like his father."

The sun shone strong in the heart of Three Arrows, because soon he would have to meet the test of strength and endurance through which the boys of his clan attained manhood. He had no fear of the outcome of the dream fast which he was so soon to take. His father was a great chief and a good man, and the boy's life had been patterned after that of his father.

When the grass was knee-high, Three Arrows left his village with his father. They climbed to a sacred place in the mountains. They found a narrow cave at the back of a little plateau. Here Three Arrows decided to live for his few days of prayer and vigil. He was not permitted to eat anything during the days and nights of his dream fast. He had no weapons, and his only clothing was a breechclout* and moccasins. His father left the boy with a promise that he would visit him every day that the ceremony lasted, at dawn.

Three Arrows prayed to the Great Spirit. He begged that soon his clan spirit would appear in a dream and tell him what his guardian animal or bird was to be. When he knew this, he would adopt that bird or animal as his special guardian for the rest of his life. When the dream came he would be free to return to his people, his dream fast successfully achieved.

For five suns Three Arrows spent his days and nights on the rocky plateau, only climbing down to a little spring for water

---

*loincloth

after each sunset. His heart was filled with a dark cloud because that morning his father had sadly warned him that the next day, the sixth sun, he must return to his village even if no dream had come to him in the night. This meant returning to his people in disgrace without the chance of taking another dream fast.

That night Three Arrows, weak from hunger and weary from ceaseless watch, cried out to the Great Mystery. "O Great Spirit, have pity on him who stands humbly before Thee. Let his clan spirit or a sign from beyond the thunderbird come to him before tomorrow's sunrise, if it be Thy will." As he prayed, the wind suddenly veered from east to north. This cheered Three Arrows because the wind was now the wind of the great bear, and the bear was the totem of his clan.

When he entered the cavern he smelled for the first time the unmistakable odor of a bear: this was strong medicine. He crouched at the opening of the cave, too excited to lie down although his tired body craved rest. As he gazed out into the night he heard the rumble of thunder, saw the lightning flash, and felt the fierce breath of the wind from the north. Suddenly a vision came to him, and a gigantic bear stood beside him in the cave. Then Three Arrows heard it say, "Listen well, Mohawk. Your clan spirit has heard your prayer. Tonight you will learn a great mystery which will bring help and gladness to all your people." A terrible clash of thunder brought the dazed boy to his feet as the bear disappeared. He looked from the cave just as a streak of lightning flashed across the sky in the form of a blazing arrow. Was this the sign from the thunderbird?

Suddenly the air was filled with a fearful sound. A shrill shrieking came from the ledge just above the cave. It sounded as though mountain lions fought in the storm; yet Three Arrows felt no fear as he climbed toward the ledge. As his keen eyes grew accustomed to the dim light, he saw that the force of the wind was causing two young balsam trees to rub violently against each other. The strange noise was caused by friction, and as he listened and watched fear filled his heart, for, from where the two trees rubbed together a flash of lightning showed smoke.

Fascinated, he watched until flickers of flame followed the smoke. He had never seen fire of any kind at close range nor had any of his people. He scrambled down to the cave and covered his eyes in dread of this strange magic. Then he smelt bear again and he thought of his vision, his clan spirit, the bear, and its message. This was the mystery he was to reveal to his people. The blazing arrow in the sky was to be his totem, and his new name—Blazing Arrow.

At daybreak, Blazing Arrow climbed onto the ledge and broke two dried sticks from what remained of one of the balsams. He rubbed them violently together, but nothing happened. "The magic is too powerful for me," he thought. Then a picture of his clan and village formed in his mind, and he patiently rubbed the hot sticks together again. His will power took the place of his tired muscles. Soon a little wisp of smoke greeted his renewed efforts, then came a bright spark on one of the sticks. Blazing Arrow waved it as he had seen the fiery arrow wave in the night sky. A resinous blister on the stick glowed, then flamed— fire had come to the Six Nations!

Source: Allan A. Macfarlan, *Fireside Book of North American Indian Folktales* (Harrisburg, PA: Stackpole Books, 1974).

THINKING ABOUT THE SELECTION

1. What test did the boys of Three Arrows' tribe have to pass to attain manhood?
2. Why did Three Arrows think he was about to receive a sign from the thunderbird?
3. **Drawing Conclusions** Why was Three Arrows afraid when he saw fire?

◆ **INTRODUCTION** When Cortés and his soldiers landed in Mexico, the Aztec emperor Montezuma showered them with gifts. In the following essay, William Carlos Williams (1883–1963), a famous American poet and writer who had a great interest in history, describes those lavish gifts. He also paints a vivid picture of the Aztec capital city Tenochtitlán and of the first meeting between Cortés and Montezuma. Yet Williams does not offer an interpretation of the events. He believed in presenting vivid images that speak for themselves.

◆ **VOCABULARY** Before you read the selection, find the meaning of these words in a dictionary: whetted, hewn, interceded, palpable, sally, semblance, aborigines, regent.

Montezuma immediately sent gifts, at the same time begging the Spaniard not to risk coming up into the back country: a gold necklace of seven pieces, set with many gems like small rubies, a hundred and eighty-three emeralds and ten fine pearls, and hung with twenty-seven little bells of gold. Two wheels, one of gold like the sun and the other of silver, with the image of the moon upon it. . . . A shield of wood and leather, with little bells hanging to it and covered with plates of gold, in the middle of which was cut the image of the god of war between four heads of a lion, a tiger, an eagle, and an owl represented alive with their hair and feathers. Twenty-four curious and beautiful shields

of gold, of feathers and very small pearls, and four of feathers and silver only. Four fishes, two ducks and some other birds of molten gold. . . . And books made of tablets with a smooth surface for writing, which being joined might be folded together or stretched out to a considerable length, "the characters inscribed thereon resembling nothing so much as Egyptian hieroglyphics."

But Cortez* was unwilling to turn back; rather these things whetted his appetite for the adventure. Without more ado he sent letters to his king advising him that having come to these lands to conquer them, in the royal name and that of the true church, he would forthwith proceed to take Montezuma, dead or alive, unless he should accept the faith and acknowledge himself a subject to the Spanish throne.

The advance was like any similar military enterprise: it accomplished its purpose. . . . Montezuma seeing that there was nothing else for it, sent envoys accompanied by three hundred warriors, who met the Spaniard advancing on the lake road and there welcomed him to the district with great ceremony and show of friendliness. . . .

The following day at noon [Cortez] arrived at the end of his journey. There it lay! a city as large as Cordova or Seville, entirely within the lake two miles from the mainland: Tenochtitlan. Four avenues or entrances led to it, all formed of artifi-

———————
*alternative spelling of Cortés

cial causeways. Along the most easterly of these, constructed of great beams perfectly hewn and fitted together, and measuring two spears-lengths in width, the Christian advanced. Running in at one side of the city and out at the other, this avenue constituted at the same time its principal street.

As Cortez drew nearer he saw, right and left, magnificent houses and temples, close to the walls of which . . . moved parallel rows of priests in black robes, and, between them, supported by two attendants, Montezuma, on foot, down the center of the roadway. Cortez stepped forward but the attendants interceded. The Emperor then advanced alone and with great simpleness of manner placed a golden chain about the Christian's neck. Then taking him by the hand, and the whole procession following, he conducted him to the quarters which had been chosen for the visitors, a great building close to the royal palaces in the center of the city. . . .

Montezuma spoke: "They have told you that I possess houses with walls of gold and many other such things and that I am a god or make myself one. The houses you see are of stone and lime and earth." Then opening his robe: "You see that I am composed of flesh and bone like yourself and that I am mortal and palpable to the touch." To this smiling sally, so full of gentleness and amused irony, Cortez could reply nothing save to demand that the man declare himself a subject to the Spanish King forthwith and that, furthermore, he should then and there announce publicly his allegiance to the new power.

Whatever the Aztec may have felt during the weeks of Cortez' slow advance upon his capital from the seashore, nothing at the present moment seemed to disturb his aristocratic reserve. He had thought and he had made up his mind. Without semblance of anger, fear or impatience; . . . he spoke again. He explained

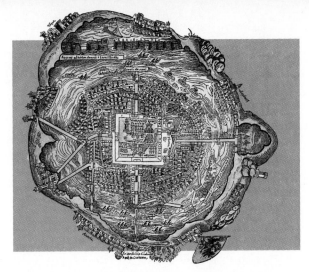

Tenochtitlán at the Time of the Spanish Conquest
Tenochtitlán, the Aztec capital, was built on an island in the center of a lake. Filled with exquisite houses and temples, it was the largest and most elaborate city in the Americas. This woodcut from a letter Cortés sent to the Spanish king shows the plan of the city at the time of his arrival. **Geography** *Why do you think the Aztecs chose to build their capital on an island?*

that his people were not the aborigines of the land but that they had emigrated there in times past and ended by accepting the Spanish Monarch as his rightful and hereditary master. After due announcements and explanations had been made to the people, Cortez became the acknowledged regent, in the name of Castile* and the true church, for all that country.

William Carlos Williams, "The Destruction of Tenochtitlan," in *The American Grain.* Copyright 1933 by WIlliam Carlos Williams. Reprinted by permission of New Directions Publishing Corporation.

THINKING ABOUT THE SELECTION

1. What kinds of gifts did Montezuma send to Cortés?
2. What demands did Cortés make?
3. **Drawing Conclusions** (a) Why do you think Montezuma sent such elaborate gifts to the Spanish? (b) Did Cortés react to the gifts as Montezuma hoped he would?

———

*a region and former kingdom in northern and central Spain

◆ **INTRODUCTION** Like its European neighbors, France wanted to find a northwest passage through or around America in order to reach Asia. This was the aim of Giovanni da Verrazano, an Italian explorer sent westward by the French king in 1524. Verrazano's ship, the *Dauphine,* first sighted land off the Carolinas and then sailed northward along the Atlantic coast. In these passages, the explorer describes the Indians, the land, and New York Harbor.

◆ **VOCABULARY** Before you read the selection, find the meaning of these words in a dictionary: russet, multitude, esteem, trifles, piteously.

The people are of color russet, and not much unlike the Saracens*—their hair is black, thick and not very long, which they tie together in a knot behind and wear it like a little tail. They are well featured in their limbs, of average stature, and commonly somewhat bigger than we. . . . We saw many of them handsome, having black and great eyes, with a cheerful and steady look, sharp witted, nimble and exceeding great runners, as far as we could learn by experience. In those two last qualities, they are like the people of the East parts of the world, and especially those of the uttermost parts of China. We could not learn of this people their manner of living, nor their particular customs, by reason of the short time we spent on the shore, . . .

Sailing forwards, we found certain small rivers . . . washing the shore on both sides as the coast lies. And beyond this we saw the open country rising above the sandy shore with many fair fields and plains, full of mighty great woods, some

very thick, and some thin. . . . And the land is full of many beasts—stags, deer and hares, and likewise of lakes and pools of fresh water, with great plenty of fowls, convenient for all kind of pleasant game.

We departed from this place, still running along the coast, . . . we saw everywhere very great fires, by reason of the multitude of inhabitants. . . .

[With the intention of sending them] things, which the Indians commonly desire and esteem, [such] as sheets of paper, glasses, bells, and such like trifles, we sent a young man, one of our mariners ashore. . . . Swimming towards them and . . . not trusting them, he cast the things upon the sand. Seeking afterwards to return to the ship, he was [beaten upon the shore by violent waves], so bruised that he lay there almost dead.

The Indians . . . ran to catch him, and drawing him out, they carried him a little way off from the sea. The young man being at first dismayed, began then greatly to fear, and cried out piteously. The Indians which did accompany him went about to cheer him and to give him courage. . . . Then setting him on the ground at the foot of a little hill against the sun, they began to behold him with great admiration, marvelling at the whiteness of his flesh. . . . They made him warm at a great fire, not without our great fear who remained in the boat, that they would have roasted him at that fire, and have eaten him.

The young man having recovered his strength, and having stayed a while with them, showed them by signs that he [wanted] to return to the ship. They with great love clapping him fast about with many embracings, accompanied him to the sea. [Then to reassure him], they went unto a high ground and stood there, beholding him until he entered the boat. . . .

———

*a tribe from Syria

Having made our abode three days in this country, and riding on the coast for want of harbors, we [traveled] along the shore . . . sailing only in the daytime, and riding at anchor by night. In the space of 100 leagues sailing, we found a very pleasant place situated among certain little steep hills.* From amidst the hills there ran down into the sea an exceeding great stream of water, which in the mouth was very deep, . . .

We [passed into] the said river, and saw the country very well peopled. . . . [But because of a sudden contrary wind coming from the sea], we were forced to return to our ship, leaving this land to our great discontentment, for the great pleasantness thereof, which we suppose is not without some riches, all the hills showing mineral matters in them.

Source: *The New Land,* compiled and edited by Phillip Viereck (New York: The John Day Company, 1967).

———

*Verrazano is describing the lower bay of New York Harbor.

THINKING ABOUT THE SELECTION

1. What features of the North American landscape most impressed Verrazano?
2. What does the incident described here suggest about the Indians' treatment of Verrazano's expedition?
3. **Drawing Conclusions** Which parts of Verrazano's narrative do you think would have been most likely to encourage further exploration?

Discovery of the Hudson River *European explorers made repeated attempts to find a northwest passage through the Americas to Asia. This painting by Albert Bierstadt depicts the expedition of the English navigator Henry Hudson, who had been hired by the Dutch. Although Hudson did not find a northwest passage, he did discover the river that now bears his name.* **Geography** *What obstacles do you imagine Hudson and his crew faced as they sailed up the river?*

UNIT 2

Colonies Take Root

The Fox Hunt: An English Tradition *Many English colonists brought their traditions to the New World. In this painting, a group of wealthy settlers are participating in a fox hunt—a popular activity among the English aristocracy.* **American Traditions** *What are some of the other English traditions that the colonists brought to the New World?.*

CHAPTER 4

Colonizing the Americas

4-1 — John Smith Saves Jamestown — FIRST PERSON

◆ **INTRODUCTION** Without John Smith, the Jamestown colony might well have died out within a few months. But he was a stern, practical man who realized what had to be done and got people to do it. This selection begins during the winter of 1608. A small fleet of English supply ships has just left; it stayed so long that the sailors ate almost all of the food they had brought with them. Note that Smith refers to himself in the third person, as the President.

◆ **VOCABULARY** Before you read the selection, find the meaning of these words in a dictionary: sloth, loiterers, deserts, weirs.

When the ships departed, all the provision . . . (but that the President had gotten) was so rotten with the last summer's rain, and eaten with rats and worms, as the hogs would scarcely eat it. Yet it was the soldiers' diet till our returns.* . . .

But now [estimating] the store, and finding sufficient till the next harvest, the fear of starving was abandoned, and the company divided into tens, fifteens, or as the business required; six hours each day was spent in work, the rest in pastime and merry exercises.

———
*That is, until the next supply ships came.

638 ◆ VOICES AND VISIONS

But the [disobedience] of the greatest number caused the President to advise as followeth:

Countrymen, the long experience of our late miseries, I hope is sufficient to persuade every one to a present correction of himself, and think not that either my pains, nor the adventurers purses,* will ever maintain you in idleness and sloth. I speak not this to you all, for [some] of you I know deserve both honor and reward, better than is yet here to be had: but the greater part must be more industrious, or starve, however you have been heretofore tolerated by the authority of the Council. . . . You see now that power rests wholly in myself: you must obey this now for a law, that he that will not work shall not eat (except by sickness he be disabled): for the labors of thirty or forty honest and industrious men shall not be consumed to maintain a hundred and fifty idle loiterers. And though you presume the authority here is but a shadow, and that I dare not touch the lives of any but my own must answer [for] it: the letters patent** shall each week be read to you, whose contents will tell you the contrary. I would wish you therefore without contempt to seek to observe these orders set down, for there are now no more Councillors to protect you, nor curb my endeavors. Therefore he that offendeth, let him assuredly expect his due punishment.

[Smith] made a [notice board], as a public memorial of every man's deserts, to encourage the good, and with shame to spur on the rest to [change]. By this many became very industrious, yet more by punishment performed their business; for all were so tasked, that there was no excuse that could prevail to deceive him. . . .

---

*The Virginia Company investors were known as adventurers; by "purses," Smith means the money they had invested.

**the official rules of the colony

Now we so quietly followed our business, that in three months we made three or four lasts* of tar, pitch, and soap ashes; produced a [test run] of glass; made a well in the fort of excellent sweet water, which till then was wanting; built some twenty houses; recovered our church: provided nets and weirs for fishing; and to stop the disorders of our disorderly thieves, and the savages, built a blockhouse in the neck of our isle, kept by a garrison to [carry on] the savages' trade, and none to pass . . . without the President's order. Thirty or forty acres of ground we digged and planted. Of three sows in eighteen months, increased 60 and odd pigs. And nearly 500 chickens brought up themselves without having any [food] given them. . . .

[In the spring of 1609, the Jamestown settlers had a rude shock.]

In searching our casked corn, we found it half rotten, and the rest so

---

*A last is a measurement of weight equal to two tons.

Survival in Jamestown *Hard work did not come easily to the first settlers in Jamestown, as John Smith noted. But under his direction, they began to clear land, build homes, and plant crops. In addition, as this 1618 engraving by Theodore de Bry shows, they also hunted and fished for food.* **Daily Life** *What other tasks do you think the Jamestown settlers had to perform in order to survive?*

consumed with so many thousands of rats that . . . we knew not how to keep that little we had. . . .

To express their loves, for 16 days' continuance, the country people* brought us 100 a day, of squirrels, turkeys, deer and other wild beasts. . . . 60 or 80 [settlers] with Ensign Laxon were sent down the river to live upon oysters, and 20 with Lieutenant Percy to try for fishing at Point Comfort. . . . Master West with as many went up to the falls, but nothing could be found but a few acorns; of that in store every man had equal proportion.

Till this present [time], by the hazard and endeavors of some thirty or forty, this whole colony had ever been fed. . . . But such was the strange condition of

———
*the Indians

some 150, that had they not been forced . . . to gather and prepare their victual they would all have starved or eaten one another.

Source: John Lankford, ed., *Captain John Smith's America* (New York: Harper Torchbooks, 1967).

THINKING ABOUT THE SELECTION

1. What work did the Jamestown colonists accomplish in the months Smith discusses here?
2. What sources of food did the colonists rely on when their "casked corn" proved inadequate?
3. **Making a Generalization** According to Smith, punishment was a more effective means of getting settlers to do their work than the notice board posted with each man's "deserts." Do you think this is generally true? Support your answer.

4-2   The Seekers   LITERATURE

◆ **INTRODUCTION** *The Seekers*, a novel by Eilís Dillon, tells of the adventures of a fictional family who left England in 1632 to settle in the Pilgrim colony at Plymouth. Their perilous journey and the hardships of life at Plymouth are described as seen through the eyes of 16-year-old Edward Deane. Soon after their arrival, Edward, his Aunt Abigail, and Abigail's brother Moses visit with a Plymouth family, the Clarks, and hear about the early years of the settlement. The following passage is about that visit.

◆ **VOCABULARY** Before you read the selection, find the meaning of these words in a dictionary: palisade, edify, pious, paganism, parson.

That was when we heard most about the early years of the settlement. My skin crawled as they talked of starvation and of trying to live on shellfish and of their

first friendship with the Indian, Squanto, long since dead of what they called the Indian sickness. Squanto knew some English, which he had learned from earlier settlers, and he was able to interpret for them so that they could begin trading with the Indians.

Because of the new audience, more and more stories came out. They told us that the first people to arrive from England had found not a soul alive on Cape Cod, nor at Plymouth, though they saw small bands of Indians from time to time. It was Squanto who told them that the whole tribe who lived on that coast was wiped out by sickness, the very winter before. Were it not for the corn those poor people had saved in pits, the men who were telling us of it would have died of starvation themselves.

The three sons-in-law, Isaac and Samuel and Richard, were only children then, but they remembered it vividly.

Indian Princess and Two Pilgrims *Shortly after their arrival at Plymouth, the Pilgrims signed a peace treaty with the Wampanoag Indians. This early needle-point captures the peaceful relationship between the Indians and the Pilgrims that the treaty tried to establish.* **American Traditions** *How might the peace treaty have benefited both the Pilgrims and the Wampanoags?*

Both had come over from England with their parents and had seen them die the very first winter. They had been taken in by other families and brought up by them as their own.

Gradually the people had built houses and the great palisade that surrounded their village and had set up trading posts up north to buy furs from the Indian hunters. The newest one was inland to the west, along a broad river on which the Indians transported the furs in canoes. Throughout the spring and summer, when the ships came out from England, they traded these for gunpowder and shot, fishing tackle and nets, nails and screws, clothing of all kinds, and the peas and beans that they had still not managed to grow themselves.

"God was with us," James Clark said. "Many a time we were near to perishing, but we were always saved in the nick of time. Every man knows that his duty is to plant the Gospel in this remote and barbarous wilderness and edify the poor savages with our wise and godly behavior. Satan is always busy, even among our company. Opposers are not wanting. In every way we strive to pacify the wrath of the Lord by humbling ourselves before him."

Everyone murmured agreement. I never saw such a serious, truly religious group of people in all my life, yet it was soon obvious that things other than religion were also on their minds.

Only two years before, no less than ten ships had arrived from England, crammed with people just as godly as our hosts, all fleeing from persecution of their religion in England. Some had settled farther north in Massachusetts, and some had gone to Charlestown in Virginia. The northern settlers were trading in furs, too, and were competing with the Plymouth ones. No one could tell what the result would be. Those who had gone south had suffered great sickness and many of them had died, so there was little to fear from them.

Aunt Abigail sat with Dinah, drinking in every word, moving her gaze from one speaker to another as if she had never heard such wisdom in all her life, nodding her head forcefully at every pious sentiment. Moses was a different story. The beer had begun to rise in his head, and he was summoning the courage to speak. As the visitors stood up to go home he said, "If you want to bring God to the savages, why were there none of them in the church?"

James turned a look of displeasure on him, then said, "Because they will not come. They still live in the darkness of paganism and ignorance. We know no' the Lord's plans for them, but we hope in time that they will come to us of their own free will. That is the way for the truly repentant sinner."

James didn't seem to hold Moses's question against him, but he clearly included him among those who had not yet repented.

Moses suffered only ten more days of hoeing before he rebelled. What finished him was the service that we were obliged to attend every Thursday evening. It was called a lecture, but it was not much different from the Sunday afternoon service. Most of the time was given to Bible reading and comments from the congregation and from Pastor Smith. And it was every bit as long.

The law of the settlement decreed that everyone who wished to have a say in the affairs of the town was obliged to attend the services, unless he was sick in bed. Those who didn't go to church were tolerated for the work they did, but they were ranked as mere servants and never consulted on important questions. Jack Cutler explained this to us, and he said,

"If you mean to live here, it would be better to keep to their rules. We always go to services when we're in town. That way we get a good welcome when we come back from a trip."

Andrew thought this a good policy, as he had no wish to offend the people of Plymouth, but he agreed with me that their idea of religion was too far from the Church of England to make us want to change. At home we were churchgoing folk, without asking too many questions, and to please Parson, and because we believed in God and Heaven and Hell.

Reprinted with permission of Charles Scribner's Sons, an imprint of Macmillan Publishing Company from *The Seekers* by Ellis Dillon. Copyright © 1986 by Ellis Dillon.

THINKING ABOUT THE SELECTION

1. According to the account of Plymouth's early years, what were the first activities of the settlers?
2. What indications are given of the importance of religion in Plymouth?
3. **Drawing Conclusions** Why do you think the Pilgrims were willing to endure tremendous hardships?

CHAPTER 5

The 13 English Colonies

5-1 — Forefathers' Song — LITERATURE

◆ **INTRODUCTION** A ballad is a type of song that tells a story and provides many descriptive details. "Forefathers' Song" is a ballad from early colonial New England. Written around 1630, it tells in plain language what life was like in the English colonies in America. Climate, food, and clothing are some of the topics discussed. Through the words of the song, you will learn more about colonial life.

◆ **VOCABULARY** Before you read the selection, find the meaning of these words in a dictionary: ponder, forfeits, clout, pottage.

New England's annoyances you that
    would know them,
Pray ponder these verses which briefly
    doth show them.
The place where we live is a wilderness
    wood,

The Beginning of New England *The early New Englanders lived in small wooden houses with thatched roofs. Most of these houses had only one room and few were more than a single story in height. This painting by Clyde O. DeLand shows a group of Pilgrims building one of these small dwellings.* **Daily Life** *What difficulties might have resulted from having an entire Pilgrim family living in a single-room house?*

Where grass is much wanting that's fruit-
   ful and good:
Our mountains and hills and our valleys
   below,
Being commonly covered with ice and
   with snow;
And when the north-west wind with
   violence blows,
Then every man pulls his cap over his
   nose:
But if any's so hardy and will it withstand,
He forfeits a finger, a foot or a hand.

But when the Spring opens we then take
   the hoe,
And make the ground ready to plant and
   to sow;
Our corn being planted and seed being
   sown,
The worms destroy much before it is
   grown;
And when it is growing, some spoil there
   is made
By birds and by squirrels that pluck up
   the blade;
And when it is come to full corn in the
   ear,

It is often destroyed by raccoon and by
   deer.

And now our garments begin to grow
   thin,
And wool is much wanted to card and to
   spin;
If we can get a garment to cover without,
Our other in-garments are clout upon
   clout:
Our clothes we brought with us are apt to
   be torn,
They need to be clouted soon after they're
   worn,
But clouting our garments they hinder us
   nothing,
Clouts double are warmer than single
   whole clothing.

If fresh meat be wanting to fill up our
   dish,
We have carrots and turnips as much as
   we wish:
And if there's a mind for a delicate dish
We repair to the clam-banks, and there
   we catch fish.
Instead of pottage and puddings and
   custards and pies,

Our pumpkins and parsnips are common
   supplies;
We have pumpkins at morning and
   pumpkins at noon,
If it was not for pumpkins we should be
   undone!

* * *

But you whom the Lord intends hither to
   bring,
Forsake not the honey for fear of the
   sting;
But bring both a quiet and contented
   mind,

And all needful blessings you surely will
   find.

Source: "Forefathers' Song," a traditional ballad.

THINKING ABOUT THE SELECTION

1. What difficulties did the early New Englanders face in trying to grow crops?
2. Why did the colonists' clothes need to be "clouted"?
3. **Drawing Conclusions** Despite the hardships the colonists faced, what attitude is expressed in the last stanza of the "Forefathers' Song"?

5-2   A Complaint From Virginia   FIRST PERSON

◆ **INTRODUCTION** Like other colonizing countries, England established settlements abroad in order to benefit its own economy. As far as trade was concerned, the policy was simple. The colonies were to ship raw materials to England, in return for which England would sell the colonies its manufactured goods.

Many colonists resented England's trade policy. In 1697, three Virginians sent a petition to the Board of Trade, the English government office that supervised the colonies. The English seemed to want nothing from Virginia but tobacco. These Virginians had other ideas.

◆ **VOCABULARY** Before you read the selection, find the meaning of these words in a dictionary: judicious, commodity.

It is astonishing to hear what contrary descriptions are given of the country of Virginia, even by those who have often seen it, and know it very well; some of them representing it as the best, others as the worst country in the world. Perhaps they are both in the right. For the most general true character of Virginia is this, that as to the natural advantages of a country, it is one of the best; but as to the improved ones, one of the worst of all the English settlements in America. When one considers the wholesomeness of its air, the fertility of its soil . . . and the temperature of its climate . . . it is certainly one of the best countries in the world. But on the other hand, if we inquire for well-built towns, for convenient ports and markets, for plenty of ships and seamen, for well improved trades and manufactures, for well-educated children, for an industrious and thriving people, or for a happy government in church and state, . . . it is certainly, for all these things, one of the poorest, miserablest, and worst countries in all America that is inhabited by Christians. . . .

It is impossible to reckon up all the improvements which might be made in such a country, where many useful inventions would present themselves to the industrious. The following ones are such as naturally offer to any judicious spectator.

The manufacture of iron and other minerals, with which that country, to all

Life on a Southern Plantation
The first African slaves were brought to Virginia during the early 1600s to work on large plantations, growing tobacco. Wealthy planters also had slaves who tended to household duties, including caring for the children. In this painting by Payne Limner, a boy, returning from a hunt, is greeted by his younger brother and the child's nurse. **Daily Life** *How do you think the lives of the boys in this painting would differ from the lives of children living in the house shown on page 643?*

appearance, is well stored, together with all the advantages of wood to burn them, and water to make the transportation easy. . . .

It is likewise very fit for potash for soap, by reason of the infinite numbers of trees, which make that country more to resemble a forest than one of the countries of Europe.

It abounds also in pitch, tar, rosin, masts, and all timbers for shipping. . . .

Wheat, rye, Indian corn, oats, barley, pease, and many other sorts of edible seeds grow there in great plenty. . . .

The country has also great advantages for the making of cider, oil, figs, raisins, and conserved fruits. . . .

We need not mention tobacco, which would likewise be an excellent staple commodity of that country, if they would make it good, without trash; but so it is at present, that tobacco swallows up all other things, everything else is neglected, and all markets are often so glutted with bad tobacco, that it becomes a mere drug, and will not clear the freight and custom.* . . .

But now, if it be inquired, what sort of a country it is? After all this, we must represent it after a quite different manner from what might be expected from the first and eldest of all the English settlements in America. . . .

The inhabitants are of three sorts, planters, tradesmen, and merchants.

Though the planters are the most numerous, perhaps not the hundredth part of the country is yet cleared from the woods, and not one foot of the marsh and swamp drained. As fast as the ground is worn out with tobacco and corn, it runs up again in underwoods. . . .

For want of towns, markets, and money, there is but little encouragement for tradesmen and skilled workers, and therefore little choice of them, and their labour very dear in the country. . . .

———

*That is, it will not bring enough return to pay for transportation and taxes.

The merchants live the best of any in that country; but yet are subject to great inconveniencies in the way of their trade, which might be avoided if they had towns, markets, and money. . . .

If towns and ports can be brought to bear, the chief obstruction to the improvement of that country will be removed. It is certain that little help towards it is to be expected from the General Assembly; unless they should come to have a Governor, in whom they have a most mighty confidence, that he acts for the public good. . . . But the members of the assembly are daily more and more adverse to living in towns together; the major part of the House of Burgesses consisting of

Virginians that never saw a town, nor have no notion of the conveniency of any other but a country life.

Source: "Large and True Account of the Present State of Virginia," Massachusetts Historical Collections (Boston, 1789).

THINKING ABOUT THE SELECTION

1. According to the authors, why is Virginia both one of the best and one of the worst regions in the world?
2. What solution does the petition recommend for Virginia's problems?
3. **Analyzing Ideas** According to the authors, why is the government of Virginia unable to solve the colony's difficulties?

CHAPTER

6

Colonial Life

6-1 A Striking Sun Dial   LITERATURE

◆ **INTRODUCTION** Perhaps no writer in colonial America was as well-known and highly regarded as Benjamin Franklin (1706–1790). Renowned as a diplomat and statesman, Franklin also made significant contributions to philosophy, literature, and science. In the following essay, written in 1757, Franklin's love of science and inventions is obvious. His wit and sense of humor are also readily apparent.

◆ **VOCABULARY** Before you read the selection, find the meaning of these words in a dictionary: impediment, annexed.

How to make a Striking Sun Dial, by which not only a Man's own family, but all his Neighbours for ten Miles round, may know what a Clock it is, when the Sun shines, without seeing the Dial.

Chuse* an open Place in your Yard or Garden, on which the Sun may shine all Day without any Impediment from Trees or Buildings.

On the Ground mark out your Hour Lines, as for a horizontal Dial, according to Art, taking Room enough for the Guns.

———

*Choose

A Lamplighter Making the Rounds in New York City
Benjamin Franklin did many things to improve city life. In Philadelphia, he had the streets paved with cobblestones. He also came up with the idea of having a person with a lantern patrol city streets at night, as shown in this painting by William Chappel. **Daily Life** *What purpose do you think lamplighters served? Why would they have made cities safer?*

On the Line for One o'Clock, place one Gun; on the Two o'Clock Line two Guns, and so of the rest. The Guns must all be charged with Powder, but Ball is unnecessary. Your Gnomon* or Style must have twelve burning Glasses annex'd to it, and be so placed that the Sun shining through the Glasses, one after the other, shall cause the Focus or burning Spot to fall on the Hour Line of One, for Example, at One a Clock, and there kindle a train of Gunpowder that shall fire one Gun. At Two a Clock, a Focus shall fall on the Hour Line of Two, and kindle another Train that shall discharge Two Guns successively: and so of the rest.

Note, There must be 78 Guns in all. Thirty-two Pounders will be best for this Use; but 18 Pounders may do, and will cost less, as well as use less Powder, for nine Pounds of Powder will do for one Charge of each eighteen Pounder, whereas the Thirty-two Pounders would require for each Gun 16 Pounds.

Note also, That the chief Expense will be the Powder, for the Cannon once bought, will, with Care, last 100 Years.

---

*the pin on the sundial that casts a shadow indicating the time of day

Note moreover, that there will be a great Saving of Powder in Cloudy Days.

Kind Reader, Methinks I hear thee say, That is indeed a good Thing to know how the Time passes, but this Kind of Dial, notwithstanding the mentioned Savings, would be very Expensive; and the Cost greater than the Advantage. Thou art wise, my Friend, to be so considerate beforehand. Some Fools would not have found out so much, till thay had made the Dial and try'd it. . . . Let all such learn that many a private and many a public Project, are like this Striking Dial, great Cost for little Profit.

Source: Benjamin Franklin, *Poor Richard Improved,* 1757.

THINKING ABOUT THE SELECTION

1. Explain how Franklin's sundial was supposed to work.
2. Why will there be a "great Saving of Powder in Cloudy Days"?
3. **Recognizing Points of View** (a) What do you think Franklin's purpose was in writing this essay? (b) What specific evidence in the essay supports your conclusion?

◆ **INTRODUCTION** In the fall of 1704, a Boston shopkeeper named Sarah Kemble Knight set out on horseback from her home to New York City. Colonial roads were little more than trails, but Madam Knight, as she is known, kept up a steady pace. She and her guide usually traveled along with the "post"—the man delivering mail. This selection from Knight's journal describes the second day of the trip, when the small group was traveling in Rhode Island.

Because people of Madam Knight's time had fewer spelling rules than we do today, you will find Madam Knight's spelling and capitalization a bit strange. If you read the selection out loud, however, you should find it easy to understand.

◆ **VOCABULARY** Before you read the selection, find the meaning of these words in a dictionary: circumspect, travail, formidable, ravenous, descents, apprehensions.

Tuesday, October the third. . . . About Three, afternoon, went on with my Third Guide, who Rode very hard; and having crossed Providence Ferry, we come to a River which they Generally Ride thro'. But I dare not venture; so the Post got a Ladd and Cannoo to carry me to tother side, and hee rid thro' and Led my hors. The Cannoo was very small and shallow, so that when we were in she seem'd redy to take in water, which greatly terrified mee, and caused me to be very circumspect, sitting with my hands fast on each side, my eyes stedy, not daring so much as to lodg my tongue a hair's breadth more on one side of my mouth than tother. . . . But was soon put out of this pain, by feeling the Cannoo on shore, which I as soon almost saluuted with my feet; and Rewarding my [boatman], again

mounted and made the best of our way forwards.

The Rode here was very even and the day pleasant, it being now near Sunsett. But the Post told mee we had neer 14 miles to Ride to the next Stage,* (where we were to Lodg.) I askt him of the rest of the Rode, foreseeing wee must travail in the night. Hee told me there was a bad River we were to ride thro', which was so very firce a hors could sometimes hardly stem it: But it was but narrow, and wee should soon be over. I cannot express the concern of mind this relation sett me in: no thoughts but those of the dang'ros River could entertain my Imagination, and they were as formidable as varios, still Tormenting me with blackest Ideas of my Approching fate—Sometimes seing my self drowning, otherwiles drowned. . . .

Now was the sun setting, leaving poor me with the rest of this part of the lower world in darkness, with which wee were soon Surrounded. The only Glimering we now had was from the spangled Skies, Whose Imperfect Reflections rendered every object formidable. Each lifeless Trunk, with its shatter'd Limbs, appear'd an Armed Enymie; and every little stump like a Ravenous devourer. Nor could I so much as discern my Guide, when at any distance, which added to the terror.

Thus, absolutely lost in Thought, and dying with the very thoughts of drowning, I come up with the Post, who I did not see till even with his Hors: he told mee he stopt for mee; and wee Rode on Very deliberatly a few paces, when we entred a Thickett of Trees and Shrubbs, and I perceived by the Hors's going, we were on the descent of a Hill, which, as wee come neerer the bottom, 'twas totaly dark with the Trees that surrounded it.

---

*a rest stop, where riders usually changed horses

Salem Witchcraft Trials *In 1692, a panic broke out over witchcraft in Salem, Massachusetts. More than 150 people were tried as witches and at least 20 were executed. This painting by T. H. Matteson shows the very emotional trial of George Jacobs, an accused witch.* **Daily Life** *How do you think the hardships faced by the colonists might have contributed to the outbreak of the Salem witchcraft hysteria?*

But I knew by the Going of the Hors wee had entred the water, which my Guide told mee was the hazzardos River he had told me off; and hee, Riding up close to my Side, Bid me not fear—we should be over Imediatly. I now ralyed all the Courage I was mistriss of. . . . So, as the Post bid me, I gave Reins to my Nagg; and sitting as Stedy as Just before in the Cannoo, in a few minutes got safe to the other side. . . .

Here We found great difficulty in Travailing, the way being very narrow. And on each side the Trees and bushes gave us very unpleasent welcomes with their Branches and bow's, which wee could not avoid, it being so exceeding dark. My Guide, as before so now, putt on harder than I, with my weary bones, could follow; so left mee and the way beehind him. Now Returned my distressed aprehensions of the place where I was: the [gloomy] woods, my Company next to none, Going I knew not whither, and encompased with Terrifying darkness; The least of which was enough to startle a more Masculine courage. . . .

Now, coming to the foot of a hill, I found great difficulty in ascending; But being got to the Top, was there amply repaid with the friendly Appearance of the moon, Just then Advancing above the Horisontall Line. The Raptures which the Sight of that fair Planett produced in mee, caus'd me, for the Moment, to forgett my present wearyness and past toils; and Inspir'd me for most of the remaining way with very divirting tho'ts. . . . Being thus agreably entertain'd without a thou't of anything but thoughts themselves, I on a suden was Rous'd from these pleasing Imaginations, by the Post's sounding his horn, which assured mee hee was arrived at the Stage, where we were to Lodg: and that musick was then most musickall and agreeable to mee.

Source: *The Journal of Madam Knight* (New York: Peter Smith, 1935).

THINKING ABOUT THE SELECTION

1. What are the main incidents that occurred during this part of the journey?
2. Do you think Madam Knight was brave or fearful? Give reasons for your answer.
3. **Linking Past and Present** A trip from Boston to New York is now a matter of hours. Do you think that in addition to being faster travel today is safer than it was in 1704? Explain.

From Revolution to Republic

Crossing the Delaware *This painting by Thomas Sully shows General George Washington just before crossing the Delaware River in December 1776. Washington and his troops launched a successful surprise attack on the British at Trenton, New Jersey.* **American Traditions** *What impact do you think that the victory at Trenton had on the colonial army? Why?*

CHAPTER

7 The Road to Revolution

7-1 What Should Colonists Do?

FIRST PERSON

◆ **INTRODUCTION** Britain's policy of taxing the colonists, begun in the 1760s, stirred up tremendous opposition. One of the many American critics was John Dickinson. His protests took the form of 12 weekly letters published in a Pennsylvania newspaper beginning in December 1767. Dickinson signed himself "a farmer in Pennsylvania." He did own country property, but he was also a lawyer and state assemblyman. The selections here are from his last letter.

◆ **VOCABULARY** Before you read the selection, find the meaning of these words in a dictionary: indelibly, frugal, goads, prudent, posterity, magnanimity.

Let these truths be indelibly impressed on our minds: that we cannot be happy without being free; that we cannot be free without being secure in our property; that we cannot be secure in our property, if, without our consent, others may take it away; that taxes imposed on us by parliament, do thus take it away; that duties* laid for the sole purposes of raising money are taxes; that attempts to lay such duties should be instantly and firmly opposed; that this opposition can

———
*Duties are taxes on imported goods. For example, the taxes imposed by the Townshend Acts were duties.

never be effective, unless it is the united effort of these provinces. . . .

As long as the products of our labours and the rewards of our care can properly be called our own, so long will it be worth our while to be industrious and frugal. But if when we plow, sow, reap, gather, and thresh, we find, that we plow, sow, reap, gather, and thresh for others, whose pleasure is to be the sole limit on how much they shall take, and how much they shall leave, why should we repeat the unprofitable toil? Horses and oxen are content with that portion of the fruits of their work, which their owners assign to them, in order to keep them strong enough to raise successive crops. But even these beasts will not submit to draw for their masters, until they are subdued with whips and goads. Let us take care of our rights, and we therein take care of our property. . . .

I shall be extremely sorry if any man mistakes my meaning in any thing I have said. Officers employed by the crown are entitled to legal obedience and sincere respect. These it is a duty to give them, and these no good or prudent person will withhold. But when these officers, through rashness or design, endeavour to enlarge their authority beyond its due limits . . . their attempts should be considered as equal injuries to the crown and people, and should be courageously and constantly opposed. . . .

You will be a "Band of brothers" cemented by the dearest ties, confederated in a good cause. Your honour and welfare will be, as they now are, most intimately concerned; and besides—you are assigned by Divine Providence, in the appointed order of things, the protectors of unborn ages, whose fate depends upon your virtue. . . .

Landing of the British Troops *In 1768, the British army occupied Boston to enforce the writs of assistance. These documents gave customs officers the right to inspect a ship's cargo without reason. This engraving by Paul Revere shows the British army arriving at Boston harbor.* **American Traditions** *What does the British action suggest about Britain's expectations of the colonists' response to the writs of assistance? How do you think colonists reacted to Revere's engraving?*

To discharge this double duty to your-selves and to your posterity; you have nothing to do, but to call forth into use the good sense and spirit, of which you are possessed. You have nothing to do, but to conduct your affairs peaceably, prudently, firmly, jointly. By these means you will support the character of freemen, without losing that of faithful subjects. . . . You will prove that Americans have that true magnanimity of soul, that can resent injuries without falling into rage; and that tho' your devotion to Great Britain is the most affectionate, yet you can make proper distinctions, and know what you owe to yourselves as well as to her. You will, at the same time that you advance your interests, advance your reputation. You will convince the world of the justice of your demands, and the purity of your intentions—while all mankind must with unceasing applause confess, that you indeed deserve liberty, who so well understand it, so passion-ately love it, so temperately enjoy it, and so wisely, bravely, and virtuously, assert, maintain, and defend it.

Source: John Dickinson, *Letters from a Farmer in Pennsylvania* (New York: Outlook Company, 1903).

THINKING ABOUT THE SELECTION

1. How does Dickinson advise the colonists to behave?
2. What is Dickinson's attitude toward British officials?
3. **Drawing Conclusions** Is Dickinson advo-cating revolution? Give reasons for your answer.

7-2 Johnny Tremain LITERATURE

◆ **INTRODUCTION** Esther Forbes's novel *Johnny Tremain* describes the life of a 14-year-old boy living in Boston in the period before the outbreak of the Revolu-tionary War. As a messenger for the Sons of Liberty, Johnny comes in contact with Paul Revere, John and Sam Adams, John Hancock, and other influential people and plays a part in some crucial events. The following passage recounts Johnny's participation in the Boston Tea Party.

◆ **VOCABULARY** Before you read the selec-tion, find the meaning of these words in a dictionary: boatswain, warped, jargon, winches, pullet.

The day had started with rain and then there had been clouds, but as they reached Griffin's Wharf the moon, full and white, broke free of the clouds. The three ships, the silent hundreds gather-ing upon the wharf, all were dipped in the pure white light. The crowds were becoming thousands, and there was not one there but guessed what was to be done, and all approved.

Rab was grunting out of the side of his mouth to a thick-set, active-looking man, whom Johnny would have known anywhere, by his walk and the confident lift of his head, was Mr. Revere. "Me Know You."

"Me Know You," Johnny repeated this countersign and took his place behind Mr. Revere. The other boys, held up by the crowd, began arriving, and more men and boys. But Johnny guessed that many who were now quietly joining one of those three groups were acting on the spur of the moment, seeing what was up. They had blacked their faces, seized axes, and come along. They were behaving as quietly and were as obedient to their leaders as those who had been carefully picked for this work of destruction.

There was a boatswain's whistle, and in silence one group boarded the *Dartmouth*. The *Eleanor* and the *Beaver* had to be warped in to the wharf. Johnny was close to Mr. Revere's heels. He heard him calling for the captain, promising him, in the jargon everyone talked that night, that not one thing should be damaged on the ship except only the tea, but the captain and all his crew had best stay in the cabin until the work was over.

Captain Hall shrugged and did as he was told, leaving his cabin boy to hand over the keys to the hold. The boy was grinning with pleasure. The "tea party" was not unexpected.

"I'll show you," the boy volunteered, "how to work them hoists. I'll fetch lanterns, mister."

The winches rattled and the heavy chests began to appear—one hundred and fifty of them. As some men worked in the hold, others broke open the chests and flung the tea into the harbor. But one thing made them unexpected difficulty. The tea inside the chests was wrapped in heavy canvas. The axes went through the wood easily enough—the canvas made endless trouble. Johnny had never worked so hard in his life. . . .

Not a quarter of a mile away, quite visible in the moonlight, rode the *Active* and the *Kingfisher*. Any moment the tea party might be interrupted by British marines. There was no landing party. Governor Hutchinson had been wise in not sending for their help.

The work on the *Dartmouth* and the *Eleanor* finished about the same time. The *Beaver* took longer, for she had not had time to unload the rest of her cargo, and great care was taken not to injure it. Just as Johnny was about to go over to see if he could help on the *Beaver*, Mr. Revere whispered to him. "Go get brooms. Clean um' deck."

Johnny and a parcel of boys brushed the deck until it was clean as a parlor floor. Then Mr. Revere called the captain

Paul Revere's Ride *Relations between Britain and the colonies grew steadily worse after the Boston Tea Party. On April 18, 1775, Paul Revere, shown here in this drawing by J. Steeple Davis, galloped along the road to Lexington, warning the colonists that the British were advancing. Thanks to Revere's warning, the minutemen were prepared for the arrival of the British forces.* **American Traditions** *What do you think would have happened if Revere had never embarked on his ride?*

to come up and inspect. The tea was utterly gone, but Captain Hall agreed that beyond that there had not been the slightest damage.

It was close upon dawn when the work on all three ships was done. And yet the great, silent audience on the wharf, men, women, and children, had not gone home. As the three groups came off the ships, they formed in fours along the wharf, their axes on their shoulders. Then a hurrah went up and a fife began to play. This was almost the first sound Johnny had heard since the tea party started—except only the crash of axes into sea chests, the squeak of hoists, and a few grunted orders.

Standing quietly in the crowd, he saw Sam Adams, pretending to be a most innocent bystander. It looked to Johnny as if the dog fox had eaten a couple of fat pullets, and had a third in his mouth.

As they started marching back to the center of town, they passed the Coffin House at the head of Griffin's Wharf. A window opened.

"Well, boys," said a voice, so cold one hardly knew whether he spoke in anger or not, "you've had a fine, pleasant evening for your Indian caper, haven't you? But mind . . . you've got to pay the fiddler yet."

It was the British Admiral Montague.

"Come on down here," someone yelled, "and we'll settle that score tonight."

The Admiral pulled in his head and slapped down the window.

Johnny and Rab knew, and men like the Observers knew, but best of all Sam Adams knew, that the fiddler would have to be paid. England, unable to find the individuals who had destroyed this valuable property, would punish the whole Town of Boston—make every man, woman, and child, Tories and Whigs alike, suffer until this tea was paid for. Nor was she likely to back down on her claim that she might tax the colonists any way she pleased.

Next day, all over Boston, boys and men, some of them with a little paint still showing behind their ears, were so lame they could scarce move their fingers, but none of them—not one—told what it was that had lamed them so. They would stand about and wonder who "those Mohawks" might have been, or what the British Parliament might do next, but never say what they themselves had been doing, for each was sworn to secrecy.

Only Paul Revere showed no signs of the hard physical strain he had been under all the night before. Not long after dawn he had started on horseback for New York and Philadelphia with an account of the Tea Party. He could chop open tea chests all night, and ride all day.

From JOHNNY TREMAIN by Esther Forbes. Copyright 1943 by Esther Forbes Hoskins. Copyright © renewed 1971 by Linwood M. Erskine, Jr., Executor of the Estate. Reprinted by permission of Houghton Mifflin Co.

THINKING ABOUT THE SELECTION

1. Why did the participants in the tea party disguise themselves?
2. Explain why the *Beaver* took longer to unload than the other two ships did.
3. **Defending a Position** Do you think the Boston Tea Party was justified? Explain.

CHAPTER

8 The War for Independence

8-1   A Teenage Prisoner of War   FIRST PERSON

◆ **INTRODUCTION** In 1774, when he was only 15, John Adlum joined a company of militia at York, Pennsylvania. Two years later he was called to active duty. Adlum fought at Fort Washington, in northern Manhattan, which the British attacked after winning the Battle of Long Island. The fort fell in November 1776. Along with some 2,800 other American soldiers, Adlum was taken prisoner. This selection from his memoirs begins as he talks to a British guard.

◆ **VOCABULARY** Before you read the selection, find the meaning of these words in a dictionary: cannonade, provincial.

I had a curiosity what they thought of our defense and observed to him that they made a great haul of us that day, to which he replied yes but it could not well be otherwise as our lines were not half manned. "When your left flank below the lines was turned, you had no other choice but to run towards the Fort or be taken prisoners in the lines."

"Then you think that if we had more men we would have made a better defense?"

"To be sure you would."

"There was a very great noise made with the artillery today."

"Yes, I was in the last war in Germany and I think I never heard so brisk a cannonade in my life."

"Then you think we behaved tolerably well?"

"Yes, considering your numbers and the badness of your cause you have done as well as could be expected." . . .

"You say you were in Germany in the last war. Were you in any of the great battles there?"

"Yes."

"From the quantity of firing with small arms, did they in Germany do as much execution* as we do?"

"No, they do not. I was in the battle of Bunker's Hill and there was more execution done there for the quantity of firing than I ever knew or heard of, except once where our regiment was attacked and, supported by some Grenadiers, we in about fifteen minutes killed near seven hundred Frenchmen."

---

*that is, kill as many soldiers

"Then you think that we might fight pretty hard upon an occasion?"

"Yes, if you were well disciplined and commanded by British officers."

"Why British officers and not our own?"

"Because there is but very few of them that appear gentlemen, consequently they cannot have a proper sense of honor."

Battle of Bunker Hill *As this painting by Alonzo Chappel suggests, the American forces fiercely resisted the British advance in the Battle of Bunker Hill. Although the British eventually won the battle, the American army proved that it was a fighting force to be reckoned with.* **Linking Past and Present** *How does this battle scene differ from the way battles have been portrayed in recent wars? What accounts for these differences?*

I felt the hit and did not ask him any more questions. . . .

[Later Adlum struck up another conversation with a British sergeant.] He observed to me, "You appear to be very young to be embarked in so bad a cause but," continued he, "I suppose you were forced into the service as most of you are."

I replied that he was mistaken and that so far from being forced there was more offered their services than arms could be procured for.

"Why," said he, "I understood that it was otherwise." He said he regretted to see so young a lad as I appeared to be opposing his King and if I would look back and see the great number of prisoners following I must be satisfied that the war was near its end, and that by the next spring we would have no troops to resist the powerful armies of the King, that this affair would prevent any but mad men from joining in the service and that he did not believe there would be much further resistance; that he remembered General Washington when he was a provincial colonel, and he regretted that so good a man should meet the fate that awaited him.

I replied (being pretty much of an enthusiast) that the reason they beat us on Long Island and now at Fort Washington was because we could not run away [to regroup] and that their shipping was the cause of all their success, and that he might depend upon it that whenever we got them from their shipping and in the country we would beat them wherever we met them. . . .

The sergeant said I was very much mistaken and he was sorry to see so young a lad as I appeared to be have such an opinion of the irresistible power of the British King, and that our fate was inevitable, for the next spring we would be a conquered people.

"But," says he, "I have no idea that many will suffer, none but the principal officers and the leading men in Congress. As for the privates and small fry, they will be treated with humanity while prisoners and will be supplied with all their wants. I shall not be surprised that after you are well fed and clothed to see General Howe send you all home with more favorable sentiments toward us (the British) than you now seem to be possessed of." But the sergeant was woefully mistaken; he calculated upon a humanity that neither General Howe nor his [troops] possessed or ever felt.

Source: Howard H. Peckham, ed., *Memoirs of the Life of John Adlum in the Revolutionary War* (Chicago: William L. Clements Library, 1968).

THINKING ABOUT THE SELECTION

1. What does the first British guard think about the colonial army's fighting ability?
2. What are the guards' attitudes toward the American cause?
3. **Defending a Position** Explain whether or not you think Adlum does a good job defending the American position.

8-2   Marion's Men   LITERATURE

◆ **INTRODUCTION** Fighting on their own soil, the Americans enjoyed a distinct advantage over the British. One military leader who used that advantage was Francis Marion, the Swamp Fox. He used guerrilla tactics in skirmishes and battles throughout South Carolina. The greatest weapons his small army had were its speed and the element of surprise. Sleeping by day and striking at night, Marion's army was very successful against the British. The following song, "Marion's

Men," gives an idea of what life was like for the followers of the Swamp Fox.

◆ **VOCABULARY** Before you read the selection, find the meaning of these words in a dictionary: legions, saber, coax, steeds, coursers.

We follow where the Swamp Fox guides,
His friends and merry men are we,
And when the Tory Legions ride
We burrow in the cypress trees.
The gloomy swampland is our bed,
Our home is in the red deer's den,
Our roof, the treetop overhead,
For we are wild and hunted men.

Chorus: We ride, we hide, we strike
again,
For we are Marion's men.

We fly by day and shun its light,
But, prompt to strike the sudden blow,

We mount, and start with early night,
And through the forest track our foe,
And soon he hears our chargers leap,
And flashing saber blinds his eyes,
And ere he drives away his sleep,
And rushes from his camp, he dies.

Chorus: We ride, we hide, we strike
again,
For we are Marion's men.

Now pile the brush and roll the log,
Hard pillow, but a soldier's head,
That's half the time in brake and bog,
Must never think of softer bed,
The owl is hooting to the night,
The cooter crawling o'er the bank,
And in that pond the plashing light,
Tells where the alligator sank.

Chorus: We ride, we hide, we strike
again,
For we are Marion's men.

Marion Crossing the Pee Dee *Francis Marion and his troops had a hideout on an island in the Pee Dee River in northeastern South Carolina. From this hideout, they made daring raids on British outposts and rescued American prisoners. This painting by William Ranney shows Marion and his troops setting out on one of their raids.* **Geography** *Why do you think Marion chose an island for his hideout?*

The Swamp Fox whistles to the scouts,
You hear his order calm and low,
Come, wave your torch across the dark,
We shall not be the last to go,
Have courage, comrades, Marion leads,
The Swamp Fox takes us out tonight,
So clear your swords and coax your
    steeds,
Tonight we right, tonight we fight.

Chorus: We ride, we hide, we strike
    again,
        For we are Marion's men.

We follow where the Swamp Fox guides,
We leave the swamp and cypress tree,
Our spurs are in our coursers' sides,
And ready for the strife are we.
The Tory camp is now in sight,
And there he cowers within his den,

He hears our shout, he dreads the fight,
He fears, and flies from Marion's men.

Chorus: We ride, we hide, we strike
    again,
        For we are Marion's men.

From SONGS OF '76: A Folksinger's History of the
Revolution by Oscar Brand. Copyright © 1972 by Oscar
Brand. Reprinted by permission of the publisher, M. Evans
& Co., Inc.

THINKING ABOUT THE SELECTION

1. Explain the meaning of the line "We fly by day and shun its light."
2. What clues do such words as *bog, pond,* and *alligator* give about the songwriter's surroundings?
3. **Linking Past and Present** Give an example of a place in the world today where guerrilla fighting is taking place.

CHAPTER 9 — Creating a Republic

9-1   Comments From a German Visitor   FIRST PERSON

◆ **INTRODUCTION** Under the Articles of Confederation, the United States set up a very weak national government. One European visitor who saw it in action was Johann David Schoepf from Germany. He first came to America during the Revolutionary War as a physician for Britain's Hessian troops. After the war, he spent two years traveling about the country.

◆ **VOCABULARY** Before you read the selection, find the meaning of these words in a dictionary: vexations, prerogatives, sovereign, indignation.

The Congress has neither the necessary weight nor the necessary solidity. It is

therefore, in the very restricted range of its activities, exposed to all manner of grievous vexations. It was to be expected of a people so enthusiastic for liberty that they should grant their Congress only a shadow of dignity, and watch its proceedings with a jealous eye.

The real business and the prerogatives of the Congress, insofar as it represents the common power of the United States, are: To declare war and conclude peace, to raise armies and give them orders, to contract alliances with foreign powers, to oversee the constitutions of all the states and preserve their relations to the whole; to call for and administer the revenues necessary to these ends, and to make public debts.

New Cities on the Frontier *Passage of the Northwest Ordinance sparked the growth of new settlements in the Northwest Territory. Some of these settlements eventually grew into large cities. One of these was Cincinnati, which is shown as it appeared in 1835 in this painting by John Casper Wild.* **Local History** *What government policies have had an important impact on the town or city in which you live? Explain.*

Insofar its activities may be compared with those of other sovereign powers, the Congress being bound to exercise care for the well-being and the safety of the community. But as regards the application of the means needed, there are a thousand difficulties in the way. Thus the United States authorized the Congress to borrow money and to pledge the honor of the nation. But to pay these debts, there is no authority granted. Each individual state has its own independent government which is concerned for its especial welfare and inner security; its own laws, police, and execution of justice. . . .

Nothing has so much damaged faith in the Congress, . . . and nothing has caused more general and bitter indignation against it, than the debts heaped by it upon the states, and especially the woeful pains left by the paper-money issued under its authority, which . . . has been the occasion of the loss of a great part or all of the property of so many once prosperous families and individuals. . . .

There was a time when printed bits of paper were to the people as valuable as hard coin. . . . At that time the paper-money issued by the Congress and the states was wholly esteemed and was reckoned without question as equal to silver and gold. But this kind of mintage was found to be so easy that new millions were struck off on all occasions in payment of the costs of the war. Thus, credit began to weaken. . . .

The value of the paper had already considerably fallen, when it was proclaimed that in the payment of old debts paper-money should be legally accepted at its full nominal value, paper dollars at the time being about as 50 to 1 of silver. Thus whoever before the war, owed 50 hard dollars could now come off by the payment of 50 paper dollars, the fiftieth part of the true worth. . . . It may easily be fancied to what great injustice and oppression such a decree must have given rise with the paper-money of the Congress sinking at last to nothing.

Source: Adapted from Johann David Schoepf, *Travels in the Confederation* (Philadelphia: William J. Campbell, 1911).

THINKING ABOUT THE SELECTION

1. What are the main powers of Congress under the Articles? What important power does it lack?
2. Why did paper money issued by the Congress lose value?
3. **Understanding Causes and Effects** Why would worthless paper money cause "once prosperous families and individuals" to lose their property?

9-2 What Is an American? LITERATURE

◆ **INTRODUCTION** As the new nation struggled to establish itself, a new breed of people was born—the Americans. A French writer, Hector St. John de Crèvecoeur (1735–1813) was one of the first to describe the new American people. His observations and experiences as he traveled throughout America and settled for a while in New York State formed the basis for his writing. He published his observations as a collection of 12 essays called *Letters From an American Farmer*. In the third of those essays, Crèvecoeur asks "What Is an American?" Part of his answer is found in this selection.

◆ **VOCABULARY** Before you read the selection, find the meaning of these words in a dictionary: haughty, magistrate, posterity, allurement, despotic, servile.

Here [a European visitor] beholds fair cities, substantial villages, extensive fields, an immense country filled with decent houses, good roads, orchards, meadows, and bridges, where a hundred years ago all was wild, woody, and uncultivated! What a train of pleasing ideas this fair spectacle must suggest. It is a prospect which must inspire a good citizen with the most heartfelt pleasure.

The difficulty consists in the manner of viewing so extensive a scene. He is arrived on a new continent; a modern society offers itself to him, different from what he had hitherto seen. It is not composed, as in Europe, of great lords who possess everything, and of a herd of people who have nothing. Here are no aristocratical families, no courts, no kings, no bishops, . . . The rich and the poor are not so far removed from each other as they are in Europe. . . .

It must take some time ere he can reconcile himself to our dictionary, which is but short in words of dignity, and names of honor. There, on a Sunday, he sees a congregation of respectable farmers and their wives, all clad in neat homespun, well mounted, or riding in their own humble wagons. There is not among them an esquire, saving the unlettered magistrate. There he sees a parson as simple as his flock, a farmer who does not exploit the labor of others. We have no princes, for whom we toil, starve, and bleed. We are the most perfect society now existing in the world. Here man is free as he ought to be. . . .

What then is the American, this new man? He is either a European, or the descendant of a European, hence that strange mixture of blood, which you will find in no other country. I could point out to you a family whose grandfather was an Englishman, whose wife was Dutch, whose son married a French woman, and whose present four sons have now four wives of different nations. He is an American, who, leaving behind him all his ancient prejudices and manners, receives new ones from the new mode of life he has embraced, the new government he obeys, and the new rank he holds. He becomes an American by being received in the broad lap of our great Alma Mater.* Here individuals of all nations are melted into a new race of men, whose labors and posterity will one day cause great changes in the world. Americans are the western pilgrims, who are carrying along with them that great mass of arts, sciences, vigor, and industry which began long since in the east; they will finish the great circle.

The Americans were once scattered all over Europe. Here they are incorporated into one of the finest systems of population which has ever appeared, and which will hereafter become distinct by the power of the different climates they inhabit. The American ought therefore to love this country much better than that where either he or his forefathers were born. Here the rewards of his industry follow with equal steps the progress of his labor. His labor is founded on the basis of nature, self-interest; can it want a stronger allurement? Wives and children, who before in vain demanded of him a morsel of bread, now, fat and frolic-

---

*literally, dear mother

Early Patriotic Symbols *Through our history, a variety of symbols have come to represent the United States and the principles of the American people. For instance, the keepsake box shown here is decorated with an eagle, a symbol that calls to mind American freedom, strength, and independence.* **American Traditions** *What other American symbols can you think of? What principles and ideals are associated with these symbols?*

some, gladly help their father to clear those fields whence exuberant crops are to arise to feed and to clothe them all; without any part being claimed, either by a despotic prince, a rich abbot, or a mighty lord. Here religion demands but little of him; a small voluntary salary to the minister, and gratitude to God; can he refuse these?

The American is a new man, who acts upon new principles. He must therefore entertain new ideas, and form new opinions. From involuntary idleness, servile dependence, and useless labor, he has passed to toils of a very different nature, rewarded by ample subsistence—This is an American. . . .

Source: Hector St. John de Crèvecoeur, *Letters From an American Farmer*, 1782.

THINKING ABOUT THE SELECTION

1. How does Crèvecoeur support his claim that equality exists in America?
2. How does he define an American?
3. **Comparing** (a) How would you define today's American? (b) How does your definition compare with Crèvecoeur's?

Daily Life in the New Nation *After winning their fight for independence, the people of the United States began forging a way of life that was distinctly American. Writers and artists created works that captured the American spirit. This painting by Francis Guy shows daily life in Brooklyn, New York, during the early 1800s.* **Linking Past and Present** *How do you imagine this part of Brooklyn has changed since the time of the painting? Explain.*

CHAPTER

10   The New Government Begins

10-1   Great Little Madison   LITERATURE

◆ **INTRODUCTION** One of the fiercest debates to take place in the first Congress concerned the funding of the debt from the Revolution. On one side of the issue was Secretary of the Treasury Alexander Hamilton. Hamilton wanted to issue new bonds to pay the national debt, and he wanted the national government to assume state debts. This plan was opposed by James Madison. Madison and others believed that assuming the states' debts was unfair to states like Virginia that had already repaid their debts. The following selection from Jean Fritz's biography of Madison presents this debate and its resolution.

◆ **VOCABULARY** Before you read the selection, find the meaning of these words in a dictionary: thronged, sheaf, secede, speculators, site.

When the debate hit the floor of the House, the country learned for the first time that Congress could at a moment's notice turn into a theater. Senators took time off so they could listen to the proceedings. Abigail Adams (wife of the vice president) and her lady friends thronged into the galleries. Alexander Hamilton could not argue his case himself, because he was not a member of the House. Still, it was clearly a fight between two of the country's leaders:

Hamilton's supporters on one side, Madison and his men on the other. Spectators looked forward particularly to the times when Mr. Madison spoke. He would shuffle a sheaf of papers, stand up, and clear his throat as if he were alerting the audience that though it might be difficult to hear him, he had something to say. Soft-spoken as he was, he tore into Mr. Hamilton's plan as if it offended every nerve in his body. And when he was reminded that this system had worked in England—well, that's when Madison's face reddened and when he began rocking back and forth in his old tense way. Who needed England to show them how to run their country? he would snap. Madison may still have borne old grudges against England, but what he particularly resented now was the way England continued to act as if the United States were a second-rate nation, hardly worth anyone's attention.

On the other hand, when Madison presented his plan for raising money, he, too, was shouted down. Why couldn't they sell land in the western territories that would eventually become part of the United States? he asked. George Clymer of Pennsylvania, a follower of Hamilton, snorted at the idea. It was "romantic," he said, to suppose that the western territories would ever agree to come into the United States. Then consider taxes. Consider tariffs, Madison suggested, Why not a whisky tax? Why not a higher tariff on American ships trading with countries having no commerical agreements with us? By this Madison meant Great Britain, which had refused to sign such an agreement, but there was an immediate outcry from New England representatives. They were the ones who did most of the trading with England; they were the ones most partial to their former enemy.

It was toward the end of the debate that Thomas Jefferson arrived back from Paris, back also from a long visit to Monticello, where Madison had seen him over the Christmas holidays. At the first opportunity Hamilton cornered him, explaining how serious the debt problem had become. Particularly the question of the nation taking over state debts. There were some states threatening to secede from the Union, he explained, if the nation did not assume their debts.

Jefferson invited Hamilton to dinner the next night. He would invite Madison too, he said.

By this time Madison realized that he could not win the debate over the funding system. Some of the speculators were themselves members of Congress. Moreover, if the country's money was largely in the hands of those who were wealthy and able to speculate, the stability of the country would be assured. That was what many believed. There remained, however, the delicate question of state debts. Hamilton needed only a few more votes to get his way on this. While Madison had no notion of changing his vote, he did agree that he might possibly arrange among his supporters to give Hamilton his victory. *If,* he said. If Hamilton for his part would see that the vote on the loca-

James Madison *James Madison was one of the most influential thinkers in the new nation. He went on to become the fourth President of the United States. This portrait of Madison by Gilbert Stuart was painted in 1820.* **Economics** *How are goverment debts paid today?*

tion of the national capital went as Madison wanted it. The Potomac River as the permanent site. A ten-year temporary site at Philadelphia. Hamilton agreed.

Still, at the end of the evening James Madison knew that he and Hamilton would never again sit and laugh together over the antics of anyone's pet monkey. He felt betrayed. Perhaps he should have paid more attention to Hamilton's outburst at the Constitutional Convention. Loyal as he was to the American cause, Hamilton, born and brought up on a British island in the West Indies, obviously still held an undue admiration for British aristocracy. He was an ambitious man, Alexander Hamilton, handsome and charming with the ability to manipulate people to do what he wanted them to do. And Madison worried about his influence over President Washington.

Actually Alexander Hamilton may himself have felt betrayed. He and Madison had both promoted the idea of a strong central government, yet in this crucial case Madison did not seem to be behind it. Madison could have pointed out, however, that he had not changed. First and foremost, he was in favor of a balance of power. If one branch of government seemed to be showing too much power, if the central government seemed to be dominating the states, he would always try to tip the scales. A few months later he would oppose Hamilton again when he succeeded in establishing a national bank. Madison advised Washington that the bank was unconstitutional and he shouldn't sign the bill. But Washington listened to Hamilton instead, just as Madison feared. And he did sign the bill.

Source: Jean Fritz, *The Great Little Madison*. Copyright © 1989 by Jean Fritz. Reprinted by permission of G.P. Putnam's Sons.

THINKING ABOUT THE SELECTION

1. What objection did Madison raise to Hamilton's plan?
2. (a) Explain Madison's plan for raising money. (b) Why was Madison's plan "shouted down"?
3. **Synthesizing Information** Briefly summarize the debt issue, Madison's and Hamilton's positions, and the outcome.

10-2   Moving Into a New House   FIRST PERSON

◆ **INTRODUCTION** John Adams was the first President to live in the White House. His family spent just a few months there at the end of his term in office. The new mansion had some drawbacks, as Abigail Adams explains in the following letter to her daughter, written in November 1800.

◆ **VOCABULARY** Before you read the selection, find the meaning of these words in a dictionary: interspersed, render, procure.

My Dear Child,

I arrived here on Sunday last, and without meeting with any accident worth noticing, except losing ourselves when we left Baltimore. . . . Woods are all you see, from Baltimore until you reach *the city,* which is only so in name. Here and there is a small [cottage], without a glass window, interspersed amongst the forests, through which you travel miles without seeing any human being. In the city there are buildings enough, if they were compact and finished, to accommodate Congress and those attached to it; but as they are, and scattered as they are, I see no great comfort for them. The river, which runs up to Alexandria, is in full view of my window, and I see the vessels as they pass and repass.

The house is upon a grand and superb scale, requiring about thirty servants to

Celebrating American Independence
Fourth of July celebrations have been an American tradition since the nation was founded. This painting by John Krimmel shows the Fourth of July celebration in Philadelphia in 1815. Philadelphia had been the nation's capital from 1790 to 1800.
American Traditions *How do you imagine the Fourth of July celebrations on the American frontier differed from the one shown here?*

attend and keep the apartments in proper order, and perform the ordinary business of the house and stables; an establishment very well proportioned to the President's salary. The lighting [of] the apartments, from the kitchen to parlors and chambers, is a [problem] indeed; and the fires we are obliged to keep to secure us from daily [chills] is another very cheering comfort. To assist us in this great castle, and render less attendance necessary, bells are wholly wanting, not one single one being hung through the whole house, and promises are all you can obtain. This is so great an inconvenience, that I know not what to do, or how to do.

The ladies from Georgetown* and in the city have many of them visited me. Yesterday I returned fifteen visits—but such a place as Georgetown appears— why, our Milton** is beautiful. But no comparisons—if they will put me up some bells, and let me have wood enough to keep fires, I [intend] to be pleased. I could content myself almost anywhere three

---

*a section of Washington, D.C.

**Milton, Massachusetts, was a simple country town near the Adams family home outside Boston.

months; but, surrounded with forests, can you believe that wood is not to be had, because people cannot be found to cut and cart it! Briesler* entered into a contract with a man to supply him with wood. A small part, a few cords only, has he been able to get. Most of that was expended to dry the walls of the house before we came in, and yesterday the man told him it was impossible for him to procure it to be cut and carted. He has had recourse to coals; but we cannot get grates made and set. We have, indeed, come into a new country.

You must keep all this to yourself, and, when asked how I like it, say that I write you the situation is beautiful, which is true. The house is made habitable, but there is not a single apartment finished, and all withinside, except the plastering, has been done since Briesler came. We have not the least fence, yard, or other convenience, [outside], and the great unfinished audience-room I make a drying-room of, to hang up the clothes in. The principal stairs are not up, and will not be this winter. Six chambers are made

---

*John Briesler was a longtime employee of the Adams family.

comfortable; two are occupied by the President and Mr. Shaw;* two lower rooms, one for a common parlor, and one for a reception room. Upstairs there is the oval room, which is designed for the drawing-room, and has the crimson furniture in it. It is a very handsome room now; but, when completed, it will be beautiful. If the twelve years, in which this place has been considered as the future seat of government, had been improved, as they would have been if in New England, very many of the present inconveniences would have been removed. It is

———

*William Shaw, a nephew of Abigail Adams, served as the President's secretary.

a beautiful spot, capable of every improvement, and, the more I view it, the more I am delighted with it.

Source: Charles Francis Adams, ed., *Letters of Mrs. Adams* (Boston: Wilkins, Carter, and Company, 1848).

THINKING ABOUT THE SELECTION

1. How does Abigail Adams describe Washington, D.C.?
2. (a) What are the chief advantages of the White House? (b) What are the main disadvantages?
3. **Analyzing Information** How does Abigail Adams contrast her present surroundings with her native New England?

CHAPTER

11

The Jefferson Era

11-1 | The Man Without a Country | LITERATURE

◆ **INTRODUCTION** During Jefferson's second term as President, his former Vice President, Aaron Burr, became involved in an unsuccessful plot to create a separate country out of lands west of the Mississippi River. Writer Edward Everett Hale used the outcome of Burr's plot as the background for his story, "The Man Without a Country." It tells of the life of Lieutenant Philip Nolan, a young soldier who became part of Burr's scheme. When Nolan was on trial for his involvement, he cried out in anger, "I wish I may never hear of the United States again." For his punishment, the court granted Nolan's wish. The remainder of his life was spent aboard ships of the U.S. Navy. For more than 50 years, he was not allowed to set foot on American soil, and no one ever spoke to him of the United States.

The following passage is taken from the conclusion of the story. Lieutenant Nolan, aware that he is near death, begs the captain of his ship to tell him everything that has happened in his former country, which he has come to love.

◆ **VOCABULARY** Before you read the selection, find the meaning of these words in a dictionary: triced, sovereignty, tyrant, expiated, manifold, transgressions.

Dear Fred: I try to find heart and life to tell you that it is all over with dear old Nolan. I have been with him on this voyage more than I ever was, and I can

An American Seascape
Following the War of 1812, the United States entered an "Era of Good Feelings." Most Americans were filled with a deep love for their country. Many American artists expressed this feeling by painting pictures that captured the beauty of the American landscape. For instance, this painting by Fitz Hugh Lane highlights the tranquil beauty of Cape Anne, Massachusetts. **Linking Past and Present** *What are some of the ways in which Americans today express feelings of patriotism?*

understand wholly now the way in which you used to speak of the dear old fellow. I could see that he was not strong, but I had no idea the end was so near. . . . Well, I went in, and there, to be sure, the poor fellow lay in his berth, smiling pleasantly as he gave me his hand, but looking very frail. I could not help a glance round, which showed me what a little shrine he had made of the box he was lying in. The stars and stripes were triced up above and around a picture of Washington and he had painted a majestic eagle, with lightnings blazing from his beak and his foot just clasping the whole globe, which his wings overshadowed. The dear old boy saw my glance, and said, with a sad smile, "Here, you see. I have a country! And then he pointed to the foot of his bed, where I had not seen before a great map of the United States, as he had drawn it from memory, and which he had there to look upon as he lay. Quaint, queer old names were on it, in large letters: "Indiana Territory," "Mississippi Territory," and "Louisiana Territory," as I suppose our fathers learned such things; but the old fellow had patched in Texas, too; he had carried his western boundary all the way

to the Pacific, but on that shore he had defined nothing.

"O Captain," he said, "I know I am dying. I cannot get home. Surely you will tell me something now? . . . Do not speak till I say what I am sure you know, that there is not in this ship, that there is not in America—God bless her!—a more loyal man than I. There cannot be a man who loves the old flag as I do, or prays for it as I do, or hopes for it as I do. There are thirty-four stars in it now, Danforth. I thank God for that, though I do not know what their names are. There has never been one taken away; I thank God for that. I know by that that there has never been any successful Burr. O Danforth, Danforth," he sighed out, "how like a wretched night's dream a boy's idea of personal fame or of separate sovereignty seems, when one looks back on it after such a life as mine! But tell me—tell me something—tell me everything, Danforth, before I die."

Ingham, I swear to you that I felt like a monster that I had not told him everything before . . . Who was I, that I should have been acting the tyrant all this time over this . . . old man, who had years ago, expiated, in his whole manhood's life, the madness of a boy's treason? "Mr. Nolan," said I, "I will tell you everything you ask about. Only, where shall I begin?". . . "God bless you! Tell me their names," he said, and he pointed to the stars on the flag. "The last I know is Ohio. . . ."

I told him the names in as good order as I could, and he bade me take down his beautiful map and draw them in as I best could with my pencil. He was wild with delight about Texas, told me . . . he had guessed at Texas. Then he was delighted as he saw California and Oregon—that, he said, he had suspected partly, because he had never been permitted to land on that shore, though the ships were there so much. . . . Then he settled down more quietly, and very happily, to hear me tell in an hour the history of fifty years.

How I wished it had been somebody who knew something! But I did as well as I could. I told him of the English war. I told him about Fulton and the steamboat beginning. I told him about old Scott, and Jackson; told him all I could think of about the Mississippi, and New Orleans, and Texas and his own old Kentucky. . . .

I tell you, Ingham, it was a hard thing to condense the history of half a century into that talk with a sick man. And I do not now know what I told him—of emigration, and the means of it—of steamboats, and railroads, and telegraphs—of inventions, and books, and literature—of colleges, and West Point, and the Naval School—but with the queerest interruptions that ever you heard. You see it was Robinson Crusoe asking all the accumulated questions of fifty-six years! . . .

And he drank it in and enjoyed it as I cannot tell you. He grew more and more silent, yet I never thought he was tired or faint. I gave him a glass of water, but he just wet his lips, and told me not to go away. Then he asked me to bring the Presbyterian "Book of Public Prayer" which lay there, and said, with a smile, that it would open at the right place—

and so it did. . . . I knelt down and read, and he repeated with me, "For ourselves and our country, O gracious God, we thank Thee, that, notwithstanding our manifold transgressions of Thy holy laws, Thou hast continued to us Thy marvelous kindness." . . . "Danforth," said he, "I have repeated those prayers night and morning, it is now fifty-five years." And then he said he would go to sleep. He bent me down over him and said, "Look in my Bible, Captain, when I am gone." And I went away.

In an hour, when the doctor went in gently, he found Nolan had breathed his life away with a smile. He had something pressed close to his lips. It was his father's badge of the Order of the Cincinnati.

We looked in his Bible, and there was a slip of paper. . . . On this slip of paper he had written:

Bury me in the sea; it has been my home, and I love it. But will not some one set up a stone for my memory at Fort Adams or at Orleans, that my disgrace may not be more than I ought to bear? Say on it:

In Memory of
PHILIP NOLAN
Lieutenant in the Army
of the United States

He loved his country as no other man has loved her; but no man deserved less at her hands

Source: Edward Everett Hale, "The Man Without a Country," 1863.

THINKING ABOUT THE SELECTION

1. How does Nolan convey the love he has developed for his former country?
2. What did Nolan want Captain Danforth to tell him?
3. **Defending a Position** Do you think Nolan's punishment was fair? Why or why not?

◆ **INTRODUCTION** One of the most vivid accounts of the Battle of New Orleans was written by a rifleman who took part in it. All that is known about the author is that he came from Kentucky.

◆ **VOCABULARY** Before you read the selection, find the meaning of these words in a dictionary: apprehend, breastwork, epaulets, cadaverous, prostrate, levee.

The official report said the action lasted two hours and five minutes, but it did not seem half that length of time to me. It was so dark that little could be seen, until just about the time the battle ceased. The morning had dawned, to be sure, but the smoke was so thick that everything seemed to be covered up in it. Our men did not seem to apprehend any danger, but would load and fire as fast as they could, talking, swearing, and joking all the time. All ranks and sections were soon broken up. After the first shot, everyone loaded and banged away on his own hook. Henry Spillman did not load and fire quite so often as some of the rest, but every time he did fire he would go up to the breastwork, look over until he could see something to shoot at, and then take deliberate aim and crack away. Lieut. Ashby was as busy as a nailor* and it was evident that the River Raisin was uppermost in his mind all the time.** He kept dashing about and every now and then he would call out, with an oath, "We'll pay you now for the River Raisin! We'll give you something to remember the River Raisin!" When the British had come up to the opposite side of the breastwork, having no gun, he picked up an empty

---

*"Busy as a nailor (nailer)" was an expression of the time meaning someone who was very active.

**A force of Kentuckians had fought, and lost, the Battle of Frenchtown, on the Raisin River near Detroit, early in 1813.

The Battle of Baltimore *This painting by Thomas Ruckle, Sr., shows American troops assembling prior to the Battle of Baltimore during the War of 1812. After launching a successful assault on Washington, D.C., the British army had begun advancing toward Baltimore. The American forces were well-prepared, however, and were able to halt the British advance.* **American Traditions** *Why is the Battle of Baltimore considered a turning point in the War of 1812?*

barrel and flung it at them. Then finding an iron bar, he jumped up on the works and hove that at them. . . .

During the action, a number of the Tennessee men got mixed with ours. One of them was killed about five or six yards from where I stood. I did not know his name. A ball passed through his head and he fell against Ensign Weller. . . . This was the only man killed near where I was stationed.

It was near the close of the firing. About the time that I observed three or four men carrying his body away or directly after, there was a white flag raised on the opposite side of the breast-work and the firing ceased.

The white flag, before mentioned, was raised about ten or twelve feet from where I stood, close to the breastwork and a little to the right. It was a white hand-kerchief, or something of the kind, on a sword or stick. It was waved several times, and as soon as it was perceived, we ceased firing. Just then the wind got up a little and blew the smoke off, so that we could see the field. It then appeared that the flag had been raised by a British Officer wearing epaulets. It was told he was a Major. He stepped over the breast-work and came into our lines. Among the Tennesseeans who had got mixed with us during the fight, there was a little fellow whose name I do not know; but he was a cadaverous looking chap and went by [the name] of Paleface. As the British Officer came in, Paleface demanded his sword. He hesitated about giving it to him, prob-ably thinking it was [insulting] to his dignity, to surrender to a private all over begrimed with dust and powder and that some Officer should show him the cour-tesy to receive it. Just at that moment, Col. Smiley came up and cried, with a harsh oath, "Give it up—give it up to him in a minute!" The British Officer quickly handed his weapon to Paleface, holding it in both hands and making a very polite bow. . . .

When the smoke had cleared away and we could obtain a fair view of the field, it looked, at the first glance, like a sea of blood. It was not blood itself which gave it this appearance but the red coats in which the British soldiers were dressed. Straight out before our position, for about the width of space which we supposed had been occupied by the Brit-ish column, the field was entirely covered with prostrate bodies. In some places they were laying in piles of several, one on top of the other. On either side, there was an interval more thinly sprinkled with the slain; and then two other dense rows, one near the levee and the other towards the swamp. About two hundred years off, directly in front of our position, lay a large dapple gray horse, which we under-stood to have been Packenham's. . . .*

When we first got a fair view of the field in our front, individuals could be seen in every possible attitude. Some laying quite dead, others mortally wounded, pitching and tumbling about in the agonies of death. Some had their heads shot off, some their legs, some their arms. Some were laughing, some crying, some groaning, and some scream-ing. There was every variety of sight and sound.

Source: "A Contemporary Account of the Battle of New Orleans by a Soldier in the Ranks," *Louisiana Historical Quarterly*, January 1926.

THINKING ABOUT THE SELECTION

1. What aspects of the battle action does the author stress?
2. How does the author describe the battle-field after the firing stopped?
3. **Expressing an Opinion** On the basis of this selection, do you think the author was a careful observer? Why or why not?

---

*Sir Edward Pakenham was the general com-manding the British forces. He was killed in the battle.

The Growing Years

12-1   Traveling Westward   FIRST PERSON

◆ **INTRODUCTION** Charles Fenno Hoffman, a New Yorker, was one of the first professional writers in the United States. He was also a hardy man. Despite the fact that he had only one leg (the result of a childhood accident), he journeyed on horseback throughout the Northwest Territory in the early 1800s. In the following selection from his book *A Winter in the West*, he describes the National Road and the pioneer families who traveled along it as they headed westward to forge new lives on the frontier.

◆ **VOCABULARY** Before you read the selection, find the meaning of these words in a dictionary: emigrants, foraging, arduous, traverse, allude.

By far the greatest portion of travellers one meets with . . . consists of teamsters and the emigrants. The former generally drive six horses before their enormous wagons—stout, heavy-looking beasts, descended, it is said, from the famous [draft] horses of Normandy. They go about twenty miles a day. . . .

Making Travel Faster and Easier *The westward expansion of the United States was made easier by many improvements in transportation during the early 1800s. This painting by Lars Sellstedt shows two steamships leaving Buffalo harbor and a canal boat being pulled into the harbor.* **Linking Past and Present** *What important advances in transportation have occurred during the 1900s?*

As for the emigrants, it would astonish you to witness how they get along. A covered one-horse wagon generally contains the whole worldly substance of a family consisting not infrequently of a dozen members. The tolls are so high along this western turnpike, and horses are comparatively so cheap in the region whither the emigrant is bound, that he rarely provides more than one miserable [horse] to transport his whole family to the far west. The strength of the poor animal is of course half the time unequal to the demand upon it, and you will, therefore, unless it be raining very hard, rarely see anyone in the wagon, except perhaps some child overtaken by sickness, or a mother nursing a young infant. The head of the family walks by the horse, cheering and encouraging him on his way. The good woman, when not engaged as hinted above, either trudges along with her husband, or, leading some weary little traveller by the hand far behind, endeavors to keep the rest of her charge from loitering by the wayside. The old house-dog—if not chained beneath the wagon to prevent the half-starved brute from foraging too freely in a friendly country—brings up the rear. . . .

The hardships of such a tour must form no bad preparatory school for the arduous life which the new settler has afterward to enter upon. Their horses, of course, frequently give out on the road; and in companies so numerous, sickness must frequently overtake some of the members. . . .

About thirty miles from Wheeling we first struck the national road. It appears to have been originally constructed of large round stones, thrown without much arrangement on the surface of the soil, after the road was first levelled. These are now being plowed up, and a thin layer of broken stones is in many places spread over the renovated surface. I hope the roadmakers have not the conscience to call this Macadamizing.* It yields like snow-drift to the heavy wheels which traverse it, and the very best parts of the road that I saw are not to be compared with a Long-Island turnpike. Two-thirds indeed of the extent we traversed were worse than any artificial road I ever travelled, except perhaps the log causeways among the new settlements in northern New York. The ruts are worn so broad and deep by heavy travel, that an army of pigmies might march into the bosom of the country under the cover they would afford. . . .

There is one feature, however, in this national work which is truly fine—I allude to the massive stone bridges which form a part of it. They occur, as the road crosses a winding creek, a dozen times within twice as many miles. They consist either of one, two, or three arches; the centre arch being sprung a foot or two higher than those on either side. Their thick walls projecting above the road, their round stone buttresses, and carved key-stones combine to give them an air of Roman solidity and strength. They are monuments of taste and power that will speak well for the country when the brick towns they bind together shall have crumbled in the dust.

Source: Charles Fenno Hoffman, *A Winter in the West,* 1835.

THINKING ABOUT THE SELECTION

1. Describe a typical pioneer family as seen by Hoffman.
2. (a) What does Hoffman dislike about the National Road? (b) What does he like?
3. **Defending a Position** As Hoffman describes them, do the settlers moving westward seem admirable? Give reasons for your answer.

---

*Macadam roads, developed about 1815, were constructed of crushed stones. They were named after their inventor, a Scot named John McAdam.

◆ **INTRODUCTION** The construction of canals was one of the major improvements in transportation in the United States in the early 1800s. Despite their importance, however, the canals also had their own unique problems. Mule drivers had to alert passengers riding on top of the canal boats to such dangers as low bridges. This warning is sounded in the refrain of the following song, "Low Bridge, Everybody Down."

◆ **VOCABULARY** Before you read the selection, find the meaning of these words in a dictionary: navigated, lock.

I've got a mule and her name is Sal,
Fifteen miles on the Erie Canal.
She's a good old worker and a good old
    pal,
Fifteen miles on the Erie Canal.
We've hauled some barges in our day,
Filled with lumber, coal, and hay,
And we know every inch of the way
From Albany to Buffalo.

    Chorus:
    Low bridge! Everybody down!
    Low bridge! We're a-coming to a town.
    You'll always know your neighbor,
      you'll always know your pal
    If you've ever navigated on the Erie
      Canal.

We'd better get on our way, old pal,
Fifteen miles on the Erie Canal.
You can bet your life I'd never part with
    Sal,
Fifteen miles on the Erie Canal.
Get us there, Sal, here comes a lock;
We'll make Rome 'fore six o'clock.
One more trip and back we'll go,
Right back home to Buffalo.

    Chorus

Source: Traditional folk song.

THINKING ABOUT THE SELECTION

1. Name some of the products transported by barge on the Erie Canal.
2. What do you think conditions must have been like on canal barges?
3. **Applying Information** On a map of New York State, locate the cities mentioned in the song.

Cultural Life in American Cities *During the Industrial Revolution, most American cities grew rapidly. The increase in population caused many problems, but it also had a number of positive effects. For instance, cities became cultural centers with theaters, museums, and concert halls. This painting by John Searle shows a New York City theater in the early 1800s.* **Daily Life** *What do you think were the main differences between city life and rural life during the early 1800s?*

Forging Trails Across the Frontier *During the early- and mid-1800s, the United States grew rapidly. A steady flow of pioneers headed westward, hoping to start new lives on the frontier. In this painting, Albert Bierstadt shows a surveying expedition heading into the Rocky Mountains.* **American Traditions** *What do you imagine it might have been like to have been one of the first settlers to arrive in the Rocky Mountains? Explain.*

CHAPTER 13 The Jackson Era

13-1 The President's Lady LITERATURE

◆ **INTRODUCTION** Irving Stone's biographical novel *The President's Lady* tells the story of Andrew Jackson and his wife, Rachel, from their first meeting until Rachel's death just before her husband's inauguration. The following passage from the novel tells of Jackson's reaction to the outcome of the presidential election of 1824.

◆ **VOCABULARY** Before you read the selection, find the meaning of these words in a dictionary: donned, greatcoat, prodigious, chagrin, castigation, morosely, pilloried, tumultuous, maraudings, ardent, booty, garner.

They awakened on the morning of February 9, the day of decision, to find snow falling heavily. Andrew donned a greatcoat and boots and left the hotel in time to reach the Capitol by noon, so that he might participate in the senatorial count which would name John Calhoun as vice-president. When Rachel asked if he were intending to remain after the Senate adjourned and the House took its seat to vote for president he replied that he did not think it proper for him to be in the House while the members were being polled.

He was back shortly after one o'clock, ordering dinner sent up to their room so they could avoid the milling crowds below in the tavern. The first course had just been set on their parlor table when Andy came in, the expression on his face clearer than any marked ballot: Mr. Adams had been elected on the first count! By prodigious efforts and brilliant maneuvering Henry Clay, singlehanded, had swung Kentucky, Ohio and Missouri behind Adams.

John Eaton [Jackson's assistant] stormed in, his face black with disappointment and chagrin, and proceeded to give Henry Clay a thorough castigation. Andrew heard him out, then said quietly:

"That's not altogether fair to Mr. Clay, John. He has a right to throw his influence to the man he thinks best for the job. You remember he once accused me, right on the floor of the House, of being a 'military chieftain who would overthrow the liberties of the people.'"

That evening they attended the last of President Monroe's regular Wednesday levees. Andrew congratulated Mr. Adams cordially. While riding back to the hotel in the Jackson carriage, John Eaton commented on how quiet the city was: no bonfires, no victory celebrations or cheering crowds.

"They wanted you, General," Eaton concluded morosely. "They feel cheated."

But nothing could shake Andrew's calm acceptance. For her own part, Rachel was content. On the whole it had been a decent election; the predictions that the Republic would fall into ruin because its Chief Executive was to be chosen by popular vote had failed to materialize; and so had her own fears of being pilloried by the opposition.

"Well, Rachel, my dear, I tried to make you First Lady of the land. You are not too disappointed, are you?"

She smiled inwardly. . . .

"Whatever disappointment I may feel is for you."

"Well, then, I'll be happy to get back to the Hermitage."

"For how long?" she asked softly. ". . . until the next election?"

His eyes met hers. They were stern.

"I will be fifty-eight in a month. Mr. Adams is certain to serve the regular two terms. Surely you don't think at the age of sixty-six . . . ? This is *forever!*"

He used that word to me at home, thought Rachel, but this time he means it. Perhaps at long last he will be content to remain a gentleman planter.

Forever lasted five days. On February 14, President-elect Adams offered the post of Secretary of State to Henry Clay. All hell broke loose, in Washington and across the nation. . . .

Every ounce of Andrew's calm and acceptance vanished. She knew from the sense of outrage that shook his long lean frame that nothing in his tumultuous career, always excepting the maraudings of the British, had ever made him so utterly determined to avenge a wrong. As

---

Hard at Work *During the Age of Jackson, a growing number of white men played a role in politics. A self-made man and a war hero, Jackson won the loyal support of common Americans, such as the blacksmith in this painting by Francis William Edmunds.* **Linking Past and Present** *How important is it for politicians today to win the support of average Americans?*

he stood in the far corner of the room surrounded by his most ardent supporters, she heard him cry:

"So the Judas of the West has closed the contract and will receive the thirty pieces of silver? The end will be the same. Was there ever witnessed such a barefaced corruption before?"

A dozen voices answered him at once.

"But surely Mr. Clay will know that the whole country is outraged?" "He can't be so stupid as to accept . . ."

"What, refuse his part of the booty?" Andrew's voice, as it penetrated to her, was shrill and cold. "But he must go before the Senate for confirmation. By the Eternal, gentlemen, I still have a vote here, and I pledge you my word that I shall unbosom myself. This barter of votes is sheer bribery, and if allowed to continue will destroy our form of government."

Three weeks later, in a slanting rainstorm, the family left the capital, all four riding in the carriage with the extra horses tied behind. Andrew was silent, his head on his chest, his eyes closed; he was still smarting from his defeat in the Senate where he had been able to garner only fourteen votes against the appointment of Mr. Clay. She had persuaded him that, as a matter of form, he should attend the inauguration. He had complained to her that Mr. Adams "had been escorted to the Capitol with the pomp and ceremony of guns and drums, which is not consistent with the character of the occasion." However, he had been among the first to shake hands with Mr. Adams, and had administered the oath to Calhoun, the new Vice-President, in the Senate.

Source: Irving Stone, *The President's Lady* (New York: Avenel Books, 1981).

THINKING ABOUT THE SELECTION

1. Why did Andrew Jackson defend Clay against John Eaton's charges?
2. What event caused Jackson to charge that there had been corruption in the election?
3. **Making Inferences** What effect do you think the election of 1824 had on Andrew Jackson's campaign for President in 1828? Explain.

13-2   Campaign Hoopla   FIRST PERSON

◆ **INTRODUCTION** In the presidential campaign of 1840, few Whigs were more enthusiastic than a prosperous New York merchant named Philip Hone. Having lost a great deal of money in the depression of the 1830s, Hone hated the Democrats. In his diary, he admiringly describes some of the meetings and parades in honor of "Tippecanoe and Tyler too."

◆ **VOCABULARY** Before you read the selection, find the meaning of these words in a dictionary: paraphernalia, appellation, scepter, prodigious, decorous.

BOSTON, THURSDAY, SEPT. 8.—The great day is over, and how shall I attempt to describe it? The weather, which was doubtful last night, was bright this morning, and the delegates from other States and from the different towns in Massachusetts began to assemble on the Common at nine o'clock, with their standards, badges, and other paraphernalia. The scene began to be very soon of the most exciting character. Crowds were pressing toward the spot from every quarter. The windows of the fine houses which surround the Common were filled with well-dressed ladies. Horsemen were galloping to and fro, and Old Men of the Revolution tottering toward the places allotted to them. . . . I was directed to join the other invited guests at the State

A Country Celebration *During the Jackson administration and the years that followed, many American painters celebrated the life of the common people. For example, this painting by William Sidney Mount shows a lively country dance.* **American Traditions** *Why is it not surprising that many American artists celebrated the lives of average Americans during the Age of Jackson?*

House, where I met Mr. [Daniel] Webster, the President of the day, and many other distinguished men. The procession did not begin to move until twelve o'clock. . . .

The procession moved up Beacon Street and down the other side of the Common . . . proceeded through Charlestown and arrived at Bunker Hill after a march of two hours and a half. . . . The ceremonies were commenced by a short address from Mr. Webster . . . after which several of the distinguished visitors were introduced to the audience, and each in turn made a short speech much to the purpose.

This honor was conferred upon me. Mr. Webster presented me as his friend, and informed the people that I was the person who first distinguished the party by the appellation of Whigs.* I spoke a few minutes and then concluded by saying that it appeared to me that all the men in the United States were present, and that they had better cut the matter short by going into the election at once. "As many of you, therefore," I said at the top of my voice, "as are willing to have William Henry Harrison for your President will please to say aye." This was responded to by a shout that rent the skies, and I came off with flying colors. . . .

WEDNESDAY, DEC. 2.—*Presidential Election.** This is the day which decides the fate of Mr. Van Buren and his Administration. The electors of President and Vice-President meet simultaneously in each of the States of the Union, and will quietly and in discharge of the constitutional rights of the people, deposit 234 votes for William Henry Harrison for

---

*Hone claimed to have been the first to use the term "Whigs" for the party of those who opposed Jackson.

*This was not when balloting took place, but rather the day when state electors met to confirm the popular vote.

President, . . . and 60 votes for Martin Van Buren for President. . . .

The party which has been in power forty years yields the scepter to its adversary, . . . There is not probably a country in the world where a change of such prodigious magnitude could have been effected in the same time, with so little apparent machinery, and in so orderly and decorous a manner.

Source: Allan Nevins, ed., *The Diary of Philip Hone* (New York: Dodd, Mead and Company, 1927).

CHAPTER 14

From Sea to Shining Sea

14-1   Death Comes for the Archbishop   LITERATURE

◆ **INTRODUCTION** Many of the novels and stories of Willa Cather (1873–1947) focus on pioneer life in the Great Plains. In *Death Comes for the Archbishop,* however, her setting is the American Southwest during the 1850s. The book's main character, Bishop Latour, journeys with his Native American guide Jacinto throughout New Mexico and Arizona and is deeply influenced by the environment and the culture of the region. In the following selection, Father Latour and Jacinto camp for the night during a journey to a distant mission.

◆ **VOCABULARY** Before you read the selection, find the meaning of these words in a dictionary: firmament, proposition, vehement.

Jacinto got firewood and good water from the Lagunas, and they made their camp in a pleasant spot on the rocks north of the village. As the sun dropped low, the light brought the white church and the yellow adobe houses up into relief from the flat ledges. Behind their camp, not far away, lay a group of great mesas. The Bishop asked Jacinto if he knew the name of the one nearest them.

"No, I do not know any name," he shook his head. "I know Indian name," he added, as if, for once, he were thinking aloud.

"And what is the Indian name?"

"The Laguna Indians call Snow-Bird mountain." He spoke somewhat unwillingly.

"That is very nice," said the Bishop musingly. "Yes, that is a pretty name. . . ."

The two companions sat, each thinking his own thoughts as night closed in about them; a blue night set with stars, the bulk of solitary mesas cutting into the

Life in San Antonio *During the mid-1800s, settlers flooded into the Southwest. By the 1840s, the population of Texas alone had swelled to 140,000. Many of these people settled in emerging cities. This painting by William G.M. Samuel shows downtown San Antonio in 1849.* **Daily Life** *How might life in San Antonio during the mid-1800s have differed from life in the large eastern cities of the time?*

firmament. The Bishop seldom questioned Jacinto about his thoughts or beliefs. He didn't think it polite, and he believed it to be useless. There was no way he could transfer his own memories of European civilization into the Indian mind, and he was quite willing to believe that behind Jacinto there was a long tradition, a store of experience, which no language could translate to him. A chill came with the darkness. Father Latour put on his old fur-lined cloak, and Jacinto, loosening the blanket tied about his loins, drew it up over his head and shoulders.

"Many stars," he said presently. "What you think about the stars, Padre?"

"The wise men tell us they are worlds, like ours, Jacinto."

. . . "I think not," he said in the tone of one who has considered a proposition fairly and rejected it. "I think they are leaders—great spirits."

"Perhaps they are," said the Bishop with a sigh. "Whatever they are, they are great. Let us say *Our Father,* and go to sleep, my boy."

Kneeling on either side of the embers they repeated the prayer together and then rolled up in their blankets. The Bishop went to sleep thinking with satisfaction that he was beginning to have some sort of human companionship with his Indian boy. One called the young Indians "boys," perhaps because there was something youthful and elastic in their bodies. Certainly about their behavior there was nothing boyish in the American sense, nor even in the European sense. Jacinto was never, by any chance, [naive]; he was never taken by surprise. One felt that his training, whatever it had been, had prepared him to meet any situation which might confront him. He was as much at home in the Bishop's study as in his own pueblo—and he was never too much at home anywhere. Father Latour felt he had gone a good way toward gaining his guide's friendship, though he did not know how.

The truth was, Jacinto liked the Bishop's way of meeting people; thought he had the right tone with Padre Gallegos, the right tone with Padre Jesus, and that he had good manners with the Indians. In his experience, white people, when they addressed Indians, always put on a false face. There were many kinds of false faces; Father Vaillant's, for example, was kindly but too vehement. The Bishop put on none at all. He stood straight and turned to the Governor of Laguna, and

his face underwent no change. Jacinto thought this remarkable.

From DEATH COMES FOR THE ARCHBISHOP by Willa Cather. Copyright 1927 by Willa Cather and renewed 1955 by the Executors of the Estate of Willa Cather. Reprinted by permission of Alfred A. Knopf, Inc.

THINKING ABOUT THE SELECTION

1. Why did the Bishop hardly ever question Jacinto about his beliefs?
2. How had the Bishop gained Jacinto's trust?
3. **Comparing** (a) Compare the Bishop's and Jacinto's beliefs concerning the stars. (b) What did each man think of the other's belief?

14-2   In the Gold Fields of California   FIRST PERSON

◆ **INTRODUCTION** One of the thousands of forty-niners drawn west by the Gold Rush was Elisha Douglass Perkins. At the age of twenty-five, he left Marietta, Ohio, to try his luck in the California gold fields. After a difficult cross-country trip that took more than four months, Perkins and the friends he was traveling with arrived in Sacramento in the fall of 1849. Soon afterward, they tried their luck prospecting. Perkins's diary ends a few months after these entries. He died in California in 1852, having never returned to Ohio.

◆ **VOCABULARY** Before you read the selection, find the meaning of these words in a dictionary: adz, commenced, sundries, accumulating, bilious.

November 1. Well here we are in the gold mines of California, & mining has been tried "& found wanting!" We left Sac. City [Sacramento] October 18, with our provisions &c in Chapins wagons en route for the Cosumne River distant some 28 or 30 miles & arrived here the 21. We are about

S.E. from the city, in a rolling country & on a small rapid stream tumbling over a rocky bed. The appearance of the country through which we passed was somewhat better than that down the Sac. River, as we saw it, but yet I have not been in any part of the "beautiful valley" of which we used to hear. On locating here we immediately went to work making "washers."* Doc & John being somewhat "under the weather" I did nearly all the work on the mine alone. I cut down a pine tree, cut it off the proper length peeled & cut down one side & with axe & adz hollowed it out till I reduced it to about 1/2 inch in thickness by nearly two days of hard labor & blistering of hands &c. . . .

The first three days Doc took hold with pick & shovel we excavated a hole about 4 feet deep & made in that time about 2.00! Here Doc broke down & was taken sick & John being about [recovered]

———
*These were wooden troughs through which water was poured to wash out sand and pebbles, leaving the heavier gold behind.

he commenced with me in another place & we have made something everyday, the highest 11.00 lowest 3 each. This won't do & we shall probably leave soon for richer diggings next week. Tis terrible hard work, & such a backache as we have every night! We are below the bed of the creek & have to bale out water from our "hole" every hour, & work in the mud & wet at the bottom.

I am pretty well satisfied that fortunes in Cal. as anywhere else, with some exceptions, take *time* & hard work to get, & I must go home without mine I'm afraid, as I would hardly lead this kind of life 5 years for any fortune, & I certainly would not be separated from H. [Harriet] for that length of time. Since we have been here every man of our company has been sick but myself. . . .

Thursday Nov. Still in our camp on the Cosumne & poor as the "diggings" have proved are likely to remain here all winter. The rains have set in in earnest & teams cannot travel. Chapins teams went to town for our provisions & sundries & are stuck fast about 5 miles from here, not able to move a step. I fear we may have difficulty in getting anything to eat. Doc has finally left us for good, & will probably go home in the next steamer, couldn't stand the hard work & went to town last week. His leaving puts the finishing stroke to my list of disappointments "& now I'm all alone." Shall have to give up my expectations of accumulating sufficient to carry me home in the spring & be thankful if I get enough to pay my expenses this winter. Well I'm here & must take the country as I find it. . . .

Christmas Day, 1849. Oh how I wish I could spend this day at home, what a "merry Christmas" I would have of it, & what happy faces I should see instead of these of the disappointed set now around me. The day here ushered in by firing of guns pistols &c & some blasting of heavy logs in lieu of cannon & this is about the amount of our celebrating. . . .

Gold Rush Sketches *Following the discovery of gold in 1848, people poured into California from all over the world. In 1849, more than 80,000 people arrived, hoping to strike it rich. These drawings by O. C. Seltzer provide a glimpse of the daily lives of prospectors.* **Linking Past and Present** *California's population has continued to grow throughout the 1900s. How might you explain this growth?*

January 8, 1850, Thursday P.M. Have just returned from assisting in the performance of the last sad duties for one of our little party which left Marietta last spring so full of health & high hopes. S. E. Cross was taken sick about two weeks since with a bilious fever. . . . Although every thing was done for him which our means permitted, [the illness] proved fatal yesterday January 7, at about 11 o'clock P.M. & we buried him today upon the hill side overlooking our little settlement. The death of one of our number here so far away from home & all that makes life dear, casts a gloom on all the survivors & we cannot but think of the possibility of a like fate being reserved for ourselves, & oh how terrible the thought. If I must die, let me but get home & die in the arms of my friends, & I'll not complain, but here with no one to care for me, or shed a tear of affection as my spirit takes its flight, tis horrible. . . . California has been, & will be the cause of many broken hearts & much grief, & I look forward to my release from it with great anxiety.

Source: Thomas D. Clark, ed., *Gold Rush Diary: Being the Journal of Elisha Douglass Perkins on the Overland Trail in the Spring and Summer of 1849* (Lexington, KY: University of Kentucky Press, 1967).

THINKING ABOUT THE SELECTION

1. What circumstances made gold mining especially difficult for Perkins and his companions?
2. What seems to have been Perkins's worst fear?
3. **Drawing Conclusions** If Perkins's diary entries had been printed in the Marietta newspaper, what effect do you think they might have had?

The Different Worlds of the North and South

15-1   American Notes   LITERATURE

◆ **INTRODUCTION** Charles Dickens, a famous English novelist, visited the United States for six months in 1842. During that time he traveled to Boston, New York, Philadelphia, Washington, St. Louis, and Cincinnati and journeyed on the Mississippi River. Dickens's keen powers of observation and subtle sense of humor are evident throughout his account of this trip. In the following selection, Dickens describes the American railroad of the 1840s.

◆ **VOCABULARY** Before you read the selection, find the meaning of these words in a dictionary: omnibuses, caravan, anthracite, interrogatively, enumerate, hewn, stagnant.

I made acquaintance with an American railroad, on this occasion, for the first time. As these works are pretty much alike all through the States, their general characteristics are easily described.

There are no first and second class carriages as with us; but there is a gentlemen's car and a ladies' car: the main distinction between which is that in the first, everybody smokes; and in the second, nobody does. As a black man never travels with a white one, there is also a negro car; . . . There is a great deal of jolting, a great deal of noise, a great deal of wall, not much window, a locomotive engine, a shriek, and a bell.

The cars are like shabby omnibuses, but larger: holding thirty, forty, fifty, people. The seats, instead of stretching from end to end, are placed crosswise. Each seat holds two persons. There is a long row of them on each side of the caravan, a narrow passage up the middle, and a door at both ends. In the centre of the carriage there is usually a stove, fed with charcoal or anthracite coal; which is for the most part red-hot. It is insufferably close; and you see the hot air fluttering between yourself and any other object you may happen to look at, like the ghost of smoke.

In the ladies' car, there are a great many gentlemen who have ladies with them. There are also a great many ladies who have nobody with them: for any lady may travel alone, from one end of the United States to the other, and be certain of the most courteous and considerate treatment everywhere. The conductor or check-taker, or guard, or whatever he may be, wears no uniform. He walks up and down the car, and in and out of it, as his fancy dictates; leans against the door with his hands in his pockets and stares at you, if you chance to be a stranger; or enters into conversation with the passengers about him. A great many newspapers are pulled out, and a few of them are read. Everybody talks to you, or to anybody else who hits his fancy. If you are an Englishman, he expects that the railroad is pretty much like an English railroad. If you say "No," he says "Yes?" (interrogatively), and asks in what respect they differ. You enumerate the heads of difference, one by one, and he says "Yes?" (still interrogatively) to each. Then he guesses that you don't travel faster in England; and on your replying that you do, says, "Yes?" again (still interrogatively), and it is quite evident, doesn't believe it. . . .

Except when a branch road joins the main one, there is seldom more than one track of rails; so that the road is very narrow, and the view, where there is a deep cutting, by no means extensive. When there is not, the character of the

The Transportation Revolution *Many advances in transportation occurred during the mid-1800s. The most significant of these was the railroad. This painted tin tray shows an early train traveling through the countryside.* **Linking Past and Present** *What do you consider to be the most important advance in transportation in the 1900s? Why?*

scenery is always the same. Mile after mile of stunted trees: some hewn down by the axe, some blown down by the wind, some half fallen and resting on their neighbours, many mere logs half hidden in the swamp, others mouldered away to spongy chips. . . . Now you emerge for a few brief minutes on an open country, glittering with some bright lake or pool, broad as many an English river, but so small here that it scarcely has a name; now catch hasty glimpses of a distant town, with its clean white houses and their cool piazzas, its prim New England church and schoolhouse; when whir-r-r-r! almost before you have seen them, comes the same dark screen: the stunted trees, the stumps, the logs, the stagnant water —all so like the last that you seem to have been transported back again by magic.

The train calls at stations in the woods, where the wild impossibility of anybody having the smallest reason to get out, is only to be equalled by the apparently desperate hopelessness of there being anybody to get in. It rushes across the turnpike road, where there is no gate, no policeman, no signal: nothing but a rough wooden arch, on which is painted "When the Bell Rings, Look Out For The Locomotive." On it whirls headlong, dives through the woods again, emerges in the light, clatters over frail arches, rumbles upon the heavy ground, shoots beneath a wooden bridge which intercepts the light for a second like a wink, suddenly awakens all the slumbering echoes in the main street of a large town, and dashes on haphazard, pell-mell, neck-or-nothing, down the middle of the road. There—with mechanics working at their trades, and people leaning from their doors and windows, and boys flying kites and playing marbles, and men smoking, and women talking, and children crawling, and pigs burrowing, and unaccustomed horses plunging and rearing, close to the very rails—there—on, on, on—tears the mad dragon of an engine with its train of cars; scattering in all directions a shower of burning sparks from its wood fire; screeching, hissing, yelling, panting; until at last the thirsty monster stops beneath a covered way to drink, the people cluster round, and you have time to breathe again.

Source: Charles Dickens, *American Notes*, 1842.

THINKING ABOUT THE SELECTION

1. According to Dickens, what is the most noticeable distinction between the men's car and the ladies' car?
2. (a) What impression does Dickens convey of the interiors of the railroad cars? (b) Which details in his account contribute to this impression?
3. **Comparing** According to Dickens, how were American railroads different from those in England?

15-2   Contrasting North and South   FIRST PERSON

◆ **INTRODUCTION** Harriet Martineau of England, who traveled widely in the United States in the 1830s, was an acute observer of the American scene. In the following passage from her book *Society in America,* she presents her contrasting impressions of the North and the South. As you read the selection, note how Martineau's personal opinions color her writing.

◆ **VOCABULARY** Before you read the selection, find the meaning of these words in a dictionary: preclude, predicament, servile, debasement, degradation, incessant.

In the north, the children all go to school, and work there, more or less. As they grow up, they part off into the greatest variety of employments. The youths must, without exception, work hard; or they had better drown themselves. Whether they are to be lawyers, or otherwise professional; or merchants, manufacturers, farmers, or citizens, they have everything to do for themselves. A very large proportion of them have, while learning their future business, to earn the means of learning. There is much manual labour in the country colleges; much teaching in the vacations done by students. Many a great man in Congress was seen in his boyhood leading his father's horses to water; and, in his youth, guiding the plow in his father's field. There is probably hardly a man in New England who cannot ride, drive, and tend his own horse. . . .

There are a few young men, esteemed the least happy members of the community, who inherit wealth. The time will come, when the society is somewhat older, when it will be understood that wealth need not preclude work. But at present, there are no individuals so forlorn, in the

Women Heading to the Factory *As northern industries grew, thousands of women went to work in factories. In this painting by Winslow Homer, a group of women are heading to work, carrying their lunch pails. The wooded setting of the factory was typical of many New England factories of the time. Yet the women who worked there usually endured harsh conditions and were badly underpaid.* **Daily Life** *What do you imagine a typical day was like for the women in this painting?*

northern States, as young men of fortune. Men who have shown energy and skill in working their way in society are preferred for political representatives. There is no scientific or literary class, for such individuals to fall into: all the world is busy around them, and they are reduced to the predicament, unhappily the most dreaded of all in the United States, of standing alone. . . .

As for the women of the northern States, most have the blessing of work, though not of the extent and variety which will hereafter be seen to be necessary for the happiness of their lives. All married women, except the ladies of rich merchants and others, are liable to have their hands full of household occupation, from the uncertainty of domestic service. . . . Women who do not marry have, in many instances, to work for their support. . . .

What is life in the slave States, in respect of work?

There are two classes, the servile and the [master], between whom there is a great gulf fixed. The servile class has not even the benefit of hearty toil. No solemn truths sink down into them, to cheer their hearts, stimulate their minds, and nerve their hands. Their wretched lives are passed between an utter debasement of the will, and a conflict of the will with external force.

The other class is in circumstances as unfavourable as the least happy order of persons in the old world. The means of educating children are so meagre that young people begin life under great disadvantages. The vicious fundamental principle of morals in a slave country, that labour is disgraceful, taints the infant mind with a stain which is fatal in the world of spirits. . . . When children at school call everything that pleases them "gentlemanly," and pity all (but slaves) who have to work, and talk of marrying early for a [home], it is all over with them. A more hopeless state of degradation can hardly be conceived of, however they may ride, and play the harp, and sing Italian, and teach their slaves what they call religion. . . .

The wives of slave-holders are, as they and their husbands declare, as much slaves as their negroes. If they will not have everything go to rack and ruin around them, they must superintend every household operation, from the cellar to the garrets. . . . The lady of the house carries her huge bunch of keys, (for every consumable thing must be locked up,) and has to give out, on incessant requests, whatever is wanted for the household. She is for ever superintending, and trying to keep things straight, without the slightest hope of attaining anything like leisure and comfort. What is there in . . . the reputation of ease and luxury, which can compensate for toils and cares of this nature?

Source: Harriet Martineau, *Society in America*, 1837.

THINKING ABOUT THE SELECTION

1. What, to Martineau, is the most striking feature of life in the North?
2. Why does she think the circumstances of the slave owners are unfavorable?
3. **Drawing Conclusions** (a) What overall impression of American life does Martineau convey? (b) Do you think that most Americans of the time would have agreed with her? Why or why not? (c) Do you agree? Explain.

CHAPTER 16

A Reforming Age

16-1   Conductor on the Underground Railroad   LITERATURE

◆ **INTRODUCTION** Harriet Tubman, who was born a slave, escaped to freedom in 1849. Anxious for others to enjoy that same freedom, she became a "conductor" for the underground railroad, escorting fugitive slaves to Canada. On one very important journey in 1854, three of her brothers were among the group of people she helped escape. The following passage from Ann Petry's biography of Tubman describes part of that journey. When it begins, Harriet and her brothers are hiding on the plantation where their parents, Daddy Ben and Old Rit, are slaves.

◆ **VOCABULARY** Before you read the selection find the meaning of these words in a dictionary: fodder, chinks, detain, jouncing.

It was still raining. From the dark, heavy look of the sky, visible through the roof of the fodder house, it would be an all-day rain. Christmas Day. And a Sunday. The beat of the rain against the roof of the fodder house, against its sides, would be their only Christmas greeting. She hoped they wouldn't resent it too much.

There were wide chinks in the walls. Through them she could see the sway-backed cabin where Daddy Ben and Old Rit lived. It looked exactly like the cabin on the Brodas plantation where she was born. A whole row of these sway-backed cabins here, too. Smoke kept pouring out of the clay-daubed chimney, hanging heavy in the air. Old Rit had probably killed her pig, and was cooking it for the Christmas dinner. The master gave her a baby pig every year, and she fattened it, saving food from her own plate to feed the pig, so that she could feed her family with a lavish hand on this one day. She'd have pork and sausage and bacon. Plenty of food. The boys said that Old Rit was expecting them for dinner. They always spent Christmas Day with her.

She had to figure out some way of letting Ben know that she was here, that the boys were with her and that they needed food. It would never do to let Old Rit know this. She would laugh and shout. Then when she learned, as she certainly would, that the boys were running away, going North, she would try to detain them, would create such an uproar that the entire quarter would know their secret.

Harriet remembered the two men, John Chase and Peter Jackson. They were strangers. She asked them to go to the cabin, to tell Ben that his children were in the fodder house, badly in need of food. She warned them not to let Old Rit overhear what they said.

John and Peter did exactly as she told them. She watched them knock on the ramshackle door of the cabin, saw the door open, saw Old Ben standing in the doorway. The men motioned to him to come outside. They talked to him. Ben

Publicizing the Abolitionist Cause *Printing played a major role in the abolition movement. Antislavery newspapers, such as* Freedom's Journal *and* The Liberator, *helped to convince thousands of Americans to join the cause. This portrait by Robert Street shows a typical printer hard at work in his shop.* **Linking Past and Present** *What impact do newspapers have on the views of Americans today? What other media also affect our views?*

nodded his head. His expression did not change at all. She thought, how wonderful he is. Then he went back inside the cabin.

Late in the afternoon, he tapped on the side of the fodder house, and then opened the door, and put part of the Christmas dinner—cooked bacon, hoecake, fried pork and roasted yams— inside on the floor. He did not look at them. He said, "I know what'll come of this and I ain't goin' *to see my children,* nohow."

Harriet remembered his reputation for truthfulness. His word had always been accepted on the plantation because he was never known to tell a lie. She felt a kind of wondering admiration for him. He had become an old man in the five years since she had seen him—an old man. Yet the integrity and the strength of his character had not changed. How badly he must have wanted to see them, four of his children, there in the fodder house, on Christmas Day; but he would not lie, and so he would not look at them. Thus, if he was questioned as to the whereabouts of his boys, he could say that he had not seen them.

He made three trips from the cabin to the fodder house. Each time he put a small bundle of food inside the door until he must have given them most of the food intended for the Christmas dinner. Harriet noticed how slow his movements were. He was stooped over. He had aged fast. She would have to come back soon for him and Old Rit. Some time very soon. She remembered his great strength, and his love for his broadax, and the stories he used to tell her about the wonderful things to be seen in the woods. She wanted to put her arms around him and look deep into his eyes and didn't because she respected his right to make this self-sacrificing contribution to their safety. How he must have wanted to look at them, especially at the daughter whom he had not seen for five long years.

They stayed in the fodder house all that day, lying on the top of the corn, listening to the drip of the rain, waiting for dark, when they would set out. They spoke in whispers.

Harriet kept reassuring them. They were perfectly safe. They would not be missed for at least two days. At Christmas everyone was busy, dancing, laughing. The masters were entertaining their friends and relatives in their big, comfortable houses. The slaves were not required to work—as long as the Yule logs burned in the fireplaces. She had never lost a passenger, never run her train off the track, they were safe with her, the Lord would see them through.

She knew they did not like this long rainy day spent inside a fodder house, rain coming through the chinks in the boards. Dainty, pretty Catherine, who had been a house servant, complained bitterly. She objected to the rough feel of the corn. She said she thought she heard the sound of rats, a dry scrabbling sound.

Harriet laughed at her, and told her this was easy, just sitting around like this, that the Underground Railroad wasn't any train ride. It means walking, and sometimes running, and being hungry, and sometimes jouncing up and down in the bottom of a farmer's wagon, but more walking than riding, rain or dry, through woods and swamps and briars and hiding anywhere that the earth offered a little shelter against prying eyes and listening ears. It meant not enough sleep because the walking had to be done at night and the sleeping during the day. Before the journey ended, Catherine would be able to sleep anywhere, on the ground, in a haystack, under a bush, and this rat-infested fodder house would loom in her memory like a king's palace. . . .

Late in the afternoon, Ben made one more trip. He pushed another bundle of food inside the door. He kept his eyes closed, tight shut. He said he would be back when it got dark and would walk with them just a little way, to visit with them. . . .

When night came, Ben tapped at the door. He had tied a bandanna tight around his eyes. Harriet took one of his arms and one of the boys took him by the other arm. They started out, walking slowly.

Harriet answered Ben's questions as fast as she could, she told him a little about the other trips she had made, said that she would be back again to get him and Old Rit, told him where some of the people were that she had piloted North, what the North was like, cold in winter, yes, but there were worse things in the world than cold. She told him about St. Catharines, in Canada, and said that she would be back—soon.

They parted from him reluctantly. Ben stood in the middle of the road, listening to the sound of their footsteps. They kept looking back at him. He did not remove the blindfold until he was certain they were out of sight. When he could hear no sound of movement, he untied the bandanna and went back to the cabin.

Source: Ann Petry, Harriet Tubman: Conductor on the Underground Railroad (New York: Thomas Y. Crowell Company,1955). Used by permission of Russel & Volkening Agency.

THINKING ABOUT THE SELECTION

1. Why did Harriet not want Old Rit to know that she and her brothers were hiding in the barn?
2. Why did Old Ben refuse to look at his children?
3. **Summarizing** Based on Harriet's comments to Catherine, explain how the underground railroad worked.

16-2 How Americans Shortchange Their Children FIRST PERSON

◆ INTRODUCTION Horace Mann had a mission. He was determined to make education in Massachusetts—and everywhere else in the United States, for that matter—worthy of a democratic people. In lectures and books, he made eloquent appeals for improvements in everything from textbooks to classrooms. This extract is from one of Mann's lectures.

◆ VOCABULARY Before you read the selection, find the meaning of these words in a dictionary: remuneration, vestments, embodiment, subordinate.

Scenes From Daily Life *During the mid-1800s, American painters, known as genre painters, focused on realistic scenes. One of the best known was William Sidney Mount, who painted these two pictures. Mount was the first American artist to show African Americans in a dignified manner.* **American Traditions** *What can you learn about life in the 1800s from paintings such as these?*

Compare the salaries given to engineers, to superintendents of railroads, to agents and overseers of manufacturing establishments, to cashiers of banks, and so forth, with the customary rates of remuneration given to teachers. Yet, does it deserve a more liberal [payment], does it require greater natural talents . . . to run cotton or woollen machinery, or to keep a locomotive from running off the track, than it does to preserve this wonderfully-constructed and complicated machine of the human body in health and vigor; or to prevent the spiritual nature,—that vehicle which carries all our hopes,—from whirling to its ruin, or from dashing madly to some fatal collision? . . .

The compensation which we give with the hand is a true representation of the value which we affix in the mind; and how much more liberally and cordially do we [pay] those who prepare outward and perishable garments for the persons of our children, than those whose office it is to [provide] their spirits with the immortal vestments of virtue? . . .

Our *works* are the visible embodiment and representation of our *feelings*. . . . Tried by this unerring standard in human nature, our *Schoolhouses* are a fair index . . . of our interest in Public Education. Suppose, at this moment, some potent enchanter, by the waving of his magic wand, should take up all the twenty-eight hundred schoolhouses of Massachusetts . . . and, whirling them through the [terrifying] air, should set them all down, visibly, round about us, in this place. . . . I ask, my friends, if, in this new spectacle under the sun, with its motley hues of red and gray, and . . . with its shingles and clapboards flapping and clattering in the wind, as if giving public notice that they were about to depart,—I ask, if, in this indescribable and unnamable group of architecture, we should not see the true image, reflection and embodiment of our own love, attachment, and regard for Public Schools and Public Education, as,

in a mirror, face to face? But, however neglected, forgotten, forlorn, these [buildings] may be, yet within their walls is contained the young and blooming creation of God. In them are our hope, the hopes of the earth. . . . Our dearest treasures do not consist in lands and [buildings], in railroads and banks, in warehouses or in ships upon every sea; they are within these doors, beneath these humble roofs; and is it not our solemn duty to hold every other earthly interest subordinate to their welfare? . . .

Within the last three years, the treasury of the Commonwealth has dispensed a bounty of about twenty-five thousand dollars to encourage the growth of wheat,—and within the last two years, of about five thousand dollars for the culture of silk,—for those goods which perish with the using; while it has not contributed one cent towards satisfying the pressing demand for apparatus and libraries for our schools, by which the imperishable treasures of knowledge and virtue would be increased a hundred-fold. The State has provided for the [free] distribution of a manual, descriptive of the art and processes of silk-culture, but made no provision for the distribution of any manual on that most difficult of all arts,—the art of Education,—as though silk-culture were more important and more difficult than soul-culture.

Source: Horace Mann, *Life and Works of Horace Mann*, 1891.

THINKING ABOUT THE SELECTION

1. What three aspects of the American attitude toward education does Mann criticize?
2. What terms does Mann use to indicate that he values children?
3. **Defending a Position** Do you agree with Mann's claim that "the compensation which we give with the hand is a true representation of the value which we affix in the mind"? Explain.

The Drums of War
When the tension between North and South erupted into war, people rushed to enlist. Many of those who volunteered were young boys, such as the one in this painting by William Morris Hunt. Tragically, tens of thousands of these boys lost their lives. ***Citizenship*** *Do you think that young men under eighteen should have been allowed to fight in the Civil War? Why or why not?*

The Nation Torn Apart

CHAPTER

17

The Road to Civil War

17-1 | Uncle Tom's Cabin

 **LITERATURE**

◆ **INTRODUCTION** Harriet Beecher Stowe's (1811–1896) novel *Uncle Tom's Cabin* is sometimes cited as an underlying cause of the Civil War. The poignant and dramatic story of Uncle Tom, a gentle, elderly slave sold to a cruel master, Simon Legree, did arouse very strong antislavery feelings in many Americans. In the following passage, Legree decides to kill Uncle Tom for helping two slaves to escape.

◆ **VOCABULARY** Before you read the selection, find the meaning of these words in a dictionary: surly, perdition, rend, ironic, despotic, degradation, paroxysm, tempest, probation, irresolute.

The escape of Cassy and Emmeline irritated the before surly temper of Legree to the last degree; and his fury, as was to be expected, fell upon the defenseless head of Tom. When he hurriedly announced the tidings among his hands, there was a sudden light in Tom's eye, a sudden upraising of his hands, that did not escape him. He saw that he did not join the muster of the pursuers. He thought of forcing him to do it; but, having had, of old, experience of his inflexibility when commanded to take part in any deed of inhumanity, he would not, in his hurry, stop to enter into any conflict with him.

Tom, therefore, remained behind, with a few who had learned of him to

Waiting for the Slave Auction *At slave markets, such as the one in this painting by Eyre Crowe, slaves were auctioned off to the highest bidder. Members of slave families were often sold to different people and were separated forever. The worst fate, however, was to be "sold down the river" to a plantation in the Deep South, where the working conditions for slaves were especially harsh.* **Geography** *Why do you think that working conditions for slaves tended to be especially harsh in the Deep South?*

pray, and offered up prayers for the escape of the fugitives.

When Legree returned, baffled and disappointed, all the long-working hatred of his soul towards his slave began to gather in a deadly and desperate form. Had not this man braved him,—steadily, powerfully, resistlessly,—ever since he bought him? Was there not a spirit in him which, silent as it was, burned on him like the fires of perdition?

"I *hate* him!" said Legree, that night, as he sat up in his bed; "I *hate* him! And isn't he mine? Can't I do what I like with him? Who's to hinder, I wonder?" And Legree clenched his fist, and shook it, as if he had something in his hands that he could rend in pieces.

But, then, Tom was a faithful, valuable servant; and, although Legree hated him the more for that, yet the consideration was still somewhat of a restraint to him.

The next morning, he determined to say nothing, as yet; to assemble a party, from some neighboring plantations, with dogs and guns; to surround the swamp, and go about the hunt systematically. If it succeeded, well and good; if not, he would summon Tom before him, and—his teeth clenched and his blood boiled—*then* he would break that fellow down, . . .

The hunt was long, animated, and thorough, but unsuccessful; and, with grave, ironic exultation, Cassy looked down on Legree, as, weary and dispirited, he alighted from his horse.

"Now, Quimbo," said Legree, as he stretched himself down in the sitting-room, "you jest go and walk that Tom up here, right away! The old cuss is at the bottom of this yer whole matter; and I'll have it out of his old black hide, or I'll know the reason why!". . .

Tom heard the message with a fore-warning heart; for he knew all the plan of the fugitives' escape, and the place of their present concealment;—he knew the deadly character of the man he had to deal with, and his despotic power. But he felt strong in God to meet death, rather than betray the helpless.

He sat his basket down by the row, and, looking up, said, "Into thy hands I commend my spirit! Thou has redeemed me, oh Lord God of truth!" and then quietly yielded himself to the rough, brutal grasp with which Quimbo seized him.

"Ay, ay!" said the giant, as he dragged him along; "ye'll cotch it, now! I'll boun' Mas'r's back's up *high!* No sneaking out, now! Tell ye, ye'll get it, and no mistake! See how ye'll look, now, helpin' [them] to run away! See what ye'll get!"

The savage words none of them reached that ear!—a higher voice there was saying, "Fear not them that kill the body, and, after that, have no more that they can do." Nerve and bone of that poor man's body vibrated to those words, as if touched by the finger of God; and he felt the strength of a thousand souls in one. As he passed along, the trees and bushes, the huts of his servitude, the whole scene of his degradation, seemed to whirl by him as the landscape by the rushing ear. His soul throbbed,—his home was in sight,—and the hour of release seemed at hand.

"Well, Tom!" said Legree, walking up, and seizing him grimly by the collar of his coat, and speaking through his teeth, in a paroxysm of determined rage, "do you know I've made up my mind to kill you?"

"It's very likely, Mas'r," said Tom, calmly.

"I *have,*" said Legree, with grim, terrible calmness, "*done-just-that-thing,* Tom, unless you'll tell me what you know about these yer gals!"

Tom stood silent.

"D'ye hear?" said Legree, stamping, with a roar like that of an incensed lion. "Speak!"

"*I han't got nothing to tell, Mas'r,*" said Tom, with a slow, firm deliberate utterance.

"Do you dare to tell me, ye old black Christian, ye don't *know?*" said Legree.

Tom was silent.

"Speak!" thundered Legree, striking him furiously. "Do you know anything?"

"I know, Mas'r; but I can't tell anything. *I can die!*"

Legree drew in a long breath; and, suppressing his rage, took Tom by the arm, and, approaching his face almost to his, said, in a terrible voice, "Hark 'e, Tom!—ye think, 'cause I've let you off before, I don't mean what I say; but, this time, I've *made up my mind,* and counted the cost. You've always stood it out agin' me: now, *I'll conquer ye, or kill ye!*—one or t'other. I'll count every drop of blood there is in you, and take 'em, one by one, till ye give up!"

Tom looked up to his master, and answered, "Mas'r, if you was sick, or in trouble, or dying, I could save ye, I'd give ye my heart's blood; and, if taking every drop of blood in this poor old body would save your precious soul, I'd give 'em freely, as the Lord gave his for me. O, Mas'r, don't bring this great sin on your soul! It will hurt you more than 't will me! Do the worst you can, my troubles'll be over soon; but, if ye don't repent, yours won't never end."

Like a strange snatch of heavenly music, heard in the lull of a tempest, this burst of feeling made a moment's blank pause. Legree stood aghast, and looked at Tom; and there was such a silence, that the tick of the old clock could be heard, measuring, with silent touch, the last moments of mercy and probation to that hardened heart.

It was but a moment. There was one hesitating pause,—one irresolute, relenting thrill,—and the spirit of evil came back, with seven-fold vehemence; and Legree, foaming with rage, smote his victim to the ground.

Source: Harriet Beecher Stowe, *Uncle Tom's Cabin,* 1852.

THINKING ABOUT THE SELECTION

1. Why did Simon Legree hate Tom?
2. Why did Tom refuse to tell Legree where the runaways were hiding?
3. **Recognizing Points of View** Do you think Harriet Beecher Stowe was concerned about the accuracy of her portrayal of slavery? Why or why not?

17-2   Lincoln's Warning   FIRST PERSON

◆ **INTRODUCTION** Abraham Lincoln delivered one of his most famous speeches in his home town of Springfield, Illinois, on June 16, 1858. He had just been nominated by the Republicans to run for the Senate against Stephen A. Douglas. Lincoln attacked not only his Democratic opponent, but also the policies of the present and previous presidential administrations. Here are some of the highlights of Lincoln's address, which came to be known as his "house divided" speech.

◆ **VOCABULARY** Before you read the selection, find the meaning of these words in a dictionary: premise, augmented, extinction, auxiliary, niche.

If we could first know *where* we are, and *whither* we are tending, we would then better judge *what* to do, and *how* to do it. We are now far into the *fifth* year, since a policy was initiated, with the *avowed* object, and *confident* premise, of putting an end to slavery agitation.*

Under the operation of that policy, that agitation has not only, *not ceased,* but has *constantly augmented.*

In *my* opinion, it *will* not cease, until a *crisis* shall have been reached, and passed.

"A house divided against itself cannot stand."

I believe this government cannot endure, permanently half *slave* and half *free.*

I do not expect the Union to be *dissolved*—I do not expect the house to *fall*—but I *do* expect it will cease to be divided.

It will become *all* one thing, or *all* the other.

Either the *opponents* of slavery, will arrest the further spread of it, and place it where the public mind shall rest in the belief that it is in course of ultimate extinction; or its *advocates* will push it forward, till it shall become alike lawful in *all* the States, *old* as well as *new*—*North* as well as *South.*

Have we no *tendency* to the latter condition?

Let any one who doubts, carefully contemplate that now almost complete legal combination—piece of *machinery* so to speak—compounded of the Nebraska doctrine, and the Dred Scott decision. . . .

The *working* points of that machinery are:

First, that no negro slave, imported as such from Africa, and no descendant of such slave can ever be a *citizen* of any State, in the sense of that term as used in the Constitution of the United States. . . .

Secondly, that "subject to the Constitution of the United States," neither

---

*Lincoln is referring here to the passage of the Kansas-Nebraska Act, in 1854.

Bleeding Kansas *During the 1850s, bloody battles erupted in Kansas over the issue of slavery. This sketch by Samuel J. Reader shows the Battle of Hickory Point, one of many skirmishes between proslavery and antislavery settlers in 1856. An opponent of slavery, Reader himself participated in the battle and later fought for the Union in the Civil War.* **American Traditions** *Why did the question of slavery provoke such strong reactions from people?*

Congress nor a *Territorial Legislature* can exclude slavery from any United States territory. . . .

Thirdly, that whether the holding a negro in actual slavery in a free State, makes him free, as against the holder, the United States courts will not decide, but will leave to be decided by the courts of any slave State the negro may be forced into by the master. . . .

Auxiliary to all this, and working hand in hand with it, the Nebraska doctrine, or what is left of it, is to *educate* and *mould* public opinion, at least *Northern* public opinion, to not *care* whether slavery is voted *down* or voted *up*.

This shows exactly where we now *are*; and *partially* also, whither we are tending. . . .

It should not be overlooked that, by the Nebraska bill, the people of a *State* as well as *Territory,* were to be left *"perfectly free"* [to adopt slavery] *"subject only to the Constitution."*

Why mention a *State?* They were legislating for *territories*, and not *for* or *about* States. . . . Put *that* and *that* together, and we have another nice little niche, which we may, ere long, see filled with another Supreme Court decision, declaring that the Constitution of the United States does not permit a *State* to exclude slavery from its limits. . . .

We shall *lie down* pleasantly dreaming that the people of *Missouri* are on the verge of making their State *free*; and we shall *awake* to the *reality,* instead, that the *Supreme* Court has made *Illinois* a *slave* State.

Source: Abraham Lincoln, Speech in Springfield, Illinois, June 16, 1858.

THINKING ABOUT THE SELECTION

1. As Lincoln sees it, what are the two alternatives the United States faces concerning slavery?
2. What legal "machinery" was set up by the Kansas-Nebraska Act and the Dred Scott decision?
3. **Evaluating Information** In Lincoln's view, what danger confronts the free states?

18-1   The Red Badge of Courage   LITERATURE

◆ **INTRODUCTION** In *The Red Badge of Courage*, novelist Stephen Crane (1871–1900) tells the story of Henry Fleming, a young volunteer for the Union army during the Civil War. Dreaming of glory and anxiously anticipating battle, Henry cannot wait to become a soldier. But the realities of war soon cause his attitude to change and Henry, gripped with fear, runs away during a battle. The following passage from an early chapter of the book describes Henry's decision to enlist and his early days in the army.

◆ **VOCABULARY** Before you read the selection, find the meaning of these words in a dictionary: lurid, ardor, diffidently, doggedly, monotonous, pickets.

[Henry] had burned several times to enlist. Tales of great movements shook the land. They might not be distinctly Homeric, but there seemed to be much glory in them. He had read of marches, sieges, conflicts, and he had longed to see it all. His busy mind had drawn for him large pictures extravagant in color, lurid with breathless deeds.

But his mother had discouraged him. She had affected to look with some contempt upon the quality of his war ardor and patriotism. She could calmly seat herself and with no apparent difficulty give him many hundreds of reasons why he was of vastly more importance on the farm than on the field of battle. She had had certain ways of expression that told him that her statements on the subject came from a deep conviction. . . .

At last, however, he had made firm rebellion against this yellow light thrown upon the color of his ambitions. The newspapers, the gossip of the village, his own picturings, had aroused him to an uncheckable degree. They were in truth fighting finely down there. Almost every day the newspapers printed accounts of a decisive victory.

One night, as he lay in bed, the winds had carried to him the clangoring of the church bell as some enthusiast jerked the rope frantically to tell the twisted news of a great battle. This voice of the people rejoicing in the night had made him shiver in a prolonged ecstasy of excitement. Later he had gone down to his mother's room and had spoken thus: "Ma, I'm going to enlist."

"Henry, don't you be a fool," his mother had replied. She had then covered her face with the quilt. There was an end to the matter for that night.

Nevertheless, the next morning he had gone to a town that was near his mother's farm and had enlisted in a company that was forming there. When he had returned his mother was milking the brindle cow. Four others stood waiting. "Ma, I've enlisted," he had said to her diffidently. There was a short silence. "The Lord's will be done, Henry," she had finally replied, and had then continued to milk the brindle cow.

When he had stood in the doorway with his soldier's clothes on his back, and with the light of excitement and expectancy in his eyes almost defeating the glow of regret for the home bonds, he had seen two tears leaving their trails on his mother's scarred cheeks.

Still, she had disappointed him by saying nothing whatever about returning with his shield or on it. He had privately primed himself for a beautiful scene. He had prepared certain sentences which he thought could be used with touching effect. But her words destroyed his plans. She had doggedly peeled potatoes and addressed him as follows: "You watch out, Henry, an' take good care of yerself in this here fighting business—you watch out, an' take care of yerself. Don't go a'thinkin' you can lick the hull rebel army at the start, because yeh can't. Yer jest one little feller amongst a hull lot of others, and yeh've got to keep quiet n' do what they tell yeh. I know how you are, Henry.

"I've knet yeh eight pairs of socks, Henry, and I've put in all yer best shirts, because I want my boy to be jest as warm and comf'able as anybody in the army. Whenever they get holes in 'em, I want yeh to send 'em rightaway back to me, so's I kin dern 'em.

"An' allus be careful an' choose yer comp'ny. There's a lot of bad men in the army, Henry. The army makes 'em wild, and they like nothing better than the job of leading off a young feller like you, as ain't never been away from home much and has allus had a mother, an' a-learning 'em to drink and swear. Keep clear of them folks, Henry. I don't want yeh to ever do anything, Henry, that yeh would be 'shamed to let me know about. Jest think as if I was a-watchin' yeh. If yeh keep that in yer mind allus, I guess yeh'll come out about right.

"Yeh must allus remember yer father, too, child, an' remember he never drunk a drop of licker in his life, and seldom swore a cross oath.

"I don't know what else to tell yeh,

Henry, excepting that yeh must never do no shirking, child, on my account. If so be a time comes when yeh have to be kilt or do a mean thing, why, Henry, don't think of anything 'cept what's right, because there's many a woman has to bear up 'ginst sech things these times, and the Lord'll take keer of us all.

"Don't forgit about the socks and the shirts, child; and I've put a cup of black-berry jam with yer bundle, because I know yeh like it above all things. Good-bye, Henry. Watch out, and be a good boy."

He had, of course, been impatient under the ordeal of this speech. It had not been quite what he expected, and he

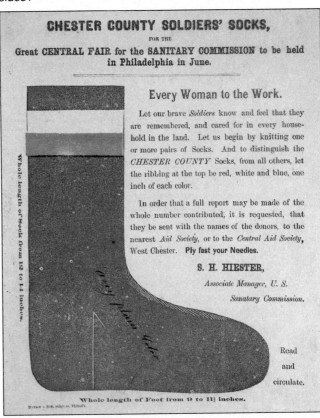

Making Socks for Soldiers *During the Civil War, civilians banded together to provide much-needed food, clothing, and medical supplies. Posters and advertisements helped stir public support for the war effort. This poster, for example, urged women to knit socks for soldiers.* **Citizenship** *Why was the support of people on the home front so important to both sides?*

had borne it with an air of irritation. He departed feeling vague relief. . . .

Still, when he had looked back from the gate, he had seen his mother kneeling among the potato parings. Her brown face, upraised, was stained with tears, and her spare form was quivering. He bowed his head and went on, feeling suddenly ashamed of his purposes. . . .

On the way to Washington his spirit had soared. The regiment was fed and caressed at station after station until the youth had believed that he must be a hero. There was a lavish expenditure of bread and cold meats, coffee, and pickles and cheese. As he basked in the smiles of the girls and was patted and complimented by the old men, he had felt growing within him the strength to do mighty deeds of arms.

After complicated journeying with many pauses, there had come months of monotonous life in a camp. He had had the belief that real war was a series of death struggles with small time in between for sleep and meals; but since his regiment had come to the field the army had done little but sit still and try to keep warm. . . .

He had grown to regard himself merely as a part of a vast blue demonstration. His province was to look out, as far as he could, for his personal comfort. For recreation he could twiddle his thumbs and speculate on the thoughts which must agitate the minds of the generals. Also, he was drilled and drilled and reviewed, and drilled and drilled and reviewed.

The only foes he had seen were some pickets along the riverbank. . . . The youth, on guard duty one night, conversed across the stream with one of them. He was a slightly ragged man, who spat skillfully between his shoes and possessed a great fund of bland and infantile assurance. The youth liked him personally.

"Yank," the other had informed him, "yer a right dum good feller." This sentiment, floating to him upon the still air, had made him temporarily regret war.

Source: Stephen Crane, *The Red Badge of Courage*, 1895.

THINKING ABOUT THE SELECTION

1. How did Henry's mother react to his decision to enlist?
2. What did Henry expect a soldier's life to be like?
3. **Understanding Causes and Effects** How and why does Henry's attitude toward war begin to change?

18-2 Lee, Dignified in Defeat FIRST PERSON

◆ **INTRODUCTION** Robert E. Lee was one of the few Civil War leaders admired and respected by both southerners and northerners. The following first-hand description of the Confederate commander the day after his surrender was written by Theodore Lyman, an aide-de-camp to Union General George Meade.

◆ **VOCABULARY** Before you read the selection, find the meaning of these words in a dictionary: florid, countenance, eccentricity, impoverished, pittance.

Monday April 10 is a day worthy of description, because I saw the remains of our great opponent, the Army of Northern Virginia. The General [Meade] proposed to ride through the Rebel lines to General Grant, who was at Appomattox Court House; and he took George and myself as aides; a great chance! for the rest were not allowed to go, no communication being permitted between the armies. At 10:30 we rode off, . . . We rode about a mile and then turned off to General Lee's Headquarters, which consisted in one fly [tent] with a campfire in front. I believe he had lost most of his baggage in some of the trains, though his establishment is at all times modest. . . . As he rode up General Meade took off his cap and said: "Good-morning, General." Lee, however, did not recognize him, and, when he found who it was, said: "But what are you doing with all that grey in your beard?" To which Meade promptly replied: "You have to answer for most of it!"

Lee is, as all agree, a stately-looking man; tall, erect and strongly built, with a full chest. His hair and closely trimmed beard, though thick, are now nearly white. He has a large and well-shaped head, with a brown, clear eye, of unusual depth. His face is sunburnt and rather florid. In manner he is exceedingly grave and dignified—this, I believe, he always has; but there was evidently added an extreme depression, which gave him the air of a man who kept up his pride to the last, but who was entirely overwhelmed. From his speech I judge he was inclined to wander in his thoughts. You would not have recognized a Confederate officer from his dress, which was a blue military overcoat, a high grey hat, and well-brushed riding boots.

As General Meade introduced his two aides, Lee put out his hand and saluted us with all the air of the oldest blood in the world.* I did not think, when I left, in '63, for Germantown, that I should ever shake the hand of Robert E. Lee, prisoner

*That is, with an aristocratic air.

Guerrilla Warfare As Union troops advanced through the South, they were plagued by attacks from Confederate guerrillas. The guerrillas were semi-independent fighters, who raided Union outposts and disrupted enemy communications and supply lines. This painting by Albert Bierstadt shows a group of Union soldiers firing at a band of Confederate guerrillas. **Geography** What advantages do you think the guerrillas might have had over the Union troops they fought against? Why?

of war! He held a long conference with General Meade, while I stood over a fire, with his officers, in the rain. . . .

We were talking there together, when there appeared a great oddity—an old man, with an angular, much-wrinkled face, and long, thick white hair, brushed *à la* Calhoun; a pair of silver spectacles and a high felt hat further set off the countenance, while the legs kept up their claim of eccentricity by encasing themselves in grey blankets, tied somewhat in a bandit fashion. The whole made up no less a person than Henry A. Wise, once Governor of the loyal state of Virginia, now Brigadier-General and prisoner of war. By his first wife he is Meade's brother-in-law, and had been sent for to see him. I think *he* is punished enough: old, sick, impoverished, a prisoner, with nothing to live for, not even his son, who was killed at Roanoke Island, he stood there in his old, wet, grey blanket, glad to accept at our hands a pittance of biscuit

and coffee, to save him and his Staff from starvation! . . .

We left Lee, and kept on through the sad remnants of an army that has its place in history. It would have looked a mighty host, if the ghosts of all its soldiers that now sleep between Gettysburg and Lynchburg could have stood there in the lines, beside the living.

Source: George R. Agassiz, ed., *Meade's Headquarters 1863–1865: Letters of Colonel Theodore Lyman from the Wilderness to Appomattox* (Boston: Little Brown & Company, 1922).

THINKING ABOUT THE SELECTION

1. How does Lyman describe Lee?
2. What does the description of Wise indicate about the state of the Confederate army at this time?
3. **Drawing Conclusions** On the basis of this selection, do you think Lyman felt vindictive toward the defeated South? Give reasons for your answer.

CHAPTER 19

Rebuilding the Union

19-1   O Captain! My Captain!   LITERATURE

◆ **INTRODUCTION** Walt Whitman (1819–1892) was one of the greatest American poets of the 1800s. Many of his poems celebrate democracy, equality, and the diversity of American life. Whitman regarded Abraham Lincoln as the personification of these ideals, and he deeply admired Lincoln for this reason. The following poem, which has become one of Whitman's most popular works, was inspired by Lincoln's tragic death.

◆ **VOCABULARY** Before you read the selection, find the meaning of these words in a dictionary: exulting, keel, trills.

O Captain! my Captain! our fearful trip
   is done,
The ship has weather'd every rack, the
   prize we sought is won,
The port is near, the bells I hear, the
   people all exulting,

Reconstructing the South
Southern cities and farmlands were devastated by the war. President Lincoln wanted to help the South rebuild. Two years after Lincoln died, however, Congress instituted a Reconstruction plan that punished the South and made its recovery even more difficult. Yet the South still managed to rebuild, as shown in this 1872 painting of Charlestown Square by Charles Hamilton.
Citizenship How might Lincoln's original plan for Reconstruction have affected the South differently?

While follow eyes the steady keel, the
    vessel grim and daring;
        But O heart! heart! heart!
            O the bleeding drops of red,
                Where on the deck my Captain
                    lies,
                    Fallen cold and dead.

O Captain! my Captain! rise up and hear
    the bells;
Rise up—for you the flag is flung—for
    you the bugle trills,
For you bouquets and ribbon'd wreaths—
    for you the shores a-crowding,
For you they call, the swaying mass, the
    eager faces turning;
        Here captain! dear father!
            This arm beneath your head!
                It is some dream that on the
                    deck,
                    You've fallen cold and dead.

My Captain does not answer, his lips are
    pale and still,
My father does not feel my arm, he has
    no pulse nor will,
The ship is anchor'd safe and sound, its
    voyage closed and done,
From fearful trip the victor ship comes in
    with object won;
        Exult O shores, and ring O bells!
            But I with mournful tread,
                Walk the deck my Captain lies
                Fallen cold and dead.

Source: Walt Whitman, *Leaves of Grass.*

THINKING ABOUT THE SELECTION

1. What "ship" is Whitman talking about?
2. What is the "fearful trip" he refers to?
3. **Making Inferences** How do you think northerners and southerners would have reacted to this poem? Why?

◆ **INTRODUCTION** The end of Reconstruction came at a high cost for African Americans living in the South. When Democrats returned to power in the South and systematically deprived blacks of their rights, few Americans protested. What this abandonment felt like is described here by John R. Lynch, an African American from Mississippi who served in his state legislature and in Congress during Reconstruction. He later fought in the Spanish-American War and was commissioned a second lieutenant on the battlefield for gallantry in action.

◆ **VOCABULARY** Before you read the selection, find the meaning of these words in a dictionary: ostracized, forfeited, odium, affiliation, oblivion, devoid.

In the elections of 1872 nearly every State in the Union went Republican. In the State and Congressional elections of 1874 the result was the reverse of what it was two years before,—nearly every State going Democratic. . . . It was the State and Congressional elections of 1874 that proved to be the death of the Republican party in the South. . . .

[After] 1872 and prior to 1875 . . . a Southern white man could become a Republican without being socially ostracized. Such a man was no longer looked upon as a traitor to his people, or false to his race. He no longer forfeited the respect, confidence, good-will, and favorable opinion of his friends and neighbors. . . . But after the State and Congressional elections of 1874 there was a complete change of front. The new order of things was then set aside. . . .

It soon developed that all that was left of the once promising and flourishing Republican party at the South was the

true, faithful, loyal, and sincere colored men,—who remained Republican from necessity as well as from choice,—and a few white men, who were Republicans from principle and conviction, and who were willing to incur the odium, run the risks, take the chances, and pay the penalty that every white Republican who had the courage of his convictions must then pay. . . .

The writer cannot resist the temptation to bring to the notice of the reader [a scene] . . . of which he had personal knowledge. Colonel James Lusk had been a prominent, conspicuous and influential representative of the Southern aristocracy of ante-bellum days. He enjoyed the respect and confidence of the community in which he lived,—especially of the colored people. He, like thousands of others of his class, had identified himself with the Republican party. . . .

After the Congressional elections of 1874 Colonel Lusk decided that he would return to the ranks of the Democracy.* Before making public announcement of that fact he decided . . . that his faithful friend and loyal supporter, Sam Henry,** should be the first to whom that announcement should be made. When he had finished, Henry was visibly affected.

"Oh! no, Colonel," he cried, breaking down completely, "I beg of you do not leave us. You are our chief, if not sole dependence. You are our Moses. If you leave us, hundreds of others in our immediate neighborhood will be sure to follow your lead. We will thus be left without

---

*That is, the Democratic party.

**Sam Henry, an African American, was president of the local Republican organization.

solid and substantial friends. I admit that with you party affiliation is optional. With me it is not. You can be either a Republican or a Democrat, and be honored and supported by the party to which you may belong. With me it is different. I must remain a Republican whether I want to or not. . . . Colonel, I beg of you, I plead with you, don't go!" . . .

Henry's remarks made a deep and profound impression upon Colonel Lusk. He informed Henry that no step he could take was more painful to him than this. He assured Henry that this act on his part was from necessity and not from choice.

"The statement you have made, Henry, that party affiliation with me is optional," he answered, "is presumed to be true; but, in point of fact, it is not. No white man can live in the South in the future and act with any other than the Democratic party unless he is willing and prepared to live a life of social isolation and remain in political oblivion. While I am somewhat advanced in years, I am not so old as to be devoid of political ambition. Besides I have two grown sons. There is, no doubt, a bright, brilliant and successful future before them if they are Democrats; otherwise, not. . . . I must yield to the inevitable and surrender my convictions upon the altar of my family's good,—the outgrowth of circumstances and conditions which I am powerless to prevent and cannot control. . . . If I could see my way clear to pursue a different course it would be done; but my decision is based upon careful and thoughtful consideration and it must stand."

Source: John R. Lynch, *The Facts of Reconstruction* (New York: Neale Publishing Company, 1913).

The Cabbage Patch *When the Civil War ended, former slaves found themselves without homes or work. They had to start new lives and find ways of supporting themselves. In this painting by Thomas P. Anshutz, freed slaves are tending a cabbage patch. **Daily Life** In what ways do you think the daily lives of southern blacks changed when they won their freedom?*

THINKING ABOUT THE SELECTION

1. How did the political situation change for southern whites between 1872 and 1875?

2. According to Lynch, why did southern blacks have no choice but to belong to the Republican party?

3. **Defending a Position** What are your reactions to the story of Colonel Lusk and Sam Henry? Explain.

REFERENCE SECTION

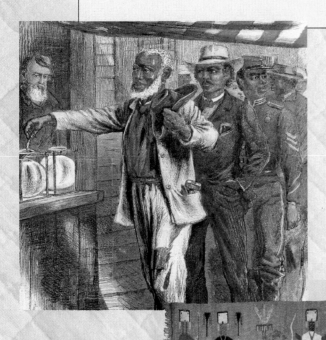

The first Americans discovered a land of endless diversity when they traveled across North America. The land itself ranges from lush coastal plains to high rugged mountain peaks, from deep forest to barren desert. As the earliest Americans spread across the two continents, they learned to use the land and what it offered. Hundreds of different cultures developed. The map at right shows some of these cultures. Study the map, chart, and illustrations. Then answer these questions:

1. Which Indian nations were part of the Southwest culture group?

2. Which illustration represents an Indian nation found in the Middle America culture group?

3. Why would the spirit of the sun be important to the Bella Coola in the winter?

4. What geographic characteristics of the Eastern Woodlands are shown in the picture of the Algonquin village?

5. Review what you learned about Native American cultures in Chapter 2. Then study the chart at right. Which pictures show the influence of climate or geography on the culture of the groups shown on the map?

Maya women were skilled weavers. Here, one end of a loom is attached to the woman's waist and the other to a tree.

This ancient bowl was found on the Hopi Mesa. The ring around the edge is called a lifeline. The Anasazi woman making the bowl left an opening in the ring because her life was not yet complete.

Environment of Early American Cultures

Culture Group	Environment
Far North	Very short summers; long cold winters
Northwest Coast	Mild, rainy; dense forests
California-Intermountain	Mild and rainy along coast; dry and hot in deserts; cold winters in mountains
Southwest	Very hot and dry in desert
Great Plains	Hot summers; cold winters; little rainfall
Eastern Woodlands	Hot summers; cold winters; dense forests
Southeast	Humid summers; mild winters

Although from the 1800s, this painting shows some ways of life on the plains that had changed little. Note the hides used for the tipi.

The Bella Coola used this wooden mask of the sun spirit during winter religious ceremonies.

This scene of an Algonquin village, painted in 1585, shows life much as it was before Europeans arrived.

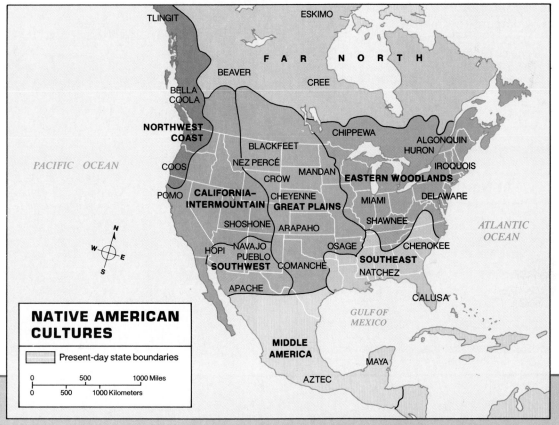

NATIVE AMERICAN CULTURES

Present-day state boundaries

0   500   1000 Miles
0   500   1000 Kilometers

ESKIMO
TLINGIT
FAR NORTH
BEAVER
CREE
BELLA COOLA
NORTHWEST COAST
CHIPPEWA
BLACKFEET
ALGONQUIN
HURON
NEZ PERCÉ
COOS
CROW
MANDAN
EASTERN WOODLANDS
IROQUOIS
POMO
CALIFORNIA–INTERMOUNTAIN
CHEYENNE
GREAT PLAINS
MIAMI
DELAWARE
PACIFIC OCEAN
SHOSHONE
ARAPAHO
SHAWNEE
ATLANTIC OCEAN
HOPI
NAVAJO
PUEBLO
OSAGE
CHEROKEE
SOUTHWEST
COMANCHE
SOUTHEAST
NATCHEZ
APACHE
CALUSA
GULF OF MEXICO
MIDDLE AMERICA
MAYA
AZTEC

Daring explorers sought adventure, wealth, and glory in North America as early as the late 1400s. Settlers soon followed. Some came in search of a better life. Many came looking for religious freedom. By 1753, English colonies flourished along the Atlantic coast. The Spanish had set up missions and towns in the Southwest. French forts lined the Mississippi River in Louisiana and the Great Lakes in New France. The map at right shows European land claims in 1753. Competition for land in North America led to war between England and France the following year, in 1754. Study the map, graph, and pictures. Then answer these questions:

1. Which nation claimed land along the Mississippi in 1753?

2. How did geographic location make conflict between France and England likely?

3. Based on the pictures, which European settlers were probably the greatest threat to Native Americans? Why?

4. Compare the map with the one on page 198. How would the wedges in the circle graph change between 1753 and 1763?

This Spanish mission at El Paso was founded in 1659. It became a gateway for Spanish settlers in the Southwest.

Settlers in Pennsylvania turned dense forests into productive farmland. This prosperous farm grew up during the mid-1750s.

Land Claims in North America, 1753

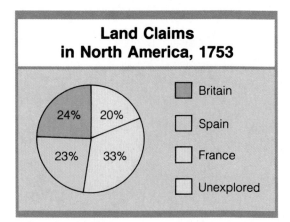

24%   20%

23%   33%

- Britain
- Spain
- France
- Unexplored

French trappers traveled far along roaring rivers. Their fur trade with Indian nations was the basis of French claims in North America.

New York was a thriving colonial port town in the mid-1750s.

The New England Primer was used in schools and homes in the English colonies. It illustrates the strong influence of religion among colonists.

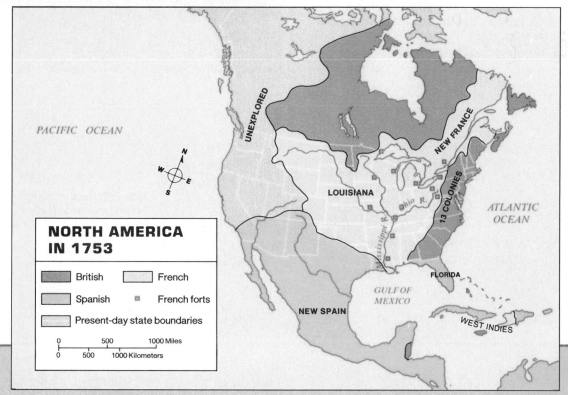

NORTH AMERICA IN 1753

British
French
Spanish
French forts
Present-day state boundaries

0   500   1000 Miles
0   500   1000 Kilometers

PACIFIC OCEAN
UNEXPLORED
NEW FRANCE
LOUISIANA
13 COLONIES
ATLANTIC OCEAN
Ohio R.
Mississippi R.
FLORIDA
GULF OF MEXICO
NEW SPAIN
WEST INDIES

709

NORTH AMERICA IN 1783

A new nation was born when the American colonists defeated Britain in the American Revolution. The United States had begun as 13 colonies wedged between the Appalachian Mountains and the Atlantic coast. In 1783, it stretched west to the Mississippi, north to Canada and the Great Lakes, and south to Florida. As settlers moved west across the Appalachians, they took along the ideals of liberty that had given birth to the country.

The French had lost their claims to land in North America during the French and Indian War. But most of the continent was still claimed by the Spanish and the British. Study the map, graph, and pictures. Then answer the questions below.

1. What nation claimed the land west of the United States in 1783?

2. Which nation claimed the largest portion of North America in 1783?

3. (a) Based on the map, which European nations might have been a threat to settlers near Fort Snelling? (b) What other groups did settlers probably consider a threat? Why?

4. What do you think American settlers would do when they reached the Mississippi River? Why?

Paul Revere made this silver bowl in 1768 at the beginning of the American colonists' struggle for liberty.

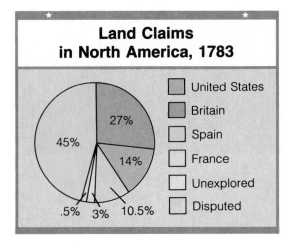

**Land Claims
in North America, 1783**

- United States
- Britain
- Spain
- France
- Unexplored
- Disputed

27%
45%
14%
.5% 3% 10.5%

Although most of North America was claimed by the United States or European nations, Native Americans lived throughout the land. In northern areas, such as Canada, snowshoes helped hunters move easily on snow.

Settlers used flatboats to move goods along the rivers of the western part of the new nation, as this painting from the 1800s shows.

After 1783, American settlers moved west in a steady stream. The army built forts to protect them. Fort Snelling, shown here, was built on the northwest frontier on the Mississippi River.

To the west of the new nation, Spanish settlers were building thriving towns and ranches.

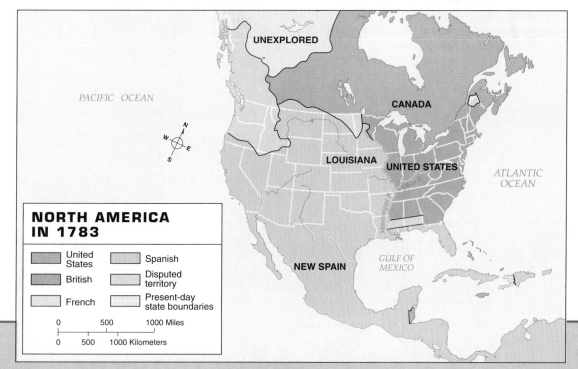

NORTH AMERICA IN 1783

- United States
- British
- French
- Spanish
- Disputed territory
- Present-day state boundaries

0   500   1000 Miles

0   500   1000 Kilometers

UNEXPLORED

PACIFIC OCEAN

CANADA

LOUISIANA

UNITED STATES

ATLANTIC OCEAN

NEW SPAIN

GULF OF MEXICO

Mississippi R.

Ohio R.

N
W   E
S

711

GROWTH OF THE UNITED STATES TO 1853

By 1853, the United States stretched from sea to sea. The nation acquired huge tracts of land through purchase, treaty, and war. This land, far from being empty, was home to many different peoples. They included Native Americans who had lived there long before Europeans arrived. Many Mexicans also had found themselves in a foreign land after the Mexican War. Plus, adventurers from all over the world had come in search of gold. The expansion of the country was to offer great opportunities and difficult challenges in the years ahead. Territorial expansion is shown on the map at right. Study the map, the graph, and the pictures. Then answer these questions:

1. (a) When did the Oregon Country become part of the United States? (b) Which picture best illustrates the trip to Oregon?

2. (a) What was the last addition to the United States shown on the map? (b) What cultural heritage was probably strongest in that area?

3. (a) Based on the graph, during which period was the most land added to the United States? (b) Which pictures help you understand the geography and culture of those areas?

Settlers began moving toward Oregon in the early 1800s. At first, they traveled by covered wagons. Later, railroads would crisscross the country.

Growth of the United States, 1790–1853

Thousands of Square Miles

Year	
1790	~850
1803	~1,750
1853	~3,100

This painting of a horse race shows the influence of Mexican culture in areas the United States acquired from Mexico. This cultural influence has remained strong in Texas and other areas of the Southwest.

These Sioux are playing lacrosse, a game that settlers learned from Indians. As settlers moved onto the plains, the lives of Indians changed forever.

The discovery of gold in California attracted people from all over the world. Miners such as these spread out in search of priceless treasure.

In the early 1800s, canals, such as the Erie Canal, became part of a vast system of transportation.

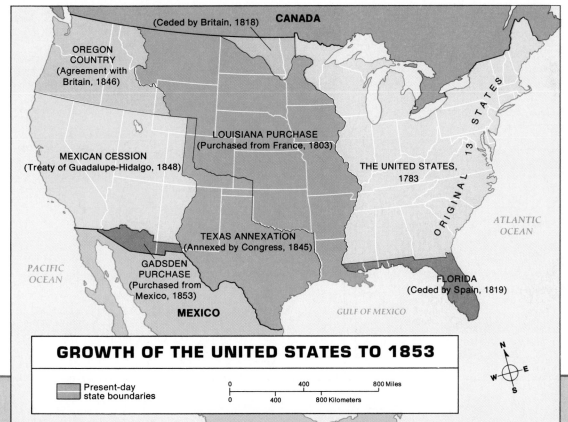

CANADA

(Ceded by Britain, 1818)

OREGON COUNTRY
(Agreement with Britain, 1846)

MEXICAN CESSION
(Treaty of Guadalupe-Hidalgo, 1848)

LOUISIANA PURCHASE
(Purchased from France, 1803)

THE UNITED STATES, 1783

ORIGINAL 13 STATES

TEXAS ANNEXATION
(Annexed by Congress, 1845)

GADSDEN PURCHASE
(Purchased from Mexico, 1853)

FLORIDA
(Ceded by Spain, 1819)

PACIFIC OCEAN

ATLANTIC OCEAN

MEXICO

GULF OF MEXICO

GROWTH OF THE UNITED STATES TO 1853

Present-day state boundaries

0   400   800 Miles
0   400   800 Kilometers

N W E S

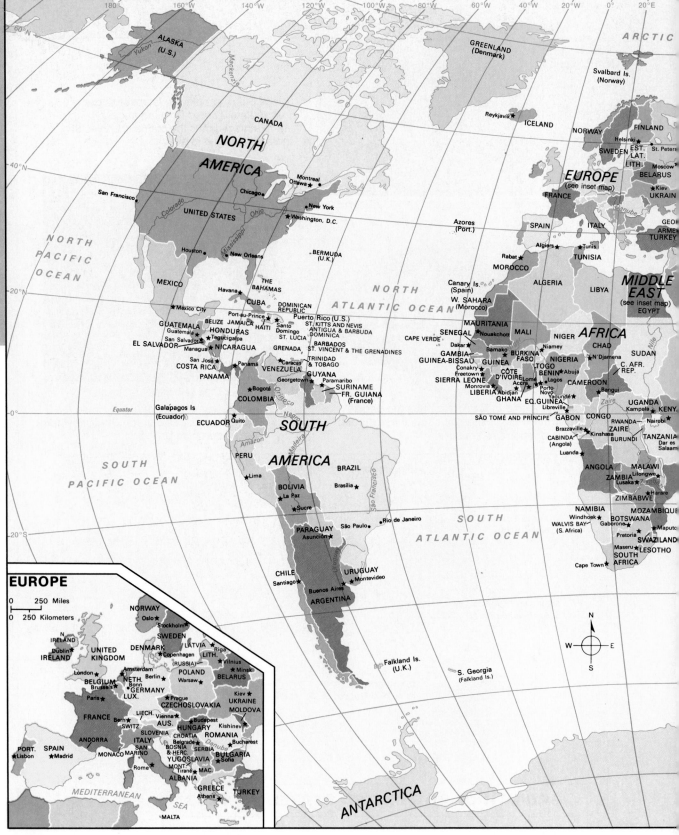

180°   160°W   140°W   120°W   100°W   80°W   60°W   40°W   20°W   0°   20°E

ARCTIC

60°N

ALASKA
(U.S.)
Yukon

GREENLAND
(Denmark)

Svalbard Is.
(Norway)

Reykjavik ★ ICELAND

NORWAY   FINLAND
SWEDEN   Helsinki ★ EST.   St. Peters
            LAT.
            LITH.   Moscow ★
EUROPE   BELARUS
(see inset map)
FRANCE   ★ Kiev
            UKRAIN

40°N

CANADA

NORTH
AMERICA

Montreal
Ottawa ●

San Francisco ●   Chicago ●   New York ●

UNITED STATES   Colorado   Ohio
Mississippi   ★ Washington, D.C.

Azores
(Port.)

SPAIN   ITALY
        GEO
        ARMEN
        TURKEY

Houston ●   New Orleans   BERMUDA
                            (U.K.)

Algiers ★ ★ Tunis
Rabat ★   TUNISIA

MEXICO   THE
        BAHAMAS

Havana ●

NORTH
ATLANTIC OCEAN

Canary Is.
(Spain)
W. SAHARA
(Morocco)

MOROCCO

ALGERIA   LIBYA

MIDDLE
EAST
(see inset map)
EGYPT

20°N

NORTH
PACIFIC
OCEAN

★ Mexico City

CUBA

GUATEMALA   BELIZE JAMAICA HAITI
Guatemala   Port-au-Prince ★   Santo
HONDURAS   Domingo
EL SALVADOR   ST. LUCIA
San Salvador ★ Managua ★ NICARAGUA
COSTA RICA   GRENADA
        Panamá ★
PANAMA

DOMINICAN
REPUBLIC
Puerto Rico (U.S.)
ST. KITTS AND NEVIS
ANTIGUA & BARBUDA
DOMINICA
BARBADOS
ST. VINCENT & THE GRENADINES
TRINIDAD
& TOBAGO

MAURITANIA   MALI   NIGER   AFRICA   CHAD
                                    N'Djamena ★
CAPE VERDE   Nouakchott ★
SENEGAL   Niamey ★   SUDAN
GAMBIA   Dakar ★ Bamako ★ BURKINA
GUINEA-BISSAU   FASO   NIGERIA   C. AFR.
                    GUINEA   REP.
                Conakry ★ CÔTE   TOGO   Abuja ★
SIERRA LEONE   Freetown ★ D'IVOIRE BENIN
                    Accra ★ Lagos   CAMEROON
            Monrovia ★ Abidjan   Porto-   Bangui ★
LIBERIA   GHANA   Novo   Yaoundé ★   UGANDA
            Lomé   Kampala ★ ★ KENY
SÃO TOMÉ AND PRINCIPE   EQ. GUINEA
                    Libreville ★ GABON   CONGO   Nairobi ●
                                RWANDA   Zaire
                    Brazzaville ★ ★ TANZANIA
                    CABINDA   Kinshasa   BURUNDI   Dar es
                    (Angola)   ZAIRE   Salaam
                    Luanda ★

EQUATOR

Tegucigalpa ★

Equator

GALÁPAGOS IS
(Ecuador)

Caracas ★
VENEZUELA
● Bogotá
COLOMBIA

GUYANA
Georgetown ★ Paramaribo ★
        SURINAME
        FR. GUIANA
        (France)

Negro

ECUADOR   Quito ★

SOUTH
AMERICA

PERU

Amazon

BRAZIL

Madeira

São Francisco

ANGOLA   MALAWI
ZAMBIA   Lilongwe ★
Lusaka ★ ★ Harare
ZIMBABWE

20°S

SOUTH
PACIFIC OCEAN

Lima ●

BOLIVIA
La Paz ★
★ Sucre

Brasília ●

Rio de Janeiro ●

São Paulo ●

SOUTH

ATLANTIC OCEAN

NAMIBIA   MOZAMBIQUE
Windhoek ● BOTSWANA
WALVIS BAY   Gaborone ● Maputo ★
(S. Africa)
        Pretoria ★ SWAZILAND
        Maseru ★ ★ LESOTHO
Cape Town ★ SOUTH
        AFRICA

PARAGUAY
Asunción ★

CHILE   URUGUAY
Santiago ★ Montevideo ★
        Buenos Aires ★
        ARGENTINA

Falkland Is.
(U.K.)

S. Georgia
(Falkland Is.)

N
W ─ E
S

ANTARCTICA

EUROPE

0   250 Miles
0   250 Kilometers

NORWAY
Oslo ★
        Stockholm ★
N   SWEDEN
IRELAND
Dublin ★ DENMARK   LATVIA
IRELAND   Copenhagen ★ Riga ★
    UNITED   LITH.
    KINGDOM   (RUSSIA)   Vilnius ★
London ★   Berlin ● POLAND   BELARUS
    Amsterdam ★   Warsaw ★
BELGIUM   NETH.   Minsk ★
Brussels ● Bonn ● GERMANY   Kiev ★
    LUX.   CZECHOSLOVAKIA   UKRAINE
Paris ★   Prague ★   MOLDOVA
            LIECH. Vienna ★ Budapest ★
FRANCE   Bern ★ SWITZ. AUS. HUNGARY   Kishinev ★
            SLOVENIA   ROMANIA
            CROATIA   Belgrade ★ Bucharest ★
ANDORRA   ITALY   BOSNIA   SERBIA
        SAN   & HERC.
MONACO MARINO YUGOSLAVIA BULGARIA
SPAIN   Rome ●   Sofia ★
PORT.   MONT.   MAC.
Lisbon ★ ★ Madrid   Tirane ★
                ALBANIA
MEDITERRANEAN   GREECE
                Athens ★ TURKEY
    SEA
        ★ MALTA

60°E 80°E 100°E 120°E 140°E 160°E 180° 160°W 140°W 120°W 100°W

60°N

OCEAN

Mackenzie

ALASKA (U.S.)

Yukon

40°N

RUSSIA

Lena

Ob

Novosibirsk

ASIA

Ulan Bator

KAZAKHSTAN

MONGOLIA

Aleutian Islands (U.S.)

UZBEK. Bishkek Alma-Ata
AZER. Tashken KYRGYZTAN
TURKMENISTAN TAJIKISTAN
Dushanbe

N. KOREA
Beijing Pyongyang
Tiarjin Seoul
S. KOREA

JAPAN

Tokyo

NORTH

IRAN AFGHANISTAN Kabul Islamabad

CHINA

Shanghai

PACIFIC OCEAN

20°N

AUDI RABIA PAKISTAN New Delhi
Kathmandu NEPAL BHUTAN
Thimphu
BANGLADESH Dacca
INDIA Calcutta

Chongqing

Mekong

Hwang

Taipei

TAIWAN

Hawaii (U.S.)

Ganges

Bombay

MYANMAR Hanoi
Rangoon Vientiane LAOS
THAILAND VIETNAM
Bangkok CAMBODIA Manila
(KAMPUCHEA) PHILIPPINES
Phnom Penh Ho Chi Minh City

HONG KONG (U.K.)

SRI LANKA
Colombo

SOMALIA Mogadishu

MALDIVES

BRUNEI

KUALA Lumpur MALAYSIA
SINGAPORE

KIRIBATI Equator 0°

SEYCHELLES

INDIAN OCEAN

NAURU

COMOROS ISLANDS

Jakarta INDONESIA

PAPUA NEW GUINEA

SOLOMON ISLANDS

TUVALU

MADAGASCAR

Port Moresby

Antananarivo

Reunion (France) MAURITIUS

VANUATU

FIJI

WESTERN SAMOA

20°S

AUSTRALIA

New Caledonia (France)

TONGA

SOUTH PACIFIC OCEAN

Adelaide Canberra Sydney

Melbourne

Wellington NEW ZEALAND

WORLD

★ National capital

● Other city

0 500 1000 1500 2000 Miles

0 1000 2000 3000 Kilometers

ANTARCTICA

MIDDLE EAST

RUSSIA

Kiev
UKRAINE
MOLDOVA

KAZAKHSTAN

ROMANIA
Bucharest

UZBEKISTAN

Sofia BULGARIA GEORGIA Tbilisi
Tirane Istanbul Baku TURKMENISTAN
ALBANIA GREECE Ankara ARMENIA AZERBAIJAN Ashkhabad
Tunis Athens TURKEY Teheran
TUNISIA CYPRUS SYRIA AFGHAN.
Beirut Damascus Baghdad
Tripoli LEB. IRAQ IRAN
Jerusalem Amman PAK.
Cairo ISRAEL JORDAN KUWAIT
LIBYA BAHRAIN
EGYPT QATAR
SAUDI ARABIA Riyadh Muscat
Mecca U. ARAB EMIR. OMAN

NIGER

CHAD Khartoum

SUDAN

RED SEA

Sana YEMEN
Aden DJIBOUTI
ETHIOPIA Addis Ababa

0 500 1000 Miles

0 500 1000 Kilometers

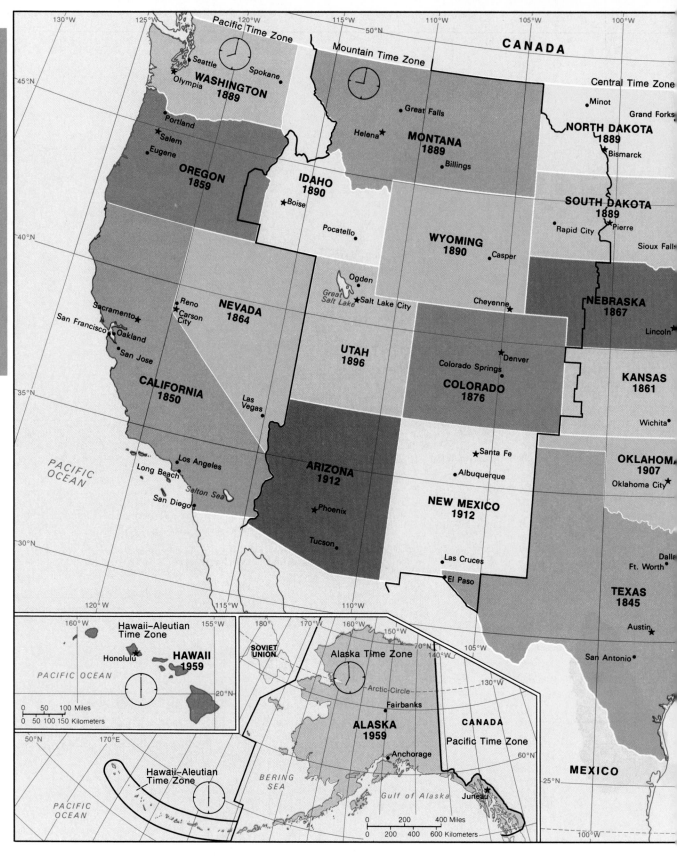

Pacific Time Zone
Mountain Time Zone
Central Time Zone

CANADA

Seattle
Spokane
Olympia
WASHINGTON
1889

Portland
Salem
Eugene
OREGON
1859

IDAHO
1890
Boise
Pocatello

Great Falls
Helena
MONTANA
1889
Billings

NORTH DAKOTA
1889
Minot
Bismarck
Grand Forks

WYOMING
1890
Casper
Cheyenne

SOUTH DAKOTA
1889
Rapid City
Pierre
Sioux Falls

Sacramento
San Francisco
Oakland
San Jose
Reno
Carson City
NEVADA
1864

Ogden
Great Salt Lake
Salt Lake City

UTAH
1896

Denver
Colorado Springs
COLORADO
1876

NEBRASKA
1867
Lincoln

KANSAS
1861
Wichita

CALIFORNIA
1850
Las Vegas

Los Angeles
Long Beach
Salton Sea
San Diego

PACIFIC OCEAN

ARIZONA
1912
Phoenix
Tucson

Santa Fe
Albuquerque

NEW MEXICO
1912

Las Cruces
El Paso

OKLAHOMA
1907
Oklahoma City

TEXAS
1845

Dallas
Ft. Worth
Austin
San Antonio

Hawaii–Aleutian Time Zone

Honolulu
HAWAII
1959

PACIFIC OCEAN

0 50 100 Miles
0 50 100 150 Kilometers

SOVIET UNION

Alaska Time Zone

Arctic Circle

Fairbanks

ALASKA
1959

Anchorage

BERING SEA

Gulf of Alaska

Juneau

CANADA

Pacific Time Zone

MEXICO

Hawaii–Aleutian Time Zone

PACIFIC OCEAN

0   200   400 Miles
0 200 400 600 Kilometers

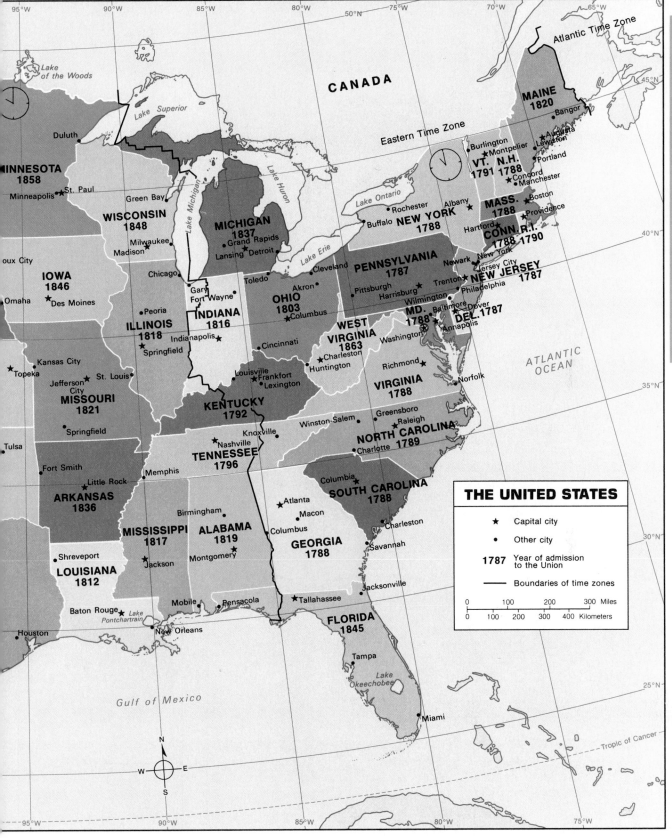

THE UNITED STATES

★   Capital city

●   Other city

1787   Year of admission to the Union

─────   Boundaries of time zones

| 0 | 100 | 200 | 300 Miles |
| 0 | 100 | 200 | 300 | 400 Kilometers |

Map labels:

Lake of the Woods, Duluth, MINNESOTA 1858, Minneapolis, St. Paul, Green Bay, WISCONSIN 1848, Milwaukee, Madison, Chicago, ioux City, IOWA 1846, Omaha, Des Moines, Peoria, ILLINOIS 1818, Springfield, Kansas City, Topeka, Jefferson City, St. Louis, MISSOURI 1821, Springfield, Tulsa, Fort Smith, Little Rock, ARKANSAS 1836, Shreveport, LOUISIANA 1812, Baton Rouge, Lake Pontchartrain, Houston, New Orleans, Mobile, Pensacola, Gulf of Mexico

MICHIGAN 1837, Grand Rapids, Lansing, Detroit, Lake Superior, Lake Michigan, Lake Huron, Lake Erie, Gary, Fort Wayne, Toledo, INDIANA 1816, Indianapolis, OHIO 1803, Akron, Columbus, Cincinnati, Cleveland, Louisville, Frankfort, Lexington, KENTUCKY 1792, Knoxville, Nashville, TENNESSEE 1796, Memphis, MISSISSIPPI 1817, Jackson, ALABAMA 1819, Montgomery, Birmingham, Columbus, GEORGIA 1788, Atlanta, Macon, Columbia, Charleston, Savannah, FLORIDA 1845, Tallahassee, Jacksonville, Tampa, Lake Okeechobee, Miami

CANADA, Eastern Time Zone, Atlantic Time Zone, Lake Ontario, Rochester, Albany, Buffalo, NEW YORK 1788, PENNSYLVANIA 1787, Pittsburgh, Harrisburg, Trenton, Newark, New York, Jersey City, NEW JERSEY 1787, Philadelphia, WEST VIRGINIA 1863, Wilmington, MD. 1788, Baltimore, Dover, DEL. 1787, Annapolis, Washington, Charleston, Huntington, VIRGINIA 1788, Richmond, Norfolk, Winston-Salem, Greensboro, Raleigh, NORTH CAROLINA 1789, Charlotte, SOUTH CAROLINA 1788, ATLANTIC OCEAN

MAINE 1820, Bangor, Augusta, Lewiston, Portland, Burlington, Montpelier, VT. 1791, N.H. 1788, Concord, Manchester, MASS. 1788, Boston, CONN. 1788, R.I. 1790, Providence, Hartford

Tropic of Cancer

N / W E / S

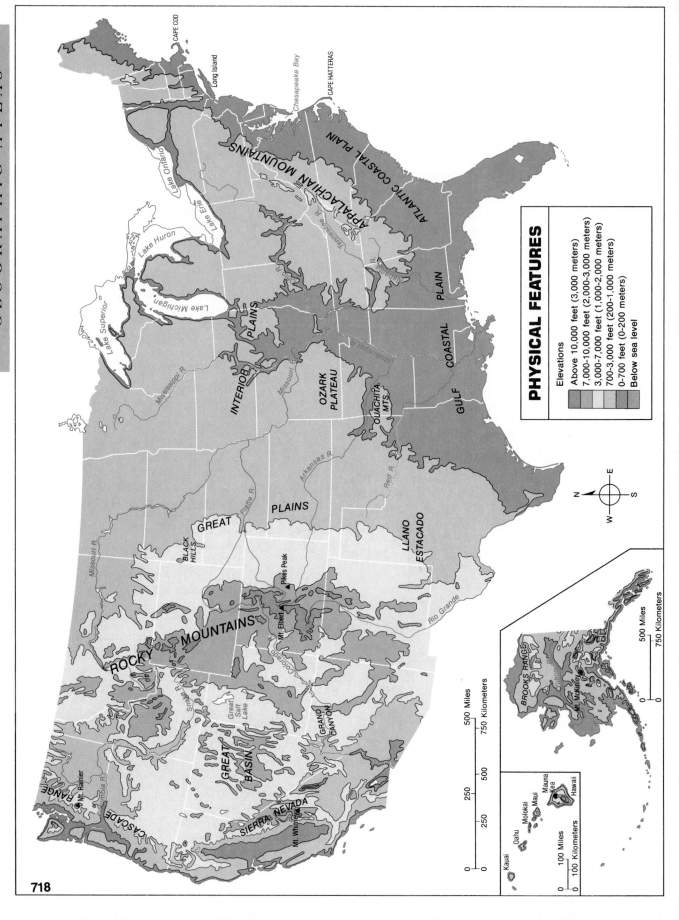

PHYSICAL FEATURES

Elevations

- Above 10,000 feet (3,000 meters)
- 7,000-10,000 feet (2,000-3,000 meters)
- 3,000-7,000 feet (1,000-2,000 meters)
- 700-3,000 feet (200-1,000 meters)
- 0-700 feet (0-200 meters)
- Below sea level

CAPE COD
Long Island
Chesapeake Bay
CAPE HATTERAS

APPALACHIAN MOUNTAINS

ATLANTIC COASTAL PLAIN

Tennessee R.

Alabama R.

GULF COASTAL PLAIN

Lake Ontario
Lake Erie
Lake Huron
Lake Michigan
Lake Superior

INTERIOR PLAINS

OZARK PLATEAU

OUACHITA MTS.

Mississippi R.

Missouri R.

Arkansas R.

Red R.

LLANO ESTACADO

GREAT PLAINS

BLACK HILLS

Pikes Peak

Mt. Elbert

Platte R.

Rio Grande

ROCKY MOUNTAINS

Colorado R.

Missouri R.

Snake R.

Great Salt Lake

GRAND CANYON

GREAT BASIN

SIERRA NEVADA

Mt. Whitney

CASCADE RANGE

Mt. Rainier

Columbia R.

N
E
S
W

0 250 500 Miles
0 250 500 750 Kilometers

BROOKS RANGE

Yukon R.

Mt. McKinley

0 500 Miles
0 750 Kilometers

Kauai
Oahu
Molokai
Maui
Mauna Kea
Hawaii

0 100 Miles
0 100 Kilometers

718

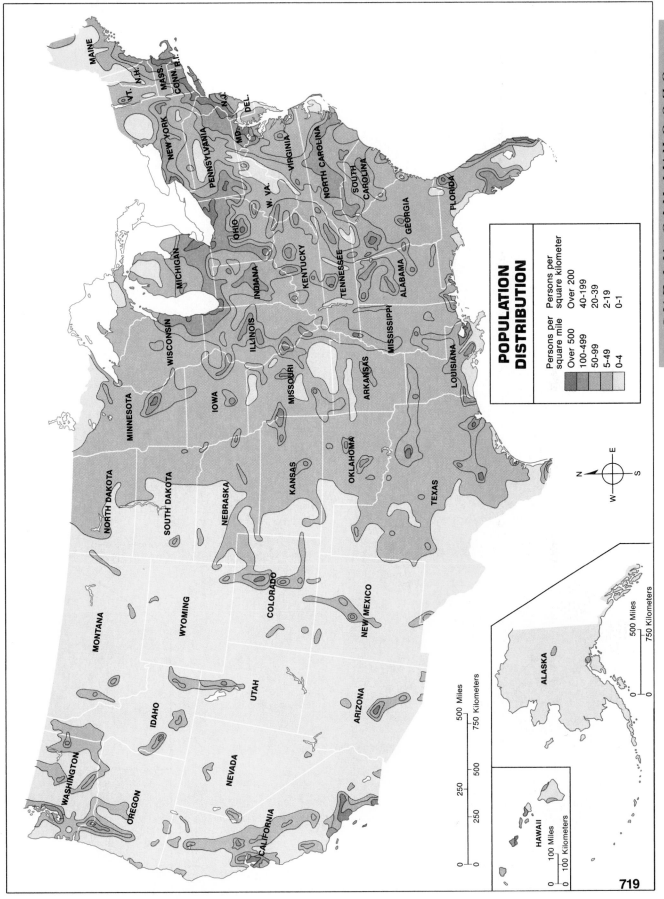

POPULATION DISTRIBUTION

Persons per square mile	Persons per square kilometer
Over 500	Over 200
100-499	40-199
50-99	20-39
5-49	2-19
0-4	0-1

N
E
S
W

MAINE
N.H.
VT.
MASS.
CONN.
R.I.
N.J.
DEL.
MD.
NEW YORK
PENNSYLVANIA
W. VA.
VIRGINIA
OHIO
MICHIGAN
INDIANA
KENTUCKY
NORTH CAROLINA
SOUTH CAROLINA
GEORGIA
FLORIDA
ALABAMA
TENNESSEE
MISSISSIPPI
WISCONSIN
ILLINOIS
MISSOURI
ARKANSAS
LOUISIANA
MINNESOTA
IOWA
NORTH DAKOTA
SOUTH DAKOTA
NEBRASKA
KANSAS
OKLAHOMA
TEXAS
NEW MEXICO
COLORADO
WYOMING
MONTANA
IDAHO
UTAH
ARIZONA
NEVADA
WASHINGTON
OREGON
CALIFORNIA

500 Miles
750 Kilometers
500
250
250
0
0

ALASKA

500 Miles
750 Kilometers
0
0

HAWAII
100 Miles
100 Kilometers
0
0

719

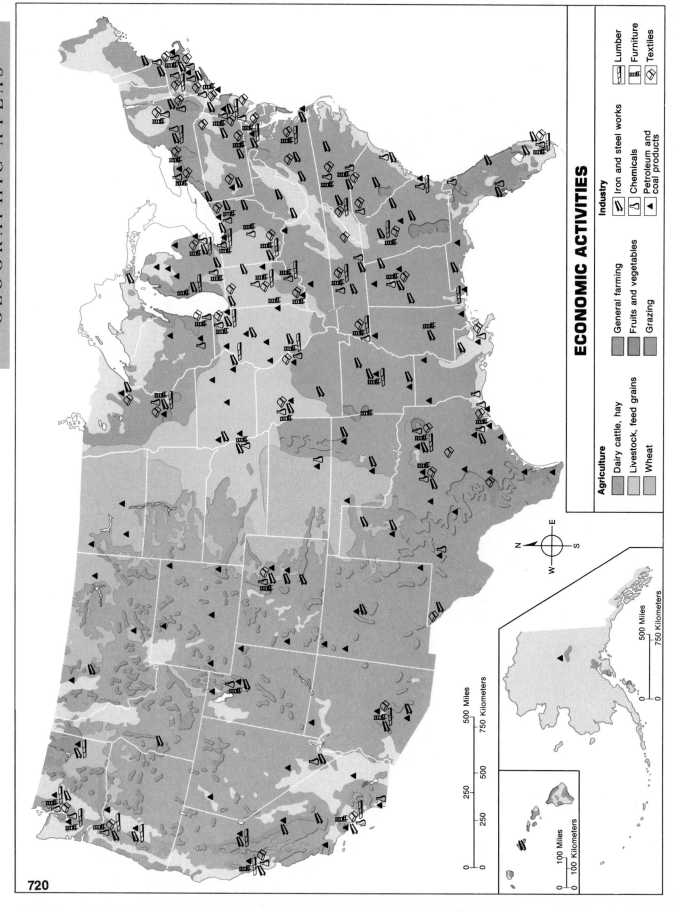

ECONOMIC ACTIVITIES

Agriculture
- General farming
- Fruits and vegetables
- Grazing
- Dairy cattle, hay
- Livestock, feed grains
- Wheat

Industry
- ⧄ Iron and steel works
- ⚗ Chemicals
- ▲ Petroleum and coal products
- ⧄ Lumber
- ⧄ Furniture
- ◇ Textiles

500 Miles
750 Kilometers

250   500
250   500   750 Kilometers

100 Miles
100 Kilometers

N
W — E
S

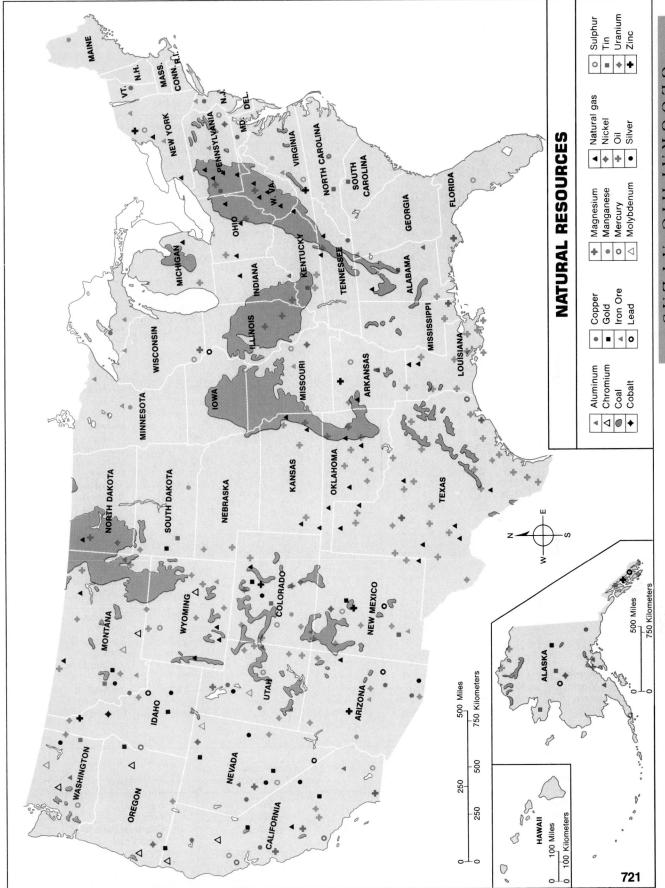

GEOGRAPHIC ATLAS

NATURAL RESOURCES

	Aluminum		Copper		Magnesium		Natural gas		Sulphur
◄		●		✚		◄		○	
△	Chromium	■	Gold	●	Manganese	◆	Nickel	■	Tin
◄	Coal	◄	Iron Ore	○	Mercury	●	Oil	◆	Uranium
◆	Cobalt	○	Lead	△	Molybdenum	●	Silver	✚	Zinc

MAINE
VT.
N.H.
MASS.
CONN. R.I.
N.J.
NEW YORK
PENNSYLVANIA
MD. DEL.
VIRGINIA
W. VA.
OHIO
KENTUCKY
NORTH CAROLINA
SOUTH CAROLINA
MICHIGAN
INDIANA
TENNESSEE
GEORGIA
ALABAMA
FLORIDA
ILLINOIS
MISSISSIPPI
WISCONSIN
MISSOURI
ARKANSAS
LOUISIANA
IOWA
MINNESOTA
KANSAS
OKLAHOMA
TEXAS
NORTH DAKOTA
SOUTH DAKOTA
NEBRASKA
MONTANA
WYOMING
COLORADO
NEW MEXICO
IDAHO
UTAH
ARIZONA
WASHINGTON
OREGON
NEVADA
CALIFORNIA

N
E
W
S

500 Miles
250
250
500
750 Kilometers

ALASKA
500 Miles
750 Kilometers
0
0

HAWAII
100 Miles
100 Kilometers
0
0

721

THE FIFTY STATES ◆

State	Date of Entry to Union (Order of Entry)	Area in Square Miles	Population 1990 (In Thousands)	Number of Representatives in House	Capital	Largest City
Alabama	1819 (22)	51,705	4,062	7	Montgomery	Birmingham
Alaska	1959 (49)	591,004	551	1	Juneau	Anchorage
Arizona	1912 (48)	114,000	3,677	6	Phoenix	Phoenix
Arkansas	1836 (25)	53,187	2,362	4	Little Rock	Little Rock
California	1850 (31)	158,706	29,839	52	Sacramento	Los Angeles
Colorado	1876 (38)	104,091	3,307	6	Denver	Denver
Connecticut	1788 (5)	5,018	3,295	6	Hartford	Bridgeport
Delaware	1787 (1)	2,044	688	1	Dover	Wilmington
Florida	1845 (27)	58,664	13,005	23	Tallahassee	Jacksonville
Georgia	1788 (4)	58,910	6,508	11	Atlanta	Atlanta
Hawaii	1959 (50)	6,471	1,115	2	Honolulu	Honolulu
Idaho	1890 (43)	83,564	1,011	2	Boise	Boise
Illinois	1818 (21)	56,345	11,466	20	Springfield	Chicago
Indiana	1816 (19)	36,185	5,566	10	Indianapolis	Indianapolis
Iowa	1846 (29)	56,275	2,787	5	Des Moines	Des Moines
Kansas	1861 (34)	82,277	2,485	4	Topeka	Wichita
Kentucky	1792 (15)	40,409	3,698	6	Frankfort	Louisville
Louisiana	1812 (18)	47,751	4,238	7	Baton Rouge	New Orleans
Maine	1820 (23)	33,265	1,233	2	Augusta	Portland
Maryland	1788 (7)	10,460	4,798	8	Annapolis	Baltimore
Massachusetts	1788 (6)	8,284	6,029	10	Boston	Boston
Michigan	1837 (26)	58,527	9,328	16	Lansing	Detroit
Minnesota	1858 (32)	84,402	4,387	8	St. Paul	Minneapolis
Mississippi	1817 (20)	47,689	2,586	5	Jackson	Jackson
Missouri	1821 (24)	69,697	5,137	9	Jefferson City	Kansas City
Montana	1889 (41)	147,046	803	1	Helena	Billings
Nebraska	1867 (37)	77,355	1,584	3	Lincoln	Omaha
Nevada	1864 (36)	110,561	1,206	2	Carson City	Las Vegas
New Hanpshire	1788 (9)	9,279	1,113	2	Concord	Manchester
New Jersey	1787 (3)	7,787	7,748	13	Trenton	Newark
New Mexico	1912 (47)	121,593	1,521	3	Santa Fe	Albuquerque
New York	1788 (11)	49,108	18,044	31	Albany	New York
North Carolina	1789 (12)	52,669	6,657	12	Raleigh	Charlotte
North Dakota	1889 (39)	70,703	641	1	Bismarck	Fargo
Ohio	1803 (17)	41,330	10,877	19	Columbus	Columbus
Oklahoma	1907 (46)	69,956	3,157	6	Oklahoma City	Oklahoma City
Oregon	1859 (33)	97,073	2,853	5	Salem	Portland
Pennsylvania	1787 (2)	45,308	11,926	21	Harrisburg	Philadelphia
Rhode Island	1790 (13)	1,212	1,005	2	Providence	Providence
South Carolina	1788 (8)	31,113	3,505	6	Columbia	Columbia
South Dakota	1889 (40)	77,116	699	1	Pierre	Sioux Falls
Tennessee	1796 (16)	42,144	4,896	9	Nashville	Memphis
Texas	1845 (28)	266,807	17,059	30	Austin	Houston
Utah	1896 (45)	84,899	1,727	3	Salt Lake City	Salt Lake City
Vermont	1791 (14)	9,614	564	1	Montpelier	Burlington
Virginia	1788 (10)	40,767	6,216	11	Richmond	Virginia Beach
Washington	1889 (42)	68,138	4,887	9	Olympia	Seattle
West Virginia	1863 (35)	24,231	1,801	3	Charleston	Huntington
Wisconsin	1848 (30)	56,153	4,906	9	Madison	Milwaukee
Wyoming	1890 (44)	97,809	455	1	Cheyenne	Cheyenne
District of Columbia		69	606	1 (nonvoting)		

Self-Governing Areas, Possessions, and Dependencies	Area in Square Miles	Population (In Thousands)	Capital
Puerto Rico	3,515	3,599	San Juan
Guam	209	127	Agana
U.S. Virgin Islands	132	106	Charlotte Amalie
American Samoa	77	46	Pago Pago

THE FIFTY STATES

722

GAZETTEER
OF AMERICAN HISTORY

This gazetteer, or geographical dictionary, lists places that are important to American history. The approximate latitude and longitude is given for cities, towns, and other specific locations. See text pages 12–13 for information about latitude and longitude. In the Gazetteer, after the description of each place, there are usually two numbers in parentheses. The first number refers to the text page where you can find out more about the place. The second number appears in slanted, or *italic*, type and refers to a map *(m)* where the place is shown.

A

Africa Second largest continent in the world. (p. 174, *m714–715*)

Alabama 22nd state. Nicknamed the Heart of Dixie or the Cotton State. (p. 722, *m716–717)*

Alamo (29°N/99°W) Mission in San Antonio, Texas, where 182 rebels died during the Texan war for independence. (p. 436, *m436)*

Alaska 49th state. Largest in size but one of the least populated states. (p. 722, *m716–717)*

Albany (43°N/74°W) Capital of New York State. Called Fort Orange by the Dutch of New Netherland. (p. 229, *m716–717)*

Andes Rugged mountain chain in South America. (p. 50, *m48)*

Antietam (39°N/78°W) Creek in Maryland. Site of a Union victory in 1862. (p. 549)

Appalachian Mountains Stretch from Georgia to Maine and Canada. (p. 20, *m18)*

Appomattox Courthouse (37°N/79°W) Small town in Virginia where Lee surrendered to Grant on April 9, 1865. (p. 565, *m565)*

Arizona 48th state. Nicknamed the Grand Canyon State. (p. 722, *m716–717)*

Arkansas 25th state. Nicknamed the Land of Opportunity. (p. 722, *m716–717)*

Asia Largest of the world's continents. (p. 58, *m714–715)*

Atlanta (34°N/84°W) Capital and largest city of Georgia. Burned by Sherman in 1864 before his "march to the sea." (p. 564, *m716–717)*

Atlantic Ocean World's second largest ocean. (p. 15, *m714–715)*

Atlantic Plain Part of the coastal plain in the eastern United States. (p. 22, *m18)*

B

Badlands Dry region of South Dakota. (p. 86)

Baltimore (39°N/77°W) Port city in Maryland. (p. 358, *m356)*

Barbary States North African nations of Morocco, Algiers, Tunis, and Tripoli. Americans had to pay a tribute to their rulers so that they would not attack American ships. (p. 347, *m347)*

Bering Sea Narrow sea between Asia and North America. Scientists think a land bridge existed here during the last ice age. (p. 5, *m30)*

Boston (42°N/71°W) Seaport and industrial city in Massachusetts. (p. 172, *m153)*

Breed's Hill (42°N/71°W) Overlooks Boston Harbor. Site of fighting during the Battle of Bunker Hill. (p. 222, *m222)*

Buena Vista (26°N/101°W) Site of an American victory in the Mexican War. (p. 444, *m444)*

Buffalo (43°N/79°W) Industrial city in New York State on Lake Erie. (p. 517, *m716–717)*

Bull Run (39°N/78°W) Small stream in Virginia. Site of Confederate victories in 1861 and 1862. (p. 546, *m547)*

Bunker Hill (42°N/71°W) Overlooks Boston Harbor. Site of an early battle during the Revolution. (p. 221, *m222)*

C

Cahokia (39°N/90°W) Fur trading post in Illinois, captured by George Rogers Clark in 1778 during the Revolution. (p. 234, *m233)*

California 31st state. Nicknamed the Golden State. Ceded to the United States by Mexico in 1848. (p. 722, *m716–717)*

Canada Northern neighbor of the United States. (p. 191, *m714–715)*

Cape Cod (42°N/70°W) Located on the coast of Massachusetts. Pilgrims on the *Mayflower* landed near here. (p. 115, *m115)*

Cape Horn (56°S/67°W) Southern tip of South America rounded by Magellan in 1520. (p. 72, *m71)*

Cape of Good Hope (34°S/18°E) Southern tip of Africa. Dias rounded this cape in 1488. (p. 64, *m65)*

Caribbean Sea Tropical sea in the Western Hemisphere. Dotted with islands of the West Indies. (p. 15, *m68)*

GAZETTEER

Central America Part of North America between Mexico and South America. (p. 26, *m714–715*)

Central Plains Eastern part of the Interior Plains. (p. 19, *m18*)

Chancellorsville (38°N/78°W) Site of a Confederate victory in 1863. (p. 561, *m547*)

Charleston (33°N/80°W) City in South Carolina. Spelled Charles Town in colonial days. (p. 138, *m138*)

Chesapeake Bay Large inlet of the Atlantic Ocean in Virginia and Maryland. (p. 111, *m115*)

Chicago (42°N/88°W) Third largest city in the United States. (p. 19, *m716–717*)

Colorado 38th state. Nicknamed the Centennial State. (p. 722, *m716–717*)

Columbia River Chief river of the Pacific Northwest. (p. 345, *m345*)

Concord (43°N/71°W) Village near Boston, Massachusetts. Site of the first battle of the American Revolution in April 1775. (p. 212, *m212*)

Connecticut One of the 13 original states. Nicknamed the Constitution State or the Nutmeg State. (p. 722, *m716–717*)

Cotton Kingdom In the 1850s, many plantations worked by slaves produced cotton in this region. Stretched from South Carolina to Georgia and Texas. (p. 469, *m470*)

Cowpens (35°N/82°W) Located in South Carolina. Site of a decisive American victory in 1781 during the Revolution. (p. 239, *m240*)

Croatoan Island Place where Roanoke settlers may have moved between 1587 and 1590. (p. 110)

Cumberland Gap (37°N/84°W) Pass in the Appalachian Mountains near the border of Virginia, Kentucky, and Tennessee. (p. 251, *m376*)

Cuzco (14°S/72°W) Inca capital. (p. 50, *m48*)

D

Dallas (33°N/97°W) City in Texas. Located on the Interior Plains. (p. 19, *m716–717*)

Delaware One of the 13 original states. Nicknamed the First State or the Diamond State. (p. 135, *m115*)

Delaware River Flows into the Atlantic Ocean through Delaware Bay. (p. 156, *m158*)

Detroit (42°N/83°W) Largest city in Michigan. (p. 356, *m716–717*)

District of Columbia Located on the Potomac River. Seat of the federal government of the United States. (p. 722, *m716-717*)

E

East Indies Islands in Southeast Asia. Source of spices in the 1500s and 1600s. (p. 62, *m59*)

El Paso (32°N/106°W) City on the Rio Grande in Texas. Settled by the Spanish. (p. 102, *m716–717*)

England Part of Great Britain. (p. 62, *m70*)

Equator Line of latitude labeled 0°. Separates the Northern and Southern hemispheres. (p. 12, *m13*)

Erie Canal Linked the Mohawk River with Buffalo and Lake Erie (p. 378, *m378*)

Europe Second smallest of the world's continents. (p. 58, *m714–715*)

F

Florida 27th state. Nicknamed the Sunshine State. (p. 75, *m716–717*)

Fort Donelson (37°N/88°W) Located in Tennessee. Captured by Grant in 1862. (p. 550, *m563*)

Fort Henry (37°N/88°W) Located in Tennessee. Captured by Grant in 1862. (p. 550, *m563*)

Fort Necessity (40°N/79°W) Makeshift stockade built by the British near the Monongahela River during the French and Indian War. (p. 194, *m196*)

Fort Pitt (40°N/80°W) British name for Fort Duquesne after its capture from the French in 1758. (p. 197, *m196*)

Fort Sumter (33°N/80°W) Guarded the entrance to Charleston Harbor in South Carolina. Confederates fired the first shots of the Civil War there in 1861. (p. 534, *m563*)

Fort Ticonderoga (44°N/74°W) British fort on Lake Champlain. Captured by Ethan Allen in 1775. (p. 220, *m223*)

France Country in Western Europe. First ally of the United States. (p. 62, *m714–715*)

Fredericksburg (38°N/78°W) Located in Virginia. Site of a Confederate victory in 1862. (p. 560, *m547*)

G

Gadsden Purchase Land purchased from Mexico in 1853. Now part of Arizona and New Mexico. (p. 446, *m445*)

Georgia One of the 13 original states. Nicknamed the Peach State or the Empire State of the South. (p. 138, *m716–717*)

Gettysburg (40°N/77°W) Small town in southern Pennsylvania. Site of a Union victory in 1863 and Lincoln's famous Gettysburg Address. (p. 561, *m547*)

Goliad (29°N/97°W) Texas town near San Antonio where Mexicans executed 300 Texans during the Texan war for independence. (p. 438, *m436*)

Gonzales (29°N/97°W) City in Texas near San Antonio. Site of the first Texan victory over Mexico in 1835. (p. 435, *m436*)

Great Britain Island nation of Western Europe. Includes England, Scotland, Wales, and Northern Ireland. (p. 193, *m714–715*)

Great Colombia Nation in Latin America in the 1800s consisting of present-day Venezuela, Colombia, Ecuador, and Panama. (p. 387, *m386*)

Great Lakes Group of five freshwater lakes in the heart of the United States. (p. 23, *m18*)

Great Plains Western part of the Interior Plains. Once grazed by large herds of buffalo. Now an important ranching and wheat-growing region. (p. 19, *m18*)

Great Salt Lake Vast salt lake in Utah. (p. 19, *m716–717*)

Great Wagon Road Early pioneer route across the Appalachians. (p. 158, *m157*)

Greenland World's largest island. Colonized by Vikings in the late 900s. (p. 58, *m714–715*)

Guatemala Country in Central America. Mayas built an advanced civilization there over 3,000 years ago. (p. 388, *m714–715*)

Gulf of Mexico Body of water along the southern coast of the United States. (p. 191, *m191*)

Gulf Plain Part of the coastal plain lowland that lies along the Gulf of Mexico. (p. 23, *m18*)

H

Haiti Country in the West Indies. Won independence from France in the early 1800s. (p. 341, *m714–715*)

Harpers Ferry (39°N/78°W) Town in West Virginia. Abolitionist John Brown raided the arsenal there in 1859. (p. 532, *m547*)

Hartford (42°N/73°W) Capital of Connecticut. (p. 358, *m716–717*)

Hawaii Newest of the 50 states. Nicknamed the Aloha State. (p. 722, *m716–717*)

Hispaniola (18°N/73°W) Island in the Caribbean that Columbus visited. Occupied today by the Dominican Republic and Haiti. (p. 69, *m68*)

Horseshoe Bend Site of American victory in the War of 1812. (p. 357, *m356*)

Hudson Bay Large inlet of the Arctic Ocean. Named for the explorer Henry Hudson. (p. 79, *m78*)

Hudson River Largest river in New York State. Explored by Henry Hudson in 1609. (p. 106, *m106*)

I

Iceland (65°N/20°W) Island nation in the north Atlantic Ocean. Settled by Vikings in the 800s. (p. 58, *m714–715*)

Idaho 43rd state. Nicknamed the Gem State. Acquired by the United States as part of Oregon Country. (p. 722, *m716–717*)

Illinois 21st state. Nicknamed the Inland Empire. Settled as part of the Northwest Territory. (p. 722, *m716–717*)

Independence (37°N/96°W) City in Missouri. Starting point of the Oregon Trail. (p. 432, *m 441*)

India Country in South Asia. (p. 64, *m714–715*)

Indiana 19th state. Nicknamed the Hoosier State. Settled as part of the Northwest Territory. (p. 722, *m716–717*)

Indiana Territory Territory east of the Mississippi River that became the states of Indiana, Illinois, and Wisconsin, and part of Minnesota. (p. 352, *m360*)

Interior Plains Region of the central United States that stretches from the Rockies to the Appalachians. (p. 19, *m18*)

Intermountain Region Rugged and mostly dry region from the Rocky Mountains to the Sierra Nevada and coastal mountains of the western United States. (p. 19, *m18*)

Iowa 29th state. Nicknamed the Hawkeye State. Acquired by the United States as part of the Louisiana Purchase. (p. 722, *m716–717*)

Isthmus of Panama Narrow strip of land joining North and South America. (p. 15, *m71*)

J

Jackson (32°N/90°W) City in western Mississippi. Captured by Grant in 1863. (p. 551, *m563*)

Jamestown (37°N/77°W) First successful English colony in North America. (p. 111, *m115*)

K

Kansas 34th state. Nicknamed the Sunflower State. Acquired by the United States as part of the Louisiana Purchase. (p. 722, *m716–717*)

Kansas Territory Territory created by the Kansas-Nebraska Act. (p. 524, *m525*)

GAZETTEER

GAZETTEER

Kaskaskia (38°N/90°W) Fur trading post on an island in the Mississippi River. Captured by George Rogers Clark in 1778. First state capital of Illinois. (p. 234, *m233*)

Kentucky 15th state. Nicknamed the Bluegrass State. Was the first area west of the Appalachians to be settled by early pioneers. (p. 542, *m716–717*)

King's Mountain (35°N/81°W) Located in South Carolina. Site of an American victory in the Revolution. (p. 238, *m240*)

L

Lake Champlain (45°N/73°W) Borders New York and Vermont. Fort Ticonderoga is at the southern end. (p. 220, *m223*)

Lake Erie One of the Great Lakes. (p. 23, *m18*)

Lake Huron One of the Great Lakes. (p. 23, *m18*)

Lake Michigan Only one of the Great Lakes located wholly within the United States. (p. 23, *m18*)

Lake Ontario One of the Great Lakes. (p. 23, *m18*)

Lake Superior Highest and farthest inland of the five Great Lakes. (p. 23, *m18*)

Lancaster Turnpike Road built in 1790 linking Philadelphia and Lancaster, Pennsylvania. (p. 375, *m376*)

Latin America Name for those parts of the Western Hemisphere where Latin languages are spoken. Includes Mexico, Central and South America, and the West Indies. (p. 386, *m386*)

Lexington (42°N/71°W) Site of the first clash between minutemen and British troops in 1775. Now a suburb of Boston. (p. 212, *m212*)

Liberia Country in West Africa. Set up in 1822 as a colony for free blacks. (p. 485, *m714–715*)

Line of Demarcation Line drawn by the Pope that divided the non-Christian world between Spain and Portugal. (p. 70, *m71*)

Lone Star Republic Another name for the Republic of Texas. (p. 438, *m436*)

Long Island Located in New York. Site of a British victory in the Revolution. (p. 228, *m230*)

Louisbourg (46°N/60°W) French fort in eastern Canada. Changed hands several times between France and Britain. (p. 197, *m196*)

Louisiana 18th state. Nicknamed the Pelican State. First state created out of the Louisiana Purchase. (p. 722, *m716–717*)

Louisiana Purchase Region between the Mississippi River and the Rocky Mountains purchased from France in 1803. (p. 342, *m360*)

M

Maine 23rd state. Nicknamed the Pine Tree State. Originally part of Massachusetts, Maine gained separate statehood in 1820 under the terms of the Missouri Compromise. (p. 516, *m716–717*)

Mali Kingdom in West Africa that reached its peak between 1200 and 1400. (p. 64, *m65*)

Maryland One of the 13 original states. Nicknamed the Old Line State or the Free State. (p. 136, *m716–717*)

Massachusetts One of the 13 original states. Nicknamed the Bay State or the Old Colony. (p. 124, *m716–717*)

Massachusetts Bay Colony Founded by the Massachusetts Bay Company and settled by Puritans. (p. 124, *m127*)

Memphis (35°N/90°W) City in Tennessee on the Mississippi River. Captured by Grant in 1862. (p. 551, *m563*)

Mexican Cession Lands acquired by the United States from Mexico under the Treaty of Guadalupe Hidalgo in 1848. (p. 446, *m445*)

Mexico Southern neighbor of the United States. Gained independence from Spain in 1821. (p. 47, *m714–715*)

Mexico City (19°N/99°W) Capital of Mexico. Was the capital of New Spain. Site of the ancient Aztec city of Tenochtitlán. (p. 96, *m97*)

Michigan 26th state. Nicknamed the Great Lake State or the Wolverine State. Settled as part of the Northwest Territory. (p. 722, *m716–717*)

Middle Colonies States of New York, New Jersey, Pennsylvania, and Delaware. (p. 130, *m135*)

Middle East Area from Afghanistan to Egypt. (p. 61, *m714–715*)

Minnesota 32nd state. Nicknamed the North Star State or the Gopher State. Most of it was acquired by the United States as part of the Louisiana Purchase. (p. 722, *m716–717*)

Mississippi 20th state. Nicknamed the Magnolia State. (p. 469, *m716–717*)

Mississippi River Longest river in the United States. Links the Great Lakes with the Gulf of Mexico. (p. 23, *m18*)

Missouri 24th state. Nicknamed the Show Me State. Acquired by the United States as part of the Louisiana Purchase. (p. 516, *m716–717*)

Missouri Compromise Line Line drawn across the Louisiana Purchase at latitude 36°30′ N to divide free states from slave states. (p. 516, *m525*)

Missouri River Second longest river in the United States. (p. 343, *m360*)

Montana 41st state. Nicknamed the Treasure State. Acquired in part by the United States through the Louisiana Purchase. (p. 722, *m716–717*)

Montreal (46°N/74°W) Major city in Canada. Located on the St. Lawrence River. Settled by the French. (p. 223, *m223*)

N

National Road Early road to the West. (p. 375, *m376*)

Nauvoo (41°N/91°W) Town founded by the Mormons in Illinois in the 1840s. (p. 448)

Nebraska 37th state. Nicknamed the Cornhusker State. Acquired by the United States as part of the Louisiana Purchase. (p. 722, *m716–717*)

Nebraska Territory Territory created by the Kansas-Nebraska Act. (p. 524, *m525*)

Nevada 36th state. Nicknamed the Sagebrush State or the Battle Born State. Acquired by the United States at the end of the Mexican War. (p. 722, *m716–717*)

New Amsterdam (41°N/74°W) Settlement founded by the Dutch on Manhattan Island. Now called New York City. (p. 107, *m106*)

New England Name for the region that today includes the states from Maine to Connecticut. (p. 124, *m127*)

Newfoundland (48°N/57°W) Island at the mouth of the St. Lawrence River. Part of Canada. (p. 79, *m78*)

New France Colony established by France in North America. (p. 103, *m104*)

New Hampshire One of the 13 original states. Nicknamed the Granite State. (p. 128, *m716–717*)

New Jersey One of the 13 original states. Nicknamed the Garden State. (p. 132, *m716–717*)

New Mexico 47th state. Nicknamed the Land of Enchantment. Acquired by the United States at the end of the Mexican War. (p. 722, *m716–717*)

New Mexico Territory Region in the Southwest including present-day New Mexico, Arizona, and parts of Utah, Nevada, and Colorado. (p. 439, *m439*)

New Netherland Dutch colony on the Hudson River. Conquered by the English and renamed New York in 1664. (p. 106, *m106*)

New Orleans (30°N/90°W) Port city in Louisiana near the mouth of the Mississippi River. Settled by the French in the 1600s. (p. 191, *m104*)

New Spain Area ruled by Spain for 300 years. Included Spanish colonies in the West Indies, Central America, and North America. (p. 96, *m97*)

New Sweden Swedish colony on the Delaware River. Taken over by the Dutch in 1655, then by the English in 1664. Now part of Pennsylvania, New Jersey, and Delaware. (p. 108, *m106*)

New York One of the 13 original states. Nicknamed the Empire State. (p. 132, *m716–717*)

New York City (41°N/74°W) Port city at the mouth of the Hudson River. Founded by the Dutch as New Amsterdam. First capital of the United States. (p. 227, *m230*)

North America World's third largest continent. (p. 15, *m714–715*)

North Carolina One of the 13 original states. Nicknamed the Tar Heel State or the Old North State. (p. 138, *m716–717*)

North Dakota 39th state. Nicknamed the Sioux State or the Flickertail State. Acquired by the United States as part of the Louisiana Purchase. (p. 722, *m716–717*)

Northwest Territory Name for lands north of the Ohio River and east of the Mississippi River. Acquired by the United States by the Treaty of Paris in 1783. (p. 253, *m254*)

Nova Scotia Province of eastern Canada. Early French, then British colony. (p. 103, *m104*)

Nueces River Claimed by Mexico as the southern border of Texas in the Mexican War. (p. 443, *m444*)

O

Ohio 17th state. Nicknamed the Buckeye State. Settled as part of the Northwest Territory. (p. 722, *m716–717*)

Ohio River Important transportation route. Begins at Pittsburgh and joins the Mississippi River at Cairo, Illinois. (p. 190, *m191*)

Oklahoma 46th State. Nicknamed the Sooner State. Acquired by the United States as part of the Louisiana Purchase. (p. 722, *m716–717*)

Oregon 33rd state. Nicknamed the Beaver State. Acquired by the United States as part of Oregon Country. (p. 722, *m716–717*)

Oregon Country Located in the Pacific Northwest. Claimed by the United States, Britain, Spain, and Russia. (p. 428, *m432*)

Oregon Trail Overland route from Independence on the Missouri River to the Columbia River valley. (p. 432, *m441*)

GAZETTEER

GAZETTEER

P

Pacific Northwest   Region along the northwest coast of North America. (p. 25)

Pacific Ocean   World's largest ocean. (p. 71, *m71*)

Pennsylvania   One of the 13 original states. Nicknamed the Keystone State. (p. 134, *m716–717*)

Philadelphia   (40°N/75°W) Major port and chief city in Pennsylvania. Second capital of the United States. (p. 135, *m135*)

Philippine Islands   (14°N/125°E) Group of islands in the Pacific Ocean. (p. 72, *m714–715*)

Pikes Peak   (39°N/105°W) Located in the Rocky Mountains of central Colorado. (p. 346, *m360*)

Plains of Abraham   Grassy field just outside of Quebec where the British defeated the French in the French and Indian War. (p. 197)

Plymouth   (42°N/71°W) New England colony founded in 1620 by Pilgrims. Absorbed by the Massachusetts Bay Colony in 1691. (p. 115, *m115*)

Port Royal   (45°N/65°W) Permanent colony founded by Champlain in Nova Scotia. (p. 103, *m104*)

Portugal   Country in western Europe. In the 1400s, sailors set out from there to explore the coast of Africa. (p. 63, *m65*)

Potomac River   Forms part of the Maryland-Virginia border. Flows through Washington, D.C., and into Chesapeake Bay. (p. 547, *m547*)

Prime Meridian   Line of longitude labeled 0°. (p. 12, *m13*)

Princeton   (40°N/75°W) Located in New Jersey. Site of an American victory during the Revolution. (p. 229, *m230*)

Puerto Rico   (18°N/67°W) Island in the Caribbean Sea. A self-governing commonwealth of the United States. (p. 69, *m714–715*)

Q

Quebec   (47°N/71°W) City in eastern Canada on the St. Lawrence River. Founded in 1608 by the French explorer Samuel de Champlain. (p. 103, *m104*)

R

Republic of Texas   Independent nation set up by American settlers in Texas. Lasted from 1836 to 1845. (p. 436, *m436*)

Rhode Island   One of the 13 original states. Nicknamed Little Rhody or the Ocean State. (p. 127, *m716–717*)

Richmond   (38°N/78°W) Capital of Virginia. Capital of the Confederacy. (p. 546, *m547*)

Rio Grande   River that forms the border between the United States and Mexico. (p. 443, *m444*)

Roanoke Island   (36°N/76°W) Located off the coast of North Carolina. Site of the "lost colony" founded in 1587. (p. 109, *m115*)

Rocky Mountains   Mountains extending through the western United States. (p. 19, *m18*)

S

Sacramento   (39°N/122°W) Capital of California. Developed as a Gold Rush boom town. (p. 447, *m716–717*)

Sagres   (37°N/9°W) Town in Portugal. In the 1400s, Prince Henry the Navigator set up an informal school for sailors there. (p. 63, *m65*)

St. Augustine   (30°N/81°W) City in Florida. Founded by Spain in 1565. Oldest European settlement in the United States. (p. 101, *m102*)

St. Lawrence River   Waterway leading from the Great Lakes to the Atlantic Ocean. Forms part of the border between the United States and Canada. (p. 79, *m78*)

St. Louis   (38°N/90°W) City in Missouri on the Mississippi River. Lewis and Clark began their expedition there. (p. 343, *m716–717*)

Salt Lake City   (41°N/112°W) Largest city in Utah. Founded in 1847 by Mormons. (p. 449, *m716–717*)

San Antonio   (29°N/99°W) City in southern Texas. Chief Texan settlement in Spanish and Mexican days. Site of the Alamo. (p. 436, *m436*)

San Diego   (33°N/117°W) City in southern California. Founded as a Spanish mission. (p. 440, *m441*)

San Francisco   (38°N/122°W) City in northern California. Boom town of the California Gold Rush. (p. 449, *m449*)

San Jacinto River   River in Texas. Site of a Texan victory in 1836. (p. 438, *m436*)

Santa Fe   (35°N/106°W) Capital of New Mexico. First settled by the Spanish. (p. 440, *m441*)

Santa Fe Trail   Overland trail from Independence to Santa Fe. Opened in 1821. (p. 440, *m441*)

Saratoga   (43°N/75°W) City in eastern New York. The American victory there in 1777 was a turning point in the Revolution. (p. 230, *m230*)

Savannah   (32°N/81°W) Oldest city in Georgia. Founded in 1733. (p. 139, *m138*)

Shiloh   (35°N/88°W) Site of a Union victory in 1862. Located on the Tennessee River. (p. 550, *m563*)

Sierra Nevada   Mountain range mostly in California. (p. 19, *m18*)

Songhai   Ancient West African kingdom. (p. 64, *m65*)

South America   World's fourth largest continent. Part of the Western Hemisphere. (p. 15, *m714–715*)

South Carolina   One of the 13 original states. Nicknamed the Palmetto State. (p. 138, *m716–717*)

South Dakota   40th state. Nicknamed the Coyote State. Acquired by the United States as part of the Louisiana Purchase. (p. 722, *m716–717*)

Southern Colonies   Maryland, Virginia, North Carolina, South Carolina, and Georgia. (p. 136, *m138*)

South Pass   Pass through the Rocky Mountains in present-day Wyoming. (p. 431, *m432*)

Spain   Country in southwestern Europe. Columbus sailed from Spain in 1492. (p. 65, *m714–715*)

Spanish borderlands   Southern half of the present-day United States. (p. 74, *m75*)

Spanish Florida   Part of New Spain. Purchased by the United States in 1821. (p. 354, *m360*)

Strait of Magellan   (53°S/69°W) Narrow water route at the tip of South America. (p. 15, *m71*)

T

Tennessee   16th state. Nicknamed the Volunteer State. Gained statehood after North Carolina ceded its western lands to the United States. (p. 722, *m716–717*)

Tenochtitlán   (19°N/99°W) Capital of the Aztec empire. Now part of Mexico City. (p. 49, *m48*)

Texas   28th state. Nicknamed the Lone Star State. Proclaimed independence from Mexico in 1836. Was a separate republic until 1845. (p. 469, *m716–717*)

Tidewater   Area of low land along the Atlantic coastal plain. Excellent farmland. (p. 160, *m162*)

Tikal   (17°N/90°W) Ancient Maya city. (p. 48, *m48*)

Timbuktu   (17°N/3°W) City on the southern edge of the Sahara Desert. Flourished as a center of trade and learning. (p. 64, *m65*)

Trenton   (41°N/74°W) Capital of New Jersey. Site of an American victory in the Revolution. (p. 229, *m230*)

U

Utah   45th state. Nicknamed the Beehive State. Settled by Mormons. (p. 722, *m716–717*)

Utah Territory   Region formed out of the Mexican Cession by the Compromise of 1850. (p. 521, *m525*)

V

Valley Forge   (40°N/76°W) Winter headquarters for the Continental Army in 1777–1778. Located near Philadelphia. (p. 231, *m230*)

Veracruz   (19°N/96°W) Port city in Mexico on the Gulf of Mexico. (p. 444, *m444*)

Vermont   14th state. Nicknamed the Green Mountain State. First new state to join the Union after the Revolution. (p. 722, *m716–717*)

Vicksburg   (42°N/86°W) Located on a high cliff overlooking the Mississippi River. Site of a Union victory in 1863. (p. 551, *m563*)

Vincennes   (39°N/88°W) City in Indiana. Settled by the French. British fort there was captured by George Rogers Clark in 1779. (p. 234, *m233*)

Vinland   Viking settlement in present-day Newfoundland. (p. 59)

Virginia   One of the 13 original states. Nicknamed the Old Dominion. (p. 137, *m716–717*)

W

Washington   42nd state. Nicknamed the Evergreen State. (p. 722, *m716–717*)

Washington, D.C.   (39°N/77°W) Capital of the United States since 1800. Called Federal City until it was renamed for George Washington in 1799. (p. 313, *m356*)

Washington-on-the-Brazos   (30°N/96°W) Town in Texas near Houston. Texans signed their declaration of independence from Mexico there in 1836. (p. 436)

Western Hemisphere   Western half of the world. Includes North and South America. (p. 15)

West Indies   Islands in the Caribbean Sea. Explored by Columbus in 1492. (p. 67, *m68*)

West Virginia   35th state. Nicknamed the Mountain State. Separated from Virginia early in the Civil War. (p. 722, *m716–717*)

Willamette River   Flows across fertile farmlands in northern Oregon to join the Columbia River. (p. 428, *m432*)

Wisconsin   30th state. Nicknamed the Badger State. Settled as part of the Northwest Territory. (p. 722, *m716–717*)

Wyoming   44th state. Nicknamed the Equality State. (p. 722, *m716–717*)

Y

Yorktown   (37°N/76°W) Town in Virginia near the York River. Site of a decisive American victory in 1781. (p. 239, *m240*)

G A Z E T T E E R

A CHRONOLOGY
OF AMERICAN HISTORY

This chronology includes some of the most important events and developments in American history. It can be used to trace developments in the areas of government and citizenship, exploration and invention, American life, and the world of ideas.

	Government and Citizenship	Explorers and Inventors
Prehistory–1499	Mayas, Aztecs, Incas build empires in Americas Crusades to Holy Land begin Rulers build strong nations in Europe	Mayas develop accurate calendar Incas use quinine to treat malaria Columbus sails to America Vasco da Gama reaches India
1500–1599	Cortés defeats Aztecs Pizarro captures Inca capital Spanish pass Laws of the Indies English colony set up at Roanoke	Spanish explore North America Magellan's expedition circles globe Cartier sails up St. Lawrence River Drake sails around world
1600–1649	House of Burgesses set up in Virginia Mayflower Compact signed Massachusetts Bay Colony founded Fundamental Orders of Connecticut written	Joint stock companies finance English settlements in North America Champlain founds Quebec West Indian tobacco brought to Virginia
1650–1699	France claims Louisiana Glorious Revolution in England Town meetings held in New England	Marquette and Joliet explore Mississippi River La Salle reaches Mississippi delta
1700–1749	Georgia founded Carolinas divided into two colonies English settlers move into Ohio Valley	Indigo developed as cash crop Benjamin Franklin invents Franklin stove
1750–1799	French and Indian War Intolerable Acts passed Declaration of Independence signed American Revolution Constitution ratified	Fitch launches first steam-powered boat Slater sets up textile mills in New England Eli Whitney invents cotton gin

Changes in American Life	The World of Ideas	
Agriculture develops in Americas Great Serpent Mound built Trade between Europe and Asia expands	Mayas develop system of writing Aztecs build Tenochtitlán Renaissance begins in Europe	**Prehistory–1499**
Native American population of Spanish America declines French develop fishing and fur trading in North America	Spanish convert Native Americans to Christianity Universities open in Spanish America John White paints in North America	**1500–1599**
Spanish, French, Dutch, and English colonists adapt to life in New World John Smith helps Jamestown survive Slavery introduced in Virginia	Religious toleration granted in Maryland Harvard College founded First public schools set up in Massachusetts	**1600–1649**
Navigation Acts passed New England becomes trade and shipbuilding center	Quakers seek religious freedom in Pennsylvania College of William and Mary founded	**1650–1699**
Triangular trade flourishes Plantations expand in South Growth of port cities	Yale College founded *Poor Richard's Almanac* published Great Awakening begins in colonies	**1700–1749**
Proclamation of 1763 Parliament passes Sugar, Quartering, Stamp, and Townshend acts Colonies boycott British goods Northwest Ordinance takes effect	Thomas Paine writes *Common Sense* Northern states ban slave trade Richard Allen organizes one of first black churches in United States National capital designed and built	**1750–1799**

	Government and Citizenship	Explorers and Inventors
1800–1824	Louisiana Purchase War of 1812 Missouri Compromise passed Monroe Doctrine	Lewis and Clark expedition Steamboats improved Eli Whitney develops interchangeable parts
1825–1849	Age of Jackson Indian Removal Act passed Texas wins independence Oregon divided along 49th parallel	Erie Canal opened Mechanical reaper, steel plow, and telegraph developed Railroads expand
1850–1874	Compromise of 1850 Civil War Emancipation Proclamation Indian wars on Great Plains	Passenger elevator, sleeping car, and air brake invented Bessemer process developed Transcontinental railroad completed
1875–1899	Battle of Little Bighorn Populist Party formed Sherman Antitrust Act passed Spanish-American War	Refrigeration developed Telephone, phonograph, and incandescent light bulb invented First skyscraper built
1900–1924	Progressive Movement Roosevelt Corollary World War I Fourteen Points United States rejects Treaty of Versailles	Panama Canal built Airplane invented Assembly line introduced Electric appliances become widespread
1925–1949	New Deal World War II Truman Doctrine and Marshall Plan NATO created	Lindbergh flies across Atlantic Antibiotics developed Atomic bomb developed First computer invented
1950–1974	Korean War Civil Rights Act passed Watergate affair Vietnam War	*Explorer 1* launched into orbit American astronauts land on moon Nuclear power plants built Vaccines increase life expectancy
1975–Present	Reagan launches conservative revolution American-Soviet relations thaw War in the Persian Gulf	Computers change the way Americans work, play, and communicate Space shuttle flights Advances in genetic engineering

732

Changes in American Life	The World of Ideas	
Henry Clay's American System Industry spreads in North Cotton growing expands in South Antislavery movement grows	"The Star-Spangled Banner" written First trade unions set up Hudson River School of painting Washington Irving is well-known writer	**1800– 1824**
California Gold Rush Temperance movement develops *The Liberator* founded Seneca Falls Convention	Mormon Church founded Idea of Manifest Destiny takes hold Mount Holyoke becomes first women's college in United States	**1825– 1849**
Thirteenth Amendment ends slavery Homestead Act passed Cattle and mining boom in West Knights of Labor founded	*The Scarlet Letter* published Free public education spreads in North *Uncle Tom's Cabin* published	**1850– 1874**
Frontier closes Trusts established Immigration grows Cities expand rapidly	Newspapers expand circulation Progressive education movement American Realists school of painting Reformers expose problems of cities	**1875– 1899**
Muckrakers expose social problems Pure Food and Drug Act passed NAACP formed Women work in war industries	Women win right to vote Jazz Age Harlem Renaissance Commercial radio begins Hollywood becomes world movie capital	**1900– 1924**
Bull market on Wall Street Great Depression Wartime production ends depression Internment of Japanese Americans	Writers and photographers describe effects of depression *The Grapes of Wrath* published WPA sponsors artistic projects	**1925– 1949**
Rapid expansion of suburbs Civil rights movement Great Society programs	Rock 'n' roll becomes popular Television age begins New emphasis on equal rights for all Americans	**1950– 1974**

Increase of women in work force
Move to Sunbelt
Nationwide campaign against
  drugs begins
	Lasers revolutionize medicine and
	  entertainment
	Physical fitness becomes popular
	Concern for environment spreads
		**1975–
		Present**

CONNECTIONS WITH AMERICAN LITERATURE

TOPIC	AUTHOR	WORK	GENRE
UNIT 1 THE AMERICAS			
Peoples of the American Southwest, pages 37–38	Zuñi Indians	The Girl Who Hunted Rabbits	myth
Settling North America, pages 39–47	Tewa Indians	Song of the Sky Loom	myth
Settling North America, pages 39–47	Ella E. Clark	The Origin of Fire	myth
Settling North America, pages 39–47	Bernard DeVoto	The Indian All Around Us	essay
Peoples of the Eastern Woodlands, pages 45–47	Iroquois Indians	The Iroquois Constitution	document
The Aztecs, pages 49–50	Juliet Piggott	Popocatepetl and Ixtaccihuatl	myth
The Spanish Set Sail, pages 65–69	Joaquin Miller	Columbus	poem
UNIT 2 COLONIES TAKE ROOT			
Trapping, Trading, and Exploring, pages 103–105	James Fenimore Cooper	The Deerslayer The Pathfinder	novels
Dutch Rule in New Netherland, pages 130–131	Washington Irving	Rip Van Winkle	tale
The Hard-Working New England Colonies, pages 152–156	Henry Wadsworth Longfellow	The Village Blacksmith	poem
Benjamin Franklin, pages 170–171	Benjamin Franklin	Poor Richard's Almanac	book
UNIT 3 FROM REVOLUTION TO REPUBLIC			
The Shot Heard 'Round the World, pages 211–213	Ralph Waldo Emerson	Concord Hymn	poem
Sounding the Alarm, pages 212–213	Henry Wadsworth Longfellow	Paul Revere's Ride	poem
Early Battles, pages 220–224	Esther Forbes	Johnny Tremain	novel
The *Common Sense* of Thomas Paine, pages 224–225	Thomas Paine	Common Sense	pamphlet
Valley Forge, pages 231–232	Maxwell Anderson	Valley Forge	play
Women in the War, pages 235–238	Phillis Wheatley	To the Right Honourable William, Earl of Dartmouth	letter

CONNECTIONS WITH LITERATURE

CONNECTIONS WITH LITERATURE

PRESIDENTS OF THE UNITED STATES

PRESIDENTS

1. **George Washington** (1732–1799)
   Years in office: 1789–1797
   No political party
   Elected from: Virginia
   Vice Pres.: John Adams

2. **John Adams** (1735–1826)
   Years in office: 1797–1801
   Federalist Party
   Elected from: Massachusetts
   Vice Pres.: Thomas Jefferson

3. **Thomas Jefferson** (1743–1826)
   Years in office: 1801–1809
   Democratic Republican Party
   Elected from: Virginia
   Vice Pres.: Aaron Burr, George Clinton

4. **James Madison** (1751–1836)
   Years in office: 1809–1817
   Democratic Republican Party
   Elected from: Virginia
   Vice Pres.: George Clinton,
       Elbridge Gerry

5. **James Monroe** (1758–1831)
   Years in office: 1817–1825
   Democratic Republican Party
   Elected from: Virginia
   Vice Pres.: Daniel Tompkins

6. **John Quincy Adams** (1767–1848)
   Years in office: 1825–1829
   National Republican Party
   Elected from: Massachusetts
   Vice Pres.: John Calhoun

7. **Andrew Jackson** (1767–1845)
   Years in office: 1829–1837
   Democratic Party
   Elected from: Tennessee
   Vice Pres.: John Calhoun,
       Martin Van Buren

8. **Martin Van Buren** (1782–1862)
   Years in office: 1837–1841
   Democratic Party
   Elected from: New York
   Vice Pres.: Richard Johnson

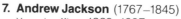

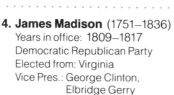

9. **William Henry Harrison***
(1773–1841)
Years in office: 1841
Whig Party
Elected from: Ohio
Vice Pres.: John Tyler

10. **John Tyler** (1790–1862)
Years in office: 1841–1845
Whig Party
Elected from: Virginia
Vice Pres.: none

11. **James K. Polk** (1795–1849)
Years in office: 1845–1849
Democratic Party
Elected from: Tennessee
Vice Pres.: George Dallas

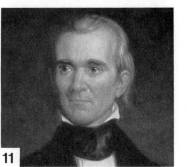

12. **Zachary Taylor*** (1784–1850)
Years in office: 1849–1850
Whig Party
Elected from: Louisiana
Vice Pres.: Millard Fillmore

13. **Millard Fillmore** (1800–1874)
Years in office: 1850–1853
Whig Party
Elected from: New York
Vice Pres.: none

14. **Franklin Pierce** (1804–1869)
Years in office: 1853–1857
Democratic Party
Elected from: New Hampshire
Vice Pres.: William King

15. **James Buchanan** (1791–1868)
Years in office: 1857–1861
Democratic Party
Elected from: Pennsylvania
Vice Pres.: John Breckinridge

16. **Abraham Lincoln**** (1809–1865)
Years in office: 1861–1865
Republican Party
Elected from: Illinois
Vice Pres.: Hannibal Hamlin,
 Andrew Johnson

*Died in office   **Assassinated   ***Resigned

PRESIDENTS

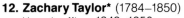

17. Andrew Johnson (1808–1875)
Years in office: 1865–1869
Republican Party
Elected from: Tennessee
Vice Pres.: none

18. Ulysses S. Grant (1822–1885)
Years in office: 1869–1877
Republican Party
Elected from: Illinois
Vice Pres.: Schuyler Colfax, Henry Wilson

19. Rutherford B. Hayes (1822–1893)
Years in office: 1877–1881
Republican Party
Elected from: Ohio
Vice Pres.: William Wheeler

20. James A. Garfield** (1831–1881)
Years in office: 1881
Republican Party
Elected from: Ohio
Vice Pres.: Chester A. Arthur

21. Chester A. Arthur (1830–1886)
Years in office: 1881–1885
Republican Party
Elected from: New York
Vice Pres.: none

22. Grover Cleveland (1837–1908)
Years in office: 1885–1889
Democratic Party
Elected from: New York
Vice Pres.: Thomas Hendricks

23. Benjamin Harrison (1833–1901)
Years in office: 1889–1893
Republican Party
Elected from: Indiana
Vice Pres.: Levi Morton

24. Grover Cleveland (1837–1908)
Years in office: 1893–1897
Democratic Party
Elected from: New York
Vice Pres.: Adlai Stevenson

25. Willam McKinley** (1843–1901)
Years in office: 1897–1901
Republican Party
Elected from: Ohio
Vice Pres.: Garret Hobart,
            Theodore Roosevelt

26. Theodore Roosevelt (1858–1919)
Years in office: 1901–1909
Republican Party
Elected from: New York
Vice Pres.: Charles Fairbanks

27. William Howard Taft (1857–1930)
Years in office: 1909–1913
Republican Party
Elected from: Ohio
Vice Pres.: James Sherman

28. Woodrow Wilson (1856–1924)
Years in office: 1913–1921
Democratic Party
Elected from: New Jersey
Vice Pres.: Thomas Marshall

29. Warren G. Harding* (1865–1923)
Years in office: 1921–1923
Republican Party
Elected from: Ohio
Vice Pres.: Calvin Coolidge

30. Calvin Coolidge (1872–1933)
Years in office: 1923–1929
Republican Party
Elected from: Massachusetts
Vice Pres.: Charles Dawes

31. Herbert C. Hoover (1874–1964)
Years in office: 1929–1933
Republican Party
Elected from: California
Vice Pres.: Charles Curtis

32. Franklin D. Roosevelt* (1882–1945)
Years in office: 1933–1945
Democratic Party
Elected from: New York
Vice Pres.: John Garner, Henry Wallace,
            Harry S. Truman

*Died in office   **Assassinated   ***Resigned

PRESIDENTS

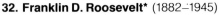

33

34

35

36

37

38

39

40

41

33. Harry S. Truman (1884–1972)
Years in office: 1945–1953
Democratic Party
Elected from: Missouri
Vice Pres.: Alben Barkley

34. Dwight D. Eisenhower (1890–1969)
Years in office: 1953–1961
Republican Party
Elected from: New York
Vice Pres.: Richard M. Nixon

35. John F. Kennedy** (1917–1963)
Years in office: 1961–1963
Democratic Party
Elected from: Massachusetts
Vice Pres.: Lyndon B. Johnson

36. Lyndon B. Johnson (1908–1973)
Years in office: 1963–1969
Democratic Party
Elected from: Texas
Vice Pres.: Hubert Humphrey

37. Richard M. Nixon*** (1913–   )
Years in office: 1969–1974
Republican Party
Elected from: New York
Vice Pres.: Spiro Agnew, Gerald R. Ford

38. Gerald R. Ford (1913–   )
Years in office: 1974–1977
Republican Party
Elected from: Michigan
Vice Pres.: Nelson Rockefeller

39. Jimmy Carter (1924–   )
Years in office: 1977–1981
Democratic Party
Elected from: Georgia
Vice Pres.: Walter Mondale

40. Ronald W. Reagan (1911–   )
Years in office: 1981–1989
Republican Party
Elected from: California
Vice Pres.: George Bush

41. George Bush (1924–   )
Years in office: 1989–
Republican Party
Elected from: Texas
Vice Pres.: Dan Quayle

*Died in office   **Assassinated   ***Resigned

PRESIDENTS

◆ GLOSSARY ◆

This glossary defines all vocabulary words and many important historical terms and phrases. These words and terms appear in blue or dark type the first time that they are used in the text.

The page number after each definition refers to the page on which the word or phrase is first discussed in the text. For other references, see the Index.

Pronunciation Key

When difficult names or terms first appear in the text, they are respelled to help you with pronunciation. A syllable printed in SMALL CAPITAL LETTERS receives the greatest stress. The

pronunciation key below lists the letters and symbols used for respelling. It also includes examples of words using each sound and showing how they would be respelled.

Symbol	Example	Respelling
a	hat	(hat)
ay	pay, late	(pay), (layt)
ah	star, hot	(stahr), (haht)
ai	air, dare	(air), (dair)
aw	law, all	(law), (awl)
eh	met	(meht)
ee	bee, eat	(bee), (eet)
er	learn, sir, fur	(lern), (ser), (fer)
ih	fit	(fiht)
i	mile	(mil)
ir	ear	(ir)
oh	no	(noh)
oi	soil, boy	(soil), (boi)
oo	root, rule	(root), (rool)
or	born, door	(born), (dor)
ow	plow, out	(plow), (owt)

Symbol	Example	Respelling
u	put, book	(put), (buk)
uh	fun	(fuhn)
yoo	few, use	(fyoo), (yooz)
ch	chill, reach	(chihl), (reech)
g	go, dig	(goh), (dihg)
j	jet, gently, bridge	(jeht), (JEHNT lee), (brihj)
k	kite, cup	(kit), (kuhp)
ks	mix	(mihks)
kw	quick	(kwihk)
ng	bring	(brihng)
s	say, cent	(say), (sehnt)
sh	she, crash	(shee), (krash)
th	three	(three)
y	yet, onion	(yeht), (UHN yuhn)
z	zip, always	(zihp), (AWL wayz)
zh	treasure	(TREH zher)

A

abolitionist person who wanted to end slavery in the United States. (p. 486)

Act of Toleration (1649) law that gave religious freedom to all Christians in Maryland. (p. 137)

Adams-Onís Treaty agreement by which Spain gave Florida to the United States. (p. 389)

adobe sun-dried clay brick. (p. 38)

Albany Plan of Union Benjamin Franklin's plan for the colonies to work together to defeat the French. (p. 195)

alien foreigner. (p. 327)

Alien Act (1798) law that allowed the President to expel foreigners thought to be dangerous to the country. (p. 327)

almanac book containing calendars and other useful information. (p. 170)

amend change. (p. 268)

amendment formal written change. (p. 291)

American Colonization Society group founded to set up a colony for free blacks in Africa. (p. 485)

American System plan devised by Henry Clay providing for high tariffs and internal improvements. (p. 383)

annex add on, such as territory. (p. 438)

Antifederalist person opposed to the Constitution during the ratification debate in 1787. (p. 266)

appeal ask that a decision be reviewed by a higher court. (p. 298)

apprentice person who learns a trade or craft from a master craftworker. (p. 168)

appropriate set aside money for a special purpose. (p. 295)

aqueduct canal that carries water. (p. 50)

archaeology study of evidence left by early peoples. (p. 36)

arsenal gun warehouse. (p. 532)

Articles of Confederation first constitution of the United States. (p. 249)

artifact object made by humans and used by archaeologists to re-create a picture of the past. (p. 36)

astrolabe instrument used by sailors to figure out their latitude at sea. (p. 61)

B

backcountry area along the eastern slopes of the Appalachian Mountains. (p. 158)

Bank of the United States national bank set up by Congress. (p. 314)

Bear Flag Republic country set up in 1846 by Americans in California. (p. 445)

bill proposed law. (pp. 264, 290)

bill of rights document that lists freedoms the government promises to protect. (p. 249)

Bill of Rights first ten amendments to the Constitution. Ratified in 1791. (p. 268)

black code laws that limited the rights of freedmen in the South after the Civil War. (p. 576)

blockade shutting off a port to keep people or supplies from moving in or out. (p. 223)

bond certificate that promises to pay the holder a sum of money plus interest on a certain date. (p. 311)

Boston Massacre shooting of five Bostonians by British soldiers on March 5, 1770. (p. 206)

Boston Tea Party protest in which Bostonians dressed as Indians dumped tea into the harbor. (p. 210)

bounty payment made to men who joined the Union army. (p. 557)

boycott refuse to buy certain goods or services. (p. 201)

burgess representative to the colonial assembly of Virginia. (p. 112)

C

cabinet group of officials who head government departments and advise the President. (pp. 294, 311)

canal channel dug and filled with water to allow ships to cross a stretch of land. (p. 378)

capital money raised for a business venture. (p. 111)

capitalist person who invests money in business to make a profit. (p. 366)

caravel ship with a steering rudder and triangular sails. (p. 63)

carpetbagger name for a northerner who went to the South during Reconstruction. (p. 582)

cartographer mapmaker. (p. 9)

cash crop surplus of food sold for money on the world market. (p. 156)

caucus private meeting of political party leaders to choose a candidate. (p. 406)

cavalry troops on horseback. (p. 231)

cede give up, as land. (p. 445)

charter legal document giving certain rights to a person or company. (p. 109)

checks and balances system set up by the Constitution in which each branch of the federal government has the power to check, or control, the actions of the other branches. (p. 264)

civilian person not in the military. (p. 554)

civil war war between people of the same country. (p. 520)

clergy religious officials and priests. (p. 60)

climate average weather of a place over a period of 20 or 30 years. (p. 24)

clipper ship fast sailing ship of the mid-1800s. (p. 461)

colony group of people settled in a distant land who are ruled by the government of their native land. (p. 69)

committee of correspondence group of colonists who wrote letters and pamphlets protesting British rule. (p. 206)

compromise settlement in which each side gives up some of its demands in order to reach an agreement. (p. 259)

Compromise of 1850 agreement over slavery that admitted California to the Union as a free state, allowed popular sovereignty in New Mexico and Utah, banned the slave trade in Washington, D.C., and passed a strict fugitive slave law. (p. 521)

Confederate States of America nation formed by the states that seceded from the Union in 1860 and 1861. (p. 534)

conquistador Spanish word for conqueror. (p. 69)

constituent person who elects a representative to office. (p. 296)

constitution document that sets out the laws and principles of a government. (p. 248)

GLOSSARY

Constitutional Convention meeting of delegates from 12 states who wrote a constitution for the United States in 1787. (p. 256)

Continental Army army set up by the Second Continental Congress to fight the British. (p. 221)

continental divide mountain ridge that separates river systems. (p. 344)

Copperhead Northerner who opposed fighting to keep the South in the Union. (p. 557)

corduroy road log road. (p. 375)

corporation business owned by investors who buy shares of stock. (p. 611)

cotton gin invention of Eli Whitney's that speeded the cleaning of cotton fibers. (p. 366)

coureur de bois French phrase meaning runner of the woods; trapper or trader. (p. 104)

creole person born in the Americas to Spanish parents. (p. 97)

Crusades series of wars fought by Christians to conquer the Holy Land. (p. 60)

culture way of life of a given people. (p. 36)

culture area region in which people share a similar way of life. (p. 39)

D

Daughters of Liberty group of colonial women who protested the Stamp Act. (p. 203)

Declaration of Independence (1776) document that stated that the colonies had become a free and independent nation. (p. 225)

democratic ensuring that all people have the same rights. (p. 336)

discrimination policy or attitude that denies equal rights to certain people. (p. 468)

domestic tranquillity peace at home. (p. 283)

draft law requiring men of a certain age to serve in the military. (p. 557)

Dred Scott decision Supreme Court decision in 1857. Stated that slaves were property, not citizens. (p. 528)

drought long dry spell. (p. 38)

due process right of every citizen to the same fair rules in all cases brought to trial. (p. 268)

dumping selling goods in another country at very low prices. (p. 383)

E

economic depression period when business activity slows, prices and wages fall, and unemployment rises. (p. 255)

electoral college group of electors from each state that meets every four years to vote for the President and Vice President. (p. 264)

elevation height above sea level. (p. 16)

emancipate set free. (p. 552)

Emancipation Proclamation (1863) Lincoln's declaration freeing slaves in the Confederacy. (p. 552)

embargo ban on trade with another country. (p. 349)

Embargo Act (1807) law forbidding Americans to export or import any goods. (p. 349)

emigrate leave one's country and settle elsewhere. (p. 124)

encomienda right to demand taxes or labor from Native Americans in the Spanish colonies. (p. 97)

English Bill of Rights (1689) document that protected the rights of English citizens. (p. 142)

Enlightenment movement in Europe in the 1700s that emphasized the use of reason. (p. 169)

enumerated article goods that Parliament said colonists could sell only to England. (p. 142)

execute carry out. (p. 249)

executive agreement informal agreement made by the President of the United States with other heads of state. (p. 296)

executive branch part of a government that carries out the laws. (p. 258)

export trade good sent to markets outside a country. (p. 141)

extended family close-knit family group that includes grandparents, parents, children, aunts, uncles, and cousins. (p. 475)

F

factory system method of producing goods that brings workers and machines together in one place. (p. 367)

famine severe shortage of food. (p. 467)

federal national. (p. 287)

federalism sharing of power between the states and the national government. (p. 262)

Federalist supporter of the Constitution in the ratification debate in 1787. Favored a strong national government. (pp. 266, 324)

feudalism system of rule by lords who owed loyalty to their king. (p. 60)

Fifteenth Amendment constitutional amendment that gave African Americans the right to vote in all states. (p. 581)

GLOSSARY

forty-niner　person who went to California during the Gold Rush in 1849. (p. 449)

Fourteenth Amendment　constitutional amendment that granted citizenship to all persons born in the United States. (p. 578)

Frame of Government　document that set up the government of the Pennsylvania colony. (p. 134)

freedman　freed slave. (p. 572)

Freedmen's Bureau　government agency that helped freed slaves. (p. 573)

French and Indian War　conflict between the French and British in North America. Fought from 1754 to 1763. (p. 193)

fugitive　runaway, such as an escaped slave in the 1800s. (p. 519)

Fugitive Slave Law of 1850　law that required citizens to help catch runaway slaves. (p. 521)

Fundamental Orders of Connecticut　system of laws in the colony of Connecticut that limited the powers of the government. (p. 126)

G

General Court　representative assembly in the Massachusetts Bay Colony. (p. 125)

general welfare　well-being of all the people. (p. 283)

gentry　highest social class in the 13 English colonies. (p. 168)

geography　study of people, their environments, and their resources. (p. 4)

Gettysburg Address　speech given by Lincoln in 1863 after the battle of Gettysburg. (p. 562)

glacier　thick sheet of ice. (p. 4)

grandfather clause　law passed by southern states after the Civil War. Excused a voter from a poll tax or literacy test if his father or grandfather had voted before 1867. (p. 589)

Great Awakening　religious movement in the colonies in the 1730s and 1740s. (p. 171)

Great Compromise　Roger Sherman's plan at the Constitutional Convention for a two-house legislature. Settled differences between large and small states. (p. 259)

H

habeas corpus　right to have charges filed or a hearing before being jailed. (p. 557)

Hartford Convention　meeting of New Englanders who opposed the War of 1812. (p. 359)

hemisphere　half of the Earth. (p. 12)

High Federalist　supporter of Alexander Hamilton against President Adams. Wanted to go to war with France. (p. 327)

hill　area of raised land. Lower, less steep, and more rounded than a mountain. (p. 16)

history　account of what has happened in the development of a people, a nation, or a civilization. (p. 5)

hogan　Navajo house built of mud plaster and supported by wooden poles. (p. 42)

House of Burgesses　representative assembly in colonial Virginia. (p. 113)

I

igloo　Eskimo house made of snow and ice. (p. 39)

immigrant　person who enters a new country in order to settle there. (p. 467)

impeach　bring charges against an official such as the President. (pp. 264, 296)

import　trade good brought into a country. (p. 141)

impressment　act of seizing men from a ship or village and forcing them to serve in the navy. (p. 348)

indentured servant　person who signed a contract to work for a certain length of time in exchange for passage to the colonies. (p. 145)

Indian Removal Act　(1830) law that forced Native Americans to move west of the Mississippi. (p. 415)

Industrial Revolution　process that completely changed the way goods were produced. (p. 366)

inflation　economic cycle in which the value of money falls and the prices of goods rise. (p. 558)

initiative　procedure that allows voters to introduce a bill by collecting signatures on a petition. (p. 615)

interchangeable parts　identical parts of a tool or instrument that are made by machine. (p. 371)

international date line　imaginary line that falls at 180° longitude. When crossing this line, one gains or loses a day, depending on the direction of travel. (p. 15)

Intolerable Acts　laws passed by Parliament in 1774 to punish colonists in Massachusetts for the Boston Tea Party. (p. 210)

irrigate　bring water to an area. (p. 7)

isthmus　narrow strip of land. (p. 15)

J

Jim Crow law　law passed by southerners that segregated public places. (p. 589)

joint committee　group of members of both the House of Representatives and the Senate. (p. 295)

joint stock company private company that sold shares to finance trading voyages. (p. 111)

judicial branch part of a government that decides if laws are carried out fairly. (p. 258)

judicial review right of the Supreme Court to review acts of the President and laws passed by Congress and declare them unconstitutional. (p. 294)

jury panel of citizens. (p. 298)

justice fairness. (p. 282)

K

Kansas-Nebraska Act (1854) law that divided Nebraska into two territories. Provided for the question of slavery in the territories to be decided by popular sovereignty. (p. 524)

kayak small boat made of animal skins. (p. 39)

Kentucky and Virginia resolutions (1798, 1799) declarations that states had the right to declare a law unconstitutional. (p. 328)

kitchen cabinet group of unofficial advisers to President Andrew Jackson. (p. 410)

kiva underground chamber where Pueblo men held religious ceremonies. (p. 41)

Ku Klux Klan secret group first set up in the South after the Civil War. Members terrorized blacks and other minority groups. (p. 584)

L

laissez faire French term meaning let alone. Referred to the idea that government should not interfere in people's lives. (p. 337)

Land Ordinance of 1785 law that set up a system for settling the Northwest Territory. (p. 254)

latitude distance north or south from the Equator. (p. 5)

Laws of the Indies laws that governed Spanish colonies in the Americas. (p. 96)

legislative branch part of a government that passes laws. (p. 258)

legislature group of people with power to make laws for a country or colony. (p. 143)

liberty freedom to live as one pleases. (p. 285)

literacy test examination to see if a person can read and write. (p. 589)

long house Iroquois dwelling. (p. 46)

longitude distance east or west from the Prime Meridian. (p. 5)

Loyalist colonist who stayed loyal to Great Britain during the American Revolution. (p. 227)

M

Magna Carta document that guaranteed rights to English nobles in 1215. (p. 113)

magnetic compass Device that shows which direction is north. (p. 61)

Manifest Destiny belief that the United States should own all the land between the Atlantic and Pacific oceans. (p. 442)

manor part of a lord's holding in the Middle Ages. (p. 60)

map projection way of drawing the Earth on a flat surface. (p. 10)

martial law rule by the military. (p. 542)

Mayflower Compact agreement signed by Pilgrims before landing at Plymouth. (p. 116)

mercantilism economic theory that a nation's strength came from building up its gold supplies and expanding its trade. (p. 141)

mestizo person in the Spanish colonies of mixed Spanish and Indian background. (p. 97)

Mexican War conflict between the United States and Mexico over Texas. (p. 443)

Middle Passage ocean trip from Africa to the Americas in which thousands of slaves died. (p. 162)

militia army of citizens who serve as soldiers during an emergency. (p. 211)

minuteman volunteer who trained to fight the British in 1775. (p. 212)

mission religious settlement. Run by Catholic priests and friars in the Spanish colonies. (p. 96)

Missouri Compromise (1820) plan proposed by Henry Clay to keep the number of slave and free states equal. Admitted Missouri as a slave state and Maine as a free state. (p. 516)

monopoly company that completely controls the market of a certain industry. (p. 611)

Monroe Doctrine policy statement of President James Monroe in 1823. Warned European nations not to interfere in Latin America. (p. 389)

Mormon member of the Church of Jesus Christ of Latter-day Saints. (p. 447)

mountain high, rugged land usually at least 1,000 feet (300 m) above the surrounding land. (p. 16)

Mountain Man trapper in the West in the early 1800s. (p. 429)

N

national debt money a government owes. (p. 311)

nationalism pride in or devotion to one's country. (p. 350)

Native American descendant of people who reached the Americas thousands of years ago. (p. 36)

nativist person who wanted to limit immigration and preserve the United States for native-born white Americans. (p. 467)

navigation practice of plotting a course at sea. (p. 63)

Navigation Acts laws that governed trade between England and its colonies. (p. 141)

neutral choosing not to fight on either side in a war. (p. 233)

Neutrality Proclamation (1793) President George Washington's statement that the United States would remain neutral in the war between France and other European nations. (p. 318)

New England Anti-Slavery Society Organized by William Lloyd Garrison to end slavery. (p. 487)

New Jersey Plan William Paterson's plan for the new government presented to the Constitutional Convention. (p. 258)

nominating convention meeting at which a political party selects a candidate. (p. 406)

nonimportation agreement promise of colonial merchants and planters to stop importing goods taxed by the Townshend Acts. (p. 202)

Nonintercourse Act (1809) law that replaced the Embargo Act and allowed Americans to trade with all nations except Britain and France. (p. 349)

Northwest Ordinance (1787) law that set up a government for the Northwest Territory. It also set up a way for new states to be admitted to the United States. (p. 255)

northwest passage waterway through or around North America. (p. 78)

nullification idea of declaring a federal law illegal. (p. 413)

Nullification Crisis tense situation created by South Carolina when it declared the tariffs of 1828 and 1832 illegal. (p. 414)

nullify cancel, such as a law. (p. 328)

O

Olive Branch Petition letter sent to King George III by the Continental Congress asking him to repeal the Intolerable Acts. (p. 221)

override overrule. Congress can override a President's veto if two thirds of both houses vote to do so. (pp. 264, 289)

P

Panic of 1837 economic crisis in which hundreds of banks failed. (p. 418)

Patriot colonist who supported the American Revolution. (p. 227)

patroon rich landowner in the Dutch colonies. (p. 130)

peninsular person sent from Spain to rule the Spanish colonies. (p. 97)

pet bank state bank used by President Jackson and Roger Taney for government money. (p. 412)

pictograph picture that represents an object. (p. 49)

plain broad area of fairly level land. (p. 16)

plantation large estate farmed by many workers. (p. 98)

plateau large raised area of flat or gently rolling land. (p. 16)

Plessy v. *Ferguson* (1896) ruling by the Supreme Court that segregation was legal as long as facilities for blacks and whites were equal. (p. 589)

poll tax fee paid by a voter in order to vote. (p. 589)

popular sovereignty practice of allowing each territory to decide for itself whether or not to allow slavery. (p. 517)

potlatch ceremonial dinner among some Native Americans of the Northwest Coast. (p. 40)

preamble opening statement. (p. 281)

precedent act or decision that sets an example for others to follow. (p. 294)

presidio fort that housed soldiers in the Spanish colonies. (p. 96)

Proclamation of 1763 British law that forbade colonists to settle west of a line along the Appalachian Mountains. (p. 199)

profiteer person who takes advantage of an emergency to make money. (p. 558)

proprietary colony English colony in which the king gave land to one or more proprietors in exchange for a yearly payment. (p. 132)

protective tariff tax placed on goods from another country to protect home industry. (p. 383)

public school school supported by taxes. (p. 167)

pueblo adobe dwelling of the Anasazis; Spanish word for village or town. (pp. 38, 96)

Puritans group of English Protestants who settled in Massachusetts. (p. 124)

Q

Quakers Protestant reformers who settled in Pennsylvania. (p. 133)

Quartering Act (1765) law that required English colonists to pay for the housing of British soldiers. (p. 204)

GLOSSARY

R

racism belief that one race is superior to another. (p. 162)

Radical Reconstruction period after the Civil War when Republicans controlled Congress and passed strict laws affecting the South. (p. 580)

Radical Republicans group of Republicans in Congress who wanted to protect the rights of freedmen in the South and keep rich southern planters out of power. (p. 577)

ratify approve. (pp. 240, 286)

recall special election that allows voters to remove an elected official from office. (p. 615)

Reconstruction period after the Civil War when the South was rebuilt; also, the federal program to rebuild it. (p. 572)

referendum process by which people can vote directly on a bill. (p. 615)

Renaissance period from 1350 to 1600 in which Europeans made great advances. (p. 62)

rendezvous Meeting where Mountain Men traded furs for supplies. (p. 430)

repeal cancel. (p. 201)

representative government system of government in which voters elect representatives to make laws for them. (pp. 113, 286)

republic nation in which voters choose representatives to govern them. (p. 261)

royal colony colony directly under the control of a king or queen. (p. 114)

S

sachem tribal chief of the Iroquois. (p. 46)

saga Viking story of brave deeds. (p. 59)

scalawag white southerner who supported Radical Republicans. (p. 582)

secede withdraw. (p. 414)

Second Great Awakening religious movement that swept the nation in the early 1800s. (p. 485)

sectionalism strong sense of loyalty to a state or section instead of to the whole country. (p. 517)

sedition stirring up rebellion. (p. 328)

Sedition Act (1798) law that allowed citizens to be fined or jailed for criticizing public officials. (p. 328)

segregation separation of people of different races. (p. 589)

Seminole War (1835–1842) conflict between the Seminole Indians and the United States. (p. 416)

Seneca Falls Convention meeting at which leaders of the women's rights movement voted on a plan for achieving equality. (p. 492)

separation of powers system in which each branch of government has its own powers. (p. 262)

serf peasant who was bound to the land where he or she was born. (p. 60)

sharecropper farmer who works land owned by another and gives the landowner part of the harvest. (p. 586)

Shays' Rebellion (1786) revolt of Massachusetts farmers. (p. 255)

skilled worker person with a trade, such as a carpenter, a printer, or a shoemaker. (p. 464)

slave code series of laws that controlled behavior of slaves and denied them basic rights. (p. 162)

Sons of Liberty group of colonial men who joined together to protest the Stamp Act and protect colonial liberties. (p. 203)

speculator person who invests in a risky venture in hopes of making a large profit. (p. 312)

spinning jenny machine that let a person spin several threads at once. (p. 366)

spoils system practice of giving government jobs to loyal supporters. (p. 409)

Stamp Act (1765) law passed by Parliament that taxed legal documents, newspapers, almanacs, playing cards, and dice. (p. 200)

standard time zone one of the 24 time divisions of the world as measured from the Prime Meridian. (p. 14)

standing committee permanent committee in the House of Representatives or the Senate. (p. 295)

states' rights idea that individual states had the right to limit the power of the federal government. (p. 413)

stocks wooden frames with holes for the arms and legs. Used to punish people found guilty of crimes during the colonial period. (p. 156)

strait narrow passage of water. (p. 72)

strike refusal by union workers to do their jobs. (p. 466)

subsistence farmer person who grows only enough food for his or her own needs. (p. 152)

suffrage right to vote. (p. 406)

Sugar Act (1764) law passed by Parliament that taxed molasses. (p. 200)

surplus amount more than needed. (p. 152)

T

tariff tax on goods brought into a country. (p. 314)

Tariff of Abominations name given by southerners to the Tariff of 1828. (p. 413)

GLOSSARY

GLOSSARY

tax-in-kind tax paid with goods rather than money. (p. 558)

Tea Act (1773) British law that let the British East India Company sell tea directly to colonists. (p. 207)

Tejano Mexican who lives in Texas. (p. 435)

telegraph machine that sends electrical signals along a wire. Invented in 1837. (p. 458)

temperance movement campaign against the sale or drinking of alcohol. (p. 497)

tenant farmer person who works land owned by another. Tenant pays rent to the landowner. (p. 157)

Ten Percent Plan Lincoln's plan for Reconstruction. (p. 572)

Thanksgiving day set aside by the Pilgrims to give thanks to God for a good harvest. (p. 117)

Thirteenth Amendment constitutional amendment that banned slavery in the United States. (p. 576)

Three-Fifths Compromise agreement of delegates to the Constitutional Convention that three fifths of the slaves in any state be counted in that state's population. (p. 259)

tipi cone-shaped tent made of buffalo hides. (p. 43)

toleration willingness to let others have their own beliefs. (p. 127)

totem pole wooden post with animals or other figures carved in it. (p. 40)

Townshend Acts (1767) British laws that taxed goods such as paper, silk, and tea. (p. 202)

trade union association of workers formed to win better wages and working conditions. (p. 466)

Trail of Tears forced march of the Cherokees to lands west of the Mississippi. (p. 415)

traitor person who betrays his or her country. (p. 225)

travois sled used by Plains people to haul gear. (p. 43)

Treaty of Ghent (1814) treaty that ended the War of 1812. (p. 359)

Treaty of Greenville (1795) treaty between the United States and 12 Indian nations of the Northwest Territory. (p. 319)

Treaty of Paris (1763) treaty that ended the French and Indian War. (p. 197)

Treaty of Paris (1783) treaty that ended the American Revolution. (p. 240)

triangular trade series of colonial trade routes. (p. 174)

tributary stream or smaller river that flows into a bigger river. (p. 23)

turnpike road built by a private company. Charged tolls to those using it. (p. 375)

tyranny cruel and unjust government. (p. 286)

U

Uncle Tom's Cabin novel written by Harriet Beecher Stowe to show the evils of slavery. (p. 522)

unconstitutional not permitted by the constitution of a nation. (p. 290)

underground railroad secret network of people who helped runaway slaves to reach freedom in the North or Canada. (p. 488)

unskilled worker person who does a job that requires little special training. (p. 466)

V

veto reject. (pp. 264, 289)

viceroy official who rules an area in the name of a king or queen. (p. 96)

vigilante self-appointed law enforcer who deals out punishment without holding a trial. (p. 450)

Vikings seagoing people from Scandinavia. (p. 58)

Virginia Company joint stock company that received a charter from King James I to start a colony. (p. 111)

Virginia Plan plan of government presented by Edmund Randolph and James Madison to the Constitutional Convention. (p. 258)

W

War Hawks members of Congress who wanted war with Britain in 1812. (p. 350)

weather condition of the air at any given time and place. (p. 24)

Whig member of a political party formed by supporters of John Quincy Adams. First called National Republicans. (p. 406)

Whiskey Rebellion (1794) revolt of farmers to protest the tax on whiskey. (p. 315)

wickiup brush hut in which peoples of the Intermountain region lived. (p. 40)

Wilmot Proviso (1846) law proposed by David Wilmot to outlaw slavery in any land won from Mexico. (p. 516)

writ of assistance legal document that let a British customs officer inspect a ship's cargo without giving any reason for the search. (p. 202)

X

XYZ Affair (1797) incident in which French agents asked American ambassadors in Paris for a bribe. (p. 326)

THE DECLARATION OF ♦ INDEPENDENCE ♦

On June 7, 1776, the Continental Congress considered a resolution that "these United Colonies are, and of right ought to be, free and independent States." Congress then appointed a committee to write a declaration of independence. The committee members were John Adams, Benjamin Franklin, Robert Livingston, Roger Sherman, and Thomas Jefferson.

Jefferson actually wrote the Declaration, but he got advice from the others. On July 2, Congress discussed the Declaration and made some changes. On July 4, 1776, it adopted the Declaration of Independence in its final form.

The Declaration is printed in black. The headings have been added to show the parts of the Declaration. They are not part of the original text. Annotations, or explanations, are on the tan side of the page. Page numbers in the annotations show where a subject is discussed in the text. Hard words are defined in the annotations.

When in the course of human events it becomes necessary for one people to dissolve the political bands which have connected them with another and to assume, among the powers of the earth, the separate and equal station to which the laws of nature and of nature's God entitle them, a decent respect to the opinions of mankind requires that they should declare the causes which impel them to the separation.

dissolve: break **powers of the earth:** other nations **station:** place **impel:** force

The colonists feel that they must explain to the world the reasons why they are breaking away from England.

The Purpose of Government Is to Protect Basic Rights

We hold these truths to be self-evident, that all men are created equal; that they are endowed by their Creator with certain unalienable rights; that among these are life, liberty, and the pursuit of happiness. That, to secure these rights, governments are instituted among men, deriving their just powers from the consent of the governed; that, whenever any form of government becomes destructive of these ends, it is the right of the people to alter or to abolish it, and to institute a new government, laying its foundation on such principles, and organizing its powers in such form, as to them shall seem most likely to effect their safety and happiness. Prudence, indeed, will dictate that governments long established should not be changed for light and transient causes; and, accordingly, all experience hath shown that mankind are more disposed to suffer, while evils are sufferable, than to right themselves by abolishing the forms to which they are accustomed. But when a long train of abuses and usurpations, pursuing invariably the same object, evinces a design to reduce them under absolute despotism, it is their right, it is their duty, to throw off such government and to provide new guards for their future security. Such has been the patient sufferance of these colonies, and such is now the necessity which constrains

endowed: given **unalienable rights:** so basic that they cannot be taken away **secure:** protect **instituted:** set up **deriving:** getting **alter:** change **effect:** bring about

People set up governments to protect their basic rights. Governments get their power from the consent of the governed. If a government takes away the basic rights of the people, the people have the right to change the government.

prudence: wisdom **transient:** temporary, passing **disposed:** likely **usurpations:** taking and using powers that do not belong to a person **invariably:** always **evinces a design to reduce them under absolute despotism:** makes a clear plan to put them under complete and unjust control **sufferance:** endurance **constrains:** forces **absolute tyranny:** harsh and unjust government **candid:** honest

People do not change governments for slight reason. But they are forced to do so when a government becomes tyrannical. King George III has a long record of abusing his power.

them to alter their former systems of government. The history of the present King of Great Britain is a history of repeated injuries and usurpations, all having, in direct object, the establishment of an absolute tyranny over these States. To prove this, let facts be submitted to a candid world:

Wrongs Done by the King

He has refused his assent to laws the most wholesome and necessary for the public good.

He has forbidden his governors to pass laws of immediate and pressing importance, unless suspended in their operation till his assent should be obtained; and, when so suspended, he has utterly neglected to attend to them.

He has refused to pass other laws for the accommodation of the large districts of people, unless those people would relinquish the right of representation in the legislature: a right inestimable to them and formidable to tyrants only.

He has called together legislative bodies at places unusual, uncomfortable, and distant from the depository of their public records, for the sole purpose of fatiguing them into compliance with his measures.

He has dissolved representative houses, repeatedly for opposing, with manly firmness, his invasions on the rights of the people.

He has refused, for a long time after such dissolutions, to cause others to be elected: whereby the legislative powers, incapable of annihilation, have returned to the people at large for their exercise; the state remaining, in the meantime, exposed to all the danger of invasion from without and convulsions within.

He has endeavored to prevent the population of these States; for that purpose, obstructing the laws for naturalization of foreigners, refusing to pass others to encourage their migration hither, and raising the conditions of new appropriations of lands.

He has obstructed the administration of justice by refusing his assent to laws for establishing judiciary powers.

He has made judges dependent on his will alone for the tenure of their offices and the amount and payment of their salaries.

He has erected a multitude of new offices and sent hither swarms of officers to harass our people and eat out their substance.

He has kept among us, in time of peace, standing armies, without the consent of our legislatures.

He has affected to render the military independent of, and superior to, the civil power.

He has combined with others to subject us to a jurisdiction foreign to our Constitution and unacknowledged by our laws, giving his assent to their acts of pretended legislation—

For quartering large bodies of armed troops among us;

For protecting them by a mock trial from punishment for

assent: approval **relinquish:** give up
inestimable: too great a value to be measured **formidable:** causing fear

This part of the Declaration spells out three sets of wrongs that led the colonists to break with Britain.

The first set of wrongs is the king's unjust use of power. The king has refused to approve laws that are needed. He has tried to control the colonial legislatures.

depository: central storehouse
fatiguing: tiring out **compliance:** giving in **dissolved:** broken up
annihilation: total destruction
convulsions: disturbances

The king has tried to force colonial legislatures into doing his will by wearing them out. He has dissolved legislatures (such as those of New York and Massachusetts. See pages 205, 210).

endeavored: tried **obstructing:** blocking **naturalization:** process of becoming a citizen **migration:** moving **hither:** here **appropriations:** grants **obstructed the administration of justice:** prevented justice from being done **judiciary powers:** system of law courts **tenure:** term (of office) **erected:** set up **multitude:** large number **swarms:** huge crowds **harass:** cause trouble **render:** make

Among other wrongs, he has refused to let settlers move west to take up new land. He has prevented justice from being done. Also, he has sent large numbers of customs officials to cause problems for the colonists.

jurisdiction: authority **quartering:** housing **mock:** false

The king has joined with others, meaning Parliament, to make laws for the colonies. The Declaration then lists the second set of wrongs—unjust acts of Parliament.

DECLARATION OF INDEPENDENCE

any murders which they should commit on the inhabitants of these States;

For cutting off our trade with all parts of the world;

For imposing taxes on us without our consent;

For depriving us, in many cases, of the benefit of trial by jury;

For transporting us beyond seas to be tried for pretended offences;

For abolishing the free system of English laws in a neighboring province, establishing therein an arbitrary government, and enlarging its boundaries, so as to render it at once an example and fit instrument for introducing the same absolute rule into these colonies;

For taking away our charters, abolishing our most valuable laws, and altering, fundamentally, the powers of our governments;

For suspending our own legislatures and declaring themselves invested with power to legislate for us in all cases whatsoever.

He has abdicated government here by declaring us out of his protection and waging war against us.

He has plundered our seas, ravaged our coasts, burnt our towns, and destroyed the lives of our people.

He is, at this time, transporting large armies of foreign mercenaries to complete the works of death, desolation, and tyranny already begun with circumstances of cruelty and perfidy scarcely paralleled in the most barbarous ages, and totally unworthy, the head of a civilized nation.

He has constrained our fellow citizens, taken captive on the high seas, to bear arms against their country, to become the executioners of their friends and brethren, or to fall themselves by their hands.

He has excited domestic insurrections amongst us and has endeavored to bring on the inhabitants of our frontiers, the merciless Indian savages, whose known rule of warfare is an undistinguished destruction of all ages, sexes, and conditions.

In every stage of these oppressions, we have petitioned for redress in the most humble terms; our repeated petitions have been answered only by repeated injury. A prince whose character is thus marked by every act which may define a tyrant is unfit to be the ruler of a free people.

Nor have we been wanting in attention to our British brethren. We have warned them, from time to time, of attempts made by their legislature to extend an unwarrantable jurisdiction over us. We have reminded them of the circumstances of our emigration and settlement here. We have appealed to their native justice and magnanimity, and we have conjured them, by the ties of our common kindred, to disavow these usurpations, which would inevitably interrupt our connections and correspondence. They, too, have been deaf to the voice of justice and consanguinity. We must, therefore, acquiesce in the necessity which denounces our separation, and hold them, as we hold the rest of mankind, enemies in war, in peace, friends.

imposing: forcing **depriving:** taking away **transporting us beyond the seas:** sending colonists to England for trial **neighboring province:** Quebec **arbitrary government:** unjust rule **fit instrument:** suitable tool **invested with power:** having the power

During the years leading up to 1776, the colonists claimed that Parliament had no right to make laws for them because they were not represented in it. Here, the colonists object to recent laws of Parliament such as the Quartering Act (page 204) and the blockade of colonial ports (page 223) that cut off their trade. They also object to Parliament's claim that it had the right to tax them without their consent.

abdicated: given up **plundered:** robbed **ravaged:** attacked **mercenaries:** hired soldiers **desolation:** misery **perfidy:** falseness **barbarous:** uncivilized **constrained:** forced **brethren:** brothers **domestic insurrections:** internal revolts

Here, the Declaration lists the third set of wrongs—warlike acts of the king. Instead of listening to the colonists, the king has made war on them. He has hired soldiers to fight in America (page 223).

oppressions: harsh rule **petitioned:** asked **redress:** relief **unwarrantable jurisdiction over:** unfair authority **magnanimity:** generosity **conjured:** called upon **common kindred:** relatives **disavow:** turn away from **consanguinity:** blood relationships, kinship **acquiese:** agree **denounces:** speaks out against

During this time, colonists have repeatedly asked for relief. But their requests have brought only more suffering. They have appealed to the British people but received no help. So they are forced to separate.

DECLARATION OF INDEPENDENCE

Colonies Declare Independence

As the representatives of the United States, they declare that the colonies are free and independent states.

The states need no longer be loyal to the British king. They are an independent nation that can make war and sign treaties.

Relying on Divine Providence, the signers of the Declaration promise their lives, money, and honor to fight for independence.

We, therefore, the representatives of the United States of America, in general Congress assembled, appealing to the Supreme Judge of the world for the rectitude of our intentions, do, in the name and by the authority of the good people of these colonies, solemnly publish and declare, that these united colonies are, and of right ought to be, free and independent states: that they are absolved from all allegiance to the British Crown, and that all political connection between them and the state of Great Britain is, and ought to be, totally dissolved; and that, as free and independent states, they have full power to levy war, conclude peace, contract alliances, establish commerce, and to do all other acts and things which independent states may of right do. And, for the support of this declaration, with a firm reliance on the protection of Divine Providence, we mutually pledge to each other our lives, our fortunes, and our sacred honor.

Signers of the Declaration of Independence

John Hancock, President   **Charles Thomson,** Secretary

New Hampshire
Josiah Bartlett
William Whipple
Matthew Thornton

Massachusetts
Samuel Adams
John Adams
Robert Treat Paine
Elbridge Gerry

Rhode Island
Stephen Hopkins
William Ellery

Connecticut
Roger Sherman
Samuel Huntington
William Williams
Oliver Wolcott

New York
William Floyd
Philip Livingston
Francis Lewis
Lewis Morris

New Jersey
Richard Stockton
John Witherspoon
Francis Hopkinson
John Hart
Abraham Clark

Delaware
Caesar Rodney
George Read
Thomas McKean

Pennsylvania
Robert Morris
Benjamin Rush
Benjamin Franklin
John Morton
George Clymer
James Smith
George Taylor
James Wilson
George Ross

Maryland
Samuel Chase
William Paca
Thomas Stone
Charles Carroll

Virginia
George Wythe
Richard Henry Lee
Thomas Jefferson
Benjamin Harrison
Thomas Nelson, Jr.
Francis Lightfoot Lee
Carter Braxton

North Carolina
William Hooper
Joseph Hewes
John Penn

South Carolina
Edward Rutledge
Thomas Heyward, Jr.
Thomas Lynch, Jr.
Arthur Middleton

Georgia
Button Gwinnett
Lyman Hall
George Walton

The Constitution is printed in black. The titles of articles, sections, and clauses are not part of the original document. They have been added to help you find information in the Constitution. Some words or lines are crossed out because they have been changed by amendments or no longer apply. Annotations, or explanations, are on the tan side of the page. Page numbers in the annotations show where a subject is discussed in the text. Hard words are defined in the annotations.

Preamble

We, the people of the United States, in order to form a more perfect Union, establish justice, insure domestic tranquillity, provide for the common defense, promote the general welfare, and secure the blessings of liberty to ourselves and our posterity, do ordain and establish this Constitution for the United States of America.

The Preamble describes the purpose of the government set up by the Constitution. Americans expect their government to defend justice and liberty and provide peace and safety from foreign enemies.

Article 1. The Legislative Branch

Section 1.   A Two-House Legislature

All legislative powers herein granted shall be vested in a Congress of the United States, which shall consist of a Senate and House of Representatives.

The Constitution gives Congress the power to make laws. Congress is divided into the Senate and House of Representatives.

Section 2.   House of Representatives

1. Election of Members   The House of Representatives shall be composed of members chosen every second year by the people of the several states, and the electors in each state shall have the qualifications requisite for electors of the most numerous branch of the state legislature.

Clause 1   *Electors* refers to voters. Members of the House of Representatives are elected every two years. Any citizen allowed to vote for members of the larger house of the state legislature can also vote for members of the House.

2. Qualifications   No person shall be a Representative who shall not have attained to the age of twenty-five years, and been seven years a citizen of the United States, and who shall not, when elected, be an inhabitant of that state in which he shall be chosen.

Clause 2   A member of the House of Representatives must be at least 25 years old, an American citizen for 7 years, and a resident of the state he or she represents.

3. Determining Representation   Representatives and direct taxes shall be apportioned among the several states which may be included within this Union, according to their respective numbers which shall be determined by adding to the whole number of free persons, including those bound to service for a term of years, and excluding Indians not taxed, three-fifths of all other persons. The actual enumeration shall be made within three years after the first meeting of the Congress of the United States, and within every subsequent term of ten years, in such manner as they shall by law direct. The number of Representatives shall not exceed one for every 30,000, but each state shall have at least one Representative; and until such enumeration shall be made, the state of New Hampshire shall be entitled to choose three; Massachusetts, eight; Rhode Island and Providence Plantations, one; Connecticut, five; New York, six; New Jersey, four; Pennsylvania, eight;

Clause 3   The number of representatives each state elects is based on its population. An *enumeration,* or census, must be taken every ten years to determine population. Today, the number of representatives in the House is fixed at 435.
   This is the famous Three-Fifths Compromise worked out at the Constitutional Convention (page 259). ***Persons bound to service*** meant indentured servants. ***All other persons*** meant slaves. All free people in a state were counted. However, only three fifths of the slaves were included in the population count. This three-fifths clause became meaningless when slaves were freed by the Thirteenth Amendment.

Delaware, one; Maryland, six; Virginia, ten; North Carolina, five; South Carolina, five; and Georgia, three.

Clause 4 *Executive authority* means the governor of a state. If a member of the House leaves office before his or her term ends, the governor must call a special election to fill the seat.

4. Filling Vacancies When vacancies happen in the representation from any state, the executive authority thereof shall issue writs of election to fill such vacancies.

Clause 5 The House elects a speaker. Today, the speaker is usually chosen by the party that has a majority in the House. Also, only the House has the power to *impeach,* or accuse, a federal official of wrongdoing.

5. Selection of Officers; Power of Impeachment The House of Representatives shall choose their Speaker and other officers; and shall have the sole power of impeachment.

Section 3.   The Senate

Clause 1 Each state has two senators. Senators serve for six-year terms. The Seventeenth Amendment changed the way senators were elected.

1. Selection of Members The Senate of the United States shall be composed of two Senators from each state chosen by the legislature thereof, for six years, and each Senator shall have one vote.

Clause 2 Every two years, one third of the senators run for reelection. Thus, the makeup of the Senate is never totally changed by any one election. The Seventeenth Amendment changed the way of filling *vacancies,* or empty seats. Today, the governor of a state chooses a senator to fill a vacancy that occurs between elections.

2. Alternating Terms; Filling Vacancies Immediately after they shall be assembled in consequence of the first election, they shall be divided as equally as may be into three classes. The seats of the Senators of the first class shall be vacated at the expiration of the second year, of the second class at the expiration of the fourth year, and of the third class at the expiration of the sixth year, so that one-third may be chosen every second year; and if vacancies happen by resignation, or otherwise, during the recess of the legislature of any state, the executive thereof may make temporary appointments until the next meeting of the legislature, which shall then fill such vacancies.

Clause 3 A senator must be at least 30 years old, an American citizen for 9 years, and a resident of the state he or she represents.

3. Qualifications No person shall be a Senator who shall not have attained to the age of thirty years, and been nine years a citizen of the United States, and who shall not, when elected, be an inhabitant of that state for which he shall be chosen.

Clause 4 The Vice President presides over Senate meetings, but he or she can only vote to break a tie.

4. President of the Senate The Vice-President of the United States shall be president of the Senate, but shall have no vote, unless they be equally divided.

Clause 5 *Pro tempore* means temporary. The Senate chooses one of its members to serve as president pro tempore when the Vice President is absent.

5. Election of Senate Officers The Senate shall choose their other officers, and also a president *pro tempore,* in the absence of the Vice-President, or when he shall exercise the office of the President of the United States.

Clause 6 The Senate acts as a jury if the House impeaches a federal official. The Chief Justice of the Supreme Court presides if the President is on trial. Two thirds of all senators present must vote for *conviction,* or finding the accused guilty. No President has ever been convicted. The House impeached President Andrew Johnson in 1868, but the Senate acquitted him of the charges (pages 580–581). In 1974, President Richard Nixon resigned before he could be impeached.

6. Impeachment Trials The Senate shall have the sole power to try all impeachments. When sitting for that purpose, they shall be on oath or affirmation. When the President of the United States is tried, the Chief Justice shall preside; and no person shall be convicted without the concurrence of two-thirds of the members present.

Clause 7 If an official is found guilty by the Senate, he or she can be removed from office and barred from holding federal office in the

7. Penalties Upon Conviction Judgment in cases of impeachment shall not extend further than to removal from office, and disqualification to hold and enjoy any office of honor, trust, or profit under the United States; but the party convicted shall nevertheless be liable and subject to indictment, trial, judgment, and punishment, according to law.

Section 4.   Elections and Meetings

1. Election of Congress   The times, places, and manner of holding elections for Senators and Representatives shall be prescribed in each state by the legislature thereof; but the Congress may at any time by law make or alter such regulations, except as to the places of choosing Senators.

2. Annual Sessions   The Congress shall assemble at least once in every year, and such meeting shall be on the first Monday in December, unless they shall by law appoint a different day.

Section 5.   Rules for the Conduct of Business

1. Organization   Each house shall be the judge of the elections, returns, and qualifications of its own members, and a majority of each shall constitute a quorum to do business; but a smaller number may adjourn from day to day, and may be authorized to compel the attendance of absent members, in such manner, and under such penalties, as each house may provide.

2. Procedures   Each house may determine the rules of its proceedings, punish its members for disorderly behavior, and with the concurrence of two-thirds, expel a member.

3. A Written Record   Each house shall keep a journal of its proceedings, and from time to time publish the same, excepting such parts as may in their judgment require secrecy; and the yeas and nays of the members of either house on any question shall, at the desire of one-fifth of those present, be entered on the journal.

4. Rules for Adjournment   Neither house, during the session of Congress, shall, without the consent of the other, adjourn for more than three days, nor to any other place than that in which the two houses shall be sitting.

Section 6.   Privileges and Restrictions

1. Salaries and Immunities   The Senators and Representatives shall receive a compensation for their services, to be ascertained by law and paid out of the Treasury of the United States. They shall in all cases, except treason, felony, and breach of the peace, be privileged from arrest during their attendance at the session of their respective houses, and in going to and returning from the same; and for any speech or debate in either house, they shall not be questioned in any other place.

2. Restrictions on Other Employment   No Senator or Representative shall, during the time for which he was elected, be appointed to any civil office under the authority of the United States, which shall have been created, or the emoluments whereof shall have been increased, during such time; and no person holding any office under the United States shall be a member of either house during his continuance in office.

future. These are the only punishments the Senate can impose. However, the convicted official can still be tried in criminal court.

Clause 1   Each state legislature can decide when and how congressional elections take place, but Congress can overrule these decisions. In 1842, Congress required each state to set up congressional districts with one representative elected from each district. In 1872, Congress decided that congressional elections must be held in every state on the same date in even-numbered years.

Clause 2   Congress must meet at least once a year. The Twentieth Amendment moved the opening date of Congress to January 3.

Clause 1   Each house decides if a member has the qualifications for office set by the Constitution. A *quorum* is the smallest number of members who must be present for business to be conducted. Each house can set its own rules about absent members.

Clause 2   Each house can make rules for the conduct of members. It can only expel a member by a two-thirds vote.

Clause 3   Each house keeps a record of its meetings. The *Congressional Record* is published every day with excerpts from speeches made in each house. It also records the votes of each member.

Clause 4   Neither house can **adjourn,** or stop meeting, for more than three days unless the other house approves. Both houses of Congress must meet in the same city.

Clause 1   *Compensation* means salary. Congress decides the salary for its members. While Congress is in session, a member is free from arrest in civil cases and cannot be sued for anything he or she says on the floor of Congress. This allows for freedom of debate. However, a member can be arrested for a criminal offense.

Clause 2   *Emolument* also means salary. A member of Congress cannot hold another federal office during his or her term. A former member of Congress cannot hold an office created while he or she was in Congress. An official in another branch of government cannot serve at the same time in Congress. This strengthens the separation of powers.

THE CONSTITUTION

755

Section 7. Law-Making Process

1. Tax Bills   All bills for raising revenue shall originate in the House of Representatives; but the Senate may propose or concur with amendments as on other bills.

Clause 1 *Revenue* is money raised by the government through taxes. Tax bills must be introduced in the House. The Senate, however, can make changes in tax bills. This clause protects the principle that people can be taxed only with their consent.

2. How a Bill Becomes a Law   Every bill which shall have passed the House of Representatives and the Senate shall, before it become a law, be presented to the President of the United States; if he approve, he shall sign it, but if not, he shall return it, with his objections, to that house in which it shall have originated, who shall enter the objections at large on their journal, and proceed to reconsider it. If after such reconsideration two-thirds of that house shall agree to pass the bill, it shall be sent, together with the objections, to the other house, by which it shall likewise be reconsidered, and, if approved by two-thirds of that house, it shall become a law. But in all such cases the votes of both houses shall be determined by yeas and nays, and the names of the persons voting for and against the bill shall be entered on the journal of each house respectively. If any bill shall not be returned by the President within ten days (Sundays excepted) after it shall have been presented to him, the same bill shall be a law, in like manner as if he had signed it, unless the Congress by their adjournment prevent its return, in which case it shall not be a law.

Clause 2 A *bill,* or proposed law, that is passed by a majority of the House and Senate is sent to the President. If the President signs the bill, it becomes law.

A bill can also become law without the President's signature. The President can refuse to act on a bill. If Congress is in session at the time, the bill becomes law ten days after the President receives it.

The President can *veto,* or reject, a bill by sending it back to the house where it was introduced. Or if the President refuses to act on a bill and Congress adjourns within ten days, then the bill dies. This way of killing a bill without taking action is called the *pocket veto.*

Congress can override the President's veto if each house of Congress passes the bill again by a two-thirds vote. This clause is an important part of the system of checks and balances (page 264).

3. Resolutions Passed by Congress   Every order, resolution, or vote to which the concurrence of the Senate and House of Representatives may be necessary (except on a question of adjournment) shall be presented to the President of the United States; and before the same shall take effect, shall be approved by him, or being disapproved by him, shall be repassed by two-thirds of the Senate and House of Representatives, according to the rules and limitations prescribed in the case of a bill.

Clause 3 Congress can pass resolutions or orders that have the same force as laws. Any such resolution or order must be signed by the President (except on questions of adjournment). Thus, this clause prevents Congress from bypassing the President simply by calling a bill by another name.

Section 8. Powers Delegated to Congress

The Congress shall have power

1. Taxes   To lay and collect taxes, duties, imposts, and excises, to pay the debts and provide for the common defense and general welfare of the United States; but all duties, imposts, and excises shall be uniform throughout the United States;

Clause 1 *Duties* are tariffs. *Imposts* are taxes in general. *Excises* are taxes on the production or sale of certain goods. Congress has the power to tax and spend tax money. Taxes must be the same in all parts of the country.

2. Borrowing   To borrow money on the credit of the United States;

Clause 2 Congress can borrow money for the United States. The government often borrows money by selling *bonds,* or certificates that promise to pay the holder a certain sum of money on a certain date (page 311).

3. Commerce   To regulate commerce with foreign nations, and among the several states, and with the Indian tribes;

Clause 3 Only Congress has the power to regulate foreign and *interstate trade,* or trade between states. Disagreement over interstate trade was a major problem with the Articles of Confederation (page 253).

4. Naturalization; Bankruptcy To establish a uniform rule of naturalization, and uniform laws on the subject of bankruptcies throughout the United States;

5. Coins; Weights; Measures To coin money, regulate the value thereof, and of foreign coin, and fix the standard of weights and measures;

6. Counterfeiting To provide for the punishment of counterfeiting the securities and current coin of the United States;

7. Post Offices To establish post offices and post roads;

8. Copyrights; Patents To promote the progress of science and useful arts by securing for limited times to authors and inventors the exclusive right to their respective writings and discoveries;

9. Federal Courts To constitute tribunals inferior to the Supreme Court;

10. Piracy To define and punish piracies and felonies committed on the high seas and offenses against the law of nations;

11. Declarations of War To declare war, ~~grant letters of marque and reprisal~~, and make rules concerning captures on land and water;

12. Army To raise and support armies, but no appropriation of money to that use shall be for a longer term than two years;

13. Navy To provide and maintain a navy;

14. Rules for the Military To make rules for the government and regulation of the land and naval forces;

15. Militia To provide for calling forth the militia to execute the laws of the Union, suppress insurrections, and repel invasions;

16. Rules for the Militia To provide for organizing, arming, and disciplining the militia, and for governing such part of them as may be employed in the service of the United States, reserving to the states, respectively, the appointment of the officers, and the authority of training the militia according to the discipline prescribed by Congress;

17. National Capital To exercise exclusive legislation in all cases whatsoever, over such district (not exceeding ten miles square) as may, by cession of particular states, and the acceptance of Congress, become the seat of government of the United States, and to exercise like authority over all places purchased by the

Clause 4 *Naturalization* is the process whereby a foreigner becomes a citizen. *Bankruptcy* is the condition in which a person or business cannot pay its debts. Congress has the power to pass laws on these two issues. The laws must be the same in all parts of the country.

Clause 5 Congress has the power to coin money and set its value. Congress has set up the National Bureau of Standards to regulate weights and measures.

Clause 6 *Counterfeiting* is the making of imitation money. *Securities* are bonds. Congress can make laws to punish counterfeiters.

Clause 7 Congress has the power to set up and control the delivery of mail.

Clause 8 Congress may pass copyright and patent laws. A *copyright* protects an author. A *patent* makes an inventor the sole owner of his or her work for a limited time.

Clause 9 Congress has the power to set up *inferior,* or lower, federal courts under the Supreme Court.

Clause 10 Congress can punish *piracy,* or the robbing of ships at sea.

Clause 11 Only Congress can declare war. Declarations of war are granted at the request of the President. *Letters of marque and reprisal* were documents issued by a government allowing merchant ships to arm themselves and attack ships of an enemy nation. They are no longer issued.

Clauses 12, 13, 14 These clauses place the army and navy under the control of Congress. Congress decides on the size of the armed forces and the amount of money to spend on the army and navy. It also has the power to write rules governing the armed forces.

Clauses 15, 16 The *militia* is a body of citizen soldiers. Congress can call up the militia to put down rebellions or fight foreign invaders. Each state has its own militia, today called the National Guard. Normally, the militia is under the command of a state's governor. However, it can be placed under the command of the President.

Clause 17 Congress controls the district around the national capital. In 1790, Congress made Washington, D.C., the nation's capital (page 313). In 1973, it gave residents of the district the right to elect local officials.

Clause 18 Clauses 1–17 list the powers delegated to Congress. The writers of the Constitution added Clause 18 so that Congress could deal with the changing needs of the nation. It gives Congress the power to make laws as needed to carry out the first 17 clauses. Clause 18 is sometimes called the elastic clause because it lets Congress stretch the meaning of its power.

Clause 1 *Such persons* means slaves. This clause resulted from a compromise between the supporters and the opponents of the slave trade (page 259). In 1808, as soon as Congress was permitted to abolish the slave trade, it did so. The $10 import tax was never imposed.

Clause 2 A *writ of habeas corpus* is a court order requiring government officials to bring a prisoner to court and explain why he or she is being held. A writ of habeas corpus protects people from unlawful imprisonment. The government cannot suspend this right except in times of rebellion or invasion.

Clause 3 A *bill of attainder* is a law declaring that a person is guilty of a particular crime. An *ex post facto law* punishes an act which was not illegal when it was committed. Congress cannot pass a bill of attainder and ex post facto laws.

Clause 4 A *capitation tax* is a tax placed directly on each person. *Direct taxes* are taxes on people or on land. They can only be passed if they are divided among the states according to population. The Sixteenth Amendment allowed Congress to tax income without regard to the population of the states.

Clause 5 This clause forbids Congress to tax exports. In 1787, Southerners insisted on this clause because their economy depended on exports.

Clause 6 Congress cannot make laws that favor one state over another in trade and commerce. Also, states cannot place tariffs on interstate trade.

Clause 7 The federal government cannot spend money unless Congress *appropriates* it, or passes a law allowing it. This clause gives Congress an important check on the President by controlling the money he or she can spend. The government must publish a statement showing how it spends public funds.

---

consent of the legislature of the state in which the same shall be, for the erection of forts, magazines, arsenals, dock-yards, and other needful buildings;—and

18. Necessary Laws To make all laws which shall be necessary and proper for carrying into execution the foregoing powers, and all other powers vested by this Constitution in the government of the United States, or in any department or officer thereof.

Section 9. Powers Denied to the Federal Government

1. The Slave Trade ~~The migration or importation of such persons as any of the states now existing shall think proper to admit shall not be prohibited by the Congress prior to the year 1808; but a tax or duty may be imposed on such importation, not exceeding $10 for each person.~~

2. Writ of Habeas Corpus The privilege of the writ of *habeas corpus* shall not be suspended, unless when in cases of rebellion or invasion the public safety may require it.

3. Bills of Attainder and Ex Post Facto Laws No bill of attainder or *ex post facto* law shall be passed.

4. Apportionment of Direct Taxes ~~No capitation or other direct tax shall be laid, unless in proportion to the census or enumeration herein before directed to be taken.~~

5. Taxes on Exports No tax or duty shall be laid on articles exported from any state.

6. Special Preference for Trade No preference shall be given any regulation of commerce or revenue to the ports of one state over those of another; nor shall vessels bound to, or from, one state, be obliged to enter, clear, or pay duties in another.

7. Spending No money shall be drawn from the Treasury, but in consequence of appropriations made by law; and a regular statement and account of the receipts and expenditures of all public money shall be published from time to time.

8. Creation of Titles of Nobility   No title of nobility shall be granted by the United States; and no person holding any office of profit or trust under them, shall, without the consent of the Congress, accept of any present, emolument, office, or title, of any kind whatever, from any king, prince, or foreign state.

Section 10.   Powers Denied to the States

1. Unconditional Prohibitions   No state shall enter into any treaty, alliance, or confederation; grant letters of marque and reprisals; coin money; emit bills of credit; make anything but gold and silver coin a tender in payment of debts; pass any bill of attainder, *ex post facto* law, or law impairing the obligation of contracts, or grant any title of nobility.

2. Powers Conditionally Denied   No state shall, without the consent of the Congress, lay any imposts or duties on imports or exports, except what may be absolutely necessary for executing its inspection laws; and the net produce of all duties and imposts, laid by any state on imports or exports, shall be for the use of the Treasury of the United States; and all such laws shall be subject to the revision and control of the Congress.

3. Other Denied Powers   No state shall, without the consent of Congress, lay any duty of tonnage, keep troops, or ships of war in time of peace, enter into any agreement or compact with another state, or with a foreign power, or engage in war, unless actually invaded, or in such imminent danger as will not admit of delay.

Article 2. The Executive Branch

Section 1.   President and Vice-President

1. Chief Executive   The executive power shall be vested in a President of the United States of America. He shall hold his office during the term of four years, and together with the Vice-President, chosen for the same term, be elected as follows:

2. Selection of Electors   Each state shall appoint, in such manner as the legislature thereof may direct, a number of electors, equal to the whole number of Senators and Representatives to which the state may be entitled in the Congress; but no Senator or Representative, or person holding an office or trust or profit under the United States, shall be appointed an elector.

3. Electoral College Procedures   The electors shall meet in their respective states, and vote by ballot for two persons, of whom one at least shall not be an inhabitant of the same state with themselves. And they shall make a list of all the persons voted for, and of the number of votes for each; which list they shall sign and certify, and transmit sealed to the seat of the government of the United States, directed to the president of the Senate. The president of the Senate shall, in the presence of the Senate and House of Representatives, open all the certificates, and the votes shall then be counted. The person having the greatest number of votes shall be the President, if such number be a majority of the whole number of electors appointed; and if there be more than one who have such majority, and have an equal

Clause 8   The government cannot award titles of nobility such as Duke or Duchess. American citizens cannot accept titles of nobility from foreign governments without the consent of Congress.

Clause 1   The writers of the Constitution did not want the states to act like separate nations, so they prohibited states from making treaties or coining money. Some powers denied to the federal government are also denied to the states. For example, states cannot pass ex post facto laws.

Clauses 2, 3   Powers listed here are forbidden to the states, but Congress can lift these prohibitions by passing laws that give these powers to the states.
  Clause 2 forbids states from taxing imports and exports without the consent of Congress. States may charge inspection fees on goods entering the states. Any profit from these fees must be turned over to the United States Treasury.
  Clause 3 forbids states from keeping an army or navy without the consent of Congress. States cannot make treaties or make war unless an enemy invades or is about to invade.

Clause 1   The President is responsible for *executing,* or carrying out, laws passed by Congress.

Clauses 2, 3   Some of the writers of the Constitution feared allowing the people to elect the President directly (page 264). Therefore, the Constitutional Convention set up the electoral college. Clause 2 directs each state to choose electors, or delegates to the electoral college, to vote for President. A state's electoral vote is equal to the combined number of senators and representatives. Each state may decide how to choose its electors. Members of Congress and federal officeholders may not serve as electors. This much of the original electoral college system is still in effect.
  Clause 3 called upon each elector to vote for two candidates. The candidate who received a majority of the electoral votes would become President. The runner-up would become Vice President. If no candidate won a majority, the House would choose the President. The Senate would choose the Vice President.
  The election of 1800 showed a problem with the original electoral college system (pages

328–329). Thomas Jefferson was the Republican candidate for President, and Aaron Burr was the Republican candidate for Vice President. In the electoral college, the vote ended in a tie. The election was finally decided in the House, where Jefferson was chosen President. The Twelfth Amendment changed the electoral college system so that this could not happen again.

number of votes, then the House of Representatives shall immediately choose by ballot one of them for President; and if no person have a majority, then from the five highest on the list the said House shall in like manner choose the President. But in choosing the President the votes shall be taken by states, the representation from each state having one vote. A quorum for this purpose shall consist of a member or members from two-thirds of the states, and a majority of all the states shall be necessary to a choice. In every case, after the choice of the President, the person having the greatest number of votes of the electors shall be the Vice-President. But if there should remain two or more who have equal votes, the Senate shall choose from them by ballot the Vice-President.

Clause 4 Under a law passed in 1792, electors are chosen on the Tuesday following the first Monday of November every four years. Electors from each state meet to vote in December.

Today, voters in each state choose **slates,** or groups, of electors who are pledged to a candidate for President. The candidate for President who wins the popular vote in each state wins that state's electoral vote.

4. Time of Elections The Congress may determine the time of choosing the electors, and the day on which they shall give their votes; which day shall be the same throughout the United States.

Clause 5 The President must be a citizen of the United States from birth, at least 35 years old, and a resident of the country for 14 years. The first seven Presidents of the United States were born under British rule, but they were allowed to hold office because they were citizens at the time the Constitution was adopted.

5. Qualifications for President No person except a natural-born citizen or a citizen of the United States, at the time of the adoption of this Constitution, shall be eligible to the office of the President; neither shall any person be eligible to that office who shall not have attained to the age of thirty-five years, and been fourteen years a resident within the United States.

Clause 6 The powers of the President pass to the Vice President if the President leaves office or cannot discharge his or her duties. The wording of this clause caused confusion the first time a President died in office. When President William Henry Harrison died, it was uncertain whether Vice President John Tyler should remain Vice President and act as President. Or should he be sworn in as President? Tyler persuaded a federal judge to swear him in. So he set the precedent that the Vice President assumes the office of President when it becomes vacant. The Twenty-fifth Amendment replaced this clause.

6. Presidential Succession In case of the removal of the President from office, or of his death, resignation, or inability to discharge the powers and duties of the said office, the same shall devolve on the Vice-President, and the Congress may by law provide for the case of removal, death, resignation, or inability, both of the President and Vice-President, declaring what officer shall then act as President, and such officer shall act accordingly, until the disability be removed, or a President shall be elected.

Clause 7 The President is paid a salary. It cannot be raised or lowered during his or her term of office. The President is not allowed to hold any other federal or state position while in office. Today, the President's salary is $200,000 a year.

7. Salary The President shall, at stated times, receive for his services, a compensation, which shall neither be increased nor diminished during the period for which he shall have been elected, and he shall not receive within that period any other emolument from the United States, or any of them.

Clause 8 Before taking office, the President must promise to protect and defend the Constitution. Usually, the Chief Justice of the Supreme Court administers the oath of office to the President.

8. Oath of Office Before he enter on the execution of his office, he shall take the following oath or affirmation:—"I do solemnly swear (or affirm) that I will faithfully execute the office of President of the United States, and will to the best of my ability, preserve, protect, and defend the Constitution of the United States."

THE CONSTITUTION

Section 2. Powers of the President

1. Commander in Chief of the Armed Forces   The President shall be Commander in Chief of the Army and Navy of the United States, and of the militia of the several states, when called into the actual service of the United States; he may require the option, in writing, of the principal officer in each of the executive departments, upon any subject relating to the duties of their respective offices, and he shall have power to grant reprieves and pardons for offenses against the United States, except in cases of impeachment.

Clause 1   The President is head of the armed forces and the state militias when they are called into national service. So the military is under **civilian,** or nonmilitary, control.

The President can get advice from the heads of executive departments. In most cases, the President has the power to grant a reprieve or pardon. A **reprieve** suspends punishment ordered by law. A **pardon** prevents prosecution for a crime or overrides the judgment of the court.

2. Making Treaties and Nominations   He shall have power, by and with the advice and consent of the Senate, to make treaties, provided two-thirds of the Senators present concur; and he shall nominate, and by and with the advice and consent of the Senate, shall appoint ambassadors, other public ministers and consuls, judges of the Supreme Court, and all other officers of the United States, whose appointments are not herein otherwise provided for, and which shall be established by law; but the Congress may by law vest the appointment of such inferior officers, as they think proper, in the President alone, in the courts of law, or in the heads of departments.

Clause 2   The President has the power to make treaties with other nations. Under the system of checks and balances, all treaties must be approved by two thirds of the Senate. Today, the President also makes agreements with foreign governments. These executive agreements do not need Senate approval.

The President has the power to appoint ambassadors to foreign countries and other high officials. The Senate must **confirm**, or approve, these appointments.

3. Temporary Appointments   The President shall have power to fill up all vacancies that may happen during the recess of the Senate, by granting commissions which shall expire at the end of their next session.

Clause 3   If the Senate is in **recess,** or not meeting, the President may fill vacant government posts by making temporary appointments.

Section 3. Duties

He shall from time to time give to the Congress information of the state of the Union, and recommend to their consideration such measures as he shall judge necessary and expedient; he may, on extraordinary occasions, convene both houses, or either of them, and in case of disagreement between them, with respect to the time of adjournment, he may adjourn them to such time as he shall think proper; he shall receive ambassadors and other public ministers; he shall take care that the laws be faithfully executed, and shall commission all the officers of the United States.

The President must give Congress a report on the condition of the nation every year. This report is now called the State of the Union Address. Since 1913, the President has given this speech in person each January.

The President can call a special session of Congress and can adjourn Congress if necessary. The President has the power to receive, or recognize, foreign ambassadors.

The President must carry out the laws. Today, many government agencies oversee the execution of laws.

Section 4. Impeachment and Removal From Office

The President, Vice-President, and all civil officers of the United States, shall be removed from office on impeachment for, and conviction of, treason, bribery, or other high crimes and misdemeanors.

Civil officers include federal judges and members of the cabinet. **High crimes** are major crimes. **Misdemeanors** are lesser crimes. The President, Vice President, and others can be forced out of office if impeached and found guilty of certain crimes. Andrew Johnson is the only President to have been impeached.

Article 3. The Judicial Branch

Section 1. Federal Courts

The judicial power of the United States shall be vested in one Supreme Court, and in such inferior courts as the Congress may from time to time ordain and establish. The judges, both of the Supreme and inferior courts, shall hold their offices during good

Judicial power means the right of the courts to decide legal cases. The Constitution creates the Supreme Court but lets Congress decide on the size of the Supreme Court. Congress has the power to set up inferior, or lower, courts. The Judiciary Act of 1789 (page 311) set up a system of district and circuit courts, or courts of appeals. Today, there are 95 district courts and 11 courts of appeals. All federal judges serve for life.

Clause 1 *Jurisdiction* refers to the right of a court to hear a case. Federal courts have jurisdiction over cases that involve the Constitution, federal laws, treaties, foreign ambassadors and diplomats, naval and maritime laws, disagreements between states or between citizens from different states, and disputes between a state or citizen and a foreign state or citizen.

In *Marbury v. Madison* (pages 338–339), the Supreme Court established its right to judge whether a law is constitutional.

Clause 2 *Original jurisdiction* means the power of a court to hear a case where it first arises. The Supreme Court has original jurisdiction over only a few cases, such as those involving foreign diplomats. More often, the Supreme Court acts as an appellate court. An **appellate court** does not decide guilt. It decides whether the lower court trial was properly conducted and reviews the lower court's decision.

Clause 3 This clause guarantees the right to a jury trial for anyone accused of a federal crime. The only exceptions are impeachment cases. The trial must be held in the state where the crime was committed.

Clause 1 Treason is clearly defined. An **overt act** is an actual action. A person cannot be convicted of treason for what he or she thinks. A person can only be convicted of treason if he or she confesses or two witnesses testify to it.

Clause 2 Congress has the power to set the punishment for traitors. Congress may not punish the children of convicted traitors by taking away their civil rights or property.

Each state must recognize the official acts and records of any other state. For example, each state must recognize marriage certificates issued by another state. Congress can pass laws to ensure this.

behavior, and shall, at stated times, receive for their services a compensation, which shall not be diminished during their continuance in office.

Section 2. Jurisdiction of Federal Courts

1. Scope of Judicial Power   The judicial power shall extend to all cases, in law and equity, arising under this Constitution, the laws of the United States, and treaties made or which shall be made, under their authority; to all cases affecting ambassadors, other public ministers and consuls; to all cases of admiralty and maritime jurisdiction; to controversies to which the United States shall be a party; to controversies between two or more states; between a state and citizens of another state; between citizens of the same state claiming lands under grants of different states, and between a state or the citizens thereof, and foreign states, citizens, or subjects.

2. The Supreme Court   In all cases affecting ambassadors, other public ministers and consuls, and those in which a state shall be a party, the Supreme Court shall have original jurisdiction. In all the other cases before mentioned, the Supreme Court shall have appellate jurisdiction, both as to law and fact, with such exceptions, and under such regulations as the Congress shall make.

3. Trial by Jury   The trial of all crimes, except in cases of impeachment, shall be by jury; and such trial shall be held in the state where the said crimes shall have been committed; but when not committed within any state, the trial shall be at such place or places as the Congress may by law have directed.

Section 3.   Treason

1. Definition   Treason against the United States shall consist only in levying war against them, or in adhering to their enemies, giving them aid and comfort. No person shall be convicted of treason unless on the testimony of two witnesses to the same overt act, or on confession in open court.

2. Punishment   The Congress shall have power to declare the punishment of treason, but no attainder of treason shall work corruption of blood or forfeiture except during the life of the person attainted.

Article 4. Relations Among the States

Section 1.   Official Records and Acts

Full faith and credit shall be given in each state to the public acts, records, and judicial proceedings of every other state. And the Congress may by general laws prescribe the manner in which such acts, records, and proceedings shall be proved, and the effect thereof.

Section 2. Privileges of Citizens

1. Privileges The citizens of each state shall be entitled to all privileges and immunities of citizens in the several states.

Clause 1 All states must treat citizens of another state in the same way it treats its own citizens. However, the courts have allowed states to give residents certain privileges, such as lower tuition rates.

2. Extradition A person charged in any state with treason, felony, or other crime, who shall flee from justice, and be found in another state, shall on demand of the executive authority of the state from which he fled, be delivered up, to be removed to the state having jurisdiction of the crime.

Clause 2 *Extradition* means the act of returning a suspected criminal or escaped prisoner to a state where he or she is wanted. State governors must return a suspect to another state. However, the Supreme Court has ruled that a governor cannot be forced to do so if he or she feels that justice will not be done.

3. Return of Fugitive Slaves ~~No person held to service or labor in one state, under the laws thereof, escaping into another, shall in consequence of any law or regulation therein, be discharged from such service or labor, but shall be delivered up on claim of the party to whom such service or labor may be due.~~

Clause 3 *Persons held to service or labor* refers to slaves or indentured servants. This clause required states to return runaway slaves to their owners. The Thirteenth Amendment replaces this clause.

Section 3. New States and Territories

1. New States New states may be admitted by the Congress into this Union; but no new state shall be formed or erected within the jurisdiction of any other state; nor any state be formed by the junction of two or more states, or parts of states, without the consent of the legislatures of the states concerned as well as of the Congress.

Clause 1 Congress has the power to admit new states to the Union. Existing states cannot be split up or joined together to form new states unless both Congress and the state legislatures approve. New states are equal to all other states.

2. Federal Lands The Congress shall have power to dispose of and make all needful rules and regulations respecting the territory or other property belonging to the United States; and nothing in this Constitution shall be so construed as to prejudice any claims of the United States, or of any particular state.

Clause 2 Congress can make rules for managing and governing land owned by the United States. This includes territories not organized into states, such as Puerto Rico and Guam, and federal lands within a state.

Section 4. Guarantees to the States

The United States shall guarantee to every state in this Union a republican form of government, and shall protect each of them against invasion; and on application of the legislature, or of the executive (when the legislature cannot be convened) against domestic violence.

In a *republic,* voters choose representatives to govern them. The federal government must protect the states from foreign invasion and from *domestic,* or internal, disorder, if asked to do so by a state.

Article 5. Amending the Constitution

The Congress, whenever two-thirds of both houses shall deem it necessary, shall propose amendments to this Constitution, or, on the application of the legislatures of two-thirds of the several states, shall call a convention for proposing amendments, which, in either case, shall be valid to all intents and purposes, as part of this Constitution, when ratified by the legislatures of three-fourths of the several states, or by conventions in three-fourths thereof, as the one or the other mode of ratification may be proposed by the Congress; provided that ~~no amendments which may be made prior to the year 1808 shall in any manner affect the first and fourth clauses in the Ninth Section of the First Article;~~ and that no state, without its consent, shall be deprived of its equal suffrage in the Senate.

The Constitution can be *amended,* or changed, if necessary. An amendment can be proposed by (1) a two-thirds vote of both houses of Congress or (2) a national convention called by Congress at the request of two thirds of the state legislatures. (This second method has never been used.) An amendment must be *ratified,* or approved, by (1) three fourths of the state legislatures or (2) special conventions in three fourths of the states. Congress decides which method will be used.

Article 6. National Supremacy

Section 1. Prior Public Debts

The United States government promised to pay all debts and honor all agreements made under the Articles of Confederation.

All debts contracted and engagements entered into, before the adoption of this Constitution, shall be as valid against the United States under this Constitution, as under the Confederation.

Section 2. Supreme Law of the Land

The Constitution, federal laws, and treaties that the Senate has ratified are the supreme, or highest, law of the land. Thus, they outweigh state laws. A state judge must overturn a state law that conflicts with the Constitution or with a federal law.

This Constitution, and the laws of the United States which shall be made in pursuance thereof, and all treaties made, or which shall be made, under the authority of the United States, shall be the supreme law of the land; and the judges in every state shall be bound thereby, anything in the constitution or laws of any state to the contrary notwithstanding.

Section 3. Oaths of Office

State and federal officeholders take an oath, or solemn promise, to support the Constitution. However, this clause forbids the use of religious tests for officeholders. During the colonial period, every colony except Rhode Island required a religious test for officeholders.

The Senators and Representatives before mentioned, and the members of the several state legislatures, and all executive and judicial officers, both of the United States and of the several states, shall be bound by oath or affirmation, to support this Constitution; but no religious test shall ever be required as a qualification to any office or public trust under the United States.

Article 7. Ratification

During 1787 and 1788, states held special conventions. By October 1788, the required nine states had ratified the Constitution.

The ratification of the convention of nine states shall be sufficient for the establishment of the Constitution between the states so ratifying the same.

Done in Convention, by the unanimous consent of the states present, the seventeenth day of September, in the year of our Lord one thousand seven hundred and eighty-seven, and of the independence of the United States of America the twelfth. *In Witness* whereof, we have hereunto subscribed our names.

Attest:　**William Jackson**　　　**George Washington**
　　　　　　Secretary　　　　　　President and Deputy from Virginia

New Hampshire
John Langdon
Nicholas Gilman

Massachusetts
Nathaniel Gorham
Rufus King

Connecticut
William Samuel Johnson
Roger Sherman

New York
Alexander Hamilton

New Jersey
William Livingston
David Brearley
William Paterson
Jonathan Dayton

Pennsylvania
Benjamin Franklin
Thomas Mifflin
Robert Morris
George Clymer
Thomas Fitzsimons
Jared Ingersoll
James Wilson
Gouverneur Morris

Delaware
George Read
Gunning Bedford, Jr.
John Dickinson
Richard Bassett
Jacob Broom

Maryland
James McHenry
Dan of St. Thomas Jennifer
Daniel Carroll

Virginia
John Blair
James Madison, Jr.

North Carolina
William Blount
Richard Dobbs Spaight
Hugh Williamson

South Carolina
John Rutledge
Charles Cotesworth Pinckney
Charles Pinckney
Pierce Butler

Georgia
William Few
Abraham Baldwin

THE CONSTITUTION

Amendments to the Constitution

The first ten amendments, which were added to the Constitution in 1791, are called the Bill of Rights. Originally, the Bill of Rights applied only to actions of the federal government. However, the Supreme Court has used the due process clause of the Fourteenth Amendment to extend many of the rights to protect individuals against action by the states.

Amendment 1
Freedoms of Religion, Speech, Press, Assembly, and Petition

Congress shall make no law respecting an establishment of religion, or prohibiting the free exercise thereof; or abridging the freedom of speech, or of the press; or the right of the people peaceably to assemble, and to petition the government for a redress of grievances.

The First Amendment protects five basic rights: freedom of religion, speech, the press, assembly, and petition. Congress cannot set up an established, or official, church or religion for the nation. During the colonial period, most colonies had established churches. However, the authors of the First Amendment wanted to keep government and religion separate.

Congress may not **abridge,** or limit, the freedom to speak and write freely. The government may not censor, or review, books and newspapers before they are printed. This amendment also protects the right to assemble, or hold public meetings. **Petition** means ask. **Redress** means to correct. **Grievances** are wrongs. The people have the right to ask the government for wrongs to be corrected.

Amendment 2
Right to Bear Arms

A well-regulated militia, being necessary to the security of a free state, the right of the people to keep and bear arms shall not be infringed.

State militia, of which the National Guard is part, have the right to bear arms, or keep weapons. Courts have generally ruled that the government can regulate the ownership of guns by private citizens.

Amendment 3
Lodging Troops in Private Homes

No soldier shall, in time of peace, be quartered in any house, without the consent of the owner; nor in time of war, but in a manner to be prescribed by law.

During the colonial period, the British quartered, or housed, soldiers in private homes without the permission of the owners (page 204). This amendment limits the government's right to use private homes to house soldiers.

Amendment 4
Search and Seizure

The right of the people to be secure in their persons, houses, papers, and effects, against unreasonable searches and seizures, shall not be violated; and no warrants shall issue but upon probable cause, supported by oath or affirmation, and particularly describing the place to be searched, and the persons or things to be seized.

This amendment protects Americans from unreasonable searches and seizures. Search and seizure are permitted only if a judge has issued a **warrant,** or written court order. A warrant is issued only if there is probable cause. This means an officer must show that it is prob-

THE CONSTITUTION

able, or likely, that the search will produce evidence of a crime. A search warrant must name the exact place to be searched and the things to be seized.

In some cases, courts have ruled that searches can take place without a warrant. For example, police may search a person who is under arrest. However, evidence found during an unlawful search cannot be used in a trial.

This amendment protects the rights of the accused. **Capital crimes** are those which can be punished with death. **Infamous crimes** are those which can be punished with prison or loss of rights. The federal government must obtain an **indictment,** or formal accusation, from a grand jury to prosecute anyone for such crimes. A **grand jury** is a panel of between 12 to 23 citizens who decide if the government has enough evidence to justify a trial. This procedure prevents the government from prosecuting people with little or no evidence of guilt. (Soldiers and members of the militia in wartime are not covered by this rule.)

Double jeopardy is forbidden by this amendment. This means that a person cannot be tried twice for the same crime. However, if a court sets aside a conviction because of a legal error, the accused can be tried again. A person on trial cannot be forced to testify, or give evidence, against himself or herself. A person accused of a crime is entitled to **due process of law,** or a fair hearing or trial.

Finally, the government cannot seize private property for public use without paying the owner a fair price for it.

In criminal cases, the jury must be **impartial,** or not favor either side. The accused is guaranteed the right to a trial by jury. The trial must be speedy. If the government purposely postpones the trial so that it becomes hard for the person to get a fair hearing, the charge may be dismissed. The accused must be told the charges against him or her and is allowed to question prosecution witnesses. Witnesses who can help the accused can be ordered to appear in court.

The accused must be allowed a lawyer. Since 1942, the federal government has been required to provide a lawyer if the accused cannot afford one. In 1963, the Supreme Court decided that states must also provide lawyers for a defendant too poor to pay for one.

Common law refers to rules of law established by judges in past cases. This amendment guarantees the right to a jury trial in lawsuits where the sum of money at stake is more than $20. An appeals court cannot change a verdict because it disagrees with the decision of the jury. It can only set aside a verdict if legal errors made the trial unfair.

Amendment 5
Rights of the Accused

No person shall be held to answer for a capital, or otherwise infamous, crime, unless on a presentment or indictment of a grand jury, except in cases arising in the land or naval forces, or in the militia, when in actual service in time of war or public danger; nor shall any person be subject for the same offense to be twice put in jeopardy of life and limb; nor shall be compelled, in any criminal case, to be a witness against himself; nor be deprived of life, liberty, or property, without due process of law; nor shall private property be taken for public use, without just compensation.

Amendment 6
Right to Speedy Trial by Jury

In all criminal prosecutions, the accused shall enjoy the right to a speedy and public trial, by an impartial jury of the state and district wherein the crime shall have been committed, which district shall have been previously ascertained by law, and to be informed of the nature and cause of the accusation; to be confronted with the witnesses against him; to have compulsory process for obtaining witnesses in his favor, and to have the assistance of counsel for his defense.

Amendment 7
Jury Trial in Civil Cases

In suits at common law, where the value in controversy shall exceed $20, the right of trial by jury shall be preserved, and no fact tried by a jury shall be otherwise re-examined in any court of the United States than according to the rules of the common law.

Amendment 8
Bail and Punishment

Excessive bail shall not be required, nor excessive fines imposed, nor cruel and unusual punishments inflicted.

Bail is money the accused leaves with the court as a pledge that he or she will appear for trial. If the accused does not appear for trial, the court keeps the money. **Excessive** means too high. This amendment forbids courts to set unreasonably high bail. The amount of bail usually depends on the seriousness of the charge and whether the accused is likely to appear for the trial. The amendment also forbids cruel and unusual punishments such as mental and physical abuse.

Amendment 9
Powers Reserved to the People

The enumeration in the Constitution, of certain rights, shall not be construed to deny or disparage others retained by the people.

The people have rights that are not listed in the Constitution. This amendment was added because some people feared that the Bill of Rights would be used to limit rights to those actually listed.

Amendment 10
Powers Reserved to the States

The powers not delegated to the United States by the Constitution, nor prohibited by it to the states, are reserved to the states respectively, or to the people.

This amendment limits the power of the federal government. Powers not given to the federal government belong to the states. The powers reserved to the states are not listed in the Constitution.

Amendment 11
Suits Against States

Passed by Congress on March 4, 1794. Ratified on January 23, 1795.

The judicial power of the United States shall not be construed to extend to any suit in law or equity, commenced or prosecuted against one of the United States, by citizens of another state, or by citizens or subjects of any foreign state.

This amendment changed part of Article 3, Section 2, Clause 1. As a result, a private citizen from one state cannot sue the government of another state in federal court. However, a citizen can sue a state government in a state court.

Amendment 12
Election of President and Vice-President

Passed by Congress on December 9, 1803. Ratified on June 15, 1804.

The electors shall meet in their respective states, and vote by ballot for President and Vice-President, one of whom, at least, shall not be an inhabitant of the same state with themselves; they shall name in their ballots the person voted for as President, and in distinct ballots the person voted for as Vice-President, and they shall make distinct lists of all persons voted for as President, and of all persons voted for as Vice-President, and of the number of votes for each, which lists they shall sign and certify, and transmit, sealed, to the seat of government of the United States, directed to the President of the Senate; the President of the Senate shall, in the presence of the Senate and House of Representatives, open all the certificates and the votes shall then be counted; the person having the greatest number of votes for President shall be

This amendment changed the way the electoral college voted. Before the amendment was adopted, each elector simply voted for two people. The candidate with the most votes became President. The runner-up became Vice President. In the election of 1800, however, a tie vote resulted between Thomas Jefferson and Aaron Burr (pages 328–329).

In such a case, the Constitution required the House of Representatives to elect the President. Federalists had a majority in the House. They tried to keep Jefferson out of office by voting for Burr. It took 35 ballots in the House before Jefferson was elected President.

To keep this from happening again, the Twelfth Amendment was passed and ratified in time for the election of 1804.

This amendment provides that each elector choose one candidate for President and one candidate for Vice President. If no candidate for President receives a majority of electoral votes, the House of Representatives chooses the President. If no candidate for Vice President receives a majority, the Senate elects the Vice President. The Vice President must be a person who is eligible to be President.

This system is still in use today. However, it is possible for a candidate to win the popular vote and lose in the electoral college. This happened in 1876 (pages 588–589).

the President, if such number be a majority of the whole number of electors appointed; and if no person have such majority, then from the persons having the highest numbers not exceeding three on the list of those voted for as President, the House of Representatives shall choose immediately, by ballot, the President. But in choosing the President, the votes shall be taken by states, the representation from each state having one vote; a quorum for this purpose shall consist of a member or members from two-thirds of the states, and a majority of all the states shall be necessary to a choice. And if the House of Representatives shall not choose a President whenever the right of choice shall devolve upon them, before the fourth day of March next following, then the Vice-President shall act as President, as in the case of the death or other constitutional disability of the President. The person having the greatest number of votes as Vice-President, shall be the Vice-President, if such number be a majority of the whole number of electors appointed, and if no person have a majority, then, from the two highest numbers on the list, the Senate shall choose the Vice-President; a quorum for the purpose shall consist of two-thirds of the whole number of Senators, and a majority of the whole number shall be necessary to a choice. But no person constitutionally ineligible to the office of President shall be eligible to that of Vice-President of the United States.

Amendment 13
Abolition of Slavery

Passed by Congress on January 31, 1865. Ratified on December 6, 1865.

Section 1. Neither slavery nor involuntary servitude, except as a punishment for crime whereof the party shall have been duly convicted, shall exist within the United States, or any place subject to their jurisdiction.

The Emancipation Proclamation (1863) only freed slaves in areas controlled by the Confederacy (page 552). This amendment freed all slaves. It also forbids *involuntary servitude,* or labor done against one's will. However, it does not prevent prison wardens from making prisoners work.

Congress can pass laws to carry out this amendment.

Section 2. Congress shall have power to enforce this article by appropriate legislation.

Amendment 14
Rights of Citizens

Passed by Congress on June 13, 1866. Ratified on July 9, 1868.

Section 1. Citizenship All persons born or naturalized in the United States and subject to the jurisdiction thereof, are citizens of the United States and of the state wherein they reside. No state shall make or enforce any law which shall abridge the privileges or immunities of citizens of the United States; nor shall any state deprive any person of life, liberty, or property, without due process of law; nor deny to any person within its jurisdiction the equal protection of the laws.

This section defines citizenship for the first time in the Constitution, and it extends citizenship to blacks. It also prohibits states from denying the rights and privileges of citizenship to any citizen. This section also forbids states to deny due process of law.

Section 1 guarantees all citizens "equal protection under the law." For a long time, however, the Fourteenth Amendment did not protect blacks from discrimination. After Reconstruction, separate facilities for blacks and whites sprang up (page 589). In 1954, the Supreme Court ruled that separate facilities for blacks and whites were by their nature unequal. This ruling, in the case of *Brown* v. *Board of Education,* made school segregation illegal.

Section 2. Apportionment of Representatives Representatives shall be apportioned among the several states according to their respective numbers, counting the whole number of persons in each state, excluding Indians not taxed. But when the right to vote at any election for the choice of electors for President and Vice-President of the United States, Representatives in Congress, the executive and judicial officers of a state, or the members of the legislature thereof, is denied to any of the male inhabitants of such state, being twenty-one years of age and citizens of the United States, or in any way abridged, except for participation in rebellion, or other crime, the basis of representation therein shall be reduced in the proportion which the number of such male citizens shall bear to the whole number of male citizens twenty-one years of age in such state.

This section replaced the three fifths clause. It provides that representation in the House of Representatives is decided on the basis of the number of people in the state. It also provides that states which deny the vote to male citizens over age 21 will be punished by losing part of their representation in the House. This provision has never been enforced.

Despite this clause, black citizens were often prevented from voting. In the 1960s, federal laws were passed to end voting discrimination.

Section 3. Former Confederate Officials No person shall be a Senator or Representative in Congress or elector of President and Vice-President, or hold any office, civil or military, under the United States, or under any state, who, having previously taken an oath, as a member of Congress, or as an officer of the United States, or as a member of any state legislature, or as an executive or judicial officer of any state, to support the Constitution of the United States, shall have engaged in insurrection or rebellion against the same, or given aid or comfort to the enemies thereof. But Congress may, by vote of two-thirds of each house, remove such disability.

This section prohibited people who had been federal or state officials before the Civil War and who had joined the Confederate cause from serving again as government officials. In 1872, Congress restored the rights of former Confederate officials.

Section 4. Government Debt The validity of the public debt of the United States, authorized by law, including debts incurred for payment of pensions and bounties for services in suppressing insurrection or rebellion, shall not be questioned. But neither the United States nor any state shall assume or pay any debt or obligation incurred in aid of insurrection or rebellion against the United States or any claim for the loss or emancipation of any slave; but all such debts, obligations, and claims shall be held illegal and void.

This section recognized that the United States must repay its debts from the Civil War. However, it forbade the repayment of debts of the Confederacy. This meant that people who had loaned money to the Confederacy would not be repaid. Also, states were not allowed to pay former slave owners for the loss of slaves.

Section 5. Enforcement The Congress shall have power to enforce, by appropriate legislation, the provisions of this article.

Congress can pass laws to carry out this amendment.

Amendment 15
Voting Rights

Passed by Congress on February 26, 1869. Ratified on February 2, 1870.

Section 1. Extending the Right to Vote The right of citizens of the United States to vote shall not be denied or abridged by the United States or any state on account of race, color, or previous condition of servitude.

Previous condition of servitude refers to slavery. This amendment gave blacks, both former slaves and free blacks, the right to vote. In the late 1800s, southern states used grandfather clauses, literacy tests, and poll taxes to keep blacks from voting (page 589).

Section 2. Enforcement The Congress shall have power to enforce this article by appropriate legislation.

Congress can pass laws to carry out this amendment. The Twenty-fourth Amendment barred the use of poll taxes in national elections. The Voting Rights Act of 1965 gave federal officials the power to register voters in places where voting discrimination was found.

Amendment 16
The Income Tax

Passed by Congress on July 12, 1909. Ratified on February 3, 1913.

The Congress shall have power to lay and collect taxes on incomes, from whatever source derived, without apportionment among the several states, and without regard to any census or enumeration.

Congress has the power to collect taxes on people's income. An income tax can be collected without regard to a state's population. This amendment changed Article 1, Section 9, Clause 4.

Amendment 17
Direct Election of Senators

Passed by Congress on May 13, 1912. Ratified on April 8, 1913.

Section 1. Method of Election The Senate of the United States shall be composed of two Senators from each state, elected by the people thereof, for six years; and each Senator shall have one vote. The electors in each state shall have the qualifications requisite for electors of the most numerous branch of the state legislatures.

This amendment replaced Article 1, Section 3, Clause 1. Before it was adopted, state legislatures chose senators. This amendment provides that senators are directly elected by the people of each state.

Section 2. Vacancies When vacancies happen in the representation of any state in the Senate, the executive authority of such state shall issue writs of election to fill such vacancies: *Provided* that the legislature of any state may empower the executive thereof to make temporary appointments until the people fill the vacancies by election as the legislature may direct.

When a Senate seat becomes vacant, the governor of the state must order an election to fill the seat. The state legislature can give the governor power to fill the seat until an election is held.

Section 3. Exception This amendment shall not be so construed as to affect the election or term of any Senator chosen before it becomes valid as part of the Constitution.

Senators who had already been elected by the state legislatures were not affected by this amendment.

Amendment 18
Prohibition of Alcoholic Beverages

Passed by Congress on December 18, 1917. Ratified on January 16, 1919.

Section 1. Ban on Alcohol After one year from the ratification of this article the manufacture, sale, or transportation of intoxicating liquors within, the importation thereof into, or the exportation thereof from, the United States and all territory subject to the jurisdiction thereof for beverage purposes is hereby prohibited.

This amendment, known as **Prohibition**, banned the making, selling, or transporting of alcoholic beverages in the United States. Later, the Twenty-first Amendment **repealed**, or canceled, this amendment.

Section 2. Enforcement The Congress and the several states shall have concurrent power to enforce this article by appropriate legislation.

Both the states and the federal government had the power to pass laws to enforce the amendment.

Section 3. Method of Ratification This article shall be inoperative unless it shall have been ratified as an amendment to the Constitution by the legislatures of the several states, as provided in the Constitution, within seven years from the date of the submission hereof to the states by the Congress.

The amendment had to be approved within seven years. The Eighteenth Amendment was the first amendment to include a time limit for ratification.

Amendment 19
Women's Suffrage

Passed by Congress on June 4, 1919, Ratified on August 18, 1920.

Section 1. The Right to Vote The right of citizens of the United States to vote shall not be denied or abridged by the United States or by any state on account of sex.

Neither the federal government nor state governments can deny the right to vote on account of sex. Thus, women won **suffrage,** or the right to vote. Before 1920, some states had allowed women to vote in state elections.

Section 2. Enforcement Congress shall have power to enforce this article by appropriate legislation.

Congress can pass laws to carry out the amendment.

Amendment 20
Presidential Terms; Sessions of Congress

Passed by Congress on March 2, 1932. Ratified on Janurary 23, 1933.

Section 1. Beginning of Term The terms of the President and Vice-President shall end at noon on the 20th day of January, and the terms of Senators and Representatives at noon on the 3rd day of January, of the years in which such terms would have ended if this article had not been ratified; and the terms of their successor shall then begin.

The date for the President and Vice President to take office is January 20. Members of Congress begin their terms of office on January 3. Before this amendment was adopted, these terms of office began on March 4.

Section 2. Congressional Sessions The Congress shall assemble at least once in every year, and such meeting shall begin at noon on the 3rd day of January, unless they shall by law appoint a different day.

Congress must meet at least once a year. The new session of Congress begins on January 3. Before this amendment, members of Congress who had been defeated in November continued to hold office until the following March. Such members were known as **lame ducks.**

Section 3. Presidential Succession If at the time fixed for the beginning of the term of the President, the President-elect shall have died, the Vice-President-elect shall become President. If a President shall not have been chosen before the time fixed for the beginning of his term, or if the President-elect shall have failed to qualify, then the Vice-President-elect shall act as President until a President shall have qualified; and the Congress may by law provide for the case wherein neither a President-elect nor a Vice-President-elect shall have qualified, declaring who shall then act as President, or the manner in which one who is to act shall be selected, and such person shall act accordingly until a President or Vice-President shall have qualified.

If the President-elect dies before taking office, the Vice President-elect becomes President. If no President has been chosen by January 20 or if the elected candidate fails to qualify for office, the Vice President-elect acts as President, but only until a qualified President is chosen.
Finally, Congress has the power to choose a person to act as President if neither the President-elect or Vice President-elect has qualified to take office.

Section 4. Elections Decided by Congress The Congress may by law provide for the case of the death of any of the persons from whom the House of Representatives may choose a President whenever the right of choice shall have devolved upon them, and for the case of the death of any of the persons from whom the Senate may choose a Vice-President whenever the right of choice shall have devolved upon them.

Congress can pass laws in cases where a Presidential candidate dies while an election is being decided in the House. Congress has similar power in cases where a candidate for Vice President dies while an election is being decided in the Senate.

Section 5 sets the date for the amendment to become effective.

Section 5. Date of Implementation ~~Sections 1 and 2 shall take effect on the 15th day of October following the ratification of this article.~~

Section 6 sets a time limit for ratification.

Section 6. Ratification Period ~~This article shall be inoperative unless it shall have been ratified as an amendment to the Constitution by the legislatures of three-fourths of the several states within seven years from the date of its submission.~~

Amendment 21
Repeal of Prohibition

Passed by Congress on February 20, 1933. Ratified on December 5, 1933.

The Eighteenth Amendment is repealed, making it legal to make and sell alcoholic beverages. Prohibition ended December 5, 1933.

Section 1. Repeal of National Prohibition The eighteenth article of amendment to the Constitution of the United States is hereby repealed.

Each state was free to ban the making and selling of alcoholic drink within its borders. This section makes bringing liquor into a "dry" state a federal offense.

Section 2. State Laws The transportation or importation into any state, territory, or possession of the United States for delivery or use therein of intoxicating liquors, in violation of the laws thereof, is hereby prohibited.

Special state conventions were called to ratify this amendment. This is the only time an amendment was ratified by state conventions rather than state legislatures.

Section 3. Ratification Period ~~This article shall be inoperative unless it shall have been ratified as an amendment to the Constitution by conventions in the several states, as provided in the Constitution, within seven years from the date of the submission hereof to the states by the Congress.~~

Amendment 22
Limit on Number of President's Terms

Passed by Congress on March 12, 1947. Ratified on March 1, 1951.

Before Franklin Roosevelt became President, no President served more than two terms in office. Roosevelt broke with this custom and was elected to four terms. This amendment provides that no President may serve more than two terms. A President who has already served more than half of someone else's term can only serve one more full term. However, the amendment did not apply to Harry Truman, who had become President after Franklin Roosevelt's death in 1945.

Section 1. Two-Term Limit No person shall be elected to the office of the President more than twice, and no person who has held the office of President, or acted as President, for more than two years of a term to which some other person was elected President shall be elected to the office of the President more than once. ~~But this Article shall not apply to any person holding the office of President when this Article was proposed by the Congress, and shall not prevent any person who may be holding the office of President, or acting as President, during the term within which this Article becomes operative from holding the office of President or acting as President during the remainder of such term.~~

Section 2. Ratification Period ~~This Article shall be inoperative unless it shall have been ratified as an amendment to the Constitution by the legislatures of three-fourths of the several states within seven years from the date of its submission to the states by the Congress.~~

A seven-year time limit is set for ratification.

Amendment 23
Presidential Electors for District of Columbia

Passed by Congress on June 16, 1960. Ratified on April 3, 1961.

Section 1. Determining the Number of Electors The District constituting the seat of Government of the United States shall appoint in such manner as the Congress may direct:

A number of electors of President and Vice-President equal to the whole number of Senators and Representatives in Congress to which the District would be entitled if it were a State, but in no event more than the least populous State; they shall be in addition to those appointed by the States, but they shall be considered, for the purposes of the election of President and Vice-President, to be electors appointed by a State; and they shall meet in the District and perform such duties as provided by the twelfth article of amendment.

This amendment gives residents of Washington, D.C., the right to vote in Presidential elections. Until this amendment was adopted, people living in Washington, D.C., could not vote for President because the Constitution had made no provision for choosing electors from the nation's capital. Washington, D.C., has three electoral votes.

Section 2. Enforcement The Congress shall have the power to enforce this article by appropriate legislation.

Congress can pass laws to carry out the amendment.

Amendment 24
Abolition of Poll Tax in National Elections

Passed by Congress on August 27, 1962. Ratified on January 23, 1964.

Section 1. Poll Tax Banned The right of citizens of the United States to vote in any primary or other election for President or Vice-President, for electors for President or Vice-President, or for Senator or Representative in Congress, shall not be denied or abridged by the United States or any state by reason of failure to pay any poll tax or other tax.

A *poll tax* is a tax on voters. This amendment bans poll taxes in national elections. Some states used poll taxes to keep blacks from voting. In 1966, the Supreme Court struck down poll taxes in state elections, also.

Section 2. Enforcement The Congress shall have power to enforce this article by appropriate legislation.

Congress can pass laws to carry out the amendment.

Amendment 25
Presidential Succession and Disability

Passed by Congress on July 6, 1965. Ratified on February 11, 1967.

Section 1. President's Death or Resignation In case of the removal of the President from office or his death or resignation, the Vice-President shall become President.

If the President dies or resigns, the Vice-President becomes President. This section clarifies Article 2, Section 1, Clause 6.

THE CONSTITUTION

773

When a Vice President takes over the office of President, he or she appoints a Vice President who must be approved by a majority vote of both houses of Congress. This section was applied after Vice President Spiro Agnew resigned in 1973. President Richard Nixon appointed Gerald Ford as Vice President. After President Nixon resigned in 1974, President Gerald Ford appointed Nelson Rockefeller as Vice President.

If the President declares in writing that he or she is unable to perform the duties of office, the Vice President serves as Acting President until the President recovers.

Two Presidents, Woodrow Wilson and Dwight Eisenhower, have fallen gravely ill while in office. The Constitution contained no provision for this kind of emergency.

Section 3 provided that the President can inform Congress that he or she is too sick to perform the duties of office. However, if the President is unconscious or refuses to admit to a disabling illness, Section 4 provides that the Vice President and cabinet may declare the President disabled. The Vice President becomes Acting President until the President can return to the duties of office. In case of a disagreement between the President and the Vice President and cabinet over the President's ability to perform the duties of office, Congress must decide the issue. A two-thirds vote of both houses is needed to find the President disabled or unable to fulfill the duties of office.

Section 2. Vacancies in Vice-Presidency Whenever there is a vacancy in the office of the Vice-President, the President shall nominate a Vice-President who shall take the office upon confirmation by a majority vote of both houses of Congress.

Section 3. Disability of the President Whenever the President transmits to the President pro tempore of the Senate and the Speaker of the House of Representatives his written declaration that he is unable to discharge the powers and duties of his office, and until he transmits to them a written declaration to the contrary, such powers and duties shall be discharged by the Vice-President as Acting President.

Section 4. Whenever the Vice-President and a majority of either the principal officers of the executive departments or of such other body as Congress may by law provide, transmit to the President pro tempore of the Senate and the Speaker of the House of Representatives their written declaration that the President is unable to discharge the powers and duties of his office, the Vice-President shall immediately assume the powers and duties of the office as Acting President.

Thereafter, when the President transmits to the President pro tempore of the Senate and the Speaker of the House of Representatives his written declaration that no inability exists, he shall resume the powers and duties of his office unless the Vice-President and a majority of either the principal officers of the executive department or of such other body as Congress may by law provide, transmit within four days to the President pro tempore of the Senate and the Speaker of the House of Representatives their written declaration that the President is unable to discharge the powers and duties of his office. Thereupon Congress shall decide the issue, assembling within 48 hours for that purpose if not in session. If the Congress, within 21 days after receipt of the latter written declaration, or, if Congress is not in session, within 21 days after Congress is required to assemble, determines by two-thirds vote of both houses that the President is unable to discharge the powers and duties of his office, the Vice-President shall continue to discharge the same as Acting President; otherwise, the President shall assume the powers and duties of his office.

Amendment 26
Voting Age

Passed by Congress on March 23, 1971. Ratified on July 1, 1971.

In 1970, Congress passed a law allowing 18-year-olds to vote in state and federal elections. However, the Supreme Court decided that Congress could not set a minimum age for state elections. So this amendment was passed and ratified, giving the right to vote to citizens age 18 or older.

Congress can pass laws to carry out the amendment.

Section 1. Lowering of Voting Age The right of citizens of the United States, who are 18 years of age or older, to vote shall not be denied or abridged by the United States or any state on account of age.

Section 2. Enforcement The Congress shall have the power to enforce this article by appropriate legislation.

An *m, c,* or *p* before a page number refers to a map *(m)*, chart *(c)*, or picture *(p)* on that page. An *n* after a page number refers to a footnote. *Painting* or *cartoon* indicates a work by the listed artist.

INDEX

INDEX

INDEX

INDEX

INDEX

INDEX

INDEX

INDEX

INDEX

INDEX

INDEX

Whitcomb; *bl* Culver Pictures; *br* The Granger Collection; **181** *t* The Granger Collection; *c* LC; *b* The Granger Collection.

UNIT 3 Page 186 *l* Independence National Historical Park Collection; *t* Independence National Historical Park Collection; *r* NMAA; **187** The Granger Collection; **188** American Antiquarian Society; **190** National Archives of Canada, Ottawa; **192** National Gallery of Canada; **194** Thomas Gilcrease Institute of American History and Art; **197** New Brunswick Museum; **200** The Granger Collection; **201** John Carter Brown Library; **204** MFA; **205** MFA; **206** Rhode Island Historical Society; **209** The Granger Collection; **211** Essex Institute, Salem, Massachusetts; **213** The Concord Museum, Concord, Massachusetts; **218** The Historical Society of Pennsylvania; **220** Fort Ticonderoga Museum; **225** Kirby Collection of Historical Paintings, Lafayette College; **226** *l* Yale; *r* J.P. Laffont/Sygma; **228** U.S. Naval Academy Museum; **229** NYSHA; **232** Florida State Archives, Tallahassee; **234** The Gilcrease Institute of American History and Art; **235** New York Historical Society; **236** The Granger Collection; **237** The Granger Collection; **239** Collection of the State of South Carolina; **246** New York Historical Society; **248** Amon Carter Museum; **249** The Granger Collection; **252** The Anschutz Collection; **253** The Granger Collection; **257** The Granger Collection; **258** State Historical Society of Wisconsin; **260** Architect of U.S. Capitol; **261** The Connecticut Historical Society; **266** The Granger Collection; **267** The Granger Collection; **269** MMA; **Gazette 274** *t* The Granger Collection; *c* The Granger Collection; *b* The Granger Collection; **275** *t* Essex Museum, Essex, Connecticut; *c* The Granger Collection; *b* The Granger Collection.

CIVICS OVERVIEW Page 280 The Nelson-Atkins Museum of Art; **283** Bill Bernstein/The Stock Market; **284** Dennis Brack/Black Star; **285** Michal Heron; **288** Michal Heron; **292** *l* Dennis Capolongo/Black Star; *r* Michal Heron; **293** Chris Sorensen/The Stock Market; **295** Dennis Brack/Black Star; **297** *l* Tom Zimberoff/Sygma; *r* Larry Downing; **299** Johnson/Gamma Liaison; **301** Daniel Brody/Stock, Boston; **302** Ted Spiegel/Black Star.

UNIT 4 Page 306 *l* NMAA; *t* White House Historical Association; *r* Museum of Art, Rhode Island School of Design; **307** *l* New York State Historical Association; *r* Museum of Fine Arts, Boston; **308** New York Historical Society; **310** NG; **312** Dallas Museum of Art; **313** *l* The Granger Collection; *r* The Granger Collection; **316** Henry Francis du Pont Winterthur Museum; **317** Musée Carnavalet; **319** Chicago Historical Society; **320** MMA; **322** Abby Aldrich Rockefeller Collection, Colonial Williamsburg; **324** The Granger Collection; **326** *l* The White House Association; *r* NYSHA; **327** Yale; **329** SI; **334** U.S. Capitol Historical Society (LC); **336** Henry Francis du Pont Winterthur Museum; **337** The Peale Museum/Baltimore City Life Museum; **338** Boston Athanaeum; **340** Maryland Historical Society; **341** The Granger Collection; **342** Missouri Historical Society; **344** Montana Historical Society; **348** Mariner's Museum, Newport, Virginia; **353** *l* Field Museum of Natural History; *r* NMAA/SI; **355** MMA; **358** Maryland Historical Society; **359** The Granger Collection; **364** MFA; **367** SI; **368** *l* The Granger Collection; *r* Ted Horowitz/The Stock Market; **370** The Granger Collection; **371** American Clock and Watch Museum, Bristol, Connecticut; **375** MMA/Rogers Fund; **377** Art Collection, Tulane University/Gift of D.H. Holmes Co.; **379** Albany Institute of History & Art; **381** *l* New York Historical Society; *r* The Cor-

coran Gallery of Art; **382** Library Company of Philadelphia; **384** MMA; **387** Laurie Platt Winfrey, Inc.; **388** LC; **Gazette 394** *t* from "The History of the Negro in America" by Langston Hughes & M. Meltzer; *c* SI; *b* Essex Institute, Salem, Massachusetts; **395** *t* The Granger Collection; *b* NMAA.

UNIT 5 Page 400 *l* Walters Art Gallery, Baltimore; *t* National Park Service, Scotts Bluff National Monument; *r* The Alamo; **401** *l* Glenbow Museum, Calgary, Alberta; *r* The Stowe-Day Foundation; **402** The Nelson-Atkins Museum of Art, Kansas City, Missouri; **405** National Portrait Gallery; **407** The Granger Collection; **409** NG/Andrew Mellon Collection; **410** The Granger Collection; **411** Terra Museum of American Art, Chicago, Illinois; **413** Gilcrease Museum; **415** Philbrook Art Center, Tulsa, Oklahoma; **417** Superstock; **419** The Cincinnati Art Museum; **420** The Granger Collection; **422** LC/Handtinting by Ladleton Studios; **426** Gene Autry Western Heritage Museum, Los Angeles; **429** Walters Art Gallery, Baltimore, Maryland; **430** Colorado Historical Society/Handtinting by Ladleton Studios; **431** Oregon Historical Society; **434** Amon Carter Museum, Fort Worth, Texas; **435** Texas State Library and Archives; **437** Art Resource (Joseph Martin/SCALA); **443** San Jacinto Museum; **446** Los Angeles County, Museum of National History; **448** Church of Latter-day Saints; **450** *l* Wells Fargo Bank Museum/Lundoff Collection; *r* California State Library; **451** Courtesy of Wells Fargo Bank; **456** MMA/Bequest of Moses Tanenbaum, 1937; **459** The Granger Collection; **460** The Chessie System, B&O Railroad Museum Archives; **463** American Steel Foundries; **465** The Granger Collection; **466** LC/Handtinting by Ladleton Studios; **468** MMA/Rogers Fund, 1942; **471** Thomas Gilcrease Institute of American History and Art, Tulsa, Oklahoma; **472** The Historic New Orleans Collection; **473** Amon Carter Museum, Fort Worth, Texas; **475** The Historic New Orleans Collection, Museum/Research Center; **477** Thomas Gilcrease Institute of American History and Art, Tulsa, Oklahoma; **482** MFA; **484** The Schomburg Center for Research in Black Culture, NYPL; **485** Kennedy Galleries; **486** National Portrait Gallery; **487** The Bancroft Library; **488** LC/Handtinting by Ladleton Studios; **490** Walters Art Gallery, Baltimore, Maryland; **491** The Granger Collection; **492** Mount Holyoke College Art Museum, South Hadley, Massachusetts; **494** The Granger Collection; **495** The St. Louis Art Museum; **496** The Granger Collection; **499** The Bostonian Society; **500** Pennsylvania Academy of Fine Arts; **501** Hood Museum of Art, Dartmouth College, Hanover, New Hampshire/Purchased through the Julia L. Whittier Fund; **Gazette 506** *t* The Granger Collection; *b* The Granger Collection; **507** *t* NYPL Picture Collection; *c* The Bancroft Library; *b* The Granger Collection.

UNIT 6 Page 512 *l* Anne S.K. Brown Military Collection; *t* Museum of American Political Life; *r* Valentine Museum, Richmond; **513** *l* MFA; *r* LC; **514** Chicago Historical Society; **517** MMA/Gift of Erving and Joyce Wolf, 1982; **518** The Granger Collection; **520** The Granger Collection; **521** The Granger Collection; **522** The Granger Collection; **523** National Portrait Gallery, Washington, D.C.; **526** Yale/The Mabel Brady Garvan Collection; **527** Anne S.K. Brown Military Collection, Brown University Library; **528** Missouri Historical Society; **531** *l* and *r* The National Portrait Gallery, Washington, D.C.; **532** MMA/Gift of Mr. and Mrs. Carl Stoeckel, 1897; **534** The Granger Collection; **535** *l* The Museum of the Confederacy, Richmond, Virginia/photo by Katherine Wetzel; *r* National Park Service, Department of the Interior; **540** MMA; **544** MFA; **545** Virginia Historical Society; **548** Museum of the Confederacy; **549** The Granger Collection;

552 The Granger Collection; 553 The Granger Collection; 555 LC; 557 LC; 559 LC; 561 New Hampshire Historical Society; 564 LC; 570 Chicago Historical Society; 573 LC; 574 Cincinnati Art Museum, John J. Emery Fund; 575 Tennessee Historical Society; 577 The Granger Collection; 578 Culver Pictures; 579 The Granger Collection; 580 LC/Handtinting by Ladleton Studio; 581 The Granger Collection; 583 The Granger Collection; 584 Culver Pictures; 586 Brown Brothers; Gazette 594 tl Culver Pictures, Inc.; tr The Granger Collection; b The Granger Collection; 595 t The Granger Collection; b The Granger Collection.

The Journey Continues Page 600 De Young Museum Society, Fine Arts Museums of San Francisco; 603 l Courtesy Edward L. Shein/Laurie Platt Winfrey, Inc.; r Andrew Holbrooke/Black Star; 604 Francis O'Brien Garfield/Saturday Review of Literature, 3/19/'46; 605 Fine Arts Galleries of San Diego/Laurie Platt Winfrey, Inc.; 607 © George Hall/Woodfin Camp and Associates; 608 Amon Carter Museum, Ft. Worth, Texas; 609 Montgomery Museum of Fine Arts; 612 l International Museum of Photography at George Eastman House; r Michal Heron; 613 The Phillips Collection, Washington, D.C.; 614 Laurie Platt Winfrey, Inc.; 615 Michal Heron; 616 Roger Ressmeyer/STARLIGHT; 618 LC; 619 Navy Combat Art Collection, Washington, D.C.; 620 Dick Halstead/Gamma Liaison; 621 Sylvia Johnson/Woodfin Camp & Associates.

VOICES AND VISIONS Page 624 t MFA; © Mead Art Museum, Amherst College; bl AMNH; br MFA; 625 tl MFA; tr MMA; bl The Granger Collection; br MFA; 626 Joslyn Art Museum; 627 Natural Museum of American Art/Art Resource; 628 Royal Ontario Museum; 631 AMNH; 632 The Granger Collection; 635 The Granger Collection; 637 The Granger Collection; 638 NG; 639 The Granger Collection; 641 MMA; 643 The Granger Collection; 645 Virginia Museum of Fine Arts; 647 MMA; 649 Essex Institute, Salem, Massachusetts; 650 MFA; 651 The Granger Collection; 653 The Granger Collection; 655 Chicago Historical Society; 657 Amon Carter Museum, Fort Worth, Texas; 659 Cincinnati Historical Society; 661 The Granger Collection; 662 The Brooklyn Museum; 663 Mead Art Museum, Amherst College; 665 Pennsylvania Academy of Fine Arts, Philadelphia; 667 Museum of Art, Rhode Island School of Design; 669 Maryland Historical Society; 671 Albright-Knox Art Gallery; 673 New York Historical Society; 674 The St. Louis Art Museum; 675 New York Historical Society; 677 MFA; 679 San Antonio Museum Association; 681 t and b Thomas Gilcrease Institute of American History and Art; 683 Edison Institute of the Henry Ford Museum and Greenfield Village; 685 Yale; 687 Atwater Kent Museum; 689 l MFA; r The Newark Museum; 691 MFA; 692 Laurie Platt Winfrey, Inc.; 695 Kansas State Historical Society; 697 Library Company of Philadelphia; 699 The Century Club; 701 Abby Aldrich Rockefeller Folk Art Collection Center, Williamsburg, Virginia; 703 MMA/Morris K. Jesup Fund, 1940.

REFERENCE SECTION Page 704 t Amon Carter Museum, Fort Worth; cl MMA; cr MFA; b Maryland Historical Society; 705 tl LC; tr The Granger Collection; b Schinler Collection, Werner Forman Archive; 706 t Laurie Platt Winfrey, Inc.; b Laurie Platt Winfrey, Inc.; 707 tl Thomas Gilcrease Institute, Tulsa, OK; bl American Museum of Natural History; r The Granger Collection; 708 t BBC Hulton/Bettmann Archive; b Prints Collection/NYPL, Miriam & Ira D. Wallach Division of Art, Prints & I. Noual MEZL + Photographs, Astor, Lenox & Tilden Foundations; 709 t Museum of Fine Arts, Boston, M. & M. Karolik Collection; bl NYHS; br Rare Book Div./NYPL, Astor, Lenox & Tilden Foundations; 710 t Museum of Fine Arts, Gift by Subscription & Francis Bartlett Fund; b Dept. of Ethnology, Royal Ontario Museum, Toronto, Canada; 711 l Minneapolis Institute of Arts, Julia B. Bigelow, Fund by John Bigelow; tr Daniel J. Terra Collection, Terra Museum of American Art; br Oakland Museum, Gift of Kahn Foundation; 712 t Nelson-Atkins Museum of Art (Nelson Fund); b Oakland Museum, Gift of Mrs. Leor. Bocqueraz; 713 t Gift of William Wilson Corcoran, Corcoran Gallery of Art; bl Laurie Platt Winfrey, Inc.; br Laurie Platt Winfrey, Inc.; 730 l Independence National Historical Park; r Thomas Gilcrease Institute of American History and Art, Tulsa, OK; 731 l The Granger Collection; r MMA, Gift of Christian A. Zabriskie; 732 l Wally McNamee, Woodfin Camp and Assoc.; r NASA; 733 l Curtis Publishing Company, r John and Kimiko Powers; 736–740 portrait nos. 1,2,4,5–7,9,10,12–18, 20,21,25–27, National Portrait Gallery, SI; portrait nos. 3,8,11,19,22–24,28–40, White House Historical Association, Photos by National Geographic Society; portrait no. 41, © Larry Downing, Woodfin Camp and Assoc.

Front Cover Art: Byron Gin
Back Cover Art: Historical handwriting—Tim Girvin Design, Inc./Seattle; Background—Ray Smith
Layout and Page Production: Function Thru Form, Inc.
Contributing Design Services: Function Thru Form, Inc., BB&K Design, Inc., McNally Graphic Design
Historical Re-creations: Ray Smith
Gazette Drawings: Don Martinetti
Text Maps: Dick Sanderson and John Sanderson, Mapping Specialists, Ltd.
Historical Atlas Maps: General Cartography, Inc.
Geographic Atlas Maps: R.R. Donnelley & Sons Company
Charts and Graphs: Function Thru Form, McNally Graphic Design
Photo Consultant: Michal Heron
Photo Researchers: Omni-Photo Communications, Inc.

The quilt that appears as background design throughout this book was made by Grace Kennedy Zimmerman of Indiana. Her father, Joseph B. Kennedy, who served in the Civil War, mustered out of Camp Stanley, Texas.